The Great Republic

A HISTORY OF THE AMERICAN PEOPLE

A HISTORY OF THE
AMERICAN PEOPLE

The Great Republic

BERNARD BAILYN
Harvard University

DAVID BRION DAVIS
Yale University

DAVID HERBERT DONALD
Harvard University

JOHN L. THOMAS
Brown University

ROBERT H. WIEBE
Northwestern University

GORDON S. WOOD
Brown University

D. C. HEATH AND COMPANY
Lexington, Massachusetts   Toronto

Acknowledgements

In the course of writing this book each of the authors has incurred debts to many individuals and institutions, but it would be inappropriate to list here six sets of personal acknowledgements. All the authors, however, owe a debt of gratitude to one individual, Ann Knight, history editor of D. C. Heath, for her diligence and skill in editing the manuscript, her assistance on a hundred details, and above all her wonderfully sensitive diplomacy.

B.B.   J.L.T.
D.B.D.   R.H.W.
D.H.D.   G.S.W.

Cover illustration from a membership certificate of the Massachusetts Mechanics Association, 1800. (Library of Congress.)

Cartography by NORMAN CLARK ADAMS

Design and layout by ROBERT AND MARILYN DUSTIN

Photo research by JUDY POE

Published simultaneously in Canada.

Printed in the United States of America.

International Standard Book Number: 0-669-86629-6

Library of Congress Catalog Card Number: 76-8738

Contents

PART ONE
SHAPING THE REPUBLIC
to 1760

INTRODUCTION   1

Chapter 1   THE BACKGROUND OF ENGLISH COLONIZATION   **4**

Points of Contrast: Spain in America   5
The Release of Enterprise   18
Personnel and the Role of the State   24
The Concept of Settlement: Ireland and America   26
Financial Limitations and the "Starving Times"   29

Chapter 2   TRANSPLANTATION   **34**

Virginia: Squalor, Struggle, and a New Way of Life   37
The Pilgrims' "Sweet Communion"   45
The Puritans and Their Progeny: Power in the Service
   of the Spirit   51
A Catholic Refuge on the Chesapeake   60
The Failure of the Dutch   64
Royal Rewards: Carolina and the Jerseys   70
Pennsylvania: A Godly Experiment and a Worldly Success   79

Chapter 3   EUROPE IN THE WILDERNESS: AMERICAN SOCIETY
IN THE SEVENTEENTH CENTURY   **85**

Population Growth and Structure   86
Economic Instability   90
Social Instability   98
Religion   108

Chapter 4 ELEMENTS OF CHANGE, 1660–1720 **123**

    Empire 124

    Anglo-American Aristocracy 134

    Rebellion: The Measure of Social Strain 147

    "Creolean Degeneracy" 153

Chapter 5 AMERICAN SOCIETY IN THE EIGHTEENTH CENTURY **163**

    The New Population: Source and Impact 164

    A Maturing Economy and a Society in Flux 170

    Religion: The Sources of American Denominationalism 180

    The Origins of American Politics 188

Chapter 6 THE ENLIGHTENMENT'S NEW WORLD **200**

    "Rule Britannia" 201

    The Alienation of the State 209

    The American 216

    CHRONOLOGY, to 1760 226

    COLOR ESSAY
    Embellishing the Wilderness Between 88 and 89

PART TWO
FRAMING THE REPUBLIC
1760–1820

    INTRODUCTION 229

Chapter 7 SOURCES OF THE REVOLUTION **231**

    The Remains of Social Dependency 231

    The Expansion of Social Independence 234

    Reorganization of the British Empire 244

    American Resistance 251

Chapter 8 THE LOGIC OF REVOLUTION **263**

    A Conspiracy Against Liberty 264

    The Imperial Debate 268

    The Popularization of Politics 272

    The War for Independence 276

Chapter 9   REPUBLICANISM   **291**

     Independent and Virtuous Citizens   292
     State Constitution Making   297
     The Articles of Confederation   301
     Republican Society   306
     The Sovereignty of the People   314

Chapter 10   THE FEDERALIST AUGUSTAN AGE   **321**

     The Critical Period   322
     The Weakness of the Confederation   325
     The Federal Constitution   330
     The Hamiltonian Program   341

Chapter 11   THE REVOLUTION RECOVERED   **352**

     The Republican Opposition   353
     Government Without Power   360
     An Empire of Liberty   368
     The Origins of Judicial Review   371
     Republican Diplomacy and War   377

Chapter 12   THE END OF THE AMERICAN ENLIGHTENMENT   **389**

     Self-Made Men   390
     The Kingdom of God in America   402
     The Popularization of American Culture   410

     CHRONOLOGY, 1760–1820   422

     COLOR ESSAY
     The Rising Glory of America   Between 312 and 313

PART THREE
EXPANDING THE REPUBLIC
1820–1860

     INTRODUCTION   425

Chapter 13   THE CONTOURS OF MATERIAL CHANGE   **428**

     Population   431
     Indians   436
     Land   442

Trade, Manufactures, and Economic Growth 453
Distribution and Opportunity 458

Chapter 14   **THE POLITICS OF OPPORTUNITY**   **465**

The End of Republican Unity 466
The Democrats in Power 473
Opposition Parties and the Realignment of the 1850s 483

Chapter 15   **ATTEMPTS TO SHAPE THE AMERICAN CHARACTER**   **496**

"We Must Educate or Perish" 497
The Evangelical Age 504
Law, Phrenology, and Self-Reliance 513
The Tensions of Democratic Art 522

Chapter 16   **THE NATURE AND LIMITS OF DISSENT**   **528**

Three Stages of Protest and Reform 529
The Mormons as a Test Case 532
The Benevolent Empire: Missions and Asylums 541
Radical Abolitionism 548
Consolidation: Political Antislavery 558

Chapter 17   **SLAVERY AND EXPANDING BOUNDARIES**   **566**

The Slave's World 567
The South as a "Slave Society" 575
"A Fire Bell in the Night": The Missouri Compromise 582
Domestic Dangers: Nullification and the Gag Rule 587
Foreign Dangers, the Monroe Doctrine, and American Expansion 592

Chapter 18   **THE BARRIERS OF POWER**   **607**

The Mexican War and Manifest Destiny 608
A Fire Bell at High Noon: The Crisis of 1850 616
The Confrontation over Kansas 624
Dred Scott and the Lincoln-Douglas Debates 630
The Ultimate Failure of Compromise 636

CHRONOLOGY, 1820–1860 644

COLOR ESSAY
The Perils of Civilization   Between 536 and 537

PART FOUR
UNITING THE REPUBLIC
1860–1890

INTRODUCTION 647

Chapter 19 STALEMATE, 1861–1862 **649**

The Rival Government 650
Winning the Border States 654
Raising the Armies 661
Financing the War 666
Wartime Diplomacy 671
Battles and Leaders 675

Chapter 20 EXPERIMENTATION, 1862–1865 **685**

Evolution of a Command System 686
The Naval War 692
The Wartime Economy 695
Inflation and Its Consequences 698
Conscription and Conflict 702
Steps Toward Emancipation 705
Europe and the War 712
Wartime Politics 713
Northern Victory 720

Chapter 21 THE LIMITS OF INNOVATION, 1865–1869 **729**

Paths Not Taken 731
Constitutionalism as a Limit to Change 735
Laissez-Faire as a Limit to Change 741
Political Parties as a Limit to Change 748
Racism as a Limit to Change 758

Chapter 22 THE AMERICAN COMPROMISE, 1865–1880 **768**

American Nationalism 769
Postwar Diplomacy 773
Toward a National Economy 777
Tariff and Currency Controversies 787
Discontent among Farmers and Laborers 792

Chapter 23 RECONCILIATION, 1865–1890   **800**
          Politics of the Gilded Age   801
          The Restoration of "Home Rule"   808
          Literary Reconciliation   813

          CHRONOLOGY, 1860–1890   822

          COLOR ESSAY
          From Eden to Babylon   Between 728 and 729

PART FIVE

NATIONALIZING THE REPUBLIC

1890–1920

          INTRODUCTION   827

Chapter 24 STABILIZING THE AMERICAN ECONOMY   **829**
          The Foundations of the American Industrial Revolution   830
          Business Fills a Vacuum   836
          The Counterrevolution Fails   843
          The Farmers' Fight Against Disorder   849
          Workers and the Challenge of Organization   856
          The Fruits of Revolution   862

Chapter 25 THE POLITICS OF REFORM   **866**
          The Politics of Equilibrium   869
          "Conditions Without Precedent"—The Populist Revolt   876
          The Great Reversal: The Election of 1896   881
          Cities in Revolt—The Rise of Urban Progressivism   890

Chapter 26 THE PROGRESSIVE IMPULSE   **903**
          The Man with the Muckrake   905
          Progressives vs Politicians   908
          Progressivism Invades the States   913
          Theodore Roosevelt: The Progressive as Hero   921
          "Wise Radicalism and Wise Conservatism"—The Square Deal   926
          The Limits of Neofederalism   933

Chapter 27 PROGRESSIVES AND THE CHALLENGE OF
          PLURALISM   **938**
          Changing the Progressive Guard   939
          Americans—New and Old   948
          The Rise of Social Feminism   959

Paradise Lost: Socialism in America 968

The New Freedom 972

Chapter 28   THE PATH TO POWER: AMERICAN FOREIGN
POLICY, 1890–1917   **979**

The Origins of American Expansionism 981

President McKinley's "Wonderful Experience" 986

Open and Closed Doors: Progressive Foreign Policy under
Roosevelt and Taft 995

"The Organized Force of Mankind": Wilsonian Diplomacy and
World War 1003

Chapter 29   PROGRESSIVISM AND THE GREAT WAR   **1014**

War and the Health of the State 1017

The Little Rebellion: Progressivism and the Challenge
of Culture 1027

Artists and Scientists: Critics of Progressivism 1034

The Ordeal of Woodrow Wilson 1038

CHRONOLOGY, 1890–1920 1050

COLOR ESSAY
Art as Urban Experience   Between 920 and 921

PART SIX

MODERNIZING THE REPUBLIC

1920 to the Present

INTRODUCTION 1053

Chapter 30   THE EMERGENCE OF MODERN POLITICS   **1056**

The Reactionary Impulse, 1920–1924 1057

The Modern Economy, 1920–1929 1061

The Politics of the New Era, 1924–1929 1066

The Crisis of Depression, 1929–1935 1073

The New Deal at the Crossroads, 1935–1936 1084

Chapter 31   THE DEVELOPMENT OF MODERN POLITICS   **1093**

The New Deal Loses Its Way, 1936–1941 1094

Wartime Prosperity and Postwar Confusion, 1941–1947 1101

Local Politics Comes to Washington, 1936–1947 1107

Solving the Riddle of Economic Policy, 1948–1954 1114

Local and National Politics Collide, 1948–1954 1119

Chapter 32   MODERN CULTURE   **1126**

     The Consumer Paradise   1126
     Modern Values   1129
     Modern Families and Careers   1133
     Response of the Traditionalists   1139
     Dangers to the Individual   1142
     Answers for the Individual   1148

Chapter 33   INTERNATIONAL POWER   **1158**

     A New International Order, 1920–1929   1159
     International Disintegration, 1930–1941   1163
     World War, 1941–1945   1172
     Cold War, 1945–1950   1182
     Containment, 1950–1953   1191

Chapter 34   THE CONSEQUENCES OF MODERNIZATION   **1199**

     Unity and Progress   1200
     World Order   1206
     Presidential Leadership   1213
     The Crisis in National-Local Relations   1218
     The Decline of Containment   1227
     The Lament of the Individual   1232
     Counterattack   1237

Chapter 35   STABILIZATION   **1245**

     National and Local Power   1246
     A Flexible Diplomacy   1250
     An Erratic Economy   1255
     A Cloudy Horizon   1259

     CHRONOLOGY, 1920 to the Present   1268

     COLOR ESSAY
     Varieties of Reality   Between 1144 and 1145

APPENDIX

     Declaration of Independence   i
     Constitution of the United States of America   iii
     Growth of U.S. Population and Area   xviii
     Presidential Elections   xxi
     Presidents and Vice-Presidents   xxii
INDEX   xxv

Maps and Charts

Spanish Conquests in America   6

Spanish and Portuguese Empires in the New World   10

Spain's Imperial Government in the New World, 1550   11

England's Overseas World, 1600   28

The Indian Paths of Pennsylvania   35

Northern British Settlements, 1700   59

Southern British Settlements, 1700   72

Land Distribution in a 17th-Century Town   106

Sources of English Emigration to New England, 1620–1650   119

Hudson River Estates in Colonial New York   141

The French Wars, 1680–1713   143

German Settlements in 18th-Century America   166

Mount Vernon Plantation   173

18th-Century Atlantic Trade Routes   175

The French and Indian War, 1755–1760   205

Concentration of Population in the Colonies, 1760   238

North America in 1763   247

Trade between Britain and the Colonies, 1763–1776   257

Northern Campaigns, 1775–1776   279

Northern Campaigns, 1777   284

Yorktown and the Southern Campaigns, 1778–1781   286

Claims to Western Lands, 1781   303

Northwest Ordinance of 1785, Land Survey   305

The Treaty of Greenville, 1795   349

The United States, 1803–1807   369

American Foreign Trade, 1790–1812   381

The War of 1812 — Major Campaigns   383

The United States, 1820–1860   430

Population, 1820   433

Population, 1860   433

Southeastern Indian Tribes Before and After Removal, 1820–1840   438

Main Canals, River and Lake Transportation, 1840s   449

Principal Railroads, 1860   451

The Election of 1828   474

The Election of 1840   489

The Election of 1844   490

The Mormon Trail   538

Geographical Distribution of Slaves in 1820   576

Geographical Distribution of Slaves in 1860   576

The Missouri Compromise, 1820–1821   586

Continental Expansion, the United States in 1819   595

Wagon Trails Westward, 1840   604

The Mexican War   611

The Oregon Controversy, 1848   613

Central America, 1850   615

The Compromise of 1850   620

The Kansas-Nebraska Act, 1854   627

The Election of 1860   639

Secession   658

Operations in the East, July 1861–November 1862   676

Operations in the West, February–April 1862   676

The Confederate Offensive in the West, August–October 1862   681

Operations in the East, December 1862–July 1863   688

Operations in the West, 1863, The Vicksburg Campaign   688

Operations in the East, May 1864–April 1865   721

Sherman's March to the Sea   722

Reconstruction   755

Black Population, 1880   761

Hayes-Tilden Disputed Election of 1876   809

Principal Railroads, 1890   832

The U.S. Economy, 1873–1900   833

Passing of the Frontier, 1870–1890   852

Dumbbell Tenement   861

The Election of 1880   870

The Election of 1892   870

The Election of 1896   888

The Election of 1912   945

Old and New Immigration, 1871–1920   948

The Lower East Side   951

Woman Suffrage Before the 19th Amendment 966
The Spanish War in the Philippines, 1898 989
The Spanish War in the Caribbean, 1898 989
The United States in the Pacific 996
The United States in the Caribbean 998
Major U.S. Operations on the Western Front, 1918 1016
The Election of 1928 1072
Index of Common Stock Prices, 1924–1932 1073
The Election of 1932 1077
Tennessee Valley Authority (TVA) 1083
Recovery of the National Economy 1103
The Growth of Union Membership 1106
Black Population, 1920–1930 1110
The Election of 1948 1114
World War II, Europe and North Africa 1177
World War II in the Pacific 1179
The Shifting Front in Korea 1192
The Election of 1960 1216
Vietnam and Southeast Asia 1231
The Election of 1968 1246

Introduction

This book is a history of the American people, from the earliest settlements in the New World to the 200th anniversary of the birth of the United States as a nation. We call our book "The Great Republic," adopting a phrase Winston Churchill used to describe the United States. No one can doubt the greatness of the American republic if it is measured in terms of the size of our national domain, the vastness of our economic productivity, or the stability of our government and basic institutions. Whether that greatness has been equaled in the realm of culture, in the uses of power, or in the distribution of social justice is more debatable; on these matters readers will make up their own minds. Our task has been to present the story of America as we have understood it—a story of great achievement, of enormous material success and of soaring idealism, but a story too of conflict, of tumultuous factionalism, of injustice, rootlessness, and rinding disorder.

Each of the six sections of the book contains its own thematic emphasis, set out in a separate introduction. But there are two general themes that unify the book as a whole. The first theme is the development and constant testing of free political institutions in America. To understand the United States today, one must analyze the conditions of life in the colonial period that made popular self-government at first possible, then likely, in the end necessary. One must see how the American Revolution expressed the longings of provincial Britons for a total reform of political culture and projected this idealism onto a nation of continental scale. One must discover how democratic institutions and practices expanded during the nineteenth century and received their crucial testing in the American Civil War. One must understand how urbanization and industrialization produced a new political culture in the United States by the beginning of the twentieth century. And one must ask how free, democratic institutions have sustained themselves through decades of international crises and world wars. Without an understanding of popular self-government, from eighteenth-century republicanism to modern political democracy, no sense at all can be made of the history of the American people.

A second theme, which has persisted from the very earliest days, is the tension between majority rule and minority rights in America. From the beginning the New World provided a feast for the ambitious, for the discontented, for the individualistic. Its vast resources, open for exploitation by the talented, the shrewd, the enterprising, and the energetic, have produced a society constantly in danger of fragmentation. The huge geographical extent of the country has nourished divisive interests of all kinds, and the admixture of peoples from every quarter of the world has led to ethnic and cultural pluralism, at times so strong as to threaten the disintegration of the social fabric. At the same time, however, there have been, from the founding of the Puritan colonies to the present, powerful forces working toward social stability and agreement.

The Founding Fathers correctly recognized that this constant struggle between the general interest and the special interests posed the most severe threat to the continuance of a self-governing democratic nation. They knew there would be no automatic harmonizing of regional, economic, and social group ambitions, no easy reconciliation of competing needs and desires. The divisive forces, they knew, would be powerful; the inevitable clashes of opinion and the conflicts of interest and ambition would be bitter and intense. At the same time they feared centralizing tendencies that might threaten despotism, and worried that minorities might become subject to the tyranny of majorities. Could public institutions sensitive to popular pressures successfully reconcile these conflicts? Could they provide the instruments of compromise that would make and remake a stable, nation-wide agreement from a tumult of clashing ambitions?

The two hundred years of our national history clearly show that the Founding Fathers did not resolve this tension between the interest of the society as a whole and the special interests of its parts, but the federal system they devised provided mechanisms for the mediation of the struggles. With the one horrendous exception of the Civil War, the institutions set up by the Founders have succeeded in harnessing the explosive energies of the American people. Often the balance has been precarious between the interest of society as a whole and that of its parts, between the needs of the nation and the rights of regions and states, between the power of majorities and the desires of minorities. From time to time the balance has tipped, first in the one direction, then in the other, yet the eighteenth-century republican design remains viable—still hopeful, still workable as a result of constant adjustment, despite the tremendous pressure that constantly threatens to overwhelm it.

The tracing of these two themes—the development of free political institutions in America and the maintaining of a balance between majority rule and minority rights—links together the six sections written by six separate authors and gives an overarching unity to the book. The sections are further unified by the authors' shared view of the nature of history. We all believe that historical knowledge is not simply the accumulation of information about the past. It is a mode of understanding. The historian is obliged not merely to describe what happened but to explain it, to make clear why things developed as they did. We share, too, an aversion to any simply deterministic interpretation of historical change. At certain junctures economic and demographic forces are dominant, but they are themselves shaped by cultural forces. Great political events are at times triggered by economic drives, but at other times they are responses to beliefs and to aspirations that are not a direct reflection of economic needs. Political decisions alter economic life, social organization, and even the way people think—yet economic, social, and intellectual forces change politics too.

History, we believe, is a complex intermingling of forces, whose relations fall into no predetermined pattern. We have sought to explore this complexity as well as to narrate the succession of important events. The book is therefore self-contained, in that it supplies the basic factual information and the essential narratives that readers will need, but it presents that information within a framework of analysis and explanation. We hope that *The Great Republic* will help readers understand why and how America developed as it did, and where, as a result of this historical evolution, we have arrived after more than three centuries of growth and two centuries of nationhood.

B.B. J.L.T.

D.B.D. R.H.W.

D.H.D. G.S.W.

C A

WASHINGTON
1889
Seattle
Tacoma
Olympia
Mt. Rainier
14,410'
Spokane
Portland
Columbia R.
Willamette R.
Salem
OREGON
1859
IDAHO
1890
Boise
Helena
Butte
MONTANA
1889
Yellowstone R.
Missouri R.
NORTH DAKOTA
1889
Bismarck
Snake R.
SIERRA
Reno
Carson
City
NEVADA
1864
WYOMING
1890
Great
Salt
Lake
Salt Lake
City
1896
UTAH
Cheyenne
SOUTH DAKOTA
1889
Pierre
1867
NEBRASKA
Platte R.
Lincoln
Sacramento
Sacramento R.
San
Francisco
CALIFORNIA
1850
NEVADA
Mt. Whitney
14,495'
ROCKY
Colorado R.
Grand
Canyon
Denver
COLORADO
1876
Pikes Pk.
14,110'
1861
K A N S
Wichita
Los Angeles
San Diego
ARIZONA
1912
Gila R.
Phoenix
Tucson
Santa Fe
NEW MEXICO
1912
Canadian R.
Oklahoma
City
OKLA
1907
PACIFIC OCEAN

El Paso
M E X I C O
Pecos R.
Rio Grande
Ft.
Worth
Brazos R.
T E X A S
Austin
Colorado R.
San
Antonio
Nueces R.

SOVIET UNION
180°
ARCTIC OCEAN
Pt. Barrow
International Dateline (U.S.S.R.)
(United States)
ARCTIC CIRCLE
Attu
BERING
SEA
Nome
Yukon R.
Fairbanks
Mt. McKinley
20,300'
Anchorage
ALEUTIAN ISLANDS
Kodiak I.
Unimak
ALASKA
1959
Juneau
CANADA
180°
PACIFIC OCEAN
0   600
Miles

KAUAI
NIIHAU
OAHU
Honolulu
MOLOKAI
LANAI
KAHOOLAWE
MAUI
PACIFIC
OCEAN
HAWAII
1959
Hilo
HAWAII
0   150
Miles

Norman Clark Adams

The United States of America
★ ★ ★ ★ ★ ★ ★ ★ ★ ★ ★ ★ ★ ★ ★

⊛ National Capital ⊛ State Capital • Other Major Cities
1845 Date of Admission to the Union

0   100   200   300   400   500
Scale of Miles

CANADA

Lake of the Woods

Lake Superior

Duluth

MINNESOTA
1858
St.Paul
Minneapolis

Quebec
St. Lawrence R.
Montreal
Ottawa ⊛

1820 MAINE
Bangor • Eastport
⊛ Augusta
Portland

L. Champlain Montpelier
VT **N.H.**
179   1788
Concord

MASS.
1788   Boston   Cape Cod

Albany ⊛
Providence
Hartford **R.I.**1790
CONN.1788

MICHIGAN
1837

Lake Huron

Toronto   L. Ontario
Rochester
Buffalo

NEW YORK
1788

New York
Long Island

Hudson R.

WISCONSIN
1848
Madison
Milwaukee

Grand Rapids   Lansing
Detroit

Lake Michigan

Lake Erie

Cleveland

PENNSYLVANIA
Harrisburg ⊛ 1787
Pittsburgh   Philadelphia

Trenton
N.J.
1787

Delaware R.

Dover
DEL.
1787

1846 IOWA
Des Moines ⊛

Omaha

Missouri R.

Chicago
South Bend
Ft.Wayne

Toledo

OHIO
1803
Columbus ⊛

Cincinnati

Baltimore
Washington D.C. ⊛
Annapolis **MD.** 1788
Potomac R.

1818 ILLINOIS
Springfield ⊛

1816 INDIANA
Indianapolis ⊛

Wabash R.

Ohio R.

Louisville
Frankfort ⊛

WEST VIRGINIA
1863
Charleston ⊛

Richmond ⊛
1788
James R.
Norfolk

Topeka ⊛

Kansas City
Jefferson City ⊛
St. Louis

MISSOURI
1821

KENTUCKY
1792
Cumberland R.

VIRGINIA

S

Roanoke I.
Cape Hatteras

Arkansas R.
Tulsa

OMA

ARKANSAS
Little Rock ⊛ 1836

Memphis

Nashville ⊛
Knoxville ▲

TENNESSEE
1796

Tennessee R.

Raleigh ⊛
NORTH CAROLINA
• Charlotte 1789

Cape Fear

Red R.

Dallas

1817 MISSISSIPPI
Jackson ⊛

Birmingham
1819 ALABAMA
Montgomery ⊛

Atlanta ⊛
1788
GEORGIA

Savannah R.

SOUTH CAROLINA
Columbia ⊛
1788

Charleston

Savannah

Sabine R.

1812
LOUISIANA
Baton Rouge ⊛
New Orleans

Pearl R.
Alabama R.

Tallahassee ⊛

FLORIDA
1845

Houston

R.

Tampa

L. Okeechobee

Miami

A T L A N T I C   O C E A N

BAHAMA ISLANDS

PUERTO RICO
San Juan ⊛

0   100
Miles

VIRGIN ISLANDS
St.Thomas I.
St. Johns I.
⊛ St.
Charlotte Amalie
St. Croix I.
(B

CARIBBEAN SEA

Havana **CUBA**

The Great Republic

A HISTORY OF THE AMERICAN PEOPLE

WEATHERVANE, BY SHEM DROWNE (MID-EIGHTEENTH CENTURY)

Swivelling atop the cupola of the Massachusetts Province House with its glass eyes flashing in the sun, this 4½-foot gilded weathervane was the work of an untutored craftsman. The visual and symbolic effect of the almost life-sized American archer swinging vigilantly year after year over the residence of the royal governors, always aiming an arrow to fly with the wind, was striking. It "bedazzled the eyes of those who looked upward," Nathaniel Hawthorne wrote in a story inspired by Drowne, "like an angel of the sun." (*Massachusetts Historical Society.*)

PART ONE

Shaping the Republic

to 1760

BERNARD BAILYN

The American Republic was created only in a legal sense in 1776. (1616) In a deeper and more general sense it was the product of a century and a half of development that preceded the establishment of American independence. The ultimate origins of this "Great Republic," as Winston Churchill called the American nation, lie far back in time—in desperate gambles of hard-pressed sixteenth- and seventeenth-century merchants involved in overseas trade; in the visions of Elizabethan dreamers who conceived of a western passage to the vast wealth of the Far East; in the courage and single-mindedness of religious refugees determined to carve a new life for themselves in the wilderness rather than compromise their beliefs; in the lifelong labors of a quarter of a million Africans transported in bondage to the New World; and in the everyday struggles of five generations of transplanted Europeans and their descendants, farmers and tradesmen for the most part, who sensed, however vaguely, that theirs was a new world, more generous to human aspirations, freer, more supportive of human dignity, and richer—for those whose risks succeeded—than any land known before.

These multitudes in colonial North America did not seek to transform the world. Though adventurous, more often than not they were conservative by instinct or became conservative as they sought to establish familiar forms of life in an unfamiliar environment. But traditions could not be maintained in wilderness communities whose basic conditions were so different from those elsewhere, and a new pattern of life slowly evolved in the course of five generations. Gradually, without theory, as matters of fact and not of design, the character of community life as it had once been known—its demographic foundations, economic processes, social organizations, religion, and politics—all of this was transformed.

Yet not by desire or will—not in an effort to attain an ideal or realize a theory. Change, in the years before the Revolution, was suspect by some, resisted in part, and confined in its effects as the colonists sought to emulate the pattern of more traditional, cosmopolitan societies. Their own provincial world was seen not as a model but as a regression to a more primitive mode of life. Behavior had changed—had had to change—with the circumstances of everyday life, but habits of mind and the sense of the rightness of things lagged behind. Many felt that the changes that had taken place in the years before the Revolution were *away from*, not *toward*, something; that they represented deviance; that they lacked, in a word, legitimacy.

For most Americans this divergence between ideals, habits of mind, and belief on the one hand, and experience and patterns of behavior on the other, was ended at the Revolution. An upheaval that destroyed the traditional sources of public authority called forth the full range of advanced and enlightened ideas. Long-settled attitudes were jolted and loosened. Suddenly it was seen that the slow erosion in patterns of social life that had taken place in the colonial period had been good and proper. In the context of Revolutionary beliefs, these changes were conceived of as steps in the direction of a new ideal—the ideal of a simpler, less encumbered existence, in which the individual would count for more and the state less; in which the weight of burdensome social institutions would be permanently lifted; in which the blight of privilege and of the misuse of power would forever be destroyed; in which corruption would be exposed before it could sap the nation's strength; and in which, as a result of all of this, the ordinary person's desire for personal fulfillment could at long last be satisfied.

Such at least were the ideals of the Revolution, formulated by a generation of brilliant political thinkers convinced that it was their great historic role to set the world on a new course. And in the context of these ideals—which, however modified, are still the highest aspirations of the American people—the changes of the colonial years took on a new meaning. The settlement of the colonies and their subsequent development, John Adams wrote, could now be seen as "the opening of a grand scene and design in providence for the illumination of the ignorant and the emancipation of the slavish part of mankind all over the earth." The glass was half-full, not half-empty; and to complete the work of fate and nature, further thought must be taken and changes accelerated rather than restrained.

Social change and social conflict took place during the Revolutionary years, but the beliefs and aspirations of the founders of the American nation, unlike those of the leaders of the French and Russian revolutions, did not require the destruction and remaking of society. The Revolution did not create new social and political forces; it released forces and intensified changes that had been developing from the day the first settlers set foot on Jamestown. Modern America, a massively developed, affluent, and tumultuous technological society of over 200 million people, is worlds away from the tiny farming hamlets and obscure port towns of the seventeenth century, huddled on the coastal fringe of an almost undeveloped continent. Yet there is a clear line of continuity in American history that links those quite primitive settlements to the sophisticated, dynamic world power of the late twentieth century. For modern America is not simply the product of modern forces—industrialism, political democracy, universal education, a consumer culture. It is the product too of the idealism of the eighteenth-century Enlightenment reinforced and intensified by the openness and affluence of American life.

It is this powerful strain of idealism flowing from the very different world of the eighteenth century into all the complexities of modern America that is the most distinctive feature of the American Republic as it enters its third century of existence. How that ineradicable strain first entered American life, how it was nourished in the soil of a strangely altered society that grew from confused seventeenth-century origins, and how the characteristic American mixture of idealism and materialism was first compounded, reaching so soon, in the subtle figure of Benjamin Franklin, an apparently absolute and perfect form—how all this took place is the central theme of the colonial period of American history.

Far from being a quaint prologue to the main story, therefore, the history of the settlement and early development of American society is a critically important phase of our history. Without an understanding of the pre-Revolutionary era none of the rest of our history can be properly understood.

1

The Background of English Colonization

The United States evolved from the British settlements on the mainland of North America, first permanently established in 1607. But a century earlier a more powerful European power, Spain, had founded an empire in the Western Hemisphere that was in a high state of development when the British first entered the colonial world. The growth of the Spanish empire in the Western Hemisphere and of Spanish-American society forms a remarkable, and revealing, contrast to the evolution of the British empire and of Anglo-American society. In some ways, to be sure, Anglo-American society in British North America and Indo-Hispanic society in Central America and South America are so different as to be incomparable. One can hardly think of any two Western cultures more distinct from each other than that of Catholic Habsburg Spain transplanted in the land of the Incas and the Aztecs and that of Protestant England and Holland resettled in North America. But there is one area at least in which extremely illuminating contrasts may be drawn: the realm of government and politics.

By the early eighteenth century, politics in British North America was distinctive in its free and fierce competition and in the institutional and cultural conditions that made such open competition possible. Nothing quite like these unconfined, brawling struggles—faction against faction, groups against the state—fought out with every weapon of publicity and manipulation, existed in any other colonial region of the world. There was certainly nothing like this politics in Spanish America; yet at one stage, strangely enough, it seems that there might have been. It is worth attempting, therefore, at the very outset to explore the underlying reasons for the absence of a free competitive political system in Spanish America at the height of the colonial period, and in doing so to isolate by contrast forces and circumstances that would later shape the dynamic political society of British America as it existed on the eve of the Revolution.

Points of Contrast: Spain in America

There are important contrasts between Spanish and British America at every stage of development. The very origins of settlement were different. Whereas it took England half a century after its first contact with the Western Hemisphere to establish even a temporary colony there, Spain proceeded swiftly after Columbus's world-transforming discovery of 1492 to exploit the territories it claimed. Led by the courageous, greedy, and often brutal *conquistadores*—adventurers for whom there are no equivalents in British experience—Spain's exploration of the Western Hemisphere, its conquest of the native peoples, and its establishment of a new civilization swept forward in three main waves.

Columbus himself explored much of the Caribbean on his four voyages (1492–1504), and within a decade of his death in 1506 Spanish adventurers seized possession of most of the coastal lands of Central America and South America. The conquest of the Caribbean basin climaxed in 1513 with Balboa's penetration of the isthmus of Panama and his discovery of the Pacific, and with Ponce de León's discovery of the Florida mainland.

The second principal wave of Spanish expansion in America was stimulated by rumors of vast treasures hidden in a highly civilized state deep in the interior, and led to the conquest, in one of the most dramatic and bloody adventures ever recorded, of the Aztec empire of Montezuma in Mexico (1519–21) by the resourceful, ruthless, and incredibly energetic Hernándo Cortés. There are no heroes in this tale of slaughter and conquest; there are only, on the one side, passionately determined adventurers, half-mad with greed, who overcame terrific adversity to plunder and ultimately to destroy an ancient civilization, and on the other side, equally courageous and brutal but bewildered and unsophisticated natives. Cortés's conquest of the Mexican world was extended to the north by others: by Cabeza de Vaca circling the northern periphery of the Gulf of Mexico and ultimately reaching the Gulf of California (1528–36); by Coronado, seeking El Dorados in the mud villages of Arizona, New Mexico, Colorado, Oklahoma, and Kansas; and by Hernando de Soto, cutting through northern Florida and the later southeastern states to discover the Mississippi (1539–41). While these conquerors were exploring and subduing what would become the northern borderlands of Spain's empire, other followers of Cortés swept through

Central America and established Spanish rule in Honduras and Guatemala.

The third great thrust of Spanish conquest was led by an illiterate adventurer, Francisco Pizarro, who propelled a series of expeditions from Panama through the jungles of Ecuador and northern Peru into the heartland of the elaborate Incan empire, then weakened by civil war. By a ruse he managed to capture the Incan emperor, whom he murdered after extracting a ransom of over twenty tons of pure gold and silver, and to destroy much of the Indian army and nobility. He then proceeded to strip city after city of their treasures, to embroil both natives and conquerors in devastating warfare, and to establish in 1535 the new central city of Lima.

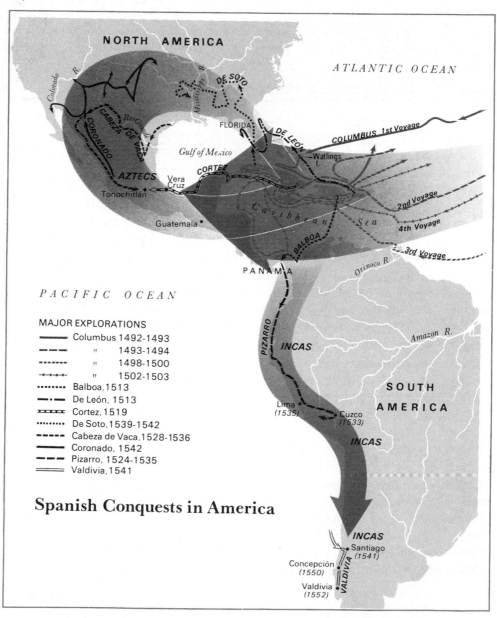

MAJOR EXPLORATIONS
- Columbus 1492-1493
- "   1493-1494
- "   1498-1500
- "   1502-1503
- Balboa, 1513
- De León, 1513
- Cortez, 1519
- De Soto, 1539-1542
- Cabeza de Vaca, 1528-1536
- Coronado, 1542
- Pizarro, 1524-1535
- Valdivia, 1541

Spanish Conquests in America

BATTLE FOR THE INCAN CITY OF CUZCO

An imaginative depiction by Flemish engraver Theodore De Bry (1528–98). Never having seen either America or an Indian, De Bry portrayed the natives as ancient Greeks, innocent but savage, and dwelt almost sadistically on cannibalism and the brutalities of the conquest. Cuzco appears as a Spanish-American walled city. (*Rare Book Division, The New York Public Library.*)

From the plundered Incan lands, further expeditions were launched, first into Ecuador, then into Chile and northern Argentina (1535–37), and finally into Bolivia (1539). The full subjugation of Chile was a vast epic in itself, the work of yet another almost unbelievably determined and ruthless *conquistador*, Pedro de Valdivia. His small troop of Spanish adventurers and Indian followers survived desert journeys, near starvation, and attacks by natives to found Santiago, Concepción, and Valdivia before succumbing to native rebellion in 1553.

Radiating out from these three main lines of conquest (first, the subjugation of the Caribbean islands and coastal areas; then the reduction of Mexico and the exploration of southern North America; and finally the invasion of Peru, Chile, and northern Argentina), Spain's empire in America expanded in all directions. By 1607, when England established at Jamestown its first permanent settlement in America, Spain's American dominion extended nearly 8000 miles, from southern California to the Straits of Magellan. Spain then controlled the largest empire the Western world had seen since the fall of Rome; its only competitor was Portugal, which then controlled the coastal areas of Brazil but little else in the Western Hemisphere. Spain's Western fabulous empire was the result of sheer lust for adventure, greed, and a passion to convert the heathen people to Christianity; it was also the result of remarkable administrative skill.

For despite the vast distances involved and all the technical impediments to the coherent management of so vast a territory, Spain's American empire by the middle of the seventeenth century was a well-organized entity. The structure of government that had evolved during the sixteenth century was elaborate, ingeniously contrived, and on the whole successful, and it was utterly different from the imperial system that Britain would devise a century later. It was most elaborately *bureaucratic*. Several echelons of full-time salaried officials enforced detailed decrees and laws governing the behavior of rulers and ruled: regulations that reached down into the daily life—economic, religious, social, political—of the meanest peasants in the most remote corners of the empire, half a world away from the central administrative agencies in Spain. And the system was *patrimonial;* that is, it was hierarchical in structure, all authority ultimately centering in the patriarchal figure of the monarch of Castile, whose rule in his kingdom of America was conceived of as personal, an extension of his dynastic and domestic authority.

THE WORLD THE SPANIARDS FOUND

The Aztec priest's skull mask was meant to be worn with an elaborate feather head-dress and rich robes. It must have had a terrifying effect on Incan worshippers. The gold Mixtec chest plate represented the god of death. Opposite, Macchu Pichu, Peru, last refuge of the Incan emperors in their flight from the Spaniards. *(Left, Copyright The British Museum; middle, National Museum of Anthropology, Mexico City; right, Braniff International.)*

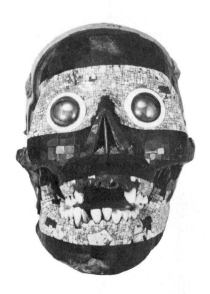

This projection of monarchical power into overseas territory by means of a complex bureaucracy had been initiated almost instantly upon the report of Columbus's discovery—a response that contrasts sharply with that of the British government a century later. In 1493, control of future expeditions to the West had been vested in the archdeacon of Seville, acting in the king's name; and as early as 1503, while Columbus was still attempting to prove that Central America was the Malay Peninsula, the first of the major imperial institutions, the *Casa de Contratación* (board of trade), had been created. From these origins, the enveloping imperial government, flung over half the globe yet bound by hundreds of

NORTH AMERICA

Santa Fe
(1609)

St. Augustine
(1565)

Havana
(1515)

Mexico
(1521)

Panama
(1519)

OCCUPIED BY SPANISH

1492-1519

1519-1543

1543-1600

1600-1743

OCCUPIED BY PORTUGUESE

1532-1543

1543-1600

1600-1743

Lima
(1535)

SOUTH AMERICA

Santiago
(1541)

Buenos
Aires
(1535-1580)

Rio de Janeiro
(1555)

Disputed by
Spain & Portugal

Demarcation Line, 1494
(Treaty of Tordesillas)

Spanish

Portuguese

**Spanish and
Portuguese Empires
in the New World**

rules and regulations enforced by an army of officials, developed within a single generation. The *Casa*, resident in Seville, licensed all equipment and operations engaged in trade with America, enforced the commercial laws and regulations, collected customs duties and colonial crown revenues, and kept the commercial accounts for the entire empire. By virtue of its power over colonial commerce and the flow of treasure that poured into Spain from America, the *Casa* became in effect a major branch of the royal exchequer.

Yet in all of this the *Casa* was subordinate to the chief regulating agency in Spain, the Council of the Indies (created in 1524), which held the decisive control, in the king's name, of both the legislative and the executive governance of the colonies, and which constituted a branch of the royal court. As the virtual monopolist of imperial power, which it exercised in the name of the king, the Council of the Indies was unconfined in its jurisdiction. All colonial laws and decrees, civil and religious, were issued by the council; and the officials, clerical and secular, who enforced the regulations were appointed by the council. It exercised a special responsibility for the spiritual and physical welfare of the Indians; it served as a court of last resort for the entire judiciary system of the colonies; it censored all publications in America; and it audited the accounts of the colonial treasurers.

(Northern Boundary
Indefinite)

AUDIENCIA OF
NEUVA GALICIA
(1548)

AUDIENCIA OF
MEXICO **VICEROYALTY OF NEW SPAIN**
(1527) **1535**

AUDIENCIA OF
SANTO DOMINGO
(1526)

AUDIENCIA OF
GUATEMALA (1543)

AUDIENCIA OF
PANAMA (1535)

AUDIENCIA OF
SANTA FE DE BOGOTA
(1549)

SOUTH AMERICA

**VICEROYALTY
OF PERU
1542**

AUDIENCIA OF LIMA

(1542)

**Spain's Imperial
Government in the
New World, 1550**

Agencies and officials resident in America were in one way or another subordinates of this supreme royal council. The chief governmental unit in America itself was the viceroyalty, of which two were created in the sixteenth century: New Spain (1535), which included all Spanish territory north of the isthmus of Panama; and Peru (1542), covering all to the south except the coast of Venezuela. These massive jurisdictions were ruled by viceroys endowed with large and somewhat ambiguous portions of royal power and established in seats of glittering splendor.

The next echelon was that of the *audiencias,* of which in the sixteenth century there were four in New Spain and five in Peru. Originally they were royal courts with direct access to the Council of the Indies and subject to its veto only; but the *audiencias* soon acquired administrative and political authority also, and they shared, or contested, those powers with the viceroys. More clearly subordinate to the viceroyalties were lesser jurisdictions—*presidencias* and captaincies general—that were deliberately created as administrative subdivisions of the larger territorial governments.

These were the main jurisdictions. Below them lay a range of inferior units, whose chief officers were usually appointed by the viceroys or *audiencias,* with the approval of the Council of the Indies, and only occasionally by the crown itself. And below them, the lowest unit of civil government was the municipal corporation, or *cabildo,* which was an urban jurisdiction of much greater importance in the hierarchy of royal government in Spanish America than its equivalent—the town or city—would prove to be in British America. Finally, in various lateral connections with the whole of this imperial hierarchy were several categories of investigating and superintending officials appointed in Spain to strengthen the crown's authority throughout its American territories.

This elaborate structure of royal government was neither altogether rational in its construction nor altogether efficient in its operation nor altogether comprehensive in its reach. There were gaps and clumsy overlaps in authority. Subordinate jurisdictions, especially in the remote territories, found many ways of ignoring the superior authorities; and corruption was widespread, at least at the lower ranges of the hierarchy. Yet despite these weaknesses, the Spanish empire did continue to function as a reasonably coherent state system, however inefficient its workings might appear to a modern analyst. For over three hundred years, it operated as a single legal jurisdiction whose ultimate power flowed from the monarchs in Spain. And this legal jurisdiction remained unchallenged. Of course there was resistance to this or that unpopular regulation and to the rule of any number of obnoxious officers sent out from Spain. But the form that resistance took was not openly organized political opposition to the state; it was evasion, the passive refusal to comply with unacceptable or unenforceable crown orders, a pattern of action that was familiarly described by the formula, "I obey but I do not execute."

There were evasions, and there were innumerable blockages in the flow of crown authority, but there was no organized and sustained opposition to the state in the colonial period of Spanish American history. No body of ideas was developed that would justify sustained opposition to the crown, and no cadre of leaders appeared who were experienced in challenging the authority of the state and motivated to do so. When in the end, more than three hundred years after its founding, Spain's empire in America succumbed to corruption, misgovernment, and rising democratic aspirations, there was no corps of native politicians fully capable of managing free governments and of creating responsible and stable self-government. Nor were the doctrines that shaped the Latin American independence movement of the early nineteenth century native to the culture. They were largely alien ideas that expressed only clumsily the particular needs of the Spanish-American people.

In all of this, the contrast with British America could hardly be sharper or more significant. There was never an effective structure of imperial government in the first British empire. The imperial authority of the British crown and of Parliament was scattered through half a dozen uncoordinated agencies of government, and it was never anything but superficial. It seldom penetrated much beyond the docks or the customs houses and its control of the American

PORTUGUESE CARRACKS OF THE EARLY SIXTEENTH CENTURY, PAINTING ATTRIBUTED TO CORNELIS ANTHONISZOON

These massive, high-built, unwieldy vessels designed for maximum freight capacity played a vital role in transoceanic shipping of the sixteenth century. The largest, over 1800 tons, could carry 700 passengers and a cargo of 900 tons. *(National Maritime Museum, Greenwich.)*

political system was weak. Yet there was organized resistance to this authority from the start. By the middle of the eighteenth century, resistance had grown into a sophisticated process of opposition politics and had bred politicians long experienced in local self-government. The transition to independence and to responsible self-government in British America was consequently smooth, and, once the War of Independence was concluded, entirely bloodless.

This stark contrast between the Spanish American and the British American patterns becomes even more vivid, and paradoxical, if one considers two underlying facts. It was Britain, whose imperial government was so weak, and not Spain, that had the advantage of easy communication with its American colonies. The British-American communities were located either in the easily accessible Caribbean island chain or along a narrow coastal strip on the North American mainland. By the early eighteenth century, after a hundred years of existence, the British settlements had barely reached the first falls of the eastern coastal rivers and hence were still in almost direct contact with the home country; even by the Revolution the British settlements had not yet crossed the Appalachian mountain barrier in significant numbers. Furthermore, the eighteenth century saw a great expansion of the British merchant fleet, which bore the main burden of communications, while the Spanish fleet declined. Yet it was Spain and not Britain that managed to keep tight control of its sprawling empire and whose governance penetrated deep into the daily life of remote communities.

Even more paradoxical is the fact that in the early years of the Spanish American empire there had existed institutions that could have developed into bases for just the kind of opposition politics that developed in North America. But these institutions, instead of maturing into centers of open competition with the state, withered and disappeared. At the start, for example, the most powerful figures in Latin America were the *adelantados*, feudal lords granted extraordinary powers by the crown to subjugate the American frontiers. Most of the famous *conquistadores* held both the title and the broad executive and judicial powers of the *adelantados*, and it was understood from the beginning that their powers, granted for several generations or in perpetuity, were essentially competitive with those of the crown. Yet few of the *adelantados* managed to transmit their authority to a second generation. The Spanish monarchs, ever fearful of the potential threat of these border chiefs, managed to eliminate them completely soon after the work of conquest was done. Similarly, the *encomiendas*, which in the sixteenth century constituted another potential threat to the overall authority of the state, were eliminated as bases of political competition. Transferred as an institution from Spain to America in 1502, the *encomienda* was a grant of the labor of a specific number of native Indians—in effect a gift of slaves or serfs— and the land they occupied. The crown had intended to protect the natives by charging the grantees with responsibility for the Indians' spiritual and physical well-being, but the *encomiendas* quickly became the instrument of the most vicious oppression. The crown, determined to eliminate the institution, gradually succeeded in reducing the powers of the 4000 or so *encomenderos*, draining away

SEVILLE, FIRST CAPITAL OF THE SPANISH-AMERICAN EMPIRE, BY
ALONZO SÁNCHEZ COELLO

Linked by short river routes and canals to the Atlantic, Seville prospered enormously in the sixteenth century. All shipping to and from America had to pass through the city. Its *Consulado*, a gild of merchant houses, enjoyed a monopoly of Spanish trade with the New World. In addition the city was the seat of the *Casa de Contratación*. (*Museo de America, Madrid; Mas/Art Reference Bureau.*)

their incomes and eliminating the heritability of the original grants. By the early eighteenth century the *encomienda* was no longer a political danger to the crown.

In similar ways the threat of other competing political authorities was eliminated or reduced. The provincial assemblies, gatherings of municipal notables summoned by the governors when funds were needed by the crown for its wars or when new policies were being introduced, contained the rudiments of popular legislatures or consultative bodies. But although in the sixteenth century about forty of these potentially important colonial assemblies were convened, some of which sought to defend local rights against the encroachments of crown officers, they never asserted their right to meet without royal orders or otherwise challenged the crown's definition of their limited role. The possibility that lay open to the members of these bodies, to form themselves into one or more parliaments in the tradition of the Spanish *Cortes,* was never developed. Similarly the independence of the municipal corporations also narrowed and weakened as the royal government took over appointment to the offices and laid down regulations of the most minute detail for governing these local communities.

Why had all of these semi-independent agencies and institutions weakened or been absorbed into the state apparatus? Why had opposition politics died almost at birth in Spanish America while in British America it grew so quickly and so strongly? There is no simple explanation for this, but there were certain circumstances in Spanish America that form at least part of an explanation, and these circumstances contrast sharply with the conditions that shaped the development of the British-American communities. With this contrast in mind one can observe some of the fundamental elements in early North American history which are otherwise lost to sight.

From the very start the crown itself—Ferdinand and Isabella in the first instance—actively sponsored exploration and settlement. Even before Columbus's discovery had been made the monarchy had asserted its rule over such conquered lands, and not merely as commercial regulation but as territorial government in depth. The Spanish monarchs declared the whole of America to be a separate kingdom of the crown of Castile, its native peoples direct subjects of the crown and its governmental jurisdictions subordinate agencies of the crown. This assertion was powerfully supported. The highest moral agency of the Western world, the papacy, reinforced it. Various papal bulls and encyclicals located the responsibility for the welfare of the natives, which meant primarily the task of converting them to Christianity, in the Castilian monarch. From that central Christian responsibility, jurists and theologians developed a massive body of legal, political, and theological commentary that strongly reinforced the claims of the Spanish monarch to personal rule in America and justified it in detail. The whole of Latin American political culture was shaped by the crown's dominance and by the flood of writing that rationalized it. There were no competing intellectual centers from which contrary ideas could develop. The Catholic church engrossed the intellectual life of Latin America, and it was a church that was conservative in doctrine and royalist in politics. Far from Spanish America

WORKING THE FABULOUS SILVER MINE
AT POTOSÍ

An imaginative depiction by De Bry (see p. 7) of the forced labor of Indian miners, thousands of whom perished in that "mouth of hell" 16,000 feet above sea level. The wealth produced at Potosí for over two centuries after the mine's discovery in 1545 was stupendous, but the cost in human suffering by whole populations of helpless natives, slaving underground by dim candlelight for days on end, was immeasureably greater. The city of Potosí itself (in modern Bolivia) had a population of 120,000 by 1572 but remained a tumultuous mining camp throughout the colonial period, swarming with gamblers, prostitutes, and adventurers of all kinds. *(Rare Book Division, The New York Public Library, Astor, Lenox and Tilden Foundations.)*

proving to be a legitimate refuge for religious dissenters, as British America would become, it developed into a more tightly controlled bastion of Catholic orthodoxy than Spain itself. Dissenters and heretics of all kinds were barred by law from emigrating to America.

Yet declarations and political theory do not in themselves create political realities. The crown's overwhelmingly powerful role in territorial government did not succeed by mere assertion. There was something in the situation in Spanish America that guaranteed a welcome for the crown's supremacy and that helped stifle competitive institutions at their birth. If one turns from institutions to population characteristics and asks what groups had the capacity to maintain an active opposition to the crown and that would have had an interest in organizing such opposition, the situation becomes clearer.

There were four principal social categories in the Spanish American population, of which the most numerous by far was that of the native Indians. The Aztecs, the Incas, and the other native Americans whom the Spanish encountered were advanced people in certain ways; but to Europeans of the time they were primitive, and they were helpless before the onslaught of the Spanish conquerers. People in good social discipline, numerous, and stable in location, the native Americans quickly became a mass laboring population, and they were incapable of organizing their own political institutions to speak against the state.

At the other extreme from the native Indians were the major imperial office-holders—the viceroys, *audiencia* judges, high church officials, and governors—who might most readily have created areas of independent authority. But the crown's policies in recruiting and controlling these officers prevented them from moving in that direction. Almost all high officers of the state who served in Spanish America in the three hundred years of the colonial period were peninsular Spaniards—that is, men born in the Iberian Peninsula, unaffiliated with American interests, and committed to returning to Spain after completing their tour of duty abroad. The figures are striking. In the entire colonial period there were only 4 American-born viceroys, and of the 602 other high civil officers whose careers have been traced, only 14 were Creoles, that is, native Americans of European descent. The church hierarchy was similarly recruited: of 706 Spanish-American bishops and archbishops, 601 were peninsular Spaniards. And as if recruitment alone were not enough, controls were devised to discipline any possible independence these officials might have developed. Their tenure in office was strictly limited; they were circulated within the imperial system to prevent their acquiring too strong an identification with any particular locality; they were dependent on the crown treasury for their salaries; and they were subjected to rigorous scrutinies of their conduct of office.

A third group was that of the Creoles, the American-born leaders of Spanish descent. Under favorable conditions they might well have provided the initiative and organization for a vigorous political life, for, as opposed to the Indians they were politically sophisticated, and as opposed to the high state officers they were closely identified with American interests. But their numbers and social characteristics shaped a dependent political role. Of the total population of more than 9 million in Spanish America in the 1570s, only 118,000 or 1.25 percent were entirely of European ancestry. And indeed in the entire three hundred years of the colonial period, only 300,000 Spaniards emigrated to America. The contrast with British America is startling. By the mid-1660s, barely fifty years after the first permanent settlement, approximately 200,000 emigrants had left the British Isles for America, a yearly average in the first century of colonization five times that of the Spanish. The occupational character of the Creole population in Spanish America followed directly from their numbers. A thin overlay on a large, stable population of natives, these Americans of European descent never constituted the mass base of the social structure. They filled the upper strata of the American communities: they were landowners, clerics, army officers, and merchants. Their identity as a ruling class, and consequently their well being, derived not from their American birth but from their European descent, which distinguished them racially from the mass of the population. As a consequence, their basic interests were always associated with Europe; they continued to identify themselves with Spain, which was the source of their status, wealth, and power.

Finally, there were the blacks, who were imported as slaves and never acquired an active political role; and, politically more important, the large segment of the population that was racially mixed. By the 1570s the racially mixed elements constituted approximately 2.5 percent of the entire populace; by the end of the colonial period that figure had risen to over 30 percent (another striking contrast to British America, where the racially mixed population was numerically insignificant). There was a great variety of racial combinations, but the most important element by far was the *mestizos,* those of mixed European and Indian ancestry. Yet, though numerous and though many of them passed into the Creole population, the *mestizos* in general were socially inferior to the dominant Spanish elements and constituted a lower middle class of small farmers and shopkeepers. Social pressures led them away from asserting their identities through politics and toward the kind of escape that came from fitting themselves as inconspicuously as possible into the situation as it existed. It would take a profound cultural evolution to release their suppressed aspirations and free them to assume effective political roles. When that took place, and only then, the colonial era of Spanish-American history was over.

These population characteristics, utterly different from the characteristics of the British-American world, go far toward explaining the failure of a free competitive political system to develop in colonial Spanish America despite the availability of institutions that originally could have supported such politics. The small elite of high state officials was bound to Spain in every way. The Creoles were a small self-conscious ruling class whose well being, in the great sea of native Indians, blacks, and racially mixed, depended on a continuing identification with the sources of authority in Europe. Only the racially mixed were disposed to move toward political autonomy, but through most of three centuries they lacked the self-esteem, the numbers, and the experience to devise effective political weapons against the overwhelming Spanish establishment.

The Release of Enterprise

In all of these circumstances and conditions, the British experience in America was altogether different. England's entry into the Western world was the very opposite of Spain's. Where Spain had been swift, England was slow; where Spain had been deliberate and decisive, England was muddled in purpose. For Spain, America almost immediately yielded immense wealth; for England, it created, at the start at least, more losses than profits. At no point were the differences more extreme and more consequential than at the very beginning of exploration and settlement.

For no less than fifty years, while Spain was conquering and exploiting vast areas of Central America and South America, England did nothing to develop its claim to North America. That claim had been established in 1497–98 when John Cabot, commissioned by Henry VII, had discovered and begun the exploration of Newfoundland, Labrador, and Nova Scotia. His son Sebastian had continued the exploration into the Hudson Bay region of Canada in 1508–9, but throughout the reign of Henry VIII (1509–47) neither the crown nor private enterprise showed any interest in developing these distant territories. The only English contact with America that remained through these years was the work of fishermen from the west country of England—Cornwall, Devonshire, Dorset-shire—who, together with fishermen from France, Spain, and Portugal, had begun to exploit the wealth of the Grand Banks off Newfoundland and the coastal waters around the mouth of the Saint Lawrence. They became familiar with the southern Canadian and northern New England coasts and built crude shacks for their immediate convenience during the fishing seasons, but they made no attempt to establish permanent settlements or otherwise assert England's claim to the land.

Then suddenly, in the early 1550s, the situation was transformed, and in this sudden reversal are to be found the beginnings of British colonization. This development was complex, and it is as important to understand what did not happen as it is to know what did happen. For there was no sudden eruption of interest in overseas settlement as such and there was no sudden determination on the part of England to assert its claim to America. Instead there were two basic shifts in orientation, both of which would eventually involve colonization but neither of which was originally directed to that goal. The first shift was in England's economy, the second in its international relations.

England's prosperity in the first half of the sixteenth century had been based on the growing European market for its raw wool and woolen cloth. The main sources of capital in England and the most skilled entrepreneurs had been in-volved in this well-established trade; the whole of the economy, as a result, had been locked into the Antwerp market, in what is now Belgium, through which England's woolen products had flowed to their eventual European consumers and which had provided the necessary mechanisms of international monetary exchange. Through the reign of Henry VIII more and more capital and labor had been involved in this dominant commercial enterprise, more and more arable land had been turned to pasturage, and England's financial stability had become increasingly dependent on Antwerp. But then in the late 1540s the financial and commercial structure began to weaken. By 1550 the Antwerp market was sat-urated; and when in 1551 a sudden revaluation of sterling upset the financial basis of the wool trade, the entire economic mechanism centering on Antwerp collapsed and with it England's economic stability. Cloth exports fell off 35 per-cent within a year and the money market was thrown into turmoil. The merchants were forced to reconsider the whole of their activities. The old patterns of trade were no longer reliable. New markets would have to be found, new routes of trade devised, and capital risked in ways that a previous generation would have thought wildly speculative.

Changes in England's international position helped channel these suddenly mobilized energies. Antagonism with France had dominated England's policies through the reign of Henry VIII, and in this rivalry Spain had been England's natural ally. As a result England had been willing to respect Spain's claim to the whole of the Western Hemisphere, which had been set out in papal bulls in 1493 and in the Spanish-Portuguese Treaty of Tordesillas (1494), assuring Spain of its title to all of the Western Hemisphere 370 leagues west of the Cape Verde Islands. England had found it diplomatically useful to support this claim, at least tacitly, and the support was confirmed by the marriage of Queen Mary (1553–58) to Philip II of Spain.

But the accession of Queen Elizabeth in 1558 began a reversal in international relations as England's Protestantism began to dominate its foreign policy. By the 1560s it was clear that Spain threatened England's independence as a Protestant nation and that England's long-range interests in Europe lay in the support of the rebellious Protestants in France and of the Netherlands struggling to free themselves from Spanish rule. From an ally of Spain, England had become an enemy, and while England felt too weak until the 1580s to engage in open warfare with the great imperial power, the country had every reason to want to harass and plunder Spanish territories in any way possible.

ELIZABETH I, AGE 41

As shrewd in politics as she was cautious in finance, Elizabeth sponsored England's overseas expansion by subtle means until she was ready to challenge Spain directly in 1585. (*National Portrait Gallery, London.*)

Thus, impelled by a sudden economic need to break out of the safe, conservative commerce of earlier years, and no longer hesitant to attack Spain's overseas territories, England entered a new phase in its history—but not by plunging directly and immediately into colonization. Its response to the economic and diplomatic shifts took several forms, and only eventually, and almost incidentally, did it involve overseas settlement. In response to the new economic pressures European merchants were expelled from the realm, and English merchants were favored in the conduct of trade. State policies forced land that had been converted to sheep grazing back into tillage, limited textile production, tightened corporate control over commerce, and blocked entry into trade by newcomers. Above all, the commercial community and its landed associates poured capital into a search for new kinds of overseas commerce and for new and distant markets independent of continental middlemen.

Expeditions that were sent to poach on the Portuguese preserves in Africa were profitable enough to justify the forming of the Guinea Company in 1555.

In the same year a highly capitalized expedition seeking a northeastern route to Asia through Lapland made sufficient contact with Russia to stimulate the formation of the Muscovy Company. In 1579 the Eastland Company organized English trade to the Baltic; in 1581 the Levant Company was created to control England's commerce with the Middle East; and a series of contacts with India and Southeast Asia led to the creation of the East India Company in 1600.

These were the more legitimate and official enterprises. During the same years, risk capital, some of it drawn secretly from royal sources, went into semi-piratical raids on Spanish commerce and Spanish shipping. These enterprises began in 1562 when John Hawkins of Plymouth broke the Spanish trade monopoly in the West Indies and the Spanish Main with the first of a series of quasi-legal and highly lucrative peddling voyages, the third of which, in 1567, led to open conflict with the Spanish. Francis Drake took up the challenge at that point and began what proved to be twenty years of wildly adventurous raids on Spanish colonial properties, the culmination of which was his famous circumnavigation of the globe in 1577–80, a joint-stock enterprise which yielded, among other results, 4600 percent profit to the shareholders.

By then English interest in the Western Hemisphere was rising, not primarily as a location for English colonies but as a route to Asian markets. The Cabots' explorations were recalled, and new information, commercial and geographical, flowed in to help justify the enthusiasm of a group of adventurers from the west of England, led by Sir Humphrey Gilbert, determined to find a northwestern passage through the Western Hemisphere into the Far East. In 1565 the Privy Council heard a formal debate on possible new routes. The Muscovy merchants, naturally enough, urged endorsement of efforts to find an *eastern* passage, north of Siberia, and to exploit the Baltic hinterland; the westcountry gentry, long familiar with the North American coastal waters, urged expeditions to the *west*, through the north of what is now Canada. Gilbert and the westerners were

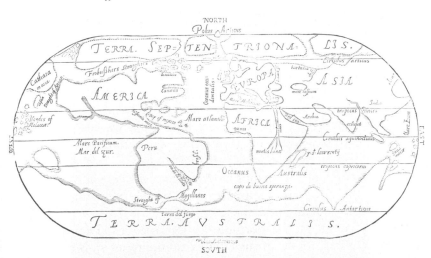

GEORGE BEST'S MAP OF THE WORLD, PUBLISHED IN HIS "TRUE DIS-COURSE OF THE LATE VOYAGES . . . UNDER THE CONDUCT OF MARTIN FROBISHER . . ." (1578)

Best, a shipmate of Frobisher's on his three voyages in search of the northwest passage, here shows "Frobussher's Straights" (which in fact is a dead-end sound near the entrance of Hudson Bay) as the hoped-for passage straight to China (Cathaia). *(By permission of the Houghton Library, Harvard University.)*

defeated in that debate, but with their support, in 1576–78, an enterprising mariner, Martin Frobisher, financed by a London group headed by a merchant, Michael Lok, led three expeditions to what would become known as Hudson Bay and organized the short-lived Company of Cathay in response to the false reports of gold that were carried back. There were continuous frustrations for all of these western initiatives, but the search for the northwest passage went on, yielding in the end, after vain and desperate efforts to get through the ice and snow of the Canadian wilderness, a reasonably clear picture of that region of the globe.

Within all of these overseas enterprises—the semipiratical raids on Spanish territory, the launching of new commercial companies, the probing of new routes to the northeast of England and northwest to the Canadian wilds—the idea of colonization slowly developed. In his appearance before the Privy Council in 1565 Gilbert had suggested the value of colonies as way stations along the proposed routes to the Far East, and in 1578 he sought and received a crown patent for establishing a colony in America.

Gilbert's efforts of 1578 to establish a colony in New England or Nova Scotia—the first English effort to colonize in the Western Hemisphere—failed almost

SIR WALTER RALEIGH AND HIS SON, 1602

Raleigh was an accomplished poet, soldier, courtier, and politician, and like many intellectuals of his time he was fascinated by geographical exploration and by the possibilities of overseas settlements—in Ireland as well as in America. He helped draw into the leadership of exploration and colonization the interrelated landed gentry of England's West Country. The failure of his Roanoke settlement showed the impossibility of financing settlements in America by individual or family efforts. *(National Portrait Gallery, London.)*

before it began. His small exploratory fleet was scattered by storms and diverted by the lure of privateering. Yet in the process of launching this first colonizing expedition, Gilbert acquired valuable experience in attempting to finance such ventures. He also engaged the enthusiasm of his gifted half-brother, Sir Walter Raleigh, in such ventures as these and drew into this realm of enterprise the two Richard Hakluyts, experts on overseas geography, who became important propagandists of colonization. The younger Hakluyt's *Discourse of Western Planting* (1584) shows the mingling of motives that existed in this advanced circle of enthusiasts. It was England's duty, Hakluyt argued, to Christianize the American pagans, especially since an American colony would provide a base for attacks on Spanish lands and Spanish treasure ships. More important would be the long-term economic gains from American colonies; they could supply England with exotic goods otherwise brought from Spain and create new markets for English consumer goods while at the same time drawing off England's unemployed workers and turning their labor to advantage. New routes to Asia, new weapons against Spain, a new source of exotic supplies, and a new market for English goods as well as a new use for England's "surplus" population—all this would justify England's support for colonization.

Raleigh's and Hakluyt's ideas were not as yet widely shared, and they in no way described state policy. In 1584, after Gilbert had died on a return voyage from Newfoundland, Queen Elizabeth transferred his patent to Raleigh, but she kept her government from directly supporting his plans for colonization. She made a minor contribution to financing a new expedition that he planned and gave his enterprise her personal blessing, but otherwise her government did nothing to help launch or sustain the famous "lost colony" that Raleigh established in America in 1585. This one English-American settlement of the sixteenth century was thus of necessity almost entirely the *private* undertaking of a group of merchants and gentlemen from the west of England.

The history of this first English colony in the Western Hemisphere is quickly told. In three successive years separate groups of settlers were landed on Roanoke Island, a heavily wooded spot off the coast of North Carolina. The first group, 108 men, arrived there in 1585. They quickly fell out with the natives, ran through their food supplies as they explored the North Carolina coastal waters, and returned to England hurriedly the next year with Francis Drake when he unexpectedly appeared on his way home from a successful raid on the West Indies. Later that year—1586—the second group, 18 men, was left behind by a party sent out to relieve the original group, but this forlorn and helpless crew was soon slaughtered by the Indians. The island was therefore deserted when, the next summer, 1587, the third and main contingent, consisting of 117 men, women, and children, arrived under Governor John White. What happened to this largest and best equipped group of Raleigh's settlers has never been discovered. White was obliged to return quickly to England to speed on more supplies, but the threat of open war with Spain and the attractions of privateering

INDIAN VILLAGE OF SECOTON AND A CHIEF'S WIFE
AND DAUGHTER

These watercolors are from a portfolio of
accurate and superbly colored scenes of Indian
life and the natural environment made by John
White on his voyages to Raleigh's "Virginia"
in 1585 and 1587. Note the three plantings of
corn, and the doll in English dress held by the
child. *(Copyright The British Museum.)*

kept relief vessels from reaching the colony. It was only in 1590 that White
finally managed to return, to find the settlers gone. Apparently they had moved
off to Croatoan Island, to the south in the outer banks of Pamlico Sound, and
White could not follow them there. Their disappearance marks the end of
Raleigh's efforts at colonization.

A fumbling, failing, almost pathetic affair, all of this, next to the bold and
hugely successful first thrusts of the Spanish in America. Yet Raleigh's Roanoke
venture is as revealing of the basic conditions that would later, in the seventeenth
century, shape the successful English settlements as it is of the limitations that
defeated colonization under Elizabeth.

Personnel and the Role of the State

Several things of permanent importance had become clear during these earliest and least successful years of English colonization in America. In England, it
developed, there was a leadership group available for colonization quite different
from the Spanish *conquistadores*, "drunk with a heroic and brutal dream," as a
Spanish poet later described them. Where the Spanish conquerors were the sons
of impoverished farmers and townsmen, many of them illiterate, the leaders of
English overseas enterprise—Gilbert, Raleigh, Grenville, Hawkins, Drake—were
the well-educated younger sons of the westcountry gentry, bred in secure landed
establishments, familiar with the sea from childhood, barred by the laws favoring
eldest sons from inheriting family properties, and eager somehow to reestablish

themselves on the land in the same genteel condition they had known before.

Second, it was clear that there was in England a mass of unemployed, uprooted, and mobile laborers available for emigration to overseas colonies. London was swollen with displaced farm workers (its population rose from 75,000 in 1500 to 200,000 in 1600); the countryside was swarming with the unemployed migrant farmhands called by contemporaries "sturdy beggars"; and in the centers of the wool industry—the west country and East Anglia (Essex, Suffolk, and Norfolk)—underemployment was already generating the discontent that would express itself forcefully in the religious protest of Puritanism. Elizabethans spoke of the "multitude of increase in our people." Responsible officials were convinced that England was overpopulated and its well-being threatened by a parasite labor force that consumed more than it contributed to the general fund of wealth: "Our land hath not milk sufficient in the breast thereof to nourish all those children which it hath brought forth." For many, the most attractive remedy was colonization and emigration. But though the population of England and Wales rose from just over 3 million in 1550 to just over 4 million in 1600 to 5.2 million in 1695, and in the next 25 years increased by another 800,000, there was no absolute "surplus" of people, as seventeenth-century English analysts came to realize. The sense of overpopulation was created by the widespread displacement of a mass population and an exceptionally high degree of geographical mobility that resulted from rapid economic growth, particularly in certain manufactures and in commerce, from inflation, and from the commercialization of agriculture. These developments—which made available for recruitment a mass of ordinary farm and town workers first in England, then in Wales, Scotland, and Ireland— were crucial to the early peopling of British North America. No such economic and demographic transformation took place in Spain, and domestic recruitment

THE CHEAPSIDE-CORNHILL DISTRICT OF LONDON, 1658

From this swarming urban concentration came hundreds of
emigrants, joining a multitude of others from the countryside to
settle England's first colonies in America. (From William Faithorne
and Richard Newcourt's *Exact Delineation of the Cities of London
and Westminster . . .*)

of an overseas population was as a consequence relatively weak there through the entire three centuries of Spanish-American imperialism.

Third, it became evident that there was capital available in sizable amounts for investment in overseas ventures, as well as entrepreneurial interest in mobilizing that capital and directing it to profitable uses in colonization. The costs of financing the Roanoke voyages and the first efforts at colonization had been borne almost entirely by the westcountry gentry, but their resources were clearly inadequate to support further, larger-scale efforts. In 1589 Raleigh transferred control of the Virginia enterprise to a London business syndicate headed by Sir Thomas Smyth, one of the most powerful merchants of the age. The capital available to these merchants was far greater than that of the westcountry gentry, and it would be these men of business who would launch the first new wave of colonization in the early seventeenth century.

It had become clear, too, that when efforts at colonization would be resumed (as plans and probes in the later years of Elizabeth's reign indicated they would be), the role of the crown would continue to be minimal. The crown would legalize exploration and settlement, and it would exert some supervision of the plans that were made, but it would initiate nothing and organize nothing, nor would it sustain or reinforce any enterprise that was undertaken. More important, the English crown had no desire to extend its direct rule of overseas territories conquered or settled by Englishmen. Some form of government would be provided, but it would not be crown government in depth. The burden of governing colonies, like the burden of financing them, would be borne not by the crown but by the entrepreneurs of settlement or by the settlers themselves. Colonial government, at the start at least, would therefore of necessity be self-government of some sort, and the imperial organization as it evolved would be a superstructure, an overlay imposed on semi-independent units of local government.

Finally, English colonizers would bring with them what might be called an ideology of colonization—a framework of attitudes and ideas concerning permanent overseas colonies, the character of colonists, and the relations of colonies to the surrounding environment—that was strikingly different from the ideas and attitudes the Spanish had brought with them and which they had put into practice in Central and South America.

The Concept of Settlement: Ireland and America

In both Spain and England the original conception of colonies had been based on prior experience; but these experiences and the ideas and attitudes they provoked could hardly have been more different. Both of these quite different models fitted smoothly into the different circumstances that the two peoples found in the Western Hemisphere, and they therefore had the most profound effect on the origins of modern American civilization. Spain's earliest experience with colonization had been gained in the reconquest of the Spanish peninsula from the sophisticated Moslems, while England's first successful large-scale efforts at colonization took place—and were still taking place when Raleigh sent his experimental colony to North Carolina—in Ireland.

For *Ireland,* strange as it may appear, was the scene of England's first concerted and sustained efforts at overseas colonization, and these efforts, which involved almost every one of the leaders of the Roanoke enterprise, took place before and during the years when the first American venture was under way. The colonization of Ireland, which at the time had far greater impact on public awareness in England than the American settlement, provided England with its model for permanent overseas settlements, just as Spain's reconquest of Iberia created a pattern for all future Spanish colonization.

In Elizabethan England there was nothing remarkable in thinking of Ireland and America as equivalent centers of overseas expansion and in transferring ideas of colonization from one to the other. The two areas were linked geographically in Elizabethans' minds. As they looked out at the world beyond England they saw a single arc of overseas territories suitable for colonization that swept north and west from Britain itself, enclosing Ireland, Newfoundland, and the mainland coast of North America, from the fishing shores of Nova Scotia and New England south to the outer banks of North Carolina. So Ireland could be described in a travel book of 1617 as "this famous island in the Virginia sea." "Virginia" and Ireland were naturally associated with each other as points on this outer periphery of the English world, and it was natural for the two regions to be developed together. Raleigh in fact concentrated his main effort at colonization not in America, interested though he was in that region, but in Cork, Ireland, where he struggled to develop a 42,000-acre estate by populating it with English settlers. At every step in Gilbert's career, Ireland had been a prior choice to America. Ralph Lane, the commander at Roanoke, had been recruited from an equivalent post he held in Ireland. And all of them—Lane, Raleigh, Gilbert, and the other leaders—brought with them to America notions derived from the peculiar situation they found in Ireland.

Henry VIII's failure to bind the Irish chiefs to him by feudal ties and gradually to infuse elements of English law and religion into the population at large had led, in 1566, to military conquest. Only by force of arms, it was felt, could England dominate Ireland, which it was feared would be a natural stepping stone for any invasion of England. And once conquered by force, Ireland could be controlled, it was agreed, only by a peculiar kind of colonization.

For the English, the native Irish were a strange and dangerous race. The English could never cease marveling at what they took to be the savagery, belligerence, and invincibility of "the wild Irish," whom they described as "unreasonable beasts . . . living without any knowledge of God or good manners, in common with their goods, cattle, women, children." They found that they could not sub-

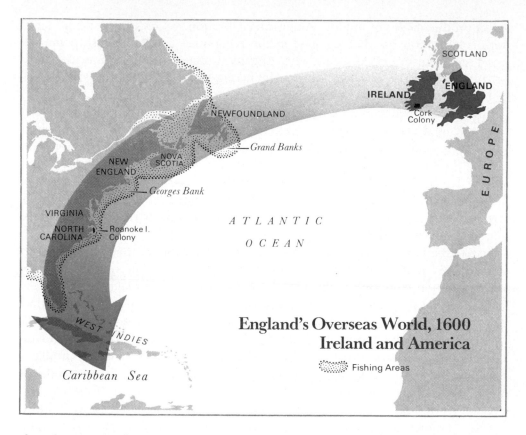

England's Overseas World, 1600 Ireland and America

Fishing Areas

due these "naked rogues in woods and bogs, whom hounds can scarce follow, and much less men" and reduce them to a useful labor force. Primitive brutes, as the Elizabethans saw them, manifestly pagan, living by codes and in tribal arrangements the English could not understand, the Irish could not be dealt with as the Spanish had dealt with the sophisticated Moslems or the Aztecs or the Incas. They could not be pacified and absorbed into a new frontier or colonial culture. Conquest must mean destruction—the devastation of native communities; and control must mean the repopulation of the land by the English themselves.

So was born the idea of "the pale of settlement," a physical separation between English colonists and barbarous natives, and with it the concept of the "plantation." It was this model of colonization, conceived of as early as the 1570s in Ireland, that dominated English attitudes to permanent overseas settlements and that was felt to be as relevant in North America as it was in southwestern Ireland where it was applied in a great colonization effort of 1585-98. A "plantation" meant a transplantation, a replantation of complete units of English society—the wholesale removal of English men and women to foreign lands. There, like Roman colonists, they would reproduce their original communities and their original way of life as closely as possible, and not merely subjugate and rule the natives. The result would be a "Nova Britannia," not merely a conquest; a displacement of native populations, not merely a reduction of them to one element in a complex colonial society; and the erection of formal barriers to be breached only as the natives might lose their original identities, adopt English law, English religion, and the ordinary ways of English life, and merge into the dominant culture.

It was no grand vision, this idea of overseas plantations, but a practical resolution of problems the English faced in their first sustained encounter with an alien native population. It was an idea that came naturally to be applied to the new American settlements that were quickly founded after 1604, when peace was concluded with Spain and when the expansionist impulses that had been building up steadily since 1550 were fully released.

Financial Limitations and the "Starving Times"

England's lunge into overseas enterprise in the reigns of James I (1603–25) and his son Charles I (1625–49) was spectacular. The famous settlements at Jamestown and at Plymouth and Boston, the latter quickly fanning out to settlements throughout New England, were only fragments of a great mosaic of efforts that reached into almost every part of the globe, that involved hundreds of thousands of Englishmen of all descriptions, and that cost millions of pounds sterling. In this great expansion, the chief center of colonization was again Ireland, this time Ulster, in the northeastern part of that island. A half-million acres of land were initially offered to prospective "planters" in Ulster, and large grants were acquired by the London city government and the largest gild corporations of the city. After the Irish rebellion of 1641 (which many likened to the Indian rebellion of 1622 in Virginia), 11 million more acres were cleared of their native inhabitants, 30,000 of whom were sold into slavery and the rest driven beyond the English pale. In all, from 1589 to 1689 approximately 100,000 Englishmen and Scotsmen were "planted" in Ireland alone, a relocated population in this one small corner of greater Britain equal to the total number of Spanish who migrated to the whole of Central and South America in the first century of Spanish colonization.

Yet the Ulster plantation was only one, if the most extensive, of the colonization efforts of the time. Besides Ireland, and besides Virginia and Massachusetts, English settlements were established in Bermuda, in the Caribbean (Providence Island, Barbados, Saint Christopher, Nevis, Montserrat, Antigua), in Newfoundland, in Canada, in Nova Scotia, and on the mainland coast of South America. In addition, fragile contacts with India were developed first into flourishing trading "factories" and then into the beginning of the network of political control that would eventually cover much of the Indian subcontinent.

In this global context, the first settlements on the mainland of North America were relatively small undertakings, and their early histories become understandable only in terms of the pattern of the greater whole. For while these American communities would ultimately acquire a unique historical importance, originally they shared characteristics common to the rest of these earliest seventeenth-century enterprises. And of these common characteristics none was more important than the way in which they were financed.

Whatever their founders' ultimate dreams may have been, these earliest English colonies—whether in Newfoundland or Barbados, Ulster, Plymouth, or Virginia—were of necessity financed at the start by profit-seeking joint-stock companies. Eleven commercial companies bore the main financial burden of the settlements launched before 1640. The capitalization of these eleven companies (an estimated £13 million) was created by the sale of stock to a remarkably broad range of the English population. Thousands invested—landowners as well as merchants, people of ordinary means as well as those of wealth. And the management of the funds generated by these investments was, for the most part, in the hands of businessmen who worked not only within the usual constraints of business operations but also under two very special pressures; and these pressures explain much of the hardship and tragedy of life in the earliest American settlements.

First, the joint stocks—the initial capital funds—of these ventures were not expected to endure. Unlike modern joint-stock companies, these colonizing organizations were not meant to survive beyond a single undertaking. Shareholders did not expect to leave their funds in these companies and draw a steady income in dividends from them, but rather to benefit from the quick liquidation of the entire enterprise at the end of a single voyage or a set number of years, at which time the original capital plus whatever profits had accumulated would be distributed. Whether there would be any further investments beyond this initial one would depend on the business prospect when this complete division of the company's assets was made. The settlers, many of whom were in effect employees of these companies for a stated term of years, were consequently placed under great pressure to produce an immediate profit for the company. If they failed to ship back tangible proof of the financial value of the settlement, they would be cut off to fend for themselves as best they could. As a consequence, instead of searching carefully into the strange American environment, they spent time scrabbling for evidence of gold in every shallow stream, searching for routes to the Pacific Ocean around the bend of every broad river, and plunging almost suicidally into the backcountry to verify garbled Indian rumors of great cities or of vast sources of furs or precious metals.

The pressure on the settlers was further intensified by the technical fact that the legal liability of stockholders in these early joint-stock companies was unlimited. The backers of the settlements were personally liable, without limit, for any debts the settlement companies might incur, and they were therefore extremely sensitive to the possibility of failure. They had no choice but to abandon doubtful enterprises as quickly as possible.

The result was desperation and starvation, at times complete chaos, in these first colonies, and bankruptcy in the companies that first colonized mainland North America. For there were only three possible sources of quick profits: surface resources of great value in proportion to weight and bulk that might simply be lifted into boats and sent back to the investors; a docile native population that might be organized quickly into labor gangs to dig out less accessible resources; and the discovery of new routes to rich, exotic markets. None of these possibilities proved realistic on the coasts of North America, and as a consequence in the early years the life-sustaining supplies, after the first shipments, were withheld from the settlements and one after another the companies failed. Sheer accident provided most of the profits that actually accrued at the start. In Bermuda, for example, ambergris, a secretion of whales used in making perfume and medicine, was found in large quantities; a shipment worth £10,000 saved the Bermuda Company, which later profited steadily from tobacco production. Similarly, the Providence Island Company had the good fortune to capture a Spanish treasure ship worth £50,000.

Such lucky accidents were rare, however. Almost every one of the companies that financed settlements in British North America failed, sooner or later, and as they did so the original investors sought desperately to find secondary sources of profit. Some of the stockholders, seeking to recover their losses, funded "magazines"—stores of goods to be sold at high prices to the desperate settlers. Some set up separately financed enterprises: glass and silk were favored in Virginia. Others attempted to develop "private plantations," that is, personal estates and jurisdictions in the new land given to them in place of the missing profits. The Virginia Company alone created fifty of these private domains. But few of these secondary enterprises succeeded. Perhaps the most successful subordinate joint stock created within the Virginia Company was the fund established to send over a hundred "maids" to Jamestown "to be made wives of." The investors in this venture realized 47 percent profit on their shares when they sold the women's work contracts to the colonists.

As the financial prospects dimmed, the investors withdrew altogether from the ventures. Often the colonists, cut off by their backers, found the transition to self-sustained community life desperately difficult. Even in the best of circumstances the first inhabitants of Jamestown or Bermuda or Plymouth would have had a shock in adjusting to the wilderness environment. Forced to search for sources of immediate profit while neglecting some of the most elemental provisions for survival, many found the struggle unendurable, and succumbed—to despair, to the ravages of disease, and to the harassment of hostile natives.

The narratives of the first settlements make painful reading. There was heroism, but there was murderous selfishness as well; there was industry, but also laziness and at times suicidal inertia. Death and misery were everywhere. It is perhaps not surprising that the best organized and most successful of the earliest communities were those dominated by passionate religious convictions. For only the transcendent goals, the fierce determination, and the inner certainty of the Pilgrim and Puritan leaders could withstand the disintegrating effects of the "starving times."

Suggested Readings

The discovery and conquest of central and south America by Spain had been the subject of some of the greatest narrative histories written in the nineteenth century, notably William H. Prescott's *History of the Conquest of Mexico* (1843) and his *Conquest of Peru* (1847). This tradition of sweeping, dramatic narratives continues in our own time in the writings of Samuel E. Morison, particularly in his biography of Columbus, *Admiral of the Ocean Sea* (2 vol. and 1 vol. eds., 1942, condensed as *Christopher Columbus, Mariner*, 1956), and his *The European Discovery of America: The Southern Voyages, AD 1492–1616* (1974), a volume crowded with maps and photographs that was written after the author retraced the routes of the Spanish discoverers by ship and plane. John H. Parry has sketched the general development of European expansion, geographical discovery, and initial overseas settlements in two very readable books, *Europe and a Wider World, 1415–1715* (1949) and *The Age of Reconnaissance* (1963).

There are several good introductory histories of Spanish America in the colonial period: Charles Gipson, *Spain in America* (1966); Hubert Herring, *A History of Latin America from the Beginnings to the Present* (3d ed., 1968), Parts I, II; Bailey W. Diffie, *Latin American Civilization: The Colonial Period* (1945); John H. Parry, *The Spanish Seaborne Empire* (1966); and Salvador de Madariaga, *Rise of the Spanish American Empire* (1947). An equivalent history of the Portuguese-American empire is C. R. Boxer, *The Portuguese Seaborne Empire, 1415–1825* (1969); on the French empire in America, see George M. Wrong, *The Rise and Fall of New France* (2 vols., 1928). The best general account of the administrative and constitutional history of Spanish America is Clarence H. Haring, *The Spanish Empire in America* (1947). See also John L. Phelan, "Authority and Flexibility in the Spanish Imperial Bureaucracy," *Administrative Science Quarterly*, 5 (1960–61), 47–65; and for a theoretical analysis of the same subject in sociological terms, see Margali Sarfatti, *Spanish Bureaucratic-Patrimonialism in America* (1966). The underlying ideas of empire are described in John H. Parry, *The Spanish Theory of Empire in the Sixteenth Century* (1940).

On economic history, there are two classic works: Clarence H. Haring, *Trade and Navigation between Spain and the Indies . . .* (1918) and Earl J. Hamilton, *American Treasure and the Price Revolution in Spain, 1501–1650* (1934). In addition, see Peter J. Bakewell, *Silver Mining and Society in Colonial Mexico . . .* (1971); Woodrow W. Borah, *New Spain's Century of Depression* (Ibero-Americana, 35, 1951); and relevant chapters in John Lynch, *Spain under the Hapsburgs* (2 vols., 1964–69).

There several studies that concentrate on the particular topics emphasized in this chapter. On race relations and population characteristics: Charles Gipson, *The Aztecs Under Spanish Rule* (1964); John H. Rowe, "The Incas under Spanish Colonial Institutions," *Hispanic American Historical Review*, 37 (1957), 156–91; Lesley B. Simpson, *The Encomienda in New Spain* (1929); V. Aubrey Neasham, "Spain's Emigrants to the New World," *Hispanic American Historical Review*, 19 (1939), 147–60; C. E. Marshall, "The Birth of the Mestizo in New Spain," *ibid.*, pp. 161–84; James Lockart, *Spanish Peru, 1532–1560, A Colonial Society* (1968) and his *Men of Cajamarca* (1972); Charles Gipson, "The

Transformation of the Indian Community in New Spain, 1500–1800," *Journal of World History*, 2 (1955), 581–607; Lyle N. McAlister, "Social Structure and Social Change in New Spain," *Hispanic American Historical Review*, 43 (1963), 349–70; and above all, Lewis Hanke, *The Spanish Struggle for Justice in the Conquest of America* (1949) and Silvio Zavala, *New Viewpoints on the Spanish Colonization of America* (1943). On politics: Woodrow W. Borah, "Representative Institutions in the Spanish Empire in the Sixteenth Century: The New World," *The Americas*, 12 (1955–56), 246–57. For an extended comparison of the Spanish-American and the British-North American colonial empires, see James Lang, *Conquest and Commerce: Spain and England in the Americas* (1975). The Brazilian comparison is also relevant, in Richard R. Beeman, "Labor Forces and Race Relations: A Comparative View of the Colonization of Brazil and Virginia," *Political Science Quarterly*, 86 (1971), 609–36. Comparisons of slavery in north and south America have been worked out in books by Frank Tannenbaum (*Slave and Citizen*), Carl N. Degler (*Neither Black nor White*), Herbert S. Klein (*Slavery in the Americas*), and most comprehensively by David B. Davis (*The Problem of Slavery in Western Culture*).

The essential writings on England's involvement in geographical discovery and overseas settlement in the sixteenth century are by David B. Quinn. His *Roanoke Voyages, 1584–1590* (2 vols., 1955) contains every document related to that enterprise, a subject he has summarized in an excellent brief account, *Raleigh and the British Empire* (London, 1947). In addition, Quinn has edited the documents of the colonizing efforts of Sir Humphrey Gilbert (2 vols., 1940), written a biography of Gilbert, edited Hakluyt's writings, and discovered the Pilgrims' original plans to settle on the islands in the gulf of the St. Lawrence. Most aspects of his writing are brought together in a volume of his essays, *England and the Discovery of America, 1481–1620* (1974). Samuel E. Morison's *The European Discovery of America: The Northern Voyages, A.D. 500–1600* (1971), covers in the same vivid fashion as *The Southern Voyages* the Cabots' voyages and all of the Elizabethan explorations, and it contains in addition an excellent account of the Roanoke expeditions. A more traditional summary is John B. Brebner, *The Explorers of North America, 1492–1806* (1933). G. R. Elton, *England Under the Tudors* (1955), chap. xii is a very brief but useful summary of Elizabethan exploration and expansionism; chap. ix contains a good sketch of the economic background. A. L. Rowse's *The Expansion of Elizabethan England* (1955) and his *Elizabethans and America* (1959) are good reading.

The important role of Ireland in the origins of Elizabethan colonization and the connections between Irish and American settlement are best described in David B. Quinn, *The Elizabethans and the Irish* (1966). Quinn has analyzed the development of English ideas of colonization in the Irish context, particularly the concept of "plantation," in "Sir Thomas Smith (1513–1577) and the Beginnings of English Colonial Theory," *Proceedings of the American Philosophical Society*, 89, no. 4 (Dec., 1945), 543–60, and in "Ireland and Sixteenth Century European Expansion," T. D. Williams, ed., *Historical Studies: I . . .* (1958).

The masterwork on the financial history of sixteenth-and seventeenth-century English exploration and colonization is W. R. Scott, *The Constitution and Finance of English, Scottish and Irish Joint Stock Companies to 1720* (3 vols., 1912). Theodore K. Rabb, *Enterprise and Empire . . . 1575–1630* (1967), demonstrates statistically the broad social basis of investment in colonization. For the financial background of England's parallel colonization of Ireland in the seventeenth century, see Karl S. Bottigheimer, *English Money and Irish Land* (1971).

2

Transplantation

In 1600 the eastern coastal region of mainland North America, some 362,000 square miles from Maine to Georgia and west to the Appalachian Mountains, was largely uncultivated, much of it covered by dense forests, but by no means an unbroken wilderness. A native population grouped in well-organized tribes and sharing approximately the same culture lived fairly sedentary lives, many in semipermanent villages of up to 1000 persons. Concentrated in the fertile coastal plain and the broad river valleys, they communicated readily along an intricate network of riverways and forest trails. They subsisted on a generally nutritious diet of fish and farm crops, principally maize, as well as on game and wild foods and they rarely suffered famines.

But the Indians' hold upon the land was light. Large areas of the Atlantic woodland region were completely uninhabited (the New England coastal population was decimated by smallpox just before the first English settlers arrived). The average population density for the entire region east of the Appalachians in the early days of European settlement has been estimated by anthropologists at thirty-four persons per hundred square miles; in the most populous region, coastal New York and southern New England, the average density was no more than four persons per square mile. Nowhere was more than one percent of all the land available for horticulture actually under cultivation, and nowhere was possession

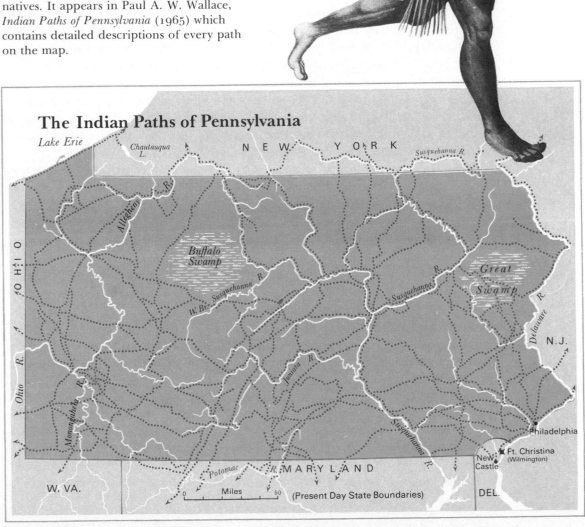

AN INDIAN SORCERER, 1585

Of this drawing by John White (see p. 24)
Thomas Hariot, one of the Roanoke settlers
of 1585, wrote: "They have sorcerers or jugglers
who use strange gestures and whose enchant-
ments often go against the laws of nature. For
they are very familiar with devils, from whom
they obtain knowledge about their enemies'
movements." *(Copyright The British Museum.)*

The map below is a composite reconstruction of
all the trails known to have been used by the
natives. It appears in Paul A. W. Wallace,
Indian Paths of Pennsylvania (1965) which
contains detailed descriptions of every path
on the map.

The Indian Paths of Pennsylvania

Lake Erie

Chautauqua L.

N E W   Y O R K

Susquehanna R.

O H I O

Allegheny R.

Buffalo Swamp

Great Swamp

W. Br. Susquehanna R.

Susquehanna R.

Delaware R.

N.J.

Ohio R.

Monongahela R.

Juniata R.

Susquehanna R.

Philadelphia

W. VA.

Potomac

M A R Y L A N D

New Castle

★ Ft. Christina (Wilmington)

0   Miles   50

(Present Day State Boundaries)

DEL.

of the land conceived of in European terms. The Indians did not view land as parcels of property held in exclusive personal possession but rather as a common resource that was inherited from ancestors, held in trust by tribal chiefs for future generations, and used by contemporaries for daily need. Nor was warfare thought of in European terms. Intertribal struggles were common and the treatment of enemies was brutal; but the Indians did not undertake war to annihilate their enemies, to create utter devastation, or to engage in wholesale massacre. Finally, only in one area of the entire Atlantic coastal region were the native inhabitants organized into a political structure effective beyond the tribal level. And even in that one famous and militarily important organization, the Iroquois Confederacy, control over the separate tribes was never secure.

By 1700 this vast coastal region had been transformed, and the foundations of British North American civilization established. The Indians had been eliminated from the seaboard lands—annihilated (destroy completely) by the invading peoples in savage local wars and driven back beyond the western fringes of European settlement. The area now contained a quarter of a million transplanted Europeans and their children and grandchildren attempting to re-create the familiar pattern of European life in this undeveloped land. Recruited principally from two of the most dynamic and economically sophisticated nations of Europe, England and Holland, they lived in communities that were parts of a commercial network spread across the entire Atlantic basin and that involved, directly or indirectly, all the nations of western Europe. Within this transplanted population, there were, mainly in Virginia and Maryland, between ten thousand and twenty thousand Africans bound in lifelong, hereditary, and debased servitude.

This transplanted population was organized into eleven provinces loosely controlled by an English government that was only beginning to understand the full importance of the colonial world it had acquired. A small proportion of the settlers, perhaps 8 percent, lived in the five main port towns (Boston, Newport, New York, Philadelphia, and Charleston) through which flowed most of the commerce and communications that linked this world to Europe. The rest lived in village communities numbering a few hundred souls, or on isolated family farms or "plantations" modeled on European agricultural establishments but different from them in fundamental ways.

These tens of thousands of transplanted Europeans and Africans, who were opening up the land to more intense cultivation than it had ever had before, had arrived in no concentrated stream, under no centralized direction, and in no limited span of years. They had arrived, and in 1700 were continuing to arrive, irregularly, in various circumstances, their migration and settlement sponsored and managed individually or by a variety of private organizations. The history of their migration and resettlement in America forms not one narrative but many. Yet these stories of colonization, for all their variety, follow a common pattern. They begin with high hopes and great plans—often utopian plans—designed by sponsoring individuals and groups whose imaginations were fired by the possibilities of starting the world anew, of creating new communities, and profiting immensely by doing so. But contact with reality in an undeveloped land brought frustration, the failure of original high hopes, and disillusion. Thereafter, however, there was a creative adaptation by those who survived. This was the persistent pattern of English colonization in the seventeenth century: soaring expectations, disappointment, frustration, disaster or near disaster, and then a slow adjustment to the grinding realities of life on the wilderness edge of the North American continent. Gradually, from this process, there emerged new forms of society made more complex by their superficial similarities to the familiar patterns of European life.

Virginia: Squalor, Struggle, and a New Way of Life

The settlement of Virginia is a classic case of high hopes shattered and a new world rescued from the ruins.

It began in 1606 when the English crown chartered the Virginia Company, which combined the ambitions of the two main groups that had already been involved in exploration and in the planning of American settlements: the gentry and merchants of the west country and the London merchants, to whom Raleigh had transferred his rights. The two groups were given separate though overlapping portions of the North American coast for settlement and instructed to appoint their own resident governments. In 1607 the Plymouth group, assigned the northern area between the Potomac River and the site of the present Bangor, Maine, attempted a settlement near the mouth of the Kennebec River, but everything went wrong. No sign of quick profits appeared, disease and Indian attacks decimated the small company huddled in the seaside fort, and within a year the effort was permanently abandoned.

The London group, assigned the southern sector, was more ambitious and better financed. Its leaders, under Sir Thomas Smith, England's most powerful merchant, were extraordinarily energetic. In December 1606 they sent out three ships, the *Sarah Constant,* the *Goodspeed,* and the *Discovery*—tiny vessels scarcely able to hold the 144 people they carried, let alone survive a midwinter crossing of the Atlantic. It was April 1607 before they reached the Chesapeake, and in May, on a low-lying island 30 miles upstream on the James River and close to the river bank, the 105 survivors of the voyage disembarked. On this spot, so permeated with stagnant water that no home site could be placed farther than 800 feet from malarial swamps, but safe from attack and believed to be close to passages through the continent to the Pacific, the Virginia Company of London established the first permanent British settlement in North America.

The colony survived, but only barely. During the eighteen years of the Virginia Company's existence (1606–24) Jamestown, the main settlement, was a disaster not only for those who lived there but for everyone in any way connected with it. Death was everywhere in the colony. Four out of five of the "planters" of the company years were victims of disease or of Indian attacks. That the company survived at all beyond its first two years was the result of the persistence of its leaders in pursuing delusive dreams of profits and of the financial support they were able to mobilize. Seldom has good money been thrown so extravagantly after bad; seldom have hard-headed businessmen been so mistaken in their expectations of success.

There are three main phases in the history of the Virginia Company's hopes and enterprises. During the first two years (1607–09) it quickly became clear that Virginia was no Mexico: there was neither easily extractable mineral wealth nor an unknown passage through the continent, nor a useful native labor force. Hope came to rest on a new idea: that if the colony could be well populated and securely financed, it might produce more ordinary goods—grapes, sugar, tobacco, cotton, dye woods—which could be sold with substantial if not sensational profits in England. Once such a reliable foundation had been laid, the search for more dramatic and lucrative possibilities could then be resumed.

It was to establish the colony on this permanent basis that in 1609 the company in London obtained a revised charter and launched a new effort that gave the moribund colony hope for the future. Without the renewed effort of 1609, Jamestown would have followed Roanoke into oblivion—which it almost did in any case.

By the terms of the new charter, the company, hitherto financed by the contributions only of its incorporators and their personal acquaintances, was recast as a seven-year public joint-stock company. In February 1609 its books were opened for public subscriptions and an elaborate publicity campaign was launched to stimulate the sale of these shares, especially in the form of pledges of personal service in the colony by prospective settlers. Such "adventurers of person" were given one or more shares of stock depending on their "quality" or special skills, each such share to be worth at least a hundred acres of land when in 1616 the com-

THE JAMESTOWN RESTORATION

(Jamestown Foundation, Jamestown, Virginia.)

pany's total assets would be divided among the stockholders. At the same time
the company's management was changed. The stockholders were organized into
a quarterly assembly with power to review the regulations laid down by the company's governor and council. And the new company management created in
turn a new resident government for the colony itself.

Under the first charter the resident government of the colony had consisted
of an appointed council that elected its own president. The result had been
wrangling among the leaders until Captain John Smith, a shrewd, hard-bitten,
and commanding war veteran, seized power. It had been Smith—a romantic,
swashbuckling, but intelligent adventurer—who by forceful leadership had kept
the forlorn band from starving to death; he had managed too, by a combination
of cleverness and brutality, to keep the neighboring Indian tribes reasonably
friendly or at least intimidated; and he had made important explorations of the
Chesapeake region and surveyed its economic possibilities. The lesson of his
leadership was not forgotten. Under the new regulations of 1609 all authority in
the colony was to be exercised by an appointed governor who was to be advised,
not controlled, by a council and whose authority was to be limited only by the
"liberties, franchises, and immunities" due all Englishmen and by the instructions
that would be issued to him by the company.

The publicity campaign of 1609 was sensational. Colonization was preached
from the pulpits of London, and the shares boomed on the merchant exchanges.
Support of the Virginia Company became, for the moment, a national cause. As
a result, in June 1609 the company was able to send out to Virginia a fleet carrying 500 men and 100 women with large quantities of equipment and supplies.
But the whole expedition seemed doomed. The vessel that carried the newly
appointed officers of the colony was blown off course and ended a wreckage in
Bermuda—an episode that is echoed in Shakespeare's *Tempest*. The 400 leader-
less settlers who arrived in Jamestown were exhausted by the long voyage and
debilitated by the putrid shipboard food. Disease was already spreading among
them when they landed. Too weak at first to work, then deeply discouraged
by the sordid prospects before them, shaken out of their normal social discipline
and confused by the disordered life around them, they fell into fierce factional
struggles, lethargy, and despair, and they failed to plant the crops they would
need for the coming year. In the midst of a rich land they starved and, unable
to withstand disease, died in droves, miserably. When the fearful winter of 1609-
10 was over only some 60 of the 500 inhabitants were still alive. In May the leaders
finally arrived from Bermuda and found a scene of utter desolation. Jamestown's
palisades were in ruins, the houses burnt for firewood, the last scraps of food—
including cattle and domestic animals—consumed; and the people spoke secretly
of cannibalism.

The ravaged settlement, still lacking the supplies that had been paid for by
the subscription of 1609, seemed hopeless. On June 7, it was abandoned. The

settlers sailed down the James in four small vessels en route to Newfoundland and home.

The colony was saved by a coincidence, which contemporaries attributed to the providence of God. For by chance the departing settlers were met near the mouth of the James by a longboat from a fleet just arrived that carried 300 men and the new governor, Lord De la Warr. The despairing and fearful settlers were ordered back, and De la Warr began the slow process of restoring discipline and confidence, creating a sound agriculture, and establishing profitable relations with the Indians. At home the company, with somewhat despairing vigor, continued its fund raising and sent further reinforcements of over 600 men with hundreds of domestic animals and shiploads of equipment. Emphasis was thrown now exclusively on the development of Virginia's agricultural, industrial, and commercial possibilities. A satellite settlement was founded at Henrico on the upper James (the site of Richmond) and two others were located at the mouth of the James. Social discipline was imposed harshly by a new code of laws published in 1612 as *Lawes Divine, Morall, and Martiall,* which organized the community into a quasi-military corps committed to compulsory service on common projects and subject to severe penalties for failure to work or to share military obligations.

Thus reinforced and thus disciplined and propelled, the colony slowly and painfully became marginally self-sustaining. Humble products—furs, timbers, sassafras, silk grass, some experimentally produced iron, and beginning in 1614 small quantities of tobacco—began to fill the holds of the returning vessels, which, it had once been hoped, would bear gold and jewels and news of river routes to the Pacific. But these cargoes, though encouraging, were not profitable enough to stimulate sizable new investments in a company whose expenses were escalating dangerously with the succession of lifesaving supply ships. More funds would have to be raised. Subscribers were dunned for further contributions, unredeemed pledges were pursued in the courts, a public lottery was authorized and launched, more pamphlets were written on Virginia's glowing promise, and once again sermons were preached on the moral obligation to support this *Nova Britannia.* But even all this could not generate the necessary support. To popularize the organization further and to broaden its base, the company obtained a third charter (1612) that increased the voice of the ordinary shareholders in the company's management. Still, the company's finances remained weak, so weak that in 1616, when the seven-year terminus of the 1609 joint-stock was reached, the company was too poor to provide the surveys necessary to make the promised distribution of 100 acres per share. By then the colony's population, despite all the recent reinforcements, was a mere 350.

One last, great effort had to be made if the company was to be saved and any profit at all realized from the tens of thousands of pounds that had been invested. In 1618 a new group of leaders headed by Sir Edwin Sandys took over control of the company from Smith and initiated the final phase of its history.

The company under Sandys's influence drew up a uniform and generous policy of land inducements for the "ancient planters" and for prospective investors and settlers. The "headright" system was devised whereby anyone who transported a settler to Virginia, including himself, would receive the right to locate, survey, and patent 50 acres of land. "Headrights" eventually became an important stimulus to immigration, though surveying and patenting land proved to be complicated and costly in fees, and ordinary settlers quickly learned to sell their claims to land brokers. More important to the immediate fortunes of the company, shareholders were allowed to pool their landholdings into jointly owned tracts within the Virginia patent, and these, together with other large personal estates that were planned, were granted minor governmental powers.

The creation of these "private plantations," or "hundreds"—seventy of them were authorized by 1663—began the uncontrolled expansion of settled territory. The lower James valley became dotted with self-contained subcolonies independent in lesser governmental jurisdiction. At the same time the rigid military discipline of the *Lawes* of 1612 was withdrawn in favor of a more normal system of civil courts bound by rules of common law, and a representative assembly—the first in American history—was provided for. At its first meeting in 1619 (its only meeting during the company's time), the Assembly, consisting of the governor and his council sitting together with representatives of each of four projected "boroughs" and of the private jurisdictions, made clear that it would not only express popular grievances, as Parliament had done time out of mind, but also protect Englishmen's fundamental rights as they were known "at home."

(Rare Book Division, The New York Public Library.)

THE INCONVENIENCIES THAT HAVE HAPPENED TO SOME PERSONS WHICH HAVE TRANSPORTED THEMSELVES from *England* to *Virginia*, vvithout prouisions necessary to sustaine themselues, hath greatly hindred the Progresse of that noble Plantation: For preuention of the like disorders heereafter, that no man suffer, either through ignorance or misinformation; it is thought requisite to publish this short declaration: wherein is contained a particular of such necessaries, as either private families or single persons shall haue cause to furnish themselues with, for their better support at their first Landing in Virginia; whereby also greater numbers may receiue in part, directions how to prouide themselues.

Apparrell.	li.	s.	d.
One Monmouth Cap	00	01	10
Three falling bands	—	01	03
Three shirts	—	07	06
One waste-coate	—	02	02
One suite of Canuase	—	07	06
One suite of Frize	—	10	00
One suite of Cloth	—	15	00
Three paire of Irish stockins	—	04	—
Foure paire of shooes	08	08	—
One paire of garters	00	10	—
One doozen of poinrs	00	00	03
One paire of Canuase sheets	08	00	—
Seuen ells of Canuase, to make a bed and boulster, to be filled in *Virginia* 8.s.	08	00	
One Rug for a bed 8. s. which with the bed seruing for two men, halfe is			
Fiue ells coorse Canuase, to make a bed at Sea for two men, to be filled with straw, iiij. s.	05	00	
One coorse Rug at Sea for two men, will			

Apparrell for one man, and so after the rate for more.

For a family of 6. persons and so after the rate for more.

Tooles.	li.	s.	d.
Fiue broad howes at 2.s. a piece	—	10	—
Fiue narrow howes at 16.d. a piece	—	06	08
Two broad Axes at 3.s.8.d. a piece	—	07	04
Fiue felling Axes at 18.d. a piece	—	07	06
Two steele hand sawes at 16.d. a piece	—	02	08
Two two-hand sawes at 5. s. a piece	—	10	—
One whip-saw, set and filed with box, file, and wrest	—	10	—
Two hammers 12.d. a piece	—	02	00
Three shouels 18.d. a piece	—	04	06
Two spades at 18.d. a piece	—	03	—
Two augers 6.d. a piece	—	01	00
Sixe chissels 6.d. a piece	—	03	00
Two percers stocked 4.d. a piece	—	00	08
Three gimlets 2.d. a piece	—	00	06
Two hatchets 21.d. a piece	—	03	06
Two froues to cleaue pale 18.d.	—	03	00
Two hand-bills 20. a piece	—	03	04
One grindlestone 4.s.	—	04	00
Nailes of all sorts to the value of	02	00	

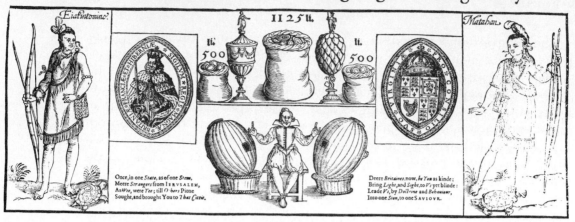

A Declaration for the certaine time of dravving the great standing Lottery.

(Copyright Society of Antiquaries of London.)

In addition to all of this, the company launched a new economic program. Some 4500 additional settlers were sent out to Virginia and through them an intense effort was undertaken to establish staple crops and products. Expert craftsmen began the manufacture of pitch, tar, ships, and other timber products, as well as iron, salt, and glass; and experiments were made with growing tropical and semitropical crops and with producing a salable wine and marketable silk.

It was all a colossal gamble by the energetic entrepreneurs who had taken over the company—and it was hopeless. Simply to launch these enterprises drained all of the company's cash, most of it produced by the lottery, which became such a public nuisance that Parliament stopped it in 1621. And there was, moreover, a growing contradiction in the failing effort. The more desperately Sandys tried to rejuvenate the company, the more he was driven to trade away the company's rights and properties to individuals in exchange for sharing the support of the colony, and hence the less likely was the company itself to reap whatever benefits might accrue. Only a miraculous parlaying of small successes into basic security could rescue the company; and with no margin for error, a single disaster would mean the end.

In March 1622 the final disaster struck. The Indians, deprived of their lands, terrorized and brutalized in a hundred ways and fearful of the sudden growth of the English population, fell on the whole string of defenseless farms along the river and killed at least 347 of the inhabitants. Not only was the colony devastated physically, it was utterly demoralized. The settlers, fearful that the slaughter would be renewed and thirsting for vengeance, abandoned their fields at the start of the planting season and took up arms. The result was both a bloody reprisal and a crop failure in the fall that created a near famine. Hundreds who had escaped butchery by the Indians' arrows, knives, and clubs died of sickness in the winter. Two years later, in 1624, when the company's charter was finally annulled and the settlement became a dependency of the crown, there remained alive but 1275 of the more than 8500 souls who had ventured to settle in Virginia. In terms of its original purpose, the company was a complete failure.

Yet in a larger sense the Virginia Company had been successful. It had opened the North American mainland to British settlement; it had peopled a small portion of it—though at a fearful cost in wasted lives, both English and Indian. It had experimented with the economic possibilities of the Chesapeake region; and it had left behind a heritage of the rule of law, within the pale, and of the practice, however rudimentary, of colonial self-government. Above all, the company had set the pattern for Virginia's future development.

The general Assembly, originally created by the company to rally support among the settlers, continued to exist in the royal colony of Virginia—because it had existed before, and because it proved useful to the crown in managing the collection of customs duties. Governor, council, and representatives (only some of whom were regularly elected deputies of the "burghs," hence "burgesses") met together as a single group. Only in the 1660s did the burgesses' interests become distinct enough from those of the council to justify their meeting as a separate body. Through most of the seventeenth century the governor and council dominated the government, especially by virtue of their control over the distribution of land and the direct regulation of the economy.

The governor and the Assembly, plus county courts that were created in 1643, were the basic governmental authorities that developed in this frontier community—a community whose everyday life was an unregulated response to the raw Chesapeake environment. By 1642, when Sir William Berkeley first arrived as governor—a position he would occupy for most of the next 34 years—the essential character of life in the first permanent British colony in America was clear.

INDIAN MASSACRE OF 1622, BY A CONTEMPORARY EUROPEAN ARTIST

By this insurrection, the English felt, the Indians became "like Cain, both murderers and vagabonds" and were morally open to unlimited retaliation. The episode, which ended all hope of the Company's survival, was the prelude to a long history of savage relations between the races. (*Rare Book Division, The New York Public Library.*)

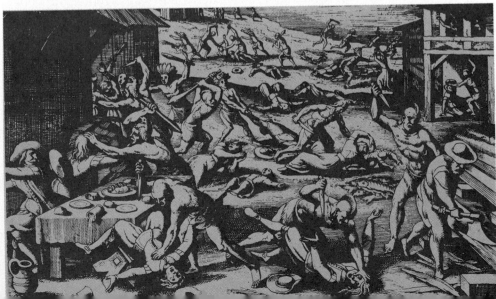

This was no life of genteel ease on gracious "plantations," and there were no "cavalier" aristocrats. True, in the first flush of the company's enthusiasm, when the settlement of Virginia was a sensational event promising all sorts of exotic rewards, the leadership of the colony had included intellectuals and sons of the nobility and of prominent churchmen and politicians. But by 1624 this early leadership had disappeared—casualties of the environment, victims of the Indians, disease, and discouragement. The new leaders established themselves by their sheer capacity to survive on rough, half-cleared tobacco farms, and to wring material gains from the raw wilderness. Former servants, yeoman farmers, and adventurers of little social status or wealth, they lacked the attributes of social authority, but by brute labor and shrewd manipulation they managed to prosper.

The leaders of Virginia in the generation after the company was dissolved were tough, unsentimental, quick-tempered, crudely ambitious men concerned with profits and increased landholding, not the grace of life. They roared curses, drank exuberantly, and gambled extravagantly, sometimes betting their servants when other commodities were lacking. They asserted their interests fiercely. They wanted an aggressive expansion of settlement and trading enterprise and unrestricted access to land no matter what objections there might be from the Indians, and they sought from such governmental agencies as existed the legal endorsement of their hard-won acquisitions. They claimed large acreage; but it was cleared land that counted, and of that there was precious little for anyone—a few hundred acres at most. For labor was in critically short supply. Every effort was made to entice over from England farm workers whose labor could be counted on for periods specified in indentures (bonds of servitude). But though an average of 1500 indentured servants arrived in the Chesapeake annually through most of the seventeenth century, their terms of bonded service were short (normally four years) and they were quickly added to the general population of free tobacco farmers seeking to expand production and competing for hired labor.

Black "slave" labor (the meaning of the term was at first ambiguous) was known in Virginia as early as 1619. But black slaves were more expensive, in the short run at least, than white servants, and their absolute foreignness—in appearance, mores, language, and abilities—offended the English whose indiscriminate suspicion of foreigners was such that they could equate "wild" Irish Catholics with Algonquins and to whom Jews seemed as alien as Eskimos. Almost all the colonists preferred white labor. A black labor force came into being only gradually. In 1640, only 150 blacks were reported in Virginia (not all of them slaves); in 1650, 300; in 1680, 3000; and in 1704, when the white population may have reached 75,600, there were roughly 10,000 blacks. And as the number of black laborers rose and as their fundamental importance to the developing economy became clear, a new status of bondage, "chattel slavery," took shape, something unknown hitherto in English law and unknown too to the Spanish and Portuguese. As servitude for whites became progressively more limited in duration and less rigorous in demands, the laws began to specify that blacks would serve for life; that their offspring would automatically become the property of their masters; that conversion to Christianity would not lead to freedom; that nothing but discretion could limit the severity of penalties imposed upon them; that racially mixed marriages were forbidden; and finally that a "slave" was no longer, as heretofore, simply a servant of lowest condition but something absolutely different in the eyes of the law, a form of property to be bought and sold, a status applicable only and necessarily to blacks and to their descendants to the ultimate degree.

Such were the main provisions of the "slave codes" so devastating in their consequences for the whole of American history. The codes originated in the latter half of the seventeenth century in response to an acute need for labor, an elemental fear of foreignness, and an insensitivity to cruelty remarkable even for that callous age. But however peculiar the conditions that gave rise to these codes, once devised they became a fundamental part of the legal fabric of community life, and they intensified and perpetuated the racial fears and hostilities that had helped shape them. By 1700 it was becoming clear, to some at least, that chattel slavery, rising like some fearful germ-laden cloud, was poisoning the very soil and roots of human relations.

The Pilgrims' "Sweet Communion"

It is difficult, perhaps impossible, for twentieth-century Americans fully to recapture the state of mind of those who led the settlement of New England. The Puritans and Pilgrims are too easily caricatured: the former as God-intoxicated demons of self-righteousness or as intellectual gymnasts cogitating day and night on exquisite subtleties of theology; the Pilgrims as altogether simple Christians spotless in their uncompromising Biblicism. But as with most caricatures there is truth behind the obvious distortions. Both groups were products of the attempted reformation of the Elizabethan Church of England and of the desire for a more direct experience of God than the church allowed. But they were otherwise very different. Their aims, their styles, their accomplishments were different, and their contributions to American life lie in altogether different spheres.

The Pilgrims were one of a series of radical "separatist" groups that first appeared in England in the 1570s. Loyal to the English state, they were determined to break altogether with the too ritualistic, too highly institutionalized, still too Catholic, Church of England. They formed their own pure and primitive churches—mere cells, conventicles, stripped bare of all ritual and institutions, unaffiliated with each other except for shared aspirations, and composed exclusively of true believers gathered voluntarily into covenanted brotherhoods. Despising alike the threat of persecution and the hope of ever forcing their views upon the world at large, yet never questioning the authority of the civil state, these fugitive groups of religious radicals were naturally drawn to the physical margins of the English world, where in isolation they might find peace to worship as they chose and yet still enjoy the protection of the English state. In the borderland regions, in fact, they might even enhance England's power.

And in this the English government itself concurred. To England, as opposed to Spain, there was from the beginning a logical and positive relationship between religious dissent and overseas settlement. As early as 1572, Elizabeth's Privy Council had endorsed the idea of relocating extreme sectarians in outlying areas where they would not contaminate the nation, yet might contribute to the general good. And it was this indulgence that the tiny brotherhood of Pilgrims that had originally gathered in the village of Scrooby in Nottinghamshire sought to take advantage of in planning their transfer to America.

Fervently pious, humble, and stubborn, these yeomen, artisans, and farm laborers under the leadership of William Brewster and William Bradford had fled first to Amsterdam, then to Leyden; but the corrupting world was with them even in that tolerant Dutch university town. They feared that their children, no longer steeled in the fires of persecution and attracted by superficial lures, would be lost to the community if nothing were done. They would have to move again, to a less comfortable, more remote site, better suited to the establishment of a pure

LEYDEN, IN THE NETHERLANDS, TO WHICH THE PILGRIMS FLED IN 1609

"A fair and beautiful city," Bradford wrote, where the Pilgrims "grew in knowledge and other gifts and graces of the spirit of God" but where their children were "drawn away by evil examples into extravagant and dangerous courses . . . so that they saw their posterity would be in danger to degenerate and be corrupted." (*Rare Book Division, The New York Public Library.*)

church of Christ. They considered various alternatives: Middleburg in Holland; Guiana, on the north coast of South America; the Magdalen Islands in the gulf of the Saint Lawrence River, which they had already investigated. They finally settled on Virginia, with whose managers, especially Sir Edwin Sandys, they had several contacts and which was then offering to groups such as theirs the semi-autonomy of private plantations.

In 1617 they obtained approval from the Virginia Company to settle within its jurisdiction and a promise from the crown not to molest them in America. But negotiations were complex, dragging out month after month, and when in 1619 the Pilgrims' patent had finally cleared through the Virginia Company, they had come under severe censure by the English crown for publishing seditious tracts. They were at the point of abandoning their project when an English investment group, headed by one Thomas Weston, that had its own patent for a plantation in Virginia proposed to join with the Pilgrims, stand between them and the authorities, and help finance their relocation in America in exchange for their labor on profitable enterprises over a seven-year period. After many hesitations, the Separatists willing to go to America sold their property to contribute to the common stock and took shares in the joint undertaking in proportion to their investments, each planter's labor being reckoned as a single share of stock.

In July 1620, 35 of the 238 members of the Leyden congregation took leave of their brethren in a scene so poignant, so prayerful and tearful, that even casual Dutch onlookers wept. They sailed to Southampton on their own small vessel, the *Speedwell*, to join an English contingent of Separatists and the 180-ton *Mayflower*, which had been rented for them by the merchants. After two false starts that led them to abandon the unseaworthy *Speedwell* and that discouraged many from completing the voyage, the remaining Pilgrims and the laborers hired by the merchants crowded into the *Mayflower*, packed high with furniture, equipment, food, and animals, and on September 16 set sail for Virginia.

There were 101 passengers in all, perhaps 87 of them Separatists or members of Separatist families. Outwardly they fared well on the overcrowded vessel: only one passenger died on the voyage and two children were born on board. But the voyage lasted over nine weeks, and by the time Cape Cod was sighted (November 9) and they debarked at Provincetown at the tip of the cape (November 11), the entire party, crew and passengers, was ridden with disease, primarily scurvy, and so debilitated by malnutrition that they were incapable of withstanding attacks of ordinary illnesses in the months that followed. The weather during this first winter in Plymouth, 1620–21, was quite mild for New England, but it proved to be one of the worst "starving times" recorded anywhere in British America. When spring at last arrived, half of those who had crossed on the *Mayflower* were dead.

They had settled, of course, in New England, though they carried with them a title to land in Virginia. But when they finally landed at Provincetown and "fell upon their knees and blessed the God of Heaven who had brought them over the vast and furious ocean and delivered them from all the perils and miseries

THE PLYMOUTH PLANTATION

Leyden Street, the view to the sea, as it appeared in the first years
of settlement. "The houses," a visitor wrote in 1628, "are constructed
of clapboards, with gardens also enclosed behind and at the sides
with clapboards, so that the houses and courtyards are arranged in
very good order." *(Plimoth Plantation.)*

thereof," they were determined to voyage no more and to ignore the legal problems that might arise from the Weston patent.

An exploring party found Plymouth Harbor on December 11, and there on a
slope rising westward from the shore, probably the site of an abandoned Indian
cornfield, they planned the town of their desires. Before the year was out they
had begun constructing homesteads and garden plots on either side of a thousand-
foot roadway running up the slope, which they fondly called Leyden Street,
crossing that broad avenue with another perpendicular to it, and enclosing the
whole village in a stockade like that of early Jamestown. A governor's house was
built at the road crossing, and at the crest of Leyden Street a solid two-story garrison was constructed; its fortified rooftop commanded the countryside and its
ground-floor chamber served as the meetinghouse of this intensely religious
community.

Plymouth's history up to 1691, when it was absorbed into the more powerful
Massachusetts Bay Colony, is a tale of modest triumphs—and a tale too of the
defeat of human aspirations by the ravages of time, growth, and decay. All of
it—the trials, the triumphs, and defeats—is recorded in Governor William Bradford's magnificent history, *Of Plymouth Plantation*, which he began in 1630 with
a review of the earlier years and continued as a documentary journal and commentary covering the next sixteen years. It is one of the most moving and

eloquent documents in the entire literature of American history. Its vivid Elizabethan imagery and its biblical cadences blend perfectly to express Bradford's
hopes and struggles and finally his sense of tragedy and defeat.

Of the blessings he recorded, one was always paramount. At long last the Pilgrims were free, Bradford wrote, "to see, and with much comfort to enjoy, the
blessed fruits of their sweet communion." The church was theirs, unfettered, un-
intimidated, and responsive to their ultimate desires. It remained the center of
the life of the Plymouth colony throughout the founding generation. But there
were severe troubles from the start. The first and most pressing was financial. For
several years they failed as businessmen, and the merchants at home, bickering
among themselves and fearful of mounting costs if they continued to resupply
the settlers, sold out or simply abandoned their investments. By 1626 the company was bankrupt, but the Pilgrims, more honest than shrewd, continued to
honor their original obligations. They struggled for years to squeeze enough
profit from fur trading, fishing, and the sale of lumber, Indian corn, and wam-
pum to pay off the original debts. By the time they succeeded, in 1648, many of
the founders were dead.

More threatening than debts was the very security that they managed to create.
A series of vessels had followed the *Mayflower* to Plymouth, and the population
had risen steadily. It reached 390 in 1630, 549 in 1637, and in 1657, the year of
Bradford's death, over 1360. By then Plymouth was not simply a single covenanted community but a colony of eleven towns that could not be enclosed
within a single purpose, infused with a single spirit. Even if the gentle leaders
had sought to impose discipline and control, they would have lacked the legal
means to do so. Their original patent from the Virginia Company was worthless in New England, and a patent they received in 1621 from the Council for

EDWARD WINSLOW, 1651

Winslow, the only Pilgrim of whom a portrait is
known, was one of the better educated and
more worldly wise of the group. His career
illustrates the cosmopolitanism of the first
generation of settlers in British America (see
p. 153). His long years of service as Plymouth's
chief business agent, Indian negotiator, and
propagandist brought him often to England
where in 1654 Cromwell engaged him on a
diplomatic mission and then appointed him to
head the expedition that seized Jamaica from
the Spanish. Governor of Plymouth for three
years, governor's assistant for over 20 years, he
was largely responsible for setting up Plymouth's
successful Indian trade and for exploring the
adjacent territories. *(Plimoth Plantation.)*

New England (which had taken over the legal rights of the old Virginia Company of Plymouth) was simply a vague land grant and an equally vague license to establish a local government. The government evolved slowly and uncertainly and was never sanctioned by charter or the approval of the crown.

The starting point was the Mayflower Compact, a document devised to control the restless noncommunicants while the Pilgrims were still at sea. It was simply an agreement—signed, on November 21, 1620, by 41 Pilgrims, hired laborers, and sailors—to obey whatever laws and officers the community would create. The signing of the Mayflower Compact in the cabin of the rocking vessel was a dramatic event. But the document was no constitution. The unsanctioned government that developed in Plymouth was as primitive an organization as could possibly govern. The freemen simply came together annually to choose a governor (Bradford was elected thirty times) and a group of assistants to support him; otherwise these electors met only on extraordinary occasions when called together by the governor.

So feeble was the colony's political structure, so weak the second and third generations' loyalty to Plymouth, that when the whole region was included within the boundaries of Massachusetts in the Bay Colony's second charter of 1691, the Pilgrims' colony slipped without a ripple into the larger jurisdiction. By then the erosion in the original purposes and piety was such that those who had inherited the leadership from Bradford could only rejoice that the government would at least continue to be in the hands of saints, even if they were not saints of the Separatists' own persuasion.

But the essential destruction of the founders' utopia had taken place years before. Bradford's "sweet communion" in its fullest form had rested on deeply shared aspirations and on isolation from the corruptions of the changing world. When town begat town and the churches multiplied, and when the ordinary world was created within Plymouth itself by strangers and by children who failed to recapture their parents' piety, the Pilgrims' hopes were shattered. It was Bradford himself who wrote the final epitaph. When in the 1650s he re-read the Pilgrims' description of themselves in Leyden as a community "knit together as a body in the most strict and sacred bond and covenant of the Lord . . . straitly tied to all care of each other's goods and of the whole, by every one and so mutually," he turned over the pages of his journal on which those words appeared and wrote in a trembling hand:

O sacred bond, whilst inviolably preserved! How sweet and precious were the fruits that flowed from the same! But when this fidelity decayed, then their ruin approached. O that these ancient members had not died or been dissipated . . . or else that this holy care and constant faithfulness had still lived. . . . But (alas) that subtle serpent hath slyly wound in himself under fair pretences of necessity and the like, to untwist these sacred bonds and ties and as it were insensibly by degrees to dissolve . . . the same. I have been happy, in my first times, to see, and with much comfort to enjoy, the blessed fruits of this sweet communion, but it is now a part of my misery in old age to find and feel the decay and want thereof (in a great measure) and with grief and sorrow of heart to lament and bewail the same. And for others' warning and admonition, and my own humiliation, do I here note the same.

The Pilgrims, lacking all instinct for power, rejecting the world rather than seeking to reform it, and tolerant of the errors of others in their humble pursuit of personal piety, were incapable of perpetuating the community they built, and their impact on American life was confined to the realm of ideals. For always, in the 350 years that have followed the founding of their fragile utopia in Plymouth, the example of their selfless pursuit of an unattainable ideal and their rejection of the satisfactions of wealth, power, comfort, and self-glory in favor of deeper, spiritual rewards have been part of America's collective memory and part of its essential culture. But this model of life, though emulated in various ways at every stage of American history, has never been dominant. Far more vital in American culture has been the very different legacy of the Puritans.

The Puritans and Their Progeny: Power in the Service of the Spirit

The Puritans, it is true, shared with the Pilgrims a desire for a direct experience of religion free from the encumbrances of an elaborate church; they shared also certain theological and ecclesiastical views as well as a stubborn moral dignity.* But the Puritans, in America as in England, were proud and driving, and as demanding of themselves as they were of the world about them. They sought power, not for its own sake, to be sure, but for Christian purposes; and they sought it relentlessly, intolerantly, and successfully. Far from forsaking the sinful world and a too worldly national church, they sought to seize them both, and control and transform them. Fiercely energetic, striving, well organized, well educated, and sophisticated, the Puritans founded colonies in New England and elsewhere whose impact on the whole of American life has been profound.

The decisions that led to this formative development in American history took place in stages within a hectic three-year period. In 1628 a group of around ninety active nonconformists, deeply troubled by the repressive tendencies of both church and state in England and well aware of the value of overseas settlements as refuges for people of their persuasion, came together as the New England Company to obtain a land patent enclosing most of the present-day Massachusetts and New Hampshire. They sent out an advance party to rebuild a settlement on Cape Ann, north of Boston, that had recently been abandoned by a Puritan fishing company, but their anxieties continued to mount. Increasingly concerned about the future of nonconformity, they sought and obtained in 1629

---

*On Puritanism as a religious movement, see Chapter 3, pages 115–121.

GOVERNOR JOHN WINTHROP

The leader of Puritan New
England in its heroic age, a
devout, able, and strong-willed
leader, Winthrop directed his
energies and talents to creating
a pure version of the Church of
England and a society directed
to God's will. The set jaw, full
but tightly drawn lips, and raised
brows suggest intense self-
discipline and resolution.
(American Antiquarian Society.)

a crown charter that created the Massachusetts Bay Company. This elaborate document, empowering them not only to trade and settle within the boundaries of their earlier land patent but "to govern and rule all His Majesty's subjects that reside within the limits of our plantation," was a legal bastion behind which a powerful social movement could organize and develop.

The new corporation's efficiency was quickly demonstrated. Within weeks of its creation it sent off five vessels bearing more than two hundred settlers to join the earlier group then living in thatched cottages on the shores of Cape Ann. But far greater enterprises were stirring beneath the surface of the Massachusetts Bay Company. In the spring and summer of 1629 political and ecclesiastical conditions in England continued to worsen for critics of the Church of England, and in addition the Puritans learned of the defeat of Protestantism throughout Europe in the international war then raging. Moreover, the king dissolved Parliament, and with it went the hope of political remedies. On top of all of this an economic depression created great distress in just the districts most prone to religious dissent.

It was in this atmosphere of social, political, and economic panic in the spring and summer of 1629 that men of experience, ability, and established position turned their thoughts to personal escape and to their own renewal in some world apart, some fresh, uncorrupted realm. Within six months of the creation of the Massachusetts Bay Company a coalition of merchants, landed gentlemen, lawyers, and minor officials alienated from their own society, turned to the new crown corporation and found in it a means of escape and of serving their own, and Puritanism's, higher purpose.

Only some of this gathering group had been directly involved in the company before. Chief among the newcomers was John Winthrop, an intensely pious, well-connected forty-one-year-old Puritan landowner and attorney recently dismissed from his government position. Faced suddenly with unemployment and with the prospect of continuing harassment, and convinced that England was being overwhelmed by corruption, he came to see a providential significance in the work of the Massachusetts Bay Company. God was clearly punishing a hopelessly corrupt world, but at the same time—Winthrop and others reasoned as the disasters of the summer of 1629 worsened—He was providing "a refuge for many whom he means to save out of the general calamity." To join personally, therefore, in creating a refuge in New England and in building a pure church and society in that distant land was a divine calling, for if indeed it were true that "the Church hath no place left to flee into but the wilderness, what better work can there be than to go and provide tabernacles and food for her against [the time] she comes thither?"

Winthrop and those like him who now took over the leadership of the Massachusetts Bay Company were no mild and passive Pilgrims; they were men of affairs, self-confident, energetic, and used to exercising authority. But their love of action in the ordinary world was disciplined by an equally powerful religious commitment. Like Winthrop, the Puritan leaders loved the everyday world, but they loved it, as they liked to say, "with weaned affection." *In* the world but not *of* the world, they sought not to abandon the Church of England but to seize it, purge it of its corruptions, and reconstruct it in the image of a pure and unadorned Christianity, if not in England then in New England. And far from withdrawing from society, they sought to seize that too and transform it—to create, by persuasion if possible, by force if force were necessary and available to them, a general pattern of behavior that would be likely to gain God's approval. They were separatists only with respect to the English state, and this they made clear in the conclusion they reached at a momentous meeting in Cambridge late in August of 1629.

The twelve leaders who assembled secretly in Cambridge pledged themselves "ready in our persons" to join the migration to New England, taking with them their families and whatever provisions they could gather, and "to inhabit and continue in New England"—*provided* that the company officially transfer itself, its charter and government, to the colony. Three days later the company concurred, in effect voting itself out of business as a commercial organization and transforming itself into a rudimentary civil government. In October, Winthrop was elected governor, and five months later, in March 1630, the great Puritan migration began. Before the year was out a fleet of 17 ships had borne well over 1000 settlers to Massachusetts. In all, during the years of the Puritan exodus, 1630–43, some 200 vessels transported over 20,000 Englishmen to the Bay Colony.

No one community could contain them all. The original settlement, Salem on Cape Ann, became a staging area for groups moving south along the coast. First Charlestown, then Boston became the central settlement. From Boston groups moved on quickly to settle a ring of satellite towns immediately around the bay. Subsequently others founded a secondary ring of communities—Haverhill, Concord, Sudbury—some 20 or 30 miles inland. Finally, beginning in 1636, the migrating subgroups of the Puritan exodus broke contact altogether with the central settlement in Boston by establishing an independent cluster of towns—Hartford, Wethersfield, Windsor—on the Connecticut River over 100 miles from Boston Bay. By banding together politically in 1639, these towns became the colony of Connecticut, which was chartered by the crown in 1662.

The dispersal of the Puritans into towns all over New England—not only west but south to the short-lived colony of New London and to Rhode Island as well as north to New Hampshire and Maine—was remarkable for its speed; it was remarkable even more for the degree to which it carried forward the purposes of the Puritans. The dispersal of the colonists was no random scattering of people but a well-organized multiplication of church societies that became political bodies and land corporations as soon as they were founded. Groups that wished to establish towns sought the approval of the colony's legislature, the General Court. When the court's franchise was granted, it carried with it not only the legal right to create a governmental jurisdiction—a town—and to send representatives to the General Court; it also carried title to a large parcel of land—a township—to be divided among the original heads of household in proportion to wealth or status. These first town leaders, consequently, owned all the land: not only their own holdings, distributed among the various fields that were opened, but all the undistributed land as well. The same men, since they were the founding members of their covenanted church, controlled too the vital area of religion, and they constituted also the initial voting membership of the town's political meeting that regulated the mundane affairs of village life. Since all of these powers, exercised at the meetinghouse center of these nucleated villages, fell to the first founders and not to others who later joined the villages, these town fathers and their direct heirs controlled full participation in all spheres of life.

Their control was not resented, in the early years at least. Later there would be opposition and factionalism as newcomers found their way into these small farming villages and as the Puritans' fierce passion to reform the world faded into mere repressive austerity. But while the fires of the original faith still burned brightly and Puritanism was still a way of embracing the world not rejecting it, these oligarchic yet democratic villages remained cohesive bodies, closely bound members of the Bible Commonwealth.

The unity of the Massachusetts colony is remarkable when one considers the rapid and wide dispersal of the settlers. It reflects not only a widespread commitment to a particular way of life and to certain beliefs but also the founders' gift for self-government and their refusal to tolerate dissent.

The Massachusetts charter, being the articles of incorporation of a commercial organization, contained, of course, no provision for a civil government; but within four years of the arrival of Winthrop's fleet a structure of public government had evolved. In Winthrop the company, now the colony, had a duly elected governor; in the seven or eight available members of the company's board of directors there was a rudimentary council of magistrates or governor's assistants; and in the adult male heads of households there were the "freemen" (once conceived of as stockholders but now as an electorate) necessary to complete the membership of the transformed General Court. Soon the perpetuation of this ad hoc government was provided for and basic rules laid down. In 1632 the freemen were given the power to choose not only the assistants but the governor and deputy governor as well. In 1634 it was agreed that taxes could be levied on the towns only by vote of the entire General Court and that in the future the entire body of freemen need not

THE
OATH
OF A
FREE-MAN

I A.B. being by Gods Providence an Inhabitant and FREEMAN within the Iurifdiction of this Commonwealth; doe freely acknowledge myfelfe to be fubject to the Government thereof.
AND therefore doe here fweare by the Great and Dreadful NAME of the Everliving GOD, that I will be true and faithfull to the fame, and will accordingly yield affiftance & fupport thereunto with my perfon and eftate as in equity I am bound; and will alfo truly endeavour to maintaine & preferve all the liberties & priviledges thereof, fubmitting myfelfe to the wholefome Lawes & Orders made and eftablifhed by the fame. +++ AND further that I will not Plot or practife any evill againft it, or confent to any that fhall fo doe: but will timely difcover and reveal the fame to lawfull authority now here eftablifhed, for the fpeedy preventing thereof.

MOREOVER I doe folemnly bind myfelfe in the fight of GOD, that when I fhall be called to give my voyce touching any fuch matter of this State in which FREEMEN are to deale +++ I will give my vote and fuffrage as I fhall judge in mine own confcience may beft conduce and tend to the publicke weale of the body without refpect of perfon or favour of any man.
So help me GOD in the LORD IESVS CHRIST.

Printed at Cambridge in New England:
by Order of the Generall Courte:
Moneth the Firft - 1639

(*American Antiquarian Society.*)

assemble in person for General Court meetings but could select representatives instead. These representatives, two or three from each town, were impowered to make laws, grant land, levy taxes, and transact whatever other business might come before the General Court.

Thus a rudimentary civil government evolved from a stockholders' meeting of a commercial company. The structure of the central government was quickly completed. Since the representatives, or deputies, as they were commonly called, met together with the assistants or magistrates, they could conclude no business without the magistrates' agreement and hence had no distinct voice of their own and no impulse to develop their own rules and procedures. In 1644 this problem was overcome. In a sensational court case that pitted popular emotions against strict legality, the views of the more numerous representatives were vetoed by the minority votes of the magistrates. In the furor that resulted the two groups drew apart, permanently as it proved, into two separate houses, each capable of expressing itself independently of the other, though the agreement of both was still needed for legislative enactments. The lower house thereupon organized itself separately, electing a speaker and working out parliamentary rules, a committee system, and other procedures modeled on those of the English House of Commons.

During the same years a court system was devised, largely copied from the local court system of England, and a code of laws agreed on. *The Lawes and Libertyes* of 1647 expressed not only the English common law in terms appropriate for life in the wilderness but also the Puritans' devotion to precepts of the Bible.

For despite all the involvements in such secular pursuits as clearing the wilderness and organizing towns, courts, and a general government, and despite the swift development of coastal and trans-Atlantic commerce that also took place in these years, Massachusetts remained a Bible commonwealth. It was not a theocracy, for it was never governed directly by the clergy. Church and state, religion and government, were inextricably bound together, but the clergy did not hold public office. The influence of the Puritan preachers, though immense, was exercised unofficially, without the sanction of law. The legal device that secured the Puritan domination was not the clergy's control of public office but the restriction of the colony's electorate to the membership of the church, a step that was taken in 1631. As a result of this measure, no matter how the population within the towns might change, or how the sources of immigration might shift, or how the people at large might drift away from the church, the central government of the colony would continue to represent primarily those loyal to the original Puritan purposes.

This arrangement was not challenged, for it expressed a broad consensus in the founding generation. The opposition to the Puritan establishment that did arise in these early years challenged not the basic religious character of the Puritan colony but specific points of doctrine; it flowed not from a deficiency of religious commitment but from an excess. Such opponents of the Puritan regime as Anne Hutchinson and Roger Williams were even more fanatical in their pursuit of religious truths, more relentless in their theology, more single-minded in their beliefs than the Puritan leaders themselves. In one way or another they went to extremes on issues the leaders felt obliged to keep in delicate balance.

Anne Hutchinson—passionate and inflexible in her convictions, brilliant in argument—was convinced that "justification," that is, the infusion of divine grace, the mysterious transfiguration by which sinful man becomes elect of God, was all; "sanctification"—that is, moral conduct, Christian behavior, piety, even prayer

RICHARD MATHER
Founder of a virtual dynasty of New England preachers and intellectuals, Mather is shown here in a woodcut by John Foster (c. 1670) which is probably the first print made in British America. Mather preached an austere Calvinism in Massachusetts for 34 years. *(American Antiquarian Society.)* In the background, notes taken on sermons heard in Boston by a spiritually tormented merchant, Robert Keayne. Convicted of overcharging and hence of greed and unchristian behavior, Keayne fell into an agony of protest and self-recrimination which he expressed in an extraordinary 50,000-word will. *(Massachusetts Historical Society.)*

we are made righteousnes in Chr: as Chr: way made ..
for this it is by Imputation. therefore looke at the as by ..
of the Covenant & they of the grace of the Covenant / ..
not to be Iustified wth owr Chr: nor by a Chr: wch is ..
not forth: or by such a Chr: as he word kindes forth: but wch ..
.. or belse faith. heare is many wayes to knew affects
in Chr: wch will euenuate owr Covenant
stand twrth by soe to grow up in Ga: Chr: & be laden of ..
all Confidence in owr owne righteousnes: or Confidence ..
god wth owr Chr: Ga: or Confidence in Chr: wch out the word ..
in Chr: wth out faythe: but see belowe & grow up in grace & ..
that we may be accepted of god in Chr

By mr Cotten at Boston. N: 2. his exposition out the
3 Chapt: of the epistle of Pawle to the Romanes. in his
Sermons. out the Lords day the aftel noones, be
ginings. on the mo 12. y.

Romanes Chapter. 3. y 1 — 4

what aduantage haue h..   .. or what proffit is
theel of Circumcission ..   .. cheiflye, becaus
unto them are committ ..   .. / for what if
some did not beleev ..   .. made he
fayth of god wh ou ..

this Chapt Consid ..
1 An Answare to an ..   .. made aga
wth his formed ..   .. 1 — 9
2 A Confirmat ..   .. heare
god did hye to ..
3 A Confirmacio ..   .. he by
inge of his ..   .. caus ..
Iustified by ..
for the first ..
made by ayns ..
.. formell ..

itself—was for her the mere husk of religion. And so, rejecting "works," rejecting in the end all ordinary worldly disciplines and responsibility, and standing only for the ravishment of the soul by God, she gathered around her a band of devotees, a church within a church, and thereby challenged the Puritan establishment to destroy her or destroy itself by tolerating her. But she could not be disposed of easily. By 1637 her following was large, especially among the women of Boston and among certain tradesmen and merchants, and the basic menace of her doctrine was difficult to disentangle from quite acceptable strands of thought. Only a microscopic theological examination would reveal the true nature of her heresy. When the General Court tried her, it brought in a battery of ministers to assist in the prosecution, but in the dramatic trial that resulted, Anne Hutchinson held them off with astonishing skill, defending herself learnedly and wittily. But at last, in exhaustion and perhaps also in exaltation, she blurted out defiantly that her knowledge of God was "an immediate revelation," free of all institutions, independent of all earthly authority. This was the ultimate heresy, condemned as "antinomianism," an arrogance of such cosmic dimensions that the court could safely and in good conscience banish her from the colony and silence her followers thereafter.

Roger Williams was more learned than Anne Hutchinson and more respectable, but he was at least as "divinely mad" as she and as passionate in his beliefs. He could never accommodate himself to the halfway reforms of the nonseparating Puritan churches and to the colony's peculiar constitutional foundation. Not only did he denounce the validity of the colony's charter, but from his Salem pulpit he challenged the mingling of church and state that was the essence of the Bible commonwealth. Civil officers, he insisted, should have power only over the civil affairs of men, over their outward state and behavior, not over matters of conscience and religion. While it would only be in later years in England and in banishment in Rhode Island that Roger Williams would develop the doctrine of religious toleration for which he would become famous, he was clearly heading in that direction, and the mere approach to such a position was intolerable to the rulers of the colony. Beyond all of that, he condemned the colony's churches for their refusal to break altogether with the polluted Church of England. Church reform was not enough he insisted; purification was not enough. *Perfection* was the goal—a church of *absolute* purity, more "primitive" even than the church of the Separatists in Plymouth.

Such a church was not to be had in Massachusetts. The colony's leaders regretfully—for Williams was a fine intellect and even to the Puritans a true Christian in his way—first corrected this wayward saint, then condemned him. Finally, finding him barred by his conscience from further relations even with his own congregation, isolated indeed from his own family, they banished him too.

Later there would be other deviants from the Puritan way, other challengers, notably Dr. Robert Child and his "remonstrants" who challenged the Puritans'

Congregational church organization, petitioned for liberty of conscience, and demanded the colony's subordination to the English government. They too were convicted of sedition, disarmed, fined, and either silenced or ejected from the colony.

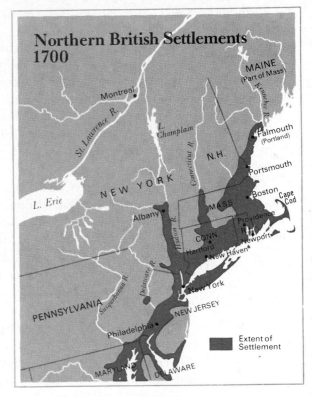

Some of these dissidents moved south to Narragansett Bay where Roger Williams, certain followers of Anne Hutchinson, a few Quakers, and other stubborn individualists unacceptable to Massachusetts were attempting to form communities in which they would be completely free to pursue their own special version of truth. But the scattered Narragansett villages were riven by discord; they splintered and regrouped repeatedly, until by the late 1640s four or five fairly stable, though quite different, communities emerged. Although the prosperous merchants who founded and dominated the island town of Newport were the most worldly of the Rhode Islanders, it was Roger Williams, the founder of Providence at the head of the bay, who recognized that only confederation of the towns and legal authorization from England would preserve the freedom of these tiny refugee settlements. And it was he who secured the colony's independence by extracting from the English government in 1644 a patent creating "The Incorporation of Providence Plantations." In 1647 representatives of these Narragansett towns, which together could not have contained more than two hundred families, came together to form a "central" government. It was the weakest and most "democratical" central government imaginable, for its essential purpose was to guarantee the independence of the towns. But it survived as an organization, to acquire in 1633 the permanent protection of a crown charter.

Connecticut and Rhode Island were both products of the Massachusetts Bay colony—the one a reproduction of the Puritans' culture, the other a rejection of it. Together, the central Puritan colony and its satellites to the west, south, and in scatterings north, formed the most vigorous transplantation of English life anywhere in the Western Hemisphere. At the heart of Puritan New England lay the determination to wipe out the corruptions of an old and oppressive world and create a new Jerusalem, in which power would not be rejected or despised but mobilized, and devoted to the service of the Lord.

A Catholic Refuge on the Chesapeake

How pervasive religion was in the establishment of British overseas settlements and how greatly America profited by England's willingness to allow its empire to develop as a refuge for religious minorities can be seen with special clarity in the founding of Maryland.

The refugee community in this case was not radical Protestant but Roman Catholic, more obnoxious to the Church of England than Protestant extremists. The dynamic force was a single family, the Calverts, enobled in 1625 as the Lords Baltimore. This family, well connected with the rulers of England and only recently converted to Catholicism, had long been involved in overseas enterprises; in 1628–29 the first Lord Baltimore had himself traveled to the Chesapeake to investigate a possible asylum for refugee Catholics. Upon his return to England he had set in motion the elaborate process of obtaining a separate royal charter for a colony that would be safe for his co-religionists, and although he died just as the charter was being approved, his project was carried through, and his ambitions fulfilled, by his twenty-six-year-old son, Cecilius Calvert, the second Lord Baltimore.

The key to much of what happened subsequently lies in the terms of the remarkable charter that was issued to the young Lord Baltimore in 1632 and in the use that the Calvert family made of the powers it bestowed. The charter granted Lord Baltimore the entire territory from the Potomac River north to the latitude of Philadelphia and west hundreds of miles to the Appalachian sources of the Potomac. The charter gave Baltimore also the extensive governmental powers of a border chieftain, powers similar to those that the Spanish crown had once bestowed on the *adelantados* and that English kings had hitherto granted only to such princely lieutenants as the bishops of Durham. As Lord Proprietor, Baltimore personally owned the land outright and could do with it what he wished; he and not the king was the source of legal authority; the government was his to shape as he chose; and he was impowered to create a system of feudal relationships through land grants if that archaic practice appealed to him.

Significantly, it did. For in this case as in so many others the barrenness of America, its openness, challenged men's imagination and led them to project their desires and their fantasies in plans for new communities.

Success came quickly at first. The young Lord Baltimore, who was the proprietor of Maryland until his death in 1675, sent his brother Leonard to the colony as governor with detailed instructions on the management of the colony. Maryland, the proprietor made clear, was to be a Catholic refuge, but Catholics, Baltimore knew, could themselves survive in the English world only as a tolerated minority, and they were therefore in no position to impose their will on others. Furthermore, he knew that the success of the colony would depend on the flow of immigrants into the area, and most of these prospective settlers would necessarily be Protestants. At the very start, therefore, Baltimore prohibited discrimination

CECELIUS CALVERT, 2D LORD
BALTIMORE

Baltimore devoted his life to
developing the colony that his
father had planned, but was
never able to visit Maryland
himself. He is pictured here
with his son, holding a new map
of Maryland ("*Nova Terrae-Mariae
Tabula*") published in 1635.
(*Maryland Historical Society.*)

of any sort against Protestants. He also forbade Catholics from engaging in public controversies on religion, and ordered them to make every effort to live at peace not only with the colony's neighbors in Virginia but with the Puritans and Dutch to the north.

This much was necessary and realistic. Fantasy entered Lord Baltimore's thinking only as he contemplated his personal proprietorship of the land and his extensive powers of government. How was one to use this princely domain and these extensive powers? What model could there be for such a vast personal estate and such extraordinary private authority? Feudalism, and its economic foundations in manorialism, provided a model of sorts for the Calverts to follow. Their provisions for land distribution, courts, and governance were the result of an effort to create some rough semblance of a feudal-manorial system.

The major subdivisions, called proprietary manors, were to be estates of 6000 acres reserved to the blood relations of the Lord Proprietor. With their land these manorial lords were to be granted the right to hold their own courts for petty misdemeanors committed on their land. Similarly privileged would be the ordinary manorial lords, but their estates would be limited to 3000 acres. It was expected that all of these manors would be populated by tenants, whose labor would produce the rents and dues necessary to support the lords. The rest of the population would be landowning yeomen and their dependents in various statuses; it was assumed that these independent farmers, whose property was not to exceed 1000 acres, would be appropriately submissive to the domination of the provincial nobility. All landowners would be required to pledge allegiance to the proprietor in exchange for their grants and to pay him a small annual fee, a "quit rent," as a "quittance" of feudal obligations. Religion would be uncoerced, Roman Catholics and Protestants living tolerantly side by side, and there would be peaceful and productive relations with the neighboring colonies and with the native Indians.

It was a reasonable design. For all its neo-manorialism it was more generous and tolerant than the designs of the Puritans, and more controlled and coherent than those of the Virginia government. Although the reality proved to be quite different from the blueprint, these original plans permanently shaped the community that developed in Maryland.

In 1632 the Calverts set up a recruiting office for settlers on the outskirts of London, advertised their colony (though not their religion) widely, and were able to induce some two hundred to three hundred settlers to join the first expedition. The prospective settlers arrived in the Chesapeake in March 1634, in good time for the year's planting and well equipped to survive the inevitable rigors of the first winter in a new colony. The Calverts located their main settlement, which they called Saint Mary's, on a creek just north of the Potomac River. There they constructed a palisaded fort similar to that of early Jamestown. After the first winter in the fort, when it became clear that the colony would have supplies sufficient for its survival and that the neighboring Indians were friendly, the distribution of land began and the inevitable dispersal of population got under way.

As planned, the proprietor's relatives were given title to 6000-acre tracts, a portion of which in each case was to be designated "the lord's demesne." Lesser manors were distributed to others, together with rights to private courts and other quasi-feudal privileges. The manorial lords, in turn, as well as the proprietor himself, began selling parcels of land to those who could afford to pay for them and renting property to others, keeping for themselves "demesne" farms and the reserves of undivided property. The Maryland records include mention of various manorial arrangements such as alienation fees and special fines and forfeitures. But none of this survived. The settlement of the countryside was in fact shaped by forces that were almost indistinguishable from those that had determined the development of Virginia.

As in Virginia, the primary cash crop was tobacco, though agriculture was generally more diversified in Maryland, and the central difficulty in expanding production was similarly the shortage of labor. Every effort was made to stimulate the importation of laborers for the farms that spread out from several centers on the mainland and on the eastern shore of Chesapeake Bay. A series of laws required prospective manor lords to import at first five workers, then ten, then twenty. Virginia's headright system was introduced in Maryland in 1640, and independent householders who settled in the colony were given special land grants for themselves and the members of their families. The population rose rapidly, partly as a result of natural increase under favorable conditions, partly due to continuing migration from England, and partly because the availability of fresh tidewater land attracted farmers from Virginia and other neighboring areas. By 1660 the population had probably reached 8000. By 1670 it had grown to over 13,000, and a contemporary map identified 823 cultivated farms in the colony, which formed a narrow but continuous strip of settled territory along the lower shores of Chesapeake Bay and the banks of the major rivers.

By then, forty years after the initial settlement, it was clear that the Calverts' efforts to reproduce elements of a manorial system had failed. They had created something simpler and more modern than a neo-feudal-manorial regime. Maryland was dominated by a landholding oligarchy with an almost monopolistic control of public offices, set off from the bulk of the population by religion as well as by wealth and power.

In the earliest years the grants of large estates had meant little since the labor shortage allowed only small segments of these properties to be cultivated. As a result the terms of servitude were generous, and freed servants acquired land and established themselves as independent farmers with ease. But property values rose as the more fertile and accessible land came under cultivation and as a growing population competed more intensely for the best of the undistributed land. Freed servants found it more difficult to establish themselves in independent households and tended increasingly to serve, for a time at least, as tenants, their labor further increasing the value of the land they worked, to the ultimate advantage of the landlords. In this situation the original "manorial" grants became increasingly valuable simply as land, quite aside from the legal privileges that were supposed to accompany them. The original grantees and their heirs—especially those closely related to the Calverts themselves—found themselves not manorial lords but well-to-do landowners in a world of tobacco farms, with control over properties valuable both for the rents they could produce and for the sale price they could ultimately command in a rising market.

The same men controlled the central offices in the government of the colony, which except for the years 1655–58 remained a legal prerogative of the proprietor, Lord Baltimore. He delegated them to his family and their close associates, most of whom were Catholic. As in Virginia, the governor's council quickly became the central governing body. But in Maryland membership on the council was less the result of achieved prominence than of personal appointment by the Lord Proprietor. As a result the earliest political struggles in Maryland were not, as in Virginia, between the governor and the councillors but between the governor and the council on the one hand and the local representatives on the other. Fiercely competitive politics was part of the life of Maryland almost from the first years of settlement.

Leonard Calvert's instructions obliged him to call an assembly of freemen and to submit all laws to that body for approval. But he retained the right to summon, adjourn, and dismiss the Assembly, and the exclusive right too of initiating all legislation, while the proprietor in England himself retained the power to veto any actions taken by the Assembly. The first full meeting of the Assembly (1638) was, like the first assemblies of Massachusetts and Virginia, a confused affair. Any freemen who chose to appear were seated. To free themselves from the dictatorial influence of the proprietary group the representatives insisted that the Assembly arrange itself like the House of Commons, take the power of convening and adjourning into its own hands, and adopt parliamentary rules. Gradually they won these demands, though the proprietor never relinquished the theoretical rights granted him in the charter. When the Long Parliament in England and the Civil War (1640–49) threw all Anglo-American relations into confusion, the Assembly seized the power of initiating legislation, and the representatives forced the Proprietor to allow them to meet independently of the council. Thereafter the representatives formed a separate lower house of the Assembly.

By 1650 the structure of forces that would persist in seventeenth-century Maryland was fully evolved. The colony was governed by an absentee proprietor, his resident governor, and his appointed council almost all of whom were Catholic. Together they monopolized the important public offices and the profits of office, and they were at the same time the major landlords. But the majority of the population, largely Protestant, had a legitimate voice in government through the lower house and maintained a continuing battle, in the Assembly and out, to force the proprietor and his followers to relinquish the privileges by which, it had once been believed, a manorial regime could be created on the Chesapeake frontier. In no other colony, by the middle of the seventeenth century, was politics so sophisticated, so bitter, and so explosive as it was in the colony that had first been conceived as an oasis of manorial harmony.

The Failure of the Dutch

Despite their differences, the early histories of Maryland, Virginia, Plymouth, and Massachusetts Bay together with its offshoots in Connecticut and Rhode Island show common characteristics. All of these colonies were originally founded as unitary communities, but in each case the original concentration of community life in a single center quickly dissolved. The population dispersed, and settlements multiplied. But as the settlers scattered, a pattern of government emerged that combined into a single structure a central executive body with representatives of the localities. And all of these colonies were culturally homogeneous: they were all overwhelmingly English, all populated by farmers and artisans together with elements of the mass of the laboring population, and they were led for the most part by members of the lesser gentry. English law was automatically put into effect and, except in Maryland, English Protestantism in some form prevailed.

The founding of what would become New York differed from this pattern on every point. As a community it was unique and it remained unique in the British North American world long after it was wholly incorporated within the British imperial system. It was the Dutch, not the English, who founded this colony; it was not originally conceived of as a community at all; its population from the start was culturally diverse; no legal system was effectively established and no government evolved comparable to the Assemblies of Virginia and Maryland and to the General Court of Massachusetts Bay.

New Netherlands, as the colony was called until its conquest by England in 1664, was an almost accidental creation of the Dutch West India Company, a worldwide trading organization, centered in Amsterdam, that was founded in 1621. The colony was never the chief concern of this complex commercial company. The company's tumultuous settlements on the Hudson and Delaware rivers were the least important, and the least successful, of all of its enterprises, which included trading forts on the Amazon River and establishments in West Africa and Brazil as well as in North America. The company set out not to create a colony at all but simply to exploit the fine fur supply and other resources of the middle Atlantic region that had been revealed by the explorations of Henry Hudson in 1609 and thereafter by voyages of a short-lived Dutch fur trading company.

In 1624 the Dutch West India Company sent over thirty Dutch and Walloon (French speaking Belgian) families to open settlements at Fort Orange and Esopus on the upper Hudson and at several points on the Delaware. Supplies, equipment, and a total of perhaps two hundred people followed in 1625. In that year too a blockhouse was built at the tip of the large island, Manhattan, that runs north and south along the mouth of the Hudson River, to protect Dutch shipping and to serve as a convenient transfer point for shipments to and from the Hudson and Delaware river posts. The next year, 1626, the beginning of a regular village was constructed around the blockhouse on Manhattan Island—windmills for sawing wood and grinding corn and some thirty log houses spaced along the west side of the island. At the same time an energetic company officer, Peter Minuit, purchased the whole of the island from the native Manhates Indians and began to consolidate in this central village, called Fort Amsterdam or New Amsterdam, the main force of the scattered Dutch settlers. He withdrew some of the settlers from the distant and exposed posts on the upper Hudson and the Delaware leaving only skeleton forces there to channel furs to New Amsterdam and to defend the Dutch claims. But the population in New Amsterdam grew very slowly, far more slowly than the population of the main English settlements, reaching only 450 in 1646 and perhaps 1500 in 1664.

By mid-century the village of New Amsterdam consisted of the original blockhouse and windmills and a number of houses, all enclosed within a palisade, or wall (which became Wall Street), the whole compound surrounded by a canal. Scattered in the open area beyond the wall and canal were about fifty farms (bouweries)—not lush, prosperous farms like those of the fertile Dutch countryside but dirt "plantations" that produced some tobacco and Indian corn and that only very gradually developed into profitable enterprises. The village of New Amsterdam itself in 1650 was a wide-open frontier community in which people of all sorts mingled, traded, and brawled. Men and women from half-a-dozen nations—Dutch, Walloons, French, English, Portuguese, Swedes, Finns, Jews, and Brazilian blacks—speaking, it was reported, eighteen different languages, and professing every religious persuasion from Catholicism to Anabaptism, flocked to the settlement seeking to turn a profit on exchanges of furs, goods, produce, or land, and occasionally setting up households and homes. It was as quarrelsome and disorderly a village as could be found in North America, torn by hostilities and constant disruption, constrained by no common purpose, disrespectful of the regulations that the company's loutish, blustering agents attempted to enforce, and above all neglected by the company that had sponsored the settlement and that remained legally responsible for its welfare.

For the company never doubted that whatever profits it was likely to make in North America would result from the fur cargoes that came in from the posts on the Hudson, Delaware, and Connecticut rivers and from nothing else except perhaps the monopolized sale of European goods to the hard-pressed settlers. The company had no intention of throwing good money after bad, as the Vir-

NEW AMSTERDAM, ABOUT THE YEAR 1650

This view appeared as a miniature inset in a large map of New Netherlands issued by Nicholas Visscher in 1655. *Legend: A:* Fort; *B:* Church of St. Nicholas; *C:* Jail; *D:* Governor's House; *E:* Gallows; *G:* West India Company's Stores; *H:* Tavern.

ginia Company had done, in the vain hope of establishing a populous and prosperous agricultural and industrial community that might in the long run repay
the original investments. It made no serious efforts to populate the colony, nor
did it have available for that purpose as mobile or alienated a population as
the English colonizers had had. To the company's directors, settlers meant
private competition for their corporate control of the fur trade. They made every
effort to monopolize that commerce, to impose heavy import and export duties
on the colonists, and to lay taxes and fees in an effort to squeeze a profit from the
settlements. Yet the profits that were made from the Dutch colony were made
not by the company itself, which never recovered its initial investment, and not
by the ordinary settlers, who lived little above the subsistence level in these early
years, but by a few Dutch middlemen in New Amsterdam. These enterprising
merchants and artisans fell in with the resident company officials to manipulate
for their own benefit the monopolized sale of goods and supplies and the prices
offered for furs and surplus farm products.

At least one of the company's directors in Holland, however, had a broader
vision of the colony's future, and his strenuous efforts made a difference. Kiliaen
van Rensselaer, a wealthy Amsterdam jeweler, argued for the creation of large-
scale private agricultural estates, like the proprietary manors in Maryland. These
farming establishments, he claimed, would not only help stabilize the colony but
provide provisions, cattle, and other necessary supplies for the Dutch ships heading for the West Indies and elsewhere in the Western Hemisphere. His efforts
resulted in the Charter of Freedoms and Exemptions issued by the company and
confirmed by the Dutch government in 1629. It authorized the creation of "pa-
troonships," large estates that would be financed by groups of investors who
would share in the profits but not in the management of these plantations, which
would be controlled by the "patroons" alone.

Ten such investment groups were created, but only one patroonship,

Rensselaerswyck, on both sides of the Hudson surrounding Fort Orange, developed in the form provided for in the charter and survived through the seventeenth century. To this huge estate van Rensselaer, the patroon, sent a flow of goods, cattle, and equipment of all sorts, and he dispatched also at his own expense farmers and miscellaneous workers to populate the grant. By 1655 he had leased sixteen farms on the estate and had developed his personal manor efficiently despite all the confusions and difficulties of managing such property through deputies. And although it is doubtful that in the end van Rensselaer recovered his heavy investment in the estate, he did establish on the upper Hudson a prosperous agricultural community.

The province of New Netherlands as a whole, however, remained ill organized, ill managed, and contentious. The continuing disorder was partly the result of the uncontrolled multiplication of thinly populated villages, poorly organized and incapable of defending themselves. They appeared on all sides: on upper Manhattan (New Haarlem); in Westchester, across the Harlem River; on Staten Island; in New Jersey (Bergen); and especially on Long Island, where five Dutch towns appeared by the 1640s. The confusion in these border towns was compounded by the agitations of the neighboring English who moved in to New Netherlands from the surrounding colonies. Attracted by the company's offer of freedom of worship, local self-government, and free land that would remain tax exempt for ten years, these migrants, while they helped populate the company's lands, created difficult administrative problems for the Dutch officials. In addition, these alien and discontented groups began agitating against the Dutch rule, advocating English conquest of the border areas if not of the whole colony. So acute were these border conflicts with the English that a formal treaty was drawn up between New Netherlands and the confederation of New England colonies that had been created in 1643. The Treaty of Hartford (1650) set the Dutch-Connecticut boundary ten miles east of the Hudson River and eliminated Dutch claims beyond that line. But the New Englanders on Long Island continued to resist the Dutch authorities, and in the South, on the Delaware River, Maryland challenged the Dutch openly. In the years preceding the English conquest of New Netherlands the English settlers in the border areas had moved to open revolt.

None of these difficulties were eased by skillful management on the part of the Dutch officials or by the effectiveness of the colony's political institutions. Of the directors general sent over by the company, only Peter Minuit (1626–32) was reasonably efficient and judicious. The first of his three successors, Wouter van Twiller (1633–38), a kinsman of van Rensselaer, was hopelessly inefficient, made more enemies than friends in the colony, and was finally removed from office in response to repeated charges that he was ruining the colony by his arrogance, corruption, indolence, and constant drunkenness. The next director general, Willem Kiefft (1638–47) may have been sober more often than van Twiller, but he too was assailed in the colony for his rapacious profiteering, half-lunatic rages, and brutish intolerance of anyone who disagreed with him. No

PETER STUYVESANT, C. 1660

Governor of New Amsterdam
for 17 years, this storming,
peg-legged war veteran swore
he would die before surrendering
New Amsterdam to the English,
but in fact he gave up the fort
quietly in 1664 and retired
peacefully to his farm in New
York City. It had become his
home, and there he died in 1672.
(*The New-York Historical Society.*)

doubt some of these charges were exaggerated, but it is certain that he personally
set on foot a savage war against the neighboring Indians.

It began in 1642, after a number of Indian raids on outlying farms, with the
slaughter of 110 unsuspecting and peaceful Indians encamped near New Amsterdam. This butchery was carried out with a barbarism that appalled even contemporary observers ("some came running to us from the country having their
hands cut off; some lost both arms and legs; some were supporting their entrails
with their hands, while others were mangled in other horrid ways, too horrid to
be conceived"). All of this set the terms of a conflict that devastated New Netherlands for three years. The Indians destroyed all the crops, buildings, and equipment they could lay hands on and killed as many settlers as they could reach.
In vengeance and in fear of total annihilation, the Dutch hired the veteran English
Indian fighter Captain John Underhill, who led 150 men in a midnight raid on
an Indian village. Some 500 Indians were shot or burned alive in the conflagration that completed Underhill's victory. The peace that was concluded in 1646
was a peace not of reconciliation but of mutual exhaustion and fear of annihilation. When in 1647 the next, and last, director general, Peter Stuyvesant, arrived, the colony was badly reduced from what it had been, hard pressed by its
competitive neighbors, and virtually abandoned by the failing company.

Stuyvesant, an autocratic ex-governor of the Dutch island of Curaçao, commissioned now to oversee all Dutch interests in the Caribbean as well as to rule
New Netherlands, plunged into a hopeless tangle of contention. Given to fits of
rage, savage in his efforts to wipe out all dissent from the colony's official Reformed Calvinism, and endowed with almost dictatorial executive powers,
Stuyvesant made little headway in solving the colony's multiplying problems.
He lacked the support of a representative assembly, but ignored a Committee of
Nine elected by the householders to represent the colony's main interests. He

failed to restrain the colonists from settling beyond defensible limits; he failed to resolve the conflicts between the ordinary settlers and the profiteering clique of officials and merchants bent on exploiting the province (indeed, he shared in the profiteering himself). He could not eliminate religious dissent or lawlessness in so tumultuous a colony. He was scarcely in a position to redress the grievances of the more affluent burghers whom he excluded from the privileges of the inner clique and who were victims of arbitrary taxation, trade monopolies, and general corruption. Least of all could he extract from the company, totally bankrupt after 1654, the subsidies needed to provide for the welfare of the colony.

In New Amsterdam a few wharves and bridges, a neglected fort, and a nondescript town hall and market area alone bore witness to the company's original support and its continuing responsibility. In 1655 the Indians, in delayed vengeance, launched a new reign of terror on the faltering and battered settlements. Farmers fled to New Amsterdam, which itself was directly attacked, and the colony's feeble resources were again drained in the effort to survive. At the same time, the English in Connecticut laid plans for seizing the colony and began more resolute encroachments on Dutch-claimed territory. By 1664, when an English fleet captured New Amsterdam, the colony as a whole was helpless and in its desolation could only look to the new English authorities with hopes that had never been stirred by the Dutch West India Company or by such storming, hard-drinking martinets as Willem Kiefft and Peter Stuyvesant.

Royal Rewards: Carolina and The Jerseys

Thus by the 1640s—within a single generation of the chartering of the Virginia Company—large-scale, permanent colonies with a total population of over 50,000 had been established in three areas of the Atlantic seaboard: along the Chesapeake Bay and the rivers of northern Virginia; at the mouth and along the banks of the Hudson River; and in central and southern New England. But no claim had yet been made to two great territories that adjoined these earliest European settlements: the mid-Atlantic region, between New Netherlands and Maryland, and the land south of Virginia to the Spanish settlement at Saint Augustine, Florida. The settlement of these two major coastal regions—from the former of which would be carved the Jerseys and Pennsylvania, and from the latter the Carolinas and Georgia—took place in very different circumstances from those of the earlier settlements. Yet the overall pattern of high hopes and imaginative designs followed by failure, disillusion, and then a slow emergence of communities in unexpected forms—this general pattern of the earlier years emerged in these later colonies as well.

Before these territories were settled, however, the greater world had been transformed. Earlier in the century, when the shores of the Chesapeake were first being opened to European colonization and villages were being founded in New England and New Netherlands, public affairs in England had been tense but relatively stable. Then in the two decades after 1640 England was convulsed by civil war, by the execution of Charles I and the exile of Charles II, and by the creation of Oliver Cromwell's republican regime, which became an autocratic protectorate. In the midst of these domestic convulsions England engaged in two international wars: one with the Dutch, largely fought at sea (1652–54), and the other with Spain (1656–59), mainly in the Caribbean. By 1658, when Cromwell died, to be succeeded briefly as protector by his son, England was exhausted by the turmoil and eager for stability and reconciliation. When Charles II, his retinue enlarged by disillusioned defectors from the conflict-torn Commonwealth, declared amnesty for all, liberty of conscience, and an endorsement of existing land titles, he was welcomed by a special parliamentary convention. He returned to England and to a restored monarchy in May 1660.

Contact had been maintained between England and the North American settlements during these two tumultuous decades, but the main flow of colonization had been interrupted. It was quickly resumed in the hugely enterprising regime of Charles II (1660–85). While still in exile he and his followers, deprived of all other properties and prospects, had eyed the colonies as a rich field for exploitation. In 1649 the king, in France, had rewarded the loyalty of seven of his close followers with the proprietorship of the Northern Neck of Virginia, a wilderness domain of 5 million acres between the Potomac and the Rappahannock rivers. Once the court was reestablished in England, it turned its attention more fully to the colonies. Enterprisers of all ranks petitioned the crown for access to the still unclaimed territories of the North American mainland. In the competitive, exuberant atmosphere of Charles II's court, a syndicate of the most powerful courtiers was formed to promote the designs of an exceptionally enterprising plantation owner of the island of Barbados, Sir John Colleton.

CHARLES II

His return from exile and restoration to the throne (1660) marked a new phase in England's overseas expansion. He chartered the Carolinas, the Jerseys, and Pennsylvania, and his government enacted legislation that turned a collection of scattered settlements into a mercantile empire (Chapter 4). *(National Portrait Gallery, London.)*

Colleton, a well-connected royalist recently returned to London, knew that Barbados, the most profitable of England's West Indian islands, was producing a surplus population of land-hungry farmers displaced by the growth of slave plantations, and he knew too that Virginians and a few New Englanders were already attempting small experimental settlements in the lands just south of Virginia. He proposed to facilitate the inevitable settlement of this region, and quickly drew into his enterprise some of the most powerful figures of the realm. Among them were his kinsman the Duke of Albemarle, who had managed Charles' return to the throne; the Earl of Clarendon, Charles II's chief minister; Lord Berkeley, brother of the governor of Virginia, Sir William Berkeley; and above all, Sir Anthony Ashley Cooper, who as the Earl of Shaftsbury would become an important political power. For these imaginative and enterprising men Colleton's proposal was irresistible. No funds, time, or effort seemed to be required of them. Since settlement was already proceeding by spillovers from the older colonies, the proprietors had merely to design a system of government and land distribution, open a land office, appoint officials, and collect the rents.

The charter that was issued to the eight partners in 1663 (extended in 1665) granted them title to all of the land lying between Virginia and central Florida and across the continent from sea to sea, and it gave them full rights of governance over the vast domain within a remarkably liberal policy of religious toleration. The management of the whole of this immense territory—many times the size of Europe—did not interest them; they were not territorial imperialists. They had their eyes on the commercial possibilities of three tiny spots on the coastal fringe: first, a northern settlement safe but isolated behind the long spits of land that formed Albemarle Sound; second, a middle settlement at the mouth of the Cape Fear River where a cluster of New Englanders had already gathered; and third, a community at Port Royal, in the deeper south, close to what would later become the colony of Georgia. From these three bustling nuclei—north, central, and south—would proliferate, the proprietors hoped, three well-populated, land-buying, rent-paying communities, and they divided the grant into three huge counties centered on these projected settlements. Then in "A Declaration and Proposals to All That Will Plant in Carolina" they designed governments patterned after the older British colonies, with veto powers retained by the

Southern British Settlements 1700

Extent of Settlement

proprietors. Freedom of religion was assured, as was a system of land distribution based on headrights of various dimensions, and large proprietary estates were reserved in every settlement.

It was a typical projection of enthusiastic colonial entrepreneurs, and it was typically unrealistic. The few Virginians in Albemarle were happy enough to organize an Assembly to protest the terms of land allotment, but their settlement, from which would eventually develop the colony of North Carolina, was isolated from transoceanic commerce by coastal sand dunes and yielded not a penny of profit. And nothing, it seemed, could induce settlers in any numbers to remain on the swampy, sandy coastal land of Cape Fear, the proposed middle settlement, which was surrounded by hostile Indians. By 1669 the enterprise of Carolina was on the point of extinction, when it was suddenly taken over by Ashley, who rescued it from failure—though not in the way he planned.

With the assistance of the philosopher John Locke, who was his secretary, physician, and general counsel, Ashley recast the assumptions and procedures of the original undertaking. Funds would have to be raised from the sponsors themselves; settlers would be sent out directly from England; and the target would be the third, most southerly location, Port Royal, the site most favored by the Barbadians. With new capital raised from the proprietors, Ashley was able to send out from England three vessels with about a hundred colonists and a large supply of equipment. The fleet was instructed to refit and to recruit more settlers in Barbados, but misfortunes of every kind befell the expedition, before and after its stopover in the West Indies. Only a handful of settlers survived to establish a settlement, which they located not where one had been planned but much farther inland, out of reach of the Spanish. In 1670 that community, isolated from principal transportation routes, was still only a palisaded garrison surrounded by

THE FIRST CAROLINA SETTLEMENT

The original Carolina fort, in an imaginative but reasonable portrayal that appeared in John Ogilby's *America, Being the Latest . . . Description of the New World* (1670). *(University of North Carolina Library.)*

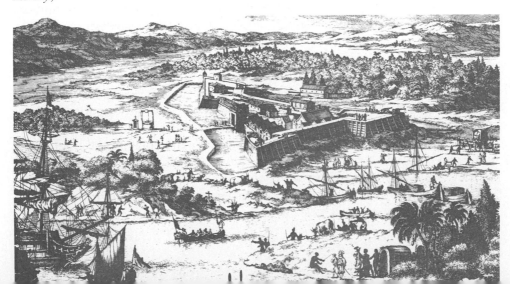

a few small subsistence farms. More vessels followed, however, especially from Barbados, and the leaders undertook a search for town sites suitable for the grand design of land distribution that had been set out by the proprietors. One of the promising sites they discovered, never contemplated by the proprietors, was Oyster Point, at the confluence of what they called the Ashley and Cooper rivers, some sixty miles from the original Port Royal. Gradually the superior attractions of this location, safe from coastal raids yet open to ocean commerce and at the hub of a network of river routes into the interior, overcame the proprietors' original plans for concentrated settlements. Family groups and individual farmers from the older mainland settlements and from Barbados began to move to this unplanned center of the colony and to establish claims to what quickly became valuable land along the banks of the rivers. By 1683 Oyster Point had been renamed Charles Town (a century later it would be called Charleston), and with a population of a thousand had become the center of a quickly growing colony altogether different from the community at Albemarle, three hundred miles to the north, and altogether different too from anything that had been contemplated by the Carolina proprietors.

Of Ashley's and Locke's hopes and plans for Carolina after the reorganization of 1669 there is an extremely detailed picture in one of the most remarkable documents of the age, the Fundamental Constitutions of Carolina, which they wrote in collaboration. Nothing shows more clearly the way in which America challenged the imagination of seventeenth-century Englishmen and evoked from them projections of their wishes and fantasies. Contemplating the socio-political chaos and the ferment of radical ideas from which England had only recently recovered, Ashley, an intellectual as well as a politician, and Locke, one of the most sophisticated minds of the century, projected for their American domain what they hoped would be a stable balance between aristocracy and democracy. They defined each of these orders by the landed property assigned to it and associated with that property a particular role in politics and administration. There would be three levels of nobility: the absentee proprietors, who were to be a final court as well as the largest landholders; the "landgraves," resident owners of very large estates who had special privileges and high public responsibilities; and the "caciques," planters of lesser though ample estates and more restricted public responsibilities but still of privileged status. These noblemen (or their deputies, in the case of the proprietors) were to administer the public affairs of the colony through eight administrative courts, and as a Council of Nobles they were to prepare legislation for the colony's parliament. Propertied freemen would participate only in the limited work of manorial courts and would vote for representatives to the unicameral parliament, which, in the early years at least, was to be limited to accepting and rejecting bills prepared by the nobility. All freeholders would pay quitrents to the proprietors at home, but the land would be worked not merely by them or by traditional tenants, but by "leetmen," whose status would be close to that of medieval serfs. Most debased of all, in this highly structured world, would be the chattel slaves, whose status as property the Constitutions formally recognized.

It was an elaborate blueprint for a hierarchical manorial world in which the association of landed property and public roles was designed to create stability. Utopian, intricately contrived, a mixture of nostalgic romanticism and hard-headed realism, the system that was detailed in the Fundamental Constitutions was a dream that could never be put into effect. The government that in fact emerged in the first decades soon came to resemble that of the other proprietary colonies, and in the eighteenth century, when the original Carolina charter was annulled, the colony's public institutions easily fell into the standard pattern of royal governments. Yet, though the romantic notions that Ashley and Locke wrote into their Constitutions died still-born or quickly fell away, a number of the document's provisions, which conformed to patterns of life that were otherwise developing in America, did become effective and did help shape the emerging community.

Religious toleration, provided for in the original Carolina charter, was rein-forced and elaborated in the Ashley-Locke Constitutions, and it contributed significantly to the development of the Carolinas. In addition, full naturalization of aliens was made extremely simple. Further, the Constitutions required that two-fifths of all the land of each county be granted in large estates to the nobility, and the way was thereby paved not so much for the creation of a landed nobility as for land speculation on a grand scale. Finally, the Constitutions established the rule of English law and outlined a structure of local administration similar to that of England—provisions that would remain fundamental to the exotic variant of British society that was developing at the end of the century in the southern part of the Carolina grant.

For what would become South Carolina *was* exotic, even in relation to the unusual communities that were elsewhere developing in mainland British America. Its quickly growing

(University of North Carolina Library.)

A Brief DESCRIPTION OF

The Province

OF

CAROLINA

On the COASTS of FLOREDA.

AND

More perticularly of a *New-Plantation* begun by the *ENGLISH* at *Cape-Feare*, on that River now by them called *Charles-River*, the 29th of *May*. 1664.

Wherein is set forth

The *Healthfulness* of the *Air*; the *Fertility* of the *Earth*, and *Waters*; and the great *Pleasure* and *Profit* will accrue to those that shall go thither to enjoy the same.

Also,

Directions and advice to such as shall go thither whether on their own accompts, or to serve under another.

Together with

A most accurate MAP of the whole *PROVINCE*.

London, Printed for *Robert Horne* in the first Court of *Gresham-Colledge* neer *Bishopsgate street*. 1666.

population, still a mere 5000 to 7000 by the end of the century, was peculiarly complex. It included not only New Yorkers, Puritan New Englanders, and Virginians, but also over 500 English Presbyterians and Baptists and also a group of Presbyterian Scots who finally managed, after earlier failures, to establish a secure if small settlement at Port Royal. Recruitment of French Huguenots from their refuge in Holland began in the earliest years and increased sizably after 1685 when these Protestant refugees lost all hope of returning to France; by 1700 at least 500 Frenchmen were settled in the colony. But the dominant element from the start was the West Indians: several thousand tough, experienced frontier farmers displaced by the growth of the plantation economy in the sugar-producing islands and determined to establish themselves and prosper in this hot, fertile, wholly unexplored land.

Experienced in the production of semitropical crops, experimental in their approach to agriculture, and familiar with slavery as a labor system, the West Indians, through the typical "starving times" of the early years, led the colony in the search for a staple crop. They tried tobacco, sugar, cotton, indigo, ginger, and a wide range of tropical fruits, while the Huguenots concentrated on silk and wine production. But like so much else in this frontier world, the economy was unpredictable. The first marketable crops were familiarly British and held no great promise: timber, cattle, and foodstuffs, all of which had to be exchanged for sugar in the West Indies and in that form redeemed in the British markets. But gradually more exotic and more lucrative possibilities became clear. The first was the trade in furs, which remained a crucial element in the economic and social life of South Carolina for half a century. As early as the 1680s pack horses could be seen hauling into Charles Town and the other coastal villages animal skins bought through a series of exchanges from Indian hunters ranging deep in the wilderness south and west of the Savannah and Altamaha rivers. The Carolina fur traders, the least squeamish of men who worked at the remote fringes of Western civilization, did not limit themselves to tracking down animals; they brought back humans as well. They led into Charles Town and the other villages troops of Indians captured from hostile tribes, and sold them into slavery at home and abroad.

Slavery—African, West Indian, American-Indian—was a basic fact of life from the earliest days of South Carolina. There is evidence that in the early years of hardship, when survival was at stake, whites and blacks, freemen and slaves, worked together—"slaved" together—in conditions of relative equality. But that did not last. By the 1690s when the first successful experiments were made in the production of rice—the crop that, with indigo and the fur trade, would ultimately secure the colony's economy and require an ever-increasing work force of slaves —their condition was reduced to absolute degradation. As early as 1708 blacks outnumbered whites in South Carolina, and by then the colony's black code, based on the savage slave laws of Barbados, was fully elaborated and rigorously enforced.

Such were the results of the enterprise of the Restoration courtiers who had been granted the great gift of Carolina in 1663. The decisive fact, at the turn of the century, was that the wide-ranging Indian trade, together with the first successes in rice production, had created a favorable balance of trade. South Carolina's survival was assured; but the colony would prosper and grow not as the nostalgic utopia of balanced orders that Locke and Ashley had dreamed of, but as a fiercely competitive world of rice plantations, savage race relations, land speculation, and commerce. Its most prominent families, as their fortunes rose, were increasingly eager for gentility, leisure, and the grace of life; but even more than the leaders of other colonies they were directly exposed to the wildness of the frontier and the barbarism of chattel slavery.

Of the Jerseys, founded at the same time as the Carolinas and under similar circumstances, less need be said. For there the proprietors' powers and claims almost immediately dissolved into an unchartable maze of divisions and subdivisions that left the territory open to largely unregulated settlement. There were, of course, high hopes at the start on the part of the two proprietors who were granted the tract of approximately 5 million acres between the Delaware and Hudson rivers by the Duke of York, overlord of the territory conquered from the Dutch. But though these first proprietors of New Jersey, Lord John Berkeley and Sir George Carteret, both of whom were already proprietors of the Carolinas, issued grandiose plans modeled on the first Carolina designs, they had even less interest in managing this province than they had in governing the Carolinas. In 1674 Berkeley sold his rights to a group of Quakers, setting in motion a bewildering selling and reselling of splintering shares, in the course of which, in 1680, the province was formally divided into two provinces, East Jersey and West Jersey. While in the eastern sector heirs of Carteret attempted vainly to organize a coherent government out of the scattered settlements that had been founded quite independently by New Englanders, Long Islanders, Barbadians, New Yorkers, and colonists sent from England, the Quaker proprietors of the western portion attempted, amid paralyzing legal complications, to establish a refuge for their persecuted community. Harassed alike by the duke's governor in New York and the government at home, the Quaker leaders, among them William Penn, issued in 1677 an extraordinarily liberal and humane document, "The Concessions and Agreements of the Proprietors, Freeholders and Inhabitants of . . . West New Jersey in America," which guaranteed a democratically elected popular assembly, individual rights including absolute freedom of conscience, and adult male participation in local and provincial government. The first West Jersey assemblies of the early 1680s attempted, with uneven success, to enact all of this into law. But though groups of settlers appeared and began the cultivation of West Jersey, the Quakers' interests in colonization soon shifted to Pennsylvania, and West Jersey followed East Jersey into the hands of land speculators interested principally in the financial value of the proprietary claims. Scottish entrepreneurs led a Scots Presbyterian migration into East Jersey where they further compounded the mixture of peoples. Gradually, as farms and towns were built in both districts, a familiarly English pattern of local government emerged, in relation to which the proprietors were quite marginal. Yet title to the undistributed land remained in the proprietors' hands, even when the crown took temporary control of the two governments (1688–92) and after the two colonies were finally and permanently rejoined into the single crown colony of New Jersey (1702).

This retention of the undistributed land by the heirs and purchasers of the original proprietary titles and the fierce political struggles that resulted when the Jersey farmers refused to pay quitrents to the proprietors or to secure their land titles with them were among the very few continuing consequences of the colony's origins. By the time of the final merger under crown auspices, the territory that the Duke of York had so casually bestowed on his two followers 38 years before, contained a population of approximately 14,000, almost all of whom lived on one-family farms of from 50 to 150 acres. The ethnic and religious diversity was extraordinary, even for a British North American colony; only New York was demographically more complex, but there a single group, the Dutch, predominated. In New Jersey no one group predominated. There were Africans, West Indians, Dutch, Germans, Huguenots, English, Scots, and Irish, worshipping as Congregationalists, Baptists, Quakers, Anglicans, Presbyterians, and Dutch and German Reformed. The colony had no particular cultural character or social organization, and its mixed farming economy was in no way distinctive in the agricultural world of the northern colonies.

Its uniqueness lay in its very lack of cultural or economic distinctiveness. New Jersey was the common denominator of the British mainland colonies, the least distinctive but by virtue of that perhaps the most typical of the earliest American communities. One can find in its later social and political history almost ideal forms of developments that elsewhere were peculiarly shaped.

(Rare Book Division, The New York Public Library,
Astor, Lenox and Tilden Foundations.)

ADVERTISEMENT,

To all Tradeſ-men, Husbandmen, Servants and others who are willing to Tranſport themſelves the Province of New-Eaſt-Jerſy in America, a great part of which belongs to Scots-men Proprietors thereof.

WHereas ſeveral Noblemen, Gentlemen, and others, who (by undoubted Rights derived from His Majeſty, a Royal Highneſs) are Intereſted and concerned in the Province of New-Eaſt-Jerſie, lying in the midſt of the gliſh Plantations in *America,* do intend (God-willing) to ſend ſeveral Ships thither, in May, June, and enſuing, 1684. from *Leith, Montroſs, Aberdeen* and *Glaſgow.* Theſe are to give notice to all Tradeſ-men, Hu men and others, who are willing and deſirous to go there, and are able to Tranſport themſelves and Families thither, upon own Coſt and Charges, to a pleaſant and profitable Countrey, where they may live in great Plenty and Pleaſure, upon far leſs and with much leſs labour and trouble then in *Scotland,* that as ſoon as they arrive there, they ſhall have conſiderable qua of Land, ſet out Heretably to themſelves and their Heirs for ever, for which they ſhall pay nothing for the firſt four or five and afterwards pay only a ſmall Rent yearly to the Owners and Proprietors thereof, according as they can agree. And all T men, Servants, and others, ſuch as, Wrights, Coupers, Smiths, Maſons, Millers, Shoe-makers, &c. who are willing there, and are not able to Tranſport themſelves, that they ſhall be carried over free, and well maintained in Meat and C the firſt four years, only for their Service, and thereafter they ſhall have conſiderable quantities of Land, ſet out to themſelve their Heirs for ever, upon which they may live at the rate of Gentlemen all their lives, and their Children after them:

Pennsylvania: A Godly Experiment and a Worldly Success

Of all the colonies, it is perhaps Pennsylvania that shows most vividly the contrast between soaring aspirations and mundane accomplishments. In part the vividness of the contrast was a consequence of the speed with which everything happened in Pennsylvania; in part too it was a reflection of the fame of the original plans and the force of the original hopes; and in part also it reflected the incongruous mixture of elements in William Penn's personality.

The founding of Pennsylvania was the accomplishment of one of the most radical religious sects of the seventeenth century. The Quakers, as religious extremists, had suffered severe persecution during their thirty years of existence as a group before the founding of Pennsylvania. Devoting themselves to finding the divine "inner light" within each soul, they practiced a religion free of all the encumbrances of church, clergy, and ritual. They were proud, courageous, and defiant of secular authority to the point of refusing to take ordinary oaths of loyalty. They advocated absolute freedom of conscience, were pacifists and political reformers.

By 1680 there were some 50,000 members of this famous radical sect in Britain, largely among the poorest elements, and there were smaller numbers scattered through continental Europe and North America. Just as in 1629–30 when the Puritans had been severely repressed by an embattled state and church, so after the hysteria of the Popish Plot (1678) when it was alleged that the country was being taken over by a French Catholic conspiracy led by the royal family, and after the Exclusion Crisis (1679–81) in which efforts were made to exclude the Catholic Duke of York from the succession to the throne, the government launched savage attacks on all dissidents, especially such extremists as the Quakers. Some 1400 of these gentle but flamboyant nonconformists were thrown in jail, and they were fined heavily both for attending Friends' meetings and for failing to attend services of the Church of England. In default of payment (and most Quakers could not meet such demands) their goods—including their means of livelihood—were seized and destroyed or carted away. Victims of such persecution were crippled not only economically but spiritually as well, for Quakers regarded work as a divine calling, and the incapacity to pursue their vocations was a further inhibition of their religious life.

William Penn, though a well-educated son of one of England's most influential naval officers and a familiar and respected figure at the court of Charles II, shared in these disabilities as he did in all the fortunes of the Quakers whom he had joined as a young man. Convinced of the truth of the Quakers' tenets, he brought to the movement great energy, high-level contacts, a lawyer's shrewdness in polemics and court proceedings, and a businesslike approach to the endless controversies in which the group was embroiled. He traveled widely as a

Quaker missionary, involved himself in every Quaker enterprise including, as early as 1674, the possibility of turning West New Jersey into a Quaker refuge; and he sought, in a series of pamphlets and court pleadings, to graft Quaker religious ideals on to liberal political principles. The West New Jersey "Concessions" of 1677 was in part his work—but only in part. For his outlook was curiously complex, and these elements of inconsistency or incongruity ultimately proved important in the history of Pennsylvania.

Penn was a radical—certainly in religion but also in politics—in that he sought every means of protecting the individual from the arbitrary power of the state and believed that government existed to improve the welfare of the masses. But though his radicalism led him to champion the notorious republican Algernon Sidney (who was executed for his political opinions in 1683) and to blast the corruption of the English government and English society under Charles II, he remained an aristocrat all his life. A political reformer and extremist in religion, he was nevertheless a monarchist, continued to believe that the well-educated and highly placed should have the decisive voices in public affairs, and though he suffered for his Quaker views, he managed to keep contact with the sources of his patronage at the court of Charles II.

It was this central ambiguity in Penn's nature and the strange variety of his associations that made possible the founding of Pennsylvania. For though by 1679 Penn was convinced that there was no future for him or his sect in England and that he had failed utterly to make headway against the complacency and corruption of the court, he retained influence enough with the king and his brother personally to turn to them successfully for the means of escape and for a refuge for the harassed Quakers.

Why Charles II granted this outspoken dissident a princely domain as a personal gift has never been fully explained. No doubt a long-standing crown debt to Penn's father played a role, and the king may have been relieved to think he could get rid of the Quakers in this convenient way; but Penn's personal relations with the royal family was probably decisive, and of that very little is known. In any case, Charles II bestowed on Penn personally in 1681 the last unassigned portion of the North American coast. The grant encompassed the entire area between New York and Maryland, stretching west almost 300 miles from the New Jersey border at the Delaware River—a total of 29 million acres, almost the size of the whole of England.

Of this territory Penn was the outright owner, and he received also the authority to form a government, make most appointments to public office, and promulgate laws subject only to the approval of an assembly of freemen and the crown's right of veto. The charter established the supremacy of Britain's mercantile regulations, but otherwise Penn was free to govern as he wished, and he immediately set forth a Frame of Government—the first of a series, as it turned out. It is a strange document: in part a code of moral principles, including absolute freedom of worship and conscience; in part an intricate formulation of traditional arrangements for civil administration, reformed to satisfy Quaker ideals; and in part a blueprint for a remarkably undemocratic government. A governor and a large council were to initiate and execute all laws, which the Assembly, elected only by property owners, might accept or reject but not amend. Thus, amid striking statements of private and public morality and appeals to humanity and decency, Penn gave power not to the people at large but to their "natural" governors, though unlike the Calverts in Maryland he never thought of himself as a feudal overlord. From this fusing of benevolence and paternalism Penn expected a community of brotherly love to emerge, tolerant, free, secure, and above all peaceful. With those hopes in mind he turned with passion and skill to making his dreams come true.

In the end he was deeply disillusioned. Simply maintaining the legal title to his colony was an endless struggle, and his relations with the settlers were profoundly embittering. His colonizing efforts, however, were extraordinarily successful, especially at the start. Immediate circulation of recruitment pamphlets through Britain and in translation in western Europe made Pennsylvania the best advertised of all American colonies. A central "city of brotherly love," Philadelphia, was founded at an excellent site one hundred miles up the Delaware River at its confluence with the Schuylkill, and a well designed street plan was laid out. A generous system of land distribution was set up; land along the Delaware south of Philadelphia (the "lower counties") was added to Pennsylvania by the Duke of York to assure the colony's access to the sea; Quaker merchants invested heavily in the colony's expenses; and an Assembly met within a year and composed a "Great Law" to serve as a temporary code of legislative and administrative principles and procedures. Above all, settlers arrived in large numbers. By 1682, when Penn visited the province, the population was already 4000—a remarkable swarming of people within a few months. There were Dutch, Swedes, and Finns from earlier settlements on the Delaware; West New Jerseyites; a large and influential influx of Welsh Quakers; Germans from the Rhineland who settled Germantown near Philadelphia; and above all English Quakers who flocked to the refuge Penn had provided for them. Fifty vessels brought 3000 more settlers in 1683. By 1700 the colony's population was a remarkable 18,000. But by then Penn knew all the difficulties that his proprietorship entailed.

He was thoroughly embroiled with Lord Baltimore over the southern boundary of the province (a dispute that would be finally settled only with the drawing of the Mason-Dixon line on the eve of the Revolution). He was faced with stiff resistance to this authority by the settlers in the newly acquired "lower counties," a district that would ultimately form the state of Delaware; he was forced to allow them their own assembly in 1701. He was unfortunate in his choice of deputy governors and suffered from their clumsiness. Above all, he was faced with fierce opposition to his concept of government, an opposition that was led by some of the most deeply committed Quakers among the settlers.

From the beginning, the colonial leaders insisted that the representative assembly, and not Penn or his deputy governors, have the determining voice in government. The house seized the power of initiating legislation and in 1696 forced Penn to concede that right; it insisted, against Penn's will, on amending bills presented to it by him; and it challenged his title to the undivided land. Pressure was maintained year after year in the 1690s until finally, after endless strain, bitter dispute, and several revisions of the original Frame of Government, Penn agreed to an altogether new Frame. Written in 1701 by a joint committee of the council and the house, this charter of liberties, which would serve as the constitution of Pennsylvania until the Revolution, embodied a total defeat of Penn's ideals. It eliminated the council altogether from the legislative process, thus constituting the only unicameral government in British America. The king's veto of laws was retained but not Penn's, and the inhabitants were explicitly freed from any special allegiance to Penn or his descendants. What remained beyond dispute to the founder and his heirs was title to the undistributed land and the sole authority to appoint the resident governors. All the other chartered powers were either eliminated or challenged, and not by a democratic, populist majority of the population but by an oligarchy of Quaker politicians and representatives elected on a limited franchise, a quarrelsome, opinionated, ambitious clique that would dominate the colony's politics for the next half-century.

Penn had lost control of the province. But though Pennsylvania had failed completely to develop into the religious utopia of its founder's dreams, it was a fabulous worldly success. Fiercely contentious in politics but populous and prosperous from the start; open and attractive equally to penniless refugees and ambitious merchants; perfectly located and peopled for maximum economic growth; the distribution center for a mass population of laborers and yet a center too of provincial high culture, Pennsylvania became within a single generation the dynamic heart of the British North American world. It was with a sure instinct in 1723 that the ambitious seventeen-year old Benjamin Franklin left Boston to seek his fortune in Philadelphia. William Penn was only five years dead, but his City of Brotherly Love had become a vigorous, prosperous community of ten thousand souls, a vital part of a colonial world that was evolving in unexpected ways.

Suggested Readings

There have been two recent efforts to summarize the English background of seventeenth-century colonization: Wallace Notestein, *The English People on the Eve of Colonization, 1603-1630* (1954) and Carl Bridenbaugh, *Vexed and Troubled Englishmen, 1590-1642* (1968). But more revealing than either of these general descriptions, which are based largely on literary sources, are studies that have nothing to do with colonization directly but make clear the disarray, mobility, and vitality of English society which underlay the extraordinary exodus of English men and women overseas: Peter Laslett, *The World We Have Lost* (1965); Peter Clark and Paul Slack, eds., *Crisis and Order in English Towns 1500-1700* (1972); and the writings of W. G. Hoskins on English local history, most of which are listed in his *Local History in England* (1959). The best introduction to the economic history of pre-industrial England is Charles Wilson, *England's Apprenticeship, 1603-*

1763 (1965), two-thirds of which is on the seventeenth century; chaps. i–iii are particularly relevant.

The starting point for all modern studies of the native North American Indian population is A. L. Kroeber, *Cultural and Natural Areas of Native North America* (1939 and later eds.), a masterwork of an anthropologist which has come into question on several points but remains fundamental. There is a vast array of historical writings on the North American Indian population, most of it discussed and listed in William N. Fenton, *et al.*, *American Indian and White Relations to 1830: Needs and Opportunities for Study* (1957) and much of it summarized in topical rather than chronological categories in Wilcomb E. Washburn, *The Indian in America* (1975). But there is no detailed historical description of the seaboard Indians on the eve of European colonization (for a sketch, see T. J. C. Brasser, "The Coastal Algonkians: People of the First Frontiers," in Eleanor B. Leacock and Nancy O. Lurie, eds., *North American Indians in Historical Perspective*, 1971), and there are sustained accounts of the conflict of races for only a few of the seventeenth-century colonies: Allen W. Trelease, *Indian Affairs in Colonial New York: The Seventeenth Century* (1960); Alden W. Vaughan, *New England Frontier: Puritans and Indians, 1620–1675* (1975); Douglas E. Leach, *Flintlock and Tomahawk: New England in King Philip's War* (1958); Nancy O. Lurie, "Indian Cultural Adjustment to European Civilization," in James M. Smith, ed., *Seventeenth-Century America* (1959); and Francis Jennings, *The Invasion of America* (1975). Jennings' book is a bitter outcry against the wrongs done the North American Indians by the Puritans (and in this, a criticism of Vaughan's more even-handed treatment) and a boiling polemic against historians' characterization of the Indians as sparce in numbers, hostile to Europeans, savage, heathen, and unsophisticated in agriculture, trade, and politics. What the Indians were, aside from the victims of Puritans and mythologizing historians, does not emerge. Jennings' bibliography is excellent.

The most detailed and comprehensive single narrative of the English settlements in the seventeenth century is Charles M. Andrews, *The Colonial Period of American History* (vols. I–III, 1934–37), which concentrates on constitutional history and the development of public institutions. A more up-to-date and broad-ranging account of the planting and early growth of the southern colonies is Wesley F. Craven, *The Southern Colonies in the Seventeenth Century, 1607–1689* (1949). The settlement stories are retold in briefer scope in John E. Pomfret, *Founding the American Colonies, 1583–1660* (1970) and Wesley F. Craven, *The Colonies in Transition, 1660–1713* (1968), both of which contain extensive bibliographies.

On the founding of Virginia, there are, besides the relevant chapters of Andrews' *Colonial Period*, vol. I, and Craven's *Southern Colonies*, a detailed narrative of public events in Richard L. Morton, *Colonial Virginia* (2 vols., 1960); an excellent short summary in Alden T. Vaughan, *American Genesis* (1975); a revealing account of the high culture of the initiators of settlement, in Richard B. Davis, *George Sandys* (1955); biographies of Pocahontas and John Smith by Philip L. Barbour; and two excellent collections of documents: L. G. Tyler, ed., *Narratives of Early Virginia, 1606–1625* (1907) and Warren M. Billings, ed., *The Old Dominion in the Seventeenth Century . . .* (1975). Sigmund Diamond's provocative essay, "From Organization to Society: Virginia in the Seventeenth Century," *American Journal of Sociology*, 63 (1958), 457–75,[1] interprets the founding as the transformation of a quasi-military organization into a fully formed society of multiple relationships. Bernard Bailyn, "Politics and Social Structure in Virginia," in Smith, ed., *Seventeenth-Century America*, pp. 90–115,* considers the development of politics in its relation to the evolving social structure. Edmund Morgan considers the human cost of the colony's success in terms of the exploitation of labor in "The First American Boom: Virginia 1618–1630," *William and*

---

[1]This essay and several mentioned in the references that follow have been reprinted in an excellent collection, *Colonial America: Essays in Politics and Social Development* (Stanley N. Katz, ed., 2d ed., Boston, 1976). Essays and selections from books that appear in this volume are indicated by an asterisk (*).

Mary Quarterly, 3d ser.,[2] 18 (1971), 169–98,* a topic discussed in a broader context in his *American Slavery, American Freedom* (1975).

The labor problem in Virginia involves the difficult question of the origins of chattel slavery. The modern debate on that question was initiated and framed by a brilliant article by Oscar and Mary F. Handlin, "Origins of the Southern Labor System," *Wm. and Mary Q.*, 7 (1950), 199–222,* reprinted as chap i of Handlin's *Race and Nationality in American Life* (1957). Handlin's view is that chattel slavery in British America was a unique institution, different from slavery in any other form or place; that the concept of "slavery" in its American meaning was created in the seventeenth-century Chesapeake; and that it arose as a legal condition, in response not so much to race prejudice as to an effort to attract voluntary white labor by debasing the condition of involuntary black labor. For differing views, emphasizing race prejudice, the fear of foreignness, and religious differences, see Winthrop Jordan, *White over Black* (1968)*, Part I, and Carl N. Degler, "Slavery and the Genesis of American Race Prejudice," *Comparative Studies in History and Society*, 2 (1959), 49–66. For a listing of recent writings on the subject, see Vaughan, *American Genesis*, p. 198.

On the Pilgrims and Plymouth, see George D. Langdon, Jr.'s general account, *Pilgrim Colony* (1966) and John Demos's social analysis, *A Little Commonwealth* (1970). George F. Willison's *Saints and Strangers* (1945) is a breezy, amusing interpretation. Bradford's great history, *Of Plymouth Plantation*, is available in a modern edition prepared by Samuel E. Morison (1952).

On the founding and early development of the Puritan colonies in New England, see, besides Andrews' chapters in *The Colonial Period*, Edmund S. Morgan's short biography of John Winthrop, *Puritan Dilemma* (1958); Darrett Rutman's *Winthrop's Boston* (1965); Samuel E. Morison's *Builders of the Bay Colony* (1930); Raymond P. Stearns, *The Strenuous Puritan: Hugh Peter* (1954); and above all, Winthrop's own *Journal . . . 1630–1649* (J. K. Hosmer, ed., 2 vols., 1908). For a theatrical and psychological account of Anne Hutchinson's career, see Emery Battis, *Saints and Sectaries* (1962), and on Roger Williams there are books by S. H. Brockunier, Perry Miller, and Edmund S. Morgan. On seventeenth-century Connecticut, besides Andrews, see Isabel M. Calder, *The New Haven Colony* (1934) and Mary J. A. Jones, *Congregational Commonwealth* (1968). On Rhode Island, see Sydney V. James, *Colonial Rhode Island* (1975), and on Maine and New Hampshire, Charles E. Clark, *The Eastern Frontier* (1970), Part I.

Maryland is well covered in Andrews' and Craven's general books, but in the case of New York the general accounts should be supplemented by Thomas J. Condon, *New York Beginnings* (1968); Van Cleaf Bachman, *Peltries or Plantations* (1969); and the early chapters of Michael Kammen, *Colonial New York* (1975). M. Eugene Sirmans, *Colonial South Carolina* (1966) and Peter H. Wood, *Black Majority* (1974) are essential on South Carolina. Hugh T. Lefler and Albert R. Newsome, *North Carolina* (1954) is a good summary of that colony's early history. Wesley F. Craven, *New Jersey and the English Colonization of North America* (1964) is the best short book on that colony, though there are a number of more detailed studies by John E. Pomfret. The most recent history of the founding of Pennsylvania is Edwin B. Bronner's *William Penn's "Holy Experiment"* (1962); on the colony's early political history, see Gary B. Nash, *Quakers and Politics . . . 1681–1726* (1968). Catherine O. Peare, *William Penn* (1957) narrates the essential facts of the founder's life in a somewhat exclamatory fashion; Mary M. Dunn, *William Penn, Politics and Conscience* (1967) is an excellent study of Penn's ideas and religious beliefs.

---

[2]This journal will be referred to hereafter as *Wm. and Mary Q.*

Europe in the Wilderness

American Society in the Seventeenth Century

Thus, through these many agencies—commercial companies, religious organizations, individual entrepreneurs, syndicates of courtiers—communities of Europeans were established on mainland North America. By 1700 these colonies formed an almost continuous line of seaboard settlements from New Hampshire to South Carolina and westward irregularly a hundred miles or so to the first falls of the coastal rivers. The total population of some 250,000 Europeans and Africans and their descendants, almost all of them English-speaking, were by no means spread evenly through this broad area. They clustered along river valleys to take advantage of the fertile soil and easy lines of communication, and they left behind large pockets of unsettled land. Even in the oldest and most densely settled communities of Massachusetts and Virginia this was still a frontier world, fundamentally shaped by its continuing encounter with the wilderness. Yet there were areas populated by native-born children of native-born parents—a third generation in America. For them, home was the colony, however much they might acknowledge a greater "home" abroad. Though they did not think of themselves as peculiarly "American," they lived settled lives in communities familiar to them from birth, and these were communities whose distinctive characteristics were becoming clear.

Newcomers to the colonies in 1700 (and immigration continued in all areas, though least in New England) were no longer faced with the bewildering disarray that earlier settlers had known. But neither did they find themselves in communities like any they had seen before. The British colonies had by 1700 acquired distinctive and permanent characteristics. A society had formed that was significantly altered from the familiar European models. There were great variations region by region and settlement by settlement, but despite the differences, common elements of a re-ordering of European life could be found in these communities.

This re-ordering of social life was not the result of design, or planning, or intent. Planning, as we have seen—elaborate designs and soaring dreams—there had been in abundance. But none of these original plans, hopes, and expectations had been fulfilled; all had been quickly destroyed or slowly dissolved upon contact with the harsh reality. The deviations from European life that developed in the course of the seventeenth century were products of the impact of circumstance upon the culture of essentially conservative immigrants, most of whom sought personal satisfactions, personal freedoms, and security within agreeable and familiar patterns of life. For many, the changes that took place were felt to be regressions rather than advances. Change was more often resisted than pursued. Only later would the alterations in community life be seen as advances toward an ideal—the ideal, expressed in the Enlightenment goals of the Revolution, of a freer, more fulfilling way of life.

Population Growth and Structure

Basic changes in community life were set in motion even before the influence of the physical environment was felt. American society in the seventeenth century was shaped most elementally by demographic characteristics that flowed from the basic conditions of immigration. Because the first American population was an immigrant population and because life in the colonies was harsh and was known to be harsh, the society that resulted was no evenly balanced re-creation of the social structure of Europe. The upper strata of traditional society were absent from the start. Of Europe's ruling nobility, there were no representatives at all. There were few even of what might loosely be called the aristocracy or of the upper gentry, few even of the professional upper middle class, if one may use these modern terms. For then, as now, society's leaders—the established and realistically hopeful—did not easily tear up their roots, migrate, and struggle to reestablish themselves in an undeveloped land.

Almost all of the free population in mainland North America was recruited from the lower working population of England and Holland—not the lowest, not destitute vagrants and outcasts, but farmers, industrial workmen, tradesmen, and artisans. In the immigrant lists of the time, the two occupations most commonly entered are "husbandman" (an independent farmer or lesser yeoman) and "servant," which included domestic, agricultural, and industrial workers, anyone dependent on another for employment. Outside of New England, between one-half and two-thirds of all white immigrants were indentured servants or convicts whose penalties were commuted to "transportation." They were bound, for four years or more, to serve some master faithfully in exchange for their trans-Atlantic passage, care and protection, and "freedom dues," which often included a small parcel of land. Averaging 2500 arrivals a year, these immigrants to the Chesapeake, originally bound in various conditions of servitude, totaled 100,000 by 1700.

Further, American society as it emerged from the seventeenth century was peculiarly mobile. The population was originally recruited, and continued to be recruited, from groups already dislodged from secure roots, often for whom resettlement in America was not a unique transplantation but a second or third uprooting. And this original mobility, renewed with each subsequent wave of immigrants, was reinforced in most places by circumstances in the colonies. Outside of New England, institutional or legal restraints on mobility, so vital a part of life in traditional European societies, scarcely existed at all. Of the annual influx of 2500 indentured servants in the Chesapeake region, an average of 2000 survived servitude to enter the community free of involvement, commitment, or obligation, free to follow the attractions of security, profit, or congeniality wherever they might be found.

More important still, the American population in the seventeenth century was unusual in its propensity for growth. The information that historians have recently gathered on the demographic characteristics of early America reveals a society remarkably fertile and healthy. In an age in which most of European society was scarcely reproducing itself, the most prolific of the settled communities in America may have reached the extraordinary growth rate of 5–6 percent a year. Until the 1640s, it is true, Virginia, and possibly Maryland too, seem to have remained a death trap of disease and malnutrition. A random list of 99 deponents before one Virginia county court shows an average age at death of only 48 in the years between 1637 and 1664. But even in Virginia the death rate fell rapidly in the later seventeenth century, and the population of that colony, supplemented by constant immigration, shot up: it stood at 8000 in 1644, quadrupled to 32,000 in the next 30 years, and then more than doubled once again in the next thirty years, reaching an estimated 75,600 in 1704. In New England, once the initial immigration was completed, the population grew during the seventeenth century at the rate of 2.6 percent or 2.7 percent a year, which meant that the settled population, quite aside from further immigration, was doubling approximately every twenty-seven years. And whatever else may be said about such a phenomenon as this, it meant that all other social changes were intensified by sheer demographic pressure.

How can this extraordinary growth rate be explained? Not, apparently, by an unusual birthrate. The birthrates available for selected American communities are similar to birthrates in French and English villages of this period. The root of the difference apparently lies in the lower death rate in the American colonies, once the original "starving times" were over and once the extended "seasoning" time in Virginia came to an end in the 1640s. The average number of recorded children in 1500 randomly selected New England families of the seventeenth century is 7.13 and the survival rate was extraordinarily high. In Plymouth, Massachusetts, the life expectancy of men who survived to the age of 21 was 69.2 years, and in Andover, Massachusetts, the average age at death of the first settlers was 71.8 years; for their sons the average was 65.2. In that same village community, one of the few that have been studied intensively, life expectancy at birth for males in the seventeenth century was longer by 12.6 years than it would be for men in England 200 years later.

How can this extraordinary survival rate be explained? Partly it appears to have been the result of the unusual age structure of the population. The Ameri-

ALICE MASON, 1670

This forthright, unpretentious portrait by an unknown artist illustrates not only the appearance of children in the seventeenth century but attitudes to children and to childhood that reflect prevailing religious ideas. This is not a child but a miniature adult, an individual who happens to be short and deficient in certain ways but fully endowed and fully responsible for her actions. The modern concept of childhood was a much later development. (*Adams' Homestead, Quincy, Massachusetts.*)

Embellishing the Wilderness

The European settlement of North America was an intrusion into the wilderness, a struggle to impose the familiar forms of an advanced civilization into an environment that was almost totally unredeemed from its natural, uncultivated state. The awareness of this struggle was as vivid to those who settled the last British colony, Georgia, and who pictured Savannah in 1734 as a tiny clearing at the edge of a vast forest as it had been to the settlers of Virginia a century and a quarter earlier. The struggle took its toll. Not only were there significant modifications in the conduct of everyday life—regressions and simplifications, it seemed—but at the margins there were complete surrenders to the wilderness. There were always frontiersmen who spent months drifting from one isolated primitive encampment to another, and emerging from time to time to buy with animal skins what they needed for survival and to tell remarkable tales of worlds beyond the mountains and the swamps. But these wandering semi-primitives were rare in British America—much rarer than they were in French Canada, where half-savage trappers and woodsmen (the famous *coureurs de bois* who roamed the wilderness for years at a time) formed a significant part of the population.

View of Savannah, 1734. The I. N. Phelps Stokes Collection, The New York Public Library.

British America from the beginning was a bourgeois society. The wilderness exerted no fatal seduction; it proved to be a challenge to the arts of cultivation, to the nesting instinct, to the impulse to domesticate and to embellish. Beauty, in European terms, was sought from the start, transferred at first from "home" and then imitated, however crudely, by local craftsmen. The artifacts of daily living had to be made from materials that lay at hand, by men whose task it was to provide the necessities of life, not the refinements. But though the products were often rough they were rarely primitive. Occasionally, even in the earliest years, some striking embellishment, some special grace of line, balance, or proportion, some flash of vivid and harmonious color, emerged to mark the point at which craft turned to art.

Above, Spindled chair, 1640–1660. *Courtesy, Museum of Fine Arts, Boston. Photo by Richard Cheek.* Below, Massachusetts press cupboard, late seventeenth century. *Courtesy, Museum of Fine Arts, Boston. Gift of Mr. & Mrs. William R. Robinson.* Right, Queen Anne chair from Philadelphia. *Courtesy, The Henry Francis du Pont Winterthur Museum.*

So furniture was crafted in the seventeenth century from local woods, its bare, hard surfaces as uncomfortable as they were serviceable and durable; but sometimes even in the earliest years the furniture was embellished too, with a conscious style, decorated and beautified. Spindled oak pieces like the Ipswich, Massachusetts, press cupboard were stained with vegetable dyes to give them tone, and their ornaments painted black to simulate ebony; the result was a complex, dappled black-brown surface. Later such embellishments grew more sophisticated as the Queen Anne chair reveals; and by the early 1700s

Above, Crewel petticoat border, mid-eighteenth century. *Courtesy, Museum of Fine Arts, Boston. Gift of Mrs. J. R. Churchill.* Right, Japanned chest, early eighteenth century. *Courtesy of the Metropolitan Museum of Art, Purchase 1940, Joseph Pulitzer Bequest.* Upper right, Silver tankard, late seventeenth century. *Courtesy, Museum of Fine Arts, Boston. Gift of Mr. & Mrs. Dudley Pickman.* Lower right, Sugar box, by John Coney, 1680–1690. *Courtesy, Museum of Fine Arts, Boston, Elliot Fund.*

japanned highboys were being produced with structural designs in classical modes and oriental scenes in brilliant color. Quite independently the Dutch in New York and the Germans in Pennsylvania developed from their own folk traditions a distinctive pattern of decoration. And everywhere craftsmen learned to produce not only beautifully designed wooden furniture in contemporary styles but upholstered pieces that were colorful as well as solid and comfortable.

Textile embellishments took many forms, from embroidered chair seats and petticoat borders to crewel bed hangings and draperies. And the skill of the silversmiths developed quickly too. By the end of the seventeenth century intricately designed and handsomely worked silver bowls, tankards, coffee pots, and sugar boxes were seen on tables in the South as in the North. Craftsmen like John Coney were creating objects in silver that would delight their users and viewers for generations to come.

Everyday life was visibly enhanced—not transformed into a wonder world of aristocratic ostentation but simply embellished, decorated, elevated above mere practicality. Clock faces and inlaid rifle stocks became minor works of art, the clock cases and gun grips beautifully worked wood. Door frames were improved by conscious imitation of metropolitan models. Glassware evolved in unexpected forms, and metal workers produced weathervanes that had the animated beauty of modern mobiles.

Left, bed hangings, c. 1745. *Old Goal Museum, York, Maine*. Right, Doorway of Fowler Tavern, mid-eighteenth century, Westfield, Massachusetts. *Courtesy of the Metropolitan Museum of Art, Rogers Fund, 1916*. Below, Glass sugar bowl, late eighteenth century. *Courtesy, The Henry Francis du Pont Winterthur Museum*.

Raleigh Tavern, Williamsburg, Virginia.
Colonial Williamsburg Foundation.

The wilderness remained—a threat to European civilization and a constructive challenge to creativity in a people conscious both of the simplicity of their lives and of the richness of their cultural heritage. Young men like Jefferson grew up in a borderland world, looking out from Queen Anne rooms of spare elegance on to a wild, uncultivated land.

Siteman/Stock, Boston.

can population was youthful. Most of the tens of thousands of indentured servants were between 18 and 24 years of age when they arrived. In Bristol, Rhode Island, 54 percent of the population were children; in seventeenth-century England the equivalent figure is 42.6 percent. The American population, being youthful, was less vulnerable to the ravages of disease than a more evenly age-distributed population would have been. The survival rate reflects too a higher proportion of women who were in the years of fertility, 15–45, and in addition a younger average age at marriage, especially for women. In England, where 15 percent of the population were servants constrained from marrying young and where socioeconomic circumstances made establishing new households difficult for those without inheritances, it appears that the average age at first marriage was 27 for men and 26 for women. For one Massachusetts community that has been closely studied (Dedham), the equivalent figures are 25.5 and 22.5. In Plymouth the average age at first marriage for women at the end of the seventeenth century was 22.3; altogether, in Bristol, R.I., before 1750, the average age for women's first marriages was 20.5.

As a result of these younger marriages women commonly bore children from their very early twenties until they were in their mid-forties. Younger marriages also assured a higher survival rate of children since the offspring of such marriages in preindustrial societies seem to have been more resistant to disease. Beyond all of these factors lay the general fact that there were fewer "demographic crises" than there were in Europe—fewer disastrous epidemics, catastrophic crop failures, and resulting voluntary restraints on childbearing.

Finally, of the population characteristics that distinguish the emerging American communities from the parent communities abroad, there is the existence of an altered sex ratio. In England through these years, as in most settled societies, there were more women than men. The figures for England in the period 1574–1821 are 91.3 men to every 100 women. In the early years of settlement in America the figures are wildly inverted. In Virginia in 1625, over 75 percent of the settlers were men, and by midcentury the proportion was still approximately 6 to 1. Even in New England, where immigration by family was more common, there were 3 men for every 2 women in the middle of the century (a ratio reached in Virginia only in 1700), and while the proportion tended to level out as the century progressed, the traditional preponderance of women was by no means reached by 1700.

One can only speculate on the consequence of this altered sex ratio, which in various degrees was repeated in each immigrant wave and in the early years of most newly opened communities. The scarcity of women no doubt tended to reduce the importance of dowries in the arrangements for marriage, and probably contributed to the gradual improvement in the legal, social, and psychological status of women. What more it may have meant in terms of sex relations, miscegenation, and perhaps the practice of religion can only be surmised, though these were areas of the most intense personal experience, then as now.

[handwritten margin note:] ← mixture of races, esp. in marriage

Economic Instability

The more manifest aspects of American society as it emerged in the early eighteenth century—economic life, social organization, and the practice of religion—varied greatly from region to region and from colony to colony. But running through each of these areas of life was a single, central characteristic, which emerges most clearly when one contrasts developments in the colonies not merely with experiences abroad but with the presumptions the colonists brought with them, their unquestioned notions and ideal expectations. In considering each of the main areas of experience, one may most profitably start by isolating these assumptions and expectations, the ideal by which reality would instinctively be measured. Against this background the departures of American life stand out most clearly, and their impact on the inner experiences of immigrants seeking to re-create a familiar and controllable world may most realistically be assessed.

The dominant view of the economy that the colonists brought with them was of a system in equilibrium, a stable system through which a more or less constant supply of goods and services flowed for the benefit of a population of relatively unchanging needs and desires. The object of individual effort in such a system was to secure oneself within it and to help preserve its organization. Difficulties, when they arose, were assumed to be disturbances in the established relations among the producing, distributing, and consuming elements, and remedies were sought that would bring the elements back into their proper proportions so as to keep the original structure intact. The object of primary concern was the consumer not the producer, and a consumer of fixed wants. Controls were assumed to be necessary to keep the economy in proper working order, especially to prevent greed or accidents from disturbing the equilibrium. Yet controls were not assumed to be solely those of the state. Lesser corporate bodies, such as gilds and municipal institutions, that stood between the individual and the state were assumed to be primary agencies of economic regulation.

Such were the ordinary presumptions and the ideal expectations of colonists still close to late medieval culture, still far from the modern world of dynamic economic systems in which an ever rising production and the manipulation of consumption are essential keys to success. How well did the nascent colonial economies conform to these traditional assumptions? The economies that developed north and south violated these expectations on every point, and in doing so created a sense of jarring disarray until, ultimately, a different kind of economic system became established and familiar and Americans learned to accommodate themselves to the high instability that lay at the heart of this new system.

In New England there had originally been little desire for or expectation of the creation of a commercial system that would link the Bay Colony's small port towns to an intricate network of Atlantic commerce and involve the Puritans in the greater world they had left behind. The original goal was economic self-sufficiency, the condition most likely to preserve the Bible Commonwealth free

SAUGUS IRONWORKS

In this perfect restoration of the works as they existed in 1650, the forge is at the left, the rolling and slitting mill at the right. *(Richard Merrill, photographer.)*

of corruption and contamination. But by the late 1650s, three stages of development had led inexorably to a complex economic pattern that would continue basically unchanged until the Revolution transformed the American economy a century and a quarter later.

During the first decade of settlement, 1630–40, the Bay Colony's economy was self-sufficient, but the conditions that made it so could not be sustained. The flow of immigrants, which continued steadily until the outbreak of the English Civil War, brought into the Puritan communities capital in the form of goods and equipment, personal effects, cash, and credit that could be used to buy goods directly from abroad. The pooled funds of the original Massachusetts Bay Company also contributed to this original capital. Once the immigration ceased, however, new capital sources had to be found to continue the development of the colony and to maintain its economic self-sufficiency.

The second-stage effort to perpetuate the colony's economic independence took two main forms. First, Puritan entrepreneurs, with the active support of the colony's government, sought to produce locally the supplies needed by the settlers, which meant establishing manufactures of iron goods and cloth. An elaborate scheme set on foot by John Winthrop, Jr., the governor's son and himself a sophisticated intellectual and public official, resulted in the establishment in Saugus, Massachusetts, of a complete iron works. It was the product of prodigious efforts by a few devoted entrepreneurs, of the investment of over £12,000 by English businessmen, and of gifts from the General Court of land, tax exemption, and a monopoly of the local markets. But although the Saugus Works was created almost overnight with generous public support, it flourished only briefly and then collapsed into a bankruptcy from which it never recovered; it was the victim of a destructive squeeze between inescapably high costs and low profits. Similarly ineffective was the colony's effort to establish a local cloth industry. A group of weavers from Rowley, England, established another Rowley in Massachusetts and sought to re-create their industry in that frontier town. A Massachusetts law of 1656 hopefully but quite unrealistically ordered all idle hands in the Bay Colony to busy themselves with spinning and weaving and assessed every family an amount of cloth proportionate to the number of available "spinners" in the household. But there were no "idle hands" in this labor-short society. Every available "hand" could find more than enough employment in the fields of the newly opened towns. There was no effective response to the government's demands and exhortations.

But if neither of the two basic manufactures could be locally produced, self-sufficiency of a sort might yet be created by discovering a commodity of high value in proportion to weight and bulk which might be exchanged directly in England for the needed goods. For a moment in the early economic history of New England it seemed as though this would be the ultimate solution. The settlers found a rich supply of fur-bearing animals in the coastal region and just beyond, and they began a quick exploitation of this highly profitable resource. The easily available beavers, otters, and raccoons were taken by the hundreds and their pelts shipped home in direct exchange for manufactures. But furs proved to be a limited resource. The animals reproduced themselves far more slowly than they were killed, and by the 1650s the supply in the immediate coastal region was

COD FISHING ON THE GRAND BANKS AND THE NORTH AMERICAN SHORE

This French print of 1705 shows all stages of the fishing industry, from catching the fish (*C*) to gutting and scaling (*F,G*) and drying and packing (*V,Q*). Fish at the upper left are being carted away for salting, and the press at lower left (*R*) is extracting oil from the cod livers, the waste draining into the tub (*S*), the oil into the barrel (*T*). *Library of Congress.)*

exhausted. The New Englanders then pressed west against the Dutch on the Hudson who blocked them from contact with the deeper sources of furs in northern New York and the Great Lakes region. Some furs continued to flow into Boston from trading posts on the Maine coast and the upper Connecticut River, but furs as a source of capital, after a decade of wonderful promise, faded from the economy of New England as it entered its third and permanent stage of development.

In place of autonomy and in place of direct exchange, a generation of small merchants in the Bay Colony worked out a system of exchanges throughout the Atlantic world that would produce the needed goods. But they did this only by involving the colony closely in the greater world beyond its boundaries. Increasingly, as the population rose, foodstuffs, fish, and timber products became available and the commercial possibilities they created became clear. These products could be sold not in England, which also produced them, but in Catholic Europe (France, Spain, and the Wine Islands of Madeira, the Azores, and the Canaries). These markets could use all the fish that could be sent, and the West Indies could absorb not only fish and other food supplies needed to feed the labor force but also timber for buildings and horses to help work the sugar mills. From the West Indies in turn sugar products could be obtained for sale elsewhere in America and in the English markets; and from Madeira, the Azores, and the Canary Islands wine could be procured for sale elsewhere in the Atlantic ports. And other contacts could be made. Tobacco could be picked up in the Chesapeake, fish in Newfoundland, and various agricultural products in New York and later in Pennsylvania. An intricate circuit of exchanges could be created — horses and fish for sugar, sugar for bills of exchange, wine, tobacco or locally produced goods. The purpose of these series of exchanges, which might go on for months or even years before being resolved, was the eventual establishment of credits on the ledgers of some merchant in London or Bristol that would finance the purchase of manufactures to be imported to the colony for profitable sale. These profits would in turn make possible ever bigger shipments in the next cycle and perhaps investment in shipbuilding as well.

So the commercial system evolved in New England, to be re-created with variations in all the northern colonies. Each colony's system was distinctive, but all were interlocked and had common characteristics. These were no stable, easily controllable commercial flows. Though patterned, they were highly unstable, driven by uncertainty and inescapable risks. Everything conspired to make this commercial world dynamic and erratic.

For, to begin with, the local production of salable commodities was unreliable and irregular. Not only were there ordinary crop failures but the hinterland farmlands were still being opened and their location and volume of production were still experimental. Even less reliable were the West Indian and Atlantic island markets, which might easily be glutted by a few shipments and from whom it was impossible to obtain reliable market information before cargoes

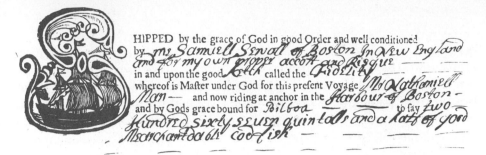

SHIPPED by the grace of God in good Order and well conditioned by *mr. Samuell Sewall of Boston In New England and for my own proper accot and Risque* in and upon the good *Ketch* called the *Fidelity* whereof is Master under God for this present Voyage *Mr. Nathaniell Man* and now riding at anchor in the *Harbour of Boston* and by Gods grace bound for *Bilboa* to say *two hundred sixty seven quintalls and a half of good Merchantable coodfish*

being marked and numbred as in the Margin, and are to be delivered in the like good Order and well conditioned at the aforesaid Port of *Bilboa* (the dangers of the Seas only excepted) unto *mr. Jnõ Short & Comp—* or to *their* Assigns, he or they paying fraight for the said Goods *a piece of Eight ℈ Quintal old pay* ———

Primage Jod. with Primage and average accustomed. In witness whereof the Master or Purser of the said *Ketch* hath affirmed to three Bills of Lading, all of this tenour and date, the one of which three Bills being accomplished, the other two to stand void. And so God send the good *Ketch* to her desired Port in safety, Amen. Dated in *Boston November 10th 1687.* *James Nathaniell Man*

SHIPPING MANIFEST, 1687 *(Massachusetts Historical Society.)*

were sent. Further, this commerce was managed not by a few big firms whose decisions and agreements might stabilize the system, but by many small and highly competitive merchants none of whom had a commanding role in the system as a whole. Finally, specialization for any of these small merchant entrepreneurs was virtually impossible if only because a chronic money shortage led to the necessity for payment in kind, with the result that every merchant had to be prepared to sell almost any commodity at any time in any market he could find.

As a result of all these conditions, it was nearly impossible to match available goods to available markets. Between the initial shipment of goods and their arrival at an ultimate destination, the entire commercial picture could change. The merchants ventured largely into the dark and were constantly victims of sudden gluts and unpredictable famines and of vicious price fluctuations. There was no fixed geometry of trade. There was no rigid "triangular" trade, in the seventeenth century or after. There were only constantly shifting polygons, forming and reforming as merchants undertook what were in effect peddling voyages up and down the North American coast and in the Caribbean and Atlantic commercial lanes.

Overseas trade proved to be a highly competitive, risky business, in which success was the result not of the conservative management of stable flows of commerce but of speculative venturing, intelligent risk taking, and driving entrepreneurship. The principle of success was not the completion of safe, carefully planned exchanges but the almost limitless accumulation of extemporized exchanges of all sorts of commodities in a great variety of markets. It was a dynamic system, impelled by powerfully expansive forces.

From this commercial system, which for over a century provided the northern colonies with the goods they needed and helped produce the material basis for a flourishing provincial culture, important social consequences flowed. In such a commercial world there could be no hard and clear definition of a merchant "class." The situation encouraged the participation of small men, newcomers who would have been rejected as interlopers in English commercial towns. There were no effective institutional boundaries that might confine the group. Neither gilds nor municipal corporations developed to limit the merchant community or to regulate its activities. Anyone's contribution to the struggling commercial economy was valuable, and the purpose of government intervention could only be to empower innovation, not limit it. A dynamic, unstable, unpredictable yet successful commercial system had produced a fluid merchant group, constantly recruiting newcomers from among successful tradesmen and farmers and seeking security and wealth in a system whose essence was risk.

No less risky, competitive, and unstable was the economic system that developed in the Chesapeake region around the production and marketing of the staple crop of tobacco. The details are of course altogether different from those of the northern commercial system, but the essence—the dynamic, risky, unstable nature of the economy—was the same. Here too success would come not from sharing in regular production and a stable process of distribution but from involvement in runaway cycles of production and a lurching, unpredictable distribution system. And in the South as in the North, a dynamic economy produced uncontrollable social consequences.

Originally there had been little enthusiasm for producing tobacco, which was considered harmful to health and was associated with general immorality. In the reign of James I (who himself wrote *A Counterblaste to Tobacco* in 1604) tobacco pipes were used as doorsigns of brothels. But then as now, however harmful it was to health, tobacco sold, and it sold extremely well in England, originally as an expensive luxury item imported from Spain. In 1620 England imported only some 60,000 pounds a year and the selling price was 8 shillings a pound. Once Americans reached this market they worked diligently to exploit it, and quickly flooded it. By 1630 the price of tobacco in England had dropped to 2 pence a pound, and then fell even lower, to a point less than the cost of production. There was a mild recovery of prices in the early 1640s and then further collapses in the 1660s as production rose still further in the Chesapeake colonies. By the end of the century, prices were still low, and a pattern of recoveries and collapses had emerged that would persist throughout the colonial period.

The low prices and the uncontrollable cycles were symptoms of profound problems in the tobacco economy. These problems were created not only by the colonial producers and by the English marketers of the crop but also by commercial and political forces at work throughout Western Europe, as American tobacco found its way into the markets of the world. One cannot understand the lives of ordinary farmers in Virginia and Maryland and the fortunes of the rising planter class, to say nothing of the fate of the slave population that provided the essential labor in the tobacco fields, without understanding such remote forces as the fiscal policies of the continental European states.

The primary problem was overproduction. By the end of the 1630s, little more than a decade after the first marketable crop had reached England, the Chesapeake colonies were producing 1.5 million pounds of tobacco a year. By 1700 the figure had risen to about 38 million pounds annually. In addition, the Chesapeake industry suffered from serious competition. Spain continued to send the best-quality crop, which commanded the highest prices, and sizable shipments also arrived from Bermuda and the West Indian islands of Barbados, Saint Kitts, and Providence. England too was a competitor, since tobacco was a well-estab-

TOBACCO PLANT, DRAWN BY KONRAD VON GESNER, 1554

This watercolor, which introduced the plant to Europe, led to its cultivation there. The habit of "drinking smoke" was believed to induce giddiness, stupors, and insanity. "What a pestiferous and wicked poison from the devil this must be!" (1565). (*Univ. Bibl. Erlangea.*)

lished crop in Gloucestershire. To compound the troubles further, American tobacco, as production rose, deteriorated in quality, and the middlemen assumed that it would fetch the lowest prices. Perhaps even more important were the technical difficulties of marketing the product of the scattered Chesapeake farms.

Initially, English merchants simply sent agents to purchase what they could from the American producers, which was bad both for the planters, who were thus selling their crop in an almost accidental and artificial market, and for the merchants themselves, who undertook the risks of these voyages with no assurance of cargoes and no way of establishing reliable schedules. But tobacco specialists appeared quickly within the London merchant community, some of them powerful figures like Sir Gilbert Heathcote, director of the Bank of England and of the East India Company, member of Parliament, later the Lord Mayor of London, and at the end of his life reputed to be the richest commoner in England. And companies were formed whose major concern was tobacco marketing: merchant houses like Perry Lane & Company, which had powerful ties to the English government and connections with the northern European states. Operators like Heathcote and companies like Perry Lane quickly transformed the marketing mechanism. They devised the consignment system, which remained the dominant merchandising mechanism until the mid-eighteenth century and which explains much of the plight of the southern planters.

In the consignment system the English merchants were primarily selling agents. The planters sent their crops to these merchants, usually on the merchants' vessels, for sale through them in the English and European markets. The English merchants advanced all the incidental charges—freight, fees, taxes, storage, and so on—and repaid themselves, with profit, when the crop was eventually sold. In addition, they advanced goods to the planters charged against the eventual sales, and so they became the planters' bankers and creditors as well as merchandisers. There was a rough efficiency in this system, but it victimized the planters. As a consequence of consignment selling, the planters were involved in endless debt cycles. Any given crop was in effect mortgaged long before it was sold. Further, the planters had no control whatever over the sale of their crops; they had no choice but to rely entirely on the merchants' goodwill. Finally, it was impossible, by this system, ever to adjust production to demand. Often two years would go by between shipment and news of eventual sale, by which time several new crops would have been produced and initially disposed of. The net result of this system was constant debts and an unmanageable rigidity in the economic process that governed the planters' lives.

As if overproduction, keen competition, deteriorating quality, and a rigid marketing system were not burdens enough, there was the ultimate and most remote but in the end most decisive problem of breaking into the markets of continental Europe. For England herself could absorb relatively little of the enormous Chesapeake production. Of the approximately 38 million pounds of tobacco exported to England in 1700, 25 million pounds were reexported to the continent. Thus these markets were crucial to the prosperity of the American farmers.

At first the continental states banned American tobacco altogether; then they imposed high duties; and finally they erected "farms," that is, state-controlled or state-owned and state-operated monopolies of imports, which determined how much tobacco would be imported, what grades would be allowed in, and what prices would be charged. And as this mechanism matured and the political complexities of tobacco marketing in Europe rose, Dutch middlemen were increasingly important in transmitting the commodity to the ultimate markets, and in doing so added still another burden to the already heavily encumbered trade.

Such was the array of problems that developed in the seventeenth century as the Southern economy took shape. Throughout the century strenuous efforts were made to overcome these problems, with only partial success. The English government taxed Spanish tobacco out of the English markets and rooted out tobacco planting in Gloucestershire; at the same time the West Indian producers were made to realize their relative weakness in this increasingly competitive industry. But Dutch shippers were shrewd competitors, and until the force of the Navigation Acts was felt toward the end of the century, they remained effective participants in the shipping trade. And neither the English nor the colonial governments could force the individual American tobacco growers to limit their production. Quite the contrary. The assumption deepened for most planters that the more they produced the greater their income; and as a consequence the system was propelled forward as if by a powerful internal accelerator. Production continued to expand, and so too did the area of land under cultivation.

The social consequences of this risky and dynamic economy were profound. The constant expansion of the area of settlement went forward without regard for the Indians, who were driven back behind the ever expanding frontiers. As the planters pressed deeper into the interior in search of fresh lands, they forced even the friendly Indians into hostility. There were frontier skirmishes long before the full-scale race war broke out that touched off Bacon's Rebellion (1676).

Further, the tobacco economy generated a desperate need for a large labor force. Hired or indentured servants were never available in sufficient numbers: there were never more than six to eight thousand free white servants in the Chesapeake area in any one time in the seventeenth century, and as a result the tobacco farms remained small (an average of 250 acres). Slavery was an obvious solution to the labor problem even if its capital costs were far greater than those of a free labor system. By the end of the century it was clear that the demands of the tobacco economy were inexorably enlarging the slave labor force and thereby compounding one of the greatest evils of early American life.

The peculiar economy of tobacco, finally, eliminated the possibility that an urban society would develop to the south of Pennsylvania. The tobacco trade prevented local merchants from developing into independent entrepreneurs since the commercial processes were provided for in England; as a consequence the secondary activities that ordinarily develop around "entrepreneurial headquarters" (shipbuilding, service trades, brokerage, and shopkeeping) were frustrated from the start. On the eve of the Revolution, Williamsburg had a total population of but two thousand, and even that small population was largely the result of the government's residence in the town. Baltimore and Norfolk, with populations of six thousand each, developed not in the heart of the tobacco country but at the borders of more diversified economies.

Social Instability

No aspect of community life was more sharply perceived by the seventeenth-century colonists and no aspect of their existences came under more complex and intense pressure than social organization. The generation that settled in America in the years before 1660 were still close to the Elizabethans, who in a period of rapid social change had spelled out clearly the traditional assumptions of an ideal community structure. The Elizabethans' acute perception of the principles of proper community organization and their elaborate articulation of these ideals in laws, treatises, sermons, poetry, and most memorably drama resulted from a sense of loss and threat and from a conservative effort to hold back change. For the early colonists, uprooted from the world they had known and committed to rebuilding their lives in a strange land peopled thinly with natives who seemed utterly primitive and frequently menacing, these fears of social disorganization were even more acute. As a result, their efforts to reknit the fabric of traditional order were even more strenuous than those that had been made by their parents and grandparents.

The ideal by which the founding generation measured the world about them was based on the Elizabethans' assumption that society was not a miscellaneous collection of people pursuing their separate goals and relating to each other haphazardly. For them, society was a disciplined organism, a fabric closely "knit together," as they liked to say, whose overall character was more meaningful than any of the separate parts that composed it. Specifically, they assumed that society would display at least three essential characteristics.

They expected, first, that the parts of a community would be functionally related, that the social, occupational, economic, and cultural elements of society would complement each other and fit together harmoniously to compose the commonwealth as a whole. They expected, too, that the structure of society would be essentially hierarchical, organized into distinct levels of inferiority and superiority, levels not of "class" but of status and dignity, characteristics related to occupation and wealth but not defined by them. And they assumed, third, that the hierarchy of society was a unitary structure in which people of superior status in one aspect of life would be superior in all others. Thus the rich would be politically powerful, educated, and dignified; leadership in public and private affairs would fall to the highborn, the firstborn, the natural leaders, equipped to rule by all the attributes of social superiority.

These were characteristics of all coherent societies, the Elizabethans believed, and those among them who voyaged to America had no intention of recasting or rejecting such fundamental notions. They did not doubt that society would display these familiar forms in the New World as it had in the Old, and confidently repeated with John Winthrop that it was simply God's will that "in all times some must be rich, some poor, some high and eminent in power and dignity, others mean and in subjection." But in fact the world that emerged in mainland North America did not conform to these ideals. To be sure, there was no total breakdown, once the horrors of the "starving times" were overcome; there was no instant transformation into a different mode of life. But from the first years of settlement there were acute stresses and strains that made social life in the colonies tense, strange, and difficult.

The sources of some of these problems were obvious. The colonists were well aware that the political and economic leadership of the communities was being assumed by people who, though capable of dealing with the raw environment,

lacked the traditional social attributes of command: a sense of natural superiority, habitual dignity, personal authority. The respect due to the leading figures was not, as a result, automatically forthcoming. Political and economic leaders were vulnerable to criticism and challenged in ways their social superiors would not have been.

In New England this general problem was peculiarly compounded. There a leadership, drawn from the lesser gentry, managed to maintain its rule for a full generation; but religious achievements, secured within the Puritans' distinctive status system, conflicted with the ordinary social dignities and led to challenges and confusions that otherwise would not have existed. Deference to traditionally recognized social superiority, which no one proposed to eliminate, was naturally subordinated where purity of religion, piety, and rectitude were expected to be decisive in establishing distinction. Every effort was made to perpetuate a familiar social structure. Allotments of land in the newly opened townships were by common agreement made larger for persons of wealth, position, and professional

NEW ENGLAND HOUSES OF THE SEVENTEENTH CENTURY

Left, the Ironmaster's House, Saugus, built in the 1630's and enlarged 20 years later, is an exceptionally imposing residence for the period. The ordinary workers at Saugus lived in thatch-roofed cottages even simpler than the houses in Plymouth (p. 48). *Above,* the Paul Revere house in Boston, 1680. The overhanging second story and heavily leaded casement windows are typical of the substantial artisans' houses of the time. *(Mark Flannery, photographer.)*

training. Even so vague a distinction as "ability" was materially rewarded. But the conflict with religious values could not be avoided.

The problem was at least clearly understood. One of the Puritans' most influential English leaders, Lord Say and Sele, considered joining the great migration in 1636, but then paused. Was it not true, he wrote the Reverend John Cotton in Boston, that men could attain the franchise in Massachusetts simply by being accepted into the church, no matter what their social condition might be? If so, what certainty was there that people like himself would be able to play their proper roles? Cotton tried to reassure him. Everyone knew that "monarchy and aristocracy are both of them clearly approved and directed in scripture" and that God never ordained democracy to be "a fit government either for church or commonwealth." So His Lordship need have no fear of finding in New England a world turned upside down. Still, Cotton had to admit, the Puritans *were* committed to the service of the Lord: religious considerations in the end would prevail and *should* prevail. For is it not better, he asked, "that the commonwealth be

fashioned to the setting forth of God's house, which is his church, than to accommodate the church frame to the civil state?" The noble lord read the message
correctly and stayed home. The Bay Colony's tumults in the founding years
continued to reflect the strange confusion and intermixture of religious and
social distinctions.

Everywhere in the colonies there were difficulties and confusions in maintaining a traditional social order in the raw wilderness world. Survival was a matter
of mutual effort, and even when the struggles of the initial settlements had passed,
the frontier had a disruptive effect on the distinctions that traditionally secured
people's sense of social order.

On the farms, whether in New England, New York, the Chesapeake colonies,
or Carolina, it was physically impossible to maintain the expected differences
in styles of life—differences not merely between masters and servants who
labored side by side, but between field workers on the one hand and preachers,
teachers, and doctors on the other. Laboring side by side day after day, masters
and servants found their lifestyles approaching each other until the differences
rested only on a legal statement, a scrap of paper establishing the servants' dependency, a formality whose force, deprived of material sanction, grew weaker
with time. There were few luxuries anywhere, and nowhere was there the material basis for leisure. The few people of professional training lived far more
primitive lives than their education and occupational roles would traditionally
have assured them.

In the towns the problems of maintaining traditional status differentiation
were especially dramatic. The standard refrain through the century was that the
free workers—the handicraftsmen, shipwrights, carpenters, shoemakers, tailors—
had lost all sense of social discipline and all respect for traditional roles and social distinctions. The wages they claimed were astronomical, it was commonly
said; their social pretensions insufferable. They refused to acknowledge their
place, flaunted their prosperity outrageously, and aped their superiors in ways
that offended all sense of decency and social order. Every effort was made to
contain the social disorder that they created by eliminating the causes of this
alleged misbehavior or by limiting its effects. Occasionally when the problem
became acute, the Assemblies sought to limit wages in order to restrict the
workers' ambitions and protect the public against their apparent greed. But such
laws could not be enforced. The workers' services were indispensable; people
would pay almost anything they demanded. And the workers' arguments were
cogent too: prices, they said, were rising; they had expenses to meet. Let prices be
fixed if wages were. But price fixing was as futile as wage fixing, and what a later
generation would call "escalator clauses" were tried with only temporary effect on
the demands and behavior of the free, self-employed workers.

By 1660 the effort to eliminate the causes of the workers' ambitions had clearly
failed, and it was left for the Assemblies to try to discipline behavior itself, to
try to confine dress and social intercourse to appropriate channels of decency.

Sumptuary legislation restricted the wearing of finery, limited display, and lectured a disordered population on the confusion of the times. The Massachusetts Bay Colony's sumptuary law of 1651 is perhaps the most eloquent testimony of the age to the founders' pervasive sense of disarray.

It was with grief, the Massachusetts General Court declared in that remarkable statute, that it had been forced to note "that intolerable excess and bravery hath crept in upon us, and especially amongst people of mean condition, to the dishonor of God, the scandal of our [religious] profession, the consumption of estates, and altogether unsuitable to our poverty." The court felt obliged to declare its

... utter detestation and dislike, that men or women of mean condition should take upon them the garb of gentlemen, by wearing gold or silver lace, or buttons, or points at their knees, or to walk in great boots, or women of the same rank to wear silk or tiffany hoods or scarves which, though allowable to persons of greater estates or more liberal education, yet we cannot but judge it intolerable in persons of such like condition.

JOHN FREAKE AND HIS WIFE ELIZABETH AND CHILD, 1674

Freake was one of the successful merchants who arrived in Boston well after the original Puritan migration and brought with them a "corrupting" luxuriance of style. His buttons are silver, his collar fine lace, his sleeves puffed muslin, and his gold brooch studded with precious stones. His wife's embroidered petticoat is carefully revealed. *(Worcester Art Museum.)*

Prohibitions and exact rules were always unfortunate, the Court confessed, but the times were deeply disordered and it therefore issued the following extraordinary declaration:

... that no person within this jurisdiction, nor any of their relations depending upon them, whose visible estates shall not exceed the true and indifferent value of £200 shall wear any gold or silver lace, or gold and silver buttons, or any bone lace above 2 shillings per yard, or silk hoods or scarves, upon the penalty of 10 shillings for every such offense.

And more than that, the court, in a devilishly clever provision, decreed that if the town selectmen apprehended anyone they judged "to exceed their ranks and abilities in the costliness or fashion of their apparel in any respect," they were ordered to increase the offender's tax rate to the level of wealth he or she pretended to—all of this *provided*, the General Court added in an afterthought that illuminates the unstable social landscape like a flare, that the law *not* apply to any of the colony's magistrates or their families, or to any regular military officers or soldiers on active duty, or to anyone else *"whose education and employment have been above the ordinary degree, or whose estates have been considerable though now decayed."*

"though now decayed"—the phrase forms a constant refrain in the records of the century. There was a pervasive sense of disordered change, of a decline of standards. And in no aspect of life was this sense more acute than in the realm of the family. Here, it seems, the erosion went deepest, the disorder was most manifest. But the reality was more complex than simple decay.

Evidences of a sense of disorder in family life are voluminous, especially in New England, where community organization remained more cohesive than elsewhere and where sensitivity to standards of behavior was more acute. The Puritan magistrates repeatedly denounced the loosening of family ties, the decline in mutual respect, and the defiance of authority in this most intimate and fundamental of all social units. Repeatedly they commanded parents to do their duty to their children and to themselves, and ordered children to respect and obey their parents and to fulfill their family obligations. The laws grew more stringent as the years passed. In New Hampshire, Massachusetts, and Connecticut, in conformity with the biblical injunction, death was decreed for children who struck or cursed their parents (the law was invoked at least once, though never enforced). In Massachusetts, tithingmen were made responsible for the good order of groups of ten families, and the church synod of 1679, blaming the evils of the time on "defects of family government," commanded the tithingmen to redouble their efforts to reinforce the failing discipline of weak-willed parents.

Such, with less extreme provisions in the other colonies, were the allegations, and such the efforts to restrain by legislation the standards that had apparently been lost through slackness, corruption, and neglect. But in fact, of course, the family was not being destroyed; the institution survived, and on the surface, at least, it was little weaker at the end of the century than it had been at the start.

But there *were* differences, and those differences, if properly understood, help explain the outcries, the sense of disarray, and the efforts to remedy what was felt by many to be a disastrous decline in the traditional good order of family life.

To understand these responses and the tensions behind them, it is necessary to note the importance of the family in the social and psychological world of the seventeenth century. Families were not merely the basic social institution; they were considered the archetype of all social order, public as well as private. In this micro-community, it was believed, all order germinated, all patterns of inferiority and superiority took shape. The political commonwealth was but an enlargement of the family. Rulers were conceived of as patriarchs whose dominance as heads of commonwealths was justified by God the Father of all. Robert Filmer's *Patriarcha,* written in the upheaval of the early '40s to justify the power of kings by analogy to the authority of patriarchs, gave full expression to what was essentially a cliché of the age. And it was a cliché that, like most commonplaces that pass unchallenged, was essentially realistic. Most Englishmen experienced a larger, more highly structured, more complex, and more disciplined family unit than now exists, but not because the nuclear family (parents and children) was significantly larger than it is now. Most completed families in seventeenth-century England contained but two or three children, though many more were born and died young. The sense of complexity, structure, and discipline grew from the fact that family meant or implied the household—all those who lived together under one roof—and not merely immediate kinship groups. It was the experience of households that formed the model of family life by which declension in America was instinctively measured, and it was the household-as-family that came under pressure in the wilderness environment.

Almost all Englishmen at some time in their lives had experienced the household-family as a complex and disciplined institution. For servants were traditionally part of this artificially extended family, and servitude was remarkably widespread. Something like a third of all English families had servants; at any one time, between 10 and 15 percent of the entire English population was serving in another's household—and serving not merely as day workers exchanging limited services for specified wages but as family members committed to total employment in exchange for maintenance, protection, and to some extent education. No less than sons and daughters, servants were members of the household and lived within its discipline. So too were the free children of other families who circulated as guests, often for long periods, in more affluent households or even in households of equivalent social position.

As a result of the widespread servitude and the circulation of free children, there was a constant flow of young people, for some period of their lives, into large households. At least 45 percent of all English people lived in households of six or more members, and consequently most people, at least in their youth, experienced families as complex units and found in this experience verification for the common image of the patriarchal family.

In traditional settings, material circumstances reinforced and helped perpetuate these extended household-families. The traditional family found circumstantial support not merely in a general low level of the economy but in specific difficulties that beset young people who attempted to break away and establish new independent households. For most people in this still largely agricultural world (over two-thirds of the entire English population derived its live-

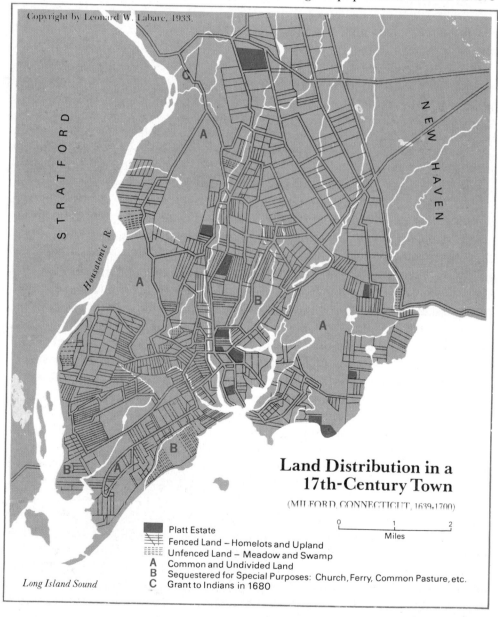

Copyright by Leonard W. Labaree, 1933.

STRATFORD

Housatonic R.

NEW HAVEN

Land Distribution in a 17th-Century Town

(MILFORD, CONNECTICUT, 1639–1700)

0   1   2
Miles

■ Platt Estate
Fenced Land – Homelots and Upland
Unfenced Land – Meadow and Swamp
A Common and Undivided Land
B Sequestered for Special Purposes: Church, Ferry, Common Pasture, etc.
C Grant to Indians in 1680

Long Island Sound

lihood entirely from the land), economic independence was made possible by the purchase, or the long-term lease, of plots of arable land, and it was extremely difficult to make such transactions in the absence of freely available public land. As a result, many servants found themselves obliged to remain dependent beyond the time of their contractual obligations; marriages were delayed, since married couples were expected to live in their own establishments and not within other households; and family discipline developed naturally and remained a familiar, accepted fact of life.

In the colonies of seventeenth-century America these material reinforcements of traditional family life were either greatly weakened or eliminated. Where land was far more freely available than in England—where, indeed, it was often available simply for the taking—the establishment of independent households became a relatively easy matter. In this frontier situation of open, new land, scarcely more effort was involved in creating a household than in maintaining one. What is remarkable in these circumstances is not that the average age at first marriage fell but that it did not fall even further and faster than it did. For there was strenuous resistance to accepting the changed circumstances. In some cases, artificially extended families were maintained despite the difficulties. More commonly, approximations to traditional forms were devised that took some account of the altered circumstances. Thus in the town of Andover, Massachusetts, when at the end of the seventeenth century the sons of the founders were comfortably established on sizable farms of their own that had been carved out of their fathers' unusably large grants, these new establishments were located immediately adjacent to the parental homes and legal titles to the sons' farms remained in the fathers' hands. How widespread such accommodations were, and how long and in what localities quasi-traditional forms were maintained, we do not know. What we do know is that everywhere in some way pressure against the simple reestablishment of the familiar household-family was created by the mere availability of land, and that with this came social and psychological tension.

But the availability of land was only one of the alterations in the material reinforcement of traditional family life that took place in the colonial setting. Equally important was the acute and continuing labor shortage, which shifted the dependency relations within the family and household. Parents and masters depended on their children and servants as never before. They needed them, sometimes desperately, to provide critically necessary labor. In this sense the parents became dependents, but not only in this sense. The young learned to cope with the environment more rapidly than their seniors; they adapted to change more easily; and in the end they inevitably became lifelines to the world for their elders. They became, in effect, their parents' teachers, despite the unquestioned and continuing assumption of parental superiority.

The consequences of the tensions and widespread sense of disarray and disorganization ran deep. Gradually, the law responded to these altered circumstances. Primogeniture—the legal requirement that real property descend only to the eldest son so that the family estate would remain intact—was commonly ignored where land was plentiful. The common practice was to divide property equally, perhaps with double portions for the wife or eldest son. Further, the law became somewhat more responsive to the interests of women. In Massachusetts, laws were passed that prohibited husbands from striking their wives—"unless it be in his own defense," a Plymouth statute cautiously added. Women were given new rights in the ownership and conveyance of property, in conducting business, and in representing themselves in court. The legal conditions of bonded servants also improved. In some places the severity of punishment was limited by law; in others, working conditions were improved; and in all the colonies every effort was made to use the law to keep servants at work despite the liberating forces that surrounded them. A case is recorded in which a servant ran away after being punished for attempting to rape his master's ten-year-old daughter—the suit being filed not to punish the culprit but to get him back and to force him to complete his term of service! Everywhere the conditions of contractual obligations grew lighter as the ease of transition to personal independence was recognized.

Social order was not destroyed in the seventeenth-century colonies, nor was the world transformed. But society had acquired a new instability which, in calmer years and in more settled circumstances, would inexorably work themselves out.

Religion

Religion was inevitably involved in the larger social changes, for the colonists' culture was still profoundly Christian and churches were still the preeminent cultural institutions as well as vital social agencies. The seventeenth century was an age of intense religious controversy; men and nations struggled savagely over differences in religious opinion. Yet if one puts aside the details of sectarian conflict, one can discover a few nearly universal presumptions shared by almost all religious groups—presumptions that illuminate the history of religion in early America particularly well.

Christians, save for the most extreme radicals, generally assumed that the principle of religious orthodoxy was valid and that religious institutions should reflect this belief. It was assumed that there was a universally true religion and that a plurality of beliefs should not be encouraged. However much most seventeenth-century Christians differed on what doctrines were orthodox, they assumed that *some* doctrines were absolutely right and others wrong and that the effort to eradicate, or at least to heavily constrain, heresy and to extend orthodoxy was altogether legitimate.

Equally axiomatic was the belief that religion was not simply a spiritual matter nor of concern only to the church. The agencies of the state were understood to have a major responsibility for the supervision of religion and the enforcement of orthodoxy. The church had its own powers, its own sources of economic support, and its own transcendent responsibility for nurturing religion; but in the

end this role was elaborately involved in civil institutions. Finally, it was assumed, as overseas emigration became a prominent part of the life of western
Europe, that the expansion of the churches overseas would be an extension of
existing orthodox forms. Church institutions established in colonial areas were
expected to follow familiar organizational patterns and fit somehow into some
larger pattern of religious institutions. There was no presumption that churches
established in the frontier borderlands would become institutions with special
characteristics.

The history of religion in the first two or three generations is the story of the
violation of these presumptions and the struggle to retain them in the face of
great adversity. Christianity in more or less familiar outward form of course
survived, but it survived with significant alterations that were forced into being
not by will or doctrine but by intractable circumstances. Not for another century
would these changes be fully accepted and incorporated into the deliberate design
of religious organization and practice. But the seeds of what would later evolve
into America's distinctive denominational organization were planted and nourished in the complex social history of the seventeenth century.

The most revealing example of the way in which environment shaped the
development of Christianity in America lies not in New England Puritanism
but in the history of the Church of England in Virginia. Here the sense of
orthodoxy was strong and free from pressures of reform and from doctrinal
conflicts; here the fullest re-creation of traditional forms was attempted; and
here the failure of expectation was most severe.

The Virginia Company and the government that followed it assumed that the
Church of England in its established form would simply be reproduced in the

ST. LUKE'S CHURCH, ISLE OF WIGHT
COUNTY, VIRGINIA (LATE
SEVENTEENTH CENTURY)

A typical Anglican parish church,
with its bell tower, arched
windows, and buttresses. (*Virginia
State Travel Service.*)

settlements along the James River, and that these local branches of the church would be easily incorporated into the national church. But there were severe problems from the start, most of which flowed from the difficulty of devising a workable economic basis for the newly founded church institutions. In England churches were usually supported by land endowments, gifts of income-producing property donated by patrons. The company, and subsequently the crown, took over the role of patron to the newly founded parishes. In 1618 the company set aside as church land 100 acres (later increased by the crown to 200 acres) in each of the still vague "boroughs." The income from this land, to be produced by the labor of tenants, was to support a minister and the institution of the church. But tenants were not easily obtainable in Virginia, and the land was worthless until some kind of labor could be provided. This left two alternatives for the support of the church. First, the clergy could become almost full-time farmworkers and produce the expected income, a prospect that in itself discouraged the recruitment of well-trained clergymen. Alternatively, a new kind of support would have to be forthcoming. This new form—taxation—was anticipated by the company when it ordered parishioners to supplement the income of the church land until its yield equaled £200 a year. Such supplements quickly became common, then universal. It soon became standard practice for the parishioners' governing body, the vestry, to vote funds for the church as an annual tax rate.

Once taxation became the financial basis of the church, the definition of the taxable unit became vitally important, and that created the besetting problem of the Anglican church in early Virginia. Church leaders were faced with a hopeless dilemma. If the parish were to be defined by the number of people, with the standard set by the population of the usual English parish, the resulting territory would spread so widely along the colony's creeks and rivers that proper ministrations would be impossible. The tobacco farmers could not gather from such distances for regular services, and the clergy would in effect become itinerants, scarcely capable of promoting full religious activities anywhere. On the other hand, if the geographical size of the parish were kept small so that the parishioners could gather easily and ministers could be in constant communication with their flocks, the per capita cost of support would be extremely high. The inevitable result, in the underdeveloped and struggling economy, was a pattern of unworkably large parishes and, because of variations in population density and wealth, great variations in the support of the clergy.

By the end of the first generation, the dilemma facing the church was officially recognized. In 1662 the Assembly tried to make all church salaries uniform at £80 a year. But this figure had to be translated into set amounts of tobacco, which was the medium of exchange, and when the real value of tobacco fell, so too did the real worth of the ministers' salaries. In any case, being paid in tobacco, the clergy were at the mercy of local variations in quality and were dependent too on the good will of their parishioners for the selection of tobacco that was made.

From this simple and fundamental economic problem flowed profoundly important consequences in the lives of the clergy and therefore in the life of religion in general. By English standards the ministers were almost everywhere grossly underpaid, and they were faced with next-to-impossible conditions of work. Further, they were stripped of economic independence because of their reliance on annual gifts of the parish. Nor did they acquire security of tenure however poor their economic condition. In England, rectors of the local parishes were nominated for their appointments by the patrons of the benefices and inducted into permanent appointments by the bishops. In Virginia, the patrons, given the tax base of the ministers' salaries, proved to be the vestries, the self-perpetuating bodies of lay leaders of the church in each parish. The vestries were instructed by the church officers in England to present their nominees for induction by the governors. But in most cases they refused (only 10 percent of the Virginia clergy in the seventeenth century were ever formally inducted into their offices), claiming that the available candidates were so inferior in quality that they did not deserve permanency of tenure.

COLLEGE OF WILLIAM AND MARY, PICTURED IN THE 1730s

Founded in large part to educate Virginians for the Anglican ministry, it was built to plans of Christopher Wren. The central building was erected by the end of the century but had to be rebuilt after a fire of 1705. *(Library of Congress.)*

It was a self-intensifying problem. The vestries refused to present candidates for formal induction to permanent tenure because the quality of the clergy was too low to justify such confidence and respect; but their refusal to present was an important reason why well-qualified candidates refused to settle in Virginia. The declining spiral fell lower and lower. Many well-qualified and able young clergymen were present in the early years of Virginia's history, but by the end of the century their numbers had declined to insignificance. Recruitment seemed to come from the dregs of the ecclesiastical barrel. Efforts of church missionaries and of the Church's Society for the Propagation of the Gospel in Foreign Parts (founded in 1701) led to a series of proposals to remedy the situation: one of them resulted in the chartering of the College of William and Mary in 1693. But it was extremely difficult to improve the situation. By 1724 the reputation of the clergy in Virginia had become so scandalous that the following almost farcical proposals were included in a comprehensive plan of reform submitted to the Bishop of London, whose jurisdiction included the American colonies.

And to prevent the scandals of bad life in the clergy, let it be enacted that whatsoever minister shall be found guilty of fornication, adultery, blasphemy, ridiculing of the Holy Scriptures, or maintaining . . . any doctrine contrary to the 39 Articles shall . . . lose his living [income] and be suspended from all exercise of the ministerial function for three years. . . . And because drunkenness is one of the most common crimes and yet hardest to be proved . . . let it be enacted that the following proof shall be taken for a sufficient proof of drunkenness, viz., first, let the signs of drunkenness be proved such as sitting an hour or longer in the company where they were a drinking strong drink and in the meantime drinking of healths or otherwise taking his cups as they came around like the rest of the company; striking, challenging, threatening to fight, or laying aside any of his garments for that purpose; staggering, reeling, vomiting, incoherent, impertinent, obscene, or rude talking. Let the proof of these signs proceed so far till the judges conclude that the minister's behavior at such a time was scandalous, indecent, and unbecoming the gravity of a minister.

The debasement of the clergy was one aspect of the general transformation of the Church of England in Virginia. Another development, in the long run equally important, was the destruction of the hierarchical structure of the church as a result of the distance from higher controls in England and by the assumption of absolute power in church affairs by the local vestries. Control fell to the parish level, and the result was in effect a congregational institution despite the official affiliation with the episcopal Church of England. Futher, the practice of religion was simplified, even secularized to some extent. Since most ministers could not reach all areas of their parishes, lay readers were appointed to fulfill certain ministerial functions. The general simplicity of life and the lack of funds for embellishments meant that the sacraments were administered without the proper vestments or ornaments of church ritual. The dead were buried in private cemeteries more often than in parish burial grounds; the holy days were neglected; and marriage was performed in private residences under lay auspices. Further, the church as a judicial body declined into insignificance, for the members of the vestries and of the local quarter courts were often the same people, and it was more reasonable, in view of the weakness of the church, for cases of moral offenses to be brought before the civil courts than before the church courts. And it was the civil courts rather than the weak parish institutions that became the repository for vital statistics.

No one, of course, doubted that the Church of England had been established in Virginia, but it was a strange establishment indeed. Conditions had led the church as an institution toward what might be called nonseparating Congregationalism—institutionally the position adopted in New England—not as a matter of doctrine but as a matter of social and institutional fact.

Maryland shared the same environmental conditions, and its religious institutions would have conformed to the same pattern except for two basic facts:

first, the government of the colony was in the hands of a Catholic Proprietor who conceived of the colony as a Catholic refuge; and second, the great majority of those available for settlement in the colony were Protestants, and the success of the colony depended on the success of recruitment. The Proprietor's Catholic interests would have to be handled with the greatest of care.

At the start, the Calverts issued to their governors instructions they thought would satisfy the conflicting demands. They ordered the Maryland officials to give no offense to Protestants because of their religion; to see to it that Catholicism was practiced as privately as possible; and to leave those who professed Christianity in any form free to worship as they chose. It was a vague, pragmatically liberal position, and it was promptly attacked from both extremes. The Jesuits who had accompanied the settlers demanded that the canon law be extended to Maryland, that the Society of Jesus be allowed to possess worldly goods, especially land, and that the pope's supreme jurisdiction over the church in Maryland be formally recognized. It took a decade of struggle on the part of the Proprietor and the help of officials in Rome to squelch this program, which if enacted would surely have led to the confiscation of the charter. In the end the Jesuits were withdrawn from the colony and their place was taken by ordinary parish priests.

More powerful were the pressures from the Protestants in the colony, who were far more numerous than the Catholics. Their power became clear in the early years of the English Civil War when a group led by William Claiborne, who had contested the Calverts' jurisdiction from the start, staged a rebellion in the colony, seized the government, and stimulated an attack on the charter in Parliament. The Calverts were obliged to appoint a Protestant governor simply to survive this assault. But the pressure continued, and it was to stabilize the situation and protect Maryland's charter that the Calverts issued in 1649 their famous Act Concerning Religion.

This document, remarkable for its era, is not an act for full freedom of religion or even full religious toleration. It begins, in fact, by ordering the death penalty for any nontrinitarian Christians who insisted on professing their religion in Maryland. But it went on to say that, in order to assure public tranquility—and for that reason alone—all trinitarian Christians were guaranteed the right to full freedom of religion. Nothing in this document, which remained in effect through the century, challenged the prevailing idea of orthodoxy. It contained no hint of the principles of the separation of church and state or of freedom of conscience and worship as good in themselves—no hint of any of the soaring ideals of liberty of thought and conscience that would later find expression in Jefferson's great Statute of Religious Freedom. The Calverts' act specified toleration on the narrowest possible ground—for just those groups whom it was expedient to tolerate: Catholics, Anglicans, and moderate Protestant dissenters. Yet it was a significant departure, if limited and pragmatic, and it fitted perfectly the decentralization of religion that was otherwise developing in the colony. For in Maryland as in Virginia the necessary tax base of church support meant full control by local authorities, in most places by the vestries. This, together with the official toleration of most differing groups, meant the emergence in this colony of a multidenominational, nondoctrinal Congregationalism.

The same result in even more extreme form emerged in New York. The Dutch, like the English, assumed at the start that their national church, Dutch Reformed Calvinist, would be re-created in America, and that it would be controlled by that church's ruling body, the Classis of Amsterdam. But from the earliest years, New Netherlands was overwhelmingly complex in its religious character, and there were no effective controls from the home country. Besides Dutch Calvinists, Jews, and a broad range of sectarian radicals that included Anabaptists and Quakers, there were Lutherans, whose insistence on the right to public worship led to their suppression and persecution by Stuyvesant. The Dutch West India Company's policy was to permit *private* worship of any kind, so long as the Dutch church was officially recognized and supported by universal taxation. The Lutherans, however, insisted on the right to public worship. The question remained unsettled, the source of fierce animosities, until after the English conquest. Then, by the Duke's Laws of 1665, the freeholders of each community in New York were ordered to vote for some one Protestant church, which would then be locally established. Once chosen, the denomination would be supported by general taxation, though private worship was allowed to continue.

The Dutch church remained dominant, of course, since most of the colonists were Dutch, and in this situation of local option it sought to perpetuate its heritage and mode of worship. But here as in the Chesapeake colonies settlements were scattered, the recruitment of properly qualified ministers was extremely difficult, and proper ministrations proved impossible to perform. Here too lay readers came to preside when ordained ministers were unobtainable, and there was a radical decline in the outward quality of religious life. Worse still, after the English conquest the Dutch church became a branch of an alien national church. How could this American branch relate to the home body? If the Dutch settlers in New York acknowledged the supremacy of the Dutch church fully, they would in effect be challenging the supremacy of the English crown; if they did not make that challenge, implicitly at least they would not be faithful to their own religious profession. It was a dilemma that could not be resolved but might be endured if the issue was never pressed.

In the context of these unexpected developments elsewhere in the colonies, the outward form of religion that became established in New England is perhaps not so unique. Everywhere the hierarchy of church organization had failed to develop, ritual had become simplified, sacramental functions of the church were reduced, and laymen shared pulpits with ordained ministers. None of this, however, had been the consequence of doctrine or belief or intent. All of it had developed in response to the circumstances of life in the new American colonies. In New England the same developments were small parts of a general plan of religious reform that was pursued almost fanatically and fortified by a theological position whose refinement was the work of men of subtle mind and great intellectual energy. But Puritanism was not only an intellectual system and it did not satisfy only the needs of theologians. It was a social movement as well as an intellectual movement, and it performed, in New England as in Old England, a notable social function.

The central character of New England Puritanism emerges most clearly if one defines it precisely; and its social role becomes apparent if one isolates the specific question of why its force continued once the original settlements were stabilized.

New England Puritanism was one specific expression of a broad movement of reform within the Church of England, a protest movement against the religious conservatism of the Church of England as it existed under Elizabeth. Those who would later be known as Puritans felt that England's break with the Roman Catholic Church under Henry VIII had been superficial. A Catholic tradition, they felt, had simply been grafted onto a national Protestant Church. The differences between the Puritan reformers and the conservative churchmen did not lie in central theological points. Both groups were predestinarian: both believed that human salvation was ultimately determined by decisions of an inscrutable God. The differences lay in two questions concerning the nature and function of the church as an institution.

The first was the question of how effective the church could be in assisting people in their search for salvation. The Anglican churchmen, like Catholics, believed that the church could be instrumental in bridging the world of ordinary, physical humanity and that of men in a state of God's grace. The difference between physical existence and true sanctity was not, the church insisted, total and absolute, bridgeable only by God's gift of regeneration; qualified priests and the procedures and rituals of the church could assist in the great search for salvation. With this, the Puritans disagreed. The gap between nature and grace was for them absolute and total, and could be mediated only by God in direct contact with an open and willing soul and by the Bible, which contained God's recorded words. The church's institutions and its ritual—all such outward "works" —merely interfered with the essential experience of religion, which for the Puritans was the experience of man struggling to make contact with an inscrutable God.

The second question that came to define Puritanism concerned the visibility of God's church. Orthodox Anglicans felt that it was impossible ever truly to tell who had achieved a state of grace and who had not. This was the ultimate mystery, and therefore the church existed for everyone, in the hope that its good offices would help some to achieve a better life and would be a natural home for those who were already members of God's elect. For them the membership of the "visible" church (that is, the worldly institution of the church) should include the whole of society; people should be born into the church as a fact of their mortal existence. The Puritans disagreed vehemently with this position. They felt that it was possible to distinguish the elect from ordinary mortals. Tests could be devised and signs detected that would distinguish these "saints" from unredeemed humanity and make it possible to confine full church membership to those visibly sanctified people. Church membership should not include everyone in society, the Puritans felt; it should be a gathering of saints. The visible church, they said, and God's church of the elect should, as far as possible, be one.

These two key issues defined the protest movement of the late sixteenth century which in the broadest sense was Puritanism: an effort to purify the Church of England of the remnants of Catholicism and to draw the deeper implications of Protestantism along these lines. But Puritanism in this broadest sense includes a variety of programs, only one of which was established in the Bay Colony.

On the far "right"—closest, that is, to the existing Church of England—were the Presbyterians. Like the Anglicans, the Presbyterians sought a hierarchical national church that would include all members of society, but they differed from the Anglicans by intrusting the direction of the church only to those manifestly elect. In the center position within the broad spectrum of Puritanism were those who hoped to confine all church membership to the elect of God but who yet continued to believe that the church, even so reduced, should control society as a whole and be responsible for creating conditions favorable to the search for salvation. On the "left" were groups who gave up all responsibility for society as a whole, who wished to draw aside from all the unregenerate and live a separate, holy life. Such were the Separatists of all sorts: such were the Pilgrims. Finally, on the extreme "left" were individuals who felt that all association of any sort, even separatist cells like those of the Pilgrims, interfered with the search for religious truth; they repudiated not only the world but voluntary associations of all kinds. Such were the Quakers, who were among the most extreme and fanatical "seekers" of the seventeenth century. Beyond their position lay only the absolute and irreducible doctrine, which Roger Williams among others ultimately maintained, that the only acceptable church was the individual himself; all groupings, all associations, no matter how "separate" and pure could only corrupt the spirit in search of salvation.

SYMBOLISM ON PURITAN GRAVESTONES

Opposite, the John Foster stone, Dorchester, Massachusetts, 1681, depicts Time holding back the hand of Death from extinguishing the flame of life atop the globe. The allegory was copied from an illustration in *Hieroglyphiques of the Life of Man* (1638) by Francis Quarles, a popular English poet, who wrote:

> Great Prince of darkness, hold thy needless hand:
> Thy captiv's fast and cannot flee,
> What arm can rescue? Who can countermand? . . .
> What need'st thou snatch at noon, what will be thine
>   at night?

Left, panel of a stone of 1692 in which the skeletal figure of Death has given way to a naked imp of the underworld carrying both Time's hour glass and Death's dart. (*Allan Ludwig, 141 Upper Montclair Ave., Montclair, N.J.*)

The settlers in Massachusetts were Puritans of the center position: they were called nonseparating Congregationalists. The visible and invisible churches should be one, but there could be no denial of responsibility for the profane world as it existed. The condition of all people was the responsibility of the saints, and the church must somehow be active in the affairs of the unredeemed.

How such a program could be effected was a matter of endless discussion and writing both in England and in America. But in England the Congregational Puritans' energies were absorbed in the struggle for survival against an authoritarian church determined to eliminate active dissent. In Massachusetts and Connecticut, however, protected from interference by the charters, the implications of the Congregationalists' position could work themselves out.

Because profoundly committed Puritans were in full charge of the community in Massachusetts and Connecticut, and because their beliefs hinged on the identification of the visible and invisible churches, the passage into full church membership took on a significance it had nowhere else. For in England, where the Congregationalist Puritans were a persecuted minority, there was no scramble on the part of ordinarily religious but unsanctified people to gain membership in these congregations. Only the fully committed and utterly sincere would have wished to join a group embattled politically and so demanding in its practices. In New England the situation was altogether different. Here the Congregational Church leaders held all the powers; they *were* the government, and the resources and power available in the community were at their disposal. Where the Congregational Church was fully established and where social rewards were attached to

membership in the church, the passage into full church affiliation became a critical issue for the society as a whole. The process had to be considered carefully and tests imposed to filter out those who were fully qualified from those who were merely ambitious. To have allowed in anyone who wished to enter would have been to defeat the central concept of Congregationalism as a gathering of proven saints; to deny entrance to all but those universally recognized as spiritual leaders would have been to cut the church off from broad social contact and ultimately from social control. Quickly, therefore, as the churches settled in the land, procedures were devised that opened access to the population at large but allowed in only those who objectively demonstrated superiority in spiritual gifts.

Candidates were obliged to make a public "profession"—to give an open account of the act of saving grace that had brought them to the condition of redemption that justified membership in the church. This was followed by a public interrogation by church officials and by experienced laymen, an inquisition, often exceedingly subtle in its demands, in which these public professions could be challenged for their authenticity on all vulnerable points and defenses made to these challenges. Finally, if this exhibit and defense had been successful, a formal ritual of acceptance was devised by which membership was officially conferred.

This was no casual procedure. Gaining entrance to the church was the central event in religious life of the Puritan communities. The subsequent history of the church in New England would be shaped by the fate of these procedures.*

Defining the process of entering into the church was one side of the central problem of the Bible Commonwealth. The other side was how to justify the rule of the saints to those who were not church members, those excluded from the social rewards the church could bestow. The intellectual justification of the rule of the elect was never in doubt. A central idea of the Puritans was the doctrine of the covenant, a conception that made clear that part of the obligation of the saved was to do whatever mortals could do to pave the way for the unregenerate to attain salvation. According to the covenant, the elect were obliged to propagate true knowledge over error, to make clear what outward sin was, and to hold sinners accountable for their conduct; in general, to expose ordinary men to truth, to remove impediments to their redemption, and to urge them to seek an ultimate salvation.

But theories do not answer people's urges and longings, their fears and aspirations. A mass population will not accept an elite rule obnoxious to them merely because a theory urges them to. No one can be argued into a willing subservience, and there is every reason to believe that the mass of the settlers accepted, indeed welcomed, the rule of the saints. We do not know exactly how many New Englanders in the first two generations reached full membership in the church. The most favorable modern estimate is 47 percent, though that is probably too high. We do know that of the twenty thousand or so immigrants of the Great Migration, few returned to England, and there were no rebellions against the

*See Chapter 5, pp. 180–183.

religious zeal of the Puritan leaders; such protests as there were mainly took the form of differing opinions on specific points of doctrine, and most often were led by individuals—Roger Williams, Anne Hutchinson—even more zealous in religion than the Winthrops.

The explanation for the Puritans' success in psychological and sociological terms is related to the sources of the Great Migration. The mass of the settlers were husbandmen and artisans drawn primarily from East Anglia and the west country of England, which were not merely the chief centers of Puritanism but the centers too of economic distress in the 1620s and 30s. Crop failures and an extended depression in the cloth industry, whose two main centers were in these regions, created a mass of discontent and severe social dislocation; and Puritanism fed on these disturbed conditions. Its teachings offered an explanation in moral terms of what was happening in the lives of this apprehensive and unrooted population. For the Puritans' social views were medieval rather than modern. They were suspicious of the life of trade, feared the effects of greed on the flow of necessary goods, and urged the necessity of subordinating the individual to the welfare of the community. Though the personality traits that Puritanism fostered—diligence, accountability, self-denial, and the scrupulous use of every God-given moment of time—would later serve to stimulate the development of an unqualified capitalism, its social doctrines confined these characteristics to goals set by the good of the whole. Puritanism stimulated acquisitiveness but at the

Sources of English
Emigration to New England, 1620-1650

same time preached the control of greed and self-satisfaction, and it sought to create a society in which social controls in behalf of the community good would predominate. The thousands of unregenerate found in Puritanism not tyranny but a source of security for which they longed. Uprooted, tossed and buffeted by economic upheaval and social dislocation, they found in New England a society that officially restrained economic appetites and translated the incomprehensible workings of the marketplace into familiar moral language. More than that, they found in close-knit village communities a system of group controls that would effectively eliminate the threat of arbitrary economic fluctuations and create the security that was one of the main goals of their existences.

By the end of the century this vital function of Puritanism was losing its power as the third generation, born secure and never steeled in the fires of social adversity as their parents and grandparents had been, lost contact with the original aims of the Great Migration. But for a moment in history—two lifetimes more or less—Puritanism had been a comfort and not an affliction, a source of security otherwise unattainable by ordinary victims of social change.

No more in religion than in social organization or economic life was this a world transformed. But everywhere—in all aspects of society in these small and obscure but swiftly growing communities—there were instabilities, uncertainties, and changes which had not yet settled into permanent new forms.

FIRST PARISH MEETING HOUSE, HINGHAM, MASS. 1681

This famous building, whose exterior is largely the work of the eighteenth century, retains much of the original seventeenth-century interior. Lacking models for the spacious but austere building they had in mind and spurning all architectural embellishments, the ship carpenters hired for the occasion simply built a ship's keel in reverse to form the interior roof. (Photos by Arthur B. Mazmanian from his *The Structure of Praise* © The Beacon Press.)

Suggested Readings

There is no single comprehensive and detailed history of American society in the seventeenth century. The subject has only recently been conceived of in the terms discussed in this chapter, and the student must draw for details on a scattering of publications. This is especially true of the first topic discussed in this chapter: population. There has recently been an extraordinary burst of interest in the field of historical demography, especially for the seventeenth century, in large part stimulated by innovating studies of the French and English populations of the same period. Their influence on early American history is summarized in Philip J. Greven, Jr., "Historical Demography and Colonial America," *Wm. and Mary Q.*, 24 (1967), 438–54. Of the older publications, two are still useful: the compilation of contemporary population estimates in Evarts B. Greene and Virginia D. Harrington, *American Population before the Federal Census of 1790* (1932) and Abbot E. Smith, *Colonists in Bondage* (1947), a study of immigrant convicts and indentured servants. The newer writings, based on statistical analysis of small communities, have so far concentrated largely on New England. A summary of that region's extraordinary growth rate appears in Daniel S. Smith, "The Demographic History of Colonial New England," *Journal of Economic History*, 32 (1972), 165–83. Other important writings on population growth are: Kenneth A. Lockridge, "The Population of Dedham, Mass., 1636–1736," *Economic History Review*, 2d ser., 19 (1966), 318–44; Philip J. Greven, Jr., *Four Generations . . . Andover, Massachusetts* (1970); and John Demos, "Notes on Life in Plymouth Colony," *Wm. and Mary Q.*, 22 (1965), 264–86.* The contrasting high death rate in the earliest years in Virginia and the eventual recovery and rapid growth of population there too are discussed in Edmund S. Morgan, *American Slavery, American Freedom* (1975). Most of these studies reveal the distorted age structure and sex ratio in the settlement years, but there is important additional information on both in John Demos, "Families in Colonial Bristol, R.I. . . .," *Wm. and Mary Q.*, 25 (1968), 40–57; in Irene W.D. Hecht, "The Virginia Muster of 1624/5," *ibid.*, 30 (1973), 65–92; and in Herbert Moller's occasionally fanciful "Sex Composition and Correlated Culture Patterns of Colonial America," *ibid.*, 2 (1945), 113–53. On migration to early New England, see T.H. Breen and Stephen Foster, "Moving to the New World . . .," *ibid.*, 36 (1973), 189–223, and Charles Banks, *Planters of the Commonwealth* (1930); on the spread of population, see Lois K. Mathews, *The Expansion of New England* (1936), ii–iii. On the peopling of the Chesapeake area, see Wesley F. Craven, *White, Red, and Black* (1971) and Arthur E. Karinen, "Maryland Population: 1631–1730," *Maryland Historical Magazine*, 54 (1959), 365–407; 60 (1965), 139–59.

There are two valuable sketches of the overall development of the early American economy: Stuart Bruchey, *Roots of American Economic Growth, 1607–1861* (1965) and George R. Taylor, "American Economic Growth before 1840," *Journal of Economic History*, 24 (1964), 427–44. The world context of American commercial development is well presented in Ralph Davis, *Rise of the Atlantic Economies* (1973).

The growth of the commercial economy in early New England is traced in Bernard Bailyn *The New England Merchants in the Seventeenth Century* (1955) and in Bernard and Lotte Bailyn, *Massachusetts Shipping, 1697–1714* (1959). The psychological turmoils of a Puritan merchant, caught between entrepreneurial and pietistic impulses, emerge in Bailyn, ed., *The Apologia of Robert Keayne* (1965). Curtis P. Nettels, *The Money Supply of the American Colonies before 1720* (1934) covers various aspects of American and Atlantic commerce as well as monetary history. For a social description of the emerging port towns, see Carl Bridenbaugh, *Cities in the Wilderness* (1938).

Many aspects of the Southern economy are described in Lewis C. Gray, *History of Agriculture in the Southern United States to 1860* (2 vols., 1933), and there is still value in Philip A. Bruce's *Economic History of Virginia in the Seventeenth Century* (2 vols., 1896). The master historian of the tobacco economy, however, is Jacob M. Price; it is from his writing particularly that one learns of the worldwide commercial network that shaped the lives of the

Chesapeake farmers. In his *The Tobacco Adventure to Russia . . . 1676–1722 (Transactions of the American Philosophical Society,* 1961), Price traces the failure of the London tobacco merchants to market Chesapeake tobacco in Russia, an effort which, if it had succeeded, would have transformed the economy and society of the American South. Price also discusses the French-American tobacco trade in *France and the Chesapeake* (2 vols., 1973).

Traditional ideals of social organization are depicted in E. M. W. Tillyard, *Elizabethan World Picture* (1943) and in Gordon J. Schochet, *Patriarchalism in Political Thought* (1975); the latter has an excellent chapter on the ideals and actuality of the family in seventeenth-century England, a subject discussed at length by Peter Laslett in *The World We Have Lost* (1965) and in his introduction to *Household and Family in Past Time* (1972). Many of the new community-demographic studies cited above, particularly those of Greven and Demos, make clear the difficulty of maintaining traditional forms in the wilderness setting. See also Sumner C. Powell, *Puritan Village* (1963) and Edmund S. Morgan, *Puritan Family* (1944). Kenneth A. Lockridge, *New England Town: Dedham . . .* (1970) locates the disarray only at the end of the seventeenth century. On social mobility there are several important writings: William A. Reavis, "The Maryland Gentry and Social Mobility, 1637–1676," *Wm. and Mary Q.,* 14 (1957), 418–28; Russell R. Menard, "From Servant to Freeholder," *ibid.,* 30 (1973), 37–64; Linda A. Bissell, "From One Generation to Another," *ibid.,* 31 (1974), 79–110; and Menard, *et al.,* "Opportunity and Inequality," *Maryland Historical Magazine,* 69 (1974), 169–84. The political consequences of social mobility and conflict are depicted in Bernard Bailyn, "Politics and Social Structure in Virginia,"* James M. Smith, ed., *Seventeenth-Century America* (1959).

On religion, Sydney E. Ahlstrom, *Religious History of the American People* (1972), surveys generally the European background as well as the transplantation of European institutions, ideas, and beliefs to the North American continent. For a particularly thoughtful overall interpretation, stressing the colonial period, see Sidney E. Mead, *The Lively Experiment* (1963). For the seventeenth century, the subject has been dominated by the prolific scholarship on Puritanism. The master scholar in that subject has been Perry Miller. His two-volume *New England Mind (The Seventeenth Century,* 1939; *From Colony to Province,* 1953); his many essays, collected in *Errand into the Wilderness* (1956) and *Nature's Nation* (1967); and his and Thomas H. Johnson's anthology of sources, *The Puritans* (1938) have made New England Puritanism one of the most absorbing subjects of modern historiography. Miller's books set in motion a flood of writing on Puritanism, which is surveyed in Michael McGiffert, "American Puritan Studies in the 1960's," *Wm. and Mary Q.,* 27 (1970), 36–67. The closest approach to a new general interpretation of Puritan thought since Miller's *New England Mind* is David D. Hall, *The Faithful Shepherd: A History of the New England Ministry in the Seventeenth Century* (1972). Among the many other important writings on Puritanism are Alan Simpson, *Puritanism in Old and New England* (1955); Edmund S. Morgan, *Visible Saints* (1963); James F. MacLear, "The Heart of New England Rent," *Mississippi Valley Historical Review,* 42 (1956), 621–52; Emil Oberholzer, Jr., *Delinquent Saints* (1955); and Timothy H. Breen, *The Character of the Good Ruler* (1970). Darrett B. Rutman, *American Puritanism* (1970) is an interesting essay of interpretation. Most recently Sacvan Bercovitch, *The Puritan Origins of the American Self* (1975) has shown the enduring impact of Puritan ideals on American self-imagery and culture.

No other religious community of the seventeenth century has received even remotely comparable study. On Anglicanism, in general, see George M. Brydon, *Virginia's Mother Church* (1947) and Elizabeth H. Davidson, *Establishment of the English Church in the Continental American Colonies* (1936); on the efforts to reform the Anglican Church in the late seventeenth and early eighteenth centuries, see Parke Rouse, Jr., *James Blair of Virginia* (1971). On the Catholics, see John T. Ellis, *Catholics in Colonial America* (1965); on the Dutch Reformed, Frederick J. Zwierlein, *Religion in New Netherland* (1910); and on the Baptists, William G. McLoughlin, *New England Dissent, 1630–1833* (2 vols., 1971).

4

Elements of Change
1660-1720

Thus, the founding of British America is the story of the efforts of private groups and individuals to profit in some way from the exploitation of the North American continent. The leading organizers had various motives. For some, the predominant goals were economic, for others, religious. For most, however, there was a mingling of religious, economic, and patriotic interests stimulated by discontent at home, lure of adventure, and the hope that in an open land, free of inherited encumbrances, their fortunes would improve. This scattering of private enterprises, some of them protected in their independence by crown charters, had developed without overall plan or general organization. By 1660 the settlements did not form an effective empire. There was little sense on either side of the Atlantic that these ill-organized, disparate settlements together constituted an overseas extension of Britain.

In the two generations that followed the restoration of the Stuarts to the throne of England (1660), efforts were made to draw these unrelated settlements into an overall governmental organization, to impose regulation and control of some sort over this miscellaneous collection of towns, villages, and farms. The way this was done, and the way in which these efforts at regulation interacted with the natural growth and maturing of the American communities, had a permanent effect on the character of American life.

Empire

Three interest groups, dominant at the Restoration court, account for the extension of the authority of the British government to America. The first were courtiers, the most active of them the Carolina proprietors, who had assisted in bringing Charles II back to the throne and had remained his key advisers. Their stake in America deepened as the possibilities of extracting profit from the settlements became more realistic. None of these influential figures at the court of Charles II conceived of themselves as potential settlers. For them America was like Ireland, where most of them had estates made profitable by the labor of tenants. And to advance their interests in the colonies most of these courtiers were willing to share in the work of devising appropriate administrative machinery and to serve as members of the agencies that were created.

A second and ultimately more influential group was composed of the merchants and their allies in government who marketed American products and sold manufactured goods to the colonists. These merchants were well aware that a significant part of the English economy had become involved in the colonies and they became leaders in the growing movement to assert British control over the American settlements—not for the sake of power, glory, and "empire" in some abstract sense, but for the sake of trade and England's economic growth.

Finally, there were the personal interests of the royal family itself, particularly those of the king's brother, James, Duke of York, and his private entourage. As proprietor of New York, an expert on naval affairs, an unusually energetic administrator, and close in temperament and religious persuasion to the continental monarchs with dynastic ambitions, James made clear soon after the Restoration that he would be a leading figure in designing an empire from among the scattered American settlements.

It was the combination of these three groups—courtiers, merchants, and the royal family itself, particularly James—all with stakes in the colonies, that accounts for the organization of the British empire at the end of the seventeenth century. Their goals were by no means identical, and there was no coordinated planning, but their interests converged in efforts at three levels.

Together they created, first, through a fumbling, pragmatic process of evolution, a network of administrative controls. Immediately after the Restoration, the Privy Council began appointing committees of its own members, occasionally supplemented by others, to deal with colonial problems as they arose. The volume and importance of the business that came before these committees soon justified the appointment of a standing committee, called the Lords of Trade (1675), composed only of members of the Privy Council itself. This committee, irregular in its efforts and lacking reliable staff, was a bridge to the permanent supervisory body, the Board of Trade and Plantations, which was created in 1696.

As an independent agency the Board of Trade, consisting of seven high state officials and eight paid members, remained the central pivot of the British imperial administration throughout the eighteenth century. But as a "Council of the Indies" it had notable weaknesses. First, the range of its duties was unrealistically broad. It was expected effectively to supervise all the trade of Britain, its fisheries, and the care of the poor throughout Britain, as well as all colonial matters; and in dealing with the colonies it was expected to have a special responsibility for reviewing all crown appointments in America and all the legislation that emerged from the colonies. Yet despite these responsibilities, the board's actual power proved to be severely limited. Other better-established branches of government took over some measure of the control of colonial affairs, and the board's power failed to mature.

The essential conflict lay between the board and the secretary of state for the Southern Department, in whose geographical jurisdiction the Western Hemisphere fell. This secretary of state was one of two chief executive officers of the government. His main responsibility lay in the area of international relations, and the center of his concerns was not the struggling settlements on the coast of North America but the glittering court of Louis XIV in Paris. Nevertheless, by 1704 the secretary of state for the Southern Department successfully challenged the Board of Trade for executive authority over the colonies, and the result was a fundamental weakness at the heart of the British

JAMES II AT THE TIME OF HIS ACCESSION

James's stubborn insistence on imposing a Catholic regime on a Protestant nation and his autocratic disregard of political realities led to his downfall in the Glorious Revolution (1688) and to a great advance in British liberalism. *(National Portrait Gallery, London.)*

overseas administration. The Board of Trade remained an information-gathering body, in effect the colonial office of that era, in charge of a substantial flow of information to and from the colonies; but it lacked the power to enforce regulations, make appointments, or otherwise direct the course of events. It could advise, counsel, admonish; but orders came from the secretary of state's office which might or might not have available to it the board's voluminous files and which tended to view colonial affairs in the context of western European diplomacy.

That significant division of authority was not the only source of administrative confusion as the empire took shape. Almost every major branch of the central government discovered some interest in the colonies and managed to secure some corner of control. The Treasury took responsibility for the colonial customs administration. The Admiralty successfully claimed jurisdiction over naval stores and other colonial products vital to the British navy, and took over the role of patrolling the coastal waters to enforce the growing body of commercial regulations. Further, the War Office took charge of army operations on the North American mainland during the many years when European international conflicts involved overseas territories. The army's contracting, like that of the navy, had a powerful influence in the economic development of the colonies, and its strategic planning involved American manpower as well. Weaving through all of these ill-assorted jurisdictions was the authority legitimately exercised by England's attorney general, solicitor general, and several auditors and collectors of the king's revenues.

By the early eighteenth century an imperial administration had taken shape in the British world. But it was a very different structure from the Spanish American empire. There was no central authority equivalent to the Spanish Council of the Indies which had at its disposal both information and executive authority and drew together all the other agencies of government that had a finger in colonial matters. The various British agencies conflicted with each other. There were overlaps in jurisdiction, and also significant gaps in authority. As a result, there was a minimum of effective central control.

Yet for Britain this administrative inefficiency was not acutely distressing. It became a matter of public concern only rarely in the years before 1760, mainly during war crises, when success depended on close coordination among the colonies. For the guiding principles behind the organization of the British empire did not require tight administrative efficiency in the years before 1760, and it did not require territorial government in depth. The colonies could largely be left alone so long as certain minimal expectations were met, and these expectations centered almost entirely on the regulation of commerce.

Britain's was a mercantilist empire: it came together not as an extension of the governance of the realm but as an extension of England's commercial growth. Its guiding principles were derived from mercantilism, the ancient doctrine that the state must intervene to regulate economic activity for the public welfare. In the heated commercial rivalries of the seventeenth century, mercantilists made two assumptions that framed the regulations of Britain's American empire: first, that the economic universe was composed of competing national states; and second, that there was a fixed amount of wealth ultimately available. According to mercantilist theory, the purpose of commercial regulation for each nation state was to secure economic self-sufficiency and, by maintaining a favorable balance of trade, to avoid falling into dependence on rival states. In this competition among nations, the colonies were fundamentally important. If they did not provide Britain with needed colonial products, these commodities would have to be purchased from other nations and hence wealth would be drained by the rival states. It followed that every effort would have to be made to direct the flow of valuable colonial products to Britain alone. Further, the colonies, as markets for the sale of manufactured goods, were to be monopolized by Britain, for every purchase of goods from a rival state meant some small drainage in the national treasure.

It was to put these ideas into effect that the famous navigation acts were passed by Parliament in three main groups beginning soon after the Restoration. By the first of these enactments (1660) the shipping and marketing of all colonial goods were made monopolies of British merchants and shippers. England alone, it was decreed, would enjoy the profits of shipping and reexporting colonial goods. To reinforce these provisions, a special list was prepared of "enumerated" commodities that could be shipped only to England or other British ports. The basic list included all the goods that England would otherwise have had to buy from other imperial powers: sugar, tobacco, cotton, indigo, ginger, certain dyes, and special wood products. Later, as other commodities became valuable, they were added to the original list: rice and molasses in 1704; naval stores in 1705 and 1729; copper and furs in 1721.

The act of 1660 was the basic law governing colonial trade. Two others completed the pattern of mercantilist regulation. The so-called Staple Act of 1663 gave England a monopoly of the sale of European manufactures to the American colonies. European goods, the law stated, could not be shipped directly to America from Europe even if the ships that carried them were British. These goods

THE LUMBER INDUSTRY ON THE NORTHERN COASTS

This detail from a map of Nova Scotia of 1750 shows timber being felled and trimmed into squared logs. Rafts of planks are being poled and towed to awaiting ships. (*American Antiquarian Society.*)

would have to be sent first to England, unloaded there, and reshipped to the colonies. Thus valuable customs duties would be produced for the English Treasury and at the same time foreign merchants would be put at a disadvantage. Certain exceptions were made, either because, like salt, they were necessary for American industry, or because like servants, horses, and provisions from Scotland and Ireland, or wines from Madeira or the Azores, they involved no competition with English production.

A final law, that of 1673, sought simply to plug gaps in the earlier legislation. As a consequence, this law was quite technical and a source of endless confusion. Its aim was to prevent colonial merchants from evading the enumeration clauses. It did this by obliging them either to take out bonds guaranteeing their compliance with the law (a cumbersome procedure particularly difficult for small merchants) or to pay on enumerated commodities a "plantation duty" equivalent to the reexport duty that would otherwise have to be paid in England. Had the act been well understood and fully complied with, it would have taken the profit out of smuggling from the colonies to Europe. In fact, it served its purpose only poorly. Nevertheless, it remained on the books as part of a growing body of mercantilist regulation that in effect defined the empire as an operating entity.

Thus, out of the convergent interests of courtiers, merchants, and the royal family itself had come the beginning of an imperial system operating at three levels: as an administrative unit; as a doctrine (mercantilism); and as a set of commercial regulations. It was, by 1700, an empire of world importance; but it was decidedly limited in effectiveness. It was limited administratively because of the ill-coordinated jumble of agencies that managed it. It was limited in theory by the mercantilist doctrines that prevailed—doctrines that demanded not territorial governance in depth but only regulation of external commerce. And it was limited also by the intricacy of the governing legislation and the great difficulty of enforcing these laws 3000 miles from home. By the early eighteenth century no one could doubt that the American colonies were part of an empire; but neither could anyone conceive of the ill-managed, superficial administration as a rigorous, centralized dominion. The passion for territorial rule was not there, nor the drive of dynastic ambition.

The limits of the British imperial system become particularly clear when one considers the efforts that were made in later years to turn the empire into something more powerful than this—something more effective than it ever in fact became. For there was one person at the center of the English government through the late seventeenth century who did have ambitions akin to those of continental monarchs, and who also had the instincts of an efficient administrator and a personal entourage capable of managing an efficient system.

The instincts that led the Duke of York, subsequently James II (1685–88) to seek to expand and deepen the controls of empire can be traced back to his childhood training as a military leader in the autocratic court of France; to his desire, as a royal refugee, to exercise the power that had been denied him; and to the fortunate position he found himself in when his brother, Charles II, returned to the throne. As Lord High Admiral with a loyal following of war-seasoned officers, James took command of garrisons all over England and appointed as governors those hungry veterans who had merged their fortunes with his. For him the colonial world was but an extension of the realm. Soon his men turned up as governors and other high officers in the Caribbean and North American governments. His base on the mainland was New York, which he ruled as proprietor from the time it was captured from the Dutch. Slowly he expanded this center into a larger imperial dominion, his efforts coinciding with the more general efforts the English government was then making to restrict the private jurisdictions that had been created in the early years of colonization.

For in the later seventeenth century and continuing into the early years of the eighteenth century, the British government, as part of its elaboration of empire, undertook to cut back the chartered powers of the private jurisdictions in America, just as the Spanish crown had cut back the independence of the *adelantados* and *encomenderos* a century earlier. Progress was slow, erratic, and in the end incomplete. Virginia, when the company failed in 1624, and New York, at the accession of James II in 1685, both automatically became crown colonies. Also, it was not difficult to separate New Hampshire from Massachusetts (1680) and assign it a royal governor. But for the rest, the charters created serious problems and they had to be attacked directly. Between 1684 and 1691 the charters of Massachusetts, Connecticut, Rhode Island, New Jersey, Pennsylvania, Maryland, and Carolina were confiscated.

It was in the early years of this campaign against these partly independent jurisdictions that James's grand and ill-fated design unfolded. As king, his ultimate ambition, it seems, was to create two centralized viceroyalties in America which would be ruled by crown-appointed governors and councils. The Delaware River at 40 degrees latitude (the division between the two original Virginia companies) was apparently envisaged as the boundary between the two great domains, and within them all the decentralizing tendencies of colonial life were to be reversed. During his short and tumultuous reign James focused his attention on the northern section, which became known as the Dominion of New England.

In a legal sense, the Dominion came together easily after 1685. To the core colony of New York were added Massachusetts, Connecticut, Rhode Island, New Jersey, and Pennsylvania as each of their charters was annulled or suspended. To rule the Dominion, in place of the existing officials, James sent over one of his closest allies and former comrades in arms, Edmund Andros, who had served him well in several other positions, particularly as governor of New York (1674–81). To assist Andros in his headquarters in Boston, James appointed a royal council which included a majority of recently arrived merchants who had struggled against the Puritan establishment, hitherto with little effect. Together, royal governor and royal council moved to work out the implications of direct and full territorial government similar to that of the Spanish crown in the Southern Hemisphere.

To the horror of the Puritans throughout New England, Andros declared toleration for all groups, and confiscated Boston's Old South Church for the use of Church of England services. Equally offensive was his disregard of the ancient principles of English self-government. He continued by mere executive declaration taxes that had originally been levied by the representative General Court. Worse still was Andros's land policy, since it affected almost the entire population. To satisfy the technicalities of crown law and to open land acquisitions to all comers, especially to his own entourage, he commanded that all town lands be regranted in the name of the king and be subject to the payment of quitrents, and that the towns' undistributed common lands be placed at the council's disposal. Finally, to complete the destruction of the local jurisdictions, he restricted the activities of the town meetings to electing officials who would help collect taxes.

Andros's efforts never reached beyond Massachusetts, indeed scarcely beyond Boston and the coastal towns. But their implications were widely known and they stimulated ferocious oppositon. His tax policy provoked an open rebellion in the town of Ipswich, led by the Reverend John Wise, and to the imprisonment of that outspoken preacher and four of his followers. Resistance grew among the Puritan leaders and the landholders throughout New England. By the time Andros's royal master was deposed in the Glorious Revolution in England, the royalist regime in Boston was so universally hated and so isolated that the rebellion that rose against it and that imprisoned the governor and his closest henchmen took place, in April 1689, almost without a struggle.

All of James's plans disappeared with his fall from power. When this high tide of imperial ambition fell back, the more permanent forms of Anglo-American relations emerged as the charters were restored, though with qualifications, and the slow, partial elimination of private jurisdictions continued. The two Jerseys were merged into a single royal colony in 1702. In the Carolinas a popular rebellion against the proprietors (1719) and constant pressure against them in England led first to the reduction of their chartered privileges and then in 1729 to the formal separation of the two districts into two royal colonies. The one residue of the Carolinas' proprietary origins was the retention of one of the eight original shares by the diplomat and politician the Earl Granville, heir of Sir George Carteret; when consolidated in 1745 his inheritance, the so-called Granville District, constituted title to the undistributed land of fully half of North Carolina on which lived perhaps two-thirds of the colony's population. The charters of Pennsylvania and Maryland were restored; but in both cases the selection of the governor had thereafter to be approved by the crown, and all legislation was subject to review by the crown's legal officers.

The result of all these developments after the collapse of James's Dominion was a limited and superficial empire—far different from Spain's, but still a visible and palpable empire. Its visibility, by the early eighteenth century, appeared most dramatically to most Americans not so much in law enforcement or in recast institutions as in the increasing number of officials sent to America to manage the new system. In most port towns there were customs collectors appointed by the Treasury who brought with them small teams of assistants. There were auditors and surveyors of the king's revenues. And there were officers of the vice admiralty courts created by the law of 1696—subordinate arms of the admiralty court system that held jurisdiction over maritime law in Britain. The judges and clerks of these "prerogative" courts (operating without juries and by rules different from those of the common law courts) were part of the imperial presence, as were, indirectly and for the limited purpose of enforcing the navigation laws, the governors and lieutenant governors of all of the royal colonies.

The importance of these officials, most of whom were newcomers to America at the end of the century, cannot be exaggerated. They represented, indeed embodied, the empire; and the way they approached their work, the attitude they brought to Anglo-American relations, and the ways in which they related to the local communities became matters of importance in the life of the American people, affecting not only the actuality of government but the image of government and of political authority more generally.

These officials were not efficient imperial bureaucrats, and they were seldom committed to promoting the strength of the empire. Their offices were minor parts of the patronage system of the English government which, like spoils systems in later phases of American history, served to cement together the various parts of the dominant political organization. Far from being viewed by their incumbents as offices demanding impartiality, efficiency, and a devotion to the public welfare, the colonial posts filled by appointment in England were seen as a kind of private property parceled out by political leaders to their deserving followers. The fortunate appointees were expected to profit by their positions through fees, gifts, and perquisites, as well as through salaries. Appointments were made almost randomly with respect to administrative ability or interest in public affairs. What counted were connections and the applicant's capacity to force his patron to reward loyalty and previous service.

At times the appointments were bizarre, even those at the highest level. The governor of New York from 1701 to 1708 was a rapacious transvestite, Lord Cornbury, a member of the Clarendon family, who traipsed around the colony in women's clothes and squeezed profit from anything he could lay his hands on. The governor of Virginia from 1705 to 1737 was the Earl of Orkney, who never had the slightest intention of setting foot in America, and never did. He had been a war companion of William III and was the Duke of Marlborough's leading infantry commander. His appointment was a reward too, however, for somewhat less heroic service. He had made what may have been a supreme sacrifice by marrying William III's mistress, Elizabeth Villiers.

Orkney's career as absentee governor of Virginia is revealing in many ways.

LORD CORNBURY, GOVERNOR OF NEW YORK, IN
FEMALE DRESS

A cousin of Queen Anne, Lord Cornbury, an
eighteenth-century historian wrote, used "to
dress himself in a woman's habit and then to
patrol the fort in which he resided. Such freaks
of low humor exposed him to the universal
contempt of the people." His avarice led the
Assembly to assert its control over tax revenues,
and his zealous Anglicanism resulted in broader
religious toleration. *(New-York Historical Society.)*

The stated salary of the position was £2,000 a year. Orkney in effect sold the office
for £1200 to a series of lieutenant governors who served in his place, with the
understanding that they were entitled to make as much out of the job as they
could. He selected, as it happens, some able men: Robert Hunter, 1706 (who,
because of accidents at sea and his wife's connections, ended up governor not of
Virginia but of New York, a post he filled with distinction); Alexander Spotswood,
in 1709; and William Gooch, in 1727. These three had only one thing in common:
they had all fought as officers under Orkney and Marlborough. Similarly, a certain Colonel Samuel Shute had been promised the command of a cavalry regiment, but being passed over for that, he was rewarded with the governorship of
Massachusetts, a post he accepted only when told that some Boston merchants
were willing to reward handsomely a governor who would assist them in founding
a bank. No less than nine veterans of the battle of Blenheim received colonial
governorships for their service.

Under these conditions, what is surprising is not that colonial offices were occasionally filled by avaricious deviants like Cornbury or by psychological cripples
like Sir Danvers Osborn, who hanged himself in a fit of melancholy a week after
his arrival as New York's governor, nor is it surprising that lesser posts were frequently held by altogether unqualified hacks. What is more remarkable is that
some appointees at all levels of the imperial system were in fact conscientious and

honest, and sought dutifully to serve the imperial interest as well as the local population.

Still, it is the randomness of these appointments, the disregard of the incumbents' ability and experience, and hence in the end the arbitrariness of the system, that had the deepest effect on American life.

The impact of this aspect of the developing imperial organization, so different from Spain's, may be seen in four important areas. First, the patronage origins of colonial appointments served to increase the superficiality of the system which had already been created by the disarray of the administrative structure and by the prevailing mercantilist goals. Appointed officeholders at all levels were always insecure in tenure. The same arbitrary movement of the patronage system that put them in office could easily eject them. Sooner or later, they knew, quite without regard to the quality of their work, they would be replaced by someone closer to the levers of power. Consequently, they were highly susceptible to compromises and vulnerable to local pressures. If the situation required speed in making a profit and in acquiring incidental benefits such as land grants, they would be quick about it, at the expense, if need be, of the strict execution of their duties.

But the consequences of the patronage control of official appointments ran deeper than that. British officialdom as it emerged from these formative years inculcated in Americans a sense that the universe of government, far from being a seamless web uniting high and low through a series of responsible links, was essentially a structure composed of two distinct and antagonistic levels, a level of local, internal government that expressed the dominant interests of the local community, and a superior, external authority which was in its nature hostile to local interests. Often this sense of disjunction took a more specific form, in which the external power became identified with executive authority and the local and benevolent authority with legislative power. Such a sharp distinction between these functions of government, which grew as the political structure matured in the early eighteenth century, was in itself extraordinary for the time and was destined to have a continuing importance in American history.

Even more general still, among the consequences of British officialdom, was the growth on the part of politically active Americans of a kind of cynicism to all government, an attitude of anti-authoritarianism stimulated by the character and behavior of these officials. These officeholders represented a great nation which was revered by most of the colonists; but in themselves they were often incompetent, poor, and supercilious, a bad enough combination made worse by their easy corruptibility. Americans could only wonder whether the power such people represented deserved automatic compliance.

Beyond all of this lay the sense, as the imperial officialdom developed, that the social and political worlds were far from unified, that social and political leadership at the highest level was dissociated. The embodiments of native social authority in the colonies were different in identity and different in interests from those who represented the state. When local leaders competed with strangers for high office in their own colony, they did so often on unequal terms, and their failures could be embittering. Thus William Byrd II, a second-generation American who spent fifteen years being educated and making contacts in England before taking over the family property in Virginia, failed in his bid to buy the lieutenant governorship from Orkney and spent years struggling with his successful rival, Spotswood, who had no original stake in the colony and no knowledge of it when he arrived on the scene. Byrd finally acquired a seat on the colony's council, but only after ten years of diligent effort. Some English officials were able to tranfer social authority quickly to the colonies or managed to gain it by working sensitively with the local gentry, but many never drew close to American life. They remained living proof that government at the highest level was not a reflection of social authority but something different, something outside the visible society and imposed upon it, something that had to be managed with caution, guarded against, and somehow bent to the community's needs.

What made all of these consequences of the growth of officialdom especially important was the fact that they coincided with the emergence of local elites in the mainland colonies. The dominance of these natural leaders within the maturing communities could not be doubted and their demands for recognition—in politics as in other spheres of life—could not easily be ignored.

Anglo-American Aristocracy

The emergence of native American elites toward the end of the seventeenth century and in the early eighteenth century was not simply the accidental product of individual ambitions and successes. For the successes that marked the rise of a provincial aristocracy were the results of the exploitation, by skillful, energetic, and ambitious men, of opportunities that suddenly became available, and these opportunities were created by structural developments in social and economic life.

The material basis for most social distinctions in the colonies, as in England, was one's position with respect to the ownership and use of land. The quarter century that bridged the turn of the century, 1689–1715, saw a significant shift in this basic relationship. Between these two dates the land area under active cultivation remained approximately the same, because of Indian wars and the difficulty of overcoming natural barriers in the way of westward expansion. But during these same years the population more than doubled: it rose from approximately 200,000 to 434,000. Land was still far easier to acquire in the colonies than it was in England, but the increasing population pressure created significant changes in social relations, and in itself accounts for the emergence of new social elites.

In New England the emergence of a landowning aristocracy in the long-settled towns was marked by dramatic conflicts almost everywhere. In its ideal, original form the New England town had been a quasi-democracy of male heads of households, all of whom shared in the governance of three main aspects of community life. They were all full church members; they were all freemen with equal voices in the town meeting; and they were all landowners with shares in the undivided common land. As time passed and movement among towns grew and immigration into the colonies continued, questions arose about how newcomers would share in these original privileges. Certain answers came quickly. Access to membership in the church was controlled by a procedure calculated to make the entry of newcomers possible but still highly selective. Access to participation in the town meeting was less easily determined but in the end was opened to all respectable male inhabitants, even to those without the land prescribed by the second charter of Massachusetts to qualify one for the colony's franchise. But there was no easy resolution of the question of control of the undivided land. The heirs of the original grantees had no desire to share their inheritances with newcomers, and they closed ranks against the claimants.

Without originally intending to do so, these second- and third-generation colonists began to form exclusive companies of proprietary landholders. Challenged in the town meeting by those excluded from sharing in the common property, they drew apart and met separately, only to have their rights to the undivided land challenged at law. In certain towns they sought compromises by allocating plots—often dismissed as bribes—to conspicuous opponents or to those with special claims. Most often, however, confrontation could not be evaded. The challenges went up to the General Court, whose decisions, after a period of uncertainty, favored the heirs of the original grantees.

The result was of great importance. Not only did the fortunate heirs continue to enjoy the increasingly valuable property that had already been opened to cultivation by their grandparents or parents, but they shared control of the still undivided common land. With this inherited capital, they were in the best possible position to build fortunes out of real estate. Those shrewd or enterprising enough to take full advantage of the opportunities that lay at hand broadened out their operations from small local transactions to large-scale land speculation; some moved into trade through successes in commercial farming; the most enterprising did both.

An inheritance was not, of course, the only road to economic success and to social eminence in early eighteenth-century New England, but for the fortunate it was the easiest and one frequently traveled. So John Winthrop's two grandsons, altogether lacking in the founder's moral, political, and intellectual stature, spent their lives attempting to cash in on the family's land claims. Both joined the Andros council in the hope of gaining confirmation of their family's claims—little enough reward, one of them said, "for the waste of that plentiful estate which my predecessors joyfully laid down to begin the growth and prosperity of this country." In Connecticut, the most successful became known as River Gods because of their valuable properties along the colony's main waterway. Everywhere in New England land claims proved a rich ore available for refinement into gold, prestige, and power.

The same was true in the South; but there, as tobacco cultivation spread westward, profits from the land were intimately tied up with the problem of labor, and that increasingly meant slavery. It was at the turn of the seventeenth century that the critical importance of slavery first emerged in Southern society. A great revolution in social relations as well as in the economy was created by the spread of the institution and the growth of the Negro population. Slavery accounted not only for the introduction of a major component of the American population but also for a basic source of social stratification within the white population. The logic of this development quickly became clear.

With profits from tobacco production small and at times nonexistent, the *extensiveness* of planting seemed increasingly important. Land was available for expansion but labor was not. In 1684 the prominent Virginian William Fitzhugh claimed title to 24,000 acres, but could cultivate only 300. Indentured servants continued to arrive and continued to form a constant if shifting part of the labor force. But there was no way to increase their numbers to serve the growing need. Slaves were the answer, it seemed; and they were increasingly available as the British slave trade entered a period of expansion and increasing efficiency. Slaves in the long run were cheap. Their upkeep, averaged over a lifetime of labor, was perhaps £1 per year, as opposed to a servant's annual maintenance cost of £2–£4. But if slaves were cheaper than servants in the long run, they were more costly in the short run because they required a higher initial investment. And costs were rising constantly. Average slave prices rose 25–30 percent between 1660 and 1700; by 1750 they had doubled, and by the revolution they had tripled. In 1700 a newly imported "prime field hand" cost £20 in Virginia, in 1750, £30. Nevertheless their numbers continued to rise as their importance in the spreading tobacco culture became clearly understood. An estimated 20,000 slaves were brought to British North America in the two decades after 1700; 50,000 arrived in the subsequent two decades. In 1715 blacks formed a quarter of Virginia's total population, by the 1730s 40 percent. In South Carolina, blacks outnumbered whites by 1708; by 1720 the ratio was almost 2 to 1, and the black population was growing at a faster rate than the white.

The growth of the slave labor force, which made possible a significant increase in tobacco cultivation and eventually in rice and indigo production, created a deepening social distinction within the white population. Capital was the critical determinant. Since profits depended on the extent of cultivation and since that in turn depended on slave labor which required high capital outlays, the line between those who had capital available and those who did not, or between those who could acquire it and those who could not, became crucial. Those with greater assets formed a new class of "great planters" in a society that as late as 1700 had consisted almost entirely of farm operations of small and medium size. In Lancaster County in northern Virginia in 1716, a majority of taxpayers owned slaves, but few had more than 2 or 3; only 4 owned over 20; one, however—Robert Carter—had 126. At his death in 1732 Robert "King" Carter—planter and above all land agent and speculator, son of a settler of 1649 who had brought capital with him and had accumulated the land claims of no less than five wives— was said to possess 300,000 acres and £10,000 in cash. Capital and inherited land claims, in a world of steeply rising land values, determined who would succeed and who would not, who would control the land and who would not, and who would live like princes on the land—bourgeois, enterprising princes, to be sure, desperately concerned with markets, prices, and the humblest details of farming, but princes nevertheless.

In the main commercial centers the merchant community as a whole remained open, free of the formal limitations of gilds and other artificial barriers to entrance. But toward the end of the seventeenth century, and increasingly in the early eighteenth century, significant differences within the merchant group appeared nevertheless, and a mercantile aristocracy of sorts began to make its appearance.

INDIGO CULTURE IN SOUTH CAROLINA

The plants of the blue dyestuff are being carried to fermenting vats, and the resulting liquid flows down the sluice at left into containers. (*Charleston Library Society.*)

As the commercial system settled into its complex pattern of oceanic routes covering the North Atlantic basin, certain portions of the network proved crucial and dominated the others. Entrance into this primary route became more and more difficult to achieve, and the colonial merchants who controlled it became dominant figures. They clustered in only two or three of the many excellent natural ports, so many of which had seemed promising at the start. In retrospect, by the Revolution, it may have seemed natural that Boston, Newport, Rhode Island, New York, Philadelphia, and Charleston would have become the commercial headquarters of the colonial world and their leading merchants the aristocrats of trade, but no one could have predicted that outcome a century before. New London, Connecticut, had had at least as much natural promise; its founders' great hopes, reflected in the name, were by no means fantastic at the time. But in fact only a few ports emerged as the central pivots of the system.

For as the magnitude of imports from England increased and as the marshaling of colonial products in ever larger quantities made greater and greater demands on colonial entrepreneurs, the whole enterprise of commerce became more complex and generated a significant degree of specialization. A multitude of small shipments of the crucial "dry goods" (iron products and textiles, primarily) to many centers in the colonies became grossly inefficient. The English specialists in North American trade began to concentrate their shipments to a few ports and to a relatively few merchants. They sought commercial correspondents whose credit was absolutely sound, whose honesty and reliability were irreproachable, and who would send payments quickly in good bills of exchange or vendible commodities. Domination of the system was ultimately theirs, and in their choices of colonial correspondents lay a measure of social as well as commercial control.

Once involved in these primary circuits of trade, colonial merchants had a cumulative advantage over others. The major profits of the commercial system tended to center in them, while the smaller merchants, confined to local routes, fell more and more clearly into subordinate roles. In this secondary network of trade—within the colonies, up and down the American coast, to and from the Caribbean—merchants and traders remained indistinguishable; shopkeeping, commercial farming, and overseas merchandising were carried on simultaneously, as in the original settling years; and commercial competition remained open to anyone willing and able to risk small shipments or who had a vessel available for hire.

But in the major ports the situation was different. There, by the early eighteenth century, were the dominant entrepreneurs who were in direct contact with the English merchants and in control of the critical goods. These few merchants, in Boston and New York at first, later in Newport, Philadelphia, and Charleston, formed an aristocracy of sorts. It was an aristocracy that was still limited in affluence, fluid in membership, and insecure, but it was a visible elite nevertheless, and its fortunes rested on the primary flows of commerce.

Thus economic developments—in the ownership of land in New England, in the expansion of the tobacco economy in the Chesapeake, and in the maturing of commerce in the main centers in the north—underlay the development of native elites. But the forces behind this development were not only economic. They were political as well. In the end, advantages flowing from the sources of political power contributed at least as much to the forming of colonial aristocracies as the development of the economy did.

As the colonial governments took firm shape in the middle and later years of the century, the value of political patronage and the yields of public office became unmistakably clear. The possibilities were seen first in Virginia, where what might be called the first "court house gang" took form during the long governorship of Sir William Berkeley (1641–52, 1659–77).

Though in general the governor's power in Virginia was limited by the countervailing power of the Burgesses, and though no effort was made in London to equip the governor with patronage sufficient to discipline the political system, in fact the offices that fell to his disposal gave him an important role in many aspects of the colony's life. He could appoint the justices of the peace, though to ignore the local notables was a risk he did not often take; he could appoint sheriffs annually, officers who were primarily responsible for collecting taxes and fees, for which they were paid substantially; above all, he had the authority to nominate members of the council, who not only enjoyed considerable prestige but benefited in material terms from the privileges available to them. Berkeley took full advantage of his patronage powers. Over the twenty-nine years of his administration he formed, by appointment to these offices, a clique of officials loyal to himself to whom he channeled these benefits.

GREENSPRING, GOVERNOR BERKELEY'S PLANTATION HOUSE

The first great house of Virginia, it was originally set in an orchard of 1500 trees. Though badly damaged by Bacon's rebels in 1676, it became the temporary seat of government after the rebellion. *(Courtesy Jamestown Restoration and Parke Rouse, Director.)*

Called the "Greenspring Faction" after Berkeley's plantation, this clique was the first in American history to gain, by the spoils of a ruling political party, a near monopoly of lucrative public offices. Privileges flowed to them. Technically, disposal of land still operated through the headright system,* but that system was clearly too complex for the speculative fever that gripped the Virginia planters well before the end of the century, and the councillors were in the best position to assure themselves title to large acreages of undeveloped property which they hoped to exploit. More immediate were the benefits from licenses to the fur trade, a commerce monopolized by the government which became increasingly concentrated in the hands of Berkeley's allies.

Benefiting from the rewards of office and the influence of political position, and beneficiaries of indirect rewards such as land grants and trading licenses, Berkeley's faction, drawn from those already distinguished in the growing plantation society, became something of an oligarchy before it was shaken up in Bacon's Rebellion. The pattern, however, was clear. A similar little oligarchy developed almost simultaneously around the proprietary interest in Maryland. Politics could help create elites in these insecure communities, or reinforce or shape leadership groups otherwise forming. While the governors were most often obliged to accept the ruling local powers, they could select among them too and hence determine in some degree who would further secure the advantages they already had.

It was not in Virginia or in Maryland, however, but in New York that these possibilities were most dramatically revealed. There in the 1690s a new land-owning elite was created almost overnight largely by a single governor attempting to make his own fortune and the fortunes of his followers as quickly as possible. In New York's tumultuous and competitive politics at the end of the century, the ruthless partisanship of Governor Benjamin Fletcher (1692–97) operated like the sword of Gabriel. Personally rapacious, surrounded by a mercenary gang of petty plunderers whom he had brought with him, Fletcher—and Cornbury after him—proceeded to buy the loyalty of the dominant group of local powers by bestowing on them enormous grants of land and confirming others previously made.

He did not invent the procedure. One patroonship had survived in flourishing shape from the Dutch period—Rensselaerswyck, a manor of close to a million acres on both sides of the Hudson—and several other great estates had been granted subsequently. Of these, the most important was Livingston Manor, a grant of 160,000 acres that had been extracted from the Dominion government by a particularly supple Scottish-Anglo-Dutch politician, Robert Livingston—a man Fletcher said, who began as "a little bookkeeper" but who "screwed himself into one of the most considerable estates in the province, . . . never disbursing

---

*See page 41 for a description of the headright system.

sixpence but with the expectation of twelve." It was just such sharp-eyed opportunists and hustling politicians, scrambling in the bonanza land grab of late seventeenth-century New York, whose appetites Fletcher fed. The estates he parcelled out in Dutchess and Westchester counties varied in size and in legal and political privileges, but almost all exceeded 100,000 acres and all elevated their owners to the apex of the community. The magnitudes in some cases were spectacular. The manor of Saint George extended for fifty miles through the full width of Long Island. Six manors covered more than one-half of the whole of Westchester County. Some grants were literally open-ended: sixteen miles, commonly, along a river bank running back indefintely into the unsurveyed countryside.

The fate of these vast New York estates and the fortunes of their owners and the tenants who helped work the land form a complex story. But it is a simple and obvious fact that the grants were extremely valuable gifts, and were destined to play a major role in the colony's subsequent history.

The results of political influence were not limited to landholding. Politics also affected the development of trade and the establishment of the merchant leadership, for at the end of the century government contracting, political in its essence, became a prime source of economic advancement, especially during war years. The colonies became involved in both of the international wars in which England fought during these years: the inconclusive War of the League of Augsburg (1689–97), in which England led a coalition against France's effort to dominate central Europe, and the more consequential War of the Spanish Succession (1702–13) in which England and Holland joined to block Louis XIV's claim to the crown of Spain. Both of these wars, whose main operations spread over large areas of Europe, led to hostili-

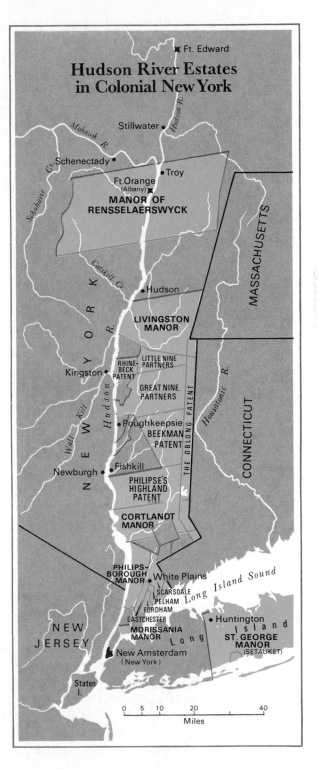

Hudson River Estates in Colonial New York

ties between the English colonies and the French in southern Canada. The slow-growing colony of New France had been settled at the same time as the English colonies; but hobbled in its development by religious restrictions on immigration, a rigid seignorial system of land distribution and social relations, and a tightly controlled colonial bureaucracy, it had achieved a population of only 6000 by 1660 and perhaps 15,000 by 1700. Nevertheless the French had been aggressive fur traders, trappers, and fishermen from the beginning, and for years there had been minor clashes between them and the English settlers, especially in Nova Scotia. Those clashes escalated into savage border warfare and extended struggles for inland territories during the two international wars of the years 1689–1713, both of which involved the English colonists as much economically as militarily.

In the first, known as King William's War in the colonies, the French, with Indian support, fought the English for control of Hudson Bay, and in 1690 fell on the exposed northern borders of English settlement with devastating raids on an arc of towns from Portland, Maine, to Schenectady, New York. The Anglo-American efforts concentrated on capturing Port Royal in Nova Scotia, which was taken but then lost by Massachusetts troops in 1690–91, and on an elaborate attack on the center of French Canada, which failed miserably. The same pattern was repeated in the second of these wars, known in the colonies as Queen Anne's War. Once again the Maine settlements were raided; and Deerfield, Massachusetts, was destroyed. In retaliation the colonists razed Nova Scotian villages and attacked Port Royal twice before finally taking that fortress. And far to the south during the same war, a force of Carolinians and Indians burned Saint Augustine and destroyed the string of Spanish missions that linked the Spanish coastal settlements to French Louisiana. By the Treaty of Utrecht (1713), whose main provisions marked a significant British victory in Europe, Britain secured permanent title to Newfoundland, Acadia (Nova Scotia), and Hudson Bay, though not all the boundaries were clear, and won a thirty-year contract to supply Spanish America with 4800 slaves and a cargo of goods annually.

All of the American efforts in these wars of the European powers made great demands on the fragile colonial economies and accounted for significant inflows of funds. Troops had to be mobilized, housed, transported, and fed; ships had to be built, equipped, and manned; and native sources of naval supplies had to be exploited. The management of these efforts during these two decades of war fell into the eager hands of a few colonial merchants. Some were experienced. Andrew Belcher, once a Cambridge innkeeper, had made his first successes in trade as a supplier to the Massachusetts government during its brief and bloody war against the local Indians, King Philip's War (1675-76). In the international conflicts that followed, Belcher became the colony's principal contractor, and by his profits established a family that would rise to the governorship and to other important offices and would enjoy grand tours of Europe and the acquaintance of monarchs. The Faneuil family, Huguenot refugees from France, also estab-

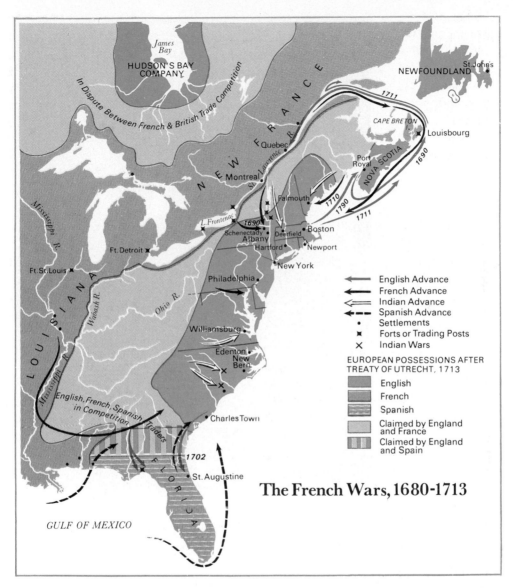

The French Wars, 1680-1713

lished itself partly through wartime contracting, and in New York another Huguenot, Stephanus DeLancey, and the Schuyler brothers in Albany, all active in a hundred enterprises, used government contracting as a major source of profits. Through that business, political in its origins, these contractors established families as important in New York as the Belchers and Faneuils were in Massachusetts.

So in these many ways the situation made possible, toward the end of the century, the growth of local elites: enterprising merchants like Belcher and Faneuil; landowning squires like the Winthrops; planters like the Fitzhughs, the Carters, and the Byrds; and manorial "lords" like the Livingstons of New York. They

PETER FANEUIL (1700–1743)

Nephew and heir of the Huguenot
refugee Andrew Faneuil, who
made a fortune in trade in
Boston in the early 18th century,
Peter devoted himself to commerce
and public affairs. In 1740 he gave
the city its famous Faneuil Hall,
which became a cockpit of
Revolutionary activity. *(Massachusetts Historical Society.)*

formed, in various centers and in scattered groups, an aristocracy of sorts, a
leadership group distinguished by wealth or substantial claims to wealth, political influence, and a superior style of life. But if there was an aristocracy, it
was a limited aristocracy indeed. The limitations of their distinctions, the essential weakness of their positions, and the instability of the membership of these
groups were as important as the eminence that they had achieved.

They formed, to begin with, no "class"—that is, no body of corporate interests,
known and acknowledged, that dominated individual or family interests. The
concerns of these striving merchants, hustling land speculators, and hard-pressed
planters were personal, local, and immediate. The groups were newly formed;
there was no sense of inherited commitments or of a corporate identity shaped
through time. These recently successful colonists identified their interests not
with the stable concerns of a particular stratum of society that had existed before
them and would persist after them and that defined each member's particular

good. Their interests were their own, only occasionally and erratically merging with the concerns of others in similar situations to form common commitments and a common program of public action.

Further, these emerging elites were distinguished from most of their contemporaries by wealth alone, and wealth of a particularly fragile kind. In education, in race, in ancestry, in cultural disposition, in speech, personal style, and public manner they were largely indistinguishable from hundreds of others who competed with them openly. They had achieved a degree of wealth, and wealth, in the colonial situation, was remarkably insecure. There was almost no way to invest a fortune securely. "Urban" properties provided perhaps the steadiest yields but were limited in scale and availability. Most capital was tied up in daily trading or planting operations or in land bought on speculation. Liquid funds scarcely existed, and momentary upsets could prove to be disasters. Bankruptcies were common occurrences. In Boston in the early years of the eighteenth century, the leading shipowner was a cooper's son, Samuel Lillie, who held shares in no less than 108 seagoing vessels, 42 of which he owned outright. But in 1707, faced with ruin by the attempted collection of a single note of a few hundred pounds, he went into hiding to escape the sheriff, and fled to England never to return. How many others there were like Lillie, tossed up by the surging economy and then cast down with equal speed, we do not know. But repeatedly names rise from obscurity only to disappear back into the population at large. Wealth, as it was achieved in these early years, remained vulnerable, and the distinctions based on wealth were equally insecure.

Even when wealth was maintained, however, it could provide no institutional protection for distinctions once they were achieved. There were no legal barriers or institutional forms that could protect these fragile aristocracies—no system equivalent to ennoblement, no institution like a House of Lords, no estate of nobles, no organization of any kind, secured in law, by which membership once created could be fixed, rendered irreversible, and transmitted across the generations. The colonial councils were political bodies, and while membership in them expressed an enviable status, seats were not heritable and membership remained open not merely to local competition by every striving merchant, planter, and landowner, but to officials sent from abroad.

Of all the limitations in the distinctions of new elites, however, the most striking was the lack of visible distance between them and the bulk of the population from which they had emerged. They had not traveled very far; in so short a time they had not been able to create a world set far apart. They built manor houses, town houses, and plantation "seats" that had some style, and they shared in other efforts to establish the outward forms of a superior way of life. But the scale, the magnitudes, of all their efforts was yet modest—lavish, perhaps, by the standards of frontier tobacco farmers and petty shopkeeper–merchants, but incomparable to the establishments of aristocracies abroad. The Van Cortlandts' manor house on their estate on the Hudson was a modest one-and-one-half story wooden building—a pleasant summer house, a farmhouse, more or less, improved for middle-class comfort but hardly suitable for an affluent country gentleman in England. 'Westover,' the Byrds' estate in Virginia, was more elegant and more substantial, with pretensions to a higher, more sophisticated style in its carved interior woodwork and up-to-date exterior brick façades. But much of its ultimate beauty was acquired gradually, in successive additions and refinements; in its original form it was a square abode of eight main rooms, and like so many of the other proud houses of the time—Carter's Grove, for example—was solidly middle class. So too the most elegant and famous house in Boston in this period, built

WILLIAM BYRD II, HIS WIFE MARIA, AND HIS ESTATE, WESTOVER

Son of a successful Virginia trader and planter, Byrd spent about 20 years in England before settling down to his inheritance. The present house was the third erected on that site, and became one of the showpieces of colonial Virginia. *(left, The Metropolitan Museum of Art; right, The Virginia Historical Society; bottom, The Library of Congress.)*

by the merchant John Foster between 1689 and 1692 and destined to descend in the Hutchinson family, seemed an immense achievement by the standard of the place and the time, but it would have been indistinguishable from the ordinary town houses of prosperous trademen in any of the major cities of Europe. There was nothing anywhere in America to compare with the great urban residences or the palatial country houses of the truly rich, or even the middling rich, of Europe —nothing to compare even with the more modest "seats" of the lesser aristocracy which were then being built with fine taste in England. Such handsome specimens of domestic architecture as the Gages' "Firle" in Sussex, which Americans of a later generation would come to know quite well, remain, in their carefully landscaped surroundings, testimonies to secure wealth and cultivated tastes.

The heights achieved by the Van Cortlandts, the Hutchinsons, the Belchers, and the Byrds were within the reach of many and never free from competition. Conversely, the surrounding ordinary world enjoyed a remarkably high level of general well-being. There was, to be sure, poverty in early eighteenth-century America. There was indigence and misery as there has been in every society that has ever existed; but among the ordinary free population there was a degree of affluence that was unique for the time. Land remained available, even if it was increasingly difficult for freed servants to rise to full independence and public influence; and entrance to wholesale trade, though narrower than before, remained open to competition. If there were a few great landlords, there were a great many independent farmers. If there were a few suddenly rich merchant "princes," there was a large number of others who had some share in the profits of trade. At the end of the seventeenth century, 65 percent of the overseas shipping registered in the port of Boston was owned by small investors—shopkeepers, prospering craftsmen, and others new to trade who committed small sums infrequently; but the top five individuals owned 18 percent of the whole, and the top two shipowners (Belcher and Lillie) together controlled no less than 11 percent. In the years of Queen Anne's War, one-third of the entire adult male population of Boston (544 individuals) were part owners of some seagoing vessel. And no fewer than 207 of these investors—12 percent of the adult male population of the town—called themselves "merchants."

Rebellion: The Measure of Social Strain

It was the sudden emergence of these new elites—proud but still striving and well within the range of effective competition by rivals close behind—that explains the intensity of the rash of rebellions that occurred in the American colonies in the later 1600s. These are very small events in the scale of early modern Western history, but seen within the context of the rapid maturing of Anglo-American society, they are extremely revealing. They show the inner seams, the strains and tensions, of communities whose social structure was still forming and in which no group s dominance and no individual's eminence were safe from effective competition.

There were five outbreaks, and their dates are significant:

Virginia	Bacon's Rebellion	1676
Carolina	Culpepper's Rebellion	1677
Massachusetts	Rebellion against Andros and the Dominion of New England	1689
New York	Leisler's Rebellion	1689
Maryland	The Protestant Association	1689

The origins of three of these rebellions—those in Massachusetts, New York, and Maryland—coincided with the arrival of news of the Glorious Revolution in England. In all three cases the insurgents explicitly associated themselves with that rebellion in England, which forced James II into exile and destroyed his incipient autocracy. But the parallels, while not altogether fanciful, are superficial. None of the basic accomplishments of the Glorious Revolution were duplicated in the colonies; they were not even wholly understood in these distant border regions. In England a king was deposed and sovereignty was shown to lie not in anointed monarchs and not in popular mobs but in Parliament and the consensus of political and social leaders. Further, the supremacy of law—statute law and common law—had been established above any action of executive and crown, and judges had been made independent of "the pleasure of the prince." The legislature, finally, had declared the independence of its existence; its elections and its convenings were fixed to regular schedules and altogether disengaged from dictates of the crown. The American rebellions duplicated none of this. Sovereignty was in no way an issue in these provincial upheavals; the American executives retained the arbitrary powers that were eliminated in England; judges remained subordinate to "the pleasure of the prince"; and the existence and convening of the representative assemblies remained subject to executive decree.

The headline issues of the various colonial insurrections differed from place to place—some were petty, some grave; some accidental, some set in the very structure of government. But whatever the incitement to rebellion, once in process these disturbances expressed the social strains of communities in which social control and political dominance were subjects of controversy, objects of challenge and continuous struggle.

Thus Bacon's Rebellion began, in a period of economic distress, as an unauthorized war against the Indians on Virginia's northwest frontier. Governor Berkeley's policy had been to stabilize the boundaries between Indians and whites and to protect the natives from depredation by land-hungry settlers. Although it was a sincere attempt to deal with an extremely difficult problem, it was also a conservative policy, favoring the well established planters and especially Berkeley's supporters and beneficiaries. As such, it was offensive to newcomers like Nathaniel Bacon, who had quarreled bitterly with the governor and had been denied the monopoly of the Indian trade he sought, and to Bacon's chief ally, Giles Bland, who had arrived in the colony in 1671 as customs collector but had been fined by the governor for "barbarous and insolent behaviors," then arrested, and finally dismissed from his post.

Around Bacon and Bland an opposition group formed. Victims of the stabilizing social and political establishment and increasingly resentful of the benefits others had acquired, they demanded land, without regard to the rights or needs of the border Indians squeezed between the double pressure of rival tribes behind them and white men before them. A violent conflict between Indians and white settlers in the border area that Bacon sought to control provided an excuse to launch a full-scale war, which became a civil war in 1676 when Berkeley repudiated Bacon and his allies and sought to bring them to justice. The rebels, having suppressed the border Indians in bloody battles, turned back upon the colony itself, seized the government, defeated and scattered Berkeley's forces, and burned Jamestown to the ground. But they could not sustain the insurrection. Bacon himself died of exposure and exhaustion in the midst of a confused military campaign. Deprived of his leadership, the rebellion faded out, and Bacon's chief allies were soon hanged for treason.

In all this turmoil the Baconites' voice rose loud and clear. Who are these men "in authority and favor," they demanded to know in their "Manifesto," to whose hands the dispensation of the country's wealth has been committed? Note, they cried, "the sudden rise of their estates compared with the mean quality in which they had first entered the country,"

. . . and let us see whether their extractions and education have not been vile, and by what pretense of learning and virtue they could [enter] so soon into employments of so great trust and consequence; let us . . . see what sponges have sucked up the public treasure and whether it hath not been privately contrived away by unworthy favorites and juggling parasites whose tottering fortunes have been repaired and supported at the public charge.

But these challengers were themselves challenged, for another main element in the upheaval, expressed in the laws of "Bacon's Assembly" of 1676, was the discontent among the ordinary settlers at the local privileges of some of the same newly risen county magnates who assailed the privileges of the Greenspring faction. At both levels, local and central, the rebellion challenged the stability of newly secured authority.

The wave of rebellion in Virginia, which broke suddenly and spread quickly, soon subsided. By the end of the century the most difficult period of adjustment had passed and there was an acceptance of the fact that certain families were indeed distinguished from others in riches, in dignity, and in access to political authority, and were likely to remain so. There had never been a challenge to British supremacy or to the idea that some people would inevitably be "high and eminent in power and dignity; others mean and in subjection." Protests and upheaval had resulted from the discomforts of discovering who was, in fact, which, and what the particular consequences of "power and dignity" were.

Infinitely more confused than Bacon's Rebellion was an almost comic-opera insurrection that took place in 1677 in Albermarle, the northern sector of Carolina, where some 3000 farmers struggled to survive in the swampy, sandy coastal lands and to profit from smuggling tobacco with the help of a few enterprising New England merchants. When the proprietary group, no less hard-drinking, ill-tempered, and ruthlessly profiteering than their opponents, attempted to collect customs, they were set upon by a gang of rivals led by a fiercely belligerent malcontent named John Culpeper who accused them of malfeasance and treason, jailed them, seized the government, and sent charges against them to England. After endless confusion and an almost farcical series of attacks and counterattacks between the two groups, the Carolina proprietors finally managed to restore order. But the rebellion died slowly, partly because the legal proceedings in England were protracted but in greater part because of the continuing uncertainty of legitimate leadership in the rough, tumultuous backwoods community.

In New York the struggle between an emerging establishment and a resentful opposition was clearer than it was in the South, but also more bitter and more permanently consequential in politics.

When word of Andros's downfall in Boston arrived in New York, the lieutenant governor, Francis Nicholson, decided to strengthen Manhattan's garrison with militia troops. The captain of the militia was a well-to-do, cantankerous merchant, Jacob Leisler. Relations between the militia and Nicholson's regular troops grew difficult, then explosive, especially since Nicholson's legal status was unclear once Andros had been deposed. When in June 1689 news of the Glorious Revolution arrived, Nicholson sailed for England, leaving the city in the hands of the militia captain. A month later, William III's message to all officers of government arrived, instructing them to retain their posts, and Leisler interpreted the directive as addressed officially to himself as the colony's governor. He drew around him what was at first a large group of supporters, who proceeded to parcel out the colony's offices and run the government, including its feeble war effort. In 1691 when the next royal governor, the well-named Henry Sloughter, arrived and demanded that Leisler surrender the city and the government, Leisler, whose support had steadily eroded in two years of erratic rule and who by then scarcely controlled any of the colony outside the city walls, refused. Sloughter's superior power prevailed, Leisler and his followers surrendered, and after a quick and legally dubious trial he and his chief assistant, his son-in-law Jacob Milbourne, were hanged for treason and their property was confiscated.

But these savage sentences, which Parliament legally annulled in 1695, hardly ended the struggle. By the time Leisler's regime ended, the political leadership of the colony was broken into two violently antagonistic parties, the Leislerians and the anti-Leislerians, who thereafter alternated in power with successive governors, each party attempting literally to annihilate the other when the opportunity arose, or failing that to crush them politically so that they would never regain power. Again, the social background is crucial. Behind this see-sawing political conflict lay a latent struggle that had been in progress since the English conquest. During those years an Anglo-Dutch leadership group took form under governors sent out by the Duke of York, and the colony's official patronage had come to center on a small group of families whose ultimate rewards would come in the land grants of Benjamin Fletcher. Gradually this Anglo-Dutch cabal—the Bayards, Van Cortlandts, Philipses, Livingstons, and Schuylers—made arrangements that satisfied their interests: a flour milling and exporting monopoly for New York City, which in effect gave them control of that vital industry; a New York City monopoly for shipping on the Hudson; and an Albany monopoly of the colony's Indian trade.

The offices were theirs, and so too was the colony's economy, to the increasing resentment of those who were excluded. Gradually a combination of alienated groups took shape. Led by the merchants, especially those of Dutch orientation, who were denied access to these

PETER SCHUYLER, MAYOR OF ALBANY, 1686–1694

Also for many years chief English negotiator with the Indians, Schuyler is pictured here around 1715, five years after he took four Iroquois chiefs to London where they were received with honor by Queen Anne. (*Albany Institute of History and Art.*)

privileges, it included the city artisans, who were indirect victims of the junto's monopolies, and the Long Island townsmen, most of whom had migrated from Connecticut. Increasingly, the focus of this rising discontent centered on Leisler, whose career encapsulates the social sources of the American rebellions. He had married a relative of the Bayards and Van Cortlandts, but had fought with those families over the terms of his wife's inheritance. He and Milbourne had been jailed for attacking the Anglican ordination of a Dutch preacher. And, in ostensible support of the Long Island opposition, he had refused to pay customs and defied all efforts to bring him into court. His associates had had similar careers.

It was this group of alienated, resentful, and enterprising outsiders who sparked the opposition to Nicholson and turned it into a rebellion against the Anglo-Dutch establishment. In principle, Leisler and his followers were no more "democrats" than were the Baconites in Virginia, but they found in the language of the Glorious Revolution a "Protestant" program—against monopolies, against autocracy, in favor of open access and a broad sharing of benefits—that served their interests well.

In Maryland, resentment, long-smoldering against the Calverts' Catholic ascendency, had erupted as early as 1676 in an obscure rebellion in Calvert County. When news of the Glorious Revolution arrived, the same small group of insurgents, further antagonized by a particularly obnoxious proprietary governor, led two hundred fifty of the settlers to seize the colony's government. Calling themselves the Protestant Association, they issued a declaration condemning the proprietary party for excessive fee taking, for resisting royal authority, and for arbitrary taxation; they identified telltale signs of an incipient papal plot; and they petitioned the crown to take over the government from the Calverts, which was promptly done.

It was only in 1715 that the Calverts' control of Maryland was returned to them, but by then the family had turned Protestant and the government had been drawn into the general pattern of colonial governance which required crown approval of executive appointments and of the colony's legislation. The rebellion had sprung out of the jostling instability of late seventeenth-century animosities, and while the proprietary group thereafter still dominated the executive government, it could no longer block the advance of the planter aristocracy or ignore a legislative body whose influence was built into the structure of government.

Though in Massachusetts there were special, local peculiarities in the rebellion that took place, there was also a similar underlying conflict. The continuing dominance of the Puritan regime, protected by the original charter, delayed the characteristic struggle of social groups. But after the confiscation of the charter in 1684 and the establishment of the Dominion, the pattern seen elsewhere quickly developed. Almost immediately, the favors of patronage and power began to flow to a small group of speculators and merchant insiders, some of them in Andros' entourage, some of them adventurous natives who gravitated to the new establishment. For four years this newly dominant group enjoyed a feast of privilege and in the process generated resentments among others which found expression in an uprising made especially bitter by the Puritan animosities that fueled it.

These rebellions are obscure events, and they are confused events, especially the last three in which the rebels claimed association with the successful revolutionaries in England. Everywhere the insurgents sought to identify themselves with the struggle for English liberty and against various forms of tyranny. None, however, questioned the basis of public authority; all submitted to legitimate crown power when it appeared; none fought for the full range of liberties that would be set out in the English Bill of Rights (1689) and the Act of Settlement (1701), which concluded the liberals' triumph in England. They questioned not the nature of government but its control; not its structure and essential character, but its personnel; not what and how, but who. Enclosed in their provincial world, they sought above all equity in the actions of government that properly reflected the balance of society as it had emerged through a period of rapid growth and change.

"Creolean Degeneracy"

These insurrections of the late seventeenth century were not only obscure events, in the scale of western history; they were also — significantly — provincial events. And as such they were characteristic of Anglo-American culture generally as it emerged in the early 1700s. For that culture had greatly changed in its relations to the parent culture from which it had developed. In the early years, the settlements, however small, distant, and isolated, had been part of a vital movement in the forefront of western European life. The key figures were products of the European world. Their lives in America were isolated physically but not psychologically or intellectually or spiritually. They never lost the sense that they were engaged in a momentous enterprise, something that mattered in an important way to the world they had left behind. They felt they could easily return, and when they did, they found themselves enhanced, not diminished, by their sojourn in the exotic frontier west. Thus the poet, traveler, and scholar George Sandys, son of the Archbishop of York, slipped back easily into Lord Falkland's literary circle after his stay in Virginia, having made good progress on his translation of Ovid's *Metamorphoses* So Roger Williams returned to Cromwell's council of state, and Winthrop's nephew George Downing, rusticated to Harvard College to improve his morals and manners, became Cromwell's chief intelligence officer, was knighted, and ended as England's ambassador to Holland. The settlements' highest meaning—as a commercial enterprise of great dimensions, as a search for information about an unknown land, as a crusade to save the pagans' souls, or as a model for the reformation of a society gone slack and corrupt—had been relevant and vital to the most forward-looking minds of the time.

By 1700 none of this was true. As the colonies grew, they grew apart, into a separate world of their own—connected with the greater world beyond, but still fundamentally removed. The success or failure of the colonists' daily affairs no longer mattered as they once had done. The settlers no longer made news; they listened for it, intently, from abroad, and imitated what they could of styles of thought, of ways of living and patterns of behavior. They knew themselves to be provincials in the sense that their culture was not self-contained; its sources and superior expressions were to be found elsewhere than in their own land. They must seek it from afar; it must be acquired, and once acquired, be maintained according to standards externally imposed, in the creation of which they had not shared. The most cultivated of the colonists read much, purposefully, determined to retain contact with the greater world at home. The diary of William Byrd II with its daily records of stints of study is a stolid testimonial to the virtues of regularity and effort in maintaining standards of civilization set abroad.

This basic transformation can be seen particularly well in the later career of the gifted and learned son of the patriarch John Winthrop. John, Jr., was educated at Trinity College Dublin and in London at the lawyers' Inner Temple. As a young man he had helped manage an English overseas military expedition, and had traveled in the Mediterranean and the Middle East. A physician, amateur scientist, and imaginative entrepreneur who served as governor of Connecticut for eighteen years, he struggled to maintain contact with the Royal Society in London of which he was the first American member. There was "a current of loneliness, almost pathos," the younger Winthrop's latest biographer writes, "in his anxiety to stay in touch." He wrote letter after letter to the society's secretary, he sent over scientific specimens—rattlesnake skins, birds' nests, plants, crabs, strange pigs; he studied the society's *Transactions* so as not to fall too far behind; and to those concerned with the propagation of the gospel he dispatched John Eliot's Algonquin translation of the Bible and two essays written in Latin by Indian students at Harvard. But these were failing efforts. In the end, loneliness and isolation overcame him. He died in 1676, venerated in the villages along the Connecticut River—themselves changing like autumn leaves from vital, experimental religious communities to sere, old-fashioned backwoods towns—but forgotten in the greater world at home. His sons, however, provincial land speculators and petty politicians, had no such memories as their father had had, and no such aspirations; they suffered, therefore, no such disappointments. They were native to the land, and their cultural horizons had narrowed to its practical demands.

This was a silent drama—of a high culture, temporarily transferred, becoming permanently provincial; and it was a drama played out most vividly in the field of education. For education, in its broadest sense, serves more than any other social process to liberate people from local, parochial environments and bring them into contact with larger worlds and broader horizons. Education is perhaps the most sensitive index to the changing character of American life as it developed in these transition years. It is also one of the most difficult subjects to interpret. For there were great accomplishments, but there were also great defeats, soaring ambitions, but serious neglect.

Certain things, however, are clear. In New England the founding generation made a remarkable effort not only to perpetuate education as it was then known but to improve it—to spread it more widely and more effectively through the entire population. In any case, that would have been extraordinarily ambitious, but it was particularly ambitious in view of the advanced state of formal education in seventeenth-century England. There, a great wave of expansion in education was under way. By 1600 England had one Latin grammar school for each 13,000 people, which is twice as many in proportion to population as there would be in the mid-nineteenth century. Almost every town of 2000 people had such a school, and almost every parish in the land had some sort of elementary school responsible for teaching simple literacy. And the universities were flourishing; in 1622, Oxford had 2850 matriculated students, Cambridge over 3000.

The Puritans' efforts in education stemmed, first, from their religious convictions, specifically their insistence that every person, saint or sinner, have personal access to the Holy Scriptures, which meant the capacity to read. That was a mere beginning, however, for to the Puritans the truly religious person was a student not only of the Bible but also of commentaries on the Bible, including those intricate oral commentaries preached at prodigious length from every pulpit in the land. To perpetuate this Biblical culture in the population at large would require schooling that went beyond the normal Elizabethan assumption that the goal of formal education was training in vocational roles. For the Puritans, there was only one essential vocation, and that was spiritual. Though true salavation was in the end a God-given grace, the preparation for grace—the opening of the mind and soul to such a possibility—was a matter of education, knowledge, and will.

It was not this central religious commitment alone, however, that led the Puritans to their remarkable efforts in education. Partly too they were driven by a sense that in their wilderness condition the family, which traditionally had borne so much of the burden of transmitting the elements of culture across the generations, had weakened and was failing in its duty and capacity. This fear bore heavily on the minds of the founding elders.* They looked ahead to the future and noted that if extraordinary precautions were not made in time they would leave behind not a Bible commonwealth but a tribe of rustic barbarians. If family discipline were loose, if parents were slack in their responsibilities, the public— the government, the magistrates, those, in Winthrop's words, who were called into office by the people and "have our authority from God, in way of an ordinance"—would have to provide for the future.

Fearful, then, of failing in their religious duty and distrustful of the private discipline of family life, the Puritans turned instinctively to the willingness of people voluntarily to establish and support formal institutions of education. For they knew that the great wave of educational foundations in England had been accomplished by private philanthropy; by gifts from institutions (gilds, universities) and even more from individual donors. Education had been largely a private enterprise, and its economic basis lay in the yields of land endowments—cultivated, tenanted land from which schools could derive their ordinary funds. In the beginning, the Puritans expected just such a pattern to develop. And in the

---

*For pressures on family life in the seventeenth century, see above, pp. 104–108.

first fifteen years, six of the ten towns whose records have survived show evidence of voluntary efforts of the relatively rich to establish schools with the traditional endowment base. But the land was wild, tenants were scarce, and endowments were worth nothing if they produced no rents. Further, the surplus funds available—especially in the new towns close to the frontier—disappeared as time went on. Other forms of financing would have to be found. In place of pleas to the rich, there must be commands. The towns ordered the wealthy to volunteer, then took to group action, assigning some of the towns' common land to schools; but the hoped-for income failed for lack of reliable tenants. In the end, there was only one resource: taxation. It began as a supplement to private gifts and ended as almost the sole and universal basis of elementary education.

So for a decade and more the Puritans struggled with the problem of education, experimented, and came to fear that their whole endeavor would fail unless some uniform provisions were made, some universal standards set, and facilities provided that would guarantee the survival of their hopes into the future. In the 1640s they made their great departure in two famous laws. By a law of 1642, the Massachusetts General Court charged all parents and ministers with the responsibility for the "calling and employment of their children, especially of their ability to read and understand the principles of religion and the capital laws of this country." Five years later, in 1647, the legislative provisions were completed: the General Court ruled that all towns of 50 families must provide for the maintenance of elementary schools, and all towns of 100 families must support Latin grammar schools. These laws became models for the rest of Puritan New England. Connecticut followed with similar provisions in 1650, and Plymouth in two stages, 1658 and 1677. Wherever these enactments remained on the books they were innovative and creative. But they are easily misunderstood.

For these laws do *not* provide for public education as it has been known since the nineteenth century. The concept of a strict distinction between "private" and "public" did not exist in the seventeenth century. Neither of these laws of the 1640s specified "public" moneys as the financial basis of the community's schools; neither made formal schooling obligatory at any level. What they *did* do was, first, to establish a minimum level of educational accomplishment (not schooling) by specifying masters' and parents' obligations and reinforcing these obligations with sanctions of fines and the threat of removing children to other households. Second, the laws required that schooling, at both elementary and secondary (Latin grammar) levels, be made universally *available* for those who wished to take advantage of it. Third, these laws established a community-wide obligation to support formal institutions of education without reference to the benefits any individual or family derived from these schools. Finally, the laws made clear that the government's role in the whole area of education would not be merely supplementary or supportive or supervisory, but positive and compelling.

All of this, written into these innovating American laws on education, was highly creative. But these famous laws are the beginning, not the end, of the historical

SONG VIII.

Praise to GOD *for learning to Read.*

THE Praises of my Tongue
I offer to the LORD,
That I was taught, and learnt so young
To read his holy Word.

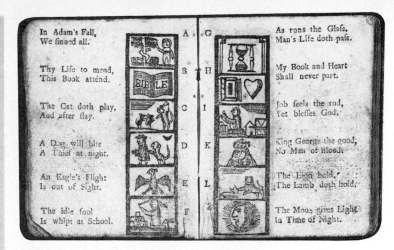

In Adam's Fall,
We sinned all.

Thy Life to mend,
This Book attend.

The Cat doth play,
And after slay.

A Dog will bite
A Thief at night.

An Eagle's Flight
Is out of Sight.

The idle fool
Is whipt at School.

As runs the Glass,
Man's Life doth pass.

My Book and Heart
Shall never part.

Job feels the rod,
Yet blesses God.

King George the good,
No Man of Blood.

The Lion bold,
The Lamb doth hold.

The Moon gives Light
In Time of Night.

Left, from Isaac Watts's *Divine and Moral Songs for Children* (1715); Above, from the "Rhymed Alphabet" of *The New England Primer*, first published in America in the 1680s. (*American Antiquarian Society.*)

development. The question is not merely what was hoped for and what was provided for, but what happened to these hopes and these provisions in later years. What effect did these remarkable provisions have on the lives of the people?

By the end of the seventeenth century it was clear that the hopes of the Puritans were not being evenly and satisfactorily fulfilled. Fines against delinquent towns were common. Subsequent revisions and codifications of the laws cite continuing neglect on the part of masters, parents, and towns. The old fears not only continued but seemed to grow more intense. In Massachusetts in 1671 the fines on towns that neglected to maintain grammar instruction were doubled. In 1689 Cotton Mather, third generation scion of a great clerical dynasty and self-appointed guardian of the ancestral hopes, bemoaned his people's fate. He doubted, he declared in a sermon of that year, if New England suffered "under an iller symptom that the too general want of education in the rising generation." If not overcome, this neglect, he said, would "gradually and speedily dispose us to that sort of Creolean degeneracy observed to deprave the children of the most noble and worthy Europeans when transplanted into America."

But even Mather's magisterial voice could not halt the movement of change. In 1718 the General Court, again raising the delinquency fines, condemned the "many towns that not only are obliged by law but are very able to support a grammar school, yet choose rather to incur and pay the fine and penalty than maintain a grammar school." In the deepening provincialism, as settlements spread throughout the countryside, as contact with the centers of high culture grew thin, and as the original fires of Puritanism cooled, the instinct somehow to modify the law or adjust it to the realities of everyday life grew bolder, stronger, and more effective, though the laws remained on the books and magistrates sought to enforce them. Sometimes there was outright evasion. A town would obey by hiring a teacher who knew no Latin to teach that subject "as far as he was able." More commonly, a new institution was used, the "moving school," which satisfied

LT. GOV. WILLIAM STOUGHTON
OF MASSACHUSETTS

In the background is the building
that this dour, wealthy, old-
fashioned Puritan gave to his
alma mater, Harvard, in 1699. It
was the first American college
building donated by an alumnus.
*(Fogg Art Museum, Harvard
University.)*

the law by providing for a schoolmaster and his equipment but distributed his
services on a circuit that moved through the town's lands in proportion to the
spread of population. Thus Gloucester, Massachusetts, had a Latin grammar
school, but the teacher and his books moved about in a cycle of three years,
settling in 7 places in these monthly proportions: 9, 7, 5½, 4½, 3, 1½. Thus even
the most remote corner of the township had contact with the "moving school,"
but it was available for children in that most isolated area only one and a half
months every three years.

Finally, by the mid-eighteenth century the towns found a permanent solution:
the district school. The towns were now formally divided into school districts,
each district drawing its proportionate share of the available funds and using it
as its own local school committee decided. School thus existed in almost every
town; but the variations were great. For the management of the schools was now
entirely in the hands of the localities, some of them limited, isolated localities,
incapable of and uninterested in transcending their narrow environments. Some
schools were excellent, some poor, some dismal. Often the Latin grammar school
proved to be a common school in which children of all ages were taught at their
own levels. Uniformity was lost, but the "Creolean degeneracy" that Mather had
feared had failed to take hold. New England emerged in the eighteenth century
still a literate culture, still open to a high level of cultural attainment.

All of this was a flame, sparked by the original creators of the Bible commonwealth, that burned fitfully at times but never failed. How remarkable an accomplishment it was may be seen by the contrast with the slow and irregular development of education elsewhere in the colonies, where the churches and a few
generous individuals sought to provide for schooling. In 1671 Governor Berkeley

of Virginia wrote about his colony, "I thank God there are no free schools nor printing," these being sources, he declared, of "disobedience and heresy and sects." By 1689 there were still only six schools of various kinds in Virginia. In the same year Maryland had one school; New York, mainly through the efforts of the Dutch church, may have had eleven.

That education at the elementary and secondary levels developed as it did in New England was in part the result of the reinforcement it received from higher education, established in the same years, which too became closely bound to the immediate needs of these provincial communities.

There can be little doubt about the Puritans' primary reason for founding in 1636 the institution that became Harvard College. They dreaded, they said, "to leave an illiterate ministry to the churches when our present ministers shall lie in the dust." There were other motives too, especially the hopes of those who sought an instrument for propagating the gospel to the native Indians through preachers trained at the college who would go out to deliver the word. But though the gospel mission failed miserably amid the general failure of civilized relations between Indians and whites, the effort to maintain a college primarily for training preachers and secondarily for educating gentlemen in the liberal arts took root and flourished. By the time the College of William and Mary, the second English colonial college, was chartered in 1693 as part of the effort to improve the condition of the Anglican clergy in Virginia, Harvard College, named after its first private benefactor, John Harvard, was a stable institution. Its influence, through its graduates, was great and its continued existence, written into the terms of the colony's second charter of 1691, was firmly guaranteed.

COLONIAL COLLEGES

COLLEGE	COLONY	FOUNDED
Harvard College	Massachusetts	1636
The College of William and Mary	Virginia	1693
Yale College	Connecticut	1701
College of New Jersey (Princeton University)	New Jersey	1746
College of Philadelphia (University of Pennsylvania)	Pennsylvania	1754
King's College (Columbia University)	New York	1754
College of Rhode Island (Brown University)	Rhode Island	1764
Queen's College (Rutgers University)	New Jersey	1766
Dartmouth College	New Hampshire	1769

Yet like so much else in American life, this college, and those that would follow it, grew apart from the models on which they were based and became something different, though familiar. The Puritan founders were well acquainted with higher education, and in founding their own college they did not seek innovation. They intended to create a familiar university-college, a residential institution whose ownership and direction would lie in the hands of the teachers—the resident tutors and professors.

The Puritans' college and those that followed it in the colonies did not develop in that way, however. Instead, by an intricate process of evolution, ownership of the property and the final direction of the educational process came to rest not in the teachers but in boards of trustees external to the educational process, who hired the teachers and supervised the work of the colleges on behalf of the founding community. In Harvard's case the emerging pattern of external control was badly confused and produced in the end two governing boards, the Overseers and the Corporation, both composed of preachers, businessmen, and lawyers uninvolved in teaching. In Virginia the evolution was clearer as the College of William and Mary's temporary Board of Visitors retained its powers permanently against the claims of the college's teachers. By the time the third colonial college was founded—Yale in 1701—there was little expectation that the English model of self-governing corporations of professors and tutors would be reproduced in the colonies. From its beginning, Yale College was governed by an external corporation, only one member of which, the president, was expected to teach.

So it was in all of the colonial colleges, and so it has been in all American institutions of higher education. For in the beginning the central impulse in creating colleges and universities was the community's concern for perpetuating a learned clergy and learning itself in the wilderness setting. Later, the definition of the founding community would shift—to denominations serving their particular concerns and to states recognizing the need for experts in technical fields and for the public's general education. But from the establishment of the first college in 1636 onward, the initiating impulse and the resources have come from groups outside the profession of teaching and learning, and the governance of higher education has reflected the groups' insistence on seeing that the institutions fulfill these community mandates. In this sense, all the American colleges and universities have been community schools—products not so much of the world of education and learning as of desires and decisions of the community at large. Control has therefore rested with the founding communities, and as, in the colonial period, the horizons of the communities narrowed, the mandates of the colleges narrowed too. A learned clergy was indeed perpetuated and higher education made generally available, not only in Massachusetts, Virginia, and Connecticut, but in New Jersey, Pennsylvania, New York, Rhode Island, and New Hampshire. Through these institutions the pursuit of learning and the cultivation of the arts were advanced and transmitted across the generations. But at the root of their foundations lay not so much a love of learning for its own sake as the parochial concerns of communities of limited horizons, determined to sustain their founders' commitments to serving local, provincial needs.

Suggested Readings

The fullest account of the origins of the British imperial system, in both theory and institutions, is Charles M. Andrews, *The Colonial Period of American History*, IV (1938). On the theory of empire, see in addition Richard Koebner. *Empire* (1961) chap. iii; on the all-important customs administration in the colonies, Thomas C. Barrow, *Trade & Empire* (1967); and on the difficulty in the late seventeenth century of imposing regulations on the scattered settlements, see Michael G. Hall, *Edward Randolph and the American Colonies* (1969). On the influence of the Duke of York (James II) and his entourage on the evolution of empire and the importance of his and his lieutenants' military background, see Stephen S. Webb, ". . . The Household of James Stuart in the Evolution of English Imperialism," *Perspectives in American History*, 8 (1974), 55–80. On the patronage sources of colonial appointments and other aspects of the politics of the early empire, see Webb's "Strange Career of Francis Nicholson" and "William Blathwayt, Imperial Fixer," *Wm. and Mary Q.*, 23 (1966), 513–48; 26 (1969), 373–415 — a subject that will be presented in full in Webb's forthcoming book, *The Governors-General*. On James II's ill-fated effort to organize a territorial government, see Viola F. Barnes, *The Dominion of New England* (1923).

The emergence of a native Anglo-American aristocracy is traced generally, in the case of Virginia, in Bernard Bailyn, "Politics and Social Structure in Virginia,"* James M. Smith, ed., *Seventeenth-Century America* (1959) and Louis B. Wright, *First Gentlemen of Virginia* (1940); in the case of commercial New England, in Bernard Bailyn. *New England Merchants in the Seventeenth Century* (1955); in the case of New York, in Thomas Archdeacon, *New York City, 1664–1710* (1976); and in the five main port towns, in Carl Bridenbaugh, *Cities in the Wilderness* (1938). The origins of rural aristocracies in New England, rooted in the shifting relations between population and land, are described in Roy H. Akagi, *The Town Proprietors of the New England Colonies* (1924) and probed analytically in Richard L. Bushman's thoughtful *From Puritan to Yankee* (1967) and in the individual community studies listed in the references to chapter III. For the reflection of this development in government, see Kenneth A. Lockridge and Alan Kreider, "Evolution of Massachusetts Town Government, 1640–1740," *Wm. and Mary Q.*, 23 (1966), 549–74; for an attempt to extend it into a general theory of regional development, see Lockridge, "Land, Population, and the Evolution of New England Society, 1630–1790," *Past and Present*, 39 (1968), 62–80. For case studies of the emergence of the Southern aristocracy, see the essays on social mobility in the Chesapeake area cited for the previous chapter; Louis B. Wright's edition of Byrd's diaries and literary writings; and Richard B. Davis, ed., *William Fitzhugh and His Chesapeake World, 1676–1701* (1963). The political aspects of a rising aristocracy are analyzed in the case of New York in Patricia U. Bonomi, *A Factious People* (1971), chaps. ii, iii; in Archdeacon's *New York City;* and in Lawrence H. Leder, *Robert Livingston* (1961).

The late seventeenth-century wars (the subject of Francis Parkman's dramatic classics, *Count Frontenac and New France under Louis XIV*, 1877; and *A Half-Century of Conflict*, 1892) are sketched briefly in Howard H. Peckham, *The Colonial Wars, 1689–1762* (1964), but their deeper significance for the development of Anglo-American politics, trade, and society is suggested in G.M. Waller, *Samuel Vetch, Colonial Enterpriser* (1960).

The colonial rebellions of the late seventeenth century are described, insofar as they relate to the English rebellion against James II, in David S. Lovejoy, *The Glorious Revolution in America* (1972); there is a documentary collection related to these events in a book of the same title edited by Michael G. Hall, Lawrence H. Leder, and Michael G. Kammen. But as social events these uprisings are to be associated with Bacon's Rebellion, which is described generally in Wilcomb E. Washburn, *The Governor and the Rebel* (1957) and analyzed in social terms in Bailyn, "Politics and Social Structure"*; in Wesley F. Craven, *Southern Colonies in the Seventeenth Century* (1949); and in Edmund Morgan, *American Slavery, American Freedom* (1975). For the social background of Leisler's Rebellion, see Archdeacon's book cited above (excerpted into essay form as ". . . The Age of Leisler in New York City,"*) and Jerome R. Reich, *Leisler's Rebellion* (1953), which exaggerates the "democratic" impulses of the rebels. On Boston's rebellion, see Barnes, *Dominion of New England.* The most exhaustive study of the social background of any of these rebellions, however, is Lois G. Carr and David W. Jordan, *Maryland's Revolution of Government 1689–1692* (1974).

The deepening provincialism of American culture in the late seventeenth century emerges in the colonists' writings, analyzed with subtlety in the opening chapter of Kenneth S. Lynn, *Mark Twain and Southwestern Humor* (1959); in the careers of third-generation Anglo-Americans such as the Winthrops (Richard S. Dunn, *Puritans and Yankees: The Winthrop Dynasty of New England, 1630–1717,* 1962, Bk. III) and the Mathers (Robert Middlekauff, *The Mathers: Three Generations of Puritan Intellectuals, 1596–1728,* 1971, Bk. III); in the missionary efforts of the Anglicans (Parke Rouse, Jr., *James Blair of Virginia,* 1971; Leonard W. Cowie, *Henry Newman: An American in London, 1708–43,* 1956); in travellers' accounts (Jasper Danckaerts [1679–80], pub. 1867; the Frenchman Durand [1687], pub. 1923; Sarah Knight [⌐704], latest pub. 1972); and above all in education.

For a comprehensive, detailed, id broadly conceived account of early American education, see Lawrence A. Cremin, *American Education: the Colonial Experience, 1607–1783* (1970), Parts I-III; for a general interpretation of the social role of colonial education, see Bernard Bailyn, *Education in the Forming of American Society* (1960); and for the deepening localization of standards, described in the text, Harlan Updegraff, *Origin of the Moving School in Massachusetts* (1907). Robert Middlekauff has traced the persistence of the classical tradition in the face of provincial difficulties in *Ancients and Axioms* (1963). James Axtell, *The School upon a Hill* (1974) shows through education in the broadest sense, how New England's culture was transmitted across the generations.

On the origins of higher education, see Samuel E. Morison's magisterial works, *The Founding of Harvard College* (1935) and *Harvard College in the Seventeenth Century* (2 vols., 1936), both summarized in his *Three Centuries of Harvard: 1636–1936* (1936). Though these learned and highly readable books remain fundamental, Morison's general interpretation has been challenged: by Winthrop S. Hudson, "The Morison Myth Concerning the Founding of Harvard College," *Church History,* 8 (1939), 148–59; and by Jurgen Herbst, "The First Three American Colleges: Schools of the Reformation," *Perspectives in American History,* 8 (1974), 7–52, in which parallels are drawn between Harvard, Yale, and William and Mary on the one hand and the "*gymnasia illustria,* academies, or *Gelehrtenschulen* on the Continent" on the other. Yale's origins have recently been detailed with great care by Richard Warch in *School of the Prophets: Yale College, 1701–1740* (1973) and The College of William and Mary in Rouse, *Blair.*

5

American Society in the Eighteenth Century

The end of the War of Spanish Succession in 1713 and the creation of a stable political regime in England under Sir Robert Walpole (1721–42) introduced a period of great expansion in all spheres of Anglo-American life. In the two generations that followed the war, despite minor involvements in other international conflicts and repeated cycles of commercial recession, the American colonies grew so rapidly and matured so fully that they came to constitute a major element not only in British life but in the life of the Atlantic world generally. Developing on scattered seventeenth-century foundations, becoming more and more distinctive though outwardly seeking to conform to the normal patterns of European life, and drawn more and more elaborately into the ill-organized structure of empire, the colonies acquired characteristics that would remain permanent in American life. The eighteenth-century world was different in a thousand ways from the nineteenth- and twentieth-century worlds that would follow, but one can nevertheless see developing in that early age certain patterns that would underlie the later evolution of American society.

The New Population: Source and Impact

Fundamental to all aspects of eighteenth-century American history was the phenomenal growth of the population. Early in the period, in 1720, the total population may have reached half a million; by 1775 it had quintupled, to 2.5 million, which was fully a third of the size of the population of England and Wales (6.7 million). A fifth of the American population was black, almost all of them slaves, nine-tenths of whom lived south of Pennsylvania. They constituted half the population of Virginia and two-thirds of the population of South Carolina.

By the start of the Revolution, the settlements formed an almost unbroken line along the seaboard, from Maine to Florida, and they reached deep into the interior. In New England, groups moving up the Connecticut River and the coastal streams penetrated into New Hampshire and Vermont. In New York, settlements spread through the rich Hudson, Mohawk, and Schoharie valleys, and in Pennsylvania and the Carolinas extended back to the Appalachians. In a few places, especially southwestern Pennsylvania, the Appalachian mountain barrier had been breached by frontiersmen who were actively opening fresh lands to cultivation in Indian territories.

The population was almost entirely rural. Of the towns, the most populous was Philadelphia, with approximately 35,000 inhabitants. The five largest communities (Philadelphia, New York, Boston, Charleston, and Newport, Rhode Island) had a combined population of 90,000, or 3.6 percent of the total. Fifteen smaller towns, ranging from New Haven, Connecticut, with 8000, to Savannah, Georgia, with 3200, account for another 77,500; but very few of the total town population of approximately 167,500 lived in circumstances that can be called "urban" in a modern sense.

The rapid increase in the size of the population—it almost doubled every twenty-five years—was in large part the result of natural growth. But in large part too it was the result of new flows of immigration. While the basic recruitment from England continued, though at a reduced rate, and while between 250,000 and 300,000 Africans were imported directly or indirectly from their homelands, altogether new elements began to make important contributions. Religious persecution in France led to the immigration of 5000–6000 Huguenots (French Protestants, forced to flee after the revocation, in 1685, of the tolerant Edict of Nantes); and from Scotland came groups of Jacobites, who had remained faithful to the exiled James II and his son, after their military defeat by the English in 1715. But the main new flows came from two quite different sources, which together supplied approximately 20 percent of the total American population when the first national census was taken in 1790.

The first new source was Ireland—not Catholic Ireland but Protestant northern Ireland, which had been the first overseas colony of the English people. The series of efforts the English had made in the early seventeenth century to colonize a great "plantation" in Ulster, the six northern counties of Ireland, had failed; but that area had become the target of a large unorganized migration from Scotland, where social and religious conditions throughout the seventeenth century were unsettled. By 1715 perhaps 150,000 Scottish families had crossed the Irish Sea to settle on Irish estates where rents were originally low. From this heartland of "Scotch-Irish" Presbyterianism a large migration to America took place in the eighteenth century. How many were involved we do not know exactly, but the best estimate is a yearly average of 4000 through most of the century, totaling a quarter of a million. In the census of 1790, 10 percent of the total population proved to be Irish, or of Irish descent, three-fifths of them from Ulster. It was said by W. E. H. Lecky, Ireland's greatest historian, that the loss of so great a number of Irish Protestants to America in the eighteenth century ended forever the hope of balancing the religious communities in that tormented island.

The other new source of the American population was the upper Rhine valley, in southwestern Germany. This area, especially the district west of the Rhine from the juncture of the River Main south to Switzerland and France, most of which formed the Rhenish Palatinate, had been badly ravaged in the religious wars of the seventeenth century and then, in 1688–89, devastated by French armies. In addition, Catholic princes, especially the Palatinate's ruling Elector, had begun persecutions of the increasingly numerous Protestant sectarians. When, further, crop disasters in 1708 and 1709 reduced much of the same population to beggary and a new English naturalization law made British territory an attractive refuge, a movement of peoples began that ended in furnishing a major component of the American population. William Penn had begun recruiting settlers in the Rhineland as early as the 1680s, and it was to his colony eventually that the greatest number of German-speaking people came. These "Pennsylvania Dutch" (*Deutsch:* Germans, that is, not Hollanders) comprised one-third of that colony's population by 1775. The census of 1790 showed almost as many German-born or German-descended Americans (9 percent of the population) as there

GERMAN PIETIST EMIGRANTS

The man carries in one hand the orthodox Lutheran "Augsburg Confession" and in the other Johann Arndt's classic of pietistic devotion, *Vom Wahren Christentum* (1605). His pack bears the motto, "God is with us in need," hers, "God has done great things for us," and between the two in the original print was the caption "Nothing but the gospel drives us into exile. Though we leave the fatherland, we remain in God's hand." *(Library of Congress.)*

were Scotch-Irish, and their influence was at least as important in the development of American society.

For in the end it is not only the numbers involved that account for the importance of immigration like these. More important are the attitudes, aptitudes, and ambitions of the immigrants and their influence on the development of the community's life. In the case of these two groups, the impact was profound. Both were alienated groups—alienated from authority both civil and ecclesiastical. Both groups were hostile to all establishments, stubborn in defense of their rights, and fiercely ambitious for economic security. Both contributed powerfully to the shaping of American social and political life.

For the Scotch-Irish, resentment if not hatred of the English establishment had long been a way of life. The Navigation Acts had excluded Irish products from sale elsewhere in British territory and thereby blighted Ireland's economic growth. Further, the Anglo-Irish landlords, mainly absentees, had increased rents whenever leases fell due, and in addition the Scotch-Irish, being Presbyterian nonconformists, were victimized by the Anglican religious establishment, which they were obliged to support by paying tithes, often extracted by professional tax collectors who profited by the amount they could gather. In 1704 a sacramental

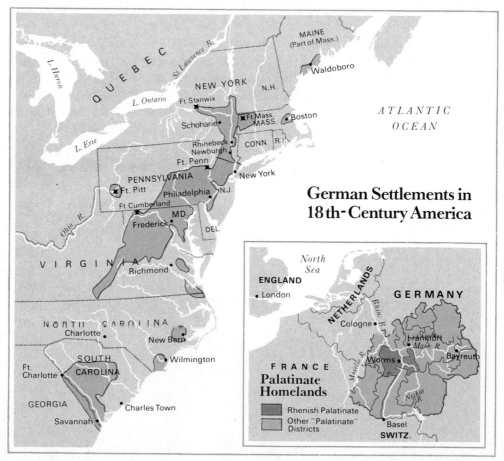

German Settlements in 18th-Century America

Palatinate Homelands

Rhenish Palatinate

Other "Palatinate" Districts

test excluded Presbyterians from all public offices, and marriages solemnized in their churches were declared invalid. The result was predictable. The first great wave of Scotch-Irish immigrants, arriving in Boston and the Delaware ports between 1717 and 1720, carried with it a burning resentment of the English establishment in all its forms. Those who followed, attracted by enthusiastic letters promising "liberty and ease as a reward of honest industry . . . without the imposition of growing rents" and an end to legal prohibitions on serving in public office, shared these attitudes in varying degrees and carried these resentments through the length and breadth of the colonies.

The Germans, as aliens, had no natural affinity with the British establishment and no political contacts to help protect them in this exploitative world. Further, their legal position in the British world was weak. Before 1740, they could become British subjects only by specific deeds of "denization" or naturalization granted by the local governments. Both were remarkably generous in the rights they bestowed, but both were revocable; neither bound the British government (hence locally naturalized Germans could not qualify as "British" subjects under the Navigation Acts); and neither was automatically accepted in any colony but the original. Many of these problems were eliminated by Parliament's general Naturalization Law of 1740, which permitted aliens who had resided continuously for seven years in any of the British colonies to become naturalized subjects of all colonies. But naturalization by this process was time consuming; excluded Catholics; involved an oath offensive to Quakers, Jews, and certain Protestants; and did not carry over fully to England itself, where naturalized colonists were not automatically entitled to own land or hold crown office.

Alienated from, if not actively hostile to, the British government, these Scotch-Irish and German newcomers had little reason to feel close to the colonial governments either, or to the groups that dominated these governments. As settlers they were often physically remote from the capitals, taking up land in backcountry areas far distant from the seats of power; at times they did not even know which governmental jurisdiction they belonged to as they moved south through the backcountry. Often their arrival preceded that of the local government, whose agents therefore appeared as carpetbaggers. And in addition, the immigrants were often deliberately exploited, not merely by land speculators and managers of the infamous trade in German "redemptioners" (those who sold themselves for a term of years in order to cover the costs of transportation) but almost officially by the colonial governments. They were not, however, active insurrectionists.

Encouragement given for People to remove and settle in the Province of New-York in America.

THE Honourable George Clarke, Esq. Lieut. Governour and Commander in chief of the Province of New-York, Hath upon the Petition of Mr. Lauchline Campbell from Isla, North-Britain, promised to grant him Thirty thousand Acres of Land at the Wood-Creek, free of all Charges excepting the Survey and the King's Quit-Rent, which is about one Shilling and Nine Pence Farthing Sterling for each hundred Acres. And also, To grant to thirty Families already landed here Lands in proportion to each Family, from five hundred Acres unto one Hundred and Fifty only paying the Survey and the King's Quit-Rent. And all Protestants that incline to come and settle in this Colony may have Lands granted them from the Crown for three Pounds Sterling per hundred Acres and paying the yearly Quit-Rent.

Dated in New-York this 4th Day of December, 1738.   GEORGE CLARKE.

In these early years of their settlement, their resentment had no ideological focus nor was it directly mobilized as a force in colonial politics. Rather, their hostilities became diffused into a general attitude of suspicion of all government and a refusal to accept the domination of any singular religious persuasion. In them, the respect for government traditionally expected of dutiful subjects was deeply eroded even before they engaged in political controversy. They were people unusually free of a sense of servility, unusually independent in mind and spirit, and these attitudes were strongly reinforced by the material conditions of life they found in the prospering and swiftly growing colonies in which they settled.

If these two major new elements in the American population, the Scotch-Irish and the Germans, were in various ways alienated from the Anglo-American establishment, they at least had access to the processes of law and ultimately of politics by which to express their grievances. In time they would blend into the general population, becoming simply Americans with friends and relatives abroad and with some special group memories and traits. But for the black population—roughly equivalent in size to each of these other new immigrant groups—there were no such possibilities of relief and assimilation. Their separate-ness was rigidly and permanently fixed by the unbridgeable alienation of race and by the hopeless debasement of slavery.

How these quarter of a million West Africans accommodated themselves to American life, the fearful human cost of that accommodation, and the character of their resistance to the brutal system that dominated their lives we do not fully know, and probably never will know. There are no documents that record di-rectly the Negroes' feelings and the intimate details of their personal lives. But from the indirect evidence that has been assembled, one catches glimpses not only of degradation but of bewildering ambiguities and paralyzing tensions in human relations, as well as heroic efforts to maintain some semblance of elemental human dignity.

On the plantations in the South two conditions shaped the character of the blacks' resistance: the degree of assimilation to white culture and the nature of labor assignments. Untrained slaves fresh from Africa were most often sent off to outlying plots of land where they lived out their lives in unending field work. Still bearing, often, the ritual face scars of their earlier tribal life, which inculcated companionship and community, and still thinking of time not in terms of hourly routines but of seasonal cycles, they ran off, frequently, seeking to return to Africa or to set up villages to re-create the life they had known. If they survived, they were returned exhausted, half-starved, and in rags after long exposure in the woods and swamps, to be punished, often by thrashings, which were part of their inescapable "seasoning." In their isolation these field hands learned English only slowly and were assimilated to Anglo-American culture only very gradually. In time, however, they found effective means of resistance—not in hopeless efforts to escape but in laziness, stealing, malingering, wasting equip-ment, damaging crops, and silently disobeying. Their rebelliousness, directed at the plantation itself and only occasionally at their overseers or masters, could have no long-term results, but at least it gave immediate relief to their feelings.

Far more complex and far more self-damaging was the resistance of the native-born slaves employed as personal servants in and around the planters' houses. Enclosed within households of patriarchal discipline, they were forced into continuous close contact with masters who were made tense and insecure by their constant presence and whose domestic lives were poisoned by the helpless availability of blacks of both sexes. The slaves, torn between hostility and fear, developed neurotic symptoms like stammering and perfected techniques of petty harassment that increased their masters' insecurity. Convenient personality disguises (the obedient "Sambo") minimized the likelihood of clashes with masters whose tensions could be released in sadistic rages.

The most openly rebellious of the eighteenth-century slaves were the most thoroughly assimilated, the highly skilled artisans, whose talents gave them a measure of independence and who could deal with the environment as effectively as the whites. They were the most likely to survive as fugitives, and the most capable of easing their everyday burdens by shrewd manipulation. Closest to the white man's world, these skilled workmen understood better than the less acculturated blacks the full meaning of their bondage, and while they lived somewhat more comfortably, they may have suffered even more.

Slavery as it developed in the eighteenth century had many shadings, many variations. Life on the swampy rice plantations of South Carolina was different from life in the Chesapeake tobacco fields. Savage overseers could make life an endless torment, but humane masters could create plantations akin to biblical patriarchies. And wise masters discovered the economic value of allowing blacks to enjoy a modicum of leisure, a semblance of independent activity, and the dignity of family life. But even in the best circumstances brutality was never far below the surface. Wherever slavery existed to any great extent, it meant degradation, fear, and hostility—for the whites as well as for the blacks.

(American Antiquarian Society.)

A Maturing Economy and a Society in Flux

The single most distinctive fact of the American economy as a whole in the eighteenth century was the broad spread of freehold tenure—the outright ownership of land—throughout the free population. In England, at the end of the seventeenth century, only one in every five people lived in families that had a claim to the ownership of land. In the mid–eighteenth century all the land of England was owned by one-tenth of the heads of households; 400 great landlords, representing a mere 3/100 of 1 percent of all families, held between 20 percent and 25 percent of all the land. Over 80 percent of the land of England was worked by tenants, whose rents constituted the income upon which the owners of the land lived. Tenancy of one kind or another formed the basic social experience of the vast majority of the English people; it shaped the structure of English society and the organization of politics, for both rested on the existence of a leisured gentry and aristocracy supported by the income that others produced from the land. And the unspoken assumption and inner force of all agrarian enterprise was that the more land one owned, the greater one's income—an assumption based on a permanent scarcity of arable land relative to the available labor force.

The situation in the American colonies was altogether different. From the beginning the great attraction had been the availability of free land, and that attraction had not proved false. Though there were important regional variations, the large majority of nonslave farmworkers owned the land they worked, even if only at the end of their working lives and even if not in the form and quantities they desired.

The constraints on wide distribution of land that had existed in the seventeenth century fell away. The headright system, which had begun in Virginia and had spread elsewhere, had concentrated land grants in the hands of shipping merchants, entrepreneurs, and officials in or close to the government. In 1705 the abuses of the system and its incapacity to satisfy the voracious land hunger of Virginia's planters led to the direct sale by the government of land warrants, or "treasury rights," which entitled the purchaser to survey and settle a designated amount of land. Maryland and the Carolinas similarly gave up the headright system in favor of direct sales.

In New England too the original, tightly controlled system of distributing land to approved groups of settlers collapsed beneath the pressure of a growing population eager for independent parcels of property. By the 1720s Massachusetts began granting townships to influential land dealers. By the 1740s town sites were being sold at public auction; and by the 1760s the public land in Massachusetts was exhausted. Connecticut had taken the same course somewhat earlier, and in Maine and New Hampshire a combination of openhanded treatment by the government and intense pressure by land speculators led to the remarkably swift distribution of hundreds of thousands of acres to dealers and independent farmers.

Freehold tenure, a dominant fact of eighteenth-century American life, created conditions altogether different from those that existed elsewhere. How unusual the resulting situation was is perhaps best seen by examining the apparent *exceptions*—situations, that is, where a re-creation, partial at least, of the traditional life of landlords would appear to have taken place.

Thus the population growth and the resulting increase in land values led those who had proprietary claims to large tracts of land derived from the original charters to cash in on them if at all possible. Four such claims were particularly imposing: those of the Penn family to the undistributed land of Pennsylvania; those of the Calvert family to Maryland's residual land; those of Earl Granville, the heir of Sir George Carteret, to one share of the original Carolina grant, a claim that was calculated to cover most of the northern half of the present state of North Carolina; and those of Lord Fairfax, as the heir to the "Northern Neck" of Virginia, the five million acres between the Potomac and the Rappahanock rivers that had originally been granted by Charles II in 1649. By the mid–eighteenth century these colossal properties were no longer wild land but territories being opened to cultivation, and they were suddenly becoming valuable to their owners. But with the exception of Fairfax, who lived in Virginia after 1753, none of these great landowners were resident landlords and none were engaged in managing and developing landed estates worked by permanent tenants. Their greatest profit came less from steady rents than from sales in rising land markets.

The operations of these great proprietary landowners were not essentially different from those of lesser land speculators throughout the colonies. Since the land was originally wild, it brought in no income at all in the form in which it had been acquired. The owner had the choice either of making a high capital investment to clear the land, improve it, and otherwise make it rentable at a profit, or of letting it out at low or no rent, and benefiting from the capital formation created by the labor of the tenants as they cleared and worked the land. The former was clearly uneconomic: investments in many other forms of enterprise were more profitable than preparing wild land for lucrative rentals. The best strategy was to rent the land at low fees to temporary tenants who would break it open to cultivation and who looked forward themselves to becoming the ultimate purchasers. Profits from such land sales, based on the initial labor of tenants, could be huge, and also continuous, since the purchasers often bought their farms on loans from the original speculators secured by mortgages on the land itself.

In a few places in the colonies there were landowners, however, who *did* seek to establish themselves as landlords in a traditional sense, and they encountered sharp and at times even violent opposition. On certain estates along the Hudson, and in New Jersey to a lesser extent, many of the traditional forms of landlordism were re-created: high perpetual rents, incidental estate burdens, alienation fees, and insecurity of tenure. These devices could be enforced because of the landlords' political influence; because of a recording system that carefully protected their land claims; and because of the landlords' control of the courts through which the tenants would normally have sought relief. But the result was not the re-creation of a traditional landlord system; it was trouble, more trouble in the end than could be easily absorbed. Many of the tenants refused to accept the burdens; they protested continually, and resorted to all sorts of devices to destroy the landlords' control. They commonly acquired dubious titles to the land they worked from Indians or from New England land speculators and sought to validate these claims in law.

By the 1750s the situation on the tenanted estates in eastern New York and in New Jersey was explosive. The tenants refused to pay rents and duties, and when the courts tried to extract the payments due, the tenants formed an armed insurrection. The climax came in 1766 in a wave of wild rioting. Tenants simply renounced their leases and refused to get off the land when ordered to do so. In Westchester County in New York, rebellious farmers, declared to be "levellers" by the landlords, formed mobs, opened the jails, and stormed the landlords' houses. It took a regiment of regular troops with militia auxiliaries to put down the insurrection; yet even then tenancy could not be uniformly enforced. Many of the farmers simply moved off to the nearest vacant land, particularly in Vermont, which as a result of this exodus from the Hudson River estates and of a parallel migration of discontented New Englanders was opened to settlement for the first time.

If, then, landlordism on the Hudson River estates was an exception to the general American pattern, it was one that could be sustained only by military force. A more glaring exception to the rule of freehold tenure was in the South, where plantations worked by slave labor would seem, in some measure at least, to have created the economic basis of a landed aristocracy. But the Southern aristocracy of the eighteenth century lived in a completely different world from that of the English gentry and aristocracy whom they sought to emulate. There were very large estates in the south (though not a great many: in Maryland only 3.6 percent of all estates were worth over £1,000), and they did support an aristocracy of sorts. But the plantation estates in the South were far different from the tenanted estates of the English aristocracy. For the estates in the South were both units of ownership and units of production, and this condition transformed their social meaning, quite aside from the obvious fact that the labor force was composed of slaves rather than of legally free tenants.

An English estate was not a single unit of production: it was a combination of many separate farms managed by individual tenants. A plantation in the eighteenth-century American South, on the other hand, was precisely a single unit of production—a unified agricultural organization of considerable size under a single management. The whole enterprise was operated as a unit in managing labor and in planning production. From this basic condition flowed the central characteristics of the life of the Southern gentry.

No more in the eighteenth century than in the seventeenth were the Southern planters leisured landowners living comfortably on profits produced by others. They were actively drawn into the process of crop management, land use, and labor direction, and they thus became the active coproducers of their own income. Even if overseers were the immediate supervisors of work on the plantations, the planters discovered at their cost that the managerial responsibility was theirs. A glance at such vivid documents as Landon Carter's diaries shows, not what Edmund Burke correctly called the prime requisite of a true aristocracy, "uncontending ease, the unbought grace of life," but the worried concerns of a hard-pressed agrarian bourgeoisie, absorbed in ledgers, profit margins, and the endless difficulties of farm production and labor management. Though the plantation owners attained a certain graciousness in style of living, that elegance was a light veneer over a rough-grained life of land dealing, ministering to the physical needs and managing the disciplinary problems of a partially dehumanized and latently rebellious slave labor force, and attempting to steer a profitable course through a commercial world that was largely insensitive to the pressures the planters might bring to bear.

The Southern plantations were closer to Russian serf-worked estates than to the tenanted lands of the English aristocracy. But the Chesapeake and Carolina plantations differed from both western and eastern European estates in that the increase in the size of the unit of ownership did not increase the real income available to the owner. The larger the plantation, the more exposed the owner was to economic dangers and the more precarious the profits he might secure. For the larger the estate, the larger the fixed charges that resulted from the purchase and maintenance of slaves and equipment. These expenses remained

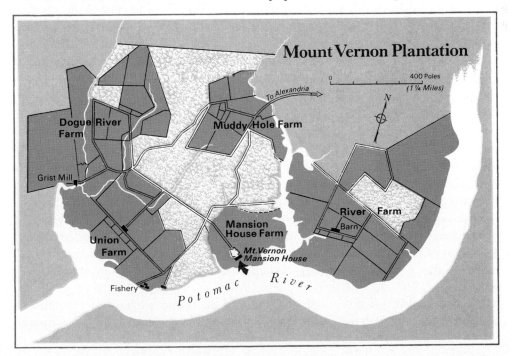

constant or grew in size no matter what the marketing situation might be, and in bad years debts could rise drastically. Indeed, once started, a marketing depression tended to deepen rapidly and uncontrollably as unsold goods carried over from one season to the next, enlarging the glut to catastrophic size.

In such periods of reversal, planters, far from enjoying the "unbought grace of life," struggled desperately to cut overhead costs or otherwise compensate for the marketing losses. Some concentrated on attaining self-sufficiency in the production of food and clothing so that indebtedness would not mean actual penury, and indeed some of the Southern plantations were almost entirely independent communities. Others turned to crop diversification. Starting on the eastern shore of the Chesapeake in the 1720s and continuing west rapidly, planters began converting to the production of grains and livestock, though the preponderance of tobacco production was never eliminated. And still others took what benefit they could from a new form of marketing introduced by Scottish entrepreneurs, whose investments in the Southern American economy in the eighteenth century were a significant new development.

The Scottish merchants and bankers, principally in Glasgow, concentrated on developing the interior of the Chesapeake region, where the units of tobacco production tended to be smaller than they were in the East, where there was very little capital to start with, and where there was no direct contact with ocean shipping. For the development of this region, the old consignment system of marketing tobacco was inappropriate. In an effort to cut costs, especially freight charges, and to increase the efficiency of the system, the Scottish firms established stores in the backcountry that were managed by "factors." These agents bought tobacco crops outright, stored them, and in the end shipped them to central distribution points where vessels sent from Scotland could take up cargoes as fast as they could load.

From the merchants' point of view, this system had the advantage of eliminating the waiting time that vessels otherwise would have in collecting a cargo, and hence a material reduction in shipping costs. For the planters, it meant somewhat greater control, since they were in a position to oversee the final sale of their crops in a situation of active competition without having to account for the complexities of the European tobacco markets. Like the tidewater planters, these inland tobacco growers also accumulated debts to the merchants, but their debts were less for consumption than for production: they took the form of loans for the purchase of slaves, equipment, and the other costs of initiating production. In making these investments the Scots became the financiers of the development of the western tobacco lands. It was estimated that in 1765 Glasgow firms had £500,000 of credits outstanding in the Chesapeake. And by then their "factors" had become prominent figures — usually unpopular figures — in the region's society.

In none of this was there a reproduction of the economic basis of a traditional landlord class. In all areas and in every subcategory of the agricultural economy, something new had evolved, and what appeared to be traditional was not. The few princely properties of the heirs of the original proprietary families were not so much tenanted estates as the capital of personal land companies whose greatest profits came from the sale of the land. The southern planters did not form a leisured aristocracy but were active, hard-pressed farm and labor managers whose profits were as likely to be threatened as to be enhanced by an increase in their holdings, and who struggled to evade the rigors of the economic system in which they were caught. In this world of widespread freehold tenure, attempted re-creations of traditional landlord systems led not to reliable incomes and a life of agrarian gentility but to controversy, even violent conflict. There were peaceable tenants, it is true, in many areas; but tenancy, far from being the normal pattern of life for those who worked the land, was an exceptional and usually transitory condition and its economic function was ordinarily different from what it traditionally had been. Above all, land speculation—the use of land as a salable commodity rather than as an income-bearing property—was an almost universal occupation.

The commercial sector of the economy was equally distinctive. Its focus lay in the larger port towns, comparable in size to the second and third rank English provincial cities. All of them but Boston (whose population was stable at around 16,000) continued to grow quickly. Though visitors often noted their outward

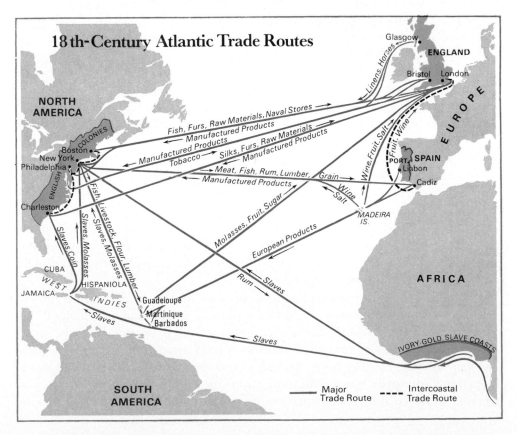

resemblance to such cities as Edinburgh and Bristol, they noted too some of the differences, which resulted from the fact that they were products of a frontier economy. There was of course, in all of these towns, a laboring population, but most of the urban workers were self-employed artisans or workmen in small-scale, often family-sized, businesses. There was a small though growing component of casual laborers—dock workers, laborers in shipbuilding enterprises, and others—who picked up what employment they could in menial tasks around the towns. They formed a volatile element in these communities, and they suffered in times of depression. But there is no evidence of mass destitution. The number of those who received charity, while it increased, never approached the figures of the dependent poor in Europe. In England at times one-third of the population was impoverished, and in the cities, where beggars crowded the cellars and attics, massed in back alleys, and overwhelmed the charitable institutions, another third was poor enough to be rendered destitute by the repeated economic crises. Poverty was the most serious and most controversial social problem of eighteenth-century England; the great "Debate of the Poor" fills the social literature of the day. But Philadelphia did not even build an almshouse until 1732; New York built one only in 1736. Rarely before 1760 were more than one hundred people supported by poor relief in Philadelphia. At no time during those years did as much as 1 percent of the population of New York and Philadelphia receive charity in any form. And even in the worst times after 1760 poor relief involved no more than 3.6 percent of New York's population, 5 percent of Philadelphia's, and 6 to 7 percent of Boston's.

A series of close statistical studies of the British mainland North American colonies in the 1700s reveals a level of living that "was probably the highest achieved for the great bulk of the population in any country up to that time," and that was as true in the towns as in the countryside. Though a relatively small part of the urban population controlled an increasing proportion of the total wealth, and though the gulf between rich and poor deepened, "the fact remains that not only were the rich getting richer but the poor were too, albeit at a slower rate." There was poverty in the pre-Revolutionary towns, but no mass starvation; there were riots, but no "bread riots"; and the "mobs" that became highly visible were not spearheads of a desperate proletariat inflamed by utopian aspirations and seeking to transform the structure of society. They were crowds of young apprentices, dock workers, and seamen temporarily idle between voyages, usually led by lesser merchants or independent craftsmen.

It would have been surprising had it not been so, for the society of the commercial towns retained the characteristics of a pioneer world. Labor remained relatively scarce, which meant that wages remained high enough to make small savings possible. Day laborers in Boston were paid twice as much as their equivalents in London. Furthermore, the scale of economic enterprise remained small. The typical enterprise was a family unit supplemented by one or two partners or a few helpers. In the typical situation the distance between employer and em-

SEA CAPTAINS CAROUSING IN SURINAM, BY JOHN GREENWOOD (1758)

Surinam (Dutch Guiana) on the northern coast of South America
was a favorite port of call for American merchants, who
exchanged horses and tobacco there for sugar products. Greenwood,
a Bostonian who lived in Surinam, painted in the faces of several
well-known Rhode Island merchants. *(The St. Louis Art Museum.)*

ployee remained relatively narrow, both objectively (in terms of lifestyle and
function) and subjectively (in terms of feelings of superiority or alienation). The
typical artisan worked closely with his employer, and their economic functions
were not unbridgeably different. Labor troubles took a quite different form from
those in modern society. There were strikes, but almost none of them were protests by urban workers against conditions or wages. They were characteristically
protests by master workers, employers, and independent artisans against price
levels set by the community for the sale of their products or efforts to stop widespread infiltration by outsiders into licensed trades. There was no solidly defined,
confined, and remediless working-class population. There were town workers
periodically distressed by the movements of the economy, which lurched through
repeated phases of bust and boom, but no permanently alienated "proletariat."

The urban communities were dominated by the merchants, who in this period
became figures of importance throughout the Atlantic world. The merchant
group as a whole developed between two quite opposite sets of pressures, two
conflicting tendencies. During the early and middle years of the eighteenth century there were forces that tended to limit and stabilize the existing mercantile
leadership—to make of them an elite merchant aristocracy. But at the same time

there were other forces tending to introduce dynamic, disbalancing elements in the commercial world, and these forces, which upset the dominance of all would-be merchant elites, were related to the deepest elements of the swiftly developing economy.

A significant degree of stability was created in the merchant group of the early eighteenth century by the political stability in England which, beginning in the 1720s, steadied the rocketing factionalism of the previous half-century. The secure arrangement of politics, patronage, and influence devised by Robert Walpole helped stabilize the organization of Atlantic commerce, involved as it was with politics and government contracting. At the same time specialization within the English mercantile establishment increased through the period, and the specialist wholesalers controlling shipments to the colonies could and did restrict access to the primary circuits of trade to selected American correspondents. And there were technical improvements in trade and finance, particularly the development of marine insurance, that helped make possible a growing concentration of commercial capital and entrepreneurial control.

All of these developments, plus the general fact that large operators could effect economies of scale, meant that the commercial community was acquiring elitist characteristics. Yet despite this emergence of dominant groups, the merchant community as a whole, and commerce as a whole, remained highly competitive and fluid in membership. For, first, as raw frontier areas matured into settled agricultural producing regions, successful farmers branched out into marketing surplus goods, became inland traders, and ultimately merchants. One critical element in the rise of these backcountry tradesmen was location, for transportation was a critical factor. It cost more to ship a unit of goods 100 miles overland, from Philadelphia to Lancaster, Pennsylvania, than 3000 miles by sea, from London to Philadelphia. Prosperous market farmers located at transfer points on the rivers or inland trade routes parlayed their advantages in goods and location into trading operations and drifted into commercial pursuits, combined often with land speculation.

But it was not only a matter of old settled areas producing surpluses from which market farmers could build careers in commerce. Wholly new hinterlands developed almost overnight, and from them emerged altogether new men who proved effective competitors indeed.

In 1720 the chief agricultural producing areas were located northeast of the Hudson and in the Chesapeake region. Thereafter the preponderance shifted to the middle colonies, the area between the Hudson and Chesapeake Bay. Surplus goods, chiefly grain, flowed to the swiftly growing port of Philadelphia from the Pennsylvania backcountry, from New Jersey, and from parts of Maryland; and this flow enriched a new mercantile aristocracy, particularly of Quakers, in that city. By the 1760s the value of their trade with England exceeded that of all of New England. Similar developments took place in other regions. Within a space of only ten years in the 1740s and 1750s Baltimore rose from a wilder-

BALTIMORE IN 1752

A sketch made at the time and subsequently corrected by David
Bewley "from his certain recollection and that of other aged per-
sons acquainted with Baltimore, with whom he compared notes."
I. N. Stokes Collection, The New York Public Library.)

ness village to a thriving urban center serving the marketing needs of a new hinterland area, and within a single generation Baltimore's merchants became
important figures in the commercial world.

The result of all these movements in agriculture and trade was a highly dynamic
mercantile world. Although conditions made possible the stabilization of a merchant leadership group, the rapid development of the economy in long-settled
areas and the constant opening of new areas of agricultural production created
a continuous recruitment of new merchants and a continuous tension of competition between established figures and newcomers. There was a widespread sense
that certain merchant families, established by the 1760s for two, three, or even
four generations, were forming into an oligarchy; but at the same time there were
always new faces, new families, capable of taking the same successful risks that
had once served to establish the older families.

Religion: The Sources of American Denominationalism

The tensions within the commercial world were moderate next to those that
developed in religion. Since American culture in the mid–eighteenth century was
still largely religious in its orientation, these tensions lay at the heart of the social
world everywhere in the colonies, North and South, seaboard and inland.

The central event in the history of religion in America in the eighteenth century was the Great Awakening, the revivalist eruptions of the late 1730s and the
1740s, which roared through the colonies like a sheet of flame and left behind a

world transformed. In part this wave of passionate evangelicalism was a typical expression of a general movement that swept through much of the Western world. The Great Awakening coincided with the first outpouring of Anglican evangelicalism in England and Wales, which would become Methodism, and with Pietism in the German-speaking world. There were direct connections between the American revivalists and their European counterparts, but there was something unique too in the American evangelical movement, and it produced quite distinctive results.

In New England the background and sources of the Awakening came closest to the usual pattern of such evangelical waves. By the early eighteenth century the Congregational churches had experienced the growth in institutional formalism and the draining away of inner fervor and emotional commitment that are typical of all long-established churches and that characteristically give rise to evangelical searchings and outbursts. It is paradoxical that this should have been so since Puritan Congregationalism had itself originally represented a protest against a formal church establishment, and it had contained two essential characteristics that had distinguished it from any ordinary church. First, membership in the Congregational churches had not been an automatic consequence of physical birth but had resulted from individual acts of association taken in public on the basis of an inner experience; and second, church institutions had been decentralized into Congregational limits.

These original characteristics did not survive. By the mid–seventeenth century the New England churches faced a crisis that arose from the failure of the second and third generations to duplicate the spiritual experiences of the founders and to come forward into membership on the basis of an act of saving grace. The founders' children had been baptized in the church on the basis of their parents' profession and the likelihood of their own ultimate conversion; full membership awaited the childrens' own personal "calling." But that promise in many cases was not fulfilled. Should, then, the children of these baptized but unconverted members of the church also be baptized?

This was the agonizing problem that had faced the Puritans in the mid–seventeenth century. If the answer were Yes, then the church as a body of converted Christians would be destroyed. But if the answer were No, then, as conversions became fewer and fewer, the church would grow apart from the society as a whole; it would become a mere sect, without the ground for social control which was so fundamental a part of Puritan life. The solution came in a convention of ministers that met in 1657 whose decision was confirmed by a synod of 1662. By the arrangement devised then, which became known as the "halfway covenant," unregenerate members *could* transmit membership in the church to their children, but only a *halfway* membership: such children would be baptised but not offered the sacrament of communion, nor would they be entitled to vote as members of the church. As halfway members, they would be required to make a public pledge to obey the rulings of the church and to bring their children up as proper

Christians. Still, they were members, if only partial, and the distinction between them and the full members who sat with them in church week after week was thin, and grew thinner and more technical as the years passed.

The "halfway covenant" was an unstable compromise, and erosions ate into it from both the liberal and conservative ends of the church spectrum, leading to the almost inevitable destruction of the Puritans' original concept of the church as a body of proven saints. Theological conservatives, like the famous Northampton, Massachusetts, preacher Solomon Stoddard, casting a cold eye on such worldly compromises as these, gave up the halfway distinction, baptized all, and sought to bring everyone to communion who was willing to accept it. The same conclusion was reached in the liberal Brattle Street Church of Boston under the Reverend Benjamin Colman. His religion was milder, less demanding, more open to various influences than the traditional Puritans', and he turned back to such banned rituals as the use of the Lord's Prayer and to the regular baptizing of all children who were put forward. Like Stoddard, he offered communion to anyone of "visible sanctity" who could sustain a proper Christian mode of conduct.

It was partly in reaction against these innovations that the more orthodox Puritan churches moved toward institutional centralization. The Mathers formed regional ministerial associations in Massachusetts which sought to impose certification and disciplinary powers over the clergy and over the general management of church affairs. Though in 1705 their effort to create such an organization in law was defeated, informal communication among the churches was strengthened, and in Connecticut a parallel effort succeeded. There, the so-called Saybrook Platform of 1708 became a public law, creating county "consociations" of the Congregational churches with disciplinary powers, regional associations of ministers, and a colony-wide general association of delegates of the ministers.

By all of these developments—a slackening in religious fervor, a growing identity of church and society, and the spread of general controls over originally independent congregational bodies—the Puritan churches increasingly approached the condition of a formalized establishment. The process had obvious limits. In the eyes of British law, Congregational churches were nonconformist and therefore their advantages as an established group in British territory could never have the full sanction of law behind them. The Church of England, a dissenting body in New England, led all opposition groups in claiming the privileges accorded nonconformists in England. And in this they were successful. In the 1720s, Anglicans, Quakers, and Baptists gained full rights of worship and of using their church taxes for their own support. They were free, too, to hold office and to attend all institutions of learning. But they still remained *tolerated* groups, obliged to register with the authorities. No one was free of the obligation to support religion, and no group but these three were allowed the privileges of dissent.

New England Congregationalism was thus a loose establishment, different in various ways from established state churches elsewhere, but it was an establish-

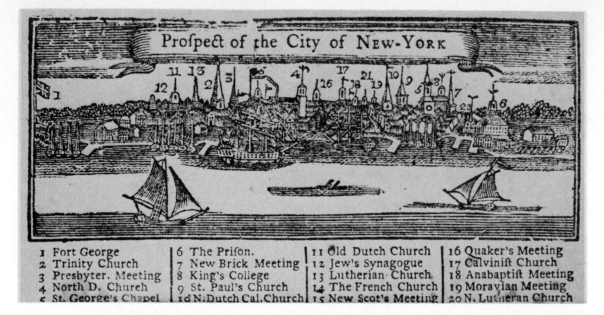

Prospect of the City of New-York

1 Fort George	6 The Prison.	11 Old Dutch Church	16 Quaker's Meeting
2 Trinity Church	7 New Brick Meeting	12 Jew's Synagogue	17 Calvinist Church
3 Presbyter. Meeting	8 King's College	13 Lutherian Church	18 Anabaptist Meeting
4 North D. Church	9 St. Paul's Church	14 The French Church	19 Moravian Meeting
5 St. George's Chapel	10 N. Dutch Cal. Church	15 New Scot's Meeting	20 N. Lutheran Church

ment nevertheless, and one in which religion as an inner experience tended to fade and in which formal observance and institutional ritual grew increasingly important. Less and less did the churches satisfy people's inner yearnings; more and more were these churches vulnerable to the charge of excessive formalism and of a deadening complacency.

Even less were the churches in the other colonies capable of satisfying the deeper needs of a still generally religious society. In Virginia the long-standing inability of the Church of England to serve the needs of the community was now compounded by its ambiguous relationship to the new settlers, almost all non-Anglicans, who moved into the backcountry in the 1720s and '30s. When the revival struck Virginia, it found a colony whose official state church was formalistic and generally ineffective but whose nonconformist churches, dominant in the west, were dynamic centers of community life. The relations between the two were likely to become embattled.

Maryland too, after 1702, had an established Anglican church, but it differed on two points from that of Virginia. First, the church's anti-Catholic animus was more meaningful there because of the presence of approximately 4000 descendants of the original Catholic settlers who adhered half-secretly and at considerable cost to the Roman communion. Second, since the Anglican community itself was numerically small, its toleration of Protestant nonconformists was greater even than the toleration shown by Virginia's Anglican church.

Elsewhere the institutional character of religious life was so chaotic and so volatile as to elude clear historical description. In the Carolinas and Georgia (the latter settled in 1732 by Anglican philanthropists as a refuge for England's paupers and as a buffer against Spanish Florida) there were Anglican establishments of sorts, but nonconformists were welcomed and little effort was made to regulate religious life as a whole, which in many areas were overwhelmingly non-

Anglican. Pennsylvania, Rhode Island, and New Jersey had no establishments at all, the first two because the very idea ran against the principles of the influential Quakers, and New Jersey because the religious diversity was so extreme and the Anglican community so small that no agreement could conceivably be reached on the definition of a privileged religion. And in New York, where dissenters outnumbered Anglicans by at least 15 to 1, the only flourishing Anglican institution was New York City's Trinity Church, which Governor Fletcher had endowed with independent financial privileges.

The overwhelming fact, amid the institutional confusion of religion in eighteenth-century America, was that the dominant churches, no matter what their definition, were failing to minister effectively to the needs of a people for whom religion continued to be a primary emotional and cultural experience. It is significant that the most vigorous branch of the Church of England in eighteenth-century America was its missionary arm, the Society for the Propagation of the Gospel in Foreign Parts. Originally formed to bring the Christian gospel to the Indians, it had instead devoted itself to guaranteeing the survival of the Anglican Church in America and strengthening it in every possible way. Under its first and most powerful leader, the Reverend Thomas Bray (1656–1730), the SPG, as it was called, launched missionary expeditions to likely points throughout the colonies, helped maintain existing parishes and organize new ones in the great desert of American noncomformity, and in its activities created the church's only effective organization above the parish level.

It was into this ill-served, parched, and questing religious world that the evangelicalism of the Great Awakening fell like a blazing torch. The revival did not begin all at once. There were premonitory stirrings in the Connecticut River valley, touched off by the remarkable young minister of Northampton, Massachusetts, Jonathan Edwards.

He was heir to a famous ecclesiastical tradition. Grandson of the powerful "Pope" Solomon Stoddard, Edwards, from the time of his graduation from Yale at the age of seventeen, devoted himself to the central philosophical and theological problems of the age. While preaching and fulfilling his other pastoral duties in Northampton, he worked out, in private notebooks and in sermons, pamphlets, and books, a body of thought so subtle and so original in reconciling uncompromising Calvinism with Enlightenment thought that it has established him as one of the original thinkers of the eighteenth century. His chief professional task, however, was more ordinary: it was to bring sinful men to a knowledge of God and to the experience of spiritual rebirth. Stoddard had stirred local revivals in the 1720s; and in 1734 and '35 Edwards, to his own great surprise and gratification, suddenly found his own people responding overwhelmingly to his closely reasoned sermons on justification by faith. Northampton was overcome with religious enthusiasm. Dozens of once complacent parishioners went through tumultuous passions of regeneration.

Word of a providential revival spread swiftly through the farming hamlets of the Connecticut River valley and then eastward along Long Island Sound, touching off similar outbreaks as it went. By the time Edwards published an account of his local revival, his *Faithful Narrative of the Surprising Work of God* (1737), the wave had passed, but it had become famous throughout the colonies and in Great Britain as well. It had stirred ministers everywhere to new exertions in bringing sinful men to an experience of God's grace, and it had created a brimming expectancy that some vast outpouring of religious zeal, if not the actual establishment of God's kingdom on earth, was about to take place. By 1740, when George Whitefield, the brilliant English preacher who had already stirred successful revivals on two tours through the middle and southern colonies, appeared in New England, anticipation was spilling over into fulfillment. It was Whitefield, following in the wake of Edwards's revival, who finally threw open the floodgates and let loose an outpouring of soul-shaking evangelicalism that flooded New England for four tumultuous years.

JONATHAN EDWARDS, BY JOSEPH BADGER

Painted a few years before Edwards was expelled from his Northampton pulpit for insisting on conversion as a basis for church membership and for attempting to discipline children of leading families. After seven years as a missionary to the Indians, Edwards died at the age of 55. *(Yale University Art Gallery.)*

Whitefield began his spectacular tour in Newport, Rhode Island, where he happily found "the word of the Lord . . . sharper than a two-edged sword." He then continued to Boston, where his effect was stupendous. Preaching first to hundreds who jammed the churches until they could hold no more, then to thousands in open-air meetings, the young, impassioned orator transfixed listeners used to hearing scholarly sermons read to them from carefully prepared texts. From Boston, Whitefield moved north to York, Maine, through a series of triumphant stopovers; he then returned to Boston, where on October 12 he delivered a farewell sermon to an audience of thirty thousand, nearly twice the population of the town, who crowded the Common to hear him. His tour turned westward to Northampton, where his preaching was so affecting that Jonathan Edwards, Whitefield reported, "wept during the whole time of exercise." After stops south along the valley towns that had already been "burnt over" by revivalism, Whitefield ended his tour in New York.

His preaching, he correctly reported, had made a great difference in the North. So too did that of the second great leader of the Awakening, Gilbert Tennant. A second-generation Scotch-Irish minister who for a decade had led the "New Light" (evangelical) party within the growing Presbyterian communities of New

Jersey and New York, he had been educated in his father's "Log College" in Neshaminy, Pennsylvania, devoted to propagating the principles of "experimental" religion—that is, deeply experienced rather than intellectual and doctrine-bound religion. Tennant's tour through southern New England lasted three months in the fall and winter of 1740–41—tumultuous months of mass excitement, profound emotional upheaval, and inner transformation. But his passionate evangelicalism, denounced by the "Old Lights" as "beastly brayings," was a model of decorum next to the wild harangues of James Davenport, who in 1741 and 1742 tore hysterically through New England, denouncing every established minister as a "dead husk" and a deceiver, and stirring crowds into frenzies. Arrested in Connecticut and deported, thrown out of Boston as a madman, Davenport reached the climax of his short and wild career in 1743 when he sponsored a public burning not only of such worldly vanities as wigs, cloaks, and rings but of books written by the most distinguished preachers. By then the most intense fires of the Awakening were fading (there were, after all, only a limited number of susceptible souls) and Davenport's cooler colleagues among the New Lights as well as declining health convinced him to moderate his attacks. His eclipse marks the passing of the most intense phase of the Awakening in New England.

Elsewhere it continued its blazing progress. It tore through the Presbyterian and Dutch Reformed communities of the middle colonies, and in the South generated a long-term missionary enterprise. Whitefield's tours in both regions were great successes, though in the South he ran into both greater apathy and greater opposition than he had in the North. The revivals split the Presbyterian churches in Pennsylvania and New Jersey. The "New Side" evangelical Presbyterians formed their own Synod in 1741 and sent out their own itinerant preachers to invade districts dominated by the "Old Side." It was these revivalist Presbyterians moving southward from Pennsylvania who had the greatest impact in Virginia. Their most effective preacher, Samuel Davies, ignited and sustained in Hanover County the most important of the Southern revivals and in the process spurred the Anglican authorities to take repressive measures against nonconformity by fining unlicensed preachers. Even more influential in the middle and Southern colonies were the evangelical Baptists. They reached out more effectively than any other church or sect to the unchurched common people of the backcountry, and undertook with great success a proselytizing effort among the new settlers on the Southern frontier. And at the end of the colonial period, evangelicals of the Church of England led by the Reverend Devereux Jarratt, who would soon organize as the Methodist Church, also began to share in the work of extending the Awakening to the settlers on the expanding frontier.

Such was the greatest event in the history of religion in eighteenth-century America. Its effect was more revolutionary by far than the parallel movements in Europe—Pietism in Germany and Methodism in England and Wales. The differences are revealing. The revivals in America were not class affairs as they were elsewhere, giving new voice to the aspirations of the socially deprived. Nor were they limited to any particular geographical group: they were as successful in the large towns as in the countryside. Their impact ran across all levels and all regions of American society, and since the institutional structures of both religion and the state in the colonies were flimsy at best, the effect could not be confined. At least four areas of American social life were irreversibly affected by the great revivalist wave.

First, the authority and status of the clergy were permanently weakened. The revivalists cared little for offices, formal status, education, learning, or even, within reasonable limits, outward behavior. For them, qualification for religious leadership was gained only by force of inner experience and by the ability to reach the populace emotionally—to unlock parishioners' spiritual aspirations. It followed naturally that they would challenge the authority of established educational institutions like Yale and Harvard whose training for the ministry seemed to them to be intellectual and formalistic. When Connecticut barred from the ministry anyone not trained at Yale, Harvard, or a foreign Protestant university, the Presbyterian New Lights not only formed a new synod devoted to evangelical preaching but in 1746 created a new college, the College of New Jersey (later Princeton), which would emphasize religion of the affections as well as of the mind. Three other colleges were founded in similar response to the revival movement (Rutgers, Brown, and Dartmouth), for the Awakening, which challenged all preachers to justify their authority by their own spiritual gifts and by their power to reach into other souls, could not tolerate merely formal qualifications of any kind.

So too the Awakening tended to destroy the stable identification of churches with particular territorial boundaries. The revivalists believed their call extended not to the few people who happened to have employed them as preachers but to anyone anywhere who would heed their word, and especially to all those whose ministers were unconverted. They therefore naturally became "itinerants," invading established parishes. If welcomed, they preached officially as visiting ministers; if not, they set up in barns or open fields and preached to anyone who came. To such invasions, the establishment vehemently objected, and "itineracy" became one of the central controversies of the revival. But it could not be stopped, and where it occurred it profoundly weakened the integrating social force of organized religion.

Related to this was a third effect of the Awakening, nothing less than the near destruction of institutional religion as the organizing framework of small-group society. For in all the new settlements, and continuously on the disorganized frontiers, the church had provided a vital center for society itself. When the Awakening hit the more vulnerable communities, a series of splits most often occurred. A split-off of a New Light faction from a stubborn Old Light group that refused to convert to evangelical principles could severely rupture a community; and even if the splinter group eventually returned, it did so more or less free of general control. Commonly, however, the splinter group would prefer another association altogether, particularly with the Baptists, whose numbers soared in this period. But often there was no point at which the disintegration could be stopped. Whole units simply disappeared in the course of successive splinterings, ending in a mere cluster of family-sized factions, unchurched and free of all constraints of church organization.

Finally, the Awakening put unsupportable pressures on what remained of church-state relations, not in doctrine but in practice. The revivalists did not believe themselves to be heterodox. Quite the contrary. They claimed that they alone represented the true orthodoxy in Protestant Christianity and denounced the establishments for their deviations. In so doing they created new grounds for challenging not the principle of religious establishment as such but the practical right of any church to claim a privileged place in the eyes of the law. They thereby moved closer to the conclusion that the very notion of an establishment of religion was false and that the only safe and correct course was to deny any and all privileges of the state to any religious group.

From all of the developments in religion that had been in motion from the time of the first settlements in British North America—developments now greatly intensified and compounded by the Great Awakening—religion in America acquired a new character. It became essentially voluntaristic even for the high church groups: Catholic, Anglican, Presbyterian, Lutheran, and Dutch Reformed—groups whose doctrines assumed a valid identification of church and society enforced by the state. Organized religion had also developed an inner emphasis on persuasion as its essential activity—an outgoing advancing of the truth as distinct from merely declaring or enjoying it. Organized Christianity, lacking the sanction of the state to guarantee membership, lacking, too, secure institutional structures and effective group discipline, swung its emphasis toward promotion and outward activity and away from the purification of doctrine and the maintenance of internal order. Finally, the role of individual decision shifted. Where in traditional situations involvement with a dominant religion was automatic, the momentous decision was to break with the association into which one was born. As a consequence, religious indifference could go hand in hand with extensive church membership. In the colonies, on the eve of the Revolution, the opposite was true: to do nothing was likely to mean to have no affiliation at all, and the momentous decision involved joining, not severing, a religious association. As a result, broad waves of religious enthusiasm could go hand in hand with low church membership.

By the end of the colonial period these characteristics were taking on a patterned and stable form, which would later be called Denominationalism. A product of the intractable realities of the colonial situation, it would find expression in theory, law, and formal doctrine during the Revolution and in the years that followed.

The Origins of American Politics

The key to much in pre-Revolutionary America was the gap that developed between expectation and reality. In no area was this discordant pattern more extreme and more consequential than in politics and government. For not only did the discrepancy between theory and expectation on the one hand and actuality on the other shape the character of American public life, but it laid the basis for the transformation of the relations between Britain and the colonies.

All formal notions of public life in the British world rested on the belief that the British political system of the mid–eighteenth century was the freest and best that existed, and that the colonial governments and political systems were more or less imperfect replicas of that world-famous model. In theory, balance was the key to the British constitution. From classical antiquity, reaffirmed in the Renaissance and in seventeenth-century England, had come the notion that there were three pure forms of government, any one of which if properly maintained could serve the people properly but all of which tended to degenerate into evil forms that created oppression: monarchy, the rule by one, which degenerated into tyranny; aristocracy, the rule of a few, which became oligarchy; and democracy, the rule of the whole political population, which declined into the rule of the mob. The challenge to political thinkers had long been the problem of devising a balance among these forms that would stabilize government and bring the degenerative processes to a halt. The most pervasive, most generally accepted presumption of eighteenth-century American politics was that the British constitution, as it had emerged from the turmoils of the seventeenth century, had achieved precisely such a stable balance of pure forms and that this balance had been securely embodied in the institutional competition among the crown, representing monarchy; the House of Lords, representing the nobility or aristocracy; and the House of Commons, representing the democracy.

It is a simple notion, but it is easily misunderstood, for while it in part incorporates the modern notion of the separation of functioning branches of government (executive, legislative, and judicial), it is distinct from that conception. It is based on the idea of balances not among the organs of government but among the social elements that participate in government, each bringing to government the interests and qualities peculiar to itself: monarchy, power; aristocracy, disinterested judgment and valor; and democracy, liberty.

Such was the theoretical explanation of the working of the British constitution in the mid–eighteenth century which was almost universally believed to explain the stability and freedom that had been achieved in Britain. Yet, as a description of the actual working of the British government it was not merely inaccurate but misleading. The balance of these elements—indeed, their very existence as distinct entities—was more apparent than real. The supposed preserves of each power were thoroughly infiltrated by the others, and their functioning was far different from the idealized description. In fact the source of the political stability of mid-eighteenth century Britain lay not in the supposed balance of these socioconstitutional orders, which Americans sought to emulate, but in two sets of conditions, the one underlying, the other manifest — both highly relevant to an understanding of the peculiar form of politics that developed in eighteenth-century America.

The main underlying condition that made Britain's stability possible was the fact that the great constitutional issues of the seventeenth century had been settled in the Glorious Revolution of 1688: the problem of the extent of crown authority and the problem of the relation of church and state. As to the first, the terms of settlement of the Glorious Revolution stipulated that the monarch would not create courts without statute or dismiss judges without formal impeachment; would not impose taxes without grant of Parliament; and would not maintain a standing army in peacetime or engage in wars for foreign territory without Parliament's consent. The crown further agreed not to limit unduly or extend the existence of a parliament or interfere with its regular meetings — elections and convenings being placed on a regular calendar schedule. In addition, it was understood, at least after 1707, that the king would not veto acts of Parliament.

As to the religious settlement after the Glorious Revolution, the Church of England was established; it enjoyed the privileges and benefits of the state, and all who did not explicitly reject it were considered to be members of its com-

THE HOUSE OF COMMONS IN THE MID-EIGHTEENTH CENTURY

The facing benches, separated only by the speaker's table and the few feet of open floor space, encouraged direct debate. Like so much of British political life, this seating arrangement was widely imitated in the colonies.

munity. But the desire for an enforced uniformity was abandoned. Dissent was tolerated, though penalized. The great majority of nonconformists were permitted to worship as they pleased; they enjoyed almost full civil rights, and in the course of the century attained most political rights as well.

These underlying conditions made stability possible. That it was actually achieved is the result of the informal accommodation that was worked out between the crown and the House of Commons. Both had extensive jurisdictions at the end of the seventeenth century, but neither was formally dominant. A working relationship between the two was achieved by a set of operating conventions so fundamental as to comprise in effect a private, informal constitution. The ministry, acting for the crown, disciplined and manipulated the House, in part by managing elections into that body through its control or outright ownership of "rotten boroughs" or other easily dominated constituencies, and in part by distributing crown patronage to Members so as to assure safe majorities on controversial issues. In the mid–eighteenth century about 200 of the 558 members of the House of Commons held crown appointments or gifts of one sort or another, and another 30 or 40 were more loosely tied to government by awards of profitable contracts. A fluctuating number of other Members were bound to the administration less directly, particularly by the gift or promise of one or more of the 8000 excise offices available.

It was this use of "influence" in managing elections and in controlling votes in the two Houses that, together with the settlement of the main policy questions, explains the stability of English political life in the mid–eighteenth century. There were certain technical requirements for such stabilizing control: an abundance of patronage available for disposal by the ministry; a small electorate, for the larger the voting population the greater the difficulty of control; and a system of representation that was not related to the shift and growth of the population or closely bound to the wishes of a broad electorate.

All of these conditions existed in eighteenth-century Britain, but none of them existed in anything like the same measure in the mainland colonies of British North America. Yet the similarity between the British constitution and the separate colonial constitutions was an axiom of political thought in eighteenth-century America. As bicameral legislatures developed in the colonies during the seventeenth century, with the lower houses more and more clearly standing for local, popular interests and the Councils appearing to approximate the classical houses of the aristocracy, the assumption grew that the colonial governments were miniatures of the British government. Dr. William Douglass of Boston explained in his *Summary, Historical and Political . . . of the British Settlements in North America* (1749–51) that, by the governor,

representing the King, the colonies are monarchical; by the Council, they are aristocratical; by a House of Representatives or delegates from the people, they are democratical: these

three are distinct and independent of one another . . . the several negatives being checks
upon one another. The concurrence of these three forms of government seem to be the
highest perfection that human civil government can attain to in times of peace.

Such irregularities and exceptions as there were in the American replicas, Douglass said, "doubtless in time will be rectified."

But while in England the mixed and balanced constitution produced a high
degree of political harmony, similar institutions in the colonies produced the
opposite. Strife was common within the provincial governments. There was
strife, first, between the branches of government—between the executive on the
one hand and the legislatures on the other—strife so rampant as to be more noteworthy by its absence than its presence and so intense as to lead on occasions to
a total paralysis of government. But it was not only a matter of conflict between
branches of government. There was, besides this, a milling factionalism that
transcended institutional boundaries and at times reduced the politics of certain colonies to an almost unchartable chaos of competing groups. Some were
personal groups, small clusters of relatives and friends that rose suddenly at
particular junctures and faded quickly, merging into other equally unstable
configurations. Others were economic, regional, and more generally social
interest groups, some quickly rising and quickly falling, some durable, persisting
through a generation or more, though never highly organized and only intermit-
tently active, and continually shifting in personnel. Still others (though these
were fewer) were groups formed to defend and advance programs that transcended immediate personal and group interests. All were vocal; most were
difficult to control; and while in certain colonies at certain times political life attained the hoped-for balance and tranquillity, there was scarcely a governor in
the eighteenth century who at one time or another did not echo the weary
question and the anguished plea of William Penn to the political leaders of the
City of Brotherly Love soon after it was founded: "Cannot more friendly and
private courses be taken to set matters right in an infant province? . . . For the
love of God, me, and the poor country, be not so *governmentish!*"

But Pennsylvania remained, in Penn's words, "noisy and open in [its] dissatisfactions," and so did most of the other colonies during the three generations that
preceded the Revolution. For beneath the apparent similarities in the formal
constitutions of government in England and America, there were basic differences
in the informal structure of politics. The similarities in government were superficial, the differences in politics so profound as to seem almost an inversion of
the universally admired British model.

The settlement of the Glorious Revolution had not extended to the colonies.
The governors in all but the chartered colonies of Rhode Island and Connecticut
had the authority to veto legislation, which was also susceptible to disallowance
by the Privy Council or the Proprietors in England. The royal governors, in

addition, had the authority to delay sittings of the lower houses of the Assemblies or dissolve them at will, and they quickly became accustomed to using those powers. Commonly, as a result, the lower houses were as dependent on executive will for their existences as the House of Commons had been under the Tudor and Stuart monarchs. Nor was the judiciary in the colonies protected as it was in England. Judges at all levels, from justices of the peace to the chief justices of the supreme courts, were appointed on nomination of the governors and dismissible by the executives' will. Similarly, the governors in all but the charter governments could create courts without statutory authority, and did so repeatedly, especially chancery courts, which sat without juries and were concerned with such unpopular matters as collecting arrears of quitrents. Associated with these "prerogative courts" in the colonists' minds were the vice admiralty courts, which operated over maritime matters, also without juries, with a jurisdiction broader than that exercised by equivalent courts in England.

Besides these powers there were also lesser powers accorded the executive in America that had been eliminated in England: power over the election of the speakers of the House; power over church appointments; power over fees. But it was in the former areas primarily—the vetoing of colonial legislation, proroguing and dissolving legislative bodies, and dismissing judges and creating courts— that the legal power of the executive was felt to be the most threatening and a source of danger to liberty and to the free constitution.

The mere existence of such powers, arbitrary and threatening to eighteenth-century Britons, generated political controversy, for they tended to mobilize the forces associated with the legislature against those associated with the executive. But what assured the actual conflict of these forces and distinguished the colonial governments from the British even more than the exaggeration of executive authority was the fact that an array of other circumstances existed that radically reduced, sometimes eliminated, the force of that "influence" by which the executive in England disciplined dissent and conflict in the political community and maintained supremacy in government. The "private" constitution, so crucial in making workable Britain's "public" constitution of mixed government, was absent in the colonies, or reduced close to the point of ineffectiveness. The paradoxical result was that while in important respects the colonial constitutions were archaic by 18th-century standards, in other respects they were radically reformed.

The political influence of the executive government was weak in the colonies, first, because the administration lacked the flexibility it needed for successful engagement in politics. The royal governors arrived in the colonies not merely with commissions that outlined their duties but with instructions that filled in the details so minutely and with such finality that in some of the most controversial and sensitive public issues the executive was politically immobilized.

Yet even the strictest of instructions would not have been burdensome to the governors if they had had the equipment they needed, and which the government at home had in such abundance, to deal effectively with the opposition.

The armory of political weapons so essential to the successful operation of the government of Walpole was reduced in the colonies to a mere quiverful of frail and flawed arrows.

Patronage was potentially the most effective weapon of all, and at the beginning of the eighteenth century the patronage available to the governors was not negligible. In the course of half a century, however, it was so ground away by forces at either extreme of the political spectrum that ultimately the governors were left, in the words of one highly placed official, "without the means of stopping the mouths of the demagogues." The expanding patronage network of England took over a number of key appointments: those of the colonial attorneys general, auditors general, receivers general, and at times the clerks of the Assemblies; later the disposal of the lucrative post of naval officer was taken over too. At the same time the colonial Assemblies took over appointments of officers of the militia, limited the governors' power over sheriffs, and monopolized the important office of colony treasurer.

By all of this the colonial governors were stripped of much of the power of patronage by which in Britain the administration could discipline dissent within the political community and maintain its dominance within Parliament. But it was not the existence of patronage alone that in Britain gave the administration its unique political advantage. The highly irregular, inequitable, and hence easily manipulated electoral system contributed greatly; and this too was absent in America.

There were no rotten boroughs in the colonies. No Assembly seats were owned outright by the government, and there were no defunct constituencies easily manipulated by the administration, for there had been no gradual accumulation of "liberties" bestowed in ancient times in recognition of once active but long since extinct political forces. While in England the House of Commons was frozen in composition throughout the eighteenth century, most of the colonial Assemblies, which were created at a stroke on general principles that implied unlimited growth — so many delegates per unit of local government — were continually expanding. So normal had the expectation of expansion become by mid-century that when governors, fearing the total eclipse of their influence in the legislatures by virtue of the increasing numbers of the country delegates, tried to stop the multiplication of constituencies and seats they found themselves involved in serious political struggles. What is important is not that by enlightened twentieth-century American standards apportionment was here and there inequitable, but that by normal eighteenth-century standards it was so remarkably equitable, adjusted to the growth and spread of population and relatively insensitive, as a consequence, to pressure from an embattled executive.

Apportionment was only one aspect of representation that created difficulties for the governors. Other practices created additional problems. From the earliest years it had been common in Massachusetts for towns to instruct their representatives on how to act in the General Court in regard to controversial issues, and this practice continued irregularly into the eighteenth century, used when the localities were committed to particular views they wished to have represented no matter what influence was brought to bear against them. Elsewhere, too, representatives were instructed on delicate issues, and often when delegates were not instructed they themselves postponed acting until—as in New York in 1734—"they had taken the sentiments of their constituents." Further, delegates were often required to be residents of the communities they represented at the time of their incumbency. Residential requirements had not been common in the colonies in the seventeenth century, but such provision increasingly appeared on the statutes. The result, the eighteenth-century historian William Smith wrote, was that the Assemblies seemed to be composed "of plain, illiterate husbandmen, whose views seldom extended farther than to the regulation of highways, the destruction of wolves, wildcats, and foxes, and the advancement of the other little interests of the particular counties which they were chosen to represent." Residential requirements were not universal in the eighteenth-century colonies, but they were common enough to contribute measurably to the enfeeblement of "influence."

But of all the underlying characteristics that distinguished politics in America

THE VIRGINIA HOUSE OF BURGESSES

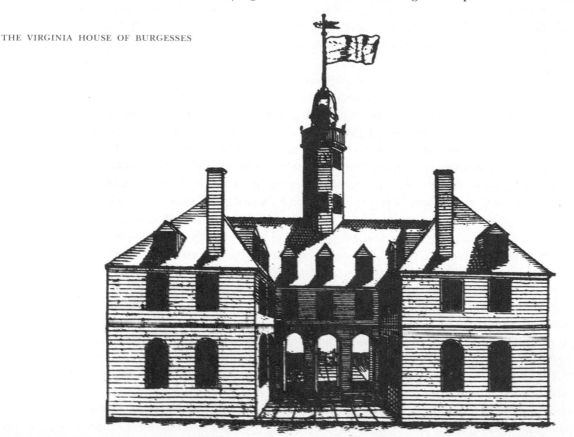

from the English model, the sheer number of those who could vote was perhaps the most dramatic. A broad franchise had not originally been planned or desired; indeed, when it appeared, it was not wholly understood for what it implied, nor used for political advantage to the extent that it might have been. Most colonies sought to do no more than re-create, or adapt with minor variations, the 40s. (forty-shilling) freehold qualification that had prevailed in the county constituencies of England for 300 years. But if ownership of land worth 40s. a year was a restrictive qualification in England, it was permissive in the colonies where freehold tenure was widespread among the white population. So ineffective was this traditional definition in excluding from voting those who appeared to be, in the jurist William Blackstone's universally approved words, "in so mean a situation as to be esteemed to have no will of their own," that most colonies went on to specify the restriction more elaborately. But everywhere the effect was to broaden the franchise rather than restrict it further. Some colonies defined the requirement in terms of acreage: in Virginia 100 acres unsettled, or 25 acres settled; in North Carolina and Georgia, 50 acres whether settled or unsettled. In other colonies permanent or even lifetime leases were declared to be as valid for the franchise as freehold property, and in some, personal property of any description, worth in some places forty, in others fifty, pounds, was allowed to serve as qualification. Inflation of local currency values further eased the restrictions of franchise qualification. In Rhode Island a £400 property "restriction," measured in local paper money, opened the franchise to 75 percent of the colony's adult males. To the disgusted Governor Thomas Hutchinson in Massachusetts, it seemed that "anything with the appearance of a man" was allowed to vote.

Generalizing across the variety of statutory provisions and practices of the various colonies, one can safely say that 50–75 percent of the adult male white population was entitled to vote—far more than could do so in Britain, and far more too, it appears, than wished to do so in the colonies themselves. Apathy in elections was common for several reasons. Besides the physical difficulty of traveling to polling places, there was a lack of real alternatives in this society dominated by the sense that the natural social leaders of society should be the political leaders. There was also a lack, in certain periods and places, of issues that seemed properly determinable at the polls. However neglected, the broad franchise was potentially a powerful weapon, certain to work against the ability of the executives to control elections and voting in the Assemblies for the interest of the state.

Given these circumstances, and in addition the uncertainty of the governors' own tenure of office and the capacity of their opponents to bypass the entire ramshackle imperial administration and appeal directly to the higher authorities in England, it is little wonder that the governors were helpless before a determined opposition and that the shifting social and economic forces in the quickly developing colonies produced a milling factionalism in politics.

The overall configuration of early American politics was a patchwork of con-

traditions. There was a firmly rooted belief that the colonial constitutions corresponded in their essentials to the English model of mixed government. That
assumption was violated, however, first, by what were believed to be excessive
powers in the hands of the executive, and second, by the absence in the colonies
of the devices by which in Britain the executive maintained discipline, control,
and stability in politics. Swollen claims and shrunken powers, especially when
they occur together, are always sources of trouble, and the political trouble that
resulted from this combination can be traced through the history of eighteenth-
century politics.

But the structure of American politics in the eighteenth century is not wholly
revealed in this. The nature of leadership too was a source of controversy.
Americans, like all Britons—indeed, like all Europeans of the eighteenth century
—assumed that political leadership was only one of a number of expressions of
leadership within society, and that in the nature of things those who enjoyed
superiority in one sphere would enjoy and exercise it in another. In the society
of stratified "dignities" (if not classes) still considered in the eighteenth century
to be normal or ideal, political leadership was expected to devolve on the natural
social leaders of the community, whose identity, it was assumed, would be steadily
and incontestably visible. And so indeed it was in America—in *some* of the colonies, in *certain* respects, at *certain* times.

In Virginia in the three generations that followed Bacon's Rebellion, a hierarchy of the plantation gentry emerged in stable form, dominated by social
and economic leaders whose roots could be traced back to the 1650s and whose
dominance in politics was largely uncontested. So too in Connecticut, a landed
gentry of "ancient" families consolidated its control in the early eighteenth century and came to dominate the political life of the colony. But even in these extreme examples there were premonitions of disturbances to come—in Virginia,
in the expansion of settlement in the west and the establishment there of new
figures of potential power and of distinctive religious interests; in Connecticut,
the growth of religious radicalism, especially in the eastern counties, which were
already nervous and unsettled as a result of the leanness of the agricultural economy and of the frustrated desire for geographical expansion.

Yet Virginia and Connecticut were colonies of the greatest stability. Elsewhere
the identity of the natural political leaders remained as it had been in the late
seventeenth century, a matter of controversy, at times the source of fierce political struggles. New figures appeared overnight, from nowhere and everywhere,
to enter the arena of politics. And always there were alien elements introduced
into the top of the political hierarchy in the form of officials sent from England in
positions of high authority.

These were the shaping elements of those "noisy dissatisfactions" that so
plagued the tranquillity of governors in eighteenth-century America. The political system was troubled and contentious—a brawling factional system in which
the will and dignity of the ill-organized imperial state embodied in harassed and

often ineffective governors were openly attacked by opposition groups. It was a free competitive politics that was the very opposite of the immobile, bureaucratized state system that prevailed in the colonies of Spain's American empire.

Such was American society in the eighteenth century, a strange society caught between traditional institutions and ways of thinking and unexpected circumstances. A motley, polyglot population lived in a community that did not recognize cultural pluralism ideologically or legally or conceive of terms by which an alien race could coexist with the dominant British except in constant conflict or absolute subjection. While one-fifth of the population was held in chattel slavery and enjoyed no more of the world's goods than well-cared-for animals, the rest enjoyed a level of affluence unknown to any other general population in the Western world. Social institutions that presumed demographic stability were subjected to extreme pressures of population growth. Land was widely distributed in freehold tenure, though efforts were repeatedly made to re-create a traditional landlord class, and tenancy was just as likely to foster land speculation, itself a new relation between individuals and the land, as to provide income for a leisured landed gentry. Transoceanic commerce was increasingly dominated by a merchant class tied securely to a traditional commercial oligarchy in Britain, but the established merchants were beset on all sides by irrepressible competition generated by the swift, uneven growth of an uncontrolled economy. Religious organization, still traditional in concept and doctrine, was so deeply eroded by altered circumstance that it seemed transformed even before the Great Awakening reduced what remained of familiar forms to an almost unrecognizable disorder. And politics was an open competition for place, profit, and power fought out within a culture that condemned factionalism as seditious and that assumed that the state was in some sense sanctified and above mere factional contention.

It was a strange world, full of incongruities, but it was moving toward a resolution of its most glaring inconsistencies.

Suggested Readings

There are several useful general surveys of eighteenth-century American society. The most valuable introduction, combining narrative and analysis, remains James T. Adams, *Provincial Society, 1690–1763* (1927); though out of date on certain matters, it touches on all major topics, includes a great deal of basic information, and conceives of society in structural and organizational terms. Lawrence H. Gipson's *British Empire before the American Revolution*, vols. II and III (1936) provides a comprehensive description from literary sources of the colonies in the years 1748–1754 and includes a full bibliography in the annotation. Volumes IV and V (1939–1942) survey the frontier areas in dispute with Spain and France and also the Caribbean colonies. An effort, the first of its kind, to bring together into a general picture the recent findings on social organization and economic development is James A. Henretta, *The Evolution of American Society, 1700–1815* (1973), chaps. i–iv. Daniel J. Boorstin's *The Americans: the Colonial Experience* (1958) is a highly personal analysis of eighteenth-century American culture, styles of life, learning, and artistic expression. Boorstin's analysis of the professions in colonial America is particularly valuable. Max Savelle, *Seeds of Liberty* (1948) is a survey of intellectual history and the fine arts.

On the eighteenth-century population, see Robert V. Wells, *The Population of the British Colonies in America before 1776* (1975), which analyses the surviving censuses. Information in Greene and Harrington, *American Population* (referred to for chap. 3) and in Stella H. Sutherland, *Population Distribution in Colonial America* (1936) remains useful. Of the new immigrations, the Irish are described in R. J. Dickson, *Ulster Immigration to Colonial America* (1966) and Wayland F. Dunaway, *The Scotch-Irish of Colonial Pennsylvania* (1944); the Germans in Albert B. Faust, *The German Element in the United States* (2 vols., 1909), F. R. Diffenderfer, *The German Immigration . . .* (1900), and Gillian L. Gollin, *Moravians in Two Worlds* (1967); the Scottish in Ian C. C. Graham, *Colonists from Scotland* (1956); and the Africans in Philip D. Curtin, *The Atlantic Slave Trade* (1969). There is very little, however, on the life of the slaves in America, aside from Peter Wood, *Black Majority* (1974) on South Carolina to 1739, and Gerald W. Mullin, *Flight and Rebellion* (1972) on slave resistance in Virginia. Winthrop D. Jordan, *White over Black* (1968), Parts I, II, scrutinizes white attitudes toward blacks. On naturalization, see Edward A. Hoyt, "Naturalization under the American Colonies," *Political Science Quarterly*, 67 (1952), 248–66, and James H. Kettner's forthcoming book, *The Development of American Citizenship, 1608–1870*.

On landowning and agriculture, see Lewis C. Gray, *History of Agriculture in the Southern United States to 1860* (2 vols., 1933) and Percy W. Bidwell and John I. Falconer's parallel book on the North. A broad survey of the opening of new frontier lands in the tradition of Frederick Jackson Turner is Ray A. Billington, *Westward Expansion* (1949), chaps. v–viii, which contains an exhaustive bibliography of writings on the westward movement. A case study of the opening of new townships in New England, contradicting the Turner view on many points, is Charles S. Grant, *Democracy in the Connecticut Frontier Town of Kent* (1961). On the opening of the land in Pennsylvania, see James T. Lemon, *The Best Poor Man's Country* (1972); on land utilization in North Carolina, Harry T. Merrens, *Colonial North Carolina* (1964).

Of the exceptions to freehold tenure discussed in this chapter, there is an excellent essay on the old proprietary estates: Rowland Berthoff and John M. Murrin, "Feudalism, Communalism, and the Yeoman Freeholder . . . ," Stephen G. Kurtz and James H. Hutson, eds., *Essays on the American Revolution* (1973). On tenancy, see Willard F. Bliss, "Rise of Tenancy in Virginia," *Virginia Magazine of History and Biography*, 58 (1950), 427–41 and Clarence P. Gould, *Land System in Maryland, 1720–1765* (1913). Plantation life and the harassed role of the large planters are vividly portrayed in Jack P. Greene, ed., *Diary of Colonel Landon Carter* (2 vols., 1965). The condition of ordinary planters is described in Aubrey C. Land, "Economic Behavior in a Planting Society . . . ," *Journal of Social History*, 33 (1967), 469–85 and "Economic Base and Social Structure . . . ," *Journal of Economic History*, 25 (1965), 639–54.* On the role of the Scottish merchants in transforming the marketing of tobacco, see Jacob M. Price, "The Rise of Glasgow in the Chesapeake Tobacco Trade," *Wm. and Mary Q.*, 11 (1954), 179–99, and on marketing in general, "Economic Growth of the Chesapeake and the European Markets, 1697–1775," *Journal of Economic History*, 24 (1964), 496–511, as well as Price's *France and the Chesapeake* (2 vols., 1973). On the difficulties of the New York landlords, see Irving Mark, *Agrarian Conflicts in Colonial New York* (1940) and Patricia U. Bonomi, *A Factious People* (1971), chap. vi.

On commerce generally, besides Emory R. Johnson, *et al.*, *History of Domestic and Foreign Commerce* (1915), see James F. Shepherd and Gary M. Walton, *Shipping, Maritime Trade, and the Economic Development of Colonial North America* (1972), a technical study with elaborate statistics on 1768–72. Arthur L. Jensen, *Maritime Commerce of Colonial Philadelphia* (1963) is an excellent account. Richard Pares, *Yankees and Creoles* (1956) and Richard B. Sheridan, *Sugar and Slavery . . . the British West Indies, 1623–1775* (1974) cover the Caribbean trade; on the timber trade and fisheries, see Joseph J. Malone, *Pine Trees and Politics* (1964) and Harold A. Innis, *The Cod Fisheries* (1940). Perhaps the best insight into the workings of commerce is provided by studies of individual merchants. There are accounts of the Hancocks by W. T. Baxter, of the Beekmans of New York by Philip L. White, of the Pepperrells by Byron Fairchild, and of the Browns of Rhode Island (a particularly vivid example of social and occupational mobility) by James B. Hedges. Life in the port towns is described in Carl Bridenbaugh, *Cities in the Wilderness* (1938), *Cities in Revolt* (1955), and *Rebels and Gentlemen: Philadelphia* . . . (1942); in Richard B. Morris, *Government and Labor in Early America* (1946); and in Gary B. Nash, "Urban Wealth and Poverty in Pre-Revolutionary America," *Journal of Interdisciplinary History*, 6 (1976), 545–84. Alice H. Jones has published the wealth estimates referred to in the text, in *Economic Development and Cultural Change*, 18, no. 4, Part II (1970) and *Journal of Economic History*, 32 (1972), 98–127.

Eighteenth-century religion is summarized in Sydney E. Ahlstrom, *Religious History of the American People* (1972), Part III. Central developments in New England are traced in Perry Miller, *New England Mind: From Colony to Province* (1953); Robert G. Pope, *The Half-Way Covenant* (1969); Robert Middlekauff, *The Mathers* (1971); Ola Winslow, *Meetinghouse Hill* (1952), and James W. Jones, *The Shattered Synthesis* (1973). There is a large literature on the Great Awakening, much of it brought together into a single brief book, J. M. Bumsted and John E. Van de Wetering, *What Must I Do To Be Saved?* (1976), which contains a good bibliography. The major works are: Edwin S. Gaustad, *Great Awakening in New England* (1957); Wesley M. Gewehr, *Great Awakening in Virginia* (1930); Charles H. Maxson, *Great Awakening in the Middle Colonies* (1920); Richard L. Bushman, *From Puritan to Yankee* (1967); C. C. Goen, *Revivalism and Separatism* (1962); and William G. McLoughlin, *New England Dissent* (2 vols., 1971). Excellent also on the complicated awakenings in the middle colonies are Leonard J. Trinterud, *Forming an American Tradition* . . . *Presbyterianism* (1949) and Martin E. Lodge, "The Crisis of the Churches in the Middle Colonies, 1720–1750," *Pennsylvania Magazine of History and Biography*, 95 (1971), 195–220. There are documentary collections on the awakenings by Richard L. Bushman and by Alan Heimert and Perry Miller; biographies of Jonathan Edwards by Miller (1949), Ola E. Winslow (1940), and Edward H. Davidson (1968); of Whitefield, by Stuart C. Henry (1957); and of the important Baptist leader Isaac Backus, by William G. McLoughlin (1967). Evarts B. Greene, *Religion and the State* (1941) and William G. McLoughlin, "Isaac Backus and the Separation of Church and State," *American Historical Review*, 72 (1968), 1392–1413 show the colonial origins of American church-state relations.

The operation of the imperial government is described fully in Leonard W. Labaree, *Royal Government in America* (1930) and Jack P. Greene, *The Quest for Power* (1963); but politics, though intimately related to government, is a different matter. Bernard Bailyn, *Origins of American Politics* (1968) is an effort at a general interpretation, stressing the relations between formal and informal organizations and between political activities and political beliefs. The role of colonial offices in the British patronage system is explained from the British point of view in James A. Henretta, *"Salutary Neglect"* (1972) and in Alison G. Olson and Richard M. Brown, eds., *Anglo-American Political Relations, 1675–1775* (1970) and from the American point of view in Stanley N. Katz, *Newcastle's New York* (1968). Michael Kammen, *Empire and Interest* (1970) is an exceptionally imaginative effort to show the changing ways in which the British political system accommodated the interests of economic and political groups in Britain and America.

Of the many thorough studies of the politics of individual colonies, several are outstanding: Bonomi, *A Factious People*; Robert Zemsky, *Merchants, Farmers, and River Gods* (1971); Charles Barker, *Background of the Revolution in Maryland* (1940); and M. Eugene Sirmans, *Colonial South Carolina* (1966). J. R. Pole, *Political Representation* (1966) covers both England and America throughout the eighteenth century.

6

The Enlightenment's New World

In 1760, when the young George III ascended the throne of Great Britain, Americans like Britons everywhere joined in the celebrations enthusiastically. Not only had the nonslave population of the colonies enjoyed with Britain the freest political conditions of the Western world, and not only had the colonists shared, though erratically, in Britain's rising prosperity, but they had participated too in Britain's recent military victories over the perennial enemy, France. Now, released from the immediate pressure of frontier wars and aware as never before of the richness of the land that lay to the west, they glimpsed a future that could be prosperous and free beyond all earlier expectations. One could reasonably conceive, the Boston preacher Jonathan Mayhew said in 1759, of "a mighty empire" in British America "(I do not mean an independent one) in numbers little inferior perhaps to the greatest in Europe, and in felicity to none." One could picture, he said, cities "rising on every hill . . . happy fields and villages . . . [and] religion professed and practiced throughout this spacious kingdom in far greater purity and perfection than since the times of the apostles."

Mayhew's buoyant sense of America's prospects as part of the British world was shared in varying degrees by many others. But beneath the glowing surface there were dark undertones in Anglo-American relations that had been developing through all the years of mutual growth and pragmatic accommodation. These countercurrents had no predictable or inevitable outcome. They could as reasonably have grown into a pattern of stable and peaceable relations as become sources of serious disruption. The future would depend on the ability of men in power to understand and manage the complex problems that faced them. In retrospect, however, one thing is clear. These latent antagonisms, rooted at three levels in the substratum of Anglo-American life, were like buried traps: to ignore them was to risk disaster.

"Rule Britannia"

At the most obvious level were the antagonisms generated by the war efforts of the mid–eighteenth century.

During the years after 1713, Britain engaged in three wars with European powers, and the colonies were involved in varying degrees in all of them. The first, the so-called War of Jenkins' Ear (1739–42) was fought with Spain over trading rights in the Caribbean and Central America. In the peace treaty of 1713 ending the War of Spanish Succession Britain had been granted the privilege of selling a limited number of slaves and a specified quantity of goods in the Spanish West Indies. The legitimate presence of British trading vessels in these otherwise closed markets had encouraged smuggling, which was countered by mutual rights of search. Spain's brutal handling of these shipboard searches had been no more improper or illegal than the British smuggling, but it had outraged British public opinion. When a certain Captain Robert Jenkins presented to a parliamentary committee one of his ears, which he said had been cut off by the Spanish seven years earlier as a punishment for smuggling, Parliament demanded a war of revenge for such atrocities, which the head of the government, Robert Walpole, who wished above all to avoid war, could not refuse.

The war, which ranged widely, was fought at first in the Western Hemisphere. A makeshift army of South Carolina and Georgia troops invaded Florida but failed to capture Saint Augustine or to relieve the pressure on the southern frontier, and the action turned to the Caribbean. There the main effort was an assault on the Spanish town of Cartagena, on the Colombian coast, for which an American regiment of 3500 men was recruited, to serve under British commanders. That campaign, in 1741, was a ghastly failure. A hopelessly slow and ill-mounted attack on the fort led to the butchery of the American troops, which was succeeded by an epidemic of yellow fever and a loss of supplies. After further failures in Cuba, the remains of the expedition, which had been largely financed as well as manned by the colonies, staggered home. The losses were shocking. Only 600 Americans survived, and they brought back with them a bitter resentment at the callousness, incompetence, and superciliousness of the British military commanders. Thirty years later Americans still recalled the agonies their countrymen had endured on this senseless campaign and the appalling waste of lives and goods.

By then the war had broadened into a general European conflict. In 1740 the young Maria Theresa had succeeded to the throne of Austria, and Frederick of Prussia had taken advantage of her inexperience to seize the Austrian province of Silesia. Britain, already at war with Spain in America, went to Austria's aid, and France joined Spain, hoping to gain Belgium for its trouble. The mere threat of French domination in Europe was intolerable to Britain. Ever fearful of a single continental power controlling Europe, Britain brought the Spanish war to a conclusion after fighting off a major Spanish attack on Georgia and South Carolina and in 1744 declared war on France. This complicated series of struggles was known in Europe as the War of Austrian Succession (1740–48) and in America as King George's War (1744–48). While its conclusion in the Treaty of Aix-la-Chapelle was no more than a truce to allow for recuperation, it left yet another source of resentment between Britain and the colonies in its abandonment of an important American victory.

SIR WILLIAM PEPPERRELL, 1747, BY JOHN SMIBERT

Pepperrell is posed on a hill overlooking Louisbourg, to which he points and into which two cannon balls are gracefully falling. An engraving of this painting of the popular hero was promptly made for wide distribution. *(Courtesy, Essex Institute, Salem, Mass.)*

The focus of conflict in the Western Hemisphere during this war was the French naval station at Louisbourg, a massive fortification on Cape Breton Island just north of Nova Scotia, which guarded the entrance to the Saint Lawrence River, sheltered French privateers, and controlled the rich fishing waters between mainland North America and Newfoundland. When Governor William Shirley of Massachusetts heard that its garrison was undermanned and dispirited and its fortifications in disrepair, he rallied support from the Massachusetts merchant community and persuaded the General Court to finance an expedition to capture the citadel. Equipment and troops were gathered from all over New England and from colonies as far south as Pennsylvania, arrangements were made for British naval support under the New Yorker, Commodore Peter Warren, and the troop command was given to a popular Maine merchant and militia colonel, William Pepperrell.

As the transports, warships, supplies, and men gathered in Boston, the campaign, in the aftermath of the Great Awakening, took on the air of a festive crusade. The clergy preached fire and destruction to the French "papists" and their pagan Indian allies. In April 1745 four thousand New England troops landed safely near the fortress of Louisbourg, turned the cannons of a captured defense battery against the central fortification, and attacked, not by sea, as the French had expected, but by weakly defended land approaches. The French held off the attackers through all of April and May while the New Englanders—who were not soldiers but undisciplined farmers, fishermen, and town workers—bumbled and stumbled their way to control of the harbor islands. Just as Warren was preparing to land an untrained amphibious force to take the partly demolished fortress, the French, hopelessly outnumbered and lacking food supplies and naval support, surrendered. On June 17 the "Gibraltar of the New World" was handed over to Pepperrell.

For New England, indeed for all of America, it was a glorious victory. Warren, who made a fortune from his capture of French merchant ships, was promoted to admiral; Pepperrell was knighted. But the war was far from over. Disease decimated the troops occupying Louisbourg, and the frontiers from Maine to New York were set aflame in savage raids. Border garrisons in Vermont, western Massachusetts, and New York were attacked, captured, retaken, and attacked again. Massachusetts, promised repayment by Parliament for its expenses in capturing Louisbourg, planned a massive assault on Quebec and then abandoned it when news arrived of a large French expedition moving to recover Louisbourg. And though that French fleet, scattered by storms and swept by disease, never made contact with the fortress, and though another French fleet on the same mission was captured by Warren, the raids continued and spilled over into Nova Scotia. In 1747 the British commanders finally induced the Iroquois to join in an attack on French positions along Lake Champlain and in Canada, but the makeshift New York army dissolved before it could get under way. The war disintegrated into miscellaneous violence. Isolated towns and farmhouses were burned and their inhabitants slaughtered, though the butchery could make no possible difference to the outcome. Prisoners were taken, then exchanged. Grand campaigns were hatched with Indian allies then dissolved before any action could be taken and for reasons that could not be clearly explained. Spain's raids on several forts along the southern British coast were equally inconclusive and equally ill designed to affect the outcome of the war.

Nothing substantial had been accomplished when in December 1748 news arrived that peace had been concluded in Europe. It brought relief from bloodshed but otherwise very little satisfaction in America, for in exchange for the return of Madras in India, which France had taken, England returned Louisbourg, the symbol of American military pride, to the French. Five hundred Americans had died in action to accomplish nothing, and twice that many had been killed by disease, exposure, and accidents. The return of Louisbourg would be recalled along with bitter memories of the Cartagena expedition—and with the memories of another famous episode of King George's War. In 1747 Commodore Knowles's naval press gangs had attempted, in the fashion of the time, to shanghai likely recruits for the royal navy on the streets of Boston. But Boston, he discovered, was not London. To his amazement, his men were fought off by an incensed mob in one of the most violent town riots of the pre-Revolutionary years. The townsmen's rampage against this flagrant though traditional invasion of civilian rights lasted for four days, and it remained a living memory for a generation to come.

The third and last of these pre-Revolutionary wars followed in part the pattern of the others. This time, however, America was the central theater of war, not a marginal one; this time too the outcome was conclusive, and the resentment generated between Britain and the colonies was of a different order of magnitude.

FRANKLIN'S SNAKE DEVICE, 1754

This famous emblem, first published by Franklin just before the meeting of the Albany Congress, was reprinted with variations throughout the colonies and became a symbol of resistance to Britain in the years preceding the Revolution. *(Historical Society of Pennsylvania.)*

The immediate cause of the Seven Years War (1756–63), known in the colonies as the French and Indian War, was a series of clashes between French army units on the one hand and Virginians on the other. The French units were trying to secure the Ohio River valley for France by establishing a string of forts there. The Virginians had claims to this territory that went back to the original charter, and these were now being advanced by a powerful group of land speculators. The French repulsed the Virginians' efforts to found a British fort at the strategic junction of the Ohio, Allegheny, and Monongahela rivers and established their own Fort Duquesne there instead. A small force under Major George Washington failed to dislodge them. Anticipating a scale of conflict greater than that of any of the previous wars, representatives of seven colonies met at Albany in 1754 in a fruitless effort to coordinate defense plans among themselves and

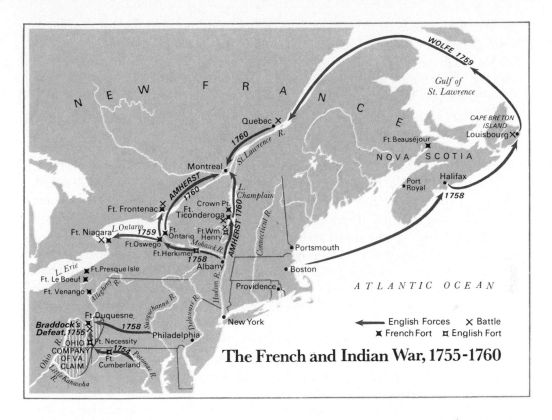

The French and Indian War, 1755-1760

with their Indian allies. Though they adopted in principle Benjamin Franklin's proposal for a political and military union of the colonies, they could not convince a single colonial assembly to ratify the detailed plan for a general government that was drawn up. Meanwhile the British government moved ahead with a design for a large-scale war that involved dispatching to America a large army, enlisting colonial troops in a complex military organization, and collecting in America quantities of provisions and equipment. Early in 1755, Major General Edward Braddock, an arrogant disciplinarian with little sympathy for difficult colonials and no sense of how to handle them, arrived with the advance regiments. He undertook, in the wilderness of western Pennsylvania, the first engagement in a war that was not formally declared until May 1756 but that, once declared, spread quickly to all points of contact among the major European powers—not only in Europe, America, and the Caribbean but in Africa, India, and the Philippines as well.

For two years the British suffered defeat after defeat. Braddock's army, moving west to eliminate Fort Duquesne, fell into confusion at the first, accidental contact with the enemy and was almost annihilated by a small French and Indian force hidden along the sides of the road. There were 1000 casualties in an army of 1400; only 23 of 86 officers survived. Washington, who helped lead the pell-mell retreat, buried Braddock in the road to keep his grave from being discovered.

To the north, Nova Scotia, whose boundaries were disputed and whose native Acadians were either pro-French or unreliably neutral, had to be retaken by the British; 6000 of the Acadians were rounded up and deported to the thirteen colonies. But though this action isolated Cape Breton and its fortress of Louisbourg, the effort by the new commander-in-chief, Lord Loudon, to capture that citadel in 1757 failed. So too did Governor Shirley's ambitious effort to force the French from the arc of forts that formed the northwest boundaries of the British colonies. Instead of the British taking the two French forts—Frontenac and Niagara—on Lake Ontario, the French under the adroit commander Montcalm took the British fort, Oswego, on the eastern side of the lake, and killed over 80 of the British after they had surrendered. Then, secure in Crown Point on Lake Champlain, the French moved deeper into New York by establishing Fort Ticonderoga to the south and in August 1757 seized Fort William Henry even farther to the south, on Lake George. Of the 2000 British who surrendered at William Henry, 200 were killed by France's Indian allies and 200 more were taken off into Indian territory as captives. But even this was not the end of the disasters. While in Europe, where Austria and Prussia had reversed sides, French and Austrian armies overran Britain's client state Hannover and threatened Prussia, the French on the American frontier penetrated to Fort Herkimer on the Mohawk River and murdered 50 of the noncombatant German farmers who lived around the fort. The whole of central New York and western New England was exposed; Albany seemed doomed.

It was at this absolute low point in British fortunes that the planning of that strange, brilliant, imaginative, half-mystical, and neurotic war minister, William Pitt, began to have its effect. Appointed secretary of state in 1757 and possessing a vision of imperial greatness that was unique for the time, Pitt conceived of something akin to a total war, with concentration on a set of coordinated American campaigns. He demanded huge government expenditures, heavy subsidies for the European allies to neutralize that zone, and large commitments by the colonies, to be financed by Parliament. He conceived of an American army of 24,000 regulars and 25,000 provincials—a very large force for the time.

Passing over established but ineffective generals in favor of younger and more energetic commanders, he launched a series of efforts to break the French arc of forts north and west of the mainland colonies. The first of his plans—an attack on Ticonderoga in July 1758—failed miserably. But that was his only failure. Later the same month, a force of 9000 regulars and 500 provincials under the young General Jeffrey Amherst and the thin, sickly, but tigerish Brigadier James Wolfe, only thirty-one years old, took Louisbourg. A month later, in a swift raid, the British swept over the critical supply depot and transfer point of Fort Frontenac, the link between the Saint Lawrence River and the French posts to the farther west and south, and with it seized control of Lake Ontario. In November a mixed force led by three excellent commanders including Colonel Washington finally redeemed Braddock's defeat by forcing the French from Fort Duquesne, thereby seizing for Britain the entire upper Ohio valley.

By early 1759, the year of Britain's greatest victories, the iron ring around the northern British colonies had been broken at three critical points: on the east (Louisbourg and Nova Scotia), the west (Frontenac and Lake Ontario), and the south (Duquesne). And there were successes not only in America but in India and Africa and at sea. Then Pitt, riding the crest of great popularity at home, planned the kill. Canada was to be sealed off in the far West by the capture of Fort Niagara; General Amherst was to invade Canada by way of Lake Champlain and the Saint Lawrence valley; and Wolfe was to take Quebec in an amphibious expedition moving west up the Saint Lawrence River. For all of this, a fortune in supplies, transports, and firearms, in addition to three large armies with substantial naval support, was required.

Somehow, these great demands were met. In July 1759 Fort Niagara, linking New France to the far West, was captured. At the same time the French destroyed and withdrew from Ticonderoga and Crown Point, leaving them to Amherst, though by the time his troops had rebuilt these forts it was too late for him to proceed with the planned thrust into Canada from the south. But Wolfe, in one of the best-organized, most daring, and luckiest exploits in British military history, succeeded in his assigned task in Pitt's strategy.

A VIEW OF THE TAKING OF QUEBEC, SEPTEMBER 13, 1759

This detail of a print of 1760 telescopes the debarking of the troops, their dislodging of the French defenders of the cliffside trail, and the final battle on the Plains of Abraham. (*Royal Ontario Museum, Toronto.*)

Moving almost 10,000 men in over 200 warships and transports to Quebec without serious loss, Wolfe fumbled for over seven weeks seeking a way to penetrate the heavily fortified city built atop the 150-foot cliffs that form the north shore of the Saint Lawrence at that point. Unable to devise a strategy of his own that would work, he agreed to one submitted by his subordinates, but himself discovered a crucial roadway running diagonally up the cliffside several miles west of the city. Through this access, on the night of September 12, 1759, he led 4500 men up the cliff and into battle formation on the Plains of Abraham just west of the city. When the French, without waiting for reinforcements, charged the carefully disposed British army rather wildly, they were met with a disciplined and efficient barrage that broke their ranks, and they were driven from the field defeated. Among the relatively few British casualties (60 dead, 600 wounded) was Wolfe; among the French, Montcalm. On September 17, Quebec surrendered.

A year later Amherst's army, moving north and east from the lakes, converged on Montreal and with contingents from Quebec forced the French governor to surrender the whole of New France. In the final peace treaty of 1763, Britain gained undisputed possession of all of North America east of the Mississippi save for New Orleans, including all of Nova Scotia and all of Canada. Furthermore, Spain, which had entered the war only in 1761, was forced to concede Florida to Britain in exchange for the return of Cuba, which a British expedition had captured in 1762; Spain's compensations were New Orleans and the land west of the Mississippi, which France had rashly pledged to Spain as a reward for its entry into the war.

It was a great triumph of British arms, and it was matched by other British successes all over the world. But there were serious hidden costs. The most obvious was the huge debt that England acquired in prosecuting the war, which set in motion a reaction against grand and costly overseas adventures (Pitt was forced to resign in 1761) and would lead the government of George III to consider new forms of taxation. Less obvious was the immediate effect of the war on Anglo-American relations. While Americans rejoiced in the victory and for the first time in their history were relieved of the threat of French and Spanish stimulation of Indian attacks on the frontiers, they learned to fear the presence of large professional armies and to insist that militias alone were forces compatible with liberty. They learned, too, to an extent they had not before, that, though they were British, they were somehow a separate people, yet not an inferior people as the professional army commanders under whom they fought so often seemed to assume. For through all these wars—from the catastrophe before Cartagena to the triumph on the Plains of Abraham—they experienced the arrogance, indifference, and often the stupidity of an officer class that was a traditional part of European life, reinforced by the social structure of Europe, but alien, abrasive, and in the end intolerable in America.

Beyond all of that there were resentments at the imperial regulations—some of them newly devised, some newly enforced during the French and Indian war. As part of his program for a total national effort, Pitt sought to eliminate all violations of the navigation acts, all smuggling, indeed all commercial contact with the enemy that might bolster his economy or help supply his troops. It was not an altogether new program. As early as 1756, the Privy Council had ordered the colonial governors to enforce the strict letter of the law and to eliminate the trade with the enemy that was well known to be taking place in neutral ports. In pursuit of these goals and in support of the efforts of the customs officials, the highest colonial courts had issued writs of assistance to customs officials. These general warrants, authorizing customs officers to command the assistance of court officials in searching for smuggled goods, were granted by the high court of Massachusetts in 1755, 1758, 1759, and 1760, and were valid throughout the lifetime of the reigning sovereign. They served their purpose well, but they were deeply resented by the merchant community, which was determined to seek relief when the opportunity arose.

Pitt's fierce insistence on enforcing the law elevated all of these efforts to a new level. In the course of his brief but powerful ministry he issued stringent orders and memoranda that closed loopholes in the regulations, brought the complex rules together into an integrated whole, and fixed responsibility for negligence. Governors were drawn directly into the business of imperial law enforcement and the navy became a more effective police arm than it had been before. Conflict was implicit in all of this. Well before 1763 certain merchants and politicians, drawn into antagonism with the imperial establishment, were learning to use the language of resistance available to them in British political culture and were beginning to question the value of a connection of which they suddenly seemed to be victims.

Yet all of this was but the tip of an iceberg. Attempts to enforce the mercantilist system during the last colonial war brought to the surface of public controversy a group of conflicts that had been built into the very structure of the imperial relation but had been hidden and submerged for a full generation.

The Alienation of the State

Long before Pitt was even involved in public affairs, three problems had arisen in Anglo-American relations that had not been solved but merely put off, patched up with makeshift solutions, and then ignored. They could be ignored because they had developed largely as a consequence of the mercantilist system, which formed the essential structure of imperial relations. So long as that system was not rigidly enforced the pressure of these problems was slight. The problems remained nevertheless, and there was a price to be paid for evasion and neglect. Even in their moderated form they created a distance, an alienation, between Britain and America, and that alienation was as much a part of the Anglo-

American world in 1760 as the universal welcome accorded the young monarch, George III.

The first of these problems arose from the fact that the rapidly increasing American population created a growing market for British goods which was not matched by an equivalent growth of a market within Britain itself for the products that the colonies could export. Through the early years of the eighteenth century, the American deficit in trade with Britain was moderate, and payments were easily balanced. But by the 1730s American consumption of British goods rose well beyond the colonists' capacity to pay for them through exchanges with Britain. By the end of the period the colonists were running a trade deficit with England of close to £1,000,000 a year, and the problem of repayment had been severe for over thirty years.

It had been solved by invisible earnings such as shipping services and by the profits of trade with southern Europe and the West Indies. The West Indies trade was particularly important in maintaining the colonies' solvency, and exchanges with the *foreign* West Indies—especially with the French sugar islands of Guadeloupe, Martinique, and Santo Domingo—had become a vital part of that trade. Dealings with the French islands were highly advantageous to the American merchants. For the French sugar plantations were subsidized by the French government and yet rum and molasses were barred from French ports to protect the French brandy industry. In addition, the French plantations tended to be more efficient since the French planters, who more often than the British were residents in the islands, plowed more of their profits back into operational improvements. As a result, the price of French sugar products was relatively low. The French planters were able to capture much of the European sugar market and at the same time sell molasses, the chief by-product of sugar, at cut-rate

SUGAR CANE AND THE MAKING OF SUGAR, FROM A PRINT OF 1749

(Library of Congress.)

prices. For this product, their best customers were the British North American merchants, who became the chief suppliers of the goods and provisions needed by the islands.

This trade with the French West Indies, in which the Americans could buy cheap and sell high, was important in making up the deficits in payments in the Anglo-American commercial world and in keeping the commercial colonies solvent. But that trade was increasingly resented by the British West Indian planters and their merchant associates in England. They recognized that the more successful this foreign trade was the higher the cost of provisions would be for their own plantations and the lower the price they could obtain for their own products.

The issue became embattled as early as 1730, and the British planters and merchants moved to correct the situation and protect themselves against French competition. They set out to place high duties on foreign sugar products imported into the mainland colonies. The American merchants and the colonial agents in London rose in opposition, claiming publicly and elaborately that such duties were more than the trade would bear, and that they would wreck the Anglo-American commercial system and bankrupt the northern colonies. A fierce debate raged in the public prints and in the House of Commons, but the result, given the power of the West Indian lobby in London, was foreordained. In 1733, Parliament passed the so-called Molasses Act, which imposed prohibitive import duties on foreign sugar products: 6 pence a gallon on molasses, 9 pence a gallon on rum, 5 shillings a hundredweight on sugar itself.

This established the terms of the problem as it existed in 1760. For the act set in motion the development of a network of illegal importations. Customs officers in the northern ports were systematically bribed, and became accustomed to being bribed, to ignore the strict letter of the law and settle for a certain percentage of the legal duties. Techniques for smuggling were perfected, known to most merchants trading to the islands even if they did not use them. Gradually a large part of the northern commercial economy developed a stake in the systematic corruption of the law—law that seemed arbitrary, the product of a distant, alien, and hostile government.

Something of the same sense developed from a second problem that arose systematically within the Anglo-American connection, and while that problem was less urgent than balancing payments between Britain and America, it contained the threat of an even more fundamental conflict of interests.

The mercantile system was based on the assumption that colonial areas were producers of exotic goods and raw materials and that they were consumers, not producers, of finished goods. Large-scale manufacturing, it was assumed, was an activity reserved to the home country, and the law reflected that assumption by prohibiting the manufacture of certain basic goods in the colonies. English statutes from the end of the seventeenth century forbade the export from England of machines or tools used in the clothing industry. The Woolen Act (1699) prohibited the export of American wool or woolen products from any one colony to another. A law of 1718 forbade the free emigration of skilled artisans from Britain, and the Hat Act (1732) barred the exportation of American-made hats from the colony of manufacture.

Yet increasingly, as the American economy developed, investments in manufactures seemed attractive and proved to be lucrative as small accumulations of capital appeared in various areas. The sums were not large by English standards, but what surplus capital was available was peculiarly disposed to such investments. For the other outlets were limited. Some profits could be, and were, plowed back into expansion of commercial enterprise. Surpluses could be invested too in urban properties, in financing land speculation, in English government bonds, and in personal loans for consumption or equipment for business. But most such investments were limited to face-to-face transactions; there were no investment institutions that could broaden the range and magnitude of the money market. In a society not prone to extravagant consumption, those who controlled the slowly growing surplus turned more and more to manufactures. There were adverse conditions that restricted what could be done: a continuing labor shortage, a poor overland transportation system, and limited markets. But wherever these disabilities were to some degree overcome, the results were impressive.

In shipbuilding the problems of both transportation and markets were eliminated, since England's need for merchant vessels was continuous and heavy. By the late colonial period approximately one-third of all British-owned merchant vessels were built in the thirteen colonies. Between 50 and 100 vessels were sold to Britain annually, worth somewhere between £80,000 and £100,000. Iron production presented greater difficulties which were only partly overcome by a dispersal into small producing units and the use of slave labor. Nevertheless iron production too rose remarkably, not only in the large Principio works in Maryland and the Hasenclever plants in New Jersey but in dozens of smaller establishments scattered through the colonies. At the end of the colonial period there were 82 blast furnaces and 175 forges in the colonies (more than existed in England and Wales), and they produced 30,000 tons of crude iron a year. This product was less than half of Britain's, but it was an imposing achievement nevertheless.

Except for shipbuilding and rum, manufacturing in the colonial period was never adequate to any single need of the colonists, but growth in this sector was continuous and the implied conflict with the mercantile system was recognized by the English authorities. Britain's restrictive legislation grew more elaborate. The manufacture or export of specific textiles was outlawed in 1750. And in that year too the most famous of these enactments, the Iron Act, was passed, which, though it removed duties on the importation of pig iron into Britain, prohibited the erection of finishing plants for iron goods in all the colonies.

The effect of these laws in economic terms is difficult to gauge. Surplus wealth available for investment in manufactures was never large, and there were other factors, quite aside from available capital and restrictive legislation, that tended to impede industrial growth. But in the less measurable area of attitudes to the authority responsible for such legislation, the impact of restrictive legislation was significant. It further heightened the awareness of hostile interests that centered in the government "at home" and deepened the sense of hostility and alienation.

The same effect resulted from the handling of the money problem, which remained an acute issue through most of the mid–eighteenth century. The problem was created by the virtual absence of specie, or coin, as a medium of exchange. The coinage of money, being a sovereign prerogative, was prohibited in the colonies after the confiscation of the charter of Massachusetts, under whose jurisdiction the "pine tree shilling" had been minted in the seventeenth century. Every effort was made thereafter to attract Spanish coin to the British colonies. But the negative balance of trade made those efforts unsuccessful. The solution was paper money—a remarkable innovation in the eighteenth-century—which entered into the economy in two forms.

The first was by issuance by the colonial governments of bills of credit to repay debts the governments owed to merchant contractors. Massachusetts began this practice in 1690, and in the years that followed before 1760 almost every other colony did the same. These bills, which were in effect IOUs to be redeemed eventually by the governments, were declared legally valid as payment for taxes, and as a consequence they entered into general circulation, their value maintained by the expectation of eventual redemption. But these bills were not generally made full legal tender (that is, valid for payment of all debts, public and private); they continued to be thought of as wartime expedients. The quantity available depended less on the needs of the economy than on the occasional demands for public expenditure.

The second source of paper money was land banks, which were in effect public loan agencies created to issue money to individuals at 5 percent interest, repayable gradually and secured against default by mortgages on land or other real property. The success of these banks, which by 1750 were in existence in every colony but Virginia, was striking. They injected a badly needed flow of currency; they reduced or even eliminated the need for taxation by the income produced from the interest on the loans; they created a source of low interest credit needed for agricultural development; and they built up purchasing power in ways that may have been crucial in softening the effects of depressions. Further, as opposed to bills of credit, the land banks put funds at low interest directly into the hands of the farmers; bills of credit went in the first instance to the merchants, who translated them into credit for the farmers on less generous terms. Both, however, provided a needed medium of exchange and, despite their experimental character, were remarkably successful. Bills of credit were especially sound in the middle colonies where both merchants and officials backed the issues and limited them carefully. In Pennsylvania the bills circulated at par, and from 1723 to the French and Indian War the interest from the loans largely supported the expenses of the government.

In parts of New England and the South, however, there was overissuance, unreliable retirement of bills, and serious depreciation. The depreciation in these areas created fear of debt repudiation by creditors facing the prospect of repayment in cheap paper. Even more apprehensive were the English merchants, who feared severe losses if their credit were in any way affected by the cheapening of currency. Together, creditors in the colonies and in England pressured the British government to send strict orders to the colonial governors not to allow bills to be issued as full legal tender and to insist that the currency laws state the times of redemption clearly, and that these specifications be honored to the letter.

But such strict controls were difficult to enforce, and a crisis arose in New England in the 1730s. Rhode Island's bills flooded the region (that colony issued £100,000 worth of paper bills in 1733 alone), and the Boston merchants refused to honor them. The pressure for more issues continued, however, and in 1739 a group of Massachusetts merchants formed a *private* land bank, which was author-

COLONIAL PAPER MONEY

The Massachusetts paper penny bears the signature of Thomas Hutchinson, the future loyalist governor, then a member of a committee in charge of issuing bills of credit. The issue of 1750 was a victory for Hutchinson's hard money policy. Based on £180,000 of silver that Parliament sent in repayment of wartime expenses, it replaced all of the colony's inflated currency in circulation. (*American Antiquarian Society.*)

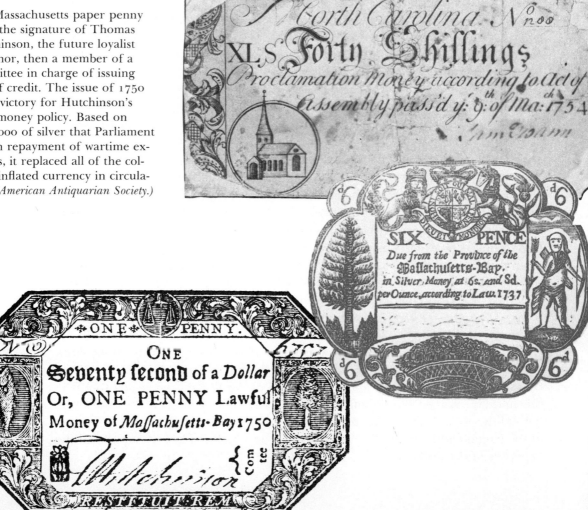

ized by the General Court to issue £150,000 worth of bills at 3 percent interest. Many members of the business community were greatly alarmed at this especially since repayment was allowed in commodities of uncertain value, and a second group formed what was called a silver bank, which would issue notes redeemable in silver, not commodities. The two groups fell into fierce controversy, which resulted in the end in the governor and the council declaring the land bank's bills invalid, although £50,000 had already been placed in circulation. The leading land bankers organized public protests, which became riotous. There were arrests and jailings, and in the end the British government adopted repressive measures. In 1741 the so-called Bubble Act was extended to the colonies, which outlawed all joint-stock companies not authorized by Parliament (in effect outlawing all private banks). The result was near-chaos and years of litigation in Massachusetts as creditors who had already accepted payment in the bank's bills demanded repayment in valid money. It was the worst upheaval in the Bay Colony between the Dominion of New England and the early years of the Revolution. Samuel Adams's father was one of the local officials removed from office for continuing to support the land bank.

But the *public* banks continued to exist, and the value of their issues continued to fluctuate. In Massachusetts, paper was discounted from par at a ratio of 9 to 1. In Rhode Island, nine issues of paper were in circulation in 1750, representing a par value of £465,000, and in addition there was £60,000 worth of bills of credit legally available. But by then more comprehensive legislation was being drafted. In 1751 Parliament passed the Currency Act, directed to the New England colonies alone. By its terms, no new land banks could be created in New England; no paper money could thereafter be made full legal tender; all bills were to be retired on the strict schedule of the original legislation; and bills could be issued to pay for government expenses only if provision were made for their redemption by taxes within two years.

Though the Currency Act applied only to New England, it constituted a warning and threat to all the colonial governments against allowing any looseness in the management of paper money. Orders went out from London severely restricting the use of this currency in all the colonies, though it had become an essential part of the American economy and though those responsible for the paper issues were by no means wildcat inflationists. Every knowledgeable merchant knew the value of sound paper money, and many, like Franklin, correctly saw that its controlled expansion could be a stimulus to the entire economy. In this case also, as in the prohibitive taxation of the trade with the foreign West Indies and in the restriction of American manufactures, the action of the British government was not merely unfairly competitive but hostile. The action seemed arbitrary and unreasonable—an imposition that called into question the grounds of loyalty. To obey such laws as these was a form of humiliation exacted by a government that seemed distant, alienated from the people it governed and unresponsive to their needs.

The American

The antagonisms of wartime collaboration and the resentments created by seemingly arbitrary and hostile legislation were problems largely of policy and management and therefore potentially, at least, within the realm of political control. A deeper and less manageable source of distance and alienation between Britain and America lay in the area of cultural perceptions—the sense Americans had of who they were in relation to the other peoples of the world, of what their life was like, and who, in contrast, the British were within the same set of considerations. In matters such as these, there are few specific events that one can point to as turning points or decisive conclusions or indisputable signs of development. Nevertheless these attitudes and perceptions are facts which in the end are as important as battles and laws and political campaigns, although they are more difficult to establish, to measure, and to describe.

Through the two generations of growth and expansion that preceded the accession of George III, Americans had gradually acquired a sense of themselves as a separate people—separate not in law or politics or constitution, but in character and culture. It was a complex image, composed of many strands, and it could be seen as positive or negative depending on the context or point of view. In its essence it was an image of a simple, rustic, innocent, uncorrupted, and unsophisticated people, an appropriate self-image for a colonial people, perhaps, but no simple reflection of reality. For it was, first, a compound of several intellectual traditions and influences; it was in addition a reflection of the ideas and attitudes of Europe's enlightened thinkers; and it was, finally, a product of certain specific political ideas of great potential power.

In its origins this image can be traced back to the ambiguous picture that Europeans first formed of American Indians soon after their first contact with the Western Hemisphere, a picture compounding simplicity and savagery, vigor and barbarism, innocence and paganism. By the eighteenth century this mingled image in the case of British North America came to be applied more to the Creoles—that is, natives of European descent—than to the Indians, whom the English had long since come to think of as unredeemably savage, if not satanic. This transfer of traits from the aborigines to the European colonists was facilitated by the common belief that the colonists had deliberately copied certain practices and skills from the Indians and as a result had acquired from them certain peculiar characteristics. Infants strapped to boards, for example, were thought to develop like Indians whatever their race or culture; American women, like Indians, were believed to be taller than European women and to suffer fewer miscarriages. This notion was reinforced by the "scientific" arguments of the environmentalists, an influential group of continental European thinkers who believed that life in all its forms was determined by the material conditions under which it was lived. It seemed reasonable to believe, from this point of view, that what had long been true of the Indians in the great American laboratory of nature would eventually, if it did not already, apply to the colonists too.

But more practical and immediate influences were also at work detailing the Americans' simplicity, innocence, and rusticity. The image of the American colonists—their own view of themselves as well as the view that others had of them—was shaped too by the recruiting propaganda that had circulated throughout Europe and America for over a century. All of these publications, from the advertisements of the Virginia Company to the publications of the German "new-landers" operating along the Rhine and the pamphlets distributed in Ireland by American land speculators, stressed the idyllic wonders of a simple, loosely institutionalized, benign society where land was free, where government scarcely existed, and where religion was practiced in absolutely uncontested freedom.

William Penn had been particularly active in recruiting settlers for his province. His two pamphlets of 1681, *A Brief Account* and *Some Account of the Province of Pennsylvania,* circulated widely through England, Wales, and Ireland, and then in translation in the Netherlands, western Germany, and France. Penn's idealistic depiction of life in his sylvan elysium was extraordinarily influential too because of the activity of his friend, chief land agent, and recruiter, Benjamin Furley. Furley was stationed in Rotterdam, in touch through correspondence with intellectuals and liberal politicians throughout Europe, and indeed personally host to political refugees like John Locke, Algernon Sidney, and Lord Shaftesbury. He was thus able to confirm the pastoral image of America in the thinking of some of the leading publicists of the time as well as in the imaginations of desperate peasants of the Rhineland.

But perhaps the greatest influence of all in propagating the image of British America as a land of simple, innocent, independent, and virtuous folk was the widespread knowledge of the kinds of people who had in fact gone there—self-respecting servants, ambitious artisans, sturdy yeoman, Puritans, and, above all and most sensationally, Quakers. The symbolic importance of the Quakers to the world at large was overwhelming. In the seventeenth century they had been thought of principally as radical exotics; they were famous throughout Britain and France for their fanatical independence of mind and their absolute refusal to respect mere earthly authorities (hence their use in addressing people of all ranks of the familiar "thee" and "thou"). In the more tolerant atmosphere of the early eighteenth century their reputation had shifted from that of defiant and fanatical seekers of religious freedom to that of genial advocates of pacifism, toleration, reasonable and simple religion, and ordinary human rights and dignity in the face of aristocratic and authoritarian impositions. It was this cluster of traits that attracted Voltaire to them during his stay in England (1726–29) and that led him to praise them extravagantly again and again. For him, the Quakers as a group were the embodiments of civic virtue; and the quintessence of their virtues, he believed, could be seen in Pennsylvania, where all their dreams and the dreams of all mankind, he thought, had reached fulfillment. Here, Voltaire wrote, an enlightened republican lawgiver had created an actual elysium. Philadelphia, he wrote in one of his *Philosophical Letters* (1734), was so prosperous that people flocked to it from all over the continent; Penn's laws were so wise that no one of them had ever been changed; the Indians had been won over to friendship; there was equality, religious freedom without priests, and peace everywhere, he believed, in this remarkable province. "William Penn could boast," he wrote, "of having brought to the world that golden age of which men talk so much and which probably has never existed anywhere except in Pennsylvania."

The world, it seemed, agreed. Montesquieu, perhaps the most widely respected and influential political analyst of the age, called Penn the greatest lawgiver since classical antiquity. The monumental French *Encyclopedia* of enlightened ideas enshrined Penn in the pantheon of Europe's heroes. And every informed person in the Western world knew something about Pennsylvania—and about America in general—through the extraordinary figure of Benjamin Franklin.

BENJAMIN FRANKLIN, BY ROBERT FEKE, AND "POOR RICHARD'S ALMANAC"

The portrait was painted about the time of Franklin's retirement from business. Thirty years later Franklin's image was completely transformed (p. 220). *(Fogg Art Museum, Harvard University; The Historical Society of Pennsylvania.)*

Poor Richard, 1733.

AN

Almanack

For the Year of Chrift

1 7 3 3,

Being the Firft after LEAP YEAR:

And makes fince the Creation   Years

By the Account of the Eaftern Greeks   7241

By the Latin Church, when ☉ ent. ♈   6932

By the Computation of W.W.   5742

By the Roman Chronology   5682

By the Jewifh Rabbies   5494

Wherein is contained

The Lunations, Eclipfes, Judgment of the Weather, Spring Tides, Planets Motions & mutual Afpects, Sun and Moon's Rifing and Setting, Length of Days, Time of High Water, Fairs, Courts, and obfervable Days.

Fitted to the Latitude of Forty Degrees, and a Meridian of Five Hours Weft from London, but may without fenfible Error, ferve all the adjacent Places, even from Newfoundland to South-Carolina.

By RICHARD SAUNDERS, Philom.

PHILADELPHIA:

Printed and fold by B. FRANKLIN, at the New Printing-Office near the Market.

Franklin, the most famous American of the eighteenth century and one of the most famous and influential Americans who has ever lived, was born in Boston in 1706, the son of a candle and soap maker. At the age of seventeen he ran away to Philadelphia, where he eventually prospered as a printer and an organizer of printing establishments in several colonies. At the age of forty-two he retired from business to devote himself to public causes, to writing, and above all to scientific experimentation. He corresponded with English scientists and intellectuals, particularly Peter Collinson, a Quaker merchant and member of the Royal Society, on the problems of electricity, and it was in the form of letters to Collinson that he published the results of his studies, *Experiments and Observations on Electricity* (1751). This book was one of the great sensations of the eighteenth century. It went through five editions in English, three in French, one in Italian, and one in German before 1800, and it elevated Franklin to the highest ranks of western thinkers. Buffon, the greatest French naturalist of the age, himself arranged for the French edition; the encyclopedist Diderot declared Franklin to be the very model of the modern experimental scientist.

And who was Franklin? A simple, unsophisticated product of the primitive society of British North America—yet he had outdone the most sophisticated intellectuals of Europe in their own field of endeavor. The implications were sensational. In the context of Enlightenment thought, Franklin's mere existence as a successful intellectual conveyed a powerful message, reinforcing the arguments of reformers everywhere and demonstrating conclusively the validity of their challenge to the establishment.

Though the great wave of reform thinking that is called the Enlightenment was complicated in its details, in its essence it was clear and simple. At its heart lay discontent with the condition of life as it was known and a general approach to improvement. All enlightened thinkers in one way or another pictured human nature as good, or if not good, then at least capable of great improvement and of far greater happiness than was commonly experienced. The evils of the world that reduced people to misery were seen mainly as artifacts—constructions of men and women themselves. To Voltaire, the chief evils, whose reform could release people's better natures and create greater happiness, were the great public institutions, especially the church and a parasitic, corrupt, and dogmatic priesthood. To the physiocrats, the French economic reformers who believed that agriculture alone produced wealth, it was the irrational constraints on agricultural production and marketing; to Locke, it was the arbitrary, authoritarian state; to Rousseau, it was civilization itself. For all, the cruelties and miseries of life were products of constructions that people themselves had made, and the solution was the reform of these structures so that human nature would be released to attain the happiness of which it was capable.

But there were powerful counterarguments. These great imposing institutions—the state, the church, the regulated economy, and the social structures that gave power over the lives of the masses to a hereditary aristocracy—were,

after all, the guardians of social order and stability; they were also the carriers
of high culture and the sponsors of the finest human achievements. To eliminate
them or change them radically might create not freedom but anarchy, not a
higher civilization but barbarism. What was needed by all the enlightened
thinkers was an example, not of thuggish primitivism but of civilized simplicity—
a Christian society free from the encumbrances of rigid and powerful institutions,
a society in which reason had been used in fashioning public institutions and in
which, despite the simplicity of life, high culture was maintained and advanced.
In British North America generally, in Pennsylvania more specifically, and
above all in the figure of Franklin—apparently an untutored genius, a simple and
unaffected but accomplished virtuoso of science, letters, and statecraft—they had
the examples they wanted. If Franklin had never existed it would have been neces-

FRANKLIN, THE ENLIGHTENMENT'S PHILOSOPHER

Left, an engraving of a drawing by Charles Nicolas Cochin,
made in 1777 shortly after Franklin arrived in Paris as representative of the new nation. It expresses perfectly the
image Franklin had projected to the enlightened world ever
since the publication of his experiments 26 years earlier.
Below right, the popularization of Franklin's image. A box
cover, probably of the 19th century, showing the great triumvirate of the Enlightenment ("The Light of the Universe"),
Voltaire, Rousseau, and Franklin. *Opposite page,* from the
French edition of Franklin's Experiments and Observations
on Electricity. *(Fogg Art Museum, Harvard University; The
Metropolitan Museum, Gift of William H. Huntington, 1883; By
permission of the Houghton Library, Harvard University.)*

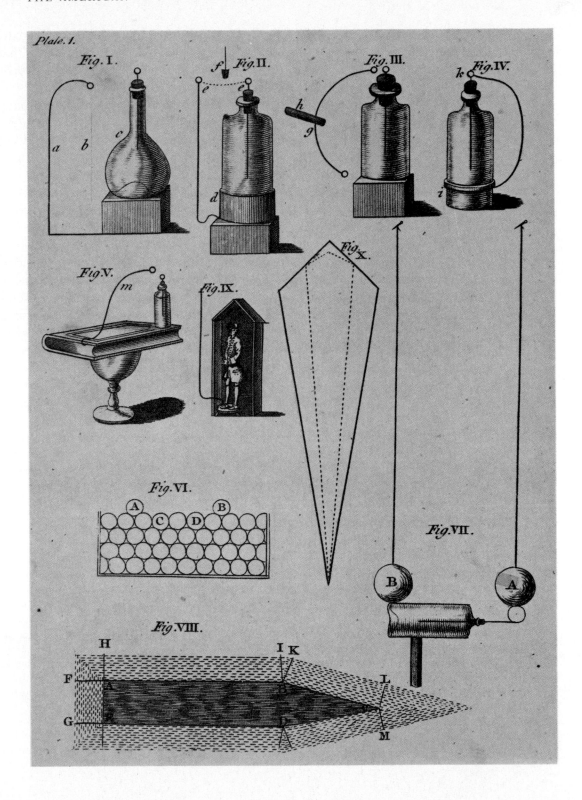

Plate. 1.

Fig. I.   Fig. II.   Fig. III.   Fig. IV.

Fig. V.   Fig. IX.   Fig. X.

Fig. VI.   Fig. VII.

Fig. VIII.

sary for the *philosophes* to invent him—a fact which Franklin understood perfectly, which he shrewdly played upon as he felt his way into the great public role that was thrust upon him, and which he fulfilled most completely in the *Autobiography* that he wrote in the later years of his life.

To much of the world, Franklin *was* America; he was the American incarnate. Caught up in the imagery of simplicity and natural gifts demanded by Enlightenment aspirations, he documented in himself the meaning of the New World to the Old, and thereby helped shape Americans' self-awareness as well as Europe's perception of the provincial society beyond the sea.

Inevitably Franklin played on the theme of the social and moral grounds of political freedom, for it was in this area that American self-imagery came into its sharpest focus and acquired its greatest relevance for the affairs of the everyday world. It was universally believed that the success of Britain's celebrated constitution, or of any constitution that protected the people's liberties, depended on the virtue of the political population. To maintain the balance of forces in government that constrained the misuse of power required eternal vigilance. Freedom from oppression rested on the ability of the people to resist the softening enticements of a privileged aristocracy and on the capacity of the aristocracy to resist the corruptions of profit and power and continue to use its privileges for the good of the whole. If the people's will to protect their own liberties weakened or if Britain's aristocracy succumbed to sloth and self-indulgence as had the aristocracies of continental Europe, freedom would be destroyed by the predictable encroachments of arbitrary power.

The signs, for Americans of the late provincial period, were worrisome. Repeatedly they found reason to question the moral qualities of English society, to doubt the independence of "the democracy" in Britain and the impartiality and responsibility of the British aristocracy. American visitors to England sent back disturbing reports. John Dickinson of Pennsylvania, in England in the election year 1754, wrote home that he was "filled with awe and reverence" by his contact with scenes of ancient greatness and by the sophistication and variety of life in London. But he was shocked too by the corruption of English politics. Over £1 million, he reported to his father, was spent in efforts to manipulate the election.

If a man cannot be brought to vote as he is desired, he is made dead drunk and kept in that state, never heard of by his family or friends till all is over and he can do no harm. The oath of their not being bribed is as strict and solemn as language can form it, but is so little regarded that few people can refrain from laughing while they take it. . . . Bribery is so common that it is thought there is not a borough in England where it is not practiced. . . . We hear every day in Westminster Hall leave moved to file information for bribery, but it is ridiculous and absurd to pretend to curb the effects of luxury and corruption in one instance or in one spot without a general reformation of manners, which everyone sees is absolutely necessary for the welfare of the kingdom. Yet Heaven knows how it can be effected. It is grown a vice here to be virtuous.

(American Antiquarian Society.)

This was not simply provincial prudery. English writers too decried the loss of virtue, warning of its implications for politics, and their voices were clearly heard in America. James Burgh's *Britain's Remembrancer* (1746) denounced "our degenerate times and corrupt nation"; the British people, he said, were wallowing in "luxury and irreligion . . . venality, perjury, faction, opposition to legal authority, idleness, gluttony, drunkenness, lewdness, excessive gaming, robberies . . . a legion of furies sufficient to rend any state or empire . . . to pieces." Burgh's pamphlet was reprinted by Franklin in 1747, by another Philadelphia printer in 1748, and again in Boston in 1759. So too Dr. John Brown's blistering attack on English corruption, *An Estimate of the Manners and Principles of the Times* (1757), found an eager audience in America—an audience convinced of the superiority and virtue of its own uncorrupted manners and of its own moral capacity to satisfy the demands of freedom if freedom were ever challenged.

So the American people entered the age of George III. Their prospects were excellent despite the troubles that lay beneath the surface of Anglo-American life and the doubts they had of the moral quality of the British people and the responsibility of the British leaders. Conscious of their characteristics as a colonial people—provincial but vigorous, unsophisticated but uncorrupted, contentious but free, undeveloped in all the main institutions of society but more prosperous than any large population in the Western world—they saw themselves growing powerful and mature as part of an enriching imperial connection.

Suggested Readings

The eighteenth-century colonial wars were the subject of Francis Parkman's most dramatic narratives—still immensely readable—in his nine-volume series, *France and England in North America*. His *Half-Century of Conflict* (2 vols., 1892) covers King George's War, and his *Montcalm and Wolfe* (2 vols., 1884) the French and Indian War. A modern, technical, scholarly work covering the same ground in greater detail but lacking Parkman's narrative style is Lawrence H. Gipson's *British Empire Before the American Revolution*, vols. VI–VIII (1946–53). Excellent also among the general works on the pre-Revolutionary military events are Stanley Pargellis, *Lord Loudoun in North America* (1933) and John Shy, *Toward Lexington* (1965), chaps. i–iii. Howard H. Peckham, *The Colonial Wars, 1689–1762* (1964) provides a brief introduction to the whole subject.

On the three problems of Anglo-American relations discussed in the second section of the chapter, the balance of payments and commerce with the West Indies are discussed in James F. Shepherd and Gary M. Walton, *Shipping, Maritime Trade, and the Economic Development of Colonial North America* (1972), esp. App. IV; Richard B. Sheridan, "The Molasses Act and the Market Strategy of the British Sugar Planters," *Journal of Economic History*, 17 (1957), 62–83 and *Sugar and Slavery* (1974); Richard Pares, *Yankees and Creoles* (1956) and *War and Trade in the West Indies, 1739–1763* (1936); and Thomas C. Barrow, *Trade and Empire* (1967). On manufactures: Victor S. Clark, *History of Manufactures in the United States* (3 vols., 1929); Eleanor L. Lord, *Industrial Experiments in the British Colonies . . .* (1898); Curtis P. Nettels, "The Menace of Colonial Manufacturing, 1690–1720," *New England Quarterly*, 4 (1931), 230–69; Arthur C. Bining, *British Regulation of the Colonial Iron Industry* (1933); Shepherd and Walton, *Shipping* (cited above), esp. App. VI. And on the money supply and banks, see E. James Ferguson, "Currency Finance . . . ," *Wm. and Mary Q.*, 10 (1953), 153–80; Theodore G. Thayer, "The Land Bank System in the American Colonies," *Journal of Economic History*, 13 (1953), 145–59; Andrew M. Davis, *Currency and Banking in . . . Massachusetts Bay* (2 vols., 1901); Richard A. Lester, *Monetary Experiments . . .* (1939); and George A. Billias, *Massachusetts Land Bankers of 1740* (1959).

On cultural relations between the colonies and Europe, see, besides the Boorstin and Savelle books cited for chapter 5, Michael Kraus, *The Atlantic Civilization: Eighteenth-Century Origins* (1949); Sacvan Berkovitch, *The Puritan Origins of the American Self* (1975); Durand Echeverria, *Mirage in the West . . . the French Image of American Society to 1815* (1957); Gilbert Chinard, "Eighteenth Century Themes on America as a Human Habitat," *Proceedings of the American Philosophical Society*, 91 (1947), 25–57; Howard M. Jones, *O Strange New World* (1964); and Bernard Bailyn, *Ideological Origins of the American Revolution* (1967), chaps. ii–iii. On Franklin's extraordinary role in cultural relations between Europe and America, see Alfred O. Aldridge, *Franklin and his French Contemporaries* (1957); Antonio Pace, *Franklin and Italy* (1958); I. Bernard Cohen's edition, *Benjamin Franklin's Experiments* (1941) and his *Franklin and Newton* (1956); and Charles C. Sellers, *Benjamin Franklin in Portraiture* (1962). The full standard biography is Carl Van Doren, *Benjamin Franklin* (1938); a shorter but well-rounded account is Verner W. Crane, *Benjamin Franklin and a Rising People* (1954).

Chronology, to 1760

1492–1504 Columbus's four voyages to New World.

1494 Treaty of Tordesillas divides non-Christian world between Spain and Portugal.

1497–98 John Cabot explores Newfoundland, Labrador, and Nova Scotia, and establishes English claim to North America.

1503 Spain establishes board of trade, *Casa de Contratación*.

1508–9 Sebastian Cabot explores Hudson Bay region.

1508–47 Reign of Henry VIII.

1513 Balboa discovers Pacific Ocean after crossing isthmus of Panama.
Ponce de Leon discovers mainland of Florida.

1519–21 Cortés conquers Mexico.

1523 Verrazano explores coast of North America, establishing French claim.

1523–30 Spaniards conquer Honduras and Guatemala.

1524 Spain creates Council of the Indies (*Consejo de las Indias*).

1528–36 Cabeza de Vaca explores northern periphery of Gulf of Mexico, west to Gulf of California.

1532–35 Pizarro conquers Peru.

1534 Cartier's explorations establish French claim to Saint Lawrence basin.

1535 Viceroyalty of New Spain created.

1535–39 Initial Spanish conquest of Ecuador, Chile, northern Argentina, and Bolivia.

1539–41 De Soto explores southeastern United States and discovers the Mississippi.

1540–42 Coronado seeks legendary cities of wealth in North American Southwest.

1540–53 Valdivia extends Spanish conquest of Chile.

1542 Viceroyalty of Peru established.

1551 Antwerp market for English woolen goods fails.

1553–58 Queen Mary reigns in England.

1624 Virginia Company charter revoked; English crown takes control of Virginia.
First settlements in New Netherlands.

1625–49 Reign of Charles I.

1626 Dutch settle Manhattan.

1629 Massachusetts Bay Company chartered.

1630 Puritan emigration from England begins; continues until 1643.

1632 Cecelius Calvert, Lord Baltimore, receives charter for Maryland colony.

1634 First settlements in Maryland.

1635 Roger Williams banished from Bay Colony.

1636 Harvard College founded.
First permanent English settlements in Connecticut and Rhode Island.

1638 Anne Hutchinson convicted of heresy in Massachusetts; flees to Rhode Island.
New Sweden founded in Delaware. (Captured by Dutch in 1656.)

1639 Fundamental Orders adopted in Connecticut.

1642 Basic literacy law passed in Massachusetts Bay.

1642–48 Civil war in England.

1643 Confederation of New England colonies.

1644 Rhode Island receives charter.

1647 Law requiring towns to maintain schools passed in Massachusetts Bay Colony.

1649 Charles I beheaded.

1650 Anne Bradstreet's *The Tenth Muse.*
Northern neck of Virginia granted to courtiers in exile.

1660 Restoration of Stuart monarchy (Charles II, 1660–85).
Basic navigation law, monopolizing colonial trade and shipping for Britain, passed by Parliament; includes "enumeration" clause.

1662 Massachusetts Bay ministers sanction halfway covenant.
Colony of Connecticut chartered by crown.

1689–97 King William's War (colonial phase of Europe's War of the League of Augsburg, 1688–97); concluded in Treaty of Ryswick.

1691 Massachusetts Bay Colony gets new charter.

1692 Witchcraft hysteria in Salem, Massachusetts; twenty "witches" executed.

1693 College of William and Mary founded.

1696 English government establishes Board of Trade and Plantations.
Passage of comprehensive navigation act, extending admiralty court system to America.

1699 Woolen Act passed by Parliament.

1701 Yale College founded.
New and permanent Frame of Government adopted in Pennsylvania.

1702–13 Queen Anne's War (colonial phase of Europe's War of Spanish Succession, 1701–13); concluded in Treaty of Utrecht.

1702 West and East New Jersey formed into single royal colony.

1702–14 Reign of Queen Anne.

1708 Saybrook Platform adopted in Connecticut.

1714–27 Reign of George I, beginning Hanoverian dynasty.

1719 Rebellion against proprietors in Carolina.

1727–60 Reign of George II.

1729 Separate royal colonies, North and South Carolina, created.

1732 Georgia established to furnish buffer against Spanish and as philanthropic effort to relocate England's paupers.

1733 Molasses Act restricts colonial importation of sugar goods from French West Indies.

1734–35 Jonathan Edwards touches off evangelical revival in Northampton, Massachusetts, and throughout Connecticut River Valley.

1735 New York jury acquits John Peter Zenger of charge of seditious libel on ground that printing truth can be no libel

America.

1566 England conquers Ireland.

1574 Gilbert leads expedition to Hudson Bay.

1577–80 Drake circumnavigates globe.

1578 Gilbert fails to establish colony in North America.

1584 Richard Hakluyt (the younger) publishes *A Discourse on Western Planting*.

1585–87 Raleigh fails to establish Roanoke Colony.

1585–98 England colonizes Ireland.

1603–25 Reign of James I.

1603–35 In eleven voyages, Samuel de Champlain establishes French colonies in Canada.

1606 Virginia Company chartered; includes two subcompanies.

1607 London subcompany of Virginia Company establishes settlement at Jamestown; Plymouth subcompany, on coast of Maine.

1608 Pilgrims flee to Holland to avoid religious persecution.

1609 Second charter of Virginia Company.

1612 Third charter of Virginia Company.

1619 First Africans arrive in Virginia. First North American representative assembly meets in Virginia.

1620 Pilgrims establish Plymouth Colony; Mayflower Compact signed.

1621 Dutch West India Company chartered.

1622 Indian rebellion in Virginia.

New navigation act (Staple Act) passed, channeling colonies' importation of European goods through England. Charter of Carolina given to eight courtiers.

1664 England conquers New Netherlands.

1665 Duke's Laws for New York promulgated. New Jersey charter issued to two courtiers.

1669 Fundamental Constitution of Carolina issued.

1673 New navigation act imposes "plantation duties." Marquette and Joliet explore Great Lakes and claim territory for France.

1674 New Jersey divided into East and West Jersey.

1675 Lords of Trade appointed as committee of Privy Council.

1675–76 King Philip's War in New England.

1676 Bacon's Rebellion in Virginia.

1677 West New Jersey's Concessions and Agreements issued. Culpeper's Rebellion in Carolina.

1680 New Hampshire given royal charter.

1680–82 LaSalle expedition descends Mississippi River to its mouth, taking possession of region for France as Louisiana.

1681 Pennsylvania charter granted to William Penn; first settlements in 1682.

1684 Massachusetts Bay charter annulled by crown (charters of Connecticut, Rhode Island, New Jersey, Pennsylvania, Maryland, and Carolina abrogated in following years, to 1691).

1685–88 Reign of James II; his accession royalizes New York.

1686 Dominion of New England established.

1688 Glorious Revolution in England drives out James II in favor of William and Mary.

1689 Successful rebellion in Boston against Dominion of New England. Protestant Association in Maryland rebels.

1689–91 Leisler's rebellion in New York.

ignites major phase of Great Awakening.

1739–42 War of Jenkins' Ear, fought with Spain principally in Caribbean and Central America.

1740–41 Private land bank created in Massachusetts; outlawed by Parliament.

1744–48 King George's War (colonial phase of Europe's War of Austrian Succession, 1740–48); concluded in Treaty of Aix-la-Chapelle.

1745 New England troops take fortress of Louisburg on Cape Breton Island (returned to France at end of war).

1750 Iron Act, limiting production of finished iron goods in colonies, passed by Parliament.

1751 Currency Act, restricting issuance and currency of paper money in New England colonies, passed by Parliament. Publication of Franklin's *Experiments and Observations on Electricity*.

1754 Albany Congress and Plan of Union. King's College (later Columbia University) founded.

1754–63 French and Indian War (colonial phase of Europe's Seven Years War, 1756–63.)

1759 Quebec falls to Britsh army.

1760 George III accedes to throne.

WOODEN FIGURE OF "VIRTUE"
CARVED BY SIMEON SKILLIN
(C. 1790)

With the creation of the United
States, republican Americans
replaced the image of the Indian
maiden with a classical goddess,
often depicted bearing a liberty
cap, which since antiquity had
been a symbol of men newly
freed from slavery. (*Yale University Art Gallery. The Mabel Brady
Garvan Collection.*)

PART TWO

Framing the Republic

1760-1820

GORDON S. WOOD

The American Revolution is the single most important event in American history. Not only did it create the United States, but it defined most of the persistent values and aspirations of the American people. The noblest ideals of Americans—the commitments to freedom, equality, constitutionalism, and the well-being of ordinary people—came out of the Revolutionary era. The Revolution gave Americans the consciousness that they were a people with a special destiny to lead the world toward liberty. The Revolution, in short, gave birth to whatever ideology Americans have had. The United States was the first nation in the modern world to make intellectual principles the foundation of its existence. A society composed of so many different races and peoples from so many different places could not be a nation in any traditional sense of the term. It was the Revolutionary experience and the ideals and beliefs flowing from it that have held Americans together and made them think of themselves as a single people.

The origins of such a momentous event necessarily lay deep in America's past. A century and a half of dynamic developments in the British continental colonies of the New World had fundamentally transformed inherited European institutions and customary patterns of life and had created the basis for a new society. In comparison with eighteenth-century England, America was disordered and turbulent, torn by competition and repeated challenges to authority.

Suddenly in the 1760s Great Britain thrust its imperial power into this chaotic world with a thoroughness that had not been felt in a century, and precipitated a crisis within the loosely organized empire. American resistance turned into rebellion; but as the colonists groped to make sense of the peculiarities of their society this rebellion became a justification and idealization of American life as it had gradually and unintentionally developed over the previous century and a half. In this sense, as John Adams later said, "the Revolution was effected before the war commenced." It was a change "in the minds and hearts of the people."

But this change was not the whole American Revolution. The Revolution was not simply an intellectual endorsement of a previously existing social reality. It was also an integral part of the great transforming process that carried America into modernity. Despite the corrosive and disruptive effects of the wilderness that by 1760 had fundamentally altered the institutions and lives of the American colonists, mid-eighteenth-century society still retained, along with powdered wigs and knee breeches, many traditional habits of behavior and dependent social relationships that separated it from the more fluid, bustling, individualistic world of the early nineteenth century.

By the early years of the nineteenth century, the Revolution had released and intensified latent forces that helped create in America a society of independent men unlike any society that had existed before, a society nearly as different from America in 1760 as colonial America was from eighteenth-century England. This complicated Revolution had several layers and successive phases that as often as not were contradictory to one another. Although its beginnings went back to the seventeenth-century settlements and its consequences are with Americans still, the Revolution can be essentially encompassed between 1760 and 1820. Some Americans thought the Revolution was over in 1776 with the Declaration of Independence and the creation of new state governments. Others, however, believed the Revolution ended only with the reconstruction of the national government in 1787; and still others thought it was not finished until the new central government was infused with strength and energy in the 1790s. Yet many other Americans saw these later centralizing developments as a repudiation of the original Revolution and thus sought to recover the spirit of 1776. For them the election of Thomas Jefferson as President of the United States in 1800 was the real fulfillment of the Revolution, a fulfillment that required ratification by another war against Great Britain in 1812.

By the end of that second war against Britain, the central impulses of the Revolution had run their course. At last the future and stability of the republic seemed secure. Democracy and equality were no longer problems to be solved; they had become articles of faith to be fulfilled. The ideological antagonisms that the Revolution had aroused had finally petered out. In place of a collection of little more than a million and a half monarchical subjects huddled along the Atlantic coast, America by 1820 had become a huge expansive nation of nearly 10 million republican citizens obsessed with their own boundlessness.

7

Sources of the Revolution

By 1760, American society had developed very differently from that of England. It was in fact remarkably modern—fragmented, highly competitive, and marked by an extraordinary degree of popular participation. At the same time, however, this new society was still pre-modern in the way it organized and justified itself. Most of the colonists' social relations and values still resembled those of the mother country.

American society was thus out of joint, torn by the discrepancy between its unprecedented circumstances and its traditional understanding of itself. Suddenly at mid-century the long-existing tendencies of a surging population and widespread egalitarian participation in commerce speeded up, further unraveling the remnants of customary social forms and habits. These dynamic social forces did not cause the Revolution. But they did affect the way the Revolution developed, and in the end they helped propel America into a new century and into a new democratic and capitalistic world.

The Remains of Social Dependency

Despite the extraordinary changes in American life that had taken place in the previous century and a half, mid-eighteenth-century society was conceived in terms that John Winthrop would have understood. It was not so much a group of separate individuals as it was an organic whole concerned with moral consensus and stability. Conflict among individuals and parties was condemned; everyone was supposed to be linked together in promoting communal interests. The goal of individuals was presumed to be finding and securing one's proper place in the social order. Although American society scarcely compared in complexity and depth with eighteenth-century English society, it was still thought to be a series of dependent ranks and degrees that ranged from the king and royal officials at the top down to the bonded laborers and black slaves at the bottom. Although Americans talked of the "better sort," the "middling ranks," and the "meaner sort," their colonial society was not yet described in modern class terms. This predominantly rural society scattered in small communities was still largely organized along lines of kinship and interest that bound superiors with inferiors in what were presumed to be paternal relationships.

The greatest social gap the free members of this society experienced was between ordinary people and gentlemen. The awareness of the "difference between *gentle* and *simple*," recalled the Methodist minister, Devereaux Jarrett, of his humble youth in colonial Virginia, was "universal among all of my rank and age." Persons in lowly stations, Jarrett remembered, were apt to be filled with consternation and awe when confronted with "what were called *gentle folks*, . . . beings of a superior order." Since this distinction has lost almost all of its older meaning (Jarrett himself lived to see "a vast alteration, in this respect"), it is difficult to recapture the significance that the eighteenth century gave to it. Southern squires often entered their churches as a body and took their front pews only after the ordinary people had been seated. Massachusetts courts debated endlessly over whether plaintiffs and defendants were properly identified as gentlemen.

Since such gentlemanly superiority was crucial to social stability, the very disorder of American life often compelled would-be gentlemen into frantic efforts to proclaim their status by all sorts of outward signs. Gentlemen sought to be recognized by their speech and bearing, the size of their houses, the number of their carriages, the style of their clothes, the nature of their table, even coats of arms. Some members of this gentry like the Tidewater planters of Virginia or the wealthy landholders of the Connecticut River valley, who were so imposing as to be called "river gods," overawed entire communities and maintained law and order without police forces or elaborate mechanisms of control. From such propertied gentlemen, lines of influence ideally branched outward into the society, connecting patrons and clients in social relationships far more personal and comprehensive than the contractual "cash nexus" of later capitalistic society. Such relationships were referred to as "connections," "interest," or even "friendship."

By the middle of the eighteenth century, the American "aristocracy," limited though it was, had become far more self-conscious and consolidated than it had been earlier. Personal correspondence, intermarriage, common education, and travel helped put gentlemen of different localities and even of different colonies in touch with one another. Those who aspired to be gentlemen required networks of kin and connections and access to markets and political and legal authority.

CHESAPEAKE TOBACCO GROWERS AND MERCHANTS SERVED BY BLACK SLAVE

With such connections they could play crucial mediating roles for numerous clients and dependents, and thus reinforce the assumption that superiority of all sorts was unitary and indivisible. Whatever acquiescence the "meaner sort" gave to those who by their wealth, influence, and independence were considered best qualified to rule was based not simply on traditional habits of deference but on mutually beneficial relations between clients and patrons. When in 1743 Henry Beekman, a large New York landowner, interceded on behalf of several small freeholders of his county, who were faced with being ejected from their property by a court suit, he was exercising the power of patronage his position gave him. Although he told the beneficiaries of his aid that he would "expect no other reward for this than your friendship," he clearly expected such "friendship" to manifest itself as political allegiance at election time.

If it were not for the remnants of personal influence of one sort or another tying people together, American society would have been more disordered than it was. Rich merchants like Thomas Hancock of Boston dispensed money and favors to important government officials and expected something in return; in Hancock's case lucrative military contracts. Young George Washington got his start as a surveyor and militia officer through the influence of Lord Fairfax and his family in Virginia. Appointments to government offices, the securing of military commissions or judgeships, the awarding of land or business contracts were only the most visible political expressions of an underlying personal system of recruitment, attachment, and reciprocity that affected all levels of life. Creditors and debtors, masters and apprentices, landlords and tenants, merchants and artisans, teachers and students, husbands and wives—all were held together by strings of interest and dependency. When people moved up within the society it was not usually because they had worked hard or had received an education, but because they had obtained the "friendship" of someone who had power and patronage—whether it was a government official offering his daughter in marriage, a merchant lending money to a tradesman, a large planter disposing of the tobacco crop of a small farmer, or a minister helping a parishoner's son get to Yale. The extraordinarily-long political career of William Shirley, who was royal governor of Massachusetts from 1741 to 1756, largely rested on the fact that, as an ambitious young lawyer named John Adams complained in 1759, "Shirley never promoted any man for merit alone."

Despite the broad participation of common people in colonial elections, politics essentially remained a contest among propertied gentlemen for the rewards of political authority. Politics was scarcely thought of as a way for ordinary people to gain social or economic power. The processes of government still depended on face-to-face relations or on the widespread use of correspondence among gentlemen. Much of the writing of pamphlets and newspaper essays was simply another form of personal correspondence among classically educated and like-thinking gentry. Politics thus involved a great deal of personal maneuvering and manipulation. It put a premium on certain traits of character—circumspection, caution, calculation—and on controlling and suppressing one's feelings for the sake of cultivating the "friendship" of those who could help or hurt one's success. Throughout the pre-Revolutionary crisis in Maryland, the elder Charles Carroll, who was raised in the old society, continually urged his impetuous son of the same name who was leading a newspaper assault on the government to move carefully and to hide his bitter antagonism to the Maryland governor. For, as the father warned, "Prudence directs you not to show that the governor's folly and want of spirit is mortifying to you. You may resolve to live in a desert if you will not generally associate with foolish, fickle, mean-spirited men." Such advice bred the civic-minded prudence and role playing that characterized that distinctive eighteenth-century world. But already a younger generation of American politicians, men like Carroll's son, were no longer willing to abide the insincerity and duplicity of that courtier-like world.

The Expansion of Social Independence

In the end, for America and for Great Britain disintegration of this older patronage society prepared the way for the liberal modern capitalistic world of the early nineteenth century. In America the disintegration had begun with the first settlements. The reordering of colonial life in the first century and a half of American history had either prohibited or inhibited a duplication of the social patterns of the mother country. To the extent to which the colonists had already destroyed or had never really established this traditional society, to the degree to which Americans were splintered by religious and ethnic diversity and were more independent, more mistrustful of one another—to that extent was eighteenth-century America already more modern than England.

With the end of the war against the French and Indians and the introduction of changes in British imperial policy, dynamic and competitive impulses long at work in American society unexpectedly accelerated and intensified. These deeply rooted impulses, particularly of population growth, not only aggravated America's alienation from British authority but put intolerable pressure on what remained of the traditional society. From 1750 especially the effects of the continued expansion of the population were felt everywhere. Disputes over the boundaries of towns, counties, and colonies increased, the overworked soil was rapidly depleted, and the consumption of imported goods greatly expanded.

For nearly a century and a half, most of the colonists had remained confined to a several-hundred-mile-wide strip along the Atlantic coast. Now, after the French had been conquered, the growing population, fed by hosts of new immigrants from abroad, was pushing farther into the west, particularly into western Pennsylvania and down the great valley of the Appalachians into the Carolinas. North Caro-

Wanted Immediately
For to go Abroad, to One of the Finest and Healthfulest Climates in
North America;

A Great number of Tradesmen of all forts to Settle, may now have an opportunity of going in a good Ship, well provided with Beds and Provisions as Passengers, not Indentured Servants, but have their Passage trusted and their own Liberty to hire themselves to the best Advantage abroad, such Passengers whom this may suit, may apply to Mr. CRISP'S Office, at No 7, in St. Michael's Alley, Cornhill, opposite the Church Yard.

N. B. Them that choose to apply will be Informed of the Terms by the Merchant's Agent, at the above Office. Some genteel Women wanted, no Objection to Men and their Wives and Children.

Some Artificers that are Masters of their Business, may meet with great Encouragement.
The Ship will Sail next Week.
This you may be sure has no Intention, but what is Fair and Just.

BAILEY, Printer, No 28, Great Tower-street.

RECRUITING EMIGRANTS TO THE COLONIES
This 1770 London poster explicitly disavows the much abused practice of making emigrants become redemptioners, that is, servants who bound themselves over to ship captains in return for passage. (*Historical Society of Pennsylvania.*)

lina itself nearly trebled its population between 1750 and 1770; by the time of the Revolution it had become the fourth largest colony. From Virginia, the most populous colony, some people moved southwest to the headwaters of the Cumberland and Tennessee rivers and others northwest into the Ohio valley and Kentucky basin. During the 1760s New England burst out in all directions. While some New Englanders went south to the lower Mississippi and western Florida, others moved up the Connecticut river valley to take advantage of grants from the royal governor of New Hampshire. In a decade's time these settlers filled what would later become Vermont with twenty thousand inhabitants. Other Massachusetts migrants streamed into Maine and founded ninety-four towns in the decade and a half before the Revolution. Connecticut farmers, under the auspices of the Susquehanna Company, flocked into the Wyoming valley in Pennsylvania and created a Connecticut county in the midst of another colony.

This explosion of migrants bewildered governments, confused boundary lines, and put pressure on the existing western colonists. In the middle and southern colonies the fanning out of settlers stirred up the Indians, leading to a series of violent clashes. In 1759, war with the Cherokees broke out in South Carolina and was suppressed only with great difficulty two years later. In 1763, Indians of various tribes in the Ohio valley followed the lead of an Ottawa chief named Pontiac and attacked white forts and settlers. Before the Indians were put down by British troops, they had penetrated deep into Virginia and Pennsylvania and killed more than two thousand colonists. By 1774, the prospect of a general Indian resistance against the steady encroachment of Virginia settlers into the frontier provided the governor of the colony, Lord Dunmore, the opportunity of leading an assault against the Shawnee and other tribes and of forcing the Indians into agreeing to white occupation of the territory of Kentucky.

It was not just the Indians who suffered from such rapid territorial expansion; government in the backcountry could scarcely keep up with the pace of settlement. In North Carolina, westerners were victimized by the excessive fees and corrupt practices of carpetbagging officials sent from the east. In the South Carolina backcountry, the new settlers found themselves without any local govern-

TREATING WITH THE INDIANS, DETAIL FROM A MAP OF 1765

Negotiations of peace treaties were marked by the smoking of pipes and the exchanging of presents, and by displays of Indian eloquence.

ment at all and at the mercy of outlaws and gangs of thieves. In Pennsylvania,
Scotch-Irish frontiersmen had little representation in the Quaker-dominated
provincial assembly in Philadelphia. In the Wyoming valley in Pennsylvania and
on the New York–Vermont border, settlers were subject to conflicting jurisdictions and land claims. As the frontier settlers organized vigilante groups and appealed for control of their local affairs or for more equal representation in the
colonial legislatures, disorder and eventually violence erupted.

Throughout the decade leading up to the Revolution, Americans carried on
intermittent battles with one another over issues that had little to do with the
controversy with Great Britain. In 1764, a group of embittered Scotch-Irish
frontiersmen of western Pennsylvania led by the Paxton Boys marched on Philadelphia. They were persuaded to withdraw only by the diplomacy of Benjamin
Franklin and the promise of a greater western voice in the colonial government.
In the late 1760s backcountry settlers of South Carolina organized themselves
as Regulators to put down lawless elements in their midst. These South Carolina
Regulators were kept from open rebellion against the provincial government
only by the institution of a new court system in the interior. Vigilantes in North
Carolina took over local government in the western counties, only to be finally
suppressed in a battle with the governor and his force of eastern militia at Alamance in 1771. By the early 1770s, the Green Mountain Boys of Vermont were
fighting all those who submitted to New York's jurisdiction, and Connecticut

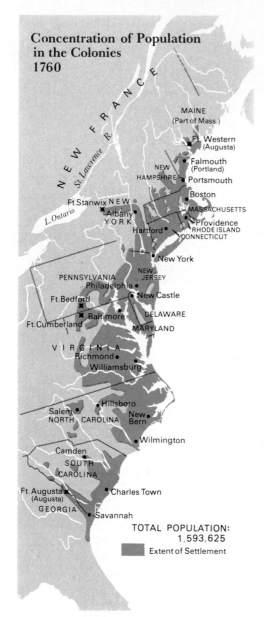

Concentration of Population in the Colonies 1760

TOTAL POPULATION:
1,593,625

Extent of Settlement

Yankees were battling Pennsylvanians for control of the settlements along the Susquehanna River. Although these violent struggles for local autonomy were not directly connected with the Revolutionary movement, they did reveal how many Americans felt about not being equitably represented in distant governments and how suspicious they were of remotely-wielded political power.

The swelling and spreading population not only affected the frontier but strained existing institutions and connections. Land speculation became a mania afflicting everyone from Benjamin Franklin to George Washington. New communities proliferated throughout the colonies. Pennsylvania experienced a town-developing fever with twenty-nine new localities created between 1756 and 1765—more in these few years than in the entire history of the colony. Throughout the scattered population of the Southern colonies, new centers for government and marketing sprang up to tie the rural countryside together in new ways. In New England, the separating, or "hiving off," of sections of townships greatly increased, further fragmenting older relationships in churches and families. New England sons for whom there was no more productive land at home yet who did not wish to migrate sought alternative careers, particularly in the ministry. Farm boys flocked to enter the established colleges of Harvard and Yale and demanded that new educational institutions be created.

Population growth speeded up the commercialization of the colonial economy and dramatically worsened the already unfavorable balance of trade. By the early 1770s, the value of American imports from England had skyrocketed to over 3 million pounds. But this swelling of American consumption of English goods was not matched by American exports to England. Only the sale of an even larger proportion of colonial exports to markets outside Britain—principally to Southern Europe and the West Indies—along with British wartime spending and huge extensions of English and Scottish credit made possible this remarkable increase in American purchasing power. By 1772 the colonists' debts to Great Britain had jumped to over 4 million pounds. British goods were flooding American markets and creating new levels of expectation and taste among the colonists.

These accelerations of long-existing commercial tendencies, together with the need to finance the war against the French and Indians, had compelled the colonial governments to expand their issuing of paper money. Established creditor-merchants on both sides of the Atlantic, who had earlier witnessed the disruptive economic and social consequences of paper money issued in New England, were not happy with the increased use of it. They were particularly disturbed by Virginia, which had never resorted to paper money before. Not only did paper money endanger the repayment of debts, but by making credit available through the more impersonal sources of the colonial loan offices or land banks, it tended to allow larger numbers of small farmers and businessmen to participate more independently in the market. Marginal businessmen appeared everywhere and began dealing directly with London merchant houses, bypassing the older commercial funnels through the big merchants of Boston, New York, and Philadelphia. Petty traders overleapt traditional retail outlets and were even auctioning goods in city streets. By the early 1760s it was not unusual for a major London merchant house to have as many as 150 correspondents in a single port. Although the American mercantile world had always been unsettled and competitive, these midcentury dynamics were remarkable. Commercialization reached deeper into the society than ever before and forced apart the relationships

MERCHANTS' COUNTING HOUSE

Merchants, defined as those involved in overseas trade, were the dominant members of the Northern cities. Dependent on them for a livelihood were great numbers of shopkeepers, vendors, sailors, sail and ropemakers, coopers, smiths, carpenters, and other artisans. (*The Library Company of Philadelphia.*)

of some colonial merchants painstakingly built up during the eighteenth century.

Suddenly in the early 1760s, with the curtailing of wartime spending and a credit crisis in Europe, the commercial boom collapsed. American markets were glutted with unsold goods at the same time as bumper tobacco crops (the result in part of new independent producers) drove tobacco prices down by 75 percent between 1760 and 1764. This collapse in turn led to soaring colonial exchange rates. In other words, to pay off English debts a much greater amount of local currency was needed to purchase an equivalent sum in sterling. Such developments threatened the entire credit structure, from London and Scottish merchant houses and colonial merchants and planters to small farmers and shopkeepers; as a result, business failures and bankruptcies proliferated. By the middle 60s the colonial market-economy was in confusion, beset by an adverse balance of trade, severe restrictions on credit, low prices, rising exchange rates, and a shortage of currency. Aggravating the collapse was the larger proportion of people who had been enticed into participating in the market during the previous decade or so.

It is not surprising that the victims of the collapse, unused to the vicissitudes of a market economy, sought to blame their shifting fortunes on the distant government in England. In fact the British government's response to the financial crisis could not have been more clumsy and provocative. In 1764, Parliament passed a new Currency Act, which extended the 1751 prohibition against New England's issuing of paper money as legal tender to all the colonies. This sweeping and simple-minded resolution of a complicated situation only ensured that more colonists than ever before would feel the effects of a remote and arbitrary power.

Certainly in the Chesapeake area of Maryland and Virginia, it was easier in the 1760s to blame the economic crisis on outside forces then it would have been several decades earlier. Substituting Scottish factors, or agents, as middlemen in the marketing of tobacco now brought both large and small planters together in this crisis as like victims of a common alien element (which helps explain Virginia's remarkable degree of unity in the face of the imperial threat).

At the same time, however, the new marketing system had deteriorated the relations between large and small planters that had contributed to the earlier stability of Chesapeake society. The appearance of the Scottish stores in the backcountry allowed many more small farmers to participate independently in the market than the old consignment system had. These ordinary farmers expressed their new independence particularly through religious dissent. To bring some measure of order into their disrupted lives, they formed new religious communities that soon challenged the established society in Virginia and Maryland. The dissenters explicitly rejected the high style and luxurious living of the Anglican gentry and sought to spread their evangelical fervor throughout the area. Throughout the 1750s and 1760s the Chesapeake gentry complained in the newspapers and their letters of the mounting defections from the Church of England, particularly among the common people. Within just a few years, succeeding waves of enthusiastic New Light Presbyterians, Separate Baptists, and finally Methodists swept up new converts from among the ordinary farmers of the Chesapeake. Between 1769 and 1774, the number of Baptist churches in Virginia alone increased from seven to fifty-four.

The Chesapeake gentry blamed this successful proselytizing by the dissenters on the long-existing laxity and ignorance of the Anglican clergy. The clergymen in turn accused the lay vestries of Anglican gentlemen of not supporting them against the evangelical threat. In this atmosphere of mutual recriminations and increased anticlericalism, planters in Virginia and Maryland attempted to lower the salaries paid to the ministers of the established Church of England. In 1755 and 1758 the Virginia House of Burgesses passed acts that fixed the standard of value of tobacco used to meet debts and public obligations at two pence a pound. Since tobacco prices were rising rapidly, this legislation, known as the "Two Penny Acts," penalized creditors and those public officials like the clergy who were used to being paid in tobacco. British merchants and the Virginia clerical establishment protested and were able to get the king's Privy Council to invalidate the act of 1758 passed by the House of Burgesses. In 1763 in one of the Virginia clergy's legal suits for recovery of wages lost by the Two Penny Act, a rising young lawyer, Patrick Henry, first made his reputation. Henry argued that, because he had disallowed the act, the king "from being the father of his people [has] degenerated into a Tyrant, and forfeits all rights to his subjects' obedience." Such struggles between Anglican gentlemen and their own clerical establishment only played into the hands of the dissenters and common farmers of the region for whom new politicians like Henry were speaking.

Perhaps even more revealing of the religious and social changes taking place was the upheaval that occurred in the Society of Friends. By the middle of the eighteenth century, the Quakers, particularly in Philadelphia, had shed much of their inward-looking and sectarian character, and had developed into well-to-do elites who dominated the political and economic life of Pennsylvania. During the Revolutionary era, however, the Society of Friends underwent a transformation. By the end of the century the Quakers had become devoted to philanthropy and reform. Older wealthy mercantile and politically-minded Quakers slipped into Anglicanism or simply retired from the scene. Sometimes their places were taken by their children who renounced the social status and refinements and the lukewarm faith of their parents in a youthful determination to take Quaker professions seriously. At other times hosts of new converts contributed to the shift in values. Most came from ordinary and middling elements of American society and sought in Quakerism and other revivalistic religious movements a resolution of the anxieties produced by their aroused aspirations and uncertain social status. By 1773, Moses Brown, the youngest brother of the raw and rapidly rising mercantile family of Providence, Rhode Island, had come to doubt the value of wealth gained so fast. Renouncing what money could buy, he converted to Quakerism, and soon became one of the

MOSES BROWN (1738–1836)

Brown, a Quaker convert and philanthropist, was one of the first Americans to become interested in cotton manufacturing. By the early nineteenth century he had become a patriarch of both commercial development and Christian benevolence in America. (*The Rhode Island Historical Society.*)

country's foremost humanitarian reformers, promoting everything from vegetarianism and antislavery to temperance.

While common people were turning to new sects, elite groups sought their own form of religious refuge, usually in Anglicanism. The Church of England had a powerful appeal to large numbers of the well-to-do distressed by evangelical enthusiasm and allured by the elegance and stability that Anglicanism, at least in the urban areas, had come to represent. In New England, liberal Congregationalism, with its softening of the harsh tenets of Calvinism, its abhorrence of pietistic revivalism, and its acceptance of the world of benevolent behavior, offered the aspiring gentility a meaningful alternative to the attractions of the Church of England—a rational supernaturalism, a dignified religion still within reformed Protestantism, and a defense of wealth without justifying the evils of luxury.

But even in New England, the lure of Anglicanism was strong. Jonathan Mayhew's bitter attacks on Anglican and royal authority were based in part on a need to save those like his wealthy and ambitious mercantile congregation of Boston's West Church, which had lost its previous minister to the Church of

England, from the temptations of Anglicanism and the aristocratic imperial circles it represented. His 1750 sermon, *A Discourse Concerning Unlimited Submission,* stridently defending the right of resistance against the tyranny of both kings and "imperious BISHOPS," seemed unaccountably exaggerated to some colonists. But Mayhew was only voicing deeply rooted anxieties shared by many Americans over the effects the steady encroachments of the Church of England were having on their society. The proposal to establish a bishop in America was especially threatening. By ordaining new ministers on this side of the Atlantic, an American bishop would enable candidates for the Anglican clergy to avoid the dangerous and expensive voyage to England. Soon, many feared, an elaborate episcopal hierarchy would be flourishing in the colonies.

The explosions in the population and in the market had an impact on politics as well as religion. Competition for political authority increased. The numbers of men eager to hold office and wield power at both the provincial and local levels of government outran the political system's capacity to absorb them. In New England, the increase in population and the

"ATTEMPT TO LAND A BISHOP IN AMERICA"

By 1768 proposals for establishing an Anglican bishop in America had become identified with British efforts to deprive the colonists of their liberties.

resultant pressure for establishing new precincts and towns, together with the emigration of thousands of inhabitants, strained family and political relationships. More and more groups and individuals scrambled for a share in political authority in order to realize or protect their interests. Securing a charter to western lands, gaining recognition of religious rights, locating a new courthouse, establishing a new college—all required access to political power. As traditional lines of authority weakened further, groups became especially anxious to secure spokesmen in government from whose "connections . . . and from whose Principles," as South Carolina craftsmen declared in 1765, they had "reason to expect the greatest assistance." By the late 1760s these Carolina artisans, like other interests elsewhere, were demanding explicit recognition of their members in political organizations as the only means of assuring that their voices would be heard.

Even in Virginia, where the common people had always acquiesced in the leadership of the planting gentry, political authority began to show signs of deterioration. The relations between the members of the House of Burgesses and their more independent constituents were no longer clear. Gentlemen voiced more and more concern over the increase in the number of competitive elections, their mounting costs, and the growing corruption in the soliciting of votes, especially, as one planter noted, by "those who have neither natural nor acquired parts to recommend them." By the late 60s and early 70s, newspapers were filled with new warnings against electoral influence, bribery, and demagoguery. Robert Munford's famous play, *The Candidates*, written in 1770, betrays the gentry's uneasiness over electoral developments in the colony, "when coxcombs and jockies can impose themselves upon it for men of learning." Although disinterested virtue eventually wins out, Munford's dramatic satire reveals the kinds of threats the established planters thought they faced from ambitious "knaves" and "blockheads" who were rapidly turning representatives in government into slaves of the people.

As patronage ties between England and the colonies began to disintegrate and many of the personal channels to imperial authority in London were closed off after 1740, more and more local leaders began to turn to the people as a counterweight to royal authority in the colonies. This increasing popularization of politics can be measured in various ways: in the multiplication of contested elections; in the broadening of voter participation; in the growing use of new political techniques and organizations, including caucuses and tickets; and in the rise of campaign propaganda and professional pamphleteering. By 1760, decades of elite competition and political wrangling, with continual invocations of the people through inflammatory radical rhetoric, had generated such a highly charged political atmosphere that it was not longer certain the dominant gentry could control the people. Not only was American politics breeding a large number of political leaders who thought their local interests were best served by antagonism to British authority, but it was also creating a popular force that was less and less susceptible to elite manipulation.

Reorganization of the British Empire

As much as these changes contributed to the character of the Revolution and the eventual transformation of American society, they were not by themselves responsible for bringing on the Revolution. The immediate origins of the Revolution lay not in any specific economic or social deprivations the colonists may have suffered, nor in any calculated efforts by planters, merchants, artisans, or farmers to improve their lives by challenging constituted authority. Like all great events, the American Revolution started from beginnings that had little to do with the results. The Revolution was precipitated by a political crisis within the British empire, and at the outset at least it was very much a colonial rebellion.

The crisis was provoked by Great Britain's attempts to reorganize its empire. From the formation of the empire in the late seventeenth century, there always had been royal officials and bureaucrats interested in rationalizing the awkwardly imposed imperial structure and in expanding royal authority over the colonists. But most of these reforming schemes had been thwarted by English ministries more concerned with the patronage and stability of English politics than with colonial reform. These ministers were anxious to keep disruptive colonial issues out of Parliament, where they might be readily exploited by opposition politicians. Under such circumstances, the empire had been allowed to grow aimlessly.

Although few imperial officials had ever doubted that the empire was supposed to be a hierarchy and that the colonies were in an inferior and dependent relationship to the mother country, the success of the accommodations worked out between England and the colonies was possible precisely because the empire was irrational and inefficient. The variety of offices, the diffusion of power, and the laxity of organization weakened the superficial imperial authority. Even in the regulation of trade, which was the empire's main business, the inefficiency, the loopholes, and the numerous opportunities for corruption prevented the coercive authority that did exist from interfering substantially with the colonists' pursuit of their own economic and social interests. Despite deeply rooted animosities against British authority, the colonists more or less accepted the imperial relationship on the loose terms that had evolved during the eighteenth century.

By the middle of the century, however, new circumstances began forcing changes in this irrational but working imperial relationship. The increasing number of British colonies—in 1760 there were twenty-two in the Western Hemisphere—demanded new attention by Great Britain. Colonial trade was making up an increasingly important segment of the English and Scottish economies. Nearly half of all English shipping was engaged in American commerce. The North American mainland alone was absorbing 25 percent of England's exports, and Scottish commercial involvement with the colonies was growing even faster. The Church of England's renewed demands for the establishment of an American bishop to oversee Anglican affairs in the colonies further enhanced the British government's interest in American affairs.

The most important event, however, that brought the colonies to the center of British concern was the Seven Years War. British experiences in the war in America had been eye-opening. The difficulties of enforcing the navigation system, the blatant trading by the colonists with the enemy, the flagrant customs violations, and the pervasive inefficiency and corruption had infuriated British military officers in America. After this wartime experience, British officials were more determined than ever to bring the colonists once and for all into proper subordination.

Yet the piecemeal reforms begun during the war and the threat of more imperial regulations through Parliament's intervention might have been stifled by the usual machinations of British politics if it had not been for the problems resulting from the Peace of Paris in 1763. The most immediate of these was the disposition of the new territory acquired from France and Spain—Canada,

East and West Florida, and all the land west of the Appalachians and east of the Mississippi. Fur traders, land speculators, and adventurers of all kinds, representing both American and British interests scrambled to control this new western territory. The traders, for their part, wanted Indian reservations established and settlers kept out, and drew upon the support of humanitarian groups. The land speculators, however, wanted to push back the Indians and open up the west to a people that had become, in the words of one participant, "land crazy." Decisions now had to be made in Britain that would reverse the careless laxity of earlier colonial policy.

An even more unsettling consequence of the war and the peace with France

North America in 1763

was the enormous expense confronting the British government. By 1763 the war debt totalled £137 million; its annual interest alone was £5 million, a huge figure when compared with an ordinary yearly British peacetime budget of only £8 million. There was, moreover, little prospect of military costs declining. Since the new acquisitions were virtually uninhabited by Englishmen, the government could not rely on its traditional system of local defense and police. Lord Jeffrey Amherst, commander in chief in North America, estimated that he would need 10,000 troops to maintain order among the French and Indians and to deal with squatters, smugglers, and bandits. Thus at the outset of the 1760s the British government made a crucial decision—a decision that no subsequent administration ever abandoned—to maintain a standing army in America. This peacetime army was more than double the size of the army that had existed in the colonies before the Seven Years War, and the costs of maintaining it quickly climbed to well over £400,000 a year. At the same time, however, the landed gentry in Great Britain felt pressed to the wall by taxes; the new English cider tax of 1763 actually required troops to enforce it. Under the circumstances—with the tales of American prosperity brought back by returning British troops, with the benefits of the new land and the peace apparently accruing to the colonists—it seemed reasonable to the British government to seek new sources of revenue in the colonies and to make the navigation system more efficient in ways that royal officials had long advocated. A half-century of what Burke called "salutary neglect" had to come to an end.

Disruptions within the delicate balance of the empire were therefore inevitable. But aggravating the changing Anglo-American relations was the accession in 1760 of a new monarch, the young and impetuous George III. George III was only twenty-two, shy, and inexperienced in politics, but he was stubbornly determined to rule personally in a manner distinctly different from that of the earlier Hanoverian monarchs. Influenced by his inept Scottish tutor and "dearest friend," Lord Bute, George aimed to purify English public life of its corruptions and factionalism and to substitute duty to crown and country for party intrigue. The results of George's good intentions were the greatest and most bewildering fluctuations suffered by English politics in a half century—all at the very moment the long-postponed reforms of the empire were to take place.

Historians no longer depict George III as a "tyrant" seeking to undermine the English constitution and destroy ministerial responsibility to Parliament by choosing his own ministers. But there can be little doubt that men of the time felt that George III, whether he intended to or not, was violating the accumulated political conventions of the day. When he chose Lord Bute, his Scottish favorite who had little political strength in Parliament to head his government, and subsequently excluded those ministers like William Pitt and the Duke of Newcastle, who did command political support in Parliament, the new king may not have been acting unconstitutionally, but he certainly was acting against the political proprieties and realities of the day. Bute's retirement in

1763 did little to ease the opposition's apprehensions that the king was seeking the advice of favorites "behind the curtain" and attempting to govern above the leading political groups in Parliament rather than through them. By diligently attempting to shoulder his constitutional responsibility for governing in his own stubborn peculiar way, George III helped to increase the political confusion of the 1760s.

A series of short-lived ministries throughout the 60s suggested that the head-strong king trusted no one who had the support of Parliament. George Grenville, as Bute's protégé, took over in 1763 because no one else acceptable to the king could be found. Grenville's ministry was maimed by the crisis over the Stamp Act, the tax measure of 1765 that so inflamed the colonists; but colonial policy had nothing to do with his personal quarrel with the king and his resignation in 1765. The Whigs connected with the Marquess of Rockingham, for whom Edmund Burke was spokesman, next formed a government, but they never had the confidence of the king and lasted only long enough to repeal the Stamp Act under the influence of their mercantile connections hurt by American economic boycotts. In 1766, George at last called upon the aged Pitt, now Lord Chatham, to

"THE COUNCIL OF THE RULERS AND ELDERS AGAINST THE TRIBE OF THE AMERICANS"

In this opposition-inspired cartoon, Lord North is pictured as too busy buying support for his government and adding to his "List of King's Friends" to pay attention to the dangerous situation in North America. (*The Library of Congress.*)

The Council of the Rulers, & the Elders against the Tribe of ye Americanites.
Sold by W. Gillman Roch
Dec.r 1775

head the government, but Chatham's illness and the bewildering parliamentary factionalism of the late 60s turned the ministry into a hodgepodge, "a Government of Departments," as Lord North later called it.

By this point no one seemed to be in charge; ministers shuffled in and out of offices, exchanging positions and following their own inclinations even against the wishes of their colleagues. Amidst this confusion only Charles Townshend as chancellor of the exchequer gave any direction to colonial policy, and he died in 1767. Not until the appointment of Lord North as prime minister in 1770 did George find a politician whom he trusted and who also had the support of Parliament. Yet North's ministry depended on the inability of the principal opposition groups, particularly the Rockingham Whigs and the Chathamites, to come together on imperial policy. While Chatham supported the American denunciation of parliamentary taxation, the Rockingham Whigs were unwilling to concede an iota of Parliament's theoretical supremacy. Such a situation precisely reversed the stability of Walpole's day when ministries kept devisive colonial issues out of Parliament. After 1765 the king's governments discovered that colonial questions were the one thing they could count on to divide those who opposed them in Parliament.

But in other ways too the instability of the British government contributed to the imperial crisis. It helped to make possible the sudden rush of long-desired but long-delayed colonial reforms. Beneath the surface of the shifting ministers and the rising and falling governments remained groups of subministers and lower-level bureaucrats who moved steadily from department to department, drawing up the various acts and putting into effect the colonial programs they had long considered essential for running the empire rationally. It is doubtful whether the influence of these bureaucrats would have been so potent or whether colonial policy would have been so coherent and consistent if ministerial politics at the top had not been so confused.

The British reforms began chaotically with the efforts to develop a policy for the new western lands. Not only were there considerable shifts among the ministers, but news of Pontiac's Indian rebellion in the Ohio valley in 1763 forced the government to rush its program into effect. The Proclamation of 1763 ran a hastily-drawn demarcation line along the Appalachians, closing the West to whites and placing the Indian trade in local hands. So crudely drawn was the line and so destructive the permissive trade policy that the British government could never convince the various contending interests that the proclamation was anything more than, in George Washington's words, "a temporary expedient to quiet the minds of the Indians." The unsteady British governments, beset by hosts of speculators and lobbyists, repeatedly shifted the line westward. But every change only whetted the appetites of the land-jobbers and led to some of the most grandiose land schemes in modern history. The Grand Ohio Company, for example, involving nearly half the members of the Privy Council, petitioned the crown in 1769 for the rights to 20 million acres in the Ohio valley. The

British government finally tried to steady its dizzy western policy with the Quebec Act of 1774. Yet that act, which transferred the land and trade between the Ohio and Mississippi rivers to the province of Quebec and allowed its inhabitants French law and Roman Catholicism, only managed to anger all American interests—speculators, settlers, and traders alike. The act also frightened American Protestants into believing this western policy was yet another attempt by the British to deprive them of their liberties.

The new colonial trade policies were more coherent than the western policy, but no less provocative. The British government issued a series of regulations designed to tighten up the navigation system and in particular to curb the colonists' smuggling and corruption. Absentee customs officials were ordered to their posts and given greater authority and protection. The jurisdiction of the vice-admiralty courts in customs cases was broadened. The navy was granted greater power in inspecting American ships. The use of writs of assistance (or search warrants) was enlarged. The list of enumerated goods that had to be brought to England was lengthened. And finally the requirements of American shippers for posting bonds and obtaining certificates of clearance were so greatly increased that nearly all colonial merchants, even those involved only in the coastwise trade, found themselves enmeshed in a bureaucratic web of bonds, certificates, and regulations.

To these frustrating rigidities now built into the navigation system were added new customs duties, which raised the expenses of American importers in order to increase British revenue. At the center of the British government's initial reform of colonial trade was the Sugar Act, or Revenue Act of 1764. The act imposed duties on foreign cloth, sugar, indigo, coffee, and wine brought into the colonies and eliminated the refunds of duties hitherto made in England on foreign goods reexported to America. Most important, the Sugar Act reduced

A TEST IMPRESSION OF ONE OF THE
STAMPS THE BRITISH GOVERNMENT
PLANNED TO USE IN THE COLONIES
IN 1765.

the supposedly prohibitory duty of sixpence a gallon on foreign molasses, set by the Molasses Act of 1733, to threepence a gallon; in 1766 the duty was further reduced to one penny a gallon on all molasses. The government assumed that with the smaller duty it would be cheaper for American merchants to import molasses legally than to resort to smuggling and bribery. The lower duty would therefore earn money for the crown. At a stroke these British reforms threatened to upset the delicately poised patterns of trade built up over the previous generation.

Such regulations and custom duties could be regarded as part of Britain's traditional authority over colonial commerce. But the next step in Britain's new imperial program could not. Grenville's ministry, convinced that the customs reforms could not bring in the needed revenue, was determined to try a decidedly different method of getting at American wealth. In March 1765, Parliament by an overwhelming majority passed the Stamp Act, which levied a tax (to be paid in sterling, like all the duties) on documents, almanacs, newspapers, and nearly every form of paper used in the colonies. Although stamp duties had been used in England since 1694 and by several colonies in the 1750s, such a parliamentary tax, directly touching the everyday affairs of Americans, exposed the nature of political authority within the empire in a way no other issue in the eighteenth century ever had.

American Resistance

The colonists' response to these initial efforts by the British government to reorganize the empire immediately brought to the surface the latent antagonisms between America and Britain. The Sugar Act, coinciding with the postwar depression and threatening economic dislocation for many, stirred up opposition and boycotts by merchants in the northern ports and provoked the first deliberately organized intercolonial protest. The assemblies of eight colonies drew up and endorsed formal petitions pleading economic injury from the Sugar Act and sent them to royal authorities in England. Britain's next step, however, Grenville's stamp tax in 1765, excited not a protest, but a firestorm that swept through the colonies with a force that amazed everyone. This parliamentary tax, however fiscally justifiable and unburdensome it may have been, posed such a distinct threat to the legislative autonomy and the liberties of the colonists that Americans could no longer contain their opposition within the traditional channels of remonstrance and lobbying.

In October 1765 thirty-seven delegates from nine colonies met in New York in the Stamp Act Congress and drew up a set of formal declarations and petitions denying Parliament's right to tax them. But remarkable as this display of colonial unity was, the Stamp Act Congress with its opening acknowledgement of "all due Subordination to that August Body the Parliament of Great Britain" could not fully express American hostility. Newspapers and pamphlets, the number and like of which had never appeared so suddenly in America before, seethed with resentment against what one New Yorker called "these designing parricides" who had "invited despotism to cross the ocean, and fix her abode in this once happy land." Meetings of towns, counties, legislatures, and other hastily convened assemblies boiled over with burning statements. When in the spring of 1765 the Virginia House of Burgesses, inspired by Patrick Henry, adopted a series of resolves denouncing parliamentary taxation, Americans announced their agreement. Although several of Henry's resolutions, including one that proclaimed the right of Virginians to disobey any law not enacted by the House of Burgesses, were too inflammatory to be accepted, colonial newspapers printed them all as though they had been endorsed by the Virginia assembly and convinced many that Virginians had virtually asserted their legislative independence from Great Britain. Such boldness was contagious. The Rhode Island assembly declared the Stamp Act "unconstitutional" and authorized the colony's officials to ignore it. Merchants in the principal ports formed associations and pledged to stop importing British goods in order to bring economic pressure on the British government.

Ultimately, however, it was the eruption of popular violence that brought down the Stamp Act in America. On August 14, 1765, a crowd destroyed the office and attacked the home of Andrew Oliver, the stamp distributor for Massachusetts. The next day Oliver promised not to enforce the Stamp Act. Twelve days later a mob gutted the home of the person who seemed to be responsible for defending the Stamp Act in Massachusetts, Oliver's brother-in-law, Lieutenant Governor Thomas Hutchinson. As news of the rioting spread to other colonies, similar violence and threats of violence spread with it. From Newport, Rhode Island to Charleston, South Carolina local groups organized for resistance. Often formed out of previously existing fire and artillery companies or artisan associations, these "Sons of Liberty" burned effigies of royal officials, forced stamp agents to resign, compelled businessmen and judges to carry on without stamps, developed an intercolonial network of correspondence, and generally took over managing and enforcing nonimportation and antistamp activities throughout the colonies.

Although Parliament, under pressure from English merchants, quickly repealed the Stamp Act, and the organized Sons of Liberty soon dissolved, the imperial relationship and American respect for British authority, indeed all authority, would never again be the same. The crisis over the Stamp Act aroused

OPPOSITION TO THE STAMP ACT

In Philadelphia, newspaper publisher William Bradford announced the suspension of publication of his *Pennsylvania Journal* while in Massachusetts, a local stamp agent was hung in effigy to protest the new tax. (*The Metropolitan Museum of Art, Bequest of Charles Allen Munn, 1924.*)

and unified Americans as no previous political event ever had. It stimulated bold political and constitutional writings throughout the colonies, deepened political participation and consciousness, and produced new forms of organized resistance. Not only did mobbing and extralegal expressions of popular power spread, but such popular resistance was now directed at English authority itself. By compelling the resignation of stamp agents and obedience to popular measures through "their riotous meetings," the people, as Governor Horatio Sharpe of Maryland observed in 1765, "begin to think they can by the same way of proceeding accomplish anything their leaders may tell them they ought to do."

Since many British officials believed that the colonists objected only to the "in-

THE

ENNSYLVANIA JOURNAL;
AND
WEEKLY ADVERTISER.

hursday, *October* 31, 1765.   NUMB. 1195.

EXPIRING: In Hopes of a Resurrection to Life again.

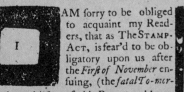

I AM sorry to be obliged to acquaint my Readers, that as The STAMP-ACT, is fear'd to be obligatory upon us after the *First of November* ensuing, (the *fatal To-mor-*...

...he Publisher of this Paper unable to ...he Burthen, has thought it expedient ...or a while, in order to deliberate, whe... ...ny Methods can be found to elude the ...s forged for us, and escape the insup-...le Slavery; which it is hoped, from ...ft Representations now made against ...Act, may be effected. Mean while, ...t earnestly Request every Individual ...y Subscribers, many of whom have ...ong behind Hand, that they would ...diately Discharge their respective Ar-...that I may be able, not only to ...rt myself during the Interval, but ...etter prepared to proceed again with ...aper, whenever an opening for that ...se appears, which I hope will be

WILLIAM BRADFORD.

And in all political Disord... under them, so much the ... the worse are we for them... stance attending public V... the more it is vilified, the... ...pears. No Falshood forme... at once detects and confute... rate Calumny. But altho... affected by the Indulgence... dom of speaking or writing... ny as it derives all its Influ... extremely benefited by the ... Countries subjected to the ... and Avarice, the first Atte... just Sense of their Conditio... Bud. It is of the last Impo... ing Men to shut up the ... Channel of Information fr... forming such Schemes as ... der to be Opposed. Bef... whole Liberty may be just... the Deprivation of any in... berty of the Press undoubte...

How amiable is the Enjo... detestable are the Bonds of ... cerly to be hoped, that the ... exemplarily free in former ... in Submission to new and ...

A Day, an Hour of vi... Is worth a whole Eter... May we all as loyal Sub... exert our utmost to preserve the Rights and Liberties of our Country, in a Manner that shall add Honour to our Endeavours; that future Posterity may reap the Benefit, and bless the Hands which were the Instruments of procuring it.---

That Glory then, the brightest Crown of Praise, Which every Lover of his Country's Wealth, And every Patron of Mankind deserves...

Stamp Master in Effigy
Massachusetts

respected as their's."

It is said the new m-----y, taking into consideration the present deplorable situation of the Canadians, have determined to take up all the Canada bills at par, with interest to the present time; and afterwards to demand, in the most spirited terms, *immediate* and *full* payment of France, under pain of all the consequences that can result from a refusal.

ternal" and "direct" nature of the stamp tax, they presumed that "external" and "indirect" taxes on trade would be more acceptable. Consequently, in 1767 Parliament, led by Chancellor of the Exchequer Charles Townshend, made new levies on glass, paint, paper, and tea imported into the colonies. Although all the new customs duties, particularly the molasses duty of 1766, began bringing in an average yearly revenue of £45,000—in contrast to only £2,000 a year collected before 1764—the yearly sums raised were scarcely a tenth of the annual costs of maintaining the army in America.

Convinced that something more drastic had to be done, the British government reorganized the executive authority of the empire. In 1767–68 the government created an American Board of Customs, located in Boston and reporting directly to the Treasury, and erected three new superior vice-admiralty courts at Boston, Philadelphia, and Charleston, besides the one already at Halifax. To cap the entire structure, in belated recognition of the importance of the colonies, it established an executive department exclusively responsible for American affairs. At the same time, for the sake of economy, the government decided to pull back much of the army from its costly deployment in the West and to close many of the remote posts. The army was now to be stationed in the coastal cities, where the colonists would be responsible for its housing and supply, according to the new parliamentary Quartering Act of 1765. Not only did this withdrawal of the troops eastward away from the French and Indians contribute to the chaos in the western territory, but concentrating a standing army in peacetime amidst a civilian population blurred the original mission of the army in America and heightened the colonists' fears of often muddled British intentions.

By 1768, some English officials were suggesting that the troops might be used to put down disorder among the Americans, while others were moving to curb the political authority of the people within the colonies themselves. Revenue from the Townshend duties was earmarked for the salaries of royal officials in the colonies so that they would be independent of the colonial legislatures. The colonial governors were instructed to maintain tighter control of the assemblies and not to agree to acts that changed popular representation in the assemblies or the length of time the legislatures sat. Some royal officials toyed with more elaborate plans for remodeling the colonial governments, proposing that the Massachusetts charter be revoked and that the royal councils be strengthened. Some even suggested introducing a nobility into America to sit in the colonial upper houses.

In the colonial atmosphere of the late 60s, these measures and proposals were not simply provocative; they were explosive. After the Stamp Act cris.s, American sensitivities to all forms of English taxation were thoroughly aroused. With the passage of the Townshend duties, the earlier pattern of resistance reappeared and expanded. Pamphlets and newspapers again leapt to the defense of American liberties. The cultivated Philadelphia lawyer John Dickinson, in his *Letters from a Farmer in Pennsylvania*, the most popular pamphlet of the 1760s, disavowed all parliamentary taxation, whether "internal" or "external," and called for reviving the non-importation agreements that had been so effective in the resistance to the Stamp Act. Following Boston's lead in March 1768, merchants in the colonial ports again formed associations to boycott British goods. By now more Americans than ever were involved in the resistance movement. Extralegal groups and committees, usually but not always restrained by popular leaders, emerged to inspect tobacco in Maryland, punish importers in Philadelphia, mob a publisher in Boston, or harass customs officials in New York.

Nowhere were events more spectacular than in Massachusetts. There the situation was so inflammatory that every move triggered a string of explosions that widened the gap between the colonists and royal authority. Forty-six-year-old Samuel Adams, with his puritanical zeal, organizational skill, and abiding hatred of crown authority, soon became a dominant political figure. It was later said that 1768 was the year Adams decided on independence for America. Given the events in Massachusetts during that year, it is easy to see why.

In February 1768, the Massachusetts House of Representatives issued a "Circular Letter" to the other colonial legislatures denouncing the Townshend duties as unconstitutional violations of the principle of no taxation without representation. Lord Hillsborough, the

SAMUEL ADAMS, BY JOHN SINGLETON COPLEY

Of all the American leaders, Sam Adams came closest to being a professional revolutionary, selflessly devoted to the cause. As "one of Plutarch's men", Adams took seriously the spartan severity of classical republicanism. (*Courtesy, Museum of Fine Arts, Boston.*)

secretary of state of the newly-created American Department, ordered the Massachusetts House to rescind its Circular Letter. When the House defied this order by a large majority of 92 to 17 (thereby enshrining the number "92" in patriot rituals), Governor Bernard dissolved the Massachusetts assembly. With this legal means for redressing grievances silenced, mobs and other unauthorized groups erupted. Boston, which was rapidly becoming a symbol of colonial resistance, ordered its inhabitants to arm and called for an extralegal convention of town delegates. Beset by mobs, customs officials in Boston found it impossible to enforce the navigation regulations, and they pleaded for military help. When a British warship arrived at Boston in June 1768, customs officials promptly seized John Hancock's ship *Liberty* for violating the trade acts. Since Hancock

THE FRUITS OF ARBITRARY POWER, OR THE BLOODY MASSACRE,

perpetrated in King-Street, BOSTON, on March 5th 1770. IN WHICH MESST SAMT GRAY: SAMT MAVERICK, JAMES CALDWELL, CRISPUS ATTUCKS & PATK CARR WERE KILLED SIX OTHER WOUNDED TWO OF THEM MORTALLY.

HOW LONG SHALL THEY UTTER AND SPEAK HARD THINGS AND ALL THE WORKERS OF INIQUITY BOAST THEMSELVES: THEY BREAK IN PIECES THY PEOPLE O LORD AND AFFLICT THINE HERITAGE: THEY SLAY THE WIDOW AND THE STRANGER AND MUR-DER THE FATHERLESS. YET THEY SAY THE LORD SHALL NOT SEE. NEI-THER SHALL THE GOD OF JACOB REGARD IT. PSALM XCIV.

"THE BOSTON MASSACRE" ENGRAVED BY PETER PELHAM

This print was scarcely an accurate depiction of the "Massacre." It aimed for rhetorical and emotional effect and became perhaps the most famous piece of antimilitary propaganda in American history. (*American Antiquarian Society.*)

and his great wealth were prominently associated with the resistance movement, the seizure was intended to be an object lesson in royal authority. Its effect, however, was to set off one of the fiercest riots in Boston's history.

Royal officials, believing virtual anarchy existed in Boston, dispatched two regiments of troops, which began arriving on October 1. By 1769, there were nearly four thousand armed redcoats in the crowded seaport of fifteen thousand inhabitants. Amid traditional English fears of standing armies, relations between townspeople and soldiers deteriorated and charged the atmosphere for the explosion of March 5, 1770. On that day, British troops fired upon a threatening crowd and killed five civilians. The "Boston Massacre," especially as it was depicted in Paul Revere's engraving, aroused American passions and inspired some of the most sensational rhetoric heard in the Revolutionary era.

This resort to troops to quell disorder was the ultimate symptom of the ineffectiveness of the British government's authority, and the government knew it. Indeed throughout the escalation of events in the 1760s many of the ministers remained confused and uncertain. "There is the most urgent reason to do what is right, and immediately," wrote Lord Barrington, secretary at war, to Governor Bernard in 1767; "but what is that right and who is to do it?" English officials advanced and retreated, cajoled and threatened in ever more desperate efforts to enforce British authority without aggravating the colonists' hostility. In the winter of 1767–68 the British responded to the disorder in Massachusetts with a series of parliamentary resolutions and addresses to the king, condemning Massachusetts' denial of parliamentary supremacy and threatening to bring the colonial offenders to England for trial. Yet strong minority opposition in the House of Commons and the ministry's unwillingness to precipitate further crises made these resolutions empty gestures. The government was content now to wage only what one Englishman called "a paper war with the colonies."

By the end of the 1760s British plans for reorganizing the empire were in shambles. Colonial legislatures and royal governors were at loggerheads; Britain's authority was denounced daily in print; and mobs were becoming increasingly common in the countryside as well as in city streets. Customs officials were under continuous intimidation and were quarreling with merchants, naval officers, and royal governors. The customs officials' entanglement in local politics made efficient or even-handed enforcement of the trade acts impossible. What enforcement there was thus appeared arbitrary and discriminatory, and drove many merchants, like the wealthy South Carolinian Henry Laurens, who had earlier been contemptuous of the Sons of Liberty, into bitter opposition. The financial returns to the British government from the customs reforms seemed in no way commensurate with the costs. By 1770, less than £21,000 had been collected from the Townshend duties, while the loss to British business from American nonimportation movements during the previous year was put at £700,000. It was therefore not surprising that the British government now abandoned the hope of securing revenue from the duties and labeled the Townshend program, in Lord Hillsborough's words, "contrary to the true principles of commerce." In 1770, after years of ministerial chaos, reorganization of the king's government

Trade Between Britain and the Colonies, 1763-1776

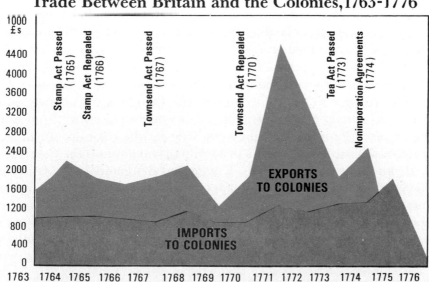

under Lord North prepared the way for repeal of the Townshend duties. Only the duty on tea was retained, in Lord North's words, "as a mark of the supremacy of Parliament, and an efficient declaration of their right to govern the colonies."

Yet the stabilization of English politics with the formation of North's ministry and the repeal of the Townshend duties could scarcely undo what had already been done since 1760. Within a decade's time, a generation of "salutary neglect" had been completely overturned. Although politicians on both sides of the Atlantic were by the early 70s calling for a return to the situation before 1763, going back was clearly no longer possible.

The tranquility of these years therefore was superficial. The royal commission sent to inquire into the sinking of the British revenue vessel *Gaspée* in Rhode Island in 1772 seemed to fulfill earlier British threats to bypass regular judicial procedures, and led Virginia to call for the creation of legislative committees of correspondence, to which five assemblies responded. Massachusetts towns, under Boston's leadership, had already begun organizing committees of correspondence to tie themselves together and to assert principles of liberty. Elsewhere royal governors were complaining how weak their remaining authority was. By the end of 1773 colonial newspapers were talking openly of independence. Since the North government was determined to uphold the sovereignty of Parliament, an eventual confrontation seemed unavoidable.

In 1773, Parliament provided the occasion by granting the East India Company the exclusive privilege of selling tea in America. Although the North government intended this Tea Act only to be a means of saving the East India Company from bankruptcy, it set off the final series of explosions. Not only did the act allow colonial radicals to draw attention once again to the unconstitutionality of the existing tax on tea, but it permitted the company to grant monopolies of selling tea to particular merchants in the colonies, thus angering those traders who were excluded. An alarm was spread throughout the colonies, and in several ports ships were prevented from landing the company's tea. When Governor Thomas Hutchinson of Massachusetts refused several ships carrying tea to leave Boston without unloading their cargo, a group of patriots on December 16, 1773, disguised themselves as Indians and dumped the tea into Boston harbor.

To the British government, the Boston Tea Party was the ultimate outrage. Angry officials clamored for a retribution that would squarely confront America with the issue of Parliament's right to legislate for the colonists. In 1774, Parliament passed a succession of laws that came to be known as the Coercive Acts. The first closed the port of Boston. The second reorganized the Massachusetts government: the Council was made appointive, town meetings were restricted, and the governor's power of appointing judges and sheriffs was strengthened. The third allowed royal officials charged with capital offenses in the colony to be tried in England or another colony to avoid a hostile jury. The fourth authorized the quartering of troops in private homes in Massachusetts. At the same time,

Thomas Gage, commander in chief of the British army in America, was made governor of the colony.

The Coercive Acts provoked open rebellion in America. Whatever influence royal authority had left in the colonies dissolved. In many areas local communities, with a freedom they had not had since the seventeenth century, began picking up the pieces and attempting to put together new popular structures of authority. Mass meetings, sometimes attracting thousands of aroused colonists as did one such Philadelphia rally in June 1774, endorsed resolutions and called for new political organizations. Committees of different sizes and names—of safety, of inspection, of merchants, of mechanics, of Fifty-One, of Nineteen, of Forty-Three—vied with each other for political control. In each colony the intensity and scope of displacing royal government differed, depending on how extensive and personal previous royal authority had been in the local communities. Thus it was greater in Massachusetts, for example, than in Virginia, where royal influence and patronage scarcely touched the planters' oligarchic control of the counties. But everywhere there was a fundamental transfer of authority that opened up new opportunities for new men to assert themselves. By the end of 1774 in many of the colonies local associations were controlling and regulating various aspects of American life. Committees overawed voters, directed appointments, organized the militia, managed trade, intervened between creditors and debtors, levied taxes, issued licenses, supervised the courts, or closed them, and, as the Tories protested, even dictated "what we shall eat, drink, wear, speak, and think." Royal governors stood by in helpless amazement as new informal governments gradually grew up around them. These new governments ranged from town and county committees and newly created provincial congresses (which often duplicated but sometimes greatly enlarged the former assemblies) to a general congress of the colonies convened in Philadelphia in September 1774.

In all, fifty-five delegates from twelve colonies (all except Georgia) participated in the First Continental Congress. Some frightened colonists and even some royal officials hoped that this Congress might work to reestablish imperial authority. Those who were eager to break the bond with Great Britain, however, won the first round. Led by the cousins Samuel and John Adams from Massachusetts, and Patrick Henry and Richard Henry Lee from Virginia, the Congress endorsed the inflammatory Resolves of Suffolk County, Massachusetts, recommending outright resistance to the Coercive Acts. But Congress was not yet ready for independence. It came very close—failing by the vote of a single colony—to considering further and perhaps adopting a plan of union proposed by Joseph Galloway, leader of the Pennsylvania Assembly and spokesman for the conservative congressional delegates from the middle colonies. Galloway's plan was radical enough as it was; it envisioned a grand colonial council along the lines earlier proposed by the Albany Congress of 1754. Enactments by either the

American grand council or the British Parliament were to be subject to mutual review and approval.

By 1774, however, too many colonists had determined that Parliament had no more right to make laws for them than it did to tax them. The Congress in its Declaration and Resolves of October 14, 1774, said as much, conceding the colonists' willingness to abide by parliamentary regulation of their external trade only "from the necessity of the case." By this date it was unlikely, even if the Congress had adopted Galloway's plan, that it could have reversed the transfer of authority that was taking place in the colonies. In the end, the Continental Congress simply recognized the new local authorities in American politics and gave them its blessing by adopting the Continental Association, which put into effect the nonimportation, nonconsumption, and nonexportation of British goods that had been agreed upon. Committees in all the counties, cities, and towns were now enjoined by the Congress "attentively to observe the conduct of all persons touching this association," to condemn publicly all violators as "enemies of American liberty," and to "break off all dealings" with them.

With the new sanction of the Congress expressed in this Association, the local committees, speaking in the name of "the body of the people," now sought to legitimize the political transformation taking place. These committees were keenly aware of the nature of the society they were assaulting. As the South Carolina General Committee told the New York Committee of Sixty in March 1775, "We are not ignorant of that crowd of placemen, of contractors, of officers, and needy dependents on the Crown, who are constantly employed to frustrate your measures." In place of these webs of personal influence, the committees offered more impersonal attachments to "the body of the people," through oathtaking, written compacts, and ideological declarations, often backed up by threats of violence. Groups of men, from a few dozen to several thousand, often showing remarkable control and direction, marched through villages and city streets searching out enemies of the people. Such suspected enemies were often forced to recant unfriendly words or designs against the public and to sign confessions of guilt and penitence. The committees bore down especially hard on key individuals like the Connecticut "river god" Israel Williams, knowing as they did the importance of the views of *a man of your place and of your ability and influence.* Once an individual's lack of commitment to the patriot cause was defined and established, whether it was drinking British tea or publicly denouncing the Continental Congress, the committees went to great efforts to get him to swear new oaths of fidelity as "marks of friendship" and "attachment" to the people.

Thus even before Independence, in some colonies American society had begun to be reordered. In such circumstances, restoring British authority without military force was impossible; it was only a matter of months before actual hostilities broke out.

Suggested Readings

A convenient guide to the historical literature on the American Revolution can be found in Jack P. Greene, ed., *The Reinterpretation of the American Revolution, 1763–1789* (1968). Although there are many short accounts of the Revolution, the student ought to begin with R. R. Palmer's monumental *The Age of the Democratic Revolution: A Political History of Europe and America, 1760–1800* (2 vols.; 1959, 1964), which places the American Revolution in a Western perspective. Stephen G. Kurtz and James H. Hutson, eds., *Essays on the American Revolution* (1973); Alfred F. Young, ed., *The American Revolution* (1976); and the five volumes from the Library of Congress, *Symposia on the American Revolution* (1972–76) are collections of original essays on various aspects of the Revolution.

Among the early attempts to treat the coming of the Revolution from an imperial viewpoint, George Louis Beer, *British Colonial Policy, 1754–1765* (1907), is still informative. Charles M. Andrews summarized his ideas on the causes of the Revolution in *The Colonial Background of the American Revolution* (1931). The most detailed narrative of the political events leading up to the Revolution, written from an imperial perspective, is Lawrence H. Gipson, *The British Empire before the American Revolution* (15 vols., 1936–70). Gipson has summarized his point of view in *The Coming of the Revolution, 1763–1775* (1954). Merrill Jensen, *The Founding of a Nation* (1968), is the fullest single volume of the pre-Revolutionary years written from an American perspective; it is especially rich in its description of the factional struggles within the separate colonies. An ingenious but sound study that combines the views of a British and an American historian on the causes of the Revolution is Ian R. Christie and Benjamin W. Labaree, *Empire or Independence, 1760–1776* (1976).

The appropriate chapters of James A. Henretta, *The Evolution of American Society, 1700–1815* (1973), discusses American society on the eve of the Revolution. Jackson T. Main, in *The Social Structure of Revolutionary America* (1965), has attempted to describe the distribution of wealth and the nature of "classes" in American society. Carl Bridenbaugh, *Cities in Revolt* (1955), attributes the Revolutionary impulse to the cities. The extent of westward migration is ably recounted in Jack M. Sosin, *Revolutionary Frontier, 1763–1783* (1967).

For efforts to connect the Great Awakening to the Revolution, see Wesley M. Gewehr, *The Great Awakening in Virginia, 1740–1790* (1930); William G. McLoughlin, *New England Dissent, 1630–1833* (2 vols., 1971); Alan Heimert, *Religion and the American Mind from the Great Awakening to the Revolution* (1966); and the articles of Rhys Isaac, especially "Evangelical Revolt: The Nature of the Baptists' Challenge to the Traditional Order in Virginia, 1765–1775," *William and Mary Quarterly*, 3d ser., 31 (1974). The transformation of the Quakers is superbly treated in Sydney V. James, *A People among Peoples* (1963). Carl Bridenbaugh, *Mitre and Sceptre* (1962), describes the growth of Anglicanism and the effort to establish an American episcopacy in the decades leading up to the Revolution. For the American reaction to these efforts, see Charles W. Akers, *Called unto Liberty: A Life of Jonathan Mayhew, 1720–1766* (1964).

The opening years of the reign of George III have been the subject of some of the most exciting historical scholarship in the twentieth century—largely the work of Sir Lewis Namier and his students. Namier and his followers have exhaustively demonstrated that George III was not seeking to destroy the British constitution, as nineteenth-century historians had argued, and that in 1760 party government with ministerial responsibility to Parliament lay very much in the future. Namier's chief works include *The Structure of Politics at the Accession of George III* (2d ed., 1957), and *England in the Age of the American Revolution* (2d ed., 1961). For detailed studies of British politics in the Revolutionary era, see P. D. G. Thomas, *British Politics and the Stamp Act Crisis* (1975); Paul Langford, *The*

First Rockingham Administration: 1765–1766 (1973); John Brooke, *The Chatham Administration, 1766–1768* (1956); Bernard Donoughue, *British Politics and the American Revolution: The Path to War, 1773–1775* (1964). The best biography of George III is John Brooke, *King George III* (1972). An excellent summary of British politics is George H. Guttridge, *English Whiggism and the American Revolution* (2d ed., 1963).

Other important studies of British imperial policy in the period 1760–1775 include Jack M. Sosin, *Whitehall and the Wilderness . . . 1763–1775* (1961); Michael Kammen, *A Rope of Sand: The Colonial Agents, British Politics, and the American Revolution* (1968); and Franklin B. Wickwire, *British Subministers and Colonial America, 1763–1783* (1966). On the military in America, see John Shy, *Toward Lexington: The Role of the British Army in the Coming of the American Revolution* (1965); and Neil R. Stout, *The Royal Navy in America, 1760–1775* (1973).

On American resistance, see especially Edmund S. Morgan and Helen M. Morgan, *The Stamp Act Crisis* (1953), which emphasizes the colonists' appeal to constitutional principles. Pauline Maier, *From Resistance to Revolution* (1972), stresses the limited and controlled character of American opposition. Oliver M. Dickerson, *The Navigation Acts and the American Revolution* (1951), argues that Americans accepted the navigation system until "customs racketeering" was introduced in the late 1760s. For a more balanced view of the navigation system, see Thomas C. Barrow, *Trade and Empire: The British Customs Service in Colonial America, 1660–1775* (1967).

On other irritants and incidents in the imperial relation see Joseph A. Ernst, *Money and Politics in America, 1755–1775* (1973); Carl Ubbelohde, *The Vice-Admiralty Courts and the American Revolution* (1960); Hiller Zobel, *The Boston Massacre* (1970); Benjamin W. Labaree, *The Boston Tea Party* (1964); and David Ammerman, *In the Common Cause: American Response to the Coercive Acts of 1774* (1974) Arthur M. Schlesinger, *The Colonial Merchants and the American Revolution, 1763–1776* (1918), schematically traces the responses of an important social group.

The loyalist reaction is analyzed in William H. Nelson, *The American Tory* (1961);Robert M. Calhoon *The Loyalists in Revolutionary America. 1760–1781* (1973); and Bernard Bailyn, *The Ordeal of Thomas Hutchinson* (1974). A vitriolic account by a loyalist of the causes of the Revolution is Peter Oliver, *Origin and Progress of the American Rebellion*, ed. Douglass Adair and John A. Schutz (1961).

Among the many local studies of American resistance are Carl Becker, *The History of Political Parties in the Province of New York, 1760–1776* (1909); David S. Lovejoy, *Rhode Island Politics and the American Revolution, 1760–1776* (1958); Theodore Thayer, *Pennsylvania Politics and the Growth of Democracy, 1740–1776* (1954); Patricia Bonomi, *A Factious People: . . . New York* (1971); Jere R. Daniel, *Experiment in Republicanism: New Hampshire Politics and the American Revolution, 1741–1794* (1970); Richard H. Brown, *Revolutionary Politics in Massachusetts* (1970); Stephen E. Patterson, *Political Parties in Revolutionary Massachusetts* (1973); and Ronald Hoffman, *A Spirit of Dissension: Economics, Politics, and the Revolution in Maryland* (1973). For biographical analyses of some of the leading Revolutionaries, see John C. Miller, *Sam Adams* (1936); Richard R. Beeman, *Patrick Henry* (1974); Merrill Peterson, *Thomas Jefferson and the New Nation* (1970); Eric Foner, *Tom Paine and Revolutionary America* (1976); Peter Shaw, *The Character of John Adams* (1976); and John R. Howe, Jr., *The Changing Political Thought of John Adams* (1966).

8

The Logic of
Revolution

Although the colonists, like other Britons, began the 1760s celebrating the accession of George III, they soon became disillusioned. Within the short span of a dozen years or so following the introduction of the imperial reforms these same British colonists were in open rebellion against Great Britain. The sudden vehemence with which Americans moved into rebellion astonished contemporaries, and it has astonished historians ever since. A series of trade acts and tax levies, however far-reaching in their implications, did not seem to justify revolution. Yet many Americans by 1776 agreed with John Adams that the colonists were "in the very midst of a revolution, the most complete, unexpected, and remarkable, of any in the history of nations." What could account for it? How was it to be justified?

The colonists admitted it was not the particular acts of the British government that explained the Revolution. It was the meaning they gave to those acts. From the outset of the controversy, Americans strove to understand the intentions of the British government and to determine their rights and liberties. The result was a phenomenal outpouring of political writings and interest in political ideas unequaled in the nation's history. These extraordinary efforts to discover the meaning of what was happening made the Revolution an unusually intellectual affair and ultimately gave it world-shattering significance.

A Conspiracy Against Liberty

Throughout their writings, American patriot leaders insisted they were rebelling not against the principles of the English constitution but on behalf of them. They assumed the name "Whigs" and branded the supporters of the crown "Tories" in order to express better their continuity with the great libertarian struggles of seventeenth-century England. By emphasizing that it was, in the words of the recent Scotch-Irish immigrant and Philadelphia lawyer James Wilson, "both the letter and spirit of the British constitution" that justified their resistance, Americans could easily believe they were simply preserving what Englishmen had valued from time immemorial; they thereby gave a curious conservative color to their Revolution.

Yet the colonists' continual talk of desiring nothing new and wishing only to return to the essentials of the English constitution was misleading. The historical traditions of the English constitution they invoked were not the "true principles" held by establishment England in the mid-eighteenth century, but were in fact, as the Tories and royal officials tried to indicate, "revolution principles" outside the mainstream of English thought. Since the colonists seemed to be reading the same literature as other Englishmen, they were hardly aware that they were seeing the English heritage differently. Amid their breadth of reading and references, however, was a concentration on a strain of thought that ultimately implicated them in a peculiar conception of English life and in an extraordinarily radical perspective on the English constitution they were so fervently defending.

The English literature of the first half of the eighteenth century, both belles lettres and political polemics, the literature the colonists read and imitated, and by which they judged English life, was above all a literature of social criticism. Most of the English writers of the Augustan age—whether notables or coffeehouse hacks, whether Tory satirists like Alexander Pope and Jonathan Swift or radical Whigs like John Trenchard and Thomas Gordon—all wrote out of a deep and bitter hostility to the great social, economic, and political changes taking place in England during the decades following the Glorious Revolution of 1688. These changes were fostered by a great financial and commercial revolution during the early eighteenth century that was as unsettling and as important as the subsequent industrial revolution for which it prepared the way. The rise of the Bank of England, powerful trading companies, and stock markets, and the growing commercialization of agriculture, the emergence of new moneyed men, and the increasing public debt—all threatened traditional values and led many English intellectuals to conclude that England, like ancient Rome, was dangerously diseased, indeed on the verge of ruin eaten away by vice, luxury, and money.

At the center of this Augustan criticism lay a fascination with politics and an intense fear that excessive monarchical or governmental power was hastening Britain's decay. Both ends of the political spectrum—both the radical Whig left, with its libertarian heritage of the seventeenth century, and the extreme Tory right, with its nostalgic image of an older rural England of independent gentry—flowed together in shrill opposition to the changes Sir Robert Walpole and his ministries were making in the conduct of the Hanoverian governments, particularly in using money and influence to manipulate or "corrupt" Parliament and the electorate. Throughout the first half of the eighteenth century this opposition, or "country," ideology kept alive an obsessive concern with English liberties and rights. Ringing proposals to control and reduce what seemed to be the enormously inflated powers of the court and the crown were directed at recovering the original principles of the English constitution. Many of the extremists' libertarian reforms were ahead of their time for England—reforms advocating adult male suffrage, less restrictive definitions of seditious libel, and greater freedom of religion. Other suggested reforms, however, were the stock proposals of opposition politicians. These aimed at prohibiting government puppets ("placemen") from sitting in the House of Commons, at reducing the public debt, and at obtaining more equal representation, the right of instructing members of Parliament, and shorter Parliaments. Such reforms easily combined with all opposition thinking to form an independent view of politics, a widely shared conception about how English public life should be organized. In this ideal nation, the parts of the constitution would be independent of one another, and members of Parliament would be independent of any connection or party; in other words, there would exist a political world in which no one was beholden to another. Such a conception, whether it was fully realized or not, struck at the heart of the traditional patronage society.

The colonists had felt the relevance of this Augustan criticism and this opposition ideology more keenly than did the English themselves. The opposition writing had made such good sense not only of the many peculiarities of American life but of the colonists' antagonism to royal power, that from the early decades of the eighteenth century, Americans had published, republished, read, cited, and even plagiarized much of it. By the middle of the century this "country" ideology, with its intense mistrust of governmental power and its suspicion of growing English corruption, had become a central part of the political vocabulary of the colonists; it constituted an emphasis of language and thought that they little sensed was different from what most other eighteenth-century Englishmen possessed.

The colonists, steeped in this English libertarian heritage, had invoked it repeatedly in the numerous conflicts between their assemblies and the governors during the first half of the eighteenth century, but indiscriminately and inconsistently. Rarely had the implications of their persistent attacks on state power been followed out. Now, however, in the years after 1763 the need for explaining and understanding politics and the ways of rulers assumed a new and vital importance. This "country" ideology, with its warning about the threats to liberty from the abuses of governmental power and its pessimistic picture of England's corruption and decay, prepared the colonists intellectually for resistance.

These inherited radical Whig ideas contained an elaborate set of rules for political action by the people: How were the people to identify a tyrant? How long should the people put up with abuses? How much force should be used? The answers to these questions came logically as events unfolded and led the colonists almost irresistibly from resistance to rebellion. Gradually, the colonists became convinced that the obnoxious efforts of crown officials to reform the empire were not simply the results of insensitivity to peculiar American conditions or mistakes of well-meant policy but rather the intended consequences of a grand tyrannical design. In Thomas Jefferson's words, the British reforms by 1774 were nothing less than "a deliberate, systematical plan of reducing us to slavery."

The crucial turning point seemed to come in the late 1760s. As Americans read of the failure of the Corsican freedom fighter Pascal Paoli, of the desperate struggles of sons of liberty in Ireland, and of the harassment and repeated exclusions from Parliament of the English radical John Wilkes, they became convinced that they were involved not simply in a resistance for their own rights but in a world-wide struggle for the salvation of liberty itself. By the early 70s a few colonists were even comparing the king with classic tyrants like Nero or the Stuarts and calling monarchy a curse visited upon the people because of their sins. The proofs of Britain's tyrannical motives were, as George Washington said, "as clear as the sun in its meridian brightness."

By 1774, there was hardly a piece of American Whig writing that did not dwell on the obsessive fear of a "Conspiracy" against America's public liberty, "first regularly formed," as John Adams confided to his diary, "and begun to be executed, in 1763 or 4." It was the cumulative momentum of this belief in a British ministerial plot against the colonists' liberties that created a revolutionary frame of mind in America. For in the Whig creed no specific acts of the government against the

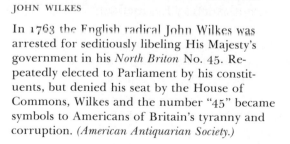

JOHN WILKES

In 1763 the English radical John Wilkes was arrested for seditiously libeling His Majesty's government in his *North Briton* No. 45. Repeatedly elected to Parliament by his constituents, but denied his seat by the House of Commons, Wilkes and the number "45" became symbols to Americans of Britain's tyranny and corruption. (*American Antiquarian Society.*)

people could sanction revolution. Only, in John Adams's words, "repeated, multiplied oppressions," placing beyond all doubt "that their rulers had formed settled plans to deprive them of their liberties," could warrant the concerted resistance of the people against constituted authority.

The pieces fell into place, as Whig leaders and writers in England and America tried to reveal the deteriorating nature of English society and the tyrannical policy of the crown under the guise of a pliant and corrupt Parliament. The multiplication of new custom offices and administrative posts in America was obviously the beginning of a ministerial plan by which, the Whigs charged, "millions of leading men's dependents shall be provided for in America, for whom places can by no means be found at home." Stationing troops in America, particularly in the settled areas, meant introducing despotism's traditional instrument, a standing army. The new admiralty courts, in which judges alone tried violators of the trade regulations, were only the first stage in the eventual elimination of trial by jury. The strengthening of the Anglican establishment and the rumor that an Anglican bishop would be appointed for America only foretold the destruction of America's religious freedom. And in such a mental atmosphere the Coercive Acts could only confirm the crown's grand strategy.

Under the pressure of this enlarging picture and drawing upon the scattered writings of disaffected Englishmen and European *philosophes*, the Americans began putting together the immense significance of what they were involved in. They could not help believing—all the evidence, all the enlightened everywhere confirmed it—that liberty was fleeing the Old World entirely and "seeking an asylum westward." Out of the tumult they could only hope that "a great and mighty empire may rise up in this western world," an empire dedicated to the principles of liberty.

This specific linkage of events, this particular conspiratorial interpretation of the crown's policy, that the Americans resorted to by the early 70s, was not a product of paranoiac or feverishly disturbed minds grappling with a series of harmful incidents. The belief in plots or designs by evil-intending men was familiar to Englishmen on both sides of the Atlantic. Not only did colonial radicals like Adams and Jefferson or harassed royal officials commonly interpret politics in terms of conspiracies but so did sophisticated English politicians like Edmund Burke and Horace Walpole. Such efforts to connect harmful events and relate them to the malevolent motives of particular individuals were in fact crude ways of explaining social and historical processes that assumed that what happened in politics or in history was always intended and managed by individuals. The pre-modern world was generally incapable of explaining evil events except in terms of the evil designs of deceitful individuals, like Shakespeare's Iago. Few in the eighteenth century had yet grasped the fundamental modern insight—that events are not necessarily the direct result of men's purposes, that it was possible for persons following their own distinct and separate plans to produce a pattern of consequences that was not part of their intentions. The eighteenth century's reliance on conspiratorial interpretations made sense of the political realities of an age of patronage where key individuals in places of power exerted great influence over events. Only later, in the early decades of the nineteenth century when this traditional hierarchical world was clearly gone, would some American and other thinkers begin to shed these eighteenth-century assumptions and move into a modern intellectual world that anticipated our own. That move was an aspect of a great intellectual transformation sweeping through the entire Revolutionary era.

The Imperial Debate

Central to this intellectual transformation were the changes Americans made in their ideas of politics. The Revolutionary era was in fact the most creative period in the history of American political thought. During three decades of controversy and constitution-making, Americans transformed their inherited classical theory of politics and made lasting contributions to Western constitutionalism. The immediate origins of this rich intellectual achievement lay in the imperial debate that accompanied the colonists' rising resistance to British authority. This debate compelled the colonists, as they had not been compelled before, to articulate their divergent political experience.

Because the colonists in the past had not generally denied Parliament's authority to regulate their trade, they offered no substantial constitutional opposition to the Sugar Act. But with the Stamp Act, the first unmistakable tax levy by Parliament, American intellectual resistance was immediately elevated to the highest plane of principle. "It is inseparably essential to the freedom of a people, and the undoubted rights of Englishmen," the Stamp Act Congress declared in 1765, "that no taxes should be imposed on them, but with their own consent, given personally, or by their representatives." And since "the people of these colonies are not, and from their local circumstances, cannot be represented in the House of Commons in Great Britain," the colonists could only be represented and taxed by persons, chosen by themselves, in their respective legislatures. This statement defined the American position at the outset of the controversy, and despite subsequent confusion and stumbling this essential point was never shaken.

Once the English ministry sensed a stirring of colonial opposition to the Stamp Act, a group of English pamphleteers connected with the government set out to explain and justify parliamentary taxation of the colonies. Although their arguments differed, they all eventually agreed that the Americans, like all Englishmen everywhere, were embraced by acts of Parliament through a system of "virtual" representation. It was this concept of virtual representation that gave Parliament its supreme authority or sovereignty. Even though the colonists, like "Nine-Tenths of the People of *Britain*," did not in fact choose any representative to the House of Commons, one government pamphleteer

wrote, they were undoubtedly "a Part, and an important Part of the Commons
of Great Britain: they are represented in Parliament, in the same Manner as those
Inhabitants of *Britain* are who have not Voices in Elections." In the eighteenth
century England's electorate comprised only a tiny proportion of the population.
Since English electoral districts were a hodgepodge left over from centuries of
history, ancient "rotten boroughs" like Old Sarum, completely depopulated
by the eighteenth century, continued to send members to Parliament while
newer large cities like Manchester and Birmingham sent none. What made
such apparent anomalies intelligible to Englishmen was the assumption, classically
voiced by Edmund Burke in 1774, that each member of Parliament represented
not any particular locality but the whole community. Hence representation in
England was virtual: it gained its legitimacy not through the process of election,
which was incidental to representation, but rather through the mutual interests
presumably shared by members of Parliament and all those Englishmen for whom
they spoke, including those, like the colonists, who did not vote for them.

The Americans immediately and emphatically rejected these British claims
that they were "*virtually* represented" in the House of Commons "in the same
manner with the nonelectors resident in Great Britain." In the most notable
colonial pamphlet written in opposition to the Stamp Act, *Considerations on the
Propriety of Imposing Taxes* (1765), Daniel Dulany of Maryland conceded the
relevence in England of virtual representation, but denied its applicability to
America. Dulany suggested in effect that America was a distinct community
from England and thus could hardly be represented by members of Parliament
with whom it had no mutuality of interests. Others pushed beyond Dulany's
argument, however, and challenged the conception of virtual representation
itself. The people, it seemed obvious to many Americans, "must be represented

THE PATRIOTIC AMERICAN FARMER.

J—N D·K·NS—N, Esq; Barrister at Law.

Who with Attic Eloquence, and Roman Spirit, hath afferted the Liberties of the British Colonies in America.

'Tis nobly done to Stem Taxations Rage,
And raise the Thoughts of a degenerate Age,
For Happiness and Joy, from Freedom spring;
But Life in Bondage is a worthless Thing.

JOHN DICKINSON'S "THE AMERICAN FARMER"

In the 1760s Dickinson was the most famous patriot-writer in all America. But by 1776 his unwillingness to endorse American independence diminished his reputation, which posterity has not yet restored. (*American Antiquarian Society.*)

actually—not 'virtually,'" and not just the colonists but people anywhere. "To what purpose," asked James Otis of Massachusetts, "is it to bring everlasting changes to the colonists on the cases of Manchester, Birmingham and Sheffield, who return no members? If those now so considerable places are not represented, they ought to be."

Many Americans, from their unusual experience in the New World, where electoral districts were not the consequence of history going back to time immemorial but recent and regular creations distinctly related to changes in population and the formation of new towns or counties, believed in a very different kind of representation from that of the English. Their belief in "actual" representation made election not incidental but central to representation and pointed toward an equal and full participation of the people in the process of consent.

Yet while Americans were denying Parliament's right to tax them, they knew that Parliament had exercised some authority over their affairs during the previous century; and they groped to explain what that authority should be. What was the "due subordination" that the Stamp Act Congress admitted Americans owed Parliament? Could the colonists accept parliamentary legislation but not taxation? In his famous *Letters from a Pennsylvania Farmer* (1767–68), John Dickinson repudiated the idea that Parliament could impose "external" taxes and made clear once and for all that the colonists opposed all forms of parliamentary taxation. Dickinson recognized nevertheless that the empire required some sort of central regulatory authority, particularly for commerce, and conceded Parliament's superintending legislative power so far as it preserved "the connection between the several parts of the British empire." The empire, it seemed to many colonists, was a unitary body for some affairs but not for others.

To all of these halting and fumbling efforts to divide parliamentary authority, the British offered a simple, formidable argument. Since they could not conceive of the empire as anything but a single, homogeneous community, they found absurd and meaningless all these American distinctions between trade regulation and taxation or separate spheres of authority. If Parliament even "in one instance" was as supreme over the colonists as over the people of England, then, wrote William Knox in a crucial ministerial pamphlet of 1769, the Americans were members "of the same community with the people of England." But if Parliament's authority over the colonists were denied "in any particular," then it must be denied in "all instances" and the union between Great Britain and the colonies dissolved. "There is no alternative," Knox concluded; "either the Colonies are part of the community of Great Britain or they are in a state of nature with respect to her, and in no case can be subject to the jurisdiction of that legislative power which represents her community, which is the British Parliament."

What made this British argument so powerful was its basis in the doctrine of sovereignty, the persuasive and pervasive belief that in every state there could be only one final, indivisible, and uncontestable supreme authority. This idea was the most important conception of English political theory in the eighteenth century; it became the single most critical abstraction of politics in the entire Revolutionary era, and the issue over which the empire was finally broken.

The concept of sovereignty had been the basis of the British position from the beginning, articulated in the Declaratory Act of 1766, which, following repeal of the Stamp Act, affirmed Parliament's authority to make laws binding the colonists "in all cases whatsoever." But now in the late 1760s its implications were drawn out fully in print. Everywhere in the late 1760s and early 70s the colonists faced what they called these "trite" but "captivating" assertions of parliamentary sovereignty based on "the well-known necessity of one central, supreme power, being somewhere lodged in every empire."

By the early 1770s many Americans despaired of breaking the unbreakable or separating the inseparable. They thus rapidly began conceding the terms of the British argument, as the Massachusetts House of Representatives did in 1773: If there was no middle ground between the supreme authority of Parliament and the total independence of the colonies from Parliament, then, the House declared, there could be no doubt that "we were thus independent." The logic of sovereignty therefore forced a fundamental shift in the American position. By 1774 the colonists, including Thomas Jefferson, John Adams, and James Wilson, were arguing that sovereignty resided in the separate American legislatures. Thus Parliament had no authority over America whatsoever, and the colonies were connected to the empire solely through the king.

Accepting one of two alternatives was not a very satisfactory explanation of past American experience in the empire, for the colonists' surrender to the logic of sovereignty made it difficult to explain Parliament's previous and acknowledged regulation of colonial trade. The best the colonists could do by 1774 was to allow Parliament the power to regulate their external commerce, as the Declaration and Resolves of the First Continental Congress put it, "from the necessity of the case, and a regard to the mutual interest of both countries."

The colonists had picked away at the unity of the empire and had sought to establish exemptions from the imperial power of Parliament. But in the end they found the doctrine of sovereignty unassailable and made it an ultimate weapon in their argument. It would take a succeeding decade of continuing debate among themselves before Americans would come to understand how two legislative authorities could exist in the same state.

The Popularization of Politics

Although ideas at times had a relentless logic of their own and carried people along through the need to work out inconsistencies and draw conclusions, the radicalization of American politics in the 1760s and 70s cannot be seen as merely an elaborate intellectual process. Beneath the surface of formal political thought existed a variety of individuals and groups whose manipulations and rivalries propelled the development of ideas and gave them meaning. So complicated and so unwitting was the process by which Americans moved from resistance into rebellion that many saw themselves, as one Marylander did in the spring of 1776, "proceeding by degrees to that crisis we so much deprecate," frightened that "in the end" they would find themselves "in a state of separation without averting to the steps by which we have arrived at it."

Many colonists argued for their rights, joined a committee, or aroused a mob not because they were planning for the future of the United States but because they believed it was in their personal, economic, social, or psychological interest to do so. Nonimportation agreements in the 1760s, for example, were often backed by artisans seeking to promote consumption of American-made products, or by illicit traders and continental and West Indian merchants benefiting from a curtailment of the transatlantic British trade, or by merchants with swollen inventories hoping to put some of their smaller, newly arrived competitors out of business. In the South, some planters even saw nonimportation as a pretext by which they might cut back on their extravagant expenses without endangering either their status or their credit. Many colonists of course acted against any such sort of narrow economic interest, but few saw accurately what their long-term interests were. Often the implications of what people did outran their intentions. Interests, passions, and ideology mingled in an intricate process, carrying Americans, as many realized when they looked back from 1776 at what had happened, "further than they intended at first setting out."

At first, politics in the 1760s seemed to be only a continuation of the earlier abrasive factionalism, involving personal contests among members of leading families for the rewards of political office and influence. But the disarray of English politics in the 1760s and the sudden injection of new imperial regulations altered political circumstances in the colonies. Such political alignments as existed — "outs" versus "ins," "country" versus "court" — hardened and grew more bitter. Royal governors, always caught between local and imperial politics, now found themselves beset and whipsawed by both sides more intensely than ever before. Suddenly they were burdened with defending and implementing the new imperial changes at the very moment that local developments were limiting and testing their capacity to govern. Thus New Hampshire under Governor Benning Wentworth had possessed the most consolidated hierarchy of royal authority in all of colonial America. But in the late 1750s and early 60s the flood of new immigrants from Massachusetts and Connecticut and the changing economy unsettled the Wentworth family's dominance over the colony. These disruptive developments gave local opposition groups in New Hampshire an opportunity for the first time in decades to move against the Wentworth government. Not only did the fluctuations in English politics weaken the influence and connections of the Wentworth family in London, but the introduction of cumbersome new imperial rules and officials curtailed the governor's political maneuverability within the colony.

Even in Virginia, where the governor's influence was relatively weak and the entrenched local oligarchies were powerful, the political and ideological forces stimulated by the imperial controversy interacted with local circumstances to create a new situation. In 1765 over one-third of the members of the House of Burgesses were replaced because they had ignored the outcry over the Stamp Act. This electoral shuffle altered the attitude of the planting gentry toward the people and gave new popular leaders like Patrick Henry and Richard Henry Lee, who had already been critical of the corrupt and secret manipulations of the dominant clique of the Virginia oligarchy, a political strength they otherwise would not have had. By 1776, popular-minded young gentry like Thomas Jefferson and James Madison rejoiced to see arrogant and illiberal elements of the Virginia aristocracy cast aside through competitive electioneering; they approved of the new men introduced into the House of Burgesses. As one Virginian gentleman observed, these new representatives were "not so well dressed, nor so politely educated, nor so highly born" as those in former as-

A WHIG VIEW OF THOMAS HUTCHINSON

Thomas Hutchinson, Governor of the Province of Massachusetts Bay, was the most learned and distinguished colonial-born official in America. Yet by the time of his exile to England in 1774 he had also become its most hated. (*American Antiquarian Society.*)

semblies, but they were trusted since "they are the People's men (and the People in general are right)." Although the imperial crisis had undoubtedly contributed to this local "political metamorphosis," to use Jefferson's term, clearly something more complicated than a simple rejection of British authority was taking place.

In other colonies, where the governors were stronger and consequently the local leaders were far more divided than in Virginia, various factions led by dominant families like the Livingstons and De Lanceys of New York whipped up Whig opposition to the imperial legislation, sought the support of extralegal popular groups, and generally worked to expand the rights and participation of the people in politics. They did this not with the aim of furthering electoral democracy but only for the tactical purpose of gaining control of the elective assemblies. While this sort of unplanned popularization of politics had gone on in the past, particularly in urban areas, the inflamed antiauthoritarian atmosphere that the imperial crisis generated gave it a new cutting edge with new unpredictable implications.

In colony after colony local quarrels, often of long standing, became so entangled with imperial antagonisms that they reinforced one another in a spiraling momentum that brought into question all governmental authority, even that not directly exercised by Great Britain. In Maryland in 1770, a proclamation by the proprietary governor setting the fees paid to government officials seemed to violate the principle of no taxation without representation made so vivid by the imperial debate. This executive proclamation provoked a bitter local struggle that forced Daniel Dulany, wealthy councilor and former opponent of the Stamp Act, into defending the governor. In the end the escalating controversy destroyed the governor's capacity to rule and made Dulany a loyalist.

By the 1770s, all these developments, without anyone's clearly intending it, were revealing a new kind of politics in America. The broadening of libertarian and antipatronage rhetoric now quickened long-existing popular political tendencies. Politicians in some colonies increasingly called for a widened suffrage, the use of the ballot, legislatures opened to the public, printed legislative minutes, and recorded legislative divisions—all in an effort to enlarge the political arena and limit the techniques of those who clung to the intricate, hidden ways of private arrangements and personal influence. Everywhere in the colonies "incendiaries," as royal officials called them, were taking advantage of the people's resentments against the British regulations to rise suddenly to political leadership. More and more "new men" were using electioneering to short-circuit the narrow and controlled channels of politics.

With an increase in literacy among some Americans, the levels of political consciousness were broadening and deepening. This development was shown perhaps most graphically in the changing nature of public rhetoric. Throughout the eighteenth century and still at the outset of the imperial controversy, most newspaper essays and pamphlets were written by gentlemen, most speeches in legislative and other public bodies were spoken by gentlemen, for restricted audiences of educated men like themselves. Their speeches and writings were often highly stylized by rhetorical rules and were usually decorated with Latin quotations and references to the literature of Western culture. The gentry's speeches and writings did not have to influence directly and simultaneously all the people but only the leaders, who in turn would bring the rest of the people with them through clientage and deferential respect. By the time of the Revolution, however, this world was beginning to change.

Part of the consternation and awe that Patrick Henry aroused by his oratory and Thomas Paine by his writing came from their deliberate rejection of traditional methods of persuasion. Particularly effective was Paine's incendiary pamphlet *Common Sense*, which helped so much to focus antimonarchical opinion in America early in 1776. Both men believed that existing conventions of speech or writing would not allow them to reach a wide audience and to express new feelings of revulsion and aspiration. Both had no formal schooling, both were accused of using ungrammatical language and coarse imagery, and both relied on their audiences knowing only one literary source, the Bible. Henry and Paine both aimed to break through the usual niceties and forms of rhetoric; and in their public expression, they meant to declare—in the words of Edmund Randolph,

THOMAS PAINE, BY JOHN WESLEY JARVIS

Paine was probably the first detached "intellectual" in American history. He belonged to no country, lived by his pen, and saw his role as the stimulator of revolutions. *(The National Gallery of Art, Washington, D.C.)*

speaking of Henry—that "it was enough to feel." Fancy words and learned citations no longer mattered as much as honesty and sincerity and the natural revelation of feelings. With this change in values, new sorts of men who held at once deep animosities and high hopes for bettering the world released their passions and enthusiasms into public life.

Tories and others who had been reared in the old ways and benefited from them stood bewildered and helpless in the face of these popularizing developments. They possessed neither the psychological capacity nor the political means to understand, let alone to deal with, this new kind of popular politics and the moral outrage and fiery zeal that lay behind it. They responded by appealing to the traditional standards of the older society by which they themselves had been raised. They intrigued and schemed, and tried to manipulate those whom they thought were the important individuals in the opposition (offering John Adams the office of advocate-general in the Massachusetts admiralty court in 1768, for example). Failing that, they accused those individuals of demagoguery or ridiculed them as upstarts. Frightened by the increased popular violence, they struck out furiously at the kinds of behavior they believed were eroding authority and causing the violence. They charged, as Daniel Dulany did in 1773, that "electioneering" and "confederated bands of politicians" were "ruinous to private attachments and good fellowship," tearing asunder "the bonds of nature," and kindling "the unextinguishable flames of hatred and animosity." Such prudent men could not accept a new and different world, and after the Declaration of Independence they either fell silent or became loyalists, determined to fight for the society that had bred them.

The War for Independence

By the beginning of 1775, the English government was preparing for military action. In February, Lord North got Parliament to pass what he regarded as a conciliatory measure. He proposed that any colony contributing its proportionate share to the common defense would not be subject to parliamentary taxation. But since the British government did nothing to resolve the issues raised by the Coercive Acts and the declarations of the Continental Congress, the colonists regarded North's efforts at reconciliation as an insidious attempt to divide them. By this date North's supporters and the king himself saw no alternative to force in bringing the colonists back into line. George III had told North as early as November 1774, "Blows must decide whether they are to be subject to the Country or Independent." The British government thus increased the army and navy and began restraining the commerce of first New England and then the other colonies.

In May 1775, delegates from the colonies met in Philadelphia for the Second Continental Congress to take up where the First Congress left off. Outwardly the Congress continued the policy of resolves and reconciliation. In July, at the urging of John Dickinson, Congress in an Olive Branch Petition professed loyalty to the king and humbly asked him to disavow his "artful and cruel" ministers who were blamed for the oppressive measures. At the same time the Congress issued a "Declaration of Causes and Necessity of Taking Up Arms" (largely the work of Dickinson and Thomas Jefferson), in which the colonies denied they had any "ambitious design of separating from Great Britain, and establishing independent states." As this superb summary of the American case against Britain demonstrated, the time for paper solutions had passed. Fighting had broken out at Lexington and Concord, Massachusetts, in April 1775, and the Second Congress now had to assume some of the responsibilities of a central government for the colonies. It created a continental army, appointed George Washington of Virginia as commander, issued paper money for the support of the troops, and formed a committee to negotiate with foreign countries.

By the summer of 1775, the escalation of actions and reactions was out of hand. On August 23, George III, ignoring the colonists' Olive Branch Petition, proclaimed the colonies in open rebellion. In October he publicly accused them of aiming at independence. By December the British government declared all American shipping liable to seizure by British warships. As early as May 1775, American forces had captured Fort Ticonderoga at the head of Lake Champlain. Out of a desire to bring the Canadians into the struggle against Britain, the Congress ordered makeshift forces under Richard Montgomery and Benedict Arnold to invade Canada. Although by the beginning of 1776 no American body had as yet formally endorsed independence, it was obviously in the air. It was left to a recent English immigrant, Thomas Paine, only fourteen months in the colonies, to express in January 1776 in his *Common Sense,* the most popular pamphlet of the entire Revolutionary era, the accumulated American rage against

THE BATTLE OF CONCORD, MASSACHUSETTS

In their march to and from Concord on April 19, 1775 the British had 73 soldiers killed and 200 wounded out of a total force of 1800. Of the nearly 4000 colonial militia who fought sometime during the day, 49 were killed and 46 were wounded. *(State Street Trust Co., Boston.)*

what Paine could now call the "Royal Brute," George III. In the early spring of 1776, the Congress threw open America's ports to the world and prepared for the Declaration of Independence, which it formally approved on July 4, 1776. In this famous thirteen-hundred word document, largely written by the graceful hand of Jefferson, the king, as the only remaining link between the colonists and Great Britain, was now held accountable for every grievance suffered by

DETAIL FROM "THE DECLARATION OF INDEPENDENCE," BY JOHN TRUMBULL

The committee that drafted the Declaration of Independence included from left to right; John Adams, Roger Sherman, Robert R. Livingston, Thomas Jefferson, and Benjamin Franklin. *(Yale University Art Gallery.)*

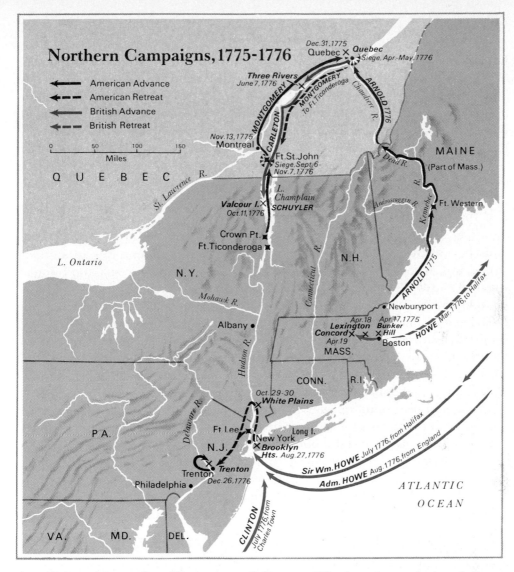

Northern Campaigns, 1775-1776

American Advance
American Retreat
British Advance
British Retreat

Americans since 1763. The reign of George III, Americans declared "to a candid world," was "a history of repeated injuries and usurpations, all having in direct object the establishment of an absolute Tyranny over these States."

The Declaration of Independence was not an American call to arms but a consequence of arms already taken up. For over a year, beginning with the hostilities in Massachusetts in the spring of 1775 and including the ill-fated American attack on Quebec in the winter of 1775–76, the American and British forces had been at war. It was a war that would eventually go on for nearly eight years—the longest war in American history, until that of Viet Nam two centuries later.

This war for independence passed through a series of distinct phases, growing and widening until what had begun in British eyes as a breakdown in governmental authority in a section of their empire became in time a world struggle.

Great Britain found itself for the first time in the eighteenth century diplomatic-ally isolated and at one point in 1779 even threatened with French invasion. The war for American independence thus eventually became an important episode in Britain's long struggle for global supremacy with France that went back a century and that would continue for another generation into the nine-teenth century.

The British military actions of 1775 grew logically out of the coercive policies of 1774, for both rested on the assumption that Boston was the center of the disruption and needed to be isolated and punished. The British thought at first that they were dealing with mobs led by a few seditious instigators who had to be arrested and tried and whose bases of insurgency had to be broken up. This view of the situation led General Gage to attempt to seize rebel munitions stored at Concord, Massachusetts, on April 19, 1775; as a result the colonial militia was called out and the harassed British had to march back to what rapidly became the besieged town of Boston. By subsequently surrounding Boston from positions in Charlestown and Dorchester Heights, the colonists cast doubt on the British view that the struggle was merely an elaborate police action. Two months later in June 1775, British regulars attempted to dislodge American fortifications on a spur of Bunker Hill in Charlestown overlooking Boston. Assuming in General John Burgoyne's words, that no numbers of "untrained rabble" could ever stand up against "trained troops," the British under General William Howe attempted a series of frontal assaults on the American redoubt that were eventually successful but only at a terrible cost of one thousand British casualties, over 40 percent of Howe's troops. In this first formal engagement at Bunker Hill the British suffered their heaviest losses of the entire war. This experience convinced the British government that it was not simply a New England mob they were up against, and it swept away almost every objection among the ministers to a conquest of the colonies.

The appointment of generals by the Continental Congress, the organization of a Continental field army under George Washington in the summer of 1775, and the American expedition to Canada were evidence to the British that they were involved in a military rather than a police action, which in turn dictated a con-ventional eighteenth-century policy of maneuver and battle. This change of strategy required that the British evacuate the hostile and peripherally located Boston in favor of New York, with its presumably more sympathetic population, its superior port, and its central position. Accordingly, in the summer of 1776 Howe, who replaced Gage as commander in chief of the British army in North America, sailed into New York harbor with a force of over thirty thousand men. Howe aimed to cut New England off from the other rebels and to defeat Wash-ington's army in a decisive battle. It was a plan that Howe was to spend the next two frustrating years trying to realize.

On the face of it, a military struggle seemed to promise all the advantage to Great Britain. Britain was the most powerful nation in the world with a popu-

GEORGE WASHINGTON, BY CHARLES WILSON PEALE

Washington's genuis lay not in his military expertise in the field but in his coolness and determination and in his extraordinary political skills. Although he lost most of his battles, he never lost the support of his officers or the Congress. *(In the Brooklyn Museum Collection.)*

lation of about 11 million, compared with only 2.5 million colonists. The British navy was the largest in the world, with nearly half its ships initially committed to the American struggle. The British army was a well-trained professional force, numbering at one point in 1778 nearly 50,000 troops stationed in North America alone; to this force were added during the war over 30,000 hired German mercenaries. To confront this military might the Americans had to start from scratch, creating eventually a small Continental Army numbering usually less than 5000 troops, supplemented by varying-sized state militia units. The whole motley collection was led mostly by inexperienced amateur officers; the commander in chief, Washington, for example, had been only a regimental colonel on the Virginia frontier, and had little firsthand knowledge of combat. Not surprisingly, then, most British officers thought that the Americans would be no match for His Majesty's troops; a veteran of many North American campaigns told the House of Commons in 1774 that with 5000 regulars he could

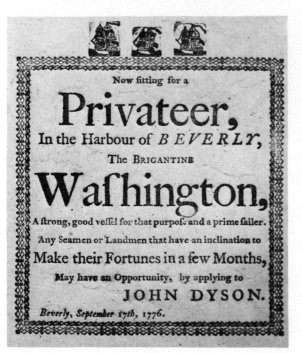

RECRUITING FOR THE AMERICAN CAUSE

Privateers were privately-owned armed vessels sailing under license (letters of marque) issued by a state or by the Continental Congress. Enemy vessels captured by privateers became the captors' "prizes." *(American Antiquarian Society.)*

march from one end of the country to the other.

Yet such a contrast of numbers was deceptive, for the British disadvantages were immense and perhaps overwhelming, even at the beginning when their opportunities to put down the rebellion were greatest. Great Britain not only had to carry on the war 3000 miles across the Atlantic with consequent problems of communications and logistics, but also had to wage a different kind of war from any the country had ever fought in the eighteenth century. A well-trained army might have been able to conquer the American forces, but, as one French officer observed at the end, America itself was unconquerable. The great breadth of territory and the wild nature of the terrain made conventional maneuverings and operations difficult and cumbersome. The fragmented and local character of authority in America inhibited decisive action by the British; there was no nerve center anywhere whose capture would destroy the rebellion. In such circumstances the prevalence of amateur militia and the weakness of America's organized army made the Americans, as a Swiss officer noted, more dangerous than "if they had a regular army." The British never clearly understood what they were up against—a revolutionary struggle involving widespread support in the population. Hence they continually underestimated the staying power of the rebels and overestimated the strength of the loyalists. And in the end, independence came to mean more to the Americans than reconquest did to the English.

From the outset, the English objective could never be as simple and clearcut as the Americans' desire for independence. Conquest was surely a prerequisite, but that by itself could not restore political relations and imperial harmony. Many people in England were reluctant to engage in a civil war, and several officers actually refused out of conscience to serve in America. Although the bulk of the Parliament and the English ministry were intent on subjugating America by force, the British commanders appointed in 1775, Sir William Howe and his brother Admiral Richard, Lord Howe, in charge of the navy, never shared this overriding urge for outright coercion. The brothers, particularly Lord Howe, saw themselves not simply as conquerors but also as conciliators. They interrupted their military operations with peace feelers to Washington and the Continental Congress, and they tried to avoid plundering and ravaging the American countryside and ports out of fear of destroying all hope for reconciliation. Such "a sentimental manner of waging war," as Lord George Germain, head of the American Department, called it, weakened the morale of British officers and troops and left the loyalists confused and disillusioned.

The Howes' policy was not as ineffectual initially as it later appeared. After defeating Washington on Long Island in August 1776 and driving him in the fall of 1776 from New York City with a series of complicated flanking maneuvers characteristic of eighteenth-century tactics designed to conserve precious manpower, General Howe had Washington in pell-mell retreat southward. Instead of pursuing Washington across the Delaware River, Howe resorted to a piecemeal occupation of New Jersey, extending his lines and deploying brigade garrisons at a half-dozen towns around the area with the aim of gradually convincing the rebels of British invincibility. Loyalist militiamen emerged from hiding and through a series of ferocious local struggles with patriot groups began to assume control of northern New Jersey. Nearly five thousand Americans came forward to accept Howe's offer of pardon and to swear loyalty to the crown. American prospects at the end of 1776 were as low as they ever would be during the war. These were, as Thomas Paine wrote, "times that try men's souls."

The Howes' policy of leniency and pacification, however, was marred by plundering by British troops and by loyalist recriminations against the rebels. But even more important in undermining the accumulated British successes of 1776 were Washington's brilliant strokes in picking off two of Howe's extended outposts at Trenton on December 25, 1776, and at Princeton on January 2, 1777. With these victories, Washington forced the British to withdraw from the banks of the Delaware and to leave the newly formed bands of loyalists to fend for themselves. Patriot morale soared, oaths of loyalty to the king declined, and patriot militia moved back into control of local areas vacated by the withdrawing British troops. The British again had to reconsider their plans.

The British strategy for 1777 involved sending an army of eight thousand under General John Burgoyne southward from Canada through Lake Champlain to recapture Fort Ticonderoga; near Albany, Burgoyne was to join a secondary force under Lieutenant Colonel Barry St. Leger moving eastward through the Mohawk Valley. The ultimate aim of the campaign was to isolate New England and break the back of the rebellion. It was assumed in England that General Howe would cooperate with this Canadian advance, but Howe's main interest, resting on his persistent assumption that there was widespread loyalist support in the middle states, was focused on capturing Philadelphia, the seat of the congressional government. After proposing a number of plans, Howe decided finally to move on Philadelphia by sea, landing after much delay at the head of Chesapeake Bay at the end of August 1777. Believing he could not give up the congressional capital without a struggle, Washington confronted Howe at Brandywine and later at Germantown and was defeated in both battles. But his defeats were not disastrous; they proved that the American army was capable of organized combat, and they prevented Howe from moving north to help Burgoyne. Howe's capture of Philadelphia demonstrated that loyalist sentiment reached only as far as British arms, and it scarcely justified the loss of Burgoyne's army in the North.

After St. Leger's force was turned back at Oriskany in the summer of 1777, Burgoyne and his huge, slow-moving entourage from Canada increasingly found

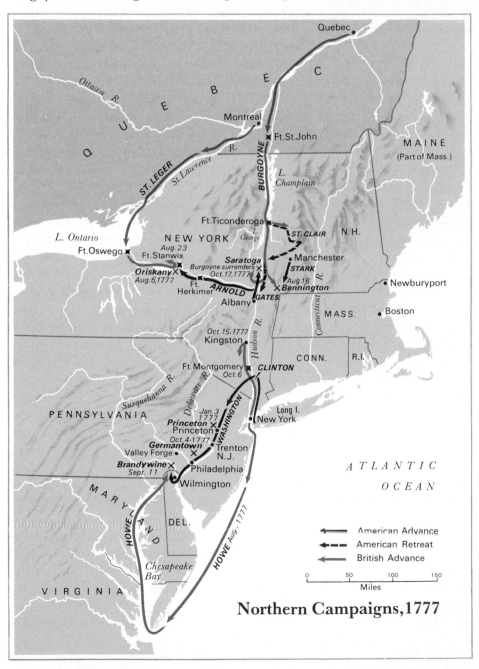

Northern Campaigns, 1777

their supply lines stretched thin and their flanks harassed by patriot militia from New England. While Burgoyne's dawdling gave the American forces in the Hudson Valley needed time to collect themselves, the British army was diminishing. While attempting to seize provisions from a patriot arsenal in Bennington, Vermont, 900 of Burgoyne's men were overcome by 2000 New England militia under John Stark. Another 900 redcoats were detached to garrison Ticonderoga. Believing that his reputation rested on the success of his Canadian invasion, Burgoyne determined to press on. On September 13–14 he crossed the Hudson, cutting off communications with his rear. When he reached Saratoga, he confronted a growing American force of over 10,000 men under General Horatio Gates. Two bloody battles convinced Burgoyne of the hopelessness of his situation, and in October 1777 he surrendered his entire army to the Americans.

Saratoga was the turning point. It suggested that reconquest of America might be beyond British strength. It brought France openly into the struggle. And it led to a fundamental alteration of British commanders and strategy. From the beginning of the rebellion France had been secretly supplying the Americans money and arms in the hope of revenging its defeat in the Seven Years War. By 1777, French ports had been opened to American privateers and French officers were joining Washington's army. It seemed only a matter of time before France recognized the new republic. The British ministry realized at once the significance of Burgoyne's surrender, and by appointing the Carlisle Commission early in 1778 made new efforts to negotiate a settlement. The British government now offered the rebels a return to the imperial status before 1763, indeed everything the Americans had originally wanted. These British overtures, which Franklin skillfully used in Paris to play on French fears of an Anglo-American reconciliation, led Louis XVI's government in February 1778 to sign two treaties with the United States, one a commercial arrangement, the other a military alliance pledged to American independence. In 1779 Spain, in the hopes of recovering its earlier losses, especially Gibraltar from England, became allied with France; and in 1780 Russia formed a League of Armed Neutrality to which nearly all of the maritime states of Europe eventually acceded—leaving England diplomatically isolated for the first time in the eighteenth century.

After 1778, putting down the rebellion became secondary to Britain's global struggle with the Bourbon powers, France and Spain. The center of the war effort in America shifted seaward and southward as Britain sought to protect her stake in the West Indies. General Howe was replaced by Sir Henry Clinton; a more ruthless policy was adopted, including the bombardment of American ports and marauding expeditions in the countryside. Philadelphia was abandoned, and the British assumed a defensive position in the North from their bases in New York and Rhode Island. From its concentration in the West Indies, the British force now aimed to secure military control of ports in the deep South, restore civil royal government with loyalist support and authority, and then methodically move the army northward as a screen behind which the gradual pacification of rebel territory by local loyalists would proceed. This strategy was based on an assumption that the South with its scattered, presumably more loyalist population living in fear of Indian raids and slave uprisings was especially vulnerable to the reassertion of British authority.

In 1779, the British captured Savannah, and on May 12, 1780 with the surrender of General Benjamin Lincoln and the American army of 5500 men they took Charleston. It was the greatest American loss of soldiers in the entire war. A new, hastily assembled American Southern army under General Gates—the victor of Saratoga—rashly moved into South Carolina to stop the British

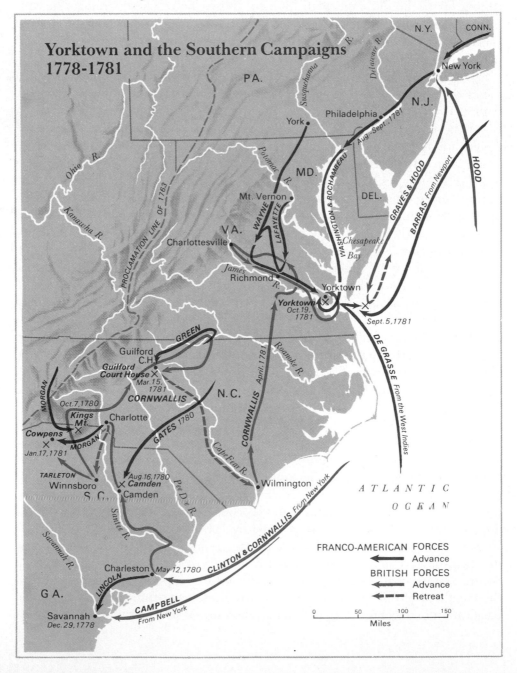

Yorktown and the Southern Campaigns 1778-1781

FRANCO-AMERICAN FORCES
← Advance
BRITISH FORCES
← Advance
⇠ Retreat

0   50   100   150
Miles

advance. On August 16, 1780 at Camden, South Carolina, Gates suffered a
devastating defeat, which destroyed not only his new American army but his
military reputation as well. But the British were not able to consolidate their
gains and give the loyalists the military protection needed for pacification to
work. Loyalist retaliations against Whigs for past harsh treatment and British
depredations, particularly those by Colonel Banastre Tarleton, drove countless
Georgians and Carolinians into partisan activity. Irregular bands of patriots,
sometimes organized under colorful leaders like Francis Marion, "the Swamp
Fox," harassed the loyalists and the British army, and turned the war in the
lower South into a series of guerrilla skirmishes.

Lord Cornwallis, now in command of the British forces in the South, was
impatient with the gradual policy of pacification and was eager to demonstrate
British strength to the undecided by dramatically carrying the war into North
Carolina. With his army constantly bedeviled by patriot guerrillas, he had just
begun moving north when word of the destruction of his left flank at King's
Mountain on October 7, 1780, forced him to return to South Carolina. In the
meantime, the Americans had begun organizing a third Southern army under the
command of a thirty-eight-year-old ex-Quaker from Rhode Island, Nathanael
Greene, recently quartermaster general of the Continental Army. Shrewdly

avoiding a direct confrontation with Cornwallis, Greene compelled the British to divide their forces. On January 17, 1781 at Cowpens in western South Carolina a detached corps of Greene's army under Daniel Morgan defeated "Bloody" Tarleton's Tory Legion and changed the course of British strategy in the South. Cornwallis cut his ties with his base in Charleston and set out after the elusive American army. After an indecisive battle with Greene at Guilford Courthouse on March 15, 1781, Cornwallis's tired and battered soldiers withdrew to Wilmington on the coast of North Carolina with the intention of moving the seat of war northward into Virginia. Thus ended the British experiment with a thorough program of pacification. During the spring and summer of 1781, patriot forces regained control of the entire lower South except for a narrow strip between Charleston and Savannah.

Although marauding by British forces in the summer of 1781 frightened Virginians and humiliated Governor Thomas Jefferson, Cornwallis could not convince his commander in chief, Clinton, in New York to make Virginia the center of British military operations. The haggling between the two generals enabled the Americans to bolster their Virginian troops under the command of the dashing French nobleman, the Marquis de Lafayette, who had been in the struggle since 1777. Cornwallis's withdrawal to the Virginia coast and his eventual isolation at Yorktown gave the combined American and French army of nearly seventeen thousand men under Washington and the Comte de Rochambeau the opportunity it was looking for. The coordinated appearance in Chesapeake Bay of the French fleet under Admiral de Grasse blocked Cornwallis's plans to escape by sea. Thus surrounded and bombarded in Yorktown Cornwallis was forced to surrender his army of eight thousand troops to Washington in October 1781. The British policy since 1778 of spreading their control along the entire Atlantic seaboard depended on maintaining naval superiority; and when this superiority was temporarily lost in 1781, the entire plan collapsed. Although the war dragged on for several months, everyone knew that Yorktown meant American independence.

The peace, nevertheless, still had to be won. The main objective of the new nation, independence from Great Britain, was clear and straightforward. But this objective and others concerning America's territorial boundaries and its rights to the Newfoundland fisheries had to be reconciled with the aims of America's ally, France, and with the aims of France's ally, Spain, which had been at war with Great Britain since 1779. The United States and France had pledged in 1778 not to make a separate peace with Britain. But since France was bound to Spain against Britain until Gibraltar was recovered, there was great danger of American interests getting lost in the machinations of the European powers. Despite the desire of France and Spain to humiliate Britain, neither Bourbon monarchy really wanted a strong and independent American republic. Spain in particular feared the spread of republicanism among its South American colonies and sought to protect its interests in the Mississippi Valley.

PRELIMINARY PEACE NEGOTIATIONS WITH GREAT BRITAIN, BY
BENJAMIN WEST

Although history painter to George III, the American-born
Benjamin West actually toyed with the idea of painting the great
events of the American Revolution. But this unfinished picture of
the peace negotiators was the only one he attempted. The picture
includes John Jay, John Adams, Benjamin Franklin, Temple
Franklin (Franklin's grandson and secretary to the delegation), and
Henry Laurens, who did not sign the final treaty. *(Courtesy, The
Henry Francis du Pont Winterthur Museum.)*

Although Franklin, John Adams, and John Jay, the American negotiators
in Europe, were only "militia diplomats," in Adams's words, they wound their
way through the intricate problems of international politics with professional
diplomatic skill. Despite instructions from the Congress to do nothing without
consulting the French, the American diplomats decided to negotiate with Britain
alone. By hinting at the possibility of weakening the Franco-American alliance,
they induced Great Britain to recognize the independence of the United States
and to agree to generous boundaries for the new country: on the west, the
Mississippi River; on the south, the thirty-first parallel; and on the north, roughly
the present boundary with Canada. The American negotiators then presented
this preliminary Anglo-American treaty to France as an accomplished fact and
persuaded the French to accept it by suggesting that allies must conceal their
differences from their enemies. The prospect of American peace with Britain
now compelled Spain to abandon its demands for Gibraltar and to settle for
Minorca and East and West Florida. In the final treaty signed on September 3,
1783, the United States, by shrewdly playing off the mutual fears of the European
powers, gained independence and a degree of concessions that stunned the
French and indeed all of Europe.

Suggested Readings

Modern interest in the ideas of the Revolution dates back to the 1920s and 1930s with the studies of constitutional law and natural rights philosophy by Carl Becker, *The Declaration of Independence* (1922); Charles H. McIlwain, *The American Revolution: A Constitutional Interpretation* (1923); Randolph G. Adams, *Political Ideas of the American Revolution* (1922); William S. Carpenter, *The Development of American Political Thought* (1930); and Benjamin F. Wright, Jr., *American Interpretations of Natural Law* (1931). While these books emphasized formal political theory, others explicitly treated the ideas as propaganda. See Philip Davidson, *Propaganda and the American Revolution, 1763–1783* (1941); and Arthur M. Schlesinger, *Prelude to Independence: The Newspaper War on Britain, 1764–1776* (1958).

In the 1950s serious attention was paid to the determinative influence of ideas in Clinton Rossiter, *Seedtime of the Republic* (1953); and especially in Edmund S. Morgan and Helen M. Morgan, *The Stamp Act Crisis* (1953). The Morgan book focuses on parliamentary sovereignty.

Only in the 1960s, however, did historians comprehend the Revolutionary ideas as ideology and begin to recover the distinctiveness of the late eighteenth-century world. The starting point now for analyzing the ideology of the Revolution—as a configuration of ideas giving meaning and force to events—is Bernard Bailyn, *The Ideological Origins of the American Revolution* (1967). Bailyn's book, which appeared initially as the introduction to the first of a four-volume edition of *Pamphlets of the American Revolution, 1750–1776* (1965–   ), was partly based on the rediscovery of the radical Whig tradition by Caroline Robbins, *The Eighteenth-Century Commonwealthmen* (1959). J. G. A. Pocock, *The Machiavellian Moment* (1975); J. R. Pole, *Political Representation in England and the Origins of the American Republic* (1966); Trevor H. Colbourn, *The Lamp of Experience: Whig History and the Beginnings of the American Revolution* (1965); and Isaac F. Kramnick, *Bolingbroke and His Circle* (1968), have further contributed to an understanding of the sources of the Revolutionary tradition. Pauline Maier, *From Resistance to Revolution* (1972); details the escalation of American fears of British policy between 1765 and 1776.

On the military actions of the Revolutionary war, the best brief account is Williard M. Wallace, *Appeal to Arms* (1951). Don Higginbotham, *The War of American Independence* (1971), and John Shy, *A People Numerous and Armed: Reflections on the Military Struggle for American Independence* (1976), best appreciate the unconventional and guerrilla character of the war. Two books edited by George A. Billias, *George Washington's Generals* (1964) and *George Washington's Opponents* (1969), contain excellent essays written by various historians on the military leaders of both sides. Eric Robeson, *The American Revolution in Its Political and Military Aspects, 1763–1783* (1955), has some penetrating chapters on the conduct of the war. For naval operations, see Gardner W. Allen, *A Naval History of the American Revolution* (2 vols., 1913). The fullest account of British strategy is Piers Mackesy, *The War for America, 1775–1783* (1964). On the British commanders in chief, see Ira Gruber, *The Howe Brothers and the American Revolution* (1972); and William Willcox, *Portrait of a General: Sir Henry Clinton in the War of Independence* (1964). Paul H. Smith, *Loyalists and Redcoats* (1964), describe British attempts to mobilize the loyalists.

On diplomacy the standard account is Samuel Flagg Bemis, *The Diplomacy of the American Revolution* (1935). See also William C. Stinchcombe, *The American Revolution and the French Alliance* (1969). Richard B. Morris, *The Peacemakers* (1965), is a full study of the peace negotiations.

9

Republicanism

A military victory over Great Britain may have been a prerequisite for the success of the Revolution, but for Americans it scarcely constituted the whole of their Revolution. Although the Revolution was precipitated by a political crisis within the empire, by 1776 it could no longer be understood as simply a colonial rebellion. The developments of the previous decades flowing into the Revolutionary era now fused with the political antagonism to Great Britain to imbue the Revolution with a universal significance. From 1774 and 1775, when independence and hence the formation of new governments became imminent, and continuing throughout the war, nearly every piece of writing about the future of the new states was filled with extraordinarily idealistic hopes for the transformation of America. Americans had come to believe that the Revolution meant nothing less than the reordering of eighteenth-century politics and society—a reordering summed up in the conception of republicanism.

This republicanism was in every way a radical ideology, comparable to the ideologies that have accompanied other revolutions in modern history. It meant more than simply eliminating a king and instituting an elective system of government. It added a moral and indeed utopian dimension to the political separation from England—a dimension that promised a fundamental shift in values and a change in the very character of American society. The republican form the Revolution had assumed by 1776 is incomprehensible unless one understands that Americans were being impelled by something more than hostility to British imperial measures. Americans found in their republican ideology a means of both expressing and alleviating the social changes and strains present by the middle decades of the eighteenth century. When republicanism was blended with the ideas of evangelical Protestantism, it became a radical transforming force. Originally designed to counter and reverse the modernizing tendencies of American life, republicanism eventually ended by quickening and magnifying them.

Independent and Virtuous Citizens

With their conventional eighteenth-century abhorrence of change, Revolutionary Americans sometimes found it difficult to admit the newness of what they were involved in. Thus the radicalness of their ideology has often been obscured. Even in the midst of declaring independence some Americans clung to the conviction that their destruction of monarchy and their institution of republicanism did not signify a repudiation of the ancient English constitution. As John Adams said in 1775, the spirit of republicanism, the spirit of the great men of seventeenth-century England—James Harrington, John Milton, Algernon Sidney—was "so far from being incompatible with the British constitution, that it is the greatest glory of it." Because republicanism could thus mean refurbishing the original English constitution, Americans could become republicans

FRONTIER FARM IN 1793

Even at the end of the eighteenth century, many American farmers continued to grow their crops Indian style, girdling and burning trees, planting between tree stumps, and allowing the fields to revert to forest when their fertility gave out. Such wasteful and shifting methods of agriculture shocked foreign observers but made sense where land was so abundant. (*Harvard College Library.*)

without doing violence to their participation in the classical and radical Whig tradition.

This tradition, like all libertarian strains of the eighteenth century, drew its inspiration from a long heritage of classical republicanism. This republican tradition had originated in the Latin literature of the century and a half spanning the birth of Christ. Writing at a time when the Roman Republic was crumbling or already gone, pessimistic Romans—Cicero, Tacitus, Plutarch, and others—had contrasted the growing corruption and disorder they saw around them with an imagined earlier republican world of simple yeomen-citizens enjoying liberty and arcadian virtue. This Latin literature and its republican vision were revived by the Renaissance and entered into the thinking of early modern Europe. By the eighteenth century, in countless writings and translations ranging from Charles Rollin's popular histories of antiquity to Thomas Gordon's *Sallust*, European and English intellectuals evoked the republican spirit and idealized images of the ancient republics as counterforces to the tyranny and luxury of the dominant monarchical society.

In the excitement of the Revolutionary movement, these classical republican values came together with the complex, long-existing image of Americans as a simple, egalitarian, liberty-loving people to form one of the most coherent and powerful ideologies the Western world had yet seen. Many of the ambiguities Americans had felt about the rustic provincial character of their society were now clarified. What some had seen as the crudities and deficiencies of American life could now be viewed as advantages for republican government. Instead of being primitive Europeans living in the backwaters of history, independent American farmers owning their own land were naturally equipped to realize the republican values intellectuals had espoused for centuries.

Inevitably, then, the new American states in 1776 became republics. Everyone knew that these new republics with their elective systems had not only political but moral and social significance. Republicanism struck directly at the older ties of patronage and dependency. It promised social relations based on natural merit and the equality of independent citizens linked to one another in harmony. Although republicanism was centrally based on individual property holding, it repudiated a narrow selfish individualism and stressed a morality of social cohesion and devotion to the common welfare or *res publica*. Several of the states in 1776 even adopted the designation *commonwealth* to express better their new dedication to the public good.

Such republican communities of independent citizens presented an inspiring but fragile ideal. History had shown republics to be the most unstable kind of state, vulnerable to foreign influence and highly susceptible to faction and internal disorder. Theorists thus concluded that republics had to be small in territory and homogeneous in character. The only existing European republican models—Holland, and the Italian and Swiss city-states—were small and compact. When a large country attempted to establish a republic, as England had tried in the seventeenth century, the experiment was sure to end in some sort of authoritarianism like that of Oliver Cromwell. Unlike monarchies, whose unitary authority and numerous dependent ranks maintained public order even over a large and diverse population, republics had to be held together from below, by the people themselves.

More than any other kind of political system, republics demanded an extraordinary moral quality in their people. The eighteenth century, like previous ages, designated this moral quality as virtue, or patriotism. If the people of a republic lost their virtue, if they became selfish and luxury-loving as the ancient Romans had, then the people's love of liberty became corrupted and the dissolution of the state inevitably followed. Americans, however, seemed nat-

TREATISE VII.

VIZ.

A NOTION of the *Historical Draught* or *Tablature*

OF THE

JUDGMENT of *HERCULES*,

According to PRODICUS, *Lib.* II. *Xen. de Mem. Soc.*

——————————————Potiores
HERCULIS ærumnas credat, sævosque Labores,
Et Venere, et cœnis, et pluma SARDANAPALI.
Juv. Sat. 10.

Paulo de Matthæis Pinx.　　　*Sim. Gribelin sculps.*

EARL OF SHAFTESBURY'S TREATISE OF 1713

The myth of Hercules confronted by Virtue and Pleasure at the youthful crossroads of his life was a convention of Western history, particularly in the eighteenth century. In 1776 John Adams proposed making "The Choice of Hercules," as it had appeared here, the device for the Great Seal of the United States. But its complexity and unoriginality made him drop the idea. *(Boston Public Library.)*

urally virtuous and thus ideally suited for republican government. Did they not possess the same hardy egalitarian character as the ancient republican citizens had? Were not the remarkable displays of popular order in the face of disintegrating royal governments in 1774–75 evidence of the willingness of the American people to obey their governments without coercion? And if such confidence was mingled with doubts, the Revolutionary leaders could exhort the American people to act patriotically, telling them, as Samuel Adams did, that "a Citizen owes everything to the Commonwealth." The citizen was in fact, as the Philadelphia physician Benjamin Rush said, "public property. His time and talents—his youth—his manhood—his old age—nay more, life, all belong to his country."

Republican citizens, in short, had to be patriots. The great social antagonists of the pre-Revolutionary period grew out of the peculiarity of that traditional social world. They were not the poor versus the rich, or democrats versus aristocrats, but patriots versus courtiers. Patriots were not simply those who loved their country but those who were free of dependent connections. Courtiers, on the other hand, were those whose corrupting dependence on the court or government, whether through appointment to offices or as recipients of favors and money, destroyed their independence. If citizens therefore were to be willing to sacrifice their selfish interests for the public good, they had to be, as the Virginia Declaration of Rights stated in 1776, "equally free and independent." As Jefferson wrote in his *Notes on Virginia*, "dependence begets subservience and venality, suffocates the germ of virtue, and prepares fit tools for the designs of ambition." Hence the sturdy independent yeomen, Jefferson's "chosen people of God," were regarded as the most incorruptible and the best citizens for a republic. The celebration of the farmer in the years following the Revolution was not a literary notion but a scientifically based imperative of republican government.

The individual ownership of property, especially landed property, was essential for a republic, both as a source of independence and as evidence of a permanent attachment to the community. Those who were propertyless and dependent could thus be justifiably denied the vote because, as a convention of Essex County, Massachusetts, declared in 1778, they were "so situated as to have no wills of their own." In Europe, corruption and dependency were common because only a few possessed property. But, as one Carolinian wrote in 1777, "the people of America are a people of property; almost every man is a freeholder." Jefferson was so keen on this point that he proposed in 1776 that the new state of Virginia grant fifty acres of land to every citizen who did not have that many.

At the heart of this republican emphasis on virtue and independence lay equality, the most powerful conception in American history. Equality was the social basis for the anticipated harmony and public virtue of the New World.

Boylston represented those wealthy
and fashionable circles surrounding royal authority that ambitious
men like John Adams simultaneously admired and resented.
"Dined at Mr. Nick Boylstones...,"
Adams in 1766 confided to his
diary with wide-eyed excitement.
"An elegant dinner indeed! Went
over the house to view the furniture, which alone cost a thousand
pounds sterling. A seat it is for a
noble man, a prince, the turkey
carpets, the painted hangings, the
marble tables, the rich beds with
crimson damask curtains and
counterpins, the beautiful chimney
clock, the spacious garden, are the
most magnificent of any thing I
have ever seen." *(The Fogg Art
Museum, Harvard University.)*

The incessant squabbling over position and rank and the bitter contentions of
factional politics in the colonies were due, it was said, to the artificial inequality of colonial society, created and nourished largely through the influence
and patronage of the British crown. "In monarchies," declared David Ramsay
of South Carolina in 1778, "favor is the source of preferment; but, in our new
forms of government, no one can command the suffrages of the people, unless
by his superior merit and capacity." With social movement both up and down
founded only on natural ability, it was assumed that no distinctions would
have time to harden and perpetuate themselves. So too it followed that all
legal and artificially created privileges would have to be abolished. In the new
Revolutionary state governments, Americans struck out at official monopolies
and at colonial laws confining the descent of property to eldest sons (primogeniture) and to a special line of heirs (entail). The goal, however, was not
to create a leveled society but an organic benevolent hierarchy led by "natural"
aristocrats. These aristocratic leaders would resemble not the luxury-loving
money-mongering lackeys of British officialdom but the stoical and disinterested
heroes of antiquity—men like George Washington, who seemed to Americans to
embody perfectly the classical ideal of a republican leader.

These republican values expressed the Americans' understanding of the special world in which they lived and their idealism in seeking to perfect it. Their republican ideology was thus as varied and complicated as that world. For those like John Adams of Massachusetts or William Drayton of South Carolina or the younger Charles Carroll of Maryland who feared that "all power might center in *one family*" and that offices of government "like a precious jewel will be handed down from *father* to *son*," republicanism offered an end to the abusive power of kinship and the undue influence of individuals. In the South, the attacks on luxury and on aristocratic pride were less the resentful protests of the socially aspiring than the uneasy introspections of the dominant gentlemen themselves, anxious about their own corruption. But everywhere the aim was to eliminate toadyism and to create a virtuous society of independent men. In its efforts to deliver America from sin and tyranny, even evangelical Protestantism became republicanized. The Puritans' "city upon a hill" now assumed a new republican character, becoming, in Samuel Adams's evocative phrase, "the *Christian* Sparta."

Obviously this Revolutionary republicanism failed to fulfill itself. Much of its communitarian emphasis flew in the face of the surging individualism of American life, and its stress on equality and new social relationships soon created a society in many respects the opposite of what had been intended. Yet whatever the ultimate results, republicanism as it was understood by Jefferson's generation colored the entire Revolutionary movement and eventually shaped much of what Americans still believe and value.

State Constitution Making

From the time royal authority disintegrated, Americans began thinking about creating new governments. During the summer of 1775 Samuel Adams and John Adams of Massachusetts, together with the Virginia delegation to the Continental Congress led by Richard Henry Lee, worked out a program for independence, involving establishing foreign alliances, creating a confederation, and most important, framing new governments. The climax of the radicals' efforts came with the congressional resolutions of May 1776, advising the colonies to adopt new governments "under the authority of the people," and declaring "that the exercise of every kind of authority under the ... Crown should be totally suppressed." Even before the Declaration of Independence, the Congress had created a committee to form a confederation, and some of the states had begun working on new constitutions. By the fall of 1777 not only had Congress drafted a plan of union, but all the former colonies had revolutionalized their ancient charters or written new constitutions.

In 1776–77, most of the Americans' intellectual attention and much of their energies were concentrated on establishing new state constitutions. The fascinating investigations of the abuses of power and the protection of liberty begun in the imperial debate now blended into the most creative period of constitutional-ism in American history. The states, not the central government or Congress, were to test the Revolutionary hopes. In fact, forming new state governments, as Jefferson said in the spring of 1776, was "the whole object of the present con-troversy." For the aim of the Revolution had become not simply independence from British tyranny, but the eradication of the possibility of future tyranny.

It was inevitable that Americans would embody their constitutions in written documents and therefore at a stroke reveal the separation of their constitutional tradition from that of Great Britain. By the word *constitution*, most eighteenth-century Englishmen meant not a written document but the existing arrangements of government, that is, laws, customs, and institutions, together with the principles these incorporated. Americans, however, had come to view a constitution in a different way. From the seventeenth century, they had repeatedly used their written colonial charters as defensive barriers against royal authority. The im-perial controversy had only reinforced this tradition. During the debate with Britain, the colonists had been compelled to recognize that laws made by Parlia-ment were not necessarily constitutional, or in accord with fundamental principles of rightness and justice. If the constitutional principles that presumably had made the English constitution a bulwark of liberty were to be protected from a sovereign legislature, then somehow they had to be lifted out of the machinery of govern-ment and set above it. Thus, unlike the English constitution, which has never been incorporated in a single document, the Americans' new state constitutions became fixed plans prescribing the powers of government and specifying the rights of citizens. Such constitutions were distinctly separate from legislation and the other ordinary workings of government.

In these new state constitutions, the Americans set about to institutionalize all that they had learned from their colonial experience and from the recent struggle with England. Although they knew they would establish republics, they did not know precisely what forms the new governments should take. The Revolution-aries' central aim was to prevent power, which they identified with the rulers or governors, from encroaching upon liberty, which the people or their representa-tives in the legislatures possessed. Somehow or other, gubernatorial power had to be offset by an increase in popular liberty. Thus the reconstruction of their governments in the year following the Declaration of Independence was carried on within the confines of the traditional theory of mixed or balanced government.

Although the constitution makers knew that the people were capable of an-archy, they also knew, as Josiah Quincy of Massachusetts declared, that it was "much easier to restrain liberty from running into licentiousness than power from swelling into tyranny and oppression." Only the Americans' deep fear of guber-natorial power—which was, in the words of a Delaware revolutionary, "ever rest-less, ambitious, and ever grasping at encrease"—can explain the radical changes they made in 1776 in the authority of their now elected governors.

The members of the various state congresses who drafted the new constitutions in 1776 were not content, as Englishmen throughout their history had been, merely to erect higher barriers against encroaching power or to formulate new and more explicit charters of the people's liberties. In their ambitious desire to root out tyranny once and for all they reduced the gubernatorial magistrate to a pale reflection of his regal ancestor. In their various constitutions they stripped the governors of much of their former power. Governors no longer would have the authority to control the meeting of the assemblies, declare war and make peace, raise armies, coin money, erect courts, lay embargos, grant dignities, or pardon crimes. In Pennsylvania, which created the most radical constitution of all the states, the Revolutionaries eliminated the gubernatorial magistrate outright. By resting the executive power in an elective council of twelve members directly elected by the people, and by maintaining only a single house legislature, the Pennsylvania radicals challenged the very idea of balanced government. While the other states still clung to the theory of some sort of mixture, in effect they destroyed the substance of an independent magistrate and turned the governor, in Jefferson's term, into an "administrator." All the governors were surrounded by controlling councils elected by the assemblies. The governors were to be elected annually, generally by the assemblies, limited in the times they could be reelected, and subject to impeachment.

However radical these changes in executive authority may have been, they did not in American minds get to the heart of the matter and destroy the most insidious and dangerous source of despotism—the executive power of appointment to offices. Since in a traditional, especially a monarchical, society the disposal of offices, honors, and favors affected the social order, American republicans were determined that their governors would never again have the capacity to dominate public life. Control over appointments and preferments was now wrested from the traditional hands of the governors and given in most cases to the legislatures. This change was justified by the principle of separation of powers, a doctrine Montesquieu made famous in the mid–eighteenth century. The emphasis in the constitutions on keeping the executive, legislative, and judicial parts of the government separate and distinct was invoked in 1776 not to protect each power from the others but to keep the judiciary and especially the legislature free from executive manipulation, the very kind of manipulation that had corrupted the English Parliament. Hence all executive officeholders and those receiving profits from the government were categorically barred from sitting in the legislatures. As a consequence parliamentary cabinet government was forever prohibited in America, and constitutional development moved off in a direction entirely independent of England.

The powers and prerogatives taken from the governors were given to the legislatures. This marked a radical shift in the responsibility of government. Traditionally in English history the "government" had been identified exclusively with the executive; representative bodies had generally been confined to voting taxes and passing corrective and exceptional legislation. But now the new American state legislatures, in particular the lower houses of the assemblies, were no longer to be merely adjuncts of governmental power or checks on it. They were to assume familiar magisterial prerogatives, including the making of alliances and the granting of pardons, that legislatures had rarely ever exercised. This transferal of political authority to the people's representatives in the legislatures led some Americans, like Richard Henry Lee, to note that their new governments were "very much of a democratic kind," although "a Governor and a second branch of legislation are admitted."

To ensure that the state legislatures fully embodied the democratic element of the societies, that is, the people, the ideas and experience behind the Americans' objections to the British theory of virtual representation were now drawn out and implemented. The new state constitutions and governments put a new emphasis on actual representation and the explicitness of consent: on equal electoral districts, on annual elections, on a broadened suffrage, on residential requirements for both electors and elected, and on the right of constituents to instruct their representatives. Earlier mid–eighteenth-century efforts by royal authority to prohibit the extension of representation to newly settled areas were now dramatically reversed. Towns and counties, particularly in the West, were granted either new or additional representation in the state legislatures, in a belated recognition of the legitimacy of the backcountry uprisings of the 1760s and 70s. Some of the new constitutions recognized the principle of numbers, as distinct from geography, as the basis of representation. Five states actually wrote into fundamental law specific plans for periodic adjustments of their representation, so that, as the New York constitution of 1777 stated, it "shall for ever remain proportionate and adequate."

In light of what would happen in the coming decade, the confidence of the Revolutionaries in 1776 in their representative legislatures was remarkable. Except among disgruntled Tories there was as yet little thought of popular tyranny by these state legislatures; for in the Whig theory of politics it did not seem possible for the people to tyrannize over themselves. Of course the people were apt to be licentious or giddy; hence the mixed republics needed not only governors but upper houses to counterbalance the popular houses of representatives. All the states, except Pennsylvania, Georgia, and the new state of Vermont, therefore provided for senates, the designation taken from Roman history. The senators were not to be any legally defined nobility but the wisest and best members of the society, who would revise and correct the well-intentioned but often careless measures of the people. Although the senators in most of the states were to be elected by the people, they were not considered in 1776, any more than were the elected governors, to be in any way "representatives" of the people. The people, although responsible for selecting all parts of the mixed republics, were still thought to be exclusively represented in the lower houses of representatives.

The Articles of Confederation

At the same time that the Revolutionaries were creating their state constitutions, they were drafting a central government. Yet this union scarcely compared in importance with the states. In marked contrast to the rich and exciting public explorations of political theory accompanying the formation of the state constitutions in the middle and late 1770s, there was little discussion of the plans for a central government. In 1776, the loyalties of most people were still concentrated on their particular provinces. The Declaration of Independence, drawn up by the Continental Congress, was actually a declaration by "thirteen united States of America" proclaiming that as "Free and Independent States, they have full Power to levy War, conclude Peace, contract Alliances, establish Commerce, and to do all other Acts and Things which independent States may of right do." Despite all the talk of union, few Americans in 1776 could even conceive of creating a single full-fledged continental republic.

Still, the Congress needed some legal basis for its authority. Like the various provincial conventions, it had been created in 1774 simply out of exigency of events, and was exercising an extraordinary degree of political, military, and economic power over Americans. It had adopted commercial codes, established and maintained an army, issued a continental currency, erected a military code

PAPER CURRENCY ISSUED BY THE CONTINENTAL
CONGRESS

(American Antiquarian Society.)

of law, defined crimes against the union, and negotiated abroad. With the approach of Independence it was obvious to many leaders that a more permanent and legitimate union of the states was necessary. Although a draft of a confederation was ready for consideration by the Congress as early as mid-July 1776, not until November 1777 and after heated controversy did Congress present a document of union to the states for their separate approval or rejection. It took nearly four years, until March 1781, for all the states to accept this document and thereby legally establish the Articles of Confederation.

The Articles created a confederacy, called "The United States of America," that was essentially a continuation of the Second Continental Congress. Delegates from each state were to be sent annually to the Congress, and each state delegation was to have only a single vote. In Article 9 Congress was granted the authority to determine diplomatic relations, requisition the states for men and money, coin and borrow money, regulate Indian affairs, and settle disputes between the states. While a simple majority of seven states was needed for minor matters, a larger majority, nine states, was required for important matters, including engaging in war, making treaties, and coining and borrowing money. There was no real executive but only a series of congressional committees with a fluctuating membership.

The degree of union that was envisioned for thirteen independent states was impressive. The states were specifically forbidden to conduct foreign affairs, make treaties, or declare war. The citizens of each state were entitled to the privileges and immunities of the citizens of all states. All travel and discriminatory trade restrictions between the states were eliminated. Extradition and judicial proceedings were made reciprocal. These stipulations together with the substantial grant of powers to the Congress in Article 9 made the United States of America as strong as any similar republican confederation in history. The Articles marked a remarkable step toward a national government.

Nevertheless, the Americans' fears of distant central authority, intensified by a century of experience in the British empire, never left any doubt that this Confederation would be something less than a full national government. Despite Congress's considerable powers, the crucial powers of commercial regulation and taxation, indeed all final ordinary lawmaking authority, remained with the states. Congressional resolutions continued to be, as they had been under the Continental Congress, recommendations that, it was assumed, the states would enforce. And should there be any doubts of the decentralized nature of the Confederation, Article 2 stated bluntly that "each State retains its sovereignty, freedom and independence, and every power, jurisdiction, and right, which is not by this confederation expressly delegated to the United States, in Congress assembled." The "United States of America" thus possessed a literal meaning that is hard for us today to appreciate. The Confederation, based as it was on the equal representation of each state, necessarily resembled more of a treaty among sovereign states than a single government. It was intended to be and remained, as

Claims to Western Lands
1781

States With Western Claims
States Without Western Claims
Western Claims
Limit of Virginia's Claims

Article 3 declared, "a firm league of friendship" among states jealous of their individuality. Not only its ratification but any subsequent changes in the Articles of Confederation required the consent of all the states.

Such state particularism prolonged the congressional debates over the adoption of the Articles and delayed its unanimous ratification until 1781. The major disputes—over representation, the apportionment of the states' contribution to the union, and the disposition of the western lands—involved concrete state interests. Large populous states like Virginia argued for proportional representation in the Congress, but had to give way to the small states' determination to maintain equal representation. The original draft of the Articles provided that each state's quota or financial contribution to the general treasury be based on its population, including slaves. Strenuous opposition from the Southern states, however, forced the Congress to shift the basis for a state's quota to the value of its land against the wishes of the New England states where land values were high.

This pitting of state particularities against one another was most evident in the long, drawn-out controversy over the disposition of the western lands between the Appalachians and the Mississippi. While those states like Virginia and Massachusetts with ancient charter claims to this western territory wanted to maintain control over the disposal of their land, those states like Maryland and Rhode Island without such claims wanted the land pooled in a common national domain under the authority of Congress. By March 1779, all the states had ratified the Articles except Maryland, which under the influence of land speculators refused to ratify until all the states had ceded their western lands to the central government. When Virginia, the state with charter rights to the largest amount of western territory, finally agreed on January 2, 1781, to surrender its claims to the United States, the way was prepared for ratification of the Articles of Confederation by all the states. But the Confederation had to promise, as part of the price paid for the cession of claims by Virginia and the other states, that the national domain would "be settled and formed into distinct republican states."

The Congress drew up land ordinances in 1784 and 1785, and in 1787 it adopted the famous Northwest Ordinance that at once acknowledged, as the British in the 1760s had not, the settlers' destiny in the West. The land ordinances of 1784 and 1785 provided for the Northwest territory to be surveyed and formed into townships of six miles square along lines running east-west and north-south. Each township was divided into 36 numbered lots, or sections of 640 acres. The Confederation, in providing for the sale of the land by auction, favored speculators and large groups by stipulating that a section was to be the smallest unit purchased, at a price of no less than a dollar an acre. In each township Congress retained four sections and set aside one other for the support of public education. The Ordinance of 1787 dealt with the political organization of the Northwest. It guaranteed to the settlers basic political rights and common law liberties and arranged for the area to be divided into not less than three nor more than five territories. When each territory reached a population of 60,000, it was to be admitted to the Union on equal terms with the existing states.

These remarkable ordinances were the greatest achievement of the Confederation outside of winning the war. They solved at a stroke the problem of relating "colonies" or dependencies to the central government that Great Britain had been unable to solve. In the succeeding decades the Land Ordinance of 1785 and the Ordinance of 1787 remained the basis for the sale and the political evolution of America's western territories. Settlers could leave the older states assured that they were not abandoning their political liberties and know that they would be allowed eventually to form new republics as sovereign and independent as the other states in the Union. Thus even the organization of this great national landed resource by the Congress was immediately devoted to the dispersion of central authority by the anticipated creation of more states, the only political units most Americans seemed to value.

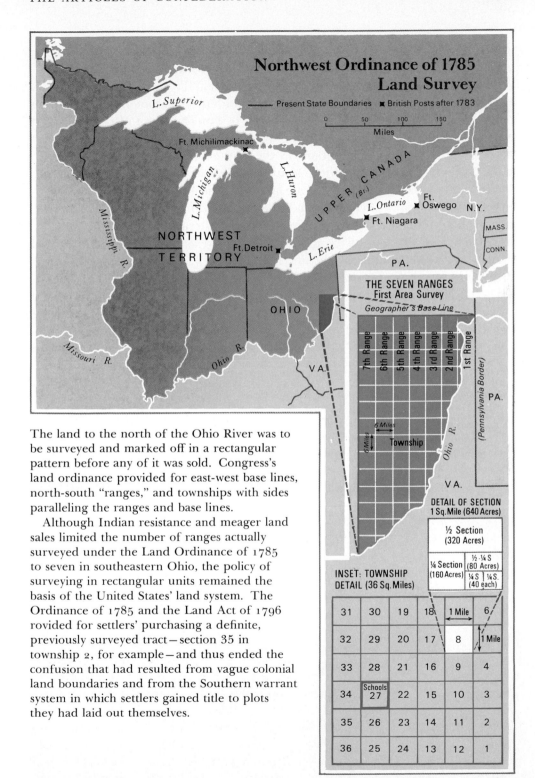

Northwest Ordinance of 1785 Land Survey

—— Present State Boundaries   ■ British Posts after 1783

0   50   100   150
Miles

L. Superior

Ft. Michilimackinac

L. Michigan

L. Huron

UPPER CANADA (Br.)

L. Ontario   Ft. Oswego   N.Y.
Ft. Niagara

NORTHWEST

Mississippi R.

TERRITORY   Ft. Detroit   L. Erie

MASS.

CONN.

PA.

OHIO

THE SEVEN RANGES
First Area Survey
Geographer's Base Line

7th Range 6th Range 5th Range 4th Range 3rd Range 2nd Range 1st Range

Missouri R.

Ohio R.

6 Miles
6 Miles
Township

V.A.

(Pennsylvania Border)

PA.

Ohio R.

V.A.

DETAIL OF SECTION
1 Sq. Mile (640 Acres)

½ Section
(320 Acres)

¼ Section
(160 Acres)

½-¼ S
(80 Acres)

¼ S ¼ S
(40 each)

INSET: TOWNSHIP
DETAIL (36 Sq. Miles)

31	30	19	18	1 Mile	6
32	29	20	17	8	1 Mile
33	28	21	16	9	4
34	Schools 27	22	15	10	3
35	26	23	14	11	2
36	25	24	13	12	1

The land to the north of the Ohio River was to be surveyed and marked off in a rectangular pattern before any of it was sold. Congress's land ordinance provided for east-west base lines, north-south "ranges," and townships with sides paralleling the ranges and base lines.

Although Indian resistance and meager land sales limited the number of ranges actually surveyed under the Land Ordinance of 1785 to seven in southeastern Ohio, the policy of surveying in rectangular units remained the basis of the United States' land system. The Ordinance of 1785 and the Land Act of 1796 rovided for settlers' purchasing a definite, previously surveyed tract—section 35 in township 2, for example—and thus ended the confusion that had resulted from vague colonial land boundaries and from the Southern warrant system in which settlers gained title to plots they had laid out themselves.

Republican Society

Beneath all these efforts to establish governments and constitutions lay unsettling changes in the nature of American society. To be sure, there was no immediate collapse of the social order, no sudden displacement of the ruling gentry, no abrupt and wholesale destruction of familiar social institutions. But everywhere the older society was being transformed, often through the accumulation of tiny, piecemeal alterations in the way people related to government, to the economy, and to each other. Many of these changes had begun long before the Revolution and were aspects of the larger modernizing process that the Revolution expressed and intensified. Yet the Revolution not only quickened these longer-range tendencies of eighteenth-century American life but had its own particular corrosive effects on the traditional society. The Revolution had scarcely begun before it was releasing and creating forces that pointed towards a new kind of republican social world.

The social movements of the pre-Revolutionary period were now propelled forward at much greater speeds. Despite a slackening of immigration and the loss of tens of thousands of loyalist émigrés, the population continued to multiply, giving the 1780s the fastest rate of demographic growth of any decade in

DETAIL FROM "THE TONTINE COFFEE HOUSE," BY GUY FRANCIS, 1797

During the Revolution fire had ravaged much of the commercial section of New York. In the following years New York's merchants enlarged the harbor facilities and rebuilt the business district, including this busy corner of Wall and Water streets. By 1797 New York had surpassed rival Philadelphia in both imports and exports. *(Courtesy of The New-York Historical Society, New York City.)*

American history. After being delayed for several years in the late 70s by inter-mittent warfare against the British and Indians, this swelling population resumed its roll westward. By 1780 the Kentucky territory had over twenty thousand in-habitants, and towns like Louisville and Nashville were being built almost over-night. Even continued British and Indian harassment in the West did not stop this outward push. General Anthony Wayne's victory over the Indians at Fallen Timbers, near present day Toledo, in 1794 and the final evacuation of the west-ern forts by the British released the greatest migration of western settlers Amer-ica had ever known. Indeed, more territory was occupied in the first post-Revolutionary generation than in the entire colonial period.

These extraordinary and mutually reinforcing demographic and geographic explosions reverberated throughout the whole society. Such a mobile population, one Kentuckian told Madison in 1792, "must make a very different mass from one which is composed of men born and raised on the same spot. . . . They see none about them to whom or to whose families they have been accustomed to think themselves inferior."

The ideology of republicanism, instead of braking these disintegrating devel-opments with its stress on social harmony and cohesion, only accelerated them. In a republic, declared a writer in 1787 in the *American Museum*, the most impor-tant of the several new American magazines created in the post-war years, "the idea of equality breathes through the whole and every individual feels ambitious, to be in a situation not inferior to his neighbour." This republican equality now became a rallying cry for aspiring middling elements, and allowed freer play than ever before to long-existing resentments of presumed social superiority. In some areas, particularly in the North, distinctions of every kind, including belonging to private social clubs and wearing imported finery, were bitterly criticized in the press. Even the term "the *better sort of people*," said one Boston newspaper in 1785, "became thoroughly contemptible and odious in the esti-mation of the people."

In such a growing egalitarian atmosphere, the creators of the Order of the Cincinnati in 1783 were audacious indeed. This hereditary society designed to perpetuate the honor of Revolutionary army officers immediately provoked a barrage of criticism throughout the country. Many Americans shared Samuel Adams's belief that the Order was making "as rapid a Stride towards an heredi-tary Military Nobility as was ever made in so short a time." In much of the public discussions of the post-Revolutionary years, "aristocrats" now replaced "cour-tiers" as the social element most vehemently feared and condemned.

"When the pot boils, the scum will rise," some Revolutionary gentlemanly leaders had warned at the outset, but few had realized how much it would rise. The turmoil of the war and the loosening of social bonds turned mobility in some areas into something of a scramble. The important distinction between gentle-men and ordinary people became blurred, with even some tradesmen now claiming gentry status. By the end of the war many like Governor James Bowdoin of Massachusetts could "scarcely see any other than new faces," a change, he said, almost as "remarkable as the revolution itself." As John Adams noted in his diary, his own deep resentment of his supposed social superiors was being echoed throughout the various strata of the society. For every brilliant provincial lawyer like Adams eager to challenge the supremacy of the imperial clique in a colonial metropolis like Boston, there were dozens of lesser men, not so brilliant, not so well-educated, and not so gentlemanly as Adams, but equally desirous of securing a local magistracy, a captaincy of the militia, something or anything that, as one Connecticut writer observed in 1786, would bring them "a little money, or what is better, a little authority."

The equality called for involved not the equitable redistribution of wealth but the obscuring and changing of older distinctions and relationships. Small-time opportunists and middling entrepreneurs challenged the gentlemanly and aristocratic order of the old society, not to destroy the economic hierarchy but to win a dominant place in it. Certainly the society was not leveled; indeed the inequality of wealth was aggravated by the Revolution. Although some poorer people were now better off than in colonial times, the gap between rich and poor was wider after the Revolution than before. But elements in the society were reshuffled and a measure of the wealth changed hands. Most important, many in the society now held their positions on new, more independent terms. Wealth increasingly became the main criterion of distinguishing one person from another.

The departure of tens of thousands of loyalists was the most obvious source of

PAUL REVERE, BY JOHN SINGLETON COPLEY

Urban artisans and craftsmen like the silversmith Paul Revere were the most important social group in the cities that emerged into political consciousness during the Revolutionary era. *(Courtesy, Museum of Fine Arts, Boston. Gift of Joseph W., William B., and Edward H. R. Revere.)*

new opportunities. The loyalists may have numbered close to half a million, or 20 percent of white Americans. Nearly twenty thousand of them fought for the crown in regiments of His Majesty's army, and thousands of others served in local loyalist militia bodies. As many as sixty thousand to eighty thousand loyalists, it is estimated, left America during the Revolution for Canada and Great Britain, although many of these returned after the war and were reintegrated into American society. Although the loyalists came from all ranks and occupations of the society, a disproportionate number of them belonged to the upper political and social levels. Many had been officeholders and overseas merchants involved with government contracting; in the North, most were Anglicans. Their regional distribution was likewise uneven. In New England and Virginia they were a tiny minority. But in western frontier areas, where hostility to eastern encroachment went back to pre-Revolutionary times, and in the regions of New York, New Jersey, and Pennsylvania, and the deep South, where the British army offered protection, loyalists made up a considerable part of the population. Their flight, displacement, and retirements created a vacuum at the top that was rapidly filled by patriots. The effects were widespread. Crown and Tory property and lands valued at millions of pounds were confiscated by the Revolutionary governments and almost immediately thrown onto the market, leading to an unsettling expansion of speculation and enterprise that accentuated the sudden rise and fall of fortunes marking the Revolutionary years.

It was in the economy that the social disorder of the Revolution expressed itself most forcefully. The Revolution at once altered the British mercantile pattern in which American commercial life had been nurtured for over a century. It released pent-up forces and stimulated a competitive spirit that spread throughout the commercial sectors of the society. Traditional markets and sources of credit were shaken or disrupted, and planters, farmers, and merchants were forced to adjust their trade relationships. However harmful to particular areas and to particular groups and individuals, the results to the economy as a whole were healthy and stimulating.

The South suffered the greatest dislocations from the war, both by losing established markets for its tobacco and other staples and by having tens of thousands of slaves freed by the British. Indeed, the British army was perhaps the greatest single instrument of emancipation in America until the Civil War. But these dislocations only accelerated an agricultural diversification that had begun before the Revolution. The upper South in particular recovered rapidly. Tobacco production in the 1780s equaled prewar levels, involving, however, many new participants and new marketing arrangements. In the North, the lines of division in the merchant communities between those involved in the British dry goods trade and others that had been apparent before the Revolution now widened, and merchants who had previously been on the periphery of economic activity were granted new openings. In Massachusetts, for example, provincial families like the Higginsons, Cabots, and Lowells quickly moved into Boston to form the basis for a new Massachusetts elite; this process was duplicated less notably but no less importantly elsewhere. New merchants pushed out in all directions in search of new markets, not only into the once restricted colonial areas of the West Indies and South America but throughout Europe and even as far away as China.

After the war, trade with Great Britain quickly reached its earlier levels; by the 1780s, aggregate figures point to an amazing recovery of commerce. Yet such gross statistics do not do justice to the extent of change involved; for in all the states there were new sources of supply, new commercial configurations, and new and increased numbers of participants in the market. Although exports soon surpassed their prewar levels, they now represented a smaller part of America's total economic activity. Already the economy was beginning to turn inward with a remarkable spread of interstate and interregional trade that would soon generate demands for new roads and canals. In these changing circumstances, towns without hinterlands to exploit began a relative decline; and a city like Newport, Rhode Island, which had been a flourishing colonial port but lacked an inland area for supply and marketing, rapidly slipped into insignificance.

The Revolutionary war itself was at once a disrupting and a creative force. Like all wars, it destroyed familiar channels of trade and produced new sources of wealth. Almost overnight the machinery of governmental finance was overhauled. During the war the Congress and the states became gigantic borrowers and buyers and dominated economic life in ways that were unfamiliar to eighteenth-century Americans. Not only did the congressional and state governments lack modern mechanisms for assessing and taxing wealth, but Congress did not even have the legal authority to tax. American governments thus had to rely largely on borrowing and on the imaginative colonial device of emitting paper currency to pay for the war. The governments sold millions of dollars of interest-bearing bonds or loan certificates and thus created important new negotiable instruments of investment and speculation for businessmen. As the war dragged on, however, such government borrowing could scarcely raise the sums needed. Both the Congress and

SCALE

OF

DEPRECIATION,

Agreeable to an Act of the Commonwealth of Massachusetts to be observed as a Rule for settling the rate of Depreciation on all contracts both publick and private, made on or since the first day of January, 1777——

One Hundred Dollars in Gold and Silver in January 1777, being equal to One Hundred and Five Dollars in the Bills of Credit of the United States.

One thousand seven hundred and seventy-seven.

January,	105	April,	112	July,	125	October,	275
February,	107	May,	115	August,	150	November,	300
March,	109	June,	120	September,	175	December,	310

One thousand seven hundred and seventy-eight.

January,	325	April,	400	July,	425	October,	500
February,	350	May,	400	August,	450	November,	545
March,	375	June,	400	September,	475	December,	634

One thousand seven hundred and seventy-nine.

January,	742	April,	1104	July,	1477	October,	2030
February,	868	May,	1215	August,	1630	November,	2308
March,	1000	June,	1342	September,	1800	December,	2593

One thousand seven hundred and eighty.

| January, | 2934 | February, | 3322 | March, | 3736 | April, | 4000 |

From April 1st, 1780, to April 20th, one Spanish milled dollar was equal to Forty of the old Emission.

April 25th,	42	May 20th,	54	June 20th,	69	Novem. 30th,	74
April 30th,	44	May 25th,	60	August 15th,	70	February 27th	
May 5th,	46	May 30th,	62	Septem. 10th,	71	1781,	75
May 10th,	47	June 10th,	64	October 25th,	72		
May 15th,	49	June 15th,	68	Novem. 10th,	73		

Depreciation of the New Emission.

From the 27th of February, 1781, to the 1st of May following, 1¼ of a Dollar of the said New Emission was equal to one Dollar in Specie.
From the 1st to the 25th of May, 2½ of the New Emission, equal to one in Specie.
From the 25th of May to the 15th of June, three of the New Emission for one in Specie.
From the 15th of June to the 1st of October, four of the New Emission were equal to one in Specie.

(American Antiquarian Society.)

the state governments therefore resorted also to the extensive printing of non-interest-bearing paper currency, which took on the character of forced loans. These bills of credit were paper promises by the governments to redeem by taxes at some future time given to citizens in return for supplies and services.

These increasing currency issues by the congressional and state governments eventually totaled nearly $400 million in paper value and led to a socially disintegrating inflation. By 1781, $167 of congressional paper was worth only $1 in specie, and the depreciation of the states' bills was nearly as bad. While creditors, wage earners, and those on relatively fixed incomes were hurt by this inflation, many of those who were most active in the economy and moving goods rapidly were able to profit. These circulating government bills, even though severely discounted, enabled countless commodity farmers and traders to break out of a barter economy and to specialize and participate more independently in the market. Of course, by the 1780s this participation for some farmers and traders had come to take the form of simply receiving promissory certificates for goods confiscated by desperate state and congressional armies. Nevertheless, generally throughout the war, government purchasing was a commercial stimulant; army commissariats became new centers of economic activity and breeding grounds for both numerous petty entrepreneurs and powerful postwar capitalists like Robert Morris of Pennsylvania and Jeremiah Wadsworth of Connecticut, who were in charge of congressional financing and contracting.

The increase of risky enterprises and insecure entrepreneurs made it necessary to form cooperative business associations that were larger and more complex than those that had existed in colonial times. These associations ranged from extensive shareholding in privateering ventures and the creation of new insurance companies to the incorporation in 1781 of the nationwide Bank of North America. Even when businesses were organized along familiar individual and kinship lines, the relationships were necessarily different—less private and stable, and more public and susceptible to the fluctuating political pressures of the state and congressional governments. These wartime experiences tended to erode the individual economic arrangements of pre-Revolutionary society. Businessmen tended to erect broader and more impersonal alignments like joint-stock companies and corporations to deal better with both the market and the new democratic legislatures. While only a half-dozen business charters had been granted in the entire colonial period, these corporate grants, or legal privileges given by government to private entrepreneurs to carry out public goals, now began proliferating. Such acts of incorporation were now granted for turnpikes, roads, canals, banking, insurance, and manufacturing. Eleven charters were issued between 1781 and 1785, 22 between 1786 and 1790, and 114 between 1791 and 1795. Everywhere members of different economic groups and occupations—creditors, debtors, overseas merchants, inland tradesmen, commodity farmers, artisans, and professionals—turned to government for protection and promotion of their special interests.

Despite repeated cries of dissatisfaction and distress, the Revolution had an invigorating and refreshing effect on American society. For everyone hurt by the instability, there were dozens touched by the new expectations of material gain aroused by the Revolution. What was truly extraordinary about the Revolution, with all its hopeful predictions of raising burdens and releasing liberty and with all its imagined dreams of ending tyranny and protecting rights, was that so much was fulfilled for so many so quickly. Nothing else but this rapid realization of the promises of the Revolution can explain the sudden emergence of that remarkable spirit of exhilaration and amelioration, that extraordinarily optimistic sense pervading the continent that there was a new era and a new kind of society being created. Such hopeful liberalizing feelings could not be confined to reforming governments or to invigorating entrepreneurial energy; they inevitably spilled out into all areas of American life.

No institution was more directly affected by this liberalizing spirit than chattel slavery. To be sure, the enslavement of nearly half a million blacks was not eradicated at the Revolution, and in modern eyes this failure amidst all the highblown talk of liberty and equality becomes the one glaring and even hypocritical inconsistency of the Revolutionary era. Nevertheless, the Revolution did suddenly and effectively end the social and intellectual environment that had allowed Negro slavery to exist in the colonies for over a century without substantial questioning.

FOLK SURVIVAL ON THE PLANTATION, C. 1777–1794

Music and dance were among the forms of African culture that survived in American slave society. *(Courtesy of Colonial Williamsburg.)*

The Rising Glory of America

Late eighteenth-century American gentlemen were sure that the United States at some not distant time would become, as one Harvard College orator said in 1797, "the seat of the Muses, the Athens of our age, the admiration of the world." Yet at the same time the adoption of republicanism heightened a deep suspicion Americans had long had of the arts. The fine arts—painting, sculpture, architecture, music, and poetry—had so often been associated with European court life and social decadence that many believed them incompatible with republican simplicity and virtue. If Americans were to exceed Europe in artistic dignity, grandeur, and taste, then they would have to create a truly republican art that avoided the corrupting vices of overrefinement and luxury.

The solution lay in the taut rationality, chaste severity, and timeless standards of a revolutionary artistic movement sweeping through Europe in the latter half of the eighteenth century, a movement that a century later came to be called neoclassicism. By redirecting the purpose of art from the private amusement of the idle rich to the civic ennoblement and civilizing instruction of the entire public, neoclassicism infused art with a new moral seriousness and high-minded idealism. Drawing from history, especially antiquity, the visual arts in particular would become public agents of social reformation and refinement. No longer would artists be craftsmen catering to a few aristocratic patrons; they would become benefactors of humanity speaking to a whole society eager to uplift its taste and cultivate its manners.

The colonial artist, John Singleton Copley (1738–1815), had longed to express these new ideas in his painting. But living in Boston for nearly two decades he had been compelled to devote his immense talent to painting portraits of the colonial gentry. By 1773 when he painted *Mr. and Mrs. Thomas Mifflin,* prominent Philadelphians visiting Boston, he was at the height of his powers and ready to escape from the stifling provincialism of the colonies.

Copley sailed for England in 1774, hoping to follow the path of an earlier Pennsylvanian emigrant, Benjamin West (1738–1820), who had become historical painter to George III. Copley left a moment too soon, for the Revolution changed everything.

Historical Society of Pennsylvania.

John Trumbull (1756–1843), member of a distinguished Connecticut family, quickly grasped that the Revolution was as much a cultural as a political event. He knew only too well that being an artist, "as it is generally practiced, is frivolous, little useful to society, and unworthy of a man who has talents for more serious pursuits. But, to preserve and diffuse the memory of the noblest series of actions which have ever presented themselves in the history of man"—that was a task that "gave dignity to the profession" and justified any gentleman's devotion.

Trumbull's use of the grand style and his attempt at an ennobling effect from history painting can be seen most vividly by comparing his *Battle of Bunker Hill* (1786) with a primitive depiction of the same event painted by an anonymous artist about 1783. Trumbull thought he would make a fortune from the sale of engravings of his paintings of the Revolution, but after an initial encouraging reception, subscriptions soon ceased. Early

nineteenth-century Americans were not much interested in history paintings, and Trumbull even had trouble getting Congress to pay for the huge commemorative scenes of the Revolution he painted in the Rotunda of the Capitol.

The National Gallery of Art, Washington, D.C.

No one responded to neoclassical ideas about art with more enthusiasm than did Thomas Jefferson. Since architecture to Jefferson was "an art which shows so much," it was particularly important for the new republican nation that appropriate inspirational forms be used. He cursed the Georgian buildings of colonial Virginia as barbaric, and aimed, through a new symbolic architecture, "to improve the taste of my countrymen, to increase their reputation, to reconcile to them the respect of the world and procure them its praise." He wanted Americans to emulate a classical art that "has pleased universally for nearly 2000 years," even at the expense of functional requirements. From France in the 1780s Jefferson badgered his Virginia colleagues into erecting as the new state capitol a magnificent copy of the Maison Carrée, a Roman temple at Nîmes from the first century A.D., and thus almost singlehandedly introduced the classical style to American public buildings. In fact there was nothing like this use of a Roman temple anywhere in the world. No matter that Richmond was still a backwoods town with mud-lined streets. No matter that a model of a Roman temple was hard to heat and acoustically impossible. For Americans other considerations counted more. By 1820 Roman and Greek revival architecture had become the official style of public buildings in the new nation.

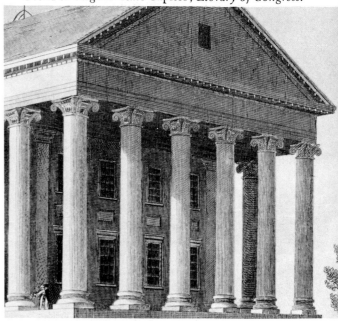

Detail of Virginia State Capitol, *Library of Congress.*

Virginia State Capitol by Benjamin Latrobe, *Maryland Historical Society.*

Excited by the new ideas about art, the Revolutionaries created a sudden outpouring of iconographic works. Statues and monuments were planned; plays, prints, and pageants were employed in support of the Revolution and the new republic. The Revolutionaries continually interrupted their constitution-making and military campaigning to design all sorts of emblems and commemorative medals and to sit for long hours having their portraits painted for history's sake.

When compared to the later extravagant French Revolutionary achievement, under the direction of Jacques Louis David, of putting the arts into the service of republicanism, the American artistic efforts seem pale and feeble. But given America's provincialism and its lack of artists and artistic experience, the Revolutionaries' aims and accomplishments are astonishing. That a monumental city like Washington, D.C., with its sweeping scale, its huge boulevards, and its magnificent parks, could have been conceived and begun in the midst of a swampy wilderness is an extraordinary tribute to the neoclassical aspirations of the Revolutionary leaders.

Yet the classical spirit that inspired Washington, D.C., the ancient place names, the Roman and Greek buildings, and the many emblems and devices was being lost even as these things were being created. Soon few Americans would know the meaning behind the Latin mottoes and the Masonic pyramid and eye appearing on the Great Seal. Indeed, many of the cultural artifacts that Americans inherited from the Revolutionary and early republican era remain only as awkward reminders of the brevity of America's classical age.

Plan of Washington, D.C., 1791, by Pierre Charles L'Enfant (Library of Congress); Great Seal of the United States of America, front and back; House of Representatives colonnade and design for female figure for the Capitol, drawn by Benjamin Latrobe, 1815 (Library of Congress); Capitol building, east and west wings, drawn by W. Thornton, 1794 (Library of Congress).

Since the arts in the new republic were to be morally instructive, many Americans whose religious scruples had formerly made them suspicious of the arts could now enlist them in the service of reform. In 1790 members of the Library Company of Philadelphia, many of whom were Quakers, commissioned Samuel Jennings (c. 1755–after 1834) to paint a picture for their new building. They recommended that "the figure of Liberty (with her Cap and proper Insignia)" be seated among the symbols of the arts, and that some scientific books be placed on a pedestal. At Liberty's feet, they suggested, the artist should put a broken chain "and in the distant back Ground a Groupe of Negroes sitting on the Earth, or in some attitude expressive of Ease & Joy," symbolizing their freedom. This was the first American painting which dealt directly with the abolition of slavery.

The Death of Jane McCrea by John Vanderlyn (1775–1852) is a good example of American efforts to put history to didactic use. The picture illustrates a well-known atrocity that occurred in New York in 1777 while an American woman was being guided through the lines by Indians to a reunion with her English financé, an officer in Burgoyne's army. Revolutionary ballads, poems, engravings, as well as this painting, quickly turned Jane McCrea into a symbol of American innocence victimized by British-inspired aggression.

Vanderlyn was trained in France and his absorption of the French neoclassical style is revealed in the sculptured figures in *The Death of Jane McCrea*. Although in need of money, Vanderlyn was very anxious to do something other than portraiture, regarded as the lowest form of painting. He painted a classical *Marius Amidst the Ruins of Carthage* (1807) and a nude *Ariadne* (1812) and then, out of frustration with the poor public reception of these in America, a 3000-square-foot panorama of Versailles on the walls of a New York rotunda built in 1818 to display his work.

Samuel F. B. Morse (1791–1872) was the son of Jedadiah Morse, Congregational minister of Massachusetts who wrote the first geography of the United States. Like Vanderlyn and many other American artists, Morse wanted to escape from the vulgarity of painting portraits, and to "elevate and refine public feelings by turning the thoughts of his countrymen from sensuality and luxury to intellectual pleasures" derived from viewing history paintings. *Congress Hall: The Old House of Representatives* was to be one such great work. The canvas measured nearly seven feet by twelve feet and cost Morse a year of labor. Although the painting was photographic in its meticulous detail, in its emphasis on classical sobriety, dignity, and decorum, it hopelessly idealized the brawling and rowdy House of Representatives that had emerged by the 1820s. Morse put the painting on tour, but the public would not pay to see its elected officials, and Congress would not buy it. In disillusionment Morse eventually turned to photography and the invention of the telegraph and the code which bears his name.

In the collection of the Corcoran Gallery of Art.

This new kind of republican portrait reveals just how far behind early nineteenth-century America had left its patrician colonial hierarchy. Although Lyon by 1826 was a rich and prominent businessman, he wanted his portrait, as he said, to depict his humble origins as a blacksmith in Philadelphia, "at work at my anvil, with my sleeves rolled up and a leather apron on." The artist, John Neagle (1796–1865), was himself something of a self-made man. His father came from County Cork and his mother was a New Jersey yeoman's daughter. He managed, however, to marry the stepdaughter of the well-known and successful portrait painter, Thomas Sully (1783–1872).

As different as the new bourgeois leaders of the early republic were from the eighteenth-century gentry, in wanting from art mainly pictures of themselves they were much the same. By the 1820s many American intellectuals were still anxiously awaiting the long-predicted westward transit of the arts across the Atlantic.

The colonists had generally taken slavery for granted as part of the natural order of society and as one aspect of the general brutality and cheapness of life in those pre-modern and pre-humanitarian times. Originally, slavery had been regarded merely as the most base and degraded status in a society of many statuses and ranks of freedom and unfreedom, and that attitude had lingered on. Bondage and servitude in many forms had continued to exist in pre-Revolutionary America, and the colonists had felt little need to defend slavery any more than other forms of debasement. Now, however, republican citizenship suddenly brought into question all kinds of personal dependency. For the first time Americans were compelled to confront the slavery in their midst as an aberration, as a "peculiar institution," and, if they were to retain it, to explain and justify it.

Even before the Declaration of Independence, the libertarian atmosphere of the imperial controversy had exposed the excruciating contradiction of slavery. The initial efforts to end the contradiction were directed at the slave trade. In 1774, the Continental Congress urged abolishing the slave trade; a half-dozen states quickly followed this advice. In 1775, the Quakers of Philadelphia formed the first antislavery society in the world, and soon similar societies were organized elsewhere, even in the South. During the war Congress and the northern states together with Maryland gave freedom to black slaves who enlisted in their armies. In various ways the Revolution worked to weaken the institution.

In the North, slavery of a less harsh sort than existed in the South had been widespread but not deeply rooted in the society or economy. Slavery in the North was thus susceptible to political pressure in a way that was not true in the South, and it slowly began to recede. In the decades following the Revolution most of the northern states moved to destroy the institution. By 1830 there were less than 3000 black slaves out of a northern black population of over

BENJAMIN BANNAKER'S ALMANAC

Between 1792 and 1797, Bannaker, an astronomer and mathematician, published six almanacs designed to demonstrate "that mental powers and endowments are not the exclusive excellence of white people." In 1791 Bannaker sent Jefferson a copy of his almanac along with a moving letter that challenged the writer of the Declaration of Independence to live up to the belief that all men were created equal. (American Antiquarian Society.)

125,000. The Revolutionary vision of a society of independent freeholders led Congress in the 1780s specifically to forbid slavery in the newly organized Northwest territory between the Appalachians and the Mississippi. The new federal Constitution promised, in 1808, an end to the slave trade, which many hoped would cripple the institution. In the South, however, despite initial criticism by enlightened *philosophes* like Jefferson and Madison, slavery was too entrenched to be legislatively or judicially abolished. Southern whites who had been in the vanguard of the Revolutionary movement and among the most fervent spokesmen for its libertarianism now began developing a self-conscious sense of difference from the rest of America that they had never had to the same degree before. By the 1790s the South was living with a growing fear, fed by the Negro insurrections in Santo Domingo, of the newly invigorated American presumption that people everywhere, white or black, yearned for freedom.

The Sovereignty of the People

Amid all this Revolutionary economic and social turmoil, the governments and constitutions created in 1776–77 could not be maintained. The ideas, passions, and interests released by the Revolution were much too dynamic to remain within the finely poised mechanism of a balanced constitution. Unlike the French and Russian revolutions, the American Revolution did not concentrate and consolidate power; it distributed it. The Revolutionary mistrust of government and the persistent calls for popular vigilance spread, eroding not only the authority of governors and magistrates but even the authority of the people's representatives in the state legislatures. The power-weakening impulse of the Revolution thus did not cease when the new state governments were established in 1776–77; it ran throughout the war and into the 1780s, leading to the creation of new institutions and new political relationships that in the end brought into question not only the Americans' classic theory of mixed government but their conventional understanding of politics.

Creating new representative governments did not end the activity of the people at large. Many Americans continued to mistrust any official institution set above the people. Some responded to this suspicion by further drawing out the logic of actual representation and resorting more and more to instructing their representatives in order to control the legislatures. Others, stimulated by the earlier Revolutionary experience, organized various committees and conventions presumably better representative of the people than the existing assemblies, and appealed to "the body of the people" to voice grievances and to seek political goals. Vigilante action of various kinds, like that of Colonel Charles Lynch of Virginia in 1780 against Tories and outlaws (from which the term *lynch law* arose), did quickly and efficiently what the new state governments often seemed unable to do. Similarly, when Revolutionary state legislatures seemed powerless to control prices or prevent profiteering and forestalling, extralegal bodies sprang up, at first under official congressional and state auspices and then un-

officially, to enforce the people's moral sense of
what the economy ought to be like. Serious
rioting under the direction of radical committees recurred in the major cities. Parts of western Massachusetts remained in turmoil from
1774 through the 1780s, as moblike committees
of debtor farmers periodically closed the courts
to protect themselves from creditors. By the
mid-eighties, local conventions and popular
associations had emerged in several states to
stifle judicial actions, resist tax collections, and
intimidate public officials. Opponents of this
popular disorder in the 1780s, including even
the old Son of Liberty, Samuel Adams, called
repeatedly for the people to obey the laws and
to show a proper respect for their own constitutionally elected legislatures.

But such appeals were often misplaced.
Popular disorder was not the most important
and most frightening source of America's
political problems in the decade following Independence. Popular disturbances were after
all an expected consequence of too much
liberty. What was new and especially alarming
to established groups was not that the people
were running into anarchy but that their representatives in the state legislatures were creating
a new, unanticipated kind of democratic despotism under the cover of law itself.

The transformation of American politics
that had begun before the Revolution was now

NEW JERSEY FARMER, 1790S

(American Antiquarian Society.)

intensified under even more indulgent popular conditions. The radical changes
in representation made by the Revolution democratized the assemblies by increasing the number of members and by altering their social character. New
men of more humble, more rural origins, less educated and with more parochial interests than those who had sat in the colonial legislatures now became
representatives. For example, in 1765 in New Hampshire the colonial house
of representatives had contained only 34 members, almost all well-to-do gentry
from the coastal region around Portsmouth. By 1786, the new state house of
representatives had increased to 88 members, most of whom were only ordinary
farmers or men of moderate wealth often from the western areas of the state.
In other states, the change was much less dramatic but no less important and was
reflected in the shifts or in the attempted shifts of many of the state capitals from
their former colonial locations on the eastern seaboard to new sites in the interior

—from Portsmouth to Concord, from New York City to Albany, from New Bern to Raleigh, from Charleston to Columbia. Electioneering and the open competition for office increased along with demands for greater popular access to governmental activities. Assembly proceedings were more and more opened to the public, and a growing number of newspapers, which now included dailies, began to report legislative debates. Self-appointed leaders, as they were called, speaking for newly aroused groups and localities, were taking advantage of the confusion, the weakened structures of social authority, the enlarged suffrage, and the annual elections of the legislatures (a radical innovation for most) to seek membership in the assemblies. New petty entrepreneurs like Abraham Yates, a part-time lawyer and cobbler of Albany, and William Findley, Scotch-Irish ex-weaver of western Pennsylvania, bypassed the traditional social hierarchy and vaulted into political leadership in the states. The number of contested elections multiplied and increased the turnover of legislative seats.

Under these circumstances many of the state legislatures could scarcely fulfill what many Revolutionaries in 1776 had assumed was their republican responsibility for promoting the general good. In every state, decisions had to be made about what to do with the loyalists and their confiscated property, about the distribution of taxes among the citizens, and about the economy. Yet with the general political instability, the common welfare in the various states was increasingly difficult to define. By 1788, James Madison concluded that "a spirit of *locality*" in the state legislatures was destroying "the aggregate interests of the Community," and that this localist spirit was "inseparable" from elections by small districts or towns. Each representative, said Ezra Stiles, president of Yale College, was concerned only with the special interests of his electors. Whenever a bill was read in the legislature, "every one instantly thinks how it will affect his constituents." Such narrow-interest politics was not new to America; it had in fact characterized the provincial assemblies. But the proliferation of such economic and social interests in the post-Revolutionary years, the heightened sensitivity of the newly enlarged and more frequently elected popular assemblies to their conflicting demands, and the lack of countervailing forces increased the importance of such parochial-interest politics. Debtor farmers urged low taxes, the staying of court actions to recover debts, and the printing of paper money. Merchants and creditors called for high taxes on land, the protection of private contracts, and the encouragement of foreign trade. Artisans pleaded for price regulation of agricultural products, the abolition of mercantile monopolies, and tariff protection against imported manufactures. And entrepreneurs everywhere petitioned for legal privileges and corporate grants.

All this political scrambling among contending interests made law making in the states seem chaotic. Laws, as the Vermont Council of Censors said in 1786 in a common complaint, were "altered—realtered—made better—made worse; and kept in such a fluctuating position, that persons in civil commission scarce know what is law." As James Madison pointed out, more laws were enacted by the states in the decade following Independence than in the entire colonial period. Many of them were simply private acts for individuals or resolves redressing minor grievances. Every effort of the legislatures to respond to the excited pleas and pressures of the various groups alienated as many as it satisfied and brought lawmaking itself into contempt.

By the mid-eighties many American leaders had come to believe that the state legislatures, not the governors, were the political authority to be most feared. Not only were some of the legislators violating the individual rights of property through their excessive printing of paper money and their various acts on behalf of debtors, but in all the states the assemblies pushed beyond the generous grants of legislative authority of the Revolutionary constitutions and were absorbing numerous executive and judicial duties, directing military operations, for example, and setting aside court judgments. It began to seem that the once benign legislative power was no different from the detested ruler's power. All parts of the government—governors, judges, and legislators—might now be regarded, in Jefferson's words, as "three branches of magistracy." No matter that the legislators were supposedly the representatives of the people and annually elected by them. "173 despots would surely be as oppressive as one," wrote Jefferson in his *Notes on Virginia*. "An *elective despotism* was not the government we fought for."

Under these circumstances, some tried to limit the legislatures by appealing to the fundamental law of the constitutions established in 1776. Since many of the constitutions had been created by simple legislative act, the distinction between fundamental and ordinary law was not easily sustained. At first several of the states had grappled with various devices to ensure the fundamentality of their constitution. Some simply declared it to be so; others required a special majority or successive acts of the legislature for amending the constitution. But none of these measures proved effective against recurrent legislative encroachments. Out of these kinds of pressures, both logical and political,

THE TRANSFORMATION OF CITY GOVERNMENT

During the 1780s the turbulence of popular government in several cities, including New Haven, Philadelphia, and Charleston, forced urban leaders to form municipal corporations, which removed government from the immediate hands of the people. *(Library of Congress.)*

Americans gradually moved toward institutionalizing the belief that if the constitution was to be truly immune from legislative tampering, it would have to be created, as Jefferson said in 1783, "by a power superior to that of the ordinary legislature." For a solution, Americans fell back on the institution of the convention. In 1775–76, the convention had been merely a legally deficient legislature made necessary by the crown's refusal to call together the regular representatives of the people. Now, however, the convention became a special alternative representation of the people with the exclusive authority to frame or amend a constitution. When Massachusetts and New Hampshire came to write new constitutions in the late 1770s and early 1780s the proper pattern of constitution making and constitution altering had become clear. Constitutions were formed by specially elected conventions and then placed before the people for ratification.

With this idea of a constitution as fundamental law immune from legislative encroachment firmly in hand, some state judges during the 1780s began cautiously moving in isolated cases to impose restraints on what the assemblies were enacting as law. In effect they said to the legislatures, as George Wythe, judge of the Virginia supreme court, did in 1782, "Here is the limit of your authority; and, hither, shall you go, but no further."

Yet many found it difficult to see how the people's representatives in the assemblies could be limited by any extralegislative body, especially by the judiciary. Americans were keenly aware of the doctrine of sovereignty as the British had used it in the debate over parliamentary authority in the 1760s and 70s; in every state, it was said, there must be one final indivisible lawmaking authority. Many were convinced that this sovereignty in America necessarily resided in the separate state legislatures. The doctrine of sovereignty dictated that unless the legislatures were free of restraints imposed by constitutions or judges and possessed the full power of the people to do what was good for the community, all legislative authority was in doubt.

Other Americans, however, were not willing to locate this sovereignty in any governmental institution, no matter how representative it might be. These critics of legislative omnipotence eventually concluded that sovereignty in America must reside only in the people at large. Relocating sovereignty in the people now helped to make theoretical sense of the Americans' political inventions—their conception of a constitution, their special constitution-making conventions, and their unusual ideas of actual representation. In Britain the people were totally embodied in the House of Commons; this embodiment gave Parliament its sovereignty. In America, however, the people were not fully or finally incorporated in any governmental body but existed outside and controlled all the institutions. Not just the houses of representatives but all parts of the government—governors, senators, members of conventions, and in time in some states even judges—were equally elective representative agents of the people.

With election being viewed more and more as the sole criterion of representation, it was now reasonable to argue, as some did, that the principle of representation should be extended throughout all parts of the government. Thus all elected, hence representative, officials—senators or others—should be elected in proportion to population (the logic of which has taken us nearly two centuries to realize). Under this kind of pressure the traditional theory of mixed government that had guided the Revolutionary constitution making slowly crumbled. The people could no longer be merely a constituent in the society alongside aristocratic and monarchical elements. In America, unlike England, the people were everything; they embraced the whole government, and no branch or part, as the House of Commons did, could speak with the complete authority of the people. Indeed, not even all parts of the government could collectively incorporate the full powers of the people. Thus legislative sovereignty, as the English had understood it, was no longer possible in America.

Suggested Readings

For a summary of the history writing covering the eighteenth-century tradition of republicanism, see Robert E. Shalhope, "Toward a Republican Synthesis: The Emergence of an Understanding of Republicanism in American Historiography," *William and Mary Quarterly*, 3d. ser., 29 (1975). Studies emphasizing the peculiar character of this tradition include Bernard Bailyn, *The Ideological Origins of the American Revolution* (1967); J. G. A. Pocock, *The Machiavellian Moment* (1975); Franco Venturi, *Utopia and Reform in the Enlightenment* (1971); Gerald Stourzh, *Alexander Hamilton and the Idea of Republican Government* (1970); and Gordon S. Wood, *The Creation of the American Republic, 1776–1787* (1969). For the influence of antiquity, see Richard Gummere, *The American Colonial Mind and the Classical Tradition* (1963); and Meyer Reinhold, ed., *The Classick Pages* (1975). For the way in which many Europeans viewed the New World in the eighteenth century, see Durand Echeverria, *Mirage in the West* (1957).

The fullest account of state constitution making and politics is Allan Nevins, *The American States during and after the Revolution, 1775–1789* (1924). Elisha P. Douglass, *Rebels and Democrats* (1955), is important in emphasizing the radical and populist impulses in the states. Among the most significant of the state studies are Philip A. Crowl, *Maryland during and after the Revolution* (1943); Richard P. McCormick, *Experiment in Independence: New Jersey in the Critical Period, 1781–1789* (1950); Irwin H. Polishook, *Rhode Island and the Union, 1774–1795* (1969); Robert J. Taylor, *Western Massachusetts in the Revolution* (1954); and Alfred F. Young, *The Democratic Republicans of New York: The Origins, 1763–1797* (1967). Jackson T. Main, *The Sovereign States, 1775–1783* (1973), describes state affairs during the war. J. R. Pole, *Political Representation in England and the Origins of the American Republic* (1966), has some excellent chapters on state politics during the Revolutionary and immediate post-Revolutionary years.

Merrill Jensen, in *The Articles of Confederation . . . 1774–1781* (1940), and *The New Nation . . . 1781–1789* (1950), describes the political and social conflicts within the Confederation government and stresses the achievements of the Articles. H. James Henderson, *Party Politics in the Continental Congress* (1974), which is the best history of the Congress, emphasizes a sectional rather than a social division among the delegates to the national government.

The starting point for appreciating the social changes of the Revolution is the short essay by J. Franklin Jameson, *The American Revolution Considered as a Social Movement*

(1926). The last two chapters of James A. Henretta, *The Evolution of American Society, 1700–1815* (1973), summarize the social effects of the war and the Revolution. J. Kirby Martin, *Men in Rebellion: Higher Government Leaders and the Coming of the American Revolution* (1973); Jackson T. Main, *The Upper House in Revolutionary America, 1763–1788* (1967); and Main, "Government by the People: The American Revolution and the Democratization of the Legislatures," *William and Mary Quarterly*, 3d ser., 28 (1966), document the displacement of elites in politics during the Revolution. Chilton Williamson, *American Suffrage from Property to Democracy, 1760–1860* (1960), describes the expansion of voting rights.

On the commercial effects of the Revolution, see Curtis P. Nettles, *The Emergence of a National Economy, 1775–1815* (1962); and Robert A. East, *Business Enterprise in the American Revolutionary Era* (1938). On the plight of the loyalists, see Wallace Brown, *The Good Americans* (1969), and Mary Beth Norton, *The British-Americans: The Loyalist Exiles in England, 1774–1789* (1972). Benjamin Quarles, *The Negro in the American Revolution* (1961), is the best study of the contribution of blacks. On slavery and opposition to it, see Winthrop Jordan, *White over Black: American Attitudes toward the Negro, 1550–1812* (1968); and David Brion Davis, *The Problem of Slavery in the Age of Revolution, 1770–1823* (1975). On the abolition of slavery in the North, see Arthur Zilversmit, *The First Emancipation* (1967).

10

The Federalist
Augustan Age

The American Revolution, like all revolutions, could not fulfill all its highest hopes in the way some of its leaders expected. Within a decade after the Declaration of Independence many of the Revolutionary leaders had come to doubt the direction America was taking. Not only was the Confederation they had established too weak to accomplish its tasks, but the new society was assuming an alarmingly unrepublican character. As they became aware of these problems, many of which were unforeseen, individuals and groups moved towards reforming not only the state governments but the central government as well. By the end of the 1780s this constitutional reform movement had created such an unprecedented concentration of power that many Americans could only conclude that something as radical as the Revolution itself had occurred. At last, in the eyes of some, the inauguration of a new federal government prepared the nation for its own Augustan age—that period of peace and stability, resembling the reign of the Roman emperor Augustus, in which a society attains its greatest glory and highest cultural expression.

The Critical Period

Through all the excitement and exhilaration of post-Revolutionary America ran a curious strain of crisis. From one point of view the Revolution was a glorious success. The war was won, independence was achieved, and the peace with Britain gained as much as could have been expected in 1776. Despite a temporary depression in the mid-80s due to an overimportation of British goods after 1783, the decade as a whole was marked by extraordinary economic and demographic growth and a broadening of prosperity and expectations to previously untouched elements of the population. Nevertheless, some Americans in the 1780s became disillusioned with the results of the Revolution and increasingly despaired of the possibilities of reforming the character of the American people. The 1780s thus became a critical period, but only to a few—some intellectuals and some influential members of the elite. To the great body of Americans the Revolution remained a marvelous accomplishment, an opening up of opportunities and a fulfilling of promises that earlier could only have been dreamed of. It was in fact the awakening of hopes and the spread of a commercial spirit among so many ordinary Americans that filled many gentlemen with so much pessimism.

Given the optimistic assumptions about the nature of American society in 1776, many political and intellectual gentry in the subsequent years could only conclude that the Revolution was going awry. It seemed that republicanism and equality were being perverted and were confusing even those natural social distinctions that gentlemen thought essential for social order. Not only were the new popular state legislatures creating a new unexpected kind of tyranny with their confusing and unjust laws, but the American people were showing by their intense interest in making money that they were not the stuff republicans were made of. Classic public spirit was being eclipsed by private interests, individualism, and selfishness. Such behavior foreshadowed the fate that had befallen the ancient republics, Great Britain, and other corrupt nations. Americans, concluded the governor of New Jersey William Livingston, in a common elitist reckoning of 1787, "do not exhibit the virtue that is necessary to support a republican government."

With these kinds of fears and anxieties multiplying in the years after Independence, American intellectual and political leaders began rethinking the political postulates of 1776, and began revising the Revolutionary state constitutions to accommodate them better to the newly appreciated character of the people. Beginning with the New York constitution of 1777 and proceeding through the constitutions of Massachusetts in 1780 and New Hampshire in 1784, constitution makers sought a very different distribution of the powers of government from that made in 1776. Instead of placing all power in the legislatures, particularly in the lower houses, and making ciphers of the governors as the early state constitutions had done, these later constitutions strengthened the executives, senates, and judiciaries. The Massachusetts constitution of 1780 especially seemed to many to have recaptured some of the best characteristics of the English constitutional balance, which had been forgotten during the popular enthusiasm of 1776. The new Massachusetts governor, with a fixed salary and elected directly by the people, now assumed much of the independence and many of the powers of the old royal governors, including those of appointing to offices and vetoing legislation. With the Massachusetts constitution as a model, other constitutional reformers, including Madison and Jefferson in Virginia and James Wilson and Robert Morris in Pennsylvania, worked to revise their own state constitutions. The popular legislatures were reduced in size and their authority curbed. Senates or upper houses were instituted where they did not exist, as in Pennsylvania, Georgia, and Vermont; and where they did exist, they were made more stable through longer terms and distinct property qualifications. The governors were freed of their dependence on the legislatures, and given the central responsibility for government. And judges became independent guardians of the constitutions. By 1790 Pennsylvania, South Carolina, and Georgia had reformed their constitutions

MASSACHUSETTS STATE HOUSE AND MEMORIAL COLUMN, 1795–1798

Bulfinch (1763–1844) was one of the first Americans to move from being a leisured gentleman with an amateur interest in building to becoming a professional architect. Everything about his State House, one of many public buildings he designed, celebrates the new classical grandeur of republican America. *(Courtesy of Bostonian Society, Old State House, Boston.)*

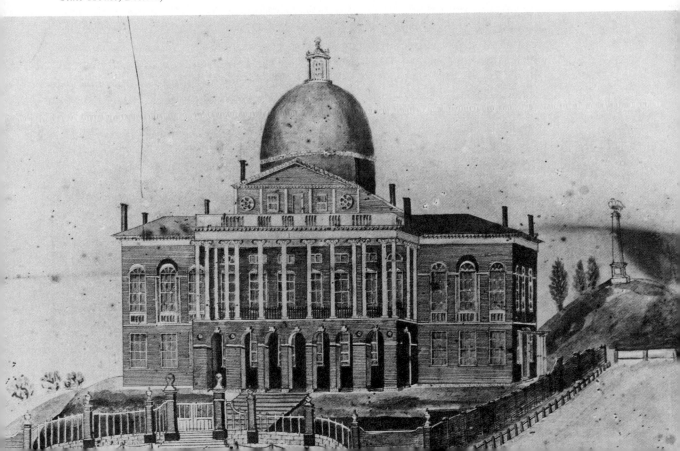

along these conservative lines; New Hampshire, Delaware, and Vermont soon followed in the early 1790s.

What helped to make these constitutional changes possible, obscuring their antipopular thrust, was the change taking place at the same time in American political thinking. By the 1780s most constitutional reformers denied that the traditional theory of mixed or balanced government applied to America. Instead, they argued that since the people were sovereign, all governmental institutions were merely different kinds of representations of the people. The governors were not elected monarchs, but, as the Massachusetts convention of 1780 declared, "emphatically the Representative of the whole People, being chosen not by one town or country, but by the People at large." The senates no longer were explained as incorporating any sort of aristocracy in the society but were widely regarded as "double representations" of the people, necessary for dividing and checking a potentially harmful legislative authority. The reformers (with some notable exceptions, including John Adams) now said that instead of redistributing the social elements — the one, the few, and the many — within the government, they were simply apportioning power among different departments of government, all equally representative of the people.

If all parts of the government — legislative, executive, and judicial — were alike, simply delegated portions of the people's sovereignty, then no part, including the once trusted houses of representatives, was to be feared less than any other. Since tyranny was not simply the abuse of executive power, as the Revolutionaries had thought, but the concentration of power in any branch of the government, the dispersion of the people's delegated power became the basis of liberty. Separation of executive, legislative, and judicial powers had been randomly invoked in 1776 to justify isolating the legislature and judiciary from the corruptive influence of executive authority. Now this once minor doctrine was applied broadly to all branches of the government in order to defend the reformers' strengthening of the governors, senates, and judiciaries at the expense of the lower houses. Even bicameralism (or having two houses in the legislature) was justified in terms of separating a mistrusted power. By 1790 the separation of powers among the various agencies of government, regardless of their former social character or special relation to the people, was elevated into what Madison called "a first principle of free government." This exclusively political principle of separation of powers in effect swallowed up the older socially conscious theory of mixed government to become the single most important attribute of American constitutionalism.

As vigorously as the constitutional reforms of the states were urged and adopted in the 1780s, however, they never seemed sufficient. By the middle 80s many reformers were thinking of shifting the arena of constitutional change from the states to the nation and were looking to some sort of modification of the structure of the central government as the best and perhaps only answer to America's political and social problems.

The Weakness of the Confederation

Already the experiences of the war had exposed the weaknesses of the Articles and encouraged some Americans to think about making changes in the central government. By 1780 the war was dragging on longer than anyone had expected and the skyrocketing inflation of the paper money used to finance it was unsettling all established business. With congressional delegates barred from serving more than three years in six, leadership in the Confederation was fluctuating and confused. The states were ignoring congressional resolutions and were refusing to supply their allotted requisitions, and the Congress stopped paying interest on the public debt. The Continental Army was smoldering with resentment at the lack of pay and was falling apart through desertions and even outbreaks of mutiny. All these circumstances were forcing mercantile and creditor interests, especially those centered in the mid-Atlantic states, to seek to add to the powers of the Congress: by broad interpretation of the Articles, by direct amendment, which required the consent of all the states, and even by the threat of military force.

A shift in congressional leadership in the early 80s expressed the increasing influence of these aggrieved national groups. Older popular radicals like Richard Henry Lee and Arthur Lee of Virginia and Samuel Adams of Massachusetts were replaced by younger men like James Madison of Virginia and Alexander Hamilton of New York, who were more interested in authority and stability than popular liberty. Disillusioned by the ineffectiveness of the Confederation, these nationalists in the Congress set about reversing the localist and power-weakening thrust of the Revolution. They strengthened the regular army at the expense of the militia and promised pensions to the Continental Army officers. They reorganized the departments of war, foreign affairs, and finance in the Congress and appointed individuals in place of committees to run them. The key individual in the nationalists' program was Robert Morris, a wealthy Philadelphia merchant who was made superintendent of finance and virtual head of the confederacy in 1781. Morris undertook to stabilize the economy and to attach financial and commercial groups to the central government. He induced Congress to recommend to the states that paper money laws be repealed and to levy its requisitions on the states in specie. And he sought to establish a bank and to make federal bonds more secure for investors.

This nationalist program depended upon getting the adoption of an amendment to the Articles giving the Confederation the power to levy a 5 percent duty on imports. Once Congress had adequate revenues independent of the states, the Confederation could pay its debts and enhance the attractiveness of its bonds. Although Morris was able to induce Congress to charter the Bank of North America, the rest of the nationalists' economic proposals narrowly failed. Not only did the states refuse to grant the unanimous consent required for the impost amend-

ROBERT MORRIS

Morris, a wealthy Philadelphia merchant, has been called "the financier of the Revolution." Land speculation in the 1790s ruined him, and he ended his career in debtors prison. *(National Portrait Gallery, Smithsonian Institution, Washington, D.C.)*

ment, but many were delinquent in supplying requisitions to Congress. Nor was Congress able to get even a restricted authority to regulate commerce.

After the allied victory at Yorktown in October 1781 and the opening of peace negotiations with Great Britain, interest in the Congress declined and some individuals became desperate. The prospect of Congress's demobilizing the army without fulfilling its promises of back pay and pensions created a crisis that brought the United States as close to a military coup d'état as it has ever been. In March 1783, the officers of Washington's army encamped at Newburgh on the Hudson issued an address to the Congress concerning their pay and actually plotted some sort of military action against the Confederation. Only when Washington personally intervened and showed his total unwillingness to support a movement designed, as he said, "to open the floodgates of civil discord, and deluge our rising empire in blood," was the crisis averted.

News of the peace in 1783 shattered much of the unionist sentiment that had existed during the war. By December 1783 the Congress, in Jefferson's opinion, had lost much of its usefulness. "The constant session of Congress can not be necessary in time of peace." After clearing up the most urgent business, the delegates, Jefferson thought, should "separate and return to our respective states, leaving only a Committee of the states," and thus "destroy the strange idea of their being a permanent body, which has unaccountably taken possession of the heads of their constituents, and occasions jealousies injurious to the public good." Congressional power, which had been substantial during the war years, now began to disintegrate, and delegates increasingly complained how difficult it was even to gather a quorum. The states reasserted their authority and began taking over the payment of the federal debt that many had earlier hoped to make the cement of union. By 1786 nearly one-third of the federal securities had been converted into state bonds, thus creating a vested interest among public creditors in the sovereignty of the individual states. Under these circumstances the temporary ascendency of those, in Hamilton's term, "who think continentally" rapidly declined, and the chances of amending the Confederation piecemeal with them. The only hope of reform now seemed to lie in some sort of convention of all the states.

International affairs after the peace further exposed the weaknesses of the Confederation. Despite strenuous efforts by American diplomats like Jefferson, minister to France in the 1780s, to develop new international commercial relationships involving the free exchange of goods, the mercantilist empires of the major European nations remained closed to the trade of the new republic. Britain recaptured its American markets without making any concessions. Lacking any authority to retaliate with trade regulations, the Confederation Congress watched helplessly as the separate states attempted to pass ineffectual navigation acts of their own.

Amid a world of hostile empires the new republican confederacy was even hard pressed to maintain its territorial integrity. Britain refused to send a minister to the United States and despite John Adams's fulminations in London ignored its treaty obligations to evacuate the posts of the Northwest, claiming that the United States had not honored its commitments. The treaty of peace had stipulated that the Confederation would recommend to the states the restoration of confiscated loyalist property and that neither side would make laws impeding the recovery of prewar debts. When the states flouted these treaty obligations, the impotent Confederation could do nothing.

While Britain was intriguing with the Indians and encouraging separatist movements in the Northwest and in the Vermont borderlands, Spain was doing the same in the Southwest. Spain in fact refused to recognize American claims to the territory between the Ohio River and Florida. In 1784 in an effort to influence the American settlers moving into Kentucky and Tennessee, Spain closed the Mississippi to American trade. Ready to deal with any government that could ensure access to the sea for their agricultural produce, many of the Westerners were, as Washington noted in 1784, "on a pivot. The touch of a feather would turn them any way." In 1785–1786 John Jay, a New York aristocrat and the secretary of foreign affairs, negotiated a treaty with the Spanish minister to the United States, Diego de Gardoqui, which opened Spain to American trade in return for America's renunciation of its right to navigate the Mississippi for several decades. Out of fear of being denied an outlet to the sea in the West,

the Southern states prevented the necessary nine-state majority in the Congress
from agreeing to the treaty. But the desire of a majority of seven states to sacrifice Western interests for the sake of Eastern merchants weakened confidence in
the existing union.

Even the rulers of the Barbary states in the Mediterranean treated the new
republic with contempt. Now lacking the earlier protection of the British flag,
American ships were seized by North African pirates and their crews sold as slaves.
Although Congress lacked the money to pay the necessary tribute and ransoms,
some American leaders like Jay did not want to bribe the pirates anyway. They
preferred to allow this national humiliation, like the indignities suffered at the
hands of Britain and Spain, to goad Americans into enhancing the power of the
central government.

By 1786 these accumulated pressures made some sort of revision of the Articles inevitable. That this revision had to take the particular form of the federal
Constitution of 1787, however, was not inevitable. The new Constitution created
in Philadelphia in 1787 established an extraordinarily powerful national government that went beyond what the difficulties of credit and commerce and the
humiliations of foreign affairs demanded in additional central powers. Given
the Revolutionaries' loyalty to the individuality of their states and their deep-
rooted fears of centralized governmental authority, the formation of the new
Constitution was a truly remarkable achievement that cannot be explained simply
in terms of the obvious weaknesses of the Articles of Confederation.

In the end it was the problems within the separate states in the 1780s that made constitutional reform of the central government possible. Only when the Americans' ingrained suspicion of political power was refocused and transferred from the Confederation Congress to the legislative oppressions in the state governments did the centrifugal movement of the post-Revolutionary years begin to turn around. The vices coming out of the state governments, Madison in 1787 informed Jefferson, who was in Paris as minister to France during the 1780s, had become "so frequent and so flagrant as to alarm the most stedfast friends of Republicanism." It was these state vices, said Madison, that "contributed more to that uneasiness which produced the Convention, and prepared the public mind for a general reform, than those which accrued to our national character and interest from the inadequacy of the Confederation to its immediate objects."

The rebellion in 1786 in western Massachusetts of nearly two thousand distressed debtor farmers led by a former militia captain, Daniel Shays, confirmed many of these anxieties about state politics. For not only did the insurrection occur in the state considered to have the best-organized constitution, but the military defeat of the Shaysites only forced them a few months later to try their strength in another way: "that is," said Madison, "by endeavoring to give the elections such a turn as may promote their views under the auspices of constitutional forms." The electoral victory of Shays's sympathizers in Massachusetts early in 1787 and their subsequently enacted debtor relief legislation convinced many that calling for obedience to law was a remedy only for uprisings; it did not solve the peculiar problem of legislative tyranny. It was obvious from the Shaysite experience that, as one Boston newspaper declared in May 1787, "sedition itself will sometimes make laws."

By 1786 the reconstruction of the central government had become the focus for most political reform. The previously frustrated efforts of public creditors and commercial interests to invigorate the national government in the early 1780s were now reinforced by new groups. Urban artisans were eager to prevent competition from British imports. Southerners, particularly in Virginia, wanted to gain proportional representation of their growing population. And most important, established elements in all regions previously suspicious of central authority were anxious to erect a national government that could counteract both popular disturbances and the abuses of legislative power within the states. Gentry up and down the continent momentarily submerged their sectional and economic differences in the face of what seemed to them a threat to individual liberty from majoritarian tyranny within the states. They urged each other to reexert their traditional political influence and rebind the social connections weakened by the Revolution. Creating a new central government was no longer simply a matter of cementing the union, or of standing up strong in foreign affairs, or of satisfying the demands of particular creditor, mercantile, and army interests. It was now a matter, as Madison declared, that would "decide forever the fate of republican government."

The Federal Constitution

The convocation of the Philadelphia Convention that drafted the federal Constitution in the summer of 1787 was very much a revolutionary movement. It was, as Patrick Henry declared, "a revolution as radical as that which separated us from Great Britain." Yet such were the circumstances and climate of the post-Revolutionary years in America that the sudden calling of a constitutional convention and the creation of an entirely new and different sort of federal republican government in 1787 seemed remarkably natural and legitimate.

There had been preliminaries. In 1786 Virginia had called for a convention of the states at Annapolis to discuss trade regulations. This meeting quickly determined that commerce could not be considered apart from other problems and called for a larger convention in 1787 in Philadelphia. After several states agreed to send delegates to Philadelphia, the Confederation Congress belatedly recognized the approaching convention and authorized it to revise and amend the Articles of Confederation. By 1787 nearly all of America's political leaders agreed that some reform of the Articles was necessary, yet very few expected what the Philadelphia Convention eventually created—a new central constitution transforming the structure of American government and promising a radical weakening of the power of the several states.

Fifty-five delegates representing twelve states attended the Philadelphia Convention in the summer of 1787. (Rhode Island refused to have anything to do with efforts to revise the Articles.) Although many of the delegates were young men—their average age was forty-two—most were well-educated and experienced members of America's political elite. Thirty-nine had served in Congress at one time or another, 8 had worked in the state constitutional conventions, 7 had been state governors, and 34 were lawyers. One-third were veterans of the Continental Army, that great dissolvent of state loyalties, as Washington once called it. Nearly all were gentlemen, "natural aristocrats," who took their political superiority for granted as an inevitable consequence of their social and economic superiority. Washington was made president of the Convention. Some of the luminaries of the Revolution were not present: Samuel Adams was ill; Jefferson and John Adams were serving as ministers abroad; and Richard Henry Lee and Patrick Henry, although selected by the Virginia legislature, refused to attend the

THE OLD STATE HOUSE OF PENN-
SYLVANIA (UNTIL 1799) LATER
CALLED INDEPENDENCE HALL

Both the Second Continental
Congress and the federal
Convention of 1787 met here.
The tower was added in the
middle of the eighteenth century
to house the Liberty Bell.

Convention, Henry saying, "I smelt a rat." The most influential delegations were those of Pennsylvania and Virginia, including Gouverneur Morris and James Wilson of Pennsylvania and Edmund Randolph, George Mason, and James Madison of Virginia.

The Virginia delegation took the lead, presenting the Convention with its first working proposal, the Virginia plan, largely the effort of the thirty-six-year-old Madison, who more than any other single person deserves the title "father of the Constitution." Short, shy, and soft-spoken, habitually dressed in black, trained to no profession but widely read and possessing an acute and questioning mind, Madison devoted his life to public service. He understood clearly the historical significance of the meeting of the Convention, and it is because of his decision to make a detailed private record of the debates of the Convention that so much is known of what was said that summer in Philadelphia.

Madison's initial proposals for reform, products of the previous year's intensive study and suggested by him in a series of letters to friends in the spring of 1787, were truly radical. They were not, as he pointed out, mere expedients or simple revisions of the Articles; they promised "systematic change" of government. While Madison knew that "a consolidation of the States into one simple republic" was politically unattainable, still he hoped that some "middle ground" might be

JAMES MADISON, 1751–1836

Madison was the greatest political thinker of the Revolutionary era and perhaps of all American history. His was the most critical and undogmatic mind of the Revolutionary leaders. More than anyone else he formulated the theory that underlay the new expanded republic of 1787. *(The Thomas Gilcrease Institute of American History and Art, Tulsa, Oklahoma.)*

found "which will at once support a due supremacy of the national authority, and leave in force the local authorities so far as they can be subordinately useful." What nationalists like Madison had in mind was creating a general government that would no longer be a confederation of independent republics but a national republic in its own right, operating directly on individuals and organized as the state governments had been organized, with a single executive, a bicameral legislature, and separate judiciary. This national republic would be somehow superimposed on the states, which would now stand to the central government, in John Jay's words, "in the same light in which counties stand to the State, of which they are parts, viz., merely as districts to facilitate the purposes of domestic order and good government." Thus the radical Virginia plan provided for a two-house national legislature with the authority to legislate "in all cases to which the states are incompetent" and "to negative all laws passed by the several states, contravening in the opinion of the National Legislature, the articles of Union."

For some in the Philadelphia Convention, the Virginia plan went much too far. Most delegates were prepared to grant substantial power to the federal government, including the right to tax, regulate commerce, and execute federal laws; but many did not want to allow such a weakening of state authority. Opponents of the nationalists, led by delegates from New Jersey, Connecticut, New York, and Delaware, countered with their own proposal, the New Jersey plan, so-called because William Paterson of New Jersey introduced it. This New Jersey plan essentially amended the Articles of Confederation by augmenting the powers of Congress and at the same time maintained the basic sovereignty of the states. With two such opposite proposals the Convention in the middle of June 1787 approached a crisis.

During the ensuing debate the nationalists, led by Madison and Wilson, were able to retain the basic features of the Virginia plan. Although the Convention refused to grant the national legislature a blanket authority "to legislate in all cases to which the separate States are incompetent," it granted the Congress (in Article I, Section 8, of the Constitution) a list of enumerated powers, including the powers to tax, to borrow and coin money, and to regulate commerce. Instead of giving the national legislature the right to veto harmful state laws, the Convention forbade the states from exercising particular sovereign powers whose abuse lay at the heart of the crisis of the 1780s: in Article I, Section 10, of the final Constitution the states were barred from carrying on foreign relations, levying tariffs, coining money, emitting bills of credit, passing ex post facto laws, or doing anything to relieve debtors of the obligations of their contracts. In contrast to the extensive fiscal powers given to the Congress, the states were rendered nearly economically incompetent. The new federal Constitution promised to do what the British government's several currency acts had failed to do—destroy the states' authority to issue paper money.

The Convention decided on a strong and single executive. The President stood alone, unencumbered by an executive council except of his own choosing. With command over the armed forces, with the authority to direct diplomatic relations, with power over appointments to the executive and judicial branches that few state governors possessed, and with a four-year term of office and perpetually reeligible for reelection, the President was a magistrate who, as Patrick Henry later charged, could "easily become king." To ensure the President's independence, he was not to be elected by the legislature, as the Virginia plan had proposed. Since the framers believed that only a few individuals besides Washington would in the future be known to the people throughout the country, they provided for local elections of "electors" equal in number to the representatives and senators from each state. These electors would cast ballots for the President, but if any candidate failed to get a majority, which in the absence of political parties and organized electioneering was normally expected, the final selection from the five candidates with the most votes would be made by the House of Representatives, with each state delegation having only one vote. The Virginia plan's suggestion of a separate national judiciary to hold office "during good behavior" was accepted without dispute. The structure of the national judiciary was left to the

Congress to devise. The right of this judiciary, however, to set aside acts of the Congress or of the state legislatures was by no means clear.

The nationalists in the Convention reluctantly gave way on several crucial issues, particularly on the national legislature's authority to veto state legislation. But they fought longest and hardest to hold on to the principle of proportional representation in both houses of the legislature, and almost stalemated the Convention. Debate between the states over the basis of taxation and representation in the central government had earlier prolonged the establishment of the Articles of Confederation. Now it was decided that both taxation and representation, at least in the House of Representatives, ought to be based on population and not on state particularity or landed wealth, with the slaves each counting as three-fifths of a person. The nationalists like Madison and Wilson, however, wanted representation in the Senate too to rest on population. For them legislative representation based directly on the people and not on the states was the foundation of the new structure. They believed that any semblance of separate state representation in the legislature, such as that which had existed under the

ROGER SHERMAN, BY RALPH EARL

Roger Sherman (1721–1793) began as a cobbler, but well before the Revolution he had become a lawyer, merchant, and substantial Connecticut official. He is best known for his introduction in the Philadelphia Convention of the "compromise" granting each state two senators. (*The Yale Art Gallery.*)

Articles, would be a recognition of the independent sovereignty of the states and would destroy at the outset the national authority of the Congress. Hence the nationalists came to regard the eventual "Connecticut Compromise" by which each state secured two senators in the upper house of the legislature as a disastrous defeat.

Yet despite the pessimism of Madison and Wilson on losing these battles over the congressional veto and proportional representation in both houses, the Federalists (as those who supported the Constitution came to call themselves) had in substance won the war even before the Convention adjourned. Once the New Jersey plan, embodying the essentials of the Articles of Confederation, was rejected in favor of the basic structure of the Virginia plan, the opponents, or Anti-Federalists, found themselves in the subsequent debates forced, as Richard Henry Lee complained, to accept "this or nothing."

Although the Articles of Confederation stipulated that amendments be made by the unanimous consent of the state legislatures, the delegates to the Philadelphia Convention decided to bypass the state legislatures and submit the Constitution to specially elected state conventions for ratification. Approval of only nine of the thirteen states was necessary for the new government to take effect. This transgression of earlier political principles was only one of many to which the Anti-Federalists objected.

Ostensibly the federal government established by the Philadelphia Convention severely violated the maxims of 1776 that had guided the Revolutionary constitution makers. Not only did the new Constitution provide for a strong government with an extraordinary amount of power given to the President and the Senate, but it created a single republican state that would span the continent and encompass all the diverse and scattered interests of the whole of American society — an impossibility for a republic according to the best political science of the day. During the debates over ratification in the fall and winter of 1787–88, the Anti-Federalists seized on these Federalist violations of the earlier Revolutionary assumptions about the nature of power and the need for a small homogeneous society in a republican state and used them to denigrate the new Constitution. They charged that not only did the new federal government with its concentration of power at the expense of liberty resemble a monarchy, but because of the extensive and heterogeneous nature of the society it was to govern, it would have to act tyrannically. Inevitably America would become a single consolidated state, with the individuality of the separate states melted down and absorbed by the federal government. And this would happen, the Anti-Federalists argued, because of the logic of sovereignty, that powerful principle of eighteenth-century political science that the English had used so effectively against the colonists in the imperial debate: the belief that no state could long possess two legislatures but must inevitably have one final, illimitable, indivisible lawmaking authority. With the preponderance of power in the new national government and the recognized supremacy of the Constitution as "the supreme Law of the Land," the doctrine of sovereignty, the Anti-Federalists said, foretold the eventual annihilation of the legislative authority of the separate states.

Despite these formidable Anti-Federalist arguments, the Federalists did not believe that the Constitution repudiated the Revolution and the principles of 1776. During the decade since Independence the political culture had been significantly transformed, and the Federalists expanded and intensified this transformation in order to make the Constitution a fulfillment of the Revolution. Like the state reformers seeking to limit the rampaging legislatures without seeming unpopular, the Federalists now resorted to the primal power of the people as the answer to all difficulties. True, they said, the Philadelphia Convention had gone beyond its instructions to amend the Articles of Confederation by drawing up an entirely new government and by providing for its ratification by special state conventions. But had not Americans learned during the previous decade that legislatures were no longer competent to create or change a constitution? If the Constitution were to be more than a treaty among separate states, if it were to be

PRO-CONSTITUTION CARTOON, 1788

(Library of Congress.)

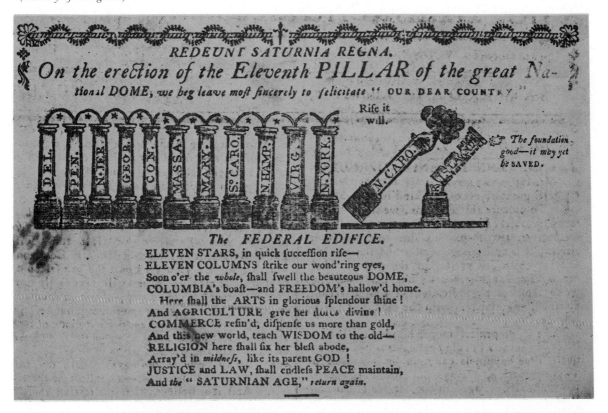

truly a fundamental law against which ordinary statute law could be declared by judges to be "null and void," then, Federalists like Madison argued, it had to be "ratified in the most unexceptionable form, and by the supreme authority of the people themselves." Hence it was "We the people of the United States," and not the states, that ordained and established the Constitution.

By locating sovereignty in the people rather than in any particular institution, the Federalists could now conceive of what hitherto had been a contradiction in politics—two legislatures operating simultaneously over the same community—and could thus answer the principal Anti-Federalist objection to the Constitution. Only by making the people themselves, and not their representatives in the state legislatures or in the Congress, the final and sovereign wielders of the lawmaking authority could the Federalists explain their emerging conception of federalism, that peculiar division of legislative responsibilities between the national and state governments that still confounds the world.

All the fast-moving intellectual developments of the previous decades were now brought to a head in the arguments over the ratification of the Constitution. These new ideas prepared Americans for a momentous reversal of the age-old Western conception of politics. During this period Americans ceased talking about politics in the way men since Aristotle had—about balancing within the state the one, the few, and the many—and they began talking about politics in a manner that is recognizably modern, about classes and interests seeking control of an autonomous state. It no longer made sense to call American governments "mixed republics," with the people, or the democracy, represented exclusively in the lower houses and balanced against the monarchical and aristocratic social elements embodied in the magistracy and in the senates. Now the American governments were increasingly described as democracies, or representative democracies, since the people participated equally and representatively through-out all branches of the governments, even in the gubernatorial and senatorial parts, and, some were saying, even in the judiciary. The Federalists, without clearly intending to, undermined the classical conception of politics and laid the basis for a new modern appreciation of the relation between society and government.

This new understanding of the relation of the society to government now enabled the Federalists to explain the expansion of a single republican state over a large continent of diverse groups and interests. Seizing on English philosopher David Hume's radical suggestion that a republican government might operate better in a large territory than in a small one, the Federalists, and in particular James Madison, ingeniously turned the older assumptions about the appropriate size of a republic on their head. Since experience in America from 1776 had demonstrated that no republic could be made small enough to avoid the clashing of rival parties and interests (tiny Rhode Island was the most faction-ridden of all), the republican state, said Madison in a series of notable letters, essays, and speeches climaxing with his most famous piece, *The Federalist,* No. 10, must be enlarged "without a departure from the elective basis of it." In this way, "the propensity in small republics to rash measures and the facility of forming and executing them" by overbearing factional majorities would be stifled.* To the Federalists, therefore, the extended territory of the new national republic to which the Anti-Federalists objected was actually its greatest source of strength. "In a large Society," concluded Madison, "the people are broken into so many interests and parties, that a common sentiment is less likely to be felt, and the requisite concert less likely to be formed by a majority of the whole." With these reformulations of older assumptions about politics, the Federalists came to a new appreciation of the dynamic realities of America's emerging market society.

Yet Madison and the Federalists did not expect this new federal government to be neutralized or paralyzed by the conflicting pressures of numerous jarring interests. Nor were they simply anticipating what has come to be called an "interest-group" theory of politics. They fully expected their new national government to possess what Madison called "an esprit de corps" and to articulate and promote vigorously the common good of the whole people. But why, Madison asked, would "private rights . . . be more secure under Guardianship of the General Government than under the State Governments, since they are both founded in the republican principle which refers the ultimate decision to the will of the majority"? What, in other words, was really different about the new federal Constitution from the earlier state constitutions that would enable it to lessen the effects of tyrannical majorities and keep it from succumbing to the same popular pressures that were besetting the state governments in the 1780s?

The answers the Federalists gave to these questions reflected their growing understanding during the 1780s of the sociology of American politics. The Federalists were opposed not as much to the governmental power of the states as to the character of the people wielding it. As the older society had disintegrated and electoral politics had expanded, the state legislatures had increasingly become dominated by localist-minded nongentry elements like Massachusetts's Samuel Nasson, a rough-hewn shopkeeper from Maine, and New York's Melancton Smith, a self-made entrepreneur from Poughkeepsie. Ordinary men like these, lacking the "enlightened" and "liberal" outlooks of the more cosmopolitan "natural aristocracy," were winning elections and enacting much of the confused and narrowly based interest-legislation of the 1780s. To the Federalists the best way to eliminate this democratic localism without repudiating republicanism and

---

The Federalist was a series of eighty-five essays published in New York in the winter of 1787–88 in defense of the Constitution. They were written under the pseudonym "Publius" largely by Madison and Alexander Hamilton, with five essays contributed by John Jay. The essays were quickly published as a book and became the most famous work of political philosophy in American history, labeled by Jefferson in 1788 as "the best commentary on the principles of government, which ever was written."

THE

COLUMBIAN MAGAZINE,

For APRIL, 1789.

Embellished with two COPPER-PLATES, representing,

I. Six Specimens of FOSSILS found in the United States.
II. A Prospect of the PAYSAIC FALLS, in New-Jersey.

CONTENTS.

History of the American war, [continued] 209
Answers to queries on the present state of husbandry and agriculture in the Delaware state, [concluded] 217
Remarks on a passage in Brydone's Travels, 220
Life of William Penn, founder of Pennsylvania 223
Description of certain American fossils 228
Address of John Doe, ib.
Description of the Dismal Swamp in Virginia; with proposals for, and observations on the advantages of draining it: by the hon. William Byrd, 230
Account of a free settlement of Negroes at Sierra Leona; in a letter from Granville Sharpe, esq; to doctor Lettsom, 234
Directions for expelling noxious vapours from wells, 240

Dissertation on the influence of the mother on the fœtus, 241
Improvement in the culture of hemp, and fitting it for use: by John Read, esq; of Massach'setts, 246
Essay on genius, [continued] 249
The Retailer, No. IX. 252
An original anecdote, 255
Literary intelligence, an account of new medical books, ib.
Recipe, 256

THE COLUMBIAN PARNASSIAD.
Sonnet on a wall-flower, 257
The happy pair, ib.
Cantata for St. Andrew's day, 259
Ossian's address to the sun, 261

THE CHRONICLE,
Containing foreign and domestic intelligence, 262
Marriages, 268
Deaths, ib.

TO WHICH ARE PREFIXED,

Tables of METEOROLOGICAL OBSERVATIONS, viz. two for the months of FEBRUARY and MARCH, made in Charleston, South-Carolina; and one for the month of FEBRUARY, made at Spring-Mill, Pennsylvania:———also,

The PRICES CURRENT of MERCHANDIZE and PUBLIC SECURITIES, and the COURSE of EXCHANGE.

PHILADELPHIA:
PRINTED FOR JAMES TRENCHARD.

PAGES FROM "COLUMBIA MAGAZINE"

Between 1775 and 1795 twenty-seven learned and gentlemanly magazines like this one were begun, six more than in the entire colonial period. The creation of these new journals was a remarkable testimony to the cultural promise of the Revolution. (*American Antiquarian Society.*)

elective government was to enlarge the arena of politics, thereby expanding the electorate and reducing the number and changing the character of those elected to legislative office. As the distinction between gentlemen and commoners became blurred and the traditional instruments of gentry patronage and influence in local affairs weakened, only conspicuous reputation, or sheer notability of name, seemed capable any longer of sustaining elite rule in politics. If the people of a state, New York, for example, had to select only ten men to the federal Congress in contrast to the sixty-six they elected to their state assembly, they were more likely in the case of the few representatives in the national government to ignore obscure ordinary men and elect only those who were well-born, well-educated, and well-known. Election by the people in large districts would inhibit demagoguery and crass electioneering and would therefore, said James Wilson of Philadelphia, whose mansion had been attacked in 1779 by a mob, "be most likely to obtain men of intelligence and uprightness." Hence through the

Constitution the Federalists hoped to restore traditional gentry dominance of government and to escape the confusion and instability created by the "wrong sorts" of people exercising political power in the state legislatures during the 1780s.

Although the Federalists in creating the Constitution may have intended to curb the populist forces the Revolution had released, the language and principles they used to defend the Constitution were decidedly popular. Indeed, most Federalists felt they had little choice in using democratic rhetoric. The proponents of the Constitution did not need John Dickinson to warn them in Philadelphia that "when this plan goes forth, it will be attacked by the popular leaders. Aristocracy will be the watchword; the Shibboleth among its adversaries." Precisely because the Anti-Federalists, as Hamilton observed in the New York ratifying convention, did talk "so often of an aristocracy," the Federalists were continually compelled in the ratifying debates to minimize, even disguise, the elitist elements of the Constitution. And in fact the Federalists of 1787–88 were not rejecting democratic electoral politics; nor were they trying to reverse the direction of the republican Revolution. They saw themselves rather as saving the Revolution from its excesses, in Madison's words, creating "a republican remedy for the diseases most incident to republican government." They shared a common American agreement that all American governments had to be "strictly republican" and derived "from the only source of just authority—the People."

In the ratifying conventions held throughout the fall, winter, and spring of 1787–1788, the Anti-Federalists were little match for the arguments and the array of talents that the Federalists gathered in support of the Constitution. Most of the Anti-Federalists were state-centered men with only local interests and loyalties, politicians without the influence and education of the Federalists, and often without social and intellectual confidence. They had difficulty making themselves heard both because their speakers, as one Anti-Federalist in Connecticut complained, "were browbeaten by many of those Cicero'es as they think themselves and others of Superior rank," and because much of the press was closed to them: out of a hundred or more newspapers printed in the late 80s only a dozen supported the Anti-Federalists.

Many of the small states—Delaware, New Jersey, Connecticut, and Georgia—which were commercially dependent on their neighbors or militarily exposed, ratified immediately. The critical struggles took place in the large states of Massachusetts, Virginia, and New York, and acceptance of the Constitution in these states was achieved only by narrow margins and by the promise of future amendments. North Carolina and Rhode Island rejected the Constitution, but after New York's ratification in July 1788 the country was ready to go ahead and organize the new government without them.

Despite the difficulties and the close votes in some states, the country's eventual acceptance of the Constitution was nearly preordained, for the alternative of governmental chaos seemed awesome to most Americans. Yet in the face of the preponderance of gentry wealth and respectability in support of the Constitution, what in the end remains extraordinary is not the political weakness and disunity of Anti-Federalism but its strength. That large numbers of Americans could actually reject a plan of government created by a body, as one Anti-Federalist said in awe, "composed of the first characters in the Continent" and backed by George Washington and nearly the whole of the "natural aristocracy" of the country said more about the changing character of American politics and society than did the Constitution's acceptance. It was indeed a portent of what was to come.

The Hamiltonian Program

The Constitution created only the outline of the new government; it remained for Americans to fill in the details of the government and make something of it. During the succeeding decade the governmental leaders, that is, the Federalists —who clung to the name used by the supporters of the Constitution—sought to build a consolidated and aristocratic empire that few Americans in 1776 had ever envisioned. The consequence of their efforts was to make the 1790s the most awkward decade in American history, bearing little relation to what went on immediately before or after.

Like the self-molded, impenetrable character of George Washington, who was the first President (1789–96) and more a monument than a person, the entire

THE INAUGURATION OF GEORGE WASHINGTON AS PRESIDENT, ENGRAVING BY AMOS DOLITTLE (1790)

This Federal Hall in New York (demolished in 1812) was designed by the French immigrant, Pierre-Charles L'enfant, in the hope that it would become the seat of the new national government. With the decision to erect the permanent capital on the Potomac, L'enfant turned to preparing the plans on which Washington, D.C., was built. *(Prints Division, New York Public Library.)*

Federalist era seems to be a sheer act of will in the face of contrary social developments. Because the Federalists stood in the way of democracy as it was emerging in the United States, they have become heretics in the story of the developing faith. Everything seemed to turn against them. They thought they were creating a classically heroic state and they attempted everywhere to symbolize these classical aims; but they left only a legacy of indecipherable icons, unread poetry, and a proliferation of Greek and Roman temples. They despised political parties, yet parties nonetheless emerged, shattering the remarkable harmony of 1790 and fomenting one of the most divisive and passionate eras in American history. They sought desperately to avoid conflict with the former mother country to the point where they appeared to be compromising the independence of the new nation, only to discover in the end that the war with Great Britain they avoided was to be fought anyway in 1812 by the subsequent administration of their opponents. By the early nineteenth century Alexander Hamilton, the brilliant leader of the Federalists, who more than anyone else pursued the heroic dreams of the age, was not alone in his despairing conclusion "that this American world was not made for me."

There was more consensus at the inauguration of the new government in 1789–90 than at any time since the Declaration of Independence. The differences among the national leaders and the states and sections they represented were temporarily obscured by a common enthusiasm for the new Constitution. The unanimous election of Washington as the first President gave the new government an immediate respectability it otherwise could not have had. With the ratification in 1791 of the first ten amendments to the Constitution—the Bill of Rights— drawn up by Madison and designed to assuage the fears of the earlier opponents of the Constitution, an optimistic sense of beginning anew, of putting the republican experiment on a new and stronger foundation, ran through communities up and down the continent. Americans talked of benevolence, glory, and heroism, and foresaw the inevitable westward transit of the arts and sciences across the Atlantic to the New World. Freemasonry and fraternity flourished. The outlook was cosmopolitan, liberal, and humanitarian; America was entering its own Augustan age.

Yet despite all this optimism the Americans of the 1790s never lost their Revolutionary sense of the fragility of republican states and the novel and tenuous nature of their boldly extended republican government. Except in the minds of a few excited poets such as Joel Barlow and Timothy Dwight, America in the 1790s was far from being a consolidated nation in any modern sense. Already separatist movements in the peripheral sections of the West threatened to break up the new country. With some Westerners even considering an allegiance to Spain in return for benefits like access to the Gulf of Mexico that the United States government could not provide, the entire Mississippi River basin was susceptible to exploitation by ambitious adventurers willing to sell their services to European nations—General James Wilkinson, soon to be commander of the army; William Blount, senator from Tennessee; George Rogers Clark, frontier

FREEMASONRY MEMBERSHIP CERTIFICATE, 1817

Freemasonry was the most important fraternal and benevolent
society of the new republic and something of a surrogate religion
for many of the Revolutionary leaders. Masonic imagery and
symbols were everywhere prevalent in the architecture and
iconography of the new nation. With the growing democratization
of America, its secrecy and elitism came under increasing attack.
(*American Antiquarian Society.*)

hero during the Revolution. Fear of this kind of intrigue and influence, to which
republican states were historically vulnerable, led to the hasty admission into the
Union during the 1790s of Vermont, Kentucky, and Tennessee. But as the grandiose western project of Jefferson's disappointed Vice-President, Aaron Burr, and
the thwarted schemes of a separate northeastern confederacy of disgruntled
Federalists in the early nineteenth century later showed, the danger of splintering remained.

Although some Americans were talking excitedly about the capacity of enlightened men to shape and control their own destiny, social change was still
widely equated with organic growth and thus eventual decay. The United States
was universally regarded as a young and rising country that would in time become
perhaps the most wealthy and illustrious empire in the world. All such exhilarating visions of future greatness, however, were tainted by the knowledge that all
empires, like that of Augustan Rome, must eventually age and die. But they also

knew that what they did now in laying the foundation for the country could accelerate or retard the inevitable process of decay. They therefore possessed an awesome sense of their responsibility for "millions yet unborn" to leave some kind of permanent legacy to the distant future, a responsibility that few generations of American leaders have ever so self-consciously shouldered.

Only in this context of uncertainty and awesome responsibility can the Federalist aims and the conflicting passions they aroused be properly appreciated. At issue in the 1790s were not simply problems of finance or foreign policy but the very character of America's emerging republican state. The Federalist leaders sought to extend the momentum that had begun in the late 1780s when the Constitution was formed. In place of the impotent confederation of disparate states that unruly popular elements had been allowed to dominate, they envisioned a strong consolidated and commercial empire, like the states of Europe, led by an energetic government composed of the best, most heroic men in the society.

In order to bolster the dignity of the new republic with some of the ceremony and majesty of monarchy, some Federalists in the Senate, led by Vice-President John Adams, sought to make "His Highness" the proper title for addressing the President. Because the future of the new republic seemed so unformed and problematical to men of the time, such an issue seemed loaded with significance and occupied the Congress in a month of debate. Although the Federalists lost this monarchical title to the republican simplicity of "Mr. President," they drew up elaborate rules concerning levees (social receptions) and the proper behavior at what soon came to be called the "republican court" at the temporary capital in New York and after 1790 in Philadelphia. At the same time plans were begun for locating and erecting a monumental "federal city" as the permanent capital of the new empire. Always acutely sensitive to the precedents being established, the Federalists also worked out the relations between the President and the Congress. Before the end of the first session of the Congress in 1789, the sparse frame of government provided by the Constitution had been filled in. Congress created the executive departments of state, war, and treasury, and a federal judiciary consisting of the Supreme Court and a hierarchy of inferior courts in which many Federalists hoped the common law would run.

As secretary of the Treasury, thirty-five-year-old Alexander Hamilton was in a crucial position to dominate the Federalist program. Since the treasury had been the foundation of power, or the source of "corruption" (in the language of opposition ideology) for the ministries of Sir Robert Walpole in Hanoverian England, the secretary of the Treasury was regarded by the first Congress with some suspicion and was thus made directly and peculiarly responsible to the Congress. With dozens of officers and well over two thousand customs officials, revenue agents, and postmasters, the Treasury was by far the largest department; and although Congress limited the capacity of these officials to involve themselves in business and trade or in buying public lands and government securities, they were an important source of patronage and influence. Hamilton in fact saw his

ALEXANDER HAMILTON (1757–1804)

Hamilton is the most controversial
of the Founding Fathers. Certainly
he was the least taken with radical
Whig ideology and the most
adventurous and heroic. As
Gouverneur Morris said, "he
was more covetous of glory than
of wealth or power." His talents,
his energy, and his clear sense of
direction awed his contemporaries,
friends and enemies alike.
*(National Gallery of Art, Washington,
D.C.)*

role in eighteenth-century English terms—as a kind of prime minister to President
Washington, whom Jefferson came to call America's figurehead king. Believing
that the "most important means of every government are connected with the
treasury," Hamilton felt justified in meddling in the affairs of the other departments and of the Congress and in taking the lead in organizing and administering
the government. While denying that he was creating a "court" party, he set out to
duplicate the great financial achievements of the early eighteenth-century English governments that had laid the basis for England's subsequent stability and
commercial supremacy.

Hamilton worked out his program in a series of four reports to the Congress
in 1790–91: on credit, on duties and taxes, on a national bank, and on manufactures. Nearly everyone admitted that the new government needed to put its
finances in order and to settle the Revolutionary debts of the United States.
Hamilton was bent on establishing the credit of the United States, but he was not
at all interested in paying off what the American governments owed their citizens
and others in the world. Instead of extinguishing these public debts, which in
1790 totaled $42 million for the federal government and $21 million for the
several state governments, Hamilton proposed that the United States government "fund" them, that is, collect all the government bonds and loan certificates,

both federal and state, into a single package and issue new federal securities in their place. Thereby the central government would create a refunded, consolidated, and permanent national debt, which would play the same continuing role for America that the English national debt had played in strengthening the former mother country. Regular interest payments were to be backed by the new government's revenues from custom duties and excise taxes; indeed, over 40 percent of these revenues in the 1790s went to pay interest on the debt. These interest payments not only would make the United States the best credit risk in the world, but would create a system of investment for American moneyed groups lacking the stable alternatives for speculation Europeans had. While land in Europe was a secure investment, in America it could be a highly risky one, as many speculators in land during the 1790s like Robert Morris, financier during the Confederation, and Henry Knox, Washington's secretary of war, eventually discovered.

Besides giving investors a secure stake in the new Constitution, these new government bonds would become the basis of the nation's money supply. Not only would the securities themselves be negotiable instruments in business transactions, but Hamilton's program provided for their forming two-thirds of the capital of a new national bank that would emulate the Bank of England. This Bank of the United States and its branches (to be established in select cities) would serve as the government's depository and fiscal agent and act as a central control on the operation of the proliferating state banks, which numbered thirty-two by 1801. But

most important, it would create paper money. The Bank would issue its notes as loans to private citizens, and these notes along with those of the state-chartered banks would become the principal circulating medium for a society that lacked an adequate supply of specie, that is, gold and silver coin, the only real money most Americans recognized. Above all, Hamilton wanted a paper money, unlike the fiat currency of the Revolutionary years, that would hold its value in relation to specie. By guaranteeing that the federal government would receive the Bank's notes at par with specie for all taxes, holders of the notes would be less likely to redeem them in coin. The notes would pass from hand to hand without depreciating, even though only a fraction of their value was available at any one time in specie. Although many American leaders continued to believe, as John Adams did, that "every dollar of a bank bill that is issued beyond the quantity of gold and silver in the vaults, represents nothing, and is therefore a cheat upon somebody," these multiplying bank notes quickly broadened the foundation of the nation's economy.

With his final report, that on manufactures, Hamilton laid out plans for industrializing the United States. In imitation of Great Britain his plan proposed a system of protective tariffs, along with bounties and incentives for developing new manufacturing techniques and labor-saving devices. Yet because American energies in the 1790s were still focused on overseas shipping and land speculation and not on domestic industry, Hamilton's complex proposals for stimulating manufacturing were ignored, with the exception of some limited tariffs on imported goods. The rest of his extraordinary financial program, however, was adopted by Congress early in the 1790s.

As much as Hamilton and other Federalist leaders envisioned and celebrated the commercial prosperity of the United States, their ultimate goals were more political than economic. Hamilton, this illegitimate son born in the West Indies of a Scottish merchant, was not a protocapitalist seeking to create America's later business culture. Deeply involved in the elegant polite world of the rich and well born, he was very much the eighteenth-century gentleman, willing to allow ordinary men their profits and property while he sought "future grandeur and

FIRST BANK OF THE UNITED STATES, PHILADELPHIA

Designed by an unsuccessful businessman from New Hampshire, Samuel Blodget, this building was essentially a three-story New England brick house with a classical portico, decorated, the *Gazette of the United States* reported excitedly, in the style of "Palmyra and Rome when architecture was at its zenith in the Augustan age." *(Library of Congress.)*

glory" for the nation. To this illustrious end America's wealth and prosperity, indeed his entire financial program, were only a means.

Like many other Federalists, Hamilton had no faith whatsoever in the idealistic hopes of the Revolution that American society could be held together solely by "virtue," by the people's willingness to sacrifice their private interests for the sake of the public good. Instead of virtue and the natural sociability of men as the adhesive force in American society Hamilton saw only the ordinary individual's selfish pursuit of his own private happiness. Lacking any modern appreciation of the ideological or emotional ties of nationalism, Hamilton and the Federalists could conclude only that the stability of such a society required harnessing this self-interest. They thus sought to use the new economic and fiscal measures to re-create in America traditional kinds of eighteenth-century connections to knit the sprawling society together.

In effect Hamilton sought to reverse the egalitarian thrust of the Revolutionary movement. Clinging to an orthodox view of an eighteenth-century hierarchical world, the Federalists believed that the federal government needed only to influence and manipulate the dominant economic and social elements of the country. These dominant elements in turn would use economic interest to bring the remaining groups and individuals beneath them along in support of the new central government. Not only did the Federalists expect the new national financial program to wean people's affections from the now economically weakened state governments, but they deliberately set out to "corrupt" the society (in the lexicon of eighteenth-century opposition thinking) into paying allegiance to the central government. In local areas they exploited previous military camaraderie and the Society of the Cincinnati, the organization of Revolutionary War officers; they appointed important and respectable individuals to the federal judiciary and other federal offices; they carefully managed the Bank of the United States and other parts of the national economic program; and they had President Washington in 1791 make a regal tour of the country.

By 1793 through the shrewd use of these kinds of influence on key individuals the Federalists had formed loosely organized "friends of government" in most of the states. The lines of connection of these centers of economic and political patronage ran from the various localities through the Congress to the federal executive, and created a vested interest in what opponents like Senator William Maclay of Pennsylvania called "a court faction"—the very thing that Madison in *The Federalist,* No. 10, had deemed unlikely in an expanded republic.

Ultimately Hamilton believed, as he declared in 1794, that "government can never [be] said to be established until some signal display has manifested its power of military coercion." From the beginning many Federalists, such as Secretary of War Henry Knox, regarded a cohesive militia and a regular army as "a strong corrective arm" necessary for the federal government to meet all crises "whether arising from internal or external causes." Following the Northwestern Indians'

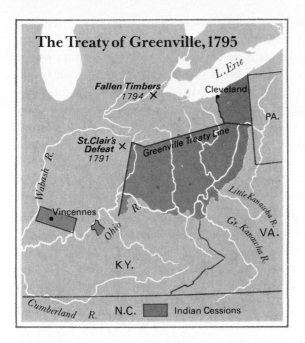

The Treaty of Greenville, 1795

annihilation of General Arthur St. Clair's motley collection of militia and levies in 1791, the army was reorganized into a legion (in emulation of classical Rome) composed of regular soldiers under General Anthony Wayne. Wayne's smashing victory over the Indians at Fallen Timbers in 1794 followed by the Treaty of Greenville a year later broke both Indian resistance and British influence in the Old Northwest and fully justified creating a permanent military establishment of regulars on the frontier. At the same time a rebellion in 1794 of some western Pennsylvania farmers, who were protesting a federal excise tax on whiskey, was met by the national government's raising of nearly 15,000 militia. This excessive show of force was essential, President Washington declared, because "we had given no testimony to the world of being able or willing to support our government and laws."

It was not just Indians and Americans who had to be impressed with the government's military might; it was the entire world. In a treaty that John Jay negotiated in 1795, Great Britain formally relinquished its hold on the Northwest posts. In another treaty that Thomas Pinckney negotiated in the same year, Spain finally recognized American claims to the Florida boundary and to navigation of the Mississippi. Both treaties thus redeemed the territorial integrity of the United States in a way the diplomacy of the Confederation had been unable to do. But the United States was still far from being a world power. Measuring American power by European standards, the Federalists were acutely conscious of the country's existing weakness in the world, and this consciousness largely determined their foreign policy. Unlike England and France, the United States as yet lacked the essential elements of state power and greatness—a well-integrated commercial nation and a modern army and navy. Since building the United States into a strong and prosperous empire rivaling the powers of Europe on their own terms might take fifty years or more, the new nation had to buy time by maintaining harmonious relations with Great Britain. Britain was the only power that could seriously hinder American development; for it was duties on British imports that supplied the national revenue on which Hamilton's entire financial program depended. Until the United States could stand up to Great Britain, the Federalists believed that the country ought to concentrate on acquiring or controlling the New World possessions of a decrepit Spain and on dominating the Western Hemisphere. The Federalists' policy of rapprochement with the former mother country thus became simply another means toward the ultimate fulfillment of their grandiose dreams of American glory.

Suggested Readings

John Fiske, *The Critical Period of American History* (1888), popularized the Federalist view of the Confederation for the nineteenth century. Merrill Jensen, *The New Nation* (1950), minimizes the crisis of the 1780s, and explains the movement for the Constitution as the work of a small but dynamic minority. E. James Ferguson, *The Power of the Purse...*, *1776–1790* (1961), also stresses the nationalists' efforts to strengthen the Confederation. Clarence L. Ver Steeg, *Robert Morris, Revolutionary Financier* (1954), is the major study of that important figure. Forrest McDonald, *E Pluribus Unum: The Formation of the American Republic, 1776–1790* (1965), describes the commercial scrambling by Americans in the 1780s. The best account of the army and the Newburgh Conspiracy is Richard H. Kohn, *Eagle and Sword: The Federalists and the Creation of the Military Establishment in America, 1783–1802* (1975). The best short survey of the Confederation period is still Andrew C. McLaughlin, *The Confederation and the Constitution, 1783–1789* (1905).

Charles Beard's *An Economic Interpretation of the Constitution* (1913) sought to explain the Constitution as something other than the consequence of high-minded idealism. It became the most influential history book ever written in America. Beard saw the struggle over the Constitution as "a deep-seated conflict between a popular party based on paper money and agrarian interests and a conservative party centered in the towns and resting on financial, mercantile, and personal property interests generally." While Beard's particular proof for his thesis—that the Founding Fathers held federal securities that they expected would appreciate in value under a new national government—has been demolished, especially by Forrest McDonald, *We the People* (1958), his general interpretation of the origins of the Constitution still casts a long shadow. Jackson T. Main, *Political Parties before the Constitution* (1974), finds a "cosmopolitan"-"localist" split within the states over the Constitution. Gordon S. Wood, *The Creation of the American Republic, 1776–1787* (1969), working through the ideas, discovers a similar social, but not strictly speaking a "class," division over the Constitution.

For a different emphasis on the origins of the Constitution, see Robert E. Brown, *Reinterpretation of the Formation of the American Constitution* (1963); and Benjamin F. Wright, Jr., *Consensus and Continuity, 1776–1787* (1958). The best history of the Convention is still Max Farrand, *The Framing of the Constitution of the United States* (1913), which sees the Constitution as "a bundle of compromises" designed to meet specific defects of the Articles. Irving Brant's third volume of his biography of *James Madison* (6 vols., 1941–1961) has a sure-footed description of the Convention.

Max Farrand, ed., *The Records of the Federal Convention of 1787* (4 vols.; 1911, 1937); and Jonathan Elliot, ed., *The Debates in the Several State Conventions on the Adoption of the Federal Constitution* (5 vols., 1876), are collections of the important documents. Jacob Cooke, ed., *The Federalist* (1961), is the best edition of these papers. Two sympathetic studies of the Antifederalists are Jackson T. Main, *The Antifederalists..., 1781–1788* (1961); and Robert A. Rutland, *The Ordeal of the Constitution* (1966). See also Robert A. Rutland, *The Birth of the Bill of Rights, 1776–1791* (1955). The papers of the Founding Fathers—Jefferson, Franklin, Hamilton, John Adams, and Madison—are currently being published in mammoth scholarly editions.

Politics in the 1790s is ably summarized in John C. Miller, *The Federalist Era, 1789–1801* (1960). Richard Buel, Jr., *Securing the Revolution: Ideology in American Politics, 1789–1815* (1972), however, better recaptures the distinctiveness of the age and the problematical character of the new national government. John C. Miller, *Alexander Hamilton, Portrait in Paradox* (1959), is the fullest biography; but Gerald Stourzh, *Alexander Hamilton and the Idea of Republican Government* (1970), better places this leading Federalist in an eighteenth-century context. In this respect, see also the collected essays of Douglass Adair, *Fame and the Founding Fathers* (1974). For single-volume studies of Washington, see Marcus Cunliffe, *George Washington: Man and Monument* (1958); and James Thomas Flexner, *Washington: The Indispensable Man* (1974).

Leonard D. White, *The Federalists: A Study in Administrative History* (1948), is the standard account of the creation of the governmental bureaucracy. Lisle A. Rose, *Prologue to Democracy* (1968), describes the formation of Federalist influence in the South during the 1790s. Richard H. Kohn, *Eagle and Sword: The Federalists and the Creation of the Military Establishment in America, 1783–1802* (1975), is important for understanding the Federalist goals. On foreign policy, see Samuel Flagg Bemis, *Jay's Treaty* (1923), and *Pinckney's Treaty* (1926). Jerald A. Combs, *The Jay Treaty* (1970), is broader than its title would suggest. A good survey is Lawrence S. Kaplan, *Colonies into Nation: American Diplomacy, 1763–1801* (1972).

11

The Revolution Recovered

The Federalist Augustan world, bred out of the reaction to the excesses of Revolutionary populism, could not endure. It ran too much against the grain of fast-moving social developments. The Federalist creators of the Constitution of 1787 had recognized the force of this populism and had made innumerable concessions to it, both political and intellectual. Yet such concessions did not satisfy American populist demands; they aggravated them. The Federalists of the 1790s refused to recognize that the people's position in American politics was no longer a debatable issue. "They have attempted," as Noah Webster observed, "to resist the force of public opinion, instead of falling into the current with a view to direct it." In the process, they "manifested more integrity than address."

Convinced that the fear of disunion was so great that almost any sort of strong national government within a republican framework would be acceptable, the Federalists sought to recapture some of the energy and authority lost in the turbulence of the Revolution. They counted on the increasing prosperity of the society to justify both their program and their reliance on rule by a traditional gentlemanly elite. But they attempted too much too late. So out of touch were they with the rapidly developing realities of American life, so counter to the libertarian impulse of the Revolutionary ideology was their program, that they provoked a second revolutionary movement that threatened to tear the republican experiment apart. Only the electoral victory of the Republican opposition in 1800 ended this threat and brought, in the eyes of many Americans, the entire Revolutionary venture of two and a half decades to successful completion. Indeed, "the Revolution of 1800," as the opposition leader and third President of the United States, Thomas Jefferson, called it, "was as real a revolution in the principles of our government as that of 1776 was in its form."

The Republican Opposition

Opposition to the Federalist program was slow in developing. Since the only prospective alternative to the new national government was the horror of disunity and anarchy, Alexander Hamilton and the Federalists were in a position at the outset to build up their system without great difficulty. During the first year of the new government (1789–90), James Madison acted as congressional leader of those forces anxious to counteract Anti-Federalist sentiment and eager to build a strong and independent executive. Not only did Madison write President Washington's first inaugural address, but he argued for the President's exclusive power to remove executive officials and worked hard to create a treasury department with a single head responsible for preparing reports on revenue and credit. Indeed, Hamilton, thinking of the collaborative atmosphere of 1786–87 in which he and Madison had written *The Federalist* papers, was so confident of the nationalism of Madison and the Southern representatives in the Congress that he felt betrayed when they did not unquestioningly support his program.

On the refunding of the debt and on the national assumption of the states' debts Madison broke with the administration. In the refunding he urged some sort of discrimination between the original purchasers of the federal bonds and their present, often Northern, speculative holders who had bought them up cheaply. Madison was also convinced that national assumption of the outstanding state debts would penalize those states, particularly Virginia, that had already liquidated a large portion of their debts. Yet congressional opposition to these measures in 1790 was still capable of compromise for the sake of federal union. Jefferson, Madison, and other Southern representatives were even willing to support national assumption of state debts in return for locating the new federal city on the Potomac on the border between Virginia and Maryland.

With the government's effort to charter the Bank of the United States in December 1790, however, the opposition began to assume a more strident and ideological character. Madison in the House of Representatives and Jefferson in the cabinet as secretary of state both urged a strict construction of the Constitution as a defense against what seemed to have become the dangerous consolidating implications of the Hamiltonian program. Washington, after asking the opinions of his cabinet members on the constitutionality of the Bank, rejected Jefferson's constitutional literalism and accepted Hamilton's broad construction of the Congress's "necessary and proper" authority to carry out its delegated powers; but this presidential decision would not quiet the opposition.

By 1791 what was called a "republican interest" was emerging in the Congress and in the country, with Madison and Jefferson as its spokesmen. By 1792 this "interest" had begun to congeal into a Republican "party," designed by its invocation of the power of the people to counter the growing "influence" of the Federalist "court" in the government.

This Republican party was composed of and supported by a variety of social elements. Foremost were Southern planters who were becoming increasingly conscious of the distinctiveness of their section and more and more estranged from the speculative world Hamilton's system seemed to be generating. Unlike Federalist gentlemen in the North these Southern gentry retained a remarkable amount of the earlier Whig confidence in the people and in what Jefferson called the "honest heart" of the common man. Part of this faith in democracy by Jefferson and his Southern colleagues came from their relative insulation from it. With the increasing questioning of black slavery in the North and throughout the world, small white farmers in the South found a common identity with large planters. Most of the leading planters therefore did not feel threatened by the democratic electoral politics that was eating away popular deference to "the better sort" in the North. In the North, especially in the rapidly growing middle states, new unconnected ambitious individuals and groups were finding in the Republican party a political mechanism by which they could challenge entrenched elites. While the Republican opposition to the Federalist program in the South was therefore largely the response of rural gentry committed to a nostalgic image of independent freeholders, the Republican party in the North was the political expression of new egalitarian social forces released and intensified by the Revolutionary assau t on the corporatism of the old society. Such rising entrepreneurs were in fact the principal contributors to the kind of world the Southern Republicans were coming to fear.

What brought these diverse and ultimately incompatible sectional and social elements together in a national Republican party was a comprehensive and common ideology. This Republican ideology, involving a deep hatred of bloated state power and of the political and financial mechanisms that created such power, had been inherited from the English "country-opposition" tradition, and sharpened and Americanized during the Revolutionary years. Now, during the 1790s, it was given a new and heightened relevance by the aggrandizing policies of the federal administration.

To those steeped in this country-Whig ideology, Hamilton's system portended the re-creation of the kind of government and society Americans had presumably eradicated in 1776—a society of cliental connections and artificial privilege sustained by magisterial powers that would in time destroy the independence of the republican citizenry. Hamilton appeared to be another Walpole, using the new economic program to corrupt the Congress and the country and create a swelling phalanx of "stock-jobbers and king-jobbers" (in Jefferson's words) in order to build up executive power at the expense of the people.

Once the Republicans grasped this ideological pattern, all the Federalist measures fell into place. The high-toned pageantry of the "court," the aristocratic talk of titles, the defense of corporate monopolies, the enlargement of the military forces, the growth of taxes, the reliance on the monarchical President and the aristocratic Senate all pointed toward a systematic plan, as Caroline County of Virginia declared in 1793, of "assimilating the American government to the form and spirit of the British monarchy." Most basic and insidious of all was the Federalist creation of a huge perpetual federal debt, which, as George Clinton, former Anti-Federalist and Republican governor of New York, explained, not only would poison the morals of the people through speculation, but would "add an artificial support to the administration, and by a species of bribery enlist the monied men of the community on the side of the measures of government. . . . Look to Great Britain."

The eruption of the French Revolution in 1789 and its subsequent expansion in 1792 into a European war pitting monarchical Britain and republican France against one another added to the quarrel Americans were having among themselves over the direction of their society and government. The meaning of the American Revolution and the capacity of the United States to sustain its grand republican experiment now seemed tied to the fate of the European antagonists.

Although the United States was ostensibly impartial as a consequence of Washington's proclamation of neutrality in 1793, the Federalists and their Republican opponents both sought to favor whichever power, Britain or France, they thought would better promote American interests. The Federalists attempted strenuously to overcome the natural sympathy most Americans possessed for France as their former Revolutionary ally and new sister republic. Citizen Genêt, the new French minister to the United States, began arming privateers in the United States for use against the British and appealed over the head of the government to the American people for support. These clumsy actions helped the Federalists to win over many Americans otherwise sympathetic to the French Revolution. With the increasing fears of spreading deistic and antireligious sentiments and of the further disintegration of American society—both now associated with the contagious excesses of the French Revolution—the Federalists recruited growing numbers of Protestant clergy and conservative groups to their cause.

The treaty negotiated by John Jay, ambassador extraordinary, with Great Britain in 1795, in which Americans abandoned many of their political and commercial claims against the former mother country, was the diplomatic expression of this Federalist perspective. Jay was burned in effigy and Republicans in the House of Representatives tried to prevent implementation of the treaty, which the Senate reluctantly ratified after a bitter struggle. Although the British conceded little to America except peace, for most Federalists this was enough. They were willing to pay a high price to stop the proliferation of what Federalist

Senator George Cabot of Massachusetts called "French principles [that] would destroy us as a society."

This rapprochement with England drove the embattled French into a series of depredations against American shipping and a refusal to treat with the United States until the new American connection with Great Britain was broken. John Adams, who had succeeded Washington as President in 1796, dealt with the crisis by sending a special mission to France. The French government, using agents designated as X, Y, and Z, tried to extort a payment from the American diplomats as a precondition for negotiations. This humiliating "X, Y, Z affair" further aroused American antagonism to France and led to the repudiation of the Franco-American treaties of 1778, the outbreak by 1798 of a "quasi-war" on the seas with France, and the opportunity for some extreme Federalists led by Hamilton to strengthen the central government once and for all.

Jefferson retired from the cabinet in 1793 but as the leader of the Republican party and as runner-up to Adams in the election of 1796, he became Vice-President. Whether in or out of office, he never let the growing anti-French atmosphere weaken his faith in the cause of the French revolutionary republic. While he supported the outward neutrality of the United States in the European war between Britain and France, he and other Republicans were bitterly opposed to Jay's treaty and convinced they could not remain impartial in a cause in which "the liberty of the whole earth was depending." Even knowledge of the bloody excesses of the French Revolution did not dampen Jefferson's enthusiasm for it. "Rather than it should have failed," he wrote in 1793, "I would have seen half the earth desolate; were there but an Adam and Eve left in every country, and left free, it would be better than it now is." Convinced that the very meaning of the United States as a republic was directly related to the conflict between Britain and France, some American public officials of both political persuasions were led into extraordinarily improper diplomatic behavior during the 1790s. Hamilton as secretary of the Treasury secretly passed on information about United States plans to the British government. Jefferson as secretary of state under Washington, Edmund Randolph, his successor, and James Monroe as minister to France, all indiscreetly sought to undermine the pro-British stand of the administration they were serving and came very close to becoming unwitting tools of French policy.

In such an inflamed atmosphere political passions ran as high as they ever have in American history. Every aspect of American life—business groups, banks, dance assemblies, even funerals—became politicized. People who had known each other their whole lives now crossed streets to avoid meeting. As personal and social ties fell apart, differences easily spilled into violence, and fighting broke out in the state legislatures and even in the Congress. With the wrestling on the floor of the House of Representatives in 1797 between Republican Matthew Lyon of Vermont and Federalist Roger Griswold of Connecticut, followed by Lyon's "outrageous" and "indecent" defense (he was reported in the

Annals of Congress to have said, "I did not come here to have my —— kicked by everybody"), some members concluded that Congress had become no better than a "tavern," filled with "*beasts,* and not gentlemen," and contemptible in the eyes of all "polite or genteel" societies.

Amid such passions the parties that emerged in the 1790s were unlike any later American political parties. Although the Federalists and the Republicans by 1796 were organized to win the presidency for their respective candidates, John Adams and Thomas Jefferson, both saw themselves in an increasingly revolutionary situation. The Federalists thought of themselves as the most enlightened and socially established members of the natural aristocracy, who by their very respectability were best able to carry out the responsibility of ruling the country. They thus affirmed that they were the government, not a "party." Parties, as Washington said in his Farewell Address, were equivalent to factions and could lead only to sedition and the disruption of the state.

Jefferson and many other Republicans shared this traditional eighteenth-century abhorrence of party, but under the extraordinary circumstances of the 1790s they had come to believe that organized opposition was justified. Because the Republicans thought the normal processes of American politics had become corrupted and poisoned by a Federalist government that had detached itself from the people, they felt pressed to create popular organizations of political opposition similar to those the Whigs had formed during the pre-Revolutionary crisis. Their goal in forming caucuses, corresponding committees, and Democratic-Republican societies was to band people together and use what they increasingly called "public opinion" to influence elections and counteract the weight of prominent individuals and the enlarged electoral districts of national politics. The

CARTOON LAMPOONING THE
LYON GRISWOLD TANGLE IN
CONGRESS IN 1797

He in a trice struck Lyon thrice
Upon his head, enraged sir.
Who seized the tongs to ease
   his wrongs,
And Griswold thus engaged, sir.
(New York Public Library.)

extralegal opposition of the Republican party would be a temporary but necessary instrument on behalf of the people to save their liberties from Federalist monarchism.

Nothing was more important in mobilizing the people into political consciousness than the press. Newspapers multiplied dramatically, from less than 100 in 1790 to over 230 by 1800; by 1810 Americans were buying over 22 million copies of 376 papers annually, the largest aggregate circulation of newspapers in any country in the world. By the late 90s many of these papers were in Republican hands, and with lower prices, with new eye-catching typography and cartoons, with the increased publication and vulgarization of political affairs, and in particular with the relentless criticism of Federalist officials, the press seemed to be single-handedly shaping American political life.

Although the Federalists began to adopt some of what they called the "petty electioneering arts" of the Republican opposition, they were not comfortable

"A PEEP INTO THE ANTIFEDERAL CLUB," 1793

This Federalist cartoon identifies the Republicans with the Anti-Federalists, or opponents of the Constitution, and with other disreputable elements.

with the new democratic politics. They saw themselves in traditional eighteenth-century terms as a gentlemanly elite to whom ordinary people, if they were only left alone, would naturally defer. The Federalists attributed the difficulties and disorder of the 1790s to the beguiling influence of demagogues and the proliferation of self-constituted extralegal associations. Republican upstarts and factions were stirring up the people's discontent against their natural rulers. They spread radical French principles, interfered with the electoral process, and herded the people, including recent immigrants, into political activity. New kinds of writers and publishers, like Congressman and editor Matthew Lyon of Vermont, were reaching out to influence an audience as obscure and ordinary as themselves. Through the scurrility and slander of their publications they were destroying the governing gentry's personal reputation for character on which popular respect for the entire political order was presumably based.

By the late 1790s, amid an economic depression and the "quasi-war" with France, all these Federalists' fears came together to justify the desperate repressive measures of 1798; this repression more than anything else has tarnished the historical reputation of the Federalists. In control of both the executive and the Congress, the Federalists contemplated various plans for strengthening the sinews holding the continental union together. They sought to augment the power of the federal judiciary, to increase the transportation network throughout the country, and to enlarge the army and navy. Above all, the Federalists aimed to end the Republicans' political exploitation of new immigrants and to stop up the flow of Republican literature that was poisoning the relations between rulers and ruled. In 1798 the Federalist-dominated Congress enacted Alien and Sedition Acts, which lengthened the naturalization process for foreigners, gave the President extraordinary powers to deal with aliens, and provided the central government with the authority to punish as crimes seditious libels against federal officials. At the same time the Congress ordered the immediate enlistment of a new regular army of 12,000 and laid plans for provisional armies numbering in the tens of thousands. Washington was to be called out of retirement as commander in chief of the new army, but Hamilton was to be actually in command. Presumably all this was done to meet the threat of a French invasion, but in the minds of some it was to deal with the domestic disorder of the United States. When the United States Army quickly suppressed an armed rebellion of several northeastern Pennsylvania counties led by John Fries in protest against the new federal direct tax on houses, land, and slaves, the advantages of federal energy were confirmed in some Federalist eyes.

For their part the Republicans in 1798–99 thought the very success of the American Revolution was at stake. In response to the Federalist repression, particularly the Alien and Sedition Acts, the Virginia and Kentucky legislatures issued resolutions, drawn up by Madison and Jefferson respectively. These resolutions proclaimed the right of the states to judge the constitutionality of federal acts and to interpose themselves between the citizenry and the unconstitutional actions of the central government. Although the other states declined to support Virginia and Kentucky, the stand taken by the two states opened a question about the nature of the union that would trouble the country for many years to come; it anticipated the far more radical effort at state nullification of federal law by South Carolina a generation later.

By the end of the decade several developments brought a measure of reconciliation. Both Madison and Jefferson were unwilling to resort to force to support their resolutions. British Admiral Horatio Nelson's naval victory over the French at the Battle of the Nile in October 1798 lessened the threat of a French invasion of either England or America. Most important in calming the crisis was the courageous decision in 1799 of President John Adams to send another peace mission to France despite the humiliating failure of his earlier effort in the X, Y, Z affair. Adams considered this decision to negotiate with France "the most disinterested, most determined and most successful of my whole life." France, now under Napoleon as first consul, agreed to make terms and in 1800 signed a convention with the United States that brought the "quasi-war" to a close. The end of the war crisis undermined the attempts of the extremist Federalists to strengthen the central government and build up the military might of the United States, and it irreparably divided the Federalist leadership between those moderates who supported Adams and those High Federalists who supported Hamilton. Although the worst was over, that was scarcely clear to everyone at the time. In 1800 the British ambassador still thought the "whole system of American Government" was "tottering to its foundations."

Government Without Power

Thomas Jefferson's election in 1800 as the third President of the United States confirmed the changing course of national developments. Despite opposition to the Federalist candidate, John Adams, from the Hamiltonians within his own party, Jefferson's electoral victory was very close, only 73 votes to Adams's 64. For a moment even that narrow victory was in doubt. Because the Constitution did not provide that the electors distinguish between their votes for President and Vice-President, both Jefferson and the Republican vice-presidential candidate Aaron Burr had received the same number of electoral votes, thus throwing the

THOMAS JEFFERSON, ARCHITECT; MONTICELLO; AND SKETCH ON THE ROTUNDA OF THE UNIVERSITY OF VIRGINIA

"Architecture," Thomas Jefferson once said, "is my delight, and putting up and pulling down one of my favorite amusements." Even as a young man, Jefferson was absorbed in designing and building his home at Monticello. He went at architecture with a mathematical precision; no detail of building — from the chemistry of mortar to the proper technique of laying bricks — was too insignificant for his attention. *(Portrait by R. Peale. Courtesy, The New-York Historical Society; Monticello, Massachusetts Historical Society.)*

election into the House of Representatives. After 35 deadlocked ballots, Hamilton and other Federalist leaders, preferring Jefferson to Burr and thinking they had assurances from Jefferson to continue Federalist policies, allowed the acknowledged Republican leader to become President. To avoid a repetition, the twelfth amendment to the Constitution, which allowed the electors to designate the President and Vice-President separately in their ballots, was quickly adopted.

In these confused electoral circumstances it is difficult to see the bold and revolutionary character of Jefferson's election. It was after all a revolution without violence—one of the first popular elections in modern history resulting in the peaceful transfer of governmental power from one "party" to another. At the outset Jefferson himself struck a note of conciliation: "We are all republicans—we are all federalists," he said in his inaugural address. Many Federalists were soon absorbed into the Republican cause. And the Republican administration did subsequently deviate from strict Republican principles. Thus the continuities are impressive, and the Jeffersonian "revolution of 1800" has blended nearly imperceptibly into the main democratic currents of American history. However, when compared with the consolidated state the Federalists tried to build in the 1790s, what the Republicans did after 1800 marked the real revolution that Jefferson said it was.

Believing that most of the evils afflicting mankind in the past had flowed from the abuses of political establishments, the Republicans in 1800 rejected outright the traditional eighteenth-century conviction cherished by the Federalists that government was the most effective mechanism of social integration. They set about deliberately to carry out what they rightly believed was the original libertarian aim of the Revolution of 1776—to reduce the overawing and dangerous power of government. They wanted to form a national republic based on their inherited country-Whig opposition ideology and cast in the image of the Revolutionary state governments of 1776 with their diluted executive powers. They envisioned a central state whose authority would resemble that of the old Articles of Confederation more than that of the European type of state the Federalists of the 1790s had thought essential in the modern world. They sought in fact to create a general government that would rule without the traditional attributes of power.

From the outset Jefferson was determined that the new government would be without even the usual rituals of power. At the very beginning he purposefully set a new tone of republican simplicity in contrast to the stiff formality and regal ceremony with which the Federalists, in imitation of European court life, had surrounded the presidency. Jefferson said that the day in March 1801 on which he became President "buried levees, birthdays, royal parades, and the arrogation of precedence in society by certain self-stiled friends of order, but truly stiled friends of privileged orders." Since the Federalist Presidents, like the English monarchs, had personally delivered their addresses to the legislature "from the throne," Jefferson chose to submit his in writing. Unlike Washington and Adams, he made himself easily accessible to visitors, all of whom, no matter how distinguished, he received, as the British chargé reported, "with a most perfect disregard to ceremony both in his dress and manner." Much to the shock of foreign dignitaries, at American state occasions he replaced the protocol and distinctions of European court life with the egalitarian rules of what he called "pell mell" or "next the door."

While Jefferson's gentlemanly tastes scarcely allowed any actual leveling in social gatherings, his symbolic transformation of manners at the capital harmonized with a changing social reality. For the Republican revolution soon brought to the national government men who, unlike Jefferson, were without the marks of gentlemen, who did not know one another, and who were decidedly not at home in polite society. During the following years of the early nineteenth century, life in the national capital became steadily vulgarized by the growing presence in drawing rooms of muddy boots, unkempt hair, and the constant chawing and spitting of tobacco.

Even the removal of the national capital in 1800 from Philadelphia, the bustling intellectual and commercial center of the country, to the rural wilderness of the "federal city" on the Potomac accentuated the transformation of power that was taking place. It dramatized the Republicans' attempt to separate the national government from intimate involvement in the society and their aim to erect the very kind of general government Hamilton in *The Federalist,* No. 27, had warned against, "a government at a distance and out of sight" that could "hardly be expected to interest the sensations of the people." This new and remote capital of Washington, D.C., utterly failed to attract the population, the commerce, and the social and cultural life needed to make it what its original planners had boldly expected, the Rome of the New World. By 1820 Washington was an out-of-the-way village of less than ten thousand inhabitants, whose principal business was keeping boardinghouses. Situated in a marsh and as one observer said, "bearing the marks of partial labour and general desertion," the federal city fully deserved the gibes of the visiting Irish poet, Thomas Moore:

> This embryo capital
> where Fancy sees
> Squares in Morasses,
> obelisks in trees.

The Republicans in fact meant to have an insignificant national government. The federal government, Jefferson declared in his first message to Congress in 1801, was "charged with the external and mutual relations only of these states." The "principal care of our persons, our property, and our reputation, constituting the great field of human concerns," was to be left to the states. Such a limited national government demanded turning back a decade of Federalism for the sake of restoring what the Virginia Republican theorist John Taylor of Caroline called the "pristine health" of the Constitution. The Sedition Act was allowed to lapse and a new liberal naturalization law was adopted. Because of what Jefferson saw as the Federalists' "dissipation of treasure," rigorous economy was invoked to root out corruption. The inherited Federalist governmental establishment was minuscule by modern standards and was small even by eighteenth-century European standards; in 1801 the headquarters of the war department, for example, consisted of only the secretary, an accountant, fourteen clerks, and two messengers; and the attorney general did not have even a clerk. Nevertheless, in Jefferson's eyes, this tiny federal bureaucracy had become "too complicated, too expensive," and offices under the Federalists had "unnecessarily multiplied." Thus the roll of federal officials was severely cut back. All tax inspectors and collectors were eliminated. The diplomatic establishment was reduced to three missions—in Britain, France, and Spain. The Federalist dream of creating a modern army and navy in emulation of Europe disappeared; the military budget was cut in half. The army, stationed only in the West, was left with 3000 regulars and only 172 officers. The navy had but a half-dozen frigates, and by 1807 these were replaced with several hundred gunboats designed only to defend the coast or to deal with the Barbary pirates in the Mediterranean. The benefits of a standing military establishment, the Jeffersonians believed, were not worth the cost either in money or in the threat to liberty it posed.

Since Hamilton's financial program had formed the basis of the heightened political power of the federal government, it above all had to be dismantled. All the internal taxes the Federalists had designed to make the people feel the energy of the national government were eliminated; for most citizens the federal presence was now reduced to the delivery of the mails. Such an inconsequential and distant government, noted one observer in 1811, was "too little felt in the ordinary concerns of life to vie in any considerable degree with the near and more powerful influence produced by the operations of the local governments." Although Jefferson's extremely able secretary of the Treasury, Albert Gallatin, persuaded the reluctant President to keep the Bank of the United States, the government was under continual pressure to reduce the Bank's influence. The growing numbers of state banking interests were resentful of the privileged and restraining authority of the Bank. By 1811 a combination of these interests and those of Southern planters, who hated all banks, eventually prevented a renewal of the Bank's charter. The federal government than distributed its patronage among twenty-one state banks and effectively diluted its authority to control either the society or the economy.

Just as Hamilton had regarded the permanent federal debt as a principal source of support for the federal government, so the Republicans were determined to pay off the debt, and quickly. By 1810 the federal debt had been reduced to nearly half of the $80 million it had been when the Republicans took office. Jefferson's lifelong desire to amortize the government's debt was not simply a matter of prohibiting a present generation from burdening posterity, but a matter of destroying an insidious and dangerous instrument of political influence. If the public debt were not extinguished, he warned Gallatin in 1809 "we shall be committed to the English career of debt, corruption and rottenness, closing with revolution. The discharge of the debt, therefore, is vital to the destinies of our government."

These destinies involved creating a new kind of government, one without preferments, privilege, or patronage. Perhaps nothing illustrates Jefferson's radical conception of government better than his problems with patronage, that powerful engine of "influence" for eighteenth-century state secretaries from Walpole to Hamilton. Not all Republicans took his assault on patronage as seriously as he did, and many were often reluctant to join a government in which they would have no sources of influence. With the slashing reductions contemplated for the navy, for example, Jefferson had to go to his fifth choice before he could get someone to serve as secretary of the navy. By the end of his second term Jefferson concluded despairingly that the removal and appointment of officeholders had been the heaviest burden of his office. Time and again he had found himself caught between his conscientious determination to avoid any semblance of Hamiltonian corruption and the pressing demands of his fellow Republicans to give them a share in the government and oust the enemy. Thus Jefferson was repeatedly forced into excruciating and sometimes contrived explanations for his removal of Federalist officeholders. Once the anti-Revolutionary Federalists were replaced by Republicans, however, it became no longer possible by republican principles to justify subsequent removals. Thus by the time of his Republican presidential successors, James Madison (1809–17), James Monroe (1817–25), and John Quincy Adams (1825–29) the government departments had become a permanent officialdom filled with men growing old in their positions.

(Courtesy of The New-York Historical Society, New York City.)

REPUBLICANS

Turn out, turn out and save your Country from ruin !

From an *Emperor*—from a *King*—from the iron grasp of a *British Tory Faction*—an unprincipled banditti of British speculators. The hireling tools and emissaries of his majesty king George the 3d have thronged our city and diffused the poison of principles among us.

DOWN WITH THE TORIES, DOWN WITH THE BRITISH FACTION,

Before they have it in their power to enslave you, and reduce your families to distress by heavy taxation. Republicans want no Tribute-liars—they want no ship Ocean-liars—they want no Rufus King's for Lords —they want no Varick to lord it over them—they want no Jones for senator, who fought with the British against the Americans in time of the war.—But they want in their places such men as

Jefferson & Clinton,

who fought their Country's Battles in the year '76

Until the new Jacksonian revolution of 1828 patronage as a means of influence in government virtually ceased.

Jefferson through a combination of this initial patronage and some improvised forms of political influence (in particular his nightly legislative dinner parties and the use of confidential legislative agents) was able to maintain a remarkable degree of personal direction over the Congress and the Republican party. Yet Jefferson's personal strength and his notable achievements as President cannot hide the remarkable transformation in the traditional meaning of government that the Republican revolution of 1800 created. During the opening three decades of the nineteenth century, particularly after Jefferson retired from the presidency, the United States government was more feeble than at any other time in its national history.

Politics became increasingly confused, and the Federalists and the Republicans did little to organize it. Although the Federalists in 1800–01 had delayed Jefferson's election by holding out for Aaron Burr, they had been willing to surrender the national ruling authority without a fight. Because the Federalist leaders considered themselves gentlemen for whom politics was not an exclusive concern, they were prepared like the Roman patriot Cato to retire to their businesses and private lives and await what they assumed would soon be the people's desperate call for the return of the "wise and good" and the "natural rulers." But the popular reaction they expected to the Republican revolution never came. Consequently, the Federalists often found themselves in a position similar to that of the Tories in 1776. Some like John Jay and John Adams retired to their country estates. Others like John Quincy Adams, the son of the former President, and William Plumer of New Hampshire eventually joined the Republican movement. Others, like Robert Goodloe Harper of South Carolina and James A. Bayard of Delaware, clung to their principles and their generally minority status in the Congress or in their state governments. And still others, like Timothy Pickering, secretary of state under Adams, and Roger Griswold, later governor of Connecticut, from their strongholds in New England dreamed of revenge and fomented separatist plots. But as a national party Federalism slowly withered under the relentless democratization of American society.

Although the Federalists and Republicans continued to compete for election (as a result there was a sudden but temporary tripling of voter participation during the first fifteen years of the nineteenth century), neither was a party in any modern sense; and it is probably anachronistic to call their electoral competition, as many historians have done, "the first party system." In 1805 and 1808 the Federalists ran Charles Cotesworth Pinckney of South Carolina for the presidency; in 1812 it was De Witt Clinton of New York, and in 1816 Rufus King of New York. But Federalist electoral strength was generally negligible and mostly confined to New England. By 1820 the Federalists were too weak even to put up a candidate.

While the declining Federalist gentry regarded themselves less as a party than as dispossessed rulers, the Republicans saw themselves as an extraordinary revolutionary movement eager to incorporate the bulk of the dissidents into the nation. Only as long as the Federalists posed a threat to the principles of free government could the Republicans remain a unified party. Therefore as the possibility of a Federalist resurgence receded, the Republican party gradually fell apart. Within the common Republican faith arose a variety of factions and groups in the Congress and in the country organized around particular individuals (the "Burrites," the "Clintonians"), around states and sections (the "Pennsylvania Quids," the "Old Republicans" of Virginia), or around ideology ("the principles of '98," the "Invisibles," the "War Hawks"). Individual politicians continued to pride themselves on their independence from influence of any sort, and "party" remained a pejorative term. In fact, until the Jacksonian era nothing approaching a stable party system developed in the Congress.

By the end of Jefferson's presidency in 1809 the balance of governmental power had slipped to the Congress, which was unequipped to exercise it. Because of the great increase in the size of Congress and its growing disintegration into diverse voting blocs, neither Madison nor Monroe was able to use any of the personal presidential charm and influence that Jefferson had used. By 1808 caucuses of Republicans within the Congress had taken over nomination of the party's candidates for the presidency, and Republican presidential aspirants soon became dependent on the legislature in the way governors in the Revolutionary state constitutions of 1776 had been. While Secretary of State James Madison was able with Jefferson's private blessing to secure the Republican nomination in 1808 and again in 1812 against only some divided opposition, in 1816 Madison's secretary of state, James Monroe, had to contend strenuously with Secretary of War William H. Crawford of Georgia for the nomination. By the early 1820s, Secretary of State John Quincy Adams, Secretary of War John C. Calhoun, and Secretary of the Treasury Crawford were all feuding with one another and seeking support in the Congress for the presidential nomination. If such political realities did not dictate presidential subservence to the legislature, Republican ideology did. Except in foreign affairs, both Presidents Madison and Monroe, the second and third members of the "Virginia Dynasty," regarded Congress as the rightful determinant of the public will free of executive influence.

As the Congress in Madison's and Monroe's administrations gathered up the power passing from the executive, it sought to organize itself into committees in order to initiate and supervise policy. But the rise of the committee system only further fragmented the government into contending interests. The executive authority itself broke apart into competing departments, each seeking its own support in the Congress and becoming a rival of the President. Congress now fought with the President for control of the cabinet and connived with executive department heads behind the President's back. At one point the Congress actually forced Madison to accept a secretary of state who was intriguing against him, and its meddling drove Monroe into bitter hostility against his secretary of the treasury, with whom he stopped speaking. Until the congressional caucus system of presidential nomination collapsed in 1824 and a new kind of democratic plebiscitary presidency emerged with the election in 1828 of Andrew Jackson, the energy of the national executive remained weak and dissipated.

But even amid this absorption in strict republican principles there were other Americans coming forth to reclaim and reenact some of the abandoned Federalist measures. A new generation of politicians, less attached to the ideology and fears of the eighteenth century and without any sense of Hamilton's driving dream to create a consolidated European-like state, now began urging a new national bank, protective tariffs, and a federally sponsored program of internal improvements. By 1815 the nation had grown faster than anyone had expected, and new states, new interests, and new outlooks had to be taken into account. By then it was becoming clear that the future of the country lay in the West.

An Empire of Liberty

While Hamilton and the Federalists had looked eastward across the Atlantic to Europe for their image of the destiny of the United States, the Republicans from the beginning had had their eyes on the West. Because they had always had, as Jefferson said as early as 1781, "a peculiar confidence in the men from the western side of the mountains," they immediately began a liberalization of federal land policy, seeing the western lands as something more than a source of revenue. For twenty years after 1800 Republican congresses lowered the price of land, reduced the size of purchasable tracts, and relaxed the terms of credit for settlers. But in fulfilling Jefferson's continental vision of an "empire of liberty" all these measures were nothing compared with his sudden acquisition in 1803 of the entire Louisiana territory, which extended from the Mississippi to the Rockies.

For decades Jefferson and other American leaders had foreseen that the natural expansiveness of this young and thriving nation would "piece by piece" inevitably take over the feebly held Spanish possessions in North America. When the Revolutionary war ended in 1783, Jefferson was already dreaming of explorations to the Pacific; and when he became President, well before he had any inkling of America's purchasing the whole Louisiana territory, he laid plans for ostensibly scientific but also military and commercial expeditions into the foreign-held trans-Mississippi West.

While several expeditions in 1804 and 1805 unsuccessfully explored the sources of the Red River, two others in 1805 and 1806 under Lieutenant Zebulon Pike went up first the Mississippi and then the Arkansas River into what is now Colorado. The most famous of these western expeditions was led by army veterans Meriwether Lewis, Jefferson's private secretary, and William Clark, younger brother of the Indian fighter George Rogers Clark. With a party of fifty-one men Lewis and Clark left St. Louis in May 1804, went up the Missouri River, and wintered in Mandan Indian villages in present-day North Dakota. In 1805 they crossed the Rockies and descended the Snake and Colorado rivers to the Pacific, returning east in 1806. The explorers brought back new scientific information about the Indians, animals, and fauna of western North America, and strengthened American claims to the Oregon territory.

At the same time that Jefferson was exploring the trans-Mississippi West, he worked out an Indian policy for those tribes living in the United States east of the Mississippi. Essentially the policy envisioned surrounding the Indians with white settlers and circumscribing their hunting lands. Jefferson expected that either such white settlements would force the Indians into farming and thus into becoming civilized citizens of the United States, or they would compel the Indians into ceding their lands and moving beyond the Mississippi. When the Indians refused to be assimilated into American society, Presidents Jefferson and Madison negotiated fifty-three treaties of land cession. Given Jeffersonian assumptions about the proper nature of a republican society, full assimilation or removal were the only alternatives. Strict republican principles demanded that the yeoman farmer, cultivating his own land and beholden to no man, be the foundation of the new nation; the open western territory guaranteed the future of that foundation.

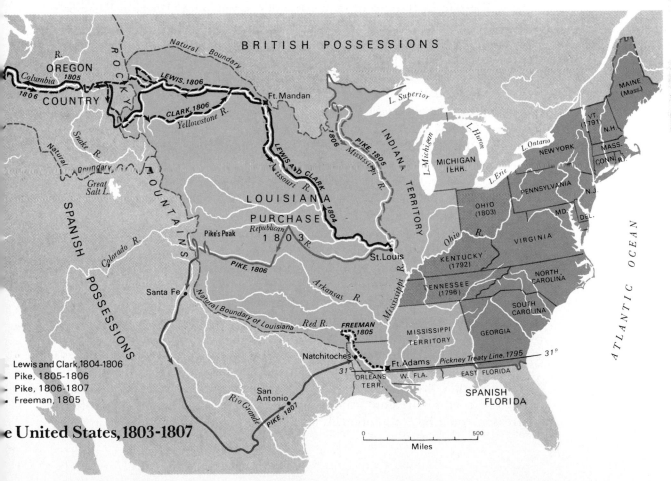

Lewis and Clark, 1804-1806
Pike, 1805-1806
Pike, 1806-1807
Freeman, 1805

e United States, 1803-1807

When in 1800 in the treaty of San Ildefonso a weak Spain ceded back to a powerful France the Louisiana territory it had formerly held west of the Mississippi, including New Orleans and the gateway to the Gulf of Mexico, a "profound reconsideration" of American prospects became imperative to Jefferson. Determined to maintain at any cost the free navigation of the Mississippi on which the livelihood of the Western farmers depended, Jefferson immediately began strengthening fortifications in the West and preparing for the worst. "The day that France takes possession of New Orleans," he informed his American minister to France, Robert Livingston, in April 1802, "we must marry ourselves to the British fleet and nation." This threat of a British alliance, together with Napoleon's reappraisal of the difficulties involved in reestablishing the French empire in the New World in the event of renewed war in Europe, led the French government in 1803 to decide to sell to the United States not just New Orleans, which Jefferson had sought to purchase, but all of Louisiana for $15 million.

Jefferson hesitated and pondered the need for amending the Constitution to justify acquiring this new territory and incorporating it into the Union. But finally and regretfully, under very intense pressure, he allowed his constitutional scruples over the limited powers of the federal government to be passed over in silence. Despite its fulfillment of his grandest dreams for America, Jefferson's agonized decision was far from suggesting any sort of concession to a broad Federalist interpretation of the Constitution. His hesitation only showed the seriousness with which he took his strict construction of the Constitution.

The purchase of Louisiana was the most popular and momentous event of Jefferson's presidency. Not only did it end the long struggle for control of the Mississippi's outlet to the sea, but also, as Jefferson exulted, it freed America from Europe's colonial entanglements and prepared the way for the eventual dominance of the United States in the Western Hemisphere. Its most immediate consequence, however, was to double the size of the United States, and to raise fears once again of the country's splitting apart. The borders of the new territory were so vague, the Spanish hold on Mexico and the Floridas so weak, and the rough and unruly frontier inhabitants so captivated by the dreams of America's destined expansion that adventurers, filibustering expeditions, and rumors of plots and conspiracies flourished throughout the South and the West.

The most grandiose of these military schemes was that of 1806–1807 involving Aaron Burr, Jefferson's former Vice-President, and (until he turned state's evidence) General James Wilkinson, commanding general of the United States Army secretly in the pay of the Spanish government, and one of the most unscrupulous and skillful adventurers in American history. In the summer of 1806 Burr and sixty men in flatboats floated down the Ohio and Mississippi towards New Orleans. When Burr learned that Wilkinson had denounced him, he fled towards Florida, probably on his way to Europe, but was captured and brought East to be tried for treason. Although Burr was acquitted because no overt act of treason could be constitutionally proved, he undoubtedly had had in mind some sort of conspiracy, involving a number of American military and civil officials, directed towards an attack on Mexico or a separation of the western areas of the United States. It was precisely these kinds of activities and the danger of splintering that caused the Congress in these years to incorporate into the Union as fast as possible the underdeveloped frontier territories of Ohio (1803), Louisiana (1810), Indiana (1816), Mississippi (1817), Illinois (1818), and Alabama (1819).

It was the Federalists who were especially alarmed by the acquisition of Louisiana. With their vision of the United States as a homogeneous and integrated nation-state like those of Europe, it was inconceivable to the Federalists that such a gigantic republic could long hold together. To the Republicans, however, with their conception of the United States as a loosely bound confederation of states, the huge expanse of territory posed no problems. "Who can limit the extent to which the federative principle may operate effectively?" asked Jefferson in his second inaugural address. Jefferson's "empire of liberty" was always one of like principles, not of like boundaries; and he was at times remarkably indifferent to the possibility that a western confederacy might break away from the eastern United States. What did it matter? he said in 1804. "Those of the western confederacy will be as much our children and descendents as those of the eastern."

The Federalists called it "a most visionary theory." Hamilton thought that the Republicans, by abandoning both force and governmental corruption, the main instruments by which eighteenth-century governments had held their growing societies together and ruled, were offering "the bewitching tenets of that illuminated doctrine, which promises men, ere long, an emancipation from the burdens and restraints of government." The consequence to the Federalists could only be eventual anarchy. But in the Republican conception, Americans were creating new bonds of social cohesion, not the virtue of classical republicanism perhaps, but, as Jefferson said, "that progress of opinion which is tending to unite them in object and in will."

The Origins of Judicial Review

In time the judiciary would become an important influence in the formation of this public opinion, but not in 1800. At Jefferson's election no institution of the national government was more detested by the Republicans than the judiciary. Not only were the appointed federal judges less susceptible to popular rule than other parts of the government, but during the 1790s the Federalists had consciously sought to strengthen the federal courts as a way of extending the central government's presence among the people. Since there was not a single Republican judge in the entire national judiciary during the 1790s, Republican newspaper editors had often been abused in the federal courts by sedition actions. Moreover, Federalist land speculators with interests that spanned state lines, like participants in the Yazoo Company of Georgia, had used the more sympathetic federal courts to resolve their conflicting claims to the anger of the often-Republican-controlled state courts. Even after the Federalists had lost the election of 1800, the lame duck Congress dominated by Federalists had passed a new judiciary act creating a system of circuit courts and broadening the jurisdiction of the federal courts. Before surrendering the presidency to Jefferson, John Adams had hastily appointed a number of judges, including John Marshall as chief justice of the United States. Jefferson could scarcely have anticipated that Marshall's career as chief justice would go on for another generation, spanning the administrations of five Presidents and helping to establish the supremacy of the national government. Yet even in 1801 he was convinced that "the remains of federalism" had "retired into the judiciary as a stronghold . . ., and from that battery all the works of republicanism are to be beaten down and erased."

To complete "the revolution," therefore, as William Brand Giles of Virginia told Jefferson, "the enemy" had to be routed from "that strong fortress." After

CHIEF-JUSTICE AND MRS. OLIVER ELLSWORTH, 1792, BY RALPH EARL

Ellsworth (1745–1807) represented Connecticut in the federal convention. He is shown with a copy of the Constitution in his hand. As Senator from Connecticut 1789 to 1796 he helped to lay out the federal court system and was chief justice of the Supreme Court from 1796 to 1801. His wife was a member of the distinguished Wolcott family of Connecticut. *(Courtesy Wadsworth Atheneum.)*

a bitter debate in the Congress, the Republicans repealed the Federalist Judiciary Act of 1801. They thus destroyed the newly created circuit courts and for the first and only time in United States history abrogated the tenure of federal judges as well. In order to bring the entire judicial establishment under greater congressional control, some Republicans proposed amending the Constitution. Others, however, fixed on impeachment for "high crimes and misdemeanors" (despite Jefferson's belief that it was a "bungling way") as the best constitutional device available for removing obnoxious Federalist judges. The Republicans in the House of Representatives first impeached and the Senate then convicted John Pickering, an alcoholic and insane judge of the federal district court of New Hampshire, even though he had committed no crimes or misdemeanors.

With this broad construction of the criminal meaning of impeachment in hand, the most rabid Republicans under the leadership of John Randolph of Virginia, the conscience of the principles of "Old Republicanism," next turned to bring down Supreme Court Justice Samuel Chase, the most overbearing Federalist on the Court. However, this perversion of the impeachment process into a mode of removal was too much for some Republicans. While a majority of the Senate in 1805 found Chase guilty, the Republicans could not muster the necessary two-thirds majority. Not only did Chase's acquittal hurt Randolph's reputation, driving him to the extremist edges of the Republican party, but it ended any further direct assault by the Republicans on the national judiciary.

In the meantime John Marshall from his position as chief justice of the Supreme Court had managed to drain some of the crisis from the controversy over the judiciary and at the same time to lay the foundation for the Court's eventual independence. Although Marshall solidified the Court by making one justice's opinion, usually his own, stand for the decision of the whole Court, he moved very cautiously. Instead of directly and disastrously confronting the Congress by declaring the Republicans' repeal of the Judiciary Act of 1801 unconstitutional, as many Federalists had urged, Marshall and the Court in the case of *Marbury* v. *Madison* (1803) chose to deal with part of the earlier Judiciary Act of 1789, which a Federalist Congress had enacted. Thus Marshall could obliquely assert the Court's role in overseeing the Constitution without the serious political repercussions involved in opposing the Republicans. Since the American people regarded their written Constitution as "the fundamental and paramount law of the nation," wrote Marshall for the Court, then it followed that "a law repugnant to the constitution," such as part of the Judiciary Act of 1789, "is void; and that courts, as well as other departments, are bound by that instrument."

Although Marshall's decision in *Marbury* v. *Madison* has since taken on immense historical significance as the first judicial assertion by the Supreme Court of its right to declare acts of Congress unconstitutional, few in 1803 saw its momentous implications. Such a right was nowhere explicitly recognized in the Constitution; and despite numerous statements justifying such a right of what came to be called judicial review, and despite examples of its use in the state courts in the years after the Revolution, such a judicial authority was by no means unquestionably established in American thinking by 1800. *Marbury* v. *Madison* was in fact the only time in Marshall's long tenure in which the Supreme Court declared an act of Congress unconstitutional.

To be sure, on many subsequent occasions the Marshall Court asserted its right to protect the power of the federal government and the property rights of individuals against the states. In *Martin* v. *Hunter's Lessee* (1816) and *Cohens* v. *Virginia* (1812), Marshall established the Court's right to review and reverse decisions of state courts involving interpretations of federal law and the federal Constitution. And in other important decisions, following the first test in *Fletcher* v. *Peck* (1810), the Supreme Court nullified state laws that violated the Constitution. In probably the most significant of these cases, *McCulloch* v. *Maryland* (1819), Marshall upheld the right of the Congress to charter a national bank as part of the "necessary and proper" authority the Constitution granted to the Congress so that it could carry its delegated powers into effect. Thus an attempt by the Maryland legislature to destroy the Bank by taxation was declared unconstitutional.

In all these judicial assertions of national authority, the Marshall Court rested its arguments, in the words of the *McCulloch* decision, on the "great principle

JOHN MARSHALL, 1755–1835, BY
WILLIAM HUBARD

Marshall is the most famous chief
Justice of the Supreme Court in
American history. During his
long tenure on the Court from
1801 to his death, this Virginia
Federalist participated in more
than 1000 decisions, writing over
half himself. In effect Marshall
created for America what came to
be called constitutional law and
transformed the meaning and
role of the Supreme Court.
*(National Portrait Gallery,
Smithsonian Institution, Washington,
D.C.)*

that the constitution and the laws thereof are supreme; that they control the constitution and laws of the respective states, and cannot be controlled by them." Although the Court clearly had a right and duty to declare what the supreme law was, it was not clear that such a role for the Court among the other parts of the national government was unique. Certainly in the *Marbury* decision Marshall's assertion of judicial authority was ambiguous and seemed to imply that the other departments in the government had an equal obligation with the courts to construe the law in accord with the Constitution. Jefferson certainly believed that the executive and the legislature had the same ultimate right as the judiciary to interpret the Constitution, and throughout his life he explicitly denied the "exclusive" authority of the judiciary to decide what laws were constitutional. Such a monopoly of interpretative power, he said in 1804, "would make the judiciary a despotic branch."

Today the right of the justices of the Supreme Court, indeed the right of all judges in all courts, both federal and state, to interpret acts of legislatures and to set aside those violating the fundamental laws—whether the federal Constitution, the state constitutions, or even at times those principles of right and justice that presumably underlie all law—this judicial authority is now so well established, so much taken for granted, that it is difficult to appreciate either its distinctiveness or the problematic character of its origins. When the Constitution was drafted, not all American leaders were ready to allow "Judges to set aside the law" made by the representatives of the people. "This," said Madison in 1788, "makes the Judiciary Department paramount in fact to the Legislature, which was never intended and can never be proper."

Only when Americans began to appreciate their newly clarified conception of the sovereignty of the people, with its implication that no legislative body no matter how representative was superior to the people who created the constitution, were they able to justify this emerging practice of judicial review. Judicial review did not "by any means suppose a superiority of the judicial to the legislative power," wrote Hamilton in *The Federalist*, No. 78. "It only supposes that the power of the people is superior to both; and that where the will of the legislature declared in its statutes, stands in opposition to that of the people, declared in the constitution, the judges . . . ought to regulate their decisions by the fundamental laws, rather than by those which are not fundamental."

But even this does not fully explain the origins of the authority wielded by American judges. For what in the final analysis gives meaning to the Americans' unusual notion of a constitution is not its fundamentality or its creation by the people but its implementation in the ordinary courts of law. The idea of fundamental law was after all an old one in Western political thought and had been invoked time and again by theorists with little sense that such a higher or natural law ought to be part of the everyday process of adjudication. Other countries since the eighteenth century have had formal written constitutions without allowing their judges in the regular court system the power of judicial review. It was not simply "the particular provisions of the Constitution of the United States" that John Marshall applied in his important 1810 decision of *Fletcher* v. *Peck*, nullifying a Georgia statute, but also, as he said, those "general principles which are common to our free institutions." In the end it was the Americans' ambiguous and instrumental conception of the law itself and not just their notion of a written constitution that lay at the heart of judicial review.

The legal confusion and uncertainties of the colonial period had exaggerated the inherent malleability of the English common law. Since the colonists had derived their law haphazardly both from their provincial legislatures and courts and from various English sources, they tended to equate law not with what English judges and legal authorities said it was, but with what made sense in America's local circumstances. Although colonial law by the middle of the eighteenth century had approached the sophistication of English law very closely, approximating the English common law forms and procedures without actually duplicating them had compelled Americans time and again to justify minor deviations and irregularities in the name of reason, justice, or utility.

Americans thus created a particularly manipulative attitude toward law that the decades following the Revolution only intensified. In the emerging business society of early nineteenth-century America, the desired predictability of law came not from strict adherence to precedent but from rapid adaptability to changing commercial circumstances. To mold the law to fit the needs of America's expanding enterprise, judges in the federal and state courts increasingly abandoned the customs and technicalities of the inherited English common law and replaced them with pragmatic and prudent regulations, justified by what jurist Jesse Root in 1798 called "the reasonableness and utility of their operation." By the second decade of the nineteenth century, American law was coming to be thought of as self-consciously changeable and man-made, as a creative instrument of social policy. And judges under fast-moving economic pressures were becoming the chief agents of legal change. Only the courts, Ezpheniah Swift, chief justice of the Connecticut supreme court, declared in 1810, "possess a discretion of shaping the rules . . . [and] furnishing remedies according to the growing wants, and varying circumstances of men, . . . without waiting for the slow progress of Legislative interference." The judicial interpretative power inherent in the plasticity of American law from the beginning was now starkly revealed and liberally expanded.

Despite continued antielitist efforts in the early nineteenth century to weaken judicial authority through codification, law in America maintained its pliable and instrumental quality. Although judges continued to deny that they made law in the way legislatures did, it was obvious that they did something more than simply discover it in the precedents and customs of the past. Law in America, rooted in the consent and sovereignty of the people, was designed to serve the needs of that people, and when it did not, it was the obligation of judges to manipulate it in such a way that it did. In fact, if neither legislatures nor judges could act fast enough to shape the law to changing circumstances, then some Americans thought that the people themselves, in extralegal groups and "mobs," had the right to take the law into their own hands and mold it as their situation demanded.

The peculiar American practices of judicial review and vigilantism were actually two sides of the same legal coin.

Republican Diplomacy and War

The dramatic culmination of the Republicans' revolution of 1800 came in the War of 1812. It was an unusual war, a "metaphysical war" John Taylor of Caroline called it, "a war, not for conquest, not for defense, not for sport" but a war on which the entire experiment in free government seemed to rest. It was a war that few wanted but that many had made inevitable. It was a war that in the end solved nothing, but that was widely regarded as a glorious victory—"the triumph of virtue over vice," as one Republican congressman from Pennsylvania said in 1815, "of republican men and republican principles over the advocates and doctrines of tyranny."

The origins of the War of 1812 lay in the drawn-out logic of American principles of foreign relations first articulated at the time of the Revolution. The American Revolution had been centrally concerned with power, not only power within a state but power among states in their international relations. Throughout the eighteenth century liberal intellectuals had looked forward to a rational world in which corrupt monarchical diplomacy and secret alliances, balances of power, and dynastic conflicts would be eliminated. In short, they had dreamed of nothing less than an end of war and a new era of peace. Just as eighteenth-century liberals like Thomas Paine believed that the harmony of society ought to rest not on artificial governmental institutions but on the natural affections among men, so too did they believe that the peace of the world ought to rely not on artificial military treaties among kings but on natural commercial relations among nations. War, the Enlightenment thought, was the product of the personal ambitions of monarchs, not of popular will. If the people of the various nations were left alone to exchange goods freely among themselves, then international politics would become republicanized and pacified.

Suddenly in 1776 with the isolation of the United States outside the European mercantile empires, the Americans had an opportunity and a need to put these liberal ideas about the free exchange of goods into practice. Thus commercial interest and Revolutionary idealism blended to form the basis for American thinking about foreign affairs that lasted until well into the first half of the twentieth century. Americans first expressed these principles during discussions over the prospective treaty with France at the time of Independence. Many in the Congress in 1776 sought to work out a model treaty to be applied to France and eventually to other states that would avoid the traditional kinds of political and military commitments and concentrate instead on an exclusively commercial connection. Ideally such a commercial relation would involve absolute reciprocity, each nation treating the traders of the other as it treated its own nationals. In time of war, neutrals would be able to trade liberally with belligerents; blockades of belligerent ports ought to be backed up by ships and not simply declared on paper; and except for a very restricted list of contraband, the goods on neutral carriers, even when they were belligerent goods, ought to be free from seizure.

Amid the unrestricted warfare that the twentieth century is used to, such rules and regulations governing belligerency, with their adjudication in the belligerents' own prize courts, seem incredibly quaint. Yet such maritime laws, despite great abuses, were taken seriously by eighteenth-century European states. In 1776 the most liberal interpretation of them—the principle that "free ships made free goods"—formed for Americans the foundation of their foreign policy, a principle that Woodrow Wilson was still trying to uphold in the general European conflict nearly a century and a half later. Not only would such a pattern of commercial treaties isolate the United States from the corrupting practices of traditional European diplomacy, but also, it was hoped, it would eventually revolutionize European international relations.

Although the Americans in the treaties of 1778 were unable to secure such an exclusively commercial arrangement with France on the liberal terms they desired, and in fact had to settle for a traditional European kind of military alliance, many never lost their enlightened hope that international politics could be made over. The Federalists, however, rejected many of these enlightened international dreams. Hamilton in particular denied the liberal assumption that republics were naturally pacific and that commerce was an adequate substitute for the power politics of traditional diplomacy. While Jefferson, Madison, and other Republicans continued to urge a policy of commercial discrimination against Great Britain in order to break the former mother country's hold on the American economy, Hamilton and the Federalists relied on the British commercial connection as the foundation of their program.

The outbreak of war between Great Britain and revolutionary France in 1792 highlighted these contrasting Republican and Federalist perspectives. The European war precipitated a struggle by Americans for a recognition of their neutral rights in a belligerent world. Unable to control the seas, France threw open its empire in the West Indies to American commerce. Britain retaliated by invoking what was called the Rule of 1756. This rule, first enunciated in the Seven Years War, enabled British prize courts, that is, courts that adjudged the legitimacy of the seizure of enemy ships or goods, to deny the right of neutral nations in time of war to trade with belligerent ports that had been closed to them in time of peace. Between 1793 and 1794 Britain seized over three hundred American merchant ships and at the same time began impressing or forcibly removing seamen from American vessels on the grounds that they were British subjects. Since Great Britain refused to recognize the right of expatriation, which was

crucial to a nation of immigrants, conflict over the nationality of American seamen, many of whom were deserters from the British navy, was inevitable. Thus
was begun the provocative British practice of impressment—"this authorized
system of kidnapping upon the ocean," John Quincy Adams later called it—
which until it was ended by the general European peace of 1815 resulted in an
estimated ten thousand sailors forcibly taken from American ships. Rather than
go to war with England and endanger their financial program, the Federalists,
with Jay's treaty of 1795, silently sacrificed America's liberal interpretation of
neutral rights for the sake of continuing trade with Great Britain.

In contrast to the Federalists, who prepared for the approaching war with
France in 1797–98 by building up the government and armed forces of the
United States in the traditional manner of European power politics, the Republicans clung to the idealistic principles of government and diplomacy they identified with the Revolution of 1776. In Republican thinking, the American republic did not need, nor could it safely afford, the conventional attributes of state
power and a European kind of army and navy; it did not even need an elaborate
diplomatic establishment. While some Republicans in the 1790s urged reducing

BUILDING THE FRIGATE "PHILADELPHIA"

All seven of the frigates of the United States Navy that
fought the War of 1812 were built in the 1790s, when war
with France threatened. The Federalists also wanted to
build some ships of the line, which had more decks and
nearly twice as many guns as frigates. Although the
Federalists acquired timber and six navy yards, the accession
of the Republicans in 1801 ended their plans for enlarging
the Navy. (*Prints Division, The New York Public Library, Astor,
Lenox and Tilden Foundations.*)

American diplomatic posts to only those in London and Paris, others favored replacing the entire American representation abroad with consuls, who were all that were required to handle matters of international trade. At times Jefferson even talked wistfully of abandoning all international commerce so that the United States might "stand, with respect to Europe, precisely on the footing of China." More often, however, he and other Republicans saw American commerce not as an object to be protected by national policy, as the Federalists did, but as a political weapon to be used as an alternative to war in the way the colonists had used nonimportation and nonexportation in the pre-Revolutionary crisis with Great Britain.

With the resumption of the conflict between Britain and France in 1803, the Republicans, now in control of the national government, at last had an opportunity to put their policies to a test. Since Britain was unable to contest on land Napoleon's domination of the continent of Europe, it was determined to exploit its supremacy on the seas to blockade France into submission. As the largest neutral carrier of goods in the world, the United States was bound to be the principal victim of such a naval blockade. In particular the British were resolved to end the enormously profitable but fictitious reexport trade that American merchants had developed between the French West Indies and Europe. By carrying belligerent goods to American ports, unloading and paying duties on them, then reloading the goods and getting a rebate on the duties before taking them on to Europe, American traders technically conformed to the British Rule of 1756. But with the *Essex* decision made by a British prize court in 1805, British judges decided that belligerent goods reexported in this manner were liable to seizure. The consequent increase in British spoliations of American shipping and the expansion of the impressment of sailors from American vessels ended the Anglo-American rapprochement that had begun with Jay's treaty in 1795.

Napoleon responded to the British blockade with commercial restrictions of his own—a "continental system" designed essentially to deprive England of markets in Europe. In his Berlin decree of 1806, he ruled that any neutral vessel stopping at an English port would be denied access to all European ports under French control. The British retaliated by requiring all neutral ships trading in the blockaded zones of Europe to stop at English ports to secure licenses. Napoleon then countered with his Milan decree of 1807, which declared that all neutral ships submitting to British search or entering British ports to secure licenses would be confiscated by the French. The net effect of these belligerent regulations was to render all neutral commerce illegal and liable to seizure. Although by 1807 the French were vigorously confiscating American ships in European ports, Britain's greater ability to capture American vessels (she was despoiling about one of every eight American ships to put to sea) and her humiliating practice of impressment made her appear the greater culprit in American eyes. British regulations seemed to strike at the heart of American independence. "They assume the principle," said John Quincy Adams in 1808, "that we shall

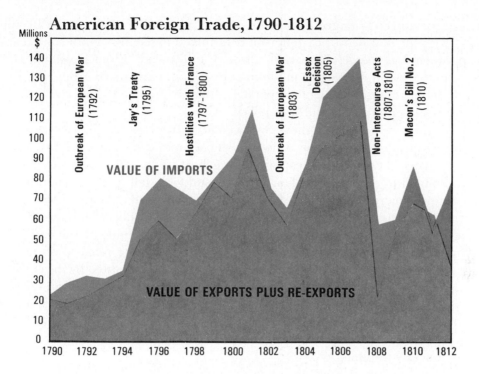

American Foreign Trade, 1790-1812

Millions $

Outbreak of European War (1792)

Jay's Treaty (1795)

Hostilities with France (1797–1800)

Outbreak of European War (1803)

Essex Decision (1805)

Non-Intercourse Acts (1807-1810)

Macon's Bill No.2 (1810)

VALUE OF IMPORTS

VALUE OF EXPORTS PLUS RE-EXPORTS

have no commerce in time of war, but with her dominion, and as tributaries to her."

The immediate response of the Jeffersonian administration to the British depradations was the nonimportation act of 1806, threatening a prohibition of certain British imports unless an Anglo-American agreement could be reached. Jefferson refused to send to the Senate for ratification a treaty with Britain that William Pinckney and James Monroe had negotiated in December 1806 not only because its commercial provisions did not go much beyond Jay's treaty, but more important because it did not renounce the British practice of impressment.

Almost immediately thereafter, in June 1807, the British man-of-war *Leopard* fired upon the American warship *Chesapeake* as it sailed out of Norfolk, killing several seamen; the British then boarded the American ship, and impressed four sailors including three Americans alleged to be deserters from the British navy. Waves of patriotic indignation swept through the United States and brought Anglo-American relations to the breaking point. "Never since the battle of Lexington," said Jefferson, "have I seen the country in such a state of exasperation as at present." Although the United States was emotionally primed for war, the Republican leaders were reluctant as yet to abandon their idealistic principles of diplomacy.

All of the strains of idealism and utopianism present in American Revolutionary thinking were now brought to a head with the Republicans' resort to a general

embargo. In 1807 Congress made a sweeping prohibition of all American shipping with the outside world. Jefferson determined to see this "candid and liberal
experiment" in "peaceful coercion" through to the end. From December 1807
to March 1809 in the face of mounting opposition, particularly from New England, Jefferson's government desperately stuck by—indeed used ever harsher
measures to enforce—its embargo policy.

While Britain and France showed few ill effects from the self-imposed stoppage
of foreign trade carried on in American ships, American commerce was thrown
into disarray. The American export and reexport trade, which between 1805–07
had doubled to over $108 million in value, suddenly fell to $22 million during
1808; and American imports declined in value from $138 million to $56 million.
Yet the economic effects were far from disastrous. Not only did numerous loopholes and violations, especially toward the end of 1808, mitigate the embargo's
depressing effect on the economy, but America's growing reliance on its own
domestic manufacturers and its internal markets was accelerated by the cutbacks
in international trade. Yet while many areas of the United States could fall back
on their domestic overland and coastwide trade, the New England ports, such as
Boston, Salem, and Providence, with their relatively meager hinterlands and their
disproportionate investment in the overseas carrying and reexport trade, were
badly hurt by the embargo.

In New England the embargo had the political effect of reviving Federalism.
With hundreds of New England petitions flooding in on the government, with
some New Englanders on the verge of rebellion, and with the Federalist governor
of Connecticut claiming the right of the state to interpose its authority between the
federal government and its citizens, some sort of retreat from the embargo became a matter of time. Hopeful of salvaging something from their policy of
peaceful coercion, the Republicans on March 1, 1809, replaced the embargo
with the Nonintercourse Act, which prohibited trade with just France and Britain
and provided that if either belligerent cancelled its blockade against American
shipping, then nonintercourse would be maintained only against the other.
Madison as President in 1809 was just as determined as Jefferson had been to
maintain this republican experiment in commercial warfare, but difficulties in
enforcing the Nonintercourse Act and growing governmental deficits from the
loss of duties on trade forced the Madison administration to turn its commercial
restrictions inside out. Macon's Bill No. 2 in May 1810 once again opened trade
to American ships with both Britain and France, with the provision that if either
belligerent revoked its restrictions on neutral commerce, nonintercourse would
be restored against the other. Intimations of a change in Napoleon's policy
against American shipping and Madison's eagerness to prove the workability
of the experiment in peaceful coercion led the Republican administration in
March 1811 into a hasty invocation of nonintercourse against Great Britain.

If the United States had to go to war, the Republicans thought, then better
to fight the country that had symbolized resistance to the experiment in popular

self-government from the beginning. Despite some strong misgivings over Napoleon's dictatorship and some weak suggestions that America fight both belligerents simultaneously, it was virtually inconceivable that the Republicans would have gone to war against France. The threat of Federalist "monarchism" tied to the former mother country was still so real to Republicans that war with Britain became a necessary product of the Republican revolution of 1800 and thus of the original Revolution itself. "We are going to fight for the re-establishment of our national character," declared Andrew Jackson.

In the end the war came because the Republicans' foreign policy left no alternative. By Republican standards America had been engaged in a kind of war with the European belligerents since 1806. The actual fighting of 1812 was only the logical consequence of the failure of "peaceful coercion." Still, many Republicans hesitated to commit the United States to a traditional sort of military conflict.

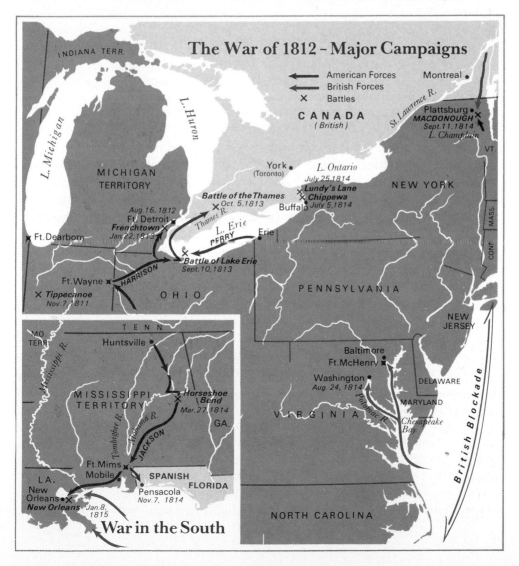

PERRY'S VICTORY ON LAKE ERIE, BY AN UNKNOWN ARTIST

Oliver Hazard Perry (1785–1819) commanded a fleet of nine vessels
built in Erie, Pa., to challenge British control of the Great Lakes in
the War of 1812. During the battle on Sept. 10, 1813 Perry's flagship
was disabled, and, as the painting depicts, he transferred to the
Niagra. Then he sailed directly into the British line and destroyed
the British ships, inspiring his famous dispatch: "We have met the
enemy and they are ours." *(New York State Historical Association,
Cooperstown, N.Y.)*

They realized, as Jefferson had warned in 1806, that "our constitution is a peace
establishment—it is not calculated for war." War, they feared, would lead to a
Hamiltonian enlargement of taxes, debt, military forces, and the executive
branch; far from saving the Jeffersonian revolution of 1800, war might ultimately
destroy republican principles. Hence even as the Republicans moved inevitably
toward war, many of them opposed all efforts to strengthen the government's
capacity to wage it. While Nathaniel Macon of North Carolina, for example,
reluctantly conceded the necessity of war, he like other Republicans urged reduction of the navy, indeed suggested abolition of the army, opposed raising
taxes, and resisted all efforts to add two assistant secretaries to the war department. Not only was the regular army cut back in favor of the popular militia,
but the Bank of the United States, the government's chief financial agency, was
allowed to expire in 1811 on the eve of hostilities. With such deliberate lack of
preparation the war that was declared in June 1812 was bound to be very different
from any that men had known.

Although by the end of 1813 the Americans had gained naval control of Lake
Erie and Lake Ontario, their militia campaigns against Canada from Detroit,
Niagara, and Plattsburg were dismal failures. On the sea American frigates, including the *Constitution,* the *United States,* the *Hornet,* and the *Wasp,* won some
notable single-ship engagements, and American privateers, the navy's militia,
captured more than thirteen hundred British merchant vessels. Eventually,

however, Britain's great naval superiority made itself felt, and by 1813 most of the American warships were bottled up in their ports and American commerce was effectively blockaded. With the abdication of Napoleon early in 1814, Great Britain was able to concentrate its military attention on America, and planned several major assaults, one designed to move down the Lake Champlain route that Burgoyne had followed in the Revolutionary war, and another aimed at New Orleans. During the summer of 1814 a British marauding force landed in the Chesapeake, entered Washington, and burned the Capitol and the White House.

Despite these humiliating circumstances, however, the American peace commissioners sent to negotiate with the British in August 1814 in Ghent, Belgium, were unwilling to make any concessions. The British, learning that their invasion from Canada had turned back as a result of Captain Thomas Macdonough's naval victory on Lake Champlain in September 1814 and increasingly anxious over the shifting situation in Europe, came to realize once again that a decentralized government and a spacious continent were not easily conquered. The peace signed on Christmas Eve, 1814, restored the antebellum status quo and said nothing about impressment and maritime rights. Andrew Jackson's smashing victory over the British invasion at New Orleans at the beginning of 1815 came after the treaty was signed and clinched it. Although the Americans had gained nothing tangible from the war, it was widely and rightly regarded a great-success.

The peace ended the threat of New England's secession and effectively destroyed Federalism as a national movement. The northeastern Federalists had repeatedly obstructed the war, refusing to comply with federal militia requisitions and discouraging loans to the United States government. While some New England extremists talked of separating from the union, other Federalists were convinced that the Republican failures in the war would justify their opposition, as the quasi-war with France in 1798 had justified the earlier Republican opposition; and that a disillusioned people would catapult the Federalist Cassandras back into national dominance. Hence the Federalist convention that met in Hartford, Connecticut, at the end of 1814 disavowed secession and contented itself with proposing a series of amendments to the Constitution. These amendments were designed to curb the power of the South in the federal government by eliminating the three-fifths representation of slaves; to prevent the admission of new states, future embargos, and declarations of war without a two-thirds majority of Congress; and to end Virginia's dominance of the executive by prohibiting the President from serving two terms and the same state from providing a President in succession. The national exuberance following the treaty at Ghent and Jackson's victory discredited these Federalist hopes and led to the enthusiastic election in 1816 of still another Republican and Virginian President, James Monroe. Thus was vindicated not the Federalists' image of a heroic state but the Republicans' remarkable experiment in governing a huge country and fighting a war without the traditional instruments of power.

Although the war seemed to settle nothing, actually it settled everything. "Notwithstanding a thousand Faults and blunders," John Adams told Jefferson in 1817, Madison's administration had "acquired more glory, and established more Union than all his three Predecessors, Washington, Adams, and Jefferson, put together." The Revolution, which had begun nearly a half century earlier, at last seemed to be over and brought to successful completion. The Federalist attempt to build a strong central government had been halted. The new national government the Republicans had created was unlike any the eighteenth century traditionally understood to be a government. Its capital was isolated from the main social and economic centers of the country; its influence was diffused throughout a rapidly expanding geographical sphere; and its effect on the daily lives of its citizens was negligible. By 1817–18 Jefferson was exultant. "Our government," he wrote in those years to his old French ally, the Marquis de

FOURTH OF JULY AT CENTRE SQUARE, 1818, BY JOHN LEWIS KRIMMEL

The day Independence was declared, John Adams wrote his wife in early July 1776, "will be the most memorable Epocha, in the History of America. . . . It ought to be solemnized with Pomp and Parade, with Shews, Games, Sports, Guns, Bells, Bonfires and Illuminations from one End of this continent to the other from this Time forward forever more." (*The Historical Society of Philadelphia.*)

Lafayette, "is now so firmly put on it's republican tack, that it will not be easily monarchised by forms." The War of 1812 and the disgrace of the Federalists, he said, had ended the need for his revolutionary party, and had in fact resulted in the "complete suppression of party." In the new "Era of Good Feelings" symbolized by Monroe's uncontested election to the presidency in 1820, the ideological passions and divisions aroused by the Revolution could at last subside. Americans could begin celebrating their own common national identity.

Suggested Readings

Much of the literature on the history of the 1790s treats the opposition of the Republicans as ordinary party activity. See William N. Chambers, *Political Parties in a New Nation...*, *1776–1809* (1963); and Noble E. Cunningham, Jr., *The Jeffersonian Republicans: The Formation of Party Organization, 1789–1801* (1957). A notable exception is Richard Buel, Jr., *Securing the Revolution* (1972). On the formation of extralegal organizations, all we have is Eugene P. Link, *Democratic Republican Societies, 1790–1800* (1942). There are a number of studies of the growth of the Republican party in the separate states. See especially Paul Goodman, *The Democratic Republicans of Massachusetts* (1964); Alfred F. Young, *The Democratic Republicans of New York* (1967); Sanford W. Higgenbotham, *The Keystone in the Democratic Arch: Pennsylvania Politics 1800–1816* (1952); and Carl E. Prince, *New Jersey's Jeffersonian Republicans* (1967). On the Whiskey Rebellion, see Leland D. Baldwin, *Whiskey Rebels* (1939).

On the foreign crisis of the late 1790s, see Alexander De Conde, *The Quasi-War: Politics and Diplomacy of the Undeclared War with France, 1797–1801* (1966). Manning J. Dauer, *The Adams Federalists* (1953), captures some of the desperation of the Federalists in 1798. The fullest study of the Alien and Sedition Acts is James Morton Smith, *Freedom's Fetters* (1956); but for a proper appreciation of the special eighteenth-century context in which freedom of speech and of the press has to be viewed, see Leonard W. Levy, *Legacy of Suppression* (1960). Stephen G. Kurtz is solid on *The Presidency of John Adams...*, *1795–1800* (1957).

The classic account of the Republican administrations is Henry Adams, *History of the United States of America during the Administration of Thomas Jefferson [and] of James Madison* (9 vols., 1889–1891). It is artful, but its obsession with the ironic turn of Jeffersonian policies subtly distorts the period. Marshall Smelser, *The Democratic Republic, 1801–1815* (1968), is a one-volume survey. Daniel Sisson, *The American Revolution of 1800* (1974), tries to recapture the radical meaning of Jefferson's election; but it does not succeed as well as James S. Young, *The Washington Community, 1800–1828* (1966), which despite an unhistorical focus rightly stresses the Republicans' fear of power. On the Republican party, see Noble E. Cunningham, Jr., *The Jeffersonian Republicans in Power: Party Operations, 1801–1809* (1963). Richard Hofstadter, *The Idea of a Party System: The Rise of Legitimate Opposition in the United States, 1740–1840* (1969), is a lucid essay that tries but does not quite break from the party conception of the secondary sources on which it is based. David Hackett Fischer, *The Revolution of American Conservatism: The Federalist Party in the Era of Jeffersonian Democracy* (1965), is an important book that compels a new look at the Republicans as well as the Federalists. On the Republicans' dismantling of the Federalist bureaucracy, see Leonard D. White, *The Jeffersonians: A Study in Administrative History, 1801–1829* (1951). On Jefferson and Madison, see the monumental multivolumed biographies by Dumas Malone and Irving Brant.

On the Louisiana Purchase, see E. Wilson Lyon, *Louisiana in French Diplomacy, 1759–1804* (1934); and the appropriate chapters of George Dangerfield, *Chancellor Robert R. Livingston of New York, 1746–1803* (1960). On Indian affairs, see Reginald Horsman, *Expansion and American Indian Policy, 1783–1812* (1967). For the tragic irony in the story of American relations with the Indians, see Bernard W. Sheehan, *Seeds of Extinction: Jeffersonian Philanthropy and the American Indian* (1973). A good, short, though unsympathetic, account of the Burr conspiracy can be found in Thomas Abernathy, *The South in the New Nation, 1789–1819* (1961).

On the politics of the judiciary, see Richard E. Ellis, *The Jeffersonian Crisis* (1971). The best biography of Marshall is still Albert J. Beveridge, *The Life of John Marshall* (4 vols., 1919). The origins of judicial review are treated in Edward S. Corwin, *The "Higher Law" Background of American Constitutional Law* (1955); and Charles G. Haines, *The American Doctrine of Judicial Supremacy* (1932). But despite all that has been written, the sources of judicial review remain perplexing. Understanding the problem requires less work on the Supreme Court and more on colonial jurisprudence. For a significant study of changes in law during the Revolution, see William E. Nelson, *Americanization of the Common Law: The Impact of Legal Change on Massachusetts Society, 1760–1830* (1975).

The underlying eighteenth-century liberal assumptions about international politics are explored in Felix Gilbert, *To The Farewell Address: Ideas of Early American Foreign Policy* (1961). Lawrence S. Kaplan, *Jefferson and France: An Essay on Politics and Political Ideas* (1967), captures the idealism of Jefferson. The best discussion of the diplomatic steps into war is Bradford Perkins, *Prologue to War: England and the United States, 1805–1812* (1961). See also L. M. Sears, *Jefferson and the Embargo* (1927); and J. F. Zimmerman, *Impressments of American Seamen* (1925). Julius W. Pratt, *Expansionists of 1812* (1925), stresses how the desire of Westerners and Southerners for land caused the war. However, A. L. Burt, *The United States, Great Britain and British North America* (1940), emphasizes the issues of impressment and neutral rights. Roger H. Brown, *The Republic in Peril: 1812* (1964), and Norman K. Risjord, *The Old Republicans* (1965), offer the best perspective on the logic of the Republicans' foreign policy that led to war.

Harry L. Coles, *The War of 1812* (1965) and Reginald Horsman, *The War of 1812* (1969) are good brief surveys. Irving Brant, *James Madison: The Commander in Chief, 1812–1836* (1961), defends Madison's wartime leadership, but Ralph Ketcham, *James Madison* (1971), is better in recovering the peculiar character of Madison's republican aims. On the Treaty of Ghent, see Bradford Perkins, *Castlereagh and Adams: England and the United States, 1812–1823* (1964). James M. Banner, *To the Hartford Convention: The Federalists and the Origins of Party Politics in Massachusetts, 1789–1815* (1970), superbly describes the Federalists' attitudes and stresses their conservative purposes in calling the Convention.

12

The End of the American Enlightenment

By the conclusion of the War of 1812, American society and culture had become very different from what they had been scarcely a half-century earlier. By 1815, Americans had moved into another century, not only in time but in the way they related to each other and in the way they perceived and valued these relationships. They had indeed undergone a revolution.

The American Revolution had seemed to give Americans the opportunity of realizing a heroic classical world, of putting the Enlightenment's ideals into practice, of creating the kind of free and ordered society and illustrious culture that people since the Greeks had yearned for. But the Revolution and the republican ideals of the Enlightenment that accompanied it contained within themselves the sources of much of their own transformation. By 1820 the cosmopolitan Enlightenment in America was over, and many of the original goals of the Revolution were changed or perverted. Yet the transformation was so complicated, so much a medley of responses to fast-moving events, that Americans scarcely sensed the revolutionary character of what they had been through. Because the future was filled with so many promises for so many people, few Americans as yet looked back with any sense of discrepancy and nostalgia to the world they had lost; and because they had escaped the violence and terror and ultimately the failure of the French Revolution, the successful radicalism of their own Revolution was obscured.

Self-Made Men

The population continued to grow spectacularly. Though immigration supplied only about 5000 a year, the total number of people in the country swelled from almost 4 million in 1790 to over 7 million in 1810 and nearly 10 million by 1820. This early nineteenth-century population was extraordinarily young and vigorous. Over one-third of the white males in the period between 1800 and 1820 were under the age of ten; two-thirds were under the age of twenty-five. And this population was extraordinarily mobile. Much of it was expanding outward, spilling over the Appalachians into the West. By 1810 the population of Kentucky was over 400,000. Between 1800 and 1810 Ohio grew from 45,000 inhabitants to over 230,000, with Cincinnati already being called by one booster, "The Great Emporium of the West."

Despite the presence of Indians even Indiana territory by 1815 had nearly 60,000 settlers. From the 1790s on, the surging migrants pushed back the Indians in the Old Northwest, mainly through a series of piecemeal cessions of land. Finally in 1805 the Shawnee chief Tecumseh and his brother the Prophet attempted to halt this steady encroachment of whites by forming an Indian confederacy. This tribal effort at organized resistance was broken by the governor of Indiana territory, General William Henry Harrison, in a battle involving 600 Indians and a mixed force of 1000 American Army regulars and Kentucky frontiersmen at Tippecanoe in 1811. Sporadic Indian fighting and raiding in the Old Northwest continued, however, but it did not stop the waves of settlers.

In the Southwestern territories the presence of Indians did divert and retard migration. Even so by 1810 Mississippi territory (much of present-day Alabama and Mississippi) had over 40,000 people, including 17,000 slaves, mainly clustered along the Mississippi River counties south of Natchez, which was fast becoming a

"YOUNG OMAHAW, WAR EAGLE; LITTLE MISSOURI AND PAWNEES," BY CHARLES BIRD KING, 1821

The Pawnees were Plains Indians. War Eagle is wearing around his neck a medal given to him by white Americans as a token of peace. In front of this symbol of the white man's yoke, however, looms the Indian's weapon. (*Smithsonian Institution, Washington, D.C.*)

UNION TEXTILE MILL, MARYLAND

Following the opening of the Slater cotton mill in Rhode Island in
1793, textile manufacturing became the prototype of mass industry
in America. Although most mills were erected in New England,
even the upper South began to engage in some large-scale
manufacturing. *(The Maryland Historical Society.)*

bustling entrepôt. In 1810 the Territory of Orleans (modern Louisiana) had over
76,000 inhabitants, more than half of whom were slaves. New Orleans with its
mixture of Spanish, French, and other nationalities in a population of over
10,000 was by far the largest and most flamboyant city of the Mississippi Valley
and on its way to becoming one of the great ports of the country. Even before the
War of 1812 pioneers were rapidly pushing beyond the Mississippi River into
what are now the states of Arkansas and Missouri, leaving behind huge pockets of
Indians—Creeks in Georgia, and Cherokees in Tennessee. By 1815 Missouri
territory had over 20,000 people.

   This fantastic mobility was ultimately fed by the expanding economy and each
individual migrant's prospect of gain. Much of the country's prosperity came from
overseas commerce and made the period between 1793 and 1807 the golden age
of American shipping. With the outbreak of the European war in the early 1790s,
American merchants gained access to the mercantile empires formerly denied
them and quickly became the largest neutral carrier of goods in the world. During
this period of European warfare, ship tonnage tripled and the value of exports
increased fivefold. Enterprising merchants, like E. H. Derby of Salem,
Massachusetts, John Jacob Astor of New York, and Stephen Gerard of Philadelphia, amassed huge fortunes. American earnings from the reexport and carrying
trade grew at an astounding rate, from nearly $6 million in 1790 to over
$42 million by 1807, and stimulated the expansion of the leading seaports of
New York, Philadelphia, Boston, and Baltimore.

   Financed by this overseas trade, commerce and enterprise reached farther and farther into the hinterlands and brought more and more Americans into the market. Therefore when the embargo and the War of 1812 suddenly curtailed the foreign carrying trade, other indigenous commercial arrangements were already emerging to take its place. The disruption of overseas trade after 1807 created a rapid rise in the cost of imported manufactured goods, which in turn led Americans to divert more and more of their capital from shipping and the foreign trade into developing native industry. While before 1808 only 15 cotton mills had been built in the United States, during 1809 alone 87 additional mills were built; and within three years the manufacturing capacity of American cotton mills grew tenfold. All over the countryside of the northern and mid-Atlantic states industries sprouted up, making everything from nails and shoes to stoves and wagons.

Much of this manufacturing began as an extension of the older household industry, drawing on the labor of women and children; thus at first it did not seem to be new and disruptive. For example, during the last decade of the eighteenth century in the little town of Franklin, Massachusetts, young Horace Mann, later to become a famous educational reformer, had along with his mother and brothers and sisters spent his spare time in the home spinning and weaving straw braids for use in making ladies' hats. At first the braids had been taken to the local general store in exchange for merchandise to supplement the father's income from farming. But by 1804 a local manufactory began buying the braids directly from families in the town and fashioning straw bonnets for sale in Boston and Providence. The Mann household and others like it were soon weaving

WORKING AT TRADES

Even by the beginning of the nineteenth century much of the manufacturing in America still came from individual craftsmen. Yet the weakness of the crafts—their lack of organized guilds and of a vested interest in specialization—made America receptive to new techniques of factory manufacturing, involving interchangeable parts and the production of standardized goods. *(American Antiquarian Society.)*

more braids than ever before. By 1812 Franklin, while still only a small and far-removed rural community, was producing six thousand hats a year and, as one observer noted, was "trading with every place in the country." Although the Mann family was now earning far more money than ever it had from farming, the effects, as Mann later saw, were unsettling. Not only was the father's influence over his wife and children weakened by the new enlarged sources of income, but the family's conception of the world now had to account for new unpredictable and uncontrollable, but decidedly man-made phenomena of the market.

This commercializing experience was duplicated and multiplied a thousand-fold all over the North. By 1820 at least 12 percent of the nation's labor force was engaged in manufacturing and construction and 28 percent in all nonagricultural occupations; but these gross figures do not cover the multitudes of households that were earning the bulk of their income from outside employment. By the early nineteenth century Secretary of the Treasury Albert Gallatin discovered that nearly every farmhouse in New Hampshire had a spinning wheel or loom and was yearly weaving hundreds of yards of salable cloth. An English visitor, Frances Wright, noted in 1819 that America was *teeming with business* and that everybody seemed to be touched with "a spirit of daring enterprise." Since such household manufacturing seemed to enhance individual independence, it posed no immediate threat to republicanism and could even be endorsed by Jefferson.

But Jefferson and other devout republicans could not have foreseen what the spread of this enterprising spirit would mean. "From one end of the continent to the other," noted the enlightened scientist and physician Samuel L. Mitchell in 1800, "the universal roar is, Commerce! Commerce! at all events, Commerce!" Although by 1820 61 towns in the United States had a population of over 2500 (though only 13 had more than 10,000), these relatively large communities scarcely suggest the degree of commercialization taking place. For every major city like Pittsburgh, whose booming productivity by 1815 promised to make it, in the eyes of *Niles' Weekly Register*, "the greatest manufacturing town in the world," there were thousands of small villages now drawn into the market and thousands of new mercantile centers springing up, even in the frontier areas of the Northwest. By 1821 Ohio was bustling with towns: 61 with a population over 200; 29 of over 500; and 22 of over 1000 — all, unlike most villages of colonial times, participating in various kinds of business and commerce.

All of these expanding economic and demographic developments indicated that a fundamental reorganization of American society was taking place, particularly in the North and the Old Northwest. The relations that had characterized eighteenth-century society were repeatedly strained and broken and great numbers of people were cut loose from their traditional ties. Foreign visitors were stunned by the unwillingness of American servants to address their masters and mistresses as superiors and by their refusal to admit that they were anything but "help." No one but black slaves could be any longer dependent, and every citizen now claimed the title "Mr." or "Mrs." It was after all, Americans said in explana-

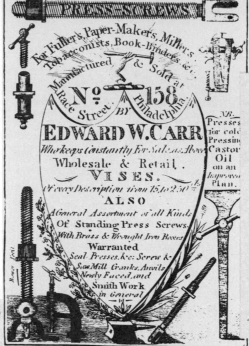

tion, a free country. And in such a free country the widely fluctuating economy and the ideology of republicanism dispersed authority of all sorts.

This prevailing competitiveness bewitched even the sturdy yeomen. In Berkshire County of western Massachusetts Elkanah Watson, the enterprising son of an artisan, discovered by 1810 that the earlier aristocratic and enlightened techniques of stimulating agricultural reform through scientific societies of gentleman-farmers would not work in America. Because American farmers were too independent for such learned paternalism, Watson devised what soon became the familiar American county fair, with exhibitions, entertainment, and prizes awarded for the best crops and livestock. By such fairs Watson aimed to excite that spirit of "envy" and "competition," and that desire for "personal interest, and personal ambition" characteristic of all Americans, which in Watson's mind was, as a "practical" source of agricultural improvement, worth all the "studied, wiredrawn books" ever written. The only way of achieving public benefits "congenial to *American habits*, and the state of our *society*," concluded Watson, was to excite individual self-interest and create "a general strife."

Others were also reaching the same remarkable conclusion. Because the people could no longer be the single homogeneous entity that republicanism had originally promised, the public good could not easily be discovered and promoted by government and enlightened political leaders. Yet somehow, men observed, "order" seemed to "grow out of chaos" and the people were guiding themselves "without the check of any controlling power, other than that administered by the collision of their own interests balanced against each other." The common good, wrote Joel Barlow in his *Columbiad*, was like a huge river formed out of the coming together of innumerable tiny and separate sources. Americans, it was now said, would never intentionally work for the public welfare, as Samuel Adams and others had hoped at the beginning of the Revolution. Only by pursuing their own individual good would Americans serve the common good.

In no area of the economy was this fragmentation of the public interest more graphically revealed than in the extraordinary multiplication of business corporations. Traditionally such governmentally chartered corporations, going all the way back to the Virginia Company at the time of the original settlements, had been instruments by which the state harnessed private enterprise to carry out public goals, like founding a colony, maintaining a college, or building a bridge. Such monopolies of legal privileges granted by the state to private individuals made sense in the older more hierarchical society. After the Revolution, however, it was no longer clear to whom the state ought to grant its legal authority. So mistrusted was governmental privilege in the egalitarian atmosphere of the early republic that all these corporate monopolies could be justified only by their proliferation. Between 1800 and 1817 the states issued nearly eighteen hundred corporate charters to groups of entrepreneurs to create banks, insurance companies, and manufactures, or to operate bridges, roads, and canals. Soon the single state of Massachusetts had more corporations than existed in all of Europe. Suppliants for these corporate charters multiplied to the point where the beleaguered state legislatures in relief eventually had to resort to general incorporation laws, making the legal powers of the corporation available to practically everyone.

The multiplication of such corporations in the early nineteenth century destroyed their exclusiveness. In 1837 in the *Charles River Bridge* case the Supreme Court legally recognized this proliferation of corporations that had been taking place in previous decades. The Jacksonian court led by Chief Justice Roger B. Taney decided that corporate grants made by the state to private entrepreneurs to build a toll bridge, for example, did not preclude the state from making subsequent grants to different groups to fulfill the same public end. The Charles River Bridge Company's charter was not abrogated, but its monopoly was lost when a second bridge was allowed to be built next to it. In a "free, active,

A VIEW OVER THE BRIDGE, CHARLES RIVER, BOSTON,
MASSACHUSETTS

(American Antiquarian Society.)

and enterprising" country like the United States, wrote Taney, the spread of such corporations was essential for "the happiness and prosperity of the community." The public good was something defined no longer by a few with a preserved right to governmental power but by the competition among various private interests.

As the states were distributing their legal powers, they lost control of what they granted. Because these corporate grants were increasingly regarded as rights, species of private property, or contracts available to all, holders argued that they were immune from legislative tampering—a view legally endorsed by the Supreme Court in the *Dartmouth College* case of 1819. In this important case the Marshall Court decided that the charter of Dartmouth College, although it was originally granted by the New Hampshire legislature and had a public purpose, was a private contract protected by the Constitution from subsequent interference by the state legislature. Orthodox republicans like Jefferson were stunned by the decision. They could not understand how "public" corporations created by a legislature were unalterable by future legislatures. Yet it was precisely the pervasive Jeffersonian fear of political power that had contributed most to this parceling of state authority and this new definition of corporate grants as rights protected from government.

These economic developments created a dizzying spiral of rising aspirations and expanding opportunities, the like of which no society in history ever experienced so intensely in so short a period. Out of these circumstances now emerged the ideal of the "self-made man," an ideal not confined to plutocrats or men of wealth but embodied in all "independent" persons whose achievement or position was due solely to personal qualities. The "self-made man" was a symbol with which Americans in time became so familiar that it has been forgotten what a novel, indeed radical, notion it originally was. There had always been social mobility in Western society, particularly in earlier American society; but it had been mobility in which the upward aspiring individual sought to acquire the attributes of the social status he strove for and at the same time tried to forget and disguise the lowly sources whence he came. Such mobility had not been universally admired; terms like *upstarts, nouveaux riches,* and *parvenus* had been used to disparage it. Now, however, in the early nineteenth century, American mobile men began boasting of their humble origins and their ability to have made it on their own, without influence and patronage, even without education, or at least not a gentleman's education. When a South Carolina politician as early as 1784 was celebrated in the press as being a self-established man, who "had no relations or friends but what his money made for him," a subtle but radical revolution in social thinking had taken place.

For many Americans it soon came to seem that wealth was the sole, and in the new republican society, the proper means of distinguishing one person from another. Catherine Sedgwick, daughter of a Tory-Federalist family, spoke for all the old gentry when she remarked of the emerging nineteenth-century entrepreneurial hierarchy: "Wealth, you know, is the grand levelling principle." Although the distribution of wealth by 1820 may have been more unequal than it was before the Revolution, many of the early-nineteenth-century holders of wealth were new, and more important, they held their wealth on new independent terms. To them and to all Americans their recent, unaided acquisition, however small, was a meaningful vindication of the egalitarianism of American society.

The radicalness of the American Revolution thus lay in the emergence of new social relationships, relationships that were revealed in every area of American life, most obviously perhaps in politics. Although egalitarian politics was intensified in the North, it was in the new territories of the Old Northwest that American democracy ran its course. There the hundreds of commercial communities were so recent and bustling, the lines of economic authority so tangled and confused, that no clear structures of political authority could be readily transplanted or created. Everyone seemed to have arrived, as it was proudly said of one Maryland printer migrating to Illinois, "without friends," more free to form new and equal connections than had been possible in the East. Would-be "great men" and landed gentry like John Cleves Symmes of Ohio, the Northwest's biggest land speculator, were no match for thousands of squatters, hustlers, and manipulators; and such grandees had barely established themselves before they found their privileges and holdings crumbling around them. In such scrambling circumstances politics was necessarily chaotic and highly popular. The new constitutions of the northwestern states of Ohio, Indiana, and Illinois provided for weak executives, white adult male suffrage, annually elected legislatures, no property qualification for officeholders, and popular election for a host of offices, including even judges. The result was that electioneering for one position or another at the state, county, or local level became a way of life in this region. As the traditional attributes of authority—breeding, education, and gentlemanly status—became liabilities in this egalitarian politics, political and social leadership was separated; and political officeholders, instead of being patrons, now often became simply clients of interests or groups within the community.

In the states of the South and the new Southwest the older society did not totally collapse. The changing nature of the tobacco trade and the diversification of Southern agriculture that had begun to appear in the upper South on the eve of the Revolution (and that had helped stimulate the development of Baltimore and Norfolk) weakened social relationships but did not change them. The declining demand for tobacco and other traditional staples and the Southern planters' heavy investment in slaves led to a frantic search for new agricultural exports. For the lower South and the new Southwestern territories in the 1790s, cotton supplied the answer, and Virginia was left with its depleted soil and declining population and wealth, slowly sinking into nostalgic dreams of the past while muttering fearful curses against the future. By the early nineteenth century the prosperity of cotton production guaranteed that the South would remain an essentially rural and agricultural society tied together by an extraordinary reliance on a single export produced by the labor of hundreds of thousands of black slaves. As the production of cotton grew from 3 million pounds in 1793 to 93 million pounds by 1815, the need for slaves increased. This slave and agricultural base of Southern society together with the peculiarities of the marketing system for cotton prevented the rise of the multitudes of small commercial com-

CINCINNATI, 1800

Cincinnati was founded in 1788 on land owned by the wealthy speculator John Cleves Symmes, who got from Congress in that year a million acres between the Miami rivers. By 1800 the population was only about 750, but, as was increasingly common for nineteenth-century Americans living in the future, the town was already being labeled "the metropolis of the north-western territory." (*The Cincinnati Historical Society.*)

munities that were fragmenting and democratizing the society of the North. Even in the new frontier areas of the Southwest, planter dominance of the society and politics was reinforced.

In contrast to the Northern states therefore politics in the South remained remarkably similar to the politics of the colonial period—dynamic, competitive, and faction-ridden but not fully democratic. To be sure, mobility especially in the raw territories of the Southwest was high, and the new states of Mississippi (1817) and Alabama (1819) adopted many of the popular and electoral features of the Northern governments. But the older structures of patronage and the older identity between social and political authority continued more or less intact. Electoral politics affected but did not disrupt what was still a society of dependent connections converging in the planter gentry. In contrast with much of the nineteenth-century North but in the manner of colonial times, the gentry in the South who dominated the economy and society, however recently arrived, however popularly elected, maintained control of the government.

It was not just in politics that social relations shifted. Wives and children became more independent. In some eastern areas, particularly in New England, the number of women outstripped the number of men and led to an increase of unmarried women who were prepared to work outside the home. Family-arranged marriages gradually gave way to ties based on romantic love. Greater restraint in courtship replaced the relative sexual freedom and candor of the eighteenth century, and chastity among young women now competing in a marriage market became more fashionable. Widening aspirations for their children made middle-class parents more self-conscious about birth control, and the size of families decreased. The breakup of marriages became more common, and more and more women came to live and maintain businesses apart from their husbands. The courts responded by granting these independent wives new rights in law to manage and convey property, to engage in litigation, and to enter into contracts. Although by modern standards the legal gains were slight, they contrasted with the legally dependent position of eighteenth-century wives.

At the same time Americans were urging the deliberate creation of new institutions—almshouses, penitentiaries, asylums, and vocational and educational organizations of all sorts—to bear the social burdens that the family had once assumed as a matter of course. As the family gradually withdrew from the society, writers began sentimentalizing it in romantic terms and stressing the domesticating roles of wives and mothers. As one Kentuckian said in 1806, women, who "would effeminate even the roughness of steel and the solidity of wood," were especially important in softening the rudeness of a frontier society and in cultivating the kind of polite refinement that new middle-class Americans increasingly desired.

There were changes too in recruiting and maintaining workers and artisans. By the end of the eighteenth-century familial contracts of apprenticeship emphasized surrogate parenthood less and economic and technical preparation more; many

ABIGAIL ADAMS, BY RALPH EARL

Though unschooled, the wife of John Adams was a confident, intelligent and widely-read woman. Occasionally she expressed her resentment at the circumscribed role allowed to women in the eighteenth century, playfully urging John in 1776 to "remember the ladies" in his plans for enhancing liberty. But generally she was very willing to sacrifice herself for her husband and to accept her femininity "as a punishment for the transgression of Eve." *(New York State Historical Association, Cooperstown, New York.)*

apprentices no longer became "children" in the master's family but were trainees in a business, now often conducted outside the household. Paternalism in labor relations now gave way to impersonal cash payments, and journeymen moved more frequently from one master to another. Both masters and journeymen in many of the crafts were beginning to perceive their interests as more distinct and conflicting than they had before; and as employers and employees they were forming new class-conscious organizations to protect these interests. Between 1786 and 1816 at least twelve strikes by various craftsmen occurred (the first major strikes by employees against employers in American history), and masters were now resorting more and more to the courts to enforce what had once been seen as a mutual and personal relationship.

In this situation of high and open competitiveness, violence became more common. Fighting in the state and federal legislatures was no longer as shocking as it had been earlier. Mobbing had always been a regular part of American life; now, however, as in the Baltimore riots of 1812, it assumed a more sinister character. Butchers, tavern keepers, and other common people were less inclined to wait for the tacit consent of elites to take to the streets to close presses, destroy property, and beat up individuals. Dueling, despite laws in many of the states against it, now occurred more often than at any time in American history. Although this aristocratic practice seemed to be one way in which gentlemen could maintain their hard-pressed sense of difference from ordinary men, the code of dueling was spreading to all ranks of the society. Even the most famous duel in American history, that in which Vice-President Aaron Burr shot and killed Alexander Hamilton in 1804, did not end the practice, although the pressure and laws against it mounted rapidly. Everything seemed to be coming apart, and murders (including those of whole families by fathers or mothers), suicides, drunkenness, and theft became increasingly prevalent responses to the burdens that individualism and the expectation of gain were placing on people.

In these quickly changing circumstances, older means of communication were democratized and dispersed. Ordinary men interested in commerce and distant markets could no longer rely on the gentry's periodically dispensing information about the outside world. Whereas Massachusetts in 1760 possessed only 5 newspapers, all located in Boston, by 1820 there were 53 dailies and weeklies published in 23 different towns. Post offices multiplied even faster than the newspapers, as every tiny hamlet sought to link itself with the larger society. In 1790 the United States had only 75 post offices, one for every 52,000 inhabitants; by 1820 there were 4500 post offices, one for every 2100 inhabitants, and the proportion was rapidly shrinking.

Isolated and independent individuals now sought to form combinations to accomplish what could not be done alone. In Boston in 1807 a group of inventors, realizing that the traditional kinds of patronage "from opulent individuals or corporate bodies" could not easily develop in America, determined "to *patronize themselves,* by associating to exchange mutual aids." In the early decades of the nineteenth century voluntary associations of all sorts—professional, civic, religious, moral, cultural, and charitable—sprang up and multiplied to an astonishing extent. By the 1820s in Massachusetts alone these personal associations of like-minded men and women were being formed at the rate of 85 a year. Tocqueville, the French commentator on Jacksonian America, claimed that no aspect of American life was more crucial to understanding America's democratic society than these voluntary associations of isolated individuals. Like the proliferating business corporations, these voluntary associations were expressions of the fragmented and diffused nature of early nineteenth-century American society. Most were small, local, and exclusive organizations of equal individuals with common concerns, freely coming together in new face-to-face relations. In

MEMBERSHIP CERTIFICATE FOR
THE MASSACHUSETTS MECHANICS
SOCIETY, 1800

(Library of Congress.)

short, they were a nineteenth-century democratic substitute for the hierarchical connections of the eighteenth-century society; they represented the only kind of association that American social conditions would now allow for fulfilling the great Revolutionary goals of communal harmony and fraternity.

The Kingdom of God in America

The most important of these new voluntary associations were those emerging in religion. The disintegrating logic of American religious development that had begun with the first settlements in the seventeenth century was now starkly revealed. No society in all of Christendom contained such a multitude and such a variety of religious groups. The age-old Christian assumptions of orthodoxy and uniformity were clearly shattered. It was not simply that the traditional identity between church, state, and society was broken up. More important, the very idea of any religious group, or "sect," demanding recognition as the true and exclusive church for the society was rendered meaningless. Religious associations in America had become something unique to Christendom: "denominations," religious groups that regarded themselves as limited and imperfect representations of Christianity and that made no claims to embodying the whole of Christian truth.

Yet such denominational fragmentation did not result in the spread of infidelity and the kind of religious neglect that some Americans and most Europeans expected. Indeed, by the early nineteenth century, American Protestantism, despite its fractionalized character, had come to be widely regarded as a significant adhesive force holding the sprawling republican society together. These clashing Christian denominations without the traditional coercive aid of the state had won a commanding control of much of American culture.

The Revolution had been central to the development of this unique religious culture. Despite all the tumult in religious life in the eighteenth century most of the colonists on the eve of the Revolution still conceived of religion ideally in orthodox terms. The concept if not the fact of church establishment was still largely acknowledged. While all colonists talked of religious toleration and even religious liberty, they had not yet worked out a full justification of the peculiarities of their religious life. What the Revolution did was clarify these confused and incomplete circumstances and give them a significance they had hitherto lacked. The Revolution endorsed the Enlightenment's faith in liberty of conscience and finally severed the increasingly tenuous connection between church and state. But the Revolution did more; it released and activated populist religious forces in the society that ultimately gave the Revolutionary momentum a special evangelical cast. By the early nineteenth century the religious liberalization begun by the Revolution had created a democratic religious world that few in 1776 had expected.

From the outset of the Revolutionary controversy American libertarian arguments had linked the dark forces of both civic and religious tyranny and had helped guarantee that all the states in their new Revolutionary constitutions would in some way affirm religious freedom. Yet such declarations, like the one of the 1776 North Carolina constitution that stated "that all men have a natural and unalienable right to worship Almighty God according to the dictates of their own consciences," did not necessarily signify any abandonment of the state's traditional role in religious matters. To be sure, the Anglican establishment, such as it existed in several of the colonies, was immediately eliminated. But in its place the Maryland, South Carolina, and Georgia Revolutionary constitutions authorized their state legislatures to create a kind of multiple establishment using tax money to support the Christian religion. Virginians especially were divided over the meaning of their 1776 declaration of religious liberty; liberals like Jefferson and Madison joined growing numbers of Presbyterian and Baptist dissenters to oppose the Anglican clergy and planters in a fierce but eventually successful struggle for the complete disestablishment of the Church of England. In 1786 this Virginia struggle was climaxed by the passage of Jefferson's memorable Act for Establishing Religious Freedom. Elsewhere, however, many of the states retained some vague or general religious qualifications for public office, and both Connecticut and Massachusetts continued to maintain their Congregational establishments.

In short, unlike the church in Europe, the American churches, developing as they had in the colonial period, were neither the enemies nor the victims of the Enlightenment and the Revolution. Except for the Anglican clergy (who inspired some anticlericalism in the South), the Protestant ministry was in the vanguard of the Revolution, perceiving no threat to religion from republicanism. Without the support of the Protestant clergy, in fact, it is difficult to see how the American people could have been as fully mobilized into Revolution as they were. Religion was after all still the means by which most ordinary Americans confronted the world and gave it meaning. For every gentleman who read a learned pamphlet and delved into Whig and ancient history for an explanation of events, there were dozens of ordinary people who read the Bible and looked to their ministers for an understanding of what was happening to America.

Much to the delight of the Protestant ministers, their message was consistent with the message of enlightened rationalists. During the controversy with Great Britain, the clergy, particularly in New England, worked out an explanation for America's difficulties in their jeremiads—their traditional admonitory sermons designed to incite reformation among the people. All the instances of British oppression were, they said in the 1760s and 70s, God's just punishment for a sinful people. What enlightened political scientists described as symptoms of corruption—the increase in luxury, acquisitiveness, and social disorder resulting from America's expanding market economy at midcentury—the clergy saw as manifestations of sin. Although a good Calvinist could never agree that the British rather than the Americans themselves were ultimately responsible for these sins, the clergy nevertheless came to see in Independence and in the morally regenerative effects of republicanism a heaven-sent opportunity to cleanse America of sin once and for all. Thus piety and politics, theology and social science, were firmly united in a common desire for moral reformation. With God's help the Revolutionaries would build a new republican society of benevolence and virtue. Some ecstatic clergymen even came to see in the Revolution the advent of the millennium itself.

Millennial thinking had long been a part of American Protestantism. Literally, millennialism referred to the doctrine some Christians held, based on the authority of Revelation 20:4–6, that Christ would establish a messianic kingdom on earth and would reign over it for a thousand years before the Last Judgment. By the 1750s many of the Protestant clergy were coming to believe that the Coming of Christ would follow, not precede, the happy and glorious final thousand years of mankind on earth. Conceived in this way, the apocalyptic hopes of the clergy came to focus on contemporary historical events as signs of the approaching age of perfection, an age that seemed first to be appearing in the New World. The millennium now became more than a stage in Christian theology; it became an anticipated part of American history. The more America progressed, the closer it was to the millennium.

This Revolutionary belief in the destiny of America to lead the world to Christian perfection was brought to a crescendo in the following decades. In 1794 in a collected edition of millennial pieces, the evangelical enthusiast David Austin pictured the biblical "eagle of liberty" fleeing the Old World to the New and taking "her station upon the broad seal of the United States" as "an emblem of this protection of Providence towards our present government, and this, our happy land." Such a millennium could not simply be prayed for; it would "be introduced," said President Eliphalet Nott of Union College to the Presbyterian General Assembly in 1806, "by HUMAN EXERTIONS." Thus every example of America's expanding enlightenment and prosperity became evidences of the millennial impulse. With Samuel Hopkins, the greatest of the post-Revolutionary millennialists, the coming New Jerusalem achieved a degree of worldly detail that made his *Treatise on the Millennium* (1793) something of a handbook to a generation of American theologians. By 1818 Joseph Emerson in his popular *Lectures on the Millennium* was prophesying that sooner or later "every cottage will be irradiated with science, as well as with religion" and "every peasant will be able not only to read the Bible but the stars." By giving the millennium such a concrete temporal and material character and by identifying the Kingdom of God with the prospects of the American republic both at home and abroad, the Protestant clergy ultimately created the most important element feeding into the Americans' gradually evolving ideas of progress and mission.

Despite the clergy's enthusiasm for the new republican experiment, however, the alliance between the Enlightenment and American Protestantism forged at the Revolution was never an easy one. Although Presbyterians and Baptists had backed Jefferson's successful effort to disestablish the Anglican church in Virginia, they could never share his rationalistic belief, expressed in his Act for Establishing Religious Freedom, that religion was only a matter of opinion, having no more relation to government than "our opinions in physics or geometry." Since religion was the principal promoter of morality and virtue, without which no republic could long exist, many of the clergy, like Henry Cumings of Massachusetts in 1783, soon began to question carrying the "idea of religious liberty so far, as . . . to rob civil government of one of its main supports." By the end of the eighteenth century and the adoption of the First Amendment, ministers could agree that "religion at all times is a matter between God and individuals"; nevertheless at the same time they welcomed "those friendly aids to the cause of our holy religion which may justly be expected from our political fathers." Even someone as passionately devoted to the separation of church and state as the Baptist leader Isaac Backus supported religious tests for governmental office and laws compelling church attendance and recognition of the Sabbath.

In the end it was not Jefferson and Madison, with their secular-minded rational religion, who spoke for the emerging competitive Christianity and separation of church and state of nineteenth-century America; it was rather Backus and other "New Lights" who represented the future. Such evangelicals came to their libertarian beliefs in the separation of church and state not out of Enlightenment rationalism but out of the exigencies of being minority sects within tax-supported established churches and out of their desires to create voluntaristic denominations of individual believers.

Yet in the immediate aftermath of the Revolution the eventual emergence of this populist pietism was obscured and retarded. The Revolution destroyed churches, scattered congregations, and politicized people's thinking and led to a precipitate decline in church membership. By the 1790s perhaps only one in twenty Americans was affiliated with a church. The earlier revivalistic enthusiasm receded under the pressure of a spreading religious rationalism, or deism, which sought to substitute reason for revelation and the science of Newton for the mysteries of traditional Christianity. In 1784 Ethan Allen published his deistic work *Reason the Only Oracle of Man,* which boldly attacked the Bible and the clergy and defended natural religion. With Thomas Paine's *Age of Reason* (1794), the Compte de Volny's *Ruins of Empire* (1791), and Elihu Palmer's attempts to organize deistic societies among urban workingmen in the 1790s, it seemed to many religious leaders that republicanism was breeding infidelity.

As long as the enlightened deism of Jefferson and the other Revolutionary leaders had been confined to the drawing rooms of the gentry and was not publicized, it had posed little threat to Protestant orthodoxy. But with the dissemination of rational and natural religion among ordinary people at the time of the French Revolution, the clergy, especially the older Calvinistic clergy, became alarmed and began a countermovement on behalf of orthodox Christianity. So identified with the excesses of the French Revolution and hence the Republican

LEMUEL HAYNES, 1753–1833, FIRST BLACK MINISTER OF THE
CONGREGATIONAL CHURCH IN AMERICA

Haynes fought in the Revolutionary War, and after he was ordained
in 1785 he became minister of the west parish of Rutland, Vermont,
where he remained for thirty years.
(Museum of Art, Rhode Island School of Design. Gift of Lucy T. Aldrich.)

party was this rational deism that even Hamilton toyed with the idea of enlisting
Christianity on behalf of the beleaguered Federalists. In the end this countermovement transcended its creators. It soon swept all before it, fusing into the
great revival known as the Second Great Awakening, which began at the end of
the eighteenth century.

The Second Great Awakening carried well into the nineteenth century and was
a radical expansion and extension of the earlier eighteenth-century revivals. It
did not simply intensify the religious feeling of existing church members; more
important, it mobilized unprecedented numbers of hitherto unchurched people
into religious communion. By popularizing religion as never before and by
bringing Christianity into the remotest areas of America, this great revival marked
the beginning of the republicanizing and nationalizing of American religion.
Thousands upon thousands of ordinary people found in evangelical religion new
sources of order and community.

In the decades following the Revolution the various Protestant churches reorganized themselves nationally and entered a period of great sectarian rivalry.
Between 1780 and 1820 the number of colleges in the United States, most of
them denominationally sponsored, grew from only 9 to over 70. With the decline in the number of college graduates among the gentry now willing to enter
the ministry, the older Calvinist churches, Presbyterians and Congregationalists,
were forced to form separate colleges and seminaries for the professional education of clergymen and to recruit increasing numbers of their ministers from lower

social levels of the population. The newer denominations, the Methodists and the Baptists,
recruited their preachers even more informally;
and rejecting as they did the idea of a settled and
learned ministry, they were more capable than
the older churches of speaking the language of
the common people they sought to evangelize.
By 1820 the Baptists and Methodists had become the largest denominations in America.

While evangelism spread throughout America, transforming the older Calvinist churches
in New England and elsewhere, it was in the new
areas of the West that the revival was most
dramatically expressed. In the first twelve years
of the nineteenth century the Methodists in
Tennessee, Kentucky, and Ohio grew from less
than three thousand to well over thirty thousand. There in the new territories the need for
some kind of community, however loose and
voluntary, among isolated men and women was
most intense; there the need for building barriers against barbarism and licentiousness was
most keenly felt. In 1801 at a meeting at Cane
Ridge, Kentucky, clergymen of several denominations cooperated in what some thought was
the greatest outpouring of the spirit since the
beginning of Christianity. Crowds estimated at
ten thousand to twenty-five thousand participated in a week of conversions that soon became a symbol of the new kind of evangelical
Protestantism spreading throughout the country. In these convulsive revivals American
religion, Calvinist included, became a participatory affair in which all who wished could
order their own salvation. As befitting an enterprising society of self-made men, sin was no
longer conceived of as something inherent in
the depravity of man but as a kind of failure
in man's will and thus fully capable of being
eliminated through exertion.

This revivalism led to a steady disintegration
of whatever orthodox authority remained, eventually breaking up the residues of establishment

A BAPTISM IN THE SCHUYLKILL RIVER

Once a small and dispised sect, the Baptists by
the early nineteenth century had become, next
to the Methodists, the second largest denomination in America. Unlike the Methodists, who
relied on a ordered authority and circuit riders,
the Baptists used independent farmer-preachers
who moved with the people into new areas or
sprang up among the unchurched in older areas.
*(Museum of Art, Rhode Island School of Design, Gift
of Lucy T. Aldrich.)*

in Connecticut (1818) and Massachusetts (1833), and to a multiplication of re-ligious groups, all intensely interested in their denominational character in order to compete more effectively in the religious marketplace. The denominations now abandoned all hope of maintaining any special identity with the society. Indi-viduals were free to join whatever religious association they wished or to change associations whenever they wished. Dissenters and schismatics were allowed to go their own separate ways without the struggles that had marked earlier Ameri-can religious life. If the role of the denominations was to contend with one an-other for souls, it was important that each denomination be as united, tightly organized, and homogeneous as possible. The consequence was a further splin-tering of religion and the increasing proliferation of new, unheard-of religious groups, such as the Stonites and Campbellites, with no connection whatsoever with the Old World.

The effects of this fragmentation were offset by a conscious blurring of theo-logical distinctions among the competing denominations. The various religious groups espoused a common creed of identity with the nation that worked to unify the culture more than any legal establishment ever could have. New sects, like the Universalists in 1810, sang hymns to God's country:

> On a delightsome spot
> From other nations free
> Lord thou hast fix'd our lot;
> We owe, we owe to thee
> The independence of our land
> How happy does our nation stand!

Both ministers and politicians in the early nineteenth century emphasized over and over that America, though without an established church, was nevertheless a nation of God, not a Newtonian god but an evangelical one. Throughout the period, religious groups resisted the secularizing effects of the Enlightenment and the First Amendment and urged the republic to recognize its basis in Chris-tianity by instituting chaplains in Congress, proclaiming days of fasting and prayer, and ending mail delivery on the Sabbath. Clergymen, said Nathaniel William Taylor of Connecticut, the most important theologian of the Second Great Awakening, had no intention of creating a new governmental establish-ment or denying the rights of conscience. "We only ask for those provisions in law . . . in behalf of a common Christianity, which are its due as a nation's strength and a nation's glory." In 1811 in the notable blasphemy decision of Chancellor James Kent, *The People of New York* v. *Ruggles*, this Christianizing of republicanism was legally acknowledged. Although the state of New York had no established church and its constitution guaranteed freedom of religious opinion, Kent de-clared, to revile the Christian religion professed by almost the whole community, as Ruggles had done, was "to strike at the root of moral obligation and weaken the security of the social ties." Pietistic Christianity seemed to the clergy to have become the main cohesive force holding the nation together, "the central attraction," Lyman Beecher, the New England revivalist and reformer, said in 1820, "which must supply the deficiency of political affinity and interest." It had become patriotism itself.

Only religion, Washington had said in his Farewell Address in 1796, was capable of supplying "that virtue or morality" that was "a necessary spring of popular government." From the outset of America's republican experiment the clergy had been repeatedly told that whatever their doctrinal differences, "you are all united in inculcating the necessity of morals," and that "from the success or failure of your exertions in the cause of virtue, we anticipate the freedom or slavery of our country." Faced with such responsibility religious groups and others responded to the cause of virtue with a stridency and zeal that went beyond what any Revolutionary in 1776 could have imagined possible. Missionary, education, tract, and Bible societies—some even composed of combinations of the various denominations—spilled out to moralize and tame the barbarians, both in the American West and throughout the world.

New middle-class people led by the evangelical clergy sought simultaneously to spread and to control the democratic forces released by the Revolution. By condemning the vices of drinking, sexual promiscuity, gambling, and other amusements associated with the behavior of the dissolute aristocracy above it and the unproductive rabble below it, the new "middle class" struck out in both social directions at once and thereby acquired its distinctiveness. Because the new moralizing spirit could no longer be enforced by law and weakened governments, the great emerging force of American democratic society, public opinion, had to be mobilized in the cause of virtue, largely through local voluntary associations. These proliferating local moral societies—"disciplined moral militia," Lyman Beecher called them—eventually became nineteenth-century middle-class replacements for the humanitarian and benevolent societies that had been founded as products of the Enlightenment by urban gentry in the immediate post-Revolutionary years. Unlike the earlier organizations, these new middle-class associations were less concerned with relieving the suffering of the unfortunate than with shaping everyone's conduct.

Under these kinds of pressures the morality of the Revolutionary era became evangelized. Virtue now lost that rational, austere, and stoical quality befitting the classical heroes the Revolutionary leaders had emulated. Temperance, for example, that self-control of the passions so valued by the ancients, became largely identified with the elimination of popular drunkenness—"a good cause," declared the Franklin Society for the Suppression of Intemperance in 1814, in which "perseverance and assiduity seldom fail of securing the denied object." Virtue no longer meant conquering the passions but intensifying them for a moral end.

A republic, wrote Parson Weems in 1802, the entrepreneurial biographer of George Washington and spokesman for the new middle-class values, was "the best government for morals." It was a traditional statement no doubt, one that Washington himself had made many times; but in Weems's updated early-nineteenth-century version the morals had become vulgarized. Simplicity meant that there was no "sordid monopolizing *aristocracy*" to judge men by the elegance of their coats. Frugality meant that "the cheapest of all governments" would allow common people to get ahead. And liberty meant that "wealth pours into every pocket." Gone was any semblance of the classically heroic republic led by a rational elite; in its place was a society of ordinary men and women with very acquisitive desires.

The Popularization of American Culture

All these developments of the early decades of the nineteenth century, so new and unforeseen, had a bewildering effect on American attitudes. Some now rejected the conventional analogy between states and human beings and thought that the United States had escaped from history. Because American minds and institutions were "susceptible of infinite improvement," America was not destined to follow the fate of the ancient republics. "We fondly believe," said one orator in 1817, "that ours will endure unhurt by the ravages of time." Others, however, continued to talk of the dangers of luxury and decay, and some even saw Americans moving backwards in the cycle of history. In other countries, wrote one analyst in 1818, "progress has been from ignorance to knowledge, from the rudeness of savage life to the refinements of polished society. But in the settlement of North America the case is reversed. The tendency is from civilization to barbarism." Under the impact of the New World environment, "the tendency of the American character is then to degenerate, and to degenerate rapidly."

Such thoughts were doubly frightening because they only confirmed what some influential European theorists had been saying about the harmful effects of the environment of the New World. The celebrated French naturalist, the Comte de Buffon, in his long rambling *Natural History of Man* (1749–1804) had concluded pessimistically that there was in the New World "some combination . . . of elements and other physical causes, something that opposes the amplification of animated Nature." The American environment—the great irregularity of its topography, the violent variability of its climate, the excessive moisture in its air, and the extent of its forests and miasmatic swamps—appeared to have a deleterious effect on all life, including human beings. Such notions, supported by others—Corneille de Pauw, the Abbé Raynal, and William Robertson—had entered the popular literature about America and were on the minds of European travelers who visited the New World.

Nothing angered Americans more than these European charges, and they replied fiercely, with indignant dismissal, scientific comparison, or exaggerated boasting. But always there was the underlying dread that the European critics might be right. The devastating epidemics of yellow fever that broke out in American cities in this early republican period, beginning with the catastrophe in Philadelphia in 1793 (which killed 10 percent of the city's population), were not duplicated elsewhere in the Western world. This led some Americans like Jefferson to conclude that the disease was "peculiar to our country," caused by the way in which the unusual American atmosphere—the cloudless skies and the intense heat and humidity—fermented the filth and putrefaction of increasingly crowded American cities.

Since all men had sprung from the same origin, as recorded in the book of Genesis, it followed that all distinctions among men were traceable to environmental influences. Some Americans believed that even the color of men's skin was a product of the environment, a position that Benjamin Rush pushed to extremes when he hypothesized in a paper delivered to the American Philosophical Society in 1799 that the Negro's blackness was the consequence of a disease, leprosy, caused by the intense heat of the African climate.

However, it was not the blacks but the indigenous inhabitants of the New World, the Indians, who became the focus of the debate over the distinctive character of the American habitat. For at the heart of Buffon's indictment of America's climate were his charges that the native Indians were physically and sexually degenerate and incapable of strong social relationships. Although Americans were anxious to distinguish themselves from the state of savagery, at the same time they felt the patriotic need to defend the prowess and virtue of the Indian. Jefferson could readily doubt the capacities of blacks, who after all came from Africa, but he could not admit any inferiority in the red men, who were products of the very environment that would mold the people of the United States.

If natural circumstances were powerful enough to create indigenous diseases, to affect skin color, and to inhibit the Indian's maturation, then obviously Americans had to learn all they could about the natural circumstances of their New World. Calls thus went out to all parts of the intellectual community for information about the American habitat. Ministers in such obscure places as Mason, New Hampshire, faithfully compiled meterological and demographic records, and exclusively literary journals like the *North American Review* published periodic weather charts sent from distant outposts in Brunswick, Maine, and Albany, New York. Temperature taking became everyone's way of participating in the Enlightenment. During the years from 1763 to 1795 Ezra Stiles filled six volumes with his daily temperature and weather readings. Volume 4 of the *Transactions* of the American Philosophical Society, published in 1799, contained no less than six papers dealing with America's climate. People grasped at the possibility that they might by their own efforts order their natural environment, and the journals and newspapers of the period were filled with accounts of how Americans, by clearing their forests and draining their marshes, had moderated their weather over the previous decades. Jefferson put his friends to work weighing and measuring American animals, "from the mouse to the mammoth." While minister to France in the 1780s, he wrote home for a variety of bones and horns to convince Buffon of his errors, apologizing to the French naturalist for the small size of the specimens when in fact he had requested the largest specimens available.

The most exciting scientific event of this early republican period was Charles Willson Peale's exhumation in 1801 of the bones of a mastodon, or mammoth, found in upstate New York. Peale, who as artist, politician, scientist, inventor, and showman was as broad in his interests as Jefferson, took the bones to his Philadelphia museum devoted to the enlightened science of nature and displayed the reconstructed American mammoth as "the LARGEST of *terrestrial* beings" and "the ninth wonder of the world!!!" In an effort to bring all this information gathering together, the Philosophical Society in 1800 formally petitioned Congress to transform the decennial census into a detailed morality and occupational survey "to determine the effect of the soil and climate of the U.S. on the inhabitants thereof," promising even before the data were in that "truths will result

"EXHUMATION OF THE MASTODON," 1806

Charles Willson Peale (1741–1827) self-portrayed here directing the excavation, began his career as a saddler and clock repairman, but soon turned to painting and science. After the Revolution he opened a museum in Philadelphia containing a conglomeration of his paintings, curious gadgets, and stuffed animals designed to teach the public the ordered beauty of the natural world. After Peale's death, however, his scientific collections passed into the entreprenurial hands of P. T. Barnum and became part of his traveling circus—a romantic ending for an Enlightenment institution. (*The Peale Museum, Baltimore, Gift of Mrs. Harry White.*)

very satisfactory to our citizens that under the joint influence of soil, climate, and occupation the duration of human life in this position of the earth will be found at least equal to what it is in any other; and that its population increases with a rapidity unequaled in all others."

All these efforts to justify the natural environment led to the excited exaggerations of America's magnificent rivers, expansive forests, and sublime cataracts. Whether it was the Hartford Wits like Timothy Dwight and Joel Barlow in their poetry, Jefferson in his *Notes on Virginia,* Jedediah Morse in his *Geography,* William Bartram in his *Travels*—leading Americans felt a need to extol the grandeur of the American landscape not only to European critics but to themselves. Always, however, these suppressed anxieties over the degenerating effects of the natural world were tempered by the enlightened realization that political and moral circumstances were ultimately more important than physical circumstances in shaping man's character. No doubt climate affected inferior animals, said one writer in the Philadelphia literary journal *Port Folio* in 1807, but surely not man, whose reason provided "expedients to soften, or means of wholly averting its sinister tendencies." Americans could thus use their liberty and their learning to overcome nature. Amidst the ameliorating and civilizing institutions of the United States, even "the negroes," prophesied the South Carolina physician and historian David Ramsay, will "lose their black color," and the Indians, predicted the Republican enthusiast and poet Joel Barlow, would gain "a fairer tint and more majestic grace."

NATURAL BRIDGE, VIRGINIA

Jefferson thought that the Natural Bridge, which was located on his property in Rockbridge County, Virginia, was "the most sublime of nature's works. . . . It is impossible for the emotion arising from the sublime, to be felt beyond what they are here; so beautiful an arch, so elevated, so light: and springing as it were up to heaven, the rapture of the spectator is really indescribable!" *(Boston Public Library.)*

Nature had been important to Revolutionary Americans too; but it was less the peculiarities of the American wilderness they had sought to celebrate than the natural order of a Newtonian universe that transcended all national boundaries. All of the many learned and scientific societies formed in the period, from the reorganized American Philosophical Society (1769) to the Literary and Philosophical Society of New York (1814), rested on the eighteenth-century assumption that science was what distinguished cultivated men from savages and made them citizens of the world. To the eighteenth-century Enlightenment, science was cosmopolitan and contemplative. The study of nature, declared a literary society orator in 1792, raised man "above vulgar prejudices" and enabled him "to form just conceptions of things." It expanded "his benevolence," extinguished "every thing mean, base and selfish in his nature," gave "a dignity to all his sentiments," and taught "him to aspire to the moral perfections of the great author of all things."

But by the early nineteenth century, scientists were urging each other to turn their backs on the generalities of European science in the name of American particularities. The contemplative and cosmopolitan sciences of the eighteenth century, physics and astronomy, now gave way to the more vital and patriotic sciences of biology and chemistry. In its search for some sort of foundation in the popular mass, science tended to sink into curiosity hunting and gimmickry. Peale, for all of his rhetorical devotion to the majesty of the natural world, loved novelties himself and used all sorts of amusements to attract customers to his museum. Dr. Benjamin Rush sought to republicanize medicine by purging it of its mysteries and making it possible to be "taught with less trouble than is taken to teach boys to draw, upon paper or slate, the figures in Euclid." He succeeded in reducing all diseases to one—to fever caused by capillary tension, with the cure being purging and bleeding; but the simplification was so extreme that the inevitable revulsion left medicine drowning in a sea of empiricism and increasing complaints against quackery. Knowledge, declared the chemist Thomas Cooper in 1817, could no longer be the business of the learned, elevated few; it belonged to everyone and had

BENJAMIN RUSH, 1745–1813

One of the most versatile figures of the American Enlightenment, Rush was a physician, scientist, and humanitarian reformer of unbounded optimism. By the early nineteenth-century, however, his earlier confidence in liberal rationalism was gone. The country's reliance on liberty "has already disappointed the expectations of its most sanguine and ardent friends." "Nothing but the gospel of Jesus Christ," could save republicanism. *(Courtesy, Pennsylvania Hospital.)*

to enter "into our everyday comforts and conveniences," chemistry even being justified by Cooper for its usefulness in preparing and marinating food.

The eighteenth century's conception of the benefaction of science to mankind became increasingly identified with hardheaded materialistic utilitarianism. The rush of technological inventions in the post-Revolutionary years—steamboats, clocks, lamps, and numerous machines for doing everything from carding wool to cutting nails—were not unexpected by Enlightenment *philosophes* like Jefferson, who too thought of knowledge as "useful"; but the business significance now given to them was new. While many of the devices of these years were the results of the detached ingenuity of enlightened gentleman-scientists like Jefferson or Peale, most were the products of bourgeois-minded men of humble background like the metal craftsman John Fitch, the glue manufacturer Peter Cooper, and the steam-engine builder Oliver Evans, seeking not fame and benevolence but more efficient and more profitable ways of doing things. Education was now explained as a way of releasing individual talents for the individual's benefit, and science was being identified solely with those who had an interest in it, an interest that was increasingly a pecuniary one. Americans lacked the "large establishments and expansive endowments" of Europeans, Jacob Bigelow, Harvard professor and the originator of the term *technology*, declared in 1816. As a consequence they had fundamentally altered the nature and sociology of scientific investigation. In America there was no place for the traditional kinds of scientific patronage. "We have had few learned men, but many useful ones," which "has entitled us to the character of a nation of inventors."

By the early nineteenth century technology and prosperity began assuming for Americans the same sublime and moral significance the Enlightenment had reserved for the classical state and the Newtonian universe. Roads, bridges, and canals were justified by the fostering of "national grandeur and individual convenience," the two now being inextricably linked. It was not virtue that held this restless and quarrelsome people together, wrote the economist Samuel Blodget in 1806; it was commerce, "the most sublime gift of heaven, wherewith to harmonize and enlarge society." If America was ever to "eclipse the grandeur of European nations," said Charles G. Haines in 1818 in an enthusiastic promotion of the Erie Canal, it had to be in America's own terms: in its capacity to further the material welfare of its citizens. The "American Athens" was thus bound to have a commercial flavor, and the nature of all the arts, fine as well as useful, had to change.

The Revolutionaries had had high expectations for the arts. Not only would the Americans' artistic achievements be evidence of their civilized character but they would also be a means of perpetuating the fame of the United States through the ages. Given the traditional association of the arts with luxury and corruption, however, the arts in America would have to be designed not for the pleasure of a few rich and aristocratic patrons but for the social benefit and moral enlightenment of the whole citizenry. Inevitably then the Revolutionaries were

Plan of Mr Fitch's Steam Boat.

John Fitch (1743–1798) was the first to produce a serviceable steamboat in America. His 45-foot craft had a successful
trial on the Delaware River in August 1787 before a group
of delegates of the Constitutional Convention. *(American
Antiquarian Society.)*

committed to emphasizing the public utility and morality of the arts. But at the
beginning of the Revolutionary era they scarcely could have foreseen to what
lengths this emphasis would eventually be carried in the efforts to make the arts
meaningful to a rapidly enlarging and democratizing public. In the process the
moral and social character of the arts was stretched and exaggerated to the point
where art as it was traditionally conceived was transformed.

To be sure, the arts had to be morally instructive and socially beneficial, but
most Revolutionaries had assumed that the attitudes to be inculcated would
embody, as the commissioners charged with supervising the construction of public buildings in Washington said in 1793, "a grandeur of conception, a Republican
simplicity, and that true elegance of proportion which correspond to a tempered freedom excluding Frivolity, the food of little minds." But in the evangelical atmosphere of the decades following the Revolution, America's classical
morality was translated into a shrill popular didacticism, close at times to mere
prudery. Apologists for the arts found themselves reduced to defending them as
simply engines of the state designed to eliminate popular vices such as drinking
or cockfighting. Instead of being benefactors to mankind, the arts were measured
by their contributions to America's material prosperity. Under these kinds of
pressures, American writers and painters like Alexander Wilson, Robert Fulton,
and Samuel F. B. Morse found it easy and more profitable to move into more
defensibly useful endeavors involving science and technology.

Behind these changing explanations of the role of the arts lay the republican
desire to bring the arts to a wider public and to involve the whole citizenry in

cultivation. But the taste of this enlarged public was not quite what was expected. No one, it seemed, wanted any sort of painting but portraits, and those who sought to commemorate great historical events on canvas had to turn their paintings into panoramas, oversized spectacles designed for carnival like exhibition. Under pressure from critics to perform nothing that "savours of indelicacy" or "tends to loosen the ties of morality," the theater in the early nineteenth century quickly degenerated into popular melodrama, whose blatant moralism and strident patriotism were in accord with the new democratic audiences. The literature most people wanted was the sentimental novel, which under the guise of moral instruction usually dealt with an illicit love affair. Susannah Rowson's tale of seduction, *Charlotte Temple*, published in 1791, became the best selling novel in America over the next fifty years with forty-two editions by 1820 alone.

By 1820 these developments were forcing a new shape and alignment to American culture, in which the modern distinction between high and popular culture was born. In the eighteenth century cultivation or learning was considered to be unitary and homogeneous, involving as it did, say, for Jefferson, all aspects of the arts and sciences, and was regarded as a personal qualification for participation in gentlemanly society. Indeed, to be a gentleman was the equivalent of being learned and a member of the republic of letters. Men of learning had no doubt of the existence of vulgar habits and customs, like bear baiting or barn dancing, but scarcely saw these as some sort of "popular culture" set in competitive opposition to the republic of letters. The Revolutionary aim of relating art to the public at large was not supposed to destroy the cultivated elite and threaten its standards but only broaden its sources of recruitment and elevate the taste of the society. Yet as the distinction between gentleman and nongentleman became blurred, cultivation itself became popularized, creating a new middle-class culture, "widely and thinly spread," the Federalists charged.

Those members of the literati who clung to the traditional humanist standards of the cosmopolitan republic of letters found themselves beset by a popular culture they could scarcely control but to which they bore a particular responsibility. Writers and artists, advised a publisher of the *North American Review*, William Tudor in 1816, "should feel something of a

(Abby Aldrich Rockefeller Folk Art Collection.)

missionary spirit" in improving "the taste of the publick." Learned academies and critical journals were formed, not for professional recognition and communication, but for the instruction and guidance of the people's artistic judgment. The traditional association of the arts with aristocracy and licentiousness created an obsession among the cultivated of making the arts "instruments of public morality." Hence Harvard professors such as Andrews Norton felt obligated in the face of the popularity of the sentimental novels of seduction to claim that such didactic authors as Maria Edgeworth and Felicia Hemans were the greatest writers in the English language. The moral and social character of art was proclaimed so strenuously that artists found it impossible to justify any sort of independent existence in defiance of the public. When Wordsworth was severely criticized for writing too solitary and too unsocial a kind of poetry, what freedom from social obligations could an American poet expect?

As a consequence of these kinds of pressures, felt by European artists also but not so intensely, artistic self-expression and the romantic movement in America were retarded. Many American artists and writers remained committed to their moral and social responsibility well into the nineteenth century; but in the end they paid a high price for this commitment in their artistic creativity and their historical reputation. The genteel culture of nineteenth-century America and the careers of such writers as Henry Wadsworth Longfellow, James Russell Lowell, and Oliver Wendell Holmes were shaped by these determined and not unworthy efforts to democratize the fine arts and relate them to the public. Whatever aesthetic judgment one may make of the artistic contributions of the post-Revolutionary generation that Emerson so scorned, it did succeed in legitimizing art in America and in transforming it into culture in the only way that American democratic society allowed.

In confrontation with what seemed to be an all-encompassing popular culture many artists and critics began throwing up their hands. "Public opinion" now seemed to be the only force that counted in American life. If people were willing to trust the clashing opinions of innumerable groups and individuals in religion, politics, and the economy, why not then in artistic taste? Ever since the debate over the Sedition Act in 1798 some Americans had been arguing that it was no longer possible in this democratic society for any institution, group, or individual, no matter how learned and rational, to determine the truth or rightness of any opinion. Although the Federalists had claimed that "truth has but one side, and listening to error and falsehood is indeed a strange way to discover truth," other Americans had concluded that opinions about all sorts of matters were many and diverse and not subject to the judgment of any individual. Not only were all opinions to be tolerated, even those that might be false, but everyone and anyone in the society should be equally able to express them. Truth was actually the creation of many voices and many minds, no one of which was more important than another, and each of which made its own separate and equally significant contribution. In the sprawling atomized society of republican America, solitary individual opinions may have counted for less, but in their collectivity they now added up to a public opinion far more significant and trustworthy than what had existed before.

Such a development was made both possible and comprehensible by the radical social changes that had taken place in America since the middle of the eighteenth century. This notion of public opinion as the transcendent consequence of many sources, none of which deliberately created it, was matched by what was happening in politics, in religion, and in the economy. In every area of American life the long-developing breakup of the older society had led to an increasing fragmentation of all sorts of power and authority and the release of individuals, parties, denominations, corporations, and other atomized units. Instead of the chaos that the eighteenth century would have expected from this individualism, something—some called it providence—was allowing these diverse and independent entities, competing freely in the open society, to arrive at a cohesive consensus that none by itself could have created.

This radically new conception of the social process was being formulated generally throughout the Western world, but it was in America that the new social reality that provoked this new thinking was most fully revealed. Under the pressure of the democratization taking place throughout Western society, people were forced to rethink the ways in which they related to government, the marketplace, and each other, and to devise new schemes for understanding the development of society. As theorists came to realize that much of what happened in history was the unintended product of numerous and diverse individual purposes, analyses of men's motives gave way to new efforts to understand the consequences of their actions. The eighteenth-century reliance on conspiratorial explanations of events now lost some of the centrality of appeal it had had for the Revolutionary generation. While conspiratorial interpretations of frightening events continued to flourish in American society, many Americans came to place a new trust in the total pattern of unintended events—the beneficent workings of providence, which was now identified with progress.

By 1815 the ways in which Americans judged their progress had fundamentally shifted. Already they were turning inward to celebrate the consequences of their Revolution and to extol the uniqueness of their society. A new generation was no longer interested in sustaining any kind of aristocracy, natural or not, no longer cared about the cosmopolitan republic of letters, and no longer dreamed of building a classical republic of austere and heroic virtue. America, it was now said, would find its greatness not by emulating Europe or the republics of antiquity, but by creating a prosperous free society rooted in individualism and acquisitiveness, overlaid by Protestant evangelical millennialism, and belonging, in a way no other society in history ever did, to obscure ordinary people. With the rise of these kinds of sentiments the Revolution and the American Enlightenment had run their course.

Suggested Readings

A helpful survey of American social history is Rowland Berthoff, *An Unsettled People* (1971). But it has not replaced the encyclopedic History of American Life Series edited by Arthur M. Schlesinger and Dixon Ryan Fox. The two volumes covering the Revolutionary era are Evarts B. Greene, *The Revolutionary Generation, 1763–1790* (1943); and John Allen Krout and Dixon Ryan Fox, *The Completion of Independence, 1790–1830* (1944). Population developments are summarized by J. Potter, "The Growth of Population in America, 1700–1860," in David Glass and D. E. Eversley, eds., *Population in History* (1965). An important social history that goes well beyond its title is David J. Rothman, *The Discovery of the Asylum: Social Order and Disorder in the New Republic* (1971).

Two surveys of economic life are useful: Stuart Bruchey, *The Roots of American Economic Growth, 1607–1861* (1965); and Douglass C. North, *The Economic Growth of the United States, 1790–1860* (1961). The essays in David T. Gilchrist, ed., *The Growth of the Seaport Cities, 1790–1825* (1967) are especially helpful. For agriculture, see P. W. Bidwell and J. I. Falconer, *History of Agriculture in the Northern United States 1620–1860* (1925); and particularly L. C. Gray, *History of Agriculture in the Southern United States to 1860* (2 vols., 1933). For manufacturing, see V. S. Clark, *History of Manufactures in the United States* (3 vols., 1928). To understand the interrelated nature of the social, economic, and political processes in this period, the student can find no better work than Oscar Handlin and Mary Handlin, *Commonwealth: A Study of the Role of Government in the American Economy: Massachusetts, 1774–1861* (rev. ed., 1969). It is especially important for its analysis of the changing nature of the corporation.

On the development of the West, see Reginald Horsman, *The Frontier in the Formative Years, 1783–1815* (1970). Stanley Elkins and Eric McKitrick, "A New Meaning for Turner's Frontier," *Political Science Quarterly*, 69 (1954), offers a scheme for understanding the differences between the northwestern and southwestern frontiers in the early nineteenth century. On the new cities of the West, see Richard C. Wade, *The Urban Frontier* (1959). Beverley W. Bond, *The Civilization of the Old Northwest: A Study of Political, Social and Economic Development, 1788–1812* (1934) is a good compilation. Land policy and land laws are covered in Malcolm J. Rohrbough, *The Land Office Business . . . 1789–1837* (1968).

On religion and the Revolution, see William W. Sweet, *Religion in the Development of American Culture, 1765–1840* (1952). The opening chapters of Perry Miller, *The Life of the Mind in America* (1965), are very helpful for understanding the emergence of evangelicism. The essays collected in Elwyn A. Smith, ed., *The Religion of the Republic* (1971), are important in relating evangelical Protestantism and republicanism. Older studies that need updating are Catherine C. Cleveland, *The Great Revival in the West, 1797–1805* (1916); and Oliver W. Elsbree, *The Rise of the Missionary Spirit in America, 1790–1815* (1928). See also John Bole, *The Great Revival in the South, 1787–1805* (1972), and especially Howard Miller, *The Revolutionary College: American Presbyterian Higher Education. 1707–1837* (1976). For secular-minded approaches to evangelicism, see Charles I. Foster, *An Errand of Mercy: The Evangelical United Front, 1790–1837* (1960); and Clifford S. Griffin, *Their Brothers' Keepers: Moral Stewardship in the United States, 1800–1865* (1960). On deism, see Gustav A. Koch, *Republican Religion* (1933); and Herbert M. Morais, *Deism in Eighteenth-Century America* (1934). On millennialism, see Ernest Lee Tuveson, *Redeemer Nation: The Idea of America's Millennial Role* (1968).

On the varying definitions of the American Enlightenment and its relation to Protestantism, see the superb study by Henry F. May, *The Enlightenment in America* (1976). Daniel Boorstin, *The Lost World of Thomas Jefferson* (1948), describes the rigidities of intellectual life in Republican circles. The standard survey is Russel B. Nye, *The Cultural*

Life of the New Nation, 1776–1830 (1960). A rich description of the cultural achievements in painting, music, literature, and theater during the Revolution is Kenneth Silverman, *A Cultural History of the American Revolution* (1976).

On the American environment, see Gilbert Chinard, "Eighteenth-Century Theories on America as a Human Habitat," American Philosophical Society, *Proceedings,* 91 (1947). Roy Harvey Pearce, *Savagism and Civilization* (1967), describes the ambiguity of American attitudes towards the Indian. On the cosmopolitanism of the Revolutionaries, see Brooke Hindle, *The Pursuit of Science in Revolutionary America 1735–1789* (1956); and Michael Kraus, *The Atlantic Civilization* (1949). The first volume of Robert E. Spiller and others, eds., *The Literary History of the United States* (3d ed., 1964), has some valuable essays on publishing and the distribution of literature. The appropriate chapters of Oliver Larkin, *Art and Life in America* (1949), are important for relating art and society. Neil Harris, *The Artist in American Society . . . 1790–1860* (1966), a pathbreaking work, is especially insightful in its understanding of the tensions between republicanism and art.

Chronology, 1760–1820

1760 George III accedes to throne.

1763 Treaty of Paris ends Seven Years War between Great Britain, and France and Spain.
Pontiac's rebellion, uprising of Indians in Ohio Valley.
Proclamation line drawn along Appalachians by British forbids settlement in West by whites.
Parson's Cause, resulting from efforts by Anglican clergy in Virginia to recover salaries lost from Two-Penny acts.
Paxton uprising by Scotch-Irish settlers in western Pennsylvania.

1764 Sugar Act passed by Parliament, reducing duty on foreign molasses.
Currency Act prohibits issues of legal-tender currency in the colonies.
Brown University founded.

1765 Stamp Act passed.
Stamp Act Congress meets in New York.

1766 Stamp Act repealed by Parliament, which adopts Declaratory Act asserting its authority to bind the colonies "in all cases whatsoever."
Antirent riots by tenant farmers in New York.

1767 Townshend Duties passed.
American Board of Customs established.
John Dickinson's *Letters from a Farmer in Pennsylvania*.
Organization of the Regulators in backcountry of South Carolina.

1768 Secretary of State for the Colonies established in England—first executive department with exclusively colonial concerns.
Circular Letter of Massachusetts House of Representatives.
John Hancock's sloop *Liberty* seized.
British troops sent to Boston.

1769 American Philosophical Society reorganized, with Benjamin Franklin as president.

1770 Lord North's ministry formed.
Townshend Duties repealed, except for duty on tea.
Boston Massacre.

1771 Benjamin Franklin begins his *Autobiography*.
Battle of Almanac, North Carolina, between western Regulators and eastern militia led by the governor.

1772 British schooner *Gaspee* burned in Rhode Island.

1778 United States concludes military alliance and commercial treaty with France. First and only military alliance by United States until North Atlantic Treaty Organization, 1949.
British evacuate Philadelphia.
British seize Savannah, Georgia.

1779 Spain enters the war against Britain.
George Rogers Clark captures Vincennes and ends British rule in Northwest.

1780 Americans surrender 5500 men and the city of Charleston, South Carolina.
Battle of Camden, South Carolina; Gates defeated by Cornwallis.
Battle of King's Mountain, South Carolina; British and Tories defeated.

1781 Battle of Cowpens, South Carolina; British under Tarleton defeated by Morgan.
Battle of Guilford Courthouse, North Carolina; outcome indecisive, but Cornwallis withdraws to coast.
Cornwallis surrenders to Washington at Yorktown, Virginia.
Articles of Confederation ratified.
Congress establishes Bank of North America.

1782 Fall of Lord North's ministry.

1783 Newburgh conspiracy of American army officers.
Society of Cincinnati founded.
Pennsylvania Evening Post, first daily newspaper in United States, begins publication.
Treaty of Peace with Britain signed.

1785 Land Ordinance for Northwest Territory adopted by Congress.

1786 Jay-Gardoqui treaty, rejected by Congress.
Virginia Statute for Religious Freedom.
Shays's Rebellion in western Massachusetts.
Annapolis Convention; adopts plan to meet in Philadelphia to revise Articles of Confederation.

1787 Federal Constitutional Convention meets in Philadelphia and drafts Constitution.
Northwest Ordinance enacted by Congress.
The Federalist papers begun by Madison, Hamilton, and Jay.
The Contrast, by Royall Tyler, first native comedy to be professionally performed.

1788 Ratification of United States Constitution by all the states except Rhode Island and North Carolina.

1802 Republican Congress repeals Judiary Act of 1801.

1803 *Marbury v. Madison*; Supreme Court upholds right of judicial review.
Louisiana Purchase.
War resumed in Europe.

1804 Hamilton killed by Vice-President Aaron Burr in duel.
Lewis and Clark expedition organized.
Impeachment of judges Pickering and Chase.
Twelfth Amendment to Constitution ratified.
Jefferson elected for second term.

1805 Pennsylvania Academy of Fine Arts formed.
Essex decision by British prize court increases British seizures of American neutral ships.

1806 Monroe-Pinckney treaty with Britain, which Jefferson refuses to send to Senate for ratification.
Burr conspiracy.

1807 *Chesapeake-Leopard* affair.
Embargo Act.
Robert Fulton's steamboat *Clermont* travels on Hudson River from Albany to New York in 30 hours.

1808 Congress prohibits Americans from participating in African slave trade.
James Madison elected President.
Embargo repealed; Non-Intercourse Act passed, prohibiting trade with Britain and France.

1810 Macon's Bill No. 2 passed, restoring trade with Britain and France, but providing for trade restrictions to be reimposed on one of the powers if other should abandon its seizure of American ships.
Connecticut Moral Society formed to combat infidelity and drinking.
West Florida annexed by Madison.
American Board of Commissioners for Foreign Missions formed.
Berkshire cattle show in Pittsfield, Massachusetts.

1811 In *Fletcher v. Peck*, Supreme Court moderates state law re *Yazoo* land claims because of impairment of contracts.
Madison, believing Napoleon has removed restrictions on American commerce, prohibits trade with Britain.
Battle of Tippecanoe, Indiana, in which

formed.

1773 Tea Act imposed.
Boston Tea Party.

1774 Coercive Acts.
Continental Congress meets in Philadelphia.
Galloway's Plan of Union.
Continental Association.

1775 Battle of Lexington and Concord.
Fort Ticonderoga taken by American forces.
Second Continental Congress meets in Philadelphia.
George Washington appointed commander in chief of Continental Army.
Battle of Bunker Hill.
Congress adopts its "Declaration of the Causes and Necessity for Taking up Arms."
George III proclaims colonists in open rebellion.
American forces fail to take Quebec; General Montgomery killed.
Pennsylvania Quakers form first antislavery society in world.

1776 Thomas Paine's *Common Sense.*
British troops evacuate Boston.
Congress calls on colonies to suppress all crown authority, and establish governments under authority of the people.
Declaration of Independence.
Battle of Long Island, New York; Americans defeated by General Howe.
British take New York City.
Battle of Trenton.
New Hampshire, New Jersey, Pennsylvania, Delaware, Maryland, Virginia, North Carolina, and South Carolina write state constitutions. Rhode Island and Connecticut change their colonial charters.

1777 Battle of Princeton.
Battle of Monmouth, New Jersey. Although outcome indecisive, Washington's troops stand up to British regulars.
Battle of Brandywine, Pennsylvania; Washington defeated.
British occupy Philadelphia.
Battle of Germantown, Pennsylvania; Howe repulses Washington's attack.
Burgoyne surrenders at Saratoga.
Articles of Confederation adopted by Continental Congress, but not ratified by all states until 1781.
Washington retires to Valley Forge for winter.
New York and Georgia write state constitutions.

Washington inaugurated as first President.
Capitol at Richmond, Virginia, built from model of Maison Carrée supplied by Jefferson.

1790 Hamilton's Report on Public Credit; Funding Bill; Assumption Bill.
Father John Carroll made first Roman Catholic bishop of United States with See in Baltimore.

1791 Bank of the United States established.

1792 First ten amendments to Constitution (Bill of Rights) adopted.

1793 Execution of Louis XVI and outbreak of European war.
Washington inaugurated for second term.
Proclamation of Neutrality by Washington.
Citizen Genêt affair.
Samuel Slater erects first cotton mill at Pawtucket, Rhode Island.
Eli Whitney applies for patent on cotton gin.
Yellow fever epidemic in Philadelphia.

1794 Whiskey Rebellion in western Pennsylvania.
Battle of Fallen Timbers, Ohio; General Anthony Wayne defeats Indians.

1795 Philadelphia-Lancaster turnpike completed.
Jay's treaty with Britain.
Treaty of Greenville, between United States and Indians of Northwest.
Pinckney's treaty with Spain.

1796 Washington's Farewell Address, warning against foreign entanglements and domestic factionalism.
John Adams elected President.

1798 XYZ affair reported by Adams to Congress.
Quasi-war with France on high seas.
Alien and Sedition acts enacted by Federalists in Congress.
Virginia and Kentucky resolutions.
Eleventh Amendment to Constitution ratified.

1799 *American Review and Literary Journal,* first quarterly literary review in America, established by the novelist Charles Brockden Brown.
Fries uprising in Pennsylvania.

1800 Washington, D.C., becomes capital.
Library of Congress established.
Convention of 1800, supplanting treaties of 1778 with France.
Thomas Jefferson elected President.

1801 Plan of Union between Presbyterians and Congregationalists to bring religion to frontier.
War with Barbary states.
Cane Ridge, Kentucky, revival meeting.
John Marshall becomes chief justice.

and prevents formation of Indian confederacy.
Charter of the Bank of the United States allowed to lapse by Congress.

1812 Congress declares war against Britain.
American Antiquarian Society formed in Worcester, Massachusetts.
Americans surrender Detroit to British.
Madison elected for second term.

1813 Battle of Lake Erie, in which Captain Oliver Perry defeats British naval forces.
Battle of the Thames, in which General Harrison defeats British and their Indian allies.

1814 Battle of Horseshoe Bend, Alabama; General Andrew Jackson defeats Creek Indians fighting for British.
British burn Washington, D.C.
Commander Thomas Macdonough defeats British fleet on Lake Champlain; invading British turned back at Plattsburgh, New York.
Hartford Convention of Federalist delegates from New England states meets.
Treaty of Ghent signed between United States and Great Britain.

1815 Battle of New Orleans; Jackson defeats British.
North American Review founded in Boston; soon becomes leading literary review in America.

1816 Second Bank of the United States chartered by Congress.
American Bible Society founded.
Protective tariff passed.
James Monroe elected President.

1817 Bonus Bill establishing fund for building roads and canals vetoed by Madison.
American Tract Society formed to circulate religious literature in the West.
Seminole War on Georgia-Florida border.

1818 General Jackson invades Florida to end Seminole War.
Rush-Bagot convention between Britain and United States establishes American fishing rights and boundary between United States and Canada.

1819 Commercial panic with many bank failures.
Adams-Onis Treaty signed between United States and Spain; Spain ceded Florida to the United States and recognized the western limits of the Louisiana Purchase.
Dartmouth College case.
McCulloch v. Maryland.

1820 Missouri Compromise.
James Monroe reelected President.

PART THREE

Expanding the Republic

1820-1860

DAVID BRION DAVIS

The end of the American Enlightenment also marked the end of attempts to model American society on European blueprints. By the 1820s it was becoming clear that the American people would quickly overleap restraints and limits of every kind. Expansive, self-assertive, extravagantly optimistic, they believed they had a God-given right to pursue happiness. In a nation of infinite promise, there could be no permanent barriers to the people's aspirations for wealth and self-improvement.

This absence of barriers, of distinctions of rank, and of prescribed identities was what Alexis de Tocqueville meant by "the general equality of condition among the people." Nothing struck Tocqueville more forcibly when he visited the United States in 1831 than this leveling of ancient and inherited distinctions of rank. He took it to be "the fundamental fact" about American society from which all other facts seemed "to be derived." Tocqueville was aware of the economic and racial inequalities of American society. Indeed, he suggested that it was precisely the lack of traditional restraints, such as those associated with a landed aristocracy, that opened the way for racial oppression and for a new kind of aristocracy created by business and manufacturing.

All societies require a system of rules, restraints, and limits. In a traditional, premodern society, such as the feudal regime to which Tocqueville looked back with some nostalgia, there was a certain stability to the territorial boundaries of a kingdom, an estate, or a people. Similarly, few people questioned the customary rules that defined social rank, the rights and duties of lords and peasants, the inheritance of land, the limits of political power and economic enterprise, and the expectations appropriate for each individual. Men and women knew what they had been born to, what place they had been assigned by fate. A close relation prevailed between the narrow boundaries of the physical environment and the social boundaries that political, legal, and religious institutions imposed.

The United States, as Tocqueville repeatedly emphasized, had thus far managed to avoid anarchy while greatly expanding most people's possibilities of life. From the time of the first colonial settlements, Americans had evolved institutions that had ensured a degree of order and stability to social life, protecting the public good from the worst excesses of acquisitive self-interest. By the early nineteenth century, however, there was a growing faith that the public good would best be served by allowing maximum freedom to the individual pursuit of self-interest.

In the period 1820–1860 this drive for individual self-betterment led to an unprecedented economic and territorial expansion, to the migration of millions of Europeans to America, and to the settlement of millions of Americans in the new states and territories of the West. Much of the nation's foreign policy was devoted to extending territorial boundaries and to preventing European attempts to impose future barriers to American influence and expansion in the Western Hemisphere. Federal land policy encouraged rapid settlement of the West. Both national and state governments committed a large share of public resources to the construction of roads, canals, and railroads that surmounted the barriers of mountains and increasing distance. Government at all levels actively sought to stimulate growth and economic opportunity. Much of the political ideology of the period was directed against forces and institutions, such as the Second Bank of the United States, which could be portrayed as restricting individual opportunity.

But for many thoughtful Americans, reformers as well as conservatives, there was a danger that these expansive energies would erode all respect for order, balance, and communal purpose; that the competitive spirit would lead to an atomized society ruled by the principle, "Every man for himself and the devil take the hindmost"; that the American people would become enslaved to money, success, and material gratification; and that the centrifugal forces of expansion would cause the nation to fly apart.

Most of the proposed remedies centered on the critical need to shape and reform individual character. Instead of looking to political institutions and governmental programs, most Americans sought social change through the moral reformation of individuals. They believed that if self-interest could be enlightened by a sense of social responsibility, the nation could be saved from the dehumanizing effects of commercialism and competitive strife. This was the great goal of the public schools, the religious revivals, and most of the new reform movements. It was a mission that gave a new importance and an educational role to mothers and to the middle-class home. In one sense, these efforts at shaping character embodied a nostalgic desire to restore a lost sense of community and united purpose. But the crusades for moral improvement were also instruments of modernization that encouraged predictable and responsible behavior and that aimed at ennobling and legitimating a market-oriented society.

It was the issue of Negro slavery that finally dramatized the conflict between self-interest and the ideal of a righteous society—a society that could think of itself as "under God." And it was the westward expansion of Negro slavery that ultimately became the testing ground for defining and challenging limits—the territorial limits of slavery, the limits of federal power, and the limits of popular sovereignty and self-determination. For most of the period an ambiguity on all these matters allowed the North and South to expand together and to resolve periodic conflicts by compromise. By the 1850s, however, Southern leaders insisted that the equal rights of slaveholders would be subverted unless the federal government guaranteed the protection of slave property in the common territories. Northern leaders, including eventually many moderates who had always favored compromise, drew a firm line against imposing slavery on a territory against the wishes of the majority of settlers. To paraphrase the poet Robert Frost, the territorial question came down to what Americans were willing to wall in or wall out. In one form or another, Americans had to face the question whether, in a free society, any limits could be imposed on the total dominion of one person over another.

13

The Contours of
Material Change

To understand the quality of American experience during the four decades preceding the Civil War one must first grasp the dimensions of demographic and economic change. Other nations have undergone brief periods of intense economic growth, industrialization, and urbanization, accompanied by painful cultural adjustment and social conflict. In general, however, this modernizing experience has occurred in regions that have been settled for many centuries, that have long been circumscribed as geographic and political unities, and that have acquired a ballast of tradition, custom, and class interest serving at once as a barrier to be broken and as a stabilizer to change. What distinguished American history, in the period 1820–1860, was that a modern market economy emerged in conjunction with the rapid settlement of virgin land and the unprecedented expansion of the Western frontier.

There were few physical, political, or cultural barriers to this double process, and the American people were determined to test, push back, and overcome what barriers there were. The American economy showed a remarkable freedom in the flow of goods, people, and capital in response to market forces. No laws restricted the influx of European and Asian laborers. By the 1850s even the federal prohibition of 1808 on further African slave importation came under sharp attack in the South. The Constitution ruled out any taxes on American

exports. Thanks largely to Southern pressure, the federal government gradually lowered protective tariffs on imports. The federal government's sale and
donation of immense tracts of public land were intended to encourage individual
enterprise in a free and unregulated market. Political stability, underscored by
the rapid and orderly creation of new states, helped to guarantee the security
of private property and the legal enforcement of contracts. Although the states
themselves actively promoted economic growth, no other society had imposed so
few fiscal, political, religious, and social restraints on the marketplace. No other
society had been so confident that market forces constituted the "invisible hand"
of a higher, cosmic order. No other society had become so committed to the
goal of maximizing individual profits by increasing productivity and lowering
costs.

The measurable changes in the economy, when viewed as segments of long-
term trends, were not revolutionary. Between 1820 and 1860 there were no
sharp breaks in development. As a result of large inputs of land, labor, and
capital, the economy experienced extremely rapid growth. But the gains in
product per capita—that is, in total national output relative to population—did

"THE CULTIVATOR"

In the Jacksonian period Americans saw
improvements in agriculture as the key
to progress and as the indispensable
support for industry, art, and science.
(Library of Congress.)

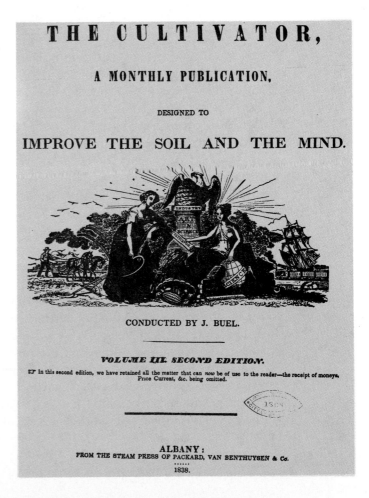

THE CULTIVATOR,

A MONTHLY PUBLICATION,

DESIGNED TO

IMPROVE THE SOIL AND THE MIND.

CONDUCTED BY J. BUEL.

VOLUME III. SECOND EDITION.

In this second edition, we have retained all the matter that can *now* be of use to the reader—the receipt of moneys,
Price Current, &c. being omitted.

ALBANY:
FROM THE STEAM PRESS OF PACKARD, VAN BENTHUYSEN & Co.
......
1838.

The United States 1820-1860

New States with Dates of Admission

not equal the high growth rates in later periods of American history or in the history of many other industrial nations. The expansion of Northeastern manufacturing led the nation through the first stages of industrialization; yet in most respects the United States in 1860 was not yet an industrial nation. The most significant structural changes included the decline of self-sufficient farming, the virtual disappearance of household manufacturing, and the growing obsolescence of independent artisans and of the apprenticeship system. American agriculture, led by the Southern slave plantations, turned increasingly toward cash crops for urban and industrial markets. Manufacturing, even when not yet mechanized, came increasingly under the control of merchant entrepreneurs who were able to reduce costs and specialize production for wider markets. Lacking other barriers, Americans could concentrate their energy and ingenuity on overcoming the nation's competitive handicaps—a relative shortage of capital and especially of cheap labor. America's great triumphs by 1860 resulted from labor-saving innovations and from the exploitation of cheap natural resources.

On the modern economist's charts, change and growth tend to flatten into orderly and predictable sequence. As perceived and experienced by living human beings, however, the changes of the period 1820–60 were both liberating and cataclysmic. The removal of former limits meant destroying family self-sufficiency, pride in craftsmanship, and personal and family ties that unified residential communities with local economic markets. Widening national markets also widened the range of individual choice. There was little choice, however, for the Indians, slaves, unskilled laborers, landless farmers, and domestic servants, in short, for those who were excluded by force, cultural differences, or lack of skill from the benefits of the market. A market society rewards certain patterns of behavior, such as risk taking coupled with a calculated intent to shape the future. It punishes others, such as living wholly in the present and submitting to fate, or equating security with loyalty to one's patron or lord. Despite a rising standard of living, Americans in the pre-Civil War decades witnessed growing economic inequalities. Success itself often appeared to increase an individual's vulnerability to impersonal forces, and to deepen anxieties over losing the reward of capricious good fortune. Above all, the triumph of market values presented the ultimate challenge to the weakening ideal of a people living in covenant under the government of God.

Population

From 1820 to 1860 America's population maintained the extraordinary rate of growth that had characterized the colonial and early national periods. The average increase by decade amounted to nearly 35 percent; the total population continued to double every twenty-three years. The United States sustained this high rate of growth until the 1860s. If the population had continued to double every twenty-three years, the nation would have passed the 1 billion mark by 1975. During the nineteenth century no European nation achieved a growth rate one-half as high as America's for even two decades.

America's population growth cannot be attributed to any significant increase in life expectancy. In the mid-nineteenth century, life expectancy in America was roughly comparable to life expectancy in northwestern Europe and was probably declining in urban areas. Before the mid-1840s most of the population growth resulted from the remarkable fertility of the American people, reinforced by a relatively low rate of infant mortality. Statistics show that the number of children under five for every thousand white women between ages twenty and forty-four was twice as great for 1840 as for 1950. Like many countries in modern Africa and South America, the United States literally swarmed with children. In 1830 nearly one-third of the total white population was under the age of ten. Yet in all parts of the country the birthrate had actually begun to decline by 1810 and continued to fall throughout the century. By 1830 the proportion of small children in urban New England had fallen below the level that could be found in many rural areas in the mid-twentieth century. For a time the high though declining fertility in the expanding West offset the more rapidly declining birthrate in the urbanizing Northeast. In the 1840s, however, it was only the influx of European immigrants, who accounted for one-quarter of the total population increase of that decade, that maintained the previous rate of national growth. After 1860 neither expanding frontiers nor succeeding waves of immigration could outweigh the continuing decline in fertility, a decline that marked a critical stage of modernization and that appeared earlier in America than in most European nations.

Immigration was partly the result of economic distress in Europe. Few Europeans would have left their homes if population growth had not pressed hard on available supplies of land, food, and jobs, and if they had not been displaced and defined as expendable by the forces of a market economy. The disastrous failure of Ireland's potato crop in 1845, followed by five years of famine, presented many Irish with little choice but emigrating or starving. And the British landlords who controlled Ireland helped to subsidize emigration in the hope of reducing taxes for the support of workhouses, which were spilling over with starving laborers who had been evicted from the land. In parts of Germany and Scandinavia, governments encouraged emigration as a way of draining off unemployed farmers, who had been displaced by the modernization of agriculture, and artisans, who had lost work when English textiles and other cheap machine-made goods were imported.

But the most important stimulus to immigration was the promise of jobs in America. Immigration rose to high levels during America's years of greatest

EMIGRANT AGENT'S OFFICE

By the 1840s the expansion of transatlantic commerce had greatly reduced the westbound steerage fare from Europe to America. Nevertheless, many emigrants, such as the Irish portrayed here, had to depend on loans, charitable gifts, or funds sent from relatives in America. (*Frank Leslie's Illustrated News, Jan. 12, 1856.*)

prosperity, and lagged during years of economic recession. Mass emigration from Europe was a direct response to the sudden demand in America for labor in construction and manufacturing, and to the supposedly limitless opportunity for land ownership in the West. American promoters, representing shipping firms, labor contractors, manufacturers, and even the governments of Western states, enticed Europeans with glowing accounts of the United States. More persuasive were the reports of fellow villagers or family members who had crossed the Atlantic and tested the terrain. In the 1830s, when northwestern Europe became aware of America's economic boom, of the North's shortage of labor, and of the canal building and other public improvements that were opening the way to vast tracts of farmland in the West, the number of immigrants rose to nearly 600,000, approximately a fourfold in-

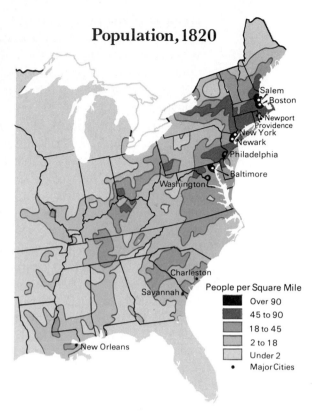

Population, 1820

People per Square Mile
- Over 90
- 45 to 90
- 18 to 45
- 2 to 18
- Under 2
- • Major Cities

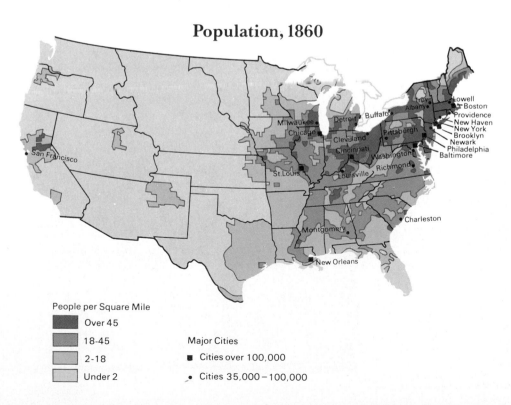

Population, 1860

People per Square Mile
- Over 45
- 18-45
- 2-18
- Under 2

Major Cities
- ■ Cities over 100,000
- • Cities 35,000 – 100,000

crease over the previous decade. In the 1840s the number soared to about 1.5 million, and in the 1850s to about 2.8 million. For each of the eight successive years from 1847 to 1854 there were over 100 immigrants for every 10,000 resident Americans, a proportion equaled only four times between 1860 and 1901.

The swelling stream, although it originated almost entirely from northwestern Europe, was anything but homogeneous. It included illiterate peasants from Germany and Ireland, highly skilled artisans from England, Germany, Belgium, and Switzerland, political refugees escaping the repression that followed the abortive revolutions of 1830 and 1848, and Jews and other victims of religious discrimination. Many of the Germans, who amounted to about 1.3 million immigrants, had sufficient funds to purchase farms in the West or at least to make their way to thriving German communities in Cincinnati, Saint Louis, and Milwaukee. The Irish, numbering some 1.7 million, had few skills and often arrived penniless, traveling steerage in the holds of westbound ships that were primarily engaged in carrying American lumber, grain, cotton, and other bulk products to Europe. Cast off by Britain as an unwanted population, the Irish peasants were in effect dumped in the Northeastern port cities or sometimes in Canada, from which they migrated southward. Gradually they found employment in heavy construction work, in foundaries and factories, and in domestic service, though for a time they enormously swelled the ranks of paupers and recipients of public and private welfare.

Before the Civil War the proportion of foreign-born, in the population as a whole, never rose above 15 percent, but in Boston and New York City by the 1850s the figure had temporarily climbed to over 50 percent. Over half the foreign-born lived in Ohio, Pennsylvania, and New York. This concentration of immigrants greatly accelerated the growth of cities in the Northeast and at strategic points along the Great Lakes and the Ohio and Mississippi rivers. In 1860

ARRIVAL OF THE GREAT WESTERN STEAMSHIP

New York harbor, always bustling with ships, was stirred to unusual excitement on April 23, 1838 by the arrival of the Great Western Steamship. Few people in the crowd could have realized that this was an omen of the eventual replacement of sailing vessels and of the decline of American shipping. *(Museum of the City of New York.)*

four out of five Americans still lived in rural environments, that is, on farms or in settlements of less than 2500. But this national figure does not show that even by 1850 over half the populations of Massachusetts and Rhode Island lived in urban centers, a proportion the nation at large did not reach until the 1920s. By 1860 eight American cities, three of them west of the Appalachians, had acquired more than 150,000 inhabitants, a population exceeded at that time by only seven cities in industrial England. Although America could boast of no metropolis equivalent to London, in 1860 the combined populations of Manhattan and Brooklyn exceeded 1 million. The Empire City, endowed with a superior harbor and with the Hudson River, which provided deepwater navigation into the interior, had won a further competitive advantage over other seaboard cities when in 1818 its merchants established the first regular and scheduled sailings to Europe. Seven years later the Erie Canal opened cheap access to the Great Lakes and to the markets of the West. Immigrants arrived and stayed in New York because it was America's great seaport and commercial center, a crucible of risk and opportunity that rewarded innovation in marketing, transportation, and public persuasion.

*The Concentration of Immigrants
in the North Accentuated
the Racial Contrast between North and South*

	Blacks per thousand whites	
	NORTH	SOUTH
1820	25	592
1860	18	582

Although the declining birthrate resulted in a slightly higher average age for the American population, the influx of immigrants greatly enlarged the number of Northeasterners between the ages of twenty and thirty. In 1850 over 70 percent of the American people were still under thirty, a figure that takes on greater meaning when compared with the 63 percent for England and the 52 percent for France. Before the Civil War the Americans remained an extraordinarily youthful people, a circumstance that helps to account for their restlessness, their venturesomeness, and their impatience with boundaries of any kind.

Alexis de Tocqueville echoed the amazement of many Europeans at the "strange unrest" of a people who could be seen "continually to change their track for fear of missing the shortest cut to happiness":

In the United States a man builds a house in which to spend his old age, and he sells it before the roof is on . . . he brings a field into tillage and leaves other men to gather the crops; he embraces a profession and gives it up; he settles in a place, which he soon afterwards leaves to carry his changeable longings elsewhere . . . and if at the end of a year of unremitting labor he finds he has a few days' vacation, his eager curiosity whirls him over the vast extent of the United States, and he will travel fifteen hundred miles in a few days to shake off his happiness. Death at length overtakes him, but it is before he is weary of his bootless chase of that complete felicity which forever escapes him.

This sense of limitless possibility helps to explain the feverish westward rush of population. By 1860 the settled area of the United States was five times what it had been in 1790, and nearly half the people lived beyond the 1790 boundaries of settlement. As late as 1820 many Americans had thought it would take at least a century to settle the vast territory east of the Mississippi. In 1860 the United States had firmly established its present continental boundaries, except for Alaska. No other nation had populated so much new territory in so short a time or absorbed so many immigrants; no other had combined rapid urbanization with the dramatic expansion of an agricultural frontier.

Indians

Long before 1820 the American people had shown an aggressive disregard for physical and social barriers, a determination to go where they pleased and to seize any chance for quick profit. They regarded the millions of acres of Western land the most valuable resource ever claimed by a republican society, a well-deserved inheritance that should be exploited as fast as possible. But in 1820 the prairies and forests east of the Mississippi still contained approximately 125,000 Indians, a population equal to that of white New Englanders in the first decade of the eighteenth century. Although millions of acres had been cleared of Indian occupancy rights, Indians blocked the way to government sale of much public land and thus to revenue, to profits from land speculation, and to the creation of private farms and plantations.

The Indians had proved to be the major losers in the War of 1812. This war, by ending the long conflict between Western settlers and European sovereigns, had removed the Indians' last hope of seeking white allies who could slow the advance of white America. The decisive victories of William Henry Harrison over the Shawnees in the Old Northwest, and of Andrew Jackson over the Creeks in the Old Southwest, had also shattered the hope of a union between Northern and Southern Indian confederations. These triumphs opened the way for exploiting tribal divisions and for gradually abandoning what Jackson termed "the farce of treating with Indian tribes" as units. Jackson thought that all Indians should be required as individuals to submit to the laws of the states, like everyone else, or to migrate beyond the Mississippi, where they could progress toward civilization at their own pace.

But land-hungry frontiersmen still faced the constraints of a federal Indian policy that had evolved from imperial, colonial, and early national precedents. This makeshift policy rested on four premises that were becoming increasingly contradictory. First, in line with Old World legal concepts, the Indian "nations" east of the Mississippi had long been treated variously as allies, enemies, and trading partners who deserved respect. The federal government continued to acknowledge that Indian tribes, while lacking many of the attributes of sovereignty, were in some sense independent nations that had acquired rights of possession by prior occupancy of the land. The continuing efforts to negotiate treaties, to purchase land, and to mark off territorial boundaries underscored the assumption that legitimate settlement by whites required at least symbolic consent from Indians. The same Old World model allowed the United States to punish "aggressor" tribes by demanding the cession of land as a legal indemnity for the damages of war.

The second premise, a product of New World experience, was that Indian "occupancy" must inevitably give way to white settlement. White Americans, like the heirs of a dying relative, had an "expectancy"—to use Jefferson's phrase—in the property that Indians held. In theory this preemptive claim did not infringe on the existing property rights of Indians. It simply gave the American government an exclusive right to purchase Indian lands, thereby blocking any future imperial designs by European powers. In practice, however, the doctrine of preemption led to the third premise of supreme federal authority over Indian affairs. Knowing the historic danger of foreign alliances with hostile Indians, the federal government had from its beginning assumed powers that would have been unthinkable in any other domestic sphere. It subjected all trade with Indians to federal licensing and regulation. It invalidated any sale or transfer of Indian lands, even to a state, unless made in accordance with a federal treaty. It guaranteed that Indians would be protected from encroachments on unceded land. Unfortunately, no federal administration had the will or military power to protect Indian rights while supervising the equitable acquisition of land by whites. In a government increasingly attuned to the voice of the people, the Indians had no voice of their own.

The fourth premise, which Jefferson had articulated and which gained momentum after the War of 1812, was that Indian culture, or "savagery," and American civilization could not permanently coexist. President James Monroe expressed the common conviction in a letter of 1817 to Andrew Jackson: "The hunter or savage state requires a greater extent of territory to sustain it, than is compatible with the progress and just claims of civilized life, and must yield to it." The government actively promoted schools, agriculture, and various "useful arts" among the Indians, hoping to convert nomadic hunters into settled farmers. This hope drew nourishment from the progress of the more populous Southern tribes, particularly the Cherokees, whose achievements in agriculture, in developing a written alphabet, and in adopting white technology seemed to meet the American tests of capability. But the government also pressured the Cherokees into ceding tracts of valuable eastern land in exchange for lands west of the Mississippi. By 1824 it was becoming clear that the five Southern confederations—Cherokees, Creeks, Choctaws, Chickasaws, and Seminoles—could not survive as even temporary enclaves without federal protection against white exploiters. The Southern tribes occupied western Georgia and North Carolina, and major portions of Tennessee, Florida, Alabama, and Mississippi, including the heart of the future cotton kingdom. In 1825 President Monroe officially proposed that these and all other remaining tribes should be persuaded to move west of the Mississippi, a plan that Jefferson and others had long regarded as the only way of saving America's original inhabitants from ultimate extinction.

Unfortunately, a commitment to individualism and state rights ruled out alternatives as well as coordinated planning for efficient removal. In Georgia, white speculators, squatters, and gold miners had no desire to see civilized Indians living on choice ancestral land. The state of Georgia complained that the United States had not fulfilled its agreement of 1802 to extinguish all Indian title to lands within the state in return for Georgia's cession of Western land claims. In 1828, after the Cherokees adopted a constitution and had claimed sovereign jurisdiction over their own territory, Georgia directly challenged federal policy by asserting that the Cherokees were mere tenants on state land, subject to the state's laws and authority. In 1832, in the case of *Worcester* v. *Georgia*,

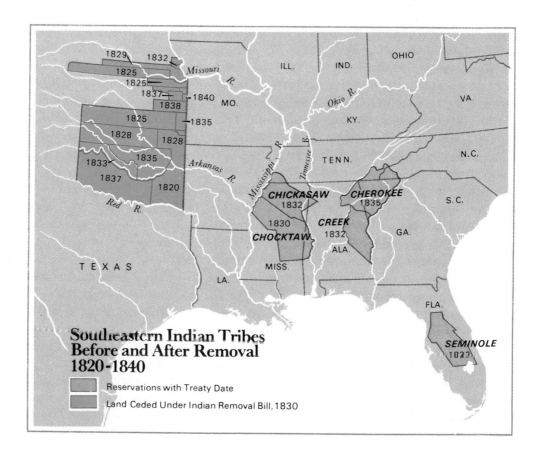

Southeastern Indian Tribes Before and After Removal 1820-1840

Reservations with Treaty Date

Land Ceded Under Indian Removal Bill, 1830

Chief Justice John Marshall ruled that Georgia had no right to extend state laws to the Cherokees or their territory. "The several Indian nations," he maintained, were "distinct political communities, having territorial boundaries, within which their authority is exclusive, and having a right to all lands within those boundaries, which is not only acknowledged, but guaranteed by the United States." But President Jackson, who had already withdrawn the federal troops earlier sent to protect Cherokee lands from intrusion, had no intention of enforcing the Supreme Court's decision.

Jackson firmly believed that Indians should be subject to state law and to the forces of a free market economy. To deal with tribes as privileged corporate groups, he thought, was simply to reinforce the power of corrupt chiefs and cunning half-breeds, who prevented tribesmen from following their own best interest. Jackson had no doubt that the vast majority of Indians, when liberated from tribal tyranny, would willingly emigrate to the West. The civilized few would be free to cultivate modest tracts of land and become responsible citizens of state and nation.

Jackson's denial of federal protection provided the needed incentives for a supposedly voluntary migration. Following Georgia's lead, other Southern states harrassed Indians with laws that few tribesmen could comprehend. White traders and lawyers descended like locusts on Indian lands, destroying tribal unity and authority. In 1830 Congress supported Jackson's policy by appropriating funds that would enable the President to negotiate treaties for the removal of all Indian tribes then living east of the Mississippi. The government still considered it necessary to purchase title to Indian land and to grant allotments of land to individual tribal leaders who could prove a legitimate claim. Federal officials even sought to protect Indians by supervising private contracts for sale. The majority of Indians, however, had no concept of land as a measurable and salable commodity. A few of the more experienced Chickasaws and other tribes men secured good prices for rich cotton land, but white speculators, who swiftly cornered between 80 and 90 percent of the Southern allotments, reaped windfall profits. Victims of wholesale fraud, chicanery, and intimidation, the great mass of Southern Indians had no choice but to follow the "Trail of Tears" to the vacant territory of Oklahoma. Subjected to disease, starvation, and winter cold, thousands died along the way. Military force gave a cutting edge to removal deadlines; in 1838 federal troops herded fifteen thousand Cherokees into detention camps. Meanwhile, Indians north of the Ohio River had earlier been demoralized as whites had cut down the supply of game, negotiated treaties with the more acculturated factions of certain tribes, and ensnared primitive societies with unfamiliar mechanisms of debt and credit. In 1832 the government crushed the resistance of Sac and Fox Indians in Illinois and Wisconsin, and in 1835 launched a long and costly war against the Seminoles in Florida. By 1844, except for a few remaining pockets mainly in the back country of New York, Michigan, and Florida, the mission of removal had been accomplished.

CATLIN'S
INDIAN GALLERY,
(FOR A FEW EVENINGS ONLY,) AT
AMORY HALL,
CORNER OF WASHINGTON AND WEST STREETS.

Mr. CATLIN, who has been for seven years traversing the Prairies of the "Far West," procuring the Portraits of the most distinguished Indians of those uncivilized regions, together with Paintings of their

VILLAGES, BUFFALO HUNTS, DANCES
LANDSCAPES OF THE COUNTRY, &c. &c.

Will endeavour to entertain and instruct the Citizens of Boston and its vicinity, for a short time, with an Exhibition of his

PAINTINGS, COSTUMES, &c.
—CONSISTING OF—

330 Portraits, and numerous other Paintings,

Which he has collected from 38 different Tribes, speaking different languages, all of whom he has been among, and Painted his Pictures from Life.——IN HIS COLLECTION ARE

Portraits of BLACK HAWK and Nine of his Principal Warriors,

Painted at Jefferson Barracks, while prisoners of war, in their War Dress and War Paint.

OSCEOLA, MICK-E-NO-PAH, CLOUD, COA-HA-JO & KING PHILIP,
Chiefs of the Seminoles.
ALSO, FOUR PAINTINGS, REPRESENTING THE

Annual Religious Ceremony of the Mandans,

Doing Penance, by inflicting the most cruel tortures upon their own bodies—passing knives and splints through their flesh, and suspending their bodies by their wounds, &c.

AND A SERIES OF

TWELVE BUFFALO HUNTING SCENES,
TOGETHER WITH
SPLENDID SPECIMENS OF COSTUME,
AND OTHER ARTICLES OF THEIR MANUFACTURE.

The great interest of this collection consists in its being a representation of the *wildest Tribes of Indians*, in America, and entirely in their *Native Habits and Costumes:* consisting of *Sioux, Puncahs, Konzas, Shiennes, Crows, Ojibbeways, Assinneboins, Mandans, Crees, Blackfeet, Snakes, Mahas, Ottoes, Ioways, Flatheads, Weahs, Peorias, Sacs, Foxes, Winnebagoes, Menomonies, Minatarrees, Rickarees, Osages, Camanches, Witos, Paware-Picts, Kiowas, Seminoles, Euchees* and others.

In order to render the Exhibition more *instructive* than it could otherwise be, the Paintings will be exhibited one at a time, and such *explanations* of their Dress, Customs, Traditions, &c. given by Mr. Catlin, as will enable the public to form a just idea of the Customs, Numbers and Condition of the Savages yet in a state of nature in North America.

☞The Exhibition, with Explanations, will commence this Evening, *(Wednesday)* August 15, and on several successive Evenings, at 8 o'clock precisely—and it is hoped and seated *as near the hour as possible,* that they may see the whole collection

Two Evenings will constitute the *course,* so that persons attending the whole, and form general and just notions of the Manners and C

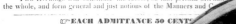

☞EACH ADMITTANCE 50 CENT

President Jackson had told the Indians that the West was a land of opportunity:

There your white brothers will not trouble you; they will have no claim to the land, and you can live upon it, you and all your children, as long as the grass grows or the water runs, in peace and plenty. It will be yours forever.

This sentiment was no doubt sincere. Jackson believed that the federal government could protect its Indian "wards" in the West without risk of encroaching on the rights of states or the opportunities of white citizens. In his "Farewell Address" of March 4, 1837, he applauded Indian removal as a great humanitarian achievement that had also happily removed the main impediment to America's economic growth:

While the safety and comfort of our own citizens have been greatly promoted by their removal, the philanthropist will rejoice that the remnant of that ill-fated race has been at length placed beyond the reach of injury or oppression, and that paternal care of the General Government will hereafter watch over them and protect them.

Ten years later, however, the government had recognized the impossibility of a "permanent Indian barrier" west of the Mississippi. Having defeated all Indian attempts to build dikes against the tides of westward migration, the government now began moving towards a policy of fencing Indians within specified "reservations" and opening the otherwise boundless territory of the great West to wagon trains, cavalry, miners, farmers, surveyors, and railroads. Even in the 1820s a few perceptive Indian chieftains had foreseen that Western lands would be no more invulnerable than the lands in the East, a conclusion soon confirmed by the destruction of tribal game reserves and by the purchase of remaining Indian lands in Missouri and Iowa. The Anglo-Saxon settlers in Texas, who won independence from Mexico in 1836, asserted the unprecedented claim that Indians had no right whatever to possession of the land. Texas reaffirmed this doctrine after being annexed as a state in 1845, and even demanded that some 25,000 Apaches and other tribesmen be removed or face extermination. Years of border warfare finally led in 1854 to the Texans' acceptance of Indian reservations

CATLIN'S AMERICAN INDIANS

Although Americans were continually reminded of the Indians' acts of cruelty, as in the torture scene in a Mandan tent, there was also a growing fascination with Indians as representatives of the exotic. Even by the early 1830s George Catlin had created a prototype for the commercial Wild West show. An accomplished painter of Plains tribesmen, Catlin also created the heroic image of Osceola, the Seminole chief who had been captured by American treachery and who posed for this portrait in prison, shortly before his death. *(Top left, American Antiquarian Society; top right, National Portrait Gallery, Smithsonian Institution; bottom, Courtesy of the American Museum of Natural History.)*

under federal jurisdiction. But the federal government found that it could not protect Texas tribes from being slaughtered by marauding whites, and therefore authorized their removal to the territory north of the Red River.

Meanwhile, from 1846 to 1860 government policy began to settle the fate of Western tribes that had previously been free to roam prairies and mountain parks without concern for the conflicting claims of white nations, tribes strong enough to lavish hospitality on the rugged traders and fur trappers who managed to penetrate their domains. The American invasion and occupation of New Mexico, in the Mexican War, led to brutal punitive expeditions against the Navajo. In 1851 Congress passed the critically important Indian Appropriations Act, designed to consolidate Western tribes on agricultural reservations, thereby lessening the danger to the tens of thousand of emigrants streaming towards California and Oregon and also to the proposed transcontinental railroad. Contrary to popular legend, there is no evidence that Indians ever attacked an emigrant wagon train, though they did demand tribute for the privilege of passing through their land and did take their toll of stragglers. Whatever the provocation, the government felt justified in building a chain of forts along the emigrant trails; it also gathered together, in 1851, some 10,000 Sioux and other Western tribes, near Fort Laramie, assigning them tribal territories and promising annual monetary compensation, a promise on which the government soon defaulted.

The degradation reached its climax in California, in the 1850s, where federal restraints on white aggression disappeared. Whites molested the Diggers and other primitive Indians, shooting the males for sport and enslaving the women and children. Farther east, the Apaches and powerful Plains tribes would continue to offer sporadic and sometimes spectacular resistance. The famed encounters between Indians and the United States Cavalry came after the Civil War. But even by 1860 the Western tribes had been demoralized, their economy had been fatally weakened when buffalo and other game became depleted, and increasing numbers of Indians had been herded into compounds with boundaries that moved only inwards. The North American aborigines had the misfortune to face not simply acquisitive settlers possessing a superior technology, but settlers whose movements and aspirations were closely tied to an economic revolution that whites themselves had only begun to understand.

Land

Throughout the pre–Civil War decades the majority of American families continued to make a living by supplying the primary human needs for food and clothing. Agriculture dominated the economy and provided the commodities for most of the nation's domestic and foreign trade. Even in towns and cities families customarily kept a vegetable garden and perhaps a pig, a cow, and chickens. Many of the most seasoned urbanites could at least remember the childhood smell of a barnyard.

What distinguished the period 1820–1860 were two trends that might seem at first to be contradictory. On the one hand, the quickening pace of urbanization and industrialization brought a decisive shift towards nonagricultural employment. This shift had actually begun in the late eighteenth century but had started to slow before 1820, when approximately 79 percent of the labor force was gainfully employed in agriculture. By 1850, however, the proportion had fallen to 55 percent. This was the most rapid structural change in the economy during the entire nineteenth century. On the other hand, the same period saw a phenomenal expansion of agriculture into the virgin lands of the West and Southwest, accompanied by revolutionary changes in transportation and marketing. The two trends were intimately related. The urban East provided the capital and markets that made the agricultural expansion possible. The food and fiber of the West and Southwest were indispensable for the industries and urban growth of the East. Western farming, fur trapping, mining, and lumbering were the spearheads of an expansive capitalist economy increasingly integrated with the great markets of the world.

Enlarge the Canals!

And thus furnish the Best and Cheapest Channel for bringing the

BREADSTUFFS

OF THE

GREAT WEST!

TO OUR DOORS.

INCREASE THE DEMAND FOR LABOR!

AUGMENT THE

Revenues of the State,

And promote our Mercantile, Mechanical, Manufacturing, Shipping and Financial Interests!

ELECTORS!

AWAKE!

To the Importance of the CANALS, and fail not to VOTE on WEDNESDAY, Feb. 15, in favor of

The Constitutional Amendment,

To provide for

THE SPEEDY ENLARGEMENT

OF THE

STATE CANALS.

Please post in a conspicuous place.

A nation of farmers is almost by definition a nation at an early stage of economic development. Yet in nineteenth-century America, agriculture did not suggest a conservative way of life limited by the entrenched customs of a feudalistic past. Farming increasingly took on the characteristics of a speculative business. The very isolation of individual farms, posted like sentries along lonely country roads, indicated that Americans placed efficiency above communal solidarity and that the individual family, practically imprisoned near the fields it worked and usually owned, had proved to be the most effective unit of production.

Four central conditions shaped America's unprecedented expansion of cultivated land. First, public policy continued to favor rapid settlement of the immense public domain, amounting to a billion acres if one includes the territorial acquisitions of the 1840s. There was no countervailing interest in conserving resources and future revenue. Second, despite population growth, agricultural labor remained scarce and expensive, especially in frontier regions. Most farm owners had to rely on an occasional hired hand to supplement the labor of their own families or of tenant families. In the South the price of slaves continued to rise. Third, the dispersion of settlement made farmers acutely sensitive to transportation facilities and thus dependent, for many decades, on navigable rivers and waterways. Fourth, the real estate mentality of earlier periods burgeoned into a national mania as the westward movement and the mushrooming of towns brought spectacular appreciation of land values. Great land companies and private investors, representing Eastern and European capital, purchased virtual empires of Western land and then used every possible device to promote rapid settlement. Even the small farmers saw that it was more agreeable to make money by speculating in land than by removing stumps or plowing up the resistant bluestem grass of the prairies.

From one point of view the pioneering outlook was progressive. There can be no doubt that the westering Americans were inventive, hardy, and willing to take risks. Often moving ahead of roads and organized government, the frontier farmers engaged in a struggle by trial and error to succeed in the face of unfamiliar climate, insects, soil conditions, and drainage. In time they experimented with different crops, livestock, and transportation routes, searching for the commodity and market that would bring a predictable cash return. Although the federal government supplied little direct knowledge to farmers, it continued Jefferson's tradition of promoting land surveys and sending paramilitary expeditions into the trans-Mississippi West to collect information on flora and fauna, geology, watersheds, and Indians. This enterprising spirit, evident in both public and private endeavors, led to the discovery and exploitation of undreamed of resources, confirming Tocqueville's judgment that "Nature herself favors the cause of the people."

But the quest for immediate returns also led to a ruthless stripping of natural resources. In the absence of national legislation and national power, the timber, grasses, and minerals of the public domain invited a headlong scramble to cut, graze, and dig. The government actually bought gold and silver that private individuals took from public property. European visitors expressed continuing astonishment at the American conviction that forests were a hostile element to be destroyed without regard for need. Trees, like the buffalo and beaver of the West, seemed so plentiful that few Americans could foresee a time of diminishing supply. In his early novel *The Pioneers* (1823), James Fenimore Cooper describes an unforgettable episode in which an entire New York village turns out with rifles and even cannon to slaughter thousands of migrating wild pigeons. When Leatherstocking, Cooper's aged and idealized forest hunter, expresses disgust over the waste, a local woodchopper replies:

"What! old Leather-stocking," he cried, "grumbling at the loss of a few pigeons! If you had to sow your wheat twice, and three times, as I have done, you wouldn't be so massyfully feeling'd toward the devils.—, Hurrah, boys! scatter the feathers."

The soil itself, the most valuable of all resources, fared no better. Except for the "Pennsylvania Dutch"—the descendants of early German immigrants who farmed the rich limestone soils of southeastern Pennsylvania—Americans lacked the incentives and patience to conserve the soil by using fertilizers and carefully rotating crops. They tended to look on land as a temporary and expendable resource that should be mined as rapidly as possible. This attitude, especially prevalent in the South and the West, reflected the common need to produce the most profitable single crop, whether wheat, corn, rice, tobacco, or cotton, in order to pay for land that could not have been purchased or settled except on credit.

The entrepreneurial character of American agriculture owed much to the way new lands were originally settled. For Americans of the late twentieth century it is difficult to grasp the significance of the fact that the chief business of the federal government, before the Civil War, was the management and disposal of public land. The government, wanting revenue as well as rapid settlement, hastily surveyed tracts of Western land, which were then sold to the highest bidder at public auction; the remainder was offered at the minimum price of $1.25 per acre. Since there was no limit to how many acres an individual or company might buy, investors eagerly bought blocks of thousands of acres, the great peaks of speculation coinciding with the expansion of bank credit in the early 1830s and in the mid-1850s. The profitable resale of such land depended on promoting settlement.

Speculators had always helped to shape the character of American agriculture. The great theme of American settlement was the continuing contest of will between absentee owners and the squatters who first developed the land and who often had some partial claim of title. Although squatters often sold their own claims to succeeding waves of migrants, they tended to picture wealthier speculators as rapacious vampires. Yet the large speculators played a key role in financing the rapid settlement of the public lands. Pooling private capital, they loaned money to squatters, often at illegally high interest rates, for the initial purchase of tools, livestock, and supplies. They extended credit for buying farms. They pressured local and national governments to subsidize canals and railroads. Railroad companies took on similar functions, especially after 1850, when Congress granted 2.5 million acres to the Illinois Central Railroad, which then offered parcels of land for a small down payment with seven years' credit. Such speculation often involved considerable risk, the returns on investment depending on the ability to predict business conditions accurately and on how fast settlement took place.

Squatters for their part yearned for economic independence. They successfully agitated for state "occupancy laws" favoring the claims of actual settlers and guaranteeing them compensation, if evicted, for their cabins, fences, outbuildings, and other improvements." Squatters also pressed for a lowered minimum in the amount of public land that could be purchased, a restriction that had fallen by 1832 to 40 acres. Above all, squatters called on the federal government to sanction squatting, formally allowing settlers to clear and cultivate tracts of public land prior to purchase. This policy of preemption, developed in limited acts in the 1830s and finally established in a general law of 1841, gave squatters the chance to settle land and then purchase as much as 160 acres at the minimum price in advance of public auction.

In practice the federal land system was a compromise between the interests of farmers and speculators. Given first claim to the land they tilled by the preemption acts, squatters failed to win national approval for free homesteads and were forced to pay rent or buy land after a limited period. Government measures did nothing to curb speculators, who were in fact favored by the requirement, beginning in 1820, of full cash payment for public land; by lavish donations of land to military veterans, railroads, and state governments; and by eventual pricing of land long unsold for as little as 12.5 cents an acre. Federal land policy allowed speculators to amass great private fortunes by acquiring valuable tracts of the public domain. Yet the wide dispersion of freehold farms gave some substance to the myth that any American could become an owner of property and an independent producer for the capitalist market.

Southern agriculture remained strikingly distinctive, although it was subject to the same public land policies. The cultivation of cotton and other staples for export depended largely on the labor of Negro slaves, whose numbers increased from 1.5 million in 1820 to nearly 4 million in 1860.* The seaboard South had long been oriented towards land speculation, soil mining, and quick profits from commercialized, single-crop agriculture. By 1820 the depletion of soil in coastal areas of Virginia and Maryland had brought prolonged agricultural depression as tobacco had given way to wheat and wheat to diminishing yields of corn. Understandably, Southerners had led the way in the rush for Western land. From 1820 on, they benefited from three advantages the North could not share. The perfection of the cotton gin and screw press, a device for compressing cotton into bales, gave them the rewards of technological change that Northern agriculture did not begin to approximate until the late 1850s. The rapid proliferation of steamboats opened the way to upriver navigation on the Mississippi and the rich network of other Southern waterways, thereby lowering transportation costs even more dramatically than the Northern canals and later the railroads did. Finally, Southern planters could take adequate supplies of labor with them to the West, or quickly move units of labor, which were also their main units of capital investment, to the most promising markets.

Accordingly, despite a sharp depression in cotton prices following the Panic of 1819, speculators swarmed to the rich cotton land of Alabama and Mississippi. English credit and capital financed much of this southwestern agricultural expansion. By 1840 the South produced over 60 percent of the world's cotton. Well over half this output went to the textile manufacturers of Great Britain, and by the 1850s American cotton also supplied the rising industries of continental Europe, including Russia. Between 1836 and 1840 cotton accounted for 63

---

*Slavery will be examined more fully in Chapter 17.

percent of the value of all America's exports. Although the proportion did not remain so high, cotton exports continued to pay for the major share of the nation's imports. For a time cotton made New Orleans the nation's leading seaport in value of exports. It contributed to the growth of New York City as a distributing and exporting center that drew income from commissions, freight charges, interest, insurance, and other services connected with the marketing of America's number one commodity. A stimulant to Northern industry and urbanization, slave-grown cotton was also the key to the great speculative boom of the early 1830s. In 1839 a temporary surplus caused the price of cotton to fall. At the same time British efforts to restrict credit diminished the flow of capital to the United States, and the nation's entire credit structure collapsed.

Neither American sellers nor British buyers felt comfortable over so concentrated a source of prosperity. British manufacturers searched unsuccessfully for alternative sources of high-grade cotton. Southern commercial conventions unsuccessfully called for a more balanced economy. It is important to stress that the South continued to export large quantities of rice, tobacco, and other staples. In Louisiana wealthy sugar planters expanded production by using new technology for the processing of cane. Planters effectively applied slave labor to culti-

"THE SQUATTERS" BY GEORGE CALEB BINGHAM

Much of the public domain was originally settled by
squatters whose claim to the land derived from their having
cleared trees, broken sod, and built cabins and fences.
(Courtesy, Museum of Fine Arts, Boston.)

vating hemp, corn, and grain; to mining, and lumbering; to building canals and railroads; and even to manufacturing textiles, iron, and other industrial products. By 1860, $252 million had been invested in Southern railroads, representing one-quarter of the nation's total railroad capital. The Southern states themselves had publicly raised over half this amount, a sign of the determination to keep abreast with the age. Yet in investment in industry, the South fell far behind the North. Except for the bustling port of New Orleans, great urban centers failed to appear. Compared with conditions in the North, internal markets languished. Investment continued to flow into slaves, whose price continued to rise, and into cotton cultivation, which remained highly profitable despite prices whose rise was sometimes limited by years of bumper crops.

   The economics of Negro slavery is still subject to much dispute. Most historians and economists agree that investment in slaves brought a profitable return, and that the slave economy was expanding throughout the pre–Civil War decades. Owning one or more large plantations often enabled a single wealthy planter to achieve the benefits of an efficient division and specialization of slave labor. Raising foodstuffs and livestock made much of the South reasonably self-sufficient, although the early Western plantations may have depended initially on imported foodstuffs from the upper Mississippi and Ohio valleys. It is true that in 1860 the South Atlantic states had a per capita income of less than half that in the Northeast. But thanks to the booming port of New Orleans, the region that included Louisiana, Texas, and Arkansas had a per capita income consider-

Steamboats, like these docked at Cincinnati, brought the markets along the upper Ohio and Mississippi river network within easy reach of New Orleans and the Lower South. *(Library of Congress.)*

ably above that of the North Central states from Ohio westward. The South as a whole was richer than most nations in Europe. In rate of economic growth, it approximated the North. Judged by productivity, it was not a backward region.

But in extreme form the South combined America's characteristics of speculative business and rural isolation. No other region contained so many farmers who merely subsisted on their own produce; yet in no other region had agriculture become so commercial—for small cotton farmers who could not afford slaves as well as for the planter elite. The South's economic opportunities resulted

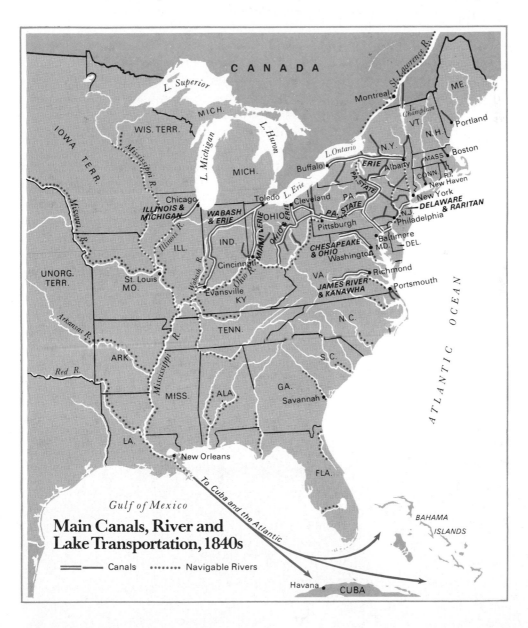

Main Canals, River and Lake Transportation, 1840s

═══ Canals ⋯⋯⋯ Navigable Rivers

from the removal of Indians and from exploitation of Negro slaves. Its prosperity, fueling the nation's expansion, depended on foreign markets. Perhaps the greatest paradox was that the national forces of industrialization and commercial agriculture, while intimately connected to the products of Southern slave labor, gradually isolated the South as a seemingly unprogressive and obstructive region.

For a time Northern agriculture faced more imposing limitations. There was no slave labor that could be applied to clearing, plowing, cultivating, harvesting, and processing. Technological improvements took the form of labor-saving tools that only gradually won acceptance and that did little to increase an acre's yield of crops. Unlike cotton, most of the North's commercial crops were perishable and had to be marketed fairly quickly. Yet the teams of horses that hauled wagons of freight over the nation's turnpikes averaged no better than two miles an hour. Worse still, the costs of wagon transport often made it prohibitive to ship corn or wheat more than the shortest of distances.

The craze during the early nineteenth century for building turnpikes, bridges, and plank roads failed to reduce significantly the cost of long distance freight. Canals were another story. The Erie Canal, completed in 1825, united East and West by providing a continuous waterway from Lake Erie to the Atlantic. In 1817 it had cost 19.2¢ per mile to ship a ton of freight overland from Buffalo to New York. By the late 1850s the cost per mile, via the canal, had dropped to 0.81¢. New York State had directed and financed this prodigious undertaking, by far the longest canal in the world, and soon reaped spectacular rewards. Foreign capital quickly flowed into the country to meet the demand of other

THE JUNCTION OF THE ERIE AND NORTHERN CANALS, C. 1838

Although canals greatly reduced the cost of overland freight, it was a slow and arduous task negotiating multiple locks and pulling barges by rope from the "tow path" alongside. (*Courtesy of the New-York Historical Society, New York City.*)

state and municipal governments, setting off a canal-building mania that soon linked Pittsburgh with Philadelphia, and the Ohio River with the Great Lakes. The high cost of building this network of waterways, undertaken for the most part by the states themselves, severely strained the credit of Ohio, Pennsylvania, and Indiana. But by dramatically lowering the costs of transport, the most successful canals had an incalculable effect on Northern agriculture and industry.

By the mid-1830s the basic pattern of internal transportation began to shift away from the traditional routes that had led from the Ohio and upper Mississippi valleys to New Orleans and ocean shipment via the Gulf of Mexico. Ohio valley farmers would continue to ship grain and pork down the Mississippi by flatboat. The richest markets, however, lay east of the Great Lakes, and for a time the richest commercial agriculture developed in regions accessible by canal to Lake Erie. By 1840 Rochester, New York, had become the leading flour-milling center of the country. The marketing of grain became more efficient as brokers and other middlemen began to arrange for storage, transport, sale, and credit. This transformation preceded the East-West railroad connections of the early 1850s.

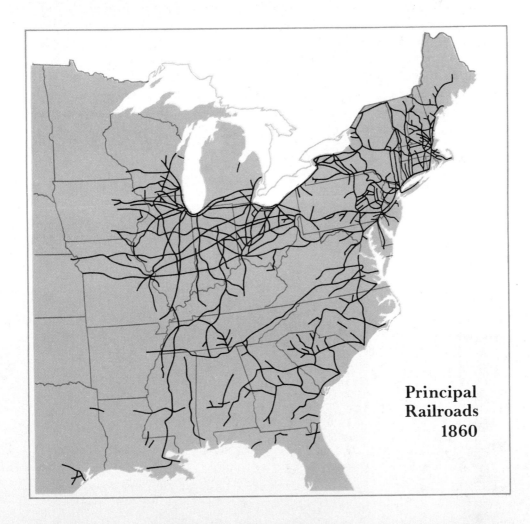

**Principal
Railroads
1860**

Although the nation's railroads equaled the canals in mileage as early as 1840, railroad lines were long concentrated in New England and in eastern Pennsylvania and New York. Baltimore became alarmed by the competitive advantage that the Erie Canal gave to New York and began constructing the first trans-Appalachian railroad in 1828; this railroad did not reach the Ohio River until 1853. By 1854, though, tracks extended from New York City to the Mississippi, and by 1860, to the Missouri at Saint Joseph. In 1860 there were still hundreds of small, independent lines with competing widths of track. But the great burst of Western railroad construction in the 1850s also led to the beginning of consolidation into trunk lines that further cemented economic ties between the West and Northeast. In that decade, Chicago emerged as the great rail center and agricultural distributor of the West. In 1860 railroads carried 20 percent of Chicago's exports of flour, 70 percent of its packing-house products, and nearly all its livestock.

This transportation revolution had momentous consequences. Agricultural regions were enabled to specialize in accordance with competitive advantage and the pressures of an increasingly national market. Western farmers began to buy trademarked tools and machines from authorized distributors. Steel plows, invented in the 1830s but widely accepted only in the 1850s, made it possible to break the tough sod and cultivate the rich but sticky soil of the prairies. Mechanical reapers had also been invented in the 1830s, but only in the 1850s did Cyrus McCormick's Chicago factory begin large-scale production and use of modern techniques of advertising and promotion. As the West proved its superiority in

DETAIL FROM "GEESE IN FLIGHT"

This imaginative painting by Leila T. Bauman captures some of the mid-nineteenth-century excitement over movement and improved transport—the steam from the train and riverboat harmonizing with the movement of horses, geese, and wind. (*National Gallery of Art, Gift of Edgar William and Bernice Chrysler Garbisch.*)

producing wheat and other grains, to say nothing of wool, corn, pork, and beef, the East turned to hay for horses and to perishable foodstuffs for urban markets.

The great railroad boom of the 1850s dramatized the growing links between agriculture and industry. In recent years there has been a highly technical debate over the contribution of railroads to economic growth, particularly in lowering costs of freight transport. There can be no question, however, that Americans eagerly chose the "iron horse" as the most expedient means of opening the prairies to agricultural settlement. By providing speedy access to isolated farms and distant markets, railroads opened new horizons and extended the risks and promises of a commercial society. By 1860 railroads had become the nation's first billion-dollar industry, spawning the first giant corporations, linking cash-crop farming with the production of iron, coal, lumber, and machine tools. The railroads, subjecting canals and even steamboats to often ruinous competition, would soon conquer the last geographic barriers of the West, compressing open space, like the power of steam, into measurable units shaped to human need.

Trade, Manufactures, and Economic Growth

The seas had been America's first economic frontier, and seaborne trade had long been essential for America's survival. But despite Yankee ingenuity and enterprise, America's deep-sea traders encountered increasing barriers. They faced a competitor, Great Britain, that was at once the world's greatest sea power and most advanced industrial nation. American shipping never recovered the central position it had occupied before the War of 1812.

The Northeastern ports flourished, nevertheless, as expansive centers of trade. Federal law barred foreign ships from the vitally important coastal trade. Swarms of brigs and schooners ferried diverse cargoes along the North American coast from Maine to Louisiana. Transatlantic packets, adopting the regular schedules of steamboats plying the Hudson and Long Island Sound, connected the main port cities with Europe. New England whalers and cargo ships began to make portions of the Pacific an American preserve. In China, American merchants simply followed the lead of Europeans who had forcibly opened certain ports to trade and had secured "extraterritorial" privileges of self-government. In 1854, however, Commodore Matthew C. Perry succeeded by diplomatic tact and a display of naval power in persuading the rulers of Japan to open that country to trade and Western influence.

America's most spectacular maritime achievement was the famed clipper ship. Blending competitive enterprise with superb art, the clippers were at first a response to the long-distance China trade, but most were built to race from New York or Boston to the California gold fields, a trip of some fifteen thousand miles around the tip of South America. With their graceful, streamlined hulls, their clouds of sail rising nearly two hundred feet above deck, the clippers seemed to

FOR CALIFORNIA!

Mutual Protection

Trading & Mining Co.

Having purchased the splendid, Coppered and very fast Sailing

Barque EMMA ISIDORA,

Will leave about the 15th of February. This vessel will be fitted in the very best manner and is one of the fastest sailing vessels that goes from this port.

Each member pays 300 dollars and is entitled to an equal proportion of all profits made by the company either at mining or trading, and holds an equal share of all the property belonging to the company. Experienced men well acquainted with the coast and climate are already engaged as officers of the Company. A rare chance is offered to any wishing a safe investment, good home and Large profits.

This Company is limited to 60 and any wishing to improve this opportunity must make immediate application.

An Experienced Physician will go with the company.

For Freight or Passage apply to 23 State Street, corner of Devonshire, where the list of Passengers may be seen.

JAMES H. PRINCE, Agent,

23 State Street, corner of Devonshire St., Boston.

For further Particulars, see the Constitution.

Propeller Power Presses, 142 Washington St., Boston.

(American Antiquarian Society.)

soar over the seas hardly touching the froth of waves. The ships of Donald McKay, Boston's master designer, occasionally sailed well over 400 nautical miles in a day. Among the clipper's incredible records was a voyage of slightly over 12 days from Boston to Liverpool. But the clipper's years of triumph, from the late 1840s to the mid-1850s, were the same years that Britain perfected steamships with unromantic iron hulls and screw propellors. Steamships could carry much larger cargoes at lower cost. The rapid decline of the wooden sailing ship also signaled a relative decline in the American shipping industry.

The more a nation earns by exports, the more it can spend on imports. The general prosperity of the pre-Civil War decades increased the American people's demand for foreign manufactured products, for iron and textiles and for foodstuffs like sugar, coffee, tea, wine, and cocoa. During most of the period the United States continued to register a negative trade balance, that is, total imports exceeded total exports in value. Despite a spectacular rise in the value of exports, Americans sold less than they bought. Merchants helped to make up the difference by selling American ships and by reexporting Cuban sugar, Canadian wheat, British manufactured goods, and Mexican silver. The nation also gained credits from the capital brought in by immigrants and from foreign investment, partly offset by the payment of interest.

The depression that followed the collapse of American credit in 1839 brought a sharp decline in imports, foreign investment, and domestic prices. But during the 1840s the United States began to export an increasing proportion of its agricultural output, partly in response to poor harvests in Europe and to England's repeal of the "Corn Laws" that had excluded American and other foreign grain. This outflow, reinforced after 1848 by hundreds of millions of dollars worth of California gold, helped to pay for America's consumption of Europe's manufactured goods. It also helped to raise the price of domestic farm products, thereby encouraging further agricultural expansion. By the 1850s American farmers had begun to prove their competitive superiority, at the expense of European agriculture. And while manufactured goods still accounted for a small proportion of the value of American exports their striking growth proved that

American industry could successfully compete for world markets. Above all, the rapid gains in manufacturing had begun to reduce the country's traditional dependence on imports, particularly textiles.

Because of scanty statistics prior to the census of 1840, there is still much uncertainty about the links between manufacturing and economic growth. In the 1820s manufacturing still mostly conformed to the literal meaning of the word—handicraft production in households and in small shops or mills. Blacksmiths, coopers, cobblers, curriers, hatters, tailors, weavers—these and other artisans and apprentices worked in central shops, mills, and stores, or moved as itinerants through the more sparsely settled countryside. Yet the 1820s may well have been America's critical decade of economic transformation. The decade marked the beginning of rapid urbanization, a decisive shift toward nonagricultural employment, and perhaps the fastest economic growth of the pre–Civil War era.

As in England, cotton textiles moved swiftly to the forefront of industrial innovation. Aided somewhat by protective tariffs, the group of wealthy merchants known as the Boston Associates pooled their capital and extended the Waltham system of large-scale factory production to new manufacturing centers like Lowell and Chicopee, in Massachusetts. The Waltham system exploited the latest English technology, such as the power loom, and continued to draw on the expertise of immigrant English artisans.

Successful competition with imported English textiles required New England manufacturers to lower the cost and increase the efficiency of labor. Traditionally, American manufacturers had cut costs by employing children or families including children. It soon became apparent, however, that children could not handle the frequent breakdowns of the new machinery or conform to the regimen necessary for increased labor productivity. The wages of adult males were too high to allow successful competition with British manufacturers. Child labor by no means disappeared from textile mills and by the late 1840s immigrants had begun to ease the general shortage of factory labor. But for a few decades the Boston Associates relied on the unique expedient of attracting adult young women by providing chaperoned dormitories and various cultural amenities. They desired, no doubt sincerely, to avoid the moral degradation that had stigmatized the English factory system. As economy-minded entrepreneurs, they also hoped to exert influence over their employees' leisure time, preventing the binges and self-proclaimed holidays that had always led to irregularity and absenteeism among the preindustrial folk. New England farm girls could be hired for less than half the wages of male factory hands, since they were secondary earners for their families and since the factory was virtually the only possible liberation from the farm. From 1815 to 1833 the cotton textile industry increased average annual output at the phenomenal rate of 16 percent. Although slackening demand soon reduced the annual rate of growth to about 5 percent, textile producers, including wool and carpet manufacturers, continued to be pioneers in mechanization, in efficiency, and in the use of steam power.

New England also gave birth to the so-called American system of manufacturing, which represented the other principal breakthrough in industrial innovation. The innovation consisted of imaginatively applying and reaping the benefits from a machine-tool technology that had first been developed in England. Unlike the English, American manufacturers could not draw on a plentiful supply of highly skilled craftsmen whose expertise required many years of training in an established craft tradition. They therefore encouraged the perfection of light machine tools that not only eliminated many hand operations but also allowed ordinary mechanics to measure within one-thousandth of an inch and to mill or cut metal with great precision. At the English Crystal Palace exhibition of 1851, American machinery astonished European experts. In 1854 one of the English commissions sent to study American achievements exclaimed over "the extraordinary ingenuity displayed in many of their labour-saving machines, where automatic action so completely supplies the place of the more abundant hand labour of older manufacturing countries."

THE NATHAN WASHBURN PLANT, WORCESTER, MASSACHUSETTS

Even an unusually large manufacturing establishment engaged in heavy industry—in this case the manufacture of railway iron and car wheels—could be portrayed in a rural, bucolic setting. In the transitional period, industry seemed to pose little threat to rural values or to the peaceful countryside. (*American Antiquarian Society.*)

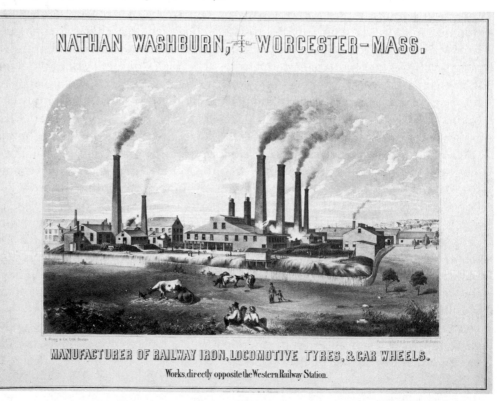

NATHAN WASHBURN, WORCESTER-MASS.

MANUFACTURER OF RAILWAY IRON, LOCOMOTIVE TYRES, & CAR WHEELS.

Works, directly opposite the Western Railway Station.

The English investigators understood the significance for the future of such seemingly prosaic devices as a machine that produced 180 ladies' hairpins every minute. As early as 1853 an exuberant writer for the *United States Review* could predict that within a half-century machines would liberate Americans from the restraints of work: "Machinery will perform all work—automata will direct them. The only tasks of the human race will be to make love, study and be happy."

In 1860 American industry was still at an early stage of transition, showing sharp contrasts according to product and level of regional development. The American iron industry, despite an impressive expansion in output, failed to follow cotton textiles in adopting and improving the latest English technology. The persistence of small blast furnaces using charcoal to produce malleable iron has been explained by the cheapness and availability of wood for charcoal; by the absence east of the Alleghenies of bituminous coal; by the belated discovery and use of anthracite; and by the particular needs of local blacksmiths. Whatever the reasons, American industry in the 1850s heavily depended on the importation of English wrought iron and railroad rails, and lagged far behind England in exploiting coal, iron, and steam. In the West, manufacturing often reverted to preindustrial methods that had almost disappeared in the East. But even in the Northeast many merchants still relied on the putting-out system, distributing raw materials to laborers who often owned their own tools and worked at home. At the same time other merchant capitalists hired laborers essentially as instruments of production, who had no share in the ownership of tools and machines, in managerial decisions, in the risks of marketing, or in the industrial product.

In 1860 American manufacturing still depended largely on water power, not steam. The typical firm employed a handful of workers, was unincorporated, and engaged in the small-scale processing of raw materials. There were at this time few industries that processed the products of other industries. The nation's largest industries included some that were thoroughly mechanized, such as the production of cotton goods, flour, and meal; some that were partly mechanized, such as the manufacture of boots and shoes; and some that were characterized by premodern technology and low labor productivity, such as lumbering and the making of men's clothing.

There is still considerable controversy over the stages of America's economic growth. Some economists have advanced the theory of a dramatic "takeoff" starting in the 1840s, in which the growth of national product shot dramatically ahead of the growth of population. The best recent evidence suggests that the economic recovery from the depression of 1819 marked the beginning of significant though gradual gains in labor productivity and per capita product. This pattern of long-term accelerated growth preceded significant industrialization and probably developed from the dynamic interaction between urbanization and Western agriculture. The inflationary boom of the 1830s, with its rapid Western settlement and expansion of the cotton kingdom, ended with the banking panic of 1837 and the more damaging depression beginning in 1839. This downturn in the business cycle was still tied to agriculture and related to English demand, English investment, and the international flow of silver. In many respects America in its economy still resembled a colony dependent on exports of raw materials. Yet the depression had far less effect on productivity and even employment than on the merchants, bankers, and Southern planters who depended on foreign credit and trade.

By 1843 the American economy had recovered its momentum and had begun a decade of rapid industrial growth, climaxed by the extension of railroads to the Great Lakes and Mississippi. Then the mid-1850s brought a slowing down of investment and of industrial production, culminating in the financial panic of 1857. For the first time the business cycle seemed to be primarily geared to the fluctuations of domestic and nonagricultural forces, such as investment in railroads. Significantly, the South suffered little from the essentially industrial depression of the late 1850s. Southern leaders could not refrain from gloating over the economic vulnerability of Northern industry and its system of "wage-slavery." Northern leaders angrily accused the South of contributing to the depression by defeating Northern moves for protective tariffs and free homesteads. The political rhetoric reflected a genuine divergence in the development of the two sections. Slave-grown cotton had been an important contributor to the North's industrial growth. But Northerners increasingly saw in the South a vestige of colonial dependency—a dependency on English markets that blocked the way to high protective tariffs and to full industrialization.

Distribution and Opportunity

There can be no question that economic growth brought impressive gains in per capita income and standard of living. By 1860, in per capita income the United States was well ahead of western Europe. But much is yet to be learned about the actual distribution of wealth in the pre–Civil War decades, to say nothing of the opportunity to acquire property or to move upward in status and occupation.

At the outset it is well to note that discussions of America's economic opportunities generally omit three groups: the Indians who were removed from their lands; the Negro slaves who had no choice of occupation and whose "income" was wholly determined by their masters; and the free blacks in both North and South whose small economic gains in various skilled trades and service industries were severely damaged by competition from white immigrants. Even excluding these oppressed minorities, one finds many indications that economic inequality increased substantially from 1820 to 1860.

According to the best recent estimates, by 1860 the upper 5 percent of families owned over half the nation's wealth: the upper 10 percent owned over 70 percent of the wealth. The disparity was far greater in the sugar-producing lands of Louisiana, but even in the relatively equalitarian farming country of the eastern

North Central states, the upper 10 percent of landholders owned nearly 40 percent of taxable wealth. The national centers of inequality, however, were the growing urban regions from Boston to New Orleans. Although much statistical research remains to be done, it is clear that between 1820 and 1860 the big cities led the nation towards the increasing dominance of the very rich. By 1860, according to one estimate, Philadelphia's top 1 percent of population owned half the city's wealth; the lower 80 percent of the city's population had to be content with 3 percent of the wealth. According to a relatively modest estimate, the richest 5 percent of American families in 1860 received between 25 and 35 percent of the national income. While these figures indicate an inequality far greater than that estimated for modern America, they are roughly comparable to the inequalities in northern Europe in the late nineteenth century.

This conclusion would not be startling if America's pre–Civil War decades had not been advertised and almost universally accepted as "the age of the common man." American politicians and journalists eagerly expanded on the theme "equality of condition," supposedly confirmed by the observations of Alexis de Tocqueville and other European travelers. On closer inspection, however, Tocqueville and other travelers claimed only that American fortunes were "scanty" compared with fortunes in Europe; that in America "most of the rich men were formerly poor"; and that in America "any man's son may become the equal of any other man's son." In other words, American inequalities were temporary and simply enhanced the incentives of a race to success in which all were free to compete.

This belief in America's unique fluidity was especially reassuring by 1850, when European industrialism had produced undeniable evidence of misery, class conflict, and seething revolution. By that date American leaders could not hide their alarm over similar contrasts of wealth and squalor, particularly when the urban poor congregated in slums beyond the reach of traditional religious and social discipline. Yet affluent Americans persuaded themselves that the poor were free to climb the ladder of success, and that the wealthiest citizens were, in the words of Senator Henry Clay, "enterprising self-made men, who have whatever wealth they possess by patient and diligent labor."

In truth, however, the fortunes of John Jacob Astor and other leading American families compared favorably with the fortunes of the richest Europeans. Notwithstanding a few astonishing examples of rags-to-riches achievement, the great majority of America's rich and successful men had benefited from inherited wealth, an affluent childhood, or a prestigious family tradition. Between 1820 and 1860 there was a marked persistence of family wealth; in effect, the rich grew richer. In the cities, at least, they constituted an elite that became increasingly segregated by exclusive clubs, high social life, intermarriage, foreign travel, and business alliances.

At the other end of the spectrum was the mass of unskilled day laborers, who took what temporary jobs they could find and whose wages, even if regular, could

not possibly support a family unless supplemented by the income of wives and
children. No one knows the size of this unskilled, propertyless population, which
drifted in and out of mill towns, flocked to the construction sites of canals and
railroads, and gravitated to urban slums. In the 1840s and 1850s the largest cities
attracted the chronic failures and castoffs who had no other place to turn. They
jammed themselves into the attics and dank, windowless basements of Boston's
Half Moon Place, where as many as one hundred people might share the same
overflowing privy; or into New York's notorious Old Brewery, a noxious tenement that supposedly housed over a thousand beggars, pickpockets, whores,
robbers, alcoholics, and starving children. In contrast to mid nineteenth-century
England, one of the meanings of America's lack of limits was the near absence of
public agencies that could enforce minimal standards of health, welfare, and
safety.

The extremes of wealth and poverty tell little about the amount of upward
movement from one class to another. Thus far, however, the available evidence
indicates that the odds were heavily against an unskilled laborer's acquiring a
higher occupational status. The overwhelming majority of unskilled workers
remained unskilled workers. It is true that in the 1850s many of the sons of unskilled workers moved into semiskilled factory jobs. But this generational advance
was amost always limited to the next rung on the ladder. It was extremely rare
for the children of manual workers, even skilled manual workers, to rise to the
levels of clerical, managerial, or professional employment.

Despite growing signs in the pre–Civil War decades of semipermanent boundaries between occupational groups, there were remarkably few expressions of
class consciousness or class interest. Historians have sometimes been misled by the

labor rhetoric of the Jacksonian period, a time when the rich felt it necessary to prove their humble origins and when everybody who could laid claim to the proud title of "workingman." The labor leaders of the era were typically artisan proprietors and small businessmen intent on fixing prices and reducing the hazards of interregional competition. This is not to deny the importance of immigrant British artisans who had been displaced by the British factory system, who reinforced the preindustrial craft traditions in the United States, and who were schooled in the techniques of secret organization and industrial warfare. Nor can one deny the courage of union organizers who faced conspiracy trials in the 1820s and 30s, who saw their gains wiped out by the depression of 1837, and who finally formed city federations of craft unions and national trades unions in the 1850s. Yet the great strikes for higher wages and for the ten-hour day were staged by skilled printers, typographers, hatters, tailors, and other artisans. Employers, who were mostly supported by the courts and who benefited from fresh supplies of cheap immigrant labor, had little difficulty in breaking strikes. Although the Massachusetts Supreme Court led the way, in *Commonwealth* v. *Hunt* (1842), in ruling that trade unions were not in themselves conspiracies in restraint of trade, in 1860 only 0.1 percent of the American labor force was organized.

Even by the 1840s America's relative freedom from class consciousness and class conflict evoked considerable comment. According to Karl Marx and other European observers, the explanation could be found in the fresh lands of the American frontier, which provided an outlet for surplus population. In America, George Henry Evans's National Reform Association referred to the West as a "safety valve" that could and should provide an escape for workers whose opportunities were limited in the East. Evans contended in the 1840s that the nation owned enough land in the West to guarantee every family a farm. In the 1850s Horace Greeley, editor of the enormously influential New York *Tribune*, popularized the Republican party's slogan, "Vote yourself a farm." More than a generation later, the historian Frederick Jackson Turner and his followers evolved a detailed historical theory that pictured the frontier as both a safety valve for the pressures of the industrializing East and a wellspring of rejuvenating opportunity.

The theory, in its simplest and crudest form, has been thoroughly demolished. The Eastern laborer, earning a dollar a day or less, could not afford to travel to the frontier and borrow funds for a farm and tools, even if he possessed the skills for Western farming. The evidence shows that Western land sales lagged in hard times, when a safety valve would be most needed, and increased when prosperity drove up the prices of wheat and cotton. Except for a few cooperative settlement

FIVE POINTS, NEW YORK CITY, 1827

For many decades the region around "Five Points," the intersection of five streets in lower Manhattan, epitomized the worst of urban degradation: poverty, prostitution, crime, drunkenness, and mob violence. Fashionably dressed gentlemen mingled with prostitutes, pigs, and racially mixed crowds. *(Brown Brothers.)*

associations and a few hundred wage earners sent by antislavery groups to settle Kansas, there are no records to show that any industrial workers were transformed into frontier farmers.

On the other hand, the westward surge of millions of Americans intensified and dramatized the central fact of American life: physical mobility. Wages in the Northeast might well have been lower if the farmers, shopkeepers, artisans, and small businessmen who did go West had stayed put. Some of these aspiring adventurers might have been forced to seek factory employment. Some might have become America's counterparts to Europe's labor organizers. Ironically, since young males predominated in the migration away from industrial New England, an increasing number of women had no prospect for marriage and thus became part of a permanent industrial labor force while living on low wages intended as a premarital supplement to their parents' income.

Intense geographic mobility reinforced the myth of America's boundlessness, of America's infinite promise. In 1850 one-quarter of the entire population born in New England had moved to other states. The south Atlantic states experienced a no less striking westward drain of whites and of Negro slaves. Each decade the Northern cities, towns, and factories witnessed an extraordinary inflow and outflow of population. These mobile Americans moved because they had hope of finding it better someplace else. And the hope may have been more significant than the reality they found. For unskilled laborers the reality was often grim, but the factories and towns they left behind had no need to worry about their accumulating grievances. The more fortunate and competitive movers could not doubt that Illinois was preferable to Ohio, or that New York City offered more opportunities than the rocky hillsides of Vermont.

It was obvious that the condition of most white Americans, except for the floating population of impoverished laborers, was improving. Even the lowliest Irish laborers in a factory town like Newburyport, Massachusetts, found that they could accumulate property if they stuck to their jobs for a decade or more. To maintain a savings account or eventually to buy a house required discipline, frugality, and multiple income from family members at the expense of education and leisure. The Irish put a greater premium on home ownership than on education or occupational achievement. The Jews, in particular, tended to make every sacrifice for their childrens' education. No cultural group, however, found confirmation of the rags-to-riches mythology. The gains, particularly for the families of manual workers, were extremely limited. But they engendered pride in achieving what others had not achieved, and were sufficient to prevent even a permanent working class from becoming a permanent and propertyless proletariat.

The incessant turnover of population, the lack of physical roots, also gave force to the ideology of an open and boundless society—an ideology repeatedly stressed by newspapers, sermons, and political speeches. Who could tell what had become of all of one's former neighbors and fellow workers? No doubt some had hit it rich. The mystery of everyone's past made it believable that most men's positions had been won according to talent and performance—that in America, where the only limits were individual will and ability, most men got what they were worth. If in time a manual worker could finally boast of a savings account of $300, of owning the roof over his head, or of a son who had moved up to the next rung on the ladder, why should he doubt the common claim, "This is a country of self-made men," where most of the rich had once been poor?

Suggested Readings

For informative surveys and detailed bibliographies, see George Dangerfield, *The Awakening of American Nationalism, 1815–1828* (1965); Glyndon G. Van Deusen, *The Jacksonian Era* (1959); Edward Pessen, *Jacksonian America: Society, Personality, and Politics* (1969); and Russel B. Nye, *Society and Culture in America, 1830–1860* (1974). Louis Hartz, *The Liberal Tradition in America* (1955), presents a brilliant and provocative interpretation of America's divergence from Old World norms. Hartz, like most interpreters of the period, draws heavily on Alexis de Tocqueville's classic work, *Democracy in America*, of which there are many editions. Daniel J. Boorstin's *The Americans: The National Experience* (1965), also emphasizes America's uniqueness. The period is illuminated in different ways by Yehoshua Arieli, *Individualism and Nationalism in American Ideology* (1964); Rowland Berthoff, *An Unsettled People: Social Order and Disorder in American History* (1971); and Fred Somkin, *Unquiet Eagle: Memory and Desire in the Idea of American Freedom, 1815–1860* (1967).

Population growth is analyzed by J. Potter, "The Growth of Population in America, 1700–1860," in *Population and History . . .* , ed. D. V. Glass and D. E. C. Eversley (1965); and Richard A. Easterlin, *Population, Labor Force, and Long Swings in Economic Growth: The American Experience* (1968). Maldwyn A. Jones, *American Immigration* (1960), is a useful introduction to the subject; it should be supplemented by Marcus L. Hansen, *The Atlantic Migration, 1607–1860* (1940); Oscar Handlin, *Boston's Immigrants* (1959); Charlotte Erickson, *Invisible Immigrants;* and Robert Ernst, *Immigrant Life in New York City, 1825–1863* (1949). For urbanization, see Sam Bass Warner, Jr., *The Urban Wilderness* (1972); and Richard C. Wade, *The Urban Frontier* (1964).

The best introduction to Indian removal is Wilcomb E. Washburn, *The Indian in America* (1975). Francis P. Prucha, *American Indian Policy in the Formative Years* (1962), is sympathetic to government policymakers. Ronald N. Satz, *American Indian Policy in the Jacksonian Era* (1975), provides an informative account of the subsequent period. There are three outstanding related works in intellectual history: Roy H. Pearce, *The Savages of America* (1965); Richard Slotkin, *Regeneration through Violence: The Mythology of the American Frontier, 1600–1860* (1973); and Roderick Nash, *Wilderness in the American Mind* (1967).

The best introduction to current views of economic growth can be found in W. Elliot Brownlee, *Dynamics of Ascent* (1974), and Stuart Bruchey, *Growth of the Modern American Economy* (1975). A more technical but very useful summary of the new economic history is Lance E. Davis et al., *American Economic Growth: An Economist's History of the United States* (1972). Douglass C. North, *The Economic Growth of the United States, 1790–1860* (1961), stresses the importance of international trade. Peter Temin, *The Jacksonian Economy* (1969), challenges many of the traditional beliefs of historians. For a fascinating discussion of the economic thought of the pre–Civil War period, see Joseph Dorfman, *The Economic Mind in American Civilization.* Vol 2 (3 vols., 1946–49).

Ray A. Billington, *Westward Expansion* (1974), presents an excellent survey of Western history as well as a comprehensive bibliography. The fullest histories of agriculture are Percy W. Bidwell and John I. Falconer, *History of Agriculture in the Northern United States, 1620–1860* (1925), and Lewis C. Gray, *History of Agriculture in the Southern United States to 1860* (2 vols., 1933). A briefer and outstanding recent survey is Paul W. Gates, *The Farmer's Age: Agriculture, 1815–1860* (1960), which can be supplemented by Clarence H. Danhof,

Change in Agriculture in the Northern United States, 1820–1870 (1969). A highly controversial work on the economics of Negro slavery is Robert W. Fogel and Stanley L. Engerman, *Time on the Cross: The Economics of American Negro Slavery* (1974). For important criticisms of this work, as well as for new information, see Paul A. David et al., *Reckoning with Slavery* (1976), and Herbert G. Gutman, *Slavery and the Numbers Game* (1975). An excellent survey of the more traditional literature is Harold D. Woodman, ed., *Slavery and the Southern Economy* (1966). The best general study is Kenneth M. Stampp, *The Peculiar Institution* (1956). For the use of slaves in nonagricultural employment, see Robert S. Starobin, *Industrial Slavery in the Old South* (1970).

The classic study of transportation is George R. Taylor, *The Transportation Revolution, 1815–1860* (1951). A monumental work, confined to New England, is Edward Kirkland, *Men, Cities, and Transportation* (2 vols., 1948). For canals, see Harry N. Scheiber, *Ohio Canal Era* (1969), and R. E. Shaw, *Erie Water West* (1966). For railroads, see Albert Fishlow, *American Railroads and the Transformation of the Ante-Bellum Economy* (1965); Alfred D. Chandler, Jr., ed., *The Railroads: The Nation's First Big Business* (1965); and Thomas C. Cochran, *Railroad Leaders, 1845–1890* (1953). The role of government is analyzed in Carter Goodrich, *Government Promotion of American Canals and Railroads, 1800–1890* (1960); Louis Hartz, *Economic Policy and Democratic Thought* (1954); and Oscar Handlin and Mary F. Handlin, *Commonwealth: A Study of the Role of Government in the American Economy* (1969).

The best works on maritime trade are Robert G. Albion, *The Rise of New York Port* (1939), and Samuel E. Morison, *Maritime History of Massachusetts, 1789–1860* (1921). For the clipper ships, see C. C. Cutler, *Greyhounds of the Sea* (1930), and A. H. Clark, *The Clipper Ship Era* (1910). L. H. Battistini, *The Rise of American Influence in Asia and the Pacific* (1960), treats an important aspect of America's commercial expansion.

On manufacturing, Victor S. Clark, *History of Manufactures in the United States, 1607–1860* (3 vols., 1929), remains indispensable. The best specialized studies are Peter Temin, *Iron and Steel in Nineteenth-Century America* (1964); Caroline F. Ware, *The Early New England Cotton Manufacture* (1931); Arthur H. Cole, *The American Wool Manufacture* (2 vols., 1926); and Nathan Rosenberg, ed., *The American System of Manufactures* (1969). Siegfried Giedion, *Mechanization Takes Command* (1948), contains a fascinating account of American technological innovation. H. J. Habakkuk, *American and British Technology in the Nineteenth Century* (1962), places American invention in a larger context, as does Carroll W. Pursell, Jr., *Early Stationary Steam Engines in America: A Study in the Migration of Technology* (1969). For a comprehensive reference work, see Melvin Kranzberg and Caroll W. Pursell, Jr., eds., *Technology in Western Civilization* (2 vols., 1967).

A pioneering study of social and economic mobility is Stephan Thernstrom, *Poverty and Progress* (1964). For disparities in the distribution of wealth and income, see Edward Pessen, *Riches, Class, and Power before the Civil War* (1973), and Lee Soltow, "Economic Inequality in the United States in the Period from 1790 to 1860," *Journal of Economic History 31* (December 1971), 822–839. The discovery of poverty is analyzed in Robert H. Bremner, *From the Depths* (1956), and Raymond A. Mohl, *Poverty in New York, 1783–1825* (1971). On working-class culture, the best guides are Herbert G. Gutman, *Work, Culture, and Society in Industrializing America* (1976); Howard M. Gitelman, *Workingmen of Waltham* (1974); Peter R. Knights, *The Plain People of Boston* (1971); and Norman Ware, *The Industrial Worker, 1840–1860* (1959). For labor movements, see Joseph Rayback, *A History of American Labor* (1966); Walter Hugins, *Jacksonian Democracy and the Working Class* (1960); and John R. Commons et al., *History of Labour in the United States.* Vol. 1 (4 vols., 1918–35).

There are two good studies of the ideology of the self-made man: Irvin G. Wyllie, *The Self-Made Man in America* (1954), and John G. Cawelti, *Apostles of the Self-Made Man* (1965). Though dealing with a later period, Richard Weiss, *The American Myth of Success* (1969), also sheds light on the earlier history of the subject.

14

The Politics
of Opportunity

The generation that came to maturity in the early nineteenth century assumed that the Founding Fathers had won the great struggle for American liberty and had bequeathed a mission of watchful preservation. But increasingly, the ideal of preserving a virtuous republic gave way to the ideal of preserving individual opportunity—of ensuring that the United States would remain a nation of self-made men.

Americans differed over specific programs for promoting opportunity and over the dangers that seemed to threaten it. Political parties emerged as crusades of "the people" against groups and "Monster Institutions" that supposedly subverted liberty and opportunity. Campaigns against the Freemasons, the Second Bank of the United States, "King Andrew" Jackson's executive power, and the Catholic church led to the formation, respectively, of the Anti-Masonic, Democratic, Whig, and Know-Nothing (American) parties. Of these parties only the Democrats and Whigs succeeded in mobilizing and preserving formidable national power.

These two major parties were coalitions—coalitions of sectional interests, class and economic interests, ethnic and religious interests. Since winning a national election required a very broad constituency, both the Democrats and the Whigs tended to avoid issues certain to alienate large groups of voters. Consequently,

465

they steered away from sectional issues, such as slavery. The two-party system became one of the strongest bonds of national unity. Unfortunately, this commitment to unity as a means of ensuring opportunity for white Americans rested on the tacit understanding that Negro slavery, the "Monster Institution" that most directly subverted liberty and opportunity, could not be questioned.

The End of Republican Unity

By 1820 the Federalist party was as good as dead. Jeffersonian Republicans congratulated themselves on having purged the nation of "artificial" principles of government copied from the British aristocratic model, and on having restored a political system attuned to the laws of nature. Despite their own jumble of shifting factions, Republicans also rejoiced over the illusion of a single national party and a new "Era of Good Feelings." President Monroe, in his second inaugural address (1821), invoked the most familiar image of harmony. The American people, he affirmed, constituted "one great family with a common interest." Four years later President John Adams, also a Republican, voiced similar sentiments and happily observed that "the baneful weed of party strife" had been uprooted. Most Americans still associated political parties with the self-serving, aristocratic factions that had dominated British politics. In a republican nation, as in a republican family, there was no room for selfish alliances representing separate interests.

But how could the idea of a common interest be squared with social reality? European travelers commented repeatedly on the centrifugal energies that seemed to be whirling Americans in all directions. In the words of Michel Chevalier, "Here all is circulation, motion and boiling agitation. Experiment follows experiment; enterprise follows enterprise." From 1820 to 1860 the contagious pursuit of wealth infected a multitude of immigrant groups, religions, social classes, subcultures, and lifestyles. The rivalries and competing interests of such groups revealed widely divergent fears, aspirations, and images of what America should be. At the same time Americans from competing localities and social groups became increasingly aware of the unequal effects of government policies concerning tariffs, banking and currency, and public land sales. Widening opportunity for some Americans could mean constricting opportunity for others.

The political parties of the Jacksonian era represented a compromise between the traditional hostility to political factions and the emerging social realities. Unlike the traditional political organizations, they were not based on family authority or elitist cliques. They transacted their business publicly, in caucuses and conventions on the local, state, and national level. Such meetings occurred so frequently that politics became a subject of popular interest and a kind of national recreation. In every case the political parties were torn between a desire to serve the special interests of their permanent constituency and a need to advocate bland, noncontroversial positions that would attract the widest possible popular following.

During the first stage of party formation, in the 1820s, most states completed the extension of suffrage to all adult white males. This extraordinary democratization of politics was accompanied by reforms providing for the popular election of governors, presidential electors, and in some states, even judges. These democratizing developments, which had roots extending back to the colonial past, proceeded peacefully except in Rhode Island, where the Dorr Rebellion of 1842 showed both the inutility of violence and the futility of conservative resistance. One consequence of this "democratic revolution" was the enormous increase in the number of voters and in the intensity of popular interest in politics. The onset of sharply contested presidential elections, beginning with Jackson's victory over John Quincy Adams in 1828, ended public apathy toward national candidates. By the presidential election of 1840 nearly 80 percent of the eligible voters went to the polls.

GEORGE CALEB BINGHAM'S "VERDICT OF THE PEOPLE"

Politics became the Americans' major public ritual. Like religious revivals, political events provided the occasion for sociability and for emotional expression. But politics also evoked the excitement that springs from looking upon or touching the levers of power. *(St. Louis Art Museum.)*

National politics receive more publicity than local politics, and historians have inevitably focused attention on the "Age of Jackson" and on the presidential elections in which two parties received the great majority of popular votes: the Democrats and the National Republicans in 1828 and 1832; the Democrats and Whigs (the successors to the National Republicans) from 1836 to 1852; and the Democrats and Republicans after 1856. These national parties acquired a certain life of their own, and were to some degree insulated from sudden gusts of regional or local excitement. Though a party's survival depended on a continuing sensitivity to the needs of its constituent groups, it also served as a disciplining and educational force, imposing definite limits to individual, local, and regional self-assertion. By 1840, for example, the majority of state legislators conformed to a strict Whig or Democratic vote even when a different position might have harmonized more with local or personal interests. The appointment of loyal party men to positions in local land offices, post offices, and customhouses established Whig or Democratic nerve centers at the grass-roots level.

Nevertheless, America's greatest political innovations have begun at the state level, and many of the significant shifts in voter loyalty have begun in local or "offyear" elections. For example, the birth of the modern political party preceded Jackson's election to the presidency in 1828 and had more to do with the political career of Martin Van Buren and the tangled struggles for local power within New York State.

Van Buren, who ultimately succeeded Jackson as President in 1837, was the son of slaveowning tavern keepers of Dutch descent (until 1827 Negro slavery was legal in New York). Lacking family prestige and connections, he became a protégé of the Clinton-Livingston faction of Republicans. Ambitious, shrewd, and exuding personal charm, the "Red Fox of Kinderhook" (also later known as the "Little Magician") climbed to prominence in state politics and finally challenged De Witt Clinton, the chief of the New York Republicans and the foremost promoter of the Erie Canal. By 1820 Van Buren's group of young "Bucktails" had captured control of the New York Republican party. Although the Bucktails included future leaders of the Jacksonian party, they did not initially favor the political reforms usually associated with Jacksonian democracy. They opposed eliminating all property qualifications for voting. They defeated proposals for the popular election of justices of the peace and other officials.

ANTI-VAN BUREN BROADSIDE

In the New York constitutional convention of 1821, Van Buren had opposed extending the suffrage to all white males. When Van Buren ran for President in 1836, his enemies accused him of having placed loyalty to property above loyalty to the white race. This broadside illustrates the ways in which racial prejudice was exploited by both parties. *(American Antiquarian Society.)*

READ!!

PAUSE and REFLECT.

Van Buren in favor of Negroes voting, and opposed to the Poor White Man's enjoying this inestimable privilege!

Extracts from the "Reports of the proceedings and "debates of the convention of 1821, assembled "for the purpose of amending the constitution of "the State of New York." These Reports were taken at the time and published in 1821.

It appears from page 178 of this volume, that on the 19th of September, 1821, the convention proceeded to consider the subject of the Elective Franchise, and that the Report upon that subject, made by Mr. Sandford, was taken up. This report proposed, as a part of the constitution, that "every "*white* male citizen of 21 years who shall have "been one year an inhabitant of this State, and for "six months a resident in the town, county or dis-"tr'ct where he may offer his vote, &c. &c., shall "be entitled to vote, &c."

In submitting this report, Mr. Sandford addressed the convention at length—and was followed by Mr. Ross, who, in the course of his argument, in favor of the Report, used the following language:

"That all men are free and equal, according to the usual declarations, applies to them only in a state of nature, and not after the institution of civil government; for then many rights, flowing from a natural equality, are necessarily abridged, with a view to produce the greatest amount of security and happiness to the whole community. On this principle the right of suffrage is extended to white men only. But why, it will probably be asked, are blacks to be excluded? I answer, because they are seldom, if ever, required to share in the common burthens or defence of the State. There are also additional reasons; they are a peculiar people, incapable, in my judgment, of exercising that privilege with any sort of discretion, prudence, or Independence. They have no just conceptions of civil liberty. They know not how to appreciate it, and are consequently indifferent to its preservation."

We have made this extract to show that, by inserting the word "*white*," it was distinctly designed to exclude "negroes" or "coloured people" from the right to vote. The Report was discussed by Mr. Rensellaer, Mr. Fairlie, Mr. Young, Mr. Root, Mr. Clarke and others.

After much debate, Mr. Jay, who is now at the head of the abolitionists in New York, moved to strike out the word "white," the effect of which would be to admit *all persons, black or white*, possessed of certain other qualifications, to the exercise of the right of suffrage. In opposing this measure, Chief Justice Spencer said:

"I have believed, and do still believe, that we are called on to extend the right of suffrage as far as the interests of the community will permit; but I do think we cannot contemplate carrying it to the full extent recommended in the report, without knowing that we are not giving to those people who

Van Buren's Negro Voters !

"*Stan bak, you poor white trash ; you got no property—we gemmen ob color votes fur Missa Van Buren and Missa Johnson; dey is our better friends and feller-citizens : Missa Van Buren he mend de constushon ob de York state to let we gemmen ob color vote, case we got $250, so you poor white bog-trotters and clod-hoppers stan back.*"

"*Massa Van Buren's frens wen dey men de Merland constushon wil please member to gib our bre'ren dere rights same as Missa Van Buren gib us in de York state.*"

will nominally enjoy the right, but to those who feed and clothe them. I shall vote against striking out the word white, on the ground that it is necessary for securing our own happiness."

The question on striking out the word *white*, (which would give all, whether black or white, the privilege of voting, if possessed of a certain amount of property,) was then taken by ayes and noes, and decided in the affirmative, as follows:

AYES—Messrs. Bacon, Baker, Barlow, Beckwith, Birdseye, Brinkerhoff, Brooks, Buel, Burroughs, Carver, R. Clark, Collins, Cramer, Day, Dodge, Duer, Eastwood, Edwards, Ferris, Fish, Hallock, Hees, Hogeboom, Hunting, Huntington, Jay, Jones, Kent, King, Moore, Munro, Nelson, Park, Paulding, Pitcher, Platt, Reeve, Rhinelander, Richards, Rodgers, Roseburgh, Sanders, N. Sanford, Seaman, Steele, D. Sutherland, Swift, Sylvester, Tallmadge, Tuttle, VAN BUREN, Van Ness, J. R. Van Renselær, Van Vechten, Ward, A. Webster, Wendover, Wheaton, E. Williams, Woodward, Wooster, Yates—63.

NOES—Messrs. Bowman, Breese, Briggs, Carpenter, Case, Child, D. Clark, Clyde, Dubois, Dyckman, Fairlie, Fenton, Frost, Howe, Humphrey, Hunt, Hunter, Hurd, Knowles, Lansing, Lawrence, Lefferts, A. Livingston, P. R. Livingston, M'Call, Millikin, Pike, Porter, Price, Pumply, Radcliff, Rockwell, Root, Rose, Ross, Russell, Sage, R. Sanford, Schenck, Seely, Sharpe, Sheldon, I. Smith, Spencer, Starkweather, I. Southerland, Taylor, Ten Eyck, Townley, Townsend, Tripp, Van Fleet, Van Horne, Verbryck, E. Webster, Wheeler, Woods, Young—59."

☞ We here see that Mr. Van Buren voted to strike out the word WHITE, so as to give the NEGRO the right of voting.

United States of America,
STATE OF MARYLAND, TO WIT:

I, Jas. B. Latimer, Notary Public in and for the city of Baltimore, do hereby certify, that I have carefully examined and compared the above extract, as printed, with the original on page 202, of the volume entitled "Reports of the Proceedings and Debates of the Convention of 1821, assembled for the purpose of amending the constitution of New York," and find the same to agree with said original in all particulars.

{ SEAL. } In witness whereof, I have hereunto set my hand and affixed my notarial seal, on this eleventh day of August, 1836.

JAMES B. LATIMER.
Notary Public.

☞ In the same Convention, (see Journal of Proceedings, pages 277, 283 and 284,) Mr. Van Buren opposed the poor man's voting if he did not own a certain amount of property [$250 worth] or paid taxes, or worked on the highways. See Mr. Van Buren's speech :

The question before the convention was to strike out the provision requiring a property qualification to entitle a man to vote :

Mr. Van Buren felt himself called upon to make a few remarks in reply to the gentleman from Delaware county, (Mr. Root.) He observed that it was evident, and indeed some gentlemen did not seem to disguise it, that the amendment proposed contemplated *nothing short of universal suffrage.* Mr. Van Buren did not believe that there

were twenty members of that committee, who, were the bare naked question of universal suffrage put to them, would vote in its favor; and he was very sure that its adoption was not expected, and would not meet the views of their constituents. Again he says,

"One word on the main question before the committee. We had already reached the verge of Universal Suffrage. There was but one step beyond, and are gentlemen prepared to take that ? We were *cheapening this invaluable right.* He was disposed to go as far as any in the extension of rational liberty, but he could not consent to undervalue this precious privilege so far as to confer it with an indiscriminating hand upon every one."—That is, if a white or a *black* man owns $250, he is to enjoy this precious privilege !

Again—Mr. Van Buren spoke against the amendment and against Universal Suffrage.

But the Van Buren faction did articulate a new conception of political parties as the impersonal agents of the people. When the Bucktails were attacked by the Clinton group as the "Albany Regency," a label suggesting the oppressive British regency of the Prince of Wales (1811–20), they replied with a strong defense of political parties, a defense that both Democrats and Whigs would subsequently echo. In America, they claimed, political loyalty could safely be extended to an egalitarian party, since it was free from the personal dominance of kings or great family magnates. American parties, far from being self-serving, required a self-less submission to the will of the organization. This respect for party discipline was later summed up by a prominent Whig, who declared that he "would vote for a dog, if he was the candidate of my party."

The Bucktails insisted that in America parties were necessarily responsible to the people. The excesses or transgressions of one party would inevitably be exposed by the opposition and brought before the bar of public opinion. The purpose of parties was essentially twofold: to win the largest possible mandate from the people; and when in power, to find the grounds of persuasion and compromise necessary for carrying out policies beneficial to the people. According to the Van Burenites, the rewards for such public service should not be confused with the corrupting privileges aristocratic patrons had traditionally bestowed on their clients. William L. Marcy, a Van Buren protégé, as he defended the new democratic meaning of patronage, felt no need to apologize for "the rule, that to the victor belong the spoils of the enemy." Finally, Van Buren envisioned national parties as antidotes to sectional division. The American people, he observed, were bound to coalesce into rival political groups, and party distinctions were infinitely safer than geographic ones. If party distinctions were suppressed, "geographical differences founded on local instincts or what is worse, prejudices between free and slaveholding states" would inevitably take their place.

Van Buren's appeal for organized political parties appeared at an opportune time. By 1821 it was evident that the "Virginia Dynasty" of Presidents would end with Monroe's second term and that the Republican party, no longer confronted by Federalist opponents, was splintering into personal and sectional factions. Some organization was necessary to preserve reasonable continuity and predictability in federal economic policy. Even more pressing was the need for suppressing the feelings of sectional animosity aroused by the controversy over admitting Missouri in 1819–1820.* The North's unexpected outrage over the admission of Missouri as a slave state convinced many Southerners of the need for cultivating alliances with Northern leaders who were unafraid of being called doughfaces, or Northern men with Southern principles. Van Buren fitted into this category, for he viewed the clamor over slavery as evidence of a dangerous breakdown in party loyalty.

---

*See Chapter 17, pp. 582–587.

There were other sources of Republican disunity. One group of Republicans responded to the vibrant nationalism of Henry Clay, John C. Calhoun, and John Quincy Adams. They favored Clay's American System—an engine for economic expansion fueled by protective tariffs, a national bank, and federal aid for internal improvements. Other "Old Republicans" like Van Buren viewed government intervention in the economy as a revival of ancient and corrupting alliances between political power and special privilege. The depression that followed the financial panic of 1819 substantiated the popular mistrust of the Second Bank of the United States and a general suspicion that state banks and other corporations were manipulating credit. By the early 1820s many Americans, particularly in the South and West, had grounds for fearing the economic dominance of a Northeastern elite.

Monroe's second administration was dominated by political maneuvering to determine who would be his successor. The proliferation of candidates signified that Monroe's "one great family with a common interest" had disintegrated. Three of the leading contenders were nationally distinguished members of Monroe's cabinet. William H. Crawford, secretary of the Treasury during several administrations, a Georgian of Virginia birth, would be heavily favored in any congressional party caucus. Crawford had won prestige as America's minister to France during the War of 1812. An advocate of state rights and limited federal power, Crawford was supported by the aged Thomas Jefferson and by Thomas Ritchie's formidable "Richmond Junto"; Van Buren led the Crawford forces in Congress. But the skeleton congressional caucus that nominated Crawford carried little weight, and an incapacitating illness further diminished his chances.

The other leading candidates sought support from state legislatures, and in that way bypassed the established procedure of nomination by congressional party caucus. Three of the four remaining aspirants were closely associated with the economic nationalism that had alienated the Old Republicans. John Quincy Adams, the secretary of state and the nation's most experienced diplomat, could expect solid support from his native New England but would always be aloof from the rough-and-tumble electioneering of the South and West. Henry Clay, the popular "Harry of the West," had won national prestige as a parliamentarian and engineer of compromise in the House of Representatives. It was expected that if no candidate should win the electoral majority the House would elect Clay President. But despite his appeal in Kentucky and other Western states, Clay ran fourth in electoral votes and was therefore excluded by the Twelfth Amendment from further consideration. John C. Calhoun, the secretary of war, had little support outside his native South Carolina. A graduate of Yale and a product of America's first small law school, in Connecticut, Calhoun was one of the few political leaders of his time who could be described as an "intellectual." Calhoun withdrew from the presidential race before the election, assuming that his almost certain choice as Vice-President would help him win the highest office in 1828.

The fourth candidate, Andrew Jackson, entered the contest unexpectedly and at a late stage. Unlike the other candidates, he had taken no clear stands on the controversial issues of the day, and his brief terms in the House and Senate had been undistinguished. Jackson's national fame arose from his victory over the British at the Battle of New Orleans, in the War of 1812, and his unswerving efforts to clear the West of Indians, thus promising limitless opportunity for white Americans. But "Old Hickory" was a good bit more than a military hero and an Indian fighter. Born on the Carolina frontier and orphaned at age fourteen, Jackson had studied law and had finally emigrated to Nashville, Tennessee, where he became attached by marriage and business connections to the local network of elite families. He prospered as an attorney, land speculator, and planter, and became the owner of over one hundred slaves. The Tennessee leaders who originally promoted Jackson for the presidency did not take his candidacy seriously, hoping only to use his popularity to neutralize the local antibank sentiment that endangered the banks they owned. In 1823 Jackson's backers were astonished when the movement caught fire in Pennsylvania and other states. The Old Hero turned out to be an astute politician, who perfectly gauged the national temper and who, once launched on the road to the presidency, skillfully took charge of his own campaign.

J. Q. ADAMS, BY DURAND

John Quincy Adams personified the intellectual as statesman. A man of learning and of wide diplomatic experience, he was more at home in the courts and capitals of Europe than in the caucuses and public forums of American politics. *(Philipse Manor Hall.)*

In the election of 1824 Jackson won a plurality of both the popular and the electoral votes, and could therefore legitimately claim to be the choice of the people. But because no candidate had won an electoral majority, the responsibility of electing a President fell on the House of Representatives. There, Clay threw his decisive support behind Adams, who was elected President and who soon appointed Clay secretary of state. This so-called corrupt bargain deeply embittered Calhoun, who was already beginning to defect from his former colleagues' economic nationalism. It also infuriated Jackson, who almost immediately launched a campaign to unseat Adams in 1828.

This final collapse of Republican unity proved to be a disaster for Adams's presidency. Adams inaugurated his administration by proposing a sweeping program of federal support for internal improvements, science, education, and the arts. He soon discovered, however, that he lacked the mandate and the power for far simpler tasks of government. One of the most intelligent and farseeing Presidents, Adams was also one of the least successful. Unfairly accused of being a monarchist with arrogant contempt for the people, he had the misfortune of inheriting the office when it had fallen into decay. His own inexperience with the realities of American political life helped to make him the unmourned victim, in 1828, of the first modern presidential contest.

The Democrats in Power

Andrew Jackson, the leader of the rising Democratic coalition, precisely fitted the need for a popular and genuinely national political leader. His stately bearing and natural dignity gave substance to the image of one of "nature's noblemen," someone who had risen to greatness without benefit of family, formal education, or subservience to any faction. Jackson's promoters disseminated the romantic mythology by every conceivable means: ballads, broadsides, barbecues, liberty pole-raisings, local committees, and militia companies. In contrast to the office-grubbing politicians and to the austere, highly cultivated John Quincy Adams, here was a frontiersman, a true self-made man, a soldier of iron will who personified the will of the people, a man without artifice or pretension who moved decisively in the light of simple moral truths. The Jackson image, in short, was an image of reassuring stability in the face of bewildering social and economic change.

Jackson also fitted the need for a leader who comprehended the new meaning of party politics. Against the Adams-Clay alliance he molded a coalition that included among other groups the followers of Calhoun (who became his running mate in 1828), the Richmond Junto of Old Republicans, former Federalists who had lost office in New Jersey, and Van Buren's powerful Albany Regency. This new Democratic party appealed to many urban workers and immigrants, to frontier expansionists and Indian haters, to many Southern planters, and to various Northeastern editors, bankers, and manufacturers who built local Democratic machines as the means of gaining or preserving power.

ANDREW JACKSON

In this homey carving President Jackson appears as a gaunt, stern, rough-hewn man of the people, a democratized Washington. *(Museum of the City of New York.)*

Jackson's state organizers, looking ahead to 1828, bypassed the local ruling gentry and concentrated for the first time on mobilizing the necessary popular vote to capture the full electoral vote of critical states. Because the new coalition contained Pennsylvanians who clamored for higher tariffs and South Carolinians who detested tariffs, keeping unity required delicate manipulation. In 1828 Jackson's leaders in Congress helped to pass the so-called Tariff of Abominations, assuming that Southern support for Jackson was secure, that the new duties on raw materials would win votes from Northern and Western protectionists, and that the most objectionable provisions could be blamed on the Adams administration. The subsequent outrage in the South suggested that Jackson as President could no longer get by with vague statements favoring a "judicious" tariff. Yet Southerners knew that a Jackson-Calhoun alliance was far more promising than the economic nationalism of Adams and Clay, who were now known as National Republicans.

The Election of 1828

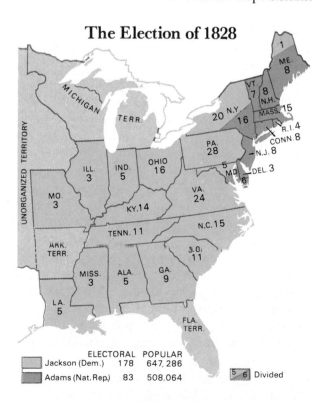

	ELECTORAL	POPULAR
Jackson (Dem.)	178	647,286
Adams (Nat. Rep.)	83	508,064

5 6 Divided

In 1828 Adams suffered a crushing defeat, receiving only 83 electoral votes to Jackson's 178. In Washington a jubilant and tumultuous mob celebrated Jackson's inauguration, and throughout the nation diverse groups rode to power on his broad coattails. In a general sense, the election of 1828 affirmed the people's rejection of government policies that were thought to encourage special privilege. The election also proved the effectiveness of the campaign organization and propaganda techniques that Jackson's managers, particularly Martin Van Buren, had perfected.

Once in power, the Democrats soon became associated with two other instruments that solidified popular support for party rule. The first was a system of patronage, or "spoils," which continued practices begun during previous administrations and tried to give them legitimacy. Jackson actually removed no more than one-fifth of the surviving federal officeholders. Yet he ardently defended the theory that most public offices required no special abilities or experience, that they should frequently rotate among loyal deserving party workers, and that party rule should prevent the establishment of a permanent and parasitic class of civil servants.

WHITE HOUSE LEVEE AFTER JACKSON'S INAUGURATION

Jackson's arrival in the White House created the image of a government accessible to the common people. (*Courtesy, The White House.*)

The second mechanism was the national party convention, which like various "Jacksonian" measures had earlier been initiated by anti-Jacksonian forces. As an alternative to nomination by legislative caucus, the "convention," by its name, suggested a return to fundamental law, to the direct voice of the people assembled in a constitution-framing body. Although party conventions could do no more than frame partisan platforms and nominate partisan candidates, they pretended to represent the true interests of the people. In theory, since they drew representatives from a broad spectrum of society, they were more democratic than legislative caucuses. In practice, they were often more subject to manipulation by political machines. But like the partisan spoils system, the party convention symbolized the central appeal of Jackson's party. It promised to break the congealing crust of privilege, eliminating all institutional barriers to individual opportunity. It also provided the assurance of solidarity with a party headed by a man of the people, a man who simply magnified the idealized self-image of millions of Americans.

Jacksonian Democrats had no monopoly on the new mechanisms for mobilizing and preserving political power. There were, however, certain principles and aspirations that distinguished the Democrats from their National Republican opponents. Jackson had long given voice to the West's demand for territorial expansion as a means of ensuring economic opportunity. As the first Westerner elected to the presidency, he symbolized a geographic shift in political power. Of course, not all Westerners supported Jackson. Those who understood that Western economic expansion depended on access to Eastern markets and on investment capital from the East and Europe favored federal aid for internal improvements, a program that Henry Clay championed. Clay's supporters were angered when Jackson, in vetoing the Maysville Road Bill, not only objected to the "partial instead of general advantage" of a road built within the borders of Kentucky, but implied that any federal support for internal improvements was unconstitutional. On the other hand, many Westerners had come to view federally supported internal improvements as sources of waste and corruption. Others were appeased when they learned that despite Jackson's pronouncements, federal support for roads and canals continued to pour in from a Congress less concerned with constitutional theory than with constituents' needs. On the whole the West cheered for Jackson because it had come to pride itself as the repository of values that Jackson fought for: an agrarian society of independent farmers, committed to individual enterprise and local self-determination.

To say that Jacksonian Democrats were advocates of laissez-faire is accurate but insufficient. They knew that on the local and state levels, economic opportunity hinged on political power. Some Jacksonian bankers worked for "free banking" laws that would eliminate the need for personal political influence in order to obtain a special charter incorporating a bank. Some Jacksonian farmers and promoters favored transferring public lands to the states and distributing surplus federal revenue to the states. Knowledgeable Americans were increasingly aware that their destinies were intertwined with local politics. Yet Democratic rhetoric and ideology refused to acknowledge the injustices and inequalities resulting from unregulated competition and justified a withdrawal of the federal government from economic responsibility. This Democratic policy rested on a faith that non-intervention would guarantee social fluidity and an expansion of limitless opportunity.

Paradoxically Jackson, the first great defender of federal laissez-faire, was the most forceful and aggressive President since Washington had held the office. During preceding administrations the chief executive's powers had been siphoned off by cabinet rivals and a jealous Congress. With the aid of party discipline, Jackson soon exerted his dominance over Congress by an unprecedented use of vetoes and pocket vetoes (the refusal to sign a bill during the last ten days of a congressional session). Except for Van Buren, whom he chose as secretary of state, Jackson treated his cabinet in the manner of the army's commander in chief. In 1831, when various personal grievances provoked a fatal split with Calhoun, his Vice-President, Jackson purged Calhoun's followers from his cabinet and administration. This bold move placed Van Buren in the position of Jackson's chosen successor. It depended on the correct assumption that Calhoun's South Carolinians could not destroy the critical alliance that Van Buren had established with Virginia's Old Republicans. Jackson, unlike his predecessors, could escape the coercions of disloyal and powerful cabinet members by relying on a group of informal advisers, the so-called Kitchen Cabinet, who could be trusted or dismissed at will.

In essence, Jackson's use of federal power was negative. As President he personified Herman Melville's exclamation "No! in thunder." (In the novel *Moby Dick* [1851], Melville addressed the "great democratic God! . . . Thou who didst pick up Andrew Jackson from the pebbles; who didst hurl him upon a warhorse; who didst thunder him higher than a throne!"). Even concerning the Indians and South Carolina's defiant Nullifiers (issues that established his forcefulness as a President and that are discussed in other chapters) Jackson's response was a thunderous "No!"—the Indians had to go, and the South Carolinians had to stay and obey. Jackson's negative policies rested on a supreme faith in America's mission. When Jackson retired from the presidency in 1837, he assured his countrymen: "Providence has chosen you as the guardians of freedom, to preserve it for the benefit of the human race." The fulfillment of this mission, he believed, required the government to prevent the growth of any artificial concentrations of power or barriers to individual enterprise.

Tariffs and fiscal policy were obvious testing grounds for defining the role of the federal government in national economic life. Because the economy was still more regional than national and because the government had so few functions, the most momentous economic issues of the era grew out of the commitment to protective tariffs and a national bank (Bank of the United States or BUS) that had followed the War of 1812. The Middle Atlantic states, the most affected by competition from European manufactured goods, had long been the political stronghold of protectionism. During the 1820s, as New England's economy became increasingly dependent on the production of wool and on textile manufacturing, New England's political leaders like Daniel Webster abandoned their traditional defense of free trade and portrayed protective tariffs as the key to economic growth and individual opportunity. Simultaneously, the Lower South became increasingly hostile to tariffs that threatened to raise the price of manufactured goods and to curtail foreign markets for cotton. For a time the Democrats attempted to arrange tradeoffs between the various interests and regions represented in the party. Beginning in 1833, however, tariff rates were gradually lowered. When the Whigs gained power and sharply reversed this trend in 1842, the tariff had become one of the many issues that divided the two parties. In 1846 President James K. Polk, a Jacksonian Democrat, signed the so-called Walker Tariff, which imposed low duties for the sole purpose of obtaining federal revenue, and these duties were even further reduced by an 1857 act. The continuation of a low-tariff policy was not only a boon to the South and a stimulant to America's foreign trade, but an indication of the growing power of the South within the Democratic party.

Jackson had long harbored a mistrust of banks and had expressed a special antipathy toward the BUS. Van Buren, Senator Thomas Hart Benton of Missouri, Amos Kendall of the Kitchen Cabinet, and other key presidential advisers shared these sentiments. To understand their "hard money" position it is important to remember that the government issued no federal bank notes like the Federal Reserve notes, or "paper money," in circulation today. Payment for goods and services might be in gold or silver coin—specie; or more likely, in paper notes issued by private commercial banks. The value of such paper currency fluctuated greatly. The hard-money Democrats realized that large commercial transactions could not be carried on with specie. But they believed that the common people, including small businessmen as well as farmers and wage earners, should not be saddled with the risk of being cheated by a speculative currency. They also knew that a policy favoring the greater circulation of gold and silver coin, which seemed magically endowed with some fixed and "natural" value, would win votes for the party.

To a large degree, however, the reserves and transfers of specie were controlled by the BUS. The BUS performed many of the functions of a truly national bank. Its own notes could be exchanged for specie, and they were accepted by the government as legal payment for all obligations to the United States. Because the BUS had large capital reserves and because it limited the issue of its own highly stable notes, it occupied a creditor position relative to the hundreds of state-chartered banks throughout the country. It served as a clearinghouse and regulatory agency for their money, refusing to accept notes that were not backed by sufficient reserves of specie. By promoting monetary stability, the BUS helped to improve the public reputation of banks in general and eased the difficulties of long-distance transfers of goods and credit. It also mobilized a national reserve of capital on which other banks could draw. Consequently, most state banks favored congressional renewal of the BUS charter, which was scheduled to expire in 1836.

Opponents of the bank feared the concentration of so much economic power in a few hands and worried that the federal government had practically no control, although it provided one-fifth of the bank's capital. They remembered that the irresponsible policies of the BUS, after the Panic of 1819, had led to widespread business failures, especially in the South and West. The bank's critics complained that, even under the expert presidency of Nicholas Biddle, this partly public institution was far more oriented to the interest of its private investors than to the interest of the general public. Senator Daniel Webster, the main lobbyist for rechartering the BUS, not only was the director of the Boston branch (the BUS headquarters was in Philadelphia), but relied heavily on Biddle for private loans and fees for legal and political services. In Jackson's eyes the BUS had become a "Monster Institution," unconstitutionally diverting public funds for private profit.

The celebrated "Bank War" erupted into open conflict in 1832, when Webster and Clay launched a legislative offensive, partly to prevent Jackson's reelection. Knowing that they could win support from many Democrats for the passage of a bill rechartering the BUS, they were confident that the President could not veto the measure without fatally damaging his chances for reelection in the fall. Jackson took up the challenge. In a masterful veto message he spelled out the principles that would be a touchstone for "Jacksonian democracy" and for populist politics in the decades to come. He denounced the BUS as a privileged monopoly, and vowed to take a stand "against all new grants of monopolies and exclusive privileges, against any prostitution of our Government to the advancement of the few at the expense of the many." Jackson in no way favored leveling wealth or other distinctions derived from "natural and just advantages." "Equality of talents, of education, or of wealth," he affirmed, "cannot be produced by human institutions." But government should provide "equal protection, and, as heaven does its rains, shower its favors alike on the high and the low, the rich and the poor." The BUS represented a flagrant example of government subsidy to the privileged, of laws that made "the rich richer and the potent more powerful." Jackson also warned of the dangerous provisions that allowed foreigners to buy BUS stock and thus to acquire influence over American policy. In defiance of the Supreme Court's decision in *McCulloch* v. *Maryland* (1819), he argued that the BUS was unconstitutional.

Although Webster and other conservative leaders immediately cried that the President was trying "to stir up the poor against the rich," the election of 1832 decisively vindicated Jackson's bold leadership and political acumen. Old Hickory would have won a sweeping victory even if the opposition votes had not been divided between Henry Clay, the National Republican candidate, and William

Major Jack Downing, I must act in this case with energy and decision, you see the downfall of the party engine and corrupt monopoly!!

Hurrah! General! if this don't beat skunkin I'm a nigger, only see that var mint Nick how spry he is, he runs along like a Weatherfield Hog with an onion in his mouth.

ORDER for the Removal of the Public Money deposited in the UNITED STATES BANK

Drawd off from Natur by Zek: Downing, Neffu to Major Jack Downing.

THE DOWNFALL OF MOTHER BANK.

Printed & Publ.d by H.R.Robinson; 52 Courtlandt St.d N.York.

"THE DOWNFALL OF MOTHER BANK"

In this popular cartoon Jackson's removal of federal
deposits from the Bank of the United States carries overtones of Christ's chasing the money lenders from the ancient
temple. Biddle, in the form of the devil, flees along with
Webster, Clay, and the various minions of the Money Power.
(Library of Congress.)

Wirt, the reluctant leader of the Anti-Masons. Confident now that the supporters
of the BUS could never override his veto, Jackson vowed to defang the Monster
Institution by removing all federal deposits.

This aggressive policy was opposed by many of the President's advisers, since
the BUS already appeared to be doomed. The removal policy also raised new
problems. According to Jackson's plan, which his secretary of the Treasury,
Roger B. Taney, soon put into execution, federal funds would be dispersed
among chosen state-chartered banks; these were soon dubbed "pet" banks. For
the policy to succeed, Jackson had to persuade the banking community that decentralization would not bring economic disaster. Nicholas Biddle, on the other
hand, needed to produce a minor financial panic to underscore the essential
role of the BUS in maintaining financial stability. Biddle could not exert his full

financial powers, however, without adding to popular hostility toward his Monster Institution. In the winter of 1832–1833 Biddle did retrench, but the constriction of credit was not serious enough to shake Jackson's resolution. The President also gained political leverage through his discriminating choice of pet banks. Many bankers who had earlier hoped to keep clear of the political struggle were eager for interest-free federal funds that would allow them to expand loans and other commercial operations. Jackson's victory was fairly complete by the spring of 1834.

Like many triumphs, the destruction of the BUS (which eventually became a state bank chartered by Pennsylvania) enmeshed the victors in a web of problems. The Democrats claimed that by slaying the Monster, they had purged the nation of a moral evil. Yet the deposit of federal funds in pet banks encouraged the expansion of credit, and in the mid-1830s the nation reeled from the intoxication of a speculative boom. Some of the orthodox Jacksonian officials even bemoaned the growing federal surplus—an unimaginable phenomenon to later generations who have only known federal deficits and mounting public debts—because there seemed to be no place to put the funds that would not corrupt the republic. Whatever the administration did invited trouble. On the one hand, if it distributed funds to the states, it fed the speculative boom by encouraging further construction of roads and canals. On the other hand, if it kept the funds in the pet banks, these banks clearly had to be regulated by the federal government, lest they too feed inflation by issuing vast quantities of paper money based on this reserve. Slowly Jackson and his successor, Van Buren, who was elected in 1836, moved towards a policy of hard money. They tried to reduce or eliminate the circulation of small-denomination bank notes and to set a minimal requirement for the pet banks' specie reserves. In 1836 Jackson also issued an executive order, the so-called Specie Circular, requiring payment in specie for purchase of public land. The Specie Circular represented a direct federal effort to curb speculation and thus to manage the fluctuations of the economy.

This controversial measure signaled the growing dominance of the antibank and hard-money faction in the Democratic party. The subsequent nomination and election of Van Buren strengthened the hand of those Democrats who found a hostility to all banks politically effective. The panic of 1837 reinforced this hostility, but also hastened the defection of many bankers and businessmen from the Democratic party. The painful downturn in investment, prices, and employment, though often blamed on the erratic inflationary and deflationary policies of the Jacksonians, was mainly the result of sudden shifts in the international flow of credit and commodities. For orthodox Jacksonians, however, the collapse of the banking structure proved the folly of government partnership with even pet banks. After three years of bitter intraparty struggle, Van Buren finally achieved a "divorce of bank and state" with the passage of the Independent Treasury Act (1840). By locking federal funds in "independent" and insulated subtreasuries, this measure deprived the banking system of reserves that might have encouraged loans and aided economic recovery. Thenceforth, Democratic policy favored moderate fiscal and banking regulations in the public interest; but this objective was largely nullified by the fear of allowing public funds to be used for private profit.

In summary, the Democrats' approach to finance can be illuminated by pointing to three inconsistencies. First, their economic policies did little to aid the groups of farmers and artisans the Democrats claimed to represent. The ultimate beneficiary was the plantation South. For the South the policy of economic laissez-faire seemed to offer assurance that the federal government would be equally averse to interfering with Negro slavery. By 1838 Calhoun and his followers, who had earlier seceded from the Democratic party, returned to the fold, and as it turned out, Calhoun's return paved the way for Southern domination of the party in the two decades to come.

Second, the nation's banking system continued to integrate and the nation's economy continued to grow with serene disregard for the vicissitudes of politics. The attempts of Jackson and Van Buren to insulate the national government

"THE TIMES"

This complex cartoon portrays the allegedly disastrous results of Democratic rule: the government's hard money policy leads to a run on the bank, which has suspended specie payments; the custom house is deserted; debtors are herded into the sheriff's office; beggars and unemployed artisans crowd the streets; scenes of drunkenness are linked with the unruliness of immigrants and Loco Foco radicals. (*Library of Congress.*)

from what they saw as an inegalitarian and corrupting economy had little effect on the general trends of economic change. Nor did the actions of John Tyler have any greater effect. Tyler became President in 1841 on the death of William Henry Harrison, who was the first Whig elected as chief executive. Tyler vetoed proposals to create a new national bank, sponsored by Henry Clay, but his negatives had more effect in disrupting the Whig party than in disturbing the economy. In 1846, when Tyler's successor, James K. Polk of Tennessee, reinstituted the Independent Treasury, the economy accepted the change with scarcely a tremor.

Finally, the Jacksonian ideal that independent yeoman farmers should exchange their produce for gold and silver coin was in one sense an anachronism. Yet Jackson thought of hard money as an essentially impersonal force that would provide the nation with stable moral as well as economic values, and thus ensure all citizens a fair return in their competitive pursuit of happiness. In this sense, the Jacksonian ideology represented a final blow against paternalistic theories of government and an unintentional sanction for the laissez-faire capitalism of the future.

Opposition Parties and the Realignment of the 1850s

For most of the thirty years following Jackson's 1828 victory the Democrats ruled the nation as the majority party. Between 1828 and 1856 their presidential nominees defeated every opposition candidate except William Henry Harrison (1840) and Zachary Taylor (1848), both of whom died in office. John Tyler, the Vice-President who succeeded Harrison only a month after the latter's inauguration, soon returned to his original Virginia Democratic loyalties and principles. Millard Fillmore, Zachary Taylor's successor, was a genial but colorless Whig party hack who began his political career as an Anti-Mason and ended it by running for President in 1856 on the nativist and anti-Catholic Know-Nothing ticket.

But the Democrats' dominance of the presidency is deceptive. By the late 1830s Whigs could match Democratic strength in most parts of the country. The South, because of the pattern of the post–Civil War politics, has commonly been pictured as a preserve for states' rights Democrats. Yet Whigs predominated as the South's representatives in three out of the five Congresses elected between 1832 and 1842. Whig strength was particularly evident on local, county, and state levels. Election contests were so close and unpredictable that no state could be taken for granted as part of a "solid" South, North, or West. Moreover, in all sections of the country the party loyalties of the 1830s held remarkably firm until the mid-1850s.

Like the Democratic party, the Whigs represented a wholly new coalition. They were not, as the Democrats charged, simply Federalists in disguise—the Democrats themselves recruited an impressive number of ex-Federalist leaders. In

Congress the Whigs coalesced as a legislative rebellion against Jackson's "Executive Usurpation." During the summer of 1832 Jackson's veto of the bill rechartering the BUS led to the temporary coalition of three of the most formidable
senators in American history. All three longed for the presidency. By 1832 they
had won fame as three mythical gods, deliverers of a kind of Olympian oratory
that dazzled aspiring young men in an era not jaded by less demanding forms of
entertainment. Daniel Webster struck the keynote when he attacked "King
Andrew" as a reincarnation of the French monarch who had declared, "I AM
THE STATE." A man of humble New Hampshire origins and aristocratic Boston tastes, Webster had risen in the legal profession by emulating and paying deference to New England's commercial elite. He was a heavy drinker, given to
extravagant living and continual debt. His sonorous voice and commanding
physical presence could never quite convey the moral sincerity that most Northeastern Whigs expected of their leaders. Yet Webster upheld their traditional
mistrust of divisive parties and their traditional ideal of government by "disinterested gentlemen." He succeeded in blending this conservative tradition
with a celebration of material and moral progress. As the agent of commercial
and manufacturing interests in Massachusetts, he was flexible enough to shift
his style of argument from the forums of the Supreme Court and the Senate to
the stump of popular politics, always pleading for the natural harmony of interests that the Democratic party threatened to undermine.

Henry Clay considered himself a Jeffersonian Republican and the leader of
the National Republicans, the label originally applied to Jackson's opponents.
The author of the American System, Clay joined Webster's assault on Jackson's
alleged despotism. Clay was a Kentuckian of Virginia birth, and had also risen
from humble origins; like Webster, he was notorious for extravagant living,
though Clay's self-indulgence took the typically Southern forms of gambling,
dueling, and horse racing. A slaveowning planter and brilliant courtroom lawyer,
Clay assumed two contradictory political roles. He competed with Jackson as a
Western man of the people, a coonskin man of nature. But Clay had also helped
to negotiate the Treaty of Ghent ending the War of 1812; he had been Adams's
secretary of state; and he represented the Western business and commercial
interests that demanded federal aid for internal improvements. One of the
greatest political manipulators in nineteenth-century America, Clay had talents
unequaled in caucuses, committee rooms, and all-night boardinghouse negotiations.

The most unpredictable member of the anti-Jackson triumvirate was John C.
Calhoun, who had shifted in the 1820s from militant nationalism to a militant
defense of slavery and state rights, and who until 1831 had been Jackson's nominal ally. Despite Calhoun's dramatic turnabouts, contemporaries admired the
clarity and logical force of his arguments and respected his earlier distinguished
service as secretary of war. But Calhoun's role in the Nullification controversy

made him a dangerous ally in the developing Whig coalition.* Unlike Calhoun, the most important Southern Whig leaders—Robert Toombs, Alexander H. Stephens, John M. Berrien, and John J. Crittenden—shared the economic and nationalistic views of their Northern brethren.

The Whig outlook on the world was almost too diffuse to be termed an ideology. Like the Democrats, Whigs gloried in the dream of America's future as the greatest nation the world had ever seen, and they found confirmation for that dream in the measurable growth of population, wealth, and power. Far more than the Democrats, they associated the "spirit of improvement" with concrete technological and social inventions. They assumed that steam power, the telegraph, railroads, banks, corporations, prisons, factories, asylums, and public schools all contributed to an advancing civilization and to an increasing equality of opportunity. Unlike the Democrats, Whigs tended to endorse an ethic geared to what modern psychologists might describe as "delayed gratifications." On both social and individual levels, they advocated saving from income, capital accumulation, budgetary planning, and fiscal responsibility. They opposed aggressive territorial expansion as a cure-all for economic problems. They insisted that America's expansion and power should be harnessed to social ends and stabilized by publicly acknowledged moral boundaries. Alarmed by the excesses of rampant individualism, they expressed continuing and sometimes hysterical concern over the loss of community—over the demagogues who won support by inciting the poor against the rich, children against parents, wives against husbands, and geographic section against geographic section.

Whigs thought of themselves as conservatives and often invoked European theories, which flourished in the post-Napoleonic decades, stressing the organic unity of society and the necessity of balancing human rights with social duties. But the Whig ideal of government was essentially optimistic and progressive. In 1825, long before the Whig party began to coalesce, John Quincy Adams advanced the central Whig proposition that the constitution had given the central government both the duty and the necessary powers to promote "the progressive improvement of the condition of the governed."

On a popular level, as distinct from alliances of congressional leaders, the Whig party began to appear by 1834 as a loose coalition of state and local groups opposed to Jacksonian Democrats. Reluctant to give the Jacksonians a monopoly over the popular label *democrat*, the anti-Jacksonians sometimes called themselves Democratic Whigs. But the final acceptance of the term *Whig* signified an important difference in the party's national and historical self-image. Superficially, the label suggested an identity with the British "Country" party of Protestant gentry, who had allegedly defended the British constitution against the despotism of the pro-Catholic Stuart kings and the later executive encroachments

---

*See Chapter 17, pp. 587–591.

of George III. This imagery linked King Andrew with the various reactionary and demagogic monarchs of Europe. If such parallels seemed farfetched, the very act of drawing parallels with Europe contained a deeper significance. Unlike the Democrats, the Whigs tended to deny the uniqueness of the American experience and to place less faith in political institutions than in economic and cultural progress. They also tended to look on Britain, despite its monarchic and aristocratic institutions, as a model of economic and cultural progress. For the most thoughtful Whig spokesmen, America was less a revolutionary departure from the rest of the world than a testing ground for progressive forces that were at once universal and dependent essentially on moral character.

In all parts of the country Whigs attracted a broad cross section of the electorate, a cross section, however, often weighted in favor of the wealthy, the privileged, the aspiring, and paradoxically the victims of overt discrimination. In the North this constituency included most of the free blacks; British and German Protestant immigrants; manual laborers sympathetic with their employers' interest; business-oriented farmers; educators, reformers, and professional people; well-to-do merchants, bankers, and manufacturers; and active members of the Presbyterian, Unitarian, and Congregationalist churches. In the South the party

"KING ANDREW THE FIRST"

The Whig image of Jackson as an autocratic king, brandishing the veto and trampling the Constitution under foot.

KING ANDREW THE FIRST.

had particular appeal to urban merchants, editors, bankers, and to those farmers and planters who associated progress with expanding commerce, capital accumulation, railroads, and economic partnership with the North.

During their initial stages of organization the Whigs faced three formidable problems. First, in the populous Northern states like New York, Pennsylvania, and Massachusetts they had to find strategies for uniting the economic interests of the National Republicans with the moral and cultural aspirations of various groups alienated by the incumbent Democrats. Second, they had to get rid of the elitist stigma that had been fastened on John Quincy Adams and then on the defenders of the BUS, and somehow prove that they were better democrats than the Democrats. Finally, they had to find delicate maneuvers for bypassing senatorial prima donnas like Webster and Clay and selecting less controversial presidential candidates who could appeal to the nation without arousing dissension and jealousy among the various state party organizations.

The way these problems were met is well illustrated by the career of Thurlow Weed of New York, who became the prototype of the nineteenth-century political boss and manipulator. A self-made man, Weed first acquired a voice in New York politics as editor of the Rochester *Telegraph* and as a bitter foe of Van Buren's Albany Regency. In 1827 Weed and his young protégé William H. Seward took up the cause of Anti-Masonry as a means of embarrassing the ruling Van Buren machine. In western New York, Anti-Masonry had suddenly erupted as a kind of religious crusade following the abduction and probable murder of a former Freemason who had sought to divulge the secrets of the fraternal society. The crusade expressed widespread popular resentment against an organization that knit many of the wealthier and more powerful urban leaders of the state into a secret brotherhood pledged to mutual aid and support. Weed and Seward succeeded in portraying the Van Buren regime as the agent of Freemasonry—a Monster Institution—intent on suppressing legal investigation and prosecution of the alleged murder,

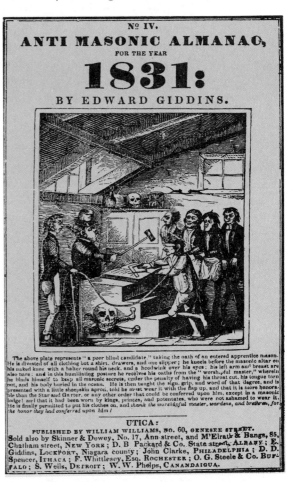

ANTI MASONIC ALMANAC

Anti-Masonic publications made much of the supposedly sinister and ridiculous initiation rituals that bound a new member "to keep all Masonic secrets, under the penalty of having his throat cut, his tongue torn out, and his body buried in the ocean." (*The New York Public Library.*)

and on disguising statewide links between Masonic political influence and economic privilege. This antielitist rhetoric helped to counteract the Democrats' claims of being the true champions of the people against the unpopular Adams administration in Washington. By 1830, when Anti-Masons captured approximately one-half the popular vote in New York State and when the movement showed increasing signs of strength in other Northern states, Weed and other strategists were working to absorb the National Republicans into a new anti-Jackson coalition.

But though the Anti-Masons organized the first national political convention in American history, Weed began to sense that the movement could be no more than a springboard for a successful national party. Weed launched his powerful *Albany Evening Journal* as an Anti-Masonic organ, but he increasingly downplayed Masonry and combined blistering attacks on the Albany Regency with the advocacy of various social reforms. To his political cronies and businessmen backers Weed kept insisting that the Jacksonians could never be beaten so long as they continued to persuade the people that they represented "the principle of democracy . . . the poor against the rich." By 1834 Weed had abandoned Anti-Masonry

"HURRAH FOR OLD TIPPECANOE"

In this Whig cartoon, "Matty" Van Buren, with Jackson's support, tries to stop the flow of Harrison's hard cider. But the people line up to receive Old Tippecanoe's "true Hospitality." (*Boston Athenaeum.*)

and had succeeded in organizing a New York Whig coalition. In 1836, when the Whigs tried to broaden their appeal by nominating various regional candidates for President, including Daniel Webster of Massachusetts and Hugh White of Tennessee, it was Weed's candidate, William Henry Harrison of Ohio, who won the most electoral votes. "Old Tippecanoe," famous for his military defeat of the Shawnee Indians in 1811, appealed to many former Anti-Masons and won strong support in the South as well as in New York, Ohio, and Pennsylvania. After years of patient organizing, wire-pulling, and passing out cigars (Weed reportedly smoked or gave away 80,000 cigars), Weed finally came into his own in 1838 when he succeeded in getting Seward elected governor of New York. As the master of patronage, the official state printer, and the "dictator" of the New York machine, Weed was now in a position to challenge his old archrival Van Buren, who claimed to be the President of the common people.

In 1840 Weed played a key role in blocking the Whigs' nomination of Clay and in opening the way for Harrison. Weed's young protégé, Horace Greeley, edited the Whigs' most influential paper, *The Log Cabin,* which set the pace in attacking President Van Buren as an affected dandy who had transformed the White House into a palace of effeminate luxury. Greeley and others cast Harrison as a frontiersman of simple tastes; his symbols were a barrel of cider (whether hard or soft depended on the locality), and a log cabin with a welcoming coonskin at the door. Harrison's victory seemed to show that strategists like Weed had overcome the Whigs' political liabilities. They could rival the Democrats in populistic appeals, in carnival-like hucksterism, and above all, in grass-roots organization.

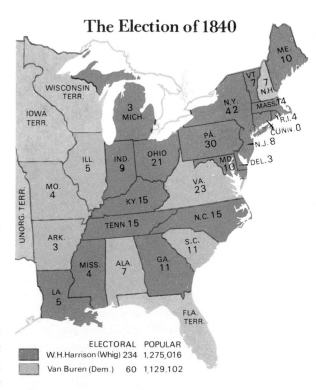

The Election of 1840

	ELECTORAL	POPULAR
W.H.Harrison (Whig)	234	1,275,016
Van Buren (Dem.)	60	1,129,102

Nevertheless, the Whigs never found a magnetic national leader who, like Jackson for the Democrats, could become a unifying symbol for their party. John Tyler, the Vice-President who succeeded Harrison, soon betrayed the economic principles of the party. In 1844 Clay went down to defeat for a third time, after which the Whigs returned to the tested expedient of nominating apolitical military heroes, Zachary Taylor in 1848 and Winfield Scott in 1852.

The Whigs' difficulties went beyond the weakness of their presidential candidates. Despite their political pragmatism and impressive party discipline, the Whigs contained a militant, reform-minded element that resented the compromises necessary for a national party.

Anti-Masonry had been one of the early expressions of such reformist and issue-oriented politics, and many of the Anti-Masons who joined the Whigs had never been comfortable with the opportunism of leaders like Thurlow Weed, who placed victory above principle. In addition to the Anti-Masons, the Whig party became the uneasy lodging place for people who wanted laws enforcing a stricter Sabbath, laws prohibiting the sale of alcohol, laws barring slavery in the territories and abolishing slavery in the District of Columbia, and laws prolonging the time before an immigrant could be naturalized or allowed to vote. These causes were nourished by the spread of Protestant religious revivals in the North.* Among Southern Whigs and hard-headed supporters of Clay's American System they had little appeal.

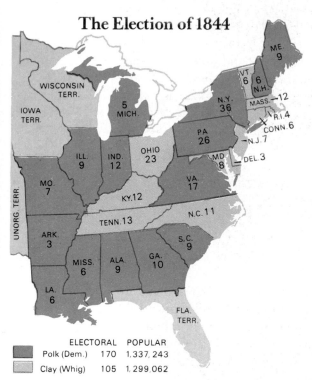

The Election of 1844

	ELECTORAL	POPULAR
Polk (Dem.)	170	1,337,243
Clay (Whig)	105	1,299,062

As early as 1844 it became apparent that as a national party the Whigs were peculiarly vulnerable to cultural and sectional tensions. In that year the issue of Texas annexation divided the party.** Enough Northern Whigs defected to James G. Birney, the candidate of the abolitionist Liberty party, to cost Clay the election, even though Birney received only 1.9 percent of the total popular vote. In the same campaign the Whigs in Philadelphia and New York City actively cooperated with the nativists and the anti-Catholic American Republican party, thereby increasing the attraction of the Democratic party to incoming waves of Irish and German immigrants (it should be added that both Seward and Weed vigorously repudiated nativism, and made heroic efforts to attract the immigrant vote).

In the 1848 campaign both Whigs and Democrats suffered from defections caused by the mounting sectional conflict over slavery in the territories. The new Free Soil party, nominating Van Buren for President, attracted voters from both the old parties. About half were former Democrats, mainly Van Buren supporters who were disappointed when the Democrats failed to renominate the "Little Magician" in 1844 and disgruntled because Polk's administration had favored rival Democratic factions in distributing patronage. The others were former Whigs, including those who had bolted to the Liberty party in 1844 and a

---

*See Chapters 15 and 16, pp. 504–512, 528–532, 541–548.
**See Chapter 17, pp. 597–604.

larger contingent of "Conscience Whigs," who declared that they placed their moral hostility toward the expansion of slavery ahead of the material and political advantages of continuing to work with Southern slaveholding Whigs. Van Buren received only 10 percent of the popular vote and won no electoral votes.

Despite these occasional defections in presidential elections, party stability among both Whigs and Democrats remained remarkably firm until 1853, surviving the shock waves of the Mexican War and the ensuing controversies over slavery in the newly acquired territories. After the debacle of 1848, Van Buren and most of his Democratic followers returned to the national party. The Conscience Whigs, for their part, mostly returned to their uneasy alliance with the "Cotton Whigs," led by such powerful New England manufacturers as Abbott Lawrence and Nathan Appleton, who looked to a continuation of their profitable trade relations with the cotton-producing South.

But between 1853 and 1856 this pattern of political stability was so severely disrupted that the national Democratic party experienced important changes in its constituency and appeals and the Whig party disappeared altogether. This political transformation was partly the result of continued agitation over the slavery issue, particularly over the Kansas-Nebraska Act.* The more immediately disruptive issue, however, was the emergence of a powerful nativist party, which appealed to hundreds of thousands of Whigs and to thousands of native-born Democrats of Protestant background. Whigs were particularly upset by the social impact of millions of Irish and German immigrants, who had begun thronging to the United States after 1845. These immigrants, with their divergent values and lifestyles, threatened the Whig vision of an ordered, morally progressive, and homogeneous society. A great majority of the immigrants were Catholics, whose acceptance of ecclesiastical authority aroused Protestant fears that had deep roots in the colonial and British past. The Protestant religious revivals of the 1820s and 30s had stimulated the "No popery!" movement, and so had the crusading missionary and Bible societies that sought to hasten the millennium by converting the world to their own brand of evangelical piety. Prominent Northern clergymen, mostly Whigs in politics, had saturated the country with lurid and often hysterical anti-Catholic propaganda, which had contributed to mob violence and church burning, culminating in a bloody Philadelphia riot in 1844.

But the appearance of a national nativist political movement was delayed until the 1850s, when a secret fraternal lodge, the Order of the Star-Spangled Banner, became the nucleus for the Know-Nothing party. In the local spring elections of 1854 entire tickets of secret Know-Nothing candidates were swept into office by write-in votes. Local party dignitaries, often confident that they were uncontested, found themselves thrown out of office by men they had never heard of. By 1855 the Know-Nothings, officially called the American party, had captured control of Massachusetts and most of New England; they had become the dominant party

*See Chapter 18, pp. 624–630.

RIOT IN PHILADELPHIA

In 1844 anti-Catholic violence reached a climax in Philadelphia, where the Catholic bishop had persuaded school
officials to allow the use of both the King James and Latin
Vulgate Bibles. After Protestant mobs had burned two
Catholic churches, a full-scale riot required the intervention
of state militia. (*The Library Company of Philadelphia.*)

opposing the Democrats in New York, Pennsylvania, California, and the border
states; they had made striking inroads in Virginia, North Carolina, Georgia, and
other Southern states. In much of the Northeast they had defeated or prevented
the spread of the new Republican party, which had been formed in 1854 to prevent the extension of slavery into the Western territories.* In effect, in two years
the Know-Nothings had replaced the Whigs as a national political force.

The causes of this dramatic realignment are difficult to assess. The spectacular
triumphs of the Know-Nothing movement had less to do with a continuing anti-
Catholic tradition than with a sudden popular yearning for change, for economic
and cultural security, and for unity. Unity is most easily achieved by joining an
alliance against people who are manifestly different. Catholic immigrants fitted
this description, and their growing numbers had encouraged them to defend
themselves by taking the political offensive. Nativism had special appeal for artisans and manual workers who associated immigrants with a new and threatening
America—an America of increasing urban poverty, of factories and railroads, of

*See Chapter 18, pp. 626–627; 633–634.

rising prices and abruptly changing markets. In the South and in the border states there was also hope that the Know-Nothing movement would finally end the needless sectional disputes over slavery. This motive probably gained force in the North as the Know-Nothings attracted conservative Whigs and lost anti-slavery members to the Republican party. Nativism was weaker in the Old Northwest, where there was a greater tolerance for immigrants; in this region, they were largely of German and Scandinavian origin. Yet there the Republicans capitalized on a similar disenchantment with the old parties. The loyalty of Western Democrats became especially strained when the Democratic administrations of Polk, Pierce, and Buchanan repeatedly blocked measures that the West demanded—a transcontinental railroad, federal aid for the improvement of river and lake transport, and free homesteads on the public domain.

In summary, the Know-Nothing movement provided the first vehicle for a widespread popular rebellion against the existing party system. Like the Anti-Masons, Democrats, and Whigs, the Know-Nothings proved to be vulnerable to political ambition and compromise. The short-lived eruption is significant because it brought a massive shift in voter identity, undermined national party discipline, and hastened the total submergence and annihilation of the Whigs. When the restraints of the Whig party were swept away, sectional conflicts could no longer be suppressed.

This broadside is an example of nativist propaganda being linked with a protest against the Fugitive Slave Law and the extension of slavery in the territories. *(American Antiquarian Society.)*

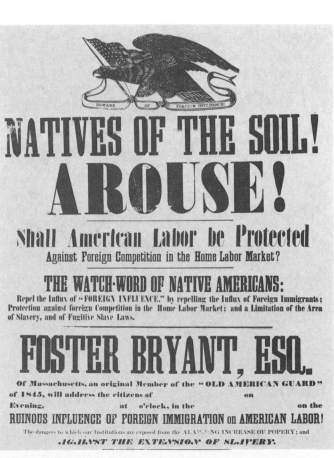

The one thread connecting all these developments was the politics of opportunity. The formative decade of the 1820s proved that subsequent political power would not be won by asserting claims to superior talent and wisdom, or even by articulating noble programs, as John Quincy Adams had done, for government-sponsored progress. Political success depended on satisfying constituents' needs on the local level, and on mobilizing the general public in crusades against incumbents, or various privileged groups, who could be pictured as thwarting equal opportunity. In New York State, for example, this was the formula used by Van Buren's Bucktails against the Clintonians, by Clinton and Weed's "People's party" against the Bucktails, by the Anti-Masons and Whigs against the Albany Regency, and by the Van Buren Democrats against the BUS. Similarly, the great appeal of Know-Nothingism lay in its ability to portray Catholic immigrants as a threat to native-born self-determination. By the mid-1850s the Southern Slave Power had come to epitomize for many Northerners all of the barriers to individual opportunity that previous Monster Institutions had foreshadowed.

But a full understanding of this political transformation requires us to examine some of the cultural forces that shaped a philosophy of opportunity, the forces that both encouraged and imposed limits on American aspirations to perfectibility.

Suggested Readings

Arthur M. Schlesinger, Jr., *The Age of Jackson* (1945), should be used with caution, but is still an indispensable introduction to political democratization. Other studies that illuminate the same subject are Shaw Livermore, Jr., *The Twilight of Federalism* (1962); Chilton Williamson, *American Suffrage: From Property to Democracy* (1960); Henry Christman, *Tin Horns and Calico: A Decisive Episode in the Emergence of Democracy* (1945); David M. Ludlum, *Social Ferment in Vermont* (1939); and Marvin E. Gettleman, *The Dorr Rebellion* (1973).

Lee Benson, *The Concept of Jacksonian Democracy: New York as a Test Case* (1961), challenges the traditional historical categories of liberalism and conservatism. Richard P. McCormick, *The Second American Party System: Party Formation in the Jacksonian Era* (1966), also deemphasizes political issues and ideology. These pioneering works should be supplemented by Richard Hofstadter, *The Idea of a Party System* (1969); Ronald Formisano, *The Birth of Mass Political Parties: Michigan, 1827–1861* (1971); Joel Silbey, ed., *Transformation of American Politics, 1840–1860* (1967); Douglas T. Miller, *Jacksonian Aristocracy: Class and Democracy in New York, 1830–1860* (1967); and Michael F. Holt, "The Antimasonic and Know Nothing Parties," and Holt, "The Democratic Party," in *History of U.S. Political Parties*, ed. Arthur M. Schlesinger, Jr., Vol. 1 (1789–1860: *From Factions to Parties*), (4 vols., 1973). For the election of 1828, see R. V. Remini, *The Election of Andrew Jackson* (1963) Two imaginative studies of Jacksonian ideology are Marvin Meyers, *The Jacksonian Persuasion* (1957); and John W. Ward, *Andrew Jackson: Symbol for an Age* (1955). For the Jacksonians in office, see Leonard D. White, *The Jacksonians: A Study in Administrative History* (1954). Informative essays on all of the presidential elections can be found in Arthur M. Schlesinger, Jr., ed., *History of American Presidential Elections, 1789–1968*. Vol. 1 (4 vols., 1971).

The standard work on the tariff issue is Frank W. Taussig, *The Tariff History of the United*

States (1931). The best introduction to the banking controversy is R. V. Remini, *Andrew Jackson and the Bank War* (1967). The main authorities on the history of banking are Bray Hammond, *Banks and Politics in America from the Revolution to the Civil War* (1957); J. Van Fenstermaker, *The Development of American Commercial Banking, 1782–1837* (1965); and Fritz Redlich, *The Molding of American Banking* (2 vols., 1947–51). Thomas P. Govan, *Nicholas Biddle* (1959), presents a strong defense of the president of the Bank of the United States. The wider political ramifications of the controversy are examined in William G. Shade, *Banks or No Banks: The Money Question in Western Politics* (1972), and John M. McFaul, *The Politics of Jacksonian Finance* (1972).

There is still no adequate history of the Whig party. Aside from the biographies of Whig Leaders, listed below, the best introduction is Lynn L. Marshall, "The Strange Stillbirth of the Whig Party," *American Quarterly 24* (Spring 1969), 24–43; Charles G. Sellers, Jr., "Who Were the Southern Whigs?" *American Historical Review 59* (January 1954), 335–46; Glyndon G. Van Deusen, "Some Aspects of Whig Thought and Theory in the Jacksonian Period," *American Historical Review 63* (January 1958), 305–32; and Thomas H. O'Connor, *Lords of the Loom: The Cotton Whigs and the Coming of the Civil War* (1968).

Ray Billington, *The Protestant Crusade, 1800–1860* (1938), provides an outstanding overview of anti-Catholic nativism. For the intellectual ties between nativism and other movements, see David B. Davis, "Some Themes of Counter-Subversion," *Mississippi Valley Historical Review 47* (September 1960), 205–24. The best studies of political nativism are Michael F. Holt, "The Politics of Impatience: The Origins of Know-Nothingism," *Journal of American History 60* (September 1973), 309–31, and Holt, *Forging a Majority: The Formation of the Republican Party in Pittsburgh* (1969).

Political history is always illuminated by the biographies of influential figures. Richard Hofstadter, *The American Political Tradition* (1948), provides brilliant sketches of a number of pre–Civil War leaders. Among the best biographies are Martin Duberman, *Charles Francis Adams, 1807–1886* (1961); Samuel F. Bemis, *John Quincy Adams and the Foundations of American Foreign Policy* (1949), and *John Quincy Adams and the Union* (1956); W. N. Chambers, *Old Bullion Benton: Senator from the New West* (1956); William E. Smith, *The Francis Preston Blair Family in Politics* (2 vols., 1933); Richard N. Current, *John C. Calhoun* (1966); C. M. Wiltse, *John C. Calhoun: Nationalist, 1782–1828* (1944); *Nullifier, 1829–1839* (1949); *Sectionalist, 1840–1850* (1951); Clement Eaton, *Henry Clay and the Art of American Politics* (1957); Marquis James, *Life of Andrew Jackson* (1938); R. V. Remini, *Andrew Jackson* (1966); Harry Ammon, *James Monroe: The Quest for National Identity* (1971); Charles G. Sellers, Jr., *James K. Polk: Jacksonian, 1795–1843* (1957); *Continentalist, 1843–1846* (1966); Jonathan Daniels, *The Randolphs of Virginia: America's Foremost Family* (1972); Glyndon G. Van Deusen, *William Henry Seward* (1967); David H. Donald, *Charles Sumner and the Coming of the Civil War* (1960); Carl B. Swisher, *Roger B. Taney* (1935); Holman Hamilton, *Zachary Taylor* (1951); William Y. Thompson, *Robert Toombs of Georgia* (1966); James P. Shenton, *Robert John Walker: A Politician from Jackson to Lincoln* (1961); Robert F. Dalzell, Jr., *Daniel Webster and the Trial of American Nationalism, 1843–1852* (1973); Sydney Nathans, *Daniel Webster and Jacksonian Democracy* (1973); Glyndon G. Van Deusen, *Thurlow Weed, Wizard of the Lobby* (1947); and John W. DuBose, *The Life and Times of William Lowndes Yancey* (2 vols., 1892).

Of the many editions of diaries and collected papers, the following deserve special notice: C. F. Adams, ed., *The Memoirs of John Quincy Adams* (12 vols., 1874–77); Thomas Hart Benton, *Thirty Years' View* (1857); Allan Nevins, ed., *The Diary of Philip Hone, 1828–1851* (2 vols., 1927); Allan Nevins and Milton H. Thomas, eds., *The Diary of George Templeton Strong* (4 vols., 1952); Horace Greeley, *Recollections of a Busy Life* (2 vols., 1868); Milo M. Quaife, ed., *The Diary of James K. Polk* (4 vols., 1910); and J. C. Fitzpatrick, ed., *The Autobiography of Martin Van Buren* (1920).

15

Attempts to Shape the American Character

During the pre–Civil War decades political and religious leaders repeatedly warned that the fate of free institutions depended on the moral and intellectual character of the American people. Religious beliefs continued to differ about man's sinfulness or inherent capacity for love and social harmony. But Americans of various persuasions agreed that human nature was much like clay that can be molded to any shape before it hardens.

This conviction could be inspiring. In 1823, for example, Charles Jared Ingersoll, a Philadelphia lawyer and former congressman, delivered the influential *Discourse Concerning the Influence of America on the Mind*. Ingersoll was confident that the average American, as a result of the free and republican environment, stood far above the average European in both intelligence and virtue. He promised that American achievements in the arts and sciences would soon show the world the full potentialities of human nature when it was not hobbled by despotism and aristocratic privilege.

But a capacity for infinite improvement might also be a capacity for infinite corruption. Even the optimists tended to worry over the growing inadequacy of local religious and social institutions in the face of America's sensational expansion. Yet Americans found a way to interpret and respond to sudden social change—by emphasizing the malleability of individual character. The need to shape or change individual character gave a new social importance to educators, religious revivalists, popular essayists, phrenologists, and other promoters of self-improvement.

"We Must Educate or Perish"

Shaping character, whether by school, church, prison, or asylum, seemed to be the only means of ensuring moral stability in an expansive and increasingly individualistic society. Lyman Beecher, best-known today as the father of Harriet Beecher Stowe but in his own day the most prominent Protestant minister in the North, viewed the rapid settlement of the West with a mixture of exhilaration and alarm. By 1835 the states west of the Appalachians had grown so rapidly that he could predict a population of 100 million by 1900: "A day which some of our children may live to see." As a "young empire of mind, and power, and wealth, and free institutions," the West contained the potential for nothing less than "the emancipation of the world." Beecher had no doubts about the West's material progress. The danger was, in his words, "that our intelligence and virtue will falter and fall back into a dark minded, vicious populace—a poor, uneducated reckless mass of infuriated animalism." Aroused particularly by the supposed threat of Catholic immigrants, whom he pictured as the agents of foreign despots intent on subverting republican institutions, Beecher urged an immediate crusade to evangelize and educate the West: "For population will not wait, and commerce will not cast anchor, and manufacturers will not shut off the steam nor shut down the gate, and agriculture, pushed by millions of freemen on their fertile soil, will not withhold her corrupting abundance. We must educate! We must educate! or we must perish by our own prosperity."

Educational reformers had some reason for alarm. Even Massachusetts, which in 1837 established the nation's first state board of education, suffered from dilapidated school buildings, untrained and incompetent teachers, and dependence on unequal and unpredictable local funding. The one-room country schoolhouse, often idealized in later years, was not only dirty, drafty, and overheated, but commonly packed with children of all ages, some old and rowdy enough to inflict beatings on male teachers and to prompt some women teachers to hide a pistol in a desk drawer. The soaring growth of Eastern cities made middle-class citizens suddenly aware of begging street urchins, teenage prostitutes, gangs of juvenile delinquents, and vagrant children who, like Mark Twain's Huckleberry Finn, had little desire to be "civilized." As early as 1820 the Boston Sunday school movement had revealed an appalling amount of illiteracy and degradation among the city's poor. The Sunday school movement had originally sought to set aside one day a week "to reclaim the vicious, to instruct the ignorant, to secure the observance of the Sabbath . . . and to raise the standard of morals among the lower classes of society." Reformers soon discovered that these objectives required a citywide system of elementary schooling at public expense.

Until the second quarter of the nineteenth century, the education of Americans was informal, unsystematic, and dependent on parental initiative and ability to pay. Even so, it is easy to underestimate the achievements of the pre-public school era. In a comparison with most Europeans, white American males had always enjoyed a high rate of literacy, especially in New England. By the early nineteenth century illiteracy was rapidly disappearing among white females. Boys and girls frequently attended the same schools, despite prejudices against sexual integration. Some "free" schools expected parents to pay a small fee, and most tax-supported schools were intended only for the children of paupers. But during the 1790s a surprising number of artisans and skilled laborers had sent their children to the "common pay schools" in New York City, where children of rich and poor backgrounds mingled. Aside from school attendance, apprenticeship long served as a noteworthy educational institution, providing the vocational skills that could not be learned in any school. Not until the mid–nineteenth century, and in the South not until after the Civil War, did education become increasingly confined to specialized institutions segregated from the mainstreams of adult social life.

SCHOOLROOM

In this curiously churchlike image of a female seminary, a globe and map of the United States are displayed on the "altar." (*American Antiquarian Society.*)

Demands for educational reform were not confined to middle-class religious reformers. In 1828 political protest erupted from the organized mechanics and journeymen of Philadelphia, most of whom were skilled artisans and craftsmen who had served their apprenticeships. As in other northeastern cities, these workers were angered by depressed wage levels, by the substitution of temporary child "apprentices" for skilled adult labor, and by the erosion of the traditional craft system that allowed apprentices and journeymen to rise within a given trade. The Philadelphia Working Men's party pressed for a broad range of economic and social reforms and showed particular sensitivity to the stigma and inferiority of "pauper schools." "The original element of despotism," proclaimed a committee in 1829, "is a monopoly of talent, which consigns the multitude to comparative ignorance, and secures the balance of knowledge on the side of the rich and the rulers."

The demand for free tax-supported schools, as a safeguard against economic debasement, became a rallying cry for the workingmen's parties and associations that sprang up in New York, Boston, Newark, and dozens of small towns throughout the country. A group of New York workers expressed the typical rhetoric when they asked in 1830 "if many of the monopolists and aristocrats in our city would not consider it disgraceful to their noble children to have them placed in our public schools by the side of poor yet industrious mechanics?" Though many of the leaders of these groups were not manual laborers, the short-lived workingmen's movement reflected an authentic desire for equal educational opportunity on the part of skilled laborers whose economic and social condition had begun to deteriorate.

For most workingmen immediate economic grievances soon took precedence over education. It should also be stressed that the economic growth of the pre–Civil War decades called for mounting supplies of unskilled laborers, but not for a significant increase in the number of skilled and nonmanual workers who might benefit materially from an education beyond the "Three Rs." In New York City, where the proportion of nonmanual and professional jobs changed very little from 1796 to 1855, working-class parents might well question the sacrifice of losing family income for an education that would equip their children for unavailable jobs. As early as 1832 the New York Public School Society pointed out: "The labouring classes of society will, to a great extent, withhold their children from school, the moment they arrive at an age that renders their services in the least available in contributing to the support of the family." Later evidence indicated that children under fifteen earned as much as 20 percent of the income expended by working-class families in Newburyport, Massachusetts. For such families compulsory attendance laws often threatened an unbearable drop in already subsistence-level income. Not surprisingly, 40 percent of Newburyport's laborers admitted to the census takers of 1850 that their school-age children had not been enrolled in any school during the previous year. And many children who were enrolled could not attend with any regularity.

"POPERY UNDERMINING FREE SCHOOLS"

A typical example of anti-Catholic iconography. While the
American eagle hovers over the schoolhouse, this bulwark of
democratic institutions is being literally undermined by
sappers working under the directions of a priest, who in
turn is executing the orders of the pope, pictured here as
a foreign potentate. (*American Antiquarian Society.*)

Moreover, by the 1840s the working class in the Northeast was becoming increasingly Roman Catholic. The values and teachings of the public schools were
unmistakably Protestant. For example, in the 1820s the New York Public School
Society had won its fight for nominally secular education, depriving denominational schools, including those of the Catholics, of public funding. But the nondenominational school society embodied the values of evangelical Protestantism,
and the same was true of the public and elected boards of education throughout
the nation. Most Americans in the mid-nineteenth century still regarded Americanism as synonymous with Protestantism. They saw nothing sectarian about
public school teachers reading aloud from the King James Bible or teaching that
the Protestant Reformation was a significant turning point in the progress of
humanity. Bishop John Hughes and other Catholic leaders saw the matter differently. In 1840, New York Catholics launched a political offensive against the
Protestant monopoly of public education. As a result of this conflict, the Catholic

church decided to construct its own separate system of schools, a costly program that took many decades to complete.

For many immigrants, Catholics, and working-class parents the school reformers threatened to impose a uniform set of values on all segments of American society. Resistance also arose from local authorities who feared any centralizing interference from a state board of education. Many conservatives insisted that parents should pay for education, if they could afford it, as they would for any other service or commodity. Others, brought up on the tradition of church schools, feared that the teaching of value-laden subjects would be catastrophic if guided only by a vaguely Protestant and nondenominational spirit.

These obstacles were finally overcome by reformers like Horace Mann, who as the chief officer of the Massachusetts Board of Education from 1837 to 1848 became the nation's leading champion of public schools. An ascetic, humorless puritan, Mann denounced intemperance, profanity, and ballet dancing along with ignorance, violence, and Negro slavery. Having personally struggled with the terrors of his New England Calvinist heritage, he had finally arrived at the conclusion that children were capable of infinite improvement and goodness. As a kind of secular minister, still intent on saving souls, he insisted that there must have been a time in the childhood of the worst criminal when, "ere he was irrecoverably lost, ere he plunged into the abyss of infamy and guilt, he might have been recalled, as it were by the saving of the hand." Mann offended the religiously orthodox by winning the fight in Massachusetts against specific religious instruction in the public schools. He outraged conservatives by asserting that private property is not an absolute right but rather a trusteeship for society and future generations. Trained as a lawyer, he decided as a young man that "the next generation" should be his clients. In pleading the cause of generations to come, he held that school taxes were not a "confiscation" from the rich, but rather a collection of the debt the rich owed to society.

Reformers placed a stupendous moral burden on the public schools. Horace Mann proclaimed the common school to be "the greatest discovery ever made by man." "Other social organizations are curative and remedial," he said; "this is a preventive and antidote." This characteristic argument suggests that the schools were to be a bulwark against undesirable change, preserving the cherished values of a simpler, more homogeneous America. Educators spoke of the frenzied pace of American life, of the diminishing influence of church and home. They held that the school should thus serve as a substitute for both church and home, preventing American democracy from degenerating into what Mann called "the spectacle of gladiatorial contests." The school, representing the highest instincts of society, could alone be counted on for cultivating decency, cooperation, and a respect for others. Women, it was believed, were best suited as teachers because they exemplified the noncombative and noncompetitive instincts. Because they also could be employed for lower wages than men, women teachers soon predominated in New England's elementary schools.

A strong element of fear gave added drive to the moral mission of public education. Again, Horace Mann's vivid imagery is particularly revealing. Speaking in 1848, a year of revolution in Europe, he observed:

A republican form of government, without intelligence in the people, must be, on a vast scale, what a mad-house, without superintendent or keepers, would be on a small one — the despotism of a few succeeded by universal anarchy, and anarchy by despotism, with no change but from bad to worse.

The reformers saw no conflict between inspiring pupils to succeed and picturing schools as serene refuges from the rough world of masculine competition; between disciplining the immigrant poor and fulfilling the aspirations of the native middle class. Advocates of mass education did not talk of equality or social democracy, but rather of ideas having to stand in the place "of bayonets and bulwarks." Yet by 1848 when the specter of class conflict in Europe underscored the dangers of concentrating wealth and knowledge, Mann expressed the common faith that public education would keep economic inequality from hardening: "For such a thing never did happen, and never can happen, as that an intelligent and practical body of men should be permanently poor."

The character traits most esteemed by educational reformers were precisely those alleged to bring material success in a competitive and market-oriented society: punctuality, cheerful obedience, honesty, responsibility, perseverance, and foresightedness. Public schools seemed to promise opportunity by providing the means of acquiring such traits. In the words of one school committee, the children "entered the race, aware that the prize was equally before all, and attainable only by personal exertion." The famed McGuffey's "Eclectic" series of readers, which after 1836 were used in countless schoolrooms and of which well over 100 million copies were eventually sold, taught young readers that no possession was more important for getting on in the world than reputation, or "a good name." On the other hand, the readers held out little hope of rags-to-riches success. When the good little poor boy sees other children "riding on pretty horses, or in coaches, or walking with ladies and gentlemen, and having on very fine clothes, he does not envy them, nor wish to be like them." For he has been taught "that it is God who makes some poor, and others rich; that the rich have many troubles which we know nothing of; and that the poor, if they are but good, may be very happy."

EDUCATING WOMEN

The pre-Civil War decades opened unprecedented opportunities for middle-class girls to advance beyond an elementary level of education. The price of this opportunity, however, was a system of strict discipline and of constant supervision of manners and morals. (*Left, American Antiquarian Society; Right, The Metropolitan Museum of Art.*)

From a present-day viewpoint, the educational reformers were often insensitive to the needs of the non-Protestants, non-Christians, nonwhites, and women. Throughout the North, except in a few scattered communities, the public schools excluded black children. Many localities made no provision for blacks to be educated. Other towns and cities, including New York and Boston, distributed a small portion of public funds to segregated and highly inferior schools for blacks. By 1850, blacks constituted no more than 1.5 percent of Boston's population, but it still required a prolonged struggle on the part of militant blacks and white abolitionists to achieve legal desegregation. In 1855 Massachusetts became the single state in which no applicant to a public school could be excluded on account of "race, color or religious opinions." In marked contrast to the public schools, Oberlin, Harvard, Bowdoin, Dartmouth and some other private colleges opened their doors to a few black students. In 1837 Oberlin also became America's first coeducational college. In general, however, American women had no opportunities for higher education except in female seminaries and, by the 1850s, in a few western state universities.

REGULATIONS

OF THE

FEMALE CLASSICAL SEMINARY, BROOKFIE

THE Principal expects of the young Ladies attending his Seminary,

1. That they will attend at the Academy, regularly and punctually, at th appointed by the Principal.

2.—That all noise and disorder in the house, before the Principal arrives, a the exercises are closed, will be carefully avoided.

3.—That, during the hours of instruction, they will give constant and dilige tion to the exercises prescribed, avoiding every thing which would be an inte to the teacher or pupils.

4.—That, during the recitations, all the members of a class will close thei except the nature of the recitation requires their being open.

5.—That the young Ladies will constantly attend public worship on the Sa

6.—That they will always board in those families, which have the approb the Principal.

7.—That they will not attend balls, assemblies, or other parties for the in of frivolous mirth.

8.—That the social visits of the young Ladies, among the families of the will be arranged by the Principal, whenever invitations are extended.

9.—That they will avoid walking or riding, with persons of the other sex seasonable hours.

10.—That they will not leave town, without permission from the Principal.

11.—That they will be subject in all respects to the superintendence and of the Principal, while belonging to his school.

TUITION, for each term. Arithmetic, Grammar, or Geography, S Rhetoric, History, or Latin, $4,50.——Geometry, Natural Philosophy, Chemist bra, Euclid, Logic, Intellectual Philosophy, or Moral Philosophy, $5,00.—— Music, and Painting will probably be taught the ensuing spring.

Sept. 1825.

By the 1850s, Massachusetts had acquired all the essentials of a modern educational establishment: special "normal schools" for training female teachers; the grading of pupils according to age and ability; standardized procedures for advancement from one grade to another; uniform textbooks; and a bureaucracy extending from the board of education to superintendents, principals, and teachers. Although Massachusetts led the nation, by the 1850s it was possible for a New York City male child to proceed from an "infant school" to a college degree without paying tuition. Educational reformers, many of them originally New Englanders, had helped to create state-supported and state-supervised school systems from Pennsylvania to the new states of the Upper Mississippi Valley. In the 1850s the same cause made some headway in the South, particularly in Virginia and North Carolina.

Whatever prejudices and blind spots the public school movement may have had, it aroused the enthusiasm of hundreds of idealistic men and women who devoted time and energy to the cause. Northern legislators committed an impressive proportion of public spending to the education of succeeding generations. The movement, particularly in the 1850s, trained a young generation of teacher-missionaries, who in time would descend on the devastated South, equipped with an ideology for "reconstruction." Above all, the movement reinforced the American faith that social problems could be solved by individual enterprise, a diffusion of knowledge, and a reconstruction of moral character.

The Evangelical Age

Americans continued to look on the church, no less than the public school, as a decisive instrument for shaping the national character. As in the early national period, religion appeared to thrive the more it achieved independence from the state.* Despite the officially secular stance of American governments, evangelical Protestantism became increasingly identified with patriotism, democracy, and America's mission in the world. Despite the continuing division and competition among religious denominations, Americans increasingly appealed to religion as the only adhesive force that could preserve a sense of community and united purpose.

During the period 1820–1860 religious revivalism became a powerful organizing and nationalizing force, permeating all parts of American life in the South as well as the North, in the great cities as well as on the Western frontier. Church membership figures can be misleading, since many people who regularly attended church could not meet the religious or financial obligations required for formal membership. It has been argued that by 1835 as many as three out of four adult Americans maintained some nominal relationship to a church. Most foreign

---

*In 1833 Massachusetts became the last state to give up an established church.

CAMP MEETING, SING SING, 1859

The religious camp meeting, originally associated with the boisterous and unruly West, became an established and well-organized institution throughout rural America. *(Library of Congress.)*

observers agreed with Tocqueville that by the 1830s there was no country in the world in which the Christian religion retained "a greater influence over the souls of men."

For the majority of adults evangelical Protestantism provided a common language and a common frame of reference, explaining not only the nature and destiny of man but the meaning of democracy and of American nationality. This point can best be illustrated by referring to the words of a non–church member, a young self-made man and future President of the United States. According to Andrew Johnson, "Man can become more and more endowed with divinity; and as he does he becomes more God-like in his character and capable of governing himself." Like millions of other Americans, Johnson believed that Christianity and political democracy were together elevating and purifying the people, working toward the day when it could be proclaimed: "The millennial morning has dawned and the time has come when the lion and the lamb shall lie down together, when . . . the glad tidings shall be proclaimed . . . of man's political and religious redemption, and there is 'on earth, peace, good will toward men.'"

In some ways this evangelical vision transcended boundaries of class and section. But though it is possible to think of America as undergoing a single Great Revival during the six decades preceding the Civil War, the revival's social significance differed according to time and place. Some socioeconomic groups were more susceptible to religious enthusiasm than others. Some personality types were likely to view revivalists as self-righteous zealots who threatened to remove all fun from life. Others were likely to seize the chance to profess faith in Christ crucified, to announce repentance for their sins, to experience the liberation of rebirth, and as the popular hymn put it, to "stand up, stand up for Jesus!" For many Americans religion provided the key to social identity. It was not that people flocked to churches to meet the right kind of people, although some no doubt had that motive. It was rather that the "right" kind of religion, as defined by employers, slaveholders, and other wielders of power, was often considered to bestow the "right" kind of character.

In the South religious revivalism depended as it did elsewhere on sensitivity to the community's norms and vital interests. Leaders of various denominations discovered that any open criticism of slavery could threaten the very survival of a church. The Baptist and Methodist churches gradually retreated from their cautious antislavery pronouncements of the late eighteenth century, which had supposedly bred discontent if not insurrection among Negro slaves. By the 1830s the most influential Southern churches had begun to deny that there was any moral contradiction between slavery and Christianity. They also insisted that Christianity, rightly understood, posed no danger to "the peculiar institution."

As a result of the evangelical revivals, Southern planters increasingly promoted the religious conversion of their slaves. Even by the first decades of the nineteenth century, a growing number of churchmen and planters had argued that religious instruction would make slaves more obedient, industrious, and faithful. The ideal Christian master would treat his slaves with charity and understanding. The ideal Christian slave would humbly accept his assigned position in this world, knowing that his patience and faithfulness would be rewarded in heaven. Servitude, in short, could be softened, humanized, and perfected by Christianity. The reality of slavery fell far short of the ideal. Religion may have induced many masters to take a sincere interest in their slaves' welfare, but it could not eliminate the cruelty and injustice inherent in the system.

No white preachers could entirely purge Christianity of its critical, subversive overtones, or prevent black preachers from converting it into a source of self-respect, dignity, and faith in eventual deliverance—the longed-for Day of Jubilee. In both North and South, free blacks responded to growing racial discrimination by forming their own "African" churches, usually Baptist or Methodist. And despite the efforts by whites to control every aspect of their slaves' religion, the

MEETING IN THE AFRICAN CHURCH

Although most illustrators tended to caricature American blacks, this wood engraving conveys some of the fervor and emotional intensity of the black churches, the churches that did so much in preserving a sense of hope and communal identity. *(Library of Congress.)*

slaves created their own folk religion and shaped it, as far as possible, to their own needs and interests. As one ex-slave from Texas recalled, "The whites preached to the niggers and the niggers preached to theyselves."

Revivalism also served as a socializing force in the nonslaveholding West, but the context and consequences were different. In the eyes of Easterners, the West had long suffered a reputation for lawlessness and sin. From the lumber camps of Wisconsin to the mining camps of California, the image presented was essentially the same: rough, dirty men who swore, gambled, got drunk, frequented houses of prostitution, and relished savage eye-gouging, knife-slashing fights. If the stereotypes were exaggerated, there could be no doubt that frontier communities were a challenge to nineteenth-century notions of decency and civilization.

The challenge of the West could not be met simply by building churches where none had existed before. When Theron Baldwin, a member of a Yale missionary group, arrived in Illinois in 1830, he was horrified by the ignorance of the settlers. Even in Vandalia, the state's capital, Baldwin discovered that most of the pupils in

his Sunday school class were illiterate. Nor could he find a literate adult in over half the families he visited in the region. Religion, Baldwin concluded, could make no headway without education and an institutional rebuilding of society. Appealing for funds from the East, he expressed the New England ideal: "We wish to see the school house and church go up side by side and the land filled with Christian teachers as well as preachers." He added, significantly, that young men could come there "and in a short time get enough by teaching to purchase a farm that would ever after fill their barns with plenty and their hands with good things." Baldwin himself worked to secure from the legislature a charter for the first three colleges in the state. As a result of the labors of Baldwin and other young missionaries, the Old Northwest became dotted with academies, seminaries, and small denominational colleges.

Easterners, who still thought of churches as fixed institutions within an ordered society, long failed to understand that religious revivals were an effective instrument for shaping and controlling character. The frank emotionalism and homespun informality of the Western and Southern revivals disguised the fact that even the camp meetings were soon stabilized by rules, regulations, and the most careful advance planning. And camp meetings were by no means the most important tool of the revivals. The power of the movement flowed from the dynamic balance between popular participation and leader control. According to the evangelical message, every man and woman, no matter how humble or mired in sin, had the capacity to say "Yes"! — to reject what was called "cannot-ism," and along with it an unsatisfying identity. Even for the poor and uneducated, consent opened the way for participation and decision making. For example, Peter Cartwright grew up in one of the most violent and lawless regions of Kentucky; his brother was hanged for murder and his sister was said to have "led a life of debauchery." But at the age of sixteen Cartwright repented his sins at a Methodist camp meeting; at seventeen he became an exhorter; at eighteen a traveling preacher; at twenty-one a deacon; and at twenty-three a presiding elder of the church. But each upward step required a probationary period, followed by an examination of the candidate's conduct, ability, and purity of doctrine. The Methodists showed particular skill in devising a meritocracy that encouraged widespread lay participation and upward mobility under hierarchical authority. But all the evangelical churches displayed the great American gift for organization. Revivals, they believed, could not be had by waiting for God to stir human hearts. Revivals required planning, efficient techniques, and coordinated effort. The need was not for educated theologians but for professional promoters.

While revivalism can be thought of as an organizing and socializing movement, it was by definition selective. The people most likely to be converted were those who had some Christian upbringing or those who were already disturbed by excessive drinking, gambling, fighting, disorder, and irresponsibility. Conversion itself reinforced crucial social distinctions. For one part of the community, religion became more than a matter of going to church on Sunday. The obligations of a new religious life required sobriety and responsibility from friends, family, employees, and business associates. The weekly "class meetings" and "love feasts" provided fellowship for the religious and helped to prevent backsliding. No doubt the solidarity of the converted brought order and discipline to the community at large. But if the evangelicals always insisted that every man and woman could say "Yes!", there were always those who said "No!" The congregations that loved to hear their preachers "pouring hot shot into Satan's ranks" knew that Satan's ranks were concentrated on the other side of the tracks.

Religious revivals could accentuate social distinctions by forging an alliance among the more ambitious, self-disciplined, and future-oriented members of a community. In the fall of 1830, for example, the leaders of Rochester, New York, invited Charles Grandison Finney to save that booming city from sin. By far the most commanding and influential evangelist of the pre–Civil War period, Finney was a tall, athletic spellbinder, a former lawyer who had undergone a dramatic religious conversion in 1823. Though lacking formal seminary training, Finney had been ordained as a Presbyterian minister and in 1825 had begun a series of highly unorthodox and spectacular revivals along the route of the newly constructed Erie Canal. In 1831 Finney's triumphs in Rochester stunned Christian America; communities from Ohio to Boston appealed to him to save their collective souls. Finney's converts in Rochester were largely manufacturers, merchants, lawyers, shopkeepers, master artisans, and skilled journeymen. He appealed to people who had profited from the commercial revolution initiated by the Erie Canal but who had become deeply disturbed by the immense influx of young and transient laborers looking for work. Over the behavior of such youths the city's leaders had no control. Significantly, Rochester's revival years brought a decline in church membership among the hotel proprietors and tavern keepers who catered to the floating population of young males traveling the Erie Canal. Rochester's Protestant churches, interpreting the revival as a sweeping popular mandate, launched a crusade to purge the city of its dens of vice and unholy amusement. They also offered a "free church," free of pew rents and other financial obligations, to the proletarians of the canal. Increasingly Rochester became divided between a Christian minority, thoroughly modernized in habits, dedicated to education and upward advancement, committed to Whig political leaders; and an essentially nonpolitical, free-floating majority of disoriented and unskilled young men.

Philadelphia differed from Rochester in important respects, but there, too, religious revivals eventually redefined the boundaries of respectable and "modern" behavior. Unlike Rochester, which grew by 512 percent in the 1820s, Philadelphia was not a new boom town. An old city by American standards, Philadelphia was relatively resistant to religious enthusiasm. Revivalism had little appeal to the wealthy Quakers and conservative Presbyterian clergy who long dominated the city's religious life. Evangelical morality had even less appeal to Philadelphia's workingmen, who preserved and cherished a traditional artisan, preindustrial culture. Largely because of irregular transportation facilities to interior markets, Philadelphia workers suffered periodic layoffs, which allowed them to enjoy traveling circuses, cockfights, drinking and gambling at the local taverns, and above all, the boisterous comradeship of voluntary fire companies. Until 1837 neither the revival nor the closely related temperance movement made much headway among Philadelphia's manual workers. The people who reformed their drinking habits and who joined the reform-minded wing of the Presbyterian church were the professional and business groups who were ushering in the new industrial order. But in 1837 the financial panic and subsequent depression began to undermine the traditional habits and culture of the working class. Waves of religious revivalism, often Methodist in character, rippled through working-class neighborhoods. A new and more powerful temperance movement developed spontaneously from the ranks of master craftsmen, journeymen, shopkeepers, and the most ambitious unskilled laborers. In Philadelphia, as in Rochester, the decision to abstain from all alcohol was the key symbol of a new morality and of a commitment to self-improvement. By the 1840s the evangelical workingmen could contrast their own sobriety and self-discipline with the moral laxity of mounting numbers of Irish immigrants. Not surprisingly, the revivalism that bolstered the self-respect of blue-collar native workers also contributed to virulent anti-Catholicism and to nativist prejudice against a population that seemed to threaten the newly won dignity of manual labor.

Revivals appeared to be the only hopeful counterforce against rampant individualism, self-serving politics, and corrupting luxury. Lyman Beecher, who for a time looked with distaste on Finney's aggressive "new measures" but who later came to accept them, put his finger on the central concern revivalists shared with educational reformers: "Our republic is becoming too prosperous, too powerful, too extended, too numerous to be governed by any power without the blessed influence of the Gospel. The bayonnette [sic] in despotic governments may for a time be a substitute; but ours must be self-government, or anarchy first, and then despotism." As Finney himself added, "the great political and other worldly excitements" of the time distracted attention from the interests of the soul. He held, accordingly, that these excitements could "only be counteracted by *religious* excitements." Only revivals could prevent the United States from sliding into the decay and collapse of ancient Greece and Rome, and prepare the nation "to lead the way," in Beecher's phrase, "in the moral and political emancipation of the world."

Revivalism absorbed and expressed the moral doubts that inevitably accompanied rapid economic growth, the disruption of older modes of work and responsibility, the sudden accumulation of wealth, and the appearance of new class divisions. Revivalist preachers denounced atheism far less than "mammonism," the greedy pursuit of riches. They voiced repeated concern over the frantic pace of American life, the disintegration of family and community, and the worship of material success.

But in America revivalism seldom led to ascetic withdrawal or to spiritualistic contemplation. Evangelical religion was above all activist, pragmatic, and oriented toward measurable results. The fame of Finney and the other great exhorters depended on the body count, or soul count, of converts. Finney proclaimed: "The results justify my methods"—a motto that could as well have come from John D. Rockefeller or other entrepreneurs in more worldly spheres. Finney confidently predicted: "If the church will do her duty, the millennium may come in this country in three years." He knew, however, that a millennium would require no revivals, and that as a revivalist, though dedicated to virtue, he needed sin much as a soldier needs war.

There was a close relation between the revivals and America's expansive economy. The exuberant materialism of American life furnished revivalists with continuing targets for attack and with vivid symbols of communal strife and moral shortcoming. Without moral crises there would be no cause for national rededica-

tion, and calls for rededication have long been America's way of responding to social change. But on another level, the revivalists had merged their cause with America's secular destiny. They had repeatedly warned that without religion, American democracy would speedily dissolve into "a common field of unbridled appetite and lust." Yet instead of dissolving, the nation continued to prosper, expand, and reveal

THE JERKING EXERCISE

The religious frenzy of whites was also subject to caricature. There can be no doubt, however, that evangelistic preaching often evoked shrieks, moans, involuntary "jerks," and other bodily contortions. (*Library of Congress.*)

new marvels. Sometimes clergymen hailed the achievements as signs of national virtue and divine favor. More important, as a reflection of their increasing respect for efficient methods and material results, they applauded technological improvements as the instruments that God had provided for saving the world.

The telegraph, railroad, and steamship all quickened the way for spreading the Gospel around the world, and could thus be interpreted as portents of the coming millennium. But America's technology and rapid westward expansion could be justified only if America took seriously the burdens of a missionary nation. Samuel Fisher, the president of Hamilton College, elaborated on the message in an address to the American Board of Commissioners for Foreign Missions:

Material activity, quickened and guided by moral principle, is absolutely essential to the development of a strong and manly character. . . . The product of this devotion to material interests is capital diffused through the masses; and capital is one of the means God uses to convert the world.

The diffusion of capital through the masses seemed to falter in 1857, when a financial crash brought a severe depression and unprecedented unemployment among factory workers. Economic insecurity formed the backdrop of what many took to be "the event of the century," the great urban revival of late 1857 and 1858. What distinguished the event from earlier religious revivals was the absence of revivalists. In Philadelphia and New York thousands of clerks and businessmen began to unite spontaneously for midday prayer. The New York *Herald* and the New York *Tribune* devoted special issues to the remarkable events—wealthy stockbrokers praying and singing next to messenger boys; revivals in the public high schools; joint services by Methodists, Episcopalians, Presbyterians, Baptists, and even the traditionally antirevivalist Unitarians. The spirit rapidly spread to manufacturing towns throughout the Northeast. Unscheduled and unconventional religious meetings sprang up in small towns and rural areas from Indiana to Quebec. "It would seem," wrote one enthusiast, "that the mighty crash was just what was wanted . . . to startle men from their golden dreams." Americans had become too overbearing, too self-confident, too complacent in their success. Yet if God had shown His displeasure, as countless interpreters maintained, He had also chosen means that underscored America's promise. He had punished Americans with economic loss, which even the hardest head among the business community could understand.

The great revival of 1858 gave a new sense of unity to Northerners who had become increasingly divided by class and religious conflict, to say nothing of the issue of slavery. It also signified the maturity of an urban, industrial Protestantism committed to material progress and self-improvement. For good or for ill, the revivals reinvigorated America's official ideal of *Novus Ordo Seclorum*—a phrase stamped on every dollar bill, conveying the message that a new social order is to exist, that Americans carry the high burden of helping to create a better world.

Law, Phrenology, and Self-Reliance

What made public schools and religious revivals seem so indispensable by the 1830s was the earlier decay of traditional communal discipline and the relative absence of authoritative institutions that could define social roles, rules of conduct, and models of character. There was no traditional standing army, for example, that could train a military class or enforce unpopular public policy. New Englanders, from the beginning of their history, had placed a high priority on the perpetuation of a learned clergy, but disestablishment of the churches gave college-trained theologians the same official status as semiliterate evangelists. Most American lawyers learned their profession by serving an apprenticeship in the office of a member of the bar, copying legal documents and studying English authorities like Blackstone and Coke. But some states guaranteed any citizen, regardless of training, the right to practice law in any court. Increasingly Americans showed little respect for any intellectual elite, religious or secular, or for any group of self-perpetuating masters who claimed to preserve and monopolize a

RURAL COURT SCENE

Some frontier regions, such as the Old Northwest, had territorial judges of extraordinary learning and ability. But the frontier also attracted judges and lawyers who were incompetent and unscrupulous. Like the frontier clergy, the legal profession endured great privations and hardships, riding "on the circuit" through the backcountry, holding court in barns, stores, or taverns. (*Museum of Art, Rhode Island School of Design.*)

body of knowledge that the public at large could not understand. Henry B. Stanton, a lawyer, an abolitionist, and a religious convert of Finney's, summed up the democratic ideal: "Would our scholars instruct and lead the national mind? Let them not strive to become an isolated class, an 'order' of society, but fused with the body of the people, giving an impulse to and receiving an impress from the mass around them."

Serious problems arose from this antielitist ideology. If lawyers and judges, for example, became wholly "fused" with the mass around them, how could they "instruct and lead the national mind"? Traditionally, the very legitimacy of law had depended on its independence from shifting public opinion and on its embodiment of some other authority besides the threat of superior physical force. At the peak of Jacksonian enthusiasm for popular democracy, Theophilus Parsons, who was soon to become a distinguished professor at Harvard Law School, insisted that the electorate should be taught "the principle that right is not their creation, and depends not on their will, but on His will who made them free." Most lawyers and judges would have agreed with this doctrine, even while acknowledging that American law had partly developed as an expression of the public will and as a response to the needs of the people. The legal profession took pride in the fact that English common law had been flexibly shaped to fit American conditions. By 1830 the common law had reputedly been purged of the irrationalities and injustices spawned by a feudal and aristocratic society. It had also been adapted to the specific circumstances of American geography, land settlement, and republican institutions. But the common law epitomized the larger difficulty of transplanting in the New World cultural systems that defined, limited, and ordered human experience. For conservatives, in the sense of those who would conserve the experience of the past, it could not be replaced or wiped away without producing chaos.

In the face of insistent demands that the law should become the monopoly of legislators or should become subject to the winds of public opinion through popularly elected judges, the legal profession succeeded in preserving an independent source of authority. The period 1820–1860 marked the triumphant growth of the common law, exemplified by James Kent's great *Commentaries on American Law* (1826–30) and Joseph Story's detailed volumes of *Commentaries* on different branches of the law (1832–45). Judges had earlier deprived juries of their customary part in determining the law, thereby limiting jury verdicts to questions of fact. Greater numbers of judicial decisions were published, thereby creating a growing and accessible body of case law dealing with questions on which no legislature had passed a statute. Statutes could not begin to cover the multitude of disputes that arose from settling new land, forming business corporations, building canals and railroads, buying and selling slaves, or engaging in new forms of commerce. Reformers continued to call for a simple and rational legal code that could be understood by all citizens. But the attempts to reduce state laws to systematic codes lagged far behind the rapidly evolving judge-made law that served the needs of an expansive, self-assertive, and extremely litigious people.

Precisely because Americans paid no homage to king, sovereign parliament, or sacred authority, it became essential to believe in a disciplining and limiting force that stood above individual or factional self-interest. Yet this rule-giving force had to be practical, relevant, and committed to material progress. The legal profession won prestige as America's dominant profession because it could make claim to disinterested reason and yet resolve disputes in ways that provided security and predictability to men who possessed or were acquiring power. For example, judges increasingly adopted principles like "no liability without culpability," stripping away the ancient legal penalties that had posed unpredictable risks for the employers of labor and the manipulators of property. The limiting of individual and corporate liability was merely one aspect of a decisive shift in the definition of the preeminent public interest. Instead of upholding the ideal of a stable and balanced social order, the law gave increasing priority to economic growth. Instead of defending traditional safeguards and privileges, it encouraged individual initiative, enterprise, and competition.

In all societies the law upholds some values at the expense of others; it rewards certain kinds of behavior and punishes others; it is thus an important instrument for shaping character. In the early nineteenth century, American courts showed a lessening interest in enforcing Christian morality—a task left to the churches and private reform societies. The law became overwhelmingly preoccupied with questions relating to property, business, and commercial contracts. The growing emphasis on contracts became the key to promoting "modern" social relations based on individual responsibility. According to Theophilus Parsons, who helped to make contracts the cutting edge of American jurisprudence, "out of contracts, expressed or implied, declared or understood, grow all rights, all duties, all obligations, and all law." By sweeping away most of the legal barriers that had restrained individuals from entering into certain kinds of risky or inequitable agreements, the American common law reinforced the one supreme social rule: promises freely made could not be broken without legal penalty. The law assumed that all society was a market of competitive exchange in which each individual calculated the probable risks of a given choice of action. Each individual carried an unmitigated burden of freedom, the burden of being responsible for his own fate.

One finds a growing awareness of this burden, quite apart from the law, in the astonishing public interest in new fads, causes, cults, and nostrums. To Americans of the late twentieth century this search for the formulas of life is no novelty, but it was something new in the 1830s. To some conservatives the fads and quackery suggested only the credulity of public opinion and a potential threat to public order. But the pervasive desire was not for reforming society but for self-knowledge—for knowing who one is and where one stands—and for self-improvement. On the broadest and most respectable level, this thirst became evident in the numerous societies and institutes for adult education and "mutual improvement" that began to spread in the 1820s from England to the United States. Tens of thousands of adults, first in New England and then in the Old Northwest, grew accustomed to attending lyceums. Lyceum lectures covered a vast range of subjects, but tended during the early years of the movement to concentrate on "useful knowledge" associated with moral improvement and popular science.

Americans generally equated the advance of science with the advance of human liberty, a linkage that was part of the heritage of the European Enlightenment. Theoretically, they believed that everyone had access to the scientific method; the marvels and secrets of nature were open to all. But what most impressed and fascinated American audiences were lectures and books on the applications of science, demonstrating the ingenious ways that human beings could master nature. As early as 1829 Jacob Bigelow's *Elements of Technology* not only helped to popularize a new word but gave impetus to the growing inclination to see invention as the key to national progress. The excitement expressed over the applications of technology and steam power was matched by a new curiosity about the human mind, which had shown that it could unlock nature's secrets. In the words of Ralph Waldo Emerson:

Man carries the world in his head, the whole astronomy and chemistry suspended in a thought. Because the history of nature is charactered in his brain, therefore is he the prophet and discoverer of her secrets. . . . The common sense of Franklin, Dalton, Davy and Black is the same common sense which made the arrangements which now it discovers.

The gap between public ignorance and the achievements of science could be bridged if someone invented the supreme technology, a technology for controlling the human mind. It was the quest for such power that gave unity to many

LYCEUM LECTURE

A caricature of the early man-of-science, pontificating to an audience of attentive women and to a few apparently inattentive men. Note that the Worcester Lyceum offered tickets to "ladies and minors" at half-price, and provided the added attraction of library privileges. *(Museum of the City of New York; American Antiquarian Society.)*

WORCESTER LYCEUM.

THE COURSE OF LECTURES
FOR THE WINTER OF 1852--3,
WILL COMMENCE ON THE 18TH NOVEMBER, AT THE

CITY HALL,

AND BE CONTINUED AS FOLLOWS, VIZ:

1st LECTURE, Nov. 18—HON. CHARLES THURBER, Worcester.   Poem.

2d   "   Dec. 2—REV. T. STARR KING, Boston.

3d   "   Dec. 16—PROFESSOR C. C. FELTON, Cambridge.

4th   "   Dec. 30—REV. THEODORE PARKER, Boston.

5th   "   Jan. 13—GEORGE R. RUSSELL, Esq., West Roxbury.

6th   "   Jan. 27—RALPH WALDO EMERSON, Concord.

7th   "   Feb. 10—WENDELL PHILLIPS, Boston.

8th   "   Feb. 24—REV. HENRY H. HUDSON.

9th   "   Mar. 10—REV. ANDREW L. STONE, Boston.

10th   "   Mar. 24—R. H. DANA, Jr., Esq., Boston.

TICKETS FOR THE COURSE

MAY BE OBTAINED OF THE TREASURER AND AT THE BOOKSTORES,
AT THE FOLLOWING PRICES:

GENTLEMEN, $1.00, ... LADIES AND MINORS, 50 cts.

Single Lectures, 12 1-2 cents—to be paid at the door.

All purchasers of tickets will be

ENTITLED TO THE USE OF THE LIBRARY,

containing about ____ es of valuable Books, for the whole year.

____ he 1____ ____losed at 7 1-2 o'clock.

____RY CHAPIN, President.

____CHARLES WHITE, Treasurer.

____et, Worcester.

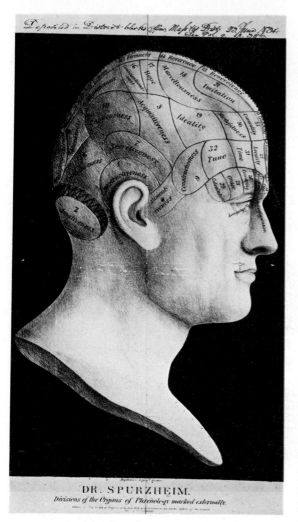

DR. SPURZHEIM.
Divisions of the Organs of Phrenology marked externally.

PHRENOLOGY CHART

This widely circulated bust of Dr. Johann Spurzheim illustrated the physical location of an amazing assortment of abilities, inclinations, and character traits. *(Library of Congress.)*

of the popular cults and fads. Mesmerists, for example, claimed to have discovered the laws of magnetic attraction and repulsion that governed relations between people. Spiritualists convinced hundreds of thousands that they had found techniques and apparatus for communicating with the dead and probing the laws of the occult. Even the manuals on self-improvement and character building, directed mainly at young men and young women, presumed definitive knowledge of the mechanics of the brain. The Reverend John Todd's *Student's Manual* (1835), which sold by the hundreds of thousands, maintained that mental power depends on a strict conservation of bodily and especially sexual energies. Todd's thesis, repeated by countless physicians and other experts, was that masturbation or sexual excess of any kind posed the gravest threats to sanity, social order, and individual achievement. Self-improvement required the rigorous avoidance of unwholesome thoughts and tempting situations.

Phrenology, however, was the most ambitious and institutionalized science of the mind. The invention of Franz Joseph Gall, a Viennese physician, phrenology identified the supposed physical location in the brain of a large assortment of human "faculties," such as firmness, benevolence, acquisitiveness, destructiveness, and Platonic love. Phrenologists claimed that they could precisely measure character from the form and shape of a head. Americans first responded to phrenology as a promising medical breakthrough. Gall's leading disciple, Johann Gaspar Spurzheim, became the first missionary for the cause. On a visit to America in 1832, he was lionized by New England dignitaries, including Justice Joseph Story and the Yale chemist Benjamin Silliman. For a time the support of Horace Mann, William Ellery Channing, and business leaders like Abbott Lawrence gave phrenology intellectual prestige. As usual, however, the American public displayed far more interest in practical application than in theory. Two skillful promoters, Orson and Lorenzo Fowler, helped to convert phrenology into a major business enterprise. In the cities audiences of thousands paid fees for lengthy lecture series expounding the new science. Thousands more flocked to salons to have their characters analyzed. Itinerant lecturers and mail-order courses enlightened the countryside. By the mid-1850s the *American Phrenological Journal* had a circulation of over fifty thousand.

In many ways phrenology perfectly suited the needs of a people devoted to technique but uncertain of their own character. In an expansive and socially disruptive economy, it provided a new set of guidelines that reduced the fear of risk. Employers, for example, no longer able to rely on long-term apprentice-ships, on personal knowledge of an employee's family, or even on a worker's reputation in the community, could request a phrenological examination. Young men who dreamed of many careers but who could decide on none wel-comed a science that would measure their talents and capabilities. The great message of phrenology was individual adjustment. In a world of confusing and fluid expectations, it furnished boundaries and specific identities. It told the individual which traits to cultivate and which to restrain. For the faithful it also made life more predictable. Criminologists not only found a physical explanation for deviant behavior, but discovered a new hope for preventing crime by identify-ing potential criminals and by teaching convicts to control their overdeveloped antisocial faculties. If Americans gradually came to realize that the results of phrenology could not substantiate its high promise, they had shown an ardent desire, which would continue to our own time, for a popular science of human behavior.

Like phrenology, the essays and lyceum lectures of Ralph Waldo Emerson, who came closer than anyone else to becoming America's official philosopher of the nineteenth century, offered something for everyone and thus nourished hope for reduced friction and for social harmony. While there is no way of know-ing how much influence Emerson actually had on American thought and culture, he helped to stimulate the great literary renaissance of the 1850s, and for decades to come was a source of inspiration for reformers, businessmen, and countless ordinary folk. It can be argued that Emerson's worship of power and of self-improvement provided the spiritual backdrop for the entire progressive era of the early twentieth century.

Yet Emerson's thought eludes all attempts at classification or categorization. The main reason, apart from the range and complexity of his mind, was his uncanny ability to play all sides at once and to ride the crest of each emerging and breaking wave. His words awakened reformers but he wrote the most pene-trating critiques of reform of his generation. He was at once the most homespun, down-to-earth, and yet stratospheric of American thinkers. An ardent champion of cultural independence, he defined the mission of native artists and writers, yet exploited his knowledge of the newest currents of German and English thought. He was the leader and spokesman for a group that domesticated German idealistic philosophy, appropriating Immanuel Kant's awkward label *Transcendentalism,* but he championed an extreme form of individualism and never felt comfortable as a member of any association. His pithy maxims on self-reliance were quoted by anarchists and were framed on the walls of the nation's business leaders.

But Emerson insisted that "to be great is to be misunderstood." To those critics who might value commitment, ideological rigor, or consistency, he replied that "a foolish consistency is the hobgoblin of little minds, adored by little statesmen and philosophers and divines." His spongelike capacity for absorption, his empathy for all sides and commitment to none, had much in common with America's greatest weaknesses and strengths. The sunny tolerance and pliant habit of mind represented by Emerson may have been as important as public schools, religious revivals, and an independent judiciary in helping American institutions to endure.

To understand Emerson's seemingly defiant rebellion against the conventions and orthodoxies of his time, it is important to know that he was descended from a long line of New England Calvinist ministers, that his father was a liberal Unitarian minister, and that his mother represented the relatively new commercial wealth of Boston. Though Emerson was trained himself to be a Unitarian minister, he found no satisfaction in the creed of his parents' generation, which seemed to express the complacency of people who had fought all the battles against Calvinism and provinciality, who had domesticated the European Enlightenment, who had achieved economic affluence and independence, and who had solved all of life's major problems. The Emerson family was in fact plagued by disease and personal tragedy, and young Emerson read and struggled with the questions posed by religious skeptics. At the age of twenty-nine, having achieved a spiritual breakthrough to faith and self-confidence, he resigned from the pulpit and began delivering secular lectures on what he called the infinitude of the private man.

In the 1830s New England was only beginning to receive the first shock waves from European literary and philosophic romanticism. The revolt of this native son, not against enfeebled Calvinism but against the rationalistic spirit of Boston's leading ministers and merchants, seemed revolutionary. In 1838 he informed the students and stunned the faculty of Harvard Divinity School: "But the word *miracle*, as pronounced by Christian churches, gives a false impression; it is Monster, it is not one with the blowing clover and the falling rain." To various audiences he proclaimed that "who so would be a man, must be a nonconformist." He said, "No law can be sacred to me but that of my nature. Good and bad are but names very readily transferable to that or this; the only right is what is after my constitution; the only wrong what is against it." To the youth of America he delivered the reassuring thought: "We but half express ourselves, and are ashamed of that divine idea which each of us represents. . . . Trust thyself: every heart vibrates to that iron string." He upbraided Americans for their single-minded pursuit of wealth and fame, for their obsession with material things: "Society everywhere is in conspiracy against the manhood of every one

RALPH WALDO EMERSON, 1803–1882
(*Library of Congress.*)

of its members. Society is a joint-stock company, in which the members agree,
for the better securing of his bread to each shareholder, to surrender the liberty
and culture of the eater. The virtue in most request is conformity."

But the point of this protest, which became clearer as both Emerson and his
audiences grew older, was the need for a continuing reshaping and reinvigoration
of the American character. The great peril that threatened the American people
was not injustice but a fragmentation of soul: "The reason why the world lacks
unity and lies broken and in heaps, is because man is disunited with himself."
The essential problem, then, was one of reconstituting character, of recovering
a sense of the whole: "We see the world by piece, as the sun, the moon, the animal,

the tree; but the whole, of which these are the shining parts, is the soul." The meaning of nonconformity and self-reliance, in other words, consisted of a detachment from society in order to achieve the sense of wholeness that flowed from unity with God, or as Emerson put it, with the Oversoul. "The relations of the soul to the divine spirit," Emerson wrote, "are so pure that it is profane to seek to interpose helps."

The notion that every "private man" possesses infinite and godlike capacities was an inspiring ideal, perfectly suited to the fantasies and aspirations of many Americans. Emerson's awe for achievement reinforced his deep native suspicion of all men who lived by their intellects. Character, "a reserved force, which acts directly by presence and without means," he associated with men of action, with "men who carry their points [without needing] . . . to inquire of their constituents what they should say, but are themselves the country which they represent." The ideal of nonconformity might inspire reformers, but Emerson's sympathies lay with the inspiration, not the reform. "No change of circumstances," he maintained, "can repair a defect of character." Precisely because Emerson wished to obliterate all partiality, all mediating and balancing forces that might stand between the individual and his fate, the champion of Transcendentalism had no ultimate standard other than power and success: "Power is, in nature, the essential measure of right."

It is one of the supreme contradictions of American cultural history that the thinker who succeeded in fusing the formal philosophy of his age with the needs of his society was both anti-intellectual and antisocial. America's leading critic of materialism and commercial values could still affirm that "money, which represents the prose of life, is in its effects and laws, as beautiful as roses." Though Emerson was a symbol of nonconformity, he idealized success in a way that encouraged acquiescence: "Divine persons are character born," he wrote, "or, to borrow a phrase from Napoleon, they are victory organized." He gave good cheer, it is true, to men of all sides, and like the revivalists he provided a vantage point for judging the sins and compromises of society. Yet he was also capable of making a statement that deflated all the manifestos on self-reliance and all the attempts to shape the national character: "Let the victory fall where it will, we are on that side."

The Tensions of Democratic Art

The continuing democratization of American culture produced a profound ambivalence toward the artistic standards and precedents of European culture, standards and precedents that had long given Americans a sense of provinciality and inferiority. On the one hand, American writers and artists felt the need to proclaim their independence from Europe and to create a genuinely native art, stripped of aristocratic associations. On the other hand, by the 1820s it was becoming clear that political independence did not guarantee cultural independence and that republican institutions would not automatically give birth to the Great American Masterwork. Improved transportation, coupled with a prolonged period of peace in Europe, made it easier for Americans to cross the Atlantic in search of inspiration and training.

Even the more ardent cultural nationalists looked on Europe with awe and fascination. Often shocked by European contrasts of elegance and squalor, they were also dazzled by the great cathedrals, castles, spacious parks, monumental public buildings, museums, and villas. From Washington Irving's *Alhambra* (1832) to Nathaniel Hawthorne's *Marble Faun* (1860), American writers expressed their enchantment with castles and ruins, with physical spaces that had been steeped in centuries of history. Whatever its evils, Europe teemed with associations that fed the imagination. It was the continent of mystery, of beauty, of romance, and in short, of culture. For many American artists it was also at least a temporary refuge from the materialism, vulgarity, and hurried pace of life they found in the United States. It is significant that Washington Irving was living in England when he created the classic American tales "Rip Van Winkle" and "The Legend of Sleepy Hollow" (1819–20). James Fenimore Cooper was living in Paris when he wrote *The Prairie* (1827). Horatio Greenough, America's first professional sculptor and a champion of democratic artistic theory, completed his gigantic, half-draped statue of George Washington, a statue commissioned by the United States government, in his studio in Florence.

It would be a mistake, however, to think of American art of the period as slavishly imitative. Although Americans tended to encase native subject matter in conventional artistic forms, they became increasingly skilled and sophisticated in their mastery of the forms. The choice of native material also affected the total character of a work. For example, space, nature, and the wilderness took on new qualities as Thomas Cole, Asher B. Durand, and other painters of the Hudson River school sought to idealize the American landscape. Cooper's five "Leather-Stocking tales," *The Pioneers* (1823), *The Last of the Mohicans* (1826), *The Prairie* (1827), *The Pathfinder* (1840), and *The Deerslayer* (1841), were far more than American versions of Sir Walter Scott's "Waverley novels." Like William Gilmore Simms's tales of the Southern frontier and backcountry, they gave imaginative expression to a distinctively American experience with Indians, violence, the law, and the meaning of social bonds in a wilderness setting. The popular New England poets and men of letters chose homey, unpretentious subjects that disguised both their literary skill and erudition. Thus Henry Wadsworth Longfellow, a translator of Dante and a master of meter, celebrated the village blacksmith. John Greenleaf Whittier sang of the barefoot boy. The highly cultivated James Russell Lowell delivered political satire in the homespun Yankee dialect of an imaginary Hosea Biglow.

By the 1820s it was becoming clear that art in America would have to be marketed like any other commodity, and that the ideal of the dabbling gentleman amateur would have to give way to the reality of the professional who wrote, carved, or painted for a living. Federal, state, and local governments did award a few commissions for patriotic and historical subjects, but political squabbles over art (including the seminudity of Greenough's Washington) dampened the attractions of government patronage. The need to compete for middle-class customers and audiences helps to explain the dominant patriotic, didactic, and sentimental themes of popular American culture. A self-consciously democratic art, as opposed to the remnants of folk art that it began to replace, had to justify itself by serving essentially nonartistic needs.

Preeminent among these needs was the shaping of character. During the pre–Civil War decades both literature and the so-called fine arts won moral legitimacy by claiming to perform educational, quasi-religious functions. They provided models to imitate, they trained and refined the emotions, and they taught that sin is always punished and virtue rewarded. Art promoted patriotism by glorifying the American Revolution and deifying George Washington. It defined idealized sex roles by identifying the American male as the man of action

"THE GREEK SLAVE" AT THE DUSSELDORF GALLERY

The traveling exhibition of Hiram Powers's "The Greek Slave" created the greatest artistic sensation of the pre-Civil War decades. The daring—and to some, immoral—display of female nudity was justified by the "ideality" of the form and by the assumption that the enslaved girl had been immodestly stripped by her brutal Turkish captors. *(The New York Public Library.)*

and conquerer of nature—hunter, trapper, scout, Mountain Man, seafaring adventurer; and by associating the American female with refinement of emotions and confinement in a home—physical frailty, periods of melancholy, and a sensitivity expressed by sudden blushing, paleness, tears, and fainting. Above all, art furnished models of speech, manners, courtship, friendship, and grief that helped to establish standards of middle-class respectability.

A few writers achieved the imaginative independence to point towards new possibilities of character and sensibility. Edgar Allan Poe, who strove for commercial success while remaining committed to the ideal of art as an autonomous craft, gave a dark transmutation to the stock themes of sentimental poetry and fiction. In a different way Nathaniel Hawthorne subtly transcended the conventions of sentimental moralism in *The Scarlet Letter* (1850), *The House of the Seven Gables* (1851), and *The Blithdale Romance* (1852). This period of creativity, later termed the American Renaissance, included Walt Whitman's *Leaves of Grass* (1855), which not only celebrated the boundless potentialities of American experience but took joy in defying the conventional limits of poetic language. Herman Melville's *Moby Dick* (1851), one of the world's great novels, also fused native subject matter with new and distinctively American artistic forms. Henry David Thoreau's *Walden* (1854) stated a goal that could be applied to many of the best works of the period. Thoreau had nothing but contempt for the conventional efforts to shape character in the interest of social conformity. But Thoreau's decision to live by himself on Walden Pond was an experiment in self-improvement. The goal of his experiment, and of the art it produced, was to break free from the distractions and artificialities that disguised "the essential facts of life" —"to drive life into a corner, and reduce it to its lowest terms." "For most men, it appears to me," he said, "are in a strange uncertainty about it, whether it is of the devil or of God."

Suggested Readings

An excellent collection of source material on children can be found in the first volume of Robert H. Bremner, ed., *Children and Youth in America: A Documentary History* (1970–71). Two recent studies of the history of juvenile delinquency are Joseph M. Hawes, *Children in Urban Society* (1971), and Robert M. Mennel, *Thorns and Thistles* (1973).

Michael Katz, *The Irony of Early School Reform* (1968), sharply challenges the self-congratulatory tradition of educational history. Two important studies, also critical but more balanced, are: Carl F. Kaestle, *The Evolution of an Urban School System: New York City, 1750–1850* (1973), and Stanley K. Schultz, *The Culture Factory: Boston Public Schools, 1789–1860* (1973). Rush Welter, *Popular Education and Democratic Thought in America* (1962), presents a more traditional approach, and so does the excellent biography by Jonathan Messerli, *Horace Mann* (1972). Among the special studies of note are Bernard Wishy, *The Child and the Republic: The Dawn of Modern American Child Nurture* (1968); Marianna C. Brown, *The Sunday School Movement in America* (1961); Ruth Elson, *Guardians of Tradition; American Schoolbooks of the Nineteenth Century* (1964); Vincent P. Lannie, *Public Money and Parochial Education* (1968); and Merle Curti, *The Social Ideas of American Educators* (1935). The best introduction to higher education is Frederick Rudolph, *The American College and University* (1962), which can be supplemented by Theodore R. Crane, ed., *The Colleges and the Public, 1767–1862* (1963), and by Richard Hofstadter and Wilson Smith, *American Higher Education: A Documentary History* (2 vols., 1961).

The most imaginative treatment of revivalism is the first section of Perry Miller, *The Life of the Mind in America* (1965). William G. McLoughlin, Jr., *Modern Revivalism* (1959), gives a more detailed and systematic account of individual revivalists. Charles A. Johnson, *The Frontier Camp Meeting* (1955), is the standard history of the subject. The wider social impact of revivalism in New York State is brilliantly traced in Whitney Cross, *The Burned-Over District* (1950).

The fullest general history of American religion is Sydney E. Ahlstrom, *A Religious History of the American People* (1972). Among the special studies of unusual interest are Henri Desroche, *The American Shakers from Neo-Christianity to Pre-socialism* (1971); Nathan Glazer, *American Judaism* (1957); Daniel W. Howe, *The Unitarian Conscience* (1970); Martin Marty, *The Infidel: Freethought in American Religion* (1961); William G. McLoughlin, Jr., *The Meaning of Henry Ward Beecher* (1970); Theodore Maynard, *The Story of American Catholicism* (1960); and Ernest L. Tuveson, *Redeemer Nation: The Idea of America's Millennial Role* (1968).

Perry Miller, *Life of the Mind in America* (1965), contains a brilliant analysis of legal thought in America. Lawrence Friedman, *A History of American Law* (1973), is a comprehensive survey. William E. Nelson, *Americanization of the Common Law* (1975), though dealing primarily with an earlier period, is a study of central importance. The standard work on the Supreme Court is Charles Warren, *The Supreme Court in United States History* (2 vols., 1926). On the political background of the Court, see Henry J. Abraham, *Justices and Presidents: A Political History of Appointments to the Supreme Court* (1974). An important aspect of constitutional development is traced in Bernard Schwartz, *From Confederation to Nation: The American Constitution, 1835–1877* (1973). Leonard W. Levy, *The Law of the Commonwealth and Chief Justice Shaw* (1957), is an outstanding study of a leading jurist. The standard biographies of Marshall and Taney are Albert J. Beveridge, *The Life of John Marshall* (4 vols., 1916–19), and Carl B. Swisher, *Roger B. Taney* (1936).

On science, the last section of Perry Miller's *Life of the Mind* contains important insights. The best general work is George Daniels, *American Science in the Age of Jackson* (1968). For medicine, see Richard H. Shryock, *Medicine and Society in America* (1960); and Martin Kaufman, *Homeopathy in America: The Rise and Fall of a Medical Heresy* (1971). Among the best biographies of individual scientists are Edward Lurie, *Agassiz: A Life of Science in America* (1960), and Frances Williams, *Matthew Fontaine Maury* (1963).

John D. Davies, *Phrenology: Fad and Science* (1955), is highly informative. Carl Bode treats the popularization of knowledge in *The American Lyceum* (1956), and reveals popular taste and culture in *The Anatomy of American Popular Culture* (1959).

The most illuminating study of Emerson's thought is Stephen Whicher, *Freedom and Fate: An Inner Life of Ralph Waldo Emerson* (1953). The best biography is Ralph L. Lusk, *The Life of Ralph Waldo Emerson* (1949). O. B. Frothingham, *Transcendentalism in New England* (1876), conveys a young participant's memories of the liberating excitement of the Transcendentalist movement. Perry Miller, ed., *The Transcendentalists* (1950), is a difficult but magnificent anthology. Walter Harding's *Thoreau, Man of Concord* (1960), and Joseph W. Krutch, *Henry David Thoreau* (1948), can be supplemented with profit by Sherman Paul, *The Shores of America: Thoreau's Inward Exploration* (1961). For individual Transcendentalists, see Charles Crowe, *George Ripley* (1967); Odell Shepard, *Pilgrim's Progress: The Life of Bronson Alcott* (1937); and Arthur M. Schlesinger, Jr., *Orestes A. Brownson* (1939). F. O. Matthiessen, *American Renaissance* (1941), is a brilliant and unsurpassed study of Emerson, Thoreau, Hawthorne, Melville, and Whitman.

Of the numerous studies of important literary figures, the following have special value for the historian: Richard Chase, *The American Novel and Its Tradition* (1957); Joel Porte, *The Romance in America: Studies in Cooper, Poe, Hawthorne, Melville, and James* (1969); Charles Feidelson, Jr., *Symbolism and American Literature* (1953); A. N. Kaul, *The American Vision: Actual and Ideal Society in Nineteenth-Century Fiction* (1963); R. W. B. Lewis, *The American Adam: Innocence, Tragedy, and Tradition in the Nineteenth Century* (1955); and David Levin, *History as Romantic Art* (1959). For Whitman, see Gay Allen, *The Solitary Singer* (1967). The best introduction to Poe is Edward Wagenknecht, *Edgar Allan Poe: The Man Behind the Legend* (1963). Newton Arvin has written two fine literary biographies: *Herman Melville* (1950); and *Longfellow: His life and Work* (1963). For Hawthorne, see Edward Wagenknecht, *Nathaniel Hawthorne: Man and Writer* (1961).

Van Wyck Brooks, *The Flowering of New England, 1815–1865* (1936), is still highly readable and informative. On the South, the best guide is Jay B. Hubbell, *The South in American Literature, 1607–1900* (1954). Henry Nash Smith, *Virgin Land: The American West as Symbol and Myth* (1950), is a brilliant study of the imaginative portrayal of the West. The early publishing industry is analyzed in William Charvat, *Literary Publishing in America, 1790–1850* (1959). For popular literature, see James Hart, *The Popular Book in America* (1950); Herbert R. Brown, *The Sentimental Novel in America, 1798–1860* (1940); and Frank L. Mott, *Golden Multitudes: The Story of Best Sellers in the United States* (1947). Mott, *American Journalism* (1962), is the standard source on newspapers. The first volume of Mott's monumental *A History of American Magazines* (5 vols., 1957), is a mine of information. For folk songs, see Alan Lomax, *The Folk Song in North America* (1969).

Oliver W. Larkin, *Art and Life in America* (1949), is the fullest and best study of the early history of art and architecture. On painting it should be supplemented by James T. Flexner, *That Wilder Image: The Painting of America's Native School from Thomas Cole to Winslow Homer* (1962). Neil Harris, *The Artist in American Society: The Formative Years, 1790–1860* (1966), is a sensitive study of art as a profession. Arthur H. Quinn, *American Drama* (2 vols., 1955), is a comprehensive introduction to the theater. A more imaginative work is David Grimstead, *Melodrama Unveiled* (1968). On architecture, see Talbot F. Hamlin, *Greek Revival Architecture in America* (1944); and Wayne Andrews, *Architecture in America* (1960). The best guides to early American music are Gilbert Chase, *America's Music* (1955), and H. Wiley Hitchcock, *Music in the United States* (1969).

16

The Nature and Limits of Dissent

The desire to transform character lay at the heart of American reform. Like other Americans, reformers rejoiced in the nation's freedom from kings and nobles, from aristocratic institutions, and from status and roles defined at birth. Yet in pursuing the good life, which had supposedly been made accessible by the sacrifices of the Founding Fathers, they discovered a society of astounding moral and physical contrasts, a society that often seemed to be ruled by no other principle besides cannibalistic self-interest and the tyranny of superior power.

The spirit of dissent centered in the Northeast and particularly in New England, the areas most prepared for the values, world view, and organizational discipline of industrial civilization. During the pre-Civil War decades this region spawned numerous missionary-like crusades to regenerate the social order. Practically all these movements, whether religious or secular, sought to orient American culture to a "higher law," the moral government of God, as a means of combating anarchy.

The expectations of the missionary reformers were often unrealistic, partly because the boundaries between the possible and impossible were still extremely uncertain. Sometimes the reformers met resistance, persecution, and violence, forcing them to retreat into their own "asylums," or protected refuges of purity. But because the structure of American society was still extremely plastic, the missionary probes also widened the boundaries of America's culture, particularly as the reformers made increasing use of modern techniques of communication. Of the more radical movements of dissent, the Mormons found that they could survive only by building their own asylum in the remote desert of the Far West. From within American society the abolitionists tested the outermost limits of permissible dissent. In the end, however, both Mormons and abolitionists were forced to accept many of the norms and common denominators of the society they had tried to transform.

Three Stages of Protest and Reform

An expanding reform impulse led in the early nineteenth century to new and complex mixtures of religious aspiration and secular organization. Throughout the ages the world had witnessed many new religions as well as crusading movements, purification movements, and monastic movements. Some of these religious groups had delivered harsh judgments on the existing social order. Some had sent out missionaries to convert the heathen. Some had sought to provide the surrounding world with a model of ascetic life, dietary discipline, and selfless commitment. History offered no precedents, however, for the kind of reform movements that began to arise in Britain, France, and the United States during the late eighteenth century. Fully developed institutions of social reform were a distinctive product of the early nineteenth century and of the Anglo-American middle class. The new movements for social betterment were almost always inspired by religious motives and ideals. Yet the organized efforts to abolish slavery, cure the insane, reform criminals, and outlaw alcoholic drinks played a critical part in secularizing Anglo-American Protestant culture.

Reform movements usually embodied a nostalgia for a supposedly simpler and more harmonious past. The evils they combated had supposedly multiplied because of an alarming disintegration of family authority and community cohesiveness. Yet in function the reform movements were agencies of modernization, striking out against the institutions, life styles, and prescribed identities that seemed to limit individual opportunity and to block the path of progress. Moreover, the character of American reform changed dramatically as a growing number of groups, particularly in the North, sought to find values and a way of life that would help them adjust to the future.

The reform movements in the early nineteenth century developed in three overlapping phases. The first phase, still closely tied to the model of the evangelical church, began with missionary campaigns to spread the message of a given cause. It was also characterized by attempts to gather the virtuous together and to expel or quarantine evil. Because Mormonism became America's first indigenous religion while also exhibiting many of the traits of a reform movement, it can introduce the theme of the gathering of the saints—that is, of converts who wished to live in accordance with a higher moral law, free from the religious and

political contaminations of their time. Reformers like Lyman Beecher, who had
no sympathy for the Mormons, embraced a similar objective of giving society a
more homogeneous moral character by restoring "the moral government of
God." This was the supreme goal of the so-called Benevolent Empire—the
coalition of home and foreign missionary societies, the American Tract Society,
the American Sunday School Union, the American Society for the Promotion of
Temperance, the American Colonization Society, the Prison Discipline Society,
and the General Union for Promoting the Observance of the Christian Sabbath.

Ideals of purification and exclusion dominated the activities of such organizations. Having already provided for the gradual but imminent extinction of
slavery in the Northern states, many antislavery reformers wanted to ship the free
blacks back to Africa. Drunkards and a drinking culture were to be banished from
the sight of respectable society. Criminals and deviants of various kinds were to
be walled off in prisons and asylums, where in the words of some New York reformers of 1822, "their stubborn spirits are subdued, and their depraved hearts
softened, by mental suffering." When deviants were institutionalized, they could
neither disturb nor contaminate a society that needed undistracted concentration
on business and moral virtue. Some enthusiastic prison reformers even argued
that society itself should be modeled on "the regularity, and temperance, and
sobriety of a good prison."

The second phase of reform, inspired by a romantic confidence in human
perfectibility, focused on the need for releasing individuals from all coercive
forces and institutions. Reformers of this phase were "immediatists," who took
their cue from the religious revivalists' faith in an immediate and total liberation
from sin. Abolitionists tried to send their message behind the South's iron curtain

and appeal directly to the Christian conscience of individual slaveholders. They also celebrated fugitive slaves, whose very existence proved that the ramparts of slavery and racial degradation could be breached. The temperance movement called for total abstinence from all intoxicating drinks and became preoccupied with the drama of former drunkards who had freed themselves from the clutches of the "demon rum." Other reformers won fame for their success in emancipating individual victims of deafness, blindness, and insanity. Samuel Gridley Howe, best known for his pioneering work with the blind and deaf-blind, expressed the growing view that even criminals were "thrown upon society as a sacred charge." He said, "Society is false to its trust, if it neglects any means of reformation." Prison reformers tried, with little success, to transform penitentiaries into communities of rehabilitation and to persuade society of the need for parole, indeterminate sentences, and sympathetic care for discharged convicts. Nativists, many of whom engaged in humanitarian causes, publicized cases of Catholic women who had escaped from supposedly tyrannical and immoral nunneries, and demanded laws that would liberate Catholic laymen from the control of their priests.

Experimental communities were the logical extreme of this assault on institutional barriers and on the constraints of past identities. By the 1840s a variety

SCHOOLROOM IN A "DEAF AND DUMB ASYLUM" AND
STATE PENITENTIARY, PENNSYLVANIA

The early nineteenth century witnessed the creation of asylums — totally planned and manipulated environments — which were intended to cure the insane, reform criminals, and liberate the handicapped from the effects of deafness and blindness. Whether liberating or repressive, these institutions exemplified the prevailing faith in the malleability of human nature. *(Culver Pictures; Pennsylvania Prison Society.)*

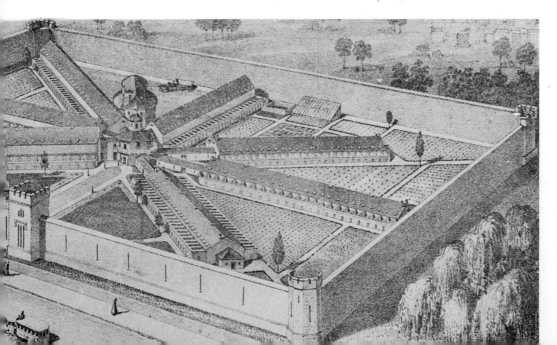

of such communities offered Americans the opportunity to lead truly new lives, free from the frustrations of competitive labor and of the private, isolated family. The members of John Humphrey Noyes's perfectionist Oneida community were convinced that all outsiders were enslaved by the bonds of private property and monogamous marriage, both of which imprisoned the human spirit behind walls of sinful possessiveness. According to Noyes, "As the doctrine of temperance is total abstinence from alcoholic drinks, and the doctrine of antislavery is immediate abolition of human bondage, so the doctrine of perfectionism is the immediate and total cessation from sin."

But the third phase of reform moved from self-assertion and experiment to consolidation and cohesion. Questions of public policy and social interest took precedence over individual freedom. This change in orientation had much to do with immigration and ethnic conflict. Nativists, for example, talked less of liberating individual Catholics than of restricting the growing power of the Catholic church. The temperance movement, having little success in converting Irish and German immigrants, worked for statewide prohibition of the sale of alcoholic drinks. On both local and state levels, bitter political conflict erupted over the passage, repeal, and enforcement of prohibition laws. Stressing the cost to taxpayers, reformers increasingly identified alcohol and immigration as the causes of crime, pauperism, and insanity. They expressed far less hope in the rehabilitative function of prisons and asylums, which were now accepted as no more than places of custody for a swelling population of immigrant and lower-class deviants. Finally, abolitionists rallied behind the slogan, "Free Soil, Free Speech, Free Labor, Free Men," and demanded the total exclusion of slavery from the Western territories. Ironically this new determination to enforce some version of liberty in a specific geographical area meant denying freedom for dissenters. In 1856, for example, the platform of the new Republican party linked the Mormons' polygamy with slavery, "those twin relics of barbarism," and asserted that Congress could and should abolish both institutions in the territories. If reform could once win a political majority, then it was the government, whether state or national, that would define alcohol, Catholicism, Mormonism, or slavery as essentially un-American.

The Mormons as a Test Case

In 1830 Joseph Smith, Jr., published The Book of Mormon in Palmyra, New York. The work purported to be a translation of mysterious golden plates containing the history of an ancient Christian civilization in the New World. It also portrayed the American Indians as the degenerate but salvageable descendants of an ancient Hebrew tribe, and foresaw a new American prophet who would discover the lost history and reestablish Christ's pure and undefiled kingdom in the New World. In 1830 Smith was an athletic, gregarious, cheerful, intensely imaginative young man of twenty-four. He was the son of one of America's many families of drifters, debtors, and habitual losers, whose poverty worsened as they drew closer to belts of commercial prosperity. Smith had been born in the hills of Vermont and his parents had migrated to that caldron of progress and poverty, of religious revivalism and new social movements—soon to be known as the "Burned-Over District" of upstate New York. Shortly after the publication of The Book of Mormon, Smith organized the Church of Christ, which in 1834 would be renamed the Church of Jesus Christ of Latter-day Saints.

Faced from the outset with religious persecution, Smith knew that the saints must ultimately move westward and build their city of Zion at some divinely appointed spot near the Indian tribes they were commissioned to convert. In accordance with his continuing revelations, he dispatched missionaries to scout out the Missouri frontier. In 1831 a few Mormons established an outpost near Independence, Missouri, which Smith designated as the site of the New Jerusalem, and which was then the eastern terminus of the Santa Fe Trail. During the same year Smith and his New York followers migrated to Kirtland, Ohio, near Cleveland, where Mormon missionaries had converted an entire community.

By 1839 the Mormons had met defeat in both Ohio and Missouri and were fleeing to a refuge of swampy Illinois farmland that Smith had bought along the eastern shore of the Mississippi. In Ohio the Mormons had experimented with communal ownership of property and with an illegal, wildcat banking venture that had brought disaster during the panic of 1837. In Missouri pro-Southern mobs, hostile to any group of nonslaveholding Yankees, and infuriated by reports that Mormons intended to bring free blacks into the state, had destroyed the settlements around Independence. A series of armed encounters, beginning with an attempt to bar Mormons from voting, led to outright warfare and to Governor L. W. Boggs's proclamation that the Mormons had to be treated as enemies, and "had to be exterminated, or driven from the state." At Haun's Mill a band of Missourians massacred nineteen Mormon men and boys. Smith himself was convicted of treason and sentenced to be shot. But Smith managed to escape, and in Illinois the Mormons finally built their model city of Nauvoo, which the legislature incorporated in 1840 as a virtually independent city-state. The Mormons' political power derived from the decisive weight they could throw in state elections that were fairly evenly balanced between Whigs and Democrats. Beginning in 1840, their numbers grew not only as the result of missionary work in the East, but as the result of the immigration of thousands who had been converted in the manufacturing districts of England. The English converts' route to the American Zion was eased by the church's highly efficient planning authority that took care of the details of travel.

By the early 1840s visitors to Nauvoo marveled at the city's broad streets, carefully laid out in neat squares; at the steam sawmills and flour mill, the factories, hotel, and schools. Though the Nauvoo temple, supported by thirty gigantic pillars and walls of hewn stone, was not yet complete, it promised to be, in the words of John Greenleaf Whittier, "the most splendid and imposing architec-

JOSEPH SMITH, REVIEWING TROOPS

While this painting exaggerates the machine-like discipline
of the Nauvoo legion, it suggests why many non-Mormons
could feel concern over Joseph Smith's private army. *(Church
Archives, The Church of Jesus Christ of Latterday Saints.)*

tural monument in the new world." Dressed in the uniform of a lieutenant general, Smith presided over a Nauvoo legion of two thousand troops. In 1843 he
dictated the official revelation, which he never made public, justifying the practice of plural marriage or polygamy. In 1844 he established the secret Council
of Fifty, a secular authority independent of the church, and gave it the mission
of building a world government that would prepare the way for Christ's kingdom.

But Smith found that he was losing the race against time. Sensing that the
surrounding non-Mormon society would not long tolerate Mormon power, he
unsuccessfully tried to persuade the new Republic of Texas to sponsor an independent Mormon colony south of the Nueces River, along the contested border
with Mexico. While also sending secret diplomatic missions to Russia and France,
he tried to influence the established order through normal political channels.
But neither the federal government nor the 1844 presidential candidates would
defend the Mormons' claims against Missouri outlaws who had seized thousands
of Mormon farms and buildings. As a gesture of protest, Smith finally announced
his own candidacy for the highest office in the land. But long before the election,
Smith ordered the destruction of a printing press set up by Mormon dissidents
who had declared: "We will not acknowledge any man as king or lawgiver to the
church." Illinois then charged Smith with treason and locked him and his brother

in the Carthage jail. On June 27, 1844, a "mob" that included many prominent non-Mormon citizens stormed the jail and killed them both.

To the Mormons the Prophet's martyrdom brought shock, division, and a struggle for power. It also temporarily appeased the aggression of anti-Mormons and gave Smith's followers time to plan an exodus. Brigham Young, like Smith a man of humble Vermont origin, soon emerged as the leader of the church and as one of the nineteenth century's greatest organizers. Aided by the elite Quorum of the Twelve Apostles and the Council of Fifty, he preserved order and morale while considering and rejecting possible refuges in British and Mexican territory. Before the end of 1845, the Mormon leadership had decided to send an advance company of 1500 men to the valley of the Great Salt Lake, then still part of Mexico. As a result of mounting persecution and harassment, the Mormons soon concentrated their energies on evacuating Nauvoo, on selling property at tremendous sacrifice, and on setting up refugee camps from eastern Iowa to Winter Quarters, a temporary destination in eastern Nebraska. The last refugees crossed the Mississippi at gunpoint, leaving Nauvoo a ghost town occupied by

THE MORMON TREK

During the 1850s and 1860s thousands of immigrants, converted to Mormonism in Europe, made the final lap of their long journey to Utah by foot, pulling handcarts over the prairies of Nebraska and the plateaus and mountains of Wyoming. *(Church Archives, The Church of Jesus Christ of Latterday Saints.)*

bands of armed men. During the summer of 1846 some twelve thousand Mormons were on the road; 3700 wagon teams stretched out across the prairies of Iowa.

In the summer of 1847 Brigham Young led a vanguard of picked men across the barren wastes of Nebraska and Wyoming to the Great Salt Lake valley of Utah. In September a second party of two thousand weary Mormons found home in the new Zion. During the same year the American defeat of Mexico brought Utah within the dominion of the United States. The Mormons had contributed a battalion of five hundred men who had marched with the American army across New Mexico to southern California, and whose pay had helped to finance the migration to Utah. Yet by 1848 the Mormons occupied an inland mountain fortress, a thousand miles beyond the Kansas frontier, and seemed at last to be the masters of their own destiny. When federal judges and other officials arrived in the territory, they found that the Mormons had held a census, adopted a constitution, elected Young governor, and established a "State of Deseret," complete with its own currency and army. The theocratic government was responsible for the remarkably rapid and orderly settlement of the valley, for the collective labor and central economic planning that brought irrigation to the dry but fertile land, and for the coordinated expansion that planted ninety-six colonies in ten years, extending in a corridor from Salt Lake City to San Diego.

Ten years before the time when South Carolina defied federal authority by firing on Fort Sumter, federal officials fled from Utah, denouncing Young's government as a theocracy fundamentally disloyal to the United States. Although the Mormons professed loyalty to the Constitution and acknowledged their territorial status, they intended to pay little attention to "carpetbag" authorities sent from Washington. When Young publicly proclaimed the sacred doctrine of polygamy, which Mormon leaders had privately practiced for over a decade, he presented a ready-made issue to outraged reformers, clergymen, and politicians. President Buchanan felt the need of appeasing this popular clamor and of forcibly establishing federal authority in Utah. In 1857 he dispatched a regular army force of 2500 men, led, ironically, by Albert Sidney Johnston, who would soon be a Confederate general resisting an invasion by the United States.

Fortunately for the Mormons, winter snows trapped the expedition in the Rocky Mountains, allowing time for behind-the-scenes negotiations. Governor Young proclaimed martial law and threatened to burn Salt Lake City to the ground and "to utterly lay waste" the land if Utah were invaded. States' rights Democrats had little enthusiasm for setting precedents that might be turned against Southern slavery, and though Buchanan had sworn that he would "put down the Mormon rebellion," he decided early in 1858 to proclaim a "pardon" to the inhabitants of Utah if they would obey United States laws and cooperate with federal officials. To prove their strength, however, the Mormons evacuated Salt Lake City. Johnston's army entered a deserted city, greeted only by squads of tough police, "glowering from beneath their hat-brims, with clubs in their

The Perils of Civilization

By the second quarter of the nineteenth century a growing number of artists were giving imaginative expression to the changing American experience. Some of these artists drew on the rich resources of "primitive" painting and popular folklore; an increasing number had received formal training in Europe and in the new artistic academies of the East. Apart from training and talent, American artists were becoming more sensitive to the opportunities and coercions of a market economy in which art competed with other luxuries. They were becoming more responsive to the exotic and romantic fashions of the time, largely derived from Europe and, above all, to America's dramatic expansion, which seemed at once both exhilarating and dangerous. For the central legacy of Old World culture, running like a blinking danger light from the ancient Greeks to Shakespeare and Milton, was the message that destruction inevitably follows excessive human pride, arrogance, or a defiance of the boundaries that God and nature had imposed on humankind.

Nature became the central theme of American art in the pre–Civil War era. It was still a nature that stood above and apart from humankind—a source of inspiration, a force to be conquered, but not a *resource* to be preserved in parks or commemorated in museums. George Caleb Bingham, who grew up on the frontier, could portray the penetration and exploitation of nature as an idyllic moment of harmony. He depicts fur traders descending the great Missouri River (not fishermen or hunters in a protected game preserve). The boat is laden with pelts and a live fox is chained to the bow. The young trapper

"Fur Traders Descending the Missouri," *The Metropolitan Museum of Art, Morris K. Jesup Fund, 1933.*

lounges over his gun and a dead waterfowl. The colorful detail and sharp, angular lines of the men and boat stand out against the feathery trees in the background. Yet Bingham has skillfully blended the human forms with the watery reflections and mist of the wild landscape. His trappers are less intruders upon nature than converts to its serenity.

Even when conflict became explicit, nature retained a sense of transcendence or "otherness." Civilization had not yet won supremacy.

In Charles Deas's melodramatic painting, *The Death Struggle,* a white trapper, still clutching a mink he has caught in a trap, is himself locked with an Indian in combat. In contrast to Bingham's peaceful mist and mirror-like river, nature now assumes the beautiful awe and terror that romantics termed the "sublime"—a boiling conflict between light and darkness that recalls nineteenth-century illustrations of Dante's *Divine Comedy* and Milton's *Paradise Lost*. Deas's painting also echoes

the themes of the contemporary *Leather-Stocking Tales* of James Fenimore Cooper. Deas's trapper, like Cooper's heroes, is in dire peril, but the white audience can confidently assume that his Indian foe will plunge into the dark abyss below.

Yet there was open space in the West that remained unconquered. The first pictorial images of conquest focused on trading posts that enclosed small fortified spaces in the midst of boundless plains and barren mountains. Alfred Jacob Miller's views of Fort Laramie represented a compromise between the harmonious blending of Bingham and the stark combat of Deas. Miller, enlisted in 1837 as the official artist for an expedition led by a British explorer and army officer, made the first on-the-spot paintings of the Rocky Mountain fur-trapping region. Fort Laramie had been built on the North Platte River (northeast of the later town of Laramie, Wyoming), at the crossroads of Indian trading routes and in the direct path of the future Oregon Trail. Miller depicted it as an outpost of white civilization, a protected space filled with rectangular lines and jutting towers reminiscent of medieval European castles. A secure oasis for tens of thousands of future overland emigrants, it was also surrounded by the tepees of nomadic Oglala Sioux. As portrayed here in *The Interior of Fort Laramie* by Miller, the fort stakes off a physical space for controlled intercourse between whites and Indians—the Indians who were sometimes allowed to enter the gate, trade, stare at the cannon, and be exploited, sexually and otherwise, by a superior power.

For pre–Civil War Americans, the Far West represented only one aspect of nature, a raw nature that sometimes seemed to threaten the moral and psychological foundations of civilization. East of the Mississippi, where civilization faced no more than a mopping-up operation, the victors could afford a certain nostalgia for the wilderness landscape that was being transformed and enclosed. Most of the East was still woodland, swamp, and pasture, but "nature," in the sense of an environment that affects man more than it is affected by man, seemed increasingly vulnerable. It could therefore be enshrined and for a time preserved in its precarious autonomy by landscape painting, a form of art that enjoyed increasing popularity. The reverent imagery of the so-called Hudson River School suggested a divine spirit within hills, brooks, forests, rocks, clouds, and illuminated skies. Building on this tradition, Martin Heade evolved an eerie realism that captured fleeting moments of changing light and atmosphere, often set off by wide horizons where civilized land gives way to a wild and ominous sea. In his *The Coming Storm,* the luminous sailboat and human figures seem almost frozen in place, yet threatened by the distant flash of lightning and heavy rain clouds. In the works of Heade and other landscape painters, nature could startle viewers, bringing a delight of recognition as well as a moment of humility. As the symbol of something beyond human reach, nature could thus serve as an aesthetic counterweight to civilization's demands for predictability, mastery, and control.

The Metropolitan Museum of Art, Gift of the Irving Wolf Foundation.

Courtesy, The National Gallery of Art, Washington, D. C.

In a way, however, American culture demanded that nature somehow assimilate and give legitimacy to the machine. This demand was most imaginatively met by George Innes, who in 1854 accepted a commission from the Lackawanna Railroad Company to paint such unorthodox subjects as a railroad roundhouse and steam locomotive. In Innes's *Lackawanna Valley* a pastoral landscape seems to embrace and merge with civilization's smoke and iron. A lone spectator, similar to the contemplative figure in Heade's *The Coming Storm,* looks out upon a peaceful valley. The train's plume

Courtesy of the New-York Historical Society.

of smoke is echoed by a distant wisp beyond the church steeple. The curving track links the background hills with the tall tree in the foreground. Despite the stumps, despite the signs of encroaching industry, the human intrusion on nature appears to be in harmony with nature's rhythms.

But antebellum artists evolved no similar formula for romanticizing the city, a subject they generally shunned. A few anonymous painters did succeed in documenting the squalor, moral degradation, and jostling confusion of New York's growing slums. It was Thomas Cole, however, the original leader of the Hudson River School and the painter who did the most to popularize the American landscape, who expressed the era's most striking vision of the consequences of "overcivilization."

Cole painted his five canvases on *The Course*

of Empire after returning from a residence in Europe, where he had contemplated the ruins of antiquity. His choice of classical imagery had special meaning for a modern republic that had taken so many of its moral and aesthetic models from classical Rome. Cole's first two canvases show the evolution from primitive origins of a pastoral, creative classical society. In *The Consummation of Empire*, however, chasteness and innocence have given way to luxurious decadence. The scene represents a total subjugation and defiance of nature. Except for a jutting cliff in the background, the landscape has become wholly encrusted with marble temples and monuments. An imperial procession on the bridge suggests the arrogance of unlimited power. The sinuous fountain and voluptuous setting at the lower right suggest moral decay.

Courtesy of the New-York Historical Society.

In *The Destruction of Empire* the viewer's perspective has shifted to the right and rear. The jutting cliff is still visible in the distance, and is the only landmark certain to survive the catastrophic destruction. Civilization is engulfed in a storm of flame and swirling smoke. People spill like ants from the bridge, while in the foreground the statue of a gigantic headless warrior holds his helpless shield above the scene of pillage and rape. On the base of the statue Cole inscribed the large numbers "1836," which was not only the date of the painting but a year when financial panic caused many Americans to ponder the future course of their own empire.

Cole's final canvas presents lifeless ruins and rubble covered by creeping vegetation—a view of nature unperturbed by the extinction of civilization. A similar theme of catastrophism, qualifying the exuberant optimism of antebellum society, was not uncommon in American literature and art. It drew on traditions of religious millenarianism as well as on the fear that any republic, no matter how virtuous its origins, might share the fate of Rome. Both models suggested the spasmodic anxieties of a people who continued to defy the limits and boundaries of their Old World heritage.

THE DESERET STORE, SALT LAKE CITY C. 1850

The Deseret Store, with the symbol of the bee hive in the middle of the sign, was owned by the Mormon church. The General Tithing Store House, at the rear, contained the agricultural produce Mormon families were required to contribute. *(Church Archives, The Church of Jesus Christ of Latterday Saints.)*

hands, and pistols ready slung at their belts." The later withdrawal of federal troops concluded the so-called Mormon War, which brought no change in the actual government of Utah. When Buchanan's successor, Abraham Lincoln, was asked what he proposed to do about the Mormons, he answered, "I propose to let them alone." Lincoln, of course, had other problems on his hands.

No story in American history is more incredible. From the outset, Mormonism embodied the longings and aspirations of people who had not shared in the growing prosperity and social modernization of the early nineteenth century and who had become increasingly disinherited from their own cultural roots. The poet Whittier observed, after listening to a Mormon service in Massachusetts: "They speak a language of hope and promise to weak, weary hearts, tossed and troubled, who have wandered from sect to sect, seeking in vain for the primal manifestation of the divine power." The new church recruited most of its members from the more remote and isolated parts of New England; from the sparsely populated southern tier of New York and adjacent parts of Pennsylvania; from the rural backwaters of the Upper South and frontier Midwest; and eventually, from both rural and manufacturing districts of Wales, Lancashire, and Scandinavia. Few of these converts were well-to-do, well educated, or well established in settled communities. They were mainly small farmers who had been displaced by commercial agriculture, and footloose tradesmen and mechanics who had been bypassed by expanding markets, a people already uprooted and highly mobile, long engaged in a search for communal and religious security.

Because the Mormon search for authority took religious form, it is easy to miss its radical challenge to American secular values and institutions. Yet religion, through previous centuries of European history, had been the vehicle for the most revolutionary movements of the common people. And in pre–Civil War America, the aspirations of dispossessed and alienated people flowed into movements like those of the Millerites, who anxiously awaited the Advent of Christ in 1843, and of the ascetic Shakers, who believed that the millennium had already begun, and whose cooperative communities promised to transcend all economic and sexual rivalry.

Of the various groups of nonconformists and "come-outers," the Mormons were the most aggressive, committed, and inventive. Against a pluralistic, permissive, and individualistic society they pitted a higher authority that rested on a rock of unswerving certainty and conviction. Divine revelation resolved all doubts. Revelation, embodied in the Doctrine and Covenants, established the church hierarchy that eventually made it easier for Brigham Young to dispense with new revelations. (As Smith's successor, he wisely limited himself to one). But institutions based on divine authority also cast doubt on the legitimacy of popular sovereignty and of all established governments. In the words of Orson Pratt, a Mormon

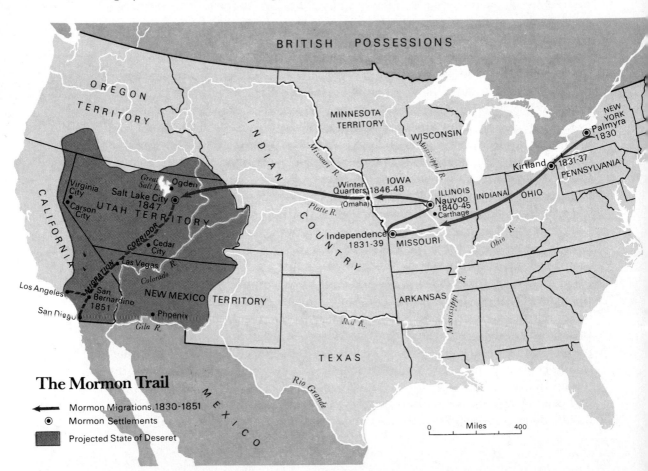

The Mormon Trail

◀── Mormon Migrations, 1830-1851
◉ Mormon Settlements
▨ Projected State of Deseret

theologian and leader: "Any people attempting to govern themselves by laws of their own making, and by officers of their own appointment, are in direct rebellion against the Kingdom of God."

From their own experience with savage persecution, the Mormons understandably took a bleak view of the morals of the unredeemed part of the world. Again, Orson Pratt went far beyond the rhetoric of the most extreme revivalists and abolitionists:

Wickedness keeps pace with the hurried revolutions of the age. Gross immoralities, drunkenness, debaucheries, adulteries, whoredoms, self-pollutions, sodomy, beastliness, thieving, robbing, murdering, have engulfed the nations in a deathly ocean of filth, and have transformed our world into a sickly, disgusting, loathsome cesspool of corruption. . . . In the midst of this overwhelming crime, millions of long-faced hypocritical, heaven-daring priests and clergy will roll up their sanctimonious eyes and insult the great Majesty of heaven, under pretense of thanking him that they live in such a glorious day of Gospel light.

At times, this angry perspective led Mormons to look forward to the day when "the United States government, and all others, will be uprooted, and the kingdoms of this world will be united in one." Yet the Mormons fervently believed that Columbus, the Pilgrim fathers, and George Washington had all been part of God's plan to prepare people to receive and understand the glorious message revealed to Joseph Smith. Mormon leaders would probably have preferred total independence from the threatening administrations of Polk and his successors, but they were confident that they represented the true interests of the United States.

On a moral and ideological level, which Protestant America reduced to the level of cheap scandal, the Mormons' defiance could not be ignored. For the Mormons, plural marriage had been sanctioned by the Bible and later revelations. To them, the institution buttressed the social order of the kingdom of God. What seemed licentious to Eastern upholders of law and morality was for the Mormons a prime support of law and morality. The Mormons could not openly defend polygamy until they had achieved geographic security in Utah. Even there they continued to mute two other doctrines that their enemies inflated into supposed evidence of outright subversion. According to their enemies, the Mormons' communal economy subverted private property, encouraged wholesale theft, and excluded non-Mormon enterprise from Utah. Far worse, the Mormons had shown little Christian forbearance in response to persecution. They had not only looked for strength from the blood of their martyrs, but had promised "blood atonement" to their enemies.

It would be a distortion, however, to think of the Mormons as would-be revolutionaries. Initially, the movement gave expression to the folk culture of rural New England and upstate New York—the legends regarding the origins of the Indians and mysterious "moundbuilders," and the popular superstitions connected with witch-hazel sticks, "seer stones," and other magic devices that might uncover riches of some sort on heavily mortgaged and unproductive farms. Smith had been engaged in such activity before he unearthed the golden plates. Digging for material treasure corresponded spiritually with a desperate quest for a better life, for the almost-forgotten security of an authoritative church, a united community. Mormonism was radical only so far as it reminded America of what the nation had lost. It was "progressive" to the extent that it prepared its disciples to adjust to the modern world. No other American denomination so fully incorporated the "Protestant ethic" of work. In "The Word of Wisdom," Smith merely advised his followers in 1833 to abstain from liquor, tobacco, and hot drinks. Three years later the church began a slow process of imposing the rule as a matter of discipline, much as the artisans of Philadelphia and other cities appropriated the cause of temperance as a symbol of their own self-discipline and modernized values.

Despite many points of dissent, Mormonism had much in common with the developing culture of pre–Civil War America. The Mormons' theocratic ideal was only an extreme version of the ideal of Lyman Beecher and countless other evangelists who insisted that rampant democracy must be guided by a higher moral force. Like other Americans, Mormons believed that mankind possessed

BRIGHAM YOUNG, 1801–1877

(Library of Congress.)

divine potentialities, that material progress prepared the way for God's kingdom on earth, and that God revealed His will through history and through natural means. Largely for these reasons, the Mormons found it possible to interpret their material success as evidence of divine favor. Not without long and bitter struggle, after the Civil War, did the Mormons finally surrender their ideals of an economic united order, plural marriage, and the political kingdom of God. What they received in exchange was confirmation that the Mormon mission had always been the mission of the United States.

In retrospect, then, Mormonism was at once a radical protest against the values of an individualistic, competitive, uprooting, and disinheriting world, and a vehicle of solidarity and authority that enabled its members to adjust to that world. During the pre–Civil War decades no other movement, with the exception of the Southern crusade to vindicate Negro slavery, posed so serious a challenge to the ideology of the industrializing, urbanizing, and modernizing North. The Mormons probed the outermost limits of tolerance, the violent limits where dissent verged on treason, and finally established their own fragile asylum beyond but soon within America's geographical frontiers. Unlike the South, they escaped the major confrontation of civil war. But their unique success required a prolonged accommodation and ultimate capitulation to the civilization against which the South finally waged civil war.

The Benevolent Empire: Missions and Asylums

Like Mormonism, the first stage of secular reform was a response to the breakdown of social rules and moral authority associated with a hierarchical, patronage society. William Lloyd Garrison, who later came to symbolize the radical liberating movements of the second stage of reform, began his career in the 1820s as a lowly but ardent champion of the societies that made up the Benevolent Empire. Like the wealthy philanthropists who supported these organizations, Garrison deplored the rising "mobocracy," the "lawless multitude" who enjoyed liquor, violence, profanity, sexual vice, and vulgar entertainment, and he embraced reform as a way of restoring "the government of God" in America. American social reform originated in the crusade to purify public morals and to find new means, such as the asylum and penitentiary, for inculcating habits of regularity, sobriety, obedience, and responsibility.

Unlike the Mormons, reformers aspired to be leaders and transformers of the dominant secular society. Although they sought to gather together like-minded promoters of virtue, they originally gave no thought to withdrawing from a sinful society in order to practice virtue. Most of the leaders of the Benevolent Empire were men of economic and educational attainment. They could think of themselves, under "normal" circumstances, as the natural leaders of their communities. They tended to idealize the New England heritage of ordered and homogeneous communities governed by educated clergy and magistrates. Above all, they looked increasingly to Britain for models of "practical Christianity" and organized reform.

Despite the wide differences between British and American society, American reform movements cannot be understood without reference to British precedents. During the turbulent years of the French Revolution and Napoleonic wars, the Evangelical party within the Church of England succeeded in identifying the cause of England with the cause of "practical Christianity"—Christianity put into practice as organized philanthropy and a reformation of public morals. Much as the American clergy had earlier succeeded in linking evangelical Protestantism with the American Revolution and with republican ideology, so the British Evangelicals succeeded in linking the defeat of Napoleon and the suppression of domestic radicalism with a staggering organizational program to Christianize the nation and the world.

Although organized philanthropy had a long history in Britain, the Napoleonic years witnessed a qualitative change as well as an explosive expansion in the number and size of organizations. Cooperating with the Quakers and other religious dissenters, the Evangelicals won the blessings of the government and the increasing support of the aristocracy for their mission to saturate the lower classes with religious literature, to bring relief to repentant sufferers, to suppress drunkenness, vice, lotteries, and ungodly amusements. One of the ultimate objectives was to unite rich and poor by an affectionate bond of philanthropy, as a substitute for the traditional deference that even in England had begun to decay.

The British and Foreign Bible Society, founded in 1804, became the model for nonsectarian organizations committed to the ideal of "Christian unity." The Bible Society also pioneered in highly specialized organization as it acquired women's auxiliaries, skilled and professional agents, and teams of "visitors" assigned to specific towns, districts, and streets to collect funds, interview poor families, and distribute Bibles. This kind of systematic division of labor, later to form the core of Mormon community organization in Utah, was soon adopted by hundreds of British societies, not all of them run by Evangelicals. There were societies to promote Christianity among the Jews, observance of the Christian Sabbath, universal peace, and the abolition of slavery; societies to suppress immorality, infidel publications, juvenile delinquency, and cruelty to animals; societies to aid the indigent blind, the industrious poor, orphans of soldiers and sailors, and "Poor, Infirm, Aged Widows, and Single Women, of Good Character, Who Have

"GO YE INTO ALL THE WORLD"

A certificate given to contributors to the Presbyterian Board of Foreign Missions. At the left are pictured a New England church and factories; at the right, scenes from Burma, the site of the most publicized early American mission. (*American Antiquarian Society.*)

Seen Better Days." The English, who seem to have outdone the Americans as a nation of joiners, even launched the Society for Returning Young Women to Their Friends in the Country.

In the early nineteenth century Britain appeared suddenly to have moved into the vanguard of humanitarianism. The Evangelicals won particular prestige from their leadership in abolishing the African slave trade, a triumph hailed in 1807 as "a Magna Charta for Africa." William Wilberforce, who for years had led the great parliamentary campaign for abolition, was known as "the conscience of his country." What made Wilberforce particularly appealing to American reformers was that he had remained independent of political parties but belonged to sixty-nine benevolent societies. Even Sir James Mackintosh, a liberal who, unlike Wilberforce, had some sympathy for French rationalism, predicted that Wilberforce's example would inspire hundreds of thousands: "How noble and sacred is human nature, when made capable of achieving such truly great exploits!"

Most Americans continued to think of England as a nation of tyranny and political corruption, and remained suspicious of any alleged humanitarian change of heart. But the New England clergy, who had fought their own battle against French atheism and rationalism, eagerly welcomed any news of England's moral

此乃神之主言未以勢未以乃也強以我靈者軍之神言是矣

This is the word of the Lord; not by might nor by power, but by my Spirit, saith the Lord of hosts.

GO YE INTO ALL THE WORLD AND PREACH THE GOSPEL

The people which sat in darkness saw great light; and to them which sat in the region and shadow of death, light is sprung up.

If any man have not the spirit of Christ, he is none of his.

transformation. Confronted by the collapse of Federalist political power, by the growing force of public opinion, and by increasing ambiguity over the relation between church and state, they seized on the organizational apparatus of British benevolence as a providential means for securing control of American culture. With the aid of allies from other parts of the Northeast, these New England ministers and reformers succeeded in domesticating the British Evangelical spirit and in institutionalizing it in New York City, Philadelphia, and regions stretching from the Erie Canal to Illinois.

Many of the original organizers of the Benevolent Empire were students or young graduates of Andover Theological Seminary in Massachusetts, founded by Congregationalists in 1809 as an antidote against Harvard's drift toward liberal, rationalistic religion (Unitarianism). The Andover group included several leaders. Adoniram Judson helped set up the American Board of Foreign Commissioners for Foreign Missions (1810), the nation's first great agency for foreign missionary work. After traveling to England to study English missionary organizations, Judson joined the nation's first group of missionaries to India and served for many years in Burma. Samuel Mills, also one of the founders of the American Board, publicized the need for domestic missions in the Mississippi valley and then helped to launch the American Bible Society (1816) and the American Colonization Society (1817). After visiting England and receiving advice and sanction from Wilberforce and the Evangelicals, Mills proceeded to West Africa, where he negotiated with tribal chieftains for the site of a colony (Liberia) for America's free blacks. Justin Edwards, one of the organizers of the New England Tract Society (1814), which soon distributed hundreds of thousands of religious tracts and moralistic books for children, in 1826 called the national convention at Boston that formed the American Society for the Promotion of Temperance. Louis Dwight, who traveled the country as an agent for the American Bible Society, became so shocked by the squalor and disorder of jails that he became a leading crusader for the Auburn penitentiary system of total silence, close surveillance, and solitary confinement at night—a system, Dwight maintained, that "would greatly promote order, seriousness, and purity in large families, male and female boarding schools, and colleges."

These Andover reformers had much in common with serious-minded young ministers and laymen who had attended Yale or Princeton, or no college at all. In the Benevolent Empire they worked closely with men like Jeremiah Evarts, a graduate of Yale and a lawyer who increasingly devoted his energies to editing the anti-Unitarian *Panoplist*, to promoting foreign missions, and to combating intemperance, Sabbath-breaking, and the government's forcible removal of Indians to the West. The same causes attracted Arthur and Lewis Tappan, wealthy New York merchants. They had received no advanced education but had grown up in Northampton, Massachusetts, having a mother who worshipped the memory and doctrines of Jonathan Edwards, and an uncle, a professor of divinity at Harvard, who hailed Wilberforce as the leading guide to "ardent piety and patriotism and philanthropy." Andover's Samuel Mills easily collaborated with the Reverend Robert Finley, a Princeton graduate, a Presbyterian evangelical, and the chief founder of the American Colonization Society ("I know," Finley said, "the scheme is from God.") One of Finley's students and disciples, Theodore Frelinghuysen, tried very hard to become the American Wilberforce. The only serious evangelical in the United States Senate, Frelinghuysen was known as "the Christian statesman" and served terms as president of most of the benevolent societies. But New Jersey elected Frelinghuysen to only one term in the Senate, and when he ran as the national Whig candidate for Vice-President in 1844, the Benevolent Empire was giving way to the Democrats' expansionist empire in the West.

The earlier movement to enforce the Christian Sabbath reveals some of the basic concerns of the Benevolent Empire as well as the obstacles that prevented the emergence of the much hoped-for "Christian party in politics." In 1810 Congress had passed a law requiring the mail to flow seven days a week, in order to meet the critical business demands for faster communication. Sunday mail service immediately drew fire from Lyman Beecher and other New Englanders, but it only provoked national debate when the completion of the Erie Canal dramatized the undesirability of continuous, week-long transportation and commerce. For devout Christians the Sabbath evoked memories of a less hurried, agrarian past. For harried merchants, uneasy over their own success and total immersion in worldly pursuits, the silent Sabbath became a reassuring symbol of moral legitimacy. This one day in the week should proclaim, as one enthusiast expressed it, "a truce to the absorbing cares and sordid passions of men; it invites them to hold communion together as fellow pilgrims of time, the heirs of immortality, the children of the skies."

It is significant that Sabbatarian reform originated in the boom town of Rochester, not in the long-settled urban areas of the seaboard. Rochester's established clergy had come from New England and New Jersey, where a quiet Sabbath had been enforced by custom and law. But the Erie Canal passed directly under the windows of Rochester's First Presbyterian Church, and the rowdy boatmen made no effort to lower their voices during the hours of Sunday prayer. In 1828 the town's leading ministers, real estate magnates, and entrepreneurs enlisted Lyman Beecher and Lewis Tappan in a national crusade to persuade Congress to enforce the laws of God. The movement was historically important because it polarized "serious Christians" against the multitude; because it prepared the way for an axis between wealthy New York philanthropists and social activists inspired by the revivals of Charles Grandison Finney; and because it marked the transition between distributing Bibles and resorting to direct political and economic action. It should also be emphasized that Rochester lay at the heart of the Burned-Over District and that the Sabbatarian movement coincided with the Anti-Masonic crusade, Finney's revivals, the perfection and extension of the Auburn penitentiary system, and the birth of Mormonism.

The more dramatic and spectacular protests of later abolitionists have tended to obscure the dissent, conflict, and testing of still flexible social rules and boundaries that the first-phase, or missionary-type, reforms involved. The Sabbatarian movement, for example, threatened financial loss to owners of boat lines, ferries, taverns, theaters, and stores, much as the temperance movement threatened not only brewers, distillers, and distributors but also thousands of grocers and store-keepers whose customers expected a free pick-me-up as a sign of hospitality. Like the more militant temperance reformers, the Sabbatarians urged true Christians to boycott offending proprietors. Between Buffalo and Albany they also established their own six-days-a-week Pioneer Stage Line, a counterpart of the special temperance hotels and of the abolitionist shops that sold only produce made by free labor. These anti-institutions, which were almost uniformly unsuccessful, were essentially asylums: they were intended to be sanctuaries—virtuous, disciplined environments set off from a chaotic and corrupting society—and models for the world to imitate. But like other reformers, the Sabbatarians were also committed to an imperial mission. Setting a precedent for later abolitionists, they organized a great petition campaign to persuade Congress to stop the Sunday mails. Like the abolitionists, they warned that unless Congress acknowledged a "higher law," the nation had little chance for survival:

If this nation fails in her vast experiment, the world's last hope expires; and without the moral energies of the Sabbath it will fail. You might as well put out the sun, and think to enlighten the world with tapers. . . . as to extinguish the moral illumination of the Sabbath, and break this glorious mainspring of the moral government of God.

As the Mormons later discovered, many Americans were suspicious of people who laid claim to the moral government of God. By 1831 the Benevolent Empire had failed in its most daring and secular missionary efforts to regenerate society. Lyman Beecher had early defined the supreme goal of the missionary and benevolent societies: to produce "a sameness of views, and feelings, interests, which would lay the foundation of our empire upon a rock." But this purpose smashed against the rocklike resistance of people who refused to be homogenized, especially under Yankee direction. In response to the Sabbatarians' petitions, Congress agreed with a Kentucky senator who drafted a report stating that the legislature was not "a proper tribunal to determine the laws of God." The colonization movement did much to unite Northern urban blacks, who angrily affirmed in conventions that they would not accept a foreign asylum as a substitute for justice: "We will never separate ourselves voluntarily from the slave population of this country." "Let not a purpose be assisted which will stay the cause of the entire abolition of slavery." Resistance also appeared in the South and Southwest, paradoxically, where an antimission movement appealed to "Hard-Shell" Baptists and rural Methodists who found no Biblical sanction for benevolent societies and who bitterly resented any attempts to bring religious instruction to the blacks. Further, as one Baptist cautioned the Sunday School Union, "our backwoods

THE FLOATING CHURCH OF THE REDEEMER

Built during the 1850s for the Churchmen's Missionary Association for seamen in the port of Philadelphia. *(Library Company of Philadelphia.)*

folks" simply could not understand the pretentious talk of the "young men come from the eastern schools."

The Benevolent Empire solved no social problems. It received no credit for legislative triumphs of the magnitude of Britain's abolition of the slave trade (1807) and gradual emancipation of West Indian slaves (1833). By 1837, moreover, internal conflicts had shattered all hope of a united front among evangelical reformers. Growing divisions over slavery simply intensified suspicions and grievances that had long been festering on every level. Sectarian rivalry weakened the supposedly nondenominational societies that Northern Presbyterians and Congregationalists had always controlled. In 1837, when the Presbyterian Church separated into conservative Old School and liberal New School camps, the economic depression also sharply reduced philanthropic gifts and thus further weakened the various organizations of the Benevolent Empire.

Nevertheless, the true revolution in American reform came in the 1820s with the militancy, the dedication, the towering expectations, and the phenomenal organization of the evangelical societies. It came when an agent of the Sunday School Union, addressing the well-to-do members of the Bible Society, repeated a British motto: "Not by exactions from the opulent but by the contributions from all"; when the organizers of foreign missions called for a "vast body like a host prepared for war"; and when the benevolent societies developed essentially the same techniques used in modern fund-raising campaigns: a week set aside for a concentrated "drive"—precise directions and goals given to teams of men and especially women who had the leisure and fortitude to canvass streets and districts building by building. The real revolution came with the mass production of literally millions of moralistic tracts, priced cheaply enough to undersell all commercial publications and marketed by discounts and other techniques that were far ahead of commercial practice. Two years before the rise of radical abolitionism, the Tappans had financed a staggering campaign to flood the entire city of New York with one tract a month. By 1830, in short, the evangelicals had devised all the apparatus needed for a massive conquest of American culture.

Although there were ethnic, class, and geographical boundaries to the conquest, few invading armies or political revolutions have had such a far-reaching effect on an entire society as the Benevolent Empire did. In 1834 the Temperance Society estimated that they had over 1.25 million members; in 1836 the American Tract Society alone sold over 3 million publications. In 1843, in response to the depression that had filled New York City's streets with thousands of beggars and vagrants, the New York Association for Improving the Condition of the Poor imitated the earlier models and sent teams of agents to gather information district by district and to distribute food, fuel, and clothing. The needy recipients could not help but be influenced, one way or another, by the association's links with the temperance movement, its conviction that poverty was a problem of individual morality, and its commitment to make the poor "respectable." The benevolent societies constituted a powerful acculturating force, in the West and parts of the South as well as in the Northeast. Though usually classified as "conservative," these missionary reformers thought of themselves as carriers of light and civilization. The liberalization of Protestantism had released them from the intellectual and theological bonds of determinism, from the notion that the social order must remain static or be convulsed in destructive change. If they harbored little sympathy for sinners who refused to be saved, their ideology rested on a belief in human perfectibility, strongly laced with hopes for an American millennium. The great missionary drives of the first stage of reform extended the frontiers of an American evangelical culture, "liberating" millions from cultures that expected less from humanity.

Radical Abolitionism

The issue of Negro slavery finally dramatized the limitations of the Benevolent Empire. Even by 1830 there was a striking discrepancy between the American missionary reformers' millenarian visions of the future and their whispered despair, usually frosted with hypocrisy, concerning Negro slavery.

Harsh facts made the discrepancy increasingly noticeable. Despite the legal prohibition in 1808 of slave imports from Africa, the number of slaves in the United States increased from approximately 1.5 million in 1820 to over 2 million in 1830. This figure represented almost one-sixth of the total United States population and more than twice the number of slaves in the British and French West Indies. The number of free blacks grew during the 1820s from about 234,000 to 320,000. The Pennsylvania Prison Discipline Society pointed out that free blacks accounted for less than 4 percent of Pennsylvania's population but made up more than half the state s prison inmates (the accuracy of these statistics is open to serious question).

In 1830 the American Colonization Society transported 259 free blacks to Liberia. Yet most missionary reformers still regarded colonization as the only solution: "We must save the Negro," as one missionary put it, "or the Negro will ruin us." Racial prejudice permeated the Benevolent Empire, and was by no means foreign to later radical abolitionists. Yet the new and significant fact was the rising tide of virulent racism among the working classes of the North. Prejudiced as they may have been, many leaders of the colonization movement were sincere opponents of slavery who abhorred the growing racism of the Northern masses and who saw deportation as the only realistic means for preventing racial war in the North and for inducing Southern planters to free their slaves.

But beginning in 1829 a series of events suggested that white America could not solve its racial problem by shipping a few hundred free blacks each year to Liberia. In 1829 David Walker, a Boston black who sold clothes and who belonged to the Massachusetts General Colored Association, published the revolutionary *Appeal,* which justified slave rebellion and which warned white Americans, "for your own good," that if justice were delayed blacks would win their liberty "by the crushing arm of power." The pamphlet created a furor and copies soon appeared among blacks in the Deep South. Then in 1831 Nat Turner led a band of fellow slaves on a rampage that killed almost sixty whites in Southampton County, Virginia. At the end of the same year the British colony Jamaica experienced one of the bloodiest slave revolts in West Indian history. In Britain, mass demonstrations continued to demand the immediate and unconditional emancipation of West Indian slaves. When Parliament responded in 1833 with monetary compensation to slaveowners to cover part of the financial loss of emancipation, and with an apprenticeship plan to prepare slaves for freedom, a few Americans concluded that effective political action of any kind required a mammoth mobilization of public opinion.

To the young abolitionists who began to appear in the early 1830s, Negro slavery was the great national sin. Lyman Beecher and other evangelical leaders had earlier perceived dueling, intemperance, and Sabbath-breaking in much the same way. Theodore Dwight Weld, the son of a Connecticut minister and a convert and close associate of Charles Grandison Finney in upstate New York, personally symbolized the fusion of American revivalism with British antislavery influence. His most intimate friend and religious model was Charles Stuart, a visiting British reformer who worked with Finney's disciples in the Burned-Over District and then in 1829 returned to England to throw himself into the battle for slave emancipation. After being exhorted by Stuart to take up the cause in

America, Weld shifted from temperance and educational reforms to abolitionism, becoming one of the most fearless and powerful lecturers in the region from Ohio to Vermont. Early in 1833 he wrote a letter to William Lloyd Garrison, whom he knew only by reputation, illuminating the meaning of slavery as sin:

> That no condition of birth, no shade of color, no mere misfortune of circumstances, can annul the birth-right charter, which God has bequeathed to every being upon whom he has stamped his own image, by making him a *free moral agent,* and that he who robs his fellow man of this tramples upon right, subverts justice, outrages humanity, unsettles the foundations of human safety, and sacrilegiously assumes the prerogative of God; and further, tho' he who retains by force, and refuses to surrender that which was originally obtained by violence or fraud, is joint partner in the original sin, becomes its apologist and makes it the business of every moment to perpetuate it afresh, however he may lull his conscience by the vain plea of expediency or necessity.

Weld's statement sums up the ethical imperative that underlay the second phase of reform. It sprang from three fundamental convictions: that all men and women have the ability to do what is right, and are therefore morally accountable for their actions; that the intolerable social evils are those that degrade the image of God in man, stunting or corrupting the individual's capacities for self-control

WILLIAM LLOYD GARRISON, 1805–1879

(Harvard College Library.)

and self-respect; that the goal of all reform is to free individuals from being manipulated like physical objects. As one Garrisonian put it, the goal of abolitionism was "*the redemption of man from the dominion of man*"

That the abolitionists were almost wholly concerned with ideals was at once their greatest strength and greatest weakness. America was supposedly a nation of doers, of practical builders, framers, drafters, organizers, and technicians. The overriding question, in abolitionist eyes, was whether the nation would continue to accommodate itself to a social system based on sheer violence. To propose rational plans or to get embroiled in debates over the precise means and timing of emancipation would only play into the hands of slavery's apologists. What the times required, therefore, was "an original motive power" that would shock and awaken public opinion, create a new moral perspective, and require legislators to work out the details, however imperfectly, of practical emancipation. In 1831 Garrison admitted: "Urge immediate abolition as earnestly as we may, it will alas! be gradual abolition in the end. We have never said that slavery would be overthrown by a single blow; that it ought to be we shall always contend." From the very outset, the abolitionism of the 1830s embodied an unseen contradiction that was intimately related to the uncertain boundaries and expectations of American society. On one level, the abolitionists realistically saw that the nation had reached a dead end on slavery. Instead of gradually withering away, as earlier optimists had hoped, the evil had grown and had won increasing acquiescence from the nation's political leaders and most powerful institutions. Therefore, the abolitionists took on the unpopular role of agitators, of courageous critics who stood outside the popular refuges of delusion, hypocrisy, and rationalization. In 1830 the acrimonious Garrison went to jail for writing libelous attacks against a New England merchant who was shipping slaves from Baltimore to New Orleans. After Arthur Tappan had paid his fine and secured his release, Garrison in 1831 founded *The Liberator* in Boston, hurling out the famous pledge: "*I will be* as harsh as truth, and as uncompromising as justice. . . . I am in earnest— I will not equivocate—I will not excuse—I will not retreat a single inch—AND I WILL BE HEARD."

Although *The Liberator* had an extremely small circulation and derived most of its support from black subscribers in the Northeast, Garrison succeeded in being heard. In the South especially, newspaper editors seized the chance to reprint specimens of New England's radicalism, accompanied by their own furious rebuttals. Even before the end of 1831, the Georgia legislature proposed a reward of $5,000 for anyone who would kidnap Garrison and bring him south for trial. Garrison also championed the free blacks' grievances against the Colonization Society, which he had once supported, and mounted a blistering attack against the whole conception of colonization. He pointed out that the hope for colonization confirmed and reinforced white racial prejudice, which was itself the main barrier the abolitionists faced in the North. Largely as a result of Garrison's early and independent leadership, the American Anti-Slavery Society, founded in 1833, committed itself to at least a vague legal equality of whites and blacks and to a total repudiation of colonization.

But having practically declared war against the values, institutions, and power structure of Jacksonian America, the abolitionists continued to think of their societies as simple extensions of the Benevolent Empire. They assumed that they could quickly win support from churches and ministers; that they could persuade the pious, influential, and respectable community leaders that racial prejudice was as harmful as intemperance. Then, after mobilizing righteous opinion in the North, they could shame the South into repentance. Abolitionists did not think of themselves as provokers of violence and disunion. Rather, it was slavery that had brought increasing violence and threats of disunion. A national commitment to emancipation would ensure harmony and national union. Nor could abolitionists think of themselves as revolutionaries; by historical definition, the evangelical conscience was an antidote to revolution. Yet the abolitionists could not move beyond the limits the Benevolent Empire had established

without losing much of their potential rearguard support and finding themselves in no-man's-land. That they made the plunge at all was a tribute to their courage and to their moral realism. That they marched forth under so many illusions was largely the result of one supreme illusion: the conviction that the same antislavery principles and determination that had triumphed in Great Britain would have similar consequences in the radically different social structure of Jacksonian America.

Like the wealthy British philanthropists, Arthur and Lewis Tappan moved from various benevolent causes to the cause of immediate emancipation. But by 1832 philanthropists in Great Britain had won the support of the established order as well as of middle-class public opinion. In America, precisely because the

Tappans had wealth and prestige, they were viciously attacked for encouraging radicals like Garrison and for betraying the common interests that had allowed elites in different sections to do business with one another. Mass rallies in the South pledged as much as $50,000 for the delivery of Arthur Tappan's body, dead or alive. In New York City, business leaders vainly pleaded with the two brothers, whose lives were being repeatedly threatened by 1834. In that year, prominent New Yorkers cheered on a mob of butcherboys and day laborers who smashed up Lewis Tappan's house and burned the furnishings. Only the unexpected arrival of troops prevented an armed assault on the Tappans' store.

Anti-abolitionists played on popular suspicions of England, charging that men like George Thompson, an English friend of Garrison's, had been sent "to foment discord among our people, array brother against brother . . . to excite treasonable opposition to our government . . . to excite our slave population to rise and butcher their masters; to render the South a desert, and the country at large the scene of fraternal war." Abolitionists continually invoked the ideals of the Declaration of Independence and portrayed themselves as fulfilling the Revolution's promise. But their enemies styled themselves as Minute Men defending American liberties. The mob riots of the Revolutionary period appeared to sanction the anti-abolitionist riots that spread across the North in the 1830s. For the most part this mob violence was carefully planned, organized, and directed toward specific goals, such as the destruction of printing presses and the intimidation of free blacks. The leaders were "gentlemen of property and standing"— prominent lawyers, bankers, merchants, doctors, and local political leaders of both parties. In most towns and cities the white abolitionists and free blacks had little chance of getting protection from the forces of law and order. The colonizationists, already weakened by financial difficulties and internal division, took the lead in accusing the abolitionists of being "amalgamationists" who would not stop short of encouraging black men to woo the daughters of white America.

It was this bugaboo that brought the Northern crowds into the streets and that also lay behind the abolitionists' most dramatic break with the Benevolent Empire. Lane Theological Seminary, in Cincinnati, was meant to be one of the Empire's crowning achievements, a beachhead of benevolence on the Ohio River, a staging ground for the missionary conquest of the West. Arthur Tappan paid Lyman Beecher's salary as president of the seminary. He also paid the way for Theodore Weld, then thirty-one, to attend the school as a student. Early in 1834 Weld conducted at Lane an eighteen-day soul-searching revival on the question of slavery. After converting many students and nonstudents, including Southerners like James G. Birney, to the doctrine of immediate emancipation, Weld led his band into the slums housing the black residents of Cincinnati, where they set up libraries, conducted evening classes, and fraternized with the city's "untouchable" caste. In Weld's view, educational institutions had a duty to train minds for the new "era of disposable power and practical accomplishment." A national meeting of college presidents and representatives of higher education, however, unanimously agreed that all antislavery agitation should be suppressed on America's campuses.

To the Tappans' dismay, Lyman Beecher, who was still a supporter of colonization, acquiesced in the decision of Lane's board of trustees to get rid of Weld and the other antislavery leaders. The break with Beecher and the Benevolent Empire was complete. Almost all the Lane students walked out of the seminary with Weld. Some ended up in Arthur Tappan's newly financed college, Oberlin. But many joined Weld as traveling agents for the American Anti-Slavery Society, of which Arthur Tappan was president, braving showers of rotten eggs and stones in order to address the American public.

As a product of the Benevolent Empire, abolitionism drew on and perfected the tested techniques of mass communication. By 1835 the new steam press and other technological improvements had reduced the cost and increased the volume of publication. In 1834, for example, the Anti-Slavery Society distributed 122,000 pieces of literature: in 1835 the figure rose to 1.1 million. Mailing lists included some 20,000 Southerners. Southern crowds seized and burned much of this mail, but they could do nothing about the itinerant abolitionist lecturers in the North, the "antislavery bazaars," the auxiliary societies for ladies and children, or the flood of propaganda in the form of medals, emblems, broadsides, bandannas, chocolate wrappers, songs, and small children's readers. The use of such media was not without effect. The number of antislavery societies grew from about 200 in the spring of 1835 to 527 in 1836.

Yet the campaign also provided a target for diffuse anxieties that had been generated by the first appearance of modern methods of organization, promotion, and manipulation.

FAIR....FAIR !!!

THE LADIES' ANTI-SLAVERY COMMITTEE are most happy to announce to the citizens of Syracuse and vicinity, that they have received very elegant additions to what has been prepared in this place, from the ladies of Rochester, Waterloo, Cazenovia, Utica, Albany, and many other places, making up in all a most desirable and splendid assortment of

USEFUL AND FANCY ARTICLES,

which will be sold at reasonable market prices. The Committee most confidently invite the patronage of the humane and philanthropic to come and buy; remembering that it is for the poorest of the poor—even the POOR SLAVE.

☞The doors will be open at 10 o'clock on Tuesday morning, August 1st, and the sales will continue two days.   Admittance 12 1-2 cents.

SOIREE.

A Soiree will be given at the Fair on the evening of August 1st, in commemmoration of the WEST INDIA EMANCIPATION.

₊ Doors open at 7 o'clock—Collation at 8.—Speeches from the most accomplished orators of Boston and other places.

ELIZABETH RUSSELL, Syracuse;
P. S. WRIGHT, Utica;
MARY SPRINGSTEAD, Cazenovia;
SARAH VAN EPS, Vernon ;
ABBY MOTT, Albany.

ANTI-SLAVERY BAZAAR BROADSIDE

The antislavery movement offered increasing opportunities for active participation and was particularly effective in mobilizing middle-class women. (*American Antiquarian Society.*)

The media, by appealing directly to women and children, bypassed the authority of fathers, husbands, teachers, and ministers. The abolitionists were, after all, applying the techniques of the Bible and tract societies to a revolutionary purpose—a purpose that threatened one of the nation's chief capital investments as well as a national system for racial control. In 1835 the nation panicked over the seemingly inexhaustible funds and propaganda machinery of the Anti-Slavery Society. From Boston to Illinois, from Albany to the Deep South, the alarm went out from governors, mayors, senators, and business leaders. Amos Kendall, the postmaster general, gave private approval to South Carolina's censorship of the mails. At the end of the year President Jackson called on the Northern states to suppress abolitionist agitation and asked Congress for a law that would prohibit, "under severe penalties," the "unconstitutional and wicked attempts" to circulate antislavery tracts through the mail.

Then in 1837 an event occurred that tested the meaning of abolitionism for American society. Elijah P. Lovejoy, a New England abolitionist who, like the Mormons, had been driven out of Missouri, tried to found a state antislavery society at Alton, Illinois, across the river from slaveholding Saint Louis. With the connivance of local authorities, who were under great pressure from Missouri, mobs destroyed two of Lovejoy's printing presses. Lovejoy and his men refused to back down, and shot a local youth while defending a new printing press still at the warehouse. The mob set fire to the warehouse and then killed Lovejoy when he ran outside. This celebrated martyrdom had two important effects. It dramatized the issue of civil liberties and won new support and sympathy for the abolitionists, who had the means to publicize the affair as the Mormons could not publicize the martyrdom of Joseph Smith. It also forced abolitionists to face the meaning of nonresistance, and thus hastened a fundamental division over principles and tactics.

The Garrisonians played a critical part in this complex division and development of American reform. Garrison, who had nearly been lynched in 1835 by a Boston mob, had become convinced that violence was a disease infecting the entire body of American society. Whenever the nation faced any issue of fundamental morality, such as the treatment of Indians, blacks, or dissenters, it resorted to the principle that might makes right. The only Christian response, Garrison maintained, was to renounce all coercion and adhere to the perfectionist ideal of absolute nonresistance. If abolitionists tried to oppose power with power, as Lovejoy had attempted, they were certain to be crushed. They would also dilute their moral argument, since the essence of slavery was the forcible dominion of man over man. In 1838 Garrison and his followers formed the New England Non-Resistance Society, a group which condemned not only defensive war and capital punishment, but every kind of coercion including lawsuits, prisons, and insane asylums, unless designed solely for "cure and restoration."

Garrison's extreme pacifism appealed to many women. Among the most important converts, for example, were Sarah and Angelina Grimké, two articulate sisters who had earlier been converted to Quakerism and abolitionism in Philadelphia, after abandoning their father's South Carolina plantation. Because they could speak of Southern slavery from personal experience, the Grimkés had a striking effect on New England audiences. But in 1837 they boldly lectured to mixed audiences of men and women, an offense that outraged clergymen and conservative reformers who believed that women should move within precisely defined boundaries. The Grimkés attacked the hypocrisy of conservative abolitionists who scoffed at biblical justifications for female subservience. The Garrisonians convinced the Grimkés that the Christian "principles of peace" were at the root of all reform; the Grimkés helped to convince the Garrisonians that the same principles applied to the "domestic slavery" of women to men.

What began to emerge in New England abolitionism, then, was a radical repudiation of all limits imposed on the individual by the threat of force. Negro slavery and racial oppression were merely extreme manifestations of an evil embodied in the patriarchal family, the criminal law, and the police power of the state. By 1843 Garrison concluded that majority rule was simply the rule of superior power, with no protection for human rights, that the Union had always been a compact for the preservation of slavery, and that the Constitution was therefore "a covenant with death, and an agreement with Hell." The Garrisonians demanded withdrawal from corrupt churches and from all complicity with the corrupt government. Calling for disunion with the South, they also crossed the threshold of symbolic treason and declared themselves enemies of the Republic.

In interesting ways the Garrisonians' rhetoric paralleled the rhetoric of the Mormons. "The governments of the world," Garrison announced in 1837, "are all anti-Christ." Yet by 1845 he also cast off the Old Testament, arguing that God could never have sanctioned slavery and violence. The Old Testament, in the words of one of his followers, was "no more the work of God than the Koran, or the Book of Mormon." Instead of moving beyond the geographic frontiers to establish his own kingdom of God, Garrison defended a pinnacle of moral independence within a hostile society. He did this by appropriating two of the society's cherished ideals and pushing them to their ultimate extreme. First, he transformed the evangelical ideal of "disinterested benevolence," or selfless love, into a doctrine of extreme pacifism. He could thus expose the worldly compromises of the Benevolent Empire and attack all forms of coercion in the name of noncoercion. Second, he defended the secular idea of freedom of speech by deliberately provoking society to define its boundaries of tolerance. In both ways he tested the outermost limits of permissible dissent.

Much of the social ferment of the 1840s had nothing to do with the Garrisonians' radical challenge, and much of the Northern population remained unaffected. Yet suddenly new things seemed possible, new ways of thinking and acting seemed worth trying. The nation had never before witnessed such frothy experimentation, such gusty defiance of received wisdom, or such faith in the spontaneous love and harmony that could arise if human nature could only be liberated from all institutional restraints.

Female abolitionists, most of whom had served apprenticeships in the temperance movement, discovered that the majority of male reformers still defended forms of bondage based on sex. In 1840 the issue of women's participation in abolitionist conventions brought an irreparable split in the American Anti-Slavery Society, which the more conservative Tappan faction abandoned to the Garrisonian radicals. By the early 1850s a bold feminist movement, led by Elizabeth Cady Stanton, Lucretia Mott, Lucy Stone, and Susan B. Anthony, focused attention on women's legal and economic disabilities, which in some respects resembled those of Negro slaves (married women, for example, had only just begun to acquire the right to own property and in most states they had yet to win a right to their own earnings, and to sue in court). Some radical feminists denounced the prevailing system of marriage as licensed prostitution and likened the family to an embryo plantation in which every woman was a slave breeder and a slave in the eyes of her husband.

Self-assertion also burst the structure of the temperance movement, which had already been weakened by bitter disputes over biblical sanctions for drinking wine. Groups of reformed alcoholics began organizing "Washingtonian societies" that appealed to classes and subcultures totally foreign to the traditional and elitist

ELIZABETH CADY STANTON

In 1840 she traveled to London with her husband, abolitionist Henry Brewster Stanton, to the first World's Antislavery Convention where the issue of women's participation sharply divided the convention. Subsequently, she and Lucretia Mott led the first women's rights convention in the U. S. held at Seneca Falls, New York, in July, 1848. (*American Antiquarian Society.*)

temperance organizations. Like fugitive slaves, the ex-drunkards told rapt audiences what hell was really like, sometimes reenacting the agonies of delirium tremens. Conservative temperance leaders tried to use and patronize the Washingtonians, much as some white abolitionists tried to use and patronize fugitive slaves. But the temperance societies never felt comfortable with the former victims of intemperance, or with the boisterous showmanship that induced thousands of disreputable-looking people to pledge themselves, at least temporarily, to total abstinence.

Consolidation: Political Antislavery

The notion of three phases of reform is helpful in giving a sense of the overall direction of change, but it cannot be rigidly applied to specific decades or movements. For example, the feminism of the 1850s typified the second-phase goal of liberating every individual from prescribed identities and from the coercions of law and custom. This goal was symbolized by the daring "bloomers," or pantalets, worn by feminist leaders. But during the same decade the temperance movement typified the third reform stage of appealing to the public interest and of pressuring various state agencies to enforce licensing or prohibition laws. The movement was dominated by the example of Neal Dow, whom Horace Mann hailed as "the moral Columbus." Dow, a combative political manipulator, secured in Maine in 1851 the first state law prohibiting the manufacture or sale of alcoholic beverages. Most Northern and Western states soon adopted their own "Maine laws." But by 1857, after bitter political struggles that overlapped those between nativists and immigrants, the laws had been repealed except in Michigan and in five New England states.

In the antislavery movement there were no clearcut lines between second and third-phase styles of reform. Nevertheless, by the mid-1840s there was a distinct shift away from anarchistic defiance and towards an accommodation to American political and religious institutions. The abolitionists' quest for political power involved both a dilution of their moral purpose and a need to capitalize on the fear that Southern expansion was a direct threat to Northern civil liberties and to all the aspirations of evangelical reform. Political antislavery soon became fused with the sectional conflicts arising from the Mexican War.*

The Liberty party, which ran James G. Birney for President in 1840, was essentially an antiparty, founded on the conviction that the regular parties had temporarily become the tools of the Slave Power, an alleged conspiratorial alliance of Southern planters and their Northern minions. The Libertymen blamed the Slave Power for the depression, for an erosion of civil liberties, and for most of the ills that the nation had suffered. They were vague on the precise measures

*See Chapters 17 and 18.

a Liberty administration would adopt for eradicating slavery, but they assumed that a victory at the polls would destroy the stranglehold of the Slave Power conspiracy and soon restore the nation to former purity. Even in 1840, however, Birney compromised the party's "one-ideaism," by giving substantive replies to questions on the tariff, bank, and other issues. After capturing only a small fraction of the potential antislavery vote in 1840 and 1844, he called for a broad "reform party" with numerous planks in its platform. An abolitionist party would thus be a recasting of the older evangelical ideal of a "Christian party."

Factional divisions actually helped to assimilate abolitionism into Northern society. Since in the 1840s there was no unified movement or common party line, Northerners were free to choose the brand of abolitionism that suited them best. They could move outside traditional church walls with Garrison or with the learned and eloquent Unitarian reformer, Theodore Parker. They could join the burgeoning groups of less militant abolitionists within the Northern Methodist and New School Presbyterian churches. They could declare themselves independent from American politics, vote for the Liberty party, Liberty League, or Free Soil party, or support Whig or even Democratic candidates who might do something tangible even if small.

By 1848 the more extreme political abolitionists had arrived at the position that the Constitution gave Congress both the power and duty to abolish slavery in the Southern states. But in that year most abolitionists saw more hope in the broadly coalitionist Free Soil party, which at most promised to remove all federal sanctions for slavery by abolishing the institution in the District of Columbia, by excluding it from the territories, and by employing all other constitutional means to deprive it of national support.

The Free Soil platform of 1848, unlike the platform of the Liberty party, ignored the legal discriminations that free blacks suffered. Many of the dissident Northern Democrats who helped form the party had consistently opposed Negro suffrage and had exploited white racist prejudices. Yet black delegates were welcomed at the party's national convention, and in Massachusetts, Free Soilers not only attacked racial segregation in public schools and transport, but also demanded repeal of a law prohibiting interracial marriage.

Northern blacks found this ambiguity of purpose increasingly frustrating. Black conventions had led the way in denouncing the Colonization Society. Black abolitionists had worked closely with the antislavery societies in New England and New York. Beginning with Frederick Douglass's celebrated escape from slavery in 1838 and enlistment as a lecturer for Garrison's Massachusetts Anti-Slavery Society in 1841, fugitive slaves performed the indispensable task of translating the abolitionists' abstract images into concrete human experience. The lectures and printed narratives of Douglass, William Wells Brown, Ellen Craft, Henry Bibb, Solomon Northup, and other escaped slaves did much to undermine Northern beliefs that slaves were kindly treated and contented with their lot. The wit and articulate militancy of black abolitionists like Henry Highland

Garnet and Charles Lenox Remond, coupled with the towering dignity of Douglass, also helped to shake confidence in the popular stereotypes of Negro inferiority.

Yet black abolitionists faced constricting walls and physical dangers that made the difficulties of white abolitionists seem like child's play. When Douglass and Garrison traveled together on lecture tours, it was Douglass who experienced constant insult, humiliation, and harassment. Black Vigilance Committees could help a small number of fugitives find their way to Canada and relative security— and blacks were the main conductors on the so-called Underground Railroad— but except in Massachusetts, black abolitionists had little leverage for loosening the rocklike edifice of discriminatory law. Instead, white abolitionists kept pressuring blacks to keep a low profile, to act the part assigned them by white directors, who presumably knew the tastes of an all-white audience, and to do nothing that might spoil the show.

THE FUGITIVE SLAVE'S SONG, 1845

Frederick Douglass's escape from slavery was celebrated in a popular song. The illustration, however lacking in skill, is notable for breaking away from the standard racist caricature of blacks. *(American Antiquarian Society.)*

THE FUGITIVE'S SONG,

WORDS
composed and respectfully dedicated, in token of confident esteem to

FREDERICK DOUGLASS
A Graduate from the
"PECULIAR INSTITUTION"
For his fearless advocacy, signal ability and wonderful success in behalf of
HIS BROTHERS IN BONDS.
(and to the FUGITIVES FROM SLAVERY in the)
FREE STATES & CANADAS.
by their friend
JESSE HUTCHINSON JUNr.

Abolitionism gradually became more acceptable in the North only by accommodating itself to white racism. Many blacks increasingly resented the attention given to women's rights, nonresistance, and communitarian experiments, and the almost conspiratorial caution that immobilized the progress of racial equality in the North. They also resented the patronizing attitudes of white abolitionists who might defend abstract equality while treating blacks as inferiors who had to be led. In the 1840s black leaders gradually cast off the yoke that had bound them to a white man's cause and tried to assert their own leadership. In 1843, at the Convention of the Free People of Color held at Buffalo, Garnet openly called for a slave rebellion, arguing that it was a sin to submit voluntarily to human bondage. Douglass adhered to his own version of nonresistance until 1847, when he broke with Garrison over the propriety of founding a black abolitionist newspaper, the *North Star*. In the same year Garrison sadly reported that Remond had proclaimed that "the slaves were bound, by their love of justice, to RISE AT ONCE, en masse, and THROW OFF THEIR FETTERS."

But speeches were one thing, action another. Black abolitionists had always looked to voting, a right few blacks possessed, as the most promising route to power. For the most part, therefore, they supported the Liberty party in 1840 and 1844, and the Free Soil party in 1848. The drift of antislavery politics, however, was away from black civil rights in the North and emancipation in the Southern states and toward a walling off to the Western territories—a walling off, in all probability, of free blacks as well as slaves. It is not surprising that by 1854 a few black leaders like Martin Delaney were talking of a separate black nation, or that blacks who had proudly defended their American heritage and right to American citizenship were beginning to reconsider voluntary colonization.

But by 1854 many Northern whites had also concluded that the Slave Power had seized control of America's manifest destiny, thereby appropriating and nullifying the entire evangelical and millennial mission.* Moreover, the Fugitive Slave Law of 1850, requiring federal agents to recover fugitive slaves from their sanctuaries in the North, directly challenged the North's integrity and its new self-image as an asylum of liberty. Even the aloof Emerson wrote in his journal: "This filthy enactment was made in the nineteenth century by men who could read and write. I will not obey it, by God." The arrival of

*For this critical contest over admitting Kansas as a slave state, see Chapter 18, pp. 624–630.

CAUTION!!
COLORED PEOPLE OF BOSTON, ONE & ALL,
You are hereby respectfully CAUTIONED and advised, to avoid conversing with the
Watchmen and Police Officers of Boston,
For since the recent ORDER OF THE MAYOR & ALDERMEN, they are empowered to act as
KIDNAPPERS AND Slave Catchers,
And they have already been actually employed in KIDNAPPING, CATCHING, AND KEEPING SLAVES. Therefore, if you value your LIBERTY, and the *Welfare of the Fugitives* among you, *Shun* them in every possible manner, as so many *HOUNDS* on the track of the most unfortunate of your race.
Keep a Sharp Look Out for KIDNAPPERS, and have TOP EYE open.
APRIL 24, 1851.

PEOPLE'S MEETING!!

CITIZENS OF CHESTER COUNTY:—The time has arrived when it is necessary to make preparations for the next general election. In view of existing circumstances, it is proper that the citizens of this County

WITHOUT RESPECT TO PARTY,

Should meet for the purpose of Conferring together, and forming such an organization as will give effect to their views on important public questions. A fixed and resolute determination has recently been manifested on the part of the

SLAVE POWER,

To extend its dominion—to carry its blighting influence to territory now free—to control the government of the nation, and make it subservient to its wicked designs. Compacts entered into, under circumstances the most solemn, have been violated; an extended territory, dedicated by the MISSOURI COMPROMISE to Freedom, in violation of faith and honor, has been thrown open to the traffickers in human flesh, who in disregard of law and order, have seized upon its fertile plains with a view of adding

OTHER SLAVE STATES TO THE UNION

And giving to the Slave Power an ascendency over freedom in the Nation. Experience has satisfied the people that while the emigration to this country of the peaceable industrious foreigner, should be regarded with favor, the facility with which persons reared abroad, under systems of government radically different from our own, approach the ballot box, and influence our elections, is an evil dangerous alike to the adopted and native citizen. A change in the

NATURALIZATION LAWS

Extending the probative period of the alien—the separation of Church and State in practice as well as in theory—the freedom of the government from all improper foreign influence—and the protection of the

AMERICAN LABORER

Are believed to be essential to the welfare of all classes of the people. All persons who are willing to co-operate upon the principles here indicated and which we believe to be those of a true democracy, are earnestly invited to meet at the

COURT HOUSE IN THE BOROUGH OF WEST CHESTER

On Saturday the 18th instant at ten o'clock A. M. August 1855.

U. V. Pennypacker,	Francis James,	Joseph Painter,	Wm. Butler,	Samuel Way,	James Sweney,
Hickman James,	William Hoopes,	Wm. Sweney,	N. Mendenhall,	John B. Brinton,	Isaac Thomas,
Jonathan T. Marshall,	Jesse C. Green,	Mordecai T. Ruth,	Wm. Darlington,	E. D. Haines,	J. B. Wood,
Joshua Darlington,	J. B. Jeffris,	Benj. J. Passmore,	Samuel S. Heed,	Wm. S. Kirk,	Reuben White,
Geo. F. Worrall,	C. P. Sweney,	Whildin M. Foster,	William Hoopes,	W. W. Sweney,	Wm. Windle,
Thos. W. Parker,	Wm. Whitehead,	C. M. Valentine,	Sam. J. Parker,	Z. C. Wollerton,	Thos. H. Hall.

Other names omitted for want of room.

federal "kidnappers" and the spectacle of blacks being seized in the streets invited demonstrations of defiance and civil disobedience. Increasing numbers of former moderates echoed Garrison's rhetoric of disunion, and an increasing number of former nonresistants called for a slave insurrection or predicted that the streets of Boston might "yet run with blood." Wendell Phillips, a Boston aristocrat and the most powerful of all abolitionist orators, rejoiced in the knowledge "that every five minutes gave birth to a black baby," for in its infant wail he recognized the voice that should "yet shout the war cry of insurrection; its baby hand would one day hold the dagger which should reach the master's heart."

In the 1850s Northern abolitionists finally learned a new and terrifying meaning of boundaries. If the Slave Power were not crushed by insurrection or expelled from the Union, they believed, it would surmount every legal and constitutional barrier and destroy the physical ability of Northerners to act in accordance with the moral ability that had been the main legacy of revivals. The Western territories were thus the critical testing ground that would determine whether America would stand for something more than selfish interest, exploitation, and rule by brutal power. All of the aspirations of the Benevolent Empire, of evangelical reformers, and of perfectionists of every kind could be channeled in a single and vast crusade to keep the territories free, to confine and seal in the Slave Power, and thus to open the way for an expansion of righteous liberty and opportunity that would transcend all worldly limits.

For large numbers of Northerners, largely Democrats by vote, this vision had little appeal. It did win the assent, however, of many other Northerners who were prepared to resist the Slave Power without believing either that slaveholding was sinful or that free blacks had a right to legal equality. Without the abolitionists, slavery would never have emerged as a moral problem. But the abolitionists finally won a hearing by dramatizing the irreconcilable conflict between the interests and cultures of North and South, not by generating a will in the North to cross the ideological borders that blocked the way to emancipating the slaves and to social justice.

Suggested Readings

David B. Davis, ed., *Ante-Bellum Reform* (1967), presents differing interpretations of reform and also an annotated bibliography. Though out of date, Alice F. Tyler, *Freedom's Ferment* (1944), is the only comprehensive survey. Whitney R. Cross, *The Burned-Over District* (1950), analyzes the origins of secular reform as well as of Mormonism and other religious movements.

Thomas F. O'Dea, *The Mormons* (1957), is the best introduction to Mormonism. Fawn M. Brodie, *No Man Knows My History: The Life of Joseph Smith* (1945), is also indispensable. Klaus J. Hansen, *Quest for Empire* (1967), is a brilliant account of the Mormons' efforts to prepare for a worldly Kingdom of God. Robert B. Flanders, *Nauvoo: Kingdom on the Mississippi* (1965), is a fascinating study of the Mormons' city-state in Illinois. A dramatic and authoritative narrative of the westward migration is Wallace Stegner, *The Gathering of Zion: The Story of the Mormon Trail* (1964). Leonard J. Arrington, *Great Basin Kingdom*

(1958), is a masterly account of the Mormon settlement of Utah. On polygamy, see Kimball Young, *Isn't One Wife Enough?* (1954). Norman F. Furniss, *The Mormon Conflict, 1850–1859* (1960), covers the so-called Mormon War.

There are no satisfactory general works on the relation between religion and secular reform. Important aspects of the subject are examined in Charles I. Foster, *An Errand of Mercy: The Evangelical United Front* (1960); Clifford S. Griffin, *Their Brothers' Keepers: Moral Stewardship in the United States* (1960); Timothy L. Smith, *Revivalism and Social Reform* (1957); and Bertram Wyatt-Brown, "Prelude to Abolutionism: Sabbatarian Politics and the Rise of the Second Party System," *Journal of American History 58* (1971), 316–41. The temperance movement, a critical link between evangelical religion and secular reform, is well described in John A. Krout, *The Origins of Prohibition* (1925). For a speculative interpretation by a sociologist, see Joseph R. Gusfield, *Symbolic Crusade: Status Politics and the American Temperance Movement* (1963).

The literature on abolitionism is voluminous. The historical precedents and background are covered in David B. Davis, *The Problem of Slavery in Western Culture* (1966); and *The Problem of Slavery in the Age of Revolution, 1770–1823* (1975). The best brief account of later abolitionism is Gerald Sorin, *Abolitionism: A New Perspective* (1972). Louis Filler, *The Crusade against Slavery* (1960), is the best comprehensive history. Gilbert H. Barnes, *The Anti-Slavery Impulse* (1933), is a dramatic and readable study, emphasizing the role of Theodore Weld and the Lane Seminary rebels. For an opposing and brilliantly argued view, see Aileen S. Kraditor, *Means and Ends in American Abolitionism: Garrison and His Critics on Strategy and Tactics* (1967). A similarly powerful and creative work is Lewis Perry, *Radical Abolitionism: Anarchy and the Government of God in Antislavery Thought* (1973). Leonard L. Richards, *"Gentlemen of Property and Standing": Anti-Abolition Mobs in Jacksonian America* (1970), keenly analyzes anti-abolition violence. Concerning civil liberties, see Russel B. Nye, *Fettered Freedom: Civil Liberties and the Slavery Controversy* (1963); and Thomas O. Morris, *Free Men All: The Personal Liberty Laws of the North, 1780–1861* (1974).

For the politics of antislavery, see Richard H. Sewell, *Ballots for Freedom* (1976), as well as the following biographical studies. Bertram Wyatt-Brown, *Lewis Tappan and the Evangelical War against Slavery* (1969); Betty Fladeland, *James Gillespie Birney: Slaveholder to Abolitionist* (1955); James B. Stewart, *Joshua R. Giddings and the Tactics of Radical Politics* (1970); Richard H. Sewell, *John P. Hale and the Politics of Abolition* (1965); Frank O. Gatell, *John Gorham Palfrey and the New England Conscience* (1963); Ralph V. Harlow, *Gerrit Smith* (1939); Edward Magdol, *Owen Lovejoy, Abolitionist in Congress* (1967); and David Donald, *Charles Sumner and the Coming of the Civil War* (1960). William Lloyd Garrison, who tried to abstain from political involvement, is the subject of two fine biographies: John L. Thomas, *The Liberator: William Lloyd Garrison* (1963); and Walter M. Merrill, *Against Wind and Tide: A Biography of William Lloyd Garrison* (1963).

Benjamin Quarles, *Black Abolitionists* (1969), is a pioneering study of a subject long neglected by historians. An important recent work is Jane H. Pease and William H. Pease, *They Who Would Be Free: Blacks' Search for Freedom, 1830–1861* (1974). For Frederick Douglass, see Arna Bontemps, *Free at Last: The Life of Frederick Douglass* (1971), and Douglass, *Life and Times of Frederick Douglass, Written by Himself* (1881).

Aileen S. Kraditor, ed., *Up from the Pedestal: Selected Writings in the History of American Feminism* (1968), is an excellent anthology. Eleanor Flexner, *Century of Struggle: The Women's Rights Movement in the United States* (1968), is a good survey, but should be supplemented by W. L. O'Neill, *Everyone Was Brave: The Rise and Fall of Feminism in America* (1970); Andrew Sinclair, *The Better Half: The Emancipation of the American Woman* (1965); and Page Smith, *Daughters of the Promised Land* (1970). For individual biographies, see Alma Lutz, *Created Equal: A Biography of Elizabeth Cady Stanton* (1973); Otelia Cromwell,

Lucretia Mott (1971); and Katharine Du Pre Lumpkin, *The Emancipation of Angelina Grimké* (1974).

David S. Rothman, *The Discovery of the Asylum* (1971), is a brilliant interpretation of reformatory institutions. The most imaginative study of early prisons is W. David Lewis, *From Newgate to Dannemora: The Rise of the Penitentiary in New York* (1965). Blake McKelvey, *American Prisons* (1936), is a more comprehensive reference. On the insane, the best guides are Helen E. Marshall, *Dorothea Dix: Forgotten Samaritan* (1937); and Gerald N. Grob, *Mental Institutions in America: Social Policy to 1875* (1973). For the reformer who did most for the deaf and blind, see Harold Schwartz, *Samuel Gridley Howe* (1956).

The classic work on the peace movement is Merle Curti, *The American Peace Crusade, 1815–1860* (1929), which should be supplemented by Peter Brock, *Pacifism in the United States: From the Colonial Era to the First World War* (1968).

On communitarian settlements, the best general works are Mark Holloway, *Heavens on Earth* (1951), and the relevant chapters in Donald D. Egbert and Stow Persons, *Socialism and American Life* (2 vols., 1952). The communitarian phase inspired by Robert Owen is masterfully covered by J. F. C. Harrison, *Quest for the New Moral World: Robert Owen and the Owenites in Britain and America* (1969). For the New Harmony experiment, see also William Wilson, *The Angel and the Serpent* (1964); and Arthur Bestor, *Backwoods Utopias* (1950). The best introduction to the Oneida community is Maren L. Carden, *Oneida: Utopian Community to Modern Corporation* (1969). Two other studies of unusual importance are Michael Fellman, *The Unbounded Frame: Freedom and Community in Nineteenth-Century Utopianism* (1973); and William H. Pease, *Black Utopia: Negro Communal Experiment in America* (1963).

17

Slavery and Expanding Boundaries

By the 1820s the institution of Negro slavery had come to dominate all aspects of Southern society. Apologies for slavery as an unfortunate though necessary evil were beginning to give way to aggressive self-justification. Paradoxically, as the South became increasingly isolated from the progressive ideology of the Western world, the rapid expansion of cotton cultivation helped to assure Southerners that their peculiar institution was indispensable to Northern and British industry. Accordingly, Southern slaveholders regarded their critics as ungrateful hypocrites who would literally bite the hand that fed them.

Although slavery had long been protected by various political and constitutional compromises, the compromises themselves rested on numerous tacit understandings. The North, for example, had accepted the legitimacy of slave property on the assumption that Southern leaders would do everything in their power to diminish and eventually eradicate the nation's moral burden. Beginning in 1820, sectional conflicts severely tested these understandings, and Southern leaders became increasingly convinced that their only security lay in fusing the expansion of slavery with America's republican mission. By portraying Britain as the chief enemy of slavery as well as of republican government, Southerners succeeded in wedding the cause of slavery with the nation's expanding "empire for liberty."

The Slave's World

During the 1820s the labor systems of North and South reached a final point of divergence. On July 4, 1827, various towns in New York State celebrated the legal emancipation of the few remaining New York slaves who had been born before July 4, 1799, and who had therefore not been freed by previous legislation. As a legal status, slavery lingered on in Pennsylvania and New Jersey, though confined to a diminishing number of aged and dependent blacks. For all practical purposes the 1820s marked the extinction of slavery in the states northeast of Delaware. The decade following the War of 1812 also witnessed the defeat of proslavery hopes in Indiana and Illinois.

But during the 1820s slave labor remained the key to agricultural expansion in the new states of Alabama, Mississippi, and Louisiana. It won national sanction in Missouri and became entrenched in the territories of Arkansas and Florida. It even spread, under the name of indentured servitude, into the fertile lands of

COTTON PLANTATION, BY C. GIROUX

Although Southern slaves cultivated sugar, rice, hemp, tobacco, and other crops, it was the cotton plantation that gave a distinctive stamp to nineteenth-century American slavery. *(Courtesy, Karolik Collection, Museum of Fine Arts, Boston.)*

eastern Texas, which Anglo-Americans were settling by invitation of the Mexican government. This southwestern expansion was fueled by the rising industrial demand for cotton and was made possible by the rapid natural increase of slave population. A self-reproducing labor force distinguished the South from the other slave societies of the New World, which remained dependent on the continuing importation of slaves from Africa.

The formative decade of the 1820s dramatically confirmed two other characteristics of American Negro slavery that had been gradually appearing since the 1790s: the peculiar institution became highly productive, efficient, and profitable as it expanded into frontier lands suitable for the cultivation of cotton; but it was now clearly sectional, having been legally confined to states and territories south of a latitudinal boundary extending from the Mason-Dixon line to the unsettled territories of the West.

In theory, the Southern slaveholder possessed all the power of any owner of chattel property. This power was limited only by state laws, which were generally unenforceable, protecting slaves from murder and mutilation; setting minimal standards for food, clothing, and shelter; and prohibiting masters from teaching slaves to read or allowing them to carry firearms or roam about the countryside. These slave codes acknowledged that bondsmen were human beings who were capable of plotting, stealing, fleeing, or rebelling, and who were likely to be a less "troublesome property" if well cared for under a regimen of strict discipline. Yet the laws also insisted that the slave was a piece of property that could be sold, traded, rented, mortgaged, and inherited. They refused to recognize the interests and institutions of slave community, to say nothing of the slave's right to marry, to hold property, or to testify in court

In practice, it proved impossible to treat human beings as no more than possessions or as the mere instruments of an owner s will. Most masters were primarily motivated by the desire for profit They wanted to maximize their slaves productivity while protecting the value of their capital investment, a value that kept rising with the generally escalating trend in slave prices. Accordingly, it made sense to provide a material standard of living that would promote good health and a natural increase in the size of slave families, and thus increase capital gains. It also made sense to keep the morale of slaves as high as possible, and to encourage them to do willingly and even cheerfully the work they would be forced to do in the last resort Convinced of the moral legitimacy of the system, most planters sincerely believed that their own best interests were identical with their slaves' best interests. They therefore sought to convince slaves of the essential justice of slavery, and expected gratitude for their acts of kindness, indulgence, and generosity, or even for restraint in inflicting physical punishment

But slaves were not passive, compliant puppets who could be manipulated at will. As human beings they had one overriding objective: self-preservation at a minimal cost of degradation and loss of self-respect. To avoid punishment and win rewards they carried out with varying degrees of thoroughness their owners'

OVERSEER DOING HIS DUTY

Benjamin Henry Latrobe, a distinguished architect and artist, captured in this sketch the arrogant power of the white overseer. *(Maryland Historical Society.)*

demands. A small minority may have been brainwashed into a submissive and childlike acceptance of their masters' authority. For the most part, however, the fawning, half-comical "Sambo" response was a role staged for a white audience. Black slaves became cunningly expert at testing their masters' will. They learned how to mock while seemingly to flatter; how to lighten unending work with moments of spontaneity, song, intimacy, and relaxation; how to exploit the whites' dependence on black field drivers and household servants; and how to play on the conflicts between their masters and white overseers. In short, they learned through constant experiment and struggle how to preserve a core of dignity and self-respect.

Although slavery "worked" as an economic system, its fundamental conflict of interests created a highly unstable and violent society. The great sugar planters in Louisiana and cotton planters in the Delta country of Mississippi, often employing over one hundred slaves on a productive unit, tried to merge Christian paternalism with a kind of welfare capitalism. They provided professional medical care, offered monetary rewards for extra productivity, and granted a week or more of Christmas vacation. Yet these same plantations were essentially ruled by terror.

Even the most humane and kindly planters knew that only the threat of violence could force gangs of field hands to work from dawn to dusk "with the discipline," as one contemporary observer put it, "of a regular trained army." Frequent public floggings reminded every slave of the penalty for inefficient labor, insubordination, or disorderly conduct. Bennet H. Barrow, a particularly harsh Louisiana planter, maintained discipline by ordering occasional mass whippings of all his field hands, by chaining offenders or ducking them under water, and even by shooting a black who was about to run away. Barrow also distributed generous monetary bonuses to his slaves and bought them Christmas presents in New Orleans. The South could point to far gentler masters who seldom inflicted physical punishment. Slaves understood, however, that even the mildest of whites could become cruel despots when faced with the deception or ingratitude of people who, regardless of pretenses to the contrary, were kept down by force, not love.

Masters also uneasily sensed that circumstances might transform a loyal and devoted slave into a vengeful enemy. It is true that white Southerners could congratulate themselves on the infrequency of serious insurrections, especially when the South was compared with Brazil and most of the Caribbean. Yet the French colony of Saint Domingue had enjoyed an even more secure history until 1791, when the greatest of all slave revolts had led to the creation of the black republic of Haiti. Toussaint L'Ouverture, the brilliant Haitian military leader, was until the age of forty-five the trusted, docile, and privileged slave of an unusually kind and indulgent master. The record showed that the South had no magic immunity from slave revolts. In 1822 South Carolina hanged thirty-five blacks after uncovering Denmark Vesey's plot for a full-scale insurrection, a plot that involved some of Charleston's most trusted household servants. Nine years later Nat Turner led some seventy slaves on a bloody rampage through Southampton County, Virginia. To the outside world Southerners presented a brave façade of self-confidence, and individual planters reassured themselves that their own slaves were happy and loyal. But rumors of arson, poisoning, and suppressed revolts continued to flourish. Alarmists frequently warned that outside agitators were secretly sowing discontent among the slaves. This widespread fantasy at least hinted at the truth; slavery not only had little sanction in the outside world, but the institution ultimately depended on the sheer weight of superior force.

The stereotyped image of the cotton plantation has distracted attention from the diversity of slave labor in the pre-Civil War South. It is too often forgotten that Negro slaves were in the vanguard of the rapidly expanding Southern frontier, clearing forests, draining swamps, plowing untilled soil, and building roads. They worked in lumber camps and sawmills; in lead mines, gold mines, and rock quarries; on river boats and cattle ranches. In the South Atlantic states slaves continued to grow rice, tobacco, wheat, and various food crops. But they also worked in textile mills, sometimes alongside free white laborers. In time they constituted nearly half the integrated work force at the Tredegar Iron Works in

Richmond and over half the four thousand iron workers in the Cumberland River region of Tennessee. In the 1850s Negro slaves were increasingly important in railroad construction and in the early industrialization of the South. In towns and cities as well as on plantations, they served as blacksmiths, carpenters, masons, and cooks. It seems likely that far more slaves would have been employed in industrial and urban occupations if there had not been a rising demand for field hands and if imported manufactured goods had not undercut traditional artisan skills.

The difficulties in generalizing about the slave's world are compounded by the geographic, climatic, and cultural diversities of the "South"—a region in which mountain highlands, pine forests, and swampy lowlands are all commonly traversed within a few hundred miles.

Almost half of the Southern slaveholders owned fewer than five slaves; 72 percent owned fewer than ten. The typical master could thus devote close personal attention to his human property. Many small farmers worked side by side with their slaves, an arrangement that might be far more humiliating for the slaves than being submerged in a field gang under delegated black authority. From the slave's point of view, much depended on the character of an owner, on the norms of a given locality, on the accidents of sale, and on the relative difficulty of harvesting cotton, rice, tobacco, or sugar.

Slave experiences covered a wide range from remarkable physical comfort and lack of restraint to the most savage and unrelieved exploitation. But to dwell on contrasting examples of physical treatment is to risk losing sight of the central horror of human bondage. As the Quaker John Woolman pointed out in the

AFRO-CAROLINIAN FACE VESSEL

During the mid-nineteenth century, slaves in Georgia and the Carolinas fashioned pottery jugs depicting the human face. Although it is difficult to assess how much of the African tradition survived in black American folk sculpture, these remarkably expressionistic pots bear strong similarities to wooden and pottery artifacts from West Africa. *(Courtesy Augusta Richmond County Museum.)*

eighteenth century, no human is saintly enough to be entrusted with total power over another. The slave is an inviting target for the hidden anger, passion, frustration, and revenge from which no human is exempt; a slave's work, leisure, movement, and daily fate depend on the will of another person.

Moreover, despite the numerical predominance of small slaveholders, most Southern slaves were concentrated on large farms and plantations. Over half belonged to owners who held twenty or more slaves; one-quarter belonged to productive units of over fifty slaves. In the South, slave ownership was the primary route to wealth, and the most successful planters cornered an increasing share of the limited human capital. Therefore, most slaves experienced fairly standardized patterns of plantation life.

By sunrise black drivers had herded gangs of men and women into the fields. The older children served as water carriers or began to learn the lighter tasks of field work. Slaves too old for field work tended the small children, along with the stables, gardens, and kitchens. This full employment of all available hands was one of the economies of the system that increased the total output from a planter's capital investment. Nevertheless, slaves often succeeded in maintaining their own work rhythm and in helping to define the amount of labor a planter could reasonably expect. Bursts of intense effort required during cotton picking, corn shucking, or the eighteen-hour-a-day sugar harvest were followed by periods of festivity and relaxation. Even in relatively slack seasons, however, there were cattle to be tended, fences mended, forests cleared, and food crops planted.

Negro slaves were saved from becoming mere robots in the field by the strength of their own community and evolving culture. There has long been controversy over the survival in North America of African cultural patterns. In contrast to Brazil, where continuing slave importations sustained a living bond with African cultures, the vast majority of Southern blacks were removed by several generations from an African-born ancestor. Yet recent research has uncovered striking examples of African influence in the Southern slaves' oral traditions, folklore, songs, dances, language, sculpture, religion, and kinship patterns. The question at issue is not the purity or even persistence of distinct African forms. In the New World all imported cultures have undergone blending, adaptation, and synthesis. The point to be stressed is that slaves created their own Afro-American culture, which preserved the most crucial areas of life and thought from white domination. Without such a culture, sustained by strong community ties, slaves could not have maintained a sense of apartness, of pride, and of independent identity.

African kinship patterns seem to have been the main vehicle for cultural continuity. As in West Africa, children were frequently named for grandparents,

SALE OF ESTATES, PICTURES AND SLAVES, NEW ORLEANS

Slaves were auctioned off along with other personal property when estates were sold to pay the taxes or other debts of a deceased planter. *(Library of Congress.)*

who were revered even in memory. Kinship patterns survived even the breakup of families. Strangers often took on the functions and responsibilities of grandparents, uncles, and aunts. The fictional portrayals of Uncle Tom and Aunt Jemima were not figments of the imagination; many younger slaves were cared and protected by "aunts" and "uncles" who were not blood kin. These older teachers and guardians passed on knowledge of a historical time, before the fateful crossing of the sea, when their ancestors had not been slaves. This historical awareness inspired hope in a future time of deliverance, a deliverance that slaves associated with the Jews' biblical flight from Egypt, with the sweet land of Canaan, and with the day of jubilee. In the words of one spiritual:

> Dear Lord, dear Lord, when slavery'll cease,
> Then we poor souls will have our peace;—
> There's a better day a-coming,
> Will you go along with me?
> There's a better day a-coming,
> Go sound the jubilee!

Historians have recently recognized how important the slave family was as a refuge from the dehumanizing effects of being treated as chattel property. The strength of family bonds is suggested by the thousands of slaves who ran away from their owners in search of family members separated by sale. The myth of weak family attachments is also countered by the swarms of freedmen who roamed the South at the end of the Civil War in search of their spouses, parents, or children, and by the eager desire of freedmen to legalize their marriages.

Nevertheless, the slave family was a highly vulnerable institution. Many slaveholders had moral scruples against separating husbands from wives or small children from their mothers, but even the strongest scruples frequently gave way to economic need. The forced sale of individual slaves in order to pay a deceased owner's debts further increased the chances of family breakups. In some parts of the South, it was common for a slave to be married to another slave on a neighboring or even distant plantation, an arrangement that left visitation at the discretion of the two owners.

In sexual relations there was a similar gap between moral scruples and actual practice. White planter society officially condemned miscegenation, and tended

DETAIL FROM "PLANTATION BURIAL." BY JOHN ANTROBUS, 1859

For the slave community no ritual was more humanizing and important than the burial of a deceased slave. (*The Historic New Orleans Collection.*)

to blame lower-class whites for fathering mulatto children. Yet there is abundant evidence that many planters, sons of planters, and overseers took black mistresses or sexually exploited the wives and daughters of slave families. This abuse of power was not as universal as abolitionists claimed, but it was common enough to humiliate black women, to instill rage in black men, and to arouse shame and bitterness in white women. At best, slave marriage was a precarious bond, unprotected by law and vulnerable to the will of whites.

The larger slave community provided some stability and continuity for the thousands of blacks who were sold and shipped to new environments. On the larger plantations one could find conjurers whose magic powers were thought to ward off sickness, soften a master's heart, or hasten the success of a courtship. There were black preachers who mixed Christianity with elements of West African religion and folklore. In the slave quarters particular prestige was attached to those who excelled at the traditional memorizing of songs, riddles, folktales, superstitions, and herb cures—who were carriers, in short, of Afro-American culture. These forms of oral communication allowed free play to the imagination, enabling slaves to comment on the pathos, humor, absurdity, sorrow, and warmth of the scenes they experienced. Together with the ceremonial rituals, especially at weddings and funerals, the oral traditions preserved a sanctuary of human dignity that survived the humiliations, debasement, and self-contempt that were inseparable from human bondage.

The South as a "Slave Society"

From 1820 to 1860 Negro slavery exemplified America's problems of defining boundaries—geographic, constitutional, cultural, and psychological. This was partly because the institution represented the most extreme form of unchecked power. For both master and slave, violence was the only ultimate appeal. The relation between master and slave was itself a continual testing of psychological boundaries, punctuated by brief intervals of compromise. On a different level, the continuing expansion of slavery as the dominant economic, social, and political institution of the South raised critical questions about the place of free blacks and nonslaveholding whites.

The meaning of the term *slave society* is best illustrated by the West Indian colonies of the eighteenth and early nineteenth centuries. There Negro slaves typically made up 90 percent or more of an island's population; political and social life was wholly dominated by large planters, their managers and agents, and the merchants who lived off the system. On the question of Negro slavery there was almost no dissent.

Parts of the South approximated this model: the swampy lowcountry of South Carolina and the Sea Islands; the fertile Black Belt, extending from Georgia to Louisiana; the Delta counties of Mississippi and the sugar parishes of lower Louisiana. At the opposite extreme, however, stood the extensive regions of

Geographical Distribution of Slaves in 1820

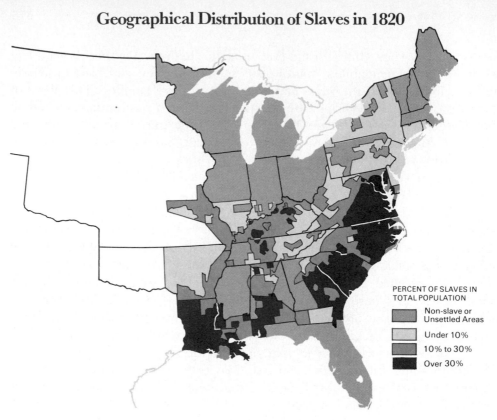

PERCENT OF SLAVES IN
TOTAL POPULATION

- Non-slave or Unsettled Areas
- Under 10%
- 10% to 30%
- Over 30%

Geographical Distribution of Slaves in 1860

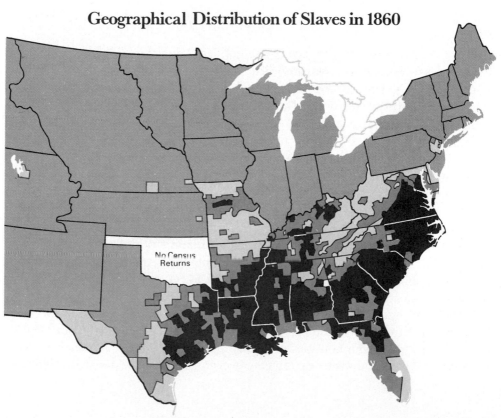

No Census Returns

eastern Tennessee and western Virginia (later to become the state of West Virginia) where Negroes, slave or free, were a rarity. Moreover, slavery was of marginal importance in large parts of Maryland, Kentucky, Missouri, and Arkansas. By 1850 there were fewer slaves in Delaware than there had been in New Jersey twenty years earlier; by 1860 fewer than two thousand slaves remained in Delaware, although the state had never enacted a law for gradual emancipation. The decline of slavery in most of the Upper South, together with attempts to legalize the institution in Indiana, Illinois, and Kansas, made it clear that the borders of the "Slavocracy" were neither permanent nor distinct.

Unlike the small and isolated West Indian islands, the sprawling South was anything but a uniform and monolithic society. In 1860 roughly ten thousand families belonged to the planter aristocracy, out of a white population of some 8 million. Fewer than three thousand families belonged to the wealthiest elite who owned over one hundred slaves. Barely one out of four white Southerners owned a slave or belonged to a family that did. Nor could most of the nonslaveholding majority be classed as hillbillies and poor whites. In addition to artisans, factory workers, and professionals, there were millions of small farmers who worked their own land or who grazed herds of cattle, pigs, and horses in the forests and open range of the public domain.

Yet except for a few isolated pockets, the South did become a slave society dominated politically and ideologically by a planter oligarchy. By 1860, millions of nonslaveholders believed that any serious threat to slavery was sufficient justification for Southern independence. Throughout the period, slaveholding remained the most widespread and obvious route to wealth and status. In the Southwest, particularly, the most enterprising nonslaveholders had reasonable hopes of acquiring land and becoming planters. In Louisiana and Texas, for example, planters often hired cowboys to herd thousands of cattle on the open range; some of these cowboys were successful enough to buy their own plantations. In other parts of the South small farmers looked with envy and admiration on the great planters, often distant relatives, who had struck it rich. Aside from kinship ties, which were stronger and more complex than in the North, small farmers often depended on a neighboring planter's cotton gin or political patronage; and they knew that in turn he depended for security on their services as armed patrols who searched the countryside for any unauthorized movement of blacks.

The planter class could also draw on a rich tradition of political leadership. In the North, possession of wealth did not ordinarily bring the obligation and privilege of personally exercising political power. But in the South the eighteenth-century connection between wealth and personal authority endured. Political leadership sprang directly from the ownership of slaves, which was supposed to provide leisure, a concern for public order, and a certain paternalistic self-assurance in exercising authority. The planter elite demonstrated skill in commanding the loyalty of nonslaveholding whites and also in imposing discipline within its own ranks. By the 1830s numerous Southern abolitionists, or simply Southerners with a strong distaste for slavery, had emigrated to the North or West after abandoning hope of challenging the dogma that Negro slavery was a necessary evil that should be discussed as little as possible. Some of these Southerners, such as Edward Coles, the Grimké sisters, and James Gillespie Birney, made important contributions to the Northern antislavery cause. But they left behind a society that increasingly preferred emigration to dissent.

The key to Southern white unity was race. Racial prejudice extended throughout the slave societies of the New World, but in Latin America prejudice was mitigated by relatively permanent social, political, and religious hierarchies that put rank above color. The South, like the rest of the United States, was an amorphous society dedicated in principle to an equality of opportunity but sensitive to the need for agreed-on boundaries. It was also a region that depended economically on a system of labor, that could easily be condemned on republican and libertarian principles. Racial doctrine, the supposed inferiority of Negroes, became the primary instrument for justifying the persistence of slavery, for rallying the support of nonslaveholding whites, and for defining the limits of dissent.

The key to racial policy was the status of free blacks. Before the nineteenth century this status had been ambiguous, the number of free blacks insignificant. By 1810, however, as a result of the emancipations that had accompanied and followed the Revolution, there were 100,000 free blacks and mulattoes in the Southern states. This group, the fastest-growing element in the Southern population, was beginning to acquire property, to found "African" churches and schools, and to assert its independence, especially in the Upper South. In response, white legislators tightened restrictions on private acts of freeing slaves in an effort to curb the growth of an unwanted population. A rash of new laws, similar to the later black codes of Reconstruction, reduced free Negroes to the status of slaves without masters. The new laws regulated their freedom of movement; prohibited their fraternization with slaves; subjected them to surveillance and discipline by whites; denied them the legal right to testify against whites; required them to work at approved employments; and threatened them with penal labor if not actual reenslavement. Paradoxically, free blacks continued to benefit from a more flexible status in the Deep South where they were fewer and where, as in the West Indies, they sometimes served as valued intermediaries between a white minority and a slave majority. Racial discrimination was most flagrant in the Upper South, where slavery was economically less secure.

This point helps to explain the fate of antislavery in the South. From the time of the Revolution a cautious, genteel distaste for slavery had been fashionable among the planters of the Upper South. This Jeffersonian tradition persisted even after the more militant abolitionists had been driven from the region and after Methodist and Baptist leaders had backtracked on various resolutions encouraging gradual emancipation. The desire to find some way of ridding the South of its "burden," or "curse," as the Jeffersonian reformers called it, was

OPERATION OF A WATERING CART, NATCHEZ, MISSISSIPPI, 1855

(The New York Public Library, Astor, Lenox and Tilden Foundations.)

perpetuated by the sons of affluent planters who went to New England to study, although it is worth noting that Jefferson himself feared the effects of such foreign study and founded the University of Virginia in part as a means of preserving loyalty to Southern institutions. The hope of removing the South's burden won assent from some of the progressive and cosmopolitan planters. Usually Whigs in politics, they shared the capitalistic values of Northern businessmen and were deeply troubled by the depletion of soil and economic decline of eastern Virginia and Maryland, to say nothing of the continuing loss of population to the Southwest. But the main foundation of this antislavery argument sprang from the conviction that Negro slavery, in the words of Thomas Marshall, son of the chief justice of the Supreme Court, was "ruinous to the whites." The institution was said to degrade the meaning of labor, thereby stifling industry, incentive, and progress. Marshall also affirmed, however, that the condition of the Negro slave compared favorably with that of "the laborer in any part of Europe," and that there was no reason for "humanity to weep for his lot." His compelling fear was that the whole country would be "inundated by one black wave, covering its whole extent, with a few white faces here and there floating on the surface."

Marshall uttered those words in 1832, in the Virginia legislature, during the only genuine debate over slavery that occurred in the pre–Civil War South. The debate was largely a response to Nat Turner's insurrection of 1831, which strengthened the hand of nonslaveholding groups who lived west of the Blue Ridge and who had various motives for challenging the political hegemony of tidewater planters. In 1832, however, there was not the slightest chance that Virginia would adopt a measure for gradual emancipation.

The Virginia legislative debates of 1832 are significant because they marked the ultimate limits to which reformers were able to push. The debates reaffirmed two cardinal rules: that Southern whites could challenge slavery only by acknowledging its relative benefits to blacks, at the supposed cost of white civilization; and that no proposal for gradual emancipation could be considered unless accompanied by assurances of compensation to slaveowners and the colonization abroad of all free blacks. The hope of deporting the entire black population continued to have some appeal in the Upper South, which could aspire to imitate the North as a "white man's country." The Lower South, however, had already committed itself to a biracial society, founded on permanent slavery, and saw colonization as abolitionism in disguise. Thus in 1832, Georgians and South Carolinians were enraged when Richmond newspapers reported to the entire South the antislavery and procolonization speeches delivered in the Virginia legislature. But by this time Northern abolitionists were also attacking the movement to colonize free Negroes, which they saw as a means of strengthening Negro slavery.

Despite their compromises and racial prejudice, Virginia's antislavery leaders found themselves in an untenable position. In 1832 the western nonslaveholding delegates suffered critical defeats, failing even to carry a resolution that would have stigmatized slavery as an evil that could not be dealt with at that time. More important, their line of argument opened the door for an aggressive defense of the peculiar institution. In an influential review of the debates, Thomas R. Dew, who taught political economy at William and Mary College, had no difficulty in exposing the total impracticality of colonization, in expanding on the admissions that slavery benefited Negroes, and in lampooning abstract notions of justice that could not consistently be applied to any concrete institution. Dew's essay provoked an eloquent rebuttal from Jesse Burton Harrison, one of the liberal young Virginians who had studied at Harvard and at Göttingen, in Germany. But Harrison soon moved to New Orleans and never again spoke out against slavery. Most Southern liberals took a similar path of retreat.

The most threatening form of Southern dissent appeared in Hinton Rowan Helper's *Impending Crisis of the South: How to Meet It* (1857), a book that assembled and updated all the traditional arguments against slavery as an economic blight and as the cause of impoverishment in the South, as compared with the North. Helper, a North Carolinian, also expressed a rabid hatred for blacks and urged that they be removed from the country. By 1857, however, even blatant racism could not prevent Helper from being branded a dangerous revolutionary. Helper fled to the North, where the Republican party exploited his book as effective propaganda.

Meanwhile, sectional conflict had committed many Southerners to the dogma that slavery was a "positive good." The proslavery argument ranged from appeals to ancient Greek and Roman precedents to elaborate biblical interpretations designed to prove that slavery had never been contrary to the laws of God. Drawing on the romantic and chivalric literary fashions of the time, Southern writers also tried to cast the plantation in the image of a feudal manor blessed with human warmth, reciprocal duties, knightly virtues, and a loyalty to blood and soil.

The most striking part of the proslavery ideology was its indictment of liberalism and capitalism, its well-documented charge that the prevailing rule in so-called free societies, as George Fitzhugh put it, was "every man for himself, and the devil take the hindmost." In his *Sociology for the South* (1854) and *Cannibals All!* (1857), Fitzhugh developed an incisive criticism of the philosophic premises of an individualistic, egalitarian society. He also examined the destructive historical consequences of dissolving the network of social and psychological boundaries that had once given mankind a sense of place and purpose. Fitzhugh's peculiar needs, as a social theorist evolving the most rigorous and consistent statement of the Southern proslavery argument, enabled him to present the master-slave relation as the only alternative to a world in which rampant self-interest had subjected a mass of propertyless workers to the impersonal exploitation of "wage-slavery." He was consistent enough to renounce racial justifications for actual slavery and to propose that the positive good of the institution be extended to white workers. But these arguments, however interesting theoretically, only showed how far Fitzhugh had moved from Southern public opinion and from social reality. Far from tolerating the enslavement of whites, the South refused to accept extremist proposals in the 1850s for expelling or reenslaving a quarter-million free Negroes. Yet nothing united the region more than its dedication to white supremacy. Fitzhugh's theories were better designed to expose the moral dilemmas of free society than to comprehend the actual complexities and contradictions of the South.

The most that can be said for the proslavery ideology is that it helped to confirm the South's more moderate conviction that even though slavery was not a positive blessing, emancipation in any form would be a disaster. Therefore those who favored emancipation were the enemies of all, including the slaves. Moral doubts persisted, especially in the Upper South. But after the 1830s the doubts were increasingly diverted from hesitant antislavery into dedicated efforts to reform, improve, and defend the peculiar institution. Owning slaves, according to the triumphant dogma, brought with it a sense of duty and burden—a duty and a burden that defined the moral superiority of the South; a duty and a burden nonslaveholders respected and were prepared to defend with their lives. That, perhaps, was the ultimate meaning of a "slave society."

"A Fire Bell in the Night": The Missouri Compromise

From the time of the Continental Congress, American leaders had understood that a serious dispute over slavery could jeopardize their bold experiment in self-government. Beginning with the Constitutional Convention, the entire structure of national politics had been designed to prevent any faction from subverting common national interests by posing a direct threat to Southern slaveholders. It is therefore not surprising that before 1819 slavery never became a central issue in national politics, though it was an issue that sat like an unactivated bomb in the minds of the foremost political leaders.

The agreement to keep the bomb unactivated rested on a number of unwritten understandings: the North would recognize the property rights of Southern slaveholders; the South would recognize slavery as an evil that should be discouraged and eventually abolished whenever safe and practicable. Changing circumstances, including the shifting balance of sectional power, required that these understandings be periodically tested. The tests took the form of brief congressional showdowns, during which representatives from the Lower South issued threats of disunion and even civil war: in 1790, over the reception of anti-slavery petitions; in 1798, over a proposal to extend to Mississippi Territory the slavery exclusion clause of the Northwest Ordinance; in 1804, over an attempt to prevent new slaves from being taken to Louisiana, which had just been purchased from France; and in 1807, over a proposal to free all slaves seized as contraband in accordance with the impending federal law prohibiting further importations from Africa. On each occasion the resulting compromise strongly favored the South. This political process demonstrated the Americans' remarkable ability to make pragmatic adjustments in the interest of national stability. Yet it depended on the dangerous assumption that Southern threats of disunion would always be met by Northern concessions, and that the threats should thus be understood as a familiar bargaining tactic.

The militancy of the Lower South's congressional leaders rested on a realistic estimate of the long-range future. For a time the North could afford concessions because Negro slavery seemed to endanger no vital Northern interests. But after 1815, humanitarian causes had increasing appeal in the North and an increasing number of Northerners expressed moral and patriotic misgivings over the westward expansion of slavery. Sooner or later the North might well acquire an anti-slavery sentiment sufficiently strong to encourage a political realignment along sectional lines. Although the Constitution had been framed to protect minorities from the tyranny of a majority, the courts alone could be of no avail against a majority coalition uniting humanitarian zeal with sectional self-interest. By 1820, as a result of rapid population growth in the North, the major slaveholding states held only 42 percent of the seats in the House of Representatives. Only the Senate could provide a firm bulwark against potential Northern encroachments, and the key to the Senate was new slave states. In the Senate, following the admission of Mississippi and Alabama, eleven slave states balanced eleven free states.

The Missouri crisis arose in February 1819, when the House was considering a bill that would enable the people of Missouri to draft a constitution and be admitted as a slave state. In 1820, slaves constituted nearly one-sixth of the territory's population. James Tallmadge, Jr., a New York Jeffersonian Republican, offered an amendment prohibiting the further introduction of slaves into Missouri and providing for the emancipation, at age twenty-five, of all children of slaves born after Missouri's admission as a state. Following prolonged and often violent debate, the House approved Tallmadge's amendment by an ominously sectional vote. The Senate, after equally violent debates, passed a Missouri statehood bill without any restrictions on slavery. The issue seemed hopelessly deadlocked.

Virginia now took the lead in militancy, trying to arouse a generally apathetic South to a common peril. "This momentous question," Jefferson announced from his retirement at Monticello, "like a fire bell in the night, awakened and filled me with terror." He feared it was the death knell of the Union, and spoke of the younger generation's betraying the sacrifices of "the generation of 1776," perpetrating "this act of suicide on themselves, and of treason against the hopes of the world." Along with Madison and other Virginia statesmen, Jefferson was convinced that the attempt to exclude slavery from Missouri was part of a Federalist conspiracy to create a sectional party and destroy the Union. He also pointed to the supreme danger of extending a boundary between free and slave territory:

A geographical line, coinciding with a marked principle, moral and political, once conceived and held up to the angry passions of men, will never be obliterated; and every new irritation will mark it deeper and deeper.

As Calhoun later observed, Jefferson's own proposed Ordinance of 1784, banning slavery from all the Western territories, was "the first blow—the first essay 'to draw a geographical line coinciding with a marked principle, moral and political.'"

The Missouri crisis was aggravated by a sense that understandings had been broken, veils torn off, and true and threatening motives exposed. The congressional debates rekindled the most divisive issues that had supposedly been settled in the Constitutional Convention, and thus raised the hypothetical question of disunion. This reenactment of 1787 was underscored by the prominence in the congressional debates of two of the Convention's surviving antagonists—Charles

Pinckney, who now insisted that Congress had no power to exclude slavery from even the unsettled territories; and Rufus King, the alleged leader of the Federalist plot, who now announced that any laws upholding slavery were "absolutely void, because contrary to the law of nature, which is the law of God."

It was a new generation of Northerners, however, who were faced with the need of reaffirming or rejecting the kind of compromises over slavery that had created the original Union. Like the Founding Fathers, the Northern majority in Congress could do nothing about slavery in the existing states. But there had been an understood national policy, they believed, enshrined in the Northwest Ordinance, committing the government to restricting the institution in every feasible way. This understanding had seemingly been confirmed by Southern avowals that slavery was an evil bequeathed by the past. The North had accepted the claims and expectations of the original slave states regarding the territories south of the Ohio River and east of the Mississippi. But Missouri occupied the same latitudes as Illinois, Indiana, and Ohio (as well as Kentucky and Virginia). To allow slavery to become legally entrenched in Missouri might thus encourage its spread throughout the entire West, to the detriment of free labor and industry. Southerners had long argued that the geographic diffusion of slavery would weaken the institution and lessen the chances of insurrection. In 1820 Daniel Raymond, a prominent political economist, gave the obvious reply: "Diffusion is about as effectual a remedy for slavery as it would be for the smallpox, or the plague." In the words of the New York *Daily Advertiser:*

THIS QUESTION INVOLVES NOT ONLY THE FUTURE CHARACTER OF OUR NATION, BUT THE FUTURE WEIGHT AND INFLUENCE OF THE FREE STATES. IF NOW LOST—IT IS LOST FOREVER.

Southerners agreed that the rules governing the admission of new states ultimately involved the self-definition of a nation, a process of legal self-definition to which no other nation had been subjected. For this very reason they were alarmed when Northern congressmen affirmed that the Constitutional guarantee to every state of "a Republican Form of Government" prohibited accepting Missouri as a slave state. The argument implied that Virginia and other Southern states fell short of "a Republican Form of Government" and would therefore not be admissible to a new Union subject to Northern definition. If this test held true, the Southern states would be reduced to a probationary and second-class status. If they accepted the Northern definition of a republican form of government, they had no choice but to take positive steps towards abolishing slavery or to face, like colonies, the punitive measures of an imperial authority.

Henry Clay, the Speaker of the House of Representatives, by exerting all the powers of his office and of his magnetic personality, finally achieved a compromise. Nearly all Southerners agreed that Congress could not impose conditions

HENRY CLAY, SPEAKING IN THE HOUSE OF REPRESENTATIVES

An idealized portrait of Henry Clay addressing an extraordinarily attentive House of Representatives. *(Library of Congress.)*

for the admission of new states without depriving them of a sovereignty equal to that of the original states. On the other side, despite Clay's efforts, Northern congressmen voted 87 to 14 to retain the restriction on slavery in Missouri. But the fourteen dissenters, coupled with four Northern absences, allowed the House to drop the antislavery clause by a close vote of 90 to 87. A small majority of Southern representatives, though very few from Virginia, were prepared as their concession to recognize the right of Congress to exclude slavery from the unorganized territories. During the initial Missouri controversy of 1819, John W. Taylor, of New York, had failed by a close vote in attaching an antislavery clause to the bill organizing Arkansas Territory. Taylor had then proposed excluding slavery from the remaining and unsettled portions of the Louisiana Purchase north of latitude 36° 30', the same latitude as the southern border of Missouri. In effect, this measure would have confined to Arkansas and Oklahoma any further expansion of slavery within the Louisiana Purchase. In 1820 the joint conference committee endorsed the proposal and both houses of Congress accepted it. These agreements also opened the way for admitting Maine as a free state,

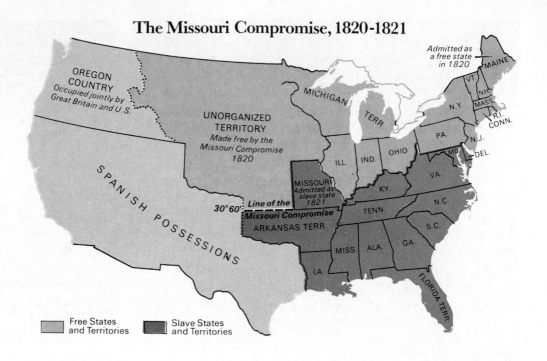

The Missouri Compromise, 1820-1821

OREGON COUNTRY
Occupied jointly by Great Britain and U.S.

UNORGANIZED TERRITORY
Made free by the Missouri Compromise 1820

SPANISH POSSESSIONS

Admitted as a free state in 1820 — MAINE

MICHIGAN TERR.

VT. N.H. N.Y. MASS. R.I. CONN.

PA. N.J.

ILL. IND. OHIO MD. DEL.

MISSOURI Admitted as slave state 1821

VA.

KY.

30°60' — Line of the Missouri Compromise

TENN. N.C.

ARKANSAS TERR. S.C.

MISS. ALA. GA.

LA.

FLORIDA TERR.

Free States and Territories   Slave States and Territories

since the Senate had refused to accept Maine's statehood until the House had abandoned efforts to restrict slavery in Missouri.

The press and legislatures of the North generally interpreted the Missouri Compromise as a victory for the South. The Northern congressmen who had yielded to Clay's blandishments were denounced as "doughfaces," a label first applied, with uncertain meaning, by John Randolph of Virginia. A new hope arose that public pressure could force Missouri to adopt a constitution providing for gradual emancipation. But the defiant Missourians drafted a constitution that prohibited the state legislature from emancipating slaves without the consent of their owners, and that barred free Negroes and mulattos from entering the state. Since free Negroes had been recognized as citizens by some of the Eastern states, this second provision violated the Constitutional guarantee that "the Citizens of each State shall be entitled to all Privileges and Immunities of Citizens in the several States." Northern congressmen now stood firm in rejecting the Missouri constitution and in effect the compromise that had already admitted Maine as a free state. Eventually, in 1821, Clay's skillful manipulation of committees produced a second compromise. Congress demanded a guarantee that no law would discriminate against the citizens of other states, a formality with which Missouri scornfully complied. The country applauded Clay as the "Great Pacificator," who had saved the Union.

But the Union would never be the same. In Southern eyes the uninhibited debates on slavery had opened a Pandora's box of dangers. The free blacks of

Washington had packed the galleries of the House and had listened intently to antislavery speeches. In 1822, during the trial of the conspirators associated with Denmark Vesey, a Charleston slave testified that Vesey had shown him an antislavery speech delivered by Rufus King, "the black man's friend." The link between the Missouri debates and a sizable slave conspiracy stunned South Carolina, confirming its worst fears. The cumulative effect was twofold: to unite all whites in the suppression of dangerous discussion, and to strengthen the hand of states' rights extremists and of the defenders of slavery as a positive good.

Domestic Dangers: Nullification and the Gag Rule

Even as early as 1820 the militant Richmond *Enquirer* proclaimed that the South and West owed it to themselves, to keep their eye firmly fixed on Texas: "If we are cooped up on the north, we must have elbow room in the West." For twenty-five years, however, the United States acquired no new territory that could upset the balance achieved by the Missouri Compromise. For a time the Old Southwest contained enough fresh land to counteract most slaveholders' fears of being walled in by geographic barriers.

Nevertheless, Southerners expressed a growing fear of federal power. Increasingly they warned one another of the inadequacy of constitutional safeguards against the hostile measures of some future antislavery national majority. Such anxieties were most explosive in South Carolina, which by 1830 had become the sputtering fuse that threatened to detonate the Union. In the 1830s South Carolina tried in particular to arouse the rest of the slaveholding South to the dangers of economic and ideological exploitation—to the dangers of being reduced economically to the status of a colony and then subjected, without defense, to the encroachments of subversive and alien ideas.

There were complex reasons for South Carolina's aggressiveness. No other state had acquired so dense a concentration of slaves or become so concerned over the peril of slave insurrection. In no other state had a planter aristocracy succeeded so well in commanding the allegiance of small slaveholding and nonslaveholding farmers; yet continuing conflicts over loyalty to state or nation dramatized the need for greater internal unity. The panic of 1819 had for a time shattered the prosperity of lowcountry planters and merchants, and economic depression persisted in the upcountry regions, which were not so fertile or productive as the cotton lands of Georgia, Alabama, and Mississippi. In both parts of the state, planters blamed protective tariffs for high consumer prices coupled with sagging foreign prices for rice and cotton. By 1832 South Carolina's anger over tariffs was aggravated by Garrisonian abolitionism, the Nat Turner insurrection, and the inflammatory debates over slavery in the Virginia legislature.

Moreover, of all Southern states South Carolina had the closest historical, geographic, and cultural ties with the British West Indies. Like the British islands, South Carolina had legally imported African slaves until a national government had prohibited the trade. South Carolinians were acutely aware that in Britain a seemingly innocuous movement to end the slave trade had been transformed, by 1823, into a crusade for slave emancipation. The West Indians, once a powerful faction in Parliament, had found no way of countering commercial policies that hastened their economic decline. By 1832 even the Constitutional checks and balances of the United States could not have protected the West Indian planters from an antislavery majority that had won control of the British government through skillful propagandizing of the middle class. The lesson was clear. The West Indian colonies had once been more valued than Canada or New England; in 1832 they faced possible devastation—a massive slave revolt broke out in Jamaica after Christmas, 1831—and certain economic ruin.

South Carolina could escape a similar fate, in the eyes of the state's leaders, only by forcing a redefinition of state sovereignty and of the limits of national power. The tariff issue made an ideal testing ground for the defense of slavery without risking the explosive effects of debating the morality of slaveholding. Because the power to tax and regulate trade could also be used to undermine slavery, the two questions had been linked in the Constitutional Convention of 1787 and in the Missouri debates Conversely, a state's power to nullify a tariff would be a guarantee not only against economic exploitation but also against direct or indirect interference with the peculiar institution. Calhoun, in his anonymous *Exposition* (1828), refined the theoretical arguments that were being put forth by South Carolina's most militant leaders. According to Calhoun the ultimate appeal, in any dispute between federal and state interests, must lie with the constituent power of a state convention, the same power that originally enabled the state to ratify the Constitution. Otherwise, a national majority, controlling the federal courts as well as Congress, could define the meaning of the Constitution and the limits of its own power. The tyranny of the majority could be curbed only if each state retained the right to consent to or nullify, within its own jurisdiction, the national majority's decisions. Calhoun carefully distinguished nullification from secession, and also granted, inconsistently, that a federal Constitutional amendment could nullify a state's nullification. He pointed to the means by which states might exercise an authentic, though limited, sovereignty while remaining within the Union.

The nullification controversy was complicated by the shifting pressures of state, sectional, and national politics. Calhoun, the Vice-President, sought to succeed Jackson as President, and many South Carolinians retained hopes of achieving their goals through Calhoun, Jackson, and the Democratic party. Calhoun did not divulge his authorship of the *Exposition* until 1831, when he had split with Jackson over personal and political issues, and when he was under mounting pressure from the "fire-eater" radicals of his own state. Even then, he continued to aspire to the presidency and looked to nullification as a means of mollifying South Carolina's extremists, establishing the Union on a more secure basis, and preserving his own national following.

By 1832 South Carolina had become increasingly isolated from the rest of the nation (the mission of the state's next generation would be to unite the rest of the South with South Carolina). South Carolina's Robert Y. Hayne, in his famous Senate debates with Daniel Webster in 1830, had failed to cement an alliance with the West against an alleged Northeastern conspiracy to discourage Western settlement. Webster had maneuvered Hayne into an eloquent defense of nullification:

Where there are conflicting interests . . . and a majority are enabled to impose burthens on the minority, to their own advantage, it is obvious that representation, on the part of the minority, can have no other effect than to "furnish an apology for the injustice."

Webster had then been able to appeal to the kind of spread-eagled nationalism that had been turned against New England during the War of 1812 and the Missouri crisis, expressing the hope that he would not live to see "the broken and dishonored fragments of a once glorious Union," and appealing, in a phrase to be memorized by countless schoolchildren in generations to come, for "Liberty and Union, now and forever, one and inseparable." Though many Southerners detested protective tariffs and maintained, especially in Virginia, that states had a right to secede from the Union, Southern legislatures turned a stony face to nullification. As a result, there was no regional convention of Southern delegates that

DANIEL WEBSTER, 1782–1852

(Culver Pictures.)

might have moderated South Carolina's suicidal course. Nor did Calhoun's theories of minority rights give any protection or encouragement to the substantial number of South Carolina unionists who risked their lives and reputations in a violent and losing struggle. In the fall of 1832 the triumphant state convention directly challenged federal authority, making it unlawful after February 1, 1833, to collect tariff duties within the state.

South Carolina chose the wrong President to test. Andrew Jackson was a wealthy slaveholder who immediately sided with South Carolina, later, in 1835, on the question of abolitionist propaganda. As a shrewd politician, Jackson had long wavered on the tariff issue, but his maturing views on tariffs and internal improvements were close·to those of South Carolina's oligarchy. But Jackson had also fought for the continental supremacy of the United States. He had crushed British and Indian armies, had hanged English meddlers in Spanish Florida, and had ordered the execution of an unruly teenage soldier. He was probably the toughest of America's Presidents. When South Carolina nullified the tariff of 1832, the old general privately threatened to lead an invasion of the state and to have Calhoun hanged. Although he sent reinforcements to the federal forts in Charleston harbor, Jackson publicly sought to avoid armed conflict by relying on

JOHN C. CALHOUN, 1782–1850

(The National Archives.)

civilian revenue agents and by warning that armed resistance would be punished as treason.

As in 1820, the crisis ended in a compromise that failed to resolve fundamental conflicts of interest and ideology. In an attempt to head off civil war, Henry Clay, assisted by Calhoun, secured the passing of a compromise bill that would gradually reduce tariff duties over a period of nine years. But this measure was accompanied by a "force bill," reaffirming the President's authority to use the army and navy, when necessary, to enforce federal laws. South Carolina's fire-eaters continued to call for armed resistance; the governor, now Robert Y. Hayne, recruited a volunteer army. Early in 1833, however, the state convention repealed its earlier nullification of the tariff and, to save face, nullified the force bill. Jackson ignored this defiant gesture. He had already proscribed as unlawful and unconstitutional the claim that any state could annul the laws of the United States. In effect, he had told rebellious states that secession was their only escape, and that secession would be met with armed force.

The compromise did not allay South Carolina's suspicions and anxieties. Although the state continued to defy federal law—for example, by jailing as security risks foreign Negro sailors who landed at Charleston—the nullification controversy had failed to provide permanent safeguards against a hostile national majority. This failure, coinciding in 1833 with the British abolitionists' success in abolishing slavery in the Caribbean colonies, made South Carolina acutely sensitive to the growing antislavery opinion in the North. Despite the Northern states' reassurances that abolitionists were a small and unpopular minority, the legislatures did not heed Jackson's call for suppressing abolitionist agitation. Moreover, Jackson's message of 1835 presupposed that Congress had the authority to bar "incendiary publications" from the mails. But as Calhoun quickly pointed out, by the same authority Congress could determine that abolitionist propaganda was not incendiary and could thus force its circulation in the South. Congress rejected Calhoun's proposal to prohibit federal postmasters from delivering mail in defiance of state law. Accordingly, Southern states had to rely on the informal and extralegal cooperation from the President and postmaster general.

In a similar test of jurisdictional boundaries, Calhoun, James Hammond, and other South Carolinians insisted that Congress had no constitutional right to abolish slavery in the District of Columbia, and could therefore not receive abolitionist petitions calling for that preliminary objective. In 1836 when the flood of antislavery petitions prevented Congress from attending to other work, the crisis was especially treacherous for Martin Van Buren. Van Buren had won out over Calhoun as Jackson's heir apparent and as the likely Democratic candidate; he had no wish of alienating either Southern slaveholders or Northern defenders of civil liberties. The compromise achieved by the Van Burenites was to deny the right of Congress to interfere with slavery in the Southern states; to affirm the *inexpediency* of interfering with slavery in the District of Columbia; and to set up a

A ROWDY HOUSE OF REPRESENTATIVES

A caricature, drawn by a famous English illustrator, Robert
Cruickshank, of the House debates on the gag rule.
(Library of Congress.)

procedure for receiving and automatically tabling abolitionist petitions. This
"gag rule" outraged Northern abolitionists. But South Carolinians also regarded
it as a defeat. For if the future should bring a shift in national opinion, the way
had been opened for formal consideration of inflammatory petitions and for the
withdrawal of all federal sanction and protection for slavery.

Foreign Dangers, the Monroe Doctrine, and American Expansion

America's foreign policy had always presupposed a federal commitment to
protect and support the South's peculiar institution. It is true that American
foreign policy reflected many other interests and motives, and that until 1844
protecting slavery was not explicitly acknowledged as a vital objective. The overriding objective in the early nineteenth century, as in the post-Revolutionary
period, was to prevent England or France from acquiring a foothold in the increasingly vulnerable Spanish territories of North America. But those territories,
including Cuba, East and West Florida, and Texas, were a threat mainly to the
slaveholding South. The War of 1812 showed that possessing the Floridas was
essential for the security of the entire Lower South. From bases in supposedly
neutral Spanish Florida, the British had incited Indian raids, had encouraged

slave desertions, and had originally planned to launch an invasion inland to cut off New Orleans from the rest of the United States. The earlier Haitian revolution had also shown that war could ignite a massive slave insurrection and totally destroy a slaveholding society.

One of the consequences of the Napoleonic wars was the fatal weakening of slaveholding regimes in most parts of the New World. Not only did France lose Haiti, the richest sugar colony in the world, but Napoleon's seizure of Spain opened the way for independence movements in the immense Spanish territories from Mexico to Chile. The prolonged wars of liberation undermined the institution of slavery and committed the future Spanish American republics to programs of gradual emancipation. This trend was reinforced by the British navy. After the British abolished the slave trade to their own colonies, they embarked on a long-term policy of suppressing the slave trade of other nations. By 1823, when little remained of the former Spanish, Portuguese, and French New World empires, slavery was a declining institution except in Brazil, Cuba (still a Spanish colony), and the United States.

This wider context dramatizes a momentous paradox of American foreign policy from the presidency of Jefferson to the Civil War. The extension of what Jefferson termed an empire for liberty was also the extension of an empire for slavery and thus a counterweight to the forces that threatened to erode slavery throughout the hemisphere. For example, Jefferson himself initiated the policy of trying to quarantine Haiti, economically and diplomatically, to end the contagion of black revolution. His successors continued to reject British requests for cooperative naval action in suppressing the slave trade. The memory of British impressment of seamen during the Napoleonic wars made Americans understandably sensitive to any treaty granting the right to seize and search American ships, yet it was precisely this immunity to British search that enabled American ships to take over much of the slave trade from Africa to Cuba. Finally, when Jefferson had exclaimed to President Madison in 1809 over America's future "empire for liberty," he was referring specifically to the annexation of Cuba, which was then on the road to becoming the world's greatest producer of slave-grown sugar. In 1820, in the midst of the Missouri crisis and in response to Spain's delay in ratifying the treaty of 1819 ceding East Florida, Jefferson privately assured President Monroe that the United States could soon acquire not only East Florida but Cuba and Texas. Texas, he confidently predicted, would be the richest state of the Union, without exception, partly because its southern part would make more sugar than the country could consume.

There is no reason to think that American statesmen consciously plotted to create a vast empire for slavery—at least until the 1840s. The paradox can be explained by examining the three basic and continuing premises that governed foreign policy. The first premise was that territorial expansion was the only means of protecting and extending the principles of the American Revolution in a generally hostile world. "The larger our association," Jefferson had predicted, "the less will it be shaken by local passions." According to this nationalist view Americans could deal with domestic imperfections once the nation had achieved sufficient power to be secure. Thus for ardent nationalists like John Quincy Adams any personal misgivings over slavery had to give way to the need for a united front against the monarchic despots of Europe. During the Missouri crisis the antislavery forces could never overcome the unfair charge that they were heirs of the Federalist Hartford Convention, serving Britain's interests by fomenting sectional discord and blocking the westward expansion of the United States.

The second premise, held with passionate conviction by every President from Jefferson to Jackson, was that England was America's "natural enemy," a kingdom ruled by selfish interest, filled with a deep-rooted hatred for everything America represented, and committed to the humiliation and subjugation of her former colonies. Anglophobia had much to do with the swift demise of the Federalist party. It was nourished by contemptuous anti-American essays in British periodicals and by unflattering descriptions written by English travelers and widely reprinted in the United States. Many Americans blamed England for the economic depressions of 1819 and 1837. Irish immigrants regarded the English as their hereditary enemies. No American politician could risk even the suspicion of being an unintentional agent of British interests. It was thus an unhappy coincidence that British interests veered increasingly toward antislavery, which American leaders interpreted, not without some reason, as a cloak for new forms of economic and ideological imperialism.

The third premise was that America's expansion should neither be so bold as to provoke unnecessary wars and European intervention, nor so cautious as to allow European powers to plant colonies or protectorates within the crumbling Spanish empire. This concern for perfect timing governed American diplomacy from the acquisition of Louisiana to the acquisition of Texas and California.

It was the takeover of Florida that established the precedents for the future and that also coincided with the dramatic southwestward expansion of cotton and slavery. As early as 1786, three years after Britain had ceded Florida to Spain, Jefferson had warned against pressing "too soon on the Spaniards." He held that those countries could not be in better hands. He feared, however, that the Spanish were, as he said, "too feeble to hold them till our population can be sufficiently advanced to gain it from them piece by piece." By 1810 there were enough American settlers in the Baton Rouge district of West Florida to stage an armed rebellion against Spanish rule. President Madison, affirming that West Florida was part of the Louisiana Purchase, promptly annexed the section of the Gulf coast extending eastward to the Perdido River. To prevent any possible transfer of West Florida to England, Congress sanctioned Madison's expansionist policy but balked at plans to seize East Florida during the War of 1812.

The postwar negotiations with Spain involved not only Florida but the entire western boundary of the United States. Spain had never recognized the validity of Napoleon's sale of Louisiana, a sale prohibited by the treaty transferring the territory from Spain to France. Luis de Onís, the Spanish minister, tried to limit

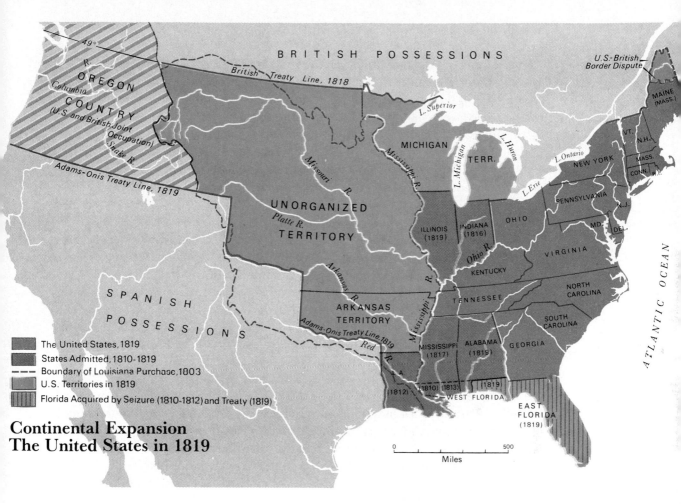

**Continental Expansion
The United States in 1819**

Legend:
- The United States, 1819
- States Admitted, 1810-1819
- --- Boundary of Louisiana Purchase, 1803
- U.S. Territories in 1819
- Florida Acquired by Seizure (1810-1812) and Treaty (1819)

American claims to the narrowest strip possible west of the Mississippi. But as the negotiations dragged on, the South American wars of independence increasingly undermined Spain's position. Secretary of State John Quincy Adams proved to be a tough and skillful bargainer, and in 1818 Andrew Jackson, then the American military commander in the South, immensely strengthened Adams's hand. Without official authorization, Jackson invaded East Florida, captured the main Spanish forts, deposed the governor, and hanged two English troublemakers. The excuse was that Florida had become a refuge for fugitive slaves and a base for Seminole Indian raids on American settlements. Faced with the temporary seizure of his main bargaining card and fearful that the United States would begin aiding the rebellious Spanish colonies, Onís agreed in 1819 to cede the Floridas to the United States in return for America's relinquishing the questionable claim that Texas was part of the Louisiana Purchase. In actuality, Onís had been desperate enough to give up most of Texas. But as President Monroe assured General Jackson, "We ought to be content with Florida, for the present, and until the public opinion . . . [in the Northeast] shall be reconciled to any further change."

For Adams the Transcontinental Treaty (ratified in 1821) was "a great epoch in our history" because it extended American territorial claims to the Pacific Ocean. Spain not only ceded to the United States her rather weak claims to the Pacific Northwest, but agreed to an international boundary that extended from the Sabine River, dividing Texas from Louisiana, westward along the Red and Arkansas rivers to the Rocky Mountains, and then along the forty-second parallel to the Pacific. Spain had hardly ratified this momentous treaty before the burden of defending its boundaries fell upon an independent, weak, and war-torn Mexico.

The collapse of the Spanish empire led directly to the Monroe Doctrine. Initially this statement of fundamental American policy had no apparent connection with slavery. By 1823 it was clear that Spain could never reduce her rebellious colonies to their former status, and Britain and America shared a common interest in preventing the autocratic nations of the Holy Alliance from intervening in Spain's behalf. Under pressure from the Russian czar, France was about to invade Spain, where a revolution had established a constitutional monarchy, in order to restore the absolutist regime of Ferdinand VII. The French foreign minister was known to have grandiose schemes for extending to the New World the Holy Alliance's crusade for monarchic legitimacy. England, though not willing to risk war, strongly opposed this French intervention in Spain. And while not a promoter of independent republics, England also had no intention of allowing antirevolutionary zeal to interfere with her growing commercial dominance in the former Spanish empire. George Canning, the English foreign minister, therefore proposed a joint British-American declaration that would disavow any British or American designs on former Spanish territory and that would warn other nations against intervention.

The British offer presented the Monroe administration with a serious dilemma. The United States was the only nation that had begun to recognize the independent republics of Spanish America, but only Britain could deter a Franco-Spanish expeditionary force from trying to subdue them. Moreover, in 1821 Russia, which was leading the crusade to reestablish monarchic rule and which had earlier expanded from Siberia into Alaska, had issued a decree claiming a monopoly over the North Pacific. Russian traders were becoming more active in the Oregon country, a region which England and the United States had agreed to occupy jointly at least until 1828. Although accepting Canning's offer would have the drawback, as Jefferson pointed out, of temporarily preventing America's annexation of Cuba, the idea of a joint declaration appealed to both Jefferson and Madison, the elder statesmen, as well as to Monroe and most of his cabinet.

The question was complicated, however, by the forthcoming presidential election of 1824. The nationalist, anti-English vote was much on the minds of the leading candidates. John Quincy Adams, the secretary of state, was already being portrayed by his rivals as a former Federalist and secret Anglophile. Despite his proved nationalism and loyal service to Republican adminstrations, Adams was vulnerable to such charges because of his New England and Federalist background. He was also the only candidate who was not a slaveholding planter. He knew that as secretary of state he would bear the largest share of political liability resulting from any Anglo-American alliance. He had long gone out of his way to publicize his resistance to English pressure for an anti-slave trade treaty that by granting the right of search would in his words "be making slaves of ourselves." Adams now insisted on a unilateral declaration against European intervention in the New World, much as he insisted on a unilateral policy against the slave trade. It would be more candid and dignified, Adams pointed out, to avow United States principles explicity to Russia and France, than "to come in as a cock-boat in the wake of the British man-of-war."

Adams's arguments prevailed, and the famous Monroe Doctrine reaffirmed America's diplomatic independence from Europe. By disavowing any American interference in "the internal concerns" of European states, Monroe in effect repudiated the popular clamor for aiding various revolutionary struggles against despotism, including the Greek war for independence from Turkey. But America's warning to Europe against future colonization in the New World extended to Britain as well as to Russia and France. And the Monroe Doctrine in no way precluded America's own expansion in the New World. Indeed, Adams had tauntingly asked Calhoun, the secretary of war and one of Adams's rivals for the presidency, whether his willingness to accept Canning's offer also meant a willingness to forfeit all claims to Cuba and Texas.

For some time the Monroe Doctrine had little practical consequence, except perhaps in vindicating Adams's reputation as a nationalist and thus in helping him win the presidency. Regardless of American pronouncements, it was British naval power that ensured the independence of Spanish America. Yet the Monroe administration, by spurning an Anglo-American alliance, also set a precedent for opposing any foreign attempts to limit the expansion of slavery. No doubt Monroe was thinking only of monarchic institutions when he warned that the United States would consider any European attempt to extend "their system" to any portions of the Western Hemisphere dangerous to America's peace and safety. By the 1830s, however, antislavery was an integral part of the British "system," and Southerners regarded the expansion of slavery as vital to America's "peace and safety."

The Texas issue eventually tested this point and led to a proslavery reformulation of the Monroe Doctrine. For abolitionists in both Britain and the United States it was not inevitable that Texas should become a slave state. In 1829 Mexico abolished slavery in all provinces (including California), providing loopholes only for the restive Anglo-American settlers in Texas. By 1830 the Mexican government had become alarmed by the growing autonomy of the Anglo-American settlements, by the intrigue accompanying the American government's secret efforts to purchase Texas, and by the agitation for annexation in the Jacksonian press. Consequently, in 1830 the Mexican government tried to prohibit the further immigration of Anglo-Americans as well as the further importation of slaves, and sought to promote the colonization of Europeans as a buffer against encroachments from the United States. Since Negro slavery had only begun to take root in Texas, English reformers were beginning to look on the province as a promising site for cultivating cotton with free labor. Benjamin Lundy, an American Quaker abolitionist, even tried in the early 1830s to establish an asylum in Texas for free blacks from the United States.

SAM HOUSTON, 1793–1863

Leader of the badly outnumbered Texans whose spectacular victory at San Jacinto in 1836 secured Texas's independence from Mexico, Houston went on to become president of the new republic, then senator from the new state. In 1861 as governor, Houston's stand against Texas's secession from the Union forced him out of office. *(Library of Congress.)*

But during his travels in Texas Lundy found evidence of growing proslavery sentiment and of various plots to throw off Mexican rule and annex Texas to the United States. The Mexican government was in fact incapable of either governing or satisfying the needs of the Anglo-Texans. In 1836, after President Antonio Lopez de Santa Anna had succeeded in abolishing the federal constitution and in asserting centralized rule, the Texans proclaimed their independence. Their new constitution, modeled on the United States Constitution, specifically legalized Negro slavery. Meanwhile, Santa Anna's army had wiped out a small band of Texas rebels at San Antonio's Alamo Mission, thereby provoking cries for revenge in the American press. Aided by a great influx of volunteers from the officially neutral United States, the Texans, led by General Sam Houston, crushed the Mexican army at San Jacinto, captured Santa Anna, and soon voted overwhelmingly to join the United States.

As late as 1835 President Jackson had tried to buy not only Texas but all the Mexican territory stretching northwestward to the Pacific, affirming the main object as securing "within our limits the whole bay of St. Francisco." By then Americans had long been engaged in trade along the Santa Fe Trail and settlers were beginning to arrive by sea in sparsely populated California. After the Texan Revolution, however, Jackson knew that a premature attempt at annexation would in all likelihood bring on a war with Mexico, which refused to acknowledge

Texan independence. It would also arouse the fury of the Northeast and lead to a sectional division, in the election year of 1836, within the Democratic party. But Jackson knew that California was important to the whaling and maritime interests of the Northeast. He therefore secretly advised Texans to bide their time and to establish a claim to California, "to paralyze the opposition of the North and East to Annexation."

The passage of time encouraged the hopes of American and British abolitionists. President Van Buren was too dependent on Northeastern support to risk agitating the question of annexation. John Quincy Adams, now a congressman from Massachusetts, had been converted to antislavery in 1836 by Benjamin Lundy's arguments and evidence. Adams's eloquent speeches popularized the view that the Southern Slave Power had engineered the Texas revolution and the drive for annexation. In 1838 Adams carried on a three-week filibuster, presented hundreds of antislavery petitions, and finally defeated a move to annex Texas by joint resolution. The rebuffed Texan leaders withdrew their formal proposal for annexation and began to think seriously of building an independent empire. As time went on, they looked to Britain and France for financial support and for diplomatic aid in ending the perilous state of war with Mexico.

The spring and summer of 1843 marked a decisive turn of events. President Tyler, having earlier been disowned by the Whig party, was courting Southern Democrats and searching for an issue that would win him reelection. Daniel Webster, the last of the Whig cabinet members, finally resigned as secretary of state after negotiating with Britain the Webster-Ashburton Treaty; this treaty settled disputed borders with Canada, provided for cooperative measures in suppressing the Atlantic slave trade, and was immediately attacked by Democrats for betraying America's interests. Through Calhoun's influence, Webster was replaced by Abel P. Upshur, a Virginian who had defended slavery as a "positive good." For the first time, an entire administration was in the hands of ardent proslavery Southerners who saw territorial expansion as the key to Southern security and Anglophobia as the key to expansion.

Anglophobia had long served many purposes; Tyler, for example, had taken the lead in 1835 in denouncing the abolitionists as agents of a British conspiracy to incite a slave insurrection and destroy the Union. The new and urgent need was to convince ardent patriots in the Eastern cities and the Old Northwest that only immediate annexation of Texas could prevent Britain from using antislavery as a moralistic front to defeat America's republican mission.

In 1843 the agitation of American and British abolitionists actually played into the hands of Tyler, Upshur, and Calhoun. In that year the World Anti-Slavery Convention assembled in London and sharply pressed the British government to make aid to Texas contingent on abolishing slavery. Although British leaders would have liked to check the territorial aggrandizement of the United States, they did not want to antagonize the South, on which England depended for cotton. They were also realistic enough to know, despite American fears to the contrary, that the European principle of "balance of power" could not be enforced across the Atlantic. But the British government was sensitive to one abolitionist argument. An independent Texas might begin importing slaves from Africa, thereby adding to Britain's difficulties in suppressing the Atlantic slave trade. The British had evidence that American officials in Cuba were conniving with slave smugglers and that American ships predominated in the illegal trade to Cuba. Texas might open another rich market for the same interests. Therefore, when Britain offered Texas a treaty of recognition and trade, it included a secret agreement to outlaw the slave trade. Otherwise, under close quesioning from abolitionists, Lord Aberdeen, the foreign secretary, conceded only two points: that in serving as mediator between Texas and Mexico, Britain hoped that any peace agreement would include a commitment to slave emancipation; and that as everyone knew, the British public and government hoped for the abolition of slavery throughout the world.

In Washington these words brought anger and alarm. The Tyler administration was convinced that West Indian emancipation had proved to be an economic and social disaster. The British, according to the prevailing Southern theory, were now determined to undermine slavery in other nations to improve the competitive advantage of their own colonies, including India. It was true that British leaders were disturbed over the economic consequences of West Indian emancipation, and that they had mixed motives for the high-handed measures used in suppressing the slave trade to Cuba and Brazil. In Cuba, British officials were attempting by the 1840s to emancipate all slaves who had been illegally imported, and in Parliament there were proposals to seize Cuba as compensation for bonds on which the Spanish government had defaulted. But what Southerners could not comprehend was the depth of antislavery sentiment among the British middle class. Having subsidized West Indian emancipation by paying £20 million in compensation to planters, British taxpayers wanted assurance that Britain's short-term sacrifices would not lead to the expansion of plantation slavery in neighboring regions of the Caribbean and Gulf of Mexico.

Regardless of the truth, however, Southerners had long been predisposed to believe that British antislavery was part of a long-term diplomatic plot to seal off and contain the United States within a crescent of British influence extending from Cuba and Texas to California, Oregon, and Canada. In 1843 this conviction was seemingly confirmed by the exaggerated reports of Duff Green, an intimate of Calhoun's and President Tyler's secret agent in England and France. According to Green, the British government was about to guarantee interest on a loan to Texas on the condition that Texas abolish slavery. The plan would make Texas a British satellite and an asylum, like Canada, for fugitive slaves from the United States. The British, by erecting a barrier of freedom across the southwestern flank of the slaveholding states, could effectively join Northern abolitionists in destroying both slavery and the federal Union.

Gradual Emancipation of Slaves Before 1860

Northeastern States	1777–1804
Old Northwest	1787
Haiti	1793–1794
British Canada	1793–1834
Central America	1824
Colombia, Venezuela, Ecuador	1821–1854
Mexico	1829
British West Indies	1833–1838
French West Indies	1848
Danish West Indies	1848

Like many myths, this elaborate fantasy rested on a thin foundation of truth. It interpreted every fortuitous incident as part of a master plan, and justified national desires that were otherwise difficult to justify. It furnished the pretext for the grand strategy that would govern American expansionist policy for the next five years. In response to an appeal for advice from Secretary of State Upshur, Calhoun in 1843 secretly spelled out the ingenious plan: Texas should be privately assured of the administration's commitment to annexation, but the question should not be pushed until a propaganda campaign, originating in Virginia, had softened Northern opposition. Calhoun suggested that in addition, annexation should be coupled with the assertion of American claims to Oregon, to win support from the Old Northwest. In the following year, 1844, the Democratic platform demanded the "reannexation of Texas" (assuming that Texas had been part of the Louisiana Purchase), and the "reoccupation of Oregon" (assuming that Britain had never had legitimate claims to the region south of 54° 40′, the border of Russian Alaska). Calhoun also proposed that America should exploit French suspicions of British intervention in Texas and promote French influence in Cuba, as a counterweight to Britain. He wanted as a preliminary step to demand a formal explanation from Britain for policies that threatened "the safety of the Union and the very existence of the South."

Calhoun himself soon had the power to press and exploit this latter tactic. Early in 1844 Upshur was killed in an accident and Calhoun succeeded him as secretary of state. Soon afterwards a Whig newspaper revealed that the administration had been engaged for months in secret negotiations with Texas and that Tyler was about to sign an annexation treaty. In response to growing Northern furor, Calhoun seized on and made public the British government's private avowal that Britain "desires and is constantly exerting herself to procure, the general abolition of slavery throughout the world." By skillfully distorting and publicizing the British diplomatic notes, Calhoun tried to identify the anti-annexation cause with a British plot to destroy the Union. He lectured the British on the blessings of Negro slavery, employing faulty statistics from the

MILITARY PLAZA, SAN ANTONIO, TEXAS.

(Library of Congress.)

census of 1840 to argue that emancipation in the North had produced Negro insanity, crime, suicide, and degeneracy. He also informed Mexico that because of the British conspiracy to subvert Southern slavery, the United States was forced to annex Texas in self-defense.

This open defense of slavery by an American secretary of state marked the beginning of a sectional conflict over slavery and expansionism that severely strained the national political parties. After the election of 1840 and especially after Tyler's defection from the Whigs, the prospect of the 1844 campaign had led to complex political maneuvering and concerted efforts to mute divisive sectional issues. But with an eye to Northern votes, Clay and Van Buren, the leading Whig and Democratic contenders, felt compelled by April 1844 to express disapproval of immediate annexation and thus of the administration's efforts to score a surprise field goal. In the Senate the Missouri Democrat Thomas Hart Benton led the onslaught against the duplicity of Tyler and Calhoun. Seven other Democratic Senators, all Northerners, joined the Whigs in a decisive rejection of the treaty.

Texas, the expansion of slavery, and America's "clear and unquestionable" title to "All Oregon" thus became issues in the election of 1844. As Calhoun had predicted, the Oregon question was an ideal means for exploiting and diffusing Anglophobia. For decades the British Hudson's Bay Company had ruled the region north of the Columbia River and had extended essential aid and hospitality to traders and settlers from the United States. In 1827 England and America had extended the joint occupation agreement of 1818, deferring the resolution of conflicting claims. What could not be foreseen in 1827, despite American success in organizing a thriving fur trade west of the Rockies, was the appeal of the fertile Willamette Valley to land-hungry farmers from the Old Northwest. Glowing reports from American missionaires to the Indians helped to spread the "Oregon fever" of the 1840s, inducing thousands of families to brave the risks and hardships of overland travel to the Pacific. 1843 marked the first of the great overland wagon migrations along the Oregon Trail, and the resulting claims to "All Oregon" acted as a political balance wheel for the annexation of Texas.

The Southern strategy on expansion contributed to the defeat of Van Buren and the choice of James K. Polk as the Democratic candidate. Although most of the electorate was less swayed by issues than by party loyalty, the Texas issue continued to embarrass Clay, Polk's Whig opponent, whose equivocations and last-minute gestures for Southern support persuaded thousands of Northern Whigs to vote for Birney, the Liberty party candidate. More popular votes were actually cast against Polk than for him, and he would have certainly lost the election if Birncy's votes in New York and Michigan had gone to Clay. Nevertheless, Tyler and the triumphant Democrats interpreted the election as a mandate for

(American Antiquarian Society.)

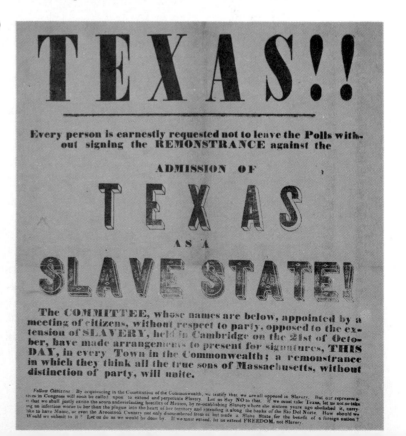

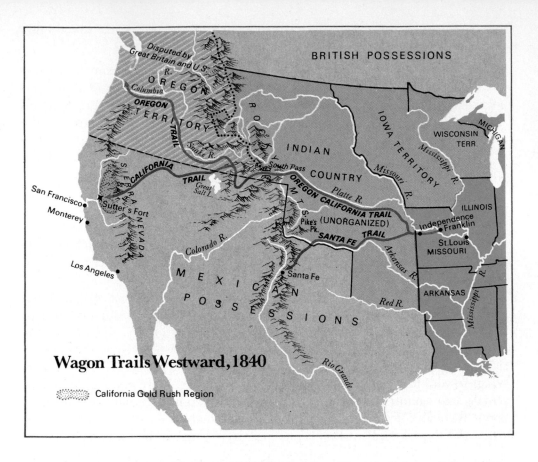

Wagon Trails Westward, 1840

California Gold Rush Region

immediate annexation. The Democrats in Congress closed ranks and allowed the retiring Tyler administration to secure annexation by joint resolution of both houses of Congress. After a tense period of international intrigue, the Republic of Texas rejected offers of peace from Mexico and of mediation from Britain. In December 1845, having bypassed territorial status, Texas entered the Union as a slave state.

In that month the pressures of over two years of expansionist policy were coming to a head. President Polk's annual message to Congress, delivered on December 2, presented an aggressive reformulation of the Monroe Doctrine. Henceforth, he warned, the United States would not tolerate any kind of European interferences designed to limit the spread of the American form of government or the right of any of the peoples of North America "to decide their own destiny," by which Polk meant the right to be annexed to the United States. In the case of Texas, whose boundaries were still extremely controversial, such annexation meant a federal commitment to support the restoration of slavery in a region in which the institution had earlier been outlawed by a foreign nation. Only the future could determine the fate of Cuba, California, and Oregon—provinces that Polk had very much in mind—or determine precisely how the people would "decide their own destiny," an ideal soon to be known as popular sovereignty.

Suggested Readings

The best general guide to sectional conflict and the coming of the Civil War is David M. Potter, *The Impending Crisis, 1848–1861* (completed and edited by Don E. Fehrenbacher, 1976). Allan Nevins, *Ordeal of the Union* (2 vols., 1947), is a highly readable and informative survey of the same subject.

Eugene D. Genovese, *Roll, Jordan, Roll* (1974), is a monumental study of Negro slavery in the South. Herbert G. Gutman, *The Black Family in Slavery and Freedom, 1750–1925* (1976), is no less impressive and innovative. For a briefer discussion of the slaves' society, based mainly on slave narratives, see John W. Blassingame, *The Slave Community* (1972). Willie Lee Rose, ed., *A Documentary History of Slavery in North America* (1976), is the richest collection of source material. See also the references on Negro slavery at the end of Chapter 13, especially Kenneth Stampp, *The Peculiar Institution* (1956), which in most respects has not been superseded.

A comprehensive picture of the South as a slave society can be found in Clement Eaton, *A History of the Old South: The Emergence of a Reluctant Nation* (1975); and Eaton, *Freedom of Thought in the Old South* (1940). The growth of sectional feeling is outlined in more detail in Charles S. Sydnor, *The Development of Southern Sectionalism, 1819–1848* (1948); and Avery O. Craven, *The Growth of Southern Nationalism, 1848–1861* (1953). Carl N. Degler, *The Other South: Southern Dissenters in the Nineteenth Century* (1974), traces the decline of antislavery protest. H. Shelton Smith, *In His Image, But...* (1972), is a fine study of the growing racism in the Southern churches. Frank Owsley, *Plain Folk of the Old South* (1949), contains valuable information on the nonslaveholding whites. A penetrating study of the mythology of the Old South, often Northern in origin, is William R. Taylor, *Cavalier and Yankee* (1961). C. Vann Woodward's essays in *The Burden of Southern History* (1960) and *American Counterpoint* (1971) are indispensable for understanding the South. The mind of the planter class is brilliantly illuminated by two accounts contemporary with the period: Mary B. Chestnut, *A Diary from Dixie* (1949); and Robert M. Myers, ed., *The Children of Pride: A True Story of Georgia and the Civil War* (1972).

The standard work on proslavery thought is William S. Jenkins, *Pro-Slavery Thought in the Old South* (1935), which can be supplemented by Harvey Wish, *George Fitzhugh* (1943). Ira Berlin, *Slaves without Masters* (1975), is a superb analysis of free blacks in the South. John H. Franklin, *From Slavery to Freedom* (1974), is the best introduction to the history of the blacks. George M. Fredrickson, *The Black Image in the White Mind: The Debate on Afro-American Character and Destiny, 1817–1914* (1971), is a brilliant study of racism in America. More specialized works of importance are Eugene H. Berwanger, *The Frontier Against Slavery: Western Anti-Negro Prejudice and the Slavery Extension Controversy* (1967); and William Stanton, *The Leopard's Spots: Scientific Attitudes toward Race in America, 1815–1859* (1960).

On the Missouri crisis of 1820, Glover Moore, *The Missouri Controversy* (1953), is still the most thorough and convincing account. William W. Freehling, *Prelude to Civil War* (1966), presents a masterful interpretation of South Carolina's growing militancy, and of the Nullification and gag-rule controversies.

The fullest history of the origins of the Monroe Doctrine is Dexter Perkins, *The Monroe Doctrine, 1823–1826* (1927). Ernest R. May, *The Making of the Monroe Doctrine* (1975), stresses the importance of domestic politics preceding the presidential election of 1824. For the European background, see E. H. Tatum, Jr., *The United States and Europe, 1815–1823* (1936); and C. C. Griffin, *The United States and the Disruption of the Spanish Empire* (1937). For a general introduction to American foreign policy, see Lloyd C. Gardner et al., *Creation of the American Empire* (1973); and for a more traditional view, Samuel F. Bemis,

A Diplomatic History of the United States (1965). The standard work on Asia is A. Whitney Griswold, *The Far Eastern Policy of the United States* (1938).

Ray A. Billington, *Westward Expansion* (1974), covers every aspect of America's westward expansion and contains an encyclopedic, relatively up-to-date bibliography. Albert K. Weinberg, *Manifest Destiny* (1935), is a fascinating study in intellectual history, but it should be supplemented by Edward M. Burns, *The American Idea of Mission: Concepts of National Purpose and Destiny* (1957). In three outstanding, revisionist studies, Frederick W. Merk reemphasizes the importance of slavery and the fear of British encroachments on the West: *Manifest Destiny and Mission in American History: A Reinterpretation* (1963); *The Monroe Doctrine and American Expansionism, 1843–1849* (1966); and *Slavery and the Annexation of Texas* (1972).

On Texas two of the standard works are by William C. Binkley: *The Texas Revolution* (1952); and *The Expansionist Movement in Texas, 1836–1850* (1925). Much can still be learned from the older, nationalistic studies: J. H. Smith, *The Annexation of Texas* (1911); and E. C. Barker, *Mexico and Texas, 1821–1835* (1928). For a meticulous portrayal of the Mexican point of view, see Gene M. Brack, *Mexico Views Manifest Destiny, 1821–1846* (1976).

Frederick W. Merk has written several superb essays on the Anglo-American diplomacy regarding Oregon: *Albert Gallatin and the Oregon Problem* (1950); and *The Oregon Question: Essays in Anglo-American Diplomacy and Politics* (1967). For general histories of the Northwest, see Norman A. Graebner, *Empire on the Pacific* (1955); Oscar O. Winther, *The Great Northwest* (1947); and Earl Pomeroy, *The Pacific Slope: A History* (1965).

Ray A. Billington, *The Far Western Frontier, 1830–1860* (1956), is a lively and scholarly survey of the exploration and settlement of the Great West. The fascinating story of government exploration is described with admirable care in William H. Goetzmann, *Army Exploration in the American West, 1803–1863* (1959). Gloria G. Cline, *Exploring the Great Basin* (1963), is an invaluable study. H. M. Chittenden, *The American Fur Trade of the Far West* (3 vols., 1935), is still the most comprehensive story of the fur trade, although important new work has long been in progress. Though sometimes scorned by professional historians, Bernard DeVoto's *Across the Wide Missouri* (1947), which deals with the Mountain Men and fur trade, and DeVoto's *The Year of Decision, 1846* (1943), which deals with the political, social, and cultural events surrounding America's war with Mexico, are exciting, readable, and basically accurate accounts of the early West.

18

The Barriers of Power

American society was expansive, plastic, and experimental. Exuberant optimism coexisted with profound collective fear. Much of the fear can be summed up by the maxim "Give him an inch, and he'll take a mile."* For Southern whites this belief applied to Negro slaves, and for American whites in general it applied to free blacks. For American expansionists a similar principle applied to the monarchic nations of Europe. England in particular, unless headed off by American expansion, would establish a crescent of power around the southern and western frontier of the United States, and then begin the fatal subversion of republican institutions. For an increasing number of Northerners the history of sectional compromise proved that the Southern Slave Power would convert every inch of Northern concession into a mile of aggressive encroachment.

The American fear of unchecked power was deeply rooted in the colonial and Revolutionary past. The fear acquired new dimensions, however, as the restraints of local customs, traditions, and privileges, never as entrenched as in the Old World, gave way to individual enterprise and the dominance of market

---

*In the original English version, the "mile" was an "ell," an archaic measurement of about forty-five inches; the American enlargement may have expressed the prevailing sense of boundless opportunity and boundless danger.

forces. Americans of the Jacksonian period voiced continuing alarm over the rise of various "powers," such as the Freemasons, the Monster Bank, the Money Power, the Catholic Church, and Slave Power, which threatened to limit individual opportunity by imposing on society their own secret designs. Such fears, if often highly exaggerated, had some basis in ethnic rivalry and economic conflict. Increasingly, these diffuse fears of unchecked power became grounded in the concrete conflict of interests between free and slave societies.

Like a magnetic field, Negro slavery polarized opposing clusters of values, interests, and aspirations—opposing versions of America's mission in the world. In Southern eyes, any withdrawal of federal sanction and protection for slavery would expose private property to the tyranny of a national majority, undermine the equal sovereignty of states, and lead America in the direction of European "wage-slavery" and class warfare, to say nothing of Negro insurrection and racial amalgamation.

By the 1850s a growing number of Northerners had become convinced that Negro slavery undermined the dignity of labor and thus threatened the indispensable faith in the self-improvement of the working class. The North offered as an alternative to the whips and chains of the South an idealized vision of prosperity and progress without exploitation—a vision of industrious farmers and proud artisans, of schoolhouses, churches, town meetings, and self-made men. The vast territories of the West, unfenced and jointly owned by the American people, would become the critical testing ground for two competing versions of the American dream.

The Mexican War and Manifest Destiny

There could be no doubt that President Polk's reformulation of the Monroe Doctrine was directed mainly at England, that it warned against economic and political interference as well as physical colonization, and that Polk interpreted the danger of foreign intervention as justification for indefinitely expanding America's boundaries. In his annual message of December 2, 1845, Polk spurned further negotiation with Britain over the Oregon question and asked Congress to give notice of the termination of the 1827 joint occupation agreement. The dismayed British government ignored the aggressive American rhetoric but commissioned new steam warships and ordered a naval force to the northeast Pacific. Commenting on Polk's message, the London *Times* indignantly proclaimed: "The rights of sovereignty are limited by the frontier of every state, and that to claim the exercise of a power of exclusion, or to assert a prospective dominion over territories beyond those frontiers, is to confuse and overthrow all the barriers of power, and to hasten the return of universal war and confusion."

Polk's primary objective was California, which he feared the British might appropriate as compensation for Mexican debts. In 1845 a British consul correctly observed that California, which contained no more than ten thousand white

TELEGRAPH HILL, SAN FRANCISCO, 1849–1850

The gold rush of 1849 transformed San Francisco into the world's most expansive and wildly speculative boom town. (*Wells Fargo Bank.*)

inhabitants, was at the mercy of whoever might choose to take possession of it. Months before Polk's December message, orders had been sent to the commodore of the American Pacific Squadron, instructing him to seize San Francisco and other ports if he could "ascertain with certainty" that Mexico had declared war against the United States. Polk's secretary of state, James Buchanan, also sent secret instructions to Thomas Larkin, the American consul at Monterey, telling him to foil British plots and to foment, as cautiously as possible, a spirit of rebellion among the Spanish Californians. Finally, only days after Polk's belligerent message, America's dashing "Pathfinder," Captain John C. Frémont, arrived in California at the head of a "scientific expedition" of heavily armed engineers. Frémont had been exploring the Mexican West without permission from Mexico, and would soon defy the Mexican authorities in California and encourage the Anglo-American settlers in an uprising, supposedly in their own self-defense.

December 1845 also marked the arrival in Mexico City of Polk's secret minister, John Slidell, who had orders to win Mexican acceptance of the Rio Grande River as the new border with the United States, and to purchase as much of New Mexico and California as possible. The instructions emphasized the determination of the United States to prevent California's becoming a British or French colony, and authorized Slidell to offer Mexico as much as $25 million, with the

RIDICULOUS EXHIBITION, OR
YANKEE-NOODLE PUTTING HIS
HEAD INTO THE BRITISH LION'S
MOUTH

In British eyes the Polk administration seemed to be arrogantly
bent on self-destruction. *(Punch,*
1846.)

additional proviso that the United States would assume the debts owed by Mexico
to American citizens. The Mexican government had earlier indicated a willingness to settle the Texas dispute, but by December, when one of Mexico's chronic
revolutions was about to erupt, the unstable government could not dare to recognize an envoy who made such sweeping demands, demands that had already been
leaked to the American press. Mexican nationalists considered Texas a "stolen
province," and especially resented the wholly unfounded claim that Texas extended to the Rio Grande. In 1816 Spain had designated the Nueces River, 130
miles north and east of the Rio Grande, as the boundary between Tamaulipas
and the province of Texas; this was the boundary that appeared on American
and European maps. In 1836, however, when the Texans had captured the
Mexican president, Santa Anna, he had been forced to agree to the Rio Grande
boundary as a condition for his release. The Mexican government had promptly
repudiated this extortionist agreement. By the end of 1845, Mexican nationalists,
hoping for European support, were eager for a war of revenge against American
imperialists.

On learning of Slidell's failure, the Polk administration was also eager for war
but wanted a pretext that would justify seizing California. In January 1846 the
President ordered General Zachary Taylor, who had long been poised for the
move, to march to the Rio Grande. Without opposition, American ships blockaded the river and Taylor took up a position across from the Mexican town
of Matamoros, towards which he aimed his cannons. By early May, however,
Washington had heard no news of hostilities and the impatient President and
cabinet decided that Mexico's unpaid debts and the rebuff to Slidell were sufficient grounds for war. Then just as Polk had drafted a war message to Congress,
news arrived that a minor skirmish had occurred between Mexican and Ameri-

can patrols. Polk could now indignantly inform Congress that war already existed. He said, "Notwithstanding all our efforts to avoid it, [war] exists by the act of Mexico herself. [Mexico] has passed the boundary of the United States, has invaded our territory and shed American blood upon American soil."

By any objective interpretation, Americans had crossed the Mexican boundary and had shed Mexican blood on Mexican soil. For American expansionists, however, the protests from Europe simply substantiated the fact that the growth of the United States was a blow to political and religious tyranny. It was America's mission to liberate the peoples of California, Mexico, Cuba, Central America, and even Canada, allowing them to share in the blessings of republican government, religious freedom, and modern technology. In 1845 an influential Democratic editor had coined the electric phrase, "manifest destiny," while denouncing the policy of other nations of

hampering our power, limiting our greatness and checking the fulfillment of our manifest destiny to overspread the continent allotted by Providence for the free development of our yearly multiplying millions.

But the crusade to prevent Europe from imposing a "balance of power" in North America brought unprecedented strains to the fragile balance on which the

The Mexican War

ST. IGNATIUS MISSION, MONTANA
TERRITORY

A small settlement in the remote
Northwest. *(Karolik Collection,
Museum of Fine Arts, Boston.)*

Union had always depended, the balance of power between North and South.
In the Northeast and particularly in New England the Mexican War provoked
thunderous outrage. From press and pulpit it was denounced as a war of brutal
aggression, plotted by the Slave Power for the purpose of extending slavery and
securing permanent control over the free states. The Massachusetts legislature
officially concurred with this view, and proclaimed the war unconstitutional.

The war remained unpopular with the great majority of Whig leaders, even in
the South, who objected to Polk's devious tactics and to the way in which Congress
had been stampeded into a declaration of war in order to rescue Zachary Taylor's
supposedly endangered army. In June 1846, a month after the war began, even
the prowar Western Democrats were angered when Polk allowed the Senate to
assume full responsibility for approving a treaty that gave Britain Vancouver
Island and all of the Oregon country north of the forty-ninth parallel. As the
Western expansionists rightly suspected, Southerners had never been enthusiastic
about adding probable free states in the Pacific Northwest, and Polk had no wish
to risk war with England when he was intent on dismembering Mexico.

Yet the nation as a whole supported the war. Mindful that opposition to the
War of 1812 had split and destroyed the Federalist party, Whigs in Congress
dutifully voted for military appropriations and congratulated themselves on the
fact that the army's two leading generals, Taylor and Winfield Scott, were also
Whigs. Taylor was the first to win glory. Within a few months, and with incredibly
few American casualties, he defeated Mexican armies much larger than his own,
crossed the Rio Grande, and captured the strategic town of Monterrey, thereby

commanding northeastern Mexico. According to Democratic critics, he then settled down to prepare for the presidential campaign of 1848, which he won. In February 1847, however, in the battle of Buena Vista, Taylor crushed another Mexican army over three times the size of his own. It was led by Santa Anna, who had been exiled from Mexico and whom Polk had allowed to enter Mexico from Cuba on the assumption that this self-styled Napoleon of the West would persuade Mexico to sue for peace.

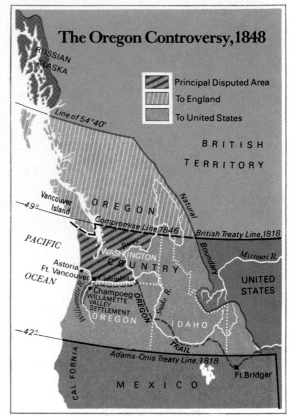

Meanwhile, by early 1847 Polk's professed objectives had been achieved. California collapsed so rapidly that the only serious conflicts stemmed from the rival and uncoordinated American onslaughts: Consul Larkin's efforts to mobilize the restive Spanish-Californians; Frémont's leadership of the Anglo-American settlers; the American navy's capture of the port towns; and the arrival of an overland force, led by Stephen W. Kearny, which conquered New Mexico on the way to San Diego.

But the war was far from over. What the Mexicans lacked in leadership and modern armament, they made up for in national pride and determination. The United States could hardly claim an efficient military machine, but the army sparkled with talent. The roster of young officers reads like a gallery of later Union and Confederate heroes: Lee, Grant, Sherman, Meade, McClellan, Beauregard, "Stonewall" Jackson, and even Jefferson Davis. For Europeans, whose memories of Napoleonic battles had receded into more than thirty years of romantic haze, the American triumphs were stupendous—without parallel, according to the Manchester *Guardian*, "except in that of Alexander the Great through Persia, Hannibal from Spain to the gates of Rome, or Napoleon over the Alps into Italy." Instead of one Napoleon, America had them "by the dozen." The *Guardian* did not consider the possibility that such a war for national grandeur might simply train America's Napoleons to fight one another.

The events that astonished even hostile Europeans began with General Scott's seaborne invasion of central Mexico in March 1847. By September, after winning a series of hotly contested battles, American troops had captured Mexico City and were relaxing in the Halls of the Montezumas. The Mexicans, however, refused to surrender and the Americans became increasingly divided over the meaning of Manifest Destiny. As the American army pushed upward to the

AMERICANS ENTER THE HISTORIC SQUARE, OR ZOCALO, OF
MEXICO CITY, MARCH 1847

(Library of Congress.)

Mexican plateau, in the caustic words of James Russell Lowell, "our Destiny higher an' higher kep' mountin'." Some Southerners believed that slavery could be extended at least into the northern states of Mexico; some antislavery Northerners believed that Mexico would be a force for freedom, and therefore favored annexing the whole country for the reasons that Calhoun opposed it. In general, however, the Democratic leaders—Polk, Buchanan, Lewis Cass, Stephen Douglas, Sam Houston, Jefferson Davis—demanded and expected to get no less than a third of the country south and west of the Rio Grande. They were therefore outraged when Nicholas Trist, whom Polk had angrily recalled as America's negotiator, proceeded to conclude the unauthorized Treaty of Guadalupe Hidalgo. Instead of capitalizing on America's conquests, Trist settled for essentially the same terms that Slidell had been prepared to offer before the war: the United States was to pay Mexico $15 million and assume up to $3.25 million in Mexican debts to American citizens in return for California, New Mexico, and the Rio Grande boundary. Polk would have liked to repudiate the treaty, but feared that further war and prolonged negotiations would split the Democratic party in an election year. Alarmed by the growing antiwar and Free Soil movement among Northern Democrats, he reluctantly submitted the treaty to the Senate, which approved it in March 1848.

But Polk also had other cards up his sleeve. In 1848 the Democratic expansionists launched an intense propaganda campaign to annex the Yucatán Peninsula, a rebellious province that had seceded from Mexico and that contained white inhabitants in danger of being exterminated by hostile Indians. Polk, fearing British intervention and mindful of the virtually unemployed American army in Mexico, invited Congress to act. But enthusiasm waned when news arrived that the Yucatán racial crisis had subsided. Polk was actually far more interested in acquiring Cuba. Like the Yucatán Peninsula, Cuba guarded access to the Gulf of Mexico; its traditional strategic importance would be increased by any future canal, about which there was already much discussion, connecting the Gulf of Mexico with the Pacific. In 1848 England was on the verge of war with Spain, and might at any time gain control of Cuba. Many of Cuba's sugar planters, who resented England's growing interference with their labor system and who feared the continuing spread of emancipation in the West Indies, hoped for annexation to the United States as their only salvation.

The Polk administration knew, however, that the North would not approve military force for acquiring over one-third of a million additional Negro slaves. Polk's only alternative was to try, with the utmost caution and secrecy, to persuade Spain that $100 million was a good price for a colony that was about to rebel or be lost to England. But Spain greatly prized the only rich remnant of her once great empire, and contemptuously rejected the bungled overtures of Polk's minister. Moreover, in the fall of 1848 Lewis Cass, the Democratic candidate who had publicly advocated the purchase of Cuba and the annexation of Yucatán, was defeated for the presidency by the nonexpansionist Zachary Taylor.

Southern hopes now turned to encouraging a Cuban revolution. Groups of Cuban emigrés, aided by American expansionists, led a series of "filibustering" invasions to liberate the Cuban people. By 1850, however, the anxieties of Cuban planters had subsided and proannexationist sentiment had waned. In 1851, in an episode that strangely anticipated the Bay of Pigs disaster of 1961, Cubans captured the entire expedition of Narciso Lopez, a Southern hero, and executed him and fifty of his American followers.

Central America, 1850

Serious efforts to acquire Cuba revived under the Democratic administration of Franklin Pierce, which contained many of Polk's more ardent expansionists. In 1854 the diplomatic intrigues culminated in the secret meetings of America's ministers to Spain, France, and England, who drafted a long memorandum to the State Department justifying the forcible seizure of Cuba if the island could not be purchased from Spain. Labeled the Ostend Manifesto, the secret memorandum was leaked to the American public at a moment of explosive sectional conflict, confirming the conviction of many Northerners that the Slave Power would continue to expand unless checked by political might. One of the authors of the Manifesto, the minister to Britain, was James Buchanan. His platform, as the Democratic presidential candidate in 1856, openly called for annexing Cuba.

A Fire Bell at High Noon: The Crisis of 1850

Meanwhile, the acquisition of vast Mexican territories required national decisions that led to the most explosive sectional confrontation since the Missouri crisis. Ralph Waldo Emerson had predicted that the United States would conquer Mexico; he said, "But it will be as the man swallows the arsenic, which brings him down in turn. Mexico will poison us." The "poison," of course, lay not in the territories acquired, but in the narrowing gap between the South's need to protect and vindicate Negro slavery and the North's need to impose limits on the South.

It is important to remember, however, that the national party systems depended on finely attuned mechanisms for avoiding sectional conflict, and that even during the 1850s both Congress and the general public were mainly preoccupied with other issues besides slavery. By 1850 the most conservative Whig leaders, including the so-called Cotton Whigs of New England, could only view slavery as an issue that had already allowed young "Conscience Whigs" to challenge their leadership and to threaten the very survival of the party. Many Democrats interpreted the political agitation of slavery as a desperate Whig ruse to promote the selfish ends of a dying party and of politicians who would otherwise have no access to power.

Nevertheless, the acquisition of new territory reactivated all the Constitutional issues as well as the political and moral arguments of the Missouri crisis. Would the South be able to maintain its balance of power in the Senate? What was the precise nature of congressional power over territories and the creation of new states? Would the government impose boundaries on the further extension of slavery? Or would it adopt a policy of "hands off," or perhaps openly sanction slavery by guaranteeing all free Americans equal protection if they took into the common territories forms of property, such as slaves, protected by the laws of their former states?

Despite the similarity of issues, political conditions had changed since the time of the Missouri debates. It was predictable that a move would be made in Congress to prohibit slavery from any of the territories acquired by the Mexican War; similar moves had been made since 1784 concerning the trans-Appalachian West, Mississippi, Louisiana, Arkansas, and Missouri. In 1846 the motion came from David Wilmot, a Pennsylvania Democrat, in the form of a proposed amendment to an appropriation bill. What made this Wilmot Proviso extraordinarily significant was its use as a testing point for challenging "Mr. Polk's War" and all that it signified. The legislatures of fourteen free states eventually endorsed the Proviso's principle; and while many Northern Senators ignored the instructions of their states, the House of Representatives several times approved the measure, which antislavery members continued to offer as an amendment.

(*American Antiquarian Society*)

The Northern determination to limit the extension of slavery sprang from many sources. Moral conviction merged with anger over the Democrats' success in lowering protective tariffs and restricting internal improvements. A growing number of Westerners, particularly those influenced by New England's mixture of business enterprise and moral improvement, were coming to view the Southern Slave Power as the chief barrier to America's progressive modernization. Moreover, the congressional deadlock over the Wilmot Proviso soon became intertwined with other matters calling for urgent decision, such as the proposed division of Texas into several slave states, the genuine prospect of armed conflict over the disputed border between Texas and New Mexico, and the extent to which the United States would fund the public debts of Texas, which as a state had been deprived of its former customs revenue as a nation. Apart from these diverse and conflicting interests, the Far West was being settled by people who resented prolonged and ineffective military government and who wanted to elect their own legislatures and draft their own constitutions. Most white settlers, having at least resided in the intensely racist states of the Old Northwest, also shared common traditions of racial discrimination. They cared very little about the fate of slaves in the South, but feared the competition of slave labor in a "land of promise" supposedly reserved for aspiring whites.

This sentiment became suddenly acute in California. The great gold rush of 1849 brought an influx of tens of thousands of settlers who clamored for instant statehood. It also brought a small influx of Southern masters and slaves and of

DIGGING FOR GOLD IN CALIFORNIA

Soon after gold was discovered in California in 1848, the news traveled quickly around the world. Although most of the prospectors came from the settled regions of the United States, the gold rush was international in scope. (*Ballou's, 1856.*)

free Negro prospectors who, according to hostile whites, were "proverbially lucky." White miners considered it unfair to compete with slave labor, and also considered it degrading "to swing a pick by side with the negro," whether free or slave. Negrophobia, particularly from the mining regions, led the California constitutional convention of 1849 to copy the sections of the newly written Iowa constitution prohibiting slavery. In Oregon the fusion of racism with antislavery was even more clear-cut. Though hardly any blacks had arrived in the territory by 1844, the provisional government followed the models of the Old Northwest and ordered the removal of both slaves and free Negroes. Until 1848 the South succeeded in delaying Oregon's elevation to territorial status, and as late as 1857 there was a concerted drive to legalize slavery in the embryonic state. After heated public debate, a referendum decisively rejected slavery and approved the constitutional exclusion of free black settlers. The referendum indicated that Oregon fell far short of being abolitionist country. The number of Oregonians who voted to legalize slavery was 2645 (7727 were opposed); only 1081 voted against the exclusion of free Negroes, a measure Congress accepted as part of the state's constitution.

By 1850, however, Southerners tended to construe any form of antislavery as abolitionism in disguise. Most Southern leaders had moved from a defensive policy of censorship and nullification to an aggressive policy of national expansion. But the Northern legislatures' demand for the Wilmot Proviso posed the threat of a permanent barrier to the expansion of slavery. Southerners feared that the Proviso would if it were ever enacted mark a critical turning point that would swing the full weight of the federal government against an institution it had always protected. Free Soil and antislavery congressmen had already linked the Proviso with demands for abolishing slavery in the District of Columbia. Northern states had adopted personal liberty laws that made it increasingly difficult to recover fugitive slaves, raising the prospect that the North would become as secure a refuge as British Canada.

Indeed, for a growing number of Southern diehards, the Northeast of the late 1840s was becoming a perfect replica of the British enemy that had first exploited her own slave colonies, and then ruined them under the influence of misguided philanthropy, finally using antislavery as a mask of righteousness in assuming commercial and ideological hegemony of the globe. The Northeast, like the more advanced industrial mother country, was attracting millions of immigrant wage earners, was acquiring vast urban complexes, and was gaining mastery over the mysterious sources of credit and investment capital. Unless Dixie made her stand, she would therefore share the fate of the exploited, debt-ridden, and ravaged West Indies. If the South were once deprived of land and labor for expansion, it would be rolled back from the west and the Gulf of Mexico as well as from the north, and would then be subjected by a tyrannical government to the ultimate fate of slave emancipation and racial amalgamation.

All these long-range fears, ambitions, and jealousies fanned the flames of the congressional debates of 1850, which for eight months blazed on like a forest fire almost out of control. In January 1850 the aging Henry Clay tried to capitalize on his reputation as the Great Pacificator by offering a series of resolutions to the Senate. Stephen Douglas, a young Democratic senator from Illinois and an ardent expansionist, had already helped to forward most of the measures, which had already been proposed independently. As an alternative to the Wilmot Proviso and to the popular Southern plan of extending the Missouri Compromise line to the Pacific, Clay favored admitting California as a free state but imposing no restrictions on slavery in the rest of the territory acquired from Mexico. Federal assumption of the Texas debt would compensate for Texas's acceptance of New Mexico's territorial claims. Congress would eliminate professional slave trading in the District of Columbia, thereby ridding the national capital of the moral eyesore of slave pens and public auctions. But Congress would allay Southern fears of an abolitionist "entering wedge" by formally denying that it had authority to interfere with the interstate slave trade, by promising that slavery would never be abolished in the District of Columbia without the consent of its citizens as well as the consent of neighboring Maryland, and by adopting a law providing severe punishment for obstructing efforts to recover runaway slaves.

The ensuing congressional struggle took place on two distinct levels. On the loftiest level, the Senate became a public forum for some of the most famous and eloquent speeches in American history, speeches that clarified conflicting principles, conflicting political philosophies, and conflicting visions of America's heritage, mission, and destiny. Calhoun, so ill and so near death that he could not personally deliver his farewell address to the nation, argued that a tyrannical Northern majority had gradually excluded their fellow Southerners from 1.25 million square miles of territory. No further compromises could save the South from a continuing loss of power or prevent the day when a hostile and increasingly centralized government would execute the demands of the abolitionists. The Union might be preserved if the North agreed to open all the territories to slaveholders and to restore, by Constitutional amendment, an equal and permanent balance of sectional power. Otherwise, self-preservation would require the South to separate, and to fight if the North refused to accept secession in peace.

Daniel Webster, in his famous reply on March 7, insisted: "There can be no such thing as a peaceable secession." Recoiling in horror from the prospects of disunion and fratricidal war, he pleaded for compromise and for a charitable spirit towards the South. He concurred with Southern complaints against the abolitionists, and supported the demand for an effective fugitive slave law. The territorial issue, he claimed, should be no cause for further discord. Convinced that slave labor could never be profitable in the territories where it had not already been permitted or excluded, Webster saw no need for a further legal exclusion that could only antagonize the South. But in the eyes of Conscience Whigs, to say nothing of abolitionists, Webster's final appeal for the Union was

The Compromise of 1850

the speech, in the poet Whittier's words, of "A fallen angel's pride of thought, still strong in chains." On March 11 this growing antislavery audience found a spokesman in William H. Seward, a Whig from New York, whom Webster had once judged "subtle and unscrupulous," bent "to the one idea of making himself President." Seward attached political force to the traditional abolitionist doctrine concerning the territories: "There is a higher law than the Constitution, which regulates our authority over the domain . . . the common heritage of mankind."

These and other great speeches raised momentous issues: Whether the Constitution could protect a sectional minority, the Southern slaveholders, who infringed upon the rights of a more powerless minority. Whether there were limits to the compromises required to perpetuate the Union. Whether, in a nation dedicated to liberty and hostile toward traditional institutional restraints, effective limits could be set on subjugating and exploiting the human personality.

But it is likely that the speeches changed few votes. The second level of struggle involved political infighting that ranged from the bribes and lobbying by speculators in Texas bonds to the patient and tireless committee work of experts committed to American political procedures and to the technicalities of Constitutional law. Apart from the moderating influence of powerful banking and business interests, four circumstances contributed to the final achievement of compromise. First, despite signs of an ominous sectional division of parties, Stephen Douglas succeeded in rallying a core of Democrats, particularly from the Old Northwest and border states, who could counteract the combined pressures of Southern and Northern extremists. Second, Douglas's simultaneous drive to win Southern support for a railroad connecting Chicago with the Gulf of Mexico (the Illinois Central), demonstrated the rewards that could be gained through sectional unity. Third, the Senate wisely abandoned an "Omnibus Bill" that combined most of the compromise in one package, and thereby allowed an alliance dominated by the North to have its way about admitting California as a free state and abolishing the slave trade in the District of Columbia. An alliance dominated by the South similarly carried the new Fugitive Slave Law. Finally, President Taylor, who had shown no sympathy for the compromise, suddenly and conveniently died in July. Millard Fillmore, his successor, was close to Webster and Clay and threw the full weight of his administration behind the compromise. In September much of the nation sank back in relief, assuming that the adoption of the proposals of Clay and Douglas marked the end of serious sectional conflict.

Although the Compromise of 1850 created the illusion of sectional peace, it left critical issues unresolved. Even the Texas debt continued to be a source of conflict. In the District of Columbia, trading and selling slaves continued though not so openly as before. Holding Negroes and particularly Indians as slaves continued on the supposedly free soil of California. The Fugitive Slave Law,

HARRIET BEECHER STOWE, 1811–
1896

The daughter of Lyman Beecher,
Harriet Beecher Stowe suddenly
became not only the most famous
member of an illustrious family
but also the world's most admired
and hated woman. Bitterly attacked in the South, she was
lionized in England and soon became an international literary
celebrity. *(Library of Congress.)*

which deprived accused Negroes of a jury trial and of the right to testify in their
own defense, dramatized the agonizing consequences of enforcing a national
commitment for which the North had little taste.* One of the Northern responses
to this law was the serial publication in 1851 of Harriet Beecher Stowe's *Uncle
Tom's Cabin,* a novel that soon reached millions in book form and stage presen-
tations. Mrs. Stowe's popular classic, often underrated as a work of literary persuasion, interpreted the moral and psychological evils of slavery in terms perfectly
attuned to the culture of Northern evangelical Protestantism. It encouraged
every reader who sympathized with the fictional fugitives, in their harrowing
ordeal of escape, to share the guilt of a compromise that gave national sanction
to slave catchers.

The territorial issue also involved national sanction, and it was here that the
Compromise of 1850 seeded the great storm clouds of the future. To pragmatists like Daniel Webster and Stephen Douglas, however, nothing could have
been more self-defeating than splitting hairs over the precise meaning of popular
sovereignty and the precise limits of congressional power over the territories.

---

*For the Northern reaction to the Fugitive Slave Law, see Chapter 16.

It seemed inconceivable that national policy of any kind could reverse the dominant Western pattern of free-labor settlement. This question was long clouded by mythology concerning the "Great American Desert" and the "natural limits" that supposedly confined slavery to the subtropics and to the wet cotton-growing lands of the Old South. In retrospect, one can argue that slavery could have been adapted to Western mining, to railroad construction, and to the kind of migratory gang labor that accompanied the development of large-scale irrigation and specialized agriculture. In the short run, however, cultivating cotton was too profitable and the value of slaves too great to encourage risky experiments in the semiarid West. It is true that in 1852 Utah legally recognized slavery and that in 1857 New Mexico adopted a slave code. Yet neither territory acquired more than a handful of Negro slaves. Southerners, long accustomed to the security of slave patrols and local law-enforcement agencies, were fearful of taking valuable human property into a region where courts might invoke the old Mexican law prohibiting slavery and where legislatures might at any time be swayed by the convictions of a free soil and anti-Negro majority.

The growing probability of such majorities underscored the South's dilemma of the 1850s. Only a few antislavery congressmen held the extreme nationalist position that Congress had the authority to exclude slaveholding states. For example, most congressmen agreed that if the voters of California had endorsed slavery, denying statehood on that ground would have deprived California of equal sovereignty with the other states. Yet the Missouri Compromise had reinforced the precedent of excluding slavery from unorganized territories, and until 1850 many Southern leaders had pressed for extending the Missouri Compromise line westward. The central problem for the South was how to delay a decision by a given territorial legislature while making certain that the territory was safe and attractive to slaveholding migrants. The sudden triumph of free soil sentiment in California swung a growing number of Southerners to the extreme position that all territories were the "common property" of the states; that the federal government, as the agent of the states, was obliged to give police protection to slaveholding minorities in all the territories throughout the period of territorial government.

Concerning territories, however, the Compromise of 1850 was deliberately ambiguous. Congress appeared to reaffirm its authority for prohibiting slavery in the territories, for it delegated this authority to the legislatures of Utah and New Mexico, subject to the possible veto by a federally appointed governor or by Congress itself. To appease the South, however, Congress publicly registered doubts about the constitutionality of this authority, which could be determined only by the Supreme Court. In effect, if territorial governments infringed on the property rights of slaveholders, the slaveholders were invited to challenge the constitutionality of any restrictions made before the state governments had been established. Southerners reluctantly accepted "popular sovereignty" because it avoided the stigma of federal exclusion and seemingly left the doors open to

slavery. Northern moderates—the "doughfaces" to their antislavery enemies—
were convinced that popular sovereignty would ultimately guarantee free states
while avoiding a congressional showdown that would lead to the South's secession.
The Compromise of 1850 narrowed the limits of further acceptable compromise.
The attempt to test the precise meaning of popular sovereignty was a main cause
of the Civil War.

The Confrontation over Kansas

Even antislavery moderates, including the Conscience Whigs, were incensed
that a Whig administration had allowed Stephen Douglas and other Democrats
to enact a compromise that included the Fugitive Slave Law and that made it
legally possible for slavery to expand into territories acquired by the Mexican
War. They were also alarmed that Douglas, Cass, and Buchanan, the three leading contenders for the Democratic presidential nomination of 1852, were all
Northern expansionists who rejected slavery as a positive good but who wholly
subscribed to the myth that even moderate antislavery measures contributed to
a British imperialist conspiracy. The actual nomination and election of another
Democrat, Franklin Pierce, signified a national desire for compromise and
mediocrity. Most Americans had little interest in slavery and were intent on making the most of an economic boom. But in the eyes of the growing antislavery
minority, it was precisely this self-serving mood that encouraged Stephen Douglas
to revive the slavery issue in 1854 and to test the meaning of popular sovereignty.

As chairman of the Senate Committee on Territories, Douglas had long been
pressing for the organization and settlement of the Nebraska territory—the
vaguely defined region west and northwest of Missouri and Iowa, an immense
portion of the Louisiana Purchase that had been reserved for Indians and thus
legally exempt from white settlement. As a senator from Illinois, Douglas had
a frank and farseeing interest in transcontinental railway routes that would make
Chicago the hub of Mid-America. He was also an ardent patriot and expansionist,
convinced that America had been commissioned to free the world from centuries
of despotism. He thought that the only serious obstacle to this mission was England, which had instigated the subversive activities of American abolitionists,
who in turn had provoked the militancy of Southern extremists. The latter had
then succeeded in blocking the organization of territories north of the Missouri
Compromise line of 36°30'. By 1854 Douglas had concluded that the Missouri
Compromise must be modified if the Nebraska country was to be opened to
settlement, if the nation was to be bound together by transcontinental railroads
and telegraph, if Americans were to fulfill their mission of driving Great Britain
from the continent, and if Douglas himself was to reunite and lead the fractured
Democratic party. He therefore drafted a bill that applied to Nebraska the
popular sovereignty provision that Congress had already applied to Utah and

New Mexico. This unexpected move destroyed nearly four years of relative sectional peace.

Douglas tried at first to play down the contradiction between popular sovereignty and the slavery prohibition of 1820. In 1850 Congress had left it to the courts to resolve any conflicts between popular sovereignty and the unrepealed Mexican law prohibiting slavery in Utah and New Mexico. Douglas hoped to bypass the Missouri Compromise in the same way. But for various motives antislavery Whigs like William Seward plotted to make the bill as objectionable as possible. A powerful group of Southern senators, the disciples of Calhoun, conspired to make repeal of the Missouri Compromise a test of Democratic party loyalty.

After a series of caucuses Douglas recognized that the bill could not pass unless Southerners were assured that all territories would be legally open to slaveholders. Aided now by his Southern allies, he helped to persuade President Pierce to throw administration support behind a new bill that declared the Missouri Compromise "inoperative and void" because it was "inconsistent with the principles of

STEPHEN A. DOUGLAS, 1813–1861

The "Little Giant" in his prime.
(*Brady Collection, National Archives.*)

nonintervention by Congress with slavery in the States and Territories, as recognized by the legislation of 1850." The new bill also provided for the organization of two separate territories, Kansas and Nebraska. By simply affirming that the rights of territorial governments were "subject only to the Constitution of the United States," the bill evaded the critical question whether popular sovereignty included the right to exclude slavery. In this form the Kansas-Nebraska Bill won almost unanimous support from Southern Whigs and Democrats and from enough Northern Democrats to pass both houses of Congress.

Southern leaders, no less than Stephen Douglas, were astonished by the outrage that exploded across the North. Opponents interpreted the bill as the violation of a "sacred compact," the Missouri Compromise, and as a shameless capitulation to the Slave Power. The legislatures of five Northern states passed resolutions condemning the Kansas-Nebraska Act. When Douglas was traveling by rail, he saw so many figures of himself hanging from trees and burned in effigy that he joked, "I could travel from Boston to Chicago by the light of my own effigy." According to the law's defenders, the cries of betrayal were sheer hypocrisy, for antislavery Northerners themselves had repudiated the principle of the Missouri Compromise by refusing to extend the compromise line to the Pacific coast. Yet the breach of faith, however interpreted, led to a rapid dissolution of other shared understandings and political restraints. For the first time, antislavery and proslavery moderates began to perceive each other as more dangerous than the extremists.

What most alarmed proslavery moderates was the sudden appearance of a new and wholly sectional party, scornfully termed the Black Republicans, who professed moderation but who sought to use the goal of excluding slavery from the territories as the means of capturing control of the federal government. Instead of being satisfied with California and the certainty of an increasing majority of free states, the self-styled Republicans (who had the gall to resurrect Jefferson's party label) seemed intent on humiliating the South and on reducing the slaveholding states to the status of a colony.

By the mid-1850s Southerners were keenly aware of the growing discrepancy in wealth between their own rural economy and the economy of the urbanizing North. The great cotton boom of the 1850s simply proved that even unparalleled Southern prosperity could not narrow the gap. Picturing themselves as the nation's true producers of wealth, slaveholders blamed Northern middlemen, epitomized by Wall Street bankers and merchants, for siphoning off their just rewards. The new Republican party represented the final and fatal spearhead of the conspiracy, allying Free Soilers, antislavery Democrats, and remnants of powerful Whig combines such as the Seward and Weed machine of New York. Whereas the earlier Liberty and Free Soil parties had never had a chance of success, the Republicans in 1856, hardly two years after their appearance, carried eleven of the sixteen free states. General John C. Frémont, the Republican presidential candidate, amassed an astonishing popular vote and would have won over Buchanan if he had carried Pennsylvania and Illinois.

Even for antislavery moderates, however, the events in Kansas following passage of the Kansas-Nebraska Act showed that compromise had only encouraged proslavery conspirators to begin to take over the Western territories. They believed that unless drastic countermeasures were taken, America's free white workers would be deprived of the land and opportunity that was their birthright. Congress, by failing to provide definite legal measures for excluding slavery from the territories, had effectively guaranteed that the issue would be decided by numerical and physical force.

"Bleeding Kansas" was actually the result of complex rivalries and aspirations. The government opened the territory to settlement before Indian treaties had been ratified and before Indian tribes, many of them recently removed to Kansas from the East, had been dispossessed and pushed onto reservations. In 1854, thousands of white settlers began the scramble for Kansas land, searching for the best town sites and the likely railroad routes of the future. Kansas, even with-

The Kansas-Nebraska Act, 1854

Free State or Territory
Slave State or Territory
Territory Open to Slavery

out the slavery issue, would have witnessed a speculative mania and a shameless defrauding of the Indians.

But the passions generated by slavery swept aside the last fragile restraints, such as the frontier's customary rules against "jumping," or disregarding prior land claims. According to Missouri's fiery Senator David R. Atchison, a free Kansas would inevitably lead to the demise of slavery in Missouri: "We are playing for a mighty stake, if we win we carry slavery to the Pacific Ocean; if we fail we lose Missouri, Arkansas and Texas and all the territories; the game must be played boldly." Atchison thus helped to organize bands of "Border Ruffians" to harass settlers from the free states. On the opposite side, New Englanders organized an emigrant aid crusade with the purpose of colonizing Kansas with free-state settlers. Although Stephen Douglas referred to the Emigrant Aid Society as "that vast moneyed corporation," the movement was in fact poorly financed and it succeeded in transporting barely one thousand settlers to Kansas. But the movement's sensational promotion fed the fantasies of Missourians and Southerners that Eastern capitalists were recruiting armies of abolitionists and equipping them with Sharps rifles.

The acts of terrorism and civil war reached a climax in 1856. Antislavery newspapers shrieked that war had actually begun when a large proslavery force, supposedly acting under the authority of law enforcement officials, sacked the free-state town of Lawrence. Even fervid Southern alarmists had not imagined anything so brutal as John Brown's retaliatory massacre at Pottawatomie Creek. Brown, a wild and messianic ne'er-do-well with an abolitionist background and abolitionist connections, led four of his sons and two followers in a night attack on an unprotected settlement. They brutally executed five men and boys who were vaguely associated with the proslavery party. Brown thought of himself as an agent of God's vengeance.

In Congress itself all pretense of civility collapsed. In 1856, speakers became inflamed, personal, malicious. After denouncing "the crime against Kansas" as "the rape of a virgin territory, compelling it to the hateful embrace of Slavery," Senator Charles Sumner of Massachusetts delivered studied insults to the elderly Andrew Butler, a senator from South Carolina. On the Senate floor Butler's cousin, Preston Brooks, later attacked the seated Sumner with a cane, leaving him unconscious and seriously hurt. This triumph of "Bully" Brooks, a congress-man from South Carolina, won applause from much of the South. For many

FORCING SLAVERY DOWN THE THROAT OF A FREE SOILER

In this striking cartoon Democratic leaders force not simply slavery but a Negro down the throat of a white Kansas settler. The image suggests the ways in which appeals for free soil could exploit racial prejudice. (*American Antiquarian Society.*)

Northerners, Sumner's Senate seat, which remained empty for over three years during his prolonged recovery, was a silent warning that Southerners could not be trusted to respect any codes, agreements, or sets of rules.

This was also the louder warning that seemed to come out of the chaos of Kansas politics. By 1857 there could be no doubt that the overwhelming majority of Kansas settlers opposed admitting the territory as a slave state. Like the white settlers in California and Oregon, they also wanted to exclude free blacks along with slaves. For most Kansans these were in themselves minor issues compared to the disposal of Indian lands, squatter rights, rival railroad routes, and the desirability of free homesteads. What made slavery an explosive question in Kansas, and what made Kansas a detonating fuse for the nation, was the federal government's effort to bypass the people's will.

A series of miscalculations led the Pierce and Buchanan administrations to this untenable position. In the first tumultuous stage of settlement, the Pierce administration had legally recognized a proslavery territorial legislature established by wholesale fraud: some 1700 Missourians had crossed the border to cast illegal votes. Many moderates hoped that the flagrant acts of this provisional legislature, such as making it a felony to question the right to hold slaves in Kansas, would soon be repealed by a more representative body. But the free-state settlers chose not only to establish their own extralegal government and constitution but to boycott later elections the official government authorized.

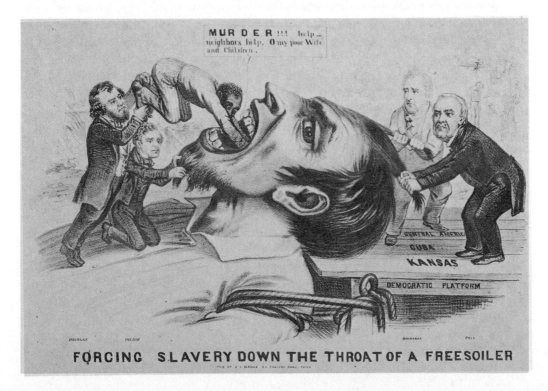

FORCING SLAVERY DOWN THE THROAT OF A FREESOILER

In 1857 the Buchanan administration was thus committed to support the outcome of an official election of delegates to a constitutional convention, in preparation for statehood, even though only one in twelve eligible voters went to the polls. By then, the South had become convinced that the security of the slave system hinged on making Kansas a slave state, and Buchanan had become equally convinced that the survival of the Democratic party hinged on appeasing the South (in 1856, 119 of his 174 electoral votes had come from slave states.) The unrepresentativeness of the Kansas territorial government simply dramatized the unrepresentativeness of the government in Washington. In Kansas, there were no moderating pressures on the proslavery convention that drafted the "Lecompton constitution." In Washington, the declining power of the Northern Democrats, largely a result of the Kansas-Nebraska Act, gave a similarly unrestrained hand to the Southern Democrats who dominated Buchanan's administration.

For Stephen Douglas the Kansas vote on the Lecompton constitution was a total subversion of popular sovereignty. The voters, instead of being allowed to accept or reject the constitution, were given two narrower options: to accept the constitution with its provision for the continuing introduction of slaves; or to accept it without that provision but with the legal recognition of slavery as it then existed. Although the free-state majority again registered their protest by abstaining from this election, Buchanan exerted all the powers of his office to pressure Congress into admitting Kansas as a slave state. This policy brought a bitter break with Douglas, who denounced the administration's attempt to "force this constitution down the throats of the people of Kansas, in opposition to their wishes." In 1858 as in 1854, Congress became the scene of a violent sectional struggle. But this time Douglas led the antiadministration forces. Buchanan stood firm, sacrificing much of his remaining Democratic support in the North. In the end, in August 1858, the administration suffered a crushing defeat when Kansas, by a vote of nearly 10 to 1, rejected the Lecompton constitution at the cost of indefinitely postponing statehood. (As it turned out, Kansas became a free state in 1861.)

Dred Scott and the Lincoln–Douglas Debates

The Lecompton struggle contributed to a fatal split in the Democratic party. As the last of the great national institutions, the Democratic party had survived the sectional division of the largest Protestant churches and benevolent societies, to say nothing of the collapse of the Whigs. The party had long given the South a disproportionate access to national power, but an access contingent on winning the support of Northern allies. As the number of such allies began to dwindle, they were partly replaced by Southern Whigs, who unlike the Northern Democrats had no need to placate antislavery constituents. Thus as the Democratic party became more Southern in character, there were fewer restraints on attempts to test the loyalty of Northern Democrats and to adopt an avowedly proslavery program. The Lecompton constitution was actually the second critical test imposed on Northern Democrats. The first test was the Dred Scott decision.

In both the Compromise of 1850 and the Kansas-Nebraska Act Congress had invited the Supreme Court to rule on the constitutionality of laws excluding slavery from the territories. Buchanan, in his inaugura address, on March 4, 1857, described how popular sovereignty had amicably settled the divisive territorial quest on. He then referred to an imminent decision of the Supreme Court that would resolve any lingering doubts about the precise time when the people of a territory could legally exclude slavery. Buchanan knew what the Court's decision would be (it came two days later), and in fact had brought pressure on one of the justices, a fellow Pennsylvania Democrat, to go along with the Southern majority. Republicans awaited the decision with foreboding, knowing that only one member of the Court, John McLean, had strongly endorsed free soil doctrines.

The Dred Scott case was extremely complex, partly because it was a test case involving many issues. Dred Scott, as the slave of an army surgeon, had been taken from Missiouri to military posts in Illinois and in a part of the Louisiana Purchase that later became Minnesota. After the surgeon-owner had died, Scott had sued in the Missouri courts for his freedom, contending that he had been liberated by his prior residence in a free state and in a territory made free by the Missouri Compromise. The case dragged on nearly eleven years, resulting in conflicting decisions and finally in a transfer from state to federal jurisdiction.

There is still controversy over the points on which the Supreme Court's majority agreed. All nine justices rendered separate opinions. Justices McLean and Benjamin Curtis presented vigorous dissents from the "Opinion of the Court," written by Chief Justice Roger Taney. In 1857, however, both Northerners and Southerners interpreted the Dred Scott decision as a judicial vindication of Calhoun's extreme proslavery position. Taney's ruling embraced three sweeping conclusions: First, he held that at the time the Constitution had been adopted, Negroes had universally been regarded as "so far inferior, that they had no rights which the white man was bound to respect; and that the negro might justly and lawfully be reduced to slavery for his benefit." Neither the Declaration of Independence nor the privileges and immunities of the Constitution had been intended to apply to Negroes, whether slave or free. Even if changed public opinion had granted citizenship to the free Negroes of certain states, they were not citizens "within the meaning of the Constitution of the United States." They were not entitled to the rights and privileges of a citizen in any other state, nor could they sue in a federal court.

Second, after denying the court's jurisdiction over Dred Scott, Taney moved on to the substantive issues. As for Scott's residence in Illinois, the Court had already recognized the principle that the status of a slave taken to a free state should be determined by the laws of the slave state to which he had returned. On Scott's residence in the federal territory north of 36°30', Taney ruled that the Missouri Compromise had been unconstitutional, since Congress had no more power in a federal territory than in a state to deprive a citizen of his property. Finally, having argued that slaves could not be differentiated from other forms of property protected by the Fifth Amendment, Taney concluded that Congress could not give a territorial government powers that exceeded those of the federal government: "It could confer no power on any local Government, established by its authority, to violate the provisions of the Constitution." This judgment struck directly at Douglas's interpretation of popular sovereignty, and affirmed the extreme Southern view that the people of a territory could not legally discriminate against slave property until they acquired the sovereignty of statehood.

Both the South and President Buchanan were jubilant. The highest court in the land had ruled that excluding slavery from the territories, the goal that had brought the Republican party into existence, was unconstitutional. Republican newspapers like the New York *Tribune* scornfully replied that the decision was "entitled to just as much moral weight as would be the judgment of a majority of those congregated in any Washington bar-room." Stephen Douglas, the leading contender for the Democratic presidential nomination in 1860, remained silent for many weeks. He wholly agreed with the denial of Negro citizenship and took credit for the congressional repeal of the Missouri Compromise. Yet his relations with Buchanan and the South were already strained, and he knew that his future career hinged on finding a way to reconcile the Southern version of popular sovereignty, embodied in the Dred Scott decision, with his own constituents' demand for genuine self-determination.

In an important speech at the Illinois statehouse, in May 1857, Douglas presented his answer. After denouncing the Republicans' disrespect for government under law, he argued that the constitutional right to take slaves into a territory was a worthless right unless sustained, protected, and enforced by "police regulations and local legislation." Douglas thus denied any contradiction between the Dred Scott decision and his own principle of popular sovereignty. Two weeks later Abraham Lincoln gave his reply to Douglas before the same forum. Terming the Dred Scott decision erroneous , Lincoln reminded his audience that the Supreme Court had frequently overruled its own decisions, and promised: "We shall do what we can to have it to over-rule this."

Since 1854, when he had attacked the Kansas-Nebraska Act, Lincoln had begun making a new career by badgering Stephen Douglas. Elected to Congress as a Whig in 1846, he had suffered politically from his opposition to the Mexican War. Lincoln was a self-educated Kentuckian, shaped by the Indiana and Illinois frontier. In moral and cultural outlook, however, he was not far from the stereotyped New Englander. He abstained from alcohol, revered the idea of self-improvement, dreamed of America's technological and moral progress, and condemned Negro slavery as a moral and political evil. "I have always hated slavery," he told a Chicago audience in 1858, "I think as much as any Abolitionist . . .   I have always hated it, but I have always been quiet about it until this new era of the introduction of the Nebraska Bill began. I always believed that everybody was against it, and that it was in course of ultimate extinction." The Kansas-Nebraska Act taught Lincoln that men like Douglas did not care whether slavery was "voted *down* or voted *up*." It also allowed him to exercise his magnificent talents as a debator and stump-speaker, talents which had already distinguished him as a frontier lawyer, a state legislator, and an attorney and lobbyist for corporations like the Illinois Central Railroad. Lincoln's humor, his homespun epigrams, his unaffected self-assurance, all diverted attention from his extraordinary ability to grasp the central point of a controversy and to compress an argument into its most lucid and striking form. In 1856, after a period of watchful waiting, Lincoln played an important part in the belated organization of

ABRAHAM LINCOLN   1809- 1865

the Illinois Republican party. Two years later the Republican state convention unanimously nominated him to succeed Douglas as United States senator.

Both in form and substance the Lincoln-Douglas contest was unprecedented. Senators were still elected by state legislatures, and no party convention had ever nominated a candidate. In an acceptance speech on June 16, 1858, Lincoln concisely and eloquently stated the arguments he would present directly to the people, appealing for a Republican legislature that would then be committed to elect him to the Senate. Since Douglas had unexpectedly repudiated the Lecompton constitution and had joined the Republican in fighting it, Lincoln needed to persuade the electorate that Douglas's own crusade for popular sovereignty had rekindled the slavery agitation and had led directly to the Dred Scott decision and the Lecompton constitution. According to Lincoln, Douglas's moral indifference to slavery disqualified him as a leader who could stand firm against the future aggressions of the Slave Power. For Lincoln was wholly convinced that the conflict over slavery would continue until a crisis had been reached and passed:

> "A house divided against itself cannot stand."
> I believe this government cannot endure, permanently half *slave* and half *free*.
> I do not expect the Union to be *dissolved* — I do not expect the house to *fall* — but I *do* expect it will cease to be divided.
> It will become *all* one thing, or *all* the other.
> Either the *opponents* of slavery, will arrest the further spread of it, and place it where the public mind shall rest in the belief that it is in course of ultimate extinction; or its *advocates* will push it forward, till it shall become alike lawful in *all* the States, *old* as well as *new* — *North* as well as *South*.
> Have we no *tendency* to the latter condition?

The "House Divided" speech signified a turning point in American political history. Lincoln identified expediency and a moral neutrality toward slavery as the forces that had undermined the Founding Fathers' expectation that slavery was "in the course of ultimate extinction." If the North continued to make compromises and failed to defend a boundary of clear principle, the South was certain to dictate "a second Dred Scott decision," depriving every state of the power to discriminate against slave property. Douglas himself, it should be noted, would soon contend that the Southern interpretation of the Dred Scott decision would in effect legalize slavery throughout the United States. But in Lincoln's view, Douglas's Kansas-Nebraska Act had been part of a master plan or conspiracy. In asserting that "the people were to be left 'perfectly free' 'subject only to the Constitution,'" it had provided "an exactly fitted *niche*, for the Dred Scott decision to afterwards come in, and declare the perfect freedom of the people, to be just no freedom at all."

Lincoln was not an abolitionist. He was convinced, like most Southern leaders, that prohibiting the further spread of slavery would be sufficient to condemn it to "ultimate extinction." Yet he insisted on a public policy aimed at that goal—a public policy similar to that of England in the 1820s, or in Lincoln's eyes, to that of the Founding Fathers. For Lincoln, repudiating popular sovereignty was repudiating moral indifference, not caring, as Douglas had said, "whether slavery be voted *down* or voted *up*"; and this was the first step towards national redemption.

Because Douglas seemed to be the nation's most likely choice for president in 1860, his struggle for reelection to the Senate commanded national attention. Making full use of newly constructed railroads, the two candidates traveled nearly ten thousand miles in four months. They crisscrossed Illinois, their tireless voices intermingling with the sound of bands, parades, fireworks, cannon, and cheering crowds. Each community tried to outdo its rivals in pageantry and in winning the greatest turnout from the countryside. Lincoln and Douglas agreed to participate in seven face-to-face debates, which are rightly regarded as classics in the history of campaign oratory. Douglas sought to make the most of his own experience as a seasoned national leader (at 45 he was four years younger than Lincoln), and to portray his opponent as a dangerous radical. According to Douglas, Lincoln's House Divided speech showed a determination to impose the moral judgments of one section on the other. Lincoln's doctrines threatened to destroy the Union and to extinguish the world's last hope for freedom. Douglas also exploited the racial prejudice of his listeners, drawing laughter from his sarcastic refusal to question "Mr. Lincoln's conscientious belief that the negro was made his equal, and hence his brother."

Lincoln searched for ways to counteract the image of a revolutionary. Always insisting on the moral and political wrong of slavery, he repeatedly acknowledged that the federal government could not interfere with slavery in the existing states. He opposed repeal of the Fugitive Slave Law. He wholly rejected the idea of "perfect social and political equality with the negro." He did maintain, however, that Negroes were as much entitled as whites to "all the natural rights enumerated in the Declaration of Independence, the right to life, liberty and the pursuit of happiness." If the Negro was "perhaps" not equal in moral or intellectual endowment, "in the right to eat the bread, without leave of anybody else, which his own hand earns, *he is my equal and the equal of judge Douglas, and the equal of every living man.* [Great applause.]"

The election in Illinois was extremely close. The Republicans did not win enough seats in the legislature to send Lincoln to the Senate, but the campaign immediately elevated him to national prominence. Lincoln had succeeded in articulating and defending a Republican antislavery ideology that combined a fixity of purpose with a respect for Constitutional restraints. Lincoln had also succeeded in magnifying the gap that separated Republicans from Douglas and other anti-Lecompton Democrats, and in further isolating Douglas from pro-slavery Democrats in the South. The latter were already embittered by Douglas's "treachery" with regard to the Lecompton constitution. They were then outraged by his response to Lincoln in the debate at Freeport, Illinois. Douglas there maintained that regardless of what the Supreme Court might decide about the abstract question whether slavery might or might not go into a territory under the Constitution, the people had the "lawful means to introduce it or exclude it" as they pleased. Repeating his familiar point that slavery could not exist "a day or an hour anywhere" unless it was supported by local police regulations, Douglas emphasized that the "unfriendly legislation" of a territorial government could effectually prevent slavery from being introduced. As Lincoln quipped, this was to say, "A thing may be lawfully driven from a place where it has a lawful right to stay."

In 1859 the breach between Douglas and the South could no longer be contained. The people of Kansas ratified a new constitution prohibiting slavery, thereby giving bite to Douglas's "Freeport Doctrine." In the Senate, where Douglas had been ousted from his chairmanship of the Committee on Territories, he led the fight against Jefferson Davis's demand for a federal slave code protecting slave property in all the territories. During a tour of the South, Douglas became alarmed by the growing movement, led by young proslavery fire-eaters, to revive and legalize the African slave trade. Looking ahead to the Democratic convention of 1860, Douglas issued practically an ultimatum about the party platform. Northern Democrats would not allow the party to be used as a vehicle for reviving the slave trade, securing a federal slave code, or pursuing any of the other new objectives of Southern extremists. Northerners would not retreat from defending genuine popular sovereignty, though popular sovereignty was clearly running against the interests of the South.

The Ultimate Failure of Compromise

By 1860 a multitude of hitherto separate fears, aspirations, and factional interests had become polarized into opposing visions of America's true heritage and destiny. Traditional systems of trust and reciprocity had collapsed.

John Brown, who had warred against slavery in Kansas, became a key symbol of this polarization. Beginning in 1857 Brown was lionized by the most eminent New England reformers and literary figures. Backed financially by a secret group of abolitionists, Brown also cultivated intimate ties with free black communities in the North. On the night of October 16, 1859, he and some twenty heavily armed white and black followers seized part of the federal arsenal at Harpers Ferry, Virginia. Brown's purpose was to begin the direct destruction of slavery by igniting a slave insurrection and creating in the South a free soil asylum for fugitives. After two days of resistance, Brown surrendered to federal troops; he was tried for conspiracy, treason, and murder and was hanged.

Brown claimed to have acted under the "higher law" of the New Testament, and insisted, "If I had done what I have for the white men, or the rich, no man would have blamed me." For Brown the higher law was not a philosophical abstraction but a moral command to shed blood and die in the cause of freedom. In the eyes of sedentary reformers and Transcendentalists, this courage to act on principle made Brown not only a revered martyr but a symbol of all that America lacked. In the eyes of Democratic editors and politicians, however, Brown's criminal violence was the direct result of the irresponsible preaching of William H. Seward and other "Black Republicans." The New York *Herald* reprinted Seward's speech on the "irrepressible conflict" alongside news accounts from Harpers Ferry. Many Southerners came to the stunned realization that Brown's raid could not be dismissed as the folly of a madman, since it had revealed the secret will of much of the North. A Virginia senator concluded that Brown's "invasion" had been condemned in the North "only because it failed." In the words of Jefferson Davis, a Mississippi senator who had been Pierce's secretary of war, the Republican party had been "organized on the basis of making war" against the South.

Paradoxically, both the Republicans and Southern extremists agreed that slavery must expand under national sanction if it were to survive. They also agreed that if the Dred Scott decision was valid, the government had an obligation to protect slave property in all the territories. This denial of any middle ground, as in Lincoln's "It will become *all* one thing, or *all* the other," made it logical for Southern fire-eaters to argue that a revived African slave trade would allow more whites to own slaves and would thus help to "democratize" the institution. Above all, both the Republicans and Southern extremists rejected popular sovereignty as Douglas had defined it. For Southerners the Constitution prohibited either Congress or a territorial legislature from depriving a settler of his slave property. For Republicans the Constitution gave Congress both the duty and power to prevent the spread of an institution that deprived human beings of their inalienable right to freedom.

Because these positions were irreconcilable, the Northern Democrats held the only keys to possible compromise in the forthcoming and possibly critical test of strength, the presidential election of 1860. But like the Republicans, the Douglas Democrats had drawn their own firm limits against further concessions to Southern extremists. Early in 1860 Jefferson Davis challenged those limits by persuading the Senate Democratic caucus to adopt a set of resolutions committing the federal government to protect slavery in the territories. For Davis and other Southern leaders a federal slave code was the logical extension of the Dred Scott decision, and the principle of federal protection of slave property an essential plank in the forthcoming Democratic platform. The Douglas Democrats knew that such a principle would completely undercut their reliance on the "unfriendly legislation" of a territory, and that such a plank would guarantee their defeat in the North. For decades the Democratic party had tried to weld slavery to America's "empire for liberty." The adhesive, popular sovereignty, had finally given way and the party itself was bursting at the seams.

THE ELECTION OF 1860

A cartoonist's view of the presidential race between
Lincoln, the tall railsplitter, and Douglas, who is weighted
down by a jug of liquor and whose record on slavery in the
territories constitutes an insuperable obstacle. (*Library of
Congress.*)

In April 1860 the fateful Democratic national convention met at Charleston,
and before considering candidates it proceeded to tear itself apart over a platform. When a majority of the convention refused to adopt a platform similar in
principle to Davis's Senate resolutions, the delegates from eight Southern states
withdrew, many of them assuming that this disunionist gesture would force
the Douglas faction to compromise. Douglas held firm to his principle of popular
sovereignty and could not muster the two-thirds majority required for nomination. In a surprise move the Northern Democrats then agreed to adjourn the
convention and to reconvene six weeks later in Baltimore.

There the Democratic party finally destroyed itself as a national force. Delegates from the Lower South again seceded, and this time adopted an extreme
proslavery platform and nominated John C. Breckinridge of Kentucky for
president. The Northern remnants of the party remained loyal to popular
sovereignty, however it might be modified in practice by the Dred Scott decision,
and nominated Douglas.

Meanwhile, the division of the Democrats at Charleston had given the Republicans greater flexibility in nominating a candidate. In 1858 Douglas had portrayed Lincoln as a flaming abolitionist, and the South had accepted the image. To the North, however, Lincoln appeared more moderate and less controversial than the better-known Senator Seward of New York. Unlike Seward, Lincoln was not popularly associated with the higher-law doctrines that had led to Harpers Ferry. Although Lincoln disapproved of Know-Nothing nativism, he was more discreet than Seward and thus stood less chance of losing the nativist vote in critical states like Pennsylvania. If some Northerners regarded him as a crude buffoon from the prairies, he appealed to many Northerners as the tall rail-splitter of humble origins, a man of the people, an egalitarian. Except for his general endorsement of the Homestead Act, protective tariffs, and a transcontinental railroad—all programs that were popular in the North and West and that had been blocked in Congress by the South—Lincoln was associated with few issues and had made few enemies. In May, at the Republicans' boisterous convention in Chicago, Lincoln finally overcame Seward's early lead and received the nomination.

Although no election in American history has been more critical, the presidential campaign of 1860 was filled with the noisy hucksterism and carnival atmosphere that had been standard since 1840. The Republicans tended to discount the warnings of serious crisis, and contemptuously dismissed Southern

The Election of 1860

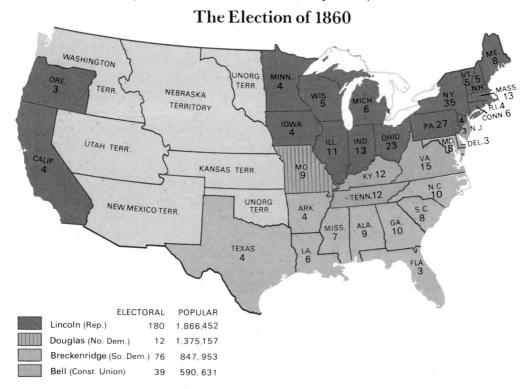

		ELECTORAL	POPULAR
	Lincoln (Rep.)	180	1,866,452
	Douglas (No. Dem.)	12	1,375,157
	Breckenridge (So. Dem.)	76	847,953
	Bell (Const. Union)	39	590,631

threats of secession as empty bluff. The Breckinridge Democrats tried to play down such threats and to profess their loyalty to proslavery conceptions of the Constitution and Union. Yet the strength in the Upper South of the Constitutional Union party, a new and antiextremist group largely made up of former Whigs, gave some indication that both the Constitution and the Union were in jeopardy. And this was the message that Stephen Douglas repeated bravely and incessantly, in the South as well as North, in the first nationwide speaking campaign by a presidential candidate.

In November the popular vote was divided among four candidates, and Lincoln received only 40 percent of the national total. Yet he received 180 electoral votes, 57 more than the combined total of his three opponents. He carried every free state except for New Jersey, and won 4 of New Jersey's 7 electoral votes. In ten of the slave states, however, he failed to register a single popular vote. Breckinridge, the Southern Democrat, captured all the states of the Lower South as well as Delaware, Maryland, Arkansas, and North Carolina. John Bell, the leader of the once powerful Whig party in Tennessee and the candidate of the Constitutional Union party, carried Tennessee, Kentucky, and Virginia. Though Douglas received approximately 525,000 more popular votes than Breckinridge, and trailed Lincoln by only 491,000, he won only 12 electoral votes (9 from Missouri and 3 from New Jersey). In many respects it was not really a national election. In the North it was essentially a contest between Lincoln and Douglas; in the South between Breckinridge and Bell.

For the South the worst fears and predictions of forty years had come true. The United States had never had an administration avowedly hostile to Negro slavery. Lincoln's reassurances regarding the constitutional protection of slavery in the existing states could not mitigate the crucial facts. The election had proved that the North was populous enough to bestow national power on a minority party that had no support in the South. The party was committed to free-labor ideology and to the proposition that slavery was a moral wrong. Slaveholders would have to take Lincoln's professions of restraint on good faith. If he or his successors should become more militant, they could not be checked by a balance of power. A dominant sectional party would control federal patronage, the postal service and military posts, the appointment of federal judges and other officeholders. Such considerations strengthened the hand of secessionists. On December 20, 1860, South Carolina crossed the threshold that had been so closely approached during the Nullification crisis. A special convention repealed the state's ratification of the Constitution and withdrew from the Union. Unlike Jackson, President Buchanan maintained that the federal government could do nothing to prevent the move.

Unionists mounted stiffer resistance to secession in the other states of the Lower South. The chief controversies, however, involved timing—whether to follow the stampede of the fire-eating militants or to wait until Lincoln had shown his true colors. By February 1, 1861, the militants had triumphed in

Mississippi, Florida, Alabama, Georgia, Louisiana, and Texas. Inevitably, the shock produced reflex actions toward the traditional saving compromise. Senator John Crittenden of Kentucky initiated the first of such moves two days before South Carolina officially seceded. Though Crittenden's proposed amendments to the Constitution were defined as moderate, they matched the most extravagant Southern demands of a few years before. Even so, the leaders of the Lower South knew that no "compromise" would be secure unless the Republican party miraculously repudiated its antislavery principles. Most Republicans could not publicly approve Crittenden's "unamendable" amendment guaranteeing the permanent security of slavery. Nor could they return to the old Democratic proposal for extending the Missouri Compromise line to the Pacific. The 1850s had shown that federal commitment to establishing and protecting slavery south of that line would only encourage Southern ambitions in the Caribbean and Latin America. As Lincoln confidentially warned William Kellogg, his mouthpiece in Congress: "Entertain no proposition for a compromise in regard to the *extension* of slavery. The instant you do, they have us under again; all our labor is lost, and sooner or later must be done over....The tug has to come and better now than later.'

By 1860 the North and South had moved beyond the reach of compromise. The United States had originally emerged from an act of secession, from a final rejection of compromise with England. Even after independence had been won, Americans continued to perceive Britain as a conspiratorial power threatening to wall in and stultify the nation's expansive energies. But despite this threat, America continued to prosper and expand. The period from 1820 to 1860 witnessed a progressive extension of limits, an overleaping of boundaries of every kind. History seemed to confirm the wish for total self-determination. The American people, like the American individual, seemed to be free from the burdens of the past and free to shape their own character. The one problem their ingenuity could not resolve was Negro slavery, which the Founding Fathers had seen as an unwanted legacy of British greed. Paradoxically, the South increasingly came to regard Negro slavery as the necessary base on which freedom must rest. For the North a commitment to slavery's ultimate extinction was the test of freedom. Each section detected a fatal change in the other, a betrayal of the principles and mission of the Founding Fathers. Each section feared that the other had become transformed into a despotic and conspiratorial power very similar to the original British enemy. And both sections shared a heritage of standing firm against despotism.

It was not accidental that the greatest novel of the period, Herman Melville's *Moby Dick* (1851), tells of the destruction that inevitably flows from denying all limits, rules, and boundaries. The novel concerns Captain Ahab's relentless and stubborn pursuit of a great white whale, a "nameless, inscrutable, unearthly thing" that becomes a symbol for all the opposing, unknown forces of life. Ahab, who commands a crew containing most of the races and types of mankind, thinks that he can become the master of his own fate. Ignoring a series of warnings and portents, he is incapable of admitting that he might be wrong or that there might be forces beyond his control.

Melville's novel is full of rich and universal meaning concerning man's heroic, yet impossible quest to know the unknowable. Since Americans of the 1850s tended to believe that men were born free and that God would ensure the triumph of democracy in the world, they could not accept Melville's brooding skepticism. Nevertheless, there was a lesson for pre-Civil War America in this tale of a highly rational but half-crazed captain—a captain who becomes so obsessed with his mission that he finally throws his navigation instruments overboard, so that he can steer only toward the visible spout of the whale. Captain Ahab seeks liberation in an unswerving pursuit and conquest of limits. In the end he dooms himself and his ship to annihilation.

Suggested Readings

David M. Potter, *The Impending Crisis, 1848–1861* (1976), continues to be the best guide to the topics discussed in the present chapter. The titles on the causes of the Civil War, listed at the end of Chapter 19 in Part Four, are also highly relevant.

J. H. Smith, *The War with Mexico* (2 vols., 1919), remains the fullest account of the Mexican War. Of the studies listed at the end of the previous chapter, Gene M. Brack, *Mexico Views Manifest Destiny* (1976), deserves special mention for its insight into the Mexican motives for war. The best recent account of the military campaigns is K. Jack Bauer, *The Mexican War, 1846–1848* (1974). For Mexican-American relations, see G. L. Rives, *The United States and Mexico: 1821–1848* (2 vols., 1913). John H. Schroeder, *Mr. Polk's War: American Opposition and Dissent, 1846–1848* (1973), is an excellent study of antiwar sentiment.

On California, the best general guide is Andrew F. Rolle, *California: A History* (1969). For the California gold rush and Western mining in general, see Rodman W. Paul, *California Gold: The Beginning of Mining in the Far West* (1947); and Paul, *Mining Frontiers of the Far West, 1848–1880* (1963). Kevin Starr, *Americans and the California Dream, 1850–1915* (1973), presents brilliant vignettes of early California history.

Holman Hamilton, *Prologue to Conflict* (1964), is the most detailed and accurate account of the Compromise of 1850. For the preceding presidential election, see Joseph G. Rayback, *Free Soil: The Election of 1848* (1970). Stanley W. Campbell, *The Slave Catchers: Enforcement of the Fugitive Slave Law, 1840–1860* (1968), traces the consequences of the most unpopular provision of the Compromise of 1850. Stephen Douglas's motives for introducing the Kansas-Nebraska Act are judiciously weighed in Robert W. Johannsen, *Stephen A. Douglas* (1973). This definitive biography is also an excellent source on the later Kansas controversy and the Lincoln-Douglas debates. Roy F. Nichols, "The Kansas-Nebraska Act: A Century of Historiography," *Mississippi Valley Historical Review 43* (September 1956), 187–212, is an invaluable guide to the controversial issues. The tangled local conflicts over land and railroad sites are illuminated in Paul W. Gates, *Fifty Million Acres: Conflicts over Kansas Land Policy, 1854–1890* (1954); and James C. Malin, *The Nebraska Question, 1852–1854* (1953). For Harriet Beecher Stowe's world-famous response to the Kansas controversy, see Philip van Doren Stern, *Uncle Tom's Cabin, an Annotated Edition* (1964); and Charles H. Foster, *The Rungless Ladder: Harriet Beecher Stowe and New England Puritanism* (1956).

The best brief account of the origins and early history of the Republican party is Hans L. Trefousse, "The Republican Party, 1854–1864," in *History of U.S. Political Parties,* ed. Arthur M. Schlesinger, Jr., Vol. 2, 1141–1172 (4 vols., 1973). See also Trefousse, *The Radical Republicans* (1969). Eric Foner, *Free Soil, Free Labor, Free Men: The Ideology of the Republican Party Before the Civil War* (1970), is a penetrating study of the Republicans' thought and values.

John Brown, a man of violence, has been the subject of violently conflicting interpretations. For traditional and hostile views, see James C. Malin, *John Brown and the Legend of Fifty-Six* (1942); and the brilliant essay by C. Vann Woodward in *The Burden of Southern History* (*1960*). More sympathetic evaluations can be found in Stephen B. Oates, *To Purge the Land with Blood: A Biography of John Brown* (1970); Benjamin Quarles, *Allies for Freedom: Blacks and John Brown* (1974); and Louis Ruchames, ed., *John Brown: The Making of a Revolutionary* (1969).

Johannsen's biography of Douglas, listed above, treats the Lincoln-Douglas debates and a penetrating analysis can be found in Don E. Fehrenbacher, *Prelude to Greatness: Lincoln in the 1850s* (1962). The debates themselves are presented in an authoritative edition by Paul M. Angle, ed., *Created Equal? The Complete Lincoln-Douglas Debates of 1858* (1958). Harry V. Jaffa, *Crisis of the House Divided: An Interpretation of the Issues in the Lincoln-Douglas Debates* (1959), gives the brilliant, far-reaching, and somewhat eccentric interpretation of a conservative political philosopher.

Most of the biographical studies of Lincoln listed in Part IV, at the end of Chapter 19, are relevant to this chapter. Fehrenbacher, cited above, is an important source, and mention should be made of James G. Randall, *Lincoln, the Liberal Statesman* (1947); Benjamin Quarles, *Lincoln and the Negro* (1962); and above all, Allan Nevins, *The Emergence of Lincoln* (2 vols., 1950).

The climactic impasse between North and South is imaginatively presented in two major studies: Roy F. Nichols, *The Disruption of American Democracy* (1948); and David M. Potter, *Lincoln and His Party in the Secession Crisis* (1942). Avery O. Craven, *The Coming of the Civil War* (1942), stresses the importance of propaganda and irrationality. For the hopes and fears of contemporaries, see J. Jeffrey Auer, ed., *Antislavery and Disunion, 1858–1861: Studies in the Rhetoric of Compromise and Conflict* (1963). No one has yet written a wholly satisfactory account of the secessionist movements in the South. For conflicting interpretations, see William L. Barney, *The Secessionist Impulse: Alabama and Mississippi* (1974); Steven A. Channing, *Crisis in Fear: Secession in South Carolina* (1970); Charles B. Dew, "Who Won the Secession Election in Louisiana?" *Journal of Southern History 36* (February 1970), 18–32; Dwight L. Dumond, *The Secession Movement, 1860–1861* (1931); William J. Evitts, *A Matter of Allegiances: Maryland from 1850 to 1861* (1974); and R. A. Wooster, *The Secession Conventions of the South* (1962).

Two works that give a fascinating picture of the Northern response to secession are Kenneth M. Stampp, *And the War Came: The North and the Secession Crisis, 1860–61* (1950); and Howard C. Perkins, ed., *Northern Editorials on Secession* (2 vols., 1942). For the election of 1860, see Elting Morison, "Election of 1860," in *History of American Presidential Elections, 1789–1968,* ed. Arthur M. Schlesinger, Jr., Vol. 2, 1097–1122 (4 vols., 1971). On the futile gestures for compromise, see Albert J. Kirwan, *John J. Crittenden: The Struggle for the Union* (1962); and Robert G. Gunderson, *Old Gentlemen's Convention: The Washington Peace Conference of 1861* (1961).

1820
Missouri Compromise.
Reelection of James Monroe without opposition symbolizes "Era of good Feelings."

1822
Denmark Vesey's conspiracy to lead massive slave uprising in South Carolina exposed.

1823
President issues the Monroe Doctrine.

1824
Congress enacts higher protective tariff.
Supreme Court, in *Gibbons v. Ogden*, extends power of Congress to regulate commerce.
John Quincy Adams elected President by House of Representatives after failure of any candidate to win electoral majority.

1825
Monroe calls for voluntary removal of Eastern Indians to lands west of the Mississippi.
Completion of Erie Canal.
Beginning of Charles Grandison Finney's religious revivals in New York State.
Founding of New Harmony community in Indiana.

1826
Disappearance and probable murder of William Morgan ignites anti-Masonic movement in New York State.
Founding of American Society for the Promotion of Temperance.

1827
Extension of 1818 United States–British agreement on joint occupation of the Oregon country.

1828
John C. Calhoun's anonymous *South Carolina Exposition and Protest*.
Congress passes "Tariff of Abominations."
Appearance of workingmen's parties in Eastern cities.
Election of Andrew Jackson as President brings triumphant victory to new Democratic party.

1829
David Walker's *Appeal to the Colored Citizens of the World*.

1830
Jackson vetoes Maysville Road Bill.
Congress passes bill authorizing Indian removal.
Webster-Hayne debate on land policy and nature of the Union.
Anti-Masonic party holds first national party convention.
Joseph Smith, Jr. publishes The Book of Mormon.
William Ellery Channing's *Remarks on National* ...

American support for Canadian insurrection worsens U.S.-British relations.
Supreme Court, in *Charles River Bridge v. Warren Bridge*, places community rights above special privileges guaranteed by contract.
Elijah P. Lovejoy is first abolitionist martyr.
Presbyterian Church divides as Old School expels much of New School faction.

1838
Massachusetts creates first state board of education; appoints Horace Mann secretary.
Emerson's address on "the American Scholar."
John Quincy Adams's filibuster defeats move to annex Texas by joint resolution.
Rift in American Peace Society leads to formation of radical New England Non-Resistance Society.
Emerson delivers "Divinity School Address," a Transcendentalist manifesto.

1839
A major depression begins, leading to widespread bankruptcies and default of several states.
Mormons establish city-state of Nauvoo, Illinois.

1840
Congress passes Van Buren's Independent Treasury Act.
Bitter conflict between Catholics and Protestants over religious instruction in New York State public schools.
Division in abolitionist ranks as conservatives withdraw from American Anti-Slavery Society.
Washingtonian temperance movement launched.
James G. Birney runs for President as Liberty party candidate.
William H. Harrison elected; Whigs in power.

1841
Harrison's death makes John Tyler President.
Frederick Douglass, escaped from slavery in 1838, begins lecturing for Massachusetts Anti-Slavery Society.
Slaves mutiny on the ship *Creole*, bound from Virginia to New Orleans; are freed when they take ship to British colony of Nassau.
Congress passes general preemption law allowing squatters to purchase 160 acres of public land at minimum of $1.25 per acre.
Dorothea Dix begins crusade in behalf of insane.

1847
General Winfield Scott captures Vera Cruz and Mexico City.
Mormons arrive in Great Salt Lake Valley.
Publicity campaign for annexation of Cuba.
Calhoun's resolutions in Senate, affirming right to take slaves into any United States territory.

1848
Treaty of Guadalupe Hidalgo ends Mexican War.
Secret attempts to purchase Cuba from Spain.
Gold discovered on American River in California.
Women's Rights Convention held in Seneca Falls, New York.
Van Buren, running for President on Free-Soil ticket, receives 10 percent of popular vote.
Zachary Taylor elected President.

1850
In Congress, violent sectional debate culminates in Compromise of 1850.
Taylor's death makes Millard Fillmore President.
Nashville convention considers the South's stake in the Union.
Clayton-Bulwer Treaty.
Nathaniel Hawthorne's *The Scarlet Letter*.

1851
Indian Appropriations Act, designed to begin consolidating Western tribes on reservations.
Herman Melville's *Moby Dick*.

1852
Massachusetts adopts first state compulsory education law.
Harriet Beecher Stowe's *Uncle Tom's Cabin*.
Franklin Pierce elected President.

1853
Upsurge of political nativism, the Know-Nothings.

1854
Gadsden Purchase from Mexico, for $10 million, of 45 thousand square miles below Gila River, needed for a railroad route from the South to the Pacific.
Spectacular Know-Nothing election victories signify critical shift in voter loyalties.
Kansas-Nebraska Bill rekindles sectional controversy over slavery.
Republican party emerges.
Railroads link New York City with the Mississippi.
Commodore Perry opens Japan to American trade.

1831 ...William Lloyd Garrison begins *The Liberator*. Finney's religious revival reaches its climax in Rochester, New York.
McCormick invents reaper.
Jackson purges Calhoun faction from his administration after Peggy Eaton affair.
Mormons migrate from New York State to Ohio; establish outpost near Independence, Missouri.

1832 Beginning of Jackson's war against Bank of the United States.
Special convention in South Carolina nullifies new protective tariff.
Virginia legislative debates over allowing a committee to report on future abolition of slavery.
Jackson reelected President.

1833 Congress provides for a gradual lowering of tariffs, but passes Force Bill authorizing Jackson to enforce federal law in South Carolina.
Formation of American Anti-Slavery Society.
Publication of New York *Sun*, first "penny press."
Emergence of Whig party, formed by Jackson's opponents.

1834 Students quit Lane Theological Seminary, in Cincinnati, after stormy debates over slavery. Abolitionist agitation intensifies.

1835 Jackson calls for suppression of abolitionist propaganda.
Garrison nearly lynched by Boston mob.
Long war against Seminole Indians, and runaway slaves begins in Florida.
Roger B. Taney succeeds Marshall as chief justice.

1836 Jackson's Specie Circular.
Congress adopts the Gag Rule, automatically tabling antislavery petitions.
Abolitionists begin to deluge Congress with petitions.
Texas proclaims independence from Mexico.
Martin Van Buren elected President.

1837 Financial panic brings many bank failures and suspension of specie payment.
The American steamer, *Caroline*, burned in Niagara River after carrying supplies to Canadian rebels.

1842 Webster-Ashburton Treaty settles disputed U.S.-Canadian boundary; provides for extradition of fugitives.
Tyler agrees to higher tariff after Whigs abandon demands for a distribution to the states of surplus federal revenue.
Dorr Rebellion in Rhode Island.

1843 Economic recovery begins.
"Oregon Fever"; first overland caravans to Oregon.
Duff Green, Calhoun, and others begin planning imperial expansion to thwart British plots to undermine American slavery.
Growing radicalism among blacks evidenced in a Convention of the Free People of Color, at Buffalo, New York.

1844 Senate rejects Calhoun's Texas annexation treaty.
Calhoun, as secretary of state, incorporates defense of slavery as part of America's foreign policy.
Congress repeals Gag Rule.
Joseph Smith, Jr., assassinated at Carthage, Illinois.
Slavery issue splits Methodist Episcopal Church into Northern and Southern camps.
James K. Polk elected President.

1845 Before Tyler retires, Texas annexed by joint resolution of Congress.
Polk gives an aggressive reformulation to the Monroe Doctrine.
John Slidell's unsuccessful mission to Mexico to negotiate purchase of New Mexico and California.
Polk risks war with England by asserting America's right to "All Oregon" and terminating joint-occupation agreement.
Failure of Ireland's potato crop marks beginning of mass emigration to United States.
Sectional division of the Baptists.
Henry David Thoreau retreats to Walden Pond.

1846 Beginning of Mexican War. General Zachary Taylor invades Mexico from the north. The "Mormon Battalion" marches with S. W. Kearney's army to southern California.
U.S.-British dispute over Oregon settled.
Wilmot Proviso fuses question of slavery's expansion with consequences of Mexican War.
Walker tariff, adopted for revenue only, eliminates principle of protection.
Elias Howe patents sewing machine.

Treaty to annex Hawaii negotiated but dropped for lack of public support.
Ostend Manifesto regarding Cuba.
Thoreau's *Walden*.
George Fitzhugh's *Sociology for the South*.
As result of election frauds, proslavery settlers in Kansas victorious.

1855 Beginning of "Bleeding Kansas."
Massachusetts desegrates the public schools.
Walt Whitman's *Leaves of Grass*.

1856 John Brown's murderous raid at Pottawatomie.
Preston Brooks's attack on Senator Charles Sumner.
James Buchanan elected President.
Democratic platform calls for annexing Cuba.
Republican platform indicts slavery and polygamy as "twin relics of barbarism."

1857 Financial panic and depression.
Dred Scott decision.
Tariff lowered to 20 percent.
Buchanan sends army to Utah to suppress Mormons.
In Kansas, Lecompton constitution ratified as free-state men refuse to vote.
Beginning of great urban religious revival.
Hinton Helper's *Impending Crisis of the South*.

1858 In Kansas referendum, Lecompton constitution overwhelmingly rejected.
Stephen Douglas joins Republicans in opposing acceptance of Lecompton constitution.
Lincoln-Douglas debates.

1859 A Southern commercial convention at Vicksburg calls for reopening African slave trade.
Kansas voters ratify a constitution prohibiting slavery.
John Brown's raid on Harper's Ferry.
Discovery of Comstock lode.

1860 Democratic party deadlocked at Charleston convention finally divides along sectional lines at Baltimore. Constitutional Union party nominates John Bell. Republicans nominate Abraham Lincoln, who wins.
Senator John J. Crittenden unsuccessfully offers series of constitutional amendments to settle the sectional controversy.
South Carolina secedes from the Union.

The Eagle, the ancient Roman symbol of Jove, was adopted in 1782 as part of the Great Seal of the United States. By the mid-nineteenth century, the eagle had become an increasingly popular symbol of power and grandeur and was used everywhere from figure heads and military insignia to the fine and decorative arts. (*The Museum of Fine Arts, Boston*).

PART FOUR

Uniting the Republic

1860-1890

DAVID HERBERT DONALD

T hese [Northern] people hate us, annoy us, and would have us assassinated by our slaves if they dared," a Southern leader wrote when he learned that a "Black Republican," Abraham Lincoln, would certainly be elected President in 1860. "They are a *different* people from us, whether better or worse and *there is no love* between us. Why then continue together?" The sectional contests of the previous decades suggested that Americans had become members of two distinct, and conflicting, nationalities. By 1860, Northerners and Southerners appeared not to speak the same language, to share the same moral code, or to obey the same law. Compromise could no longer cobble together a union between two such fundamentally different peoples. "I do not see how a barbarous and a civilized community can constitute one state," Ralph Waldo Emerson gravely concluded for many Northerners. "The North and the South are heterogeneous and are better apart," agreed the New Orleans *Bee*. "We [Southerners] are doomed if we proclaim not our political independence."

On first thought, the four-year civil war that broke out in 1861 seems powerfully to confirm this idea that the Union and the Confederacy were two distinct nations. Yet the conduct of the war suggested that Northerners and Southerners were not so different as their political and intellectual leaders had maintained.

At the beginning of the conflict both governments tried in much the same ways to mobilize for battle their invertebrate, unorganized societies. As the war progressed, both Union and Confederacy adopted much the same diplomatic, military, and economic policies. By the end of the war both governments were committed to abolishing slavery, the one institution that had most clearly divided the sections in 1860.

The events of the postwar period gave further evidence that the inhabitants of the North and the South were—what they had always been—part of the same nationality. Though some Republicans wanted a radical revolution in the social and economic system of the conquered Confederacy, there were relatively few, and only limited, social experiments or political innovations during Reconstruction. In both the North and the South, shared beliefs in limited government, in economic laissez-faire, and in the superiority of the white race blocked drastic change, while shared economic interests and national political parties pulled the sections back into a common pattern of cooperation.

In the backward glance of history, then, the conflicts and the quarrels of the Civil War era take on a significance different from their meaning to participants and contemporaries. In retrospect it is clear that the Civil War was not so much a contest between two separate nations as a struggle within the American nation to define a boundary between the centralizing, nationalizing tendencies in American life and the opposing tendencies toward localism, parochialism, and fragmentation. The issue, then, was the familiar one of majority rule and minority rights: How could a society follow the dictates of the majority of its members without infringing on the essential interests of those who were in the minority? For Americans in the 1860s, this was no new question; it had been the central concern of American political philosophers from James Madison to John C. Calhoun. Even today, when the balance of power has shifted so markedly toward a national, centralized society, the rights of regional and ethnic minorities remain a topic for hot dispute.

Perhaps there can be no final resolution to the problem of reconciling, in a single nation, the interests of the whole and those of the parts. Certainly the Civil War generation did not find one. But the painful experience of war and its aftermath led them to work out a series of informal agreements and understandings that, on the one hand, guaranteed to the national government sufficient strength to sustain the interests of the country as a whole. On the other hand, this loose set of compromises secured some degree of autonomy to many—but not all—local and parochial groups adversely affected by centralization. After decades of strife and years of bloodshed, Americans, both in the North and the South, came to accept this pragmatic compromise. It was a solution that was neither completely satisfactory nor wholly logical. It rested less upon reason than upon emotion. It reflected the hard-learned lesson of the Civil War that Americans were, after all, one people.

19

Stalemate
1861-1862

During the first two years of the Civil War, as the Union and the Confederacy grappled with each other inconclusively, it seemed that two distinct and incompatible nations had emerged from the American soil. Certainly the aims announced by their leaders were totally inconsistent. President Abraham Lincoln announced that the United States would "constitutionally defend, and maintain itself"; the territorial integrity of the nation must remain inviolate. For the Confederate States, President Jefferson Davis proclaimed that his country's "career of independence" must be "inflexibly pursued." As the rival governments raised and equipped armies, attempted to finance a huge war, and sought diplomatic recognition and economic assistance abroad, the people of the two nations increasingly thought of each other as enemies: "Yankees" and "Rebels." It is easy to understand why Lord John Russell, the British foreign minister, concluded: "I do not see how the United States can be cobbled together again by any compromise. . . . I suppose the break-up of the Union is now inevitable."

A shrewder observer might have reached the opposite conclusion. Perhaps the most striking thing about the war in America was the fact that both sides carried it on through virtually identical methods. The Union and the Confederate governments faced the same wartime problems and arrived at the same wartime solutions. Northerners and Southerners on the battlefields found each other not two alien peoples but mirror images. That identity made the conflict truly a brother's war.

The Rival Governments

The government of the Confederate States was in most respects a duplicate of that of the United States, from which the Southern states had just withdrawn. Framed by delegates from six states of the Lower South (delegates from Texas, which seceded on February 1, 1861, arrived late), the Constitution largely followed the wording of the one drawn up in Philadelphia in 1787. To be sure, the new charter recognized the "sovereign and independent character" of the constituent states, but it also announced that they were forming "a permanent federal government," and it listed most of the same restrictions on state action included in the United States Constitution. Unlike that document, it used no euphemism about persons "held to Service or Labour" but recognized explicitly "the right of property in negro slaves." Otherwise, the two documents were substantially and intentionally identical. As secessionist Benjamin H. Hill of Georgia explained, "We hugged that [United States] Constitution to our bosom and carried it with us."

For President of the new republic, the Montgomery convention chose a man distinguished for his moderation in the secession crisis and for his slowness in concluding that breakup of the Union was inevitable.* If the crowds that thronged Montgomery's streets on February 18, 1861, to watch the procession of military companies wearing red jackets, battle-green jackets, and gray jackets and flashing their shiny new bayonets hoped to hear a stirring inaugural from the South's new head of state, they were disappointed. Stepping forward on the portico of the Alabama statehouse, Jefferson Davis, of Mississippi, gave a long, legalistic review of the acts of Northern aggression that had led to the formation of the new state. While Davis pledged he would, if necessary, "maintain, by the final arbitrament of the sword, the position which we have assumed among the nations of the earth," he spoke in a tone more melancholy than martial. He saw himself as the leader of a conservative movement. "We have labored to preserve the Government of our fathers in its spirit," he insisted.

Just two weeks later, from the portico of the yet unfinished Capitol in Washington, another conservative took his inaugural oath. The capital was thronged, as Nathaniel Hawthorne wrote, with "office-seekers, wire-pullers, inventors, artists, poets, prosers (including editors, army correspondents, attachés of foreign journals, and long-winded talkers), clerks, diplomatists, mail contractors, [and]

---

*The Montgomery convention drew up a provisional constitution of the Confederacy, constituted itself the provisional legislature of the new republic, and named Jefferson Davis the provisional president. It also drew up a permanent constitution, which was submitted to the states for ratification. After that, regular elections were held in the fall of 1861 both for members of the Confederate Congress and for President. Reelected without opposition, Davis was formally inaugurated as the first and only regular president of the Confederate States on February 22, 1862.

ALEX. H. STEPHENS. WM. L. YANCEY. JEFF. DAVIS. HOWELL COBB.
Vice-President *Leader of the Secession Party* *First President* *President of the Senate*

THE STARTING POINT OF THE GREAT WAR BETWEEN THE STATES.

INAUGURATION OF JEFFERSON DAVIS

INAUGURATION OF JEFFERSON DAVIS

On February 18, 1861, Jefferson Davis, standing in front of the state capitol at Montgomery, Alabama, took the oath of office as the first—and, as it proved, only—President of the Confederate States of America. Davis is the thin, tall figure behind the lectern. To his right is William L. Yancey, a leading secessionist; to his right, Howell Cobb, president of the Confederate Senate, who administered the oath. *(Library of Congress.)*

railway directors." On public buildings along the route of the inaugural procession, sharpshooters were strategically placed, to prevent any pro-Southern interruption of the proceedings. Doubtless few in the crowd could hear Abraham Lincoln's words, but when they read his address in the newspapers, they might have been struck by its similarity in tone to Davis's. Vowing that the Union would be preserved, Lincoln gave a low-keyed version of the previous sectional quarrels, explained his personal views on slavery, and pledged that he contemplated "no invasion—no using of force" against the seceded states. In a warning softened by sadness, he reminded his listeners of the oath he had just taken to preserve, protect, and defend the government of the United States and entreated his Southern fellow citizens to pause before they assailed it. "In *your* hands, my dissatisfied fellow-countrymen," he concluded, "and not in *mine*, is the momentous issue of civil war."

In the weeks immediately following the two inaugurations, the central problem confronting both Davis and Lincoln was not so much whether either should start a civil war but whether they could form viable governments. In Davis's Confederacy, everything had to be started afresh. Even the most routine legal and governmental matters could not be taken for granted. For instance, it was not certain, until the Confederate Congress passed an act, whether the laws of the United States passed before 1861 and the decisions of the United States courts were binding in the seceded states. The new nation had to choose a flag—over the opposition of some purists who claimed that the Confederacy, representing the true American spirit, ought to retain the Stars and Stripes and let the Union look for a new banner. It had to provide for the printing of money and postage stamps—no small undertaking in a land where engravers were so few and incompetent that their unprepossessing likenesses of Jefferson Davis and other Confederate worthies caused suspicion about the loyalty of the artists.

In selecting his cabinet advisers, President Davis theoretically had a free hand, but in fact his range of choice was severely limited. No man of doubtful loyalty to the new government could be permitted a place in his cabinet; no Southern Unionist in the tradition of Henry Clay, John J. Crittenden, and John Bell was invited. On the other hand, because Davis wanted the world to see that the Confederacy was governed by sober, responsible men, he excluded from his council all the most conspicuous Southern fire-eaters. Then, too, he had to achieve some balance between former Whigs and former Democrats, and he felt obliged to secure a wide geographical spread by appointing one member of his original cabinet from each of the seven Confederate states, except Mississippi, which he himself represented. As a result of these elaborate calculations, Davis's cabinet consisted neither of his personal friends nor of the outstanding political leaders of the South, except for Secretary of State Robert Toombs, of Georgia, who served only briefly.

Such a cabinet might have sufficed in a country where administrative procedures and routines were firmly rooted. Instead in the Confederacy there was everywhere a lack of preparation, a lack of resources for running a government. Typical was the Confederate Treasury Department, which initially consisted of one unswept room in a Montgomery bank, "without furniture of any kind; empty . . . of desks, tables, chairs or other appliances for the conduct of business." The secretary of the treasury had to pay for the first rickety furniture out of his own pocket.

Disorganization and improvisation also characterized Lincoln's government in Washington. The Union had the advantage of owning the Capitol, the White House, and the permanent records of the United States government, and it had a recognized flag and a postal system. But in other respects it was thoroughly demoralized. Lincoln's government had no clear mandate from the people, for the President had received less than 40 percent of the popular vote in the 1860 election. It had an army of only 14,657 men, and every day army and navy officers announced that they were defecting to the South. Its treasury was empty. Some of the most experienced clerks in the Washington offices were leaving to

ABRAHAM LINCOLN

"Probably," wrote Walt Whitman, "the reader has seen physiognomies . . . that, behind their homeliness or even ugliness, held superior points so subtle, yet so palpable, making the real life of their faces almost as impossible to depict as a wild perfume or fruit taste . . . such was Lincoln's face—the peculiar color, the lines of it, the eyes, mouth, expression. Of technical beauty it had nothing —but to the eye of a great artist it furnished a rare study, a feast, and fascination." (*The National Archives.*)

join the Confederacy, and others who remained were of suspect loyalty. Adding to the confusion was the fact that Lincoln's was the first Republican administration and under the prevailing spoils system, party workers who had helped elect the Republican candidate now flocked to Washington, expecting to oust Democratic officeholders. The claimants for patronage ranged from elegant Brahmins, like the historian John Lothrop Motley, who sought a diplomatic appointment, to Lincoln's rough frontier acquaintances, but they all shared one characteristic, persistence. Accompanied by their representative or senator and bearing huge rolls of recommending letters, the office seekers besieged Lincoln in the White House. Wryly the President likened his plight to the problem of the innkeeper whose clients demanded that he rent rooms in one wing of his hotel even while he was trying to put out a fire in the other.

To add to the confusion, not one member of the Lincoln administration had previously held a responsible position in the executive branch of the national government, and many, including the President himself, had no administrative experience of any sort. Like Davis, Lincoln made no attempt to form a coalition government; for his cabinet he did not choose leaders of the Douglas Democracy or the Constitutional Union party. Nor after a few unsuccessful efforts did he name Unionists from the South. Instead, all members of his cabinet were Republicans. That fact, however, scarcely gave his government unity, for several of Lincoln's cabinet appointees had themselves been candidates for the Republican nomination in 1860 and hence were rivals of Lincoln and of each other. The most conspicuous member was Secretary of State William H. Seward, wily and devious, extravagant in utterance but cautious in action, who felt that he had a duty to save the country through compromise and conciliation despite its bumbling, inexperienced President. Seward's principal rival in the cabinet was Secretary of the Treasury Salmon P. Chase, pompous and self-righteous, who had an equally condescending view of Lincoln's talents and who lusted to become the next President of the United States. The other members, with whom Lincoln had had only the slightest personal acquaintance, were appointed because they were supposed to have political influence or to represent key states.

Winning the Border States

Desperately needing time to get organized, these two shaky rival administrations immediately confronted a problem and a crisis, which were intimately interrelated. The problem concerned the future of the eight remaining slave states, which had not yet seceded. Though tied to the Deep South by blood and sentiment and fearful of abolitionist attacks upon their "peculiar institution" of slavery, these states had refused to rush out of the Union. In January 1861, Virginia had elected a convention to consider secession, but it dillydallied and did nothing. In February, North Carolinians and Tennesseans voted against holding secession conventions. When the Arkansas and Missouri conventions did meet in March, they voted not to secede. Up to April 1861, Kentucky, Maryland, and Delaware held no elections or conventions. But the loyalty of all these states to the Union was clearly conditional upon the policy Lincoln's government adopted towards the Confederacy.

The crisis was the first test of that policy. It concerned the fate of the United States installations in the seceded states that still remained under Federal control. At Fort Pickens in Pensacola Bay, an uneasy truce held between the Union troops in the garrison and the Confederate force on the mainland. The real trouble spot was Fort Sumter, in the harbor of Charleston, South Carolina. Its garrison, which consisted of about seventy Union soldiers and nine officers under the command of Major Robert Anderson, was no serious military threat to the Confederacy, but its presence at Charleston, the very center of secession, was an intolerable affront to Southern pride. Confederates insisted that President Davis demonstrate his devotion to the Southern cause by forcing Anderson and his men out immediately. Many Northerners, who had despairingly watched during the final months of the Buchanan administration as fort after fort was turned over to the Confederates, also saw Sumter as a test of the strength and will of the Lincoln administration.

Despite these pressures, there were in both governments powerful voices that urged compromise or at least delay. All but two members of Lincoln's cabinet initially thought that Sumter should be evacuated. Davis's secretary of state was equally adverse to hasty action. When the Confederate cabinet discussed attacking Anderson, Toombs solemnly warned: "The firing upon that fort will inaugurate a civil war greater than any the world has yet seen."

But Anderson's situation made some action necessary. After Charleston authorities prohibited further sale of food to the troops in the fort, his men faced starvation. The day after Lincoln was inaugurated he learned that the garrison, unless supplied, could hold out no longer than April 15. Since Lincoln had just pledged that he would "hold, occupy, and possess" all places and property belonging to the government, he promptly directed his secretary of the navy to begin outfitting an expedition to provision Fort Sumter. At the same time, recognizing how dangerously explosive the Charleston situation was, he explored alternatives. One possibility was to reinforce Fort Pickens, in the relatively calm area of Florida; that would allow Lincoln to demonstrate his firmness of purpose, even if he was obliged to withdraw Anderson from the Charleston harbor. But the naval expedition sent to Florida miscarried, the Union commander at Pickens misunderstood his orders, and the planned reinforcement could not be completed in time for Washington to know about it before Anderson's deadline for surrender. Another possibility was to consent to a peaceable withdrawal from Fort Sumter in return for assurances that the still vacillating border states would remain in the Union. "If you will guarantee to me the State of Virginia, I shall remove the troops," Lincoln confidentially promised a prominent Virginia Unionist. "A State for a fort is no bad business." But the Virginians delayed, a rainstorm kept a delegation of Unionists from reaching Washington, and they could give no firm promises. Seeing no other possible course Lincoln let the expedition bearing food and supplies sail for Sumter.

President Davis understood that in merely supplying Fort Sumter Lincoln was not committing an act of aggression. Indeed, he predicted that for political reasons the United States government would avoid making an attack so long as the hope of retaining the border states remained. But the Confederate President's hand was forced too. Hot-headed Governor Francis Pickens and other South Carolina extremists, impatient with Davis's caution, prepared to attack the fort. Rather than let Confederate policy be set by a state governor, Davis ordered General P. G. T. Beauregard, in command of the Confederate forces at Charleston, to demand the surrender of Fort Sumter. Anderson responded that he would soon be starved out, but he failed to promise to withdraw by a definite date. Beauregard's officers felt they had no alternative but to reduce the fort. At 4:30 A.M. on April 12 firing began. To the aged Virginia secessionist Edmund Ruffin, who for a generation had crusaded for the creation of a separate Southern nation, was entrusted the honor of firing one of the first shots against the flag of the United States. Outside the harbor the relief expedition Lincoln had sent watched impotently while Confederates bombarded the fort. After thirty-four hours, with ammunition nearly exhausted, Anderson was obliged to surrender.

Promptly Lincoln called for 75,000 volunteer soldiers to put down the "insurrection" in the South. On May 6 the Confederate Congress countered by formally declaring that a state of war existed. The American Civil War had begun.

Both at that time and later there was controversy about the responsibility for precipitating the conflict. Critics claimed that Lincoln by sending the expedition to provision Fort Sumter deliberately tricked the Confederates into firing the first shot. Indeed, some months after the event Lincoln himself told a friend that his plan for sending supplies to Major Anderson had "succeeded." "They attacked Sumter," he explained; "it fell, and thus, did more service than it otherwise could." That statement clearly reveals Lincoln's wish that if hostilities began, the Confederacy should bear the blame for initiating them, but it does little to prove that Lincoln wanted war. It is well to remember that throughout the agonizing crisis the Confederates took the initiative at Sumter. It was Charleston authorities who cut off Anderson's food supply; it was Confederate authorities who decided that, though the fort offered no military threat, Anderson must surrender; and it was the Southerners who fired the first shot. Writing privately to the Confederate commander at Fort Pickens, President Davis acknowledged that there would be a psychological advantage if the Southerners waited for the Federal government to make the initial attack; but, he added, "When we are ready to relieve our territory and jurisdiction of the presence of a foreign garrison that advantage is overbalanced by other considerations." These other considerations impelled Davis to take the initiative at Sumter.

If intent can be tested by consequences, it is evident that, initially at least, it was the Confederacy, not the Union, that benefited from the attack upon Fort Sumter. The slave states still in the Union had now to make a choice of allegiances, and for a time it seemed that all would join the Confederacy. Virginia Governor John Letcher spurned Lincoln's call for troops as a bid "to inaugurate civil war," and on April 17 the state convention hastily passed a secession ordinance. Technically it was subject to popular ratification, but in actuality it immediately linked to the Confederacy the most populous and influential state of the Upper South, with its long tradition of leadership, its vast natural resources, and its large Tredegar Iron Works.

Other border slave states acted only a little less precipitously. On May 6 the Arkansas convention voted, with only five dissenters, to withdraw from the Union. When Lincoln's call for troops reached Governor Isham Harris of Tennessee, he replied haughtily: "In such an unholy crusade no gallant son of Tennessee will ever draw his sword," and began private negotiations with Confederate officials. On May 7 the Tennessee state legislature ratified the arrangements Harris had already made and voted to secede. On May 20 the North Carolina convention, under pressure from pro-Confederate newspapers to withdraw forever from the "vile, rotten, infidelic, puritanic, negro-worshipping, negro-stealing, negro-equality . . . Yankee-Union," unanimously adopted a secession ordinance.

Far to the west, the Confederacy scored another victory in the Indian Territory (later to become the state of Oklahoma). Confederate commissioner Albert Pike had little success with the Plains Indians there, but he won over most of the so-called civilized tribes, many of whom were slaveholders. The Confederacy agreed to pay all annuities that the United States government had previously provided, and it allowed the Choctaws, Chickasaws, Creeks, Seminoles, and Cherokees to send delegates to the Confederate Congress. In return these tribes promised to supply troops for the Confederate army. Most of them loyally supported the Southern effort throughout the war, and the Cherokee chief, Brigadier General Stand Watie, did not formally surrender until a month after the war was over. A rival faction among the Cherokees, headed by Chief John Ross, and most of the Plains Indians favored the Union cause.

Elsewhere along the border, the Confederacy fared less well. Though it was a slave state with sentimental ties to the South, Delaware never really contemplated secession. To Lincoln's call for troops, the Delaware governor replied that his state had no standing militia, but he unenthusiastically recommended that citizens could form volunteer companies, which had the "option of offering their services to the general government for the defense of its capital."

Much more painful was the decision of Maryland, a state bitterly divided. On April 19 a pro-Confederate mob in Baltimore fired upon a Massachusetts regiment en route to Washington, and communications were then cut between the Union capital and the rest of the country. For a time it seemed highly probable that Maryland would secede. But Lincoln arranged for further shipments of

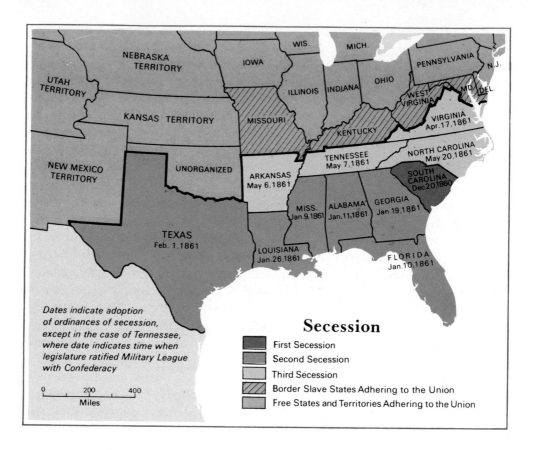

Union troops to bypass Baltimore until passions could cool. Tactfully reassuring the timorous governor, the President did everything possible to strengthen Unionist sentiment in Maryland. By May, Baltimore was back under Federal control, and the mayor, along with nineteen members of the state legislature, was unceremoniously arrested and jailed without trial. In the 1861 fall elections, Maryland soldiers who wanted to go home and vote received furloughs, while provost marshals kept from the polls any persons believed to favor disunion. As a result, Maryland elected an uncompromising Unionist as governor, and thereafter there was no further question of secession.

In Missouri the Union cause was managed with less skill. Though the pro-Southern governor denounced Lincoln's call for troops as "illegal, unconstitutional, revolutionary, inhuman, [and] diabolical," public opinion was so evenly divided that no steps towards secession probably would have occurred had it not been for the hasty action of Unionist leaders. Union commander Nathaniel Lyon precipitated hostilities by overrunning an encampment of pro-secessionist militia near Saint Louis. Confederate sympathizers rallied to protect them, and for two days there was bloody street fighting in the city. Open warfare followed. Union forces controlled the area around Saint Louis; secessionists commanded by Sterling Price, most of the rest of the state. After General John C. Frémont became commander of the department of the West, with his headquarters in Saint Louis, the territory under Union control was gradually extended, although Lyon, in a rash attempt to drive the secessionist forces from the state, was defeated and killed at the battle of Wilson's Creek on August 10. During the next three years, guerrilla warfare devastated the Missouri countryside, as neighbor fought neighbor. The bitterness was further aggravated when free-soil men from Kansas, remembering how Missouri "border ruffians" had once tried to extend slavery into their state, crossed the border to take revenge upon secessionist sympathizers. In turn, Confederate gangs, the most notorious led by the horse thief and murderer William C. Quantrill, preyed upon Missouri Unionists.

Far more skillful was Lincoln's handling of Kentucky, which was his native state as well as that of Jefferson Davis. As in Missouri, the governor was an outright seccessionist, but strong Unionist sentiment prevented the calling of a state convention. Out of this stalemate rose the anomalous situation of Kentucky declaring itself neutral in any conflict between the United States and the Confederacy. Between May and September of 1861 both the Lincoln and the Davis governments ostensibly acquiesced in this policy of neutrality; at the same time, each tried quietly to strengthen the hands of its partisans in Kentucky. Finally, suspecting that Federal forces were about to seize a position in Kentucky, the Confederates moved first and took Columbus. Union troops then entered Paducah, and neutrality was dead. These months of indeterminate status gave Kentucky Unionists a chance to plan and organize, so that the state did not, like Tennessee, join the Confederacy nor, like Missouri, become a fierce battleground. In bringing about this outcome, Lincoln himself played a large role, for he gave Kentucky affairs close attention and took pains to assure prominent Kentuckians in private interviews that he "intended to make no attack, direct or indirect, upon the institution or property [meaning slavery] of any State."

Against the major Confederate victory in Virginia, the Union could count a lesser success in the western counties of that state, long disaffected from the planter oligarchy of the Tidewater region and little interested in slavery. When the Virginia convention voted for secession, a sizable minority of the delegates, mostly from these western counties, were opposed, and they went home vowing to keep their state in the Union. A series of exceedingly complex maneuvers followed, including the summoning of several more or less extralegal conventions and the creating of a new government for what was termed "reorganized" Virginia, rivaling that at Richmond. This "reorganized" government then gave permission—as required by the United States Constitution—for the counties west of the mountains to form a new and overwhelmingly Unionist state of West Virginia. Not until 1863, when all these steps were completed, was the new state admitted to the Union. Thus by that date there were no fewer than three state governments on Virginia soil: the pro-Confederate government at Richmond; the "reorganized" pro-Union government, which had only a small constituency and huddled under the protection of Federal guns at Alexandria; and the new Union government of West Virginia.

In summary then, after the firing of Fort Sumter, the border slave states divided. Virginia, Arkansas, Tennessee, and North Carolina went with the Confederacy; Delaware, Maryland, Missouri, and Kentucky remained in the Union, where they were presently joined by West Virginia.

It is impossible to exaggerate the importance that these decisions, made early in the conflict, had upon the conduct of the Civil War. For the Confederacy, the accession of states from the Upper South was essential. For all the brave talk at Montgomery, the Confederacy was not a viable nation so long as it consisted only of the seven states of the Deep South. So limited, the Confederate States could not dream of carrying on a war for independence. Its population was only one-sixth of that of the remaining states of the Union. In all the Gulf states in 1861 there was not a foundry to roll heavy iron plate or to cast cannon, nor a large powder works, nor indeed a single factory of importance. But when Virginia, North Carolina, Arkansas, and Tennessee joined the Confederacy, they almost doubled its population. What is more, they brought to the new nation the natural resources, the foundries and factories, and the skilled artisans that made it possible to rival the Union. To recognize the economic and psychological strength added by these states of the Upper South—and also to escape the sweltering summer heats of Montgomery—the Confederacy in May 1861 removed its capital from Montgomery to Richmond.

If the states of the Upper South brought the Confederacy strength they also limited its freedom of action. So important were Richmond and Virginia that defending this area became the passion of the Confederate government, so absorbing that it neglected the vital Western theaters of military operations.

For Lincoln's government, too, the border states were vital. If Maryland had seceded, the capital at Washington would have been surrounded by enemy territory, cut off from the Union states of the North and the West. Confederate control of Kentucky would have imperiled river transportation along the Ohio, and the secession of Missouri would have endangered Mississippi river traffic and cut off communication with Kansas and the Pacific coast. While Lincoln grieved over the secession of the states that joined the Confederacy, he could take comfort in the fact that by keeping four slave states in the Union he was preventing the Southern armies from recruiting from a population that was three-fifths as large as that of the original Confederacy.

So important were the border states for the Union government that special pains had to be taken not to disturb their loyalty. In particular, Lincoln saw that there must be no premature action against slavery. European nations might fail to understand the nature of the American Civil War and Northern abolitionists might denounce their President as "the slave-hound from Illinois," but Lincoln knew that to tamper with slavery would result in the loss of the border states, particularly Kentucky. "I think to lose Kentucky is nearly the same as to lose the whole game," he wrote to a friend. "Kentucky gone, we cannot hold Missouri, nor, as I think, Maryland. These all against us, and the job on our hands is too large for us. We would as well consent to separation at once, including the surrender of this capitol."

Raising the Armies

While Lincoln and Davis were moving in parallel fashion to win the support of the border states, ordinary folk, North and South, were rallying around their flags. Here too, the pattern of response was remarkably similar in the Union and in the Confederacy. On both sides the firing on Fort Sumter triggered a rush to enlist. "War! and volunteers are the only topics of conversation or thought," an Oberlin College student reported when the news reached Ohio. "The lessons today have been a mere form. I cannot study. I cannot sleep, I cannot work, and I don't know as I can write." An Arkansas youth recorded identical emotions: "So impatient did I become for starting that I felt like a thousand pins were pricking me in every part of the body and [I] started off a week in advance of my brothers."

Ordinarily a volunteer offered to enlist in one of the regiments that was being raised in his community. Wealthy citizens and prominent politicians usually took the lead in recruiting these companies. The South Carolina planter Wade Hampton, for example, raised, organized, and equipped at his own expense the Hampton Legion of one thousand men. Inevitably these regiments displayed a wide variety of arms and accoutrements, ranging from rusty flintlocks to the latest sharpshooting rifles. Often their uniforms bore distinctive insignia; for instance, a Louisiana battalion recruited from the daredevil roustabouts of the New Orleans levees called themselves the Tigers, and their scarlet skullcaps bore mottoes like "Tiger on the Leap" and "Tiger in Search of a Black Republican." Perhaps the most colorful, and impractical, uniforms were those of the Northern Zouave regiments, dressed in imitation of the

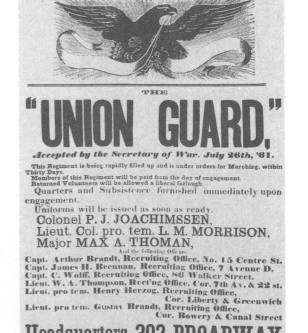

UNITED STATES VOLUNTEERS

In both the Union and the Confederacy the first step in raising a regiment was often the publication of a broadside like this one calling for volunteers. *(Library of Congress.)*

French troops in North Africa. These soldiers, wearing their red fezzes, scarlet baggy trousers, and blue sashes, were magnificent in a military review, but when they had to wade across a stream, their baggy garments ballooned around them and they floated down the current like so many exotic waterlilies. When a regiment's ranks were filled, there was invariably a farewell ceremony, featuring hortatory addresses, lengthy prayers, and the presentation of the regimental flag, often handsewn by patriotic wives and sweethearts of the enlisted men. Then, loaded with hams, cakes, and sweetmeats provided by fond mothers and wives, the men went off to war.

Neither Union nor Confederate war departments knew what to do with this

AN ILLINOIS VOLUNTEER OF 1861 (LEFT) AND PRIVATE JOHN WERTH, RICHMOND HOWITZER BATTALION, C.S.A. (RIGHT)

As soon as volunteers were sworn in and received their uniforms and equipment, most rushed to photographers' studios to have pictures made for their loved ones. *(Left, Library of Congress; right, The Museum of the Confederacy, Richmond.)*

flood of volunteers. Leroy P. Walker, the first Confederate secretary of war, held office because the leading Alabama secessionist, William L. Yancey, recommended him; he had had no military training and no administrative experience. An amiable Southern gentleman of the old school, fond of prolonged conversation with visitors, of writing discursive three-page business letters, and of filing his correspondence by piling it in a chair after he had read it, Walker was wholly unable to cope with the situation. Complaining that he lacked equipment and arms, he refused the services of regiment after regiment. Perhaps 200,000 Confederate volunteers were thus rejected during the first year of the war.

The Northern war office was equally chaotic. Simon Cameron, the secretary

of war, had been forced upon Lincoln as part of a political bargain. Known as "The Great Winnebago Chief" because of frauds he allegedly committed while an Indian agent, Cameron's main objective was to become the undisputed boss of Pennsylvania politics. There is no evidence that he used his cabinet position to line his own pockets, but he did employ his huge patronage to strengthen his faction of Pennsylvania Republicans. Lacking administrative talent, Cameron, like Walker, simply could not deal with the flood of volunteers, nor could he supervise the hundreds of contracts his office had to make for arms, ammunition, uniforms, horses, and dozens of other articles for the army. Inevitably there was haste, inefficiency, and corruption. For instance, in October 1861, General Frémont, desperately needing mounts for his cavalry in Missouri, contracted to purchase 411 horses. Subsequent investigation proved that 350 of the beasts supplied him were undersized, under or overaged, ringboned, blind, spavined, and incurably unfit for service; 5 were dead. Unable to equip the Union volunteers as they rushed to defend the flag, Cameron thought it was his principal duty "to avoid receiving troops faster than the government can provide for them."

As the war wore on, the initial enthusiasm for volunteering abated, and many of the men rejected by Walker and Cameron in the early months of the conflict were never available again. Soon even those whose services had been accepted began to exhibit less enthusiasm for the war. Most had expected the army to be like the peacetime militia, to which all able-bodied white men belonged; the monthly militia rallies had been the occasion for fun and frolic, punctuated by a little, uneven military drill, a considerable amount of political oratory, and a great deal of drinking. Now they discovered that war was not a lark. Belonging to the army meant discipline, spit-and-polish cleaning of equipment, and hours of close-order drill. A soldier's life was one of endless monotony, punctuated occasionally by danger from enemy bullets and more frequently by disease resulting from inadequate food and clothing, lack of vaccination, filthy drinking water, and open latrines. By the end of 1861, many Union volunteers were beginning to count the weeks until the end of their three-year term of enlistment. Confederate regiments, which had been enrolled for twelve months, were about ready to disband in the spring of 1862.

Of necessity, then, Lincoln and Davis moved, almost simultaneously, to strengthen their war departments in order to give more central direction to their armies. In January 1862, having persuaded Cameron to become American minister to Russia, Lincoln named a former Democrat, Edwin M. Stanton, to the war department. Brusque and imperious, Stanton was also hard-working, efficient, and incorruptible. Quickly he reorganized the war department, regularized procedures for letting war contracts, and investigated frauds. Standing behind an old-fashioned writing desk, looking like an irritable schoolmaster before a willful class, Stanton heard all war department business in public. Patronage seekers, even when accompanied by congressmen, he brusquely dismissed; contractors had to state their prices in clear, loud voices; and even a petitioner bear-

PRESENTATION OF COLORS OF 1ST MICHIGAN INFANTRY

Regiments were raised under state, not national, auspices.
Before a regiment left home to join the Union or Confederate army, there was usually a formal ceremony, where
the governor or some other high-ranking state official made
a patriotic speech and presented the fighting men with
their regimental flag. (*Detroit Public Library.*)

ing a letter of introduction from the President might be abruptly shown the door.
Working incessantly, Stanton saw to it that the Union army became the best
supplied military force the world had ever seen.

It took a bit longer for Davis to find a war secretary to his liking. When Walker,
to everyone's relief, resigned in September 1861, Davis replaced him briefly with
Judah P. Benjamin, who subsequently became Confederate secretary of state, and
then with George Wythe Randolph, who did much to see that Robert E. Lee and
Thomas J. ("Stonewall") Jackson had the necessary arms and supplies for their
1862 campaigns. But when Randolph and Davis disagreed over strategy, the
secretary had to go, and in November 1862 James A. Seddon succeeded Randolph. Sallow and cadaverous, looking, as one of his clerks remarked, like "an
exhumed corpse after a month's interment," Seddon was nevertheless diligent
and efficient. Moreover, he had the good sense to give solid support to subordinates of great ability. Perhaps the most competent of these was General

Josiah Gorgas, head of the Confederate ordnance bureau. Thanks to Gorgas's exertions, the Confederacy, which in May 1861 had only about 20 cartridges for each musket or rifle, had by 1862 built powder plants capable of producing 20 million cartridges—enough to supply an army of 400,000 men for twelve months.

While both Presidents were strengthening their war departments, they also moved, in 1862, to take a more active role in recruiting troops. Because the twelve-month period of enlistment of Confederate troops expired in the spring, Davis warned that the Southern army would be decimated just as Federal forces were approaching Richmond. Uncomfortably ignoring the principle of state sovereignty proclaimed in the Confederate Constitution, the Southern Congress on April 16, 1862, passed a national conscription act, declaring every able-bodied white male between the ages of eighteen and thirty-five subject to military service. This first conscription law in American history was, however, less Draconian than it seemed. It allowed for numerous exemptions, ranging from druggists to Confederate government officials; and a subsequent law excused from military service planters or overseers supervising twenty or more slaves. The purpose of the Confederate conscription act was less to raise new troops than to encourage veterans to reenlist. If the men stayed in the army, the law provided, they could remain in their present regiments and elect new officers; if they left, it threatened, they could be drafted and assigned to any unit that needed them.

Lincoln's government moved toward conscription a little more slowly. After the bloody campaigns in the summer of 1862, volunteering all but stopped, and the army needed 300,000 new men. Union governors suggested to the President that a draft would stimulate volunteering, and on July 17 the Federal Congress passed a loosely worded measure authorizing the President to set quotas of troops to be raised by each state and empowering him to use Federal force to draft them if state officials failed to meet their quotas. Intentionally a bogeyman, which the governors used to encourage enlistments, this first Union conscription law brought in only a handful of men.

Financing the War

If it became hard for both the Union and the Confederate governments to raise troops, it was even harder to supply and pay them. Though the United States in 1860 was potentially one of the great industrial nations of the world, it was still primarily an agricultural country, with five out of six of its inhabitants living on farms. The factories that would be called upon to supply vast armies were mostly small in scale. Some 239 companies manufactured firearms in 1860; their average invested capital was less than $11,000. Textile mills, especially for the manufacture of woolens, were larger, but ready-made clothing was still sewn in small shops. The country produced an abundance of foodstuffs, but there was no effective wholesale marketing system for meat and grain. Maps showed that by 1860 the country was crisscrossed by 30,000 miles of railroads, but most of these were in fact short spans, each under its own corporate management, often not connected to other lines at common terminals and even having different rail gauges. The sending of a boxcar from, say, Baltimore to Saint Louis was an undertaking that required diplomacy, improvisation, frequent transshipment, long delays, and a great deal of luck. Commercial transactions were impeded by the fact that the United States in 1860 had no national bank; indeed, it did not even have a national currency, for the bills issued by the numerous state banks, depreciating at various rates, formed the principal circulating medium.

Yet Union and Confederate leaders had somehow to mobilize this invertebrate economy so that it could support an enormous war effort. Both governments made a basic initial decision to rely primarily upon privately owned factories to supply their armies, rather than upon government-operated ones. Necessity more than a theoretical preference for free-enterprise lay behind this choice. If individual businessmen and corporations had little experience in the large-scale production of goods, the civil servants at Washington and Richmond had even less. Where it seemed useful, both governments supplemented the output of private industry with production from government-owned plants. While the Lincoln administration was purchasing firearms from Colt, Remington, and dozens of other manufacturers, it continued to rely upon its armories, especially the one at Springfield, Massachusetts, for some of its best weapons. Because the South was even more largely rural and agricultural than the North, it had to be more active in establishing government-owned plants, the most successful of which was the huge powder factory at Augusta, Georgia. But both governments contracted with private individuals and corporations for most of the arms, clothing, and other equipment needed for the armies.

It was easier to contract for supplies than it was to pay for them. Both Union and Confederacy began the war with empty treasuries. When Secretary of the Treasury Chase took up his duties in Washington, he was horrified to discover that between April and June 1861 the expenses of the Union government would exceed its income by $17 million. Inexperienced in financial matters, Chase, whose reputation had been built on his work as an antislavery lawyer and politician, desperately cast about for solutions. He managed to keep up a good façade, for visitors to his office thought this tall, broad-shouldered, and proudly erect statesman was the incarnation of "intelligence, strength, courage, and dignity"; yet inside, Chase was a jelly of confusion and uncertainty. So wavering was the advice he offered in cabinet that some of his own colleagues thought he was pursuing some devious goal of his own, and Secretary of the Navy Gideon Welles concluded that he was "cowardly and aspiring, shirking and presumptuous, forward and evasive." But Chase's real problem was that he was an incompetent financier, placed in charge of unmanageable financial problems.

Even so, Chase's difficulties were nothing compared to those of his Confederate counterpart, Christopher G. Memminger, who had to make bricks without clay as well as without straw. Like Chase, Memminger had no extensive experience in financial matters, and his neat, systematic mind was troubled by the free and easy ways of government finance during wartime. He did what he could to bring about order—by requiring Confederate Treasury employees to keep regular 9-to-5 hours, by outlawing traditional Southern sociability in the Treasury offices, including drinking on the job, and by insisting that his visitors curb their customary garrulity and state their business. Such measures, however, did little to solve Confederate financial difficulties and only increased Southerners' suspicion of a man who had been born in Germany and raised in a South Carolina orphanage and who was not, therefore, a proper gentleman.

However dissimilar personally, Chase and Memminger faced similar financial problems and finally opted for the same solutions. Neither secretary seriously thought of financing the war through levying taxes. For either the Union or the Confederacy to impose heavy taxation in 1861 might well have killed the citizens' ardor for war. Americans simply were not used to paying taxes to their national government; there had been no federal excise duties during the thirty-five years before the war. In 1860 the United States Treasury had no internal revenue division, no assessors, no inspectors, and no agents. Since tariffs were a more familiar method of raising revenues, both secretaries hoped for large customs receipts. But when Republicans in the Union Congress passed the highly protective Morrill Tariff in 1861 and raised rates even higher in 1862, they effectively killed that source of revenue. Similarly, the Union blockade of the South

26TH NEW YORK INFANTRY AT FORT LYON, VIRGINIA

Once accepted into the Union or Confederate army, volunteers found they had a great deal still to learn before they were soldiers. These New York volunteers, manning the fortifications surrounding Washington, were receiving lessons in close-order drill. *(Library of Congress.)*

reduced the amount and value of goods brought into Confederate ports and cut the Southern income from tariffs. In desperation the Union government resorted to a direct tax (levied upon each state in proportion to population) of $20,000,000 in August 1861; much of it was never collected. The same month the Confederates imposed a "war tax" of 0.5 percent on taxable wealth. Davis's government, like Lincoln's, had to rely upon the states to collect this tax, and most of them preferred issuing bonds or notes rather than levying duties upon their people.

In neither country was borrowing a realistic possibility for financing the war. Products of the Jacksonian era with its suspicion of paper certificates of indebtedness, Americans of the 1860s were a people who preferred to hoard rather than invest their surplus funds. The rival Union and Confederate governments were themselves affected by this same suspicion of paper and trust in specie. In the North, Secretary Chase insisted that the banks of New York, Philadelphia, and Boston subscribe to a $150 million federal bond issue, but he was unwilling to take anything but gold or silver in payment. The drain on the banks' reserves, coupled with uncertainty over the course of the war, forced Northern banks to suspend specie payment for their notes in December 1861. Nor was Chase more successful in his early attempts to sell Union bonds directly to small investors. The Confederacy followed much the same course in its borrowing. An initial loan of $15 million was quickly subscribed to, with the result that Southern banks, including the strong institutions of New Orleans, were obliged to give up virtually all their specie to the new government; consequently they could no longer redeem

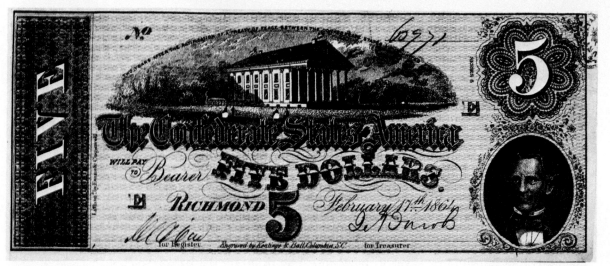

CONFEDERATE PAPER MONEY

Both the Confederacy and the Union were obliged to resort
to paper money in order to finance the war. In the South
engravers were few and incompetent. As a result the likenesses they produced of President Davis and other Confederate officials were so unprepossessing as to raise doubts
about the artists' loyalty to the Southern cause.

their notes in gold or silver. Memminger's attempt to sell subsequent Confederate bonds directly to the Southern people ran into the difficulty that nobody
had any specie. Urged by Vice President Alexander H. Stephens and other Confederate orators, planters in the fall of 1861 subscribed tobacco, rice, cotton, and
other commodities to purchase bonds. Since the Union blockade cut off the market for these products, the Confederate government realized little from the loan.

In consequence, by early 1862 both governments moved to the issue of paper
money, backed only by the promise that it would some day be redeemed in
specie. Both Treasury secretaries came reluctantly to this policy. Memminger, a
prominent hard-money advocate before the war, was obliged to resort to the
printing presses in 1861. The Confederacy issued $100 million in paper money
in August 1861 and the next year it printed millions of dollars more. So crude
were these Confederate notes that counterfeits could be readily detected, since
they were obviously superior in quality and design. Having denounced "an irre-
deemable paper currency, than which no more certainly fatal expedient for im-
poverishing the masses and discrediting the government of any country, can
well be devised," Chase found it even more embarrassing than Memminger to
resort to treasury notes. But by January 1862 he had no alternative. Declaring
that an issue of paper money was now "indispensably necessary," he persuaded
Congress to authorize the printing of $150 million in non-interest-bearing

United States treasury notes (which were promptly dubbed "greenbacks," because of their color). Rarely does history provide such a tidy illustration of how huge impersonal forces overrule the preference and will of individual statesmen.

Wartime Diplomacy

In diplomacy as in economic policy the Union and the Confederacy moved along parallel paths during the first two years of the war. Neither Lincoln nor Davis had much knowledge of diplomacy or took an active role in the conduct of foreign policy. Both, however, had difficulties with their secretaries of state. Seward, Lincoln's principal adviser, would ultimately rank as one of the greatest secretaries of state, but in the early stages of the Civil War he gave evidence of wild eccentricity, coupled with personal ambition. At the height of the Sumter crisis, he submitted to Lincoln a private memorandum complaining that the government as yet had no policy for dealing with secession, announcing his readiness to take over the President's function and shape a suitable policy, and suggesting that the proper course for the administration was to "change the question before the public from one upon slavery . . . for a question upon union or disunion" by precipitating a confrontation with foreign powers. If allowed, Seward would "seek explanations from Great Britain and Russia"—for what offenses he did not specify; he "would demand explanations from Spain and France, categorically, at once," presumably over their threatened intervention in the affairs of Santo Domingo and Mexico; and if Spain and France did not respond forthwith, he would urge a declaration of war against these powers. Lincoln, to his enduring credit, quietly filed away this memorandum, refrained from dismissing a secretary who planned to bring on a world war, and allowed Seward time to return to his senses.

Despite Lincoln's reticence, word of Seward's bellicosity leaked out in conversation at Washington dinner tables, and diplomats at the capital soon had a pretty good idea of what was in the secretary's mind. From the diplomatic dispatches, European governments during the first two years of the war learned to view all Seward's policies with skepticism, even after the secretary had returned to sobriety and moderation. Perhaps, however, the awareness of Seward's hair-trigger temper did something to make those governments more cautious in their relations with the United States and less willing to recognize the Confederacy.

Davis, too, had trouble with his state department. Toombs, the first Confederate secretary of state, was as ambitious and overbearing as he was able. It was a relief when he decided that the path to glory lay on the battlefield rather than in the cabinet and resigned to take a commission in the Southern army. His successor, R. M. T. Hunter, was equally ambitious, and—perhaps with an eye on the 1868 Confederate presidential election—he too promptly resigned, to become senator from Virginia. In March 1862, Davis finally found his man in

Judah P. Benjamin, who had already been Confederate attorney general and secretary of war. Serving until the end of the war, Benjamin cleverly reflected the changing moods of his chief, but he was not an innovator in foreign policy. In the words of a critical Northerner who visited Richmond during the war, Benjamin had a "keen, shrewd, ready intellect, but not the stamina to originate, or even to execute, any great good, or great wickedness."

Union and Confederate diplomatic appointments abroad were rather a mixed lot. If Lincoln lacked tact in appointing Carl Schurz, considered a "red republican" for his participation in the German revolution of 1848, as minister to conservative, monarchical Spain, Davis showed a total failure to understand British antislavery sentiment by sending Yancey, the most notorious Southern fire-eater, as first Confederate commissioner to London. On the positive side, the Union minister to Great Britain, Charles Francis Adams, exhibited the patience and restraint required in his difficult assignment; and the pride, the chilly demeanor, and the punctiliousness of this son and grandson of American Presidents made him a match even for the aristocratic British foreign minister, Lord John Russell. Of the Confederate emissaries abroad, probably John Slidell of Louisiana proved ablest; wily, adroit, and unscrupulous, he was perfectly at home in the court of Napoleon III.

Much to the disappointment of Americans on both sides, the attitudes of European powers toward the Civil War were not primarily shaped by the actions of American ministers, secretaries of state, or even Presidents. Nor, during 1861 and 1862, were they shaped by appeals to economic self-interest. Southerners, firmly believing that cotton was king, expected that pressure from British and French textile manufacturers would compel their governments to recognize the Confederacy and to break the blockade. But as it happened, European manufacturers had an ample stockpile of cotton, purchased before the outbreak of hostilities, and were therefore not much affected when Southern cotton was cut off in 1861. By 1862, cotton mills in both Britain and France were suffering, but Union and Confederate orders for arms, ammunition, and other equipment counterbalanced these losses. There was great hardship among the workers in the cotton mills, especially in the Lancashire district of England, where unemployment was high, but their complaints were relatively ineffectual since Britain still did not allow these men to vote.

Northerners were equally disappointed in their belief that European powers would see the American conflict as a war against slavery and would consequently condemn the Confederacy. Since Lincoln had announced that he would not interfere with slavery where it existed, since Seward in his dispatches called abolitionists and "the most extreme advocates of African slavery" equally dangerous to the Union cause, and since Union generals in the field were still returning runaway slaves to their Southern masters, it was unrealistic to expect European antislavery forces to rally behind the Union. Yet when Britons failed to see that the South represented "the cause of chaos against that of harmony, of anarchy against order, of slavery against freedom," even such conservative Northerners as the New York diarist George Templeton Strong denounced their "monstrous and incredible blindness."

What Northerners and Confederates alike failed to understand was that the policy of European states towards the Civil War would be determined largely by considerations of national self-interest. Since the Crimean War, an uneasy balance of power had prevailed in Europe, and no nation was eager to upset it by unilateral intervention in the American conflict. But concerted action by the European powers was always difficult because of mutual suspicion, and in the 1860s it was virtually impossible because of the nature of the British government. The British prime minister, Lord Palmerston, who was nearly eighty years old, headed a shaky coalition government, which was certain to fall if it undertook

"COTTON IN THE STOCKS"

The Union blockade sealed off Southern exports of cotton and helped produce severe hardships in the textile-producing regions of Great Britain and France. This 1862 cartoon shows the French minister to Washington, Henri Mercier, threatening Uncle Sam with European intervention if the blockade is not lifted. *(Library of Congress.)*

COTTON IN THE STOCKS.

M. Mercier:—"HOW MUCH LONGER IS THIS TO LAST? OR ARE YOU WAITING UNTIL WE INTERFERE?"

any decisive action. With the British government immobilized, the Russians largely favorable to the Union cause, and the Prussians and the Austrians mostly indifferent to the conflict, the inclination of the ambitious Napoleon III to meddle in favor of the Confederacy was effectively curbed.

As a result, European nations announced their neutrality early in the war. Queen Victoria's proclamation of May 13, 1861, was typical in recognizing that a state of war existed between the United States and "the states styling themselves the Confederate States of America" and in declaring British neutrality in that war. Recognition as a belligerent—not as a nation—meant that the Southerners had a right to send out privateers without their being considered pirate ships and that the Union blockade of the South would have to be effective if other nations were to respect it. Initially these proclamations seemed a great Confederate success. In fact, however, they were both necessary and warranted by international law and, despite Seward's rantings, were truly impartial.

In November 1861, the rash action of a Union naval officer threatened to upset this neutrality. Learning that Davis was replacing the temporary commissioners he had sent to France and Britain by permanent envoys, John Slidell and James M. Mason, Union Captain Charles Wilkes decided to capture these diplomats en route. Off the shore of Cuba on November 8, 1861, his warship stopped the British merchant ship, the *Trent,* Union officers boarded and searched the vessel, and Mason and Slidell were unceremoniously removed, to be transported to Boston for imprisonment. When news of Wilkes's action, in clear violation of international law, reached Europe, hostility toward the Union government flared up. "You may stand for this," Palmerston told his cabinet, "but damned if I will!" Russell drafted a stiff letter demanding the immediate release of the envoys. It was clear that the Lincoln government faced a major crisis if it held its prisoners. After conferring with cabinet members and senators, Lincoln decided on Christmas day to release the Southern envoys. He would fight only one war at a time.

Even with the firm intention of remaining neutral, European powers found their patience tested as the American war stretched on without apparent chance of ending. International relations were disturbed, commerce was disrupted, textile manufacturing was suffering, and neither North nor South seemed able to achieve its goal. Increasingly, support built up in both France and Britain for offering mediation to the combatants, and such an offer inevitably involved recognition of the Confederacy as an independent nation. In September 1862, Palmerston and Russell agreed to explore a mediation plan involving France and Russia as well as Great Britain, but pro-Union members of the British cabinet, like the Duke of Argyll and George Cornewall Lewis, replied with strong arguments against mediation. Faced with dissension within his unstable coalition and given no encouragement by Russia, Palmerston by October 1862 changed his mind and concluded that the European states must continue to be lookers-on till the war should have taken a more decided turn.

Battles and Leaders

But on the battlefields in 1861 and 1862 there were no decided turns. Engagement followed engagement, campaign followed campaign, and neither side could achieve a decisive victory. The stalemate was baffling to many armchair strategists, in both the South and the North, who had been sure that the war would be short and decisive, ending in an overwhelming victory for their own side.

Confederate war planners counted among their assets the fact that some of the best graduates of West Point led their armies and that President Davis himself had military training and experience. They believed that Southern men had more of a fighting spirit than Northerners, and they were probably correct in thinking that Southerners had more experience in handling firearms and were better horsemen. They knew that the Confederacy would generally act on the defensive and assumed that the offensive Union army would have to be at least three times as large as that of the South. Since Southern forces could operate on interior lines, they could move more quickly and easily than Union forces, which would have to travel longer distances. While recognizing the superiority of the Union navy, Southerners knew that the Confederacy had 3500 miles of coastline, with innumerable hidden harbors and waterways through which shipping could escape. When Confederate strategists added to all these assets the fact that Southern soldiers were fighting on their home ground, where they knew every road and byway, they saw no reason to doubt ultimate victory.

But an equally good case could be made for the inevitability of a Union victory. The population of the Union in 1860 was about 20.7 million; that of the Confederacy, only 9.1 million. Moreover, 3.5 million of the inhabitants of the South were blacks, mostly slaves, who, it was presumed, would not be used in the Confederate armies. Along with this superiority in manpower, the North had vastly more economic strength than the Confederacy. The total value of all manufactured products in all eleven Confederate states was less than one-fourth of that of New York alone. The iron furnaces, forges, and rolling mills in the United States were heavily concentrated in the North. The North in 1860 built fourteen out of every fifteen railroad locomotives manufactured in the United States. Northern superiority in transportation would more than compensate for Southern interior lines, as only 30 percent of the total rail mileage of the United States ran through the Confederacy. The Union navy, which experienced few defections to the South, was incomparably superior, and the blockade President Lincoln announced at the outbreak of hostilities would cut off, or at least drastically reduce, Southern imports from Europe. When Northern planners added to the advantages of their side the possession of the established government, the recognition of foreign powers, and the enormous enthusiasm of the people for maintaining the Union, they could not doubt that victory would be sure and swift.

In fact, these assets substantially cancelled each other during the first two years of the war and produced not victory but deadlock. As the armies engaged in

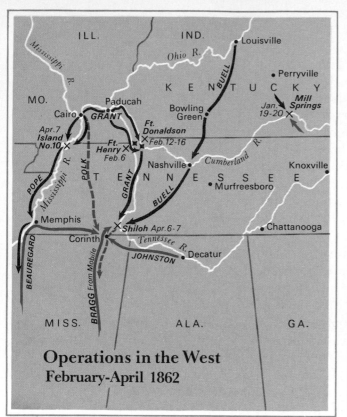

Operations in the West
February–April 1862

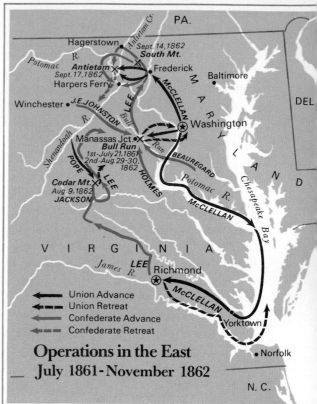

Union Advance
Union Retreat
Confederate Advance
Confederate Retreat

Operations in the East
July 1861–November 1862

complex maneuvers and in indecisive battles, they demonstrated not only that they were fairly evenly balanced but also that even on the battlefield, Americans from the North were very much like Americans from the South.

It is hardly surprising that Union and Confederate commanders largely employed the same strategic plans, for most had been taught the art of war by the same teachers at West Point. In fifty-five of the sixty biggest battles of the war, the generals on both sides had been educated at West Point, and in the remaining five, a West Pointer led one of the opposing armies. At the military academy they had studied the theories of the French historian and strategist Baron Henri Jomini. Some read Jomini's works in the original French or in translation; more, doubtless, absorbed his ideas from the abridgement and interpretation of his work *Elementary Treatise on Advance-Guard, Outpost, and Detachment of Service of Troops* (1847), written by Dennis Hart Mahan, who for a generation taught at the academy and greatly influenced his students.

Although in fact a complex body of doctrine, subject to many differing interpretations, Jomini's military theories as understood by American commanders stressed the importance of the conquest of territory and emphasized that the seizure of the enemy's capital was "ordinarily, the objective point" of an invading army. Jomini envisaged a battle situation in which two armies were drawn up in opposing lines, one offensive, and the other defensive, and he even prepared a set of twelve diagrams showing the possible orders of battle. In all twelve, a major determinant of victory was the concentration of force—the bringing to bear of a powerful, united force upon the enemy's weakest point. Warfare was thus something like an elaborate game of chess, an art that only professional soldiers could fully master.

Most of the military operations during the first two years of the Civil War can best be understood as a kind of elaborate illustration of Jomini's theories, slightly modified to fit the American terrain. The first big battle of the war occurred on July 21, 1861, when Union General Irwin McDowell, under much pressure from Northern newspapers and much badgered by exuberant politicians in the Congress, reluctantly pushed his poorly organized army into Virginia. He expected to encounter the Confederates, under General Beauregard, near Centreville. In the ensuing battle of Bull Run (or Manassas), both armies tried to apply the same battle plan from Jomini's treatise; each attempted a main attack upon the enemy's left flank, to be followed by a secondary thrust at his center and right wings. If completely executed, the two plans would have had the amusing result of leaving each army in its opponent's original place. But the Confederates also followed another of Jomini's principles, that of concentration of force and, using the railroad, rushed General Joseph E. Johnston's troops from

GENERAL GEORGE BRINTON MCCLELLAN

Union General McClellan, the "Little Napoleon" of the Civil War, seemed to have everything it took to make a great general. He was handsome and brave; he was a superb organizer and administrator; and he knew all that the books taught about the art of war. But, as Lincoln painfully found out, McClellan had one great fault: he had "the slows." (*National Archives.*)

the Shenandoah Valley to join Beauregard's main force. The Union troops fought bravely and initially seemed to be carrying the day, but after Johnston's men were in position, the Union army was thrown back and then routed. Weary and disorganized, Federal troops limped back to the Potomac and to safety. The Confederates were almost equally demoralized by their victory and were unable to pursue. The South's easiest opportunity to follow Jomini's maxim and seize the enemy's capital had to be given up.

After this initial engagement, it was clear that both armies needed reorganization and training before either could attempt further campaigns. As a result, despite growing impatience for action, there was little significant military action during the rest of 1861, except for minor engagements in Kentucky and Missouri. During this period General George Brinton McClellan, who was credited with some overrated small successes in western Virginia, was summoned to Washington to bring order to the Union army. With enormous dash and enthusiasm, the young commander began to whip the Federal regiments into fighting shape. He insisted on careful drill and inspection; he demanded the best of food and equipment for his men; and he refused to move forward until his army was thoroughly prepared.

By early 1862, Union armies, not merely those in the East but in all the theaters of war, were ready to advance, and, taking advantage of numerical superiority, Union commanders concentrated their forces on a series of weak spots in the Confederate defenses, just as Jomini had directed. In January, General George H. Thomas defeated a Confederate force at Mill Springs, Kentucky, and made an important break in the Southern defense line west of the mountains. The next month General Ulysses S. Grant made an even more important breach in that line, when in collaboration with the Union gunboats on the Tennessee and Cumberland rivers, he captured Fort Henry and Fort Donelson, requiring the Confederate army in the latter fort to accept his terms of unconditional surrender.

The Southerners now had to abandon Tennessee. Union armies under Grant and Don Carlos Buell pushed rapidly after them, so rapidly indeed that for the moment they forgot Jomini's maxim about concentration and allowed the Confederates a chance for victory. On April 6, while Buell's troops were still some distance from Grant, the Confederates, who had concentrated their forces in the West under Generals Beauregard and Albert Sidney Johnston, fell on Grant's unsuspecting army at Shiloh Meeting House and during the first day's

UNION ORDNANCE READY FOR TRANSPORTATION FROM YORKTOWN

For McClellan's push up the Peninsula in the hope of capturing Richmond, the Union war department assembled the largest collection of men and materiel ever collected on the American continent. But, as events proved, Union generalship did not equal Union resources. (*National Archives.*)

fighting came near to pushing it into the river. But the death of General Johnston, the demoralization of the victorious Confederates, and the timely arrival of Buell's forces meant that on the second day the Federal forces, now fully concentrated, were able to sweep back the enemy and reclaim the field. Dissatisfied with Grant's generalship, General Henry Wager Halleck, who was the Union commander for the entire Western theater, took personal charge of the army after Shiloh. A dedicated disciple of Jomini, whose works he had translated, Halleck concentrated his force for a push on Corinth, Mississippi, in order to break the important rail connection that linked Memphis and the Western portion of the Confederacy with the East.

Meanwhile in March Union forces had decisively defeated the Confederates at Pea Ridge in northwestern Arkansas, and organized Southern armies had to be withdrawn from Missouri. Even farther west, Union forces captured Santa Fe and compelled Confederate General Henry Hopkins Sibley to withdraw from New Mexico. To the south, Flag Officer David Glasgow Farragut daringly pushed his fleet up the Mississippi and in April captured New Orleans, the largest city in the Confederacy.

A Union advance in the eastern theater promised to be equally successful. After long delays, McClellan began his offensive against Richmond, not by going directly overland, but by transporting his troops to Fort Monroe, on the peninsula between the York and James rivers. Bitterly complaining because Lincoln violated the principle of concentration and held back 40,000 troops to defend Washington, McClellan nevertheless prepared to follow Jomini's maxims and seize the Confederate capital.

At this point in the gigantic, synchronized Union offensive, designed to crush the Confederacy, everything began to go wrong. The difficulties stemmed partly from human inadequacies. Although good theoreticians and able administrators, Halleck and McClellan were indecisive fighters. Halleck took nearly two months to creep from Shiloh to Corinth, stopping to fortify his position each night so that there could be no repetition of Confederate surprise. By the time he reached his destination, the Southern army had moved south with all its provisions. Equally cautious was McClellan's advance on the Peninsula, where he allowed 16,000 Confederate soldiers under General John B. Magruder to hold up his magnificent army of 112,000 until the Confederates could bring reinforcements to Richmond. The trouble was partly that these Union campaigns attempted to coordinate movements of forces larger than anything seen before on the American continent, though few of the commanding officers had ever led anything larger than a regiment. But chiefly the Union failure was due to the fact that able Confederate generals had read the same books on strategy as the Union commanders and knew how to fight the same kinds of battles.

While McClellan slowly edged his way up the Peninsula, Confederate commander Joseph E. Johnston, who had rushed in with reinforcements, kept close watch until the Union general injudiciously allowed his forces to be divided by the flooded Chickahominy River. Applying Jomini's principle of concentration on the enemy's weakest spot, Johnston on May 31–June 1 fell upon the exposed Union wing in battles at Fair Oaks (or Seven Pines), which narrowly failed of being a Confederate triumph. When Johnston was wounded in this engagement, Davis chose Robert E. Lee to replace him.

Lee quickly revealed his military genius by showing that he knew when to follow Jomini's principles and when to flout them. Remembering from his days at West Point how slow McClellan was, Lee allowed "Stonewall" Jackson to take 18,000 men from the main army for a daring campaign through the Shenandoah Valley. Jackson defeated and demoralized the Union forces in the Shenandoah and so threatened Washington that Lincoln withheld reinforcements that he had promised McClellan. When Jackson had accomplished this objective, Lee reverted to the principle of concentration and ordered Jackson promptly to rejoin the main army before Richmond. The combined Confederate force fell upon McClellan's exposed right flank at Mechanicsville. Since Jackson was not fighting at his best and his soldiers were exhausted, Lee failed to crush McClellan; but in a series of engagements known as the Seven Days (June 25–July 1), he forced the Union army to beat a slow, hard-fought retreat to the banks of the James River, where it lay under the protection of Federal gunboats. Lee had saved Richmond.

As the Union advances ground to a halt by midsummer, 1862, the Confederates planned a grand offensive of their own. In the West, two Southern armies

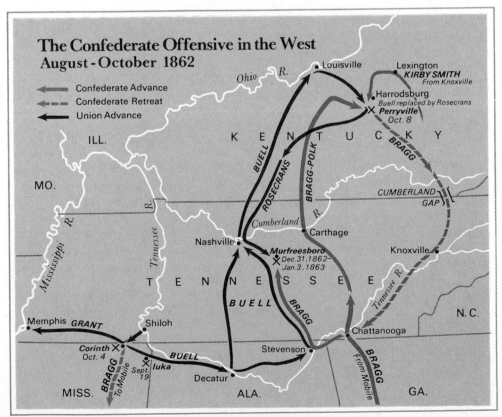

under Generals Braxton Bragg and Edmund Kirby-Smith in August swept through eastern Tennessee; by September, they were operating in Kentucky, where they were in a position to cut the supply line for Buell's army in Tennessee. The early phases of their offensive were brilliantly successful, but the campaign as a whole was fruitless because of a lack of coordination between the two Southern armies and because of Bragg's indecisiveness. After a bloody battle at Perryville (October 8), the Confederate forces withdrew toward Chattanooga, followed, at a very respectful distance, by the Union army.

The more daring part of the Confederate offensive was in the East. While McClellan's army was slowly being withdrawn from the Peninsula, Lee turned quickly upon Union forces in central Virginia under the braggart General John Pope, and concentrating his entire strength upon this segment of the Federal army, scored a brilliant Confederate victory in the second battle of Bull Run (August 29-30). Free then to push into the North, Lee crossed the Potomac into Maryland, where he hoped to supply his ragged army and to rally the inhabitants of that state to the Confederate cause.

Lee's invasion of Maryland ended with the battle of Antietam (September 17), an indecisive engagement whose very inconclusiveness clearly demonstrated the impossibility of ever ending the war so long as it was fought by the conventional rules. Union General McClellan, again in command, moved slowly to catch up

"CAVALRY OFFICER" BY WINSLOW HOMER

Even after a year of combat, Americans, North and South, could not reconcile themselves to the fact that modern war requires regimentation. They continued to think of themselves as individualists, like this dashing union cavalry officer, sketched by Winslow Homer. *(The Cooper Union Museum.)*

with Lee's army, because he wished to concentrate all his forces for an attack. Lee in turn waited in a defensive position behind Antietam Creek at Sharpsburg, Maryland, because he too needed to concentrate his troops, a portion of whom had been sent on a successful expedition to capture Harpers Ferry. When McClellan was finally ready to take the offensive, he followed one of Jomini's battle plans precisely, and Lee defended his position by the same rules. The result was the bloodiest day of the Civil War. In areas of the battlefield like the cornfield, the Dunkard church, the Bloody Lane, and Burnside's bridge, men fell as in windrows. By the end of the day, there were more than 25,000 casualties, with at least 5000 dead. The next day an eyewitness noted "the most appalling sights upon the battle-field . . . the ground strewn with the bodies of the dead and the dying . . . the cries and the groans of the wounded . . . the piles of dead men, in attitudes which show the writhing agony in which they died—faces distorted . . . begrimed and covered with clotted blood, arms and legs torn from the body or the body itself torn asunder."

Quietly Lee slipped back into Virginia, and McClellan did not pursue him. The Confederate offensive was over, and with it ended an era. If Jomini's strategy could only lead to stalemate, it was time for both Union and Confederacy to experiment with modern, organized warfare.

Suggested Readings

There are two excellent guides to the vast literature on the causes of the Civil War: Howard K. Beale, "What Historians Have Said about the Causes of the Civil War," in *Theory and Practice in Historical Study* (Social Science Research Council *Bulletin*, no. 54 [1946], 55–102), and Thomas J. Pressly, *Americans Interpret Their Civil War* (1954). Edwin C. Rozwenc, ed., *The Causes of the American Civil War* (1972), and Kenneth M. Stampp, ed., *The Causes of the Civil War* (1974), offer extensive extracts from writings by contemporaries and subsequent historians.

Peter J. Parish, *The American Civil War* (1975), is the best one-volume history. *The Civil War and Reconstruction* (1969), by J. G. Randall and David Donald, is more comprehensive and has a fuller bibliography. Of the older large-scale studies, James Ford Rhodes, *History of the United States from the Compromise of 1850 . . .*, Vols. 3–5 (1895–1904), remains valuable. The fullest modern account is Allan Nevins, *The War for the Union* (4 vols., 1959–71), a work of enormous scholarship, which, however, concentrates on the North. Bruce Catton, *The Centennial History of the Civil War* (3 vols., 1961–65), is eloquent and imaginative but of uneven quality.

Mark M. Boatner, III, *The Civil War Dictionary* (1959), is a useful, accurate reference work. For maps, see Vincent J. Esposito, ed., *The West Point Atlas of American Wars* (2 vols., 1959).

The best Civil War anthologies are Henry S. Commager, ed., *The Blue and the Gray* (2 vols., 1950), and William B. Hesseltine, ed., *The Tragic Conflict* (1962). Francis T. Miller, *The Photographic History of the Civil War* (10 vols., 1911), offers the most complete pictorial coverage, but the photographs are poorly reproduced. Better pictorial histories, using modern photographic techniques, are David Donald, ed., *Divided We Fought* (1952), and Richard M. Ketchum, ed., *The American Heritage Picture History of the Civil War* (1960).

On the Sumter crisis, see David M. Potter, *Lincoln and His Party in the Secession Crisis* (1942), Kenneth M. Stampp, *And the War Came* (1950), and Richard N. Current, *Lincoln and the First Shot* (1963). The secession of the states of the upper South is treated in Dwight L. Dumond, *The Secession Movement* (1931), and Ralph A. Wooster, *The Secession Conventions of the South* (1962).

There are several good general histories of the Confederacy: E. Merton Coulter, *The Confederate States of America* (1950); Clement Eaton, *A History of the Southern Confederacy* (1954); Nathaniel W. Stephenson, *The Day of the Confederacy* (1919); and Charles P. Roland, *The Confederacy* (1960). Albert D. Kirwan, ed., *The Confederacy* (1959), is a valuable anthology.

There is no satisfactory life of the Confederate president. The best of a rather poor lot is Hudson Strode, *Jefferson Davis* (3 vols., 1955–64). Students will learn more from Rembert W. Patrick, *Jefferson Davis and His Cabinet* (1944). Three Confederate diaries are invaluable: Mary B. Chesnut, *A Diary from Dixie* (1949); John B. Jones, *A Rebel War Clerk's Diary* (2 vols., 1866); and Robert G. H. Kean, *Inside the Confederate Government*, ed. Edward Younger (1955).

Abraham Lincoln has been the subject of many distinguished biographies. The best one-volume life is that by Benjamin P. Thomas (1952); Reinhard H. Luthin, *The Real Abraham Lincoln* (1960), is also valuable. The fullest and most flavorful of the biographies is Carl Sandburg, *Abraham Lincoln: The War Years* (4 vols., 1939). The most scholarly and critical is *Lincoln the President* (4 vols., 1945–55), by J. G. Randall and Richard N. Current. Several volumes of essays deal with important and controversial aspects of Lincoln's career: Richard N. Current, *The Lincoln Nobody Knows* (1958); David Donald, *Lincoln Reconsidered* (1956); Norman A. Graebner, ed., *The Enduring Lincoln* (1959); and J. G. Randall, *Lincoln the Liberal Statesman* (1947). See also Edmund Wilson's thoughtful essay on Lincoln in his *Patriotic Gore* (1962). The diaries of three of Lincoln's cabinet officers are indispensable: Howard K. Beale, ed., *The Diary of Edward Bates* (1933); David Donald, ed., *Inside Lincoln's Cabinet* (Salmon P. Chase) (1954); and Howard K. Beale and Alan W. Brownsword, eds., *Diary of Gideon Welles* (3 vols., 1960).

The standard work on Anglo-American relations remains Ephraim D. Adams, *Great Britain and the American Civil War* (2 vols., 1925). Frank L. Owsley, *King Cotton Diplomacy* (1959), is more recent and more controversial. Lincoln's role in foreign policy is over-dramatized in Jay Monaghan, *Diplomat in Carpetslippers* (1945). For correctives, see Glyndon G. Van Deusen, *William Henry Seward* (1967), Martin B. Duberman, *Charles Francis Adams* (1961), and David Donald, *Charles Sumner and the Rights of Man* (1970). Franco-American relations are admirably covered in Lynn M. Case and Warren F. Spencer, *The United States and France: Civil War Diplomacy* (1970), and Daniel B. Carroll, *Henri Mercier and the American Civil War* (1971).

On social and economic conditions, see Paul W. Gates, *Agriculture and the Civil War* (1965), and Mary E. Massey, *Bonnet Brigades: American Women and the Civil War* (1966). Developments on the Southern home front are sketched in Charles W. Ramsdell, *Behind the Lines in the Southern Confederacy* (1944), and Bell I. Wiley, *The Plain People of the Confederacy* (1943). Emerson D. Fite, *Social and Industrial Conditions in the North during the Civil War* (1910), remains the best survey. For the continuing debate on the effect of the war on Northern economic growth, see Ralph Andreano, ed., *The Economic Impact of the American Civil War* (1962), and David T. Gilchrist and W. David Lewis, eds., *Economic Change in the Civil War Era* (1965).

Studies dealing with other aspects of the Civil War are listed at the end of the following chapter.

20

Experimentation
1862-1865

"I have been anxious and careful," President Lincoln announced in his December 1861 message to Congress, that the present war "shall not degenerate into a violent and remorseless revolutionary struggle." Both he and President Davis assumed at the outset that the conflict would be a brief and limited one, waged in a conventional fashion by armies in the field and having little impact on the economic, social, and intellectual life of their sections. The events of 1861–62 proved these expectations utterly wrong. It slowly became clear that to carry on the war Americans, in both North and South, had to break with tradition and engage in broad experimentation. They had to try new forms of government action, new modes of social and economic cooperation, and new patterns of thought.

Since the Union was ultimately victorious, it would be easy to conclude that Northerners were more willing to experiment, better able to mobilize all their resources, for what has been called the first modern war. But such a judgment makes the historian the camp follower of the victorious army. The record shows, instead, that both the Confederacy and the Union attempted innovations that for the time were daringly original. It also shows that both combatants during the final years of the war resorted to much the same kinds of experimentation. Thus even while devising novel means for destroying each other, Northerners and Southerners showed themselves to be fundamentally similar.

Evolution of a Command System

The bloody and indecisive campaigns of 1861 and 1862 made innovators out of both Union and Confederate soldiers. Experience under fire convinced them not to follow Jomini's tactics. The French writer had conceived of a tactical situation where infantrymen, drawn up in close, parallel lines, blazed away at each other with muskets capable of being loaded perhaps twice a minute and having an effective range of one hundred yards. But Civil War soldiers were equipped with rifles, which not only were more quickly loaded but had an effective range of about eight hundred yards. In Jomini's day the offensive force had the great advantage; rushing forward, with bayonets fixed, charging troops could break the defenders' line before they had time to reload. In the Civil War, on the other hand, the advancing force was exposed to accurate fire during the last half-mile of its approach. In consequence, nine out of ten infantry assaults failed, and the Civil War soldier had little use for his bayonet—except perhaps as a spit on which to cook meat.

Soldiers on both sides rapidly learned how to make defensive positions even stronger. At the beginning of the war, most military men were scornful of breastworks and entrenchments, arguing that they simply pinned down a defending force and made it more vulnerable to a charge. When Lee, upon assuming command of the Army of Northern Virginia in 1862, ordered his men to construct earthworks facing McClellan's advancing troops, Confederate soldiers bitterly complained and called their new general the King of Spades. But when they saw how entrenchments saved lives, they changed their tune, and Lee became to the Confederate common soldier "Marse Robert," the general who looked after his men's welfare. What Confederate generals started, Union commanders imitated. Even William Tecumseh Sherman, who feared fortifications would make his men cowardly, changed his mind after the Confederates swept through his unprotected camp at Shiloh. By the end of 1862, both armies dug in wherever they halted. Using spades and canteens, forks and sticks, soldiers pushed up improvised earthworks and strengthened them with fence rails and fallen logs.

Experience also quietly killed off Jomini's view that warfare was restricted to professionals. In the early days of the conflict, commanders believed warfare should not injure civilians. When McClellan's army pushed up the Peninsula, the general posted guards to keep his soldiers from raiding Confederate farmers' cornfields. Similarly Halleck permitted slaveowners to search his camp in order to reclaim their runaway slaves. By the end of 1862, such practices vanished. Soldiers joyfully foraged through civilians' watermelon patches, cornfields, and chicken roosts, while their officers ostentatiously turned their backs. Northern generals exhibited a growing reluctance to permit the recapture of fugitive slaves who had fled to the Union lines. As early as May 1861, General Butler at Fortress Monroe, Virginia, refused to return three such fugitives on the ground that they were contraband of war. *Contrabands* became a code name for escaped slaves, and in 1862 the Federal Congress showed what it thought of Jomini's notion of limited warfare by prohibiting any Federal military officer from returning runaways.

The deadlock of 1861–62 also brought about a transformation of the command systems of both Union and Confederate armies. Because the Union lost so many battles during the first two years of the conflict, Lincoln was forced to experiment first. His initial venture came in mid-1862. Since he distrusted McClellan's capacity to keep an eye on the general progress of the war while also leading a campaign to capture Richmond, he brought in Halleck from the West to serve as his military adviser and gave him the grand title of general-in-chief. The position was not a viable one, for it placed Halleck in conflict with the other generals, especially McClellan; it also often put him at odds with Secretary of War Stanton, and exposed him to what he called the "political Hell" of pressure from congressmen. In addition, Halleck's slowness, his indecisiveness, and his rigid adherence to Jomini's principles made him hostile to all innovation, and Lincoln soon concluded that he was of little more use than a clerk.

Seeing no alternative, Lincoln, after McClellan's withdrawal from the Peninsula and Pope's defeat at Second Bull Run, again tried to direct military operations himself; his efforts proved the desperate need for a unified system of command. For the rest of 1862 and most of 1863, individual Northern generals managed their own armies and planned their own campaigns, with Lincoln, Stanton, and Halleck providing only loose supervision and frequent injunctions to win speedy victories.

In the eastern theater Lincoln replaced McClellan, after his failure to follow up his partial success at Antietam, with that bumbling incompetent, Ambrose E. Burnside, whose one redeeming feature was that he knew he was bumbling and incompetent. Burnside led the Army of the Potomac into the battle of Fredericksburg on December 13, 1862, one of the most disastrous, and surely the least necessary, Federal defeats of the war. Replacing Burnside with "Fighting Joe" Hooker, a boastful egotist fond of the bottle, brought no better luck to the Union cause. The battle of Chancellorsville (May 1–4, 1863) was still another Confederate victory—but one won at a great price, for "Stonewall" Jackson was accidentally fired upon by his own Southern soldiers and mortally wounded.

Still trying to direct military operations himself, Lincoln watched anxiously as Lee in midsummer of 1863 began his second invasion of the North, this time pushing into Pennsylvania. When Hooker appeared unable or unwilling to pursue the Confederates, Lincoln replaced him with the shy, scholarly George Gordon Meade, who assumed command of the army only three days before the climactic battle of Gettysburg (July 1–3, 1863). Rushing all available forces to that Pennsylvania town, Meade succeeded in turning back the invaders. At last the Army of the Potomac had won a victory—but Meade failed to pursue, and Lee's army recrossed the Potomac to safety. "We had them within our grasp,"

Operations in the West, 1863
The Vicksburg Campaign

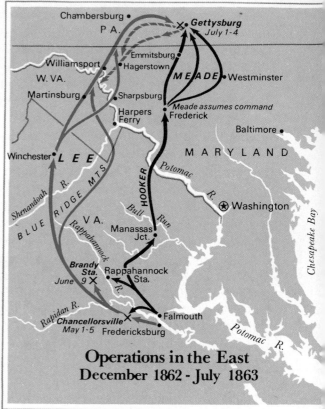

Operations in the East
December 1862 – July 1863

Lincoln lamented. "We had only to stretch forth our hands and they were ours. And nothing I could say or do could make the Army move."

When Lincoln tried personally to plan strategy for the trans-Appalachian theater of war, he was no more successful. After the battle of Perryville, it was clear that Buell must be replaced, and Lincoln chose W. S. Rosecrans, suspected of having military ability and known to have political connections. If Buell had been slow and cautious, Rosecrans proved to be slow and careless. Lincoln urged him to push on to Chattanooga, the rail hub of the Confederacy, but en route Rosecrans encountered Bragg's army in the bloody and indecisive battle of Murfreesboro (December 30, 1862–January 2, 1863). Though Rosecrans claimed victory, his army was so badly mauled that he could not advance for another six months. Finally, in June 1863 he maneuvered the Confederates out of Chattanooga, but in pursuing Bragg's army he received a smashing defeat at Chickamauga (September 19–20). Only the rocklike determination of General George H. Thomas prevented the reverse from becoming a rout, and Rosecrans's army limped back into Chattanooga. Disoriented by defeat, Rosecrans, as Lincoln said, behaved "like a duck hit on the head," and allowed Bragg to invest the city.

Farther west, Lincoln's personal direction of the Union armies proved equally ineffectual. Here the main objective was Vicksburg, the last major city on the

Mississippi River still in Confederate hands; when it fell, the eastern part of the Confederacy would be severed from the trans-Mississippi region. At first Lincoln thought Grant, who commanded Union forces in this area after Halleck's departure, ought to push overland from his base in northern Mississippi, but when a Confederate raid destroyed the Union base of supplies, that approach had to be abandoned. Next Grant tried a frontal assault upon Vicksburg. Bringing his troops down the river from Memphis, Sherman, Grant's ablest lieutenant, attempted to scale the virtually impregnable bluffs on which the city was situated, and the Confederates, commanded by General John C. Pemberton, drove him back. Growing dissatisfied with Grant's management of the campaign, Lincoln authorized former Democratic Congressman John A. McClernand to raise a new army in the Northwestern states for use against Vicksburg.

Grant now reached the turning point in his career. Unwilling to be ousted from command and knowing that he outranked McClernand, he moved his headquarters and his troops down the Mississippi to Young's Point, on the west bank just above Vicksburg. When the Illinois congressman arrived, along with the troops he had raised, Grant quietly took over, informing McClernand that he would be one of his corps commanders. But retaining command of the army did not solve Grant's problem. If he made another frontal attack upon Vicksburg, he would surely be defeated. If he withdrew his troops up the river to Memphis for a fresh start overland, Lincoln was sure to remove him from command. Reviewing the situation, Grant saw only one solution. "There was," he concluded, "nothing left to be done but to *go forward to a decisive victory.*"

To win that victory, Grant devised, without aid from Washington, a bold plan. Using the navy's gunboats and transports to run his ammunition and supplies past the Vicksburg batteries, he marched his army to a point on the west bank below the city, staged a rapid amphibious crossing, and before the Confederates could recover from their surprise, pushed inland. To the dismay of Washington, he thus abandoned his base of supplies, announcing that he planned to live on the countryside. First he struck at Jackson, the capital of Mississippi, to drive back the small Confederate force General Joseph E. Johnston had collected there, and then he turned on Pemberton's army and forced it into Vicksburg. After two ill-advised assaults, the Union army settled down to besiege the city, while from the river the Union gunboats kept up a constant bombardment. As civilians in the city took to caves for safety and as starvation made mule meat a delicacy, Pemberton fought back as well as he could, but on July 4, 1863 — the day after Gettysburg — he had to surrender his army and the city.

When the news reached Washington, Lincoln, who had distrusted Grant's strategy, wrote the general a handsome apology: "I now wish to make the personal acknowledgment that you were right, and I was wrong." The President was happy to be proved wrong, for Grant's success meant that he finally had a general who knew how to plan a campaign and fight it. Putting Grant in command of all the troops in the West, Lincoln directed him to relieve the army cooped up in Chattanooga. Quickly Grant and Sherman came to the rescue, opened up a line of communication to the starving Union troops in Chattanooga, now commanded by Thomas instead of the inept Rosecrans, and brought in reinforcements. On November 23–25 the combined forces routed Bragg's encircling army and forced it back into Georgia.

This further victory gave Lincoln a solution to the problem of command, which had so long vexed him. Early the next year he brought Grant to Washington, where he received the rank of lieutenant general, and assigned him to command all the armies of the United States. Initially Washington observers thought the burden might be too much for this "short, round-shouldered man," of whom they now received their first glimpse. One observer reported that the new lieutenant general "had no gait, no *station*, no manner, rough, light-brown whiskers, a blue eye, and rather a scrubby look withal . . . rather the look of a man who did, or once did, take a little too much to drink." But appearances were deceiving, for in the next few days Grant set forth a broad strategy for winning the war. Taking advantage of Northern superiority in manpower, he planned a simul-

MAJOR GENERAL ULYSSES SIMPSON GRANT, U.S.A., IN THE FALL OF 1863

Grant lacked the polish of McClellan, the brilliance of Sherman, and the flamboyance of Sheridan. But he had one quality more important than any of these. As Lincoln concisely put it: "I can't spare this man — he fights." *(Library of Congress.)*

taneous advance of all Union armies, so that the Confederates must divide their forces or else leave their territory open to invasion. The idea of involving all the Federal forces at once made sense to Lincoln. "Oh, yes! I can see that," he exclaimed. "As we say out West, if a man can't skin he must hold a leg while somebody else does." Accepting Grant's plan, Lincoln created a modern command system for the United States army, with the President as commander in chief, Grant as general in chief, and Halleck as essentially a chief of staff, while Stanton as secretary of war ably supported all the others.

Meanwhile the Confederate command system was also evolving through experimentation. The tremendous victories won by Lee and the Army of Northern Virginia obviated the need for constant changing of command in the East, but by 1863 it was evident that there must be a reorganization of Confederate commanders in the West. Davis instituted what was, in effect, a theater command system, with Lee in control of the forces in Virginia, Joseph E. Johnston, now recovered from his wound, in command of the troops between the mountains and the Mississippi River, and Edmund Kirby-Smith in charge of all troops in the vast trans-Mississippi region.

The new system was only partially successful. Made a kind of super-commander of the trans-Mississippi theater, which was becoming increasingly isolated as Union forces captured point after point along the Mississippi, Kirby-Smith did an effective job of recruiting and reorganizing the troops in his region. He stepped up trade with Mexico, so that impressive amounts of European munitions and supplies were brought in by way of Matamoras. So strengthened, "Kirby-Smithdom," as it was popularly called, fared better than most of the rest of the South, and the Confederate armies in this area were able to repel General N. P. Banks's invasion up the Red River in 1864 and also to blunt General Frederick Steele's push through Arkansas. But Kirby-Smith linked his fortunes with a group of trans-Mississippi sectionalists, who did not want to see their region bled to help the rest of the South, and he did little to make the vast resources of his command available to the government at Richmond.

In the central theater a strong Confederate command system failed to emerge. Suspicious of Davis and the Confederate war department, aware that his subordinates had the authority to report directly to Richmond, Johnston claimed he did not know the extent and nature of his duties. Repeatedly he asked whether he was supposed to take field command of the widely separated armies of Bragg, near Chattanooga, and of Pemberton, at Vicksburg, or was merely to serve as advisers to those generals. Knowing that both were protégés of the President, he did not dare give a positive order to either. In consequence, he made only a feeble effort to replace the unpopular Bragg and diverted a few of his troops to support Pemberton. Unable to persuade Pemberton to leave Vicksburg while there was still time, Johnston watched in impotent impatience as the Confederate army was cornered and starved into surrender.

The brilliant successes of Lee and his lieutenants in the Eastern theater allowed the Army of Northern Virginia to operate pretty much as it wished, without much regard for the needs of the Confederacy elsewhere. There were some exceptions to this generalization, as when Lee permitted General James A. Longstreet's corps to join Bragg's army in time to win the Confederate victory at Chickamauga. But mostly Lee, who had direct access to President Davis, resisted any attempt to weaken his force. In mid-1863, rather than attempt to relieve Vicksburg, Lee deliberately chose to stage a new invasion of the North, in the vain hope that it would relieve pressure on Confederate armies elsewhere. The result was the defeat at Gettysburg and the capture of Vicksburg.

Even so, Lee was by 1864 the only Confederate commander who retained the confidence of the country and of his troops. As Southern defeats became more numerous than victories, a strong demand swelled up in the Confederate Congress for coordinated direction of all the Southern armies, and men naturally looked to Lee. The general was, however, averse to these broader responsibilities and did all that he could to discourage the plan. When the Congress in January 1865 passed an act requiring the appointment of a commander in chief of all the armies, it clearly had Lee in mind, and Davis named him. In accepting the new position, Lee made it clear that he would continue to be essentially a theater commander, responsible only to Davis. The Confederacy thus reached Appomattox without ever developing a truly unified command system, comparable to that of the Union.

The Naval War

In naval warfare necessity compelled the Confederates to take the lead in experimentation. Southerners were not a seagoing people, with a tradition of shipbuilding. Secretary of the Navy Stephen R. Mallory had initially not a single ship at his command. He had to improvise, and he did so with imagination and remarkable success.

In the early months of the war the long Southern coastline seemed to be at the mercy of the Union fleet, which could pick the most vulnerable points for attack. In November 1861, a Union flotilla commanded by Flag Officer Samuel F. DuPont routed the weak Confederate defenders of Port Royal Sound, and Federal troops occupied Beaufort and the adjacent South Carolina Sea Islands. The victory gave the vessels in the Atlantic blockading fleet a much needed fueling station, and it also brought freedom to the numerous slaves of the area. In February and March 1862, another Union expedition easily reduced Confederate positions on Roanoke Island and at New Bern, North Carolina, and enabled the Federal blockaders to keep a closer watch on Hatteras Sound. Farragut's fleet in April 1862 helped capture New Orleans, the Confederacy's largest city.

By this time the Confederacy had greatly strengthened its coastal defenses, and further Union successes came slowly and at great cost. In April 1863 the Confederates repelled a vast Union armada, commanded by DuPont, which tried to capture Charleston. That citadel of secession remained in Confederate hands until nearly the end of the war, when Sherman's advance compelled Southern troops to abandon it. Equally effective were the Confederate defenses of Wilmington, North Carolina, which became the main Southern port on the Atlantic through which supplies from Europe were imported. Not until January 1865 could Federal troops capture Fort Fisher, the principal defense of Wilmington. The powerfully protected harbor of Mobile remained in Southern hands until August 1864, when the 63-year-old Admiral Farragut, lashed in the rigging of his flagship so that he would not fall to his death if wounded, led his fleet past the defending Confederate forts to stop the last remaining major Southern port on the Gulf.

To supplement the coastal batteries that protected these and other harbors, the Confederate navy experimented with new weapons. They used torpedoes extensively for the first time in warfare. These "infernal machines," constructed of kegs, barrels, and cans filled with explosives, were sometimes anchored at the entrance of Southern harbors, at other times were turned loose to float with the tide toward attacking Union vessels, and on still other occasions were propelled at the end of a long pole by a small boat, whose crew was willing to undertake the suicidal risk. Even more risky were the several Confederate experiments with submarine warfare. The most successful of these novel vessels was the *H. L. Hunley,* propelled under water by a crank turned by its eight-man crew. After four unsuccessful trials, in which all members of the crews were lost, the *Hunley* in February 1864 sank the Union warship *Housatonic* in Charleston harbor, but the submarine itself was lost in the resulting explosion.

Quickly comprehending that the Confederacy could never build as large a fleet as the Union, Secretary Mallory early in the war urged the construction of iron-armored ships, against which the wooden vessels of the North would stand no chance. Despite shortages of iron and lack of rolling mills, the Confederacy developed a surprising number of these vessels. The most famous of the Confederate ironclads was the *Virginia,* originally the United States warship *Merrimack,* which the Federals sank when they abandoned Norfolk navy yard at the beginning of the war. Raised and repaired, the *Virginia* had her superstructure covered with four-inch iron plate, and she carried a cast-iron ram on her prow. On March 8, 1862, just as McClellan began his campaign on the Peninsula, the *Virginia* emerged and began attacking the wooden vessels of the Union fleet at Hampton Roads. In her first day's action she destroyed two of the largest ships in the squadron and ran a third aground. Reappearing the second day, she found her way barred by a curious Union vessel, the *Monitor,* which looked like a tin can on a raft. Belatedly contracted for by the slow-moving Union navy department, the *Monitor,* designed by John Ericsson, was a low-lying ironclad with a revolving gun turret. The battle between the *Virginia* and the *Monitor* proved a draw, but the Confederate ship had to return to Norfolk to repair her defective

"ENGAGEMENT BETWEEN THE MONITOR AND THE MERRIMACK"
BY J. G. TANNER

Lacking a fleet, the Confederacy was early forced to improvise
in naval warfare. Its ironclad, the C.S.S. *Virginia* (formerly
the U.S.S. *Merrimack*) wrought havoc among the wooden
ships of the Union navy at Hampton Roads in March 1862.
But the opportune arrival of the Union ironclad, the
Monitor — which looked, as a contemporary said, "like a
cheesebox on a raft" — checked the Confederate vessel.
The engagement between the two ironclads opened a new
era in the history of naval warfare. *(National Gallery of Art.)*

engines. Two days later, when forced to abandon Norfolk, the Southerners ran
the *Virginia* ashore and burned the vessel to prevent its capture. The South's
most promising hope for breaking the blockade was lost.

Mallory was equally prompt in purchasing or commissioning conventional
vessels for the Confederate navy, ships designed not to combat Union warships
but to harass the United States merchant marine. The most successful of these
vessels was the *C. S. S. Alabama*, built to Southern specifications at the Laird shipyards in Liverpool and commanded by Raphael Semmes. Ranging over the Atlantic, Indian, and Pacific oceans, the *Alabama* between 1862 and 1864 hunted
down and destroyed sixty-nine Union merchantmen, valued at more than $6
million. Not until nearly the end of the war could the Union navy corner and sink
the raider. By this time, however, the *Alabama*, along with other Confederate
cruisers, had virtually exterminated the United States carrying trade.

However imaginative and innovative, Confederate navy officials could not keep pace with the growth of the Union navy, under the slow but honest direction of Gideon Welles. Drawing upon the vast industrial resources of the North and upon the experience of its seagoing population, Welles was able to build up the United States navy from its 42 active vessels in 1861, only 26 of which had steam power, to 671 ships in December 1864, of which 71 were ironclad. Navy personnel rose from 7400 at the start of the war to 68,000 at its end. Superbly equipped and managed, the Union fleet maintained an ever tightening blockade of the Southern coast. According to the best, but not wholly reliable, statistics, the Union fleet captured not more than 1 in 10 blockade runners in 1861, and not more than 1 in 8 in 1862. But by 1864 they caught 1 in 3, and by 1865 every other one. When dispirited by their exhausting but unpublicized duties, Union blockaders could take comfort in the knowledge that they were helping to strangle the Confederacy.

The Wartime Economy

Inevitably these huge military and naval operations put a heavy strain upon the economic resources of the combatants. In the Confederacy one result was a sharp shift in the nature of Southern agriculture. When the outbreak of war cut off Northern markets and the blockade increasingly sealed off European outlets for cotton and tobacco, farmers, at the urging of the Confederate and state governments, turned to producing grain and other foodstuffs. Cotton production in the South dropped from 4 million bales in 1861 to 300,000 in 1864.

In the North, too, farmers began producing more grain. Partly because of inflation, the price of wheat rose from 65¢ a bushel in December 1860 to $2.26 in July 1864, and farmers, especially in the Middle West, saw a chance to make money. At first the labor shortage kept them from expanding their acreage, for many farmhands enlisted in the Union army at the outbreak of the war, but machines soon made up for the absent men. One of Cyrus Hall McCormick's reapers could replace from 4 to 6 farmhands, and McCormick sold 165,000 of his machines during the war.

Industry in both the Union and the Confederacy also grew. The amount and significance of this growth has become a matter of controversy among economic historians. Rejecting the traditional view that the Civil War enormously accelerated American economic growth, some scholars, using statistics only recently made available, have concluded that, on the whole, the war years retarded growth. It is difficult to resolve the controversy because statistics from this period are incomplete, because the South is omitted from many of the calculations, and because many aspects of economic growth, such as entrepreneurship and organizational skill, are not readily quantified. It seems safe to conclude, however, that the Civil War years did not witness a dramatic growth of the American economy but saw a continuation and extension of trends evident before 1861.

However absorbing this controversy over economic growth is to the economist, the historian is more interested in the experimentation and innovation in industry that the war produced and in the striking similarity of these changes in the Union and the Confederacy. In the South, which had previously had little manufacturing, the war served as a hothouse for industry. The Union blockade unintentionally protected infant Southern manufactures by cutting off imports, and the demands of the army and the needs of the civilians provided an insatiable market. It is hard to measure Southern industrial growth, both because there was no Confederate census and because inflation affected all prices, yet there are some clues to show that manufacturing could be very profitable. For instance, the 1862 conscription acts exempted the owners of certain basic industries provided that their annual profits were no more than 75 percent. Under the astute management of Joseph Anderson, the Tredegar Iron Works at Richmond, the largest privately owned factory in the South and the primary source for Confederate cannon, made profits of 100 percent in 1861 and of 70 percent in 1862.

Northern manufacturing was equally profitable, especially when it produced items needed for the army. With the demand for uniforms, woolen mills, which had averaged dividends of only 9 percent for the years before the war, by 1865 were able to pay 25 percent dividends, and the number of woolen mills more than doubled. Investors were willing to pour money into such industries more confidently because Congress raised tariffs to levels that virtually excluded competing European products. War demands made the mass production of ready-made clothing profitable, and the army's need for shoes speeded the introduction of Gordon McKay's machine for sewing soles to uppers. Simultaneously, in an unrelated development, the discovery of oil at Titusville, Pennsylvania, in 1859, led to a wartime boom in the new petroleum industry.

If these changes signified no acceleration of American economic growth, they had an important impact on the structure of the American economy. The increase in the number of factories, particularly in the Confederacy, encouraged entrepreneurship. In the North, men like John D. Rockefeller and Andrew Carnegie, who started their fortunes during the war, continued to dominate the industrial scene after 1865. When the South began rebuilding its industry in the 1870s and 1880s, it looked for leadership to its wartime entrepreneurs and to the Confederate commanders who likewise had experience in directing the labor of large numbers of men. The war also encouraged the growth of large, rather than small, factories. Obliged to contract for huge shipments, both Union and Confederate governments naturally turned to the manufacturing companies financially and physically able to handle them. The selective process was accelerated because larger firms could pay an agent in Washington or Richmond who understood the requirements of the army and navy—as well as those of influential Congressmen and bureaucrats.

Most important of all, the wartime experience changed attitudes toward the role of the national government in the economy. Since the destruction of the second Bank of the United States in the Jackson era, the national government had done little to regulate or control the economy; investment in railroads and canals, regulation of working conditions for certain laborers, and supervision of the quality of milk and other foods were regarded as functions of the state and local authorities. But during the war both the Union and the Confederate governments took steps that affected every branch of economic life. In passing the Homestead Act of May 20, 1862, which offered any citizen 160 acres of the public domain after five years of continuous residence, the Union Congress signaled its intention henceforth to give more attention to the nation's farmers, as it did in

MAKING GUNS FOR THE NEW MONITORS AT PITTSBURGH, PENNSYLVANIA

The success of the North was due in considerable measure to its economic superiority over the South. The Fort Pitt ironworks at Pittsburg, which manufactured guns for the fleet of monitors, had their counterparts in a dozen other Northern cities. Confederate ordnance depended almost entirely upon imports from Europe and the output of the Tredegar ironworks in Richmond. (*Carnegie Library of Pittsburgh.*)

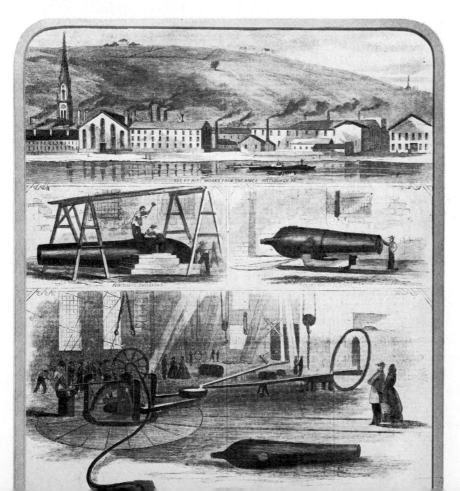

creating a federal department of agriculture that same year. The Morrill Act of 1862, giving vast tracts of the public domain to endow agricultural (land grant) colleges, was further evidence of the same purpose. Both governments found it necessary to regulate transportation, especially railroads, during the war. Davis, despite his strict interpretation of the Confederate Constitution, urged his Congress to finance the construction of some missing links in the Southern rail system. Lincoln in July 1862 signed the Pacific Railroad Act, giving enormous tracts of the public land to support the construction of a transcontinental rail route.

In both the United States and the Confederacy, private citizens became aware, often for the first time, of the economic impact of their national governments. In the Confederacy, the Impressment Act of March 1863 authorized government agents to seize civilians' food, horses, wagons, or other supplies if required for the army and to set an arbitrary price for the confiscated goods. In the Union the creation of a new national banking system in 1863 (amended and strengthened in 1864) meant, among other things, that a uniform national currency began to replace the dozens of issues by local banks. Citizens, paying national taxes in national currency, grew accustomed to the idea that their national government would henceforth play a positive role in the economic life of the country.

Inflation and Its Consequences

During the desperate final years of the Civil War, both Union and Confederate Treasury departments had to experiment with new ways to finance the war. Both imposed broad excise duties. The Union internal revenue act of July 1, 1862, has been fairly characterized as an attempt to tax everything. Duties were imposed upon all sorts of manufactures, with a fresh duty levied each time the raw material underwent a new process. In a carriage, for instance, the leather, the cloth, the wood, and the metal would each be taxed; then the manufacturer was taxed for the process of putting them together; the dealer was taxed for selling the carriage; and the purchaser, having paid a sufficient price to cover all these duties, was taxed in addition for ownership. Heavy duties fell upon luxuries, like billiard tables and yachts, and taxes upon professions and occupations covered, as Representative James G. Blaine said, "bankers and pawn brokers, lawyers and horse-dealers, physicians and confectioners, commercial brokers and peddlers." Ultimately these taxes brought in about 21 percent of the total wartime expenditures of the Union government.

The Confederacy moved more slowly, but on April 24, 1863, it too adopted a comprehensive tax measure, which included an income tax, occupational and license taxes ranging from $40 for bowling alleys to $500 for bankers, and what a later generation would call an excess profits tax. A unique feature of the Confederate legislation was the tax-in-kind, which compelled producers of wheat, corn, oats, potatoes, sugar, cotton, tobacco, and other farm products to pay one-tenth of their crop each year to the government. A last, desperate attempt in March 1865 to tax all coin, bullion, and foreign exchange was made too late to have any effect. All told, the Confederacy raised only about 1 percent of its income from taxes.

The sale of bonds contributed little more to the Confederate treasury. Values were so uncertain in the wartime South that investors were afraid to tie up their money in such rigid investments, and doubts spread as to when and whether the Confederate government would even pay the interest on its obligations. In the Union, on the other hand, bonds became a major source of revenue. Unable initially to sell bonds even at a discount, Secretary Chase appointed his friend, Jay Cooke, the Philadelphia banker who also had an office in Washington, special agent of the Treasury Department. Using high-pressure advertising, Cooke launched an extensive propaganda campaign, extolling the merits of the "five-twenties" (bonds bearing 6 percent interest, which could be paid off at the expiration of five, and must be redeemed in twenty, years). He was so successful that between 600,000 and a million citizens were persuaded to invest in the public debt, and the entire loan of half a billion dollars was oversubscribed. But in 1864, as the war stretched on endlessly and victory appeared nowhere in sight, the market for bonds collapsed. Resigning for political reasons, Chase left office at an opportune moment to preserve his reputation as a financier, and Cooke went with him. Chase's successor, William Pitt Fessenden, could only raise money through short-term loans at an exorbitant rate of interest. Not until the very end of the war, when victory was obviously near, did the sale of Union bonds pick up, and Cooke, reappointed special agent, attracted large additional numbers of investors.

Necessarily, therefore, both governments continued to depend upon paper money. The Union treasury, which had cautiously issued its first greenbacks in 1862, continued to print more and more during the rest of that year and during

UNION PAPER MONEY: A "GREENBACK"

Secretary Chase decided to print Union legal-tender notes with a patented green ink. Consequently they became known as "greenbacks."

1863 as well, until most of the $450 million authorized by Congress were in circulation. The value of the greenbacks gradually declined. A Union treasury note with a face value of one dollar was worth 99.86¢ in gold in 1862, but by 1864 it was worth only 62.66¢ and by early 1865, 50.3¢. In the Confederacy, where the printing presses never stopped, paper money had even less value. Perhaps $2 billion in unredeemable paper was issued in all. A Confederate treasury note for one dollar, worth 82.7¢ in gold in 1862, dropped to 29¢ in 1863 and to 1.7¢ in early 1865. In a desperate attempt to check the slide, the Confederate Congress in February 1864 undertook a partial repudiation of these notes, but the confusing and complex legislation was badly administered and served further to undermine trust in the government and its money. Having lost the confidence of the country, Memminger resigned in the summer of 1864 — at about the same time that Chase left the Union treasury department. His successor, the South Carolina banker and businessman, George A. Trenholm, could devise no better solution for the Confederacy's financial woes than to urge citizens to donate to the government their money, jewels, gold and silver plate, and public securities.

The excessive amount of paper money was only one of many factors that produced runaway inflation in both the North and the South. With importations largely cut off, in the North by the highly protective tariff and in the South by the Union blockade, with the productive labor force sharply reduced because of the number of men in military service, and with a huge portion of all goods required to supply the armies and navies, civilians had to expect shortages and high prices.

In both sections there were some who profited from the wartime economy. War contracts helped pull the Union economy out of a sharp depression, and higher prices spurred on manufacturers, who could now look for higher profits. The demand for grain, along with the Homestead Act, encouraged new settlers to begin farming, and the development of new industries, like petroleum, made for quick fortunes. The wartime boom in the North had a hectic quality about it, and men spent their easily earned money quickly lest it be worth less in the future. Many of the new rich were extravagant and hedonistic. Censoriously the *New York Independent* asked in June 1864:

Who at the North would ever think of war, if he had not a friend in the army, or did not read the newspapers? Go into Broadway, and we will show you what is meant by the word "extravagance." Ask [A. T.] Stewart [the department-store owner] about the demand for camel's-hair shawls, and he will say "monstrous." Ask Tiffany what kinds of diamonds and pearls are called for. He will answer "the prodigious," "as near hen's-egg size as possible," "price no object." What kinds of carpetings are now wanted? None but "extra." . . . And as for horses the medium-priced five-hundred-dollar kind are all out of the market. A good pair of "fast ones" . . . will go for a thousand dollars sooner than a basket of strawberries will sell for four cents.

But not all elements in the North shared in this wartime prosperity. Wages lagged sadly behind prices, so that in real income a worker between 1861 and

1865 lost 35 percent of his wages. Women, who composed one-fourth of the nation's manufacturing force in 1860, were especially hard hit. As more and more wives and mothers found it necessary to work, since soldiers could only send them a pittance for support, employers actually cut their wages. Even the United States government participated in this practice. At the Philadelphia armory, the government in 1861 paid a seamstress 17¢ for making a shirt; three years later, when prices were at their highest, it cut the wage to 15¢. Meanwhile private contractors paid only 8¢.

Suffering in the North was, however, relatively minor when compared to that in the South. To be sure, residents of some parts of the agricultural South who were never disturbed by Union troops had only minor shortages to complain of. As imported goods disappeared from the grocers' shelves, they resorted to sassafras tea and to "coffee" made of parched rye, okra seeds, corn, and even sweet potatoes, the grounds of which were said to form a remarkable cleaning agent for curtains and carpets. Since salt was in short supply, meat could not be preserved, and Southerners ate more chicken and fish. As clothing wore out, they increasingly turned to homespun, and velvet draperies and brocaded rugs found new use as gowns and overcoats.

The thousands of Southerners in the path of the armies had to think not just of shortages but of survival. Hundreds of families fled before the invading Union armies, often attempting to take their slaves with them, but nowhere could these refugees find assurance of safety. Their lives took on a desperate, nightmarish quality, and merely existing from one day to the next was a struggle. There was never enough of anything, including food. Recalling these unhappy days, one writer declared that "the Confederacy was always hungry."

The greatest destitution appeared in towns and cities, where supplies had to be brought in over the rickety Southern railroad system. White-collar workers, especially those on fixed salaries from the government, were especially hard hit. The celebrated diary of J. B. Jones, a clerk in the Confederate War Department at Richmond, is a melancholy record of shortages and high prices. In May 1864, he reported that beans in Richmond were selling for $3 a quart, meal for $125 a bushel, and flour $400 a barrel. Richmond, he observed, was an astonishingly clean city, since "no garbage or filth can accumulate." The citizens of the Confederate capital were obliged to be "such good scavengers" that there was "no need of buzzards."

Deprivation was the more painful because, as in the North, some made enormous profits from the war. The blockade runner, who preferred to bring in compact, expensive items like silks and jewels rather than bulky supplies for the army, often reaped fantastic profits. Speculators also flourished. As early as the winter of 1862, the governor of Mississippi learned that the families of volunteers in his state were seriously suffering for want of corn and salt, while rich planters held back their ample supply of both commodities, waiting for the inevitable rise in prices. Even more remunerative was trading with the enemy, a practice completely illegal but tacitly condoned by both Confederate and Union officials. Southern women and men who were initiated into the mysteries of the trade bought up as much cotton as they could find in their neighborhoods and took it to convenient exchange points like Memphis and Natchez to sell to the Yankees for coffee, clothing, and luxuries. Late in the war they accepted payment in United States greenbacks, which Southerners valued more than their own depreciated money.

Conscription and Conflict

Along with economic inequity, the unfairness of conscription was the subject of bitter complaints on the part of both Northerners and Southerners during the Civil War. The Confederate conscription act of 1862 ostensibly made all able-bodied white males between the ages of eighteen and thirty-five equally eligible for military service, but the Southern Congress promptly began exempting large categories of men.

As men rushed to enter "bombproof" occupations and claim exemptions, the outcry against the Confederate conscription system grew louder. One of the most vociferous critics was Governor Joseph E. Brown of Georgia, who protested, "The conscription Act, at one fell swoop, strikes down the sovereignty of the States, tramples upon the constitutional rights and personal liberty of the citizens, and arms the President with imperial power." After attempting unsuccessfully to induce the Georgia supreme court to declare conscription unconstitu-

THE NEW YORK DRAFT RIOTS: BATTLE IN SECOND AVENUE AND 22ND STREET AT THE UNION STEAM WORKS, JULY 14, 1863

Conscription triggered resistance in the North. The largest riot was in New York City, where Federal troops, fresh from the Gettysburg campaign, had to be called in to restore order. (*Frank Leslie's Illustrated Newspaper.*)

tional, Brown proceeded to undermine the policy by naming his supporters to state jobs exempt from military service. According to some estimates he put 15,000 able-bodied Georgians into this exempt category; certainly he created 2000 justices of the peace and 1000 constables, none of whom had to serve in the army. Less prominent than Brown but equally potent were the critics who complained that conscription was class legislation that benefited the educated and the wealthy. They raised especial objection to the so-called "twenty-nigger" provision, which clearly favored planters at the expense of farmers. "Never did a law meet with more universal odium than the exemption of slave owners," wrote Senator James Phelan of Mississippi to President Davis. "It has aroused a spirit of rebellion . . . and bodies of men have banded together to desert."

Despite intense criticism and dubious results, the Davis administration continued conscription, for it saw no other way to raise the needed number of men. Indeed, as the war progressed, it was obliged to experiment with even more stringent legislation. In a new conscription act of February 17, 1864, the Confederate Congress declared that all white males between the ages of seventeen and fifty were subject to the draft, with the seventeen-year-old boys and the men above forty-five to serve as a reserve for local defense. As a concession to small planters, the act exempted one farmer or overseer for every plantation with fifteen slaves, but it abolished most other exemptions, on the theory that once skilled laborers were in the army the government could detail them to the forges and factories where they were most needed. Total mobilization of manpower was, however, far beyond the competence of the shaky Confederate government,

and in practice the industrial-detail system never worked. As the Confederacy scraped the bottom of the barrel, more and more white Southerners began thinking about the one group of able-bodied males who did not serve in the armies, the Negroes.

In the North, too, conscription evoked bitter criticism. The first effective Northern draft act, passed by the Union Congress on March 3, 1863, was patently unfair. Declaring that all able-bodied males between the ages of twenty and forty-five (except for certain high governmental officials and the only sons of widows and infirm parents) were liable to military service, the act promptly contradicted itself by permitting those who could afford to do so to hire substitutes. In an effort to keep the price of substitutes down, it also permitted a man to purchase outright exemption from military service for $300.

As in the South, there was immediate and widespread hostility toward conscription. Since there was a social stigma attached to being drafted, nobody wanted to be forced to serve in the army. This reluctance was magnified when it became evident that the system favored the wealthiest citizens and the most prosperous sections of the country. A well-to-do citizen like George Templeton Strong of New York, for example, did not dream of serving in the army; he paid $1100 for a substitute, "a big 'Dutch' boy of twenty or thereabouts," who, as Strong remarked complacently, "looked as if he could do good service." Rich towns and counties raised bounty funds to encourage volunteering, so that none of their citizens would have to be drafted, and as the war progressed, they offered higher and higher bounties. The volunteers they sought were by no means all local residents who needed a little financial inducement; many of them were professional bounty hunters, who went from place to place, enlisting, receiving bounties, and promptly deserting. Perhaps the record for bounty jumping was held by one John O'Connor, who when arrested in March 1865 confessed to thirty-two such desertions.

Part of the outcry against conscription in the North stemmed from the inequity of the quotas the President was authorized to announce for each state, presumably giving credit for the number of volunteers it had previously supplied. The Democratic governor of New York, Horatio Seymour, engaged in acrimonious correspondence with Lincoln and finally forced the President to admit that the quota assigned to the Empire State was excessive. Such concessions, however, came too late to placate those threatened by the draft. In Wisconsin, Kentucky, and Pennsylvania, in Troy, Newark, and Albany, there was outright resistance to the enrolling officers, and in several instances federal troops had to be brought in to quell the insurgents. None of these outbreaks compared in extent or ferocity to that in New York City, where the drawing of the first draftees' names triggered a three-day riot (July 13–15, 1863) by a mob of predominantly Irish workingmen. Turning first against the enrollment officers and the police, the rioters then exhibited their animus against the rich by plundering fine houses and rifling jewelry stores. Toward Negroes, whom the rioters feared as economic competitors and blamed for the war and hence for conscription, the mob acted with hideous brutality. After sacking and looting a Negro orphan asylum they chased down any blacks unwary enough to appear on the streets and left those they could capture hanging from lampposts. The Union government had to rush in troops from the Gettysburg campaign to stop the rioting and disperse the mob.

Despite all resistance, Lincoln's government continued conscription because, as in the Confederacy, there seemed to be no other source for soldiers. Even so, the draft remained cumbersome and often ineffectual. In 1864, for instance, 800,000 names were drawn, but so many were exempted because of health or occupation and so many others hired substitutes or paid the commutation fee that only 33,000 were actually inducted into the army. As conscription proved both unfair and ineffective, citizens in the North, like those in the South, began to think of the value of black soldiers.

Steps Toward Emancipation

Just as the Negro played a central part in causing the Civil War, so was he to play a major role in determining its outcome. At the outset there was a tacit agreement that the Civil War was to be a white man's fight, and both Union and Confederate governments in 1861 refused to accept black regiments. In the Confederacy during the first two years of the war, virtually nobody questioned the correctness of this decision. After all, as Vice-President Alexander H. Stephens announced, slavery was "the real 'corner-stone'" upon which the Confederate States had been erected, and few Southern whites could even contemplate the possibility of putting arms into the hands of slaves or of freeing blacks who became soldiers.

In the Union, on the other hand, there were from the beginning powerful voices urging the emancipation of slaves and the enlistment of black men in the army. Frederick Douglass, the leading spokesman of blacks in the North, constantly insisted: "Teach the rebels and traitors that the price they are to pay for the attempt to abolish this Government must be the abolition of slavery." Abolitionists, white and black, repeatedly instructed Lincoln that he could win the war only if he emancipated the slaves. Urging the President to make his cardinal rule that *Nothing against Slavery can be unconstitutional*," Senator Charles Sumner of Massachusetts visited the White House almost daily in his efforts to persuade Lincoln that emancipation was the *"one way to safety,* clear as sunlight — pleasant as the paths of Peace."

So influential was this antislavery sentiment that several of the President's subordinates who fell into disfavor with the administration tried to appeal to it. When General Frémont was in deep trouble over his maladministration in

Missouri, he suddenly announced in August 1861 that the property of all rebels in his region would be confiscated and their slaves freed. Similarly in December 1861 when Secretary of War Cameron came under fire for inefficiency and possible corruption, he surprisingly declared himself in favor of freeing and arming the slaves. In May 1862 General David Hunter, in command of the Union troops occupying the Sea Islands, proclaimed the emancipation of the slaves in Florida, Georgia, and South Carolina. But President Lincoln, aware of the dangerous complexity of the issue, patiently overruled each of these subordinates, declaring that emancipation was a question "which, under my responsibility, I reserve to myself."

Unwillingness to arm or emancipate the slaves did not signify any reluctance to employ blacks in nonmilitary service. Slaves were the backbone of the Confederate labor force. Had blacks not continued to till and harvest the grain, the Confederacy could never have fielded so large an army. Equally important was the role played by blacks, slave and free, in the industrial production of the Confederacy. In the Tredegar Iron Works, for example, half the 2400 employees were blacks; they included not merely unskilled workers but puddlers, rollers, and machinists. Blacks also performed indispensable service for the quartermaster and commissary departments of the Confederacy, serving as teamsters, butchers, drovers, boatmen, bakers, shoemakers, and blacksmiths, and they formed the backbone of the nursing staff of many Confederate hospitals.

So essential was Negro labor to the existence of the Confederacy that President Davis had to ensure that enough blacks were available for this service. From the beginning of the war, Confederate authorities from time to time impressed slaves to work on fortifications, and some states, notably Virginia, moved promptly to require owners to lease their slaves to the government when needed. But the Confederate government itself did not act until March 1863, when the Confederate Congress, despite much opposition from planters, authorized the impressment of slaves, whose owners were to receive $30 a month. In February 1864 it permitted military authorities to impress more slaves, with or without the consent of the owners.

Meanwhile the Union was also making full use of the labor of blacks. As slaves fled from their masters to the camps of the Union army, they were put to use as teamsters, cooks, nurses, carpenters, scouts, and day laborers. Perhaps half a million blacks crossed over to the Union lines, and nearly 200,000 of these performed labor for the army. Many of these "contrabands" brought with them valuable information about the disposition of Confederate troops and supplies. Occasionally some brought even more valuable assets. Robert Smalls and his

A BLACK FAMILY ON THE J. J. SMITH
PLANTATION, BEAUFORT, SOUTH CAROLINA, 1862.

(Library of Congress.)

brother, who were slaves in Charleston, South Carolina, in May 1862 daringly seized the Confederate sidewheel steamer *Planter,* navigated it out of the harbor ringed with Confederate guns, and delivered it to the blockading Union fleet.

When the war appeared to have reached a stalemate, Northern sentiment in favor of freeing and arming the slaves grew. Republican congressmen were ahead of the President on these questions. As early as August 1861, they had passed an act declaring that slaves used to support the Confederate military were free. In March 1862, Congress forbade the return of fugitive slaves by the military. And on July 17, 1862, in a far-reaching confiscation act, it declared that slaves of all persons supporting the rebellion should be "forever free of their servitude, and not again [to be] held as slaves." These measures were, however, poorly drafted and not readily enforced, so that they had little practical consequence. More effective was the act of April 16, 1862, abolishing slavery in the District of Columbia.

But powerful forces in the North were opposed to emancipation. The border states, where slavery still prevailed, were of such uncertain loyalty that they might try to break away from the Union if emancipation became a Northern war aim. In the free states, anti-Negro prejudice was rampant, and many feared that emancipation would produce a massive migration of blacks to the North, where they would compete with white laborers for jobs. Belief in the inferiority of the Negro race was general, and the experience of Union soldiers in the South often strengthened this stereotype, for the fugitives who fled to their camps were mostly illiterate, ragged, and dirty. "The contrabands are numerous," callously wrote one soldier in Hunter's army in South Carolina, "and ought all to be drowned."

During the initial stages of the war Lincoln, who hated slavery, had to take these racist attitudes into account, and he knew he could move toward emancipation only in a circuitous fashion. In early 1862 he made an earnest, though ultimately unsuccessful, plea to the border states to devise plans of gradual, compensated emancipation, for which he promised federal financial assistance. At the same time he took anti-Negro sentiment into account by favoring plans to colonize freedman in Central America and in Haiti. To a group of black leaders who visited him in the White House, the President explained his position frankly: "You and we are different races. We have between us a broader difference than exists between almost any other two races. Whether it is right or wrong I need not discuss, but this physical difference is a great disadvantage to us both. . . ." "It is better for us both," he concluded, "to be separated."

By the fall of 1862, however, Lincoln felt able to act decisively against slavery. By failing to adopt his program of gradual emancipation, the border states had lost their chance. Blacks showed little interest in his plans for colonization, which in any case were poorly thought out and could only lead to disaster. As casualties mounted, Northern soldiers, without necessarily shedding their prejudices against Negroes, came to think it was time to enroll blacks in the army. But most influential in changing Lincoln's mind was his grim recognition after eighteen months of combat that the war could not be ended by traditional means. "We . . . must change our tactics or lose the war," he concluded.

Waiting only for McClellan to check Lee's invasion at Antietam, Lincoln issued, on September 22, 1862, a preliminary emancipation proclamation announcing that unless the rebellious states returned to their allegiance he would on January 1, 1863, declare that "all persons held as slaves" in the territory controlled by the Confederates were "then, thenceforward, and forever free." Since the President justified his action on the ground of military necessity, it was appropriate that the definitive Emancipation Proclamation at the beginning of the new year officially authorized the enrollment of black troops in the Union army.

Promptly the war department began to accept Negro regiments. These were not, to be sure, the first black soldiers to serve in the war, for a few Negroes had been enrolled without permission from Washington in the Federal forces on the Sea Islands, in Louisiana, and in Kansas, but now large numbers of blacks joined the army. They were enrolled in segregated regiments, in nearly all cases with white officers, and they received less pay than did white soldiers. By the end of the war, the number of Negroes in the Union army totalled 178,895 — more than twice the number of soldiers in the Confederate army at Gettysburg.

At first most Union officials thought black regiments would be useful only for garrison duty, but in bitterly contested engagements such as Fort Wagner and Port Hudson, Millikin's Bend and Nashville, they demonstrated, as Lincoln said, how well, "with silent tongue, and clenched teeth, and steady eye, and well-poised bayonet," they could and would fight. The battle record of these black troops did much to change popular Northern stereotypes of the Negro. In the early stages of the war, cartoonists and caricaturists portrayed blacks as invisible men; their faces were vague and featureless blobs of black, hardly human. But with emancipation and the enrollment of Negroes in the army, war artists began to take a closer look, to depict blacks with distinctive, recognizably human features, and finally, in a kind of perverse tribute to their merit, to sketch them with Nordic profiles.

Meanwhile, and much more slowly, sentiment was growing in the Confederacy for the military employment of blacks. Support for arming the slaves emerged first in those areas scourged by Northern armies. After Grant's successful Vicksburg campaign, the Jackson *Mississippian* boldly called for enrolling slaves as soldiers in the Confederate army. Though other Mississippi and Alabama newspapers echoed the call for black recruits, the most powerful voice for arming the slaves was that of General Patrick R. Cleburne, who witnessed how easily the powerful Union army broke the thin Confederate line at Chattanooga. Seeing no other source of manpower, Cleburne, together with his aides, addressed a long letter to General Joseph E. Johnston, who had succeeded Bragg as commander of the army of Tennessee, urging "that we immediately commence training a large reserve of the most courageous of our slaves, and further that we guaran-

tee freedom within a reasonable time to every slave in the South who shall remain true to the Confederacy in this war."

So drastic a proposal was bound to rouse strong opposition, and President
Davis, upon learning of Cleburne's letter, ordered it suppressed. But the subject
would not die. As Union armies moved closer to the Confederate heartland, Virginia editors also began to urge arming the blacks, and at an October 1864 meeting Southern governors proposed "a change of policy on our part" as to the
slaves.

Finally, on November 7, 1864, President Davis, in a deliberately obscure message to Congress, put himself at the head of the movement. Urging further impressment of blacks for service with the army, Davis argued that the Confederate
government should purchase the impressed slaves. Having state-owned slaves
would be, Davis admitted, a "radical modification" of Confederate policy, and he
pondered the future of such a bondsman: "Should he be retained in servitude, or
should his emancipation be held out to him as a reward for faithful service, or
should it be granted at once on the promise of such service. . .?"

However obscurely phrased, Davis's proposal clearly looked toward the end
of slavery, and it at once encountered powerful resistance. Davis, said his enemies, proposed the confiscation of private property; he was subverting the Constitution. His plan would be a confession to the world of the South's weakness.

CHANGING NORTHERN IMAGES OF THE BLACK MAN

The Dis-United States: a Black Business   Cutting His Old Associates

It would deplete the labor force needed to feed the army. And most frightening of all, it would arm black men, who at best might desert to the Union armies and at worst might use those arms against their masters. "The African is of an inferior race, whose normal condition is slavery," insisted the Charleston *Mercury*. "Prone to barbarism, and incapable of any other state than that of pupilage, he is at his best estate as the slave of the enlightened white man of this country."

Despite all opposition, the Confederate government pushed ahead with the plan, for it had no other reservoir of manpower. In February 1865, the scheme received the backing of General Lee, who wrote that employing blacks as soldiers was "not only expedient but necessary" and announced plainly that "it would be neither just nor wise . . . to require them to serve as slaves." The next month the Confederate Congress passed, by a very close vote, an act calling for 300,000 more soldiers, irrespective of color. No provision was made in the act to free blacks who enrolled, but the Confederate war department in effect smuggled emancipation into the measure through the orders it issued for its enforcement. Promptly the recruiting of black troops began, and some black companies were raised in Richmond and other towns. By this time, however, it was too late, even for such a revolutionary experiment, and none of the black Confederate soldiers ever saw service.

Teaching the Negro Recruits the Use of the Minié Rifle   The Escaped Slave in the Union Army

Europe and the War

Though the Union and Confederate governments moved toward emancipating and arming the blacks because of military necessity, both recognized how profoundly their actions affected the continuing struggle for European recognition and support. Well informed Americans were aware of the intensity of European antislavery sentiment. But so long as neither government took a bold stand against the South's peculiar institution, European antislavery leaders were puzzled and divided by the war. In Great Britain, for example, some important spokesmen, like John Bright, Richard Cobden, and John Stuart Mill, from the beginning supported the Union cause, confident that Southern defeat would end slavery. But Lord Russell, on the other hand, predicted that if the South should be conquered and the United States be restored without emancipating the blacks, "slavery would prevail all over the New World. For that reason," he concluded, "I wish for separation."

Lincoln's emancipation proclamation ended the confusion. Though some complained that it promised freedom only to slaves whom the Union army could not reach and denied it to those in areas under Union control, European antislavery spokesmen soon recognized that the proclamation marked a new era. Within three months after the final emancipation proclamation was issued, fifty-six large public meetings were held in Great Britain to uphold the Northern cause.

Union diplomacy had need of such popular support, for there still lurked the possibility of European intervention in the war. Though the gravest threat had passed in the fall of 1862, before the full effect of the emancipation proclamation could be sensed abroad, the French emperor continued to contemplate the advantages that might come of meddling in American affairs. Hoping that a divided United States would assist his mad enterprise of establishing a puppet empire under the Emperor Maximilian in Mexico, Napoleon in February 1863, when Northern military fortunes were at their nadir after Fredericksburg, offered to mediate between the two belligerents. Shrewdly judging that Great Britain and Russia were not behind the French move, Secretary of State Seward spurned the offer, declaring "that peace proposed at the cost of the dissolution [of the Union] would be immediately, unreservedly, and indignantly rejected by the American people."

More dangerous to the Union cause than Napoleon's clumsy diplomacy were the warships being built for the Confederacy in British shipyards. Supplying either belligerent in a war with armed ships was contrary both to international law and to British statutes, but through a loophole in the law it was legal to sell separately unarmed vessels and the armaments that would convert them into men of war. In March 1862 the ship that became the *C. S. S. Florida* sailed from a British shipyard, and in July of that year the more powerful *Alabama* set forth to begin her depredations. Even as these raiders swept the Union merchant marine from the high seas, a more formidable Confederate naval threat, this time to the blockade itself, was being forged in the form of two enormous ironclad steam rams under construction at the Laird yards in Liverpool.

The British government wished to observe its neutrality laws, but the legal machinery was slow and cumbersome. When Union minister Charles Francis Adams called the attention of the foreign office to the rams, Lord Russell replied that he could not act to detain them unless there was convincing evidence of Confederate ownership. Adams and his aides rushed to secure affidavits to prove that the vessels were intended for the Confederacy, but British law officers were unconvinced since other sworn testimony claimed the rams were being constructed for the French emperor or the Pasha of Egypt. Finally, in utter exasperation, Adams on September 5, 1863, sent Russell a final warning against permitting the ships to sail, adding: "It would be superfluous in me to point out to your Lordship that this is war." Fortunately, two days before receiving Adams's ultimatum, Russell had already decided to detain the rams, and the Confederates' final hope of breaking the blockade was lost.

With that crisis, the last serious threat of European involvement in the American war disappeared. A few months later Henry Adams, the son of the United States minister, wrote from London: "Our whole question is now old and familiar to every one, so as to have become actually a bore and a nuisance. The enthusiasm for the slaveholders has passed away. . . ." So indifferent, or even hostile, to the Southern cause was the British cabinet that late in 1863 Confederate Secretary of State Benjamin ordered Mason, his envoy, to leave London on the grounds that "the Government of Her Majesty [Queen Victoria] . . . entertains no intention of receiving you as the accredited minister of this government."

Keenly aware of the influence that emancipation had exerted in uniting European opinion against the South, President Davis sought similarly to capitalize on the actions that the Confederate States took against slavery during the final months of the war. In January 1865, he sent Duncan F. Kenner, one of the largest slaveholders in Louisiana, on a secret mission to Europe, authorizing him to promise the emancipation of the slaves in return for European recognition and aid to the Confederacy. The experiment came too late, for now it was evident that Northern victory was inevitable. Neither the French nor the British government expressed interest in Kenner's proposal.

Wartime Politics

The military and diplomatic advantages resulting from emancipation were to a considerable extent counterbalanced by its political disadvantages. The steps that Lincoln and Davis took toward freeing and arming the slaves enormously increased the opposition to their administrations and provided their domestic enemies a fresh supply of ammunition.

In the Confederacy there had been from the beginning of the war a sizable disloyal element. Unionism was strong in the Upper South, in the mountain regions, and in some of the poorer hill counties. Some white Southerners expressed their hostility toward the Confederate government by enlisting in the Union armies; others, by volunteering information to advancing Union forces; still others, by supplying provisions for the Federal troops. As the war progressed, some of these disaffected Southerners joined secret peace societies, such as the Order of the Heroes, which had its following in the Carolinas and Virginia. Disloyalty extended into the ranks of the Confederate army, especially after conscription was initiated, and desertion was widespread. About one out of every nine soldiers who enlisted in the Confederate army deserted. Sometimes they formed guerrilla bands that preyed equally upon Confederate and Union sympathizers. When halted by an enrolling officer and asked to show his pass to leave the army, a deserter would pat his gun defiantly and say, "This is my furlough."

Probably no action of the Davis administration could have won over these actively disloyal citizens, but the policies of the Confederate government alienated also a large number of entirely loyal Southerners. Some of these critics complained that President Davis was timid and tardy. He was sickly, neurasthenic, and indecisive, they said; he could not tolerate strong men around him and relied for advice upon sycophants; he did not know how to rouse the loyalty and the passions of the Southern people; he lacked courage to put himself at the head of the Southern armies and lead the Confederacy to victory. "Oh, for a man at the helm like William of Orange," exclaimed diarist Robert Kean, "a man of steadfast calm temper, heroic character and genius, a man fertile in resources, equal to emergencies. This, it is quite evident, Mr. Davis is not."

A much larger group of Confederates censured their President for exactly opposite reasons. Davis's plan to arm and free the slaves reinforced their conviction that he intended to undermine the principles upon which the Confederacy had been founded. Conscription, they argued, had begun the subversion of state sovereignty, guaranteed by the Constitution. They found evidence of Davis's dictatorial ambitions in his requests that Congress suspend the writ of habeas corpus, so that the disloyal could be arrested and imprisoned without trial. Grudgingly Congress agreed to the suspension for three limited periods, but late in 1864 it rejected Davis's appeals for a further extension on the ground that it would be a dangerous assault upon the Constitution. Although infringements of civil liberties were infrequent in the Confederacy and no Southern newspaper was suppressed for publishing subversive editorials, the critics warned that Davis was reaching after imperial powers. If the South was to have an absolute ruler, announced Senator William L. Yancey, he preferred Lincoln, "not a Confederate dictator."

Leading this group of Davis's critics was none other than the Vice-President of the Confederate states, Alexander H. Stephens, who spent most of the final years of the war not in Richmond but in Georgia, stirring up agitation against the President's allegedly unconstitutional usurpation of power and simultaneously complaining of Davis's "weakness and imbecility." The Vice-President was ably supported by his brother, a leader in the Georgia legislature, who believed Davis was "a *little, conceited, hypocritical, snivelling, canting, malicious, ambitious, dogged,* knave and fool," and by Governor Brown, who deplored the President's "bold strides toward despotism."

The congressional elections of 1863, held after Southerners had begun to realize the gravity of their defeats at Gettysburg and Vicksburg, greatly strengthened the anti-Davis bloc. During the following year, the President was often able to muster a majority in Congress only because of the consistent support of representatives from districts overrun or threatened by advancing Federal armies. In some instances these districts were unable to hold regular elections in 1863 and their incumbent congressmen, chosen in the early days of complete commitment to the Confederate cause, remained in office; in any case, representatives from these occupied regions had little to lose from measures that taxed and bled the rest of the Confederacy. But by the desperate winter of 1864–65, not even this support could give Davis control of Congress. Now in a majority, his critics refused his request for control over the state militias and rejected his plea to end all exemptions from conscription. Even as Sherman's army advanced through the Carolinas, Congress endlessly debated his plan for arming the slaves. It passed, over Davis's opposition, an act creating the post of general in chief, advising the President to name Lee, and urging him also to give Joseph E. Johnston an important command. Fearful of attacking the President directly, congressional critics began investigations of several of his cabinet officers, and they introduced resolutions declaring that the resignation of Secretary of State Judah P. Benjamin, Davis's closest friend and most trusted adviser, would be "subservient of the public interest." Secretary of War Seddon also came under fire, and when the Virginia delegation in Congress called for his resignation, he felt obliged to leave the cabinet. In January 1865, for the first and only time the Confederate Congress overrode a presidential veto.

Meanwhile in the North, Abraham Lincoln and his government were subjected to the same kinds of criticism. In the Union as in the Confederacy there were some who were outright disloyal. Pro-Confederate sympathy was strongest in the states of the Upper South that remained in the Union, in those parts of the Old Northwest originally settled by Southerners, and in cities like New York, where the Irish immigrant population was bitterly hostile to blacks. Relatively few Northerners enlisted in the Confederate army, but many joined secret societies, such as the Knights of the Golden Circle and the Order of American Knights, devoted to bringing about a negotiated peace, which inevitably would entail recognizing Confederate independence. The purposes and indeed the very existence of these secret "Copperhead" organizations have become a matter of historical controversy, for it is clear that many members intended nothing more subversive than replacing a Republican administration with a Democratic one. It nevertheless remains certain that a sizable number of Northerners were hostile to the war and were ready to accept a dissolution of the Union. Some idea of the extent of this disaffection can be gained from the figures on desertion. One out of every seven men who enlisted in the Union armies deserted.

Much of the criticism of the Lincoln administration came from those who were entirely loyal to the Union but who deplored the measures the President took to save it. They bitterly complained when Lincoln, without waiting for congressional approval, suspended the writ of habeas corpus so that suspected subversives could be arrested without warning and imprisoned indefinitely. Though Chief Justice Roger B. Taney protested against the unconstitutionality of these arrests, Lincoln refused to heed his objections, and more than 13,000 persons were thus arbitrarily imprisoned. Critics also complained when the Lincoln administration curbed the freedom of the press. Because of the publication of allegedly disloyal and incendiary statements, the Chicago *Times,* the New York *World,* the Philadelphia *Evening Journal,* and many other newspapers were required to suspend publication for varying periods of time.

Lincoln's emancipation proclamation, followed by the arming of black soldiers, gave his critics further evidence of his ambition to become dictator and of his diabolical plan to change the purpose of the war. The emancipation proclamation

EMANCIPATION PROCLAMATION: A NORTHERN VIEW AND A SOUTHERN VIEW

"PRESIDENT LINCOLN WRITING THE PROCLAMATION OF FREEDOM," BY DAVID GILMOUR BLYTHE

A Northern artist shows Lincoln consulting the history of the United States, United States court decisions, Daniel Webster's views of the Constitution, and other documents in preparing his Emancipation Proclamation. A bust of the ineffectual President Buchanan hangs by a noose from the book case. *(Library of Congress.)*

convinced the Newark *Evening Journal* that Lincoln was "a perjured traitor, who
. . . betrayed his country and caused the butchery of hundreds of thousands of
the people of the United States in order to accomplish either his own selfish purpose, or to put in force a fanatical, impracticable idea."

So unpopular was the policy of emancipation that Lincoln's preliminary proclamation, together with the inability of Union generals to win victories, seriously
hurt his party in the congressional elections of 1862. In virtually every Northern
state there was an increase in Democratic votes. New York, Pennsylvania, Ohio,
Indiana, and Illinois, all of which had voted for Lincoln in 1860, went Democratic. The Republican majority in Congress was now paper-thin, and the administration kept that lead only because the army interfered in the Maryland,
Kentucky, and Missouri elections. Just as Jefferson Davis's control of the Confederate Congress after 1863 depended upon the votes of border state representatives, so Abraham Lincoln's majority in the Union Congress rested upon the
support of representatives from the same region.

If Democrats complained that Lincoln acted arbitrarily and too swiftly, critics
within his own party held that he was too slow, too cautious, and too indecisive.
His own attorney general, Edward Bates, felt that Lincoln had the ability to cope
with "neither great *principles* nor great *facts*." He lacked "practical talent for his
important place," concluded Senator Sumner, since in inertia and indecisiveness
he resembled Louis XVI more than any other ruler in history. The President's

"WRITING THE EMANCIPATION
PROCLAMATION," BY ADALBERT
VOLCK

A Confederate caricaturist depicts
Lincoln with his foot on the
Constitution, sitting beneath a
painting of slave insurrection in
Santo Domingo, as he dips his pen
into an inkwell held by Satan to
draft the proclamation of freedom.
*(Karolik Collection, Boston Museum
of Fine Arts.)*

former law partner, William H. Herndon, angrily berated "Old Abe" for his shameful want of courage: "Does he suppose he can crush—squelch out this huge rebellion by pop guns filled with rose water? He ought to hang somebody and get up a name for will or decision. . . . Let him hang some Child or woman, if he has not courage to hang a *man*."

So widespread was dissatisfaction with Lincoln that when Congress reassembled in December 1862, after the fiasco at Fredericksburg, the Senate Republican caucus tried to force the President to change his cabinet. Just as Davis's critics made Benjamin their target, so Republican senators blamed Secretary of State Seward for the weakness of the Lincoln administration and the maladministration of the war. By forcing Seward's resignation, they hoped to make Chase, who had fed them stories of Lincoln's incompetence, in effect premier. Deeply distressed by this maneuver, Lincoln thwarted it with great adroitness, by securing Seward's resignation and forcing Chase also to offer his. "I can ride now," he declared, remembering his days on the farm; "I've got a pumpkin in each end of my bag." Announcing that either resignation would leave his cabinet unbalanced, he declined them both. His cabinet remained intact, and the President remained responsible for Union policy.

Such sleight of hand was not enough to make dissent within Lincoln's own party disappear, and there gradually emerged two rival Republican factions, the Conservatives (or Moderates) and the Radicals (or "Jacobins," as their enemies called them). Represented by Seward in the cabinet and by Senator James R. Doolittle of Wisconsin in Congress, the Conservatives continued to think the war could be won by conventional means, and were opposed to such experiments as emancipation, the arming of slaves, and the confiscation of rebel property. The Radicals, on the other hand, represented by Chase in the cabinet and by Sumner and Thaddeus Stevens in the Congress, were eager to try more drastic experiments; they demanded that the entire Southern social system be revolutionized, that Southern slaveholders be punished, and, increasingly, that blacks should have not merely freedom but civil and political equality.

Lincoln refused to align himself with either faction and tried to be even-handed in distributing federal patronage to both. He shared the desire of the Conservatives for a speedy peace and a prompt reconciliation between the sections, but he recognized that in casting about for votes to carry through their plans, they would be "tempted to affiliate with those whose record is not clear," even persons infected "by the virus of secession." As for the Radicals, he conceded that "after all their faces are set Zionwards," but he objected to their "petulant and vicious fretfulness" and thought they were sometimes "almost *fiendish*" in attacking Republicans who disagreed with them. For his neutrality, the President gained the distrust and abuse of both factions.

The schism within the Republican party was the more serious because the presidential election of 1864 was approaching. In General George B. McClellan the

Democrats had a handsome, glamorous candidate, and they had a powerful set of issues. They could capitalize upon war weariness. They made much of Lincoln's arbitrary use of executive power and the infringement of civil liberties. They objected to the unfairness of the draft. They showed how the Republican Congress had benefited the Northeast by enacting protective tariffs, handing out railroad subsidies, and creating a national banking system. Democratic Senator Thomas A. Hendricks of Indiana warned his fellow Westerners that Republicans intended them to become "the 'hewers of wood and drawers of water' for the capitalists of New England and Pennsylvania." Endlessly the Democrats rang the changes on the anti-Negro theme, charging that the Lincoln administration had changed a war for Union into a war for emancipation. If Lincoln was reelected, they charged, Republicans were planning to amalgamate the black and white races; the word *miscegenation* made its first appearance in an 1864 campaign document.

Even in the face of such powerful opposition, the Republicans in the winter of 1863–64 divided sharply when Lincoln in December 1863 announced a plan for reconstructing the Southern states. Promising amnesty to all Confederates except a few high government officials, the President proposed to reestablish civilian

JEFF DAVIS'S NOVEMBER NIGHTMARE

A Northern cartoon shows Lincoln's reelection in 1864 as evidence that there would be no letting up in pressure upon the Confederacy. *(Library of Congress.)*

government in the conquered areas of the South when as few as 10 percent of the number of voters in 1860 took an oath swearing future loyalty to the United States Constitution and pledging acceptance of emancipation. Fearing that this program would replace the antebellum leadership in control of the South and would leave freedmen in peonage, the Radicals pushed through Congress the Wade-Davis bill, requiring that over half the number of 1860 voters in each Southern state swear allegiance and participate in drafting a new constitution before it would be readmitted to the Union. When Lincoln killed this measure, passed at the very end of the 1864 congressional session, by a pocket veto, Radicals were furious. Senator Benjamin F. Wade and Representative Henry Winter Davis, the sponsors of the vetoed bill, issued a manifesto, accusing the President of "usurpations" and claiming that he had committed a "studied outrage upon the legislative authority of the people."

Because Lincoln had control of the federal patronage and of the party machinery, he was readily renominated in June 1864 by the Republican national convention, which selected Andrew Johnson of Tennessee as his running mate, but the unanimity of the vote was only a façade. After an unsuccessful attempt to run Chase as a rival to Lincoln, some ultra-Radicals had already thrown their support to a third-party ticket headed by General Frémont, who had been hostile to the President since his removal from command in Missouri. Other Radicals tried, even after Lincoln had been renominated, to persuade the party to pick a new candidate. As late as September 1864 a move was afoot to reconvene the Republican convention for this purpose. A questionnaire sent to Republican governors, leading editors, and prominent congressmen elicited a virtually unanimous response that if Lincoln could be persuaded to withdraw from the race, Republicans should name another standard-bearer. As Massachusetts Governor John A. Andrew expressed the general sentiment, Lincoln was "essentially lacking in the quality of leadership." So bleak was the outlook that the President himself a few weeks before the elections conceded that McClellan was likely to win.

Northern Victory

Until the fall of 1864, then, the wartime history of the United States and of the Confederate States moved in parallel lines as each government improvised experiments that might lead to victory. But in the final months of the struggle the course of the two rivals markedly diverged. Increasing dissension and disaffection marked Jefferson Davis's last winter in office, while Abraham Lincoln won triumphant reelection in November 1864. By April 1865 the Confederacy was dead, and a month later Davis was in irons, like a common criminal, at Fortress Monroe. The Union was victorious, and Lincoln, killed by the bullet of the mad assassin, John Wilkes Booth, lived in memory as the nation's martyred President who freed the slaves and saved the Union.

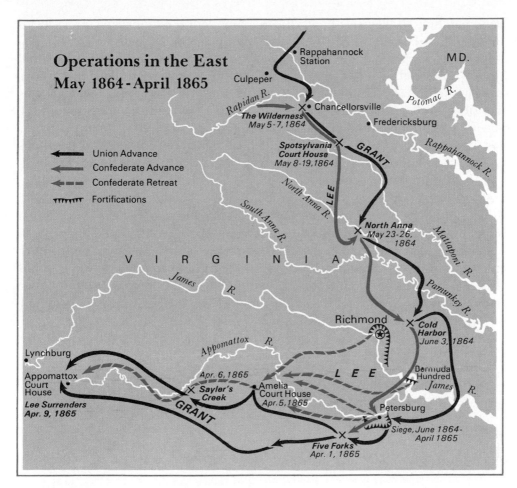

Operations in the East
May 1864 - April 1865

Though historians sharply disagree in explaining why the North won the Civil War, it is clear that the very different fates of the Lincoln and Davis administrations were decided, in major part, on the battlefield. When Grant became general in chief of the Union armies in 1864, he determined to make his headquarters not in Washington but with the often defeated Army of the Potomac. Working closely with Meade, the actual commander of that army, he developed a plan for pushing Lee back upon the defenses of Richmond. Checkmated in the bloody battle of the Wilderness (May 5–7), Grant did not retreat, as previous Union generals had done, but pushed around Lee's right flank, attempting to get between him and the Confederate capital. Checked again at Spotsylvania (May 8–12), Grant again did not retreat but sent word to Washington: "I propose to fight it out along this line if it takes all summer." In an unwise reversion to Jomini's tactics, he next ordered a direct assault upon the Confederate lines at Cold Harbor (June 3). Union soldiers, who had learned the lessons of the war better than their commander, wrote their names on slips of paper and pinned them to their uniforms, so that their corpses could be identified; they knew they were marching to their deaths. In the first month of the campaign Grant's losses amounted to sixty thousand—approximately Lee's total strength.

Ignoring charges that he was a mere butcher, Grant again skillfully maneuvered around Lee's right flank, crossed the James River, and joined the Union troops already there under General Butler. He then instituted what became known as the "siege" of Petersburg and Richmond—incorrectly so, since the two cities were not fully surrounded and since supplies continued to come in from the South and West. But as Grant's lines constantly lengthened, he cut these access routes one by one. Pinned down before Richmond, Lee remembered "Stonewall" Jackson's brilliant diversionary campaign of 1862 and sent what men he could spare under Jubal A. Early into the Shenandoah Valley. Though Early achieved initial success and even pushed on to the outskirts of Washington, Grant did not loosen his grip on Richmond. Instead he sent brash, aggressive Philip H. Sheridan to the Shenandoah Valley, ordering him not merely to drive out the Confederates but to devastate the countryside so that thereafter a crow flying over it would have to carry its own rations. Sheridan followed his orders explicitly, and Early's army was smashed. More than ever before, the fate of the Confederacy was tied to Richmond and to Lee's army.

Meanwhile, on May 7, 1864, Sherman began his slow progress through north-

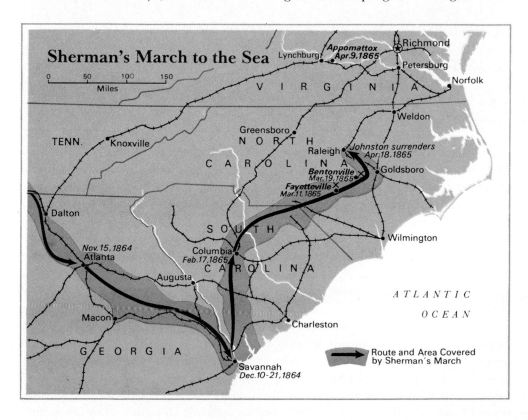

western Georgia, opposed by the wily Joseph E. Johnston, who made the Union troops pay for every foot they advanced. But as Sherman neared the railroad hub of Atlanta, President Davis, who had never trusted Johnston, removed the general and put John B. Hood in command. In a series of attacks upon overwhelmingly superior Union forces—exactly the sort of engagement Johnston had so skillfully avoided—Hood was defeated; and on September 2 Sherman occupied Atlanta. News of the victory reached the North just before the presidential election and made a farce of the Democratic platform's assertion that the war was a "failure."

Next, casually dispatching Thomas to fend off Hood and to hold Tennessee, Sherman turned his back on the smoking ruins of Atlanta and set out on a march toward Savannah and the sea, where he knew that a Union fleet was waiting with supplies.* Meeting only desultory resistance, Sherman's men cut a swath through central Georgia, destroying railroads, military supplies, and even many private houses. Sherman's objective was as much psychological as military. "I can make the march," he had promised Grant, "and make Georgia howl!"

Offering captured Savannah to Lincoln as a Christmas present, Sherman turned his army north, pushing aside the depleted Confederate forces, again under the command of Johnston. His men took Columbia, South Carolina, which was burned either by intention or by accident, and drove on into North Carolina. Grant, meanwhile, clamped down ever tighter on Richmond. At last, on April 2, 1865, Lee found his position untenable, and warning President Davis and his government to flee, he tried to lead his ragged troops to join Johnston's dwindling force. Cut off by Grant, he had no alternative but to surrender, and on April 9 at Appomattox Courthouse he told his weary, hungry men to lay down their arms. On April 26 Johnston followed by surrendering to Sherman, and when the news reached the trans-Mississippi region, Kirby-Smith capitulated in June. The war had lasted almost precisely four years.

The Union cause, and the Lincoln administration, were the beneficiaries of these victories. The critics of the government had been most vocal, their opposition most powerful, in the heartbreaking summer months of 1864, when Grant seemed to be getting nowhere in Virginia and Sherman appeared unable to bag his enemy in Georgia. Northern morale and support for the President mounted perceptibly at the news of Sherman's success at Atlanta and of Farragut's victory at Mobile Bay. Conversely, support for Davis's administration dwindled and critical voices became louder as Confederate reverse followed reverse. In a certain sense, then, victory begot victory, and defeat defeat.

---

*Attempting to force Sherman to turn back, Hood invaded Tennessee but was checked in the battle of Franklin (November 30, 1864) and routed in the battle of Nashville (December 15–16).

Yet this is circular reasoning and does not explain the final Union triumph after so many earlier Confederate successes. For a fuller understanding one must turn to the slow but steady mobilization of the North's infinitely superior economic resources and to the gradual erosion of those in the South. The effect of Northern economic and industrial superiority was not fully felt until after more than two years of war; it took time to award contracts, to expand factories, to recruit skilled laborers, and to deliver the products. But by 1863, observers noted that Lee's veterans invading Pennsylvania looked like a gaggle of "barefooted, ragged, lousy, [but] disciplined, desperate ruffians," so badly supplied and so poorly fed that their line of march was "traceable by the deposit of dysenteric stool the army leaves behind it." By 1863 the Union armies, on the other hand, were so completely equipped that their paraphernalia became a hindrance. When Northern soldiers advanced, they shucked off layers of greatcoats, blankets, and other unnecessary supplies. Nowhere was Northern economic superiority more evident by the end of the war than in its transportation system. By that time Southern railroads simply had worn out because, as the Confederate railroad coordinator, Captain F. W. Sims, reported in February 1865, "not a single bar of railroad iron has been rolled in the Confederacy since [the beginning of] the war, nor can we hope to do better during the continuance." In the Union,

on the other hand, some 5000 more miles of railroad were in operation in 1865 than at the start of the war—a figure that does not include the numerous military railroads operated in the South—and, under the necessity of linking up with the newly authorized Union Pacific Railroad, Northern lines all converted to a standard rail gauge.

But supplies do not fight wars, nor do trains; men do. From the start the overwhelming numerical preponderance of the Northern population counted heavily against the Confederacy, and during the conflict that advantage increased. During the four years of war more than 180,000 male immigrants of military age settled in the North, while there was virtually no immigration to the Confederacy. In addition, the black population of the country became another vast source of Union manpower. Cherishing the institution of slavery and correctly fearing that armed Negroes might point their guns in the wrong direction, Confederates dared not tap this source until their cause was already lost.

But men, no matter how numerous, fight well only if ably led by their military commanders and inspired by their political leaders. It would be hard to argue that Northern generalship was superior to that of the South. While Grant has his admirers, to most students Robert E. Lee is unquestionably the greatest Civil War commander. Nor is it easy to maintain that the political leadership of the North was markedly superior. Later generations, recalling the eloquence of the Gettysburg address and the mystical beauty of the second inaugural address, have found it difficult to remember that for most of his administration Lincoln was considered uninspiring and ineffectual. Had Lincoln been defeated for re-election in 1864, he would doubtless be rated as an honest but unsuccessful President. On the other hand, had the Southern states been able to win their independence, Jefferson Davis would undoubtedly rank as the George Washington of the Confederacy.

There were, of course, important differences between the two wartime Presidents, but these were of less significance than the differences in the political systems in which they had to work. Like many more recent emerging nations, the Confederacy tried to present a facade of unity to the world. It was a one-party, or more properly, a no-party state. Southerners blamed the antebellum political parties for encouraging anti-Southern and antislavery sentiment and they feared that party divisions would suggest they were less than unanimous in seeking in-

A DEAD CONFEDERATE SOLDIER AT FORT MAHONE, NEAR
PETERSBURG, VIRGINIA, APRIL 2, 1865

In the final bloody battles of the war the Confederacy lost
men who could not be replaced. "Where is this to end?"
asked General Josiah Gorgas. "No money in the Treasury—
no food to feed Gen. Lee's army—no troops to oppose
Gen. Sherman—what does it all mean . . . ? Is the cause
really hopeless?" (Library of Congress.)

dependence. The most careful analysis of the voting records of Confederate congressmen has been able to show, at most, only incipient party lines. Senators and representatives were former Whigs or former Democrats, secessionists or opponents of secession, spokesmen for overrun districts or voices from the Southern heartland; but these divisions never coalesced, and small, temporary factions rather than permanent political parties dominated Congress. President Davis's enemies were many, and they were constantly attacking him from all directions, like a swarm of bees; his friends were divided, and he could never rally them into a unified cohort. As with the Congress, so with the people. It is safe to guess that if at any point the voters of the Confederacy had been asked to endorse their President or to topple him, Davis would have received overwhelming support. But lacking political parties, Southerners had no way of making this sentiment felt.

In the Union, on the other hand, the two-party system remained active. Even at the outbreak of the war, when Stephen A. Douglas, who died within a few months, pledged Democratic support of President Lincoln, he reserved the right to lead an opposition to measures he thought wrong. The Democrats remained a formidable, if not always united, force throughout the war. They came close to winning a majority in Congress in the 1862 elections; even in 1864 McClellan

"GENERAL ROBERT E. LEE LEAVING THE MCLEAN HOUSE AFTER HIS SURRENDER AT APPOMATTOX" BY A. W. WAUD

After accepting Grant's terms of surrender, Lee stepped out to the porch of the McLean House and signaled his orderly to bring up his horse. While the animal was being bridled, one of Grant's aides remembered, Lee "gazed sadly in the direction . . . where his army lay—now an army of prisoners. He thrice smote the palm of his left hand slowly with his right fist in an absent sort of way." Then he mounted, and Grant saluted him by raising his hat. "Lee raised his hat respectfully, and rode off at a slow trot to break the sad news to the brave fellows whom he had so long commanded." (*Library of Congress.*)

received 45 percent of the popular vote—at a time when the strongest opponents of the Republican party were still out of the Union and, of course, not voting. Such a powerful opposition party compelled the Republican factions, however bitterly at odds with each other, to work together. Conservatives and Radicals might disagree over slavery, emancipation, and reconstruction, but they all agreed that any Republican administration was better than a Democratic one. It was, then, the absence of political machinery in the South that weakened Davis's regime and rendered him unable fully to mobilize the material and spiritual resources of the Confederacy. And it was the much maligned two-party system that allowed Lincoln, despite quarrelsome and impassioned attacks from fellow Republicans, to experiment boldly and to grow into the most effective wartime leader the United States has ever produced.

Suggested Readings

The studies listed at the end of the previous chapter continue, for the most part, to be pertinent to the topics discussed in the present chapter.

Of the enormous literature on the military operations during the Civil War, only a few of the most important titles can be listed here. On the Northern armies, the most comprehensive works are Kenneth P. Williams's five-volume study, *Lincoln Finds a General* (1949–59), and Bruce Catton's absorbing trilogy: *Mr. Lincoln's Army* (1951); *Glory Road* (1952); and *A Stillness at Appomattox* (1953). Among the best biographies of Union generals are Warren W. Hassler, Jr., *General George B. McClellan* (1957); Bruce Catton, *Grant Moves South* (1960), and *Grant Takes Command* (1969); and Lloyd Lewis, *Sherman* (1932).

The most elaborate account of military operations from a Southern point of view is Shelby Foote, *The Civil War* (3 vols., 1958–74). Douglas S. Freeman, *Lee's Lieutenants* (3 vols., 1942–44), is an important examination of Confederate commanders in the eastern theater, while western operations receive excellent treatment in Thomas Connelly, *Army of the Heartland* (2 vols., 1967–71). Among the most significant biographies of Confederate generals are Douglas S. Freeman, *R. E. Lee* (4 vols., 1934–35), Frank E. Vandiver, *Mighty Stonewall* (1957), and Grady McWhiney, *Braxton Bragg and Confederate Defeat* (1969).

On the recruitment of the Northern armies, see Fred A. Shannon, *The Organization and Administration of the Union Army* (2 vols., 1928), and Eugene C. Murdoch, *One Million Men: The Civil War Draft in the North* (1971). Adrian Cook, *Armies of the Street* (1974), is the definitive treatment of the New York City draft riots. A. B. Moore, *Conscription and Conflict in the Confederacy* (1924), is still the best study of its subject.

Two books by Bell I. Wiley provide a fascinating social history of the common soldier of the Civil War: *The Life of Johnny Reb* (1943), and *The Life of Billy Yank* (1952).

The best accounts of Civil War naval operations are Virgil C. Jones, *The Civil War at Sea* (3 vols., 1960–62), and Bern Anderson, *By Sea and By River* (1962). See also John Niven's fine biography, *Gideon Welles: Lincoln's Secretary of the Navy* (1973).

On the function played by political parties in the Union and the Confederacy, see Eric L. McKitrick's brilliant essay, "Party Politics and the Union and Confederate War Efforts," in William N. Chambers and Walter D. Burnham, eds., *The American Party Systems* (1967), pp. 152–81. The story of Confederate politics has to be pieced together from Wilfred B. Yearns, *The Confederate Congress* (1960); Frank L. Owsley, *State Rights in the Confederacy* (1925); Georgia L. Tatum, *Disloyalty in the Confederacy* (1934); and James Z. Rabun, "Alexander H. Stephens and Jefferson Davis," *American Historical Review 58* (1953), 290–

321. On Union politics, see William B. Hesseltine, *Lincoln and the War Governors* (1948); T. Harry Williams, *Lincoln and the Radicals* (1941); Grady McWhiney, ed., *Grant, Lee, Lincoln and the Radicals* (1964); Hans L. Trefousse, *The Radical Republicans* (1969); James A. Rawley, *The Politics of Union* (1974); and William F. Zornow, *Lincoln and the Party Divided* (1954). For conflicting interpretations of the amount of disaffection and disloyalty in the North, see Wood Gray, *The Hidden Civil War* (1942), George F. Milton, *Abraham Lincoln and the Fifth Column* (1942), and Frank L. Klement, *The Copperheads in the Middle West* (1960).

Benjamin Quarles, *The Negro in the Civil War* (1953), is a comprehensive study. James M. McPherson, ed., *The Negro's Civil War* (1965), is a valuable set of documents, skillfully interwoven. Bell I. Wiley, *Southern Negroes, 1861–1865* (1938), is the standard account; on Confederate moves toward emancipation it can be supplemented by Robert F. Durden's excellent study, *The Gray and the Blacks* (1972). Benjamin Quarles, *Lincoln and the Negro* (1962), and John H. Franklin, *The Emancipation Proclamation* (1963), are both valuable. James M. McPherson, *The Struggle for Equality* (1964), is a fine account of abolitionists' efforts during the war and afterwards. The authoritative account of Negro troops in the Union army is Dudley T. Cornish, *The Sable Arm* (1956).

For varying explanations of the collapse of the Confederacy, see Henry S. Commager, ed., *The Defeat of the Confederacy* (1964); David Donald, ed., *Why the North Won the Civil War* (1960); Charles H. Wesley, *The Collapse of the Confederacy* (1922); and Bell I. Wiley, *The Road to Appomattox* (1956).

From Eden to Babylon

Just as the Civil War required Americans to reconsider the meaning of national loyalty, so it compelled them to rethink the bases of a good society. Before the war their vision of America was primarily agrarian. Most of the inhabitants of the United States lived on farms, plantations, and ranches. Of course there were bustling cities, but most city dwellers had been born in the countryside, whether in the United States, Ireland, Germany, or England. It was natural, then, that when mid-century Americans portrayed themselves, it was as farmers, herdsmen, trappers, and explorers—not as businessmen, factory laborers, or clerks.

Just before the outbreak of the war Emanuel Leutze accurately recaptured the Americans' definition of themselves in *Westward the Course of Empire Takes Its Way,* which filled a six-hundred-square-foot panel in the rotunda of the national Capitol. It was not a great painting, not even a good painting; in it, as one contemporary remarked, "confusion reigns paramount." But it did serve to perpetuate the myth that Americans were a people close to the land, who drew their strength from nature.

Courtesy of National Collection of Fine Arts, Smithsonian Institution.

Nature had a special place in the thought of antebellum Americans. The most influential American philosophical work published in the first half of the nineteenth century was Ralph Waldo Emerson's essay on that topic. "Nature," to Emerson and the thousands who read his essays and heard him lecture, included those "essences unchanged by man: space, the air, the river, the leaf." It was to be distinguished from "art," the imposition of man's will upon nature that resulted in "a house, a canal, a statue, a picture." "Nature," then, had emotional and moral primacy over "art," and most Americans believed, with Emerson himself, that by shedding all artifice man could again become part and parcel of nature itself.

A self-taught Massachusetts painter, Erastus Salisbury Field, perfectly recaptured the spirit behind Emerson's ideas. With only three months of informal training as an artist, Field personified the spirit of spontaneity and improvisation that Emerson extolled. More important, his early paintings showed an attachment to, and a meticulous interest in, nature. The land he portrayed was a tidied-up, New England version of Leutze's sprawling continent. Field's *The Garden of Eden* did not have a specifically American setting, though his neatly paired animals of peculiar anatomy and his trees with their improbable fruit might have flourished in America, if anywhere. There is, however, a distinctively American note in Field's treatment of nudity in the Garden of Eden: a clump of strategically placed lilies preserves Adam's modesty, and Eve lurks behind some unlikely blossoms. Clearly for Field, as for Emerson, man is at his best when most closely linked to nature, in a scene unmarred by human artifice or ingenuity.

Yale University Art Gallery, Mabel Brady Garvan Collection.

During the Civil War years Americans' perception of the good society dramatically changed. The war may not have stimulated economic growth, but it did promote mechanization. Steam power largely replaced horse power and water power. Machines of ever increasing complexity, with fascinating gears and gauges, replaced men. The vast foundries and rolling mills that had turned out cannons during the war were diverted to the production of structural iron girders, and later steel beams, which made possible a new American architecture. No longer was it necessary to erect buildings out of huge piles of masonry, and no longer was it dangerous to build them too high. Using steel beams, innovative architects like Louis Sullivan invented the skyscraper, a triumphant fusing of form and function. The skyscraper, Sullivan proclaimed, "must be every inch a proud and soaring thing, rising in sheer exultation that from bottom to top it is a unit without a single dissenting line." Imaginative engineers, like Samuel B. B. Nowlan of New York, foresaw the day when whole cities would be made of steel, and Nowlan's sketch, *Proposed Arcade Railroad under Broadway*, looked ahead to a new era in urban design.

Magnum.

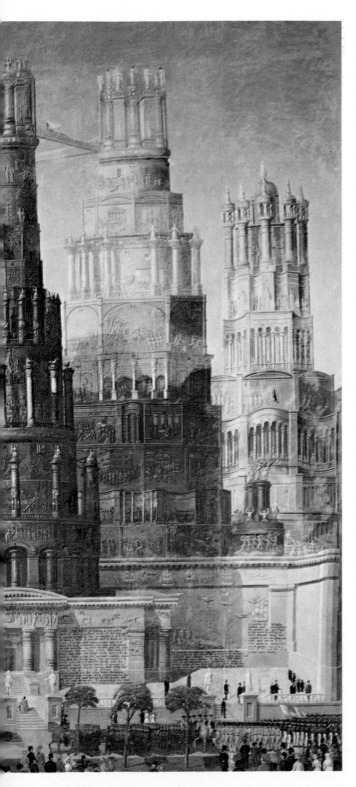

Postwar Americans found the new technology exhilarating to the point of intoxication. Gone now was the day when Erastus Field portrayed man in the bosom of nature. Instead, looking forward to the Centennial Exposition in Philadelphia, the aging Field painted his *Historical Monument of the American Republic*. Field's picture showed America as wholly urban, entirely built over with huge towers, with round or octagonal sides, rising in diminishing stages. The central and tallest tower commemorated Abraham Lincoln and the Constitution. Near the top, several of these towers were joined together with vaulting steel bridges, along which steam railroad trains puffed. As a significant reminder of Civil War days, soldiers paraded the avenue in front of Field's monumental vision of America as Babylon.

By 1876, then, Field's ideas, like those of most Americans, had completely shifted. Rural peace paled beside the attractions of mechanized urban life. The machine was now the magnet of the American mind. When the novelist William Dean Howells visited the Centennial Exposition, he, like thousands of other Americans, was most impressed by the gigantic Corliss engine, which gave power to the 8000 other machines, large and small, that sewed cloth, printed newspapers, made shoes, and pumped water on the thirteen-acre Exposition grounds. After comparing the displays of painting and sculpture with the Corliss engine, Howells concluded: "It is in these things of iron and steel that the national genius most freely speaks."

The greatest painter of the postwar period, Thomas Eakins of Philadelphia, shared Howells's admiration of the machine and his respect for the scientific knowledge that it represented. Just as the Corliss engine was "an athlete of steel and iron, without a superfluous ounce of metal on it," so a painting, thought Eakins, should be lean and objective. In order to portray the human figure scientifically, he studied anatomy at Jefferson Medical College. Eakins also linked painting with mathematics, because both were disciplines in which "the complicated things are reduced to simple things." Eakins's portrait, *Max Schmitt in a Single Skull,* shows how perfectly he fused art, anatomy, and the mathematics of perspective. More subtly it also speaks of the changed values of postwar American society. In decisive contrast to the absence of all man-made artifacts in Leutze's painting and in Field's *The Garden of Eden,* a superb steel bridge is a vital part of Eakins's portrait. More emphatically than any number of words, the presence of that bridge shows that, by the end of the Civil War era, Americans had come to think of nature as something to be spanned, conquered, and controlled.

Metropolitan Museum of Art, Alfred N. Punnett Fund and Gift of George D. Pratt, 1934.

21

The Limits of Innovation, 1865-1869

"A house divided against itself cannot stand," Abraham Lincoln prophesied in 1858. The Civil War proved that the United States would stand, not as a loose confederation of sovereign states but as one nation, indivisible. Never again would there be talk of secession. The war also ended slavery, the most divisive institution in antebellum America. Weakened by the advances of the Union armies and undermined by Lincoln's Emancipation Proclamation, slavery received its death blow in February 1865, when the Congress adopted the Thirteenth Amendment, outlawing slavery and involuntary servitude. Ratified by three-fourths of the states, the amendment became a part of the Constitution in December 1865.

But the Civil War did not settle the terms and conditions on which the several states, sections, races, and classes would live in the firmly united "house." Those problems formed the agenda of the Reconstruction era, one of the most complex and controversial periods in American history. During these postwar years some basic questions had to be answered: What, if any, punishment should be imposed on Southern whites who had supported the Confederate attempt to disrupt the Union? How were the recently emancipated slaves to be guaranteed their freedom, and what civil and political rights did freedmen have? When and on what conditions were the Southern states so recently in rebellion to be readmitted to the Union—that is, entitled to vote in national elections, to have Senators and Representatives seated in the United States Congress, and, in general, to become once more full-fledged, equal members in the national body politic?

The initial moves to answer these questions came from the President, whose powers had been greatly expanded during the war years. President Lincoln in December 1863 announced a generous program of amnesty to repentant rebels and inaugurated a plan for reorganizing loyal governments in the South when as few as 10 percent of the voters in 1860 were willing to support them. After the assassination of Lincoln in April 1865, President Andrew Johnson, his successor, continued the process of Reconstruction under a similar plan. Although Johnson required former Confederate leaders and Southerners with estates worth more than $20,000 to make individual applications for pardon—applications that were for the most part promptly granted—he, like Lincoln, expected Southern whites to take the lead in establishing new state governments loyal to the Union. To initiate the process he appointed a provisional governor for each of the former Confederate states (except those where Lincoln had already initiated Reconstruction) and directed them to convene constitutional conventions. These were expected to adopt the Thirteenth Amendment ending slavery, nullify or repeal the ordinances of secession, and repudiate state debts incurred for the prosecution of the war. By early 1866 each of the states that had once formed the Confederacy completed these required steps, and the President viewed the process of Reconstruction as concluded. He recommended that the senators and representatives chosen by these reorganized governments be promptly given their rightful seats in Congress.

From the outset presidential Reconstruction had its critics. If Lincoln's plan met opposition, Johnson's program was certain to be fiercely attacked. For one reason, Congress, which had jealously watched the executive branch augment its power during the war, was ready to reassert its equality, if not its hegemony. For another, Andrew Johnson, a Tennessee Democrat and former slaveholder, had no popular mandate, as had President Lincoln, nor did the taciturn, inflexible, and pugnacious new occupant of the White House understand that politics is the art of compromise.

After an initial attempt to cooperate with the new President, Republican leaders in 1866 began to devise their own plans for Reconstruction. The first congressional plan was embodied in the Fourteenth Amendment to the Constitution, which made it clear that blacks were citizens of the United States and tried to define the rights and privileges of American citizens. When the Southern states refused to ratify this amendment, congressional Republicans moved in 1867 to a more stringent program of reorganizing the South by requiring Negro suffrage. Under this second plan of congressional Reconstruction, every Southern state (except for Tennessee, which had been readmitted to the Union in 1866) received a new constitution that guaranteed to men of all races equal protection of the laws, and between 1868 and 1871 all were readmitted to the Union. Republican governments, which depended heavily on Negro votes, controlled these states for a period ranging from a few months in the case of Virginia to nine years in the case of Louisiana.

Paths Not Taken

Contemporaries called this the period of Radical Reconstruction or, very often, Black Reconstruction, and it is easy to understand why many Americans of the 1860s and '70s viewed these changes as little short of revolutionary. To their Constitution, which had not been altered since 1804, were added during the five years after the Civil War the Thirteenth Amendment, ending slavery, the Fourteenth Amendment, defining the rights of citizens, and the Fifteenth Amendment (1870), prohibiting discrimination in voting on account of race or color. The national government, so recently tottering on the edge of defeat, was now more powerful than in any previous point in American history. The Southern ruling class of whites, lately in charge of their own independent government, were petitioners for pardon. More than 3 million blacks, slaves only a few months earlier, were free men, entitled to the same privileges as all other citizens. Americans fairly gasped at the extent and the speed of the transformation wrought in their society, and it is hardly surprising that most subsequent historians accepted this contemporary view of the Reconstruction era as one of turbulent disorder.

Without denying that real and important changes did occur during the Reconstruction period, it might help to put these into perspective by inventing a little conterfactual history, a recital of conceivable historical scenarios that were never acted out. For instance, it would be easy to imagine how the victorious North might have turned angrily on the prostrate South. In 1865, Northerners had just finished four years of war that cost the Union army more than 360,000 casualties. To destroy the Confederacy required Americans of that and subsequent generations to pay in taxes at least $10 billion. Northerners had reason to believe, moreover, that their Confederate opponents had prosecuted the war with fiendish barbarity. Sober Union congressmen informed their constituents that the Confederates employed "Indian savages" to scalp and mutilate the Union dead. Reliable Northern newspapers told how in April 1864 General Nathan Bedford Forrest and his Confederates overran the defenses of Fort Pillow, Tennessee, manned by a Negro regiment, and, refusing to accept surrender, deliberately beat, shot, and burned their prisoners. The influential *Harper's Weekly Magazine* carried apparently authentic drawings of a goblet that a Southerner had made from a Yankee soldier's skull and of necklaces made of Yankee teeth that Southern ladies wore. When Union armies liberated Northern prisoners from such hell-holes as Andersonville, Georgia, pictures of these half-starved skeletons of men, clad in grimy tatters of their Union uniforms, convinced Northerners that Jefferson Davis's policy had been "to starve and freeze and kill off by inches the prisoners he dares not butcher outright."

When the murder of Abraham Lincoln by the Southern sympathizer, John Wilkes Booth, added to this hyperemotionalism, an outraged North could easily have turned on the conquered Confederacy in vengeance. The victorious Northerners might have executed Jefferson Davis, Alexander H. Stephens, and a score of other leading Confederates and might have sent thousands more into permanent exile. The triumphant Union might have erased the boundaries of the Southern states and divided the whole region into new, conquered territories. They might have enforced the confiscation acts already on the statute books and have seized the plantations of rebels, for distribution to the freedmen. In short, the North could very easily have adopted the policy advocated by the generally cautious, middle-of-the-road Senator from Ohio, John Sherman: "We should not only brand the leading rebels with infamy, but the whole rebellion should wear the badge of the penitentiary, so that for this generation at least, no man who has taken part in it would dare to justify or palliate it."

No such drastic course was followed. With the exception of Major Henry Wirtz, commandant of the infamous Andersonville prison, who was hanged, no Confederate was executed for "war crimes." A few Southern political leaders were imprisoned for their part in the "rebellion," but in most cases their release was prompt. To be sure, Jefferson Davis was kept in shackles for two years at Fortress Monroe, and he was under indictment for treason until 1869, when all charges were dropped. His case was, however, as unusual as it was extreme, and one reason for the long delay in bringing him to trial was the certainty that no jury,

Northern or Southern, would find him guilty. There was no general confiscation of the property of Confederates, no dividing up on plantations.

Equally conceivable is another scenario—another version of history that did not happen—this time featuring the Southern whites. For four years Confederate citizens, like their counterparts in the Union, had been subjected to a barrage of propaganda designed to prove that the enemy was little less than infernal in his purposes. Many believed the Southern editor who claimed that Lincoln's program was "Emancipation, Confiscation, Conflagration, and Extermination." According to the North Carolina educator Calvin H. Wiley, the North had "summoned to its aid every fierce and cruel and licentious passion of the human heart"; to defeat the Confederacy it was ready to use "the assassin's dagger, the midnight torch, . . . poison, famine and pestilence." Such charges were easy to credit in the many Southern families that had relatives in Northern prison camps, such as the one at Elmira, New York, where 775 of 8347 Confederate prisoners died within three months for want of proper food, water, and medicine. The behavior of Union troops in the South, especially of Sherman's "bummers" in Georgia and the Carolinas, gave Southerners every reason to fear the worst if the Confederate government failed.

RUINS OF RICHMOND

When the Confederate government evacuated Richmond on April 3, 1865, orders were given to burn supplies that might fall into the enemy's hands. There were heavy explosions as ironclads, armories, and arsenals were blown up. The next morning, as the fires spread, a mob of men and women, whites and blacks, began to plunder the city. (*Library of Congress.*)

It would therefore have been perfectly reasonable for Confederate armies in 1865, overwhelmed by Union numbers, to disband quietly, disappear into the countryside, and carry on guerrilla operations against the Northern invaders. Indeed, on the morning of the day when Lee surrendered at Appomattox, Confederate General E. P. Alexander advocated just such a plan. He argued that if Lee's soldiers took to the woods with their rifles, perhaps two-thirds of the Army of Northern Virginia could escape capture. "We would be like rabbits and partridges in the bushes," he claimed, "and they could not scatter to follow us." The history of more recent wars of national liberation suggests that Alexander's judgment was absolutely correct. But even had his strategy not proved practicable, it would have given time for thousands of leading Southern politicians and planters, together with their families, to go safely into exile, as the Tories did during the American Revolution.

But, once again, no such events occurred. Lee firmly put down talk of guerrilla warfare and reminded his subordinates that they must henceforth think of "the country as a whole." To Virginia soldiers who pressed around him after the surrender, he gave the advice: "Go home, all you boys who fought with me, and help to build up the shattered fortunes of our old state." Following Lee's example, commanders of the other Southern armies also quietly surrendered, and Confederate soldiers promptly became civilians. Some few Confederate leaders did go into exile. For instance, General Jubal A. Early fled to Mexico and thence to Canada, where he tried to organize a Southern exodus to New Zealand; but finding that nobody wanted to follow him, he returned to his home and his law practice in Virginia. A few hundred Confederates did migrate to Mexico and to Brazil. But most followed the advice of General Wade Hampton of South Carolina, who urged his fellow Southerners to "devote their whole energies to the restoration of law and order, the reestablishment of agriculture and commerce, the promotion of education and the rebuilding of our cities and dwellings which have been laid in ashes."

Still a third counterfactual historical scenario comes readily to mind. Southern blacks, who had been for generations oppressed in slavery, now for the first time had disciplined leaders in the thousands of Negro soldiers who had served in the Union army. They also had arms. Very easily they could have turned in revenge on their former masters. Seizing the plantations and other property of the whites, the freedmen might have made of the former Confederacy a black nation. If the whites had dared to resist, the South might have been the scene of massacres as bloody as those in Haiti at the beginning of the nineteenth century, when Toussaint L'Ouverture and Dessalines drove the French out of that island.

Many Southern whites feared, or even expected, that the Confederacy would become another Santo Domingo. For more than a year after the war, Northern reporters in the South noted "a general feeling of insecurity on the part of the whites," derived from their "vague and terrible fears of a servile insurrection." Whites were much troubled by reports that blacks were joining the Union League, an organization that had originated in the North during the war to stimulate patriotism but during the Reconstruction era became the bulwark of the Republican party in the South. The secrecy imposed by the League on its members and its frequent nocturnal meetings alarmed whites, and they readily believed reports that the blacks were collecting arms and ammunition for a general uprising. Fearfully, Southern whites read newspaper accounts of minor racial clashes. Indeed, whites were told, racial tension was so great that blacks "might break into open insurrection at any time."

But no such insurrection occurred. Though the freedmen unquestionably coveted the lands of their former masters, they did not seize them. Indeed, black leaders consistently discouraged talk of extralegal confiscation of plantations. Nor did freedmen threaten the lives or the rights of whites. One of the earliest black political conventions held in Alabama urged a policy of "peace, friendship, and good will toward all men—especially toward our white fellow-citizens among whom our lot is cast." That tone was the dominant one throughout the Reconstruction period, and in many states blacks took the lead in repealing laws that disfranchised former Confederates or disqualified them from holding office.

The point of these three exercises in counterfactual history is to suggest the inadequacy of traditional accounts of the Reconstruction era as a period of revolutionary change. To those who lived through these years change did seem to come swiftly and drastically, but in retrospect it is clear that Southern society was transformed only to a quite limited degree. The unprecedented conditions of the Reconstruction era required innovation, but the shared beliefs and institutions of the American people, North and South, black and white, restricted the amount of change that would be tolerated.

Constitutionalism as a Limit to Change

One set of ideas that sharply curbed social experimentation and political innovation during the Reconstruction period can be labeled constitutionalism. It is hard for twentieth-century Americans to understand the reverence with which their nineteenth-century ancestors viewed the Constitution. In a country that lacked a ruling family, a hereditary aristocracy, and an established church, that document, next to the flag, was the most powerful symbol of American nationhood. Tested in the trial of civil war, the Constitution continued to command respect approaching veneration during the Reconstruction era.

Among the most sacrosanct provisions of the Constitution were those that separated the powers of the state and the national governments. Although the national government greatly expanded its role during the war years, Americans still tended to think of it as performing only the specific functions enumerated in the Constitution, which granted it virtually no authority to act directly on any individual citizen. The national government could not, for instance, prevent or punish crime; it had no control over public education; it could not outlaw discrimination against racial minorities; and it could not even intervene to maintain public order unless requested to do so by the state government. Virtually everybody agreed, therefore, that if any laws regulating social and economic life were required, they must be the work of state and local, not of national, government.

Nobody, consequently, even contemplated the possibility that some federal agency might be needed to supervise the demobilization after Appomattox. Everybody simply assumed that after some 200,000 of the Union army volunteers bravely paraded down Pennsylvania Avenue on May 23–24, 1865, and received applause from President Johnson, the cabinet, the generals, and the members of the diplomatic corps, the soldiers would disband and go back to their peaceful homes. This is precisely what they did. Of the more than one million volunteers in the Union army on May 1, 1865, two-thirds were mustered out by August, four-fifths by November. Of the 68,000 sailors, artisans, and laborers in the Union navy at the beginning of 1865, only 12,000 remained in active service by December. To the demobilized soldiers and sailors, the United States government offered no assistance in finding jobs, in purchasing housing, or in securing further education. It paid pensions to those injured in the war and to the families of those who had been killed, but beyond that it assumed no responsibility. Nor did anybody think of asking the national government to oversee the transition from a wartime economy to an era of peace. Without notice the various bureaus of the army and navy departments by the end of April 1865 simply suspended requisitions and purchases, government arsenals slowed down their production, and surplus supplies were sold off.

Hardly anybody had the thought that the national government might play a role in rebuilding the wartorn South. Everybody recognized that the devastation in the South was immense and ominous. The Confederate dead totaled more than a quarter of a million. In Mississippi, for instance, one-third of the white men of military age had been killed or disabled for life. Most Southern cities were in ruins. Two-thirds of the Southern railroads were totally destroyed; the rest barely creaked along on worn-out rails with broken-down engines. But none of this was thought to be the concern of the United States government.

The failure of the national government to come to the rescue was not caused by vindictiveness. To the contrary, Union officials often behaved with marked generosity toward Confederates. After Lee's hungry battalions surrendered at Appomattox, Grant's soldiers freely shared with them their rations. All over the South, Federal military officials drew on the full Union army storehouses to feed the hungry. In distributing these necessities, the Union army made no discrimination; newly freed slaves stood in line with former Confederate soldiers, all with bags to be filled. But beyond these attempts to avert starvation the Federal government did not go, and very few thought that it should. Not until the twentieth century did the United States make it a policy to pour vast sums of money into the rehabilitation of enemies it had defeated in war.

Rebuilding had, therefore, to be the work of the Southern state and local authorities, and this task imposed a heavy tax on their meager resources. In Mississippi, one-fifth of the entire state revenue in 1866 was needed to provide artificial limbs for soldiers maimed in the war. For the larger tasks of physical restoration, the resources of the South were obviously inadequate. Borrowing a leaf from antebellum experience, Southern governments did the only thing they knew how to do—namely, they lent the credit of the state to back up the bonds of private companies that promised to rebuild railroads and other necessary facilities. Since these companies were underfinanced and since the credit of the Southern state governments after Appomattox was, to say the least, questionable, these bonds had to be sold at disadvantageous prices and at exorbitant rates of interest. In later years, when many of these companies defaulted on their obligations and Southern state governments had to make good on their guarantees, these expenditures would be condemned as excessive and extravagant, and Democrats blamed them on the Republican regimes established in the South after 1868. In fact, however, the need for physical restoration immediately after the war was so obvious and so pressing that nearly every government, whether controlled by Democrats or Republicans, underwrote corporations that promised to rebuild the region.

Even in dealing with the freedmen—the some 3 million slaves emancipated as a result of the war—the United States government tried to pursue a hands-off policy. Few influential leaders, either in the North or in the South, thought that it was the function of the national government to supervise the blacks' transition from slavery to freedom. Politicians did not foresee that freedmen would require guidance, counseling, and, most of all, education in order to become free and equal citizens. Even abolitionists, genuinely devoted to the welfare of blacks, were so accustomed to thinking of the Negro as "God's image in ebony"—in other words, a white man in a black skin—that they had no plans for assisting him after emancipation. In 1865, William Lloyd Garrison urged the American Anti-Slavery Society to disband, since it had fulfilled its function, and he suspended the publication of *The Liberator*. Sharing the same point of view, the American Freedmen's Inquiry Commission, set up by the Union war department in 1863, unanimously opposed further governmental actions to protect the blacks. "The negro does best when let alone," argued one member of the commission, Samuel Gridley Howe, noted alike for his work with the deaf, dumb, and blind and for his hostility to slavery; "we must beware of all attempts to prolong his servitude, under pretext of taking care of him. The white man has tried taking care of the negro, by slavery, by apprenticeship, by colonization, and has failed disastrously in all; now let the negro try to take care of himself."

But the problem of the care of the freedmen could not be dismissed so easily. Wherever Union armies advanced into the South, they were "greeted by an irruption of negroes of all ages, complexions and sizes, men, women, boys and girls . . . waving hats and bonnets with the most ludicrous caperings and ejaculations of joy." "The poor delighted creatures thronged upon us," a Yankee soldier reported, and they insisted: "We'se gwin wid you all." "What shall be done with them?" commanders in the field plaintively wired Washington.

The administration in Washington had no comprehensive answer. Initially it looked to private philanthropic organizations to rush food, clothing, and medicine to the thousands of blacks that thronged in unsanitary camps around the headquarters of each Union army. The New England Freedmen's Aid Society, the American Missionary Association, and the Philadelphia Society of Friends promptly responded, but it was soon clear that the problem was too great for private charity.

Slowly, and without much guidance from Washington, Union commanders in the field began to improvise plans to assist the blacks clustered about their camps. In Louisiana, General N. P. Banks told freedmen that they had to support themselves, either by working on the levees or at other public employment or by returning to labor on the plantations, where, Banks said, "they belong." Farther north, Grant named Chaplain John Eaton general superintendent of all freedmen in his military department, which consisted mostly of Mississippi and Tennessee, and directed him to supervise the freedmen's camps, to provide for their education and health, and to set them to work picking cotton on abandoned plantations.

As such piecemeal and often inconsistent programs for dealing with the freedmen got under way, sentiment grew in the North for the creation of a general "Emancipation Bureau" in the federal government—only to conflict directly with the even stronger sentiment that the national government had limited powers. Out of this conflict emerged the Freedmen's Bureau Act of March 3, 1865. Congress established, under the jurisdiction of the war department, the Bureau of Refugees, Freedmen, and Abandoned Lands and entrusted to the new agency, for one year after the end of the war, "control of all subjects relating to refugees and freedmen." To head the new organization, Lincoln named Oliver O. Howard, a Union general less conspicuous for military skill than for devotion to Christianity and for paternalistic views toward blacks.

At first glance, the Freedmen's Bureau seems to have been a notable exception to the rule that the national government should take only a minor, passive role in the restoration of the South. Howard had a vision of a compassionate network of "teachers, ministers, farmers, superintendents" working together to aid and elevate the freedmen, and, under his enthusiastic impetus, the bureau appointed agents in each of the former Confederate states. The most urgent task of the bureau was issuing food and clothing, mostly from surplus army stores, to destitute freedmen and other Southern refugees. This action unquestionably prevented mass starvation in the South. The bureau also took the initiative in getting work for freedmen. Fearful on the one hand that Southern planters would attempt to overwork and underpay the freedmen, troubled on the other by the widespread belief that blacks, once emancipated, were not willing to work, the bureau agents brought laborers and landlords together and insisted that workers sign labor contracts.

No part of the bureau's work was more successful than its efforts in the field of education. The slow work of educating the illiterate Southern blacks had already begun under the auspices of army chaplains and Northern benevolent societies before the creation of the bureau, and Howard's bureau continued to cooperate with these agencies, providing housing for black schools, paying teachers, and helping to establish normal schools and colleges for the training of black teachers. All these educational efforts received an enthusiastic welcome from the freedmen. During the day, classrooms were thronged with black children learning the rudiments of language and arithmetic; in the evenings they were filled with adults who were "fighting with their letters," learning to read so that they would not be "made ashamed" by their children. "The progress of the scholars is in all cases creditable and in some remarkable," reported one of the teachers. "How richly God has endowed them, and how beautifully their natures would have expanded under a tender and gentle culture."

Even more innovative was the work of the bureau in allocating lands to the freedmen. During the war many plantations in the path of Union armies had been deserted by their owners, and army commanders like Grant arranged to have these tilled by the blacks who flocked to his camp. The largest tract of such abandoned land was in the Sea Islands of South Carolina, which were overrun by Federal troops in the fall of 1861. Though speculators bought up large

PRIMARY SCHOOL IN CHARGE OF MRS. GREEN — VICKSBURG, MISSISSIPPI

Freedmen were avid for learning. In schools sponsored by the Freedmen's Bureau, grandparents sat alongside toddlers, as all sought knowledge.

amounts of this land during the war, sizable numbers of black residents were able to secure small holdings. When General W. T. Sherman marched through South Carolina he ordered that the Sea Islands and the abandoned plantations along the river banks for thirty miles from the coast be reserved for Negro settlement and directed that black settlers be given "possessory titles" to tracts of this land not larger than forty acres. The act creating the Freedmen's Bureau clearly contemplated the continuation of these policies, for it authorized the new bureau to lease confiscated lands to freedmen and to "loyal refugees." The bureau could also sell the land to these tenants and give them "such title thereto as the United States can convey."

But if the Freedmen's Bureau was an exception to the policy of limited federal involvement in the reconstruction process, it was at best a partial exception. Though the agency did invaluable work, it was a feeble protector of the freedmen. Authorized to recruit only a minimal staff, Howard was obliged to rely heavily on Union army officers stationed in the South—at just the time when the Union army was being demobilized. Consequently the bureau never had enough manpower to look after the rights of some 3 million freedmen; toward the end of its first year of operation it employed only 799 men, 424 of whom were soldiers on temporary, assigned duty. Important as the work of the bureau was in Negro education, its chief function was to stimulate private philanthropy in this field. In providing land for the freedmen, the bureau was handicapped because it

CELEBRATION FOR NEWLY MARRIED BLACK COUPLES

Legally slaves could not marry. When blacks became free, they sought to regularize their marital arrangements and to legitimatize their children. Many Southern states passed blanket laws for this purpose, but thousands of Negroes desired formal wedding ceremonies. *(Frank Leslie's Illustrated Newspaper, August 19, 1871.)*

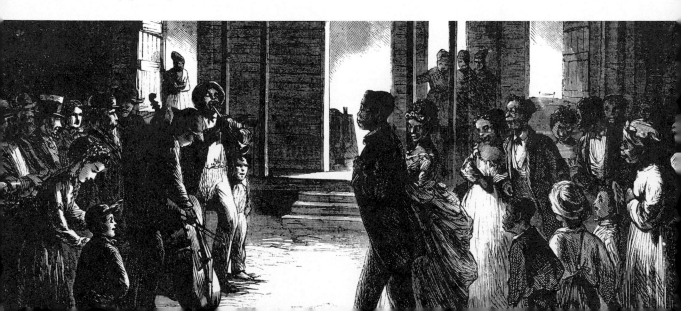

controlled only about 800,000 acres of arable land in the entire South, enough at best for perhaps one black family in forty. Moreover, its efforts to distribute lands to the Negroes were repeatedly undercut both by the Congress and the President. The very wording of the act creating the bureau suggested congressional uncertainty about who actually owned deserted and confiscated lands in the South. General Sherman announced that the "possessory titles" he had issued were valid only so long as the war lasted; and President Johnson issued pardons to Southerners that explicitly included "restoration of all rights of property." In October 1865, the President directed Howard to go in person to the Sea Islands to notify blacks there that they did not hold legal title to the land and to advise them "to make the best terms they could" with the white owners. When blacks bitterly resisted what they considered the bureau's betrayal, Union soldiers descended on the islands and forced blacks who would not sign labor contracts with the restored white owners to leave. Elsewhere in the South the record of the bureau was equally dismal.

In short, belief in the limited role to be played by the national government affected the rehabilitation of the freedmen, just as it did the physical restoration of the South and the demobilization in the North. In all these matters, the United States government was supposed to play the smallest possible part, and its minimal activities were to be of the briefest duration.

It is certain that most whites in the North and in the South fully approved these stringent limitations on the activities of the national government. What the masses of freedmen thought is harder to determine. On the one hand stands the protest of Sea Island blacks when they learned they were about to be dispossessed: "Why, General Howard, why do you take away our lands? You take them from us who have always been true, always true to the Government! You give them to our all-time enemies! That is not right!" On the other is Frederick Douglass's reply to the question, "What shall we do with the Negroes?" The greatest black spokesman of the era answered: "Do nothing with them; mind your business, and let them mind theirs. Your *doing* with them is their greatest misfortune. They have been undone by your doings, and all they now ask and really have need of at your hands, is just to let them alone."

Laissez-Faire as a Limit to Change

Along with the idea of limited government went the doctrine of laissez-faire ("let things alone"), which sharply limited what the government could do to solve economic problems that arose after the Civil War. Except for a handful of Radical Republicans, such as Charles Sumner and Thaddeus Stevens, most congressmen, like most academic economists, were unquestioning believers in an American version of laissez-faire. Though they were willing to promote economic growth through protective tariffs and land grants to railroads, they abhorred governmental inspection, regulation, and control of economic activities. These

A GROUP OF FREEDMEN IN RICHMOND, VIRGINIA, 1865

A central problem of the Reconstruction years was the future of the freedmen. Nobody had made any plans for a smooth transition from slavery to freedom. Consequently, when emancipation came, as one former slave recalled, "We didn't know where to go. Momma and them didn't know where to go, you see, after freedom broke. Just like you turned something out, you know. They didn't know where to go." *(Library of Congress.)*

matters were ruled by the inexorable laws of economics. "You need not think it necessary to have Washington exercise a political providence over the country," William Graham Sumner, the brilliant professor of political and social science, told his students at Yale. "God has done that a great deal better by the laws of political economy."

No violation of economic laws was deemed more heinous than interference with the right of private property—the right of an individual or group to purchase, own, use, and dispose of property without any interference from governmental authorities. There was consequently never a chance that congressmen would support Thaddeus Stevens's radical program to confiscate all Southern farms larger than 200 acres and to divide the seized land into 40-acre tracts among the freedmen. "No man in America," announced the *Nation,* a journal that spoke for educated Republicans, "has any right to anything which he has not honestly earned, or which the lawful owner has not thought proper to give him." Stevens's plan could lead only to socialism, or worse. "An attempt to justify the confiscation of Southern land under the pretense of doing justice to the freedmen," declared the New York *Times,* "strikes at the root of all property rights in both sections. It concerns Massachusetts quite as much as Mississippi."

Informed opinion in the North held that the best program of Reconstruction was to allow the laws of economics to rule in the South with the least possible interference by the government. Behind this theory lay the judgment, accepted by Republicans long before the Civil War, that the South was a land on which slavery had brought "the calamity of premature and consumptive decline, in the midst of free, vigorous and expanding states." The war served as drastic surgery to remove the cancer of slavery. Now it was reasonable to expect that, though there might be some soreness and subsequent healing, Southerners, white and black, should, without further governmental meddling, set about making money and acquiring property just like the free men in the northern and western states.*

Obsessed by laissez-faire, Northern theorists left out of their calculations the physical devastation wrought in the South by the war, and they did not recognize how feeble were the section's resources to rebuild its economy. Even excluding the loss of property in slaves, the total assessed property evaluation of the Southern states shrank by 43 percent between 1860 and 1865.

Northern pundits also failed to take into account the psychological dimensions of economic readjustment in the South. For generations Southern whites had persuaded themselves that slavery was the natural condition of the black race, and they truly believed that their slaves were devoted to them. But as Union armies approached and slaves defected, they were compelled to recognize that they had been living in a world of misconceptions and deceits.

So shattering was the idea that slaves were free that some Southern whites simply refused to accept it. Even after the Confederate surrender, some owners would not inform their slaves of their new status. As late as July 1865, according to officials of the Freedmen's Bureau, planters in Mississippi were resorting to "whipping and the most severe modes of punishment . . . to compel the Freedmen to remain at the old plantations and the negro [was] kept in ignorance of his real condition." A few planters angrily announced they were so disillusioned that they would never again have anything to do with blacks, and they sought, vainly, to persuade European immigrants and Chinese coolies to work their fields.

---

*Discussion of economic changes and problems in the North is reserved for the following chapter.

Even those whites who overtly accepted the reality of emancipation betrayed the fact that, on a deeper emotional level, they still could only think of blacks as performing forced labor. "The general interest both of the white man and of the negroes requires that he should be kept as near to the condition of slavery as possible, and as far from the condition of the white man as is practicable," explained Edmund Rhett of South Carolina. "Negroes must be made to work, or else cotton and rice must cease to be raised for export." The contracts that planters in 1865, under pressure from the Freedmen's Bureau, entered into with their former slaves were further indications of the same attitude. Even the most generous of these contracts provided that blacks were "not to leave the premises during work hours without the consent of the Proprietor," that they would conduct "themselves faithfully, honestly and civilly," and that they would behave with "perfect obedience" toward the land owner.

Blacks, too, had difficulties in adjusting to their new status that were never anticipated by the devotees of laissez-faire. *Freedom*—that word so often whispered in the slave quarters—went to the heads of some blacks. A few took the coming of "Jubilee," with the promise to put the bottom rail on top, quite literally. Nearly all blacks had an initial impulse to test their freedom, to make sure it was real. As Patience Johnson, a former slave in the Laurens District of South Carolina explained when her mistress asked her to continue working for wages: "No, Miss, I must go, if I stay here I'll never know I am free." During the first months after the war there was, then, much movement among Southern blacks. "They are just like a swarm of bees," one observer noted, "all buzzing about and not knowing where to settle."

Much of this black mobility was, however, purposeful. Thousands of former slaves flocked to Southern towns and cities where the Freedmen's Bureau was issuing rations, for they knew that food was unavailable on the plantations. Many blacks set out to find husbands, wives, or children, from whom they had been forcibly separated during the slave days. A good many freedmen joined the general movement of Southern population away from the seaboard states, devastated by war, and migrated to the Southwestern frontier in Texas. Most blacks, however, did not move so far but remained in the immediate vicinity of the plantations where they had labored as slaves.

The reluctance of freedmen in 1865 to enter into labor contracts, either with their former masters or with other white landowners, was also generally misunderstood. Most blacks wanted to work—but they wanted to work on their own land. Freedmen knew that the United States government had divided up some abandoned plantations among former slaves, and many believed that on January 1, 1866—the anniversary of their freedom under Lincoln's Emancipation Proclamation—all would receive forty acres and a mule. With this prospect of having their own farms, they were unwilling to sign contracts to work on somebody else's plantation.

Even when the hope of free land disappeared, freedmen were averse to signing labor contracts because, as has been noted, so many white landowners expected to continue to treat them like slaves. Especially repugnant was the idea
of being again herded together in the plantation slave quarters, with their communal facilities for cooking and washing and infant care, and their lack of privacy. Emancipation did much to strengthen the black family. Families divided
by slave sales could now be reunited. Marital arrangements between blacks,
which had had no legal validity during slavery, could be regularized. Freedmen's Bureau officials performed thousands of marriage ceremonies, and some
states passed general ordinances declaring that blacks who had been living together were legally man and wife and that their children were legitimate. This
precious new security of family life was not something blacks were willing to
jeopardize by returning to slave quarters. Before contracting to work on the
plantations, they insisted on having separate cabins, scattered across the farm,
each usually having its own patch for vegetables and perhaps a pen for hogs or a
cow.

When these conditions were met, freedmen in the early months of 1866 entered into labor contracts, most of which followed the same general pattern.
Rarely did these arrangements call for the payment of wages, for landowners
were desperately short of cash and freedmen felt that a wage system gave planters too much control over their labor. The most common system was sharecropping. Although there were many regional and individual variations, the
system usually called for the dividing of the crop into three equal shares. One of
these went to the landowner; another went to the laborer—usually black, though
there were also many white sharecroppers in the South; and the third went to
whichever party provided the seeds, fertilizer, mules, and other farming equipment.

For the planter this system had several advantages. At a time when money was
scarce, he was not obliged to pay out cash to his employees until the crop was
harvested. He retained general supervision over what was planted and how the
crop was cultivated, and he felt he was more likely to secure a good harvest because the freedmen themselves stood to gain by a large yield. Blacks, too, found
the sharecropping system suited to their needs. They had control over how their
crops were planted and when they were cultivated and harvested. They could
earn more money by working harder in the fields. And, best of all, they could
live in individual family units scattered over the plantation, each cabin having
some privacy.

To some observers the disappearance of the slave quarters and the resettling
of families in individual. scattered cabins seemed to mark a revolution in the
character of Southern agriculture. According to the United States census, the
number of Southern landholdings doubled between 1860 and 1880 and their
average size dropped from 365 acres to 157 acres. In fact, the census figures

were misleading, because the census takers failed to ask farmers whether they owned their land or were sharecroppers. An examination of tax records, which show land ownership, in the representative state of Louisiana helps correct the distortion of the census. Between 1860 and 1880 in Louisiana the number of independently owned farms of less than 100 acres actually dropped by 14 percent, while during the same period the number of plantations increased by 287 percent. By 1900, plantations of 100 acres or more encompassed half the cultivated land in the state, and more than half the farmers were not proprietors.

If the postwar period did not see the breakup of large plantations, it did bring some significant changes in ownership and control of the land. Hard hit by debt, by rising taxes, and by increasing labor costs, many Southern planters had to sell their holdings, and there was an infusion of Northern capital into the region after

THE SAME GEORGIA PLANTATION IN 1860 AND IN 1880

Before the Civil War slave quarters were located close together, all near the white master's house, so that he could impose order and prevent secret meetings of the blacks. After emancipation freedmen insisted upon scattering out over the plantation, so that each family could have its own house and some privacy.

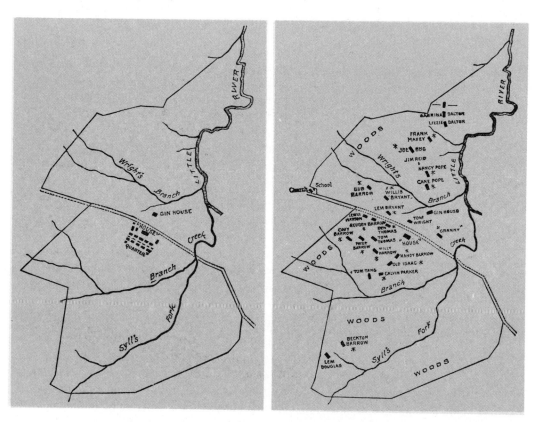

the war. More tried to cling to their acres by going heavily into debt. Since the banking system of the postwar South was inadequate, the principal source of credit was the local merchant, who could supply both the landowner and his sharecroppers with clothing, shoes, some food, and other necessities to tide them over the lean months between the planting of the tobacco or cotton crop and its harvest. On each sale the merchant charged interest, to be paid when the crop was sold, and he also charged prices ranging from 40 percent to 110 percent higher for all goods sold on credit. It is hardly surprising that those planters who could afford to do so set up their own stores and extended credit to their own sharecroppers, and quite soon they discovered they were making more profits on their mercantile enterprises than from farming. Planters who could not make such arrangements frequently had to sell their lands to the neighborhood merchant. It is not accidental that in William Faulkner's fictional saga of Southern history the power of planter families like the Compsons and the Sutpens diminished during the postwar years, while the Snopes family of storekeepers, hard-trading, penny-pinching, and utterly unscrupulous, emerged prosperous and successful.

It would be a mistake, however, to accept the novelist's hostile characterization of the Southern merchant without reservation. If the storekeeper insisted on a crop-lien system, which required the farmer legally to pledge that the proceeds from his crop must go first to pay off his obligation to the merchant, it was because he was aware that, as in both 1866 and 1867, crops throughout the South could fail. And if the merchant urged farmers to forget about soil conservation, diversification, and experimentation with new crops, it was because he knew that the only way to pay his own debts was to insist that his debtors must raise cotton and tobacco, for which there was a ready cash market.

Thus merchants, landowners, and sharecroppers, thus white Southerners and black Southerners, became locked into an economic system that, at best, promised them little more than survival. At worst, it offered bankruptcy, sale of lands, and hurried nocturnal migrations in an attempt to escape from a set of debts in one state but with little more than the hope of starting a new set in another.

By the 1880s, then, the South had become what it remained for the next half-century, the economic backwater of the nation. In 1880 the per capita wealth of the South was $376, that in the states outside the South $1,086. Yet it was this impoverished region that had to deal with some of the most difficult political and racial problems that ever have confronted Americans. In attacking these problems, Southerners, black and white, could expect no assistance from the government, since such intervention would violate the immutable laws of laissez-faire economics. Even the most humane national leaders could discover no way to help this backward region. They could only agree with Whitelaw Reid, editor of the influential New York *Tribune*, who concluded after his tour of the South in 1879, "Manifestly something is wrong," and gave as his diagnosis: "Economic laws are violated in some way."

Political Parties as a Limit to Change

Of the institutions that checked radical change during Reconstruction, none were more influential than the national political parties. The fact that both parties were conglomerates of disparate and often competing sectional and class interests meant that party policy had to be arrived at through compromise and concession. In that process extreme and drastic measures were nearly always screened out.

Nationally the Democratic party during the postwar years was torn by two conflicting interests. On the one hand Democrats sought the immediate readmission of the Southern states under the governments President Johnson had set up. Controlled by whites hostile to the Republican party, these states would surely send Democrats to Congress and support Democratic candidates in a national election. Even during the 1850s, the South had increasingly become a one-party region; now the goal of a solidly Democratic South appeared within reach. On the other hand, too enthusiastic advocacy of the Southern cause could hurt Democrats in the North by reviving talk of disloyalty and the Copperhead movement during the war. Throughout the Reconstruction era, Democrats remained vulnerable to charges like those brought by Governor O. P. Morton of Indiana during the 1868 campaign: "Every unregenerate rebel . . . every deserter, every sneak who ran away from the draft calls himself a Democrat. . . . Every man who labored for the rebellion . . ., who murdered Union prisoners by cruelty and starvation . . . calls himself a Democrat. . . . In short, the Democratic party may be described as a common sewer and loathsome receptacle, into which is emptied every element of treason North and South, every element of inhumanity and barbarism which has dishonored the age." To minimize the effectiveness of such attacks, Democrats had no choice but to mute their defense of the South and to urge restraint on their colleagues in the former Confederacy.

Among Republicans, similar constraints operated to dampen any ideas of taking vengeance on the South or of encouraging blacks to seize control of that region. From its inception the Republican party had been an uneasy admixture of antislavery men, former Whigs, disgruntled Democrats, and Know Nothings. How tenuous were the ties that bound these groups together became evident in the factional disputes that racked Lincoln's administration, and for the party it was a bad omen that the sharpest area of disagreement between Radical and Conservative Republicans concerned Lincoln's plan to reorganize the Southern states.

During the first year after Lincoln's death, quarrels between the Radicals and the Conservatives were somewhat muted because practically all Republicans could join in opposing President Johnson's program of Reconstruction. Followed only by Secretary of State Seward, Navy Secretary Gideon Welles, and a handful of other very cautious Republicans, Johnson began to work closely with the Democrats of the North and South. He announced that the Southern states had never been out of the Union, and he insisted that, under the provisional governments he had set up, they were ready to reclaim their right to be represented in Congress.

It is easy to understand why almost all Radical and Conservative Republicans rejected the President's argument. Regardless of faction, they were outraged when the Southern elections in 1865, held at the direction of the President, resulted in the choice of a Confederate brigadier-general as governor of Mississippi, and they were furious when the new Georgia legislature named Alexander H. Stephens, the Vice President of the Confederacy, to represent that state in the United States Senate.

What made these newly elected Southern officials more threatening to Republicans was the fact that (though many had been Whigs before the war) they clearly contemplated allying themselves with the Democratic party. However much Republicans disagreed among themselves, they all agreed that their party had saved the Union. They believed, with Thaddeus Stevens, "that upon the continued ascendency of that party depends the safety of this great nation." Now that ascendency was threatened. What made the threat so grave, and so ironic, was the fact that when the Southern states were readmitted to the Union they would receive increased representation in Congress. Prior to the ratification of the Thirteenth Amendment, only three-fifths of the slave population of the South had been counted in apportioning representation in the House of Representatives; but now that the slaves were free men, all would be counted. In short, the Southern states, after having been defeated in the most costly war in the nation's history, would have about fifteen more representatives in Congress than they had had before the war. And under the President's plan, all of the Southern Congress unquestionably would be Democrats.

Equally troubling to Republicans of all factions was the fear of what white Southerners, once restored to authority, would do to the freedmen. The laws that the Southern provisional legislatures adopted during the winter of 1865–66 gave reason for anxiety on this score. Not one of these governments considered treating black citizens just as they treated white citizens. Instead, the legislatures adopted special laws, known as the Black Codes, to regulate the conduct of freedmen. On the positive side, these laws recognized the right of freedmen to make civil contracts, to sue and be sued, and to acquire and hold most kinds of property. But with these rights went restrictions. The laws varied from state to state, but in general they specified that blacks might not purchase or carry firearms, that they might not assemble after sunset, and that those who were idle or unemployed should "be liable to imprisonment, and to hard labor, one or both, . . . not exceeding twelve months." The Mississippi code prohibited blacks from renting or leasing "any lands or tenements except in incorporated cities or towns." That of South Carolina forbade blacks from practicing "the art, trade or business of an artisan, mechanic or shopkeeper, or any other trade, employment or business (besides that of husbandry, or that of a servant)." So clearly did these measures seem designed to keep the freedmen in quasi-slavery that the Chicago *Tribune* spoke for a united, outraged Republican party in denouncing the first of these Black Codes, that adopted by the Mississippi legislature: "We tell the white men of Mississippi that the men of the North will convert the state of Mississippi into a frog-pond before they will allow any such laws to disgrace one foot of soil over which the flag of freedom waves."

Unwilling, for all these reasons, to recognize the regimes Johnson had set up in the South, all Republicans easily rallied in December 1865, when Congress reassembled, to block seating of their senators and representatives. All agreed to the creation of a special joint committee on Reconstruction to handle questions concerning the readmission of the Southern states and their further reorganization. In setting up this committee, congressional Republicans carefully balanced its membership with Radicals and Moderates. If its most conspicuous member was the Radical Stevens, its powerful chairman was Senator William Pitt Fessenden, a Moderate.

Congressional Republicans found it easier to unite in opposing Johnson's plan of Reconstruction than to unite in devising one of their own. Throughout the winter of 1865–66, the joint committee met to consider various plans for reorganizing the South. With its evenly balanced membership, the committee dismissed, on the one side, the President's theory that the Southern states were, in reality, already reconstructed and back in the Union. On the other side, it discarded the theory of Thaddeus Stevens that the Confederacy was conquered territory over which Congress could rule at its own discretion, and it rejected Charles Sumner's more elaborate argument that the Southern state governments had committed suicide when they seceded, so that their land and inhabitants now fell "under the exclusive jurisdiction of Congress." More acceptable to the majority of Republicans was the "grasp of war" theory advanced by Richard Henry Dana, Jr., the noted Massachusetts constitutional lawyer, who was also the author of *Two Years before the Mast*. Dana argued that the federal government held the defeated Confederacy in the grasp of war for a brief and limited time, during which it must act swiftly to revive state governments in the region and to restore promptly the constitutional balance between national and state authority. Dana's theory was an essentially conservative one, in that it called for only a short period of federal hegemony and looked toward the speedy restoration of the Southern states on terms of absolute equality with the loyal states.

Finding in Dana's theory a constitutional source of power, the Joint Committee after much travail produced the first comprehensive congressional plan of Reconstruction in a proposed Fourteenth Amendment to the Constitution, which was endorsed by Congress in June 1866 and submitted to the states for ratification. Some parts of the amendment were noncontroversial. All Republicans recognized the need authoritatively to overturn the Supreme Court decision in the Dred Scott case (1857), which had declared Negroes were not citizens of the United States, and consequently accepted the opening statement of

RECONSTRUCTION.

Uncle Sam—"WELL, ANDY, DO YOU THINK THAT YOU CAN GET MY COAT TOGETHER BEFORE YOU CLOSE SHOP?"
Andy—"WELL, IT'S BEEN TORN PRETTY BADLY, BUT I GUESS ME AND MUM SEWARD CAN GET IT TOGETHER BEFORE WE CLOSE SHOP."

RECONSTRUCTION: A DIALOGUE BETWEEN
UNCLE SAM AND A. JOHNSON, TAILOR

Taking off from Andrew Johnson's
frequent bragging about his humble
origins as a tailor, this cartoon shows
the President and Secretary of State
Seward busily mending Uncle Sam's
coat, badly torn by the recently ended
Civil War. (*American Antiquarian Society.*)

the amendment: "All persons born or naturalized in the United States, and subject to the jurisdiction thereof, are citizens of the United States and the State
wherein they reside." There was also no disagreement about the provision declaring the Confederate debt invalid.

All the other provisions, however, represented a compromise between Radical
and Moderate Republicans. For instance, Radicals wanted to keep all Southerners who had voluntarily supported the Confederacy from voting until 1870, and
the arch-Radical Stevens urged: "Not only to 1870 but 18070, every rebel who
shed the blood of loyal men should be prevented from exercising any power in
this Government." Moderates favored a speedy restoration of all political rights
to former Confederates. As a compromise the Fourteenth Amendment included
a provision to exclude high-ranking Confederates from office but one that did
not deny them the vote.

Similarly, the Fourteenth Amendment's provisions to protect the freedmen
represented a compromise. Radicals like Sumner (who was considered too radical
to be given a seat on the joint committee) wanted an unequivocal declaration of
the right and duty of the national government to protect the civil liberties of the
former slaves. But Moderates drew back in alarm from entrusting additional
authority to Washington. The joint committee came up with a provision that
granted no power to the national government but restricted that of the states:

RETURN OF THE PRODIGAL SON—NEW VERSION.

KIND-HEARTED DEMOCRAT "THERE, MOTHER, THERE'S YOUR BOY COME HOME AGAIN; MAKE HIM WELCOME."
PENITENT SOUTH "YES, BY THUNDER, I'VE COME BACK; AND D'YE HEAR? HURRY UP THEM CAKES AND HOT WHISKY, AND DON'T LET US SEE
ANY DARND NIGGERS AROUND."

"RETURN OF THE PRODIGAL SON — NEW VERSION"

This Republican view of Reconstruction depicts the
unregenerate South — still bullying, whiskey-loving, and
Negro-hating — welcomed as the prodigal son by Northern
Democrats. *(American Antiquarian Society.)*

"No State shall make or enforce any law which shall abridge the privileges and
immunities of citizens of the United States; nor shall any State deprive any person of life, liberty, or property, without due process of law; nor deny to any
person within its jurisdiction the equal protection of the laws."

Finally, another compromise between Radicals and Moderates resulted in
the provision of the amendment concerning voting. Though Sumner and other
Radicals called Negro suffrage "the essence, the great essential," of a proper
Reconstruction policy, Conservatives refused to give to the national government
power to interfere with state requirements for suffrage. The joint committee
thereupon devised a complex and, as it proved, unworkable plan to persuade
the Southern states voluntarily to enfranchise blacks, under threat of having
reduced representation in Congress if they refused.

The efficacy of the Fourteenth Amendment as a program of Reconstruction
was never tested because of the deterioration of relations between Congress
and the President. While the joint committee was deliberating, Johnson further
alienated the Republicans, who were already distrustful of his policy. Recognizing that a constitutional amendment would take time for ratification, congressional
leaders early in 1866 tried to pass interim legislation to protect the freedmen.

One bill extended the life and expanded the functions of the Freedmen's Bureau, and a second guaranteed minimal civil rights to all citizens. Contrary to expectations, Johnson vetoed both these measures. Incorrectly terming these bills the work of Radical Republicans who wanted "to destroy our institutions and change the character of the Government," the President publicly announced that he intended to fight these enemies of the Union just as he had once fought secessionists and traitors in the South. Congress sustained Johnson's veto of the Freedmen's Bureau bill (a later, less sweeping measure extended the life of that agency for two years), but it passed the Civil Rights Act over his disapproval.

From this point, open warfare existed between the President and the majority of the Republican party that had elected him Vice-President in 1864. During the summer of 1866, Johnson and his friends tried to create a new political party, which would rally behind the President's policies Conservative Republicans, Northern Democrats, and Southern whites. With the President's hearty approval, a National Union Convention held in Philadelphia in August stressed the theme of harmony among the sections. The entry into the convention hall of delegates from Massachusetts and South Carolina, arm in arm, seemed to symbolize the end of sectional strife. The President himself went on a "swing around the circle" of leading Northern cities, ostensibly on his way to dedicate a monument to the memory of another Democrat, Stephen A. Douglas. In his frequent public speeches he defended the constitutionality of his own Reconstruction program and berated the Congress, and particularly the Radical Republicans, for attempting to subvert the Constitution. In a final effort to consolidate sentiment against the Congress, he urged the Southern states not to ratify the proposed Fourteenth Amendment. With the exception of Tennessee, which was controlled by one of Johnson's bitterest personal and political enemies, all the former Confederate states rejected the congressional plan. In ten Southern legislatures not a single vote was cast in favor of it.

When Congress reassembled in December 1866, the Republican majority had therefore to devise a second program of Reconstruction. Cheered by overwhelming victories in the fall congressional elections, Republicans were even less inclined than previously to cooperate with the President, who had gone into political opposition, or to encourage the provisional regimes in the South, which had unanimously rejected their first program. Republican suspicion that Southern whites were fundamentally hostile toward the freedmen was strengthened by reports of a race riot in Memphis during May 1866, when a mob of whites joined in a two-day indiscriminate attack on blacks in that city, and of a more serious affair in New Orleans four months later, when a white mob, aided by the local police, attacked a black political gathering with what was described as "a cowardly ferocity unsurpassed in the annals of crime." In New Orleans, 45 or 50 blacks were killed, and 150 more were wounded.

Once again, however, the Republican majority in Congress found it easier to agree on what to oppose than what to favor in the way of Reconstruction legis-

lation. Stevens urged that the South be placed under military rule for a generation and that Southern plantations be sold to pay the national debt. Sumner
wanted to disfranchise large numbers of Southern whites, to require Negro
suffrage, and to create racially integrated schools in the South. Moderate Republicans, on the other hand, were willing to retain the Fourteenth Amendment
as the basic framework of congressional Reconstruction and to insist on little
else but ratification by the Southern states.

The second congressional program of Reconstruction, embodied in the Military Reconstruction Act of March 2, 1867, represented a compromise between
the demands of Radical and Moderate Republican factions. It divided the ten
former Confederate states that had not ratified the Fourteenth Amendment into
five military districts. In each of these states, there were to be new constitutional
conventions, for which black men were allowed to vote. These conventions must
draft new constitutions that had to provide for Negro suffrage, and they were
required to ratify the Fourteenth Amendment. When thus reorganized, the
Southern states could apply to Congress for readmission to the Union.

The radical aspects of this measure, which were pointed out by Democrats
during the congressional debates and were denounced by President Johnson in
his unsuccessful veto of the act, were easy to recognize. In particular, the requirement of Negro suffrage, which Sumner sponsored, seemed to Radicals "a prodigious triumph."

In fact, however, most provisions of the Military Reconstruction Act were more
acceptable to Moderate than to Radical Republicans. The measure did nothing
to give land to the freedmen, to provide education at national expense, or to
end racial segregation in the South. It did not erase the boundaries of the Southern states, and it did not even sweep away the provisional governments Johnson
had established there, though it did make them responsible to the commanders of
the new military districts. So conservative was the act in all these respects that
Sumner branded it as "horribly defective."

Intent on striking some kind of balance between the Radical and Conservative
wings of the Republican party, the framers of the Military Reconstruction Act
drafted the measure carelessly, and it promptly proved, as Sumner had predicted,
"Reconstruction without machinery or motive power." Facing the acceptance of
military rule or Negro suffrage, the provisional governments in the South chose
the former, correctly believing that army officers were generally in sympathy with
white supremacy. To get the Reconstruction process under way, Congress had
therefore to enact a supplementary law (March 23, 1867), requiring the federal
commanders in the South to take the initiative, when the local governments did
not, in announcing elections, registering voters, and convening constitutional
conventions. During the summer of 1867, as the President, the attorney general,
and Southern state officials tried by legalistic interpretations to delay the Reconstruction program, Congress had to pass two further supplementary acts, explaining the "true intent and meaning" of the previous legislation.

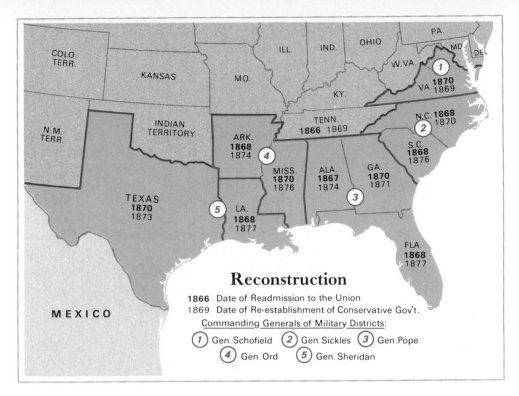

Reconstruction

1866 Date of Readmission to the Union
1869 Date of Re-establishment of Conservative Gov't.
Commanding Generals of Military Districts:
(1) Gen. Schofield (2) Gen. Sickles (3) Gen. Pope
(4) Gen. Ord (5) Gen. Sheridan

With these measures, the fabric of congressional Reconstruction legislation as it affected the South was substantially completed. Both the first and the second congressional plans of Reconstruction were compromises between the Radical and the Moderate factions in the Republican party. The Radicals' insistence on change was essential in securing the adoption of this legislation, but the Moderates blocked all measures that would have revolutionary social or economic consequences in the South.

The same need to compromise between the factions of the Republican party shaped the relation between Congress and the other two branches of the national government during the Reconstruction era. Many Republicans in both factions were profoundly suspicious of the Supreme Court, because of its decision in the Dred Scott case before the war. Not even Lincoln's appointment of Salmon P. Chase in 1864, to succeed Roger B. Taney as Chief Justice, removed their doubts about the judiciary. They grew alarmed when the Court in 1866 handed down its decision in *ex parte Milligan*, a landmark case in the history of American civil liberties, which denied the power of a Civil War military tribunal to try the Indiana Copperhead conspirator Lambdin P. Milligan, and held that he should have been brought before a civil tribunal. Some Republicans in Congress feared— quite incorrectly—that the Court was getting ready to invalidate military rule in the South and thus destroy the main protection for the freedmen's rights.

Timorous Republicans watched in something approaching panic as the provisional governments in both Georgia and Mississippi brought suit to test the constitutionality of the Military Reconstruction Act, and they were relieved when the Supreme Court refused to hear these cases. When, however, one McCardle, a Mississippi editor arrested and tried by military commission for publishing criticism of the congressional Reconstruction policy, succeeded in bringing his case before the Court, Republicans in Congress acted swiftly to deprive the Court of jurisdiction in such cases.

This step was highly exceptional, and Republican fulminations against the Court were largely a matter of Radicals' letting off steam. Moderate Republicans were always numerous enough to block Radical proposals to hobble the judiciary. Congress did reduce the number of justices from ten to seven, but this was a nonpartisan move, approved by President Johnson himself, which was designed to increase the efficiency of the Court, not to undermine its authority. Even the Radical success in the McCardle case was of little significance, since, as the Court promptly demonstrated in *ex parte Yerger* (1869), another case involving a Mississippian, that its jurisdiction derived not from an act of Congress but from the Constitution itself, and it freed Yerger from the prison to which a military court had sentenced him. Radicals stewed impotently, while Moderates prevented them from taking further measures against the Court.

The same balance between Radical and Moderate Republican factions dictated the policy of Congress toward the President during the Reconstruction years. Almost all Republicans were suspicious of the President and were fearful that he intended turning the South over to Confederate rule. Most were angered by Johnson's repeated veto messages, assailing carefully balanced compromise legislation as the work of Radicals and attacking the Congress itself as an unconstitutional body, since it refused to seat congressmen from all the states. Republicans of both factions were, therefore, desirous of keeping a close eye on the President and were willing to curb executive powers that had grown during the war. In 1867, fearing that Johnson would use his power as commander in chief to subvert their Reconstruction legislation, Republican factions joined to pass an army appropriations bill that required all military orders to the army, including those of the President himself, to go through the hands of General Grant. Suspecting that Johnson wanted to use the federal patronage to build up a political machine of his own, they adopted at the same time the Tenure of Office Act, which required the President to secure the consent of the Senate not merely when he appointed officials but when he removed them.

Up to this point the Republicans in Congress were prepared to go in striking unanimity—but no further. When Radical Republican James M. Ashley in January 1867 moved to impeach the President, he was permitted to conduct a serio-comic investigation of Johnson's alleged involvement in Lincoln's assassination, his purported sale of pardons, and other trumped-up charges; but when Ashley's motion reached the floor of the House of Representatives Moderate Republicans saw that it was soundly defeated.

A subsequent attempt at impeachment fared better, but it also revealed how the Radical and Moderate factions checked each other. In August 1867, President Johnson suspended from office Secretary of War Edwin M. Stanton, whom he correctly suspected of having collaborated closely with the Radicals in Congress, and, as required by the Tenure of Office Act, he asked the Senate to consent to the removal. When the Senate refused, the President removed Stanton and ordered him to surrender his office. News of this seemingly open defiance of the law caused Republicans in the House of Representatives to rush through a resolution impeaching the President, without waiting for specific charges against him to be drawn up.

The trial of President Johnson (who was not present in court but was represented by his lawyers) was not merely a test of strength between Congress and the chief executive, but between the Radical and the Moderate Republicans. Impeachment managers from the House of Representatives presented eleven charges against the President, mostly accusing him of violating the Tenure of Office Act but also censuring his repeated attacks upon the Congress. With fierce joy Radical Thaddeus Stevens, who was one of the managers, denounced the President: "Unfortunate man! thus surrounded, hampered, tangled in the meshes of his own wickedness—unfortunate, unhappy man, behold your doom!"

But Radical oratory could not persuade Moderate Republicans and Democrats in the Senate to vote for conviction. Though Sumner, like a handful of other Radicals, was prepared from the outset of the trial to pronounce that Johnson was "guilty of all, and infinitely more," most senators were open-minded. They listened as Johnson's lawyers challenged the constitutionality of the Tenure of

AWKWARD COLLISION ON THE GRAND TRUNK COLUMBIA R. R.
A. J. (driver of Engine "President")—"LOOK HERE! ONE OF US HAS GOT TO BACK."
THADDEUS (Driver of Engine "Congress")—"WELL, IF AIN'T ME THAT'S GOING TO DO IT—YOU BET!"

"AWKWARD COLLISION ON THE GRAND TRUNK COLUMBIA RAILROAD"

In this cartoon "A. J[ohnson]." personifies presidential Reconstruction and "Thaddeus [Stevens]" congressional Reconstruction. The two plans are obviously on a collision course. which led ultimately to the impeachment of the President. *(Library of Congress.)*

Office Act, showed that it had not been intended to apply to cabinet members, and proved that, in any case, it did not cover Stanton, who had been appointed by Lincoln, not Johnson. When the critical vote came, Moderate Republicans like Fessenden voted to acquit the President, and Johnson's Radical foes lacked one vote of the two-thirds majority required to convict him. Several other Republican Senators who for political expediency voted against the President were prepared to change their votes and favor acquittal if their ballots were needed.

Nothing more clearly shows how the institutional needs of a political party prevented drastic change than did this decision not to remove a President whom a majority in Congress despised, hated, and feared. The desire to maintain the unity of the national Republican party, despite frequent quarrels and incessant bickering, overrode the wishes of individual congressmen. Moderate Republicans felt that throughout the Reconstruction period they were constantly being rushed from one advanced position to another in order to placate the insatiable Radicals. With more accuracy, Radical Republicans perceived that the need of retaining Moderate support prevented the adoption of any really revolutionary Reconstruction program.

Racism as a Limit to Change

A final set of beliefs that limited the nature of the changes imposed upon, and accepted by, the South during the Reconstruction period can be labeled racism. In all parts of the country, white Americans looked with suspicion and fear on those whose skin was of a different color. For example, in California white hatred built up against the Chinese, who had begun coming to that state in great numbers after the discovery of gold and who were later imported by the thousands to help construct the Central Pacific Railroad. White workers resented the willingness of the Chinese to work long hours for "coolies'" wages; they distrusted the unfamiliar attire, diet, and habits of the Chinese; and they disliked all these things more because the Chinese were a yellow-skinned people. Under the leadership of a newly arrived Irish immigrant, Dennis Kearney, white laborers organized a workingman's party, with the slogan, "The Chinese must go."

The depression of 1873 gave impetus to the movement, for day after day thousands of the unemployed gathered in the sand lots of San Francisco to hear Kearney's slashing attacks on the Chinese and on the wealthy corporations that employed them. In the summer of 1877 San Francisco hoodlums, inspired by Kearney, burned 25 Chinese laundries and destroyed dozens of Chinese houses. Politically the movement was strong enough to force both major parties in California to adopt anti-Chinese platforms, and California congressmen succeeded in persuading their colleagues to pass a bill limiting the number of Chinese who could be brought into the United States each year. Since the measure clearly conflicted with treaty arrangements with China, President Rutherford B. Hayes vetoed it, but he had his secretary of state initiate negotiations leading to a new treaty that permitted the restriction of immigration. Congress in 1882 passed the Chinese Exclusion Act, which suspended all Chinese immigration for ten years and forbade the naturalization of Chinese already in the country.

If white Americans became so agitated over a small number of Chinese, who were unquestionably hard-working and thrifty and who belonged to one of the most ancient of civilizations, it is easy to see how they could consider blacks an even greater danger. There were more than 3 million Negroes, most of them recently emancipated from slavery. The exploits of black soldiers during the war—their very discipline and courage—proved that Negroes could be formidable opponents. The fact that blacks were no longer portrayed as invisible men but now, in photographs and caricatures, had sharply etched identities exacerbated, rather than allayed, white apprehensions. More clearly than ever before Negroes seemed distinctive, alien, and vaguely menacing. After all, according to the defective ethnology of the day, they were lazy and improvident by nature, the descendants of barbarous African tribes that had never shown a trace of civilization.

THE MARTYRDOM OF ST. CRISPIN.

"THE MARTYRDOM OF ST. CRISPIN"

Racism in postwar America took many forms. Here the artist Thomas Nast shows the obviously 100 percent American "St. Crispin," the patron saint of shoemakers, threatened by the cheap labor of Chinese immigrants. (*American Antiquarian Society.*)

Most American intellectuals of the Civil War generation accepted unquestioningly the dogma that blacks belonged to an inferior race. Though a few reformers like Charles Sumner vigorously attacked this notion, a majority of even philanthropic Northerners accepted the judgment of the distinguished Harvard scientist Louis Agassiz that while whites during antiquity were developing high civilizations "the negro race groped in barbarism and never originated a regular organization among themselves." Many accepted Agassiz's conjecture that Negroes, once free, would inevitably die out in the United States. Others reached the same conclusion by studying the recently published work of Charles Darwin, *Origin of Species* (1859), and they accepted the Darwinian argument that in the inevitable struggle for survival "higher civilized races" must inevitably eliminate "an endless number of lower races." Consequently the influential and tender-hearted Congregational minister Horace Bushnell could prophesy the approaching end of the black race in the United States with something approaching equanimity. "Since we must all die," he asked rhetorically, "why should it grieve us, that a stock thousands of years behind, in the scale of culture, should die with few and still fewer children to succeed, till finally the whole succession remains in the more cultivated race?"

When even the leaders of Northern society held such views, it is hardly surprising that most whites in the region were overtly anti-Negro. In state after state whites fiercely resisted efforts to extend the political and civil rights of blacks, partly because they feared that any improvement of the condition of Negroes in the North would lead to a huge exodus of blacks from the South. At the end of the Civil War only Maine, New Hampshire, Vermont, Massachusetts, and Rhode Island allowed Negroes to have full voting rights, and in New York blacks who met certain property-holding qualifications could have the ballot. During the next three years in referenda held in Connecticut, Wisconsin, Kansas, Ohio, Michigan, and Missouri, constitutional amendments authorizing Negro suffrage were defeated, and New York voters rejected a proposal to eliminate the property-holding qualifications for black voters. Only in Iowa, a state where there were very few blacks, did a Negro suffrage amendment carry in 1868, and that same year Minnesota adopted an ambiguously worded amendment. Thus at the end of the 1860s most Northern states—and all of the Northern states that had substantial numbers of Negro residents—refused to give black men the ballot.

In words as well as in votes, the majority of Northerners made their deeply racist feelings evident. The Democratic press constantly preyed on the racial fears of its readers, and they regularly portrayed the Republicans as planning a "new era of miscegenation, amalgamation, and promiscuous intercourse between the races." From the White House, denouncing Republican attempts "to Africanize the [Southern] half of our country," President Andrew Johnson announced: "In the progress of nations negroes have shown less capacity for self-government than any other race of people.... Whenever they have been left to their own devices they have shown an instant tendency to relapse into barbarism." Even Northern Republicans opposed to Johnson shared many of his racist views. Radical Senator Timothy O. Howe of Wisconsin declared that he regarded "the freedmen, in the main . . . as so much animal life," and Senator Benjamin F. Wade of Ohio, whom the Radical Republicans would have elevated to the presidency had they removed Johnson, had, along with a genuine devotion to the principle of equal rights, an incurable aversion to blacks. Representative George W. Julian of Indiana, one of the few Northern congressmen who had no racial prejudice, bluntly told his colleagues in 1866: "The real trouble is that *we hate the negro*. It is not his ignorance that offends us, but his color. . . . Of this fact I entertain no doubt whatsoever."

Both personal preferences and the wishes of constituents inhibited Northern Republicans from supporting measures that might alter race relations. When Sumner sought to expunge federal laws that recognized slavery or to prohibit racial discrimination on the public transportation in the District of Columbia, his

Black Population, 1880

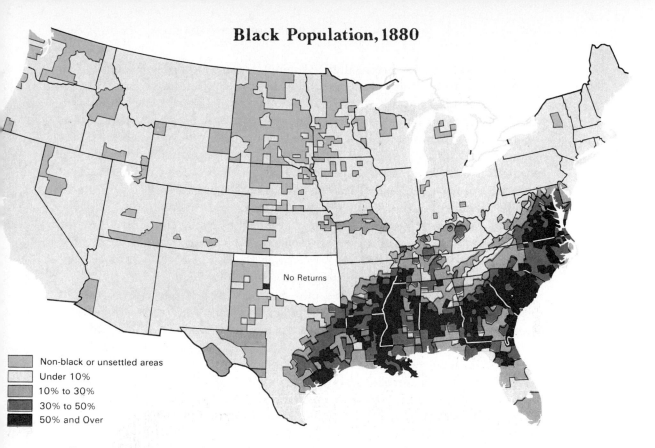

No Returns

- ☐ Non-black or unsettled areas
- ☐ Under 10%
- ☐ 10% to 30%
- ☐ 30% to 50%
- ☐ 50% and Over

colleagues replied: "God has made the negro inferior, and . . . laws cannot make him equal." Such congressmen were hardly in a position to scold the South for racial discrimination or to insist on drastic social change in that region.

If racism limited the innovation that Northerners were willing to propose during the Reconstruction period, it even more drastically reduced the amount of change that white Southerners were prepared to accept. The note of racial bigotry runs through both the private correspondence and the public pronouncements of Southern whites during the postwar era. "Equality does not exist between blacks and whites," announced Alexander H. Stephens. "The one race is by nature inferior in many respects, physically and mentally, to the other. This should be received as a fixed invincible fact in all dealings with the subject." A North Carolina diarist agreed: "The Anglo-Saxon and the African can never be equal . . . one or the other must fall." Or, as the Democratic party of Louisiana resolved in its 1865 platform: "We hold this to be a Government of white people, made and to be perpetuated for the exclusive benefit of the white race; and . . . that people of African descent cannot be considered as citizens of the United States, and that there can, in no event, nor under any circumstances, be any equality between the white and other races." The Black Codes were the legal embodiment of these attitudes.

These racist views shaped the attitude of most Southern whites toward the whole process of Reconstruction. They approved of President Johnson's plan of

Reconstruction because it placed government in the Southern states entirely in the hands of whites. They rejected the Fourteenth Amendment primarily because it made blacks legally equal to whites. They watched with incredulity bordering on stupefaction as Congress passed the 1867 Military Reconstruction Act, for they simply could not believe that the freedmen were to vote. Stunned, they watched army officers supervise the process of voter registration, a process that excluded many prominent whites who had participated in the Confederate government but included more than 700,000 blacks, who formed a majority of eligible voters in South Carolina, Florida, Alabama, Mississippi, and Louisiana. Knowing that these Negro voters were well organized by the Union League, often with the assistance of agents of the Freedmen's Bureau, whites were more apathetic than surprised when the fall elections showed heavy majorities in favor of convening new constitutional conventions.*

With hostile and unbelieving eyes, most Southern whites observed the work of these conventions, which between November 1867 and May 1868 drafted new constitutions for the former Confederate states. To Southern whites unaccustomed to seeing blacks in any positions of public prominence, the presence of freedmen in these conventions meant that they were Negro-dominated. In fact, except in the South Carolina convention, in which blacks did form a majority, only between one-fourth and one-ninth of the delegates were Negroes. Whites ridiculed the Negro members' ignorance of parliamentary procedures, and they laughed sardonically when they read how the "coal black" temporary chairman of the Louisiana convention put a question by asking those who favored a motion "to rise an stan on der feet" and then directing "all you contrairy men to rise."

The reactions of Southern whites to the constitutions these conventions produced were also determined by their racial prejudice. Generally they denounced these new charters as "totally incompatible with the prosperity and liberty of the people." In fact the constitutions, often copied from Northern models, were generally improvements over the ones they superseded. In addition to requiring Negro suffrage (as Congress had directed), they promised all citizens of the state equality before the law. They reformed financial and revenue systems, reorganized the judiciary, improved the organization of local government, and, most important of all, instituted a state-supported system of public education, hitherto notably lacking in most Southern states.

Because these constitutions guaranteed racial equality, Southern whites tried, without great success, to block their ratification. In Alabama, whites boycotted the ratification election; in Mississippi, they cast a majority of votes against the new constitution. In Virginia, ratification was delayed because the conservative army commander of that district discovered that there was no money to hold an

---

*The Texas election was not held until February 1868. Tennessee had no election, because it had already been readmitted to the Union.

election, and in Texas all moves toward the creation of a new government lagged several months behind those in the Eastern states. Despite all the foot-dragging, new governments were set up, and in June 1868 Congress readmitted representatives and senators from Alabama, Arkansas, Florida, Georgia, Louisiana, North Carolina, and South Carolina. Two years later the reconstruction of Virginia, Mississippi, and Texas was completed, and in early 1870 these states were also readmitted. Meanwhile Georgia underwent one further reorganization after the legislature of that state attempted to exclude Negroes who had been elected to that body. But by 1871, when Georgia senators and representatives again took their seats in Congress, all the states of the former Confederacy had undergone the process of Reconstruction and had been readmitted to the Union.

With bitter hostility, most Southern whites witnessed this reorganization of their state governments, and the name "Black Reconstruction," which they gave to the ensuing period of Republican ascendency in the South, reveals the racial bias behind their opposition. In fact, these Southern state governments were not dominated by Negroes, and blacks generally held fewer offices than their numbers entitled them to. Only in South Carolina did the legislature have a black majority. No Negro was elected governor, though there were black lieutenant governors in South Carolina, Louisiana, and Mississippi. Only in South Carolina was there a black state supreme court justice. During the entire Reconstruction period only two blacks, Hiram R. Revels and Blanche K. Bruce, both from Mississippi and both men of exceptional ability and integrity, served in the United States Senate, and only fifteen blacks were elected to the House of Representatives.

Even to the most racist Southern whites it was obvious that most of the leaders of the Republican party in that section, and a large part of the Republican following as well, were themselves white. To those white Republicans born in the North, racists gave the label Carpetbaggers, because they allegedly came South with no more worldly possessions than could be packed into a carpetbag, or small suitcase, ready to live on and to exploit the prostrate region. The term, with its implication of corruption, was applied indiscriminately to men of Northern birth who had lived in the South long before the war as well as to newly arrived fortune hunters, many of them recently discharged Union army officers.

Southern-born white Republicans were called Scalawags, a term that cattle drovers applied to "the mean, lousy and filthy kine that are not fit for butchers or dogs." Again the term was used indiscriminately. Southern racists applied it to poor hill-country whites, who had long been at odds with the planters in states like North Carolina and Alabama and now joined the Republican party as a way of getting back at their old enemies. But other "Scalawags" were members of the planter, mercantile, and industrial classes of the South; many of these were former Whigs who distrusted the Democrats, and they felt at home in a Republican party that favored protective tariffs, subsidies for railroads, and appropriations for rebuilding the levees along the Mississippi River. A surprising number of Southern-born white Republicans were former high-ranking officers in the

COLORED RULE IN A RECONSTRUCTED (?) STATE

As postwar racism mounted, cartoonists no longer depicted
Negroes as handsome, intelligent fighters for freedom but
painted them as grotesque and animal-like. In addition to
perpetuating racial stereotypes, this drawing of Thomas
Nast's exaggerates the number and influence of blacks in the
Southern legislatures. (*American Antiquarian Society.*)

Confederate army, like General P. G. T. Beauregard and General James Longstreet, who knew at first hand the extent of the damage wrought by the war and
were willing to accept the victor's terms without procrastination.

Bitterly as they attacked these white Republicans, Southern Democrats reserved their worst abuse for Negroes, and they saw in every measure adopted by
the new reconstructed state governments evidence of black incompetence, extravagance, or even barbarism. In truth, much that these state governments did
supplied the Democrats with ammunition. The postwar period was one of low
political morality, and there was no reason to expect that newly enfranchised
blacks would prove any less attracted by the profits of politics than anybody
else. Petty corruption prevailed in all the Southern state governments. Louisiana legislators voted themselves an allowance for stationery—which covered

purchases of hams and bottles of champagne. The South Carolina legislature ran up a bill of more than $50,000 in refurbishing the statehouse with such costly items as a $750 mirror, $480 clocks, and 200 porcelain spittoons at $8 apiece. The same legislature voted $1,000 to the speaker of the House of Representatives to repay his losses on a horse race.

Bad as these excesses were, Southern Democrats were angered less by them than by the legitimate work performed by the new state governments. Unwilling to recognize that Negroes were now equal members of the body politic, they objected to expenditures for hospitals, jails, orphanages, and asylums to care for blacks. Most of all they objected to the creation of a public school system. Throughout the South there was considerable hostility to the idea of educating any children at the cost of the taxpayer, and the thought of paying taxes in order to reach black children seemed wild and foolish extravagance. The fact that black schools were mostly conducted by Northern whites, usually women, who came South with a reforming mission, did nothing to increase popular support; too many of the teachers stated plainly and publicly their intention to use "every endeavor to throw a ray of light here and there, among this benighted race of ruffians, rebels by nature." Adding to all these hostilities was a fear that a system of public education might some day lead to a racially integrated system of education. These apprehensions had little basis in fact, for during the entire period of Reconstruction in the whole South there were significant numbers of children in racially mixed schools only in New Orleans between 1870 and 1874.

Not content with criticizing Republican rule, Southern Democrats organized to put an end to it. Theirs was a two-pronged attack. On the one hand they sought to intimidate or to drive from the South whites who cooperated politically with the Republican regimes; on the other, they tried to terrorize and silence blacks, especially those active in politics. Much of this pressure was informal and sporadic, but much was the work of racist organizations that sprang up all over the South during these years. The most famous of these was the Ku Klux Klan, which originated in 1866 as a social club for young white men in Pulaski, Tennessee. As the Military Reconstruction Act went into effect and the possibility of black participation in Southern political life became increasingly real, racists saw new potential in this secret organization with its cabalistic name and its mysterious uniforms of long flowing robes, high conical hats that made the wearers seem preternaturally tall, and white face masks. In 1867 the Klan was reorganized under a new constitution that provided for local dens, each headed by a Grand Cyclops, linked together into provinces (counties), each under a Grand Titan, and in turn into realms (states), each under a Grand Dragon. At the head of the whole organization was the Grand Wizard, who, according to most reports, was former Confederate General Forrest. Probably this elaborate table of organization was never completely filled out, and certainly there was an almost total lack of central control of the Klan's activities. Indeed, at some point in early 1869 the Klan was officially disbanded. But even without central direction its members, like those of the Order of the White Camellia and other racist vigilante groups, continued in their plan of disrupting the new Republican regimes in the South and terrorizing their black supporters.

Along with other vigilante organizations, the Klan was an expression of the traditional racism of Southern whites. They were willing to accept the defeat of the Confederacy, and they were prepared to admit that slavery was dead; but they could not bring themselves to contemplate a society that would treat blacks and whites as equals. As a group of South Carolina whites protested to Congress in 1868: "The white people of our State will never quietly submit to negro rule. . . . We will keep up this contest until we have regained the heritage of political control handed down to us by honored ancestry. That is a duty we owe to the land that is ours, to the graves that it contains, and to the race of which you and we alike are members—the proud Caucasian race, whose sovereignty on earth God has ordained."

The appeal was shrewdly pitched, for the Southern racist knew how to reach his Northern counterpart. Joined together, their fears of men with darker skins helped to undercut the Reconstruction regimes in the South and to halt any congressional efforts at further innovative Reconstruction legislation.

Suggested Readings

The Civil War and Reconstruction (1969), by J. G. Randall and David Donald, continues to be useful, especially for its full bibliography. Three modern treatments of the postwar period are John H. Franklin, *Reconstruction after the Civil War* (1961), Kenneth M. Stampp, *The Era of Reconstruction* (1965), and Rembert W. Patrick, *The Reconstruction of the Nation* (1967).

The best account of steps taken during the Civil War to reorganize the Southern states is Herman Belz, *Reconstructing the Union* (1969). William B. Hesseltine, *Lincoln's Plan of Reconstruction* (1960), argues that Lincoln had not one but many approaches to Reconstruction, all of them unsuccessful.

Robert W. Winston, *Andrew Johnson, Plebeian and Patriot* (1928), is the best of several unsatisfactory biographies of that President. More valuable are the markedly favorable estimates of Johnson's program in George F. Milton, *The Age of Hate* (1930), and Howard K. Beale, *The Critical Year* (1930), and the strongly critical analyses in Eric L. McKitrick, *Andrew Johnson and Reconstruction* (1960), LaWanda Cox and John H. Cox, *Politics, Principle, and Prejudice* (1963), and W. R. Brock, *An American Crisis* (1963).

Four major studies of postwar constitutional changes are Harold M. Hyman, *A More Perfect Union* (1973), Stanley I. Kutler, *Judicial Power and Reconstruction Politics* (1968), William Gillette, *The Right to Vote* (1965), and Charles Fairman, *Reconstruction and Reunion* (1971).

George R. Bentley, *A History of the Freedmen's Bureau* (1955), is a standard work, but it should be supplemented by William S. McFeely, *Yankee Stepfather: General O. O. Howard and the Freedmen* (1968), and Louis S. Gerteis, *From Contraband to Freedman* (1973).

Four perceptive and sympathetic analyses of blacks' responses to emancipation are Willie Lee Rose, *Rehearsal for Reconstruction* (1964), Joel Williamson, *After Slavery* (1965), Peter Kolchin, *First Freedom* (1972), and Vernon L. Wharton, *The Negro in Mississippi* (1947).

Fred A. Shannon, *The Farmer's Last Frontier* (1945), is an excellent discussion of postwar Southern agricultural problems. There is much information on Southern economic life in E. Merton Coulter, *The South during Reconstruction* (1947), and in C. Vann Woodward, *Origins of the New South* (1951). On the alleged breakup of the plantation system, see Roger W. Shugg, *Origins of Class Struggle in Louisiana* (1939).

Two articles provide the best brief introduction to the modern interpretation of Reconstruction politics: Larry G. Kincaid, "Victims of Circumstance: An Interpretation of Changing Attitudes toward Republican Policy Makers and Reconstruction," *Journal of American History* 57 (1970), 48–66, and Michael L. Benedict, "Preserving the Constitution: The Conservative Basis of Radical Reconstruction," ibid., *61* (1974), 65–90. See also Hans L. Trefousse, *The Radical Republicans* (1969), David Donald, *The Politics of Reconstruction* (1965), and Michael L. Benedict, *A Compromise of Principle* (1974). Among the fullest biographies of Radical leaders are Fawn M. Brodie, *Thaddeus Stevens* (1959), David Donald, *Charles Sumner and the Rights of Man* (1970), and Benjamin P. Thomas and Harold M. Hyman, *Stanton* (1962).

David M. DeWitt, *Impeachment and Trial of Andrew Johnson* (1903), is the standard account, strongly pro-Johnson in tone. Michael L. Benedict's book of the same title (1973) is a useful, anti-Johnson corrective. The best explanation of why impeachment occurred when it did is to be found in Hans L. Trefousse, *Impeachment of a President* (1975).

On American racial attitudes, George M. Fredrickson, *The Black Image in the White Mind* (1971), is excellent. On Northern racism, see V. Jacque Voegeli, *Free but Not Equal* (1967), and Forrest G. Wood, *Black Scare* (1968). A thoughtful and provocative essay is C. Vann Woodward, "Seeds of Failure in Radical Race Policy," *American Philosophical Society Proceedings 110* (1966), 1–9.

On the work of the Reconstruction governments in the South, see W. E. B. DuBois, "Reconstruction and Its Benefits," *American Historical Review* (1910), 781-99, and DuBois, *Black Reconstruction* (1935). The best accounts of Reconstruction in individual states are Francis B. Simkins and Robert H. Woody, *South Carolina during Reconstruction* (1932), Jerrell H. Shofner, *Nor Is It Over Yet: Florida in the Era of Reconstruction* (1974), Thomas B. Alexander, *Political Reconstruction in Tennessee* (1950), James W. Garner, *Reconstruction in Mississippi* (1901), and Joe G. Taylor, *Louisiana Reconstructed* (1974).

On the education of blacks after the war, see Henry A. Bullock, *A History of Negro Education in the South* (1967), William P. Vaughn, *Schools for All* (1974), and Roger A. Fischer, *The Segregation Struggle in Louisiana* (1974).

Southern white resistance to the Reconstruction process is the theme of Michael Perman, *Reunion without Compromise* (1973). Allen W. Trelease, *White Terror* (1971), is a harrowing account of white vigilantism, as carried on by the Ku Klux Klan and less formally organized groups.

The American Compromise, 1865-1880

An exclusive focus on the Southern states during the postwar years obscures the fact that Reconstruction was a national, not just a sectional, process. In both sections the nationalistic impulses unleashed by the war portended revolutionary consequences. Just as some Radical Republicans sought to overturn the entire Southern social system, so other postwar nationalists yearned to expand the role of the federal government and to integrate the hitherto inverterbrate American economy. Many Northerners considered the changes introduced into their section during the Civil War and Reconstruction period as offensive and unacceptable as most white Southerners found the program of the Radical Republicans. In the South, plans for drastic social and economic change ran headlong into long-established institutions and values, so that the amount of innovation tolerated was limited. A similar fate met schemes to transform the ideas, the society, and the economy of the North and the West. Here, too, deeply rooted local and parochial interests resisted the forces of nationalism.

The resolution of this conflict was what can be called—for lack of a better phrase—"The American Compromise." The term does not refer to formal agreements or legislative enactments embossed on parchment. Instead, it embraces a whole series of loose, informal, and frequently tacit understandings that by the 1880s legitimated the broader role played by the national government and the national economy but also protected the states and local or regional economic interests. To an observer from Bismarck's recently reunited Germany, these arrangements would doubtless have seemed chaotic and incomprehensible, for, like most American solutions to difficult problems, they were entirely pragmatic and not alway logical or consistent. But, like many other such informal American agreements, the American Compromise rested upon a broad popular consensus, and it worked. This uneasy equilibrium between national and local interests, achieved by the 1880s, served for a generation as the basis for the country's social and political order.

American Nationalism

The Civil War strongly encouraged the sentiment of nationalism among Northerners. The primary Northern war aim was not to guarantee equal rights to all men nor even to end slavery; it was to preserve the Union. By that often repeated phrase, men and women of the war years meant something more than merely maintaining the country as a territorial unit. Attached to the idea of union was an almost mystical sense of the wholeness of the American people. Americans viewed themselves as a chosen people, selected to conduct an experiment in self-government, to be a test case as to the viability of democratic institutions. As Lincoln declared, the United States was nothing less than "the last, best hope of earth."

That faith in the special destiny of the United States gave courage and hope to Northerners during the darkest hours of the war. Defeats on the battlefield, properly understood, were the fire that served to burn away the dross and impurities in American life. As the Reverend Marvin R. Vincent of Troy, New York, announced: "God has been striking, and trying to make us strike at elements unfavorable to the growth of a pure democracy; and . . . he is at work, preparing in this broad land a fit stage for a last act of the mighty drama, the consummation of human civilization." A similar inspiration moved Julia Ward Howe to draw on the imagery of the Book of Revelations in composing the most powerful and popular battle hymn ever written:

> Mine eyes have seen the glory of the coming of the Lord:
> He is trampling out the vintage where the grapes of wrath are stored;
> He has loosed the fateful lightning of his terrible swift sword:
> His truth is marching on.

Northerners believed that the Union would emerge from the war more powerful, more cohesive than ever before. They expected that the United States would no longer be a confederation or a union of states but, in the fullest sense a nation. A small shift in grammar tells the whole story. Before the Civil War many politicians and writers referred to the United States in the plural, but after 1865 only a pedant or the most unreconstructed Southerner would have dreamed of saying "the United States *are*."

The word *nation* came easily now to American lips. Unlike his predecessors who generally avoided the term, Lincoln regularly referred to the United States as a nation. For example, he used the word no fewer than five times in his brief Gettysburg Address, most eloquently in the concluding pledge: ". . . that this nation, under God, shall have a new birth of freedom." In 1865 when Republicans agreed to establish a weekly journal that would reflect their views, they called it, as a matter of course, *The Nation,* and it became, as it has remained, one of the most influential periodicals in the country. In 1867 when Sumner took to the lecture circuit to supplement his senatorial salary, he chose for his topic, "Are We a Nation?" The answer, he believed, was obvious. Americans were "one people, throbbing with a common life, occupying a common territory, rejoicing in a common history, sharing in common trials." Never again should any "local claim of self-government" be permitted "for a moment [to] interfere with the supremacy of the Nation." He concluded: "Such centralization is the highest civilization, for it approaches the nearest to the heavenly example."

Political theorists as well as public men in the postwar generation exalted American nationalism. In 1865 Orestes Brownson, the former Jacksonian spokesman, published the first book-length contribution to the bibliography of American nationalism, *The American Republic: Its Constitution, Tendencies, and Destiny.* "Nations are only individuals on a larger scale," Brownson argued, and his treatise was designed to resolve the identity crisis of the Civil War by persuading the American nation to "reflect on its own constitution, its own separate existence, individuality, tendencies, and end." Even more soaring were the claims of the Reverend Elisha Mulford's *The Nation: The Foundations of Civil Order and Political Life in the United States* (1870). The nation, Mulford argued in terms of Hegelian philosophy, was a mystic body, endowed with a spirit and a majesty of its own. "The Nation," he concluded, "is a work of God in history. . . . Its vocation is from God, and its obligation is only to God."

It would be easy to believe from such statements that Americans of the post–Civil War generation, rejoicing in the newly restored unity of their country, were swept up into an ultranationalistic frenzy comparable to that of the Germans, who almost simultaneously achieved national unity under Bismarck, or of the Italians, who were being reunited under Cavour. But a moment's reflection shows the weakness of these historical parallels. After all, the federal structure of the American government survived the Civil War. The national government continued to consist of three separate centers of power, which often checked each other. If there was no further talk of secession, there was frequent invocation of state rights, and regionalism and localism did not disappear from American life. The very fact that the Reconstruction policies imposed on the conquered South were so limited in scope and so brief in duration is the best evidence that the high priests of American nationalism did not have things their own way.

Indeed, if the works of these nationalistic writers are read carefully, they convey an ambivalent message. While rejoicing in the growth of American na-

MENDING THE MAPS OF THE WORLD.

KING OF PRUSSIA—"AHA! MAD'MOISELLE! WHAT YOU THINK OF MY NEEDLE-GUN WORK?"
COLUMBIA—"WELL I THINK I CAN PRODUCE A BETTER THING WITH MY UNION SEWING-MACHINE."

"MENDING THE MAPS OF THE WORLD"

Conveniently forgetting the bloodshed of the Civil War, an American cartoonist contrasts the restoration of the American Union with Bismarck's unification of Germany. (*American Antiquarian Society.*)

tionality, Brownson warned that this could lead to "consolidation," which might result in "socialism, or centralized democracy." Nationalism, then, needed to be checked, not, as in the past, by state sovereignty, which led toward disintegration, but by state rights. One of Brownson's admirers, the able lawyer J. C. Hurd, warned even more vigorously against the dangers from a despotic national government. In *The Theory of Our National Existence* (1881), Hurd strongly endorsed national sovereignty, but he also sought liberty, under the national aegis, for the growth of localism and particularism. Too much concentration of power in Washington, he feared, might lead to another civil war; and the next time it would be truly internecine, not a contest between sections but a war of interest groups and classes that would divide the American people "as the constituent members of States, cities, towns, communes, families, and even households."

The most successful attempt to work out a political theory that would at once safeguard the gains made by American nationalism during the Civil War and also recognize the wide diversity of regional, class, and ethnic interests in American society was that of Professor Francis Lieber, whose career, appropriately enough, was a kind of epitome of the American national experience. As a lad this Prussian-born savant had wept when he saw the troops of Napoleon overrun his native land, and he had been old enough to fight against the French at Waterloo. But he had also experienced the repressive side of nationalism when the Prussian government arrested him for harboring dangerous, liberal ideas. After a disillusioning experience in the war for Greek independence, Lieber came to the United States, where he founded and edited the *Encyclopaedia Americana* (13 volumes, 1829–33). Unable to find an academic or literary position in New England, he accepted a professorship at South Carolina College (now the University of South Carolina), where he taught history and political economy. Suspected by Southerners because of his friendship for Charles Sumner and other abolitionists and distrusted by Northerners because he did not speak out against the South's peculiar institution—indeed, he even owned slaves—Lieber felt caught in the middle, and he found no escape until 1857, when he was appointed professor at Columbia College (later Columbia University) in New York. When war broke out, one of Lieber's sons joined the Confederate army and was killed in action; the other two fought for the Union, and one lost an arm at Fort Donelson.

A passionate American nationalist, Lieber did all he could to sustain the Union government during the war. Highly respected in Washington, he became an adviser to the war department, and he drafted for the guidance of the Union army General Orders No. 100, the first codification of military law ever published. Alarmed at the lack of popular support for the national government, he helped found the Union League; he was also instrumental in setting up the Loyal Publication Society, for which he and other nationalists prepared pamphlets to promote the Union cause. Lieber's wartime message was consistent: "The people are conscious that they constitute and ought to constitute a nation, with a God appointed country, the integrity of which they will not, and must not, give up, cost what it may."

But along with Lieber's exaltation of nationalism went warnings against excess. He opposed efforts of the Radical Republicans, like his friend Sumner, to permit the national government to supervise the daily activities of citizens in the South. These attempts would "run the [national] cart into such a mire that we shall be able to extricate it only by sacrificing a good deal of our best baggage." Lieber's concern became greater when he observed how Bismarck's triumphant reuniting of Germany was followed by curbs on civil liberty. The United States, he feared, might face a similar danger.

To forestall this threat, Lieber reverted to arguments that he had earlier developed in his influential book *On Civil Liberty and Self-Government*, which had gone through two editions before the war. Without disavowing his nationalism, he sought to distinguish it from centralism. "Centralism is the convergence of all the rays of power into one central point," Lieber wrote; "nationalization is the diffusion of the same life-blood through a system of arteries, throughout a body politic. . . . " Nationalism was to be encouraged, centralism to be avoided. The most effective restraint on despotism, toward which centralism tended, lay in what Lieber called Institutional Liberty. Seeing that mechanical checks and balances between the various branches of government had already proved themselves ineffectual limits on power, Lieber looked instead to organically related institutions—the family, the churches, the scientific community, the business community, the literary world, and the like—to provide "a union of harmonizing systems of laws instinct with self-government." Such "self-evolving," "interlimiting," and "inter-guaranteeing" institutions could supply "the negation of absolutism" and thus lead to "the only self-government, or self-government carried out in the realities of life."

Lieber's theory of Institutional Liberty was thus a compromise, one particularly congenial to the postwar generation. So popular was it that when Lieber died in 1872, President Theodore Dwight Woolsey of Yale willingly undertook the preparation of a new edition of *On Civil Liberty,* for he enthusiastically endorsed both Lieber's high nationalism and his fear of "a more centralized government." That ambivalence, indeed, was the special attraction of Lieber's theory. He exalted American nationalism—but encouraged autonomy for local and particularistic interests. He upheld the Union—but sought to prevent its powers from becoming despotic. His solution for the theoretically unresolvable antagonism between liberty and authority was pragmatic; he allowed Americans to eat their cake and have it.

Postwar Diplomacy

American diplomacy during the post–Civil War generation followed a pattern that Lieber undoubtedly would have approved. On the one hand, it was vigorously nationalistic, even at times bellicose; on the other, it drew back from conflict with foreign powers, and it refrained from pursuing goals strongly opposed by influential interest groups. In short, American foreign policy showed how Lieber's Institutional Liberty worked. It showed the American Compromise in action.

During the decade after Appomattox, hardly a year passed without some significant American diplomatic initiative. With President Johnson's willing acquiescence, Secretary of State Seward maneuvered skillfully to force the withdrawal of French troops from Mexico, and he tried unsuccessfully to persuade Queen Victoria's government to pay for the damages British-built Confederate cruisers inflicted on Union shipping during the war. Seward also promoted the construction of a canal across the isthmus of Panama, the annexation of all or part of Santo Domingo, the acquisition of the Danish West Indies, and the purchase of Russian North America. There was no diminution of America's outward thrust during the first five years of President Grant's administration. His able secretary of state, Hamilton Fish, succeeded in settling the Alabama claims (as the whole groups of shippers claims against Great Britain came to be called), in adjudicating the long-standing controversy between Canadians and Americans over fisheries in the North Atlantic, and in demarcating the disputed boundary between British Columbia and the state of Washington. The President himself took a deep interest in the efforts of Cuban insurgents to oust their Spanish rulers, and at one point Spain and the United States came close to war. Grant also took the lead in seeking the annexation of the Dominican Republic.

These foreign policy initiatives received considerable popular support. After Appomattox there was a general feeling that the United States, with a million seasoned veterans under arms, was in a position to humiliate the French Emperor Napoleon III, to have a showdown with John Bull, and to pick up any adjacent territory that it pleased. The old spirit of Manifest Destiny, quiescent during the war, sprang to life again. Even those who feared it anticipated its triumph. The more optimistic rejoiced in the prospect. Advocating the annexation of both Haiti and the Dominican Republic and hoping for the future acquisition of the Kingdom of Hawaii, President Johnson's 1868 annual message to Congress concluded: "The conviction is rapidly gaining ground in the American mind that with the increased facilities for intercommunication between all portions of the earth the principles of free government, as embraced in our Constitution, if faithfully maintained and carried out, would prove of sufficient strength and breadth to comprehend within their sphere and influence the civilized nations of the world."

Despite both fears and hopes, the accomplishments of American foreign policy during the Reconstruction years were few. From the point of view of national security the most important feat was Seward's success in getting French troops

THE LAST ACT OF THE MONROE DOCTRINE

Reflecting exuberant postwar American nationalism, this artist in 1866 predicts the simultaneous expulsion of the French (personified by an effete Emperor Maximilian) from Mexico and of the British (represented by a corpulent John Bull) from Canada. (*American Antiquarian Society.*)

removed from Mexico. Introduced into Mexico during the Civil War, ostensibly to compel the bankrupt Mexican government of President Benito Juarez to pay its debts, French troops in 1864 provided the support for the installation of the Archduke Maximilian of Austria as emperor of Mexico. Unable to do more than protest against this violation of the Monroe Doctrine while the war was going on, Seward adopted a more vigorous tone after Appomattox. Yet, knowing the French emperor was a proud and volatile man, he refrained from direct threats and allowed Napoleon to discover for himself how expensive, unpopular, and unsuccessful his Mexican adventure was proving. By 1867 Napoleon finally decided to cut off further financial support for Maximilian's shaky regime and, under steady American pressure, withdrew his troops. Captured by Juarez's troops, Maximilian was shot by a firing squad on June 19, 1867. Never again would a European power so openly challenge the Monroe Doctrine.

A second diplomatic achievement of the Reconstruction years was the settlement of the Alabama claims. Immediately after the war it probably would have been possible to clear up this controversy speedily and inexpensively, had not the British government haughtily denied that it had violated international law in permitting Confederate raiders to be built in its shipyards. With delay, American grievances festered. Sumner, the powerful chairman of the Senate Committee on Foreign Relations, began to argue that the British owed not merely repayment for actual damages done by the *Alabama* and other vessels; they were also responsible for protracting the war, for the "immense and infinite" cost of the entire last two years of the conflict. The failure of Reverdy Johnson, Seward's special envoy to Great Britain, to secure an apology or expression of regret from the stubborn British government further exacerbated American feelings. Not until after Hamilton Fish took charge of the American State Department and not until after there was a change of government in Great Britain could a settlement be worked out. In the Treaty of Washington of 1871 Great Britain admitted negligence in permitting the Confederate cruisers to escape and expressed regret for the damages they had caused; and the United States tacitly abandoned the extravagant claims put forward by Sumner and agreed that the amount of damages should be assessed by a commission of arbitration representing five nations. Ultimately damages to American shipping were estimated at $15.5 million and the British government paid this amount. More important than any monetary settlement was the precedent set for arbitrating international disputes, and the Treaty of Washington paved the way for the rapprochement of the two greatest English-speaking nations. Not until the two world wars of the twentieth century would the full consequences of this development emerge.

Apart from the almost unnoticed American occupation of the Midway Islands in August 1867, the sole territorial acquisition of the United States during the Reconstruction era—and it was a very considerable addition—was the purchase of Alaska. There was little public enthusiasm for Seward's 1867 treaty to buy Russian America for $7.2 million. Newspapers called the territory "a national

RUSSIAN AMERICA — CANVASSING
THE STATE TICKET

Critics of the purchase of Alaska in
1867 called the Russian territory
"Seward's Icebox" or Andrew Johnson's
"Polar Bear Garden." (*American
Antiquarian Society.*)

icehouse" consisting of nothing but "walrus-covered icebergs." Congressmen were
equally unenthusiastic. Yet after much grumbling the Senate finally ratified the
treaty and the House reluctantly appropriated the money for the purchase.
Seward's success was due in part to his ability to convince senators that Alaska
had vast hidden natural resources; in part it was due to the judicious payments of
money to American congressmen by the Russian minister in Washington. More
influential than either of these factors, however, was the general feeling that
rejecting the treaty would alienate Czar Alexander II, who alone of the important European rulers had been sympathetic to the Union cause during the
Civil War.

Nothing came of the other postwar plans for expansion. Each of them ran into
snags that made American diplomats draw back. For instance, the desire of many
United States politicians, including Grant, Fish, and Sumner, to annex Canada
had to be abandoned when it became clear that the British would not withdraw
a fight. Grant's plan to acquire the Dominican Republic aroused the opposition
of Sumner, who considered himself the senatorial voice of the blacks and wanted
the island of Santo Domingo to become not an American possession but the center
of "a free confederacy [of the West Indies], in which the black race should predominate." Seward's treaty for the purchase of the Danish West Indies was
pigeonholed by the Senate when those unfortunate islands were visited by a
hurricane, a tidal wave, and a series of earthquake shocks.

It would, however, be a mistake to put too much stress on these idiosyncratic
factors that stopped American expansion, for there were broader forces at work.
The American people, exhausted by four years of fighting, were not prepared to
support a vigorously nationalistic foreign policy if it threatened another war.

Northern businessmen felt that it was more important to reduce taxes and to return to a sound monetary policy than to engage in foreign adventures. Because of the difficulties of racial adjustment in the South, increasing numbers of politicians hesitated before agreeing to annex additional populations of dark-skinned inhabitants. During Johnson's administration, many Republicans opposed all Seward's plans for expansion because they might bring credit to that unpopular President. During Grant's tenure, disaffected Republicans, who by 1872 joined the Liberal Republican party and opposed Grant's reelection, had similar motives for blocking his diplomatic schemes. So powerful were these combined elements of opposition that after 1874 there was little further talk of a vigorous nationalistic foreign policy or of American expansionism.

American foreign policy during the Reconstruction generation, then, illustrates the operation of Lieber's principle of Institutional Liberty. On issues that clearly touched the national security, those that affected the existence of the nation itself —such as the presence of French troops in Mexico and the difficulties with Great Britain that might have resulted in war—there was a consensus sufficiently strong to permit the national government to act. Even the purchase of Alaska, which seemed to involve the friendship between the United States and the powerful Russian empire, fell into this category. But where there was no clear, overriding national interest, local, sectional, racial, and class objections to expansion prevailed. Though Presidents and secretaries of state might fume, there was a tacit agreement that the wishes of these minorities must be respected. To use Lieber s phraseology, American foreign policy during the postwar years was an expression of nationalism but a rejection of centralism.

Toward a National Economy

The years immediately following the Civil War witnessed an enormous boom in the American economy. Except for the South, still recovering from the ravages of war, every region of the country prospered during the eight years after Appomattox. Except for the merchant marine, which never recovered from the damages inflicted by Confederate raiders, every branch of commerce, industry, and agriculture flourished.

The age was an expansive one, and Americans rushed to settle vast tracts of hitherto uninhabited land in the West. In 1860 the western frontier of settlement lay near the Missouri River, and between eastern Kansas and California there were hardly any white inhabitants except in the Mormon settlement in Utah and in the Spanish-speaking community at Santa Fe. Thirty years later, immigrants pushing west into the Great Plains and Rocky Mountain region and pushing east from California formed a virtually uninterrupted pattern of settlement across the continent. In 1890 the superintendent of the United States census announced— a bit prematurely—that the frontier was gone: "Up to and including 1880 the country had a frontier settlement, but at present the unsettled area has been so broken into by isolated bodies of settlement that there can hardly be said to be a frontier line."

To some extent the peopling of the West was triggered by the passage in 1862 of the Homestead Act, which offered free of charge to any citizen who was over 21 or the head of a family 160 acres of public lands if he resided on them for five continuous years. As an alternative, a homesteader could purchase his land from the government for $1.25 an acre after six months' residence. Between 1862 and 1900 about 400,000 families received free homesteads under this program, but the dream that free public land would siphon off industrial workers from the overcrowded cities of the East was not realized. Very few urban artisans could afford to transport themselves and their families to the frontier, pay the necessary fees at the land office, to construct a cabin, to purchase the necessary tools and seeds, and buy food during the long growing season before the wheat or corn was harvested. Even fewer knew how to farm. Consequently the great majority of homesteaders were men and women who had spent all their earlier years on the land. Even experience was no guarantee of success, for fully two-thirds of all homestead claimants before 1890 failed at the venture.

Most settlers in the West did not stake claims under the Homestead Act but continued, as they had always done, to purchase land directly from the government. Thousands more bought land from the railroad companies, which received from state and national governments enormous tracts of land, equal to more than twice the acreage made available to homesteaders. For instance, Congress gave the Union Pacific and the Central Pacific lines ten square miles of public land for every mile of track completed in the states, twenty square miles for every mile built in the territories.

However Western settlers secured their land titles, they looked to the national government to protect their farms from the Indians, about 225,000 of whom roamed the Great Plains and Rocky Mountains. In the north the Sioux, Arapaho, Cheyenne, and Nez Percé were the most powerful tribes; to the south the most warlike were the Comanches, Apaches, and Utes. Intrepid and hardy, the braves of all these tribes were fine horsemen and superb marksmen; they were exceedingly dangerous foes of the whites who penetrated their territory to build railroad lines, to mine for gold, or to farm. Hostilities between white settlers and Plains Indians, which broke out during the Civil War, continued almost without interruption for a quarter of a century, with the most barbarous atrocities committed by both sides. After the war, the army slowly but ineluctably forced the tribes into ever smaller reservations. Some desperately resisted, as did the Sioux led by Sitting Bull and Crazy Horse, who tried to keep the Black Hills, their tribal holy grounds, from spoliation by gold miners. In 1876, when the army attempted to disperse the Sioux, the Indians succeeded in massacring the whole force of 264 officers and men commanded by the dashing, golden-haired Civil War hero, George A. Custer, at Little Big Horn. Such Indian successes were, however, at best temporary, for the army ultimately subdued such great tribal leaders as Chief Red Cloud of the Sioux, Chief Joseph of the Nez Percé, and Geronimo of the Apaches. The final victory of the white settlers was symbolized in the Dawes Act of 1887, which allotted the lands within the still further restricted Indian reservations in 160-acre parcels to Indian residents and thus anticipated an end of the traditional Indian tribal relationship. The West, it was clear, would belong to the white settlers, whose numbers were mounting astronomically.

Indeed, the whole country was growing at a fantastic pace. During the decade

WAGON TRAIN CROSSING THE PLAINS DURING THE 1870S

For able-bodied single men a pack train was the most efficient way of moving West. But for families, undertaking a trip that might last from three to five months, a wagon train was more practicable. The covered wagon, or prairie schooner, usually pulled by oxen, had iron tires four inches wide and held up to 7,000 pounds. Such a wagon allowed a family to bring along its cherished possessions, and it also offered a place where the pregnant mother could rest, the children could sleep, or a sick member of the family could recuperate. (*University of Washington.*)

CHIEF JOSEPH OF THE NEZ PERCÉ

After white squatters committed
repeated outrages upon the Nez
Percé Indians, Chief Joseph was
reluctantly drawn into hostilities
with the United States army.
Realizing that he could not cope
with the whites' superior manpower and firepower, he led his
people in a brilliantly executed
retreat toward the safety of the
Canadian border. In October 1877,
only thirty miles from his
destination, he was cornered,
besieged, and defeated.
(*Smithsonian Institute.*)

from the end of the Civil War to 1876, when the Republic celebrated its centennial
year, the population of the United States jumped by 30 percent, from 35.7 million to 46.1 million. During these same years more than 3 million immigrants,
mostly from Europe, poured into the country. Railroad mileage increased by 111
percent during the decade, the number of bushels of corn by 100 percent, and
production of bituminous coal by 163 percent. Almost no American steel was
manufactured at the end of the war; 390,000 tons were made ten years later.

This phenomenal rate of growth fostered a tendency to consolidate the American economy into one huge functional unit. This had been the dream of some
businessmen long before the war, but after 1865 for the first time the necessary
preconditions for economic integration existed. Never before had the United
States had a national currency, and earlier businessmen had been obliged to
settle their obligations with an assortment of state bank notes, local script, and
coin; but passage of the National Banking Act of 1864 created a uniform circulating medium. Banks chartered by the national government were allowed, in return for purchasing government bonds, to issue the new national bank notes
supplied by the federal comptroller of the currency. A tax placed on state bank

notes in 1865 ensured that these national bank notes would thereafter have no competition.

For the first time, too, the United States after 1865 was bound together by a modern communications network. Before the Civil War, a number of rival telegraph companies had been constructing lines but their efforts had been sporadic and uncoordinated. Thanks in part to the extensive military use of the telegraph during the war, the Western Union Telegraph Company grew strong enough to absorb smaller rivals, extended a line across the continent to San Francisco, and secured a virtual monopoly in the field. Western Union made it possible for a citizen in almost any part of the country to communicate almost instantaneously with his fellows in any other part of the reunited nation. After Alexander Graham Bell invented the telephone in the 1870s, and particularly after he demonstrated the miraculous ability to transmit the human voice by electrical current at the great Centennial Exhibition at Philadelphia in 1876, a second communications network appeared. By the 1880s most city physicians

SIOUX INDIAN ENCAMPMENT, DAKOTA TERRITORY, 1891

The Sioux, led by such chiefs as Crazy Horse and Sitting Bull, fiercely resisted white settlement of the northern Great Plains. *(Library of Congress.)*

A BRIGHT, HEALTHFUL SKIN AND COMPLEXION ENSURED BY USING PEARS' SOAP. Recommended as "A BALM FOR THE SKIN" by the greatest English Authorities on the Skin, Prof. Sir ERASMUS WILSON, F. R. S., L. L. D., Pres. of the Royal Col. of Surgeons, England, and other eminent men. COUNTLESS BEAUTEOUS LADIES, INCLUDING Mrs. LILLIE LANGTRY, M'lle ADELINA PATTI, Miss MAY FORTESCUE, and others praise its virtues and prefer Pears' Soap to any other, which is the purest and best for the skin and the most economical in use. This Soap has been established in London nearly 100 years and has received 15 International Awards. The Proprietors, Messrs. A. & F. Pears, are Soapmakers by sealed appointment to H.R.H., The Prince of Wales.

PEARS SOAP ADVERTISEMENT, 1887

The completion of a national system of transportation and communication encouraged the sale of nationally known, brand-name products. One of the first of these was Pears Soap, the nationally circulated advertisements for which managed simultaneously to titillate and to convey the impression of purity and cleanliness. *(Culver Pictures.)*

had telephones, and during President Hayes's administration an instrument was installed in the White House. The telephone was still such a novelty that, when it rang, the President himself was likely to pick up the receiver.

An improved transportation network also cemented the nation together. A transcontinental railroad, long advocated but repeatedly postponed because of sectional controversies, received the support of Congress in 1862, when it incorporated the Union Pacific Railroad Company. Financed by vast tracts of public lands, the Union Pacific began constructing a line from western Iowa to join the Central Pacific Railroad, which was pushing eastward from San Francisco. In 1869 the two roads met at Promontory Point, Utah, and it became possible to move passengers and freight by rail from the Atlantic Ocean to the Pacific. Less dramatic but more economically significant was the simultaneous coordination and consolidation of rail lines in more settled areas. Before the Civil War, there had been eleven different rail gauges in use on northern roads; President Lincoln's choice of the 4-foot 8½-inch gauge for the Union Pacific led to the standardization of all roads at this width. Before the war, rail travel from New York to Chicago had been barely possible by using eight or ten independent lines, with repeated transfers. In 1869, Commodore Vanderbilt consolidated the New York Central and the Hudson River railroads to give continuous service from New York to Buffalo, and five years later he completed arrangements with western railroads to offer through service to Chicago. At about the same time the Pennsylvania Railroad, the Erie Railroad, and the Baltimore and Ohio Railroad also completed connections with Chicago.

A national communications and transportation network encouraged businessmen to seek national markets for their products. Business consolidation, already under way before the war, proceeded rapidly, and a striking number of new entrepreneurs—"robber barons," as later critics called them—were men whose wartime experience had taught them the advantages of technological innovation and large-scale management. For instance, Andrew Carnegie, who came to the United States as a poor Scottish immigrant and trained himself to become a skilled telegraph operator, served during the war as aide to Thomas A. Scott, the assistant secretary of war in charge of all government railroads and transportation lines. From this vantage point, Carnegie shrewdly foresaw the postwar expansion and reorganization of the railway system, and he invested his early savings in the company that owned the patents for Pullman sleeping cars. When these cars became standard equipment on railroads, Carnegie was on his way to acquiring his huge fortune, with which he subsequently helped build the steel industry in the United States.

John D. Rockefeller, the pious young Baptist from Cleveland, Ohio, got his start through handling wartime government contracts for hay, grain, meat, and other commodities. Quickly he learned how a company that was managed with order and enterprise could drive inefficient competitors out of business, and he decided to apply this lesson to the new petroleum industry. Astutely recognizing that the way to dominate the industry was to control the refining process, Rockefeller in 1863 constructed the largest refinery in Cleveland, and two years later he built a second one. His brother, William, developed the Eastern and the export market for their products. Enlisting Harry M. Flagler as a partner in 1867, Rockefeller worked systematically to cut costs and to rationalize an industry hitherto unstandardized and intensely competitive. By 1870, Rockefeller's company, Standard Oil of Ohio, made its own barrels, built its own warehouses, and owned its own fleet of tankers. Because of the volume of his business, Rockefeller was able to force the railroads to give his firm lower rates, or rebates, on all his shipments. Then, as his power grew, he compelled the railroads to turn over to Standard Oil "draw-backs," or a portion of what other oil companies had to pay in the way of freight. As a consequence of these business practices, which were at once shrewd and unscrupulous, Standard Oil by 1880 controlled 95 percent of the refining business of the country and practically all the transportation of oil in the United States, whether by pipeline or railroad.

While businesses that operated on a nationwide scale were emerging, so was a national labor movement. There were several attempts to organize labor on a national scale. One of the earliest was the eight-hour movement, led by Ira Steward, a Boston machinist, who sought legislation to limit the work day to eight hours without reduction of wages. Under this pressure the United States established an eight-hour day for its employees in 1868, and legislatures in six states passed acts to make eight hours a legal day's work. In private industry these laws proved ineffectual because they instituted the eight-hour restriction only "where there is no special contract or agreement to the contrary." Consequently most businessmen required employees to agree to work longer hours as a condition of employment.

The National Labor Union, created in 1866 at a Baltimore conference of delegates from various unions, proved little more successful. It was headed by William H. Sylvis, a dedicated propagandist and a superb speaker, whose interests, however, were not in conventional labor issues like hours and wages but in cooperatives and currency reform. Sylvis recruited many members for the National Labor Union—it claimed 640,000 in 1868—but whether these were

SPECIMEN DIAL FOR MECHANICSVILLE TOWN HALL—HANDS EMPLOYED TO WORK EIGHT HOURS ONLY

The eight-hour movement was the most popular of the early postwar labor reform drives. Its slogan was: "Eight hours work a day leaves eight for sleep and eight for play." (*American Antiquarian Society.*)

actual workingmen is questionable. A scornful observer remarked that the National Labor Union was made up of "labor leaders without organizations, politicians without parties, women without husbands, and cranks, visionaries, and agitators without jobs." After Sylvis's death in 1869, the organization began to decline, and it disappeared during the depression of 1873.

A more successful labor movement was the Knights of Labor, founded in 1869 by Uriah Stevens and other garment workers of Philadelphia. It grew slowly at first and, like the National Labor Union, received a serious setback in the depression. By the 1880s, however, its membership increased in a spectacular fashion as it attempted to create a broad union of all workingmen, skilled and unskilled. But its leadership, like that of the National Labor Union, was averse to discussing hours, wages, and working conditions and was reluctant to call strikes. After 1879, the General Master Workman of the Knights of Labor was the idealistic, eloquent, and neurasthenic Irishman Terence V. Powderly, who preferred to think of himself as the head of a national educational institution rather than of a labor union. Indeed, Powderly never behaved like a labor leader but, as an analyst has said, "acted more like Queen Victoria at a national Democratic convention." Consequently, size failed to bring strength to the Knights of Labor, and until the organization of the American Federation of Labor in 1886 there was no national organization that could rightfully claim to speak for the labor movement.

While industry was expanding to reach a national market, other segments of the economy were becoming integrated into the national system. In the post-Civil War years a huge Western range-cattle industry became the prime supplier of beef for the East, and also for Europe. Even before the Civil War, cattle raising had become a major occupation in the Great Plains area, stretching from Texas to Canada. There hardy cattle, descendants of Mexican longhorns, fed on open ranges. At yearly roundups calves were branded so that their owners could identify them, and cowboys selected the strongest steers for the long drive east. Since the war cut off markets for Texas cattle, herds became uncomfortably large, and as soon as peace was restored Texas cattlemen renewed their annual drive of cattle at an unprecedented scale. Initially these vast herds headed for the railhead at Sedalia, Missouri, where they could be transported to Chicago, Saint Louis, and other Eastern markets, but when the Kansas Pacific Railroad reached Abilene, Kansas, in 1867, cattlemen found a shorter, safer route to market. From Texas alone, 35,000 head of cattle came to the new railhead in its first year of operation; 350,000 in 1869; and 700,000 in 1871. Thereafter, as the national rail network extended farther west, Wichita and Dodge City came to rival, if not to replace, Abilene. These were rowdy frontier towns, where the cowboys, black as well as white, lonely after long months on the range, could let off steam in the dance halls, the saloons, and the red-light districts. But these cattle towns also served a basic economic function by tying the range cattle industry into the national economy.

TRANSPORT OF TEXAS BEEF ON THE KANSAS-PACIFIC RAILWAY,
ABILENE

Beginning in 1867 Abilene, Kansas, became the principal
railhead to which Texas ranchers brought their long-horn
cattle, after the long drive, for shipment to the East. By
1871 1,460,000 head of cattle were shipped out of Abilene.
(*Library of Congress.*)

Farmers, too, became part of that national network in the postwar era. The first few years after the war were boom times for Northern and Western farmers. With the growth of American cities, the domestic demand for grain constantly increased, and at the same time Great Britain was becoming more dependent on American harvests. By 1880, for the first time, the value of American wheat and flour exports nearly equaled that of exported cotton.

Heartened by rising prices, Northern and Western farmers expanded their operations. Using new and improved farm machinery, such as Cyrus Hall McCormick's reaping machine, they were able to cultivate and harvest large crops with fewer workers. Since this machinery was expensive and since it operated best on large, level tracts of land, small, self-sufficient farmers, chronically short of cash, were at a disadvantage. The future seemed to belong to large producers, and confident Western farmers went heavily into debt to buy more land and better machines. More than in any previous era they were now tied into a national market economy. Their fortunes depended not alone on the land, the weather, and their efforts, but on the grain elevators, the railroads, and the national and international markets.

Tariff and Currency Controversies

The movement toward a national economy in the post-Civil War decades encountered opposition. It rapidly became evident that complete integation could be achieved only at enormous economic, social, and psychological costs. Not even the business interests of the Northeast, which tended to be the primary beneficiaries of a national economic system, were unanimously in favor of integration. If New York City grew because of the increasingly centralized financial and transportation networks, that growth was at the expense of such former rivals as Boston and Philadelphia. If Standard Oil benefited by Rockefeller's rationalization of the refining industry, hundreds of less successful oil men were forced into failure. If mass production of nails at Andrew Carnegie's massive J. Edgar Thompson steel mill made building construction cheaper and safer, it also cost local blacksmiths and ironmongers their markets.

These tensions within the business community rarely surfaced as issues of public policy to be settled in the political arena. During the Gilded Age—so called from the novel by Mark Twain and Charles Dudley Warner depicting the boom-and-bust speculative mentality of businessmen of the post–Civil War era and the willing complaisance of the politicos who served their interests—almost everyone agreed that the role of government, and especially of the national government, in economic life should be minimal. In only two principal fields was it considered proper for the national government to act in a way that affected the economy: the tariff and the currency. Disagreements among business interests were therefore usually voiced in connection with these two endlessly troublesome, highly technical questions, so complex that only a handful of congressmen fully understood them.

The tariff was rarely debated in terms of free trade versus protection. Except for a few doctrinaire economic theorists, virtually everybody recognized that some tariff barrier was needed to protect some American industries. The debates in Congress revolved about which industries and how much protection. At the end of the Civil War the high tariffs of the war period, enacted in part to protect heavily taxed American industry from untaxed foreign competition, were clearly out of date.

Seeking some reasonable compromise, the New England economist David A. Wells, who was appointed Special Commissioner of the Revenue in 1866, drafted a bill to reduce duties upon imported raw materials such as scrap iron, coal, and lumber, to eliminate arbitrary and unnecessary duties on items like chemicals and spices, and to lower slightly duties on most manufactured articles. Virtually all lawmakers admitted the theoretical excellence of Wells's bill—and virtually all opposed the provisions that lessened or removed protection for their own constitutents' businesses. Consequently Wells's bill was defeated, and during the next fifteen years there was no general revision of the tariff legislation.

The absence of general tariffs acts did not mean that discussion of tariff rates

PIONEER RUN, 1865

The discovery of petroleum in western Pennsylvania led to
its rapid and wasteful exploitation. Not more than one well
out of twenty was properly sunk and carefully managed.
(*American Petroleum Institute.*)

was at an end. To the contrary, there was throughout the period an endless pulling and hauling between economic interests that stood to gain or lose from
changes in duties on specific imported items. For example, during the war a considerable copper industry had grown up in Boston and Baltimore that smelted
and refined Chilean ore, which paid a very low tariff duty. But in the late 1860s,
the great copper mines around Lake Superior began to be worked on a large
scale, and their owners asked Congress to protect their product by raising duties
on imported ore. After sharp disagreement, in which President Johnson took the
side of the refiners and most congressional Republicans the side of the ore producers, the tariff on copper ore was increased in 1869 to a point at which most of
the Eastern smelting firms had to go out of business.

Other tariff changes were the consequence of combined efforts by the producers and processors of raw materials. An 1867 act revising the duties on raw
wool and on woolen cloth was drafted at a convention of wool producers and
manufacturers at Syracuse, and it was lobbied through Congress by the indefatigable and effective secretary of the Wool Manufacturers' Association, John
L. Hayes.

Some of the minor adjustments made in the tariff during the postwar years
reflected political pressures. In a general way Republicans, with some notable
exceptions, tended to favor high protective tariffs, and Democrats, especially

PETROLEUM GALLOP

Petroleum seized the American imagination. Poets waxed rhapsodic about the soft kerosene light that was weaving a "golden web" over all America. The refrain of a popular song was "Oil on the Brain." The cover of this sheet music, by the pseudonymous "Oily Gammon"—i.e., bacon—captures the frenetic spirit of the oil fields. *(American Antiquarian Society.)*

those in the South who needed foreign markets for their cotton, wanted to reduce duties. But the issue was rarely clear-cut, for Democrats in manufacturing states like Pennsylvania were high-tariff men. Moreover, both parties tinkered with the tariff issue at election time. In 1872, for instance, the Republican party faced a split, when many tariff reformers in the Liberal Republican movement were preparing to join the Democrats. Attempting to check the bolt, the Republican-dominated Congress rushed through a bill reducing all duties by 10 percent. Once Grant was triumphantly reelected, the Congress promptly repealed the reduction. Again in 1883, when it seemed likely that in the next election Democrats would elect Grover Cleveland President and would win majorities in both houses of Congress, Republicans hurriedly enacted the first general tariff act since the Civil War. They claimed that it reduced duties by an average of 5 percent, but in fact the measure was so complex and so contradictory that nobody could predict its impact. John L. Hayes, now president of the United States Tariff Commission, gave the secret away when he explained, shortly after the passage of the 1883 act: "In a word, the object was *protection through reduction.* . . . We wanted the tariff to be made by our friends."

The whole complex history of tariff legislation during the Gilded Age, then, demonstrates the continuing strength of the highly nationalistic impulse toward protectionism. At the same time it shows how powerful regional and economic interests adversely affected by excessively high duties were able to secure concessions that gave relief without compromising the general protective framework.

The debate over currency during the post–Civil War generation was more complex, but in general it illustrates the same point. Unless a historian is prepared to write a book about these monetary issues, perhaps he ought to confine his account to two sentences: During the generation after the Civil War there was constant controversy between those who wished to continue, or even to expand, the inflated wartime money supply and those who wanted to contract the currency. Most debtors favored inflation, since it would allow them to pay debts in money less valuable than when they borrowed it; and creditors favored contraction, so that the money they received in payment of debts would be more valuable than when it was loaned.

But those two sentences, accurate enough in a general way, fail to convey the full dimensions of the controversy. They make the whole argument seem a purely economic question of profit and loss. In fact, for many people the resumption of specie payments—that is, the redemption of the paper money issued by the United States government in gold, at face value—involved the sanctity of contracts, the reliability of the government's pledges, and the rights of private property. Indeed, the return to the gold standard seemed to have almost a religious significance. Probably most economists of the period shared the conviction of Hugh McCulloch, Johnson's secretary of the treasury, that "gold and silver are the only true measure of value. . . . I have myself no more doubt that these metals were prepared by the Almighty for this very purpose, than I have that iron and coal were prepared for the purposes for which they are being used." On the other hand, the advocates of so-called soft money argued that it was downright un-American to drive greenbacks out of circulation and return to the gold standard. "Why," asked the promoter Jay Cooke, "should this Grand and Glorious Country be stunted and dwarfed—its activities chilled and its very life blood curdled—by these miserable 'hard coin' theories, the musty theories of a bygone age?"

That two-sentence summary also ignores the fact that the currency controversy involved economic interests falling into more sophisticated categories than debtors and creditors. Merchants in foreign trade were ardent supporters of resumption because fluctuations in the gold value of United States paper money made the business of these importers and exporters a game of chance. On the other hand, many American manufacturers, especially iron makers, were stanch foes of resumption because they needed an inflated currency to keep their national markets expanding.

Finally, that two-sentence summary does not indicate that attitudes toward these monetary policies changed over time. Throughout the postwar period farmers were mostly debtors, but they were primarily concerned with such issues as railroad regulation and until 1870 showed little interest in the currency. Creditor interests of the Northeast were indeed mostly supporters of resumption, but when the depression began, they unsuccessfully urged President Grant to sign a so-called Inflation Bill of 1874, which would have slightly increased the amount of paper money in circulation. In other words, they preferred mild inflation to economic collapse. Moreover, by the late 1870s, inflationists were no longer calling for additional greenbacks; instead, they joined forces with Western mining interests to demand that the government expand the currency by coining silver dollars. When they discovered that, partly by oversight, partly by plan, the Coinage Act of 1873 had discontinued the minting of silver, they were outraged. Protesting the "Crime of '73," they demanded a return to bimetallism (both gold and silver being accepted in lawful payment of all debts) and the free and unlimited coinage of silver dollars.

With so many opposing forces at work, it is scarcely surprising that the history of currency policy and financial legislation in the postwar years is one of sudden fits and starts. Right after the war, Secretary McCulloch assumed that everybody wanted to return to specie payments promptly, and, as a means of raising the value of the paper currency, he quietly sequestered greenbacks paid into the United States treasury for taxes and for public lands. His mild contraction of the currency checked business expansion, and Congress forced him to desist. Subsequently the sequestered greenbacks were reissued, and in the total amount of $382 million they remained in circulation for the next decade.

In an indirect fashion, the currency became an issue in the presidential election of 1868. During the previous year, what became known as the Ohio Idea gained popularity in the Middle West. Critics of hard money objected to the government's practice of paying interest on the national debt in gold—which was, of course, much more valuable than greenbacks. Since the bonds had been purchased with greenbacks, they argued, it would be entirely legal and proper to pay their interest in the same depreciated currency. In this way the crushing burden of the national debt on the taxpayer would be reduced. So attractive was this argument that the Democratic national convention incorporated a version of the Ohio Idea in its 1868 platform, but it negated this move by nominating Governor Horatio Seymour of New York, an earnest hard-money man, for President. The Republican national convention, against the wishes of many Western delegates, sternly rejected the Ohio Idea, and Grant was nominated with a pledge to reject "all forms of repudiation as a national crime.'

Despite this commitment, Grant's administrations witnessed the completion of a series of compromises on currency. The new President announced that he favored a return to the gold standard; but at the same time he warned: "Immediate resumption, if practicable, would not be desirable. It would compel the debtor class to pay, beyond their contracts, the premium on gold . . . and would bring bankruptcy and ruin to thousands.' But, lest anyone think that this last statement meant he desired further issues of paper money, Grant vetoed the Inflation Bill of 1874, against the advice of many of his advisers.

It was within this broad policy of affirmation checked by negation that John

Sherman, the Senate expert on finance, persuaded Congress in 1875 to pass the Resumption Act, announcing the intention of the United States government to redeem its paper money at face value in gold on or after January 1, 1879. Ostensibly a victory for hard-money interests, the act was, in fact, a brilliant compromise. It did commit the United States to resumption—but only after a delay of four years. Sherman sweetened this pill for the silver mining interests by providing that "as rapidly as practicable" silver coins would be minted to replace the "fractional currency"—notes of postage-stamp size in 3, 5, 10, 15, 25, and 50-cent denominations—issued during the war. To placate the greenback interests in the South and West, Sherman's measure made it easier to incorporate national banks, which had the right to issue treasury notes, in those regions.

Though attempts were made after 1875 to repeal the Resumption Act, it was such a carefully constructed compromise that they all failed. Sherman, who became Secretary of the Treasury in President Hayes s cabinet, skillfully managed the transition in 1879 so that resumption took place without fanfare and without economic disturbance. The whole controversy over currency during the Gilded Age was thus another illustration of the kind of compromises Americans of this generation worked out. The national policy of resumption, desired by most businessmen and needed if the United States was to play a part in world trade, was sustained; but local business interests were able to delay and modify implementation of the policy so that it did not impose too sudden or heavy a burden on groups adversely affected by hard money.

Discontent among Farmers and Laborers

If the emergence of a national economy produced strains within the business community, it created severe problems for farmers and laborers, who felt that they were not fairly sharing its rewards. Discontent became vocal first among farmers. Even in the buoyant years immediately after the Civil War, the life of the Northern and Western farmer was often lonely and dull. On the western plains, where farmers lived miles from stores, schools, and churches, where there were often no near neighbors, and where there was no regular mail service, even the prosperous lived stunted lives. Perhaps farm women felt the isolation even more deeply than the men.

In an effort to remedy these problems, Oliver Hudson Kelley, a clerk in the United States Department of Agriculture, in 1867 founded a secret society called the Patrons of Husbandry. Kelley, who had lived in Massachusetts, Iowa, and Minnesota and who had traveled extensively in the South after the war, knew at first hand the bleakness and the deprivation of rural living, and he wanted to give farmers all over the country a broader vision and a livelier social and intellectual life. The Patrons of Husbandry was intended to stimulate farmers thinking through lectures, debates, and discussions, and it was designed to promote a sense of social solidarity through group singing, picnics, and other family entertainment. Each local unit of Kelley's society was called a Grange, and women as well as men belonged as equal members. So new was the whole idea to American farmers that the organization got off to a slow start, and at the end of 1868 only ten Granges had been established.

In the following year, when the price of farm commodities dropped sharply, agrarian discontent mounted, and by the mid-1870s about 800,000 farmers, mostly in the Middle West and South, joined the Granger movement. Though the Granges never abandoned their social and intellectual objectives, the meetings came increasingly to focus on economic issues important to farmers, such as the declining price of wheat and the mounting costs of railroad transportation. Forbidden by the constitution of the Patrons of Husbandry to engage in politics, the Grangers found it easy after the recital of the Grange litany and the standard literary or musical program to move that the meeting be adjourned; then, technically no longer Grangers but simply farmers gathered together, they discussed politics and endorsed candidates who favored the farmers' cause.

That cause embraced a variety of discontents with the operations of the national economy. Farmers in Iowa, Nebraska, and Kansas complained that it took

The Patrons of Husbandry (the Grange) had a double function. Officially the organization was designed to promote better methods of agriculture and to improve the social and intellectual life of farmers. Unofficially Grangers often supported independent political candidates pledged to regulate rates charged by railroads and grain elevators. (*American Antiquarian Society.*)

The Granger at Home.   The Granger abroad.

the value of one bushel of corn to pay the freight charges for shipping another bushel to Eastern markets; farmers in Minnesota and Dakota said the same of wheat. Middle Western farmers protested the policy of the grain elevators, used to store their wheat and corn until it could be picked up for rail shipment. Elevator operators frequently misgraded grain, offering the farmer with superior produce only the price for a lower grade, and the farmer usually had to accept, for he could not dump his grain on the ground. Southern and Western farmers also objected to the limited bank credit available in their regions. When the national banking system was set up, the war was still going on, and no provision was made for establishing national banks in the South. In the West there were few national banks because Congress required a minimum capital of $50,000, which few Western towns could raise. Consequently, the circulation of national bank notes, and hence the availability of loans, were grossly inequitable. Connecticut alone had more national bank notes in circulation than Michigan, Wisconsin, Iowa, Minnesota, Kansas, Missouri, Kentucky, and Tennessee.

Farmers dissatisfaction with the national economy blended into a more general pattern of Middle Western discontent. It was not farmers alone who objected to high and discriminatory railroad rates; businessmen in Middle Western cities and towns, especially those served by only one rail line, also protested. Because the railroads set rates that favored large grain terminals, wheat produced twenty miles from Milwaukee might be diverted to Chicago. Because railroads gave special preference to long-distance shippers, lumber merchants in Clinton, Iowa, found that Chicago lumber dealers could undersell them; trainloads of lumber rumbled in from Chicago on the way to central and western Iowa without even slowing down at Clinton. The inequities in the national banking system affected Western businessmen at least as much as they did farmers, for the absence of credit crippled business expansion in the South and West.

Out of these general Western grievances emerged what came to be known, somewhat inaccurately, as the Granger laws. Between 1869 and 1874, legislatures in Illinois, Iowa, Wisconsin, and Minnesota set maximum charges for grain elevators and railroads, and some of these states established regulatory commissions with broad powers. Though farmers supported this legislation, it was actually framed by Western lawyers and pushed by Western businessmen; only in Wisconsin were the Grangers the principal advocates of regulation. Promptly the railroad and grain elevator companies challenged the constitutionality of these acts, but the United States Supreme Court in *Munn* v. *Illinois* (1877) upheld the right of states to regulate railroads, even to the point of setting maximum rates.

In the long run, state regulation of railroads and grain elevators proved ineffectual, and the Granger laws were repealed or seriously modified. Nevertheless, their temporary success marked a victory for the forces of localism injured by a national economy. The Supreme Court's decision, in effect, endorsed Lieber's theory of Institutional Liberty: Middle Western farmers and businessmen made no attempt to dismantle the national system of transportation, communications, and marketing, but that system was required to concede some autonomy to localities and interests harmed by economic consolidation.

Far different was the outcome of labor protests against a national economic system during these same years. Labor discontent became articulate and forceful when the panic of 1873, precipitated by the failure of Jay Cooke and Company, led into the longest and most severe depression Americans had yet experienced. As business activity declined about one-third between 1873 and 1879 and the number of bankruptcies doubled during the same period, workers were laid off. During the winter of 1873–74 about one-fourth of all laborers in New York City were unemployed, and during the following winter the number increased to one-third.

While private charities did what they could to relieve distress, nobody seemed to know how to end the depression. Informed opinion tended to view the panic and the subsequent unemployment and suffering as part of the natural workings of the national economic order, necessary to purge unsound businesses and speculative practices. Economists warned that "coddling" laborers would only retard this inevitable and necessary process. Blaming the depression on the wartime habit of looking to the federal government for leadership, Democratic Governor Samuel J. Tilden of New York called for a return to "government institutions, simple, frugal, meddling little with the private concerns of individuals . . . and trusting to the people to work out their own prosperity and happiness."

Labor leaders were not much more helpful. For one reason, the national labor movement collapsed during the depression, and many local unions disappeared as well. In New York City, for example, membership in all unions dropped from 45,000 in 1873 to 5000 in 1877. Those labor spokesmen who remained active tended to advocate panaceas. A writer in the *Radical Review* found the cause of the depression in the private ownership of land, which in his words, "begets . . . ground rent, an inexorable, perpetual claim for the use of land, which, like air and light, is the gift of Nature." In 1879, Henry George made that proposition the basis for the economic system proposed in *Progress and Poverty* Other labor voices supported the Socialist Labor movement, founded in 1874, which foresaw the ultimate overthrow of the capitalist system through a socialist revolution; it advocated, as interim measures to combat the depression, federal aid for education, industrial accident compensation, and women's suffrage. The movement attracted a minuscule following.

Some labor spokesmen sought the way out of the depression by supporting independent political parties pledged to protect labor's position in the national economy. There was considerable labor support for the Greenback, or National Independent, party, which was organized in 1874 at Indianapolis. The party's national platform opposed the resumption of specie payments, recently voted by Congress, and advocated further issues of paper money to furnish relief to the depressed industries of the country. That the Greenback party was not a labor movement exclusively is attested by the fact that its presidential candidate in 1876 was the 85-year-old New York iron manufacturer, Peter Cooper. The 80,000 votes Cooper received came mostly from Middle Western farm states. In the congressional elections two years later, however, more laborers supported the National Independent party as it campaigned for government regulation of the hours of labor and for the exclusion of Chinese immigrants. Like other advocates of inflation, the party by this time had moved beyond favoring greenbacks and urged expansion of the currency through silver coinage. Candidates endorsed by the National Independent party received more than a million votes in the 1878 congressional elections.

Other laborers during the depression rejected politics in favor of direct action. With the collapse of the trade union movement, the "Molly Maguires," a secret ring that controlled the popular fraternal society, the Ancient Order of Hibernians, gained power in the anthracite coal region of Pennsylvania. Soon mine owners reported a "crime wave" in collieries, as the Mollies allegedly intimidated

THE GREAT RAILROAD STRIKE

Labor unrest mounted during the severe depression that began in 1873. The most severe outbreak of violence was in Pittsburgh, to which federal troops were dispatched after rioters set fire to the Pennsylvania Railroad roundhouse. *(New York Public Library.)*

and even murdered bosses and superintendents they considered unfair. Eventually, on the dubious testimony of a paid infiltrator, a number of the ringleaders were arrested, and when twenty-four of them were convicted in late 1876, the disturbances ended.

Labor unrest reached its peak in 1877, the worst year of the long depression. Railroad managers precipitated a crisis when, without warning, they cut wages on most railroads east of the Mississippi River by 10 percent. On July 17, the day after the cut became effective, workers on the Baltimore and Ohio Railroad went on strike, took possession of the railyards at various points, and refused to let any freight trains depart. Promptly employees of other Eastern railroads also went on strike, and traffic on the four trunk lines connecting the Atlantic coast and the Middle West was paralyzed. Shortly afterward, the strike spread to some of the roads beyond the Mississippi and in Canada.

Local and state governments proved unable or unwilling to cope with the crisis. The governor of Maryland called out the state militia, but these civilian soldiers fraternized with their friends and relatives among the strikers. In Pittsburgh, the strikers had the sympathy of the local government, for the city fathers had long felt that the Pennsylvania Railroad was discriminating against their city. Employees of nearby iron works joined the railroad men in blocking all traffic on the Pennsylvania. When the governor sent in state militia companies from Philadelphia to clear the tracks, they succeeded in dispersing a large mob by killing twenty-six persons, but their action roused so much additional hostility that the troops were obliged to retreat into the roundhouse, which the mob promptly surrounded and set on fire. The next morning the Philadelphia soldiers fought their way out of the roundhouse and retreated from the city, leaving it in control of a mob of strikers, sympathizers, and looters, who proceeded to destroy railroad property worth some $5 million.

To protect the national system of transportation so essential to the national economy, President Hayes sent in regular army troops. This was the first time in American history that the army had been used on any extensive scale to crush a labor disturbance. Promptly the army restored order, and the strike collapsed. Deeply disturbed members of the business community took steps to prevent any recurrence of such labor violence. State legislatures began passing conspiracy laws directed against labor organizations, and the courts began to invoke the doctrine of malicious conspiracy to break strikes and boycotts. Throughout the North the state militia, which had so often proved untrustworthy during the 1877 crisis, was reorganized and given stricter training. Cyrus Hall McCormick personally purchased equipment for the Second Regiment of Illinois militia because it had "won great credit for its action during . . . disturbances and can be equally relied on in the future."

Thus labor protests against the national economy failed at just the time that farm protest movements largely succeeded. This different outcome is attributable, in part, to the fact that there was a long history of agrarian discontent in the

United States, and the Granger movement seemed as American as apple pie. Urban labor, labor unions, and massive strikes were, on the other hand, something novel to most Americans, and no doubt all three seemed the more dangerous since so many industrial laborers were immigrants with strange-sounding names and alien ways of behavior. In part, too, the differences stemmed from the fact that farmers and their allies lived in a distinct region of the United States, where they were strong enough to control local and state governments in the South and Middle West; industrial laborers were scattered geographically and the labor movement nowhere had political power commensurate with its numbers.

More important than either of these differences was the fact that agrarian discontent did not pose a basic threat to the structure of the national economy. The imposition of limits on the power of railroads and a few other monopolies was an idea that many businessmen also thought desirable. Labor unrest, on the other hand, appeared to strike at the heart of the national economic system. A popular Boston minister declared that the rioting of "the lawless classes at the

THE EMANCIPATOR OF LABOR AND
THE HONEST-WORKING PEOPLE

To terrified conservatives, like the cartoonist Thomas Nast, labor organizers were "Communists," with "foreign" ideologies, intent upon leading honest American working people to death and destruction. *(Harper's Weekly, February 7, 1874.)*

bottom of our cities" had been instigated by "secret socialistic societies." The prominent financial editor, W. M. Grosvenor, spoke for much of the business community when he announced that "the light of the flames at Pittsburgh" portended "a terrible trial for free institutions in this country." He warned: "The Communist is here."

In short, Lieber's theory of Institutional Liberty worked only within limits. Advocates of a national economy could accept compromise when various segments of the business community differed over particular legislative issues, such as the tariff or the currency. They could coexist with the local autonomy demanded by the Granger movement. But they could not tolerate the fundamental threat that insurrectionary labor seemed to pose to the capitalist system.

Suggested Readings

The best general treatment of social and economic change during the post–Civil War period is Allan Nevins, *The Emergence of Modern America, 1865–1878* (1927). There is an enormous amount of unassimilated data in Ellis P. Oberholtzer's *History of the United States Since the Civil War*, Vols. 1–4 (1926–31).

On the growth of American national sentiment, see Hans Kohn's *American Nationalism* (1957) and Herbert W. Schneider, *A History of American Philosophy* (1946). George M. Fredrickson, *The Inner Civil War* (1965) is indispensable on intellectual developments. Frank Freidel's *Francis Lieber* (1947) is authoritative, but there is also an important discussion of Lieber in Philip S. Paludan, *A Covenant with Death* (1975).

Foreign affairs during the Reconstruction era are treated in Glyndon G. Van Deusen, *William Henry Seward* (1967), Allan Nevins, *Hamilton Fish* (1936), and David Donald, *Charles Sumner and the Rights of Man* (1970). Ernest N. Paolino, *The Foundations of the American Empire: William Henry Seward and U.S. Foreign Policy* (1973), and Milton Plesur, *America's Outward Reach* (1971), are both valuable. Adrian Cook's *The Alabama Claims* (1975), is authoritative. On expansionism, the standard work is A. K. Weinberg, *Manifest Destiny* (1935). For opposition to Manifest Destiny, see Donald M. Dozer, "Anti-Expansionism during the Johnson Administration," *Pacific Historical Review 12* (1943), 253–76.

Fred A. Shannon, *The Farmer's Last Frontier* (1945), and Edward C. Kirkland, *Industry Comes of Age* (1961), are admirable studies of postwar economic change. Joseph F. Wall, *Andrew Carnegie* (1970), and Allan Nevins, *Study in Power, John D. Rockefeller* (2 vols., 1953), are excellent biographies. The classic account of unionization during this period is Norman J. Ware, *The Labor Movement in the United States, 1860–1890* (1929). Walter P. Webb, *The Great Plains* (1931), contains a brilliant account of the range cattle industry; also see Robert R. Dykstra, *The Cattle Towns* (1968).

Three modern, sophisticated accounts of the currency controversy are Robert P. Sharkey, *Money, Class, and Party* (1959), Irwin Unger, *The Greenback Era* (1964), and Walter T. K. Nugent, *The Money Question during Reconstruction* (1967).

Solon J. Buck, *The Granger Movement* (1913), continues to be a standard work; but George H. Miller, *Railroads and the Granger Laws* (1971), shows the influence of Western businessmen on the so-called Granger legislation. Samuel Rezneck, "Distress, Relief, and Discontent in the United States during the Depression of 1873–78," *Journal of Political Economy 58* (1950), 494–513, is exceptionally helpful, and there is much information about labor unrest in John R. Commons et al., *History of Labor in the United States,* Vol. 2 (1918).

23

Reconciliation
1865-1890

It is evident, then, that the nationalistic impulse stimulated during the Civil War lost much of its momentum during the Reconstruction years. In both the North and the South, long-established institutions, deeply rooted interests, and ingrained American values limited innovation and slowed down the tendency toward centralization. By the 1870s the forces of nationalism and localism reached equilibrium. The American Compromise between these forces guaranteed, within a sphere much broader than before the war, the supremacy of the national government and the primacy of the nationally integrated economy. It also protected, though within limits more constricted than in 1860, the rights of regions and states and localities.

So long as this American Compromise was simply the result of a balance between opposing forces, it was a fragile arrangement. Any change in the business cycle, any significant shift of voters, could easily upset it and again set North against South, East against West, hard-money advocate against inflationist, businessman against farmer. In order to endure, the American Compromise had to be legitimated. Politicians of both national parties had to agree not to consider these informal arrangements as issues in elections. Equally important, these agreements had to find a place in the minds and hearts of the American people. A lasting compromise had to rest not on calculation but on consensus. The times called for reconciliation.

Politics of the Gilded Age

In this process of reconciliation, the politicians during the final years of the Reconstruction era played a vital part. On first thought this may seem an odd idea to advance, since the 1870s and '80s are generally considered a singularly uninteresting period in American political history, when the holders of public office appeared as interchangeable as Tweedledum and Tweedledee. Many historians have written of the Gilded Age as a time of mediocre Presidents, uninspired congressmen, and unimportant legislation.

That verdict fails to take into account the fact that these politicians most effectively gave legitimacy to the American Compromise by not upsetting the balance. Their most useful role was the one W. S. Gilbert attributed to the British peers:

> The House of Lords throughout the war
> > Did nothing in particular,
> And did it very well.

It must be conceded that the success of the politicos of the Gilded Age was in large measure inadvertent. Many of them professed to have policies they wished to pursue, but fortunately they failed to receive any popular mandate for action. Most of the Presidents of the period barely squeaked into office. Grant's success in 1868 was a popular tribute to a great military leader, not an endorsement of the policies of the Republican party that nominated him. Even so, he received only 53 percent of the popular vote. Grant's reelection by a huge popular margin in 1872 was due chiefly to the fact that his opponents committed political suicide. Dissatisfied members of Grant's own party joined the Liberal Republican movement, which agitated for lower tariffs and for reconciliation with the South—and then proceeded to nominate for President the erratic New York *Tribune* editor, Horace Greeley, famed as a protectionist and noted for his prewar denunciations of slaveholders. Holding its nose, the Democratic party also endorsed Greeley, but thousands of Democrats and Liberal Republicans stayed away from the polls. In 1876, Rutherford B. Hayes received a minority of the popular vote and, after prolonged controversy, was elected by a majority of only one vote in the electoral college. Hayes's successor, James A. Garfield, had a plurality of 9000 votes over his Democratic rival in the 1880 presidential election, when over 9 million votes were cast. Chester A. Arthur, who became President in 1881 after Garfield's assassination, clearly had no mandate from anybody. In 1884 Grover Cleveland, the first Democrat elected President after the Civil War, received less than a majority of the total popular vote and only 70,000 votes more than his Republican rival. Four years later, in 1888, that rival, Benjamin Harrison, defeated Cleveland by winning a majority in the electoral college, although the Democratic candidate had a plurality of the popular votes.

Even had these Presidents been elected by overwhelming majorities in order to carry out ambitious programs, they would have been frustrated by the fact that

THE PHILOSOPHER'S STONE.

A Republican cartoon shows the difficulties Horace Greeley
had in uniting the anti-Grant forces in 1872. Sitting on the
political fence are the laboring man, hostile because of
Greeley's opposition to strikes, and the Negro, distrustful
because Greeley favors amnesty for the Confederates. The
German voter, beer in hand, sits the election out because
Greeley supports prohibition. (*American Antiquarian Society.*)

control of Congress was usually in the hands of their political enemies. To be
sure, Grant started with safely Republican majorities in both houses of Congress,
but Carl Schurz, Charles Sumner, and other leading Republicans soon joined the
Liberal Republican movement, voted with the Democrats, and blocked the administration's favorite measures. In the congressional elections of 1874, Democrats for the first time since the Civil War won a majority in the House of Representatives, and, except for two years (1881–83), they retained control of the
House until 1889. It was not, therefore, until the inauguration of the Democratic
President Grover Cleveland in 1885 that the executive and the legislative branches
of the national government represented the same political party. Given these
facts, it is easy to understand why the politicians of the Gilded Age accomplished
so little and why the few measures they succeeded in adopting had to be compromises.

Though untutored in politics, Grant seems to have sized up the political situation at once. The same strategic sense that dictated his offensive campaign against Vicksburg suggested his defensive, compromising role as President. "Let us have peace," the President urged in his inaugural address—but it was not clear whether he was addressing the white Ku Kluxers who were trying to overthrow the Reconstruction governments in the South or the Northern Radicals who wanted to impose further conditions on the Southern states. As it proved, Grant had both extremes in mind. On the one hand, the President warmly supported the immediate and unconditional readmission of Virginia to the Union, even though Radicals like Sumner warned that the Virginia legislature was "composed of recent Rebels still filled and seething with that old Rebel fire." On the other, Grant was outraged by the terrorism rampant in the South, and he insisted that Congress pass a series of Enforcement Acts (1870–71) enabling him to crush the Ku Klux Klan. Under this legislation, the President proclaimed martial law in nine South Carolina counties where white terrorists were most active, and federal marshals arrested large numbers of suspected Klansmen in North Carolina, Mississippi, and other Southern states. In brief, then, Grant's policy was to warn Southern whites that the national government would not tolerate overt violence and organized military activity—but to let them understand that at the same time they would not be harassed if they regained control of their state governments through less revolutionary tactics.

Though a few old Radicals like Sumner attacked Grant's Southern policy and blamed him for shedding the blood of innocent white and black Unionists in the South, most Northerners accepted the President's program without difficulty. They were growing tired of the whole question of Reconstruction. Other issues claimed their attention, as debates over the resumption of specie payments and the annexation of Santo Domingo pushed stories about the South off the front pages of the newspapers.

Especially diverting were the revelations that newspapers began to make about corruption at all levels of government. The Civil War inaugurated a period of low public morality in the United States, and wartime patterns of favoritism, fraud, and bribery continued into the Reconstruction era. Then, about 1870, reformers and crusading newspaper editors started to expose the scandals. The earliest revelations concerned New York City, which had fallen under the control of "Boss" William Marcy Tweed, who proceeded joyfully to loot the taxpayers. Tweed's ring began construction of a new county courthouse, on which $11 million was spent. Nearly $3 million went to a man named Garvey for plastering; after the amount of his fees leaked out, he became known as the "Prince of Plasterers." Tweed approved the purchase of so many chairs, at $5 each, that if placed in line they would have extended seventeen miles. In 1871 when the New York *Times* began to expose the ring's padded bills, faked leases, false vouchers, and other frauds, the attention of the whole nation was attracted, and when

Harper's Weekly started carrying Thomas Nast's devastating caricatures of the Boss, Tweed's face became more familiar to Americans than that of any other man except Grant. As readers followed the stories of Tweed's arrest, trial, escape from detention, flight to Spain, and return to a New York prison, they had little time or interest in the customary tales of terrorism in the South.

Soon revelations about the national government began to make equally fascinating reading. Shortly before the 1872 election, the New York *Sun*, a Democratic paper, exposed the workings of the Credit Mobilier, the construction company that the Union Pacific Railroad Company paid to build its transcontinental route. Investigation proved that members of the Credit Mobilier were also members of the board of directors of the Union Pacific, who were thus paying themselves huge profits. What was even more damaging was the revelation that, in

"BOSS TWEED" BY THOMAS NAST

Thomas Nast's caricatures of the corrupt William M. Tweed of New York were devastatingly effective. When the "Boss" fled the United States to escape prosecution, a Spanish immigration official identified him on the basis of Nast's drawings, and he was sent back to New York to serve his prison sentence. (*American Antiquarian Society.*)

order to avert public inquiry, the Credit Mobilier offered stock to Vice-President Schuyler Colfax, Representative (and future President) James A. Garfield, and other prominent politicians. They were allowed to "purchase" the stock on credit, the down payment being "earned" by the high dividends that the stock began to pay.

Though Republicans found it advisable to drop Colfax from their ticket in 1872, scandal did not seriously touch the Grant administration until after the election. Then, in short order, stories of fraud began to appear about practically every branch of the executive offices. In the Treasury Department unscrupulous customhouse officers, especially in New York, preyed on importers. Merchants who failed to pay off the brigands had their shipments delayed, their imported goods subjected to minute, time-consuming inspection, and their crates and boxes that were not immediately removed from the docks stored at exorbitant rates. Corruption was rampant in the Navy Department, where political favoritism dictated everything from the employment of workers in the shipyards to the contracts for the construction of new vessels. Secretary of War William W. Belknap was proved to have accepted bribes from Indian traders, who had the exclusive and remunerative franchise to sell goods to Indians and soldiers at frontier posts.

Of all these scandals, the closest to the White House was the Whiskey Ring. In order to avoid heavy excise taxes, first levied during the war, whiskey distillers, especially those at St. Louis, had for years been conspiring with officials of the internal revenue service. During Grant's administration they secured the cooperation of none other than Orville E. Babcock, the President's private secretary, who warned the swindlers whenever an inspection team was sent out from Washington. In return for his assistance, Babcock received such favors as a $2,400 diamond shirt stud, which he found defective and asked to have replaced with another, more expensive one, and from time to time the ministrations of a "sylph." When Grant first learned of the scandal, he urged, "Let no guilty man escape." But as it became clear that his close friends and his personal staff were involved, he did everything possible to block further investigation. When Babcock went on trial, the President of the United States offered a deposition expressing "great confidence in his integrity and efficiency." Babcock was acquitted, and Grant retained him on the White House staff.

As news of these shabby scandals—and there were scores of others, on all levels of government—spread, large numbers of Northerners came to think it was more important to set their own house in order than to tell Southerners how to behave. As early as 1867, *The Nation* announced: "The diminution of political corruption is the great question of our time. It is greater than the [question of Negro] suffrage, greater than reconstruction. . . ."

The desire to reduce political corruption led to the emergence of the civil service reform movement during the Gilded Age. Though voices had been raised against the spoils system long before the Civil War, it was not until after Appomattox that an organized reform drive appeared. Knowledge of widespread corruption among government officials, fear that President Johnson might convert the government bureaucracy into a tool to promote his renomination, and the example of the British system of appointing civil servants after competitive examinations gave strength to the movement. Early efforts to require federal appointees to pass competitive examinations failed in Congress, but the reformers, led by the politically ambitious George William Curtis, editor of *Harper's Weekly,* and by E. L. Godkin of *The Nation,* hoped for success under Grant's administration.

They were doomed to disappointment, for on this, as on all other controversial topics, Grant perfectly understood that compromise was the mood of the age, and he straddled. He made no mention of civil service reform in his first message to Congress, and Henry Adams—the son of Lincoln's minister to Great Britain and the grandson and great-grandson of American Presidents—remarked in his supercilious way that Grant was inaugurating "a reign of western mediocrity." But when disgruntled civil service reformers began to talk loudly about joining the Liberal Republican movement, Grant moved swiftly to head them off. In 1871 he pressured Congress into creating the Civil Service Reform Commission, and he neatly co-opted his chief critic by naming Curtis chairman. Though the commission had little power and achieved less success, the move kept Curtis and a sizable number of reformers as supporters of Grant's reelection. Once the election was over, Grant lost interest in the commission and so blatantly violated its rules that Curtis had to resign.

Strengthened by the news of the scandals that rocked Grant's second administration, civil service reformers claimed some of the credit for the nomination of Hayes in 1876, but they found him as difficult to manage as Grant. On the one hand, the new President did take on the powerful political machine of New York's Senator Roscoe Conkling, and he succeeded in ousting some of Conkling's supporters, including future President Chester A. Arthur, from the New York customhouse. On the other hand, at election time the President wanted his own appointees to contribute to Republican campaign funds and to help organize Republican state conventions, much as their predecessors had done. "I have little or no patience with Mr. Hayes," exclaimed the reforming editor of the New York *Times.* "He is a victim of . . . good intentions and his contributions to the pavement of the road to the infernal regions are vast and various."

Hayes's successor, Garfield, gave civil service reformers little more satisfaction. With cruel accuracy one Massachusetts reformer characterized the new President as "a grand, noble fellow, but fickle, unstable, . . . timid and hesitating." Civil service reform advocates noted suspiciously that Garfield's Vice-President was Arthur, named by the Republican national convention in a vain attempt to placate Conkling. Consequently reformers felt no special sense of victory when

IN MEMORIAM—OUR CIVIL
SERVICE AS IT WAS

Thomas Nast proposes a substitute for Clark Mills's famous
equestrian statue of Andrew
Jackson, in Lafayette Square
across from the White House.
Nast incorrectly attributes to
Jackson the phrase, "To the
Victors belong the Spoils," which
was a remark of William L. Marcy,
a New York Democrat. (Harper's
Weekly, April 28, 1877.)

Garfield began to oust more of Conkling's "Stalwarts" from the New York customshouse. Conceited and imperious, Conkling resigned in a huff from the Senate and rushed to Albany seeking vindication through reelection. To his surprise, the removal of his friends from federal office undercut his support, and
the New York legislature failed to send him back to the Senate. Shortly afterward,
a crazed office seeker named Charles Guiteau assassinated Garfield, shouting that
he was a Stalwart and rejoicing that Arthur was now President. Shocked by Garfield's assassination, Congress in 1883 passed the Pendleton Act, which required
competitive examinations of applicants for many federal jobs. Though the
measure covered only a fraction of all government employees, it was a genuine
measure of civil service reform and permitted the emergence of a professional
government bureaucracy.

The Restoration of "Home Rule"

While Northern opinion was focused on corruption and civil service reform, and while it was further diverted by the depression, unemployment, and strikes, state after state in the former Confederacy was restored to what was euphemistically called home rule—which meant the rule of native white Democrats. The Redeemers, as they called themselves, gained power first in Virginia, North Carolina, Tennessee, and Georgia. In 1875 they won control of Alabama, Mississippi, Arkansas, and Texas, and early in 1877 they ended Republican rule in Florida.

To the relatively few Northerners who were concerned about these developments, the new rulers of the South seemed much like the antebellum slavocracy. All stanch Democrats, the Redeemers sported the traditional Southern mustacios and goatees, they bragged about their records in the Confederate army, and they erupted in florid Southern oratory. In fact, however, they represented a very different interest from the plantation oligarchs of the prewar era; they allied themselves instead with the factory owners, railroad men, and city merchants of the New South. In public stance, the Redeemers identified themselves with the romantic cult of the Confederacy and yearned over "the dignifying memories of the war," but they were really in favor, as a Vicksburg, Mississippi, editor admitted, "of the South, from the Potomac to the Rio Grande, being thoroughly and permanently Yankeeized."

But the process of creating a Yankee South, the Redeemers made very clear, had to be directed by Southerners like themselves. Their experience during the Reconstruction years taught them to distrust Northerners, even Northerners of their own economic backgrounds and viewpoints. Consequently, in state after state, the Redeemers systematically went about overthrowing Republican rule. The tactics varied according to the locality, but the strategy was everywhere the same. White Republicans were subjected to social pressure, economic boycott, and outright violence; many fled the South. Redeemers exercised economic pressure on blacks by threatening not to hire or extend credit to those who were politically active. In several states whites organized rifle clubs, which practiced marksmanship on the outskirts of Republican political rallies. When the blacks attempted to defend themselves, whites overpowered them and slaughtered their leaders. In state after state Republican governors appealed to Washington for additional federal troops, but Grant, convinced that the public was tired of "these annual autumnal outbreaks" in the South, refused. In consequence, by the end of Grant's second administration, South Carolina and Louisiana were the only Southern states with Republican governments.

The fate of these two remaining Republican regimes in the South became intricately connected with the outcome of the 1876 presidential election. The Democratic nominee, Samuel J. Tilden, undoubtedly received a majority of the popular votes cast—though, equally undoubtedly, thousands of blacks who would have voted for his Republican rival, Hayes, were kept from the polls. But Tilden lacked one vote of having a majority in the electoral college unless he received some of the votes from South Carolina, Florida, and Louisiana, all of which submitted to Congress competing sets of Democratic and Republican ballots. (There was also a technical question of the eligibility of one Republican elector from Oregon.)

Consequently when Congress assembled in December 1876 it confronted a crisis. If it decided to accept the disputed Democratic electoral votes, Republican control of the White House would be broken for the first time in a quarter of a century and the Reconstruction in the South would be ended. If Congress accepted the Republican electoral votes, that decision would run counter to the will of a majority of the voters in the country.

To resolve the impasse required a compromise—not a single compromise, but a complicated, interlocking set of bargains. After intricate and secret negotiations, several agreements were reached. First, Congress decided that the disputed electoral votes should be referred to a special electoral commission, which should consist of five members from the House of Representatives, five members from the Senate, and five associate justices from the Supreme Court. This body was composed of eight Republicans and seven Democrats, and on every disputed ballot the commission ruled in favor of Hayes by that same vote. In consequence of these decisions, Tilden's electoral vote remained at 184, while Hayes's slowly mounted to 185. In March 1877, for the fifth time in succession, a Republican President was inaugurated.

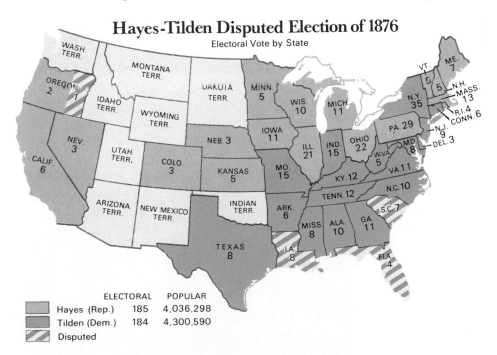

Hayes-Tilden Disputed Election of 1876
Electoral Vote by State

	ELECTORAL	POPULAR
Hayes (Rep.)	185	4,036,298
Tilden (Dem.)	184	4,300,590
Disputed		

Democrats reluctantly accepted the election of Hayes because of some other bargaining that took place while the electoral votes were being counted. One set of compromises came to be known as the Wormley agreement, because it was negotiated in the luxurious Washington hotel owned by the Negro restaurateur, James Wormley. Representing Hayes at these sessions were Senator Sherman, Representative Garfield, and other prominent Republicans. Across the table sat Southern Democratic leaders, including Senator John B. Gordon, the former Confederate general who now represented Georgia in Congress, and L. Q. C. Lamar, once Confederate minister to Russia, who was senator from Mississippi. The Republicans promised the Southerners that, if allowed to be inaugurated, Hayes "would deal justly and generously with the south." Translated, that meant that Hayes would withdraw the remaining federal troops from the South and acquiesce in the overthrow of the Republican regimes in South Carolina and Louisiana. The Southerners found the terms acceptable, and they promptly leaked the news of the agreement, so as to protect themselves from charges that they had betrayed their section.

Behind the Wormley agreement lay other, less formal, compromises. Hayes's backers promised that the new President would not use federal patronage in the South to defeat the Democrats. They further pledged that he would support congressional appropriations for rebuilding levees along the flood-ridden Mis-

"WE'LL SHOW YOU WHEN WE COME TO VOTE"

The attitude of Northern women contributed to the declining interest in the problems of the South. Many women who had loyally supported the war and emancipation felt that they, as well as the freedmen, should have been enfranchised under the Reconstruction amendments to the Constitution. In 1869 Elizabeth Cady Stanton, Susan B. Anthony, and others organized the National Woman Suffrage Association to promote a sixteenth amendment to the Constitution, enfranchising women. (*American Antiquarian Society.*)

sissippi River and for constructing a transcontinental railroad along a Southern route. In return, Southerners agreed to allow the Republicans to elect Garfield speaker of the new House of Representatives, with the power to determine the membership of congressional committees. More important, they promised to protect the basic rights of blacks, as guaranteed in the Thirteenth, Fourteenth, and Fifteenth Amendments to the Constitution.

Once Hayes was inaugurated, virtually all these informal agreements were flouted by both sides. Hayes, for his part, ordered the removal of federal troops from the South and did appoint a Southerner, former Confederate David M. Key, to his cabinet as postmaster general. But two-thirds of the federal office-holders in the South remained Republicans. Hayes changed his mind about supporting a Southern transcontinental railroad. To "make possible any more Credit Mobilier operations," he said piously, "would be a serious mistake."

Southern Democrats for their part reneged on their promise to support Garfield for speaker, and, once the House was organized under Democratic leadership, they eagerly joined in an investigation of alleged fraud in Hayes's election. Only a very few Southern Democratic politicians, like Governor Wade Hampton of South Carolina, remembered their promises to respect the rights of blacks. Instead, almost all took the final withdrawal of federal troops from the South as a signal that the Negro, already relegated to a position of economic inferiority, could be excluded from Southern political life. Southern whites had to act cautiously, so as not to offend public opinion in the North or to invite renewed federal intervention, but they moved steadily and successfully to reduce Negro voting. One of the simplest devices was the poll tax, adopted by Georgia in 1877 and quickly copied by other Southern states. To Northerners the requirement that a voter had to pay $1 or $2 a year did not seem unreasonable, yet in fact, since three-fourths of the entire Southern population had an average income of only $55.16 in 1880, the poll tax was a considerable financial drain, especially to poverty-stricken blacks. More imaginative was the "eight box" law, adopted by South Carolina in 1882 and imitated by North Carolina and Florida. Under this system ballots for each contested race had to be deposited in separate boxes. Thus a voter must cast in one box his ballot for governor, in another box his ballot for sheriff, and so forth. The system frustrated the illiterate Negro voter, who could no longer bring to the polls a single ballot, marked for him in advance by a Republican friend. To make the task of semiliterate voters more difficult, election officials periodically rearranged the order of the boxes. Still another device, which did not become popular until the late 1880s, was the secret, or Australian, ballot. Ostensibly introduced in the South, as in the North, in order to prevent fraud, the secret ballot actually discriminated heavily against blacks, for as late as 1900 the number of illiterate adult Negro males ranged from 39 percent in Florida to 61 percent in Louisiana.

Despite all these devices, Southern blacks continued to vote in surprising numbers. In the 1880 presidential election, for example, more than 70 percent of the eligible Negroes voted in Arkansas, Florida, North Carolina, Tennessee, and Virginia, and between 50 percent and 70 percent voted in Alabama, Louisiana, South Carolina, and Texas. To the Redeemers these black voters posed a double threat. They were numerous enough that ambitious Northern Republicans might be tempted again to try federal intervention in state elections, with the hope of breaking the now solidly Democratic South. Even more dangerous was the possibility that poor whites in the South, whose needs for public education and welfare the business-oriented Redeemers consistently neglected, might find common cause with their black peers.

The Redeemers saw both these dangers materialize after 1890. Shortly after the Republicans gained control of the House of Representatives in 1889, Representative Henry Cabot Lodge of Massachusetts introduced a strong bill for federal control of elections, which was promptly christened the Force Bill. Though Democrats in the Senate defeated Lodge's bill in January 1891, Redeemers saw in it a threat to renew "all the horrors of reconstruction days.' Their fear was doubtless the greater because the almost simultaneous rise of the Populist movement threatened, as never before, to split the white voters of the region. Appealing to farmers and small planters, the Populist party was the enemy of lawyers and bankers and of the rising commercial and industrial spokesmen of the "New South.' Some of the Populist leaders, like Thomas Watson of Georgia, were openly critical of the Redeemers' policy of repressing the blacks and seemed to be flirting with the Negro voters.

Faced with this double threat, Southern states moved swiftly to exclude the Negro completely and permanently from politics. Mississippi led the way with a constitutional convention in 1890 that required voters to be able to read and interpret the Constitution to the satisfaction of the white registration officials. It is not hard to imagine how difficult even a graduate of Howard University Law School would have found the task of satisfactory constitutional exegesis. In 1898 a Louisiana constitutional convention improved on the Mississippi example by requiring a literacy test of all voters except the sons and grandsons of persons who had voted in state elections before 1867. Since no Louisiana Negroes had been permitted to vote before that date, this provision allowed illiterate whites to vote, while the literacy test excluded most Negro voters.

State after state across the South followed, or elaborated on, these requirements. South Carolina held a disfranchising convention in 1895. North Carolina amended its constitution to limit suffrage in 1900. Alabama and Virginia acted in 1901–02, and Georgia adopted a restrictive constitutional amendment in 1908. The remaining Southern states continued to rely on the poll tax and other varieties of legislative disfranchisement. When opponents of these measures accused their advocates of discriminating against the Negroes, Carter Glass of Virginia replied for his entire generation: "Discrimination! Why that is precisely what we propose; that exactly is what this convention was elected for.'

It took time, then, for the complete working out of the political compromises of the Reconstruction era. Not until the end of the nineteenth century did white Southerners receive the full price they had exacted in permitting the election of Rutherford B. Hayes. But by 1900 that payment had been made in full. The Negro was no longer a political force in the South, and the Republican party was no longer the defender of Negro rights.

Literary Reconciliation

These political arrangements, which, in effect, ratified the American Compromise and excluded the Negro question from national politics for more than a generation, were probably less important in bringing the Civil War era to a close than the changes that were simultaneously occurring in the minds of Americans. If the American Compromise was to hold, it had to rest on a fundamental consensus, a desire to forget or ignore the differences that had hitherto divided sections, interests, and races. In short, the theme of reconciliation had to dominate the world of ideas as it did the world of economics and politics.

During the first few years after the Civil War, it was not at all clear that such an intellectual reconciliation could occur. Northern writers and intellectuals during the war had been intensely patriotic and highly nationalistic. Even the best of their productions were suffused with a tone of Northern superiority. Although he was compassionate toward the fallen soldiers of the South, Walt Whitman never concealed his belief in the righteousness of the Union cause, and his greatest war poems, "O Captain! My Captain!" and "When Lilacs Last in the Dooryard Bloom d," were tributes to Lincoln, the fallen leader of the national cause. Similarly Herman Melville's *Battle Pieces and Aspects of the War* (1866), spare, gnomic verses whose greatness was not to be recognized until a later generation, exulted in Union victory even while expressing sympathy for individual Rebels. James Russell Lowell also turned literary nationalist. His second series of *Biglow Papers* used Yankee dialect to explain why Southerners had to give up their sectional identity:

> Make 'em Amerikin, an' they'll begin
> To love their country ez they loved their sin;
> Let 'em stay Southun, an' you've kep' a sore
> Ready to fester ez it done afore.

In fiction as in verse Northern writers during and immediately after the war insisted that Southerners must repent and accept Northern values. That was the central theme of *Miss Ravenel's Conversion from Secession to Loyalty,* John W. DeForest's 1867 novel, which remains perhaps the best novel ever written about the Civil War. A native of Connecticut, DeForest had spent some time in the South before the war, commanded a company of Union volunteers in Louisiana and in the Shenandoah Valley, and after Appomattox served with the

BLUE AND GRAY MEET AT SEVEN PINES BATTLEFIELD AFTER
THE WAR

As the bitterness of the Civil War years faded, Union
soldiers and Confederate veterans began to hold joint
reunions on the battlefields, where they engaged in
reminiscences about a struggle they increasingly
romanticized. Note that each of the veterans here shown
has lost an arm. *(Valentine Museum, Richmond.)*

Freedmen's Bureau in South Carolina. He was not, therefore, ignorant of the
South, and some aspects of Southern life seem to have had sensuous charm for
this straitlaced New Englander. The most credible characters in his novel are
the corrupt, whiskey-drinking Virginian, Captain Carter, whose animal mag-
netism is so strong that Lillie Ravenel marries him against her own better judgment, and the lurid Creole, Mrs. Larue, with whom Carter continues to carry on a
torrid affair even after his marriage. But in the end it is not these Southern-born
characters who have the strength to win victory. After Carter's fortunate death in
battle, Lillie weds her patiently waiting Northern lover, Captain Colbourne—as

stiff and as formal as DeForest himself. Sententiously, Colbourne and Miss Ravenel's father discuss the significance of the romances that have occurred, and of the war itself. "The right always conquers because it always becomes the strongest," Dr. Ravenel suggests. "In that sense 'the hand of God' is identical with 'the heaviest battalions. "' Agreeing, Colbourne summarizes in a sentence the theme of Northern superiority: "The Southern character will be sweetened by adversity as their persimmons are by frost."

Like DeForest, Whitman initially assumed that the national sentiment aroused by the Civil War would erase sectional feelings and ultimately would produce a national literature, which could provide for America's democratic society "that glowing, blood-throbbing, religious, social, emotional, artistic, indefinable, indescribably beautiful charm and hold which fused the separate parts of the old feudal societies together.' But by the time Whitman got around to elaborating his theory in his strange, rambling essays, *Democratic Vistas*, published in 1871, his confidence had begun to wane. "Society, in these States, is cankered, crude, superstitious and rotten," he judged, and he feared that America might be suffering from "the lack of a common skeleton, knitting all close." On all levels government was "saturated in corruption, bribery, falsehood, maladministration," and the cities reeked "with respectable as much as non-respectable robbery and scoundrelism.' Despite obvious signs of material progress, he was tempted to conclude that the United States was "so far, an almost complete failure in its social aspects, and in really grand religious, moral, literary, and aesthetic results." But that "so far" suggested that there was a possible remedy. It was the emergence of a powerful national literature, and Whitman longed for the appearance of "a single great literatus," who could issue a clarion call for American culture.

Whitman's hopes were not to be fulfilled. The giants of American literature belonged to a previous generation. Whitman himself was too exhausted, too old, to serve as "literatus' of the new age; in 1873 he suffered a stroke of paralysis and retired to Camden, New Jersey. Melville after the war sank into decades of silence, only to complete the manuscript of *Billy Budd* just before his death in 1891. Ralph Waldo Emerson, who during the pre–Civil War period had come nearest to fulfilling Whitman's specifications for an American "literatus," was now slowly slipping into senility.

The new generation of Northeastern writers offered little more hope for literary leadership. Once the intellectual capital of the country, New England was now stagnant. Its ablest poet, Emily Dickinson, lived a recluse in her house in Amherst, Massachusetts, her verse unseen by the public until after her death. Its ablest novelist, the transplanted New Yorker Henry James, found the American scene uncongenial and fled to Europe. Its supply of local talent was so bankrupt that in 1871 the editorship of the *Atlantic Monthly* went to a Middle Westerner, William Dean Howells. The New York publishing scene was, as always, bustling, but Whitman correctly dismissed the now deservedly forgotten poets and essayists of the era as "a parcel of dandies and ennuyees, dapper little gentlemen from

"WALT WHITMAN" BY THOMAS EAKINS

Old and ill, Whitman longed for the appearance of a "literatus," who could write the story of "the actual Soldier of 1862–'65, North and South, with all his ways, his incredible dauntlessness, habits, practices, tastes, language, his appetite, rankness, his superb strength and animality, lawless gait, and a hundred unnamed lights and shades of camp." But, he feared, this history "will never be written—perhaps must not and should not be." *(Pennsylvania Academy of the Fine Arts.)*

abroad who flood us with their thin sentiments of parlors, parasols, piano songs, [and] tinkling rhymes. '

Instead of the national literature for which Whitman hoped, there emerged between 1865 and 1890 strong regional schools of literature—"local colorists," as they have somewhat condescendingly been called. It was in the Far West, where a motley group of Indians, Mexicans, Chinese, Yankees, and Southerners were engaged in the experiment of constructing an instant society, that the first of these regional writers appeared. The center of the group was the dapper, elegant New Yorker Bret Harte, who had moved to California in the 1850s and, with the support of a lucrative but undemanding job in the United States mint at San Francisco during the 1860s, wrote prolific verse and fiction. Not until Harte became editor of the *Overland Monthly* in 1868, however, did he turn his imagination to the local area, and the publication of "The Luck of Roaring Camp" and "The Outcasts of Poker Flat" proved that he had struck a literary pay dirt in the garish, tawdry, but deeply romantic adventurers in the California mining country. Immediately lionized by both English and Eastern literary circles, Harte generously assisted his fellow Western local colorists. It was with Harte's encouragement that Mark Twain (Samuel L. Clemens) published *The Celebrated Jumping Frog of Calaveras County and Other Stories* (1867), a transposition of the traditional American tall tale to a Far Western setting, and became a world celebrity. Less enduring was the fame of another Harte protégé, Joaquim Miller, who compensated for his limited literary talents by self-dramatization; appearing at London dinner parties in his sealskin coat, his red plaid shirt, and his hip boots, Miller seemed so completely the personification of the Wild Westerner that the English forgot his limping rhymes.

A second regional school of writers emerged in the Middle West in the 1870s. Stimulated by reading Bret Harte, Constance Fenimore Woolson—the grandniece of James Fenimore Cooper—sought in her stories of French voyageurs, of fur trappers and traders, and of rough lumbermen to recapture the traditions and the color of the Great Lakes region where she was brought up. In 1871 John Hay, who had served as Lincoln's private secretary, succumbed to the regional impulse and published his *Pike County Ballads*, which reproduced in frontier dialect both the crudeness and the humor of early Illinois. More prolific was Edward Eggleston, a Methodist minister who made a systematic study of life and language in his native southern Indiana before writing *The Hoosier Schoolmaster* (1871), *The Circuit Rider* (1874), and other novels that attempted to re-create life on a frontier that was beginning to slip from memory. Soon that frontier would be romanticized and subdued in the ever popular verse of the Hoosier poet James Whitcomb Riley, who wrote his jingles about "just plain folks.'

Regional writing emerged in the South more slowly than that in other sections. Some older Southern writers could not break themselves of the habit of writing polemics in defense of slavery. Others were too embittered by the war to appeal to a national audience. Younger writers were for the most part less sore, but they were too exhausted to write the kind of regional romance that a national audience sought. Paul Hamilton Hayne, the Charleston poet who saw his house and library burned in the bombardment of his city and had his silver stolen by Sherman's "bummers," lived out his days in north Georgia, in a rough "shanty of uncouth ugliness," so dilapidated that he tried to paper over the holes in the walls with pictures his wife cut from magazines. Henry Timrod, the South Carolina poet who died of tuberculosis at the age of thirty-nine, summarized his life after the war as "beggary, starvation, death, bitter grief, utter want of hope." The ablest of Southern poets, Sidney Lanier, whose health had been broken during service in the Confederate army and who was also destined for a premature death from tuberculosis, epitomized in a sentence the experience of Southern writers in the 1860s: "Pretty much the whole of life has been merely not dying."

Thanks largely to the enterprise of Northern magazine editors, Southern writers fared very differently during the 1870s and '80s. The warm reception readers gave Western local color fiction and verse led the editors of *Scribner's Monthly Magazine* (after 1881, *The Century Magazine*) and of *Lippincott's Magazine* actively to solicit contributions from Southern authors. Early successes in these journals brought offers to Southern writers from *Harper's Monthly Magazine* and finally even from the formerly antislavery journal *The Atlantic Monthly.* Publication of stories or serialization of novels in these prestigious monthlies usually led to successful book publication by a major Northern firm, so that for the first time writing became a remunerative occupation in the South.

The successful Southern writer had first to meet terms and conditions of his Northern editors. *Scribner's,* which set the standard, sought to promote "a sane and earnest Americanism" and constantly "to increase the sentiment of union throughout our diverse sisterhood of States." Southern writers were tacitly barred from any expression of the old hostility between the sections. Northern editors wanted no polemics defending slavery or justifying secession, no jeremiads about what the North had done during the war, no objective reporting on the

workings of Reconstruction. Instead, they sought stories set in the South, long on local color, heavy in Southern dialect, ingenious in plot, and romantic in tone.

These were terms that Southern writers of the new generation found easy to accept. Most young Southerners were prepared to admit that they were glad the Confederacy had failed; nearly all felt that their section had a brighter future in the Union. Many consciously sought in their writing to bring about sectional reconciliation. The Virginia novelist Thomas Nelson Page declared that he had "never wittingly written a line which he did not hope might tend to bring about a better understanding between the North and the South, and finally lead to a more perfect Union." They agreed that regional literature must be part of a broad national literature. Joel Chandler Harris, author of the Uncle Remus stories, spoke for his generation in asserting "that whatever in our literature is distinctly Southern must . . . be distinctly American."

In return for accepting American nationality, Southern writers were allowed great freedom in their choice of subjects. George Washington Cable's fiction explored the mysteries of that least American of cities, New Orleans, where Creoles and Yankees, 'Cajuns, quadroons, and slaves mixed together in a cosmopolitan and fascinatingly decadent society. Mary Noailles Murfree wrote of Southern Appalachian folk, so isolated from the American mainstream that their dialect, which she laboriously attempted to reproduce, was full of Elizabethan idioms. Harris wrote scores of conventional novels and stories about Southern life, but his readers identified him as author of the Uncle Remus tales, about Br'er Rabbit, that defenseless yet preternaturally clever animal, who was able—perhaps like the slaves who had originally told Harris the tales—to outwit his more powerful enemies like Br'er Fox and Br'er Bear. Page's stories had a courtly Virginia setting, and the lush bluegrass country of Kentucky was the scene of James Lane Allen's impressionistic tales.

In all this postwar Southern writing, the Negro played a surprisingly small part. As in the Uncle Remus stories, a black was often allowed to be the narrator, a gentle, aged former slave, full of folk wisdom and glowing with happy memories about "dose times befoah de wah." "Dem wuz good ole times, marster," said Sam, the former slave who narrated Page's most popular story, *Marse Chan* (1884), "de bes' Sam uver see! Niggers didn' hed nothin' 'tall to do. . . . Dyar warn' no trouble nor nuthin'." Though the point was never made explicitly, the implica-

UNCLE REMUS

In the Southern literature of reconciliation, the Negro played a surprisingly small role. Often he appeared as the narrator of tales, like Joel Chandler Harris's Uncle Remus. Even more frequently he reminisced happily about "dose times befoah de wah." *(American Antiquarian Society.)*

tion was that race relations in the South had been exemplary until disrupted by Northern invaders. Though the recommendation was never given overtly, the promise was that if white Southerners were left alone there would be a return to the good old days.

If slaves and slavery were peripheral in this Southern literature, the theme of reconciliation was central. Again and again the stories dealt with the Civil War as the result of misunderstanding, of a failure of Northerners and Southerners to recognize how much they had in common. In one of Harris s stories, a wounded Union officer, captured by a black "mammy" and nursed back to health by her white mistress, proved to have such a noble character as to shatter the Southerners' stereotypes about Yankees. "He gave . . . a practical illustration of the fact that one may be a Yankee and a Southerner too, simply by being a large-hearted, whole-souled American." Typically in these romances, understanding leads to marriage. Time and again the Union officer, befriended by a Southern planter's family during the conflict, returns South after Appomattox to claim the hand of the planter's daughter and to save the plantation from foreclosure for debts.

The product of changing sectional sentiment after the Civil War, Southern fiction also helped to produce that change. Both sides in the recent conflict had been right. Both sides shared equally in the glory and the gallantry. To Northern readers, as well as to Southern, these were ideas immensely appealing, immensely consoling. They permitted the Civil War generation to gloss over the brutal past, and they allowed the postwar generation of Northerners to shed any guilt it felt at abandoning the Negro. Indicative of the power of Southern romance was the response of Thomas Wentworth Higginson to Page's *Marse Chan*, a tale about a political quarrel that kept two Southerners from marrying before the young man rode away to the war. By the time the girl's father relented, the hero had bravely died on the battlefield, and shortly after, the girl too expired of grief. Sitting in his study in Cambridge, Massachusetts, Higginson—who had once organized an attempt to free a fugitive slave, who had been a confidant of John Brown, who had heroically commanded a regiment of Negro soldiers during the Civil War—let the tears trickle down his face as he grieved over the death of a fictional Southern slaveholder.

Thus Americans of the postwar generation became emotionally reconciled to a series of compromises that ended decades of conflict between national interests and local concerns. In foreign policy and in economic organization, in race relations and in politics, informal agreements were hammered out that served to guarantee the primacy of the nation but also to protect local and regional rights. These compromises made no provision to protect the Indians, who were being ruthlessly pushed into barren reservations. They systematically relegated blacks to the category of second-class citizens. They took little account of the needs of labor. But, especially when veiled by literary sentimentality, the compromises seemed to most white middle-class Americans to provide a tolerable way of life that preserved both the national Union and their own individual freedom.

Suggested Readings

Volumes 6–8 of James Ford Rhodes's *History of the United States* (1906–19) chronicle political history from Grant to McKinley. H. Wayne Morgan, *From Hayes to McKinley* (1969), is a modern treatment. The best account of Grant's presidency remains William B. Hesseltine's unsatisfactory *Ulysses S. Grant, Politician* (1935). Ari A. Hoogenboom, *Outlawing the Spoils* (1961), is a superior account of the civil service reform movement. Earl D. Ross, *The Liberal Republican Movement* (1919), remains a standard account. Harry Barnard, *Rutherford B Hayes and His America* (1954), is the best biography of that President, and Thomas C. Reeves, *Gentleman Boss* (1975) is a fine life of Chester A. Arthur.

C. Vann Woodward, *Reunion and Reaction* (1951), is a highly original account of the compromises of 1876–77. On the Redeemer regimes, see Woodward's authoritative *Origins of the New South* (1951). The best account of the disfranchisement of the Negro is J. Morgan Kousser, *The Shaping of Southern Politics* (1974).

Robert E. Spiller et al., *Literary History of the United States*, Vol. 2 (1948), is a good introduction to its subject. Edmund Wilson, *Patriotic Gore* (1962), and Robert A. Lively, *Fiction Fights the Civil War* (1957), are thoughtful studies. On the local colorists, there is much in Van Wyck Brooks, *New England: Indian Summer* (1940) and *The Times of Melville and Whitman* (1947). The best account of the literary reconciliation between North and South is Paul H. Buck's *The Road to Reunion* (1937).

Chronology, 1860–1890

1860 Democratic party deadlocked at Charleston convention finally divides along sectional lines at Baltimore. Constitutional Union party nominates John Bell for President. Republicans nominate Abraham Lincoln, who wins. Senator John J. Crittenden unsuccessfully offers series of constitutional amendments to settle the sectional controversy. South Carolina secedes from the Union.

1861 Secession of remaining states of deep South (Mississippi, Florida, Alabama, Georgia, Louisiana, and Texas). Jefferson Davis inaugurated provisional president of the Confederate States of America. Morrill Tariff Act, first of a series of highly protective tariff acts. Firing on Fort Sumter precipitates war. Secession of Virginia, North Carolina, Tennessee, and Arkansas. Union army routed at first battle of Bull Run (Manassas). George B. McClellan becomes Union commander in chief. Captain Charles Wilkes (USN) stops British steamer *Trent* on high seas and removes Confederate envoys James M. Mason and John Slidell. War with England avoided when Lincoln's government releases envoys.

1862 General U. S. Grant captures Fort Henry and Fort Donelson, breaking Confederate line in the West. Further Union advance halted by Confederates at Shiloh. First battle of ironclads, *Merrimack* v. *Monitor*. McClellan's Peninsula campaign brings Union army to outskirts of Richmond. Robert E. Lee becomes commander of Army of Northern Virginia. T. J. ("Stonewall") Jackson's raid in Shenandoah Valley prevents Union reinforcement of McClellan, who is

Jefferson Davis installed for six-year term as president of Confederacy. Union forces capture New Orleans. Confederacy adopts its first conscription act. Union Congress passes Homestead Act, Internal Revenue Act, Morrill Act creating land-grant colleges, and Pacific Railroad Act, authorizing transcontinental railroad.

1863 Bragg's army defeats Union forces under Rosecrans at Chickamauga; General George H. Thomas saves Union army from rout. Reinforced by Grant and W. T. Sherman, Union army defeats Confederates in battle of Chatanooga (Lookout Mountain and Missionary Ridge).
Lincoln announces lenient program of amnesty and pardon and introduces 10 percent plan for reconstructing Southern states.

1864 Grant named Union general in chief. Union Congress passes Wade-Davis bill, a more stringent reconstruction plan. When Lincoln pocket vetoes it, Radical Republicans angrily denounce him.
Grant's direct advance on Richmond checked in the battles of the Wilderness, Spotsylvania, and Cold Harbor. Grant moves south of James River to begin "siege" of Petersburg. Sherman pushes back Confederates under Joseph E. Johnston and captures Atlanta. Farragut captures Mobile. Lincoln reelected President over Democratic candidate McClellan. Sherman marches from Atlanta to the sea, devastating Georgia.

1865 Sherman pushes northward through South Carolina and North Carolina. Cut off from supplies and nearly surrounded, Lee gives up Petersburg and Richmond, and Confederate government flees. Lee surrenders at Appomattox. Johnston surrenders to Sherman. Kirby-Smith surrenders Confederate forces west of the Mississippi. Lincoln assassinated; Andrew Johnson becomes President. Walt Whitman publishes *Drum Taps*. Johnson moves for speedy, lenient restoration of Southern states to Union. Congress creates Joint Committee of Fifteen to supervise reconstruction process. Thirteenth Amendment ratified.

1866 Johnson breaks with Republican majority in Congress by vetoing Freedmen's Bureau bill and Civil Rights bill. Latter is passed over his veto.

1869 Congress passes Fifteenth Amendment and submits it to states for ratification.
Transcontinental railroad completed.
Public Credit Act affirms government's obligation to pay its debts in gold, not in depreciated paper money.

1870 First Ku Klux Klan (or Enforcement) Act gives Grant power to move against white terrorists in South. A second act in 1871 further strengthens President's hand.
Grant's proposal to annex the Dominican Republic leads to feud with Senator Charles Sumner and break in Republican party.
Incorporation of Standard Oil Company of Ohio.
Grant names G. W. Curtis to head Civil Service Commission.

1871 Treaty of Washington, settling differences between United States and Great Britain, signed.
Knights of Labor formed.
Tweed Ring in New York City exposed.
Whitman publishes *Democratic Vistas*.
Edward Eggleston publishes *The Hoosier Schoolmaster*.

1872 Liberal Republicans and Democrats nominate Horace Greeley for President; Republicans renominate Grant, who is elected.
Exposure of Credit Mobilier scandal shows prominent Republican politicians tainted by graft.

1873 Coinage Act demonetizes silver in so-called Crime of '73.
Panic of 1873 begins long economic depression.
In Slaughterhouse Cases, Supreme Court begins narrow interpretation of Fourteenth Amendment.

1874 Grant vetoes Inflation Act.
Greenback party founded.
Democrats, for first time since 1860, secure majority in House of Representatives.

1875 Specie Resumption Act provides for return to gold standard by 1879.

1876 Exposure of Whiskey Ring reveals further corruption in Republican administration.
Custer and his men slaughtered at battle of the Little Big Horn.

liberating slaves of all persons supporting the rebellion.

C. S. S. *Alabama*, built in British shipyards, begins its career of devastating United States merchant marine.

Lee and Jackson defeat Union General John Pope at second battle of Bull Run (Manassas).

Lee's invasion of Maryland halted at Antietam (Sharpsburg), the bloodiest day of the war.

Lincoln issues his preliminary Emancipation Proclamation, promising to free slaves in rebellious region on January 1.

Gravest threat of Anglo-French intervention in American Civil War averted because of dissension in British cabinet.

1863 Confederate invasion of Kentucky, led by Braxton Bragg and Edmund Kirby-Smith, halted at Perryville. Union General William S. Rosecrans forces Bragg to withdraw from central Tennessee in battle of Murfreesboro (Stones River).

Lee defeats Union commander Ambrose P. Burnside at Fredericksburg.

Cabinet crisis in Union government as Radical Republicans attempt to oust Seward; Lincoln remains in control.

Napoleon III offers to mediate American quarrel; rebuffed by Seward.

Union Congress adopts first real conscription act.

Confederate Congress passes broad internal revenue taxes.

Lee defeats new Union commander, Joseph Hooker, at Chancellorsville.

Grant captures Vicksburg.

Lee invades the North but is checked by General George G. Meade at Gettysburg.

Draft riots throughout the North, especially in New York City.

Union Congress passes National Banking Act (strengthened in 1864).

Union minister Charles Francis Adams persuades British government to prevent sailing of Laird rams.

In the Prize Cases, the United States Supreme Court upholds legality of the war and of Lincoln's actions to subdue the Confederates.

submits it to states for ratification.

Herman Melville publishes *Battle-Pieces*.

National Labor Union organized at Baltimore.

Johnson tries to form new Union party of conservative Republicans, Democrats, and white Southerners. Despite "arm-in-arm" convention at Philadelphia and Johnson's speeches on his "Swing around the Circle," Republicans win fall congressional elections.

In *ex parte* Milligan, Supreme Court forbids military trials in areas where civil courts are functioning.

Southern whites in Pulaski, Tennessee, organize Ku Klux Klan, which rapidly spreads over the South.

1867 Congress passes Military Reconstruction Act over Johnson's veto. (Two supplementary acts in 1867 and a third in 1868 passed to put this measure into effect.)

Congress passes Tenure of Office Act and Command of Army Act to reduce Johnson's power.

Annexation of Alaska.

Execution of Emperor Maximilian marks end of French adventure in Mexico.

John W. DeForest publishes *Miss Ravenel's Conversion*.

Samuel L. Clemens (Mark Twain) publishes *The Celebrated Jumping Frog of Calaveras County*.

O. H. Kelley founds Patrons of Husbandry (Granger movement).

1868 Former Confederate states hold constitutional conventions, for which former slaves are allowed to vote, and adopt new constitutions guaranteeing universal suffrage.

Arkansas, Alabama, Florida, Georgia, Louisiana, North Carolina, and South Carolina readmitted to representation in Congress. Because of discrimination against Negro officeholders, Georgia representatives are expelled. (State is again admitted in 1870.)

President Johnson impeached. Escapes conviction by one vote.

Republicans nominate Grant for President; Democrats select Governor Horatio Seymour of New York. Grant elected President.

Middle Western states begin passing Granger laws, regulating railroads and grain elevators.

In *Texas* v. *White*, Supreme Court declares Union indissoluble and affirms authority of Congress to reconstruct Southern states.

Republicans nominate Rutherford B. Hayes for President; Democrats nominate Samuel J. Tilden. Tilden secures majority of popular vote but electoral vote in doubt because of disputed returns from three Southern states.

1877 After elaborate political and economic bargaining, Congress creates an electoral commission, which rules that all disputed ballots belong to Hayes, who is inaugurated President.

In *Munn* v. *Illinois*, Supreme Court upholds Granger legislation.

Nationwide railroad strike and ensuing violence lead to first significant use of federal troops to suppress labor disorders.

1878 Bland-Allison Act requires United States Treasury to purchase $2 to 4 million of silver each month and coin it, thus slightly inflating the currency but not assuring unlimited coinage as silver interests demanded.

Hayes ousts Chester A. Arthur and Alonzo B. Cornell from New York customshouse and precipitates break with "Stalwart" Republican faction of Roscoe Conkling.

Timber and Stone Act permits inexpensive sale of public lands considered unfit for cultivation. Miners, lumbermen, and speculators reap huge profits.

1879 As authorized by the 1875 act, Secretary of the Treasury John Sherman begins resumption of specie payments.

Terence V. Powderly elected head of the Knights of Labor, which enters a period of great expansion until by 1886 it has more than 700,000 members.

The First Church of Christ, Scientist, opened in Boston. This is the mother church of the Christian Science faith established by Mary Baker Eddy.

Henry George publishes *Progress and Poverty*.

1880 In the presidential contest, Republicans nominate James A. Garfield and Chester A. Arthur; Democrats choose Winfield Scott Hancock and William H. English; Greenback Labor party selects James B. Weaver and B. J. Chambers. Garfield elected President.

Joel Chandler Harris publishes *Uncle Remus*.

1881 Charles J. Guiteau assassinates Garfield. Chester A. Arthur succeeds Garfield as President.
Publication of Helen Hunt Jackson's *A Century of Dishonor* calls attention to serious defects in United States Indian policy.
Publication of *The Portrait of a Lady* inaugurates Henry James's major phase as a novelist.

1882 Chinese Exclusion Act restricts immigration of Chinese laborers for ten years.
In *San Mateo County v. Southern Pacific Railroad Company*, Supreme Court accepts Roscoe Conkling's argument that word *persons* in the Fourteenth Amendment was deliberately chosen to extend protection of due process clause to corporations.

1883 In the Civil Rights Cases Supreme Court declares unconstitutional 1875 Civil Rights Act, because it protected social rather than political rights.
Anticipating Democratic control of Congress, Republicans pass the Tariff of 1883, which nominally makes some reductions in rates but firmly keeps protectionist principle.
In reaction to assassination of Garfield by a disappointed officeseeker, Congress passes Pendleton Act, setting up Civil Service Commission and requiring many future federal appointees to take competitive examinations.
Congressional authorization to build three steel cruisers begins renovation of the United States navy.
James Whitcomb Riley publishes *The Old Swimming Hole.*
Mark Twain publishes *Life on the Mississippi.*

1884 In the presidential campaign Republicans nominate James G. Blaine, Democrats Grover Cleveland, Prohibitionists John P. St. John, and National Greenback Labor party Benjamin F. Butler. Cleveland narrowly wins, becoming the first Democrat to be elected President since Buchanan.

1885 Founding of Leland Stanford, Junior, University (now Stanford University).
Mark Twain publishes *Huckleberry Finn.*

1886 After police break up an anarcho-communist rally in Haymarket Square, Chicago, a bomb explodes among the police, who then open fire. In ensuing trials, August Spies, Albert Parsons, and other radical agitators sentenced to death. Petitions circulated by William Dean Howells and other intellectuals convince Governor John Peter Altgeld of Illinois that the trial was unfair, since the identity of the bomb thrower was never established, and in 1893 he frees the surviving prisoners.
American Federation of Labor organized; Samuel Gompers, first president.
In *Wabash, St. Louis & Pacific Railroad Company v. Illinois*, the Supreme Court invalidates state regulation of railroads when it affects interstate commerce, thus weakening Court's previous ruling in *Munn v. Illinois* (the Granger Cases, 1877).

1887 To fill gap in railroad regulation left by Wabash decision, Congress creates Interstate Commerce Commission, first federal regulatory commission in United States history.
Cleveland vetoes Dependent Pension Bill and numerous individual pension bills, declaring that they would make the pension roll a refuge for frauds rather than a "roll of honor."
Congress repeals 1867 Tenure of Office Act.
Looking toward the dissolution of the Indian tribes, Congress passes the Dawes Severalty Act providing for the division of tribal lands among individual members.

1888 In the presidential campaign, Democrats renominate Grover Cleveland and Republicans nominate Benjamin Harrison. Harrison elected President by a majority in the electoral college but receives fewer popular votes than Cleveland.
Edward Bellamy publishes *Looking Backward.*

1889 Department of Agriculture raised to cabinet status.
Omnibus Act admits North Dakota, South Dakota, Montana, and Washington as states.
Germany, Great Britain, and United States agree to set up a tripartite protectorate over Samoa.
United States calls together first International American Conference; leads to creation of

1890 Sherman Anti-Trust Act passed in attempt to regulate monopolies in restraint of trade.
Sherman Silver Purchase Act passed, resulting in depleted gold reserves.
McKinley Tariff raises duties to average 49.5 percent.

Descended from "Uncle Sam"
Wilson, a real-life butcher
from Troy, New York, who
provisioned the militia in the
War of 1812, the symbolic
Uncle Sam was born during the
Age of Jackson and was raised
by politicos in the Whig and
Democratic parties. During the
Gilded Age the pictorial Uncle
Sam spent most of his time
enforcing the law, punishing
political miscreants, and
lecturing the rest of the world
on the blessings of democracy.
Even his recreation was grimly
purposeful: in this piece of
folk sculpture he is seen on his
bicycle riding hell-bent for
prosperity. *(Courtesy Mr. & Mrs.
Leo Rabkin.)*

PART FIVE

Nationalizing the Republic

1890-1920

JOHN L. THOMAS

As the American people completed their industrial revolution in the half-century following the Civil War, they continued to celebrate unprecedented growth even as they were driven to experiment with new ways of regulating it. In 1900 as in 1850 most Americans saw cause for national self-congratulation in the numerous signs of prosperity all around them: an improved standard of living; rapid population growth; the rise of great cities; and an ever-growing stock of consumer goods. More thoughtful observers, however, noted that all of these achievements had come at a high social price: the sudden uprooting of a rural people and the disruption of their communities; the forced mobility of new masses of underprivileged; deplorable working conditions for too many Americans; and the persistence of a conspicuously unequal distribution of wealth. Still, for most people caught up in America's industrial transformation the benefits of rapid material growth clearly outweighed its costs.

For economic growth continued to verify earlier predictions of illimitable progress, and most Americans, whether they consulted population statistics or production charts, still sought confirmation of their cherished ideal of progress. The key concept in this doctrine of progress—freedom from external restraints on individual ambitions and energies—had survived the Civil War, if not unscathed at least intact. A simple faith in the individual continued to claim the allegiance of a majority of Americans in 1900 just as it had an earlier generation.

Yet in spite of the optimum mood of the country, reform-minded citizens in all walks of life by 1880 were beginning to note the signs of mounting social disorder. Under the triple impact of industrialization, modernization, and urbanization a growing number of leaders in all parts of the national community came to recognize the need for controls and system as new means of acquiring efficiency and stability. Businessmen sought consolidated power within their firms with which to improve their operations and increase their profits. Farmers quickly discovered an urgent need for better credit facilities and marketing mechanisms. Social theorists and urban reformers began to adjust their vision to the requirements of systematic planning. By 1890 what had once been considered a self-regulating device for producing happiness automatically had come to be seen as a machine badly in need of repair if not a complete overhaul.

Not all these would-be reformers of American society after 1890 agreed either on priorities or means. But the thrust of their ideas and programs pointed unmistakably toward the construction of a new national order. The historical meaning of this new vision declared itself in a repudiation of the permissive philosophy of Thomas Jefferson and the refurbishing of the original nationalist model of Alexander Hamilton. In the fields of law and constitutional theory the change brought replacement of outworn formal definitions of rights and duties with more flexible concepts of social utility requiring new roles for lawyers and legislators alike. In social reform the steady drift away from midcentury absolutes was accompanied by a new emphasis on training, expertise, and the predictive functions of science. To politics, the organizational revolution brought new styles of leadership and new approaches to the workings of government.

The distance the nation had traveled by 1920 could be measured in two widely different assessments of American politics and society, the first by the individualist prophet Ralph Waldo Emerson in the salad days of moral reform before the Civil War. Emerson located the national genius in the "wise man" with whose appearance "the state expires." "The tendencies of the times," Emerson predicted, "favor the idea of self-government, and leave the individual . . . to the rewards and penalties of his own constitution; which works with more energy than we believe whilst we depend on artificial restraints." Three-quarters of a century later the progressive sociologist Charles Horton Cooley took the measure of Emerson's prophecy only to discard it. Cooley dismissed Emerson's self-enclosed individual as a moral abstraction unknown to history. "In a truly organic life the individual is self-conscious and devoted to his work, but feels himself and that work as part of a large joyous whole. He is self-assertive, just because he is conscious of being a thread in the great web of events." The story of the years separating the sage of Concord from the progressive social scientist is the account of the American discovery of the great social web and the multitude of connecting threads that composed it.

Stabilizing the American Economy

     The American people greeted the arrival of the twentieth century by con-
sulting the facts and figures they hoped would explain the abundance heaped
upon them by their industrial revolution. Looking back across the previous decade, they could trace the rise of their country's wealth from $65 billion to $90 billion and the growth of their national income from $12 billion to $18 billion. If
progress could be measured in dollars and cents, then who could quarrel with the
obvious?

     Nowhere was the American faith in the quantitative more evident than in the
popular account of the recent economic growth of the nation. From a new breed
of economic experts, from professional economists and financial commentators,
from statistical compilations and industrial reports came reams of data, which,
Americans reasoned, could tell them not simply where they had been but where
they were headed. The mass of statistics distinguished two phases of growth in
American industry and agriculture in the sixty years before 1900. The first
phase had begun well before the Civil War, gathered momentum in the decades
following it, and culminated in the year of the Republican presidential triumph
of William McKinley, 1896. In business this first stage of economic growth was
typified by the startling success of John D. Rockefeller's Standard Oil Company
in gaining control over the oil industry; in agriculture, by the appearance of

mammoth ten-thousand-acre "bonanza" farms run with new mechanical seeders and harvesters. The second and still developing phase of economic consolidation was marked by the growth of industrial and financial mergers that, beginning in 1898 demolished the brownstone order of Gilded Age capitalism and cleared the ground for twentieth-century skyscrapers housing new corporate giants.

By 1900, most Americans looked to the merger movement for the clues to their recently acquired munificence. From one angle, the great merger movement appeared to be a towering peak of corporate consolidations. The number of mergers traced a sharp trajectory from 69 in 1897 to 303 a year later to 1,208 in 1899, before leveling off in the next three years at between 350 and 425. By 1900, there were already 73 so-called trusts, with capitalizations of over $10 million, and two-thirds of them had been established within the previous three years.

Viewed negatively, the merger movement looked like nothing so much as a gigantic hole into which some 300 businesses tumbled each year, swallowed by huge new combinations like United States Steel and General Electric. United States Steel absorbed over 200 manufacturing and transportation companies and quickly won control over two-thirds of the steel market. American Tobacco combined 162 independent companies and ruled all but 10 percent of the tobacco market. By 1904, the approximately 2000 largest firms in the United States composed less than 1 percent of the total number of the nation's businesses yet produced 40 percent of the annual value of the nation's industrial goods. By 1910, monopoly (domination of an industry by a single firm) and oligopoly (control established by a few large firms) had secured the commanding positions from which they would continue to dominate twentieth-century American life.

The merger movement that ended a half-century's search for economic order was both the logical outgrowth of rapid industrial development and at the same time an unsettling departure from remembered ways, the forerunner of massive changes in the way Americans lived and worked. The reorganization of the national economy after 1900 generated hopes and fears, made promises and raised doubts as it worked a revolution in the habits and values of the American people. How did it happen? What forces accounted for it?

The Foundations of the American Industrial Revolution

The key factor in the earlier phase of the economic transformation of the United States in the thirty years following the Civil War was the unprecedented growth of American cities. An enormous demographic shift had piled native-born citizens and recently arrived immigrants into metropolitan areas where they furnished vast new markets for consumer goods of all kinds, both basic necessities like food and clothing and newly developed products like sewing-machines, typewriters, and cigarettes. In the four decades surrounding the Civil

CITY TRAFFIC IN THE NINETIES

Trolleys, horse-drawn cabs, delivery wagons, and wary
pedestrians compete for space on Chicago's Clark Street.
(*Library of Congress.*)

War, the population of American cities rose at the rate of 4 percent per decade;
by 1880 over a quarter of the nation's people lived in urban areas. In the remaining years of the century, the urban population grew even faster—at the phenomenal rate of 6 percent per decade, until by 1900 a full 40 percent of the American
people lived in cities. Even more important, they tended to concentrate in giant
metropolitan centers like New York, Chicago, Philadelphia, and Detroit. "We
cannot all live in cities," Horace Greeley complained to a younger generation
headed toward the metropolis, "yet nearly all seem determined to do so. . . . 'Hot
and cold water,' baker's bread, the theatre, and the streetcars . . . indicate the
tendency of modern taste."

As cities grew at a pell-mell pace, pushing the boundaries of old commercial centers into surrounding suburbs along elevated railroads and trolley lines, they themselves became consumers of heavy industrial goods—electric dynamos, telephone wire, lead pipe and copper tubing, streetcars and the motors to run them. Cities, whether underwriting large public constructions like John and Washington Roebling's magnificent Brooklyn Bridge or encouraging private ventures like Louis Sullivan's steel-framed Wainwright Building in Saint Louis, supplied an insatiable appetite for all the products turned out by the American industrial machine. And with huge concentrations of "new immigrants" from southern and eastern Europe, cities also became producers as well as consumers of industrial abundance.

It was not only the mushroom growth of cities that made an economic revolution, but also the continuing expansion of a transcontinental railroad network. Railroads fed growing heavy industry with orders for equipment, triggered a process of large-scale formation of investment capital, and linked the cities of the nation, first in a loose network of commercial centers and then in the outlines of a national market system. Total railroad mileage rose from 35,000 miles of track in 1865 to 166,000 a quarter-century later. Transcontinental lines became primary arteries for distributing consumer goods. By 1890 railroad transporta-

Principal Railroads, 1890

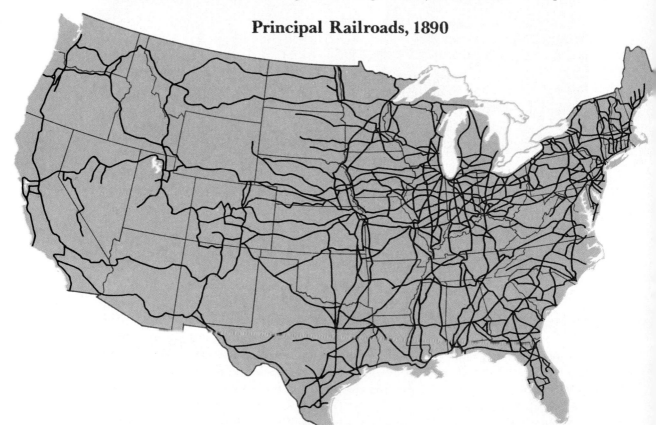

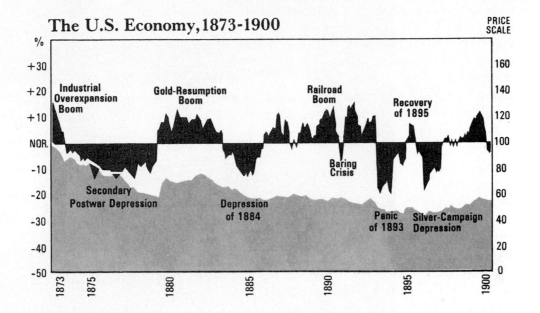

The U.S. Economy, 1873-1900

tion was dominated by a small group of integrated lines like the New York Central and the Pennsylvania roads in the East, the Burlington system in the Midwest, and the Union Pacific, Northern Pacific, and Great Northern routes to the West Coast. Once an efficient distributing system complete with telegraph network had been built, American businessmen were able to envision for the first time a national complex of large integrated firms, practicing economies of scale and passing these savings along to consumers in all parts of the country in lower prices for their goods they sent rolling along the nation's railroad tracks. Both as fact and as organizational idea, the railroad played a major role in the economic transformation of the country.

Still another component of economic growth was the steady increase in labor-saving machinery that eventually and often unintentionally led to better working conditions and a growing investment in education. Technological development and managerial innovation worked together to improve the quality and performance of American labor. Throughout the nineteenth century, a huge reservoir of unskilled labor was considered essential to economic expansion, and as late as the First World War the national economy continued to depend on the unskilled labor of women and children. But propelled by technology, the long-term trend pointed in another direction. Despite the willingness of native-born youths fresh from the farm and young immigrants just off the boat to feed the furnaces and sweep the floors, it was machines that sent American productivity soaring after the turn of the century. And it was machines that accounted for the annual increase of 1 percent in the physical output per man-hour between 1889 and 1919.

Equally important in quickening the rate of national economic growth was the increasing availability of large amounts of investment capital. By the 1880s the

EDGAR THOMSON STEEL WORKS,
BRADDOCK, PENNSYLVANIA, 1908

Rapid industrialization was not
gained without high ecological
costs. (*Library of Congress.*)

rate of savings of Americans, which had doubled in thirty years, was helping to
form a huge pool of investment funds that began to flow into industry in increasing volume. Technology bred great expectations and with them a mounting demand for capital. In the early years of the oil business just after the Civil War,
John D. Rockefeller was able to acquire a small refinery for $10,000 and a large
one for $50,000. Twenty-five years later, it took over $200 million to incorporate
Federal Steel. In steel production, the expensive Bessemer process turned brittle
iron into flexible steel and transformed the industry. In oil, the development of
refining techniques accompanied the discovery of new uses for petroleum. In
nearly every industry—meat-packing with the refrigerated car, the electric industry with alternating current, the railroads with the air brake—technology
brought ever greater efficiency as it created ever greater demands for capital. On
the eve of the Civil War a total of $1 billion was invested in the nation's manu-
facturing plants, which turned out a collective product worth $1.8 billion and
employed 4.3 million workers. By 1900 the size of the work force had grown
fivefold and the total value of products nearly tenfold; at the same time, the
amount of invested capital had multiplied twelvefold.

Thus the merger movement at the end of the century seemed to have a logic
all its own. Mergers, with their vast concentration of power and control, appeared
to mark the emergence of a stable corporate society from the chaos of small-
scale competitive capitalism. Big businessmen and the new investment bankers
presumably held the answers to the pressing problems of economic disorder,
which was no longer seen as the price of progress.

The continuing instability of the American economy between 1870 and 1900—itself the most persuasive argument for economic concentration—was no mere figment of the business imagination but a hard-edged reality. For every year of upswing and expansion in this thirty-year period there was another of downturn and contraction. The American economy moved like a pendulum from flush to hard times and back again. The Panic of 1873 plunged the country into six years of depression, with mass unemployment, wage cuts, and price decline. Following a short season of recovery, a second recession buffeted the economy in 1884 and again sent prices skidding and workers into the ranks of the unemployed. Once more, after a brief respite, the Panic of 1893 brought four years of economic paralysis, from which the country had just recovered at the end of the century.

All three depressions were triggered by financial panics—the collapse of the investment houses of Jay Cooke in 1873 and of Grant and Ward in 1884, and of nearly the entire railroad empire in 1893. But satisfactory explanations of the causes of depressions were hard to come by. Whether they compared them to the swing of a pendulum, the breaking of a wave, or the onset of a fever, most American observers despaired of controlling the business cycle or easing the effects of periodic slumps. Despite the lessons in the need for economic planning that the Civil War had taught, the great majority of Americans still held fast to a Jacksonian faith in the self-regulating market, with which, conventional wisdom declared, government interfered at its peril.

The result of this popular belief in untrammeled business opportunity was a national government in the Gilded Age that frequently subsidized but seldom regulated. Politicians vied with businessmen in predicting marvelous achievements for a new industrial statesmanship left to its own devices. Corporations, Abram S. Hewitt, the wealthy iron-master told the Chicago Board of Trade in 1885, were the "best friends" the American people had. Farseeing industrialists were now "doing the work which was done by Jefferson and Madison in the early years of the Republic."

Politicians deferred to such business leadership, and the directive force of government at all levels tended to disappear in misty hopes for ever growing prosperity. The great steel manufacturer Andrew Carnegie explained the terms of the new social contract in language that a business civilization readily understood. It would be a mistake, Carnegie insisted, for the American community to shoot its millionaires, since after all they were the "bees that [made] the most honey. "Under our present conditions the millionaire who toils on is the cheapest article which the community secures at the price it pays for him, namely, his shelter, clothing and food." Carnegie need not have worried; there would never be an open season on American millionaires.

Business Fills a Vacuum

The renunciation of public authority over industrial growth cast the burden of creating economic stability on American businessmen themselves. Blessed with innovative talent, abundant material resources, and the nearly total freedom to use them, American businessmen were the first to respond to the challenge of disorder with new devices for securing stability and increasing profits. But businessmen after the Civil War tended to direct the diagnostic skills they possessed to specific problems only. In their view, the troubles besetting the American economy required, not a public policy designed to regulate growth, but short-term survival strategies to protect the individual firm against fate.

Chief among the most obvious threats to American prosperity was a long-term drop in prices in the last three decades of the nineteenth century. In these years the wholesale price index fell from a high of 174 in 1866 to 135 four years later and then to 100 by 1880 and 82 in 1890. Although scarcely continuous—as consumers knew full well—this general downward trend of prices clearly showed the effects of two new factors in the national economy. Production costs were declining, and competiton for markets was increasing dramatically. Threatened with recurrent panics, intense competition, collapsing prices and the prospect of shrinking profits, the more innovative of the nation's business leaders began to experiment with a variety of techniques for gaining greater control over their industries. Their inventions were the structural improvisations of a business community confronted with severe problems but left to find its own solutions. In deciding to replace a small business economy with its free market system, Amer-

On the Promenade, Brooklyn Bridge, New York, U. S. A.
Copyright 1897 by Strohmeyer & Wyman.

ON THE PROMENADE, BROOKLYN BRIDGE, 1897

In this stereopticon view New Yorkers enjoy a Sunday afternoon stroll. (*Library of Congress.*)

ican business leaders quickly came to play, however reluctantly, a revolutionary role.

Attaining stability in major industries required increasingly sophisticated techniques. The earliest and most primitive forms of organization, necessitating the least amount of change, were *cartels*, loose trade associations (pools) of independent business firms joined together to dominate an industry. The organizer of the Wire Nail Association explained the case for cartels with disarming candor:

There is nail machinery enough in this country to produce four times as many nails as can be sold. When there is no pool the makers simply cut each other's throats. Some people think there is something wicked about pools. When we were trying to get up the nail pool, I talked with directors of companies who held up their hands against going into any sort of combination. I said to them, "How much did you make last year?" "Not a cent." "Are you making anything now?" "No." "Well, what do you propose to do? Sit here and lose what capital you have got in the business . . . ?" There is only one way to make any money in a business like the nail business, and that is to have a pool.

Cartels met the problem of overproduction and falling prices through gentlemen's agreements; independent competitors agreed among themselves to accept quotas and refrain from price cutting. In organizing a pool in 1881 the whiskey distillers, for example, agreed that "only 28 percent of the full capacity [of member firms] shall be operated, and no stocking up beyond this amount under any circumstances." To tighten sagging steel prices, the steel rail manufacturers in 1887 formed the Steel Rail Association, one of the few genuinely successful pools, which established a strict quota system and instituted a series of stiff fines for uncooperative members. Although the Steel Rail Association continued to deny charges of price fixing, it nevertheless enjoyed a period of remarkable price stability thereafter.

Yet cartelization had distinct liabilities. Pools and trade associations flourished in good times but fell apart during recessions. Their agreements were unenforceable in the courts, and in general they tended to assume the community of interests they were in fact designed to create. American consumers, moreover, regarded such combinations an undue restraint of trade and scrutinized their operations with an ever more jaundiced eye.

Recognizing the limitations of pools, and confronted with aroused public opposition to secret agreements, pioneer reorganizers like John D. Rockefeller turned to "horizontal" combinations in the form of the trust. The trust was the brainchild of a member of Standard Oil's legal staff, the affable and shrewd Samuel C. T. Dodd, who patiently explained its advantages to his hesitant colleagues. Since state laws prohibited outright ownership by one company of the stock of another, Dodd admitted, there was no foolproof way of consolidating, holding and managing a string of separate companies.

But you could have a common name, a common office, and a common management by means of a common executive committee. . . . If the Directors of one of the companies and their successors shall be made Trustees of all such stock, you thus procure a practical unification of all the companies.

The idea worked. In 1882, forty-one stockholders in the Standard Oil Company of Ohio signed an agreement creating a board of nine trustees to whom they transferred all the properties and assets of their own companies in exchange for trust certificates. The trust agreement declared that "it shall be the duty of said Trustees to exercise general supervision over the affairs of said Standard Oil Companies, and as far as practicable over the other Companies or Partnerships, any portion of whose stock is held in said trust." The visible signs of this financial feat were 700,000 hundred-dollar certificates, the price of consolidated control over the oil industry. The corporate spirit had wrought its first miracle.

Many trusts and holding companies (integrated firms allowed to hold the stocks of other corporations), having won formal control over production and prices, were content to operate as loose cartels, simply parceling out shares of the market to their newly acquired properties without trying to impose a centralized management and authority. But soon the largest and most powerful businesses began to follow the examples of the Carnegie Steel Company, and of Gustavus Swift in meatpacking, by achieving "vertical" integration of their industries. They sought to combine under a single management all the processes of production and distribution—from sources of raw material to new marketing mechanisms. Increasingly after 1890, big business sought control that extended "backward" to resources and transportation as well as "forward" towards market control maintained by research departments and the development schemes of central business offices.

Financing this corporate revolution required immense sums of money, much of it recently made available in new forms. For the first seventy-five years of the nineteenth century, most of the capital for industrial investment had come out of the savings of the firms that used it. By 1900, however, the stock market had established itself as the main mechanism for exchanging securities and mobilizing the vast funds large-scale integrated businesses demanded. By the time the United States entered the First World War, Wall Street had succeeded in creating a genuine national capital market. Part of this growing supply of capital was derived from foreign investment, which increased from $1.5 to $3.5 billion between 1870 and 1900. Even more important was the dramatic rise in the personal savings of Americans, which peaked in the 1870s and 1880s and provided large reserves of investment capital eventually flowing into the new "industrials."

The increase in personal savings was accompanied by the rapid growth of financial institutions—commercial banks, savings banks, and life insurance companies—that served as intermediaries between the investor and the business firm. Above all, the stock market facilitated the work of promoters and investment bankers by mobilizing buyers of stock and stimulating demand through overcapitalization. Growing numbers of investors, responding to the lure of profits, became buyers of more and more securities. "Probably four-fifths of the companies that are organized," Roger Babson reported, "whether in the transportation, electric power, or industrial field, are organized primarily not to transport passengers or generate power or manufacture goods, but to get securities to sell." Between 1896 and 1900 the number of new industrials listed on the board of the New York Stock Exchange more than doubled—from 20 to 46—with the securities of integrated corporations leading the way.

It was natural for a new generation of promoters and investment bankers to discern in industrial combination, if not the hand of God, at least an inexorable law of nature at work ordering the business affairs of the world. Samuel C. T. Dodd, Rockefeller's counsel, warned of the futility of tinkering with the celestial machinery. "You might as well endeavor to stay the formation of the clouds, the falling of the rains, or the flowing of the streams as to attempt by any means or in any manner to prevent organization of industry, association of persons, and the aggregation of capital to any extent that the ever growing trade of the world may demand."

And indeed, the success of mergers was difficult to deny. The facts of industrial and financial combination seemed to emphasize several practical advantages of monopoly and oligopoly. By 1895, the remarkable growth and swelling profits of Standard Oil, American Sugar Refining, and American Tobacco had marked out what appeared to be a sure route to salvation through combination. John W. "Betcha-Million" Gates, the flamboyant president of the newly fashioned American Steel and Wire Company, boasted of the blessings conferred on his trust by integration. "We are the owners of iron mines, miners of ore, owners of coal mines, burners of coke." Judge Elbert Gary explained Federal Steel's sudden success in similar terms: "It takes the ore from the ground, transports it, manufactures it into pig iron, manufactures pig iron into steel, and steel into finished products, and delivers those products." Even more impressive was the formation of United States Steel (1901), into which went some 200 manufacturing plants and transportation companies, 1000 miles of railroad, 112 blast furnaces, and 78 ore boats. Soon U.S. Steel was employing 170,000 workers as it gathered control over 60 percent of the country's steel capacities. Its initial capitalization at $1.4 billion was three times the annual expenditure of the federal government.

Increased efficiency, elimination of waste, bigger shares of the market, and anticipated though not always actual economies of scale—all were factors that ensured larger profits and convinced adventurous businessmen of the need to pursue mergers. By 1910, mergers had spread to all the principal sectors of the economy, and many of the twentieth century's most powerful corporations had been formed: Swift and Armour, Standard Oil and Texaco, General Electric and Westinghouse, International Harvester and DuPont. When the first great wave of mergers receded, it left standing the institutional forms of a new corporate

capitalism; they were the mammoth integrated enterprises with interlocking structures, managed by professionals with newly acquired expertise, selling their increasing variety of products in shared markets at administered prices. The great merger movement declared the bankruptcy of laissez-faire competition and announced the imminent arrival of a modern corporate society in need of new definitions to replace the outworn pieties of pluck and luck. In place of a host of small- and medium-sized business firms scrambling for a share of the market and justifying their rivalry with clichés drawn from classical economy, there stood an increasing number of huge unified structures based on the bureaucratic values of efficiency and predictability. The corporate revolution was by no means over by 1914, and the nation in the Progressive years continued to support a dual economy of big and little business. But the meaning of the merger movement was unmistakable: most Americans believed that bigger was better.

Organizing the mergers and raising the capital to launch them quickly became the specialty of investment bankers like J. P. Morgan and Jacob Schiff, who dominated the American economy in the first years of the twentieth century as they never would again. While taking a handsome slice of stock in the consolidations they created, they became powerful middlemen between an eager investing public and an expansive business community. They arranged the mergers and floated the stock, stabilizing the workings of their new creations, and manufacturing favorable publicity. Their success could be read in the achievements of the House of Morgan, which by 1912, together with the Morgan-controlled First National

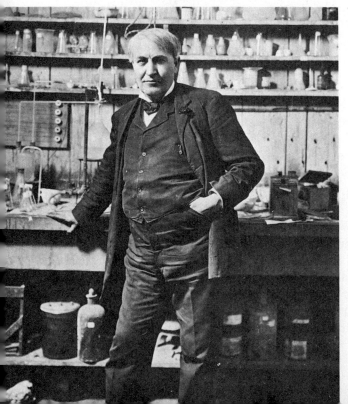

TWO AMERICAN HEROES

Edward Steichen's portrait of J. Pierpont Morgan as the awesome financial wizard (left) contrasts sharply with Thomas A. Edison in his laboratory in the legendary pose of the native American genius (right). (*Left, The Museum of Modern Art; right, Courtesy of National Park Service.*)

Bank of New York and the Rockefeller-managed National City Bank, held 341 directorships in 112 national corporations worth $22.2 billion.

In the public imagination the entire merger movement became personified in the investment banker, part savior of a threatened economy, part devil in disguise. For their everyday heroes, Americans might prefer the inventor and the engineer — Thomas Edison, Alexander Graham Bell, George Westinghouse; but they also admired, feared, envied, and puzzled over the new industrial and financial moguls who now presumably managed the economy of the country. The awesome J. P. Morgan, the circumspect Jacob Schiff, and their clients and lesser breeds of big businessmen seemed to embody the combination of inventive energy and financial shrewdness, the drive for power and the pursuit of profits, an alternating boldness and extreme caution that mirrored an American public's ambivalence towards industrial plenty and the concentrated power needed to produce it.

The heroes of the new corporate age, like their many admirers, were never entirely clear about their aims. The president of the newly formed International Silver Company, an amalgam of 16 former independents, as he testified before the Industrial Commission in 1899, betrayed the confusion of motives underlying the merger movement. To his persistent questioners, he unwittingly confessed the difficulty of distinguishing between scale economies and the desire for monopoly control as the primary incentive for combination.

Q. What was the purpose of your combination — to repress this competition, or to make economies of manufacturing?

A. That was what we were trying to do; both.

Q. Both?

A. To make economies and put the thing under one administration, just as I said before. That was all there was to it.

None of the new men of business — corporate executive, financial mogul, professional manager — was very explicit about the ultimate meaning of his vision of an industrial heaven on earth. Heavy capital investment, rapid plant expansion, increased production and reduced overhead, economies of scale, market control — all to what greater good? For profits, surely, and for rising quantities of consumer goods for more and more people. But beyond that? What did the manufacture and constant manipulation of consumer demand mean for individual freedom of choice? Was standardization of products and prices really so desirable? How were Americans to equate rising standards of living with loss of control over production? How could big business be called to account and made to deliver on its promise of economic security for all citizens? Were huge industrial and financial combinations compatible with political democracy and social responsibility? These were questions that neither the corporate revolutionists nor their uneasy admirers equipped with production statistics could quite answer. Such fundamental questions posed a continuing twentieth-century dilemma.

The Counterrevolution Fails

The same questions troubled the opponents of big business, whose numbers and influence also grew rapidly after the Civil War. Ultimately the antimonopolists failed, but not for lack of numbers. The antimonopoly army in the last quarter of the nineteenth century included at one time or another farmers and workingmen clinging to a belief in equal opportunity; small businessmen with their dreams of sudden fortune; and liberal publicists, country lawyers, clergymen, and academicians who enjoyed a traditional and honorable status and feared losing it to new big businessmen. Antimonopoly found a congenial home in the major protest parties of the period, from the Grangers and the Greenbackers of the 1870s to the Populists of the 1890s. According to their sharpest antagonists, trusts held the people's hands while they picked their pockets. Other critics pointed to the political depredations of monopolies, "these unnatural and unnecessary monsters" roaming the American terrain. A Populist editor in 1891 summed up the frustration of discovering that monopoly was the "logical result of the individual freedom which we have always considered the pride of our system." Americans, he added, had always subscribed to the "very greatest degree of liberty" and the "very least legal restraint," a creed which, paradoxically, had encouraged a predatory big business to preempt the powers of the community and defy the public will.

Most of the opposition to bigness was based on apprehension rather than solid evidence. The antimonopoly indictment tended to dissolve into charges of conspiracy and denunciations of greed precisely because the facts of economic concentration seemed so inconclusive. Monopolies, it was widely held, misallocated and underused resources and thus kept the nation's total output lower than it might have been. If pools, trusts, and all the other instruments of business collusion did not actually raise prices, they at least had the power to do so at will. Their power, moreover, had been acquired by driving out the small competitor, another good reason for demanding their dissolution.

Trusts, according to still another group of critics, were socially inefficient. They protected the weak at the expense of the strong. They sheltered inefficient producers within vast integrated structures where their inefficiencies went unnoticed. Not all the opponents of monopoly agreed that the business world should be ruled by the law of the survival of the fittest, but the word *unnatural* struck a universal chord of response on whose notes hung the real meaning of the case against big business.

Beneath the antimonopolist account of the recent past lay the presumption of a "natural development" that trusts were violating. For social prophets like Henry George and Edward Bellamy, whose bestsellers *Progress and Poverty* (1879) and *Looking Backward* (1888) commanded national attention, for countless other publicists and popularizers of the case against monopoly, "natural" economic growth meant a steady rate of development accompanied by full employment and

LOUIS SULLIVAN BUILDINGS

By 1880 Chicago had become the center of a new "commercial style" of city architecture, the home of the steel-framed tall office building that frankly combined the commercial and the functional. The city boasted Henry H. Richardson's mammoth Marshall Field Warehouse, the pioneer William L. Jenney's Home Insurance Company, and impressive commercial structures by Daniel Burnham, William Holabird, John W. Root, and, the greatest of the Chicago school, Louis Sullivan. Three of Sullivan's most famous buildings are shown here. On the opposite page, the Guaranty Building, Buffalo, New York. (*Chicago Architectural Photo Co.*) On this page right, the Carson, Pirie, Scott Department Store, Chicago. (*Chicago Architectural Photo Co.*) On this page below, the "Golden Door" entrance to the Transportation Building, Chicago World's Fair. (*Brown Brothers.*)

widespread consumption. According to this reasoning, healthy societies like the United States enjoyed a "normal" pace of growth with which monopolies played havoc by accelerating the growth rate and stimulating speculation. If trusts, pools, and all other artificial contrivances could simply be dismantled and their privileges annulled, the American economy would return to a steadier rate of "real growth" that would spread the benefits of industrialism evenly throughout society.

This fiction of the "natural economy," which Americans had inherited from midcentury, tended to direct attention away from the central problem of stabilizing the economy and towards peripheral matters of morality. Monopolies, the indictment went, choked off inventions and bottled up technological improvement. They fixed prices, rigged markets, and hoodwinked consumers. They gave to selfish men the power to direct and dispose of the wealth of an entire society. They corrupted the political process. Total moral collapse would surely follow the arrival of corporate consolidation. Not all these charges were wide of the mark, but they offered little in the way of useful strategy. Stability, in the view of the antimonopolists, was generally assumed to be an automatic by-product of a free market. Because the opponents of monopoly refused to consider controls on the business cycle or a consistent policy of business regulation, they let the initiative fall into the hands of the nation's industrial and financial leaders.

Before 1890 opposition to monopoly proved largely ineffective. In the 1870s, the Patrons of Husbandry, or the Grange, as the national farmers' organization was called, turned to politics in states like Illinois and Wisconsin and passed laws regulating the rates charged by railroads for hauling freight and storing grain. Although the Supreme Court had originally upheld these so-called Granger laws, in 1885 the Court made it painfully clear that individual states were forbidden to regulate rates for interstate carriers.

Nor on the federal level was the Interstate Commerce Act (1887) much more successful in bringing the railroads to heel. The act prohibited pools, rebates, and rate discrimination and set up a commission to investigate violations, but the commission's findings could be enforced only in the courts, a costly and cumbersome procedure. Although the Interstate Commerce Act marked the beginning of the public's acceptance of federal government intervention, it did not establish an effective policy of rate regulation.

By the time Congress responded to the public clamor to "do something about the trusts" by passing the Sherman Antitrust Act in 1890, more than a dozen states had already attempted some kind of antitrust legislation aimed at making restraint of trade "illegal, actionable and indictable." Big business, however, countered these attempts by moving into more permissive states like New Jersey, where they secured generous enabling laws. Henry Demarest Lloyd, perhaps the severest critic of monopoly, complained that Standard Oil, in its bid for preferential treatment, had done everything to the Pennsylvania legislature except refine it.

The Sherman Act brought no antimonopoly millennium. The bill, which John Sherman of Ohio introduced in the Senate, quickly found its way to the Judiciary Committee, which rewrote it before sending it to the full Senate where it passed by a vote of 52 to 1. The House, in turn, passed the measure unanimously. The Sherman Act was an honest if confused effort to create legislation that was more than symbolic. Yet big business could take heart from the long list of unanswered questions concerning enforcement. Article I declared "every contract, combination in the form of trust or otherwise, or conspiracy in restraint of trade or commerce among the several States . . . illegal." But what was "unreasonable restraint"? What constituted monopoly? How much directive power over an industry spelled "control"? More difficult still, how was the government to proceed in breaking up monopolies?

These questions the Sherman Act left to the government attorneys and the judges, who at least during Cleveland's and McKinley's administrations in the 1890s were not disposed to halt the merger movement. Richard Olney, Cleveland's waspish attorney general, spoke the collective mind of business when he approved the Supreme Court's refusal to break up the sugar trust in the E. C. Knight case. "You will observe that the government has been defeated in the Supreme Court on the trust question. I always supposed it would be, and have taken responsibility of not prosecuting under a law I believed to be no good."

MADISON SQUARE PARK CAB STAND, 1900

New York shows its best face along a fashionable boulevard. (*Museum of the City of New York.*)

Labor unions, on the other hand, seemed to Olney and his masters thoroughly objectionable conspiracies against trade. When Eugene Debs' American Railway Union in its epochal battle with the Pullman Company in Chicago in 1894 refused to move the mails, Olney drew up an injunction declaring the union in restraint of trade and successfully prosecuted Debs for contempt of court in violating the injunction. On appeal, the Supreme Court upheld the application of the Sherman Act to labor unions.

The Sherman Act was applied adversely in two railroad cases in 1897 and 1898 and again, more notably, in the Northern Securities case in 1903, which put an end to J. P. Morgan's dream of merging the Northern Pacific, Union Pacific, and Burlington railroads. Yet only eighteen cases were initiated in the first ten years following the passage of the Act, and in the crucial Knight case a poorly drafted brief allowed a conservative Court to declare the American Sugar Refining Company—a trust controlling 98 percent of the industry—not technically in restraint of trade.

When Theodore Roosevelt arrived in office as the new century began, the fortunes of the antimonopolists appeared to improve. Moreover, Roosevelt's successor, William Howard Taft, continued to initiate suits against monopolies. The Sherman Act, besides breaking up the Northern Securities Company, was applied successfully in 1911 against the Standard Oil and American Tobacco companies. Still, by that time it was all too evident that the Act, far from achieving the results its framers intended, was strengthening rather than checking the forces behind the merger movement. By making it clear that not every restraint of trade was unreasonable, and further, by ruling cartel behavior unacceptable but full-blown mergers legitimate, the courts invited big business to abandon looser forms of organization for tighter and more controlling ones.

Battered but durable, the spirit of antimonopoly survived down to the First World War, kept alive by various reform enthusiasms like those of Wisconsin's Governor Robert LaFollette and by new energies generated in the Democratic South during the first administration of Woodrow Wilson. Gathering coherence from the economic analysis and social theory of several of Wilson's advisors, in particular Louis Brandeis, antimonopoly sentiment supplied the impetus for the passage in 1914 of the Clayton Antitrust Act. Yet while the Clayton Act duly defined certain unfair practices like interlocking directorates and price discrimination, and a supplementary Federal Trade Commission act provided for publicity and prosecution of violators, the momentum of business combination was scarcely broken. The advantages of bigness now appeared compelling, a fact attested to by the incorporation of the giant General Motors soon after the Clayton Act was passed. With these meager accomplishments to show for forty years of continual agitation, the opponents of monopoly quit the field to await another call to battle in the waning years of the New Deal. The counterattack against big business had failed.

The Farmers' Fight Against Disorder

Although American farmers were loath to admit it, their problems from 1870 to 1900 were not very different from the problems that industry confronted—enormously increased production, falling prices, and inefficient and generally inequitable marketing processes. Just as technology revolutionized industrial production after 1870, so mechanical reapers, harrowers, spreaders, and harvesters dramatically expanded agricultural productivity. With a cradle scythe, a wheat farmer could cut two to three acres a day; with a self-raking reaper he could cut twelve. By 1880 a full 80 percent of American wheat was being harvested by machine. Farm machinery, valued at $42 million in 1870, surpassed the $100 million mark thirty years later.

Another important cause of increased productivity was regional crop specialization—wheat and hogs in the trans-Mississippi West, dairy products in the Old Northwest, and cotton in the South—encouraged by the railroads and new machinery. Beyond these two factors, however, lay a startling increase in world demand for staples after 1870 which acted much like growing American cities in

POPULIST COUNTRY

Beyond the 100th meridian rain was scarce, trees non-existent, neighbors few, and life bleak. (*National Archives.*)

providing markets for industrial goods. The two developments were related. As American staples flooded Europe, prices for foodstuffs fell sharply there, an event quickly followed by collapsing land prices. The agricultural depression in Europe drove millions of peasants and small farmers out of the countryside and into seaports, the first stopping point en route to American cities. Both in Europe and in America, cheaper food hastened industrial transformation, but in the United States the farmers also paid a large part of the bill for modernization by ensuring a favorable balance of trade with massive exports of staple crops at declining prices.

From one vantage point, the American farmer's shift from subsistence farming to specialized commercial farming meant progress toward a higher standard of living. But this advantage was soon offset by the commercial farmer's suspicions that he had become a prisoner of the market, locked into a price structure from which there was no ready means of escape. With the onset of the world agricultural depression in the 1870s, the price curve for staple crops dropped precipitously and the income of the farmer slid down it. Wheat plummeted from $1.19 a bushel in 1881 to a low of 49¢ in the depression year 1894. Corn fell in the same period from 63¢ a bushel to 18¢. Buying in a protected market and selling in an unprotected one, the staple-crop farmer saw himself as the victim of a logical absurdity: he was forced to overproduce while someone else walked off with his dwindling profits. Why, he asked, as the producer of the largest share of the nation's abundance, should his burdens grow heavier every year? Why, while the rest of the country advanced towards prosperity, was he going backwards? A Kansas farmer in 1891 summarized these feelings of betrayal.

At the age of 52 years, after a long life of toil, economy, and self-denial, I find myself and family virtually paupers. With hundreds of hogs, scores of good horses, and a farm that rewarded the toil of our hands with 16,000 bushels of golden corn we are poorer by many dollars than we were years ago. What once seemed a neat little fortune and a house of refuge for our declining years, by a few turns of the monopolistic crank has been rendered valueless.

As God's chosen, the American farmers were being sorely tried.

To increase output and cut costs, many staple-crop farmers, like their counterparts in business, borrowed heavily to buy mechanized equipment only to find themselves faced with high interest rates and tight money. Currency contraction, they reasoned, lay at the root of their troubles; it cut consumption, and so prices fell. Economists and eastern financial experts might assure the American public that price decline was a natural result of overproduction, but farmers in the trans-Mississippi West and the South explained their difficulties in terms of "underconsumption" and blamed hard-money "gold bugs" and the bankers.

As staple-crop farmers singled out the gold standard as their chief enemy, and identified their own distress with the plight of debtors everywhere, they dreamed of forging a common cause of "true producers" on which to build a new national economy. When prices decline, so their reasoning went, all little people, the urban as well as the rural, find themselves in exactly the same predicament, squeezed between the fixed costs of borrowing capital and the slumping prices resulting from the tight money policies of an unresponsive federal government. Though this reasoning was accurate in a way, the hopes for a national coalition of farmers and industrial workers foundered on the rocks of cultural and religious as well as regional and economic differences. American farmers never would succeed in converting city workers to their cause.

Meanwhile tight money and sharp price drops combined, first in the 1870s and then again in the 1890s, to drive the farmer into protest politics and third parties. Reform politics came first to the farmers of the Old Northwest in the aftermath of the Panic of 1873, as the Grangers began to experiment with cooperative storage and marketing schemes. At the same time these Western farmers together with businessmen of the region conducted forays into state politics to force passage of railroad regulation. Yet significant rate regulation would be late in coming to the rescue of farmers; when it did, it was more a result than a cause of their improved bargaining power.

The 1880s saw the growth of regional farm organizations like the Agricultural Wheel and the National Farmers Alliance, which joined in 1888 to form the Southern Alliance boasting more than a million members. In the Great Plains states the Northern Alliance became the mouthpiece of staple-crop producers. Even though the South and West agreed on diagnosis and prescription—antimonopoly, producers' and marketing cooperatives, and cheap money—only with reluctance did they enter the political arena together as a third party. Out of their agreement at Omaha in 1891 came the Populist crusade, which rallied agrarian discontent around the symbols of conspiracy and decline while advancing specific interest-group demands. This coupling of rhetorical excess and hard-nosed analysis had scarcely altered in twenty years even though farmers' attitudes had swung from an initial nonpartisanship to intense political involvement. Until the defeat of William Jennings Bryan by McKinley in 1896 shattered the farmer's dream of national redemption, recurrent apocalyptic fantasies and millennial hopes continued to characterize his discontent Populism when it arrived drew on profound convictions of betrayal.

The basic insight of American farmers throughout the nineteenth century was the moral primacy of agriculture. This view was stated most eloquently by William Jennings Bryan in his famous "Cross of Gold Speech," at the Democratic convention in 1896. "You come to us and tell us that the great cities are in favor of the gold standard," the Great Commoner declaimed. "We reply that the great cities rest upon our broad and fertile prairies. Burn down your cities and leave our farms, and your cities will spring up again as if by magic; but destroy our farms and grass will grow in the streets of every city in the country." Bryan confirmed the farmer's own belief, borne out by the record, that he had indeed built America. He had cleared and cultivated the land, raised the foodstuffs, supplied

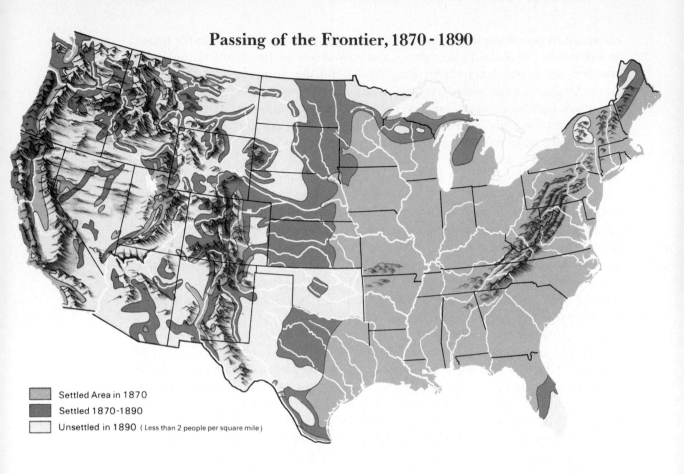

Passing of the Frontier, 1870 - 1890

Settled Area in 1870
Settled 1870-1890
Unsettled in 1890 (Less than 2 people per square mile)

the foreign trade, and constructed the material base on which a modern industrial society rested. The land, in spite of the violence methodically visited upon it,
remained foremost in the American moral imagination. "On the land we are
born, from it we live, to it we return again — children of the soil as truly as is the
blade of grass or the flower of the field," Henry George wrote in *Progress and
Poverty* in celebrating the redemptive power of the American land. George's
message reached millions of already converted farmers who sought only endorsement of their faith.

In more measurable terms the American land produced the agricultural
abundance with which the United States paid for the European goods and capital
needed to modernize. Farmers, who still considered themselves the owners of
the Garden of the World, lashed out with mounting frustration as an ungrateful
urban society denied their achievements, neglected their interests, ridiculed
their proposals for reform, and mocked their provincial ways and narrow lives.
Out of this massive loss of confidence came a compensatory politics of alienation
in Populism. The Populists gathered their forces for the presidential election of
1892 determined to rescue the nation from moral and material ruin. "A vast

conspiracy against mankind has been organized on two continents and is taking possession of the world," their Saint Louis platform declared. "If not met and overthrown at once it forbodes terrible social convulsions, the destruction of civilization, or the establishment of an absolute despotism." With the advent of Populism, the American farmer's twenty-year crusade became a holy war.

By 1900, however, the predicted end of the world had failed to materialize. In the sharp upturn of the economy that opened the twentieth century, American farmers appeared willing to relinquish their millennial expectations for the more immediate gains that rising farm incomes furnished. The advantages of organization, consolidation and integration, which were the lessons being taught by big business, had now become too obvious for the farmer to ignore. He too could learn to read the statistics that told him what to do. The cheering figures on production and price that he began to consult were being compiled by the Division of Statistics of the Department of Agriculture whose other departmental divisions—soils, chemistry, pomology, and animal industry—attested to the effects of the continuing bureaucratic revolution in American agriculture. These figures, whether for soaring staple prices, or declining shipping costs, or estimates of rising production, continued to assure the farmer down to the First World War of the reality of his new-found prosperity. Between 1900 and 1910, the price of corn shot up from 35¢ to 52¢ a bushel, wheat from 62¢ to 91¢, as the wholesale farm price index jumped 50 percent and the average price of farm land doubled from $20 to $40 an acre. As staple-crop farmers remembered with chagrin, if it had not been a frantic third-party politics that had accomplished all this, nevertheless the national economy was at last responding to their needs and demands. Just as American business opened the twentieth century by applying the lessons of consolidation with a will, so American farmers were beginning to follow the seemingly simple directives for finding safety in system and security in organization.

The most durable of the early twentieth-century farm organizations were producers' cooperatives that concentrated on solving the problems of price stability and marketing procedures. Except for their official nonprofitmaking status and their democratic voting procedures, cooperatives were modern corporations that became as streamlined and efficient as their counterparts in business. They also came to rely on experts and specialists, trained managers and accountants, legal advisers, lobbyists, and public relations men. Like the integrated industrial enterprise, they also achieved the equivalent of forward integration and market control by building their own facilities at railroad terminals and by writing ironclad contracts with their members compelling them to withhold their crops until the price was right. By 1910 the antimonopoly scruples of big farmers were already disappearing.

Prosperous farmers, like the big businessmen they were fast becoming, designed and built cooperatives as interest-group devices for solving particular problems. The Grangers, Knights of Labor, and Populists, who pioneered with

IN THE FIELDS OF WESTERN CALIFORNIA, 1902

Bonanza farms brought an end to the day of the self-sufficient yeoman but also the beginning of agricultural abundance. (*Library of Congress.*)

commodity cooperatives, envisioned the preservation of earlier conditions of independence and equality. The new farm organizations that accompanied the rise of Progressivism professed no such grandiose social aims but were content, with the return of flush times, to perfect the means the bureaucratic revolution had assigned to them. Why replace an economic system capable of producing the abundance that, however belatedly and unaccountably, was now being showered upon Jefferson's chosen people?

The leading advocates of the organizational revolution in American agriculture were not the staple-crop farmers in the trans-Mississippi West but the dairy, poultry, and fruit and vegetable farmers in the older sections of the East and Northwest and their competitors on the Pacific Coast, whose fortunes had risen steadily with the growth of metropolitan markets. With the return of prosperity, these groups put aside their interest in protest politics, never very strong, in favor of scientific methods and interest-group associations. By 1914 the cooperative marketing movement was in full swing, and dozens of livestock unions, dairymen's leagues, grain exchanges, cotton cooperatives, and tobacco pools were being founded each year. Cooperatives in turn spawned new pressure groups— the Farmers' Equity Union, the Farmers' Mutual Benefit Association, the Farmers' Social and Economic Union, the Farmers' Relief Association—all of them proclaiming as their own the slogan of the American Society of Equity: "What the farmer wants to produce is not crops, but money." In 1912, cooperatives secured the blessing of the Department of Agriculture, which provided them with their own fact-finding agency, the Bureau of Markets. Eight years later the formation of the American Farm Bureau Federation announced the arrival of modern agriculture as a national political force. Although the chief gains in numbers and influence were not to come until the 1920s, the commercialization of the American farmer had begun in earnest.

The dramatic shift in agrarian perceptions that accompanied the return of prosperity could be read in the changed outlook of one of the farmers' most impassioned spokesmen. Returning home to the Middle Border in 1889 at the height of the agrarian distress, Hamlin Garland, still an unknown but aspiring young writer, found his old neighbors caught up in social crisis and engaged "in a sullen rebellion against government and against God."

Every house I visited had its individual message of sordid struggle and half-hidden despair. . . . All the gilding of farm life melted away. The hard and bitter realities came back upon me in a flood. Nature was as bountiful as ever . . . but no splendor of cloud, no grace of sunset, could conceal the poverty of these people; on the contrary, they brought out, with a more intolerable poignancy, the gracelessness of these homes, and the sordid quality of the mechanical routine of these lives. I perceived beautiful youth becoming bowed and bent.

Convinced that "men's laws" rather than God's were responsible for "industrial slavery" as well as the degradation of the farmer, Garland brought to the Populist cause an enthusiasm for root-and-branch reform and an aesthetic theory to match. Yet fifteen years later with the Populist years behind him, Garland left the main traveled thoroughfares of agrarian protest for nostalgic excursions into the romantic high country of the Far Northwest, abandoning reform to settle in the bureaucratic environs staked out by Theodore Roosevelt's Country Life Commission. The commission, itself proof of the revival of the farmers' influence, was appointed in 1908 and charged with the task of improving rural life in the United States. The commissioners concluded, after taking the pulse of rural America and listening to a recital of its ailments, that what the farmer needed was simply to catch up with his city cousin, to "even up" the distribution of amenities between town and country. This recovery, according to the commission's diagnosis, involved agricultural credits, a highway program, rural free delivery, better schools, a country church movement to rescue "lost sheep," and very little else. Prosperity had soothed old discontents. By 1910, Hamlin Garland's outraged cry for justice "for the toiling poor wherever found" had receded into memory as American farmers settled in to enjoy their golden age, which statistics, government recognition, and their own pocketbooks told them had come at last.

Workers and the Challenge of Organization

Of all the groups enmeshed in the American economic revolution, the industrial workers depended the least on statistics to confirm what they already knew. And what they knew was that their rewards for tending the American industrial machine hardly matched their services. From assembled data at the end of the century, workers could have verified their impressions that the workweek for the "average" worker in industry was little less than 60 hours and that the "average" wage for skilled workers was about 20¢ an hour and for unskilled workers just half that amount. Annual wages for the factory worker in 1900 came to an average of $400 to $500, from which a working family saved an average $30 after spending nearly half the remainder for food, another quarter on rent, and the balance on fuel, light, and clothing. Earnings for workers engaged in manufacturing went up 37 percent between 1890 and 1914, but the cost of living between 1897 and 1914 rose 39 percent.

If there was a certain grim satisfaction in the knowledge that others shared their straitened circumstances, there was considerably less in the daily reminder that in spite of growing national abundance American workers and their families managed on very narrow margins. Their share of the pie, though larger than it had been a half-century earlier, was still comparatively small. A statistical breakdown of national income, had they consulted it, would have strengthened their conviction that workers, too, must organize for bargaining power. The richest tenth of the population received 33.9 percent of the nation's income, the poorest, 3.4 percent. The wealthier half of the country's income recipients accounted for over 70 percent of all income. The rich were certainly getting richer in 1900 while the American workers, if not absolutely poorer, were still not enjoying much of the wealth they were helping to create. Nor had they yet found the organizational power with which to counter the growing strength of big business. In 1900 a full 95 percent of the labor force in the United States remained unorganized, captive still of public opinion dead set against unions.

Prospects for the American worker had not always seemed so dim. As late as the 1880s, the goal of industrial unionism had remained within sight. The tradition of the solidarity of true producers, like the American farmers' myth of the chosen people, had originally been assembled by the Jacksonians and had survived the Civil War. This utopian ideal, foreshadowed in the National Labor Union in the early 1870s, was most eloquently stated in the platform of the Knights of Labor. There was no good reason, Terence V. Powderly, the mercurial president of the Knights insisted, why American workers building unions and cooperatives, owning and operating mines, factories, and railroads, should not usher in a new age of harmony and cooperation. This was the dream he held before his membership, which reached a peak of 700,000 in 1886.

In fact there were excellent reasons why the Knights of Labor failed to sustain its reform crusade. The attempt to organize workers by industry rather than craft put the organization in direct competition with skilled workers who resented its efforts. Powderly's antistrike policy seriously impaired the leaders' control

A HOT-WEATHER NIGHT ON NEW YORK'S LOWER EAST SIDE

For this father and his children, the sidewalk provided cooler sleeping quarters than the tenement apartment above. (*Brown Brothers.*)

over an increasingly militant rank and file. Cooperatives, overly ambitious and badly underfinanced, collapsed one after another, and the general executive board of the union could not meet the demands for support thrust upon it by hard-pressed locals determined to strike. "The number of appeals for assistance," Powderly complained in 1883, "now being showered on the board is frightful, and nothing but a treasury of millions could stand it. My advice to the board is to shut down on all appeals and stick to the original plan of the order, that of educating the members as to the folly of strikes."

Education converted neither businessmen, who were inclined to equate union leaders with secessionists in the late War of the Rebellion, nor local members, who were anxious to test their strength in encounters with railroad management. A series of strikes culminated in the disastrous contest with Jay Gould's Texas Pacific Railroad in 1886, and thereafter the Knights entered a period of sharp decline, a victim of business antagonism, craft union fears, and not least, its own illusions of grandeur. With the retreat of the Knights of Labor before the steady advance of the American Federation of Labor, the torch of industrial unionism and radical reform after 1900 passed to militant but marginal organizations like the Western Federation of Miners and its stepchild, the Industrial Workers of the World. The narrowed field of craft unionism was left to the country's skilled workers, who were not averse to a labor caste system, as it soon became apparent.

The American Federation of Labor (AFL), a flexible organization of craft unions formed in 1886, represented a new generation's capitulation to the corporate revolution. Labor too could learn the lessons of consolidation. "It is our purpose and a large part of our work has been devoted to gathering and concentrating the forces of labor into compact National Unions, and that work has been crowned with a success never before equalled," Samuel Gompers, the founder and longtime president of the AFL, reported in 1892. Gompers and his lieutenant, Adolph Strasser, readily confessed that their sole concern was for the skilled trades they represented and the immediate welfare of their members. Asked to define the "ultimate ends" of "pure and simple unionism," Strasser replied at once that the two terms were contradictory. "We have no ultimate ends. We are going on from day to day. We are fighting for immediate objects— objects that can be realized in a few years."

The new union leaders reminded businessmen that they too were "practical men," neither theorists nor reformers but pragmatists and opportunists, like their employers, organizers with their eyes on the main chance. The distance separating the AFL from its now moribund rival, the Knights of Labor, was best measured in Gompers's reply to the Socialist Morris Hillquit, who was bent on discrediting his rival. Hillquit demanded to know whether the president of the AFL really believed that American workers received the "full product" of their labor. Gompers brushed aside the question as meaningless in terms of the new industrial instrumentalism. "I will say," he replied, sidestepping the rusty ethical trap his interrogator had set, "that it is impossible for anyone to definitely say what proportion the workers receive as a result of their labor, but it is the fact that due to the organized-labor movement they have received and are receiving a larger share of the product of their labor than they ever did in the history of modern society." Accused by irate socialists and labor radicals of having betrayed the labor movement by refusing to develop a genuine social philosophy, Gompers and his craft unionists cheerfully admitted to a belief in half a loaf and a willingness to follow "the lines of least resistance."

"Least resistance" for organized labor as the twentieth century opened meant accepting the merger movement and closing a bargain with big business. The trusts, Gompers announced, "are our employers, and the employer who is fair to us, whether as an individual, or a collection of individuals in the form of a corporation or a trust, matters little to us so long as we obtain fair wages." As for the wage system on which capitalism rested, there was little, he thought, to be gained by quarreling with it or dreaming up half-baked substitutes. Trade unionists should rest content with the argument that the right to strike was itself the greatest preventive of strikes.

The American Federation of Labor, modest in its aims and moderate in its counsels, overcame employer resistance only with difficulty and gained the leverage it sought at great cost. Although membership grew from 140,000 at its founding in 1886 to over 2 million in 1914, less than a third of the country's skilled workers could be found in its ranks by 1900. When war broke out in Europe in 1914, only 15 percent of the nonagricultural workers in the United States were members of any union.

With the banner of industrial unionism in tatters and the craft unions besieged by business opponents armed with new weapons like the injunction and the yellow-dog contract, American workers faced the prospect of increased control. Small businessmen sought to curtail their organizational freedom. This strategy promised a vigorous campaign of union-busting as the National Association of Manufacturers (NAM) in 1903 formed and funded the Citizens Industrial Association to spread the gospel of the open shop under the brand name "The American Plan." The success of their American Plan, conservative businessmen promised, would spell the doom of labor unions.

Big business hoped to control labor through the concepts of guided democracy. It offered a paternal concern for the American worker along with the concepts of arbitration and "responsible" leadership. The response of big business, unlike the NAM's unwieldy counteroffensive, recognized that labor's grievances were real and its demands for redress legitimate—an acknowledgment that workers' needs for security and stability were not so very different from the needs of management. In 1900, the agents of big business, led by progressive industrialists like George E. Perkins and financiers like J. P. Morgan, struck a bargain with

Gompers and founded the National Civic Federation on the proposition that labor, like business, must be encouraged to organize its interests and rally its forces for participation in the new corporate society.

The strategy of enlightened business interests required, first of all, vastly improved working conditions. Factory work was still alarmingly dangerous. A survey of industrial accidents for the year 1913 showed that some 25,000 workers had been killed on the job and another three-quarters of a million seriously injured. Then there were the problems of incentive, alienation, and the loss of community resulting from increased scale of business and the impersonality of the assembly line. These were eloquently described to the Industrial Commission in 1899 by a veteran shoe worker, who recalled the day of a rough shop-floor socialism before the advent of the giant mechanized factory. "In these old shops, years ago," he told the commissioners, "one man owned the shop; and he and three, four, five or six others, neighbors, came in there and sat down and made shoes right in their laps, and there was no machinery. Everybody was at liberty to talk. . . ."

But could this idyll be recovered or recreated? "We do not want to go back to the time when we could do without the sewing machine, or the machinery for manufacturing purposes, or the large aggregations of capital," a shoemaker replied, "but we want capital controlled in such a way that it will not result in the

SLUM INTERIOR

New Americans experienced various kinds of exploitation, among them unhealthy and expensive living quarters.

displacement of three-fourths of the population for the increased wealth of one-fourth of the population." In grudging admissions like this lay the secret of big business's success.

Workers packed in slums and ghettos of center cities in the opening years of the twentieth century knew precisely how far they stood from the margins of plenty. The quality of life in the working-class districts of most American cities was appalling. In 1915, President Wilson's Industrial Commission, still another investigatory body appointed to examine the causes of continuing industrial unrest, concluded: "A large part of the industrial population are . . . living in actual poverty." Exactly what proportion of the nation's working class lived below the subsistence level the commissioners did not care to estimate; they added, however, "It is certain at least one-third and possibly one-half of the families of wage earners employed in manufacturing and mining earn in the course of the year less than enough to support them in anything like a comfortable and decent condition." Urban housing for the new arrivals from Europe and the American countryside—whether three-story wooden firetraps in Boston's South End or

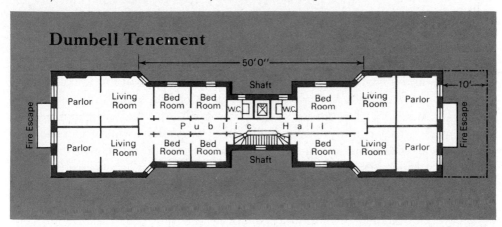

dumbbell tenements on New York's lower East Side or dilapidated single-family shanties in Cincinnati, St. Louis or Chicago—was generally deplorable and, worse still, expensive. Gas, water, electricity, sanitation, and transportation—all of the services needed to make the life of the city worker tolerable—were in short supply and of poor quality as late as 1900. These inadequacies, in fact, were the basis of the original reform challenge for urban coalitions of dissatisfied consumers.

The main surge in urban improvement began with the new century, and within a decade had succeeded in providing improved municipal services, better sanitation and health care, parks and recreational facilities, libraries and museums, giving cities a public face-lifting and genuine rejuvenation. But housing and personal standards of living improved much more slowly. The public life of American cities responded to the work of urban reformers with their vision of a renovated democratic purpose; yet blighted neighborhoods, fractured communities, crumbling apartments, and stunted lives continued to pose a stark reality for too many American workers. The environmental exploitation of American labor was not a major factor included in the pragmatic assessments of union organizers, but it was real nonetheless.

For recently arrived immigrants who endured these conditions and who comprised the major portion of the industrial labor force by 1900, there was yet another and more subtle kind of exploitation in the cultural drive to "Americanize" them as quickly as possible. All the ethnic groups arriving in such great numbers after 1880—Italians, Greeks, Poles, Russian Jews—were viewed at one time or another as dissidents and potential bomb throwers in need of the ministrations of cultural counterrevolutionaries teaching a kind of "Americanism" indistinguishable from conformity. Status anxieties, religious fears, a distrust of cultural pluralism, and nostalgia for a largely imaginary age of stability—all the yearnings of older American groups—combined with recurrent malfunctionings of the economy to intensify the desires of native-born Americans for unity and homogeneity.

Where the previous generation had singled out the political party as the chief agent of acculturation, reformers emphasized the school. As one observer explained to the readers of *World's Work* in 1903, "The results shown by the public schools seem little short of marvellous. There are many things in which, as a rule, the public consider that the public schools fail, but the one thing that cannot be denied—and it is the greatest—is that these boys and girls of foreign parentage catch readily the simple American ideas of independence and individual work and, with them, social progress." "Social progress," in the half-century after 1880, meant social equilibrium through Americanization: widespread literacy, technological education, elimination of child labor, cultural conformity, and last but not least, cultivation in an aspiring working class of a hearty appetite for all the consumer goods produced by the huge American industrial machine.

Thus the stabilization of big business in patterns of monopoly and oligopoly and the organizational revolution in American agriculture had their equivalent for industrial workers after 1900 in an effort to adjust them both as producers and consumers to necessary but subordinate roles in a corporate capitalistic society. In largely ignoring the alternatives posed by socialism, and in seemingly accepting their assignments, American workers added their share to the impression of inevitability created by production statistics.

The Fruits of Revolution

The glowing statistics of a materialistic society seemed to establish beyond question the reality of American progress and unity. For at least the first half of the nineteenth century Americans had been intoxicated with a sense of boundlessness of time and space, of individual opportunity and the national future. They had ritualized freedom as providential and pointed proudly to the absence of social and geographical fixity. By midcentury, however, the nation's physical boundaries had been virtually settled, and the Civil War overturned the last barriers to rapid modernization. By 1870 American energies at last could be fully devoted to mining the country's vast material treasures. At first, no price seemed too great for sustained economic growth. But then, by 1880, the costs began to seem excessive, first to businessmen and then to farmers and workers, who eventually became uneasy partners in completing the organizational revolution.

Like all revolutions, the economic transformation of the United States had unintended consequences. Used as an index of national prosperity, the statistics of growth seemed a simple instrument for measuring the accomplishments of a whole people. The national wealth, $16 billion in 1860 according to the estimate of government statisticians, had grown by 1900 to $88 billion, a per capita increase from $500 to $1,110. But these figures effectively masked differences of class, region, occupation, and the persistence of a grossly uneven distribution of income. Americans were being affected by the organizational revolution in drastically different ways. Yet the American dream of 1900 remained what it had been a half-century earlier, a vision of a people uniquely equipped to create and enjoy abundance. Economic integration itself seemed convincing proof of the near approach of "the promise of American life." A national market had been built and the nation's shelves stocked with an incredible variety of goods. In this sense the economic well-being of the nation appeared to be exactly what a new generation of American businessmen pronounced it, that is, a single economic system binding citizen and nation in a network of mutual benefits.

But beneath the surface, as the new century opened, lay not unity but multiplicity; not a single national purpose but competing and even warring interests; not pressures unifying American society but forces that threatened to fling it apart; not the conservation of national energies but their diffusion in politically volatile forms. Americans in the opening years of the twentieth century thus confronted a paradox capping a half-century of growth: the economic integration that had seemingly rescued them from chaos had set in motion cultural and political counterforces that threatened fragmentation, dispersion, diffusion, and isolation. To cope with these threats to national order the American people would require new and more sophisticated conceptions of social and political organization, and the capacity somehow to use them.

Suggested Readings

There are two outstanding accounts of the organizational revolution in American society in the half-century after 1870. Brief but still the model for more recent interpretive work is Samuel P. Hays, *The Response to Industrialism* (1957). Robert Wiebe, *The Search for Order* (1968) traces the shift from small-town America to modern bureaucratic society in terms of political institutions and social values as well as economic reorganization. John A. Garraty, *The New Commonwealth, 1877–1890* (1968) focuses on the crucial decade of the

1880s. Ray Ginger, *The Age of Excess* (1965) is a lively and impressionistic survey, and so is Howard Mumford Jones, *The Age of Energy: Varieties of American Experience, 1865–1915* (1970).

The technical literature on the developing economy in this period is extensive. Among the most useful studies of aspects of American economic growth discussed here are Clarence D. Long, *Wages and Earnings in the United States, 1860–1900* (1960); Albert Rees, *Real Wages in Manufacturing, 1890–1914* (1961); Rendig Fels, *American Business Cycles* (1959); and Milton Friedman and Anna J. Schwartz, *A Monetary History of the United States, 1867–1960* (1963). The early chapters in Alfred D. Chandler, Jr., *Strategy and Structure: Chapters in the History of American Industrial Enterprise* (1966) provide a compact summary of the first phase of business concentration. Ralph L. Nelson, *Merger Movements in American Industry* (1959) gives a detailed account of the great merger movement at the end of the nineteenth century, and Hans B. Thorelli, *Federal Antitrust Policy: The Origination of an American Tradition* (1955) traces the origins and development of the countermovement against monopoly. These and other recent findings are ably synthesized in Stuart Bruchey's brief but perceptive essay, *Growth of the Modern Economy* (1975) and in greater detail in W. Elliot Brownlee, *Dynamics of Ascent: A History of the American Economy* (1974).

The industrial transformation of the United States is characterized as a success story in Edward C. Kirkland's survey, *Industry Comes of Age: Business, Labor, and Public Policy, 1860–1897* (1961), which should be supplemented with Thomas Cochran, *The Inner Revolution* (1964). The development of the oil industry is exhaustively treated in Harold F. Williamson and associates, *The American Petroleum Industry* (2 vols., 1959–63), and Ralph W. Hidy and Muriel E. Hidy, *Pioneering in Big Business, 1882–1911: History of Standard Oil (New Jersey)* (1955). For changes in American banking practices in this period, see Fritz Redlich, *Molding of American Banking: Men and Ideas: Part II: 1840–1910* (1951), and for railroads, George R. Taylor and Irene Neu, *The American Railroad Network, 1861–1890* (1956), and Oscar O. Winther, *The Transportation Frontier: Trans–Mississippi West 1865–1890* (1964). Julius Grodinsky, *Transcontinental Railway Strategy, 1869–1893* (1962), analyzes the ideas and plans of the railroad builders and organizers; Lee Benson, *Merchants, Farmers, and Railroads* (1955), explores the movement for increased regulation; and Robert Fogel, *Railroads and American Economic Growth* (1964), offers an econometric revision of the role of the railroads in stimulating American economic growth. For an account of iron and steel, see Peter Temin, *Iron and Steel in Nineteenth-Century America: An Economic Inquiry* (1964).

The connections between economic theory and social policy are explored in Sidney Fine, *Laissez-Faire and the General Welfare State* (1956). Richard Hofstadter, *Social Darwinism in American Thought* (1945), and Robert McCloskey, *Conservatism in the Age of Enterprise* (1951), are highly readable accounts of economic and social conservatism in the Gilded Age. James Weinstein, *The Corporate Ideal in the Liberal State, 1900–1918* (1960), is a carefully documented study of a central organizational concept and its wide social and political meanings. Irvin G. Wyllie's *The Self-Made Man in America* (1954), scrutinizes a resilient American myth, and Edward C. Kirkland's lively essays in *Dream and Thought in the Business Community, 1860–1900* (1956), describe the utopian musings of American businessmen.

Biographies of the leading figures in the American industrial transformation are legion. Among the best are three monumental studies: Joseph Wall, *Andrew Carnegie* (1970); Alan Nevins, *Study in Power: John D. Rockefeller, Industrialist and Philanthropist* (2 vols., 1953); and Matthew Josephson, *Edison* (1959). Frederick Lewis Allen, *The Great Pierpont Morgan* (1940), takes the measure of the great financier in a colorful portrait, and Edward C. Kirkland, *Charles Francis Adams, Jr., 1835–1915* (1965), gives sympathetic treatment to a frustrated planner and organizer. Keith Sward, *The Legend of Henry Ford* (1948), and Frank E. Hill, *Ford: The Times, the Man, the Company* (1954), provide useful estimates of the automative pioneer.

The recent literature on American urbanization is admirably synthesized in two recent studies: Howard Chudacoff, *Evolution of American Urban Society* (1975), and Zane Miller, *Urbanization of America* (1973). Constance Green, *The Rise of Urban America* (1965), and A. T. Brown, *A History of Urban America* (1967), are also helpful surveys. For a model study of urban spread in this period see Sam Bass Warner, *Streetcar Suburbs: The Process of Growth in Boston, 1870–1900* (1971). The pervasive antiurbanism of American intellectuals is documented in Morton and Lucia White, *The Intellectuals vs. the City* (1962). Charles N. Glab, ed., *The American City: A Documentary History* (1963), offers a wide range of source materials. David Ward, *Cities and Immigrants: A Geography of Change in Nineteenth-Century America* (1971), traces the patterns made by the new arrivals from Europe, and Stephen Thernstrom, *The Other Bostonians* (1973), and Howard Chudacoff, *Mobile Americans: Residential and Social Mobility in Omaha, 1880–1920* (1972), are two important studies of urban mobility.

The story of agrarian developments after the Civil War is told in Fred A. Shannon, *The Farmer's Last Frontier* (1963). Two older works—Solon J. Buck, *The Granger Movement* (1913), and John D. Hicks, *The Populist Revolt* (1931)—are still useful surveys of their subjects. Irwin Unger, *The Greenback Era* (1964), and Walter T. K. Nugent, *Money and American Society, 1865–1880* (1968), examine monetary policy as it affected the farmer. For an illuminating discussion of agrarian politics in the South, see Theodore Saloutos, *Farmer Movements in the South, 1865–1933* (1960). Eric E. Lampard, *The Rise of the Dairy Industry in Wisconsin: A Study in Agricultural Change, 1860–1920* (1963), studies developments in a single industry, and Joseph C. Bailey, *Seaman A. Knapp* (1945), presents a profile of a "new" farmer. Harold Barger and H. H. Landsberg, *American Agriculture, 1899–1939: A Study of Output Employment and Productivity* (1942), traces the continuing rise of agricultural productivity in the early twentieth century. Allen G. Bogue, *Money at Interest: The Farm Mortgage on the Middle Border* (1955), offers a revisionist account of agrarian distress in that region. Grant McConnell, *The Decline of Agrarian Democracy* (1953), describes the growth of commercial farming, and Reynold M. Wik, *Steam Power on the American Farm* (1953), treats early technological change and its effect on American agriculture. The elimination of the Indian in the trans-Mississippi West is chronicled in two readable studies: Ralph K. Andrist, *The Long Death: The Last Days of the Plains Indians* (1964), and Dee A. Brown, *Bury My Heart at Wounded Knee* (1971).

Two brief surveys of American labor, Joseph G. Rayback, *A History of American Labor* (1959), and Henry Pelling, *American Labor* (1959), should be supplemented with the older but still valuable Norman J. Ware, *The Labor Movement in the United States, 1860–1896: A Study in Democracy* (1929). The conflict between the Knights of Labor and the new trade unions is explored in Gerald N. Grob, *Workers and Utopia* (1961). Philip Taft, *The A.F. of L. in the Time of Gompers* (1957), is an authoritative study of the organization in its formative years. Bernard Mandel, *Samuel Gompers, A Biography* (1963), and Stuart Bruce Kaufman, *Samuel Gompers and the Origins of the American Federation of Labor* (1973), focus on the problems of leadership. The role of the immigrant in the American industrial revolution is explored in Charlotte Erickson, *American Industry and the European Immigrant* (1957), and Rowland Berthoff, *British Immigrants in Industrial America, 1790–1950* (1953). A brilliant article that points towards a new synthesis of cultural and labor history is Herbert G. Gutman, "Work, Culture, and Society in Industrializing America, 1815–1919," *American Historical Review* 78 (June 1973), 531–88.

The Politics
of Reform

Politics in the quarter-century following the Civil War gave Americans the sense of equilibrium that their economic system lacked. The Jacksonian generation had discovered in the idea of party a way of controlling the disruptive forces of modern democracy. Now their sons, the professional managers of the Republican and Democratic parties after 1865, perfected the machinery of party, which they proceeded to run with skill and zest until the very end of the century.

Political equilibrium depended, first of all, upon restoring a regional balance of power within both parties. A stable party system rested on regional interests as well as state machines. Republicans throughout the Gilded Age confronted the task of including the urban working classes in the Northeast and the farmers of the Midwest in their plans for industrial development and business enterprise. Democrats were busy repairing the broad Jacksonian coalition of Southern planters and Northern city bosses that had been smashed by the war. The primary unit in this renovated political system remained the state party machine, and both national parties continued to operate as loose assemblages of largely autonomous state organizations. But states also comprised regions, each with its own cultural identity and economic concerns that demanded attention. Increasingly after 1870 national tickets were arranged and party slates balanced with regional preferences as well as state claims in mind.

The smooth operation of American politics in the Gilded Age also depended on the mastery of a few basic rules. Chief among these was the assumption shared by political managers in both parties that their organizations differed, not so much in class or economic interests, which were often quite similar, as in religious, ethnic, and cultural values. Both parties, in fact, were supported by wealthy citizens whose opinions the party leaders duly acknowledged while maintaining an egalitarian posture before the rest of the country. Both parties operated as broad-based, nonideological coalitions that appealed to businessmen, farmers, professionals, and workers. What separated them at a deeper level was neither wealth nor status but differing clusters of values.

The Republican party was dominated until late in the century by values that could be called "pietistic." Democrats, except in the South where questions of race and economic recovery took precedence, were generally ruled by values that have been called "ritualistic" or "liturgical." Pietism pointed towards a politics of strict morality; ritualism, towards a politics of traditionalism and toleration. The original Whig party and its stepchild, the Republican party before the Civil War, had been governed by the forces of pietism. Party members were primarily Protestant, predominantly of native stock or Anglo-Saxon descent, aggressively evangelical and reformist, equipped with a keen sense of morality, and eager to use government at all levels to enforce their behavioral standards on the rest of the American community. Republicans assembled all of these cultural ingredients in their attack on slavery. Despite the steady infiltration of the party by business interests after the Civil War, Republicans continued to attract and hold in uneasy alliance a broad range of social moralists—prohibitionists, sabbatarians, blue law advocates, and moral reformers of all persuasions. Only at the very end of the century had such groups become marginal enough in the party as a whole for the managers to cast them aside as liabilities.

The Democratic party in respect to these values often seemed the precise opposite of the Republican. It embraced Catholics as well as Protestants, and professed a tolerance of immigrants who lacked the compulsive morality of the native-born. The party preached a "personal liberty" deemed safest when government was kept local and minimal and practiced a cultural as well as an economic laissez-faire. While Republicans expected government to be generous and active, Democrats hoped to keep it grudging and stingy, if only to check the cultural imperialism of its pietist foes. Thus the differences between the two parties in 1880 were real, but they concerned cultural outlook even more than economic interest or crude social differences, a distinction professional politicians in both camps fully appreciated.

Party managers also realized that the voters seldom approached political questions like the tariff or the currency as simple issues having scientific solutions, but instead responded to them as symbols that could be mobilized for the support of the party and its candidates. The skilled practitioners of Gilded Age politics

knew that the electoral behavior of most American voters was ultimately determined by images and impressions, prejudices and predilections. Voters
might consider themselves both rational and fully informed, but woe to any
office-seeker who really believed them such!

This configuration of a balanced and highly competitive politics lasted until the
last decade of the nineteenth century when the very idea of party rule came
under concerted attack by a younger generation of political reformers. By 1890,
the old pattern of political stability was breaking up, old loyalties were being discarded and traditional assumptions reversed as new political leaders in all sections of the country began to experiment with new techniques and devices for
modernizing government and making it more accountable and efficient.

UNVEILING A STATUE

Patriotism and purity combined readily in the Gilded Age
imagination. (*Pennell Collection, University of Kansas.*)

On the national level, the Republican party, casting off its pietistic garb, stepped forth as the champion of the workingman in the nation's cities. The Democrats, abandoning their urban base, embarked on an ill-fated alliance with agrarian reformers and Populists marching to battle beneath the symbolic banner of free silver. Their defeat under William Jennings Bryan at the hands of William McKinley in the election of 1896 left them stranded in the wilderness from which they would not emerge until the election of Woodrow Wilson sixteen years later.

Meanwhile in states like Wisconsin, California, and New York younger reformers like Robert LaFollette, Hiram Johnson, Charles Evans Hughes, and Theodore Roosevelt were clashing with railroad, lumber, oil and traction "interests" in their attempts to seize the political control of their states needed to launch experiments in economic and social legislation. And in the nation's cities, social reformers and charity organizers, urban planners and settlement-house workers, public health officials, university professors, and new business leaders were busy assembling urban coalitions for an assault on the citadel of Gilded Age politics, the "machine" presided over by the sinister figure of the "boss."

By 1890, rural Populists and urban progressives, in their separate attacks on the politics of equilibrium, were challenging the code of the old professionals and forcing them to respond to new pressures for change. Out of this revolt against the Gilded Age came a transformation of politics that paralleled the revolution in the American economy and brought new assessments of the American political process and new ways of ordering it.

The Politics of Equilibrium

The Civil War shaped the thinking and molded the political behavior of Americans for a generation. The success of Gilded Age politics in tapping the emotional reserves once monopolized by the war could be read, first of all, in the remarkably high levels of voter participation. In the six presidential elections between 1876 and 1896 an average 78.5 percent of the eligible voters of the country actually voted, and an equally impressive 62.8 percent turned out for off-year elections. If political democracy implies a high rate of voter participation, then the Gilded Age, despite its confused responses to industrialization, remained flamboyantly, defiantly democratic.

Americans in exercising their right to vote also remained stubbornly consistent. Whether they marched to the polls behind the "bloody shirt" of wartime Unionist fervor or stirred to the memories of the Lost Cause, voters in all sections of the country kept alive the spirit of the War between the States. Joining enthusiastically in campaigns complete with military mounted troopers and fancy drill teams, they made national elections extremely close. Sixteen states could always be counted on to go Republican; fourteen just as regularly voted Democratic. Elections usually hung on the disposition of voters in five key states—Connecticut,

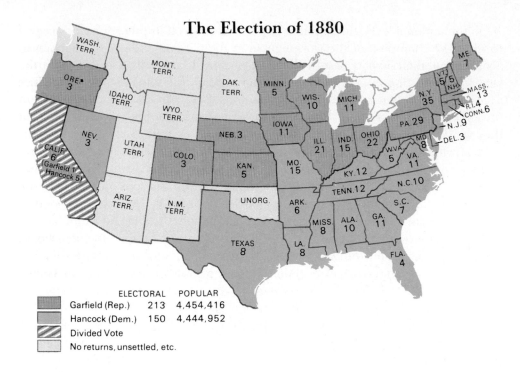

The Election of 1880

	ELECTORAL	POPULAR
Garfield (Rep.)	213	4,454,416
Hancock (Dem.)	150	4,444,952
Divided Vote		
No returns, unsettled, etc.		

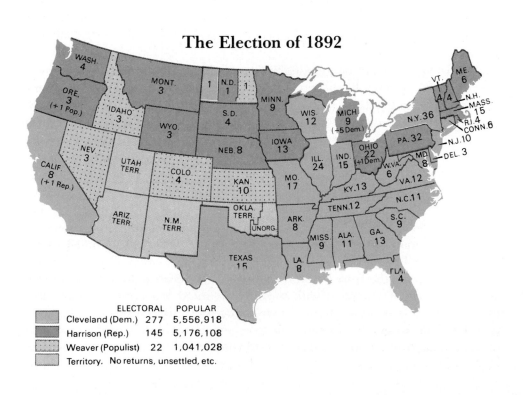

The Election of 1892

	ELECTORAL	POPULAR
Cleveland (Dem.)	277	5,556,918
Harrison (Rep.)	145	5,176,108
Weaver (Populist)	22	1,041,028
Territory. No returns, unsettled, etc.		

New York, Indiana, Nevada, and California. Although the Republicans' control of the presidency from 1872 to 1912, broken only by Cleveland's two victories in 1884 and 1892, seemingly established them as the majority party, in fact the Democrats, who controlled the House of Representatives with sizable majorities in seven out of ten congressional elections, secured their claims to dominance at the grass roots of politics. Pluralities in pivotal states were perilously slim, in New York and Indiana particularly. With intense competition and close elections the rule, winners were not only lucky but frequently surprised. In the presidential elections of 1880 and 1884, for example, fewer than fifty thousand votes separated the candidates. In the Hayes-Tilden contest of 1876 and again in the first Harrison-Cleveland election in 1888, the winners received fewer popular votes than the losers.

The two parties were drawn up against each other across the political terrain like equally matched armies, their battles resembling the engagements of a too familiar war. Even the language of politics was borrowed from recent martial exploits:

From the *opening gun* of the *campaign* the *standard bearer*, along with other *war-horses fielded* by the party, *rallied* the *rank and file* around the party *standard*, the *bloody shirt*, and other *slogans*. Precinct *captains aligned* their *phalanxes shoulder to shoulder* to mobilize votes for the *Old Guard*. Meanwhile the *Mugwumps* warned that the *palace troops* sought to *plunder* the treasury; their *strategy* was to *crusade* against the *myrmidons* of corruption. Even a *man on horseback* could not have saved the *lost cause* with his *jingoism*. But party *headquarters* changed *tactics* and emptied its *war chest* to buy *mercenaries* and *Hessians*. Finally the *well-drilled fugelmen* [sic] in the *last ditch* closed *ranks*, overwhelmed the enemy *camp*, and divided the *spoils* of victory.

Military figures invaded the campaign ceremony with songs, war whoops, and hours of speechifying from bewhiskered colonels "late of the Confederate Army" or beribboned commissary generals of the GAR (Grand Army of the Republic). The median age of voters in the Gilded Age was thirty-seven, and so they had generally arrived at political maturity under the tutelage of fathers who had fought to preserve the "glorious Union" or to rescue a "prostrate nation." In circumstances reminiscent of battlefield conditions, ticket splitting suggested a lack of patriotism, and the ingrate who switched parties was regarded as little better than a bounty jumper.

Yet politics in this era, stripped of its gaudy regalia, was a business in the same stage of early development as small-scale entrepreneurial capitalism. Recently arrived immigrants may have performed like well-drilled foot soldiers on election day, but they were also urban consumers needing jobs, favors, and services. Such voters created a vast human market in which a judicious investment of limited political capital could pay off handsomely. The business of politics, unlike the more established concerns, stayed open at the bottom to new talent and offered unlimited opportunity to get ahead and make good. Caught in the posture of go-getter, the professional politician—ward heeler, precinct captain, county chairman, state assemblyman, or senatorial aspirant—resembled a salesman with a territory to cover that was filled with prospective customers whose buying habits he had better know thoroughly.

In this sense the professional politician's motto had scarcely changed in the half-century or more separating Martin Van Buren's Albany Regency and George Washington Plunkitt's Tammany Hall. "I seen my opportunities and I took 'em," Plunkitt recalled for a progressive generation fully prepared to be outraged. "Ain't it perfectly honest to charge a good price and make a profit on my investment? Of course, it is. Well, that's honest graft." Plunkitt and his colleagues described the political district in terms familiar to every drummer out of New York or Chicago with a territory to cover, and concluded: "If he holds his district and Tammany is in power, he is amply rewarded by a good office and the opportunities that go with it." The Gilded Age politician's true American was Horatio Alger in ward heeler's attire and sporting a campaign button. "Yes, many of our men have grown rich in politics," Plunkitt admitted. "I have myself. I've made a big fortune out of the game, and I'm gettin' richer every day." The shortest route to success in the business of politics lay through the upstairs rooms at party headquarters, where the sign over the door read "Never Closed."

IMMIGRANTS ARRIVING AT ELLIS ISLAND, NEW YORK CITY

New recruits for the American political army. (*Culver Pictures, Inc.*)

Politics in the Gilded Age, from the city to the Senate, constituted a revitalized patronage society bearing some of the marks of its eighteenth-century ancestor. Under the guiding hand and sharp eye of the boss, power was organized vertically within the machine in a hierarchical system of patrons and clients. The style of the Gilded Age boss was innovative, coarse, and raw, at once more personalized, direct, and cynical than the style of his predecessors. To his critics, like Moisei Ostrogorski, whose *Democracy and the Organization of Political Parties* summarized the reformers' indictment of machine politics, the political boss was Machiavelli's prince come to life, an all-powerful leader, unsleeping, devious, and ruthless, who commanded through his "strength of will, his cleverness, his audacity and his luck."

To this one he lends a dollar; for another he obtains a railroad ticket without payment; he has coal distributed in the depth of winter; he makes gifts of other kinds; he sometimes sends poultry at Christmas time; he buys medicine for a sick person; he helps bury the dead by procuring a coffin on credit or half-price. He has a kind heart in virtue of his position and his position gives him the means of satisfying his need for kindness: the money which he distributes comes from the chest of the Machine; the latter has obtained it by the most reprehensible methods . . . but no matter. With this money he can also dispense an ample hospitality in the drinking-saloons. As soon as he comes in, friends known and unknown gather round him, and he treats everybody, he orders one drink after another for the company; he is the only one who does not drink; he is on duty.

The party machine's stock in trade was supplied by jobs and appointments in increasing numbers, transit franchises, paving contracts, public construction bids, licenses, permits and a hundred other salable items needed to conduct the business of the nation's cities.

Urban machines formed the base of the political pyramid on which state party bosses built organizations that dutifully sent their men to Washington to fill seats in the Senate. The new ruling heads of state politics—Tom Platt in New York, Nelson Aldrich in Rhode Island, and Justin Morrill in Vermont—conducted national business in Washington while they kept an eye on the statehouse gang back home, mediating patronage quarrels, settling factional disputes, and smoothing discontents. For all this continuing process, system and organization provided the answers. The Michigan boss, James McMillan, explained that his rise to the United States Senate only proved "what quiet work and an active continuance of party organization can accomplish." Running the state machine was half the battle. "When party organization is perfect, campaigns are more easily conducted and victory more certain." Democratic party bosses—Maryland's Arthur Pue Gorman, New York's David Hill, Virginia's Thomas Martin—perfected their control over their states more slowly than Republicans, and, particularly in the one-party South, kept a looser grip on the party reins. But in both parties, as in the business world after 1880, consolidation and concentration of power became the order of the day.

This recognition of the need for order and control led the boss to consider himself both a professional and a practical reformer. "Politics," Plunkitt reminded his enemies, "is as much a regular business as the grocery or dry goods or the drug business. You've got to be trained up to it or you're sure to fail." The besetting sins of the do-gooder, Plunkitt insisted, were amateurism and innocence. "He hasn't been brought up in the difficult business of politics and he makes a mess of it every time." From at least midcentury, bosses like New York City's William Marcy Tweed and Philadelphia's James McManes had watched the aimless spreading of their cities and understood the growing problem of managing them. Tweed frankly admitted that New York's population was "too hopelessly split into races and factions to govern it under universal suffrage, except by bribery of patronage and corruption." Their cities, the bosses realized, were fragmented like giant jigsaw puzzles. The boss alone could provide the liberal application of patronage to glue them together, though his workmanship might be both slipshod and expensive.

Tweed's reign in New York City immediately after the Civil War saw authority centralized in the city government, a new county courthouse built, Central Park in the planning stage, and a transit system begun. All this had been achieved at the cost of widespread corruption and an astronomical increase in the city's bonded debt. In Washington, D.C., Alexander Shepherd, real estate speculator-turned-boss, supervised the building of a new drainage system for the capital, constructed miles of paved streets, installed a new lighting system, and leveled and landscaped the center city. Bosses seldom achieved the efficiency and system they sought; at best, they acquired an oligarchy for managing loose federations of their constituents. Their failings in efficiency and accountability would subsequently provide progressive reformers with most of their ammunition in their attacks on the urban machines in the 1890s. In the absence of a genuine science of administration and a corps of professional managers, the bosses, improvising lavishly and corruptly with materials at hand, at least gave their cities a minimum of order and necessary services.

The politics of equilibrium pressed the strenuous life into service in behalf of spoilsmen preaching a joyful acceptance of the facts of political life, whether a bit of bribery or orders from above to stuff the ballot box. The cult of moral strenuosity, once the mark of the lone observer situated on the outskirts of society, was now enlisted on the side of political expediency—the need to win at any cost. The world of the professionals was a masculine one though it also appeared at times to be grossly sentimental. For the professionals, politics could not be cut and trimmed by the moral shears of women or patched together with the tiny needles of the men-milliners of reform. Gilded Age politicians, in claiming the political arena as an aggressive male preserve, repudiated the original alliance of women and reformers that had precipitated the very war the professionals now sought to mythologize. Dismissing feminine activism and moral reform as contrary to human nature, and ridiculing their champions as long-haired men and short-haired women, the politicians added their testimony to the

THE WOMAN'S SPHERE

For the Gilded Age politician the woman's proper
occupations were domesticity and motherhood.
(*Culver Pictures, Inc.*)

conservative meaning of the Civil War. The exquisite moral sensibilities of a
William Lloyd Garrison appeared unaffordable luxuries in a materialistic age,
the reformer a biological sport in a society that considered politics masculine,
culture feminine, and the gulf between them permanent. So orders came down
from party headquarters: Let the women and their carpet knights remain in
their well-appointed parlors where they could exchange rumors of political misbehavior while sipping lemonade. The real world, the Blaines and Conklings,
Aldriches and Hannas insisted, was their own world of cigar smoke and fifteen-
dollar votes, rolling logs, and brimming pork barrels.

But there were still deeper worlds stirring by the 1890s. In agrarian revolts
in the provinces and civic campaigns in the metropolis, reformers were beginning
to draw on the resources provided by two alternative traditions of American
politics that had survived the spoilsmen. The Populist movement in the trans-
Mississippi West and the South renewed a millennial vision promising the triumph

of political righteousness. And by 1895, in the nation's cities progressive reformers were drawing on patrician fears, business notions of efficiency, and the scientific hopes of new professionals and academics. Working in tandem in the midst of industrial unrest and agrarian discontent, these two groups of reformers, Populists and urban progressives, shattered the confidence of party professionals by confronting them with different interpretations of the American dream.

"Conditions Without Precedent"— The Populist Revolt

The first reform tradition to challenge the politics of equilibrium as the nineteenth century drew to a close stemmed from a millennial outlook that had long flourished in a Protestant frontier democracy. This reform model was constructed according to utopian blueprints for a world beyond politics in which power and strife were finally relinquished for the righteous rule of "good men." Those who envisioned this utopia, the political pietists, tended to personalize evil and corruption and to define their task as essentially a religious undertaking aimed at conversion and regeneration. The language of political pietism, unlike the vocabulary of the professionals, was openly evangelical: A new heaven on earth awaits the coming of the new dispensation; social salvation requires men of Old Testament vision who will lead true believers through the political wilderness into the promised land where they will need none but the Lord to rule over them. Secular politics as practiced by the ungodly is an abomination, and party leaders the willing instruments of the devil. Good politics is "no politics," as simple and direct as the Golden Rule.

Part metaphor, part literal reading of religious promise, the millennial reform tradition had continued to tantalize Americans throughout the nineteenth century. Translated into action, it had spawned a variety of third-party movements before the Civil War, beginning with the anti-Masonic outbreak in the 1820s, gathering force with the abolitionist campaigns and communitarian experiments in the following decades, and fixing on the issue of slavery in the Free Soil and Republican parties soon thereafter.

Pietists demanded a complete change in the rule of conventional political behavior. Instead of the easy tolerance of broker politics they advocated cultural and political uniformity. In place of competing interest groups they proposed a national congregation of the right-minded. No more minor skirmishes between equally corrupt contestants, but the last mighty battle for the Lord: Armageddon. Pietism invited total participation at the grass roots, chiefly in the form of camp meetings of the faithful to support the few correctives considered necessary for defeating corruption. Pietists promised to restore a lost community, a preindustrial solidarity that depended on the recovery of abandoned values. In its purest form, pietism promoted counterrevolution—the overthrow of the modern, secular, boss-run, or bureaucratic state and a return to the Golden Age.

Pietism's moral rejection of modernity, however, was not matched by its economic program, which remained solidly *petit bourgeois*, bearing all the marks of small-scale capitalism with its hopes for the independent producer, regional markets, and steady growth rate. These wish-pictures once had sustained the North in its war against slavery. Instead of the millennium, however, the Civil War brought business consolidation and the rule of the Spoilsmen, and the original vision dimmed until it guided only such marginal groups as the prohibitionists and the Greenbackers. It was from the margins, therefore, that the first calls for a "new politics" were heard—from Henry George's legion of single-taxers, the Nationalist recruits in Bellamy's industrial army, and converts to the "New Conscience" of the Social Gospelists. Pietist grievances in the 1880s continued to center on issues with social and cultural as well as economic meaning: cheap money, the power of monopoly, and Wall Street conspiracies, which all underscored the isolation and marginality of the little man in a rapidly industrializing society. Here, then, in the mounting frustrations of staple-crop farmers who were certain they had been victimized lay the deepest seedbed of Populism.

Populist grievances were real enough. In the trans-Mississippi West they were chargeable mainly to the hectic pace of economic development; in the South they resulted from the workings of a quasi-feudalized agricultural system complete

THE SOD-HOUSE FRONTIER

Picknicking in the front yard, Custer County, Nebraska, 1886. (*Solomon D. Butcher Collection, Nebraska State Historical Society.*)

with tenancy, a crop lien system, and a large submerged class of dirt-poor farmers, both black and white. In the West, exorbitant shipping charges and extortionate mortgage rates were compounded after 1887 by a series of crop failures that sent land prices and farm income skidding downhill. Years of retrenchment followed, and destitute farmers trekked back eastward from the sod-house frontier, leaving behind ghost towns with gilded opera houses and empty storefronts. Western Kansas lost half its population between 1882 and 1892, South Dakota some 30,000 people, while the number of prairie wagons lumbering back to Iowa from the Nebraska frontier in 1891 was estimated at 18,000. A sign on an abandoned farmhouse in Blanco County, Texas, in the drought year 1886 read: "200 miles to the nearest post office; 100 miles to wood; 20 miles to water; 6 inches to hell. God bless our home! Gone to live with the wife's folks."

The ebbing human tide left dark pools of discontent in isolated bypassed communities, where bitter men and women were determined to stick it out, blindly, uncomprehendingly. From the beginning, Populism required terms and symbols sufficiently stark to explain to the disinherited the cause of their affliction. Kansas Populist Mary E. Lease put it this way:

We were told two years ago to go to work and raise a big crop, that was all we needed. We went to work and plowed and planted; the rains fell, the sun shone, nature smiled, and we raised the big crop they told us to; and what came of it? Eight-cent corn, ten-cent oats, two-cent beef, and no price at all for butter and eggs—that's what came of it. Then the politicians said that we suffered from over-production.

Populism in the South, while plagued by many of the same problems, displayed regional features that had characterized the nonslaveholding farmer's struggle for survival before the Civil War. Tenancy and crop liens continued to exploit an underclass of blacks and whites, whose awareness of their plight was matched by their fears of challenging a Bourbon dynasty based on white supremacy. Western Populists risked little more than failure in organizing a third party. Southern farmers, in attacking the political establishment, put their personal security and sometimes their lives on the color line.

In both regions, Populism emerged rapidly from a nonpartisan background in 1890 and drew into protest politics groups that had previously been inarticulate if not inert. Some of the new recruits were women: Mary Lease, who harangued country audiences on their subservience to monopoly; Annie L. Diggs, a strict prohibitionist bent on saving the West from alcohol as well as Wall Street; Sarah Emery, whose tract *Seven Financial Conspiracies* traced the national decline along a descending curve of democratic participation. For every seasoned veteran of third-party politics like Minnesota's Ignatius Donnelly, the Sage of Nininger, there were three new converts like Georgia's Tom Watson fired by Populist speeches for campaigns "hot as Nebuchadnezzar's furnace."

The atmosphere at Populist meetings was heavy with the spirit of revivalism—"a pentecost of politics," according to observers, "in which a tongue of flame sat upon every man." Recruits, like converts, came from everywhere: farmers, hard-pressed local merchants, cattlemen, miners, small-town editors; men with chin whiskers, broad-brimmed hats and muddy boots, accompanied by wives "with skin tanned to parchment by the hot winds, with bony hands of toil, and clad in faded calico." Quickly they became stereotypes—comic hayseeds to the political opposition, heroic figures in the folklore of Populism with nicknames to match: "The Kansas Pythoness," "Bloody Bridles," "Sockless Socrates." Behind the mask frequently appeared the original types, biblical figures like Senator William A. Peffer, for example, a Topeka editor elected to the Senate who reminded Hamlin Garland of Isaiah. "His general appearance is that of a clergyman," full beard, steel-rimmed glasses and frock coat, with the "habitual expression" of gravity on an otherwise inscrutable countenance. "He made a peculiar impression upon me, something Hebraic," Garland recalled, "something intense, fanatical."

The People's party yoked political opposites to the vehicle of reform. Southern Populists listened to the saving word not only from "Stump" Ashby, the Texas cowpuncher, and "Cyclone" Davis toting his volumes of Jefferson, but also from Virginia patricians bearing the names of Page, Beverly, and Harrison. In Minnesota, Ignatius Donnelly's mercurial style was offset by the sensible advice of Charles H. Van Wyck, the party's candidate for governor in Nebraska, who singled out solid issues like railroad regulation for his campaign. For the most part, however, Populists were political innocents, and innocence was widely deemed a virtue. To Eastern professionals in the major parties, Populism, under banners urging the steadfast to vote as they prayed, presented the strange spectacle of an embittered interest group talking in tongues.

New to the work of organizing a national party, the Populists encountered formidable obstacles to building a platform designed to advance farmers' interests and at the same time attract the worker in the city. They discovered that appeal for votes could be made in two distinct ways: first, by explaining their problems as staple-crop farmers and calling on the federal government to help, and second, by avoiding interest-group tactics and waging a campaign against modernity in the name of the "true producers" all over the country. It was the peculiar mark of Populism that it sought to undertake both of these assignments simultaneously.

The interest-group program of the Populists grew out of the reasoning of political leaders like Governor Lorenzo D. Lewelling of Kansas, who demanded a federal government responsive to the needs of all its citizens. "If the Government fails in these things, it fails of its mission.' Several of the party's planks rested on this construction: a graduated income tax to lift the financial burden from the shoulders of farmers and workers; postal savings banks and a flexible currency; and a subtreasury system to stabilize prices and provide agricultural credits. All of these demands, calling the federal government to the rescue, could be defended as protective measures for producers who lacked the privileges already accorded more favored industrial interests. Another and different set of demands

—for immigration restriction, antimonopoly legislation, and farmer-labor cooperation—suggested eternal brotherhood for those who lived by the sweat of their brows. Party delegates to the convention in Omaha in 1892 cheered lustily as their leaders denounced the "governmental injustice," which was dividing the nation into two great classes, "tramps and millionaires." To postpone the day of wrath, the Omaha platform called for the people to seize power in a new constituent act:

Assembled on the anniversary of the birthday of the nation, and filled with the spirit of the grand general and chieftain who established our independence, we seek to restore the government of the Republic to the hands of the plain people with whose class it originated. . . . We declare we must be in fact, as we are in name, one united brotherhood of freemen.

In the society envisioned by the Populists righteousness would infuse God's chosen with high purpose. In the recesses of the Populist imagination lay hopes for a transpolitical realm of permanent harmony, where peace and virtue reigned supreme over a vast fee-simple empire of rejuvenated yeomen. However differently they were heard, the millennialist strains in Populism sounded the call for a counterrevolutionary crusade. The triumph of American justice would come only when the people themselves had purified national life at its wellsprings. Only a small part of such a gigantic task required the passage of "wise and reasonable legislation." A much larger part involved a moral crusade "to bring the power of the social mass to bear upon the rebellious individuals who thus menace the peace and safety of the state."

Populism transcended conventional politics in declaring itself "not a passing cloud on the political sky" nor a "transient gust of political discontent" but "the hope of realizing and incarnating in the lives of common people the fulness of the divinity of humanity." With this shift in political perception came glimpses of catastrophe should the people's courage fail—the swift approach of the "last days, nightmares of "men made beastlike by want, and women shorn of the nobility of their sex" pouring through city streets past plutocrats who stand "grabbing and grinning" as the mob rushes to its destruction.

In this realm of the apocalyptic, the ordinary political rules of the road no longer applied. If the crisis facing the nation could be reduced to a simple choice between justice and injustice, liberty and slavery, what was the need for reasoned proofs and analysis? "The very fact of widespread suffering," a Nebraska Populist insisted, "is sufficient evidence that the whole system under they have lived is a lie and an imposture." Once allow the people to destroy the Money-Power, and politics as a selfish pursuit of wealth and power would disappear.

The Populist call for an evangelical politics violated a cardinal rule of the professionals, which Ohio's John Sherman once invoked in reminding his Republican colleagues that "questions based upon temperance, religion, morality, in all their multiplied forms, ought not to be the basis of politics." Populists flatly disagreed, and like the abolitionists before the Civil War, rested their case on symbolic issues—the Money Question and Free Silver—as explanations of their plight.

For Western Populists and silver interests, fusion with the Democrats offered the only alternative to continued failure. In 1892, the Populist party won over a million popular votes and 22 electoral votes and sent a dozen congressmen to Washington while securing the governor's chair in Kansas, North Dakota, and Colorado. As the Panic of 1893 tipped the country into the deepest depression it had ever known, the Populists sought to reach into the industrial masses for support. But underfinanced, lacking a roster of attractive candidates, and beset with severe organizational and financial problems, the party had made few electoral gains in 1894 even though it increased its total vote by nearly 50 percent.

As the election of 1896 approached, Populists split into two camps, one led by fusionists ready to join the Democrats on a platform of free silver, the other headed by diehard reformers who agreed with Ignatius Donnelly that while the Democratic party had learned at least some of its lessons, Populists ought not to "abandon the post of teacher and turn it over to [a] slow and stupid scholar." For Southern Populists fusion seemed an invitation to a suicide since it meant rejoining the establishment whose ranks they had so recently deserted. But for a majority of the delegates to the convention in Saint Louis in 1896, a "Demopop" ticket headed by William Jennings Bryan seemed to offer the only sure passage out of the political wilderness. Following a rancorous debate, in which it was charged that the People's party had become "more boss-ridden, gang-ruled, gang-gangrened than the two old parties of monopoly," the convention agreed to unite with their former rival under the banner of free silver.

The Great Reversal: The Election of 1896

By 1896 the Democratic party, bitterly divided between agrarians and Eastern business interests, needed all the support it could get. Cleveland's return to office four years earlier had been greeted with a series of industrial strikes that seemed to many Americans the opening shots of a class war. The first of these upheavals came at Homestead, outside of Pittsburgh, in 1892, when Andrew Carnegie sailed for Europe and left Henry Clay Frick, his hard-driving manager and an implacable enemy of labor unions, in charge of his steel company. Frick took advantage of his chief's absence by attempting to break the Amalgamated Iron and Steel Workers Union, which two years earlier had won a favorable wage settlement from the company. Frick decided on a wage cut as the best weapon for destroying the union; when the Amalgamated refused his terms, he cut off negotiations and hired a private police force to take over the plant at Homestead. The union retaliated by calling a strike and preparing to repel the Pinkertons who had been dispatched by barge up the Monongahela with orders to seize the plant. The invaders, numbering some three hundred, were met with a hail of bullets from the workers lining the shore, and in the pitched battle that followed they were routed by the angry mob and their barges burned to the waterline. But final victory, as Frick had foreseen, lay with the company, which prevailed on the governor of Pennsylvania to send in the militia to open the plant. Frick nearly paid for his union-busting with his life when a young anarchist, Alexander Berkman, attempted to assassinate him but bungled the job. Frick's principle of the open shop, however, emerged triumphant. After five months out on strike the Homestead workers were forced to accept the harsh new terms of the settlement, suffering a defeat that ended effective organizing in the industry for nearly half a century.

In the Pullman strike in 1894, Grover Cleveland threw his considerable weight on the side of management against the forces of organized labor. Like Homestead, the Pullman strike grew out of the antiquated notions of a business paternalist whose sense of duty to his employees included building them a model company town but did not extend to their right to negotiate their wages. When workers in the car shops went on strike, George Pullman, president of the Pullman Palace Car Company and chief planner of the company town named after him, sent instructions to his managers to refuse to bargain and to evict the strikers from their homes. Then in the late spring of 1894, Eugene V. Debs and his newly organized American Railway Union, fresh from a victory over the Great Northern Railroad, came to the rescue of the Pullman strikers with funds and an offer to help settle their grievances. When the company once again declined arbitration, the ARU voted to boycott all Pullman cars by refusing to couple them to any trains, even those carrying the mail. Here was the issue that the Pullman Company, now supported by the railroads' General Managers Association, seized on in seeking an injunction and the dispatch of federal troops to Chicago. Over the vehement protests of Governor John P. Altgeld, Cleveland obliged. Faced with a choice between the rights of labor and the rights of property, Cleveland unhesitatingly elected to uphold the latter.

In 1894 the American economy hit bottom. Five hundred banks closed their doors, sixteen thousand business firms collapsed, and unemployment stood at nearly 20 percent. New issues on the New York Stock Exchange plummeted from $100 million to $37 million as 2.5 million jobless men tramped winter streets in the nation's cities looking for work. Neither municipal governments nor private charity organizations could cope with such numbers of desperate men who wandered aimlessly from city to city in search of a job. Everywhere the migrants found factory gates closed and crowds of unemployed workers whom they joined in long lines in front of soup kitchens. Not since the dark days of the Civil War had the country seemed so threatened.

DEPRESSION LANDSCAPE

Pennsylvania coal miners' housing with outhouses and railroad tracks. (*Carnegie Library, Pittsburg.*)

Workers met the depression with the only weapon at their disposal, the strike. In 1894 alone there were over thirteen hundred strikes, of which the confrontation at Pullman was only the most publicized. The mining industry, for example, was hit by a wave of strikes rolling across the country from the coalfields in the East to Coeur d'Alene in Idaho, where besieged miners fought back with sticks of dynamite, and Cripple Creek, Colorado, where armed deputies broke up demonstrations. For such economic distress, Cleveland prescribed heroic remedies of self-denial, and dispensed terse reminders that while it was the clear duty of citizens to support their government, the obligation was by no means reciprocal.

The spectre of masses of starving men marching on the nation's cities to plunder and pillage in an uprising of the dispossessed assumed the shape of farce in the spring of 1894 with the arrival in Washington of Coxey's Army, a "petition in boots" come to the capital to ask for work. The leader of the few hundred jobless men who straggled into the city was the self-appointed "General" Jacob Coxey, a small-town businessman from Massillon, Ohio, who simply wanted

to present his plan for solving unemployment with a "good roads bill," which would finance public improvement with $500 million worth of government bonds. The Cleveland administration's response to this "living petition" mirrored its fear of mass upheaval; Coxey's followers were dispersed and their leader jailed on a technicality, while rumors of revolution swept through the city.

For Coxey's futile gesture and also for the state of the economy Cleveland blamed the nostrums of the free silver forces. In 1890 Congress, responding to the clamor of bimetallists and inflationists, had passed the Sherman Silver Purchase Act, which required the government to buy 4.5 million ounces of silver each month and to pay for it with treasury notes redeemable in gold. The Sherman Act precipitated a sudden rush on the gold reserves of the United States, which declined from $190 million in 1890 to just over $100 million three years later. Confronted with an unfavorable balance of trade, depleted gold reserves, and industrial stagnation, Cleveland moved quickly to persuade Congress to repeal the Silver Purchase Act, a decision that seriously weakened his control over his own party. He succeeded in shutting off the flow of silver from the mines in the West but in doing so lost the support of the agrarian half of the Democratic party. By 1895 the President was complaining that there was "not a man in the Senate with whom I can be on terms of absolute confidence."

In calling on the banking syndicates of J. P. Morgan and August Belmont to help check the outflow of American gold, Cleveland only compounded his political problems. The administration and the bankers, working together, arranged a sale of government bonds for gold on terms that allowed the banking houses to manipulate exchange rates in their own favor. To Populists and irate Democrats in the South and West, Cleveland's deal was proof that their suspicions of a Wall Street conspiracy to rig the economy against them were firmly grounded in fact.

The issues of sound money and free silver involved choosing between a deflationist monetary policy and an inflationist one for economic recovery. Silver and gold quickly became the organizing symbols for diametrically opposed strategies for solving the depression. Cleveland chose "sound money,' the gold standard and currency restriction as the safest course. For bankrupt farmers and Western miners, on the other hand, gold was a "crown of thorns" pressed on the brow of the honest laborer who was being crucified by the money lenders. In fact, Cleveland's monetary policy did aggravate the effects of the depression by widening the gap between fixed costs and income and accentuating the long-term price decline. More important, it provided farmers with a highly visible target for their grievances. The South Carolina demagogue, Ben Tillman, denounced the President to his back-country constituents as a Judas who had thrice betrayed the Democracy. "He is an old bag of beef, and I am going to Washington with a pitchfork and prod him in his fat ribs."

Democrats gathered in Chicago for the convention in 1896 with similar intentions. Southern and Western Democrats saw that by repudiating Cleveland's policies and by advocating the free and unlimited coinage of silver they had an opportunity to win the support of the Populist movement. Bryan quickly emerged as the choice of the agrarian wing of the party, which rode roughshod over the defenders of "sound money" and drove them out of the convention to form their own splinter organization. Bryan spoke the mood of his followers in sounding a new note of resistance:

We have petitioned, and our petitions have been scorned; we have entreated, and our entreaties have been disregarded; we have begged and they have mocked when our calamity came. We beg no longer; we entreat no more; we petition no more. *We defy them!*

The Eastern press, both Republican and Democratic, replied with charges of anarchy and treason. "The Jacobins are in full control at Chicago," an editor announced. "No large political movement in America has ever before spawned such hideous and repulsive vipers." Both the promise and the danger of a Bryan victory seemed to increase after the Populists' convention in Saint Louis endorsed the Democrats' choice for President. Not since 1860 had the fate of the nation appeared to hang in the balance of a single election. In 1896, as in 1860, the differences were sectional and economic, but they were also social and cultural, as two fundamentally opposed views of politics competed for the allegiance of the American voter.

Bryan and McKinley between them gave over nine hundred speeches in the campaign of 1896, the Republican from his front porch in Canton, Ohio, to throngs of admiring visitors shipped in by party managers, and the "Boy Orator of the Platte" at every whistlestop in the West where local leaders could collect a crowd. Their speeches riveted national attention on the money question, which quickly brought into focus cultural and social disagreements between urban and rural America. Behind the façade of monetary policy a "new politics" of pietism competed against an equally new political coalition of pragmatists and pluralists. Bryan was soon forced to expand his economic indictment to a plea for moral revival. Republicans, capitalizing on an upturn in the economy late in the summer, continued to denounce the Democratic platform as "revolutionary and anarchistic . . . subversive of national honor and threatening to the very life of the Republic."

A powerful orator and an appealing political figure, Bryan was new to the business of presidential campaigning, and in casting his party adrift from its Eastern financial moorings, he was driven to improvise. The professionals, frightened by the prospect of free silver, withheld their support, and Bryan rejected the offers of those few regulars who remained loyal. Sensing the need for new rules and definitions, Bryan cast himself in the role of the crusading prophet who could purify both his party and his country—eliminating corruption in Democratic ranks, paring the campaign budget, purging the party of hacks, and emphasizing principles rather than men. As the new leader he appeared an avenging angel of the outraged American yeomanry, the people's savior stepping

THE TWO PRESIDENTIAL
CONTENDERS IN THE ELECTION OF
1896

McKinley waged his campaign
from his front porch in Canton,
Ohio, while Bryan took to the
hustings. (*Left, Ohio Historical
Society; right, Brown Brothers.*)

off his campaign train for just one more sermon to his flock. To his listeners he
invariably apologized by confessing that "a large portion of my voice has been
left along the line of travel, where it is still calling sinners in repentance." His
speeches drew on a fund of stock pietist images as he mixed indictments of the
money power, the tariff, and the gold standard with allusions to the Old Testament. His message was everywhere the same: the people must arise in their
majesty and smite the money-lenders and destroy their temple. Audiences came
to know the arguments by heart and gathered to hear confirmation of their beliefs in the Protestant virtues of hard work and a just reward. When their leader
assured them that "every great economic question is in reality a great moral
question," they understood instinctively and they cheered. As Bryan preached
the saving word of free silver his audiences saw the stone suddenly rolled away
and "the door   opened for a progress which would carry civilization up to
higher ground."

Republicans, following the orders of new party managers like Mark Hanna of
Ohio, willingly exchanged places with their rivals. Tossing aside their pietistic
heritage as a burden, party leaders embarked on a pragmatic course directed at
a coalition of business and labor in the urban centers of the country where most

of the votes lay. Recent Republican recognition of the need for organizational efficiency and a full party chest also dictated the choice of McKinley, bland, amiable, a solid public figure with no strikingly original ideas but plenty of presumed common sense. To McKinley's front porch in Canton came some three-quarters of a million people carried there on nine thousand railroad cars paid for by the party, to stand behind a white picket-fence and listen to homilies on the honest dollar and the full dinner pail.

McKinley's image was the invention of younger Republican managers who had come to acknowledge the liabilities of pietism in an age of industrial organization and also the need for full-time professionals, a permanent headquarters, forceful propaganda, and a full campaign chest. During the campaign, the party released an unprecedented volume of campaign literature that reached every corner of the country. Speeches, pamphlets, and newspaper editorials were carefully orchestrated to the themes of cultural and ethnic pluralism, arranged to make interest-group appeals to farmers and workers, small businessmen and big bankers, shippers, consumers, Catholics as well as Protestants, and a variety of ethnic groups to whom the gold standard was offered as the last best hope of democracy.

As election day approached, Republican leaders realized that the battle for the gold standard consisted of a number of skirmishes fought for the allegiance of a wide variety of interest groups whose loyalty could be gained and held by arguments specifically tailored to their needs. Such a strategy entailed a platform of cultural and social tolerance, ethnic and religious variety, and political flexibility, an approach that contrasted dramatically with the Democratic countercrusade for unity. It also meant a forced retreat from the military style of campaigning that had characterized the politics of equilibrium. McKinley himself summed up the new Republican mood of toleration for his followers: "We have always practiced the Golden Rule. The best policy is to 'live and let live.'" With their candidate's blessing, the Republicans turned their backs on their pietistic heritage and assumed the task of engineering a consensus sufficient to guarantee winning the election.

The returns verified the reversal of political roles. With 7 million popular and 271 electoral votes, McKinley swept the entire East and Middle West, carried California and Oregon, and held onto Minnesota, North Dakota, and Iowa. Bryan, with 6.5 million popular votes and 176 electoral votes, won the Solid South together with the plains and the mountain states.

Beneath the regional features of the election lay the deeper meaning of the political realignment. As one student of the election has noted: "The realignment of the 1890s meant that the major parties faced the new century as much different social entities than the ones that had done battle in the 1850s. The Republican

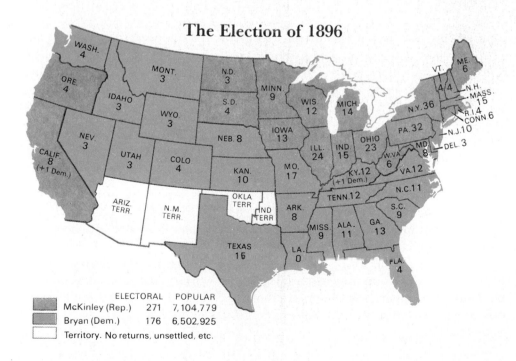

The Election of 1896

	ELECTORAL	POPULAR
McKinley (Rep.)	271	7,104,779
Bryan (Dem.)	176	6,502,925
Territory. No returns, unsettled, etc.		

party was no longer a narrowly based social vehicle in the hands of evangelical crusaders. It was a functioning integrative mechanism with a much broadened social base of support. The Democracy of Bryan was not the party of 'personal liberty,' but the instrument in the hands of 'reformers' who aimed at the creation of a moral social order." With their votes a majority of Americans declared their preference for pluralism and pragmatic accommodation and left the Democratic party to repair the damages while pondering the meaning of its defeat.

The meaning was sufficiently clear: the American electorate had repudiated the pietist countercrusade. Reforms there would undoubtedly be as the twentieth century opened, but they would not be the handiwork of a millennialist dream of purity and perfection. Political parties would have to consider and cater to the wishes of a multitude of social interests, welcoming newcomers under a broad canvas covering a wide diversity of social and cultural groups, meeting their demands, registering their complaints, and serving their needs.

Second, the election of 1896 made it clear to Americans that the organizational revolution that was transforming business and finance had also invaded politics. Just as both houses of Congress were beginning to modernize their procedures for doing the nation's business, so the two principal parties themselves had learned the value of efficient organization, continuing communications, flexible and sophisticated leaders, and above all, money with which to run their political machinery.

Finally, and most significant for the immediate future, the election of 1896 broke the grip of party regularity that had long been considered a permanent feature of the politics of equilibrium. It freed the American party system for a long-term realignment of voting patterns that would reveal the average voter as considerably more independent than the professionals had once assumed him to be. Absolute party loyalty and sustained political interest could no longer simply be assumed; voting behavior suddenly seemed more volatile and capricious than anyone had imagined. In the future, parties would have to reckon with the habits of their members, inclinations that often made them doubt the value of party rule and even mistrust the whole political process.

In defeat Bryan had uncovered a latent American suspicion of politics, a set of misgivings that had apparently been buried under the rubble of the Civil War. In his unsuccessful campaign, Bryan located this skepticism in the agrarian mind, attempted to exploit it, and failed. But by 1896 in the cities of the nation, new urban forces were already responding to a similar distrust of entrenched power and beginning to experiment with alternative ways of playing politics.

The political program of the new urban reformers, while it too promised to end machine politics and return power to the people, envisaged, not the triumph of righteousness but the rule of professionals. Experts would replace boss politics with scientifically designed administration, provide efficient and economical urban services, and stabilize the American city with man-made rather than God-given controls. The vision of social reformers organizing in American cities after 1890 centered on creating the "organic city" and liberating citizens' energies. With the stirring of these reform activities came a second and more powerful challenge to the old politics, the challenge of progressivism.

Cities in Revolt — The Rise of Urban Progressivism

The challenge of the city, announced the reformer Frederic C. Howe in 1906 after a decade of studying urban life, "has become one of decent human existence." Everywhere urban social reformers looked in the closing years of the century, they saw compartmentalization and fragmentation. Wealthy neighborhoods with million-dollar mansions were screened by parks and boulevards from teeming ghettos with dilapidated tenements and filthy streets — all too visible proof of the immense distances, social and psychological as well as economic and geographical, separating rich from poor.

It was to close the distance between urban affluence and poverty that in 1889 Jane Addams, the pioneer settlement-house worker, had moved into Hull House, a battered mansion on the corner of Polk and South Halstead streets in the heart of Chicago's Nineteenth Ward. "The streets are inexpressibly dirty," she reported, "the number of schools inadequate, factory legislation unenforced, the street-lighting bad, the paving miserable and altogether lacking in the alleys and smaller streets, and the stables defy all laws of sanitation."

Hundreds of houses are unconnected with the street sewer. . . . Back tenements flourish; many houses have no water supply save the faucet in the back yard; there are no fire escapes; the garbage and ashes are placed in wooden boxes which are fastened to the street pavements. . . . Our ward contains two hundred and fifty-five saloons; our own precinct boasts of eight. . . . There are seven churches and two missions in the ward.

In listing the needs of the Nineteenth Ward, Jane Addams summarized the main points in the urban progressive indictment of boss politics. Progressivism began as a spontaneous revolt of city dwellers convinced that they were being denied their share in the American social fund. The drive to reform the nation's cities opened with a pragmatic assessment of urban needs and quickly spawned broad coalitions of voters demanding immediate solutions to a wide range of problems: tax reforms, health regulations, streetcar fares, utility services, and city governments dominated by corrupt bosses and predatory "interests."

TENEMENTS, WASHINGTON, D.C.

Lewis W. Hine's famous photograph of the capital's black slums documents the urban progressive challenge. (*George Eastman House Collection.*)

By 1895 urban progressivism had drawn together the separate strands of a reform impulse that had originated, in the years following the Civil War, in piecemeal demands for civil service reform, railroad rate regulation, the eight-hour day, and factory legislation. The depression of the 1890s, by placing new burdens on urban consumers, bred a sudden sense of urgency and focused public attention on the shortcomings of machine rule. The key to the urban reform program, and itself the most powerful weapon in the progressive arsenal, was "invisible government," the sinister alliance between municipal authorities and business interests. The connection between "corrupt government" and "corporate arrogance" was a simple one of mutual need. In attempting to modernize their cities, machine politicians had discovered in secret agreements with transit and utility interests a handy device for supplying minimal service while lining their own pockets. At the same time, a new and unstable industry undergoing rapid reorganization saw in monopoly franchises, wholesale bribery, and kickbacks a measure of certainty in an otherwise unpredictable world. By 1890 the bargain had been sealed in most of the major cities of the country. The only real loser in this arrangement was the public.

Thus progressivism first appeared as a "people's movement" aimed at eliminating corruption and providing better services in urban transportation and other public facilities. Cutting across class and occupational lines and fastening on specific issues like dangerous railway crossings, improved sanitation facilities, or lower streetcar fares, the progressive movement in this early campaign developed a rhetoric and a style that was democratic and moralistic. The twin villains in the reformers' morality play were the businessman and the boss. His experiences as reform mayor of Detroit, Hazen Pingree concluded, had convinced him that monopolistic corporations were responsible "for nearly all the thieving and boodling with which cities were made to suffer from their servants." The muckraker Lincoln Steffens pronounced the American businessman "a self-righteous fraud." "I found him buying boodlers in Saint Louis, defending grafters in Minneapolis, originating corruption in Pittsburgh, sharing with bosses in Philadelphia, deploring reform in Chicago, and beating good government with corruption funds in New York." From the beginning progressives developed an antibusiness style that continued to obscure the real contributions of businessmen to urban reform.

The bosses offered even more enticing targets. According to Frederick Howe, Cincinnati's Boss George Cox ruled the city "as a medieval baron did his serfs."

He rose to this eminence by binding together and to himself the rich and powerful members of the community, for whom he secured and protects the franchises of street-railway, gas and electric lighting companies. They, in turn, became his friends and protectors, and through him, and for him, controlled the press and organized public opinion.

According to urban reformers, the only remedy for boss rule lay in fostering citizen coalitions to unite a fragmented community. "The very nature of city life," one progressive commentator insisted, "compels manifold cooperation. The individual cannot 'go it alone'; he cannot do as he pleases; he must conform his acts in an ever increasing degree to the will and welfare of the community in which he lives." This concept of the organic city fitted neatly the interests and ambitions of a new group of reform mayors in the 1890s who launched individual campaigns to overhaul their cities.

The first of the new reform mayors who succeeded in assembling dissatisfied urban consumers behind his reform program was Hazen Pingree, mayor of Detroit from 1889 to 1896 when he was elected governor. Pingree, who was a wealthy shoe manufacturer with a yen for politics, quickly mastered the role of "reform boss," campaigning vigorously in all the wards of the city and studiously avoiding issues of moral reform like prohibition and parochial schools, concentrating instead on the hard economic issues calculated to win him the greatest support. In the course of his several administrations, Pingree exposed bribery in a local electric light company's dealings with his predecessors and embarked on an extensive program of school and park construction. After a prolonged battle with the transit and utility interests, he succeeded in reducing streetcar and gas rates while building the city's municipal lighting plant. During the depression he initiated work relief for Detroit's unemployed and extended a variety of social service programs. Attacking Detroit's "invisible government" and replacing it with an efficient and responsive administration, Pingree set a pattern for his successors by collecting loose coalitions of voters behind a series of significant if unspectacular urban reforms.

It remained for Tom Johnson, the mercurial mayor of Cleveland from 1901 to 1909, to exploit most fully a whole new range of possibilities for leadership. Johnson had made his fortune reorganizing transit systems, and had been converted to reform on reading Henry George's *Social Problems*. After two successful terms in Congress as a reform Democrat, he returned to Cleveland to assemble the coalition with which to fight Mark Hanna and the traction interests. Energetic, tough-minded, and a consummate politician right down to the unlit cigar he waved from the nearest handy soapbox, Johnson borrowed all the techniques of the machine and improved on them. Like Pingree, he instinctively shied away from moral issues and inaugurated his reform program by arranging for a regulated system of prostitution free from police graft. Like Pingree too, he confronted the transit interests with the prospects of regulation. His most widely acclaimed achievement was the "three-cent fare," but he continued to agitate for municipal ownership of utilities, and provided the city with free public bathhouses, recreational facilities, and effective sanitary inspection.

Reform mayors who launched their careers from a platform of pragmatic opposition to the "interests" were frequently forced to confront broader questions of social welfare. Some of them, like Pingree and Johnson, and later Brand Whitlock in Toledo and Mark Fagan in Jersey City, were driven to adjust to shifting interests within their reform coalitions and to support welfare measures that extended far beyond the political and structural reforms they originally had called for. The "social justice" mayors, as they have been called, also came to question the value of strict party identification; increasingly they came to rely on the advice and services of new professionals and experts in municipal management, whose scientific concerns centered on finding more efficient and economical ways of running the city. "The fact of the matter is," "Golden Rule" Jones, reform mayor of Toledo, admitted late in his career, "that there is little hope for improvement, for progress, in the direction of scientific government in our municipalities until we shall first get the people freed from the baneful superstition of partisan politics." One route to nonpartisanship lay through increased dependence on experts; another through alliances with humanitarian reformers with their base in urban slums.

Streetcar politics was only the most visible sign of the urban revival in the 1890s. City churches, suddenly conscious of their declining membership among the working class, responded to the perceived crisis with the "institutional church" in lower-class neighborhoods. They hoped thus to spread the "social gospel" of Christianity through devices like lodging houses, reading rooms, recreational halls, and day nurseries. Then too, by 1890, groups of earnest young college graduates, many of them women, were moving to the slums to live in settlement houses modeled on London's famed Toynbee Hall. In New York in 1886, the young seminary graduate Stanton Coit founded the Neighborhood Guild on the Lower East Side, a center that soon became known as University Settlement as it began to attract young recruits from Columbia University uptown. Three years later, Jane Addams and Ellen Gates Starr moved into Hull House, where with the financial help of Chicago matrons they gathered a staff of idealistic young college graduates and set to work building a kindergarten and a day nursery for working mothers, and organizing a variety of youth clubs and an employment bureau.

By 1895 there were over fifty such settlements in major cities around the country. Settlement-house workers were invariably young (the great majority under thirty), religious (predominantly Congregationalist and Presbyterian), college-educated, single, and overwhelmingly from genteel middle-class homes. For such young intellectuals and would-be professionals, many of them with advanced training in the new social sciences taught in German universities, the city settlement offered an escape from gentility and from feelings of superfluousness and provided the chance to practice their new skills. Settlements freed their members from what Jane Addams called "the snare of preparation" for unknown careers. More important, they became the focus for a new sense of the complex social and cultural relations that defined the organic city. Teachers, housing reformers, charity organizers, health inspectors, and visiting nurses all found a congenial home in the settlements, which suddenly seemed to them miniature models of the good society. By 1900, the settlement house had established itself as an indispensable laboratory of social reform, its success measured in the years that followed by the alacrity with which city administrations institutionalized their improvements.

In experimenting with urban reform, these social pioneers discovered new techniques for coping with the bewildering variety of urban problems. In the first place, they came to rely heavily on new methods of research and fact gathering as essential to the task of re-ordering urban society. One of Jane Addams's first assignments was to collect and collate the raw data on the surrounding neighborhood; and in 1895, *Hull House Maps and Papers* appeared as the first detailed account of an immigrant community published in the United States. In 1903, Lawrence Veiller and Robert W. DeForest published their two-volume *Tenement-House Problem,* an attempt to relate urban housing to the larger city setting through the use of statistics and first hand observation. Perhaps the most ambitious project for examining the city in its entirety was the six-volume *Pittsburgh Survey* (1909–1914) which treated politics, crime, prostitution, the family, housing, and working conditions as aspects of a functioning organism.

Social surveys underscored the need for trained personnel and scientific management. The autonomous commission staffed by trained professionals and given power to revamp tax structures, regulate transit and utility rates, and provide efficient city services quickly became the principal agency of effective urban reform. With the commission came another type of progressive reformer, the expert who saw his job as imposing order on the city in much the same way corporate businessmen were regularizing their procedures.

Still another sign of the growth of bureaucratic values was the spectacular increase in professional organizations. Economists, sociologists, political scientists, tax reformers, charity organizers, settlement-house workers, and dozens of other specialized professions had formed national societies by 1900, each with its own publications and communications network. These national organizations, besides strengthening a sense of professional community, cemented an alliance with the new universities providing the training and the facilities for scientific investigation of urban problems. In Chicago, the residents of Hull House quickly established close connections with William Rainey Harper's new University of Chicago through reform-minded academics like John Dewey, Albion Small, William I. Thomas, and Charles Merriam. In New York, economists and sociologists from Columbia University joined freelance writers and publicists at the University Settlement in analyzing city problems and working out solutions.

The settlement connection proved vital for young academicians by providing laboratories for testing new concepts of behavior and by drawing them into the exciting world of reform politics beyond university walls. Charles Merriam, the ambitious young political scientist who had trained under John W. Burgess and William A. Dunning at Columbia before joining Harper's faculty at Chicago, explained the urban challenge and the urgent need for formulating a new political science to cope with it. "The new techniques of the new time must be adapted to the new background, social and intellectual, of the new world we live in," Merriam told fellow reformers. "Politics as the art of the traditional advances to politics as the science of constructive, intelligent social control."

Businessmen and academicians often parted company, however, on the question of applying Merriam's new critical spirit. By 1900 the university had come to house historians, economists, political scientists and social theorists equipped with sharp analytical tools for dismantling old conservative myths. Charles A. Beard was only the best known of the young academicians who were beginning to question the hide-bound interpretations of American law and the Constitution as well as the penchant for ancestor-worship they encouraged. Beard's own Columbia University typified the new iconoclastic spirit. There the economist Edwin Seligman, the earnest advocate of the "New History," James Harvey Robinson, and pioneer students of administrative law like Frank Goodnow were busy probing the economic roots of political behavior. In another setting and from a different direction the political scientist Arthur F. Bentley in *The Process of Government* (1908) approached political decision-making as a pluralistic process subject to the shifting strengths of interest groups. At the University of Washington the radical historian J. Allen Smith in a book entitled *The Spirit of American Government* (1907) dismissed the Constitution as a "reactionary document" de-

MYTHS AND REALITIES

The Gilded Age abounded in racial and social stereotypes, always crude and often vicious. On the cover of the song sheet at left the Irishman wears a dog's face while the advertisement for rat poison promises to rid the country of rats along with the Chinese who presumably eat them. The corrective facts appear in the photographs above: Boss "Tim" Sullivan gives his annual dinner for the poor; American flags fly in New York City's Chinatown. (*Top left, Brown Brothers; top right, Library of Congress.*)

signed to check the forces of democracy. After 1900 the partnership between highly critical academicians and their corporate financial supporters grew increasingly strained as the professors began to question the very business civilization on which their universities now depended.

With the appearance of concepts like "social control" and "scientific efficiency," however, progressive reformers made contact with another nineteenth-century reform tradition, one that was alien to the open tolerance of reform politicians and to the democratic and humanitarian hopes of social workers. This distinctive component of urban progressivism was the belief in the transcendent importance of remodeling American city governments on the principles of efficiency and economy.

Municipal reform as a scientific movement matured in 1893 with the Conference for Good City Government, out of which came the National Municipal League. Soon a range of specialized organizations demanding the overhaul of municipal government sprang up; they combined the interests of academics and new political professionals with those of progressive businessmen intent on applying their own methods to the management of cities. The organizational zeal for scientific reform with its emphasis on economy, efficiency, and stability was part of the bureaucratic revolution that had overtaken all American society, but it was not altogether new in intent or spirit. The political goals of the scientific reformers were as old as the nation itself, and they had been renewed in various forms, generation after generation. In this latest phase, however, patrician reformers joined new businessmen in broadening their vision to include politicians who promised to return strict accountability to government at all levels. By the nineties, reform-minded Republicans, new academic specialists in tax reform and municipal affairs, and business spokesmen were busy brewing an elixir of scientific efficiency and business economy with which to restore the health of the American cities.

Constant in all phases of the movement for good government was the belief that simply by tightening the system of expenditures, consolidating power in the hands of experts, and revising the political system without particular regard for human needs and demands, reformers could manage the city. Good government, the scientific reformers reasoned, would be rigorously honest, determinedly efficient, resolutely frugal, and strictly accountable. In its initial formulation, scientific reform was neo-Federalist, designed as a check on democratic participation and aspirations; it was a modernized version of virtual representation for limiting the influence of uninformed voters whose numbers it sought to reduce through literacy tests and voter registration laws.

By the end of the century, the ancient patrician model of good government had been adapted to the modern demands of professional politicians and sophisticated businessmen. Rule by the talented few had become management by trained administrators and experts. Efficiency and economy had come to be equated with business practices of budget paring, cost cutting, tax trimming, and service chopping according to a "ledger-book ethics" of corporation accountants. To be allowed to practice as well as to preach their revivified civic morality, scientific reformers needed to win office, and this recognition led to experiments with a variety of political and structural reforms ranging from the Australian ballot, at-large elections, and voter registration laws to new commission forms, investigative bureaus, and the extension of civil service. By 1900, the original reform design had acquired the outlines of a utopia promising the extinction of parties and politics as a way of life, rule by disinterested experts supervising a trimmed-down government and using the latest scientific procedures. "Scientific" government promised a self-perpetuating bureaucratic system whose frictionless operation would ensure the efficient dispensing of goods and services.

Good government reformers considered the city a challenge that was not very different from the need for business integration and corporate merger confronting new industrialists and financiers. "Municipal government is business, not politics" read the slogan of the scientific reformers. The shaping power of the modern corporation in determining the outlook of the structural progressive reformers was reflected in their vocabulary, built on a set of useful analogies.

THE PROGRESSIVE SOCIAL WORKER'S
CLIENTS

While social workers recognized that reforms ultimately depended upon the votes of men, they concentrated their efforts for immediate improvement on women and children. (*George Eastman House Collection.*)

The mayor served as *chairman of the board* of an urban *corporation* comprising big and little *stockholders,* who were expected to vote their *proxies* at annual meetings and accept their *dividends* without constantly interfering with the *managers* of the *enterprise.* It was hardly a coincidence that the waning years of the century, which saw the triumph of the corporation and the advent of scientific municipal reform, also witnessed the opening assault on the concept of a rational "public opinion," once considered the cornerstone of democratic politics. In dismissing that opinion as frivolous or perverse, scientific reformers betrayed what Frederick Howe called a "distrust of democracy," for in declining to take their instructions from the "people" they echoed the sentiments of their Federalist predecessors a century earlier in calling for the reduction of popular influence in the governing of the community. The first order of reform business, insisted Frank Goodnow, a spokesman for the scientific reformers, was recruiting cadres of loyal and politically unambitious civil servants whose combined efficiencies would permit "the business and professional class of the community to assume care of public business without making too great personal sacrifice."

For business-dominated mayors who tried to clean up city politics after 1900, urban reform meant an opportunity for Americans of the middle and upper classes, armed with new bureaucratic techniques and procedures, to repossess the field of urban politics that their predecessors had abandoned to the bosses fifty years earlier. Some of the participants in the revolt against machine politics professed not to see the contradictions between scientific efficiency and the superior claims of social democracy. Robert Merriam, a leading spokesman for a scientific politics and an active office seeker, called for "the organization of public authority" in a system linking administrative freedom with long-term democratic directives. Merriam continued to define the problem of the city as repair of the "institutional forms of democracy," and saw the progressive task as one combining the conflicting principles of autonomy and accountability in the experimental process itself.

The case for democracy was most forcefully put by Brand Whitlock, novelist, social welfare reformer, and mayor of Toledo from 1905 to 1913. Whitlock defined the "city sense" as democracy and "the spirit of goodwill in humanity" and predicted the coming of cities that should "express the ideals of the people and work wonderful ameliorations in the human soul."

This will not be accomplished by the triumph of one class over another, or by any *bouleversement* in which the processes of despotism will be reversed. . . . It will not descend upon the cities from any feudal lord or industrial baron of our time, whether in the hall of legislature or in the counting-house, however gracious and benevolent he may be. It must come up from the people themselves through patient study and careful experiment . . . and be the expression of their own best longings and aspirations.

But the great majority of reformers recognized the progressive problem for what it was, a value choice involving two widely divergent estimates of democracy and human nature. Some reformers, like the sociologist Edward A. Ross, frankly rejected the idea of democratic participation in favor of elitism. Politically, Ross argued, democracy meant not the sovereignty of the average citizen, "who is a rather narrow, shortsighted, muddleheaded creature," but the "mature public opinion" of an educated elite.

'One man, one vote,' does not make Sambo equal to Socrates in the state, for the balloting but registers a public opinion. In the forming of this opinion the sage has a million times the weight of the field hand. With modern facilities for influencing mind, democracy, at its best, substitutes the direction of the recognized moral and intellectual elite for the rule of the strong, the rich, or the privileged. . . . Let the people harken a little less to commercial magnates and a little more to geologists, economists, physicians, teachers and social workers.

The legacy of urban progressives to the twentieth century was thus a divided one. Even with the development of overlapping groups and ideas among scientific and humanitarian reformers a dual tradition emerged, polarized around conflicting values of social efficiency and democratic liberation. These contesting principles, which had combined briefly in the 1890s to unsettle the politics of equilibrium, would continue to diverge in the twentieth century, creating tensions within progressivism that would make it a varied, confused, and contradictory movement.

Suggested Readings

There are several useful guides to the politics of the Gilded Age. Leonard D. White, *The Republican Era, 1869–1901* (1958) examines the workings of the federal government. H. Wayne Morgan, *From Hayes to McKinley: National Party Politics, 1877–1896* (1969), concentrates on political organization. Daniel J. Elazar, *The American Partnership* (1962), treats federal-state relations in detail, and David J. Rothman, *Politics and Power: The United States Senate, 1869–1901* (1966), presents a fascinating account of the organizational changes in the upper house. Robert D. Marcus, *Grand Old Party: Political Structure in the Gilded Age, 1880–1896* (1971), analyzes the workings of the Republican party, and Horace Samuel Merrill, *Bourbon Democracy of the Middle West, 1865–1896*, gives a regional account of the Democrats for the same period. Vincent P. DeSantis, *Republicans Face the Southern Question* (1959) and Stanley P. Hirshson, *Farewell to the Bloody Shirt: Northern Republicans and the Southern Negro, 1877–1893* (1962), consider the race issue as it affected Republican strategy. Southern politics is perceptively treated in four important works: C. Vann Woodward, *The Origins of the New South, 1877–1913* (1951); Dewey W. Grantham, Jr., *The Democratic South* (1963); Albert D. Kirwan, *Revolt of the Rednecks: Mississippi Politics: 1876–1925* (1951); and Morgan Kousser, *The Shaping of Southern Politics: Suffrage Restriction and the Establishment of the One-Party South, 1880–1910* (1974). Mary R. Dearing, *Veterans in Politics* (1952), recounts the activities of Civil War veterans, and Marc Karson, *American Labor Unions and Politics, 1900–1918* (1958), discusses unions and politics in the opening years of the twentieth century.

A number of studies examine electoral behavior in crucial elections. Among the best are Paul W. Glad, *McKinley, Bryan, and the People* (1964); Stanley Jones, *The Presidential Election of 1896* (1964); J. Rogers Hollingsworth, *The Whirligig of Politics: The Democracy of Cleveland and Bryan* (1963). Two challenging studies, Paul Kleppner, *The Cross of Culture: A Social Analysis of Midwestern Politics, 1850–1900* (1970), and Richard J. Jensen, *The Winning of the Midwest* (1971), examine cultural factors operating in Midwestern politics during the Gilded Age and perhaps elsewhere as well.

Political biography abounds. Two of the best studies of Bryan are Paolo E. Coletta, *William Jennings Bryan: Political Evangelist, 1860–1908* (1964), and Paul Glad, *The Trumpet Soundeth: William Jennings Bryan and His Democracy, 1896–1912* (1964). For McKinley, see H. Wayne Morgan, *William McKinley and His America* (1963). On Cleveland, Horace Samuel Merrill, *Bourbon Leader: Grover Cleveland and the Democratic Party* (1957), supersedes Allan Nevins, *Grover Cleveland* (1932). Biographies of other important figures include numerous older works: Ray Ginger, *The Bending Cross: A Biography of Eugene V. Debs* (1948); Herbert Croly, *Marcus Alonzo Hanna* (1912); Nathaniel W. Stephenson, *Nelson W. Aldrich* (1930); Francis Butler Simkins, *Pitchfork Ben Tillman* (1944); Leland L. Sage, *William Boyd Allison* (1956); and Harry Barnard, *"Eagle Forgotten": The Life of John Peter Altgeld* (1938).

On the troubled 1890s, a good overview is Harold U. Faulkner, *Politics, Reform and Expansion, 1890–1900* (1959). The intellectual and cultural climate of the decade is analyzed in the idiosyncratic and amusing Thomas Beer, *The Mauve Decade* (1925), and Lazar Ziff, *The American 1890s: Life and Times of a Lost Generation* (1966). For contemporary accounts that treat the social and cultural issues in nostalgic fashion, see Harry Thurston Peck, *Twenty Years of the Republic, 1885–1905* (1907), and the first volume of Mark Sullivan, *Our Times* (6 vols., 1926–35).

Local politics continues to attract the attention of historians, and the recent literature on bosses and machines is impressive. Alexander B. Callow, Jr., *The Tweed Ring* (1966) and Seymour J. Mandelbaum, *Boss Tweed's New York* (1965) offer penetrating analyses of machine politics in New York, and so does Theodore J. Lowi, *At the Pleasure of the Mayor: Patronage and Power in New York City, 1898–1958* (1964) for a later period. For Chicago, Harold F. Gosnell, *Machine Politics: Chicago Model* (1935), is still useful but should be supplemented with Lloyd Wendt and Herman Kogan, *Bosses in Lusty Chicago: The Story of Bathhouse John and Hinky Dink* (1943), and Joel A. Tarr, *A Study of Boss Politics: William Lorimer of Chicago* (1971). Other big American cities are analyzed in Zane L. Miller, *Boss Cox's Cincinnati* (1968); Lyle Dorsett, *The Pendergast Machine* (1968); and Walton E. Bean, *Boss Ruef's San Francisco* (1952). The effect of progressive reforms is described in Melvin Holli, *Reform in Detroit: Hazen Pingree and Urban Politics* (1969); James B. Crooks, *Politics and Progress: The Rise of Urban Progressivism in Baltimore, 1895–1911* (1968); and William D. Miller, *Memphis During the Progressive Era, 1900–1917* (1957). A good study of Tammany in this period is Nancy Weiss, *Charles Francis Murphy, 1858–1924: Respectability and Responsibility in Tammany Politics* (1968). Jack Tager, *The Intellectual as Urban Reformer: Brand Whitlock and the Progressive Movement* (1968), is a sharply etched portrait of a recognizable progressive type.

The Progressive
Impulse

In 1915, as progressive reform neared its zenith, a young professor of government at New York University, Benjamin Parke DeWitt, published a book entitled *The Progressive Movement*, in which he catalogued the political and social reforms in the United States since 1900 and pointed to their underlying unity. DeWitt, a fervent admirer of Theodore Roosevelt and an active reformer, looked behind recent campaigns and elections and discovered three interlocking progressive tendencies:

The first of these tendencies is found in the insistence by the best men in all political parties that special, minority, and corrupt influence in government—national, state, and city—be removed; the second tendency is found in the demand that the structure or machinery of government, which has hitherto been admirably adapted to control by the few, be so changed and modified that it will be more difficult for the few, and easier for the many, to control; and, finally, the third tendency is found in the rapidly growing conviction that the functions of government are too restricted and that they must be increased and extended to relieve social and economic distress.

In identifying the most urgent reform task as the redesign of American government and the recruitment of new personnel to run it DeWitt summarized the progressive belief in the primacy of politics. The progressives' reasoning made a tidy syllogism: Government at all levels was both inefficient and corrupt; because it was corrupt it neglected the needs and demands of the people, who accordingly must seize the initiative in repairing the entire system. According to this logic, the first reform task was removing unworthy and inept politicians and replacing them with trained public servants drawn from the popular ranks and equipped with the needed expertise. These new bureaucrats would see to it that government—city, state and national—performed an expanding range of functions efficiently and responsibly. Progressive reformers, in short, discovered in the uses of scientific government the materials for building a common national movement.

The progressives' keen sense of their renovative mission helped them to ignore the bewildering variety of factors that determined their goals. In the first place, there was no single "progressive type," among the leaders or the rank and file whose age, status, background, religion, and education were remarkably similar to those of their opponents. Progressives simply composed the vital center of the native-born, middle-class establishment that dominated American politics in the first two decades of the twentieth century. Educated, articulate, and eager to apply their ideas for reforming society and politics, they held no monopoly on political gentility and could be found in equal numbers in the reform wings of both major political parties.

Progressives, moreover, offered an impressive array of reform proposals: initiative, referendum, and recall; corporate regulation and social legislation of all kinds; tariff reform and banking laws; city manager plans and new budgetary procedures; immigration restriction and even prohibition. Progressive priorities differed widely according to region and interest. Farmers fought strenuously for regulation of railroad rates but ignored the plight of the industrial worker. Southern progressives rallied behind tariff and banking reform as they proceeded to disfranchise the black. Settlement-house workers grappled with the bosses for control of their cities but neglected the problems of the small-town businessman. For every progressive reformer with a comprehensive platform there were ten would-be saviors of American society with a single nostrum.

With this shifting fault line running through the first two decades of the twentieth century, it has sometimes seemed more useful to write the "obituary" of progressivism as a collectivity, approaching it, instead, as simply another form of "aggregative politics," a patchwork of divergent interest groups willing occasionally to agree on specific measures but generally unable to combine in a coherent movement.

Most progressives, however, thought otherwise. They recognized that the United States had entered a new century of consolidation, one demanding new techniques for managing what they agreed was a flourishing national enterprise. Although they admitted that there was still much wrong with America, they saw little that could not be mended by applying public authority and scientific efficiency. In the spirit of the Founding Fathers, whose buoyant nationalism they so admired, progressive reformers considered themselves the architects of a stable social order based on many of the same principles that had guided the work of their Federalist ancestors, who in their time had sought to impose system and control on a prodigal democratic people.

With their use of new political techniques and behavioral concepts, progressives were innovators, but at a deeper level of social perception they were restorationists, picking up the promise of American life where their eighteenth-century forebears had dropped it — with the creation of a strong national government capable of directing the energies of its citizens. If part of the progressive message calling on the "people" to seize power from their corrupt rulers seemed to invoke the spirit of Jefferson, the heart of the progressive program was the Hamiltonian demand for a new national leadership capable of composing discord and providing direction. The ghosts of Hamilton and Jefferson fought over the progressive terrain with much the same intensity the two statesmen had contested each other's principles a century earlier. To the delight of his numerous progressive followers Hamilton won the victory denied him during his lifetime. If not in intent, at least in effect, progressivism marked the rebirth of original Federalist hopes for a managed republic in which men of talent and training guided the affairs of a prosperous people. After a century-long aberration chargeable to the pernicious enthusiasms of Jefferson, progressivism promised a return to order.

The Man with the Muckrake

The Muckrakers supplied progressivism with an agenda. The name was a label affixed to a new brand of reform journalists by President Theodore Roosevelt who complained that their relentless exposure of corruption in high places hindered rather than helped him in his work of improving American society. Comparing the group of headstrong publicists to Bunyan's gloomy figure who refused a celestial crown for a muckrake, the President denounced their "crude and sweeping generalizations" and their penchant for pointing the finger of civic shame. For their part the Muckrakers — Lincoln Steffens, Ida Tarbell, Ray Stannard Baker, David Graham Phillips, and half a hundred colleagues — accepted the label and wore it proudly as proof of their devotion to the Jeffersonian principle of a free and vigilant press.

Muckraking was the commercial product of two forces that had combined by the end of the nineteenth century: significant advances in the technology of printing that made it possible for the first time to produce an inexpensive, illustrated popular magazine; and the simultaneous arrival on the metropolitan scene of the reform reporter sensitive to the new social concerns of his middle-class readers and eager to exploit them. By 1900, rotary presses, linotype machines, and photoengraving had caught the attention of a group of aggressive editors whose magazine bore their personal stamp and often their names. Frank Munsey and S. S. McClure were only two of the pioneer explorers of this lucrative field, and they were quickly joined by dozens of competitors drawn to social criticism by their keen sense of the market and the prospect of sizeable profits. From the outset

Muckraking proved that reform could be a paying proposition. Gathering a staff of trained, well-paid newspapermen whom they set loose on the national community, the Muckrake editors launched an attack on the underside of American life with articles on sweatshops, tainted meat, the white slave traffic, insurance company scandals, labor racketeering, city bosses, and high finance. Effectively, they were compiling a list of all the social wrongs that enlightened readers would presumably set right.

McClure's quickly became the leader of the Muckrake pack. In the January 1903 issue of the magazine there appeared three articles exposing American social sins: Lincoln Steffens's "The Shame of Minneapolis"; an installment of Ida Tarbell's accusatory history of Standard Oil; and Ray Stannard Baker's account of the nonunion victims of the closed shop, "The Right to Work." Steffens singled out business as the cause of the nation's woes: "That's what's the matter with it. That's what's the matter with everything—art, literature, religion, journalism, law, medicine,—they're all business. . . ." More soberly Tarbell weighed the

ethical costs of monopoly and the sanctifying of business success, while Baker drew sharply etched portraits of scabs and racketeers. In an accompanying editorial McClure himself sounded the central theme in the Muckraking appeal: "There is no one left; none but all of us. . . . We all are doing our worst and making the public pay. The public is the people. We forget that we all are the people. . . ."

Beyond such moral exhortation it was difficult for the Muckrakers to go in examining the causes of the American malaise. Upton Sinclair and Charles Edward Russell urged a mild form of socialism as a corrective for predatory business behavior, and George Kibbe Turner preached salvation through business responsibility. The exuberant David Graham Phillips, whose discovery of treason in the Senate first called down the presidential wrath, warned of a power-hungry plutocracy invading the halls of state, while Steffens concentrated on municipal graft and misbehavior of statehouse rings. The thematic thread connecting their various indictments was a carefully cultivated hard-boiled tone. "If our political leaders are to be always a lot of political merchants," Steffens declared, "they will supply any demand we may create. All we have to do is to establish a steady demand for good government."

Muckraking, as Theodore Roosevelt denounced it and millions of readers reveled in it, offered both a new kind of factual reporting and an old form of moral publicity. Always extravagant and frequently sensational, the Muckrakers perfected the uses of contrast and contradiction in pointing to the disparity between venerable American fictions and startling social facts. In an article for *Cosmopolitan* on child labor in Southern cotton mills, for example, the poet Edwin Markham depicted "The Hoe Man in the Making" in the faces of "ill-fed, unkempt, unwashed, half-dressed" children penned in the narrow lanes of the mills, little victims whose dreary lives mocked the "bright courtesy of the cultured classes." The social gospelist Ernest Crosby contrasted the "appearance" of a majestic United States Senate with the reality of a "House of Dollars," a political monopoly modeled on an industrial trust. Samuel Hopkins Adams explained the national failure to regulate the food and drug industries as the result of "private interests in public murder" when "everybody's health is nobody's business."

Muckraking thus presented a technique rather than a philosophy, a popular style rather than a coherent analysis. As social critics, the journalists were curiously Janus-faced, on the one side seemingly tough-minded and factual, and on the other, romantic, moralistic, and more than occasionally sentimental. Like their millions of readers, they were the beneficiaries of a fundamental change in the idea of publicity, which they conceived of as an open-ended process of fact gathering that reflected the shifting nature of social reality. Read in this subdued light, their articles could be considered wholesome remedies and useful correctives for particular problems. Their work, the Muckrakers insisted, was never done, since an unfolding social process required constantly accommodating accepted theory to recently acquired facts, old values to new conditions.

Yet Muckraking tapped traditional moral reserves and exploited the conventional reform roles of the disinterested observer and the clear-eyed, hard-nosed investigator with his fierce desire to get "all the facts" and expose them to the sanitizing rays of moral publicity. Muckrakers liked to think of themselves as brave detectives, dashing from one hidden clue to another looking for the fragments of information that once collected and arranged would tell them what to do. Their appeal to the awakened conscience of the "people" was pure myth, serviceable enough as propaganda but scarcely an adequate description of political reality. There was also a strong bias against party government in the Muckrakers' reading of American politics as well as a weakness for conspiratorial interpretations. Their tendency to assign vast restorative powers to the masses of American voters served to justify their own roles as indispensable fact finders. Tell the people the truth, they seemed to say, and they will correct injustice forthwith! Conscience, duty, character, virtue—these were the watchwords of the Muckrakers and also a measure of their limited understanding of the problems confronting progressive America. Muckrakers identified the symptoms of disorder, but they could not isolate its causes or prescribe effective remedies. For these a clearer understanding of the workings of industrialized society was needed.

Progressives vs Politicians

The most powerful force for reforming American society came from another direction—from the ranks of businessmen, academicians, and professionals who had lately received an education in new organizational methods and now sought to apply them to the conduct of politics. These key groups in early twentieth-century America were already developing more systematic ways of doing their work along with new attitudes towards it and more sophisticated standards for measuring its performance. By 1900, professionals and businessmen were busy as never before organizing themselves according to discipline, specialty, or interest. The advantages of combination had now become obvious to groups as different as the American Sociological Association and the National Association of Manufacturers. The rise of organization was largely the work of new specialists—municipal tax experts, city planners, corporation lawyers, public health officials, market analysts, efficiency experts, and public relations men—all bent on modernizing their professions and enjoying newly acquired prestige.

Progressive businessmen and professionals shared a set of values and goals that redirected their careers and reshaped their priorities into concepts of

BOSS POLITICS: PROGRESSIVE TARGET

Progressive reformers found it difficult to compete with the city boss whose services to his clients, like those of Tammany Hall, included free barbecues. (*Brown Brothers.*)

system, control, stability, and predictability. Charity organizers realized the pressing need for accurate data and scientific procedure in drafting workable solutions to social disorganization. A giant lumber company like Weyerhaeuser came to appreciate the importance of planning and cooperation with the new experts in the Forestry Service. College professors and high school teachers now recognized the need for professional solidarity to protect their rights. Public-service lawyers, like young Louis Brandeis, suddenly realizing the complexities of new legal relations, began to experiment with the role of "counsel to the situation" and with new techniques of arbitration.

The social perceptions of this middle-class vanguard of the bureaucratic revolution stemmed from their sense of American society as a collectivity—whether a complete organism or an intergrated piece of machinery. To implement their bureaucratic values they fashioned new "scientific" operating procedures: centralizing authority in a hierarchical order rather than a democratic one; concentrating decision-making power in an energetic executive; establishing impersonal relations marked by bureaucratic function; and above all, planning for maximum efficiency. Although the bureaucratic ideal was seldom achieved either by businessmen or professionals, after 1900 it commanded increasing attention with its promise of replacing ceremonial loyalties to party and private interest with a new spirit of professional purpose and civic responsibility.

These values and procedures assumed concrete form for large numbers of progressives in the image of the modern corporation. The picture of the efficient, impersonal corporation was not drawn by big businessmen alone; it was a widely accepted model of organization that appealed to intellectuals and professionals as well as to industrialists and financiers who recognized its uses in rebuilding American politics. Progressive criticism of the trust was largely directed towards its misuse by unscrupulous promoters, not towards its seemingly rational structure. "The trust is the educator of us all," Jane Addams announced in explaining the need for new kinds of collective action. Seen in this light, the corporation appeared as a corrective of the waste and the inefficiencies of an earlier age, an actual model of organizational reform extendable, like the utopian communities before the Civil War, to a larger American society. Advocates of technology and economic innovation maintained that the new procedures had outstripped political developments, which now must catch up. Reformers had first to demolish the crumbling foundations of party politics and begin their rebuilding program by vesting power in an informed electorate willing to grant a new managerial class the power to lead.

The conservative bias of many progressive reformers could be most clearly seen in their attacks on the boss and the machine while their real intentions were frequently obscured, even to themselves, by their seemingly democratic enthusiasm. "The people are finding a way," exclaimed the progressive publicist William Allen White, who pointed in astonishment to the rapid growth of "fundamental democracy" in the American soul. A whole roster of progressive proposals for open government were billed as democratic devices for ensuring popular control at the grass roots. The direct primary and direct election of senators would release the stranglehold of the bosses on the electoral process. Referendum would send important questions of policy straight to the people over the heads of unresponsive legislators. Recall would return the power to remove officeholders to the voters, with whom it belonged. Many progressives, contemplating improvements like these, were inclined to agree with William Allen White that the machine was in "a fair way to be reduced to mere political scrap iron by the rise of the people."

Urban progressives were not hypocrites in advertising their reforms as democratic, but they did not always make it clear that by "the people" they meant not the huddled masses in center cities but solid citizens with sensible views and sober habits who had previously abdicated in favor of the bosses and their benighted clients. Below the blaring trumpets of democracy could be heard, subdued but distinct, the progressive call for the politically vanquished to return to the fray armed with new weapons.

The nerve center of urban progressivism after 1900 consisted of municipal leagues, civic federations, citizens' lobbies, commercial clubs, and bureaus of municipal research. These civic groups provided forums for the lively exchange of ideas between academicians operating out of the urban university and businessmen eager to try out their own ideas of efficiency and economy in managing their cities. From organizations like the National Municipal League and the National Civic Federation poured a flood of proposals and plans for repairing urban administrations: home rule and charter revision, ballot reform and literacy tests, citywide election schemes and city-manager plans, all of them aimed at the power base of the boss. Urban progressives, as one municipal leaguer explained, sought to make the city "an efficient business enterprise . . . a simple, direct, businesslike way of administering the business of the city." Social scientists sharpened the progressive indictment of machine politics by emphasizing waste

PROGRESS AMERICAN-STYLE

"If God had meant man to fly. . . ." But woman? (*Library of Congress.*)

as well as corruption, denouncing the politicians' "extravagant measures" that mulcted the taxpayers. According to these new scientific experts, machine politics represented the vestiges of a nineteenth-century "sectionalism" with its futile "treaty-making by factionalism."

At first the reformers concentrated on procedural improvements. They proposed segregated budgets for economy. They introduced time clocks, work sheets, job descriptions, and standardized salaries. They developed systematic ways of letting contracts in place of the old patronage methods. But the heart of their reform program was the commission and city-manager plans, modeled on the corporation. The original idea for the city commission was the work of John H. Patterson, president of the National Cash Register Company in Dayton, Ohio, who described the ideal city as "a great business enterprise whose stockholders are the people" but one that ought to be run by "men who are skilled in business and the social sciences." Combining executive and legislative functions in a single board, at once more economical and more efficient, the commission plan spread rapidly until by 1913 over 300 cities in the United States had adopted it. The city-manager plan, a refinement of the original commission idea, further consolidated decision making in the municipal government, and by the 1920s it too had been widely adopted.

Urban progressives never succeeded in putting the political boss out of business. The profitable "business of politics" was never forced into bankruptcy, and reformers never managed to establish a permanent receivership. Nevertheless, progressivism successfully challenged boss politics by confronting it with another way of doing the business of the city. The machine's power lay in the center city, with its immigrants and working classes. Middle-class reformers generally operated from power bases in the suburban periphery. Boss politics, for all its various sins, was marked by a high degree of accountability and popular participation in the wards and precincts. Progressives tried to reduce direct popular involvement at both the voting and the officeholding level. Bosses were prodigal but democratic; reformers were economical and bureaucratic. In the tradition of the Federalists, urban progressives attempted to bring democratic society under control by arrogating the directive power in an industrial society to themselves.

Progressive success was limited. All too often procedures changed but official policy did not. Still, if the boss and his underlings proved remarkably adept at parrying the electoral thrusts of reform candidates, they could no longer ignore the increasingly strident cries for more effective government. By 1920 neither side could claim victory. The progressives' dream of a shiny, streamlined, nonpartisan administration rationally measuring and meeting citizen demands never materialized. Yet the modernizing of American cities proceeded with or without the politician's blessing. In their partial overhaul of the nation's cities the progressives scored important gains for the new bureaucratic order.

Progressivism Invades the States

The progressives who set out to reform state politics after 1900 built on urban achievements. Beginning in 1900 with the first administration of Wisconsin governor Robert M. LaFollette, reform swept across the country in the next decade transforming the conduct of state politics and bringing a change of outlook that was long overdue.

Although progressivism varied widely in the three major sections of the country, there were enough similarities to give political reform the appearance of a national movement. In the South, progressives, inheriting a number of Populist grievances, often wore the one-gallus trappings of a redneck revolt against business-minded Bourbons. By the opening years of the century one governorship after another was falling to economy-minded agrarians from upcountry or downstate—Jeff Davis's punitive rule in Arkansas, Hoke Smith's rural ascendency in Georgia, Ben Tillman's pitchfork politics in South Carolina. The Southern rebellion against the alliance of big business and Democratic regulars drew on popular sympathies and brought railroad and corporate regulation, antimonopoly laws and insurance company controls, improved public education and child labor reforms, all at the price of total disfranchisement of the Negro.

Progressivism in the Midwest and on the Pacific Coast also grew out of insurgency, usually within a Republican party perceived as too generous to railroads and corporations. Midwestern progressives drew more heavily from the arsenal of democratic political reforms like the initiative and the referendum than their counterparts in the East, who tended to rely more on administrative reforms. But everywhere the political control of state legislatures by big business made an inviting target. In New Jersey, corporate dominance by 1900 was all but complete. "We've got everything in the state worth having," a spokesman for the state's corporate interests boasted. A compliant legislature regularly dispatched two senators to Washington to represent the utility interests and the insurance companies. The chief justice of the state supreme court, the commissioner of banking and insurance, the state comptroller, the attorney general, and a majority of the state board of taxation were all former employees of the Pennsylvania Railroad.

The governors who organized the revolts against these statehouse rings headed the cast of new progressive folk heroes as tough-minded reformers who combined a proper democratic outrage with a shrewd sense of the possible. Not all progressive governors were charismatic figures; New York's Charles Evans Hughes, for example, made his reputation as a low-keyed, genteel reformer specializing in repairing the state's administrative structure. But all the progressive governors capitalized on their independence from the "interests" and organized labor and featured themselves as representatives of all the people.

The most popular of the reform governors cast themselves as Western heroes, riding into office with a mandate to clean up the state, setting about their work with grim determination, and moving on to bigger things when their job was done. Denied office by the state party machine, the reformer collected his small band of insurgents and attempted, at first without success, to take over the party. To help him in his fight he enlisted other mavericks in his posse and began to explore electoral reforms, like the primary and the direct election of senators, fixing his sights on the "interests" and eventually unhorsing the party regulars.

Once elected, the progressive governor moved quickly to neutralize his opposition by absorbing some of their numbers into his own reform coalition. He quickly learned to wield patronage with a surprising ruthlessness, and with secure majorities in the legislature proceeded to enact his reform program. His list of reforms generally included strict regulation of railroads and public service corporations, a revamped tax structure, and major pieces of social legislation to improve working conditions in the state. After a hectic term or two in which he managed to complete at least part of his rebuilding program the

"BATTLING BOB" LAFOLLETTE CAMPAIGNING

LaFollette was famous for his style of political barnstorming. (*State Historical Society of Wisconsin.*)

progressive governor moved on to the Senate where he was joined by other like-minded rebels from similar backgrounds who had the same hopes of imposing their reform designs on national politics. The career of one such progressive hero, Robert M. LaFollette, illustrates the main features of this legend of progressive reform.

LaFollette, an intense, unsmiling, self-made man in the Horatio Alger mold, was a small-town lawyer who struggled to the top of the political heap in Wisconsin and in his three terms as governor after 1900 enacted a reform program that became the envy of progressives across the country. Born in Primrose, Wisconsin in meager circumstances, the young LaFollette was a walking example of the Protestant ethic. He put himself through the new state university by teaching school, and dutifully prepared himself for a career in politics by studying for the bar. At the University of Wisconsin he came under the reform influence of President John Bascom who was just beginning to build a public service institution, a task that LaFollette himself would complete a quarter of a century later.

Short, wiry, with a shock of bristling iron-gray hair, LaFollette combined a rock-hard moralism with a combativeness difficult to match in progressive circles. He won his first office as district attorney, without the endorsement of the Republican machine, by barnstorming the countryside and haranguing rural audiences on the need for integrity and independence. In 1884, he was elected, again without the support of party regulars, to the first of three terms in Congress as the youngest member of the House. After six years as a useful but undistinguished member of the Republican contingent in Washington, LaFollette was defeated in the Democratic landslide of 1890 and came home to a lucrative law practice.

The Republican party in Wisconsin, as in a number of other states, was the effective instrument of conservative Stalwarts representing the railroad and the lumber companies. Faced with a recovery suit against their state treasurers, who had regularly dipped into the public till for twenty years, the party bosses sent an emissary to LaFollette with a bribe to secure his influence with the judge, who happened to be his brother-in-law. LaFollette promptly cried havoc and later reckoned the attempted bribe the turning point of his career. "Nothing else ever came into my life that exerted such a powerful influence upon me as that affair." In exposing the machine's crime to the voters he effectively isolated himself from the party leaders and spent nearly a decade trying to collect enough votes from Scandinavian farmers and industrial workers in Milwaukee to overthrow the machine. By 1900 he had succeeded.

LaFollette's victory won him instant national acclaim. After destroying the power of the old machine by detaching some of its leaders to his own cause, he set out to modernize Wisconsin. The "Wisconsin idea," as it came to be known, depended on a firm progressive majority in the state legislature, and this the new governor secured by campaigning personally for his supporters and then holding them strictly accountable. Soon his opponents were complaining that he had made himself the "boss" of a ruthlessly efficient machine of his own. The substance of the Wisconsin idea consisted of a set of related reforms: a direct primary law, an improved civil service, a railroad rate commission, an equitable tax program, state banking controls, conservation measures, a water power franchise act, and labor legislation. At the center of LaFollette's reform complex stood the independent regulatory commission, staffed by the new experts supplied by the state university and given wide administrative latitude. Another of LaFollette's proudest achievements was a legislative reference bureau to help amateur lawmakers draft their bills in proper form. The bureau maintained its reputation for nonpartisan service to the very end, even drafting the bill for its enemies that put it out of business.

To his many admirers across the country, LaFollette appeared a political anomaly, at once a popular leader with his feet firmly planted in the grass roots and an enthusiastic convert to scientific government. Exacting, fiercely partisan, and a consummate hater, he often seemed to view the world as a gigantic conspiracy to do in "Battling Bob." He kept ready for display at a moment's notice the image of the sea-green incorruptible who preached the virtues of direct democracy and constantly urged his followers to "go back to the people." "Selfish interests," he declared, "may resist every inch of ground, may threaten, malign and corrupt, they cannot escape the final issues. That which is so plain, so simple, and so just will surely triumph."

The other half of LaFollette's reform equation, however, was filled with facts and figures his investigatory commissions collected. His own interminable speeches came heavily freighted with statistics and percentages provided by a corps of tax experts, labor consultants, industrial commissioners, and social workers. These facts he hammered at the voters of Wisconsin in the belief that the people, once apprised of their unmistakable meaning, would hardly fail him. The conflicting principles of divine-right democracy and government by an expert elite—principles that sat uneasily on the progressive conscience—caused LaFollette little distress, convinced as he was that once they were properly informed the people would accept his proposals. The commission form, central to the implementation of the Wisconsin idea, also answered another vexing question, what to do about increased social fragmentation and incipient class conflict. Positioned above the battle of parties and interests, the commission seemingly embodied the very disinterest and altruism it was designed to foster in the people. LaFollette's growing national reputation, in fact, rested on the confidence he inspired in the belief that democracy and scientific government were not simply compatible but complementary.

An integral part of progressive reform programs in the states was a package of new laws drawn up by civic groups, women's organizations, and consumer interests that finally humanized working conditions. As late as 1900 over half of the states had no laws establishing a minimum age for workers. By 1914 every

"SHUCKING" OYSTERS, OYSTER HOUSE, BALTIMORE, MARYLAND

After 1900 progressive legislation in the states was aimed at protecting working women like these. (*Culver Pictures, Inc.*)

state but one had set an age limit on the employment of children. In most states a social justice crusade for the protection of women in industry paralleled the drive to abolish child labor. Illinois led the way in 1892, by limiting hours for women. New York and Massachusetts followed suit, and thereafter the movement spread rapidly westward. When the Supreme Court upheld the principle of state regulation of hours for women in the celebrated case of *Muller* v. *Oregon* in 1908, barriers collapsed, and by the time America entered the First World War thirty-nine states had written new laws protecting women or significantly strengthening old ones while eight of them had gone even further by enacting minimum wage laws for women. A third feature of the progressive social reform program

(Right, Culver Pictures; below, George Eastman House Collection; opposite page, Library of Congress.)

was the campaign for employers' liability laws and industrial accident insurance, which did away with the worst of the inequities of the old common-law doctrines of the "fellow-servant" and contributory negligence. By 1916 nearly two-thirds of the states, responding to the mounting pressure of progressive reformers, had established insurance programs.

Progressivism, taking different forms in different states, everywhere signified a shift of power within the American political system from cumbersome, interest-dominated legislatures to a new public authority vested in the executive and its supporting administrative agencies charged with the enforcement of a revitalized general will. To justify their roles as custodians of this general will, progressives unearthed a national-interest theory of politics as old as the Founding Fathers. "I would not be a dredger Congressman, or a farm Congressman, or a fresh egg Congressman," a typical progressive told his constituents in summoning up the spirit of Edmund Burke and virtual representation. "I would like to be an American Congressman, recognizing the union and the nation." If warring economic interests were chiefly responsible for the lack of direction and the low tone of American politics, progressives reasoned, then it was wise to ignore them and appeal instead to a latent public virtue. "Progressivism believes in nationalism, in individual citizenship," another reformer added. "It opposes class government by either business, the laboring, or any other class. . . ." The tendency to reject interest-group government (government as a bargaining process between blocs of big business, big labor, and big agriculture) drove progressives to embrace the concept of leadership from above—from those "good men" in whom altruism presumably ran deeper than selfishness. "While the inspiration has always come from below in the advance of human rights . . ." the California progressive William Kent insisted, the real accomplishments in the improvement of American society must always be "the disinterested work of men who, having abundant means, have ranged themselves on the side of those most needing help." In the progressive interpretation of American politics underdogs announced their needs but topdogs filled them.

Draped with the mantle of disinterested benevolence, progressivism looked like nothing so much as a renovated model of Federalism, suitably altered to fit a modern bureaucratic society. Progressives, like their Federalist ancestors, came to fear the idea of party government and class division, and sought to take the politics out of American life in the name of scientific management. For an eighteenth-century rule by republican notables they substituted leadership by experts whose skills would command the allegiance of all enlightened citizens. Most of the progressive political reforms, an analyst of American politics has noted, were "devices of political stabilization and control, with strongly conservative latent consequences if not overt justifications, and with an overwhelming non-partisan bias." In similar fashion the progressive social justice programs initiated by the states were designed to strengthen corporate capitalism by empowering

Art as Urban Experience

The great Chicago architect, Louis Sullivan, summed up the meaning of the twentieth-century city for a progressive generation of Americans when he defined it as a scene of "strife"—at once an "arena" for contending social energies and the center of a new democratic culture. For Sullivan a "culture of democracy" meant a "culture of action." His tall office buildings, as he called them, embodied the "mobile equilibrium" that symbolized for him the fusion of individual genius and the massed energies of a whole people. The architect, he explained, "causes the building by acting on the body social" following a design "struck out at a single blow." As for the building, "the force and power of altitude must be in it, the glory and pride of exaltation must be in it. It must be

every inch a proud and soaring thing, rising in sheer exaltation that from bottom to top it is a unit without a single dissenting line." Sullivan's own buildings with their sharp verticality, contrasting piers and planes, hard-edged mouldings and exuberant ornamentation represented the encased energy and power of "becoming" which their creator identified with the democratic spirit and the city.

American artists in the opening years of the century shared Sullivan's vision of the city as the focus of national life and the center of a new culture. For Robert Henri and his "black gang" of realists who gloried in their name as the Ashcan School, New York City served as a backdrop for an exciting procession of urban scenes and types which they recorded in the documentary style they had perfected

Detail from "Stag at Starkey's," George W. Bellows, *The Cleveland Museum of Art, Hinman B. Hurlbut Collection.*

"The Speilers," George B. Luks, Addison Gallery of American Art, Phillips Academy, Andover, Mass.

as newspaper illustrators—swirling crowds on gusty street corners, slum kids swimming in the East River, working girls drying their hair on a sunny tenement roof, ragamuffins gaily dancing the two-step on a crowded pavement —all the "drab, happy, sad and human" moments in the life of the metropolis. Henri's student, John Sloan, took West Fourteenth Street for his reporter's beat and painted the

energy he discovered in ordinary people and familiar neighborhood scenes. George Bellows extended the idea of energy from subject to slashing technique in his famous *Stag at Sharkey's* with its two faceless fighters straining against each other. "Who cares what a prize fighter looks like," Bellows exclaimed. "It's his muscles that count."

The New York Eight were boisterously

"Cliff Dwellers," George W. Bellows, *Los Angeles County Museum of Art*.

"Election Night in Herald Square," John Sloan, *Memorial Art Gallery of the University of Rochester, R. T. Miller Fund.*

"Steaming Streets," George W. Bellows, *Santa Barbara Museum of Art.*

"Hammerstein's Roof Garden," William J. Glackens,
Whitney Museum of American Art.

democratic and proletarian in sympathy. "A child of the slums will make a better painting than a drawingroom lady gone over by a beauty shop," insisted George Luks, the most colorful and obstreperous of the Eight. In the city's "incredible panorama" of clattering els and gigantic excavations, towering skyscrapers and shabby tenements, vaudeville houses and open-air markets, the Eight discovered an infinitely renewable America. "What a mistake we have made in life seeking for the finished product," Henri scoffed. "A thing that is finished is dead." To the Ashcan School, as to Louis Sullivan, the city promised a democratic immortality.

Another group of younger and more adventurous American artists fresh from encounters with European post-Impressionism, who exhibited at Alfred Stieglitz's Photo-Secession Gallery at 291 Fifth Avenue, also responded to the clashing energies of the city which they caught and fixed in abstract patterns and bold colors. Like the Ashcan School, the new abstract painters sought vitality in

"Hester Street," George Luks,
The Brooklyn Museum, Dick S. Ramsay Fund.

their work in the conviction, as Stieglitz put it, that "it is the spirit of the thing that is important. If the spirit is alive, that is enough for me." But John Marin, Georgia O'Keeffe, Marsden Hartley, Max Weber, Arthur Dove and the other modernists gathered at 291 to celebrate, not the Eight's triumph of life over art, but the liberating forces of the esthetic experience itself. The modernists, unlike the Ashcan School, were defiantly *avant garde,* and the freedom they sought was freedom from the conventions of pictorial art and the chance to experiment with new forms with which to record a kaleidoscopic urban world. "I see great forces at work, great movements," John Marin declared, "the large buildings and the small buildings, the warring of the great and the small.... While these powers are at work ... I can hear the sound of their strife, and there is a great music being played."

"Rush Hour, New York," Max Weber, National Gallery of Art, Washington, D. C., Gift of the Avalon Foundation.

"Lower Manhattan," by John Marin, *Collection, The Museum of Modern Art, New York, Lillie P. Bliss Bequest.*

The modernists, in the spirit of the progressives who often failed to understand them, approached their art as a process of experimentation and research, one demanding innovative technique and bold improvisation. "There was life in all these new things," Marsden Hartley explained in recalling the years before the First World War. "There was excitement, there was healthy revolt, investigation, discovery, and an utterly new world out of it all." Art, as the modernists conceived it, was what the instrumentalist John Dewey called "a process of doing or making," a confrontation with partially disorganized nature with its "breaks and reunions" that plunged the viewer into "the ongoing world around him." The young abstract painters were struck with the action, clash, and tension of city life which they captured in new dynamic patterns quite unlike the static forms of European cubists such as Georges Braque and

"Battle of Lights, Coney Island," Joseph Stella, *Yale University Art Gallery, Gift of the Collection of the Société Anonyme.*

Juan Gris. The Futurist Joseph Stella found the most powerful image of conflicting urban forms in the Brooklyn Bridge, with its "massive dark towers dominating the surrounding tumult of surging skyscrapers . . . the eloquent meeting point of all the forces arising in a superb assertion of their powers, an Apotheosis." His *Coney Island,* an arrangement of splinters of light, Stella entitled "Battle of Light." Georgia O'Keeffe confessed to a fascination with New York's skyscrapers and determined to make her flowers "big like the huge buildings going up. People will be startled and look . . . ."

With the arrival of the twentieth century, the city came to dominate the imagination of artists and architects who continued to seek in it the source of a vital American art.

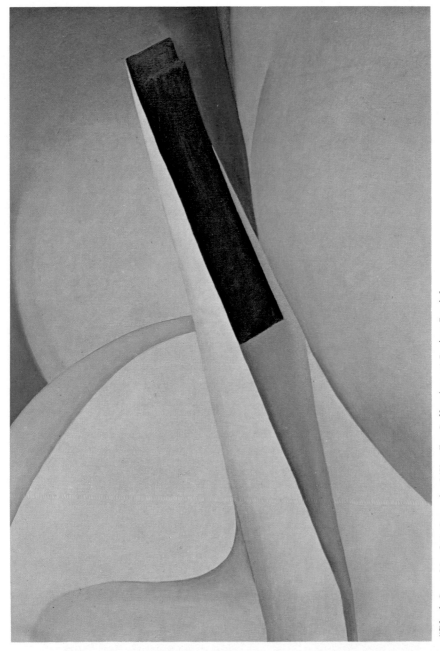

"Black Spot No. 2," Georgia O'Keeffe, *Collection of Irving Levick.*

government to help reassign responsibilities and temper the harshness of the American industrial environment. To carry out their containment policy at the national level, the progressives looked to the figure of the new statesman, and in Theodore Roosevelt they found their earthly paragon.

Theodore Roosevelt: The Progressive as Hero

In September 1901, President William McKinley died in Buffalo of an assassin's bullet, and Theodore Roosevelt, "this crazy man," as Republican managers thought him, was catapulted from his "utterly anomalous office," the vice-presidency, into the post of national leader. Blueblood, historian, student of the classics, amateur naturalist, cowpuncher and Rough Rider, Roosevelt at forty-two appeared to his millions of admirers as the last of the universal men, and to uneasy Republican managers like Mark Hanna as "that damned cowboy." With an audible sigh of relief Old Guard Republicans heard the new President announce his intentions "to continue, absolutely unbroken, the policy of President McKinley." McKinley had meant high tariffs, the gold standard, and a not-too-vigorous prosecution of the trusts. The prospect of a continuing custodial presidency reassured those congressional standpatters who feared above all a rambunctious executive. Yet within the year Roosevelt had begun to challenge congressional ascendency, and by the time he retired from his second term in March 1909, he had succeeded in creating a national progressive movement, reinvigorating American foreign policy, and laying the foundations of the twentieth-century welfare state. Well might the professionals have wondered what manner of man had fallen heir to the presidency.

Roosevelt was the product of patrician New York society, the son of a banker-philanthropist who had dabbled in genteel reforms and organized the city's upper-class contribution to the cause of the Union during the Civil War. A graduate of Harvard, where he amused his classmates with his odd earnestness and vibrancy, he immediately settled on a life in politics among the "kittle-kattle" of Spoilsmen and Mugwumps. For the moral chaos of Gilded Age politics he held the comfortable classes chiefly responsible, and with a highly developed sense of noblesse oblige he entered the New York State Assembly as a representative from one of the city's Republican silk-stocking districts. In the Assembly, where he served a single term from 1882 to 1884, he displayed the singular mixture of social conservatism, pugnacity, and political acumen that was to become his distinguishing mark. In 1886 he accepted the Republican nomination in the three-cornered mayoralty race in New York City and ran a respectable third behind winner Abram S. Hewitt and Single-Taxer Henry George. The 1880s also saw the growth of a sizable body of historical work—*The Winning of the West*, a biography of Gouverneur Morris, and another of Thomas Hart Benton—in which Roosevelt proclaimed his unqualified approval of the nationalist designs of the

Federalists, denounced Jefferson as a hypocrite, and hymned the glories of west-ward expansion and the fulfillment of a continental destiny.

When his first wife died in 1884, Roosevelt retired to the frontier he had de-scribed so eloquently, finding solace in Dakota ranch life filled with cowboys, frontier justice, and manly virtues. As a steadfast if unpredictable young Re-publican he was appointed to the United States Civil Service Commission by Pres-ident Benjamin Harrison in 1889 and served in Washington until 1895, when he returned to New York to head the Board of Police Commissioners and make a name for himself with late-night prowls on the lower East Side with his journalist friend Jacob Riis in futile attempts to enforce the city's blue laws. McKinley re-warded such misplaced energy by appointing him assistant secretary of the navy despite rather than because of Roosevelt's outspoken views on behalf of Amer-ican military power.

The Spanish-American War in 1898 drew Roosevelt out of the shadows of appointive office and into the limelight of electoral politics to play the nation's hero. As self-appointed leader of the Rough Riders, the First Regiment of the United States Cavalry Volunteers, he caught the fancy of a patriotic public that

followed with keen interest his dramatic if somewhat superfluous exploits in charging up San Juan Hill, pausing now and then to exult over all "those damned Spanish dead" as he rallied his disorderly troops. Disembarking to the tune of "There'll Be a Hot Time in the Old Town Tonight," he was promptly elected governor of New York and as quickly discomfited party bosses by taking a firm progressive stand on a state factory inspection act and on another law regulating the hours of state employees. "If there is going to be any solution of the big social problems of the day," he warned his supporters, "it will come, not through a sentimental parlor socialism, but through actually taking hold of what is to be done working right in the mire." Republican leaders in New York, however, were content to lift their governor out of the slough of reform politics and into the clean and safe office of the vice-presidency, a piece of political miscalculation made clear to them by an assassin's bullet.

In seeking to learn what kind of President they had acquired Americans did not lack for answers, for Roosevelt had strong opinions on every conceivable subject and delighted in publishing them in pungent and readable phrases. The objects of presidential scrutiny ranged from the novels of Emile Zola (which he

THE TWO SIDES OF THEODORE ROOSEVELT
Surrounded by the paraphernalia of patriotism, Roosevelt campaigns in New Castle, Wyoming, in 1903. The more reflective man appears in the doorway of his Dakota ranch-house. (*Left, Library of Congress; right, Theodore Roosevelt Collection, Harvard College Library.*)

generally disliked) to the "full baby carriage" (which he heartily endorsed); and his advice ranged from conduct becoming both football players and would-be reformers ("Don't flinch, don't foul, hit the line hard!") to what one observer called an "unflagging approval of the Ten Commandments." A vigorous intellectual himself, with interests in birds and political bosses, trusts and big game, divorce and "practical idealism," Roosevelt collected hundreds of willing contributors to a mind already well stocked with ideas that he regularly assembled in print—not writing with a pen, as one reader put it, so much as charging with it.

Roosevelt's forceful and sometimes contradictory opinions revealed two distinct personalities. The first one was once described by a New York boss as "the most indiscreet guy I ever met," the keeper of the national conscience always ready to speak his mind. This public Roosevelt served as the confident spokesman of an aggressive American nationalism—prophet of a coming Anglo-Saxon supremacy, celebrant of military valor, unblushing advocate of power politics, and true believer in the American mission to order the affairs of the rest of the world. The national hero—"Teddy," a name he disliked—looked the part. With pince-nez adorning a bulbous nose, toothy grin stretched tight in a near grimace, a full square face with its several chins resting on heavyset shoulders, and reedy voice and pump-handle gestures, he was a cartoonist's dream!

In the role of the mad American of his generation, as he has been called, Roosevelt could and frequently did talk great nonsense. He lashed out at "radical fanatics" and the "lunatic fringe" of soft-headed reformers with equal contempt. "Sentimental humanitarians" he denounced as "a most pernicious body, with an influence for bad hardly surpassed by that of the professional criminal classes." He stressed the importance of "good blood" flowing in the veins of well-bred, self-denying gentlemen. He predicted race suicide for any of the world's people who preferred "effeminacy of character" to the "rougher and manlier virtues." For handling mobs he recommended "taking ten or a dozen of their leaders out, standing . . . them against a wall, and shooting them dead." For anarchists and socialist agitators a similar prescription—troops supplied with real bullets and "the most wholesome desire to do them harm." Americans, whether delighted or appalled by such balderdash, recognized in Roosevelt the authentic American hero, the compulsive man of action who shot from the hip and whose motto read: "Get action; do things; be sane."

The other Roosevelt, unlike the trigger-happy dispenser of justice, was a thoughtful if highly partisan student of American history with a keen appreciation of the original work of the Founding Fathers. Young progressives entering the political arena after 1900 with credentials from the new university brought with them training in new disciplines like economics and sociology. But for the slightly older progressive leaders, the study of history was still the primary tool for examining American society. Despite the rapid growth of "scientific history" in the nation's graduate schools and the appearance of the specialized monograph, much of the popular history written after 1880 continued to be the work of gentleman amateurs like Roosevelt himself, or his friends Henry Adams and the retired industrialist James Ford Rhodes, who measured the achievements and noted the shortcomings of nineteenth-century American democracy. The thrust of much of this popular history was towards political nationalism and social conservatism, whether in John Fiske's account of the Founding Fathers' rescue operation during the "critical period" or Henry Adams's search for the principles of "scientific government" in his magnificent nine-volume history of the administrations of Jefferson and Madison, or in Roosevelt's hymns to national valor in *The Naval War of 1812* and *The Winning of the West.*

This reflective, historically minded Roosevelt was the first President after Lincoln and the last of the moderns with an understanding of the eighteenth century. Beneath his dramatic account of America's rise to greatness lay a clear grasp of the original Federalist design and the men who fashioned it. National greatness, then as in his own time, seemed to Roosevelt to rest on the "power to attain a high degree of social efficiency," by which he meant "love of order" and the "capacity to subordinate the interests of the individual to the interests of the community." The Federalists, led by farseeing nationalists like Hamilton and Gouverneur Morris, had tried to teach the first Americans the same lessons that his own generation had just learned, that "the sphere of the State's action may be vastly increased without in any way diminishing the happiness of either the many or the few."

The American people, Roosevelt was convinced, had been given the wrong

"TEDDY" CORRECTS THE
HISTORICAL RECORD

George Washington is now "*Second* in war, *second* in peace, and *second* in the hearts of his countrymen." (*Library of Congress.*)

directions by a demagogic Jefferson and had drifted steadily towards the smashup of the Civil War even as they expanded and enriched their domain. From Jefferson and his Jacksonian heirs they had acquired the illusions of little government and the self-regulating moral order. Despite their magnificent material accomplishments in filling out a continent and building an industrial empire they had failed to devise the political means of managing it. Only briefly during Lincoln's war administrations had Americans caught a glimpse of true national unity and the statesmanship required to create it. With the onset of the Great Barbecue the original statesman's question "Will it work?" had given way to the commercial demand "Does it pay?" and the national energy had been squandered in money grubbing. One fact was clear at last—that Americans had to "abandon definitely the *laissez-faire* theory of political economy, and fearlessly champion a system of increased Governmental control." The opening years of the twentieth century, Roosevelt was sure, represented "an era of federation and combination" that had been foreshadowed by the age of the Founding Fathers. The President, like his Federalist mentors, deplored class politics and called for the rule of enlightened men of integrity whom, for the moment, he identified with the better half of the Republican party. But wherever found, the disinterested patriot held the key to the future. "A simple and poor society can exist as a democracy on the basis of sheer individualism. But a rich and complex society cannot so exist. . . ." By the time Roosevelt took over the presidency, he had acquired a clear definition of his role as general manager of the United States even though the details of his plan for its "orderly development" emerged only gradually from the recesses of his conservative mind.

"Wise Radicalism and Wise Conservatism"— *The Square Deal*

The Roosevelt presidency saw the establishment of the regulatory principle and the arrival of twentieth-century administrative government. What Roosevelt and the country came to call the Square Deal, as he campaigned for reelection in 1904, began as a loose collection of proposals for regulating national economic development. The President inherited from Gilded Age Republicanism an old guard of party conservatives who had built their stronghold in the Senate, where they kept firm control over the legislative process and saw to it that any President followed their dictates. Roosevelt was immediately forced to bargain with their leader, Senator Nelson W. Aldrich of Rhode Island, and to agree to keep his hands off the tariff question in exchange for a limited freedom to pursue his interventionist concerns elsewhere. These concerns, like the interests of several of his progressive followers, centered on the trusts.

Roosevelt shared the progressives' ambivalent views of big business. "Nothing of importance is gained," he admitted in reviewing his policy of regulation, "by breaking up a huge inter-State and international organization which has not offended otherwise than by its size. . . . Those who would seek to restore the days of unlimited and uncontrolled competition . . . are attempting not only the impossible, but what, if possible, would be undesirable." Roosevelt followed most progressive thinking in considering behavior rather than mere size of the new conglomerates the test of their social utility, and in declaring it the job of the federal government to require them to operate "in the interest of the general public," whatever that might mean. To ensure their proper conduct and prevent them from fixing prices and manipulating the market, he proposed a watchdog agency modeled on the Interstate Commerce Commission, an appointive body staffed by "trained administrators, well known to hold the scales exactly even in all matters. . . ." After a sharp skirmish with big business and its spokesmen in Congress, he succeeded in 1903 in establishing the Bureau of Corporations within the new Department of Labor and Commerce to police business practices and report its findings to the public.

Publicity formed the keystone of Roosevelt's regulatory arch, and he himself perfected the art of disclosure in launching a series of actions under the Sherman Act, advising the Beef Trust of his intentions to "Destroy the Evils in Trusts, But Not the Prosperity" and insisting publicly on settling in the Northern Securities Case "the absolutely vital question" of federal power to regulate the trusts. The Northern Securities Company, together with its partners in monopoly, the United States Steel Company and the American Tobacco Company, Roosevelt considered potential forces for evil. While it was clearly impossible to "restore business to the competitive conditions" of the middle of the previous century, he considered it essential for the federal government to maintain "strict supervision" of the trust to see that it did not go wrong.

In applying his interventionist strategy, Roosevelt gave the signal to the Department of Justice in 1902 to move against J. P. Morgan's railroad combine. Morgan, he recalled with relish, "could not help regarding me as a big rival operator who intended to ruin all his interests or else could be induced to come to an agreement and ruin none." But it was power that concerned the President, who viewed the clash as one between rival sovereignties. The Supreme Court, in upholding the government's case against the railroad merger, gave Roosevelt his precedent. In the E. C. Knight case, he announced with obvious satisfaction, the Court had erroneously decided that the federal government lacked the power to break up dangerous combinations. "This decision I caused to be annulled." He failed to add what soon became obvious—that he had not thereby annulled the force of the merger movement.

Roosevelt more nearly approximated the progressive ideal of government by administration and arbitration in his handling of labor problems which he also approached with a divided mind. The test of his opinion on unions, strikes, and injunctions came early in his first administration, when the United Mine Workers struck against the anthracite coal operators, a confrontation that alarmed the whole country and provided Roosevelt with welcome public support. The miners, led by the canny union leader John Mitchell, demanded a pay increase and an eight-hour day along with acknowledgement of their right to organize the coal industry. George Baer, president of the Reading Railroad, bungled the case for the operators from the outset. He proclaimed it his "religious duty" to defeat the strikers, insisting that "the rights and interests of the laboring men will be protected and cared for—not by labor agitators, but by Christian men to whom God in his infinite wisdom has given control of the property interests of the country." Roosevelt, his interventionist hand strengthened by the obstinacy of the operators, moved quickly by calling for an investigation by his labor commissioner and using his findings to force the coal companies to compromise. When they refused, Roosevelt ordered both parties to a conference in Washington, where the operators, under the presidential threat to send in troops, finally agreed to an arbitrational panel. The Anthracite Coal Strike Commission awarded a 10 percent pay increase and a reduction in hours to the miners while refusing their demand for a closed shop. Once again, as in regulating the trusts, it was principle and procedure—the orderly disposition of grievances by disinterested men—that concerned the President.

Roosevelt's views on organized labor mirrored his convictions on big business: the ultimate test for both sides was a willingness to furnish order and stability of their own volition. If trusts tended to threaten the balance of economic power with their irresponsible aggrandizements, Roosevelt reasoned, labor also could prove disruptive and greedy. If there were "good" and "bad" trusts, there were also dependable labor leaders like Samuel Gompers and dangerous visionaries like Eugene Debs. In either case, he concluded, it was the President who had to distinguish legitimate demands from crackpot notions, and the only standard he could finally invoke was conduct. "Where in either one or the other, there develops corruption or mere brutal indifference to the rights of others, and shortsighted refusal to look beyond the moment's gain, then the offender, whether union or corporation, must be fought." Since it was the government that would have to do the fighting, the President as its principal officer must avail himself of every opportunity to consolidate his power. Roosevelt missed few such oppor-

PORK-PACKING IN CINCINNATI

The Meat Packing Act was aimed at established practices and methods like those shown in this engraving. (*The Cincinnati Historical Society.*)

tunities. "I don't think that any harm comes from the concentration of power in one man's hands," he protested to his critics, "provided the holder does not keep it for more than a certain definite time, and then returns to the people from whom he sprang." Yet winning presidential power, he would learn, was easier than relinquishing it.

Roosevelt's theory of expanded executive power proceeded logically from his belief that only "a great exertion of federal authority" could meet the needs of all the people. The most vulnerable members of a still largely unregulated commercial society were American consumers, who needed all the help they could get. In the field of consumer legislation as in his negotiations with big business and labor Roosevelt assumed the leadership of forces that had already begun to organize by 1900. The Pure Food and Drug Law, for example, passed in 1906, was the result of a carefully orchestrated public outcry and shrewd presidential timing. The law, limited though it was in providing coverage and effective procedures, capped a strenuous campaign for effective legislation by Harvey Wiley, chief chemist of the Department of Agriculture, who twice had seen his recommendations accepted in the House only to languish in the Senate, where the food and drug interests held court. Aided by a series of lurid exposés furnished by the Muckrakers, Roosevelt finally collected the votes needed to prohibit the manufacture and sale of misbranded or adulterated foods and drugs, a power wielded cautiously ever since.

Support for the Meat Packing Act (1906) also came from consumers, many of whom learned of the appalling conditions in the industry from Upton Sinclair's sensational novel *The Jungle.* In indicting the packers Sinclair traced the shipment from prairie to slaughterhouse of cows "that developed lumpy jaw, or fell sick, or dried up of old age," carcasses "covered with boils that were full of matter."

It was a nasty job killing these, for when you plunged your knife into them they would burst and splash foul-smelling stuff into your face. . . . It was enough to make anybody sick, to think that people had to eat such meat as this; but they must be eating it—for the canners were going on preparing it, year after year.

Though annoyed by Sinclair's fictionalized account, Roosevelt promised him: "The specific evils you point out shall, if their existence be proved, and if I have the power, be eradicated." An investigation by the commissioner of labor verified most of Sinclair's charges in a fact-studded report, which the President, indulging in a calculated bit of blackmail, threatened to release unless the packers accepted minimum regulation. The final bill, like most of Roosevelt's Square Deal legislation, represented a series of trade-offs—increased appropriations for inspection against removing inconvenient requirements for enforcement—and left the matter of appeal to the courts in what the President called "purposeful ambiguity." Once the industry had accepted the legitimacy of any form of federal regulation, the big packers welcomed those requirements that could be expected to drive out their small competitors. For his part Roosevelt was perfectly willing to compromise on details in order to gain the principle of federal control.

In an eagerness to sacrifice specifics for precedent, Roosevelt frequently disappointed his more determined progressive supporters who complained that he gave in too easily on points that might have been won with more determination. In the tug of war over the Hepburn Act regulating railroad rates they appear to have won their case. The Elkins Act (1903), a piece of symbolic legislation supposedly prohibiting discriminatory rebates, had been drafted by the railroad senators who refused to grant the government effective control over rate making, and Roosevelt now meant to acquire this authority. Since transportation lay at "the root of all industrial success," he explained, the need for an "orderly system" was obvious. "It is far better that it should be managed by private individuals than by the government," he admitted. "But it can only be so managed on condition that justice be done the public."

Effective regulation basically meant strengthening the Interstate Commerce Commission by investing it with the power to fix rates and make them stick, and this an administration measure passed by the House in 1905 was designed to do. In the Senate, however, Roosevelt's plans for securing what he called "additional power of an effective kind" met the stubborn opposition of Aldrich and his group of railroad senators, who decided to teach the President a lesson in the limits of executive power. Aldrich and his conservatives quickly bottled up the bill in committee, where they conducted lengthy hearings for the benefit of its enemies. Roosevelt tried a second time the next year with another bill, this one sponsored by Representative William P. Hepburn of Ohio, empowering the ICC to set reasonable rates after hearing complaints from shippers. Again Aldrich stepped in, allowed the bill to go to the floor without Republican endorsement, and looked on with detachment as one amendment after another stripped the bill of its original intent. Roosevelt countered with a hastily assembled coalition of faithful Republicans and disgruntled Democrats, only to see it collapse; he then reversed his field and managed to win over enough moderate Republicans to force Aldrich to a compromise. The final version of the Hepburn bill increased the powers of the ICC but left intact the injunction against enforcing new rates in cases under court appeal. At best the President had won a limited victory.

Roosevelt's critics accused him of violating his own standards of political morality in accepting considerably less than half a loaf. In fact the terms agreed to by the railroads and their representatives entirely satisfied him. "I want to get something through," he told Senator LaFollette, who correctly pointed out that without actual physical evaluation of railroad properties the ICC could hardly be expected to supervise the setting of rates. To those doubters who insisted that the Hepburn Act did not go far enough the President expounded his own philosophy of reform: "I believe in the men who take the next step; not those who theorize about the two-hundredth step." With the Hepburn Act the President and his progressive contingent administered a mild corrective but gained a principle.

In the case of conservation, the last main item on the Square Deal agenda, compromise again weakened principle. Though Roosevelt himself was a nature lover and preservationist by inclination, he abandoned the tradition of Thoreau and John Muir for a developmentalist strategy designed for the multiple use of the nation's natural resources. "We are prone to speak of the resources of this country as inexhaustible; this is not so," he informed a reluctant Congress in his annual message of 1907. Calling on citizens to look ahead to "the days of our children," he warned against the waste and destruction that would "result in undermining . . . the very prosperity" that ought to go down to them "amplified and developed." Yet his formula for conservation remained the same as for other national needs: expert advice from scientists committed to development rather than preservation, and a permissive governmental oversight of private interests.

These long-term limitations were obscured for the moment in the flurry of executive actions during his second term as he added 43 million acres to the national forests, withdrew from entry over 2500 water power sites and 65 million acres of coal lands, and established 16 national monuments and 53 wildlife refuges. Conservation as an issue assumed crucial significance in Roosevelt's mind as he found himself blocked by a dilatory Congress from pursuing other social justice goals. He turned, accordingly, to the management of natural resources as "the fundamental problem which underlies almost every other problem in National life," the acid test of executive power. He flouted the congressional will with a "midnight proclamation" setting aside 23 new forest reserves and then threw down his challenge: "If Congress differs from me . . . it will have full opportunity in the future to take such positions as it may desire anent the discontinuance of the reserves." While Congress fumed, he moved rapidly ahead with plans for his conservation empire. His instruments consisted of bureaus and commissions operating under executive supervision and filled with geologists, hydrologists, foresters, and engineers taking their orders from Gifford Pinchot, his volatile but capable chief forester. In 1908, sensing widespread public interest, Roosevelt called the National Conservation Congress, which was attended by 44 governors and over 500 conservation experts and out of which came the National

JOHN MUIR AND HIS LUMBERMAN ENEMIES

The naturalist and preservationist John Muir fought, with limited success, to save the wilderness from the depredations of the lumber companies. (*Above, Culver Pictures, Inc.; right, Courtesy of the Sierra Club.*)

Country Life Commission and the Inland Waterways Commission, deprived of congressional support but enjoying a hearty presidential blessing.

In spite of its appearance as a popular crusade Roosevelt's conservation program was less a grass-roots movement to save the environment than an executive scheme for national resource management imposed from above. The President envisioned a grand design "systematically and continuously carried forward in accordance with some well-conceived plan" in which irrigation, flood control, forestry, and reclamation would be treated as "interdependent parts of the same problem' of American regional development. He was forced to settle for much less. Government experts and lumber company executives, for example, could agree on the need for less wasteful methods of harvesting the national abundance, but they also shared a strong distaste for the purist notions of the preservationists. Moreover, the new federal agencies, understaffed and underfinanced, quickly found themselves dependent on the services and the good will of the very private interests they were charged with policing, and soon there arose a developmental accord between them that made effective regulation difficult. Small operators, whose reputation for gouging the landscape was well earned, were sometimes driven out, but the large concerns continued to swap their expertise for the privilege of exploiting national resources under a government seal of approval. From the perspective of three-quarters of a century Roosevelt's national conservation program, like the original Federalist partnership between wealth and government, appears to have assumed rather than protected the public interest which it identified with the welfare of private groups.

The Limits of Neofederalism

Roosevelt embarked for Africa in the spring of 1909, leaving in the White House his hand-picked successor, the ponderous William Howard Taft, to "carry on the work substantially as I have carried it on," by which he meant steering both party and country between the reactionary policies of Nelson W. Aldrich and the "fool radicalism" of insurgents like Robert LaFollette. In many ways the conservation issue, soon to give Taft the first of his numerous political headaches, symbolized both the success and the limitations of Roosevelt's attempt to forge a new national purpose. Central to his plan was infusing the American electorate with the meaning of national unity and strong government, an educational task Roosevelt had performed admirably for seven years. The conservation campaign, which gradually moved to the center of the progressive consciousness, had meant a fight against sectionalism, states' rights, business particularism, and a Congress that gave them voice. To check these divisive forces and hold the allegiance of his reform followers Roosevelt revitalized the presidential office and buttressed it with new concepts of civic duty and loyalty. "I believe in a strong executive; I believe in power. . . ," he announced and then proceeded to use his power in ways that no President since Lincoln had contemplated. "Under this interpretation of executive power," he boasted in summing up his accomplishments, "I did or caused to be done many things not previously done. . . . I did not usurp power, but I did greatly broaden the use of executive power." To aid him in his work of executive renovation, he drew heavily from the ranks of progressive experts and professionals whose cause of scientific government he championed with enthusiasm. His reform program, for all its timid approach to the regulatory principle and its deference to vested interests, marked at least a step toward the orderly republic he envisioned.

If Roosevelt's utopia still lay well over the horizon in 1909, it was because he intentionally set conservative limits to the application of governmental power, and in the last analysis firmly believed in the democratic process, guided though it might be. Although he chafed under the restraints placed on him by his party and a laggard Congress, he managed both of them with consummate skill, alternately bullying and cajoling both but breaking with neither. In negotiating his limited reforms he was willing more often than not to take the shell and leave the kernel, concerned as he was with winning a principle. Yet his presidency was no mere exercise in educational politics. Roosevelt wanted results that the country would accept, and to get them he willingly used traditional political methods. When he left office, these results remained clearly etched in the minds of his progressive followers. He had raised his office to its twentieth-century position of dominance. He had laid the foundation for a governmental bureaucracy and collected the presumably disinterested professionals to manage it. And finally, he had preached with unflagging zeal the traditional virtues of altruism, integrity, and independence as indispensable to the new citizenship.

Further than this neither Roosevelt nor the nationalist-minded progressives could well go. For it was the continuing engagement in the political process—the on-going encounter with power to which he called his supporters—that all along defined his concept of the strenuous life and formed the core of his appeal for reform. Roosevelt spoke for progressives everywhere in demanding the return to service of "the man of business and the man of science, the doctor of divinity and the doctor of law, the architect, the engineer and the writer," all of whom owed a "positive duty to the community, the neglect of which they cannot excuse on any plea of their private affairs." The ordinary citizen, "to whom participation in politics is a disagreeable duty," had long since been defeated by the "organized army" of political hacks. Now, Roosevelt and the progressives believed, it was time to try the *extra*ordinary citizen wherever he could be found. Neither he nor they would have been surprised to learn that the average citizen in the common walks of life was already taking less rather than more interest in politics if the act of voting were any test. Voter turnout, which in the Gilded Age had averaged nearly 80 percent in presidential years and over 60 percent in off years, fell a full 15 percent after 1900. Whether disenchanted with the prospects of a managed republic that progressive reformers held before them or simply because they were discovering their most pressing concerns outside the political arena, the fact was that fewer Americans were troubling themselves with the duty of taking what Roosevelt called "their full part in our life."

Here indeed lay the outermost reaches of Roosevelt's progressive domain. If Jefferson's political formula had long since proved hopelessly inadequate for managing an industrial society, his original estimate of the diverse sources of American energy had not. Jefferson, never inclined to overestimate the fragility of American society, had counted the advantages as well as the dangers of sectional division, religious variety, ethnic diversity, and even class disagreement. With Roosevelt's retirement these forces of social and cultural pluralism began to take revenge on his promise of national unity as if to fulfill the original Jeffersonian pledge, first shaking the party structure and then disrupting the national social consensus which Rooseveltian progressivism had attempted to construct. In a revived Democratic party the American people would find a different variety of progressive reform, and in Woodrow Wilson a very different kind of leader.

CONEY ISLAND, 1905

The original wonderland. (*Culver Pictures, Inc.*)

Suggested Readings

An assessment of progressivism properly begins with Benjamin Parke DeWitt, *The Progressive Movement* (1915), a contemporary account that emphasizes structural reforms. John Chamberlain, *Farewell to Reform: The Rise, Life and Decay of the Progressive Mind in America* (1932), records the New Deal disillusionment with early twentieth-century reform nostrums, and Otis L. Graham, Jr., *An Encore for Reform: The Old Progressives and the New Deal* (1967), explains the opposition of many of the progressives to later and (to them) more drastic reforms. Harold U. Faulkner, *The Quest for Special Justice, 1898–1914* (1931), defines the movement as a liberal response to social problems incident to rapid industrialization and urbanization. Read together, George E. Mowry, *The Era of Theodore Roosevelt, 1900–1912* (1958), and Arthur S. Link, *Woodrow Wilson and the Progressive Era, 1900–1917* (1954), provide an excellent survey of the politics of the Progressive period. Robert H. Wiebe, *Businessmen and Reform* (1962), and Gabriel Kolko, *The Triumph of Conservatism* (1963), make parallel observations concerning the role of businessmen in the progressive enterprise but draw different conclusions. Recent interpretive essays include William L. O'Neill, *The Progressive Years: America Comes of Age* (1975); Lewis L. Gould, ed., *The Progressive Era (1973)*; and David M. Kennedy, ed., *Progressivism: The Critical Issues* (1971).

Still the best discussions of muckraking are two older works: Louis Filler, *Crusaders for American Liberalism* (1938), and C. C. Regier, *The Era of the Muckrakers* (1932), which should be supplemented by David M. Chalmers, *The Social and Political Ideas of the Muckrakers* (1964). Peter Lyon, *The Life and Times of S.S. McClure* (1963), and Harold S. Wilson, *McClure's Magazine and the Muckrakers* (1970), provide readable accounts of the career of the pioneer muckraking editor. Arthur Weinberg and Lila Weinberg, eds., *The Muckrakers* (1961), and Harvey Swados, ed., *Years of Conscience: The Muckrakers* (1962), cover a wide range of muckraking reporting. For the autobiographical accounts of two of the leading journalists, see Lincoln Steffens, *The Autobiography of Lincoln Steffens* (1931), and Ida M. Tarbell, *All in the Day's Work* (1939).

There are several good state studies of progressivism—among them George E. Mowry, *The California Progressives* (1951); Robert S. Maxwell, *LaFollette and the Rise of Progressivism in Wisconsin* (1956); Herbert Margulies, *The Decline of the Progressive Movement in Wisconsin, 1890–1920* (1968); Ransom E. Noble, *New Jersey Progressivism before Wilson* (1946); Richard M. Abrams, *Conservatism in a Progressive Era: Massachusetts Politics, 1900–1912* (1964); Hoyt L. Warner, *Progressivism in Ohio* (1964); Irwin Yellowitz, *Labor and the Progressive Movement in New York State, 1897–1916* (1965); Robert F. Wesser, *Charles Evans Hughes: Politics and Reform in New York State, 1905–1910* (1967). David Thelen, *Robert LaFollette and the Insurgent Spirit* (1976), is a brief biography of an influential Progressive leader.

Biographies of other major political figures in the Progressive era are numerous. For Roosevelt, see the lively but biased Henry Pringle, *Theodore Roosevelt: A Biography* (rev. ed., 1956); also consult the more judicious William H. Harbaugh, *The Life and Times of Theodore Roosevelt* (1961), the brief but perceptive essay by John Morton Blum, *The Republican Roosevelt* (1954), and George E. Mowry, *Theodore Roosevelt and the Progressive Movement* (1946). G. Wallace Chessman, *Theodore Roosevelt and the Politics of Power* (1969) is a short, balanced account. On Taft, Henry Pringle, *The Life and Times of William Howard Taft* (2 vols., 1939) completes his account of the two Republican Presidents; a more useful study is Donald E. Anderson, *William Howard Taft* (1973). Norman Wilensky, *Conservatives in the Progressive Era: The Taft Republicans of 1912* (1965), is a good study of the Republican regulars, and James Holt, *Congressional Insurgents and the Party System, 1909–1916* (1969), covers the careers of leading Insurgents. Biographies of other important figures include Alpheus T. Mason, *Brandeis: A Free Man's Life* (1946); Paolo E. Coletta,

William Jennings Bryan (3 vols., 1964–69); Lawrence W. Levine, *Defender of the Faith: William Jennings Bryan The Last Decade* (1965); Dexter Perkins, *Charles Evans Hughes and American Democratic Statesmanship* (1956); Richard Lowitt, *George W. Norris: The Making of a Progressive* (1963); John A. Garraty, *Right-Hand Man: The Life of George W. Perkins* (1960); Richard Leopold, *Elihu Root and the Conservative Tradition* (1954); M. Nelson McGeary, *Gifford Pinchot: Forester-Politician* (1960).

Progressive issues have been exhaustively treated in numerous recent works. James H. Timberlake, *Prohibition and the Progressive Crusade, 1900–1920* (1963), explores connections between progressive politics and moral reform. Jack Holl, *Juvenile Reform in the Progressive Era* (1971), examines a hitherto neglected aspect of progressivism. The progressive concern with eugenics and birth control is described in Donald K. Pickens, *Eugenics and the Progressive Era* (1971); Mark H. Haller, *Eugenics: Hereditarian Attitudes in American Thought* (1963); and David Kennedy, *Birth Control in America: The Career of Margaret Sanger* (1970). C. Roland Marchand, *The American Peace Movement and Social Reform, 1898–1918* (1973), traces the varied fortunes of the progressive advocates of peace. Changing patterns of morality emerge clearly from William L. O'Neill, *Divorce in the Progressive Era* (1967), and crucial developments in progressive education from Lawrence Cremin, *The Transformation of the School: Progressivism in American Education, 1876–1956* (1961). Samuel P. Hays, *Conservation and the Gospel of Efficiency* (1959), provides a revisionist account of the conservation movement, and James Penick, Jr., *Progressive Politics and Conservation: The Ballinger-Pinchot Affair* (1968), effectively recounts an imbroglio. Albro Martin, *Enterprise Denied: Origins of the Decline of American Railroads, 1897–1917* (1971), reverses a number of long-held assumptions about the regulation and management of railroads in the Progressive era. Mary O. Furner, *Advocacy and Objectivity: A Crisis in the Professionalization of American Social Science, 1865–1905* (1975), treats perceptual contradictions inherited by Progressives.

The intellectual climate of Progressivism has been described in several excellent studies. David Noble, *The Paradox of Progressive Thought* (1958), is a stylistically dense but highly rewarding examination of representative progressive intellectuals and professionals. Charles Forcey, *The Crossroads of Liberalism: Croly, Weyl, Lippmann and the Progressive Era, 1900–1925* (1961), offers a lively account of three leading Progressive publicists. Edward Moore, *American Pragmatism* (1950), is useful for understanding the reform outlook of the Progressives. Robert W. Schneider, *Five Novelists of the Progressive Era* (1965), examines the connection between reform and new American fiction. Frederic C. Jaher, *Doubters and Dissenters: Cataclysmic Thought in America, 1885–1918* (1964), traces a persistent theme of apocalypticism in a handful of nay-sayers in the Progressive years. Thomas F. Gossett, *Race: The History of an Idea in America* (1963), and I. A. Newby, *Jim Crow's Defense* (1965), follow the history of another tenacious and socially destructive myth. The best introduction to the writing of Progressive history is Richard Hofstadter, *The Progressive Historians* (1968). R. Jack Wilson, *In Quest of Community: Social Philosophy in the United States, 1860–1920* (1968), and Jean B. Quandt, *From the Small Town to the Great Community* (1970), give accounts of still another central Progressive concept. Samuel J. Konefsky, *The Legacy of Holmes and Brandeis* (1956), examines the instrumentalist heritage. Samuel Haber, *Efficiency and Uplift: Scientific Management in the Progressive Era, 1890–1920* (1964), explains the many uses of Taylorism in reshaping Progressive values. For perceptive discussions of three key intellectuals, see David Riesman, *Thorstein Veblen: A Critical Introduction* (1963); Ralph Barton Perry, *The Thought and Character of William James* (2 vols., 1935); and Sidney Hook, *John Dewey: An Intellectual Portrait* (1939).

Reflections — sometimes illuminating, always entertaining — on the meaning of Progressivism by two active Progressives are collected in William Allen White, *The Autobiography of William Allen White* (1946), and Frederic C. Howe, *The Confessions of a Reformer* (1925).

27

Progressives and the Challenge of Pluralism

In 1910 Theodore Roosevelt, after a year's trek through Africa and the capitals of Europe, returned home to a rebellion in his own party. Once apprised of the Republican split between President William Howard Taft's regulars and his own progressive followers, the "Colonel" moved quickly to return the party to his original vision of a unified national purpose. In a speech in 1910 dedicating a state park in Osawatomie, Kansas, where John Brown had clashed with Missouri ruffians a half-century earlier, he gave his program a name—the "New Nationalism." In part, Roosevelt's speech owed its clarity to his recent reading of Herbert Croly's *The Promise of American Life* (1909), a powerful indictment of American political drift with which the former President fully agreed. But in a broader sense both Croly's lengthy analysis and the clarion call at Osawatomie summarized the arguments for an organized national society that Roosevelt had formulated years before.

It was not "overcentralization," Roosevelt announced, but "a spirit of broad and far-reaching nationalism" that must guide the American people "as a whole." The New Nationalism, putting national needs before sectional interest or personal advantage, promised to bring order out of "the utter confusion that results from local legislatures attempting to treat national issues as local issues."

After enumerating the many unfinished tasks awaiting federal action Roosevelt drove home his point with a comparison still familiar to the few aging veterans of the Grand Army in his audience. "You could not have won simply as a disorderly mob," the Rough Rider reminded them. "You needed generals; you needed careful administration of the most advanced type. . . . You had to have the administration in Washington good, just as you had to have the administration in the field. . . . So it is in our civil life."

Unfortunately for Roosevelt in 1910, administration of the most advanced type was not yet a fact, as the man who was to be his chief rival in the election of 1912 correctly sensed. Woodrow Wilson, as a Southerner and a Democrat, drew on both these traditions in sounding the principal countertheme of progressivism. Wilson, a former professor of political science and president of Princeton, currently the reform governor of New Jersey, was fully Roosevelt's match as an historian and an intellectual, and in appraising the American system in 1910 he came closer to understanding the complexity of social forces at work in the nation than either of his Republican rivals.

Whereas Roosevelt's New Nationalism called for an immediate ordering of American forces and the acquiring of new duties and habits, the New Freedom, as Wilson came to call it, offered a variant reading of progressivism as a liberation movement. Wilson envisioned an open society filled with immigrants and women as well as native-born white males, Catholics and Jews along with Protestants, reformers together with politicians, and visionaries of all sorts to balance the offerings of self-proclaimed realists. In the election year 1912 the broader strokes of Wilson's New Freedom seemed to present a truer picture of American life than the more stylized renderings of the New Nationalists. But it remained to be seen whether the Democratic party, emerging from sixteen years of enforced retirement, could succeed in turning its estimate of the "generous energies" of the American people into a political program.

Changing the Progressive Guard

By 1910 it seemed that reform had slowed, as the forces of pluralism—both social and political—applied the brakes to the progressive engine. Republicanism stood in disarray, the President besieged by liberal critics within and without the party. The Democratic party showed few signs of wanting to become a national contender again. Congress, continuing to house a bipartisan faction of conservatives, appeared in no mood to complete the tasks of building a national banking system and assembling a program of business regulation. To one side stood a watchful Supreme Court, always ready to disapprove any further advances toward the social service state.

Of all the branches of the federal government, the Supreme Court was the least responsive to the problems confronting industrial society. Although it agreed to the Roosevelt administration's attempt to break up the Northern

Securities combine and the oil and tobacco monopolies, the Court was considerably less enthusiastic about the new progressive forms of administrative government. The struggle for administrative autonomy after 1890 often seemed to be waged between a handful of justices clinging tenaciously to the right of review and a clique of frustrated congressional reformers seeking to strengthen the administrative arm of government. To disgruntled reformers the judiciary's stubborn defense of its prerogatives seemed an act of usurpation, taking away from federal agencies like the Interstate Commerce Commission the power to do their job. In late progressive memory, moreover, the Court had also declared a federal income tax unconstitutional and set severe limits on the powers of the states to enact social legislation.

Progressivism invaded the Supreme Court with the appointment of Oliver Wendell Holmes, Jr. Chosen by Roosevelt in the belief he would reeducate his colleagues in judicial restraint and bring a more enlightened view of regulatory power to the Court, Holmes was already acknowledged as the most articulate of the new legal instrumentalists. Holmes, as he had repeatedly made clear, considered the Constitution not a yardstick for measuring the shortcomings of imperfect laws but a flexible instrument for meeting the "felt necessities" of the age. For Holmes, the life of the law inhered not in absolute truth—cold, formal-

TWO VIEWS OF NEW YORK AT THE OPENING OF THE CENTURY

The New York Stock Exchange on Wall Street contrasts with
Mulberry Street on the Lower East Side. (*Library of Congress.*)

istic, and abstract—but in attributes of utility—relative, approximate, and experimental. Those justices who still professed belief in natural law Holmes dismissed as willing captives of "that naive state of mind that accepts what has been familiar and accepted by them and their neighbors as something that must be accepted everywhere." As for himself, the outspoken newcomer readily admitted, "I . . . define truth as the system of my limitations and leave absolute truth for those who are better equipped."

Holmes attempted to explain his belief in the necessity of social experimentation in the famous *Lochner* case in 1905, a decision involving a New York law that reduced the workweek for bakers to 60 hours. In a five-to-four decision the majority declared that the law, as another of the recent "meddlesome interferences with the rights of individuals," was unconstitutional. In his dissent Holmes lectured his colleagues on the inadvisability of intruding their laissez-faire views into the legal process. The Constitution, he declared, had not been intended "to embody a particular economic theory, whether of paternalism and the organic relation of the citizen to the state or of laissez-faire." Instead it was made for "people of fundamentally differing views, and the accident of our finding certain opinions natural and familiar, or novel and even shocking, ought not to conclude our judgment upon the question whether statutes embodying them conflict with the Constitution of the United States." In a series of similar dissents over the next two decades Holmes—together with Louis Brandeis, who joined the liberal side of the court in 1916 after an epochal confirmation battle—argued the tradition of judicial restraint against an activist conservatism of a majority intent on checking the progressive drift toward a managerial society.

Congress, frequently at loggerheads with itself after 1909, made little headway against such certainty of conservative purpose. Both the Senate and the House, in fact, saw a series of encounters between aggressive Insurgents and stubborn conservatives over tariff and reciprocity matters, conservation policy, and governmental reorganization. Without the support of the President, who chose to back the Republican regulars in their holding action against the Insurgents, the immediate prospects for further reforms grew dim.

Meanwhile Taft's personal bulk and political lethargy made an inviting target for the barbs of the Insurgents. Though he came recommended as a reformer, Taft lacked Roosevelt's concern with strengthening the federal government as well as the former President's skill in managing his party. Ponderous, stubborn, unschooled in the arts of political persuasion and with none of the Colonel's popular appeal, Taft quickly made it clear that he was no crusader.

Taft's administration, accordingly, was marked by a series of political explosions. The first one was touched off by the Pinchot-Ballinger imbroglio over conservation policy. Gifford Pinchot, "Sir Galahad of the Woods," as Harold Ickes called him, accused Taft's secretary of the interior, Richard Ballinger, of neglecting his duties, and further, of unsavory conduct in validating the Bering River coal claims that had mysteriously come into the possession of the Morgan-Guggenheim syndicate. Although a congressional investigation exonerated Ballinger of any suggestion of fraud, and though the feisty Pinchot overplayed his accusatory hand by appealing to the American public, Taft's administration lost face along with the loyalty of a sizable contingent of Roosevelt progressives.

Taft compounded his political troubles with his handling of the tariff. After promising meaningful downward revision, he backed away from the ensuing congressional donnybrook and sat by while the high-tariff forces of Aldrich and the Old Guard loaded the bill with higher schedules. To the consternation of the Insurgents the President hastened to their midwestern camp, where he pronounced the Payne-Aldrich Act the "best tariff ever passed by the Republican party."

Roosevelt watched Taft's maladroit handling of his party with growing disdain that soon hardened into conviction; "a lawyer's administration" was proving itself "totally unfit" to lead the country. For like-minded progressives, who had recently formed the Progressive Republican League, there were two choices, the first to appeal to Roosevelt to intervene in party councils in their behalf and help them replace Taft with a candidate of their own, the second and more desperate measure, to bolt the Republican party and set up shop for themselves as a reform party. By 1912, Republican progressives remained sharply divided on this question.

As the election year approached, Roosevelt himself was of two minds about the best course. For two years after his retirement he remained dubious about the prospects of any "back from Elba movement" in his behalf. On the one hand, he was convinced that under the "Taft-Aldrich-Cannon regime," as he now called it, there had been little understanding of the "needs of the country." On the other, he confessed to little enthusiasm for "staggering under a load on my shoulders through no fault of my own."

Whether Roosevelt knew it or not, he had practically declared himself available with his "New Nationalism" speech at Osawatomie in 1910 as he began to assemble the pieces of the original Square Deal into an even bolder nationalist design. Composed of plans for improved regulation of corporations, physical evaluation of railroads, a graduated income tax, a refurbished banking system, labor legislation, the direct primary plus a corrupt practices act, the former President's new program, so reassuring to his nationalist followers, seemed nothing less than revolutionary to the Old Guard. Far from closing the breach

WOMEN SWIMMING IN THE SURF, CONEY ISLAND, 1910

(*Brown Brothers.*)

between the two factions of the party, the New Nationalism speech in effect threw down the gauntlet to Taft and his conservatives.

Taft's refusal "to step out of the way of Mr. Roosevelt" along with LaFollette's rival bid for progressive support finally determined Roosevelt, and he entered the contest. Six months before convention time the Colonel announced that he would accept the offer if there were signs of "a real popular movement" in behalf of his nomination and if it were tendered to him. It never was. Taft regulars, with a secure hold on the Southern "rotten boroughs," put them to good use against their old adversary. Roosevelt's hopes at the convention rested on some 252 contested seats, at least 100 of which he needed to secure his candidacy. With the credentials committee and the whole party apparatus in the hands of the regulars he succeeded in winning exactly 14 of them. Consulting hurriedly with his financial backers, George W. Perkins and Frank Munsey, who promised to see him through his long night of opposition, Roosevelt agreed to call his own convention of the vanquished to protest Taft's grand larceny by launching an independent Progressive party.

The loyal ten thousand who gathered in the Chicago Auditorium in August 1912 to hear their leader pronounce himself as fit as a "Bull Moose" and to sing with him the "Battle Hymn of the Republic" comprised a motley collection of mavericks and reformers, nationalists and big businessmen, social workers and intellectuals, all determined to stand at Armageddon. Conspicuously absent were most of the original Insurgents, who declined to make an investment in third party politics. Although the spirit of the old progressivism enveloped the Bull Moosers at Chicago and lifted their nationalist hopes, winning the necessary votes, as the Colonel and his advisers realized, would prove another matter. As Roosevelt intoned the Eighth Commandment and called down divine judgment on his betrayers, he must have known secretly that a Democratic victory that fall was all but inevitable.

If fortune was about to shine its face on the Democratic party in the election of 1912 it gave no sign. Democrats carried their own pluralist liabilities into the convention, and chief among them was their titular head and perennial candidate, William Jennings Bryan, who had labored sixteen years to undo the damages of his ill-fated experiment in political pietism. In the center ring at the 1912 Democratic Convention stood "Champ" Clark, speaker of the House and veteran Southern politician backed by the party's agrarians; William Randolph Hearst, the demagogic publisher and would-be reformer; and Woodrow Wilson, the shining knight of New Jersey progressivism. Fresh from a series of legislative encounters that had seen the passage of a direct primary law, railroad regulation, workmen's compensation, and a corrupt practices act, Wilson represented the hopes of urban progressives. Clark upheld the time-honored particularism of the Democracy.

The Democratic Convention in Baltimore in 1912 was every bit as uproarious as the Republican Convention. Clark, armed with preconvention pledges, jumped out to an early lead, which he maintained until the Wilson contingent finally broke his hold. On the forty-sixth ballot, following some timely arrangements with Alabama Senator Oscar Underwood and a deal with Chicago boss Roger Sullivan, the deadlock was ended and Wilson won the nomination. Before the Democrats adjourned, they patched up their differences in a platform that roundly condemned Republican centralization—as all Democratic platforms had unfailingly done since Reconstruction—and advertised its own brand of progressivism guaranteed to lower tariffs, break up trusts, give the banks back to the people, and destroy all special privilege.

The Election of 1912

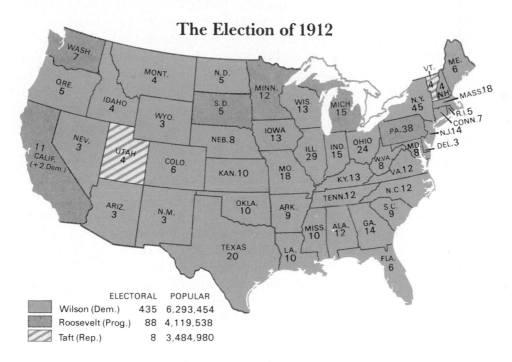

	ELECTORAL	POPULAR
Wilson (Dem.)	435	6,293,454
Roosevelt (Prog.)	88	4,119,538
Taft (Rep.)	8	3,484,980

But the heart of the Democratic promise in 1912 lay in its candidate's call for liberation from the rule of big business and big government. Wilson pictured Democratic deliverance as "coming out of a stifling cellar into the open" where the people could "breathe again and see the free spaces of the heavens." Taft's official Republicanism, according to Wilson, spelled business domination, and Roosevelt's plan for monitoring trusts simply added the power of the national government to the power of the monopolists. "We design that the limitations on private enterprise shall be removed, so that the next generation of youngsters, as they come along, will not have to become the protégé of benevolent trusts, but will be free to go about making their own lives what they will. . . ."

Whether or not American voters considered an escape from economic and political consolidation likely, enough of them—6,286,214, or 42 percent—elected Wilson President. Even with the split among Republicans, who gave Taft some 3.5 million votes, and Roosevelt's Progressive party, which garnered just over 4 million, the changing of the political guard was easily effected. It remained to be seen to what purpose.

If the intellectual roots of Roosevelt's New Nationalism reached back into the eighteenth century world of the Founding Fathers, the roots of Woodrow Wilson's New Freedom were firmly planted in Victorian verities. Wilson, who was born in Staunton, Virginia, in 1856, grew up in the heart of the Confederacy, briefly attended Davidson College, and graduated from Princeton in 1879. After a year spent studying law, for which he had no particular liking, he turned to his real interest, political science and history, studying with the great institutionalist historian Herbert Baxter Adams at Johns Hopkins and earning a doctorate there in 1886. Then came several years of climbing the academic ladder, with appointments at Bryn Mawr, Wesleyan, and Princeton where he taught for twelve years before becoming president in 1902. Wilson's books, polished though not sparkling pieces of political science and history, made a varied collection: *Congressional Government* (1885); an extended essay, *The State* (1889); a history of the Civil War years, *Division and Reunion* (1893); the five-volume *History of the American People* (1902); and *Constitutional Government in the United States* (1908).

By temperament as well as training Wilson was an academician, an educator-scholar whose calling it was to instruct a progressive generation in the science of good government. As schoolmaster to the nation, he looked the part—with a lean, angular face, a long aquiline nose adorned by a pince-nez, full pursed lips, and eyes that seemed to look through his visitors rather than at them. Distant, formal, somewhat austere in his relations with the public, he often appeared correct but cold. He recognized this reserve in himself and considered it a weakness. "I have a sense of power in dealing with men collectively," he once confessed, "which I do not feel always in dealing with them singly." There was little familiarity in the man and no feelings of camaraderie. As president of Princeton, governor of New Jersey, and chief executive, Wilson was a man one worked *for* but not *with*. Both as pedagogue and as administrator, he had a problem not so much in disciplining his followers, at which he excelled with a politeness occasionally frosty, as in gaining control over a high-voltage temper and a tendency to bridle when challenged. When opposition to his plans mounted, as it did at Princeton over the issue of the graduate school, Wilson would dig in his heels, personalize the conflict, and impute malice to his opponents while avowing the purity of his own motives.

At his best, however, Wilson could be a superb leader, directing the work of his subordinates with cool precision, holding their loyalty with ideals, and winning the American public over with his convictions of rectitude. In the few moments when his self-confidence flagged in the face of enemy attack he could be petty, vindictive, and ultimately self-destructive. But at all times he lived the role of the statesman as educator, standing before and slightly above the people to whom he sought to teach the meaning of effective government.

WOODROW WILSON CAMPAIGNING, 1912

Although his style differed markedly from Theodore
Roosevelt's, Wilson was an effective and persuasive speaker.
(*Drown Brothers.*)

   Some of the lessons Wilson taught were curiously old-fashioned—moral precepts rather than operational concepts. For him words like *liberty, justice* and
progress still possessed their mid-nineteenth-century clarity, connected as they
were in his mind with the Christian principles of "obligation," "service," and
"righteousness" that his father preached from his Presbyterian pulpit. These
were the skeletal truths around which Wilson packed such flesh-and-blood meaning as his Southern Democratic heritage afforded. His intellctual origins predisposed him to an individualist and pluralist view of American politics, one in
which John Stuart Mill's definition of liberty as the absence of external restraint
ideally held sway. A Southern upbringing also left him with a generally unen-
lightened outlook on race and a quiet respect for the reasoning that had once
upheld the Lost Cause.
   Wilson sensed clearly that American life in the opening years of the twentieth

century was too amorphous, its forms too protean, to be encased in any national-istic formula. "The life of the nation has grown infinitely varied," he reminded his fellow Democrats in pointing to a flourishing cultural diversity. "It does not centre now upon questions of governmental structure or of distribution of gov-ernmental powers. It centres upon the questions of the very structures and opera-tions of society itself...." In Wilson's view the most urgent American reform task was releasing the creative impulses of a free people. Nations, he argued with Jeffersonian logic, are renewed from the bottom up, from "the great strug-gling unknown masses of men" at the base of society.

If America discourages the locality, the community, the self-contained town, she will kill the nation. A nation is as rich as her free communities; she is not as rich as her capital city or her metropolis.... The welfare, the very existence of the nation, rests at last upon the great mass of the people; its prosperity depends upon the spirit in which they go about their work in the several communities throughout the broad land.

What the nation most needed, Wilson announced, was the revival of the common counsel of the working men and women in their many communities.

Americans — New and Old

Many of the men and women who did the daily work of the nation were recent arrivals from Europe. The decade after 1900 saw the climax of a century-long European exodus in the cresting of a wave of new immigrants from new sources. Until roughly 1890 the great majority of immigrants had come from northern and western Europe. Although these newcomers in their time had posed acute prob-lems of cultural identity for native-born Amer-icans, these paled in comparison with those accompanying the so-called "new immigration." In the first place the very numbers of these newcomers appeared overwhelming to the nativists: statistics confirmed their worst fears. In the quarter-century before the First World War 18 million newcomers poured down the gangplanks, 80 percent of them from southern and eastern Europe. In the first decade of the century alone some 5.8 million people arrived from Austria-Hungary, Spain, Italy, and Russia.

Another set of figures reinforced the fears of native-born Americans. In the peak nineteenth-century year, 1882, when more than three-quarters of a million immigrants had disem-barked at Atlantic ports, a third of their numbers had come from Germany while Italy sent only 32,000 people and Russia not quite 17,000. The

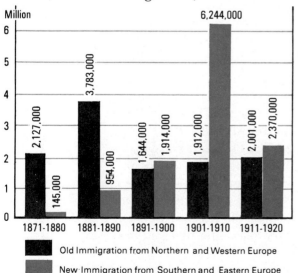

Old and New Immigration, 1871-1920

Million

■ Old Immigration from Northern and Western Europe
■ New Immigration from Southern and Eastern Europe

peak year in the progressive era, 1907, reversed this balance: Germany sent only 37,000 while Italy dispatched 285,000 of its citizens, the Austro-Hungarian empire another 338,000, and Russia together with the Baltic states still another 250,000 people. For the entire period 1881–1910 Italy headed the list of European exporters with 3 million immigrants. Next came the Jews, most of them from Russia, numbering about 2 million, followed by 1 million Poles by 1914. These three main groups, then, together with Magyars, Greeks, Armenians, Syrians, and Turks, attested to the results of leaving the gates ajar.

Four out of five of the new arrivals settled in the industrial cities of the Northeast and the Midwest, concentrating in areas where the jobs were. Their collective impact on these cities became clear when native-born Americans suddenly realized that 75 percent of the populations of New York, Chicago, Cleveland, and Boston were immigrants or children of immigrants. Like it or not, progressives faced a bewildering ethnic variety in the sudden presence of so many new arrivals eager to get ahead in their new land.

Economic opportunity magnetized the new immigrants as it had the old, drawing them off worn-out lands and out of the ghettos of European port cities

PASSENGERS WHO MISSED THE MAYFLOWER

Immigrants arrive in steerage. (*Culver Picture, Inc.*)

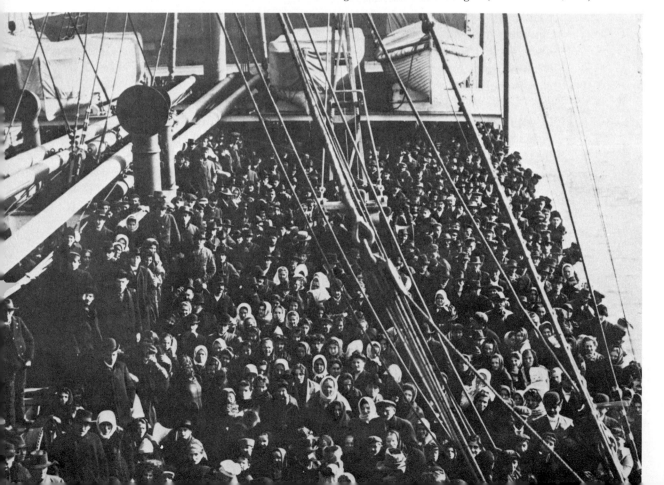

into an American setting of deprivation that at first seemed all too familiar. Once arrived, they started at the bottom of the occupational ladder doing the nation's dirty work—construction, mining, smelting, factory work, and domestic service. They usually arranged themselves in tight ethnic communities around their work, finding security in an enforced segregation. This pattern of inner-city concentration fed old-stock American fears even as it removed the "foreigners" from the suburban field of vision. Frequently, too, the newcomers elbowed their predecessors out of their neighborhoods, sending them further out along the city's extremities.

Old-stock Americans tended to assign the new arrivals a national identity that most of them did not yet possess. The vast majority of the "new immigrants" came from cultures that had long been narrowed to the locale, the region, or the village. However compact and homogeneous the immigrant enclaves in American cities seemed to outsiders, they were in fact fractured into blocks of ethnic and religious experience, each neighborhood boasting its own churches and patron saints, feast days and civic associations. In trying to impose an institutional order on their new surroundings, the new Americans mirrored the progressive search for order, but under adverse conditions and with improvised methods. By 1910, urban America had become a patchwork quilt of tightly knit and sharply contrasted peoples and cultures.

Packed into slums, exploited by native-born employers and their own contractors alike, harassed by nativist groups and earlier arrivals, fighting among themselves for a foot on the economic ladder, millions of the new immigrants at first lived marginal lives close to the edges of defeat. The going rate for piecework for young Jewish girls in New York's garment industry was 8¢ an hour. Slovak steel workers in Pittsburgh sweated a 60-hour week for $12.50. A German husband and wife team on Tenth Street on the lower East Side in 1900 could expect $3.75 for every 1000 cigars they wrapped. By working 15 hours a day the two of them could turn out 3000 cigars. Leisure for cultural and educational pursuits was a scarce commodity in America's Little Italys and Little Warsaws.

Slowly these immigrant communities acquired a measure of stability. They developed lively subcultures of their own through churches, foreign language newspapers, service organizations like the Sons of Italy and the Pan-Hellenic Union, and a growing variety of social agencies and immigrant aid societies. Edward Corsi, who became Hoover's commissioner of immigration and naturalization, recalled the clotted tenement-house life of New York's East Harlem with "five thousand human beings in one city street, as many as fifteen to a four-room flat; two, three, and even four hundred to a tenement intended for fifty." Twenty-seven nationalities all told, with Chinese laundrymen, Syrian shopkeepers, and gypsy phrenologists tossed in for good measure. On the East River the Italians; along Pleasant Avenue, the Poles, Austrians, and Hungarians; over on the West Side, Jewish shopkeepers besieged by Turks and Spaniards. And descending from the north like a new Mongol horde driving all before them, the blacks, turn-

The Lower East Side

The Jewish Immigrant
District of New York City
1910

Legend:
- – – – Hungarian Jews
- –·–·– Galician Jews *(From Northwest Spain)*
- ----- Rumanian Jews
- –•–•– Levantine Jews *(From E. Mediterranean Seacoast)*
- ——— Russian Jews

ing the retreat of the Irish and Germans into a rout. Scattered here and there were lonely islands of old-stock Americans "like refugees in exile."

Corsi's East Harlem supported a lusty popular culture, not the imposing façades of "opera houses, theaters, and hotels," but the reenactment of Old World pageants in cafes, rathskellers, spaghetti houses, cabarets, and dance halls. "We have Yiddish theaters and Italian marionette shows, not to mention movie and vaudeville houses. Our secondhand book shops are as good as those of Paris. So are our music stores."

Mystified by the teeming variety of immigrant life, most progressive Americans fell back on increasingly irrelevant schemes for "Americanizing" the new arrivals. At dockside civic aid societies handed out pamphlets printed in English admonishing the newcomers to be "honest and honorable, clean in your person, and decent in your talk," but these scattered in the swirl of numbers like so many pious hopes. Restrictionists followed Theodore Roosevelt in deploring the "tangle of squabbling nationalities" as "the one certain way of bringing the nation to ruin," yet the fact remained that hyphenated Americanism was the only clear avenue to full citizenship. Even the hopeful immigrant Israel Zangwill, looking forward to the day of total assimilation, described a dream rather than reality. The composer-hero of Zangwill's popular play *The Melting Pot* hears the melodies for his "American symphony" in the "seething crucible—God's crucible," where a new amalgam, "the coming superman," is being forged over divine fires. Yet Zangwill told progressive audiences what they wanted to hear, not what they saw around them.

A clearer assessment of the forces of cultural pluralism came from the more reflective of the immigrants themselves, who exposed the progressive persuasion as the myth that it was. "There is no such thing as an American," a Polish priest informed the genteel social worker Emily Greene Balch. Poland, he explained, was a nation, but the United States was simply a country—in the beginning an empty land open to all comers in turn. Immigrants, according to the newly arrived Mary Antin, were just people who had missed the *Mayflower* and taken the next available boat.

A growing number of younger progressive intellectuals responded enthusiastically to the promise of cultural pluralism. In the variety and excitement of cultural clash they found an escape from the stifling middle-class gentility of Gilded Age homes. One of them, a young radical student of John Dewey's at Columbia University, Randolph Bourne, found a title for this cultural diversity—"Trans-National America"—and hailed the United States as the "intellectual battleground of the world . . . a cosmopolitan federation of national colonies, of foreign cultures, from whom the sting of devastating competition has been removed."

Bourne's concept of America as a world federation in miniature ran headlong into the barriers of exclusivist fears. The myth of the "new immigrants" assumed a variety of ugly shapes: they were dangerously illiterate and culturally deprived; they brought with them either a benighted Catholicism or private visions of the overthrow of capitalist society; they were doomed to a permanently inferior place in the Darwinian scale of races and could never master the skills democracy demanded. Amateur and professional sociologists, Cassandras all, consulted the numbers and predicted "race suicide." The sociologist Franklin Giddings announced hopefully but somewhat ambiguously that the "softening" of the traits of "preeminently an energetic, practical people, above all an industrial people" would continue as Mediterranean instincts insinuated themselves into the American character until the original Baltic and Alpine stock had become transformed into "a more versatile, a more plastic people," at once gentler and more poetic. Giddings's prophecies raised the inevitable question that a progressive reformer put in *Charities:* "Are we not, most of us, fairly well satisfied with the characteristics, mental and physical, of the old American stock? Do we not love American traits as they are?"

The Dillingham Commission placed the imprimatur of the federal government on these progressive anxieties by making an official distinction between the already assimilated "old immigration" and the patently unassimilable "new immigration." The commission, a joint House-Senate inquiry that Roosevelt appointed in 1907, took four years to complete its 42-volume report. Although it amassed much useful information on the work patterns and living conditions of immigrants, the Dillingham Commission took for its controlling assumption the need to check the flood of new arrivals, if not with a literacy test, then through a quota system. When Congress promptly obliged by passing a literacy bill in 1913, Taft vetoed it in deference to Republican employers who still found merit in a supply of cheap labor. But the quota scheme survived the prewar debate and reemerged in postwar legislation establishing strict limits. The Dillingham Report marked a reversal in American attitudes toward cultural minorities: by 1910 restrictionist hopes flared as the more cosmopolitan aims of the pluralists flickered and died.

In the case of black Americans, white fears produced an even harsher doctrine of reaction. The progressive generation had inherited most of the ingredients for a racist myth from the nineteenth century but improved the formula with new "scientific" evidence of the biological inferiority of the Negro race. Not surprisingly, the opening years of the twentieth century saw the nearly total disfranchisement of black voters in the South. Exclusionist techniques varied from state to state: poll taxes, grandfather clauses, literacy tests, white primaries— all served effectively throughout the South to bar the great majority of Negroes from the polls. Southern liberals and progressives justified the purge with a variant of the argument Northern reformers used to exclude the immigrant, that good government required the political elimination of the inferior and the unfit. The Southern progressive Edgar Gardner Murphy pronounced sentence on the civic performance of Southern blacks when he dismissed them as a "backward and essentially unassimilable people."

Most Northern liberals continued to regard the Negro as a peculiarly Southern problem, despite mounting evidence to the contrary. "The popular mind in the old free states," lamented the progressive publicist Walter Weyl, ". . . has retreated from its uncomfortable dictatorial attitude and thrown the whole matter over to the States of the South." But it was South Carolina's racist demagogue Ben Tillman who probed the softest spot in the progressive plan for regeneration,

The pioneer documentary photographer Lewis W. Hine (1874–1940) had acquired a degree in sociology from Columbia when in 1908 he joined the staff of the National Child Labor Committee as investigator-photographer. For the committee he compiled the first American photographic documentary, "Neglected Neighborhoods of Our National Capital," and also served as staff photographer for *Charities* as well as for the Russell Sage Foundation whose six-volume *Pittsburgh Survey* contained a number of his photographs. Hine's primary subjects throughout the progressive years remained children and immigrants whose drab lives and harsh routines he caught with unforgettable clarity. (*George Eastman House, Inc.*)

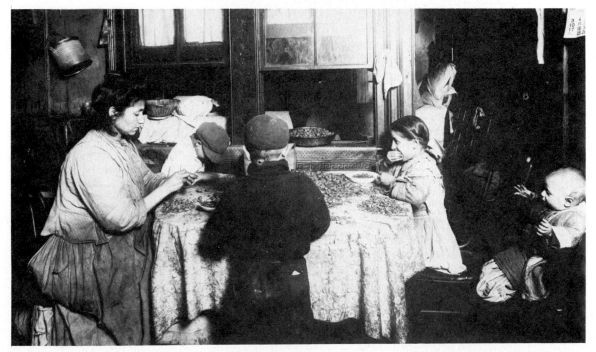

its lack of moral certainty. "Your slogans of the past—brotherhood of man and fatherhood of God—have gone glimmering down the ages," Tillman chortled. A progressive age, stripped of the moral absolutes that once sustained the abolitionist crusade, the more easily accepted the racist conclusions seemingly established by its up-to-date social science.

For the moment, however, statistics obscured the long-term meaning of the effect of industry on Southern blacks, most of whom as late as 1900 were tied to the land by tenancy and sharecropping. In that year there were less than 1 million Negroes north of the Mason-Dixon Line, and thirty years later a full 80 percent of all blacks in the United States still lived below it. Still, the intervening years saw a net gain to Northern cities of 1.4 million as even before the First World War the often illusory lure of economic opportunity and personal freedom drew blacks northward. Herded into big-city ghettos—New York's black community numbered 70,000 by the turn of the century—they were met with proscription and wholesale discrimination. As lynchings in the South slowly declined, they were replaced by their Northern counterpart, the race riot—in the small Indiana town of Greensburg in 1906; in Springfield, Illinois, two years later; and in explosive racial tensions in New York, Chicago, and Philadelphia. Blacks paid a high price for their escape from sharecropping.

Black Americans attempted to counter political proscription and economic exploitation with two limited strategies, neither very successful in overcoming white progressive prejudices. The official black spokesman, the "office broker for the race" as admiring white liberals called him, was Booker T. Washington. The son of a slave, Washington learned the gospel of self-help at Hampton Institute and put it into practice at Tuskegee, where he trained thousands of young men and women in the industrial and domestic arts. Washington presented the philosophy underlying his educational program in his famous address at the Atlanta Exposition in 1895. He urged black listeners to strike their roots in Southern soil by "making friends in every manly way of the people of all races by whom we are surrounded." To whites he offered the same suggestion, urging them to cast down their buckets among a race "whose habits you know, whose fidelity and love you have tested."

Most white liberals took Booker T. Washington to their hearts as a "credit to his race," although not all of them approved of President Roosevelt's inviting him to lunch at the White House. Washington became the symbol of the "good Negro," who knew his place and aspired only to keep it—the man of sorrows who accepted the fact of race prejudice while rejecting all its assumptions and working patiently to lift his people the few notches a dominant white society allowed them. The question Washington's program did not answer, however, was the one the Muckraker Ray Stannard Baker asked in his pessimistic analysis of American race relations, *Following the Color Line* (1908): "Does democracy really include Negroes as well as white men?"

The photographer Francis Benjamin Johnson posed this picture of a carpentry class at Hampton Institute to illustrate the kind of "useful" vocational training for blacks offered at the school. The black women going to work at the Libby, McNeill and Libby plant in Chicago during the Stockyards Strike in 1904 were probably hired as strikebreakers. (*Top, Library of Congress; bottom, Chicago Historical Society.*)

By 1900 the black progressive William E. B. DuBois, together with several Northern liberals of both races, had concluded that until Negroes gained full political rights democracy would never be theirs. Northern black leadership in the big cities appealed to a different constituency from Booker T. Washington's and offered another approach to black advancement. DuBois, a New Englander and a graduate of Harvard, followed the typical progressive route to professionalism by studying in Berlin before returning to an academic career at Atlanta University in 1897. Like his white counterparts, he recognized the pressing need for scientific data on the actual conditions of Negro life in America. "We must not forget," he reminded his students, "that most Americans answer queries regarding the Negro a priori, and that the least that common courtesy can do is to listen to the evidence." To provide this evidence DuBois pioneered with a sociological study of the Philadelphia Negro, in which he presented a clear picture of life in the ghetto. In *Souls of the Black Folk* (1903) he appealed to a latent black solidarity and cultural consciousness in criticizing Washington's "gospel of work and Money." He suggested, instead, cultivating the "higher aims of life" with his plea for the "Talented Tenth," calling for programs to train and equip a black intellectual vanguard. In this early phase of his career DuBois developed an undisguised progressive program aimed at substituting "man training" for moneymaking and at cultivating "intelligence, broad sympathy, knowledge of the world" in a new elite. Increasingly after 1900 DuBois turned to the small group of progressives in the North who agreed with him in defining black issues as the need for leadership, organization, and political activism.

Although DuBois's elitist strategy and Washington's accommodationist tactics complemented each other in theory, a bitter rivalry developed between the Tuskegee Machine and the Niagara Movement of Northern radicals seeking full political and social equality. By the time the National Association for the Advancement of Colored People was founded in 1910 through the joint efforts of white neo-abolitionists like Mary Ovington and Oswald Garrison Villard and the black liberal followers of DuBois, neither moderate nor militant efforts had succeeded in denting the prejudices of most white Americans. For them the "race problem" was best solved by a system of strict segregation and the fiction of "separate but equal."

The Jeffersonian tradition of decentralization and localism worked to the distinct disadvantage of black Americans throughout the progressive years. It perpetuated sectional patterns of discrimination and fostered a national disregard for what had clearly become a fundamental challenge to democracy. Down to the New Deal of the 1930s the progressive compromise with the forces of bigotry and prejudice blocked any real hopes for a federal program to equip Negroes with political rights or to open the door for them to full economic opportunity. In the last analysis progressivism rested on racist assumptions and a supportive doctrine of localism, which had changed little since the Civil War.

The Rise of Social Feminism

The arrival of large numbers of American women on the social and industrial scene after 1900 also disrupted nationalist-progressive plans for completing the ordered society. The percentage of working women rose most spectacularly in the first decade of the century; gainfully employed women between the ages of 16 and 44 composed 21 percent of the work force in 1910. Their rapid recruitment into industry effectively dismissed the question of their suitability for factory and office work, and raised other issues in its stead. Were there certain "natural" occupations for them? Did they have the right to organize? to strike? For a raw industrial society that had not yet fashioned a general labor policy, these questions became increasingly urgent as a small group of women workers began to raise them in militant fashion after 1910.

Even more perplexing to American men in the progressive age was the question of the proper role and acceptable functions of the "New Woman," the young, educated, unmarried woman in revolt against a smothering gentility and the prospects of perpetual domesticity. In the beginning, feminist protests against an American society that seemingly offered no useful work for talented women did not threaten to disarrange the ideological formulations of progressivism. Some of the most articulate new social feminists echoed progressive demands for greater efficiency in managing American society. The radical feminist Charlotte Perkins Gilman, for example, indicted the American home for its shocking waste of human energies. The home, she scoffed, was a case of arrested development. "Among the splendid activities of our age it lingers on, inert and blind, like a clam at a horse race." By reducing the wife to a "social idiot" and subjecting the child to the constant care of an ignorant "primeval mother," the home acted as the chief deterrent to progress.

Equally subversive of the progressive program for social order was the feminist theme of liberation that Jane Addams and the legions of settlement-house women sounded in announcing the need for new social outlets for feminine energies. Addams cited not simply the inefficiencies of family arrangements but the waste of individual lives in enforced domesticity. In her widely read account of social settlements, *Twenty Years at Hull House*, she duly acknowledged the objective conditions in urban slums demanding remedial action, but also stressed the "subjective necessity" for useful work to fill the empty lives of educated women languishing in the family circle. While admitting the need to expand social democracy, she was also worried lest the feminine personality, denied a full range of experience, atrophy. Where efficiency-minded reformers like Gilman called for better organization of public resources, Jane Addams and her colleagues emphasized the release of vital creative forces.

Yet viewed as either an efficiency or a liberation movement, social feminism collected little in the way of an ideology. Even in its attempts to improve the lot of working women it mounted no concerted assault on corporate capitalism or the profit motive. Its power to unsettle an American male order stemmed from a different source. Nineteenth-century feminism had concentrated for the most part on removing legal barriers to full citizenship for women—on winning the vote and acquiring the right to hold and bequeath property. The new social feminism, fed by the ideas of European artists and intellectuals like Ibsen, Nietzsche, and Bergson, postulated a new kind of individualism and self-realization. The Western revolt against positivism and the discovery of the irrational that swept across the Atlantic in the last years of the nineteenth century provided women as well as men with new standards of social and sexual behavior not fully legitimized by the moral politcs of progressivism. It was precisely here that the challenge of feminism seemed so disquieting.

The revolt began inauspiciously as an uprising of young educated women against the concept of self-denial. When Theodore Roosevelt, as was his wont, spoke of duty as involving "pain, hardship, self-mastery, self-denial," he presumably prescribed for both sexes. It was against this male-imposed definition of duty as circumscribed by hearth and home that young middle-class women suddenly began to rebel. One of the leaders of this feminist revolt, appropriately named Lydia Commander, pointed to the decline of the Victorian ideals of humility, obedience, and self-sacrifice once "assiduously cultivated as the highest womanly virtues." Now, she declared, these qualities had fallen from grace, and the "principle of self-development" reigned supreme in the soul of the new woman. Gone too, feminists agreed, was the obsolescent notion of female innocence. "What good does it do her?" snapped Charlotte Gilman.

Subjectivity proved a two-edged sword for would-be liberated women. With the one hand it could be used to carve out blocks of experience for women that were manifestly different from men's, and with the other to cut away piled-up deprivations. The sense of victimization could lead to the demand for special protection from the oppressive force of industry—for compensatory laws against long hours, dangerous conditions, and exhausting routines. In this sense social feminism aimed not so much at equality of treatment as at special consideration. But for a more privileged class of leisured women the feminist impulse was more purely egalitarian—the demand for equal access to all the opportunities of modern life. By 1910, the "New Woman," after countless repeat performances in popular fiction and middle-class magazines, had become a stereotype. "This young person," one mother complained, "with surprisingly bad manners—has gone to college, and when she graduates is going to earn her own living . . . she won't go to church; she has views upon marriage and the birthrate, and she utters them calmly, while her mother blushes with embarrassment; she occupies herself, passionately, with everything except the things that used to occupy the minds of girls." To the late Victorian mother it seemed that her home was passing out of vogue.

One of the outlets for the growing social concerns of women before the

First World War was the women's club movement, which provided a useful if limited perspective on the problems of industrial society. The General Federation of Women's Clubs grew rapidly from an initial membership of 20,000 in 1890 to nearly a million twenty years later. The clubs were thoroughly genteel organizations, devoted, at least in the beginning, chiefly to self-culture. At no time did the federation encourage a high level of political consciousness. Nevertheless, individual branches took up issues like factory inspection and child labor, lobbied for criminal justice reforms, and even experimented with tenement-house improvements. In a variety of "study groups" middle-class women discovered an expanding range of problems: the poor quality of municipal services; urban political graft; the need for pure food and drug laws; conservation; and belatedly, the importance of the vote for women.

Women's clubs popularized rather than initiated reforms. Ultimately their most important contribution lay in their support, however tardy, for women's suffrage. Neither innovative nor consistently liberal, the General Federation of Women's Clubs did, however, succeed in shifting the interests of well-to-do women outside the home and settling them in the center of the national social spectrum.

EAST SIDE SETTLEMENT CLASS, CIRCA 1910

A settlement teacher and her pupils. (*Brown Brothers.*)

A second, more sharply focused women's organization, which gave a practical point to the humanitarian concerns of the women's clubs, was the National Consumer's League. Modeled on English precedents, the NCL grew out of the early work of the patrician charity organizer Josephine Shaw Lowell, who took up the cause of New York City's working girls late in her career. Out of her efforts in the 1890s came a small group of upper-class women who decided to use their buying power to enforce an enlightened labor policy on the city's employers. As the consumer movement spread to other cities, a national league was formed in 1899, with the remarkable administrator Florence Kelley to head it. The daughter of an abolitionist congressman, a graduate of Cornell University with advanced training in Zurich, a socialist and Illinois's first factory inspector, Florence Kelley brought impressive credentials and the skills of a superb lobbyist to her job. Under her firm guidance the National Consumers' League grew rapidly until it numbered 60 local branches in 20 states, all applying the league's White Label to approved products.

The league specialized in protective legislation for women and children, lobbying successfully for the Ten-Hour Law in Oregon and retaining Louis Brandeis to argue its constitutionality before the Court. The league also joined the campaign for establishing the Children's Bureau within the Department of Labor, and it helped its sister organization, the National Child Labor Committee, to press Congress for a child labor law. Working together in a new spirit of professionalism, the social feminists built staffs of dedicated administrators like Frances Perkins and the Goldmarks, Pauline and Josephine, who would carry their crusade against child labor and social abuse into the 1920s. These women reformers, in separating their bureaucratic methods from the profit motive, were experimenting, however provisionally, with an alternative to what the feminist Rheta Childe Dorr called the "commercial ideal" of American business.

This same spirit of education and a distaste for the commercial life also distinguished the settlement house. In contrast to England, where young men from Oxford and Cambridge took the lead in founding settlements in London's East End, women dominated the American wing of the movement from the outset. The settlements themselves, shabby remnants of a genteel society that had long ago moved out, stood in the middle of sprawling slums and quickly became the focal points for the public activities of their inhabitants. To the busy complex at Hull House, for example, or to New York's Henry Street Settlement or Boston's South End House came children of the neighborhood to nurseries and playgrounds, their mothers for classes in hygiene and domestic economy, and in the evenings, the men for lessons in English and discussions of politics.

The impulse behind settlements was religious though not sectarian, and the atmosphere in all of them—Graham Taylor's Chicago Commons, New York's University Settlement, Kingsley House in Pittsburgh—was redolent with Christian ethics. Inevitably the earnestness of young college women bent on lifting the tone of immigrant neighborhoods with lectures on Ruskin and displays of pre-Raphaelite reproductions gave rise to sneers. Thorstein Veblen dismissed the settlements as "consistently directed to the incubation, by precept and example, of certain punctilios of upper-class propriety in manners and customs." But it was not long before the settlement-house workers learned to estimate the needs of their neighbors more accurately, and cultural uplift gave way to hard practicality.

The restless energies of the residents combined with their vagueness about political means and an absence of ideology to give the settlement houses all the features of an alternative form of community. Turnover remained high, and a constant lateral mobility into the furthest reaches of the city often made them mere collecting points for members whose jobs as teachers, social workers, visiting nurses, architects, and planners kept them out in city streets. For both men and women, settlements provided a halfway house between the closed intellectual communities of college or university life and the fragmentations of a professional career, fluid arrangements of work and leisure held together by a sense of social sharing.

Education formed the core of the settlement-house experience. The educational process was initially conceived of as a one-way street down which the immigrants would march toward citizenship. Under the pressures of adversity, however, it was quickly redefined as a mutual learning experiment, one that involved genuine exchange and not simply bestowal. As Jane Addams explained to an increasingly receptive progressive public, "A settlement is a protest against a restricted view of education."

Frequently settlement-house workers borrowed and applied the progressive scientific methods of fact gathering and data analysis. And as professionals they looked out on an indeterminate world of the city, one that required continual adaptation and manipulation of means. There the similarity to progressive political reform stopped; instead of accepting specialization and compartmentalized functions they tried to transcend them or at the very least to humanize them. Their instrument was the new educational theory of John Dewey, which in defining learning as a social experience cemented together the various pieces of city life into the concept of the settlement school extending into and in turn penetrated by the larger community. The settlement-house women sought to perform their new roles as social teachers with every device at their disposal— nurseries, evening classes, lectures and lunch programs, health care and slum clearance.

When the women first founded their settlements, they carefully avoided clashes with the city bosses on the theory that urban politics was hopelessly corrupt and that their own redemptive task lay elsewhere. Soon however, they came to agree with Jane Addams that "to keep aloof from it [politics] must be to lose one opportunity of sharing the life of the community." Still, they found it difficult and often impossible to work with the unsympathetic ward boss, who distrusted them as do-gooders and rivals for the affections of his clients. Cooperation turned to confrontation over matters of garbage removal, street lighting, police protection, or the location of a neighborhood park. The most adventurous residents were driven to oppose the boss, but the contest was unequal, as Jane Addams learned to her chagrin in trying to unseat Alderman Johnny Powers in Chicago's Nineteenth Ward. She attacked Powers with every argument she could muster, capping her indictment with the charge that although he dispensed free turkeys at Christmastime he gave notoriously poor service. Yet turkeys continued to turn the political trick, and the likes of Johnny Powers generally held on to their fiefdoms.

Struggling to fend off the counterthrusts of the politicians, the settlement-house women deliberately fashioned their institutions into public forums where social opinions of every stripe could be heard. Chicago Commons, for example, featured a weekly "Free Floor Discussion" billed as "self-conscious democracy,"

SACRED MOTHERHOOD POSTER OF THE WOMEN'S TRADE UNION LEAGUE OF CHICAGO, 1908

(*State Historical Society of Wisconsin.*)

in which a labor leader, a college professor, an anarchist, and a businessman disposed of the future of the capitalist system. From these discussions the women themselves learned valuable political lessons as the logic connecting reform to the vote suddenly became too obvious to ignore. As Maude Nathan, an active member of the Consumers' League and a supporter of settlements, pointed out, women needed the vote to make good on their promise to improve American life. Without the franchise they were left with little more than moral suasion, while manufacturers and merchants used their voting power "to hold in terror" over the politicians. By 1910, mounting frustrations had led many of the settlement-house women to join the drive for woman's suffrage. With their discovery of the political dimension of their reform work, social feminists struck an alliance with political feminists.

The two main agencies of the suffrage movement after 1912 were the staid and cautious National American Woman Suffrage Association, headed by Carrie Chapman Catt, and its more militant offshoot, the National Women's Party, which had been organized by the formidable Quaker agitator Alice Paul. Suffragists presented two fundamentally different and even contradictory arguments. The first was well suited to the progressive temper, a conservative appeal to the instincts for order and control. Mary Putnam Jacobi, a veteran suffragist and leading woman doctor, summarized the case for women as willing instruments of political correction:

No matter how well born, how intelligent, how highly educated, how virtuous, how refined, the women of today constitute a political class below that of every man, no matter how base born, how stupid, how ignorant, how vicious, how poverty-stricken, how brutal.

The second suffragist argument singled out the interests and capabilities of women that were in need of recognition. According to this reasoning, women were uniquely endowed with humane qualities that could soften the rigors of industrial society and nurse the American polity back to health. Such was Jane Addams's explanation for women's political role: "If women have in any sense been responsible for the gentler side of life which softens and blurs some of its harsher conditions, may not they have a duty to perform in our American cities?" In arguing for the vote middle-class women could take their choice between a demand for a simple justice and the promises of a regenerative creed.

At the other end of the social spectrum stood Margaret Dreier Robins and her National Women's Trade Union League. Robins argued that the vote was essential for the working women of the nation since, she said, "The power of the police and of the courts is against them in many instances, and whenever they try to meet that expression of political power, they are handicapped because there is no force in their hands to help change it." Whatever the case for the vote for women, idealistic or purely practical, it was strengthened by the more glaring absurdities of its opponents, one of whom, a worried military officer, warned

Woman Suffrage Before the 19th Amendment

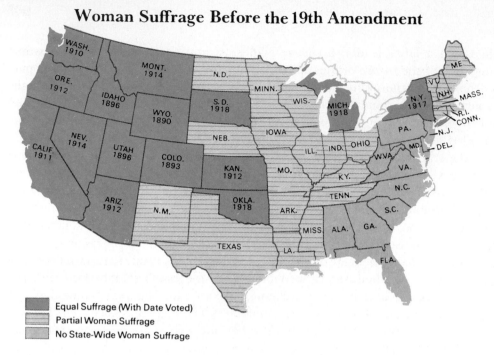

Equal Suffrage (With Date Voted)
Partial Woman Suffrage
No State-Wide Woman Suffrage

against "the dilution with the qualities of the cow, of the qualities of the bull upon which the herd's safety must depend."

The suffrage movement gathered its momentum for the assault on the federal government in the states. In 1910, Washington state gave the vote to women, and the next year California, succumbing to a high-pressure campaign, also awarded women the vote. In 1912, Arizona, Kansas, and Oregon capitulated as Theodore Roosevelt's Bull Moose party, despite the initial reservations of its leader, adopted a plank calling for national suffrage. With the presidential election of 1912 a more militant feminist strategy emerged, which concentrated on Congress and the President, neither of which was particularly sympathetic to the suffrage cause.

The leader of a small band of radicals who began to demonstrate their refusal to accept federal proscription was Alice Paul, a grimly determined feminist who had earned a doctorate at the University of Pennsylvania and spent five years in England studying Emmeline Pankhurst's disruptive tactics before returning home to try them out for herself. Intense, untiring, a stickler for principle and an able tactician, Alice Paul promptly singled out Woodrow Wilson and the occasion of his inauguration for a giant protest parade involving 5000 women, which ended in a near riot. Then, in applying the ideas of the English suffragettes, she organized an aggressive lobby, which three years later became the National Woman's party, dedicated to direct action. The National American Women's Suffrage Association, challenged by the successes of its aggressive rival, revived under Mrs. Catt's able leadership, and a reorganized board of directors redoubled its efforts to reach women at the state and local levels.

By 1917, as the country prepared for war, Wilson's administration faced two

The Lower East Side

The Jewish Immigrant
District of New York City

1910

Madison Square

Union Square

GREENWICH VILLAGE

Wholesale Garment District

Galicians

Rumanians

Levantines

Hungarians

Russians

City Hall

East River

Houston St. Ferry

Williamsburg Bridge, 1903

Grand St. Ferry

Manhattan Bridge 1909

Brooklyn Bridge 1882

East R.

- - - - Hungarian Jews
- · - · Galician Jews (From Northwest Spain)
- - - - Rumanian Jews
-·-·- Levantine Jews (From E. Mediterranean Seacoast)
——— Russian Jews

ing the retreat of the Irish and Germans into a rout. Scattered here and there were lonely islands of old-stock Americans "like refugees in exile."

Corsi's East Harlem supported a lusty popular culture, not the imposing façades of "opera houses, theaters, and hotels," but the reenactment of Old World pageants in cafes, rathskellers, spaghetti houses, cabarets, and dance halls. "We have Yiddish theaters and Italian marionette shows, not to mention movie and vaudeville houses. Our secondhand book shops are as good as those of Paris. So are our music stores."

Mystified by the teeming variety of immigrant life, most progressive Americans fell back on increasingly irrelevant schemes for "Americanizing" the new arrivals. At dockside civic aid societies handed out pamphlets printed in English admonishing the newcomers to be "honest and honorable, clean in your person, and decent in your talk," but these scattered in the swirl of numbers like so many pious hopes. Restrictionists followed Theodore Roosevelt in deploring the "tangle of squabbling nationalities" as "the one certain way of bringing the nation to ruin," yet the fact remained that hyphenated Americanism was the only clear avenue to full citizenship. Even the hopeful immigrant Israel Zangwill, looking forward to the day of total assimilation, described a dream rather than reality. The composer-hero of Zangwill's popular play *The Melting Pot* hears the melodies for his "American symphony" in the "seething crucible—God's crucible," where a new amalgam, "the coming superman," is being forged over divine fires. Yet Zangwill told progressive audiences what they wanted to hear, not what they saw around them.

A clearer assessment of the forces of cultural pluralism came from the more reflective of the immigrants themselves, who exposed the progressive persuasion as the myth that it was. "There is no such thing as an American," a Polish priest informed the genteel social worker Emily Greene Balch. Poland, he explained, was a nation, but the United States was simply a country—in the beginning an empty land open to all comers in turn. Immigrants, according to the newly arrived Mary Antin, were just people who had missed the *Mayflower* and taken the next available boat.

A growing number of younger progressive intellectuals responded enthusiastically to the promise of cultural pluralism. In the variety and excitement of cultural clash they found an escape from the stifling middle-class gentility of Gilded Age homes. One of them, a young radical student of John Dewey's at Columbia University, Randolph Bourne, found a title for this cultural diversity— "Trans-National America"—and hailed the United States as the "intellectual battleground of the world . . . a cosmopolitan federation of national colonies, of foreign cultures, from whom the sting of devastating competition has been removed."

Bourne's concept of America as a world federation in miniature ran headlong into the barriers of exclusivist fears. The myth of the "new immigrants" assumed a variety of ugly shapes: they were dangerously illiterate and culturally deprived; they brought with them either a benighted Catholicism or private visions of the overthrow of capitalist society, they were doomed to a permanently inferior place in the Darwinian scale of races and could never master the skills democracy demanded. Amateur and professional sociologists, Cassandras all, consulted the numbers and predicted "race suicide." The sociologist Franklin Giddings announced hopefully but somewhat ambiguously that the "softening" of the traits of "preeminently an energetic, practical people, above all an industrial people"

organizations of political feminists with distinctly different views of the world conflict: a small group of militants who vehemently protested American participation and demonstrated against "Kaiser Wilson" with marches and hunger strikes; and a much larger group of moderates who supported the war in the belief that peace would bring victory to women as well as to the cause of democracy. In June 1919, Congress rewarded the patience of the moderates by passing the Nineteenth Amendment, thereby giving the vote to all adult Americans regardless of sex. Yet the cause of democracy and reform, American women would soon learn, was not to be determined one way or the other by their sudden invasion of the polls. A genuine pluralist alternative to rule by male politicians never really materialized. Women, their arguments to the contrary notwithstanding, did not compose an interest group with special needs and talents, nor did their egalitarian arguments alter the course of progressivism. Proposals for a great recasting of industrial society and the reordering of American priorities properly belonged only to the socialists.

SUFFRAGETTE AT WORK

(*Brown Brothers.*)

Paradise Lost: Socialism in America

American socialism in the years before the First World War presented the odd spectacle of a lively critique of the capitalist system developed by an inventive but faction-ridden party drifting steadily away from its nineteenth-century European revolutionary moorings. Despite a collectivist ideology, socialism in action embodied a Jeffersonian pluralism that defied the bidding of progressive nationalists. In its salad days between 1900 and 1914, the socialist movement followed a pattern of checkered regionalism as old as the nation itself. Party members included industrial workers in the cities of the Northeast, old ethnics in the urban enclaves of the upper Midwest, agrarians with memories of Populism in the Plains States, hard-bitten miners and lumber stiffs from the Rocky Mountains and the Pacific Northwest, and a cadre of college-trained intellectuals preaching everything from Fabianism and Christian Socialism to revolution-for-the-hell-of-it. If socialists never quite lived up to their reputation as the chief American menace to order and decency, they nevertheless presented a case against corporate capitalism that progressives found deeply disturbing.

Socialism as a significant political force dated from the turn of the century. In 1901 disgruntled members of the Socialist Labor party, fed up with the dictatorial ways of its hard-lining Marxist leaders, bolted, and collecting other splinter groups like Eugene Debs's Social Democratic party, formed the Socialist party of America. The 94,000 votes Debs won in the presidential election of 1900 marked the beginning of a revisionist drift among a majority of American socialists towards the center and of a theory of nonviolent parliamentary socialism, a move not always clear to the embattled participants themselves.

American socialism showed two faces. To progressive outsiders it continued to threaten the replacement of their capitalist system. According to socialists, capitalism was traveling a historically determined route to oblivion, destroying small-scale enterprise, saturating international markets, and establishing spheres of influence along the way. Although the socialist account of the rise and fall of industrial capitalism touched a few raw nerves, most progressives comforted themselves with the conviction that neither class war nor the degradation of the working class in the United States appeared very likely. Yet to most Americans before the First World War the very vehemence of the socialist prophecy constituted a menace that appeared to stem from an organized conspiracy of malcontents and madmen. Accordingly, progressive society prepared to deal with its enemy and to dispose of it in the best way it knew how, by intimidation and suppression.

Socialists themselves, on the other hand, seemingly confronted the riddle of the Sphinx propounded by American developments. Their list of unanswered questions lengthened as capitalism continued to display surprising powers of recuperation. Did the immediate gains of shorter hours and improved working conditions strengthen class solidarity or simply adjust workers to a wage system over which they could exercise no real control? Could socialists accomplish more through political action—running candidates of their own—or was such politicking tantamount to betraying the interests of the working class? Was the overthrow of the capitalist order imminent, or would the takeover proceed only gradually, following the education of the workers? The socialist failure to reach agreement on such matters was taken by most progressives as proof of the absurdity of their ideas but also as a warning to a society willing to tolerate their foolishness.

Gradually, however, the center of the Socialist party began to be occupied by solid and sensible moderates—men like Milwaukee's shrewd tactician Victor Berger; New York's scarred veteran of innumerable ideological campaigns Morris Hillquit; and the "Pennsylvania Dutchman" James Hudson Maurer, who looked to an alliance with the AFL. This moderate center hoped to educate the country out of its capitalistic habits with the lessons of evolutionary socialism. They were bitterly opposed, from without by diehard members of the militant Socialist Labor Party, and also from within by their own left wing, which had converted to industrial unionism and direct action. In the years after 1900 the Socialist Party, far from solving its theoretical and organizational problems, continued to divide into camps of pragmatists and doctrinaires, "impossibilists" and "opportunists." The party, Algie Simons complained to fellow moderate William English Walling, was a precariously balanced seesaw with "a bunch of intellectuals" at one end, and on the other "a bunch of never-works, demagogues and would-be intellectuals, a veritable 'Lumpen Proletariat.'"

Of all the dissident left-wing groups careering out of the socialist orbit, the most alarming to progressives was the Industrial Workers of the World, a faction of industrial unionists led by "Big Bill" Haywood. The "Wobblies," as they were called by a derisive but apprehensive American public, rejected all forms of political action and recommended strikes and sabotage as the only way to build "the one big union." The IWW roused fear and resentment far out of proportion to its membership, which was mostly made up of unskilled and migratory workers, lumber stiffs, ore-boat hands, and all the other rejects of organizational society. The Wobblies saw their historic mission as the total destruction of capitalism and the forming of the new society "within the shell of the old." Progressives shuddered at the prospect.

During a brief and stormy existence, the Wobblies waged a bitter struggle for survival. Although they scored short-lived victories in strikes in the Pennsylvania steel town of McKees Rocks in 1907 and again in the Lawrence, Massachusetts mills in 1912, they lacked the funds and the organization for sustained unionizing drives. Their myth of the "general strike" and the vision of "One Big Union" served chiefly to rally the spirits of marginal men who dreamed of participatory democracy among the uprooted. At no time did the Wobblies threaten the American capitalist order.

Seen in proper historical perspective, the Wobblies represented the last futile attempt of a nineteenth-century frontier mentality to recover an imaginary world

without politics, where abundance automatically rewarded the natural cooperation of free men. "Big Bill" Haywood could have been addressing an audience
of progressives when he confessed his hopes for a future America:

I have had a dream that I have in the morning and at night and during the day, that there
will be a new society sometime in which there will be no battle between capitalist and wage-
earner . . . there will be no political government . . . but . . . experts will come together for
the purpose of discussing the means by which machinery can be made the slave of the
people instead of part of the people being made the slave of machinery.

Ironically, it was a progressive majority bent on finding another way of transcending politics with the rule of the experts that clubbed the Wobblies' dream to
death.

Socialists themselves were burdened with many of the same liabilities as their
more radical competitors—a tradition of local autonomy, fierce rivalries for leadership, and a host of competing views on the verdict of history. The choice of
Eugene Debs, with his enduring popularity, as the spokesman for a splintered
party was proof of Socialist divisions. Tall, angular, with a shambling gait and an
easy-going manner, Debs served the party faithfully as a national walking-delegate,
captivating hundreds of thousands with homely speeches punctuated by allusions
to America's past. When Debs walked out of Woodstock jail after serving a term
for violating a federal injunction during the Pullman strike, he left a confirmed
but confused socialist. His were the home-grown talents of the moral agitator,
his heroes the abolitionists Wendell Phillips and William Lloyd Garrison. When
it came to formulating a workable collectivist strategy, Debs vacillated between

EUGENE V. DEBS CAMPAIGNING

The Socialist party candidate
makes one of his innumerable
speeches in behalf of a lost cause.
(*Brown Brothers.*)

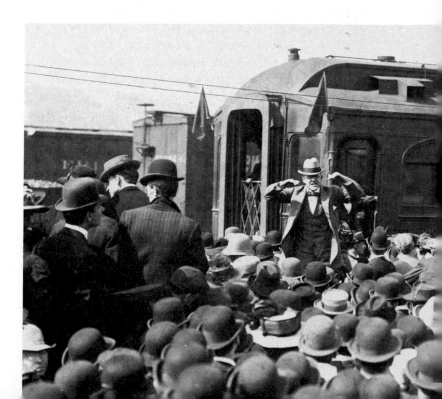

supporting left-wing industrial unionism and endorsing the moderate parliamentarians. A spellbinder with no large fund of useful ideas, he was nevertheless an able conciliator and a durable campaigner. In 1904 he won some 400,000
votes for his party, and four years later duplicated the feat with a whirlwind tour
by rail across the country in his "Red Special," giving up to twenty speeches a
day. The big leap in Socialist party totals, however, came in 1912 when voters
gave Debs nearly a million votes in his fourth try for the presidency.

Debs personified both the ethical force of the socialist critique of capitalism
and also its besetting organizational weakness. He cared little for the hard work
of running the party and warmed to the myths of participatory democracy. "I
never had much faith in leaders," he once admitted. "I am willing to be charged
with almost anything, rather than to be charged with being a leader. . . . Give me
the rank and file every day." Even though both wings of the party criticized his
leadership, Debs remained the choice of his rank and file from the halcyon prewar days through the lean years of socialist martyrdom during and after the war.

The chief socialist contribution to the American pluralist tradition was the
example it set of the open society it sought to create. The party posed as a model
of pluralism in action—a loosely organized, tactically divided intellectual community in rough agreement in its ethical condemnation of capitalism but unable
to unite on its application. These disagreements crystallized in the lives of the
young academics, artists, and intellectuals who were drawn to socialism as much
by its promise of cultural revolution as by its economic platform. Socialist intellectuals soon made it clear that they opposed both the moral pieties of progressivism and the bureaucratic collectivism of party centrists. They made their
spiritual home in the Intercollegiate Socialist Society, the brainchild of Upton
Sinclair, which was primarily composed of students and their teachers, artists,
and intellectuals.

The membership rolls of the ISS listed some of the most impressive and varied
intellectual talent in the country and proffered a range of critical analysis extending from the Fabianism of John Spargo to the protocommunism of Louis Budenz,
the civil liberties concerns of Roger Baldwin and Alexander Meiklejohn to the
protest fiction of Ernest Poole and Zona Gale, the latent progressivism of defectors
like Walter Lippmann to the pacifism of A. J. Muste and Jessie Wallace Hughan.
Connecting these diverse personalities was a strong distaste for the commercial
spirit generated by capitalism and an abiding fear of privilege. While the solid
burghers at the center of the party fed on the ordinary fare of meat-and-potato
socialism, the intellectuals preferred the lighter diet served up by Max Eastman's
The Masses, in which variety abounded and readers were admonished to "enjoy
the revolution." More serious moderates struggling for control of the movement
objected that such lightheartedness smacked of frivolity, not to say heresy. They
railed constantly at the inhabitants of "that nebulous middle world which lies
somewhere between the Socialist movement and the world of bourgeois complacency," a never-never land where undisciplined enthusiasts mixed "Socialism,

Anarchism, Communism, Sinn Feinism, Cubism, sexism, direct action and sabotage into a more or less harmonious mess."

Such complaints of workaday socialists were not altogether misguided although they betrayed a bias toward bureaucracy uncomfortably close to that of the progressives. In their most inspired moments Socialist intellectuals argued not merely the case against economic injustice but an ethical and an aesthetic set of perceptions as well. They found a Marxist world view less helpful than the pragmatic guidelines of William James and John Dewey. To them, socialism signified the preconditions for an age of altruistic experimentation, a conviction they had reached less through the study of Marx than an appreciative reading of Anglo-American revisionists like George Bernard Shaw, H. G. Wells, Graham Wallas, and Thorstein Veblen. Their expectations for socialism were as much psychological as sociological, and they combined their insights into the social creation of personality with an open-ended experimental outlook. Socialism, as redefined by the intellectuals, came to mean a rational, peaceful method of securing economic justice and social harmony.

The striking variety of American socialism, its shifting assessment of ends and means, and its inventiveness in tapping the rich reserves of American dissent made it a lively if not ultimately a powerful opponent of progressivism. Despite its brief successes on the local level the Socialist party was never a genuine political contender even before the First World War, and its greatest days were spent in vocal but isolated opposition to that war and the mindlessness of superpatriots. Its real role, like the role of the Populist party before it, was largely educational. And what it taught, more by example than by design, was the uses of secular, permissive open society. In so doing it supplied useful correctives for a compulsive progressive order from which Americans might have profited. Its disruption and decline with the coming war dealt a major setback to the Jeffersonian tradition.

The New Freedom

Woodrow Wilson's New Freedom followed the design outlined by his academic career and rested on his hopes for a strong presidency. The second half of Wilson's intellectual heritage, his scholarly background, led him to a prolonged examination of American institutions and leadership. His training at Johns Hopkins had come at a time when political scientists were beginning to set aside their preoccupation with constitutional questions and matters of sovereignty but had not yet acquired the economic and sociological techniques for examining how institutions really functioned. Wilson shared the progressive fascination with institutional politics, but his treatment of it remained curiously abstract. "My purpose," he announced in one of his books, "is to show . . . our constitutional system as it looks in operation." Yet the workaday reality of American politics was precisely what his analysis always lacked, the linking of larger social forces with political action. Despite frequent promises to "look below the surface" of American institutions Wilson was at his best in expounding a philosophy of politics that Theodore Roosevelt would have endorsed: "All the country needs is a new and sincere body of thought in politics, coherently, distinctly and boldly uttered by men who are sure of their ground." Like Roosevelt too, Wilson held that the key to effective democratic government rested in the hands of a powerful executive who offered "the best chance of leadership and mastery."

For Wilson, then, leadership, whether as head of a university, governor of a state, or President, involved a preference for governing attached to a contrary urge to dismantle concentrated federal power. These seeming contradictions— strong presidential leadership and diminution of regulatory power—were yoked together in his mind by the figure of the plebiscitarian leader like the great English prime minister, William Gladstone, who could sense the aspirations of the common people and give voice to them as commands to the parliamentarians. Yet there was a vacuum at the center of Wilson's liberalism in 1912, one that could not be filled with nineteenth-century pieties. More would be required than restoring old liberties and appealing to the "generous energies" of citizens. The federal government, in particular the power of the President, had its uses, as he clearly sensed. But the real question was whether it could be used to elimi- nate business coercion, break up communities of privilege, restore competition, and rescue the little man from the clutches of impersonal economic forces.

The chief architect of the New Freedom citadel was Louis Brandeis, the nation's leading progressive lawyer, who had made a career of tilting with big business. In the course of this prolonged combat Brandeis had worked out a full-blown alternative to Roosevelt s New Nationalism. His program rested on the conviction, reached by watching corporate capitalists play with other people's money, that the country was drifting steadily toward oligarchy. Financial oligar- chy, he predicted, would soon become political despotism through the same processes that once had made Caesar Augustus master of Rome. In alluding to the fate of Rome, Brandeis touched a sensitive Democratic nerve in Wilson, who also feared monopoly but had not yet devised an effective plan for controlling it. Brandeis supplied the guiding concepts for Wilson's first administration. The core of Brandeis's program was a dismantling operation that would ensure the survival of regulated competition by shoring up the small businessman, breaking up the new conglomerates, returning the marketplace to free enterprise, dispersing wealth more widely, and reaching down a helping hand to the working classes.

Out of the collaborative thinking of Wilson and Brandeis came the New Freedom's arraignment of monopoly and a not altogether convincing distinction between acceptable and antisocial business behavior, which recalled Roosevelt's similar attempts. Big business, Wilson agreed, was natural and thus inevitable, but trusts, on the other hand, were artificial and wholly undesirable. "A trust is an arrangement to get rid of competition, and a big business is a business that has survived competition by conquering in the field of intelligence and economy," the President announced, in explaining how it was that he could support big business and yet oppose monopoly. Wilson was further convinced of the impracticality of Roosevelt's plans for a regulatory commission to oversee the operations of big business. "As to the monopolies, which Mr. Roosevelt proposes to legalize and welcome, I know that they are so many cars of juggernaut, and I do not look forward with pleasure to the time when juggernauts are licensed and driven by commissioners of the United States." But could the New Freedom offer a better solution? Was destroying monopoly by antitrust suits really feasible?

Before Wilson tackled the monopolies he decided, with the aid of a sizable Democratic majority in the House and a solid contigent of party stalwarts in the Senate, to make good on the perennial promise to lower the tariff. Calling Congress into special session and breaking precedent by appearing in person, he called for immediate downward revision. The Underwood Tariff slid through the House on rails greased by a willing Democratic majority but in the Senate ran into a barrier erected by Republicans and party members representing sugar and wool interests. Using patronage adroitly, Wilson turned aside the attacks of the protectionists. The Underwood Tariff lowered duties a general 10 percent, placed the manufactured goods of the trusts on the free list, and added a small income tax as compensation. Wilson had redeemed an old party pledge but had also encountered the force of an interest-group pluralism different from the single grassroots impulse he had formerly envisioned.

Tariff reform tested Wilson's talents as an honest broker, but banking reform strained them to the limit. Most Americans were mainly interested in getting more flexible credit than the Eastern banking establishment was currently providing. But there were also vestiges of Andrew Jackson's Bank War in the revived contest between big bankers in the East with their hopes for a central banking system under their direct control and smaller regional bankers in the hinterland, who sought freedom from Wall Street in a thoroughly decentralized system. Ranged between these contenders was a third group of progressives in both parties who wanted a genuinely national system under government management that would ensure stability.

The Federal Reserve Act was thus the product of conflicting interest groups with diametrically opposed notions of what the country needed. Establishing twelve districts, each with a member-owned and member-directed Federal Reserve Bank, argued, in theory at least, a certain degree of decentralization and autonomy. But the creation of a new currency—Federal Reserve notes—and a supervisory seven-member board in Washington gave the federal government an effective instrument of monetary control.

Big bankers, however, need not have fretted. Much depended on the willingness of the Federal Reserve Board to interpret its powers generously, but the urge to direct the financial working of the nation proved not very vigorous in the next two decades. The immediate effect of the Federal Reserve Act was to strengthen rather than weaken the control of New York banks by consolidating their partnership with the government. Somewhere Wilson's concept of the "people" became lost. As a stabilizing device for corporate capitalism involving a minimum amount of government interference and direction, the Federal Reserve System worked with reasonable efficiency. As a "democratic" reform intended to parcel out financial power to the people, it was an illusion. "Like most other progressive regulatory measures," a recent student of progressivism has concluded, "the banking reform of 1913 replaced uncoordinated strivings with an orderly, more centralized apparatus very friendly to the industry it was mandated to guide. The gain for efficiency was immediate, but the gain for other social goals took years and a different climate to materialize."

Wilson's approach to the trusts also represented a capitulation to the logic of the New Nationalism. The confusions of a quarter-century's attempted enforcement of the Sherman Act had made clarification essential. The question was how to proceed? What degree of monopolistic control was permissible, and what constituted undue restraint? These questions the Clayton Act, as originally drafted in 1914, tried to answer with an interminable list of "thou shalt nots." The bill listed unfair trade practices in tedious and confusing detail. Congressional debate, however, along with the anguished cries from big business made it increasingly obvious that a complete list of forbidden practices was an impossibility and that any attempt to compile such a catalogue amounted to legislative insanity. Yet if it was impossible to specify each and every example of wrong conduct—to name the particular sin—then the only alternative lay in vesting a regulatory commission with the discretionary power to make concrete applications of a very general rule. Here was the course Roosevelt and his New Nationalists had advised all along, regulation rather than proscription and dismantlement.

In reluctantly agreeing to the commission proposal, Wilson jettisoned the moral compass of the New Freedom and steered for the shores of administrative government. His intentions in securing passage of the Federal Trade Commission Act in 1914 closely paralleled Roosevelt's, a scheme he had once so airily dismissed: the creation of an objective body of dispassionate experts whose ad hoc judgments rested on scientific evidence.

As a regulatory agency empowered to mediate conflicts between public efficiency and private economic opportunity, the Federal Trade Commission disappointed its progressive champions. During the First World War its functions in checking business concentration were greatly curtailed, and after the war even its fact-finding powers invited the wrath of both big business and Congress itself. Congressional conservatives demanded an investigation of its methods.

The courts, in a series of adverse decisions, stripped the FTC of its power to define unfair practices. Business simply defied it by denying it access to company records and ignoring its rulings. Only when a much chastened commission, staffed with compliant members agreed to serve as the handmaiden of big business instead of the policeman did the attacks cease. Government by commission in the 1920s provided no cure for a raging speculative fever.

In other areas of national life as well, Wilson's pluralistic dreams of liberating the energies of "the great struggling unknown masses of men" ended in perplexity and defeat. Not the "people" of his earlier progressive imaginings but highly organized interest groups, exacting and clamorous, descended on Washington seeking protection and advancement of their affairs. In some cases Wilson's administration prove openhanded. For newly organized farmers, rural credit facilities. For labor, a workman's compensation act for federal employees. For consumer groups, a National Child Labor Act. There were limits to Wilson's receptivity to interest-group politics, however; notably, he disapproved of women's suffrage, and he refused to lift the burden of antitrust suits from the backs of labor organizations. He also tacitly supported the secretary of the interior and the postmaster general in instituting segregation in their departments and only reluctantly reversed himself when liberals objected. Not all interests, it was clear, could command the attention of a broker president.

By 1916, as Americans watched the war in Europe settle into a protracted and bloody stalemate, the Wilson administration had largely completed its progressive program. The President's initial promise of reversal and restoration had met an early death. In each of his major attempts at reform—lowering the tariff, building the Federal Reserve System, controlling the trusts—the President, although he preferred dispersion, had been driven in precisely the opposite direction. A Tariff Commission to systematize the nation's trade policies. A Federal Reserve Board to manage the monetary affairs of the country. A Federal Trade Commission to police big business. The meaning of these reforms was unmistakable. More not less government. An increase rather than a decrease in governmental agencies. A greater instead of a lesser reliance on experts and bureaucratic procedure. A supportive relation rather than a supervisory one between government and the large, organized interest groups, whose activities it presumably sought to regulate in the name of the people. And presiding over this new system of interest-group competition a President fully as powerful as the most ambitious New Nationalist could have wished.

Pluralism of a different sort from that with which Wilson entered the presidency strengthened the federal government under the New Freedom and completed Roosevelt's bureaucratic revolution. By the time America entered the World War in 1917, progressivism had erected the foundations of a democratic state capitalism designed to house a people of abundance. No one could yet foresee how the forces of the administrative state would erode nineteenth-century values. It would take the war itself to drive that lesson home.

Suggested Readings

Two good general introductions to the study of immigration and assimilation are Maldwyn A. Jones, *American Immigration* (1960), and Leonard Dinnerstein and David Reimers, *Ethnic Americans: A History of Immigration and Assimilation* (1975). The hostile reactions of native Americans is chronicled in John Higham, *Strangers in the Land: Patterns of American Nativism* (1955), and Barbara Solomon, *Ancestors and Immigrants* (1965). Their conclusions are documented in Stanley Feldstein and Lawrence Costello, eds., *The Ordeal of Assimilation* (1974), and Leonard Dinnerstein and Frederic C. Jaher, eds., *The Aliens: A History of Ethnic Minorities in America* (1970). Oscar Handlin, *The Uprooted* (2d ed., 1973), though challenged on many points by more recent studies, is nevertheless a classic; also see Philip Taylor, *The Distant Magnet* (1971), particularly for the European setting. Milton Gordon, *Assimilation in American Life: The Role of Race, Religion and National Origins* (1964), and Nathan Glazer and Daniel Moynihan, *Beyond the Melting Pot: Negroes, Jews, Italians and Irish of New York City* (1963), correct old American myths of easy assimilation.

The literature on specific minorities is extensive. Among the best collective portraits are Moses Rischin, *The Promised City: New York's Jews, 1870–1914* (1970); Arthur S. Goren, *New York Jews and the Quest for Community: The Kehillah Experiment, 1908–1922* (1970); Irving Howe, *World of Our Fathers: The Journey of the East European Jews to America and the Life They Found and Made* (1976); Humbert Nelli, *The Italians of Chicago, 1880–1920* (1970); Richard Gambino, *Blood of My Blood* (1974); Roger Daniels, *The Politics of Prejudice* (1968); Stanford M. Lyman, *Chinese Americans* (1974); Stephan Thernstrom, *The Other Bostonians: Poverty and Progress in the American Metropolis, 1880–1970* (1973).

August Meier, *Negro Thought in America, 1880–1915* (1963), is the best general assessment of black aspirations and programs during these years. George Fredrickson, *The Black Image in the White Mind, 1817–1914* (1972), contains several enlightening chapters on responses of the whites to the "race problem," and Jack Temple Kirby, *Darkness at the Dawning: Race and Reform in the Progressive South* (1972), gives an accurate estimate of the social price of progressive reform. The story of Harlem is well told in Gilbert Osofsky, *Harlem, The Making of a Ghetto, 1890–1930* (1966). For the Chicago equivalent, see Allan H. Spear, *Black Chicago* (1967). Louis R. Harlan, *Booker T. Washington: The Making of a Black Leader, 1856–1901* (1972), is a definitive account of the early years of that leader, and Elliot M. Rudwick, *W. E. B. DuBois: Propagandist of the Negro Protest* (1969), analyzes the early contributions of a mercurial black Progressive. Organizational problems and institutional developments are thoroughly covered in Charles F. Kellogg, *NAACP: A History of the National Association for the Advancement of Colored People, 1909–1920* (1970); Nancy Weiss, *The National Urban League, 1910–1940* (1974); and Joyce Ross, *J. E. Spingarn and the Rise of the NAACP* (1972).

Two readable surveys of women's rights and social feminism are Eleanor Flexner, *Century of Struggle: The Woman's Rights Movement in the United States* (1959) and Lois Banner, *Women in Modern America* (1974). Aileen Kraditor, *The Ideas of the Women's Suffrage Movement, 1890–1920* (1965), is indispensable for understanding the ideology but should be supplemented by Alan P. Grimes, *The Puritan Ethic and Woman Suffrage* (1967). William O'Neill presents an impressive range of individual portraits in *Everyone Was Brave: The Rise and Fall of Feminism in America* (1969). David Morgan, *Suffragists and Democrats: The Politics of Woman Suffrage in America* (1972), thoroughly analyzes political developments. For a useful study of the problem of work, see Robert Smuts, *Women and Work in America* (1959).

American socialism has been fully treated in a number of solid monographs: Ira A. Kipnis, *The American Socialist Movement, 1897–1912* (1952); Howard Quint, *The Forging of*

American Socialism (1953); David Shannon, *The Socialist Party of America: A History* (1955); James Weinstein, *The Decline of Socialism in America* (1967); and Daniel Bell, *Marxian Socialism in the United States* (1967). Donald D. Egbert and Stow Persons, eds., *Socialism and American Life* (2 vols., 1952), contains much useful documentary material. John H. M. Laslett, *Labor and the Left: A Study of Socialist and Radical Influences in the American Labor Movement, 1881–1924* (1970), explains a limited socialist impact on American workers. David Hereshoff, *American Disciples of Marx: From the Age of Jackson to the Progressive Era* (1967), covers a range of contributors to American socialism.

A brief but excellent survey of the rest of the radical spectrum is contained in John P. Diggins, *The American Left in the Twentieth Century* (1973). Melvyn Dubofsky, *We Shall Be All: A History of the Industrial Workers of the World* (1969), is a brilliant history of the movement; Paul F. Brissenden, *The IWW: A Study of American Syndicalism* (1919), provides useful documentation in addition, and Patrick Renshaw, *Wobblies: The Story of Syndicalism in the United States* (1967), is also valuable. Joseph R. Conlin, *Big Bill Haywood and the Radical Union Movement* (1969), improves on "Big Bill's" *Autobiography* (1929). Christopher Lasch, *The New Radicalism in America, 1889–1963* (1965), presents a persuasive indictment of cultural radicalism in the Progressive era.

On the intellectual and cultural transformation of American society after 1912 Henry F. May, *The End of American Innocence* (1959), is now standard. Lawrence Veysey, *The Emergence of the American University* (1970), analyzes the institutional growth of American higher education, and Richard Hofstadter and Walter Metzger, *The Development of Academic Freedom in the United States* (1955), recounts the struggle for academic autonomy. Joseph Blau, *Men and Movements in American Philosophy* (1952), covers the contributions of the pragmatists, and Nathan G. Hale, Jr., *Freud and the Americans: The Beginnings of Psychoanalysis in America, 1876–1917* (1971), is a detailed discussion of the development of Freudianism in the United States. Literary histories of the Age of Realism are numerous. Still the best discussions of important writers are Alfred Kazin, *On Native Grounds* (1942), and two volumes by Maxwell Geismar, *Rebels and Ancestors: The American Novel, 1890–1915* (1953), and *The Last of the Provincials: The American Novel, 1915–1925*. Jay Martin, *Harvest of Change: American Literature, 1865–1914* (1967), is a generally informative survey with good discussions of Henry James and Henry Adams. Michael Millgate, *American Social Fiction* (1964), traces the rise of a genre. Kenneth S. Lynn, *William Dean Howells: An American Life* (1970), is a sympathetic if critical assessment of a fractured artistic sensibility.

For illuminating discussions of significant contributors to the Progressive reform outlook, see two particularly valuable studies: Daniel M. Fox, *The Discovery of Abundance: Simon Patten and the Transformation of Social Theory* (1967), and Barry D. Karl, *Charles E. Merriam and the Study of Politics* (1974). James Gilbert, *Designing the Industrial State: The Intellectual Pursuit of Collectivism in America, 1880–1940* (1972), is an informative study.

Indispensable for an understanding of Wilson and the New Freedom is the magisterial Arthur S. Link, *Wilson* (5 vols., 1947–65), although the hostile John Blum, *Woodrow Wilson and the Politics of Morality* (1956), and John A. Garraty, *Woodrow Wilson* (1956), offer critical insights unavailable to the sympathetic Link; so does the psychoanalytical portrait, Alexander and Juliette George, *Woodrow Wilson and Colonel House: A Personality Study* (1956). William Diamond, *The Economic Thought of Woodrow Wilson* (1943), examines the shaky theoretical underpinnings of the New Freedom, and Melvin Urofsky, *Big Steel and the Wilson Administration* (1969), canvasses aspects of the Wilsonian labor policy.

Biographies of other important figures during the New Freedom years include Dorothy Rose Blumberg, *Florence Kelley: The Making of a Social Pioneer* (1966); Charles Larsen, *The Good Fight: The Life and Times of Ben Lindsey* (1972); Julius Weinberg, *Edward Alsworth Ross and the Sociology of Progressivism* (1972); Robert C. Bannister, *Ray Stannard Baker: The Mind and Thought of a Progressive* (1966); and H. C. Bailey, *Edgar Gardner Murphy* (1968).

28

The Path to Power

American Foreign Policy

1890-1917

For most of the nineteenth century Americans managed their affairs without a foreign policy. The defeat of Napoleon and the success of the American peace commissioners following a nearly disastrous war with England closed an era of diplomatic defeat for the new nation perched precariously on the rim of the Atlantic world and subject to the buffetings of the two major European powers. After 1815, geographical and ideological separation gave the American people an open continental field to explore and exploit. By midcentury George Washington's original prediction of a peculiar American destiny had seemingly become a providential fact. Secure in its continental fastness, its hemispheric dominance guaranteed by English sea power, the United States turned inward to expand its borders and develop its resources.

This favorable international climate together with unlimited opportunity at home fostered extravagant versions of an American 'Manifest Destiny, which at one time or another pointed to the annexation of Canada, the acquisition of Cuba, and the taking of "all Mexico." Geopolitical prophets dreamed of the Caribbean as an American lake or of the Mississippi valley as the center of a vast heartland empire that extended eastward across the Atlantic and westward to

China shores. But these flickering dreams of empire, like the immoderate reck-
onings of the farmers and the conjectures of manufacturers and shippers, were
predictions rather than policy directives for a people busy planting the Garden
of the World and producing an increasing variety of manufactured goods.
In spite of sporadic American interest in the fate of republican movements in
Europe, Manifest Destiny remained mostly an article for home consumption—
exuberant and aggressive but not really for export

The slavery question also checked the American expansionist appetite after
the Mexican War as the debate over its future in the territories monopolized the
national attention. With mounting ferocity planters and free soilers charged
each other with clandestine schemes for spreading or checking slavery in the
territories. Americans, who were confronted with an insoluble moral problem,
prepared for war and forgot about foreign affairs.

By the last quarter of the nineteenth century, however, the belief in a separate
American destiny was being overturned by a series of developments that began
to draw the United States into the vortex of international power politics. The
most ominous of these signs was the sudden imperialist activity of the major
European powers—first England, then France, Germany, and Russia—who
proceeded to carve generous colonial portions for themselves out of the hinterland of Asia and Africa. American diplomats and their political masters
in Washington watched with growing apprehension as the European powers,
following the dictates of capital investment, scrambled for possessions and spheres
of influence in the undeveloped regions of the world.

Still, in the course of his inaugural address in 1885 President Grover Cleveland
could pause to say only a brief word about his foreign policy. His words were
reassuring to those Americans who still considered foreign affairs a distraction.
The genius of American institutions and the real needs of the people, Cleveland
explained, dictated a "scrupulous avoidance of any departure from that foreign
policy commended by the history, the traditions, and the prosperity of our Republic." In case his audience might have forgotten their primary responsibilities
in contemplating European imperialism the President restated the traditional
policy of the United States towards the rest of the world. "It is the policy of
independence, favored by our position. . . . It is the policy of peace suitable to
our interests. It is the policy of neutrality, rejecting any share in foreign broils
and ambitions upon other continents and repelling their intrusion here,"

Cleveland's attitudes were embodied in the dilapidated foreign-policy establishment over which he presided. A casual and still largely amateur operation,
it had no very effective fact-gathering apparatus, and although it boasted a handful of able diplomats, was saddled with a great many more political friends and
nonentities. Most of the useful information trickling back to Washington from
European capitals came from cosmopolitan private citizens concerned with the
shifting scenes of international politics as the vast majority of their countrymen
obviously were not. Until 1890, Europe seemed willing to take the American pro-

fession of international disinterest at face value as a declaration of intent to remain a second-class power. The diplomatic corps resident in Washington was not on the whole a distinguished one, and on more than one occasion a European state simply neglected to fill a vacant post that had come to appear superfluous.

Yet at the very moment when Cleveland spoke the platitudes that had passed for a foreign policy throughout the nineteenth century, new intellectual forces were beginning to collect around a different set of propositions drawn directly from a scrutiny of European imperialist scrambles. Lord Bryce, whose perceptive analysis of American government and society, *The American Commonwealth*, appeared in 1888, noted the difference between the foreign-policy influentials in England and their counterparts in the United States. In America, Bryce explained, "there are individual men corresponding to individuals in that English set, and probably quite as numerous." There were a sizable number of journalists of real ability, a handful of literary men, and not a few politicians who understood the mechanisms of power politics. Yet this American intellectual class remained isolated and disorganized, constantly subject to popular pressures and mass opinion as the "first set" in England clearly was not. "In England the profession of opinion-making and leading is the work of specialists; in America . . . of amateurs. By the time Bryce published his observation, however, a small group of congenial amateurs were already at work in Washington building the foundations of a foreign-policy establishment and beginning to call for a more active pursuit of world power.

The Origins of American Expansionism

By 1890 it began to dawn on an American foreign-policy public only recently recruited to the standards of national interest that the United States was in danger of being left behind in the race for territory and markets. A decade later the unblushing expansionist Senator Albert J. Beveridge summed up the lessons of the intervening years with the reminder that, like it or not, the American people had become the trustees "under God" of world civilization. "He has made us the master organizers of the world to establish system where chaos reigns." Not all Beveridge's countrymen agreed that destiny had mapped an imperial course for their country, but it was clear to them that they could no longer view the international scene with indifference.

A second force propelling the United States into the imperialist scramble, concern with world markets, was less easy to measure precisely. After 1875, American businessmen, bankers, industrialists, and shippers began to call for ready access to the markets of the world; their demands were given dramatic point by periodic depressions and doubts concerning the capacity of domestic markets to absorb what was generally considered a glut of manufactured goods and staples.

Still, the size of the American foreign market in the undeveloped areas of the

SENATOR BEVERIDGE'S "TRUSTEES" PACIFYING THE PHILIPPINES

(*Oregon Historical Society.*)

world remained relatively small as late as 1900, and the recurrent demand for enlarging it often spoke to promise rather than current realities. The discussion of markets provided an idiom for popular debate—a political grammar with which expansionists and antiexpansionists, interventionists and isolationists, realists and idealists, argued the proper role of the United States in world affairs. No one denied the importance of foreign markets as visible symbols of American prosperity and the chief instrument for spreading the blessings of democracy. But did the search for markets mean intervening in the domestic affairs of undeveloped and unstable countries? Did it require outright annexation? Were markets for investment capital different from markets for manufactured goods? And most troublesome of all, how could the spokesmen for expanded foreign markets catch and hold the attention of an unresponsive federal government?

A third force propelling the United States into the world arena could more properly be called a condition. The 1890s in many ways made up an American social crisis comprising severe economic dislocation, class conflict, political instability and intellectual discord. The cumulative effect of these tensions was a vague but intense popular conviction that the United States had passed the point of no return on its march to modernity. Whether or not they pondered Frederick Jackson Turner's warnings of the social consequences of the closing of the frontier, many Americans were acutely aware of the passing of an era of development in which free land and geographical mobility had been determinative. Viewed as fact or metaphor, the frontier had dominated the American imagination for two centuries, and the announcement of its closing, no matter how premature, reinforced a sense of irreversible change. In the twentieth century the concept of the frontier would enter the popular vocabulary in mythological form as the "urban frontier" and the various "frontiers" of science, technology, and education. But for the generation of the 1890s the simple extension of the concept out into space towards the equator and across the Pacific quickened a sense of mission and released pent-up feelings of humanitarianism as though the answer to their loss of certainty at home was a vigorous pursuit of democratic purpose abroad.

Across the rising ground of ideological debate leading to war with Spain in 1898 and the winning of empire, two traditional sets of partisans struggled to control an emergent American foreign policy. The actual contestants appeared in a number of guises in the quarter-century before American entrance into the First World War: upholders of international law and advocates of national power; preachers of pacifism and sponsors of preparedness; champions of arbitration and defenders of American honor. However distinct in style and manner, the participants in the great debate over the proper role for the United States ranged themselves behind two conflicting formulations of power and responsibility.

The first view of the nature of power and the future of the national state was admirably summarized for his generation by Captain Alfred Thayer Mahan, naval strategist and geopolitical theorist, in his *The Interest of America in Sea Power, Present and Future* (1897). Since governments, Mahan argued, could not be expected to act on any ground except national interest, it followed that patriotism and the will to fight were the indispensable attributes of a great people.

Not in universal harmony, nor in any fond dream of unbroken peace, rest now the best hopes of the world. . . . Rather in the competition of interests, in that reviving sense of nationality . . . in the jealous determination of each people to provide first for its own . . . are to be heard the assurance that decay has not touched yet the majestic fabric erected by so many centuries of courageous battling.

For a convincing explanation of the second and opposing view of the American mission, William Jennings Bryan reached down to the rich metaphorical soil of the Midwest. Nations, Bryan insisted, redeem only by force of example. "Example may be likened to the sun, whose genial rays constantly coax the buried seed into life, and clothe the earth, first with verdure, and afterward with ripened grain; while violence is the occasional tempest, which can ruin, but cannot give life."

Mahan's invitation to national greatness took precedence, at least for the moment, over Bryan's warnings as to its costs. Mahan had spent most of his career wandering about the world observing the kaleidoscopic patterns of European imperial politics, and now his warning to Americans was unequivocal. The United States, he announced, must quickly formulate and apply an aggressive expansionist policy based on naval supremacy and undisputed control of the world's sea lanes, a vigorous development of foreign markets, and an energetic cultivation of the domestic spiritual resources needed to sustain the new national mission.

To most Americans accustomed to the comforts of isolationism, Mahan's message came as a shock. In a Darwinian world of clashing national states, he argued, the United States must organize itself into a spiritual and military garrison ready to defend its interests with power. Mahan did not deny the existence of a universal law of conscience, but he anchored it in the concept of the national state fully apprised of its duty and prepared to perform it. In his view the "evils of war" paled before the dangers of "moral compliance with wrong." In the last analysis all depended on the disposition of the American people to take up their appointed tasks as the democratic saviors of the world and the guarantors of a Pax Americana. "The sentiment of a people is the most energetic element in national action," he insisted. The meaning of Mahan's argument was unmistakable: "Whether they will or no, Americans must now begin to look outward."

Mahan's arguments won him enthusiastic support in England and Germany, and were also warmly received by a small circle of American influentials whose own estimates of the international situation had led them to conclude that the

THE GREAT WHITE FLEET AND DIRTY BLACK SMOKE

In 1907 President Roosevelt dispatched the new American navy on a world cruise as a display of American strength. (*Brown Brothers.*)

United States must take its place among the imperialist powers. "You are head and shoulders above us all," wrote Roosevelt in promising Mahan to do all he could "toward pressing your ideas into effect." Roosevelt was joined by other important converts to the captain's doctrines: John Hay, soon to become McKinley's acerbic secretary of state; the freewheeling radical-reactionaries Brooks and Henry Adams and their protégé, Massachusetts Senator Henry Cabot Lodge; young, aggressive cosmopolitans like Richard Olney and staid conservatives like Joseph Choate; the academic popularizer John Fiske with his own version of the new Manifest Destiny; and the social-gospelist-turned-jingo, Josiah Strong, whose best-selling *Our Country* (1885) developed the evangelical case for renewal through expansion.

Until 1895 and the eruption of the Cuban crisis, however, the influence of these ambitious formulators of a "large policy" for the United States remained limited chiefly to those members of Congress with an interest in shipbuilding and naval rearmament and to a few career diplomats like William Rockhill, an old China hand with grandiose visions of his own. But gradually from this ideological core there developed a loose network of informed opinion concerning the need for expanding American opportunity, views increasingly expressed in metropolitan dailies and liberal journals and calling for a more realistic appraisal of America's needs. Still, not until 1896 and the election of McKinley would this rudimentary foreign-policy establishment gain a hearing for its proposals, and by that time it too was caught up in a mass popular uprising, partly humanitarian, partly chauvinist, demanding the rescue of the Cuban insurgents.

In the meantime the temperature of American diplomacy continued to rise alarmingly as though events in Latin America and the Pacific were responding to American demands by providing a hothouse climate for nourishing hardier

strains of diplomacy. A series of minor crises early in the 1890s served notice of America's intentions to take a firmer hand in managing international relations by asserting national interests and defending national honor whenever opportunity arose. In Samoa it was the threat of a German protectorate that brought United States naval forces steaming into the harbor at Apia in time to be destroyed by a typhoon. In Chile a barroom brawl involving American sailors ended in an American ultimatum to Valparaiso. And in Venezuela in 1895 a boundary dispute between England and an unstable and improvident Latin American state called forth a declaration of American omnipotence in the Western Hemisphere. "Today," Richard Olney, Cleveland's secretary of state, boasted to the startled British, "the United States is practically sovereign on this continent, and its fiat is law upon the subjects to which it confines its interposition . . . its infinite resources combined with its isolated position renders it master of the situation and practically invulnerable against any or all other powers." By 1896 events like these, evoking a disproportionate American belligerence, had paved the way for a popular crusade in behalf of Cuban independence.

The limits of popular pressure for expanding United States commitments, however, became clear in the abortive attempt to annex Hawaii following an American-engineered coup in the islands in 1893. Commercial interests pressed hard for annexation; Protestant missionaries welcomed the chance to finish the job of converting the heathen; global strategists stressed the key location of Hawaii athwart the trade lanes to the Asian mainland; and only a tiny group of anti-annexationists led by the venerable Carl Schurz objected on grounds of principle to taking the islands. The *Independent* summed up the traditional arguments for annexation in a timeworn metaphor: "The ripe apple falls into our hands, and we should be very foolish to throw it away."

President Cleveland, however, was fully prepared to resist the public outcry and called for an investigation of the circumstances of the recent revolution against the native queen. Convinced that the coup had been the work of a small group of powerful white planters and businessmen and that the great majority of the native population remained loyal to the monarchy, he preemptorily withdrew the treaty of annexation from the Senate. Without the overwhelming support of an aroused public and confronted by an executive firmly opposed to their designs, the annexationists were forced to bide their time. Hawaii in 1893 afforded neither the right time nor the right place for flexing American muscles. In Cuba five years later it would be different.

President McKinley's "Wonderful Experience"

In 1895, the Cuban revolution, which had been smoldering for nearly a quarter of a century, flared once again, and Spain dispatched fifty thousand soldiers to extinguish it. American sympathies, a mixture of humanitarian outrage and "jingo" bluster, instinctively went to the underdogs, who were widely credited with a wholesome intent to establish a Yankee-style republic. The insurrectionists responded to this encouragement pouring in from the North by dispatching a high-powered lobby to New York City with instructions to raise money and supplies while keeping William Randolph Hearst's and Joseph Pulitzer's reporters amply provided with atrocity stories. It was not long before the Cuban junta in New York received support from unexpected quarters—from Latin American trading interests, promoters of an isthmian canal, a variety of patriotic groups, and even trade unions. Carefully planned "spontaneous" rallies across the country whipped up sentiment for American intervention as Democrats and Populists joined their Republican rivals in denouncing Spain and calling for a declaration of support for the Cubans.

This mounting popular clamor was echoed in Congress, where two resolutions were reported out of the Senate Foreign Relations Committee: a majority report recommending immediate recognition of Cuban belligerency, and a minority report calling for active intervention. It soon became obvious to the incoming McKinley administration that the President would have to move quickly to avoid capture by a bellicose public mood that could give force but not direction to his policy.

In 1896 the exact meaning of this public concern for the fate of the Cuban revolution was not altogether clear. To the small group of advocates of the "large

THE SPANISH BRUTE
ADDS MUTILATION TO MURDER.

"THE SPANISH BRUTE ADDS MUTILATION TO MURDER"

The jingoistic tone of the American press during the Spanish-American War is revealed in this cartoon. (*Culver Pictures, Inc.*)

policy," intervention appeared a foregone conclusion. Roosevelt, who admitted to being "a quietly rampant 'Cuba Libre' man," informed Mahan that intervention was inevitable if the country was to retain its self-respect as a nation. Many expansionists agreed: the Cuban business would afford a heaven-sent opportunity for annexing Hawaii. But as for Cuba itself, no one could predict. Roosevelt himself, while angrily discounting "the craven fear and brutal selfishness of the mere money-getters" who opposed American intervention, doubted the wisdom of annexing Cuba "unless the Cubans wished it." "I don't want it to seem that we are engaged merely in a land-grabbing war," he admitted. Until war was declared there was little support for the idea of continuing United States involvement in the island even among the most vocal enthusiasts for intervention.

In the fiercely contested presidential election of 1896 the issue of Cuba had given way to domestic problems of free silver and the tariff. It took the renewed campaigns of the insurrectionists in December 1896, and the murder of their leader, Maceo, to raise the ire of an American public once again. This time the pattern of response was different; instead of planned demonstrations and organized rallies there were outbursts of protest across the country, genuinely spontaneous meetings in which businessmen joined patriots and humanitarians in demanding an end to Spanish rule. From now on McKinley's administration would have to contend with a powerful popular indignation.

At this point Spain added fuel to the interventionist fire as her troops in the island began to enforce a brutal program of reconcentration, herding suspected Cubans into makeshift camps, where they died by the thousands. Meanwhile an irresolute government in Madrid continued to agonize over the dwindling number of options left to it. A decaying monarchy, torn between rival factions of liberals and conservatives, unable to pacify the island but unwilling to give it up, Spain temporized hopelessly. Confusion was nearly as great within the McKinley administration, as the President found himself already caught in a verbal crossfire between Republican jingoes crying for justice at the point of an American sword and his conservative business backers fearful of the effects of a war on economic recovery. As popular pressure for intervention mounted, McKinley was also driven to temporize, publicly demanding promises of instant reform from Madrid while quietly reining in the jingoes in his party with promises of his own.

By 1897 the horrors of the reconcentration program had forced the President to press for firmer Spanish concessions when a series of incidents further strained relations between the two countries. First came the release of an indiscreet letter from the Spanish minister in Washington to his government in which he ungenerously but not inaccurately characterized McKinley as "weak" and "a bidder for the admiration of the crowd, besides being a would-be politician who tries to leave a door open behind him while keeping on good terms with the jingoes of his party." Then came the explosion in Havana harbor that destroyed the battleship *Maine* and multiplied rumors of Spanish complicity in what Senator Lodge called a "gigantic murder, the last spasm of a corrupt and dying society." Now at last the jingoes formed the vanguard of an aroused American public demanding retaliation in the name of justice and democracy.

McKinley's dilemma became more painful as conflicting reports of Spanish intentions came flooding in, accounts of the ministry's complete intransigence on the one hand, and assurances of its willingness to comply with demands for "full self-government" on the other. Given the choice between waiting and taking immediate action, McKinley finally capitulated. Two days after Spain had agreed to his demands for an immediate armistice and an end to reconcentration —while still declining to grant Cuban independence—the President sent a message to Congress requesting authority to intervene and restore peace in the island. By the time word of Spain's partial compliance reached Washington it was already too late: McKinley could now admit formally what had been obvious for some time, that the issue rested with Congress. Intervention, he realized, was tantamount to war, and Congress made the decision official on April 19, 1898, by recognizing that a state of war existed. Lacking a clearly defined set of goals and the diplomatic means of implementing them, caught in a domestic political crossfire, McKinley was forced to accept the prospect of what John Hay called a "splendid little war" for no very compelling reasons of national interest.

In the brief contest that followed, the United States made short work of Spain's decrepit navy and demoralized army. Commodore George Dewey's Asiatic squadron promptly demolished the monarchy's Pacific fleet in the Battle of Manila Bay, and the Atlantic squadron as easily penned up Cervera's ships in Santiago and systematically destroyed them. Spanish troops scarcely improved on this

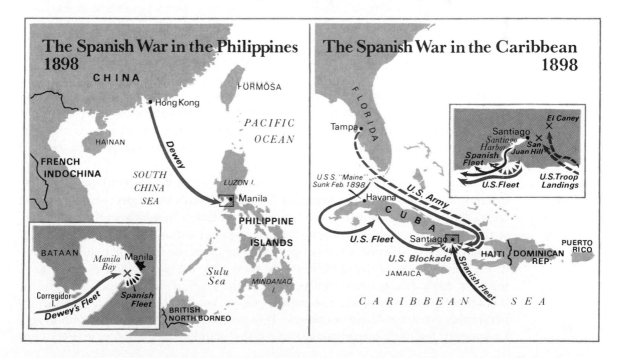

performance against poorly trained, badly equipped, disorganized American forces. After endless confusion General William R. Shafter finally succeeded in assembling some eighteen thousand troops for an invasion of Cuba and managed to land his army, complete with press corps, foreign dignitaries, and well-wishers, near Santiago, where Roosevelt and his Rough Riders seized the lion's share of the glory in what the Colonel called a "bully fight." The Battle of Santiago capped the successes of the navy, and American soldiers settled in on the jungle heights above San Juan, where more of them died from disease than in actual combat. A small expeditionary force dispatched to nearby Puerto Rico encountered no real resistance. By August 1898, its meager military resources entirely spent and its morale shattered, Spain gave up and signed the peace protocol.

The problem of disposing of the remnants of the Spanish empire caught McKinley's administration by surprise. In the case of Cuba, Congress in an unaccountable burst of altruism had rushed through the Teller Amendment, declaring the island free and independent and disavowing any American intentions of annexation. Not for conquest nor for empire had American soldiers fought so bravely, but, as one Republican senator put it, "for humanity's sake . . . to aid a people who have suffered every form of tyranny and who have made a desperate struggle to be free." Within a year these professions of disinterest would be strained to the breaking point.

The new problem of the Philippines together with the old question of Hawaii compounded McKinley's difficulties. "If old Dewey had just sailed away when he smashed the Spanish fleet, what a lot of trouble he would have saved us," the President grumbled, confessing that he "could not have told where those darned islands were within 2000 miles"—a not entirely candid remark, since he had ordered an invasion force to Manila even before Dewey announced his victory. But with the quick collapse of Spain the barriers to empire began to fall, both within the administration and in the country at large, as groups once hostile to the idea of acquiring new territory suddenly began to weigh its advantages. Business opinion, banking and mercantile interests, church organizations, and even social reformers joined in calling for the retention of the Philippines, if not as a permanent possession, at least as a temporary way station on the route to vast Asian markets.

When the Senate came to debate the merits of annexation, the opponents of the new imperialism argued strenuously that "political dominion" was not "commercially necessary" and that the United States ought to satisfy itself with a few coaling stations and naval yards. But the logic of expansion ran against these anti-imperialists. If commercial opportunity dictated the need for political stability in both Hawaii and the Philippines, then why not go the full distance and secure it while lifting untutored peoples to the level of democratic self-government? McKinley now spoke the popular mood as previously he had failed to in presenting a narrow range of choices. It would be "cowardly and pusillanimous," he insisted, for the United States "to turn the islands back to Spain, giving them

The battleship *Maine* on the morning after the explosion, and Theodore Roosevelt surrounded by his Rough Riders. (*Above, The National Archives; left, Theodore Roosevelt Collection, Harvard College Library.*)

power again to misrule the natives." Equally "despicable" was the thought of handing them over to England or allowing Japan to take them by default.

There is only one logical course to pursue. Spain has shown herself unfit to rule her colonies, and those [that] have come into our possession as a result of war, must be held, if we are to fulfill our destinies as a nation . . . giving them the benefits of a christian civilization which has reached its highest developement [*sic*] under our republican institutions.

For the moment the benefits—spiritual and material—appeared to outweigh the costs of empire.

With the debate over the peace terms there emerged a small but vocal group of "anti-imperialists," hastily assembled and representing a wide variety of arguments against seizing new territory. The nucleus of this anti-imperialist opposition consisted of a group of venerable mid-nineteenth-century liberals whose advanced age and recent Mugwump obsessions with political corruption constituted their distinguishing mark and their chief liability. The veteran antislavery campaigner Carl Schurz was 71; the free trader Edward Atkinson, 73; the Republican maverick George F. Hoar, 74; the steelmaker Andrew Carnegie, 65. Most of the anti-imperialists hovered on the outskirts of government and party holding long and honorable records in the cause of dissent against the Gilded Age. As an imperial ambition caught up the majority of their countrymen they found themselves severely handicapped in preaching a doctrine of self-denial. Unskilled in the new arts of mass propaganda, saddled with a negative program, often distrustful of the democratic forces ranged behind the President, they were soon outmanned and outmaneuvered by the expansionists even though they scored some telling ideological hits on their victorious opponents.

The anti-imperialist manifesto expressed racist doubts about the wisdom of incorporating dark-skinned, unschooled peoples. But the core of their case against empire was the charge of betrayal of that cherished principle of national self-determination embodied in the Declaration of Independence. It was Charles Eliot Norton, high priest of American gentility, strangely enough, who made this charge most indignantly:

We believe that America had something better to offer to mankind than those aims she is now pursuing, and we mourn her desertion of her ideals which were not selfish nor limited in their application, but which are of universal worth and validity. She has lost her unique position as a potential leader in the program of civilization, and has taken up her place simply as one of the grasping and selfish nations of the present day.

Some of the anti-imperialists looked back to a less complex world of a half-century earlier, when the United States, as one defender of tradition put it, was "provincial, dominated by the New England idea." These New England worthies, however, were joined by younger, pragmatic critics of imperialism, like William James who deftly probed the false "realism" of the expansionists and dissected their specious reasoning. As the bloody and inconclusive pacification campaign in the Philippines dragged on and the native freedom fighter Emilio Aguinaldo gave American troops a lesson in guerrilla warfare, James centered his own attack on the American penchant for substituting "bald and hollow abstractions" for the "intensely living and concrete situation." An unchecked appetite for power, he scoffed, had caused the country to "puke up its ancient soul . . . in five minutes without a wink of squeamishness."

Could there be a more damning indictment of that whole bloated idol termed "modern civilization" than this amounts to? Civilization is, then, the big, hollow, resounding, corrupting, sophisticating, confusing torrent of mere brutal momentum and irrationality that brings forth fruits like this?

Until the Philippine insurrection gave the lie to American professions of altruism, the opponents of expansion made very little headway against the winds of imperial destiny. McKinley, after wrestling with his conscience, announced that "without any desire or design on our part" the war had brought new duties for the United States to "meet and discharge" as became "a great nation." Accordingly he instructed his peace commissioners to stand firm against Spanish protests. By the terms of the peace treaty signed late in 1898 Spain agreed to dismemberment, relinquishing Cuba, the Philippines, Puerto Rico, and Guam.

In the Senate the treaty was taken in hand by the Republican faithfuls—Lodge, Spooner, Nelson, and Beveridge—who were aided in their work by Bryan's odd notion that the course of empire could only be determined in the elections of 1900. The inclination of the majority of senators for striking a balance between immediate material gains and long-term spiritual rewards was best summarized by the jingo Albert J. Beveridge: "It is God's great purpose made manifest in the instincts of the race whose present phase is our personal profit, but whose far-off end is the redemption of the world and the Christianization of mankind." Despite the warnings of the anti-imperialists that their country was descending from the "ancient path" of republican rectitude into the "cesspool" of imperialism, the Senate voted 57 to 27 to accept the treaty. Hawaii became an incorporated territory under the Organic Act of 1900. Guam was acquired as a naval station administered by the Navy Department. And Puerto Rico under the Foraker Act was attached as unincorporated territory with an elective legislature and a governor appointed by the President.

With the gathering of the colonial fruits of war with Spain and the arrival of Theodore Roosevelt in the White House, the initiative in formulating foreign policy fell to the activists who supported the President in his belief that national interest afforded the only sound base for a democratic foreign policy. "If we stand idly by," Roosevelt warned as the century opened, "if we seek merely swollen, slothful ease and ignoble peace, if we shrink from the hard contests where men must win at hazard of their lives and the the risk of all they hold dear, then the bolder and stronger people will pass us by. . . . Let us therefore boldly face the life of strife." Strife marked and not infrequently marred Roosevelt's

THE PATTERN OF UNITED STATES INVOLVEMENT IN THE
CARIBBEAN

U.S. Marines stationed in Nicaragua. (*U.S. Marine Corps.*)

conduct of foreign policy from first to last — in Cuba and Panama and throughout
Latin America, and in American dealings with China and Japan. National interest in the Roosevelt years came to mean national egoism.

In Cuba the occupation by American forces continued as the United States
launched a program of administrative and public health reforms that culminated
in a successful campaign against yellow fever. With the Platt Amendment in 1901
the "ties of singular intimacy" connecting the United States and Cuba were drawn
even tighter by provisions for American intervention in case an unstable new
government failed to protect life, liberty, and property. Following the application of heavy pressure on the Cuban leadership this provision was written into
the constitution of the new republic in 1901 and incorporated into the treaty
between Cuba and the United States two years later. By 1903 the United States,
despite earlier disavowals, had established a virtual protectorate in the island
and reserved for itself the right of intervention in the internal affairs of its new
neighbor, a privilege it would invoke with regularity in the next half-century.

In the Philippines imposing American control awaited the outcome of the
insurrection, which dragged on until March 1901, when Aguinaldo was captured

and his scattered forces surrendered. Under the terms of the Philippine Organic Act of 1902 the United States provided a bicameral legislature and an appointed governor with broad executive powers. Although there would be numerous modifications of American rule in the islands during the next three decades, Philippine independence would not be achieved until 1946. Within a decade the dreams of a handful of "large policy" advocates had become a reality. The United States, without actually willing it, had acquired an imperial base for commercial and ideological expansion throughout the world.

Open and Closed Doors: Progressive Foreign Policy under Roosevelt and Taft

If a "splendid little war" had suddenly thrust the United States into the ranks of the world's big powers, its aftermath taught corrective lessons in the limits of American influence. The United States proved a slow and often recalcitrant pupil in the school of international power politics, and as late as the outbreak of war in Europe in 1914 still had much to learn about world affairs and the proper role of a democracy in managing them.

American education in the limits of power began in China at the turn of the century. The dream of a China market, rich and limitless, was older than the nation itself, a prime motive for original colonizing ventures and the search for a Northwest Passage. After the Revolution the dream became reality as the new nation opened markets in the Far East to compensate for the loss of old ones; and the subsequent age of clipper ships continued to feed American hopes for untold riches in the fabled Orient. Still, by century's end less than 2 percent of the foreign trade of the United States involved China, and it was with expectations of expanding this slim total that commercial and banking interests, concession hunters and investment seekers apprehensively watched European power rise rapidly in the Far East. If the United States meant to establish its own foothold on the Chinese mainland, it would have to move quickly.

The fatal weakness of the Manchu dynasty had recently become apparent in China's disastrous war with Japan in 1894–95. In the wake of China's defeat, the chief European powers joined Japan in descending on the moribund empire with demands for extended spheres of influence, trade concessions, and leases. Once again, as in the case of the Monroe Doctrine seventy-five years earlier, American and British interests coincided on the point of equal market opportunity. Again the British Foreign Office proposed a joint statement, only to be met by the preference of McKinley's administration for a unilateral American pronouncement. The result was a series of notes dispatched to the European capitals and Tokyo by Secretary of State John Hay that took the form of a self-denying ordinance binding the major powers not to interfere with vested rights within their spheres of influence or to infringe the tariff rights of the Chinese

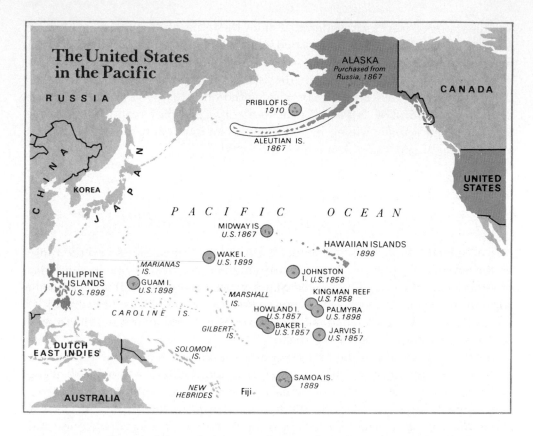

The United States in the Pacific

government. On receiving what were at best equivocal responses, Hay boldly proclaimed a general acceptance of his principles of the Open Door that he welcomed as "final and definitive."

Hay's optimistic reading of the intentions of the major powers with respect to China was soon tested by the Boxer Rebellion, a series of militant antiforeign riots that isolated the international community in Peking and invited a retaliatory rescue expedition (including 2500 American soldiers fresh from the Philippines) to lift the siege and punish the Chinese nationalists. Again the road lay open to further Chinese concessions leading to the dismantlement of the empire. Now Hay was forced to improvise a second circular note, this one announcing that the United States intended to maintain the territorial integrity of the Chinese empire. Here was a radical departure in American diplomacy—not simply a commitment to preserve equal economic opportunity on the mainland but a pledge to uphold the sovereignty of China. The American education in the limits of unilateral assertion was about to begin.

The Open Door policy, it was clear from the outset, would be just as controlling of imperialistic ambitions as the determination of England and the United States could make it. Events quickly dispelled American hopes for equal investment opportunity. The Chinese empire lay in shambles, its days numbered before revolution toppled the dynasty in 1911. England, accepting the inevitable, hastened to make overtures to Japan acknowledging that country's predominant interests on the mainland. Meanwhile rivalry between Russia and Japan over railroad and mining concessions in Manchuria led to the outbreak of war. Japan in a series of smashing victories played to perfection the role of "underdog," so attractive to Americans, and forced Russia to accept the mediational offices of Roosevelt, who suddenly appeared in the unfamiliar guise of peacemaker.

Although the Portsmouth Treaty, which Roosevelt forced on an unhappy Russia, established Japan as the dominant power in the Far East, the principles of the Open Door were scarcely advanced. In a secret agreement in 1907 Russia and Japan agreed to divide Manchuria, Mongolia, and Korea into dual spheres of influence with "special interests." Roosevelt, in recognizing Japan's special interests in Manchuria in the Root-Takahira Agreement (1908), presided over the ceremonial closing of the Open Door. Conceding that the Open Door was "an excellent thing" so far as it could be upheld by general diplomatic agreement, Roosevelt admitted that the policy simply disappeared once a nation like Japan chose to disregard it. The Open Door had ended in failure. It would take the Taft administration's abortive attempt to send American capital by diplomatic pressure "into a region of the world it would not go of its own accord" to revive interest in prying open the door to Manchuria, and here too hopes for American economic penetration would outstrip performance.

In the Moroccan crisis of 1905–06 Roosevelt managed to salvage at least some of the splinters of the Open Door as he improved his performance as peacemaker. The crisis grew out of conflicting French and German interests in North Africa, a clash in which American concern, according to Roosevelt's secretary of state, Elihu Root, was not strong enough "to justify us in taking a leading part." Nevertheless, Roosevelt broke a century-long tradition of nonintervention by actively directing the Algeciras Conference (1906). The terms of settlement, following Roosevelt's intentions, checked German penetration of North Africa for the moment, united France and England in solid opposition to the kaiser, and reaffirmed for the United States the principles of the Open Door. Roosevelt, who already distrusted German military power, professed himself entirely satisfied with the outcome at Algeciras and boasted of having stood the kaiser on his head "with great decision." Yet imperial Germany soon righted itself, and it was clear that a temporary departure from a policy of nonentanglement in European affairs was not to be repeated in the second Moroccan crisis of 1911, which Taft studiouly avoided. Despite Roosevelt's assertion of an American interest in the European balance of power, he was unable to overturn a century-long tradition of isolation or to provide compelling reasons for abandoning it. An American foreign policy of realism reached its outer limits at Algeciras.

No such doubts concerning the United States role as policeman inhibited progressive foreign policy in the Caribbean, where economic interests and preponderant American power combined in a shortsighted policy of constant intervention. In Latin America interference in the internal affairs of unstable republics quickly became a habit. Behind this pattern of continual interference lay rapidly expanding American economic interests, not simply in trade but in banking, investments, and the development of natural resources, all of which seemingly required a favorable political climate and the willingness to grant generous economic concessions to the Colossus of the North.

Troubles for Progressive policymakers began in that "infernal little Cuban republic," as Roosevelt called it in confessing to a recurrent urge to "wipe its people off the face of the earth." Four years after the removal of American forces in 1902 the troops were back again in another attempt to restore order. A policeman's lot, the President agreed, was not a happy one. "All that we wanted from them was that they would behave themselves and be prosperous and happy so that we would not have to interfere." Instead, the Cubans persisted in playing at revolution and "may get things into such a snarl that we have no alternative save to intervene—which will at once convince the suspicious idiots in South America that we do wish to interfere after all, and perhaps have some land hunger." The President neglected to add what was beginning to be obvious to interested European observers—that it was not land hunger but the hope of establishing economic hegemony in Latin America that dictated an interventionist strategy.

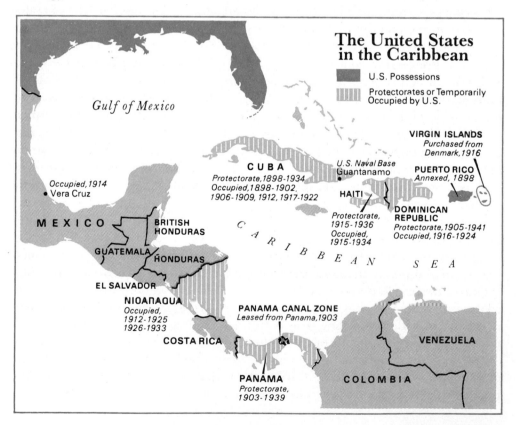

The United States in the Caribbean

■ U.S. Possessions

▥ Protectorates or Temporarily Occupied by U.S.

Gulf of Mexico

Occupied, 1914
• Vera Cruz

MEXICO   BRITISH HONDURAS

GUATEMALA   HONDURAS

EL SALVADOR

NICARAGUA
Occupied,
1912-1925
1926-1933

COSTA RICA

PANAMA
Protectorate,
1903-1939

CUBA
Protectorate, 1898-1934
Occupied, 1898-1902,
1906-1909, 1912, 1917-1922

U.S. Naval Base
Guantanamo •

HAITI
Protectorate,
1915-1936
Occupied,
1915-1934

VIRGIN ISLANDS
Purchased from
Denmark, 1916

PUERTO RICO
Annexed, 1898

DOMINICAN REPUBLIC
Protectorate, 1905-1941
Occupied, 1916-1924

C A R I B B E A N   S E A

PANAMA CANAL ZONE
Leased from Panama, 1903

VENEZUELA

COLOMBIA

A policy of constantly interfering in the domestic affairs of neighbors required an explanation from the United States; and Roosevelt provided this in the famous "corollary" to the Monroe Doctrine in his annual message to Congress in 1905. The occasion once again as in Cleveland's administration ten years earlier was a fiscal crisis in Venezuela, where a chronically unstable and corrupt dictatorship refused to honor its debts. In 1903 Germany took it upon herself to nudge the Venezuelan government toward a more conciliatory stance by bombarding Fort San Carlos and was dissuaded from further reprisals only by prompt American condemnation of the "outrage." To forestall similar European moves to protect investors, Roosevelt offered his corollary. "Chronic wrong-doing," he admitted, would inevitably invite the wrath of "civilized" nations determined to safeguard their investments in Latin America. Since the Monroe Doctrine effectively prevented them from intervening directly, the United States, "however reluctantly," might be forced to step in "in flagrant cases of such wrongdoing or impotence." In short, denying to the major powers spheres of influence in China under the Open Door was to have no equivalent in Latin America, which rightfully belonged to the United States even if it had to undertake the work of an "international police power" itself.

The meaning of the Roosevelt "corollary" immediately became clear in the Dominican Republic in 1905, when after considerable urging from the United States the government agreed to request American assistance in straightening out its finances, advice which Roosevelt, despite congressional reservations, was more than willing to provide. With the control of the Dominican customshouse safely in American hands the United States had succeeded in forestalling German intervention once more but at the cost of a policy that would continue to breed hemispheric ill will throughout the twentieth century.

The problem of Panama and American acquisition of the rights to an isthmian canal offered the clearest example of a Progressive foreign policy based on narrow and shortsighted national interest. The decision to abandon the Nicaraguan route, which had intrigued America for over a century, was made at the behest of high-powered lobbyists of the New Panama Canal Company, successor to the defunct French company that had tried and failed to complete the Panama enterprise. The ingenious combination of French adventurers and American entrepreneurs succeeded in convincing Roosevelt, Mark Hanna, and other Republican leaders of the distinct advantages of the Panama route, and managed, with the help of a few carefully placed investments in the future of the Republican party, to win congressional support for their lucrative deal. By 1902 all that remained was to convince the inept government of Colombia of the benefits about to be conferred on it by civilization.

For a while negotiations proceeded smoothly The Hay-Herran Treaty of 1903 tendered to the United States the rights to a canal zone six miles wide for the bargain-basement price of $10 million plus an annual rental of $250,000. Then

DIGGING THE PANAMA CANAL

(*Panama Canal Company.*)

suddenly Colombian patriots, preparing to overthrow a corrupt dictatorship and awakening to the fact that they were being swindled, forced the Colombian Senate to withdraw the treaty. Colombia, it became clear to Roosevelt, was about to up the ante even if it meant incurring the famed presidential wrath.

Roosevelt denounced his new opponents as "inefficient bandits" and "contemptible little creatures" who were willfully blocking the march of progress. His initial scheme frustrated, the President accepted an alternative plan for a pocket revolution engineered by the promoters of the canal and a handful of native dissidents, who proceeded to establish Panamian independence with the blessings of the United States and the help of the American navy. The new state of Panama, following hasty recognition by the United States, willingly obliged her benefactor by granting the terms for the canal that Colombia had refused. Roosevelt had his canal project, the Panamanian patriots their revolution, and the canal promoters their prospects of profits. Roosevelt never ceased defending his part in the affair. "If I had followed traditional conservative methods I would have submitted a dignified State paper of probably 200 pages to Congress and the debates on it would have been going on yet; but I took the Canal Zone and let Congress debate; and while the debate goes on the Canal does also."

With this bald assertion of executive power and national egoism Roosevelt drew together the strands of his progressive diplomacy. His diplomatic style, in the first place, was a highly personal one, proceeding from the assumption that most of the issues in foreign affairs were best handled, as he said, "by one man alone." Although he used his secretaries of state John Hay and Elihu Root effectively on occasion, just as frequently he bypassed them and seldom gave them credit for decisions that rightly or wrongly he considered his own. Determined to play a lone hand, he also fumed at the constant interference of the Senate and its tampering with what he considered an executive prerogative. Deliberative bodies, he insisted, were virtually useless when there was "any efficient work" to be done. It was for the President alone to take charge of foreign policy in the same way that he formulated domestic priorities of reform and reorganization. After he had retired from office, Roosevelt compiled for his admirers a list of the Latin American countries in which he had been forced to intervene, and prefaced his remarks with the boast that given the opportunity, he would have intervened in a number of others. Such actions, he boasted, would have been "simply in the interest of civilization, if I could have waked up our people so that they would back a reasonable and intelligent foreign policy which would have put a stop to the crying disorders at our very doors."

"Crying disorders"—here was the key to the passageway leading from domestic to foreign policy. Order in Asia, Roosevelt was to learn, lay beyond the reach of American power. In Europe, where his leverage was greater, Roosevelt could combine plans for a balance of power with predictions of a perpetual Anglo-American ascendency throughout the world. But it was at home in the Western Hemisphere that the benefits of order and stability seemed to him greatest even though the long-term costs in good will eventually proved prohibitive.

Although it fell to Roosevelt to preside over the transformation of territorial imperialism into a policy of economic penetration, his language betrayed an ignorance of his historical function. He spoke constantly of "honor, territorial integrity and vital interests" as the only basis for an American foreign policy, but his concepts lacked substance. His speeches rang with the clichés of "righteousness" and "duty," as he mixed moralism and nationalism in a blend of power politics that glossed over the economic motives he never clearly acknowledged. The central theme running through his pronouncements on foreign policy concerned the dangers of American preoccupation with domestic prosperity that threatened to turn righteous citizens into a mere "assemblage of well-to-do hucksters" who cared nothing for what happened beyond their borders. But to argue the case for an aggressive foreign policy purely in terms of altruism was to ignore the very economic forces that increasingly determined American activities, particularly in Latin America, namely, investment opportunity, concessions, corporate resource development, and other forms of economic penetration—all requiring political and economic stability essential to the continued exploitation of colonial economies. Roosevelt's rhetoric tended to conceal the fact that as President he became if not the captive at least the confederate of the very economic forces he presumably distrusted. In substituting dollars for bullets the Taft administration displayed no such squeamishness in confronting the reality of economic imperialism.

The marriage of economic policy and power politics that Roosevelt had failed to legitimize received its awaited sanction from the Taft administration. Taft's choice of a secretary of state, the corporation lawyer Philander C. Knox, was itself proof of the growing intimacy between the investment community in Wall Street and the State Department. Knox, who was given a freer hand in formulating policy than Roosevelt had accorded his predecessors, was the chief architect of a democratic state capitalism that came to be known as "dollar diplomacy." Dollar diplomacy involved using American export capital together with preponderant political power to appeal, as Taft explained, "alike to idealistic humanitarian sentiments, to the dictates of sound policy and strategy, and to legitimate commercial aims."

Dollar diplomacy also represented the extension of the principles of domestic progressivism into foreign policy. Investment capitalists were instructed to pursue a policy of development and economic penetration in undeveloped areas under conditions of stability and profitability to be ensured by the government. Knox himself explained how the system worked to the advantage of all parties: "If the American dollar can aid suffering humanity and lift the burden of financial difficulty from States with which we live on terms of intimate intercourse and earnest friendship, and replace insecurity and devastation by stability and peaceful self-development, all I can say is that it would be hard to find better employment." Yet Knox was not always successful at convincing American capitalists that his course was wise.

Even though the Taft administration proved more willing than its predecessor to declare openly an economic motive, it did not alter the pattern of success and failure—conspicuous success in attracting investment in Latin America, where the bankers were more than willing to go, and nearly total failure in the Far East, where they were not. In attempting to open China once more to American capital Taft met the determined resistance of British, French, and German bankers against including their American counterparts into a consortium to finance and build the Hukuang Railway in China, an ill-considered project that was never completed. By dint of considerable diplomatic pressure applied to the Chinese emperor Knox succeeded in gaining admission to the consortium but needlessly made trouble for himself by a carelessly conceived experiment in state capitalism in Manchuria. The scheme backfired when both Russia and Japan objected and American bankers lost interest. Like Hay's original scheme, the Taft administration's attempt to open the door to American capital in Asia ended in complete failure.

No such difficulties were encountered in Latin America, where American capital was already streaming in. Here a combination of supersalesmanship and regular government intervention to protect American investments—in Nicaragua, Guatemala, the Honduras, and Haiti—continued to open the sluice gates to American capital.

The legal framework within which dollar diplomacy sought to realize its economic objectives was provided by the progressive faith in arbitration with which Taft hoped to defuse international crises in much the same way mediational panels in domestic affairs theoretically depoliticized economic conflict. Twenty-five arbitration treaties had been signed in the last days of the outgoing Roosevelt administration, and Taft sought to extend the application of the principle to all "justiciable" issues. The Senate, however, promptly eliminated the procedures for discussion in every case in which the United States might be presumed to have a "vital interest." Nevertheless, an arbitration scheme designed to complement dollar diplomacy lived on as a progressive panacea, drawing the immediate attention of Woodrow Wilson and his secretary of state—the "Prince of Peace," William Jennings Bryan. There would be continuities as well as new departures in the missionary diplomacy of Woodrow Wilson.

"The Organized Force of Mankind": Wilsonian Diplomacy and World War

The progressive years saw internationalists, peace groups, and idealists regroup into a broad coalition behind the principles of missionary diplomacy, moral publicity and open covenants. In repudiating both Roosevelt's role of big brother to the benighted and Taft's "dollar diplomacy," Woodrow Wilson entered office with an appeal to national altruism that warmed the hearts of moralists everywhere. "My dream is that as the years go on and the world knows more and more of America," Wilson told a Fourth of July audience in 1914, "it . . . will turn to America for those moral inspirations which lie at the basis of all freedoms . . . and that America will come into the full light of day when all shall know that she puts human rights above all other rights and that her flag is the flag not only of America but of humanity." Yet three months earlier Wilson had ordered the occupation of Vera Cruz to vindicate American honor.

It was not the least of early twentieth-century American paradoxes that both these widely divergent formulations of foreign policy led unerringly to a continuing involvement of the United States throughout the world and direct, forcible intervention in the affairs of neighboring states almost constantly. Both the demands of national interest and the less precise requirements of moral mission ended in the application of raw power. By 1917, America's arrival as a world power had long been established, but it remained to be seen what uses would be made of the material resources of the United States in reordering a world at war. Americans joined the fighting still seeking an answer to this question.

Like most Americans before 1914, Woodrow Wilson had given little serious thought to the specifics of an American foreign policy. Diplomatic problems had not figured prominently in the campaign of 1912, and to their solution Wilson brought only a widely shared set of assumptions which constituted the conventional wisdom of an active peace movement in the United States. In the years that followed, the President served as the mouthpiece of this movement, taking many of its principles for his own and fashioning them into a theoretical alternative to balance-of-power politics.

By 1910 a belief in a coming age of international harmony had become a staple item in the ideological stock of numerous progressive intellectuals and professionals for whom worldwide communications, an international technology, and the uses of arbitration seemed to point to a new world order. The American peace movement consisted of a variety of groups and interests: traditional church-affiliated peace societies and new secular foundations like Andrew Carnegie's Endowment for International Peace; students of international law intent on building new legal frameworks; preachers of disarmament; and prophets of a vast people-to-people crusade. Common to many of these peace advocates was a peculiarly American set of assumptions that made their movement an adjunct to domestic progressive reform. There was the belief, for example, that the path to world order had been first discovered by the United States as it progressed from a loose confederation of sovereign states to a genuine union of loyal citizens. From similar beginnings, the promoters of peace reasoned, might well come an age of international harmony and democratic striving.

Attached to this golden vision of an Americanized world order was a faith in arbitration itself as a transnational mechanism for resolving tensions and conflicts, whether in a Hague Court, a body of international law, or bilateral "cooling off" treaties. Much of the appeal of the peace movement lay in its remoteness from the realities of clashing national ambitions that descended on an unsuspecting American public in 1914.

These progressive preferences led Wilson to examine the hopes of the peace advocates at just the time when many of them were beginning to retreat to a more comfortable faith in enlightened national self-interest. Wilson's language, like the vocabulary of his chief rival, Theodore Roosevelt, was unrelievedly abstract. But whereas Roosevelt, a self-declared "realist," argued the unexamined propositions of national "honor" and "integrity," Wilson translated these terms into the language of altruism. National interest narrowly construed he equated with "selfishness" and the rule of unbridled materialism. "Balance of power," in his mind, meant unstable coalitions of aggressive interests. The outlook of "average" people the world over, on the contrary, was becoming "more and more unclouded" as national purposes fell more and more into the background and the "common purpose of enlightened mankind" took their place. The time was not far distant when these "counsels of plain men" would come to replace the "counsels of sophisticated men of affairs" as the best means of securing peace. Then the statesmen of the world would be forced to heed the "common clarified thought" or be broken.

Here in embryonic form lay Wilson's plan for an alternative system of world politics, which had begun to take shape in his mind even before war broke out in Europe. Wilson's language proved fully equal to his vision as he assumed what critics called his "papal role" in preaching a humanitarian theology. "I do not know that there will ever be a declaration of independence or grievances for mankind," he told a Fourth of July audience at Independence Hall in Philadelphia in 1914, scarcely a week before the outbreak of war, "but I believe that if any such document is ever drawn it will be drawn in the spirit of the American Declaration of Independence, and that America has lifted high the light which will shine unto all generations and guide the feet of mankind to the goal of justice and liberty and peace." The President, noted the editors of the *New Republic* wryly, uttered nothing that might sound trivial at the Last Judgment.

The first fruits of this Wilsonian "missionary" spirit were bitter ones for the promoters of Dollar Diplomacy. Wilson quickly dashed the hopes of the outgoing Taft administration for continued economic penetration in China as he denounced the scheme for railroad financing as a violation of Chinese sovereignty. In the delicate negotiations over the Panama Canal tolls he argued that American exemption betrayed a "dishonorable attitude" on the part of the United States, and at the risk of dividing his own party he secured a repeal. Then in October 1913, in his famous Mobile address, he completed the reversal of Dollar Diplomacy by promising to emancipate Latin America from its "subordination" to "foreign enterprise."

Yet in Latin America, where the interests of business were real and compelling, Wilson found it impossible to reverse his predecessors' policy of intervention, and his formal disavowal of American interference ended in bitter irony. The chief contradiction of missionary diplomacy lay in the fact that under Wilson the United States intervened in the affairs of its neighbors more often than ever before. Military occupation of Haiti in 1915. Financial supervision in the Dominican Republic in 1916. Renewed controls in Cuba in 1917. And minor meddling in behalf of American investors throughout the Caribbean. Moralistic though he was, Wilson was not blind to the operation of economic motives nor deaf to the appeals of investors. His difficulties in Latin America largely resulted from his tendency to identify the beneficent workings of American capital with the welfare of "the submerged eighty-five per cent" of native populations to whom he wanted to bring the blessings of parliamentary democracy. This was the real meaning of his announced intention "to teach the South American republics to elect good men."

Mexico served as the testing ground for these theories of moral diplomacy and proved them wanting in political realism. In 1911, following a quarter-century's oppressive rule, moderate constitutionalists led by Francisco Madero overthrew the Mexican dictator, Porfirio Diaz. The new government received the prompt recognition of the Taft administration. Then, less than two years later, Madero himself fell victim to a counterrevolutionary coup directed by one of his lieutenants, Victoriano Huerta, who murdered his former chief and seized the presidential office. This was the situation confronting Wilson as he took office.

Wilson, outraged by Huerta's brutality, lost no time in denouncing him as a thug and a butcher, and refused to recognize his government. His refusal rested partly on a genuine moral revulsion and partly on the knowledge that England had accorded Huerta recognition in the hope of gaining further economic concessions. Although economic and strategic concerns usually appeared on the periphery of Wilson's moral vision, they were never quite out of sight. He continued to insist that the United States must never abandon morality for expediency and "never condone iniquity because it is convenient to do so." But in Mexico profits for American investors and parliamentary democracy for the Mexican people seemed to him wholly compatible.

Wilson's heroic remedy for Mexico mixed strong disapproval of a "government of butchers" with plans for replacing Huerta with the liberal rule of Venustiano Carranza, another constitutionalist who had succeeded in rallying opposition to the dictator. The President seized the occasion for toppling Huerta when a boatload of American sailors were arrested and unlawfully detained in Tampico. Wilson demanded an immediate apology, and his administration found itself in the strange diplomatic posture of demanding a twenty-one-gun salute from a government it would not recognize. When Huerta predictably refused, Wilson ordered the occupation of Vera Cruz, an exercise that cost the lives of nineteen Americans and a great many more Mexicans. Under relentless pressure from the United States and besieged by the forces of the constitutionalists, Huerta resigned and fled to Spain in 1914. Yet Carranza's liberal regime proved no more willing to tolerate American intervention than the deposed dictator had. Only the timely offer of the ABC Powers (Argentina, Brazil, Chile) to mediate the dispute allowed Wilson to withdraw the American forces and save diplomatic face temporarily.

The second act of the diplomatic crisis in Mexico opened with the attempt of Pancho Villa, bandit leader and unsavory associate of Carranza, to overthrow his chief and take power by provoking a war with the United States, a piece of strategy that very nearly worked. On January 10, 1916, Villa and his band stopped a train at Santa Ysabel in the northern provinces, took 17 Americans off, and shot 16 of them. Then in March, Villa raided the tiny New Mexico town of Columbus, burned it flat, and killed 19 more American citizens. Wilson responded, as Villa had hoped he would, by dispatching General John J. Pershing

MEXICAN-AMERICAN RELATIONS, 1916–1917

Pancho Villa's raid on a New Mexico town and his murder of American citizens called for a U.S. punitive expedition led by General John J. Pershing. (*Left, Brown Brothers; below, Culver Pictures, Inc.*)

on a punitive expedition, which chased the bandit chief some three hundred miles back into Mexico without managing to catch him.

Once again Carranza's diplomatic temper flared, and his government demanded the immediate withdrawal of American troops. Faced now with the nearly certain prospect of war with Germany, Wilson could only comply. "We shall yet prove to the Mexican people that we know how to serve them without first thinking of ourselves," he had promised. But in 1917 Villa roamed the Mexican countryside, an unstable Carranza government lurched toward yet another constitutional crisis, and Wilson had little to show for his five-year labor in the Mexican vineyard. Now, however, his attention was fixed on Europe.

The outbreak of the First World War caught the Wilson administration and the entire country by surprise. At first the news that Austria had invaded tiny Serbia occasioned little American concern beyond traditional sympathy for the underdog. Since neither European nor American diplomats yet realized the scale of the coming catastrophe, it was not difficult for Wilson to declare American neutrality and call on all citizens to remain "impartial in thought as well as in action." Behind the proclamation of neutrality lay the President's belief that the war would be short and end in a settlement that the United States, from its Olympian station above the battle, could help arrange. And behind that sanguine expectation lay still another conviction that the terms imposed by America would usher in a new moral order.

As the war dragged into its second year, all of Wilson's hopes for remodeling the world of power politics came to hinge on a doctrine of neutrality that itself depended on two misconceptions. First, developments quickly showed that the United States was not and could not be unconcerned with the outcome of the war. The fact was, as shrewd observers had pointed out before war broke out, that England, in upholding the European balance of power from the early 1800s, had directly contributed to American growth and well-being. An Anglo-German conflict was thus bound to affect the United States in crucial ways.

The first year of the war drove home the force of this observation. England monopolized access to the information defining the meaning of the war and skillfully manipulated its advantage until the President and his advisers came to realize, as one of them put it, that "Germany must not be permitted to win this war." By 1915 the administration began, half consciously, to act on this assumption. The American economy was placed at the disposal of the Allies, who despite the embarrassing presence of imperial Russia, were presumed to be fighting autocracy and militarism in the name of democracy. Trade with the Allies was proclaimed "legal and welcome." When Allied credit soon evaporated, American bankers rushed to the rescue with credits and loans that totaled $2.5 billion by the time America entered the war in 1917. Wilson continued to press both England and Germany for a settlement, but when neither side agreed, he tended to excuse the former and blame the latter for the disastrous military stalemate.

The second misconception underlying Wilson's doctrine of neutrality grew out of his failure to credit the logic of total war or to acknowledge the effect of modern technology. The submarine had made the traditional rights of neutrals obsolete. Both combatants as they grappled for an economic stranglehold on the other were forced to resort to novel practices that were clear violations of established precedent. England extended the right of search and visit to new lengths and established a paper blockade that virtually extinguished the rights of neutrals. Yet diplomatic exchange with England settled into a predictable pattern of violation, protest, discussion, and eventual resumption of the objectionable practice.

With Germany, on the other hand, diplomatic exchange soon grew brittle and strained as Wilson's language became increasingly terse. The use of submarines, which struck without warning or provision for the safety of passengers and crew, touched a raw nerve in the American people as yet unacquainted with the techniques of total war. When in May 1915, a German U-boat without warning torpedoed the British liner *Lusitania* with the loss of 128 American lives, Wilson initiated an angry dialogue that became more and more strident in the next year and a half. Germany quite correctly pointed out that the ship carried contraband of war, but that fact hardly weakened Wilson's determination to apply the old rules. For the President the sinking of the *Lusitania* demonstrated "the practical impossibility of employing submarines in the destruction of commerce without disregarding those rules of fairness, reason, justice and humanity, which all modern opinion regards as imperative." In resolving to hold Germany "strictly accountable" Wilson put the United States on a collision course: if the German government decided that unrestricted submarine warfare was worth the risk of bringing the United States into the war against it, the President would have little freedom to maneuver. By 1917 he had lost that initiative.

In the meantime, following the *Lusitania* incident, Germany agreed to comply with Wilson's terms. Then in 1916, with the attack on the unarmed French passenger ship *Sussex* in the English Channel, which resulted in injury to American citizens, the meaning of "strict accountability" suddenly became clear to the President. Submarine warfare, he informed Germany, "of necessity, because of the very character of the vessels employed," was "incompatible" with the "sacred immunities of noncombatants." Unless the imperial government agreed to abandon its methods forthwith, the United States would have no choice but to sever relations preparatory to declaring war. Germany agreed to discontinue the practice but only with the proviso that the United States call on England to lift the blockade. The German government reserved the right to rescind its pledge until Britain agreed. The President's options were dwindling fast.

Wilson's growing indignation reflected another, more personal anxiety. For three years he had continued to pile on the conventional concept of neutral rights a load of moral principles that the original construction had not been designed to carry. Now he was forced to admit that the United States might not be able to impose its will on warring Europe without joining the Allies. A nation that had been "too proud to fight" and had reelected him on the slogan "He kept us out of war" now faced the prospect of securing a "peace without victory" only as a participant. The meaning of this new commitment was not lost on Wilson, who now sought to define his mission to his countrymen as nothing less than the building of a system of collective security to replace a bankrupt system of balance of power. If compelled to fight, the United States would fight for utopia.

In January 1917, a week before Germany announced its decision to resume unrestricted submarine warfare, Wilson described his vision of a new world order to the Senate. The United States, prepared by "the very principles and purposes" of its humanitarian policy, must rebuild the machinery of diplomacy. Its terms for peace would "win the approval of mankind" and not merely "serve the several interests and immediate aims of the nations engaged." Wilson proposed a perpetual league of peaceful nations as an integral part of the settlement, a collective instrument, which he described as "so much greater than the force of any nation now engaged or any alliance hitherto projected" that governments and their leaders would bend to its dictates. The future of the world would thus come to depend, not on a balance of power, but on a community of opinion, not on "organized rivalries," but on an "organized peace." He proposed, in short, a concert of moral force made up of peoples who with their open covenants openly arrived at could enforce their collective will for national self-determination, democratic government, and lasting peace. To skeptical senators, particularly those in the Republican ranks, Wilson explained that his were at once "American principles" and "the principles of all mankind."

A week later the German imperial government renewed its submarine attacks in a desperate gamble to win the war before the United States could rescue England and France. In March, German submarines without warning sank four unarmed American merchantmen, and on April 2, 1917, Wilson appeared before a joint session of Congress to request that it accept the war that had been "thrust" upon the United States. By a vote of 82 to 6 in the Senate and 373 to 50 in the House, Congress agreed to the presidential request.

The United States, its citizens would learn from a year and a half of war and another year of peacemaking, had arrived at a position of world power that only a few of their number would have predicted thirty years earlier. The nation had gone to war with Spain on the flimsiest of pretexts and built an empire on its victory. But in the intervening years, most Americans, far from accepting imperial responsibilities, had agreed to neglect the chores of maintaining an empire, and except at home in their own hemisphere, had conveniently forgotten their regenerative mission. Now as their President called on them to fight another and infinitely greater war, the precise nature of their moral contribution still eluded them. For a sense of the right direction they still relied on Wilson.

WAR BOND RALLY

The American people prepare for war. (*Brown Brothers.*)

The President, for his part, having determined on war as the only option left open to him, indulged in a prophecy and a private confession in contemplating his course. "We are at the beginning of an age," he told the country, "in which it will be insisted that the same standards of conduct and of responsibility for wrong done shall be observed among nations and their governments that are observed among individual citizens of civilized states." But privately in the solitude of the White House on the eve of his appearance before Congress, he made another prediction. To Frank Cobb, the editor of the New York *World*, he admitted to fears about the unintended effects of going to war. "Once lead this people into war," he told Cobb, "and they'll forget there ever was such a thing as tolerance. To fight you must be brutal and ruthless, and the spirit of ruthless brutality will enter into the very fibre of our national life, infecting Congress, the courts, the policeman on the beat, the man in the streets." The meaning of his prophecy of a new international order awaited the outcome of the war, but the prediction of the domestic dangers in fighting it proved all too accurate.

Suggested Readings

The boundaries of scholarly criticism of American foreign policy after 1890 are established in two different surveys. George F. Kennan, *American Diplomacy, 1900–1950* (1951), points to consistently unprofessional and uninformed leaders as the chief difficulty, while William Appleman Williams, *The Tragedy of American Diplomacy* (1959), cites economic expansion as the source of a peculiar kind of American imperialism. Robert E. Osgood, *Ideals and Self-Interest in America's Foreign Relations* (1953), evaluates the assumptions of both parties to the great debate over means and ends. Richard W. Leopold, *The Growth of American Foreign Policy* (1962), is an excellent survey, which should be combined with John A. S. Grenville and George B. Young, *Politics, Strategy, and American Diplomacy, . . . 1873–1917* (1966). Two other readable accounts of the emergence of an American foreign policy are Foster R. Dulles, *America's Rise to World Power, 1898–1954* (1955), and for backgrounds Richard W. Van Alstyne, *The Rising American Empire* (1960). Rubin F. Weston, *Racism in U.S. Imperialism: The Influence of Racial Assumptions on American Foreign Policy, 1893–1946* (1972), examines race prejudice as a component of U.S. foreign policy. William Appleman Williams, *The Shaping of American Diplomacy* (1956), is a highly useful source.

The origins of the American expansionism in the 1890s are carefully examined in Walter LaFeber, *The New Empire: An Interpretation of American Expansion, 1860–1898* (1963), and Milton Plesur, *America's Outward Thrust, 1865–1890* (1971). David Pletcher, *The Awkward Years: America's Foreign Relations under Garfield and Arthur* (1962), offers a meticulous analysis of early fumblings in the 1880s.

There are several excellent studies of the rising diplomatic crisis in the 1890s—among them Ernest R. May, *Imperial Democracy: The Emergence of America as a Great Power* (1961), and the same author's exploratory essay, *American Imperialism: A Speculative Essay* (1968); H. Wayne Morgan, *America's Road to Empire: The War with Spain and Overseas Expansion* (1965); David Healy, *United States Expansionism: The Imperialist Urge in the 1890's* (1970). The influence of the navy and the role of Mahan are explored in Peter Karsten, *The Naval Aristocracy* (1972), and William Livezey, *Mahan on Sea Power* (1947). Charles H. Brown, *The Correspondents' War: Journalists in the Spanish-American War* (1967), covers the reporters' beat. Robert L. Beisner, *The Anti-Imperialists, 1898–1900* (1968), and E. Berkeley Tompkins, *Anti-Imperialism in the United States: The Great Debate, 1890–1920* (1970), assess the arguments and futile activities of the opponents of expansionism. Leon Wolff, *Little Brown Brother* (1961), gives an outraged account of the Philippine insurrection and the American pacification program.

Areas of growing American interest and control have been well covered in a number of careful monographs: Merze Tate, *The United States and the Hawaiian Kingdom* (1965); Howard F. Cline, *The United States and Mexico* (1953); A. Whitney Griswold, *The Far Eastern Policy of the United States* (1938); Charles Vevier, *The United States and China, 1906–1913* (1955); Charles E. Neu, *The Troubled Encounter: The United States and Japan* (1975); and Samuel F. Bemis, *The Latin American Policy of the United States* (1967). John Hay's intentions in announcing the Open Door policy are thoroughly canvassed in Tyler Dennett, *John Hay* (1933), and the unforeseen results in Marilyn B. Young, *The Rhetoric of Empire: American China Policy, 1893–1901* (1968); Warren Cohen, *America's Response to China* (1971); Thomas McCormick, *China Market: America's Quest for Informal Empire, 1893–1901* (1967); Jerry Israel, *Progressivism and the Open Door: America and China, 1905–1921* (1971); and Paul A. Varg, *The Making of a Myth: The United States and China, 1899–1912* (1968). Other detailed studies of aspects of progressive foreign policy include Charles E. Neu, *An Uncertain Friendship: Theodore Roosevelt and Japan* (1967); Akira Iriye, *Across the*

Pacific: An Inner History of American–East Asian Relations (1967); and Edward Berbusse, *The United States in Puerto Rico* (1965).

On Roosevelt's foreign policy formulations, Howard K. Beale, *Theodore Roosevelt and the Rise of America to World Power* (1956), is still standard; see also Raymond A. Esthus, *Theodore Roosevelt and the International Rivalries* (1970). Robert A. Hart, *The Great White Fleet: Its Voyage Around the World* (1965), is a highly readable account of Roosevelt's colorful gesture. Dwight C. Miner, *Fight for the Panama Route* (1966), tells a complicated story well, and Akira Iriye, *Pacific Estrangement: Japanese and American Expansion, 1897–1911* (1972), explains Roosevelt's many problems in that area. Walter V. Scholes and Marie V. Scholes, *The Foreign Policies of the Taft Administration* (1970), analyzes the workings of Dollar Diplomacy, and Dana G. Munroe, *Intervention and Dollar Diplomacy in the Caribbean, 1900–1921* (1964), examines its consequences. Sondra R. Herman, *Eleven Against War: Studies in American Internationalist Thought, 1898–1921* (1969), studies a variety of peace types, and Bradford Perkins, *The Great Rapprochement: England and the United States, 1895–1914* (1968), is indispensable for understanding American attitudes towards the First World War.

The most comprehensive discussions of Wilsonian diplomacy from a presidential perspective are to be found in the volumes of Link's *Wilson*. P. Edward Haley, *Revolution and Intervention: The Diplomacy of Taft and Wilson with Mexico, 1910–1917* (1970), is an even-handed examination of Mexican policy, and so is Robert Freeman Smith, *The U.S. and Revolutionary Nationalism in Mexico, 1916–1932* (1972), for the later period. Robert E. Quirk, *An Affair of Honor: Woodrow Wilson and the Occupation of Veracruz* (1962), criticizes the President for his misguided actions in that unfortunate affair, and Clarence C. Clendenen, *The United States and Pancho Villa* (1961) is adequate. Hans R. Schmidt, *The United States Occupation of Haiti, 1915–1934* (1971), surveys the problems presented by the unstable republic in the Progressive search for order in the Caribbean. Harley Notter, *The Origins of the Foreign Policy of Woodrow Wilson* (1937), tests the theoretical underpinnings of Wilsonian diplomacy.

Neutrality and American intervention in the First World War fascinated a Depression generation preparing for war and produced a number of notable accounts, from the acerbic Walter Millis, *The Road to War* (1935), to the scholarly Charles Seymour, *American Neutrality, 1914–1917* (1935), and Edwin Borchard and W. P. Lage, *Neutrality for the United States* (1940). More recent literature on Wilsonian neutrality and its premises is extensive. Among the best accounts are Ernest R. May, *The World War and American Isolation, 1914–1917* (1959); John M. Cooper, Jr., *The Vanity of Power: American Isolation and the First World War, 1914–1917* (1969); Ross Gregory, *The Origins of American Intervention in the First World War* (1971); Daniel M. Smith, *The Great Departure: The United States in World War I, 1914–1920* (1965); and Carl P. Parrini, *Heir to Empire: U.S. Economic Diplomacy, 1916–1923* (1969). Link's *Wilson* contains a meticulous account of the gradual shift in the President's assessment of the war, and Edward Buehrig, *Woodrow Wilson and the Balance of Power* (1955), examines his various strategies.

29

Progressivism
and the Great War

By the time the United States entered the war in April 1917, all the European powers were rapidly approaching exhaustion. After three years of stalemate Germany was suffering from starvation and the imminent collapse of civilian morale. Austria-Hungary managed to continue the war only by imposing martial law. Russia, crippled by astronomical losses that had led to the overthrow of the czarist regime a month earlier, stood on the brink of a second Bolshevik revolution. France, its national will shattered, faced widespread mutiny in her armies. England, having sacrificed an entire generation of young men to German machine guns since 1914, was beset with severe manpower shortages both at home and in the field.

The original predictions and plans of both sides—Germany's for a six-week war and the Allies' for rolling back the enemy on two vast fronts—had long since been buried under mounds of casualties. Both sides, driven by contrasting but strangely complementary illusions, had succeeded in proving that in total war it is the war that wins. Shared strategic obsessions with artillery barrages and massed infantry assaults on entrenched positions had created a mirror image war of appalling senselessness and butchery. Two million casualties on the Western Front in 1916 had failed to move the line of advance for either side, and the war had descended once again into the trenches that stretched in an unbroken line from the sea to the mountains. A week after Wilson addressed Congress in April 1917, the British launched still another frontal attack in the Ypres sector of the front, and in five days gained 7000 yards at the cost of 160,000 dead and wounded.

Although the United States entered the war late and suffered proportionately fewer losses, the meaning of the slaughter lingered in the American imagination for a generation. In a scene in F. Scott Fitzgerald's *Tender Is the Night,* one of the characters leads a party of sightseers across the Somme valley after the war. "See that little stream," he says, "We could walk to it in two minutes. It took the British a whole month to walk to it—a whole empire walking very slowly, dying in front and pushing forward behind. And another empire walked very slowly backward a few inches a day, leaving the dead like a million bloody rugs." American soldiers in the last year of the war followed the footsteps of their British and French predecessors. In joining the Allies, the United States committed its forces to a war in which a grisly paradox awarded ultimate defeat to the side that won the most battles. Woodrow Wilson's hopes for a just peace, it is clear in retrospect, died along with more than 100,000 American soldiers on the Western Front.

It took eight months for American troops to join in the fighting on the Western Front in effective numbers and nearly a year before they were decisively engaged in helping to turn back the final German offensive. In the meantime the Allied cause hung in the balance. In November 1917, Lenin and the Bolsheviks overthrew the provisional government, established a party dictatorship and took Russia out of the war, releasing badly needed German divisions for a last offensive on the Western Front. In the spring drive along the Somme beginning in March 1918, the Germans routed the British and penned up the French but without making a decisive breakthrough. In May and June the American Second Division was dispatched to the Marne, where it bolstered sagging French defenses. In the first big American engagements of the war, United States forces halted a German advance at Château-Thierry and slowly drove the enemy out of the Belleau Wood. These American actions were only preliminaries to the great Allied counteroffensive, which in the late summer began to push the German army back toward its frontier. By September the American commander, General John J. Pershing, who had stubbornly held out for an independent command, had over a half a million men at his disposal, a number that would double by the end of the war. In October, Pershing, in concert with British and French offensives elsewhere along the line, opened a massive American drive out of the Argonne Forest aimed at the railhead at Sedan—the last sustained American action of the war. On November 3, Austria-Hungary collapsed, and on the same day the German navy mutinied at Kiel, thus raising the specter of another communist revolution. Six days later a general strike in Germany led by the

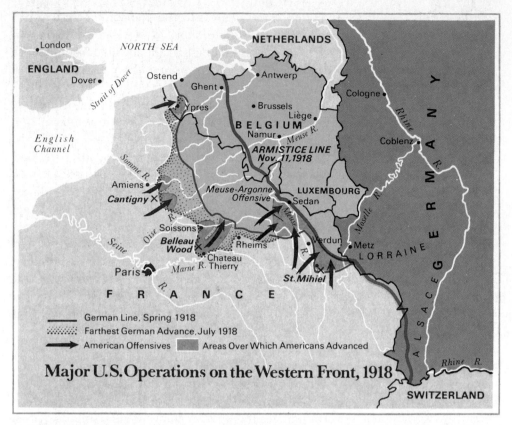

Major U.S. Operations on the Western Front, 1918

Legend:
- German Line, Spring 1918
- Farthest German Advance, July 1918
- American Offensives
- Areas Over Which Americans Advanced

Independent Socialists forced the Kaiser to abdicate, and a coalition of socialists and liberals proclaimed the republic that forty-eight hours later accepted Wilson's Fourteen Points as the basis for an armistice. The Great War was over.

The American entry, it was immediately clear, had brought badly needed troops and supplies to the Allies at a critical moment. American soldiers had supplied the preponderance of power needed to win the war. Equally important was the contribution of the United States in replenishing reduced stockpiles of food and materiel with its "bridge of ships," replacing the merchantmen sunk by German submarines, and experimenting successfully with the convoy system, which in the last analysis saved the Allies. The American contribution was essential, and it came at a crucial time. Yet despite the provisional German acceptance of the Fourteen Points as the agenda for peacemaking, the American war effort had not wiped out the national fears and hatreds embodied in wartime secret agreements and arrangements among the partners nor had it established the moral climate either at home or in Europe that, as Wilson knew, was essential to lasting peace.

With the American entrance a conflict which had already grown fiercely ideological became a crusade for democracy. All the powers had secured control over the actions and opinions of their civilian populations as they accepted the logic of total war. But the United States action completed an ideological shift for the Allies by defining the struggle in religious terms as one between the forces of peace and democracy against the dark powers of militarism. In submitting his Fourteen Points, and by explaining American war aims as nothing less than "the right of those who submit to authority to have a voice in their own government" and "a universal dominion of right by . . . a concert of free peoples," Wilson hardened the resolve of his allies to seek an unconditional surrender and a punitive peace. Perhaps the greatest irony of the First World War lay in the President's determination to inject into it a democratic ideology, which would make his own role as the even-handed peacemaker an impossible one.

Total war also imposed an organizational logic on the participants, all of whom were forced to adjust to the national need for centralization and control. Early in the war Germany recruited civilian administrators for its War Raw Materials Department, which established efficient mechanisms for allocating manpower and materiel. England organized its dwindling resources under the Defense of the Realm Act, which provided for full mobilization of all available manpower. France, its Northern industrial provinces lost for the duration, used the powers of government to relocate factories and regulate the production of food. Once in the war, the United States followed the same pattern in building a war machine, enlisting civilians in the war effort, and improvising the bureaucratic controls demanded by the emergency. By the time the war ended in November 1918, Wilson's administration had completed an organizational revolution that brought the power of government into nearly every phase of American life.

War and the Health of the State

For some progressives the coming of the war seemed a heaven-sent opportunity to consummate the American promise. The war, they confidently predicted, would bring genuine national unity and an end to class and ethnic division. It would discredit dangerous radicalism by infusing the citizens of the nation with a new spirit of patriotism. The demands of the war, moreover, would destroy all selfish materialism and preoccupation with profits and replace them with the higher goals of service and sacrifice. National preparedness and mobilization, central features of the New Nationalism, would foster moral virtue and civic purity in soldiers and civilians alike. Those progressives who continued to define their basic purpose as creating a new American morality saw in the impending war effort the outlines of what one of them called a "true national collectivism" to be built out of efficiency, social control, altruism, and revived moral purpose.

On a less ethereal plane many more progressives responded with enthusiasm to the organizational and reform opportunities furnished by the war. Those

AMERICAN BOYS AT WAR

Above, Fifteenth regiment on Fifth Avenue. (*Library of Congress.*) Top left, American field hospital in church ruins at Neuilly in the Argonne Forest. (*Library of Congress.*) Top right, American forces move up on the road to Grand Pré. (*Library of Congress.*) Bottom, A machine-gun platoon advances on a German entrenched position. (UPI *photo.*)

reformers who approached their work as a form of moral cleansing—of vice, alcohol, and prostitution—viewed the war as a chance to purify democracy at home while saving it abroad. "Long live social control," one of them exclaimed, "social control, not only to enable us to meet the rigorous demands of the war, but also as a foundation for the peace and brotherhood that is to come."

In fact, the war advanced the more restrictive progressive hopes in measurable ways. The preparedness campaign furthered the ideal of universal military service as a school of citizenship. The various Americanization programs aimed at controlling the immigrant took on new life. Prohibitionist hopes soared, and women's suffrage suddenly seemed a near thing. Even city planners, social justice workers, child labor reformers, and other progressive humanitarians warmed to the prospects of a domestic reformation in the midst of foreign war.

The war seemed to hold the greatest promise for progressives in administration and public policy, in closing the distance between the original New Nationalist emphasis on efficiency, administrative centralization, and executive power and the New Freedom faith in fact-finding, voluntary cooperation, and democratic participation. "We must speak, act, and serve together," Wilson reminded the nation. Efficiency quickly became the watchword for a new managerial elite that came to Washington with proposals for a planned war effort. Wesley C. Mitchell, a professor-turned-bureaucrat who joined the Division of Planning and Statistics of the War Industries Board, explained the appeal of government service to the professionals and businessmen who signed up for the duration. "Indeed I am in a mood to demand excitement and make it up when it doesn't offer of itself. I am ready to concoct a new plan for running the universe at any minute. . . ." Efficiency as the dominant progressive ideal attached itself to the image of the war machine turning out men and materiel automatically without the interference of politcs or partisanship. Slogans defined the renewed progressive purpose—"Elimination of Waste," "Standardization of Production," "Conservation of Resources," "Centralized Control," and above them the Wilsonian device "Democratic Autocracy."

The American performance fell far short of the progressive ideal. The most urgent task for the war state was mobilizing industry. Even before war was declared, Congress established the Council of National Defense, an advisory body composed of cabinet members and industrial and labor leaders charged with taking an inventory of the national resources. Out of the council's preliminary survey came the War Industries Board, which attempted. at first without success, to control production, arrange purchases, allocate scarce resources, and regulate labor relations. The War Industries Board failed to function effectively until Congress overhauled it, conferring near dictatorial powers on the President. Wilson brought the Wall Street banker Bernard Baruch to Washington to head the agency early in 1918 and gave him sweeping powers to establish priorities and increase production. Baruch's agency, however, was hampered in its work throughout the war by inadequate information. The continuing lack of needed data, Baruch complained, was "the greatest deterrent to effective action." By the end of the war the WIB was just beginning to unsnarl the problems of production.

In addition to regulating industrial production Wilson moved quickly to bring food and transportation under control. To head the Food Administration he appointed Herbert Hoover, who used his powers under the Lever Act to extend government control over the production and distribution of staples. Hoover's problems were complicated by poor harvests, and he was forced to experiment with price-fixing devices and a massive consumer education campaign to limit consumption. The strategy succeeded, first in doubling and then in trebling the amount of food that could be exported to starving Europe. Hoover's management of food production represented the primary accomplishment of wartime progressivism.

Managing the nation's railroads proved even more difficult, as Wilson first experimented unsuccessfully with a voluntary system under the Railroads War Board. Attempts to increase rolling stock and equalize traffic broke down completely in December 1917. Congress demanded an investigation, out of which came a revised United States Railroad Administration given effective power. Gradually the Railroad Administration extricated itself from confusion, and by

THE WAR ON THE HOME FRONT

Victory gardens were one way Americans at home could contribute. (*Brown Brothers.*)

the end of the war it too, like the War Industries Board, was beginning to function efficiently.

The Fuel Administration, headed by the progressive Harry A. Garfield, followed Hoover's lead in the Food Administration by seeking to stimulate coal production with price supports designed to guarantee profits, and less successfully, with schemes for rationalizing production and distribution. Shipping and the construction of a carrying fleet presented the Wilson administration with its most difficult problems. Here the challenge was deceptively simple: to build or commandeer ships faster than German U-boats could sink them. The progressive solution—the Emergency Fleet Corporation, originally an adjunct of the United States Shipping Board—proved inadequate. Divided leadership played havoc with planning, and the heads of the competing administrative agencies spent half the war quarreling over priorities and conflicting programs. Wilson finally removed them and put the competing interests under a single head. By September 1918 the Emergency Fleet Corporation had built only 500,000 tons of new shipping, less than German submarines had sunk in an average month in early 1917.

The labor policy of the Wilson administration was aimed at including the American workingman into the wartime partnership of business and government, as a junior partner but one entitled to his fair share of war prosperity. Yet here too a workable labor policy was slow in developing. Not until April 1918 did Wilson move to establish the National War Labor Board, with the power to adjudicate disputes between labor and management. Under the direction of ex-President William Howard Taft and the progressive labor lawyer Frank P. Walsh, the National War Labor Board heard over a thousand cases during the war involving three-quarters of a million workers. In general, Wilson's labor policy was a generous one designed to tolerate if not encourage unionism, establish an eight-hour day, avert strikes through arbitration, and provide limited increases in wages. The WLB also attempted to extend its influence into policymaking, with the creation of the War Labor Policies Board under the direction of Felix Frankfurter who sought to regularize and direct the flow of labor into crucial war industries. Frankfurter, however, like Baruch in the WIB, lacked the data needed to devise an effective plan, and once again progressive hopes outdistanced bureaucratic performance.

The progressive experiment in wartime planning was hardly an unqualified success. Lacking more than the rudiments of a national bureaucracy at the outset, Wilson's administration necessarily fumbled and temporized, dispersing rather than centralizing power through a host of overlapping and competing agencies. Not surprisingly, confusion and inefficiency resulted, as progressive bureaucrats groped their way toward centralization, learning slowly from their many mistakes. When the Armistice came the American war machine was just beginning to produce at a level approaching full capacity.

The most important consequence of the national war effort was the completion of the alliance between big business and the government. To an extent the pact was inevitable since it was only within those consolidated national industries that needed managerial talent could be recruited. To Washington accordingly, came the leaders of business and industry primed with patriotism but also determined to advance the interests of their sector, which they quickly identified with the national good. Wilson's appointment of Bernard Baruch was only the most visible symbol of this new alliance. From the ranks of railroad management, from big steel, heavy industry, finance, and banking came the self-appointed leaders of national mobilization, all bringing a measure of expertise but with it demands for stability and predictability in their industries that could only be furnished them by government.

Big business profited from the war directly and indirectly—directly in the form of arrangements like the cost-plus contract guaranteeing high levels of profit, indirectly in an education in the uses of government power to provide incentive and reward. Labor fared less well. Wartime inflation, climbing from a cost-of-living base of 100 in 1913 to 203.7 in 1920, cut deeply into wage increases. Farmers benefited from a substantial rise in real income during the war, a gain that would quickly disappear with the return of peace. But corporate profits skyrocketed in the years between 1914 and 1919, increasing threefold by the time America entered the war and leveling off in the following years at an annual 30 percent. Gains in the steel industry ranged from 30 percent to 300 percent. In the lumber industry they averaged 17 percent. In oil, 21 percent. In copper, 24 percent. Even with the moderate excess-profits tax and steeper levies on higher incomes the war made an estimated 42,000 new millionaires. If the progressive programs of Theodore Roosevelt and Woodrow Wilson had sought, at least in part, a more equitable distribution of American wealth, the war tended to reverse their hopes by piling up profits in the upper reaches of the economy.

A second limitation of the wartime experiment with state capitalism stemmed from the limited progressive experience with bureaucratic management before the war. American bureaucracy in 1917 was still in its infancy, and the relative handful of federal agencies at the policymaking level—the Federal Reserve Board, the Federal Trade Commission, and other fledgling agencies—had yet to assert their powers fully. Inevitably, the wartime administrative apparatus creaked and strained under the pressures of mobilization. Ambitious reorganizational schemes were never carried out. Programs broke down. Authority almost always overlapped, and agencies collided over matters of precedence and priority. By a method marked by more trial and error than most progressives expected, the United States moved hesitantly from administrative chaos to some bureaucratic order at war's end. The wartime administrative apparatus could the more readily be dismantled once the war ended because it had never really functioned efficiently in the first place. Businessmen, convinced of the advantages accruing to the wartime partnership with government, were nevertheless willing

AMERICAN WOMEN WAGE WAR

New York chorus girls prepare to defend the city. (*Brown Brothers.*)

to dissolve the formal ties, leaving in their place a gentlemen's agreement that promised the benefits of government support without the threat of regulation.

If the gains for the federal bureaucracy brought by the war proved partial and temporary, the same was not true of the wartime campaign for loyalty and uniformity. Here the original progressive dream of an aroused and patriotic citizenry turned into a chauvinist nightmare, and the country experienced a crisis of civil liberties.

The American people responded to the war with a spontaneous burst of nationalist fervor, which triggered a chain reaction of repression and hysteria. In the first months of the war hundreds of thousands of self-styled patriots banded together in vigilante-like groups bearing impressive titles—the American Defense Society, the National Security League, the American Anti-Anarchy Association, even the Boy Spies of America—and dedicated to hunting out heresy wherever they found it. The leaders of these grassroots purges were usually the "leading men" in the local community, businessmen, professionals and merchants, who combined more useful work for the Red Cross and Y.M.C.A. with the witch-hunting escapades common to superpatriots in any age. Wilson's administration, unable or unwilling to check such popular excesses, joined in purging dissent. The result was a fevered public uprising against nonconformity of all kinds and the ruthless suppression of American liberties.

The war hysteria fed a progressive appetite for national unity that had gone unchecked by a tradition of civil liberties. The absence of a libertarian concern with protecting basic freedoms, the central weakness in the progressive program, made a domestic war on liberalism all but inevitable. Patriots and vigilantes, equipped with ropes, whips, tar and feathers, and all the other instruments of intimidation, enjoyed a ritualistic field day complete with flag-kissing ceremonies and forced declarations of loyalty. The victims of this reign of righteous terror were mainly marginal people, uneducated or disaffected, isolated and without power. In Bisbee, Arizona, the "best" people rounded up some 1200 striking miners led by the IWW, piled them into freight cars, and sent them across the state line into the desert, where they were left stranded. In Montana a mob dragged the Wobbly organizer Frank Little out of his boardinghouse and hanged him from a railroad trestle. Soon the federal government itself joined in the campaign to crush radical dissent: in September 1917, Justice Department agents rounded up 113 officers and organizers of the IWW and impounded five tons of material with which to arraign and convict them.

Out of these spontaneous acts of suppression came loose national organizations and federations, perversions of the original progressive consumer and reform leagues, dedicated to rooting out subversion and punishing disloyalty. With support from local and state law-enforcement agencies the National Security League and the Council of Defense fixed on new targets—the Non-Partisan League in North Dakota, intent on nothing more seditious than interest-group politics; and the People's Council of America for Peace and Democracy, a band of pacifists widely condemned as "traitors and fools." Within six months of Wilson's declaration of war a rigid censorship combined with political repression had reached into the American press, schools and universities, the churches, and even the new movie industry.

This mass popular reaction formed the base of a pyramid of repression supporting a middle range of official and semiofficial bodies from citizens councils to state administrative agencies, like the Minnesota Commission of Public Safety, which became a model for the rest of the country. Other states passed criminal syndicalism laws aimed primarily at left-wing dissenters but designed as dragnets for a variety of nonconformists as well. Soon the traditional American distinction between public and private had dissolved in a welter of competing patriotic agencies.

The apex of the national system of extralegalism was completed by the federal government itself with an increasing range of agencies and activities, chief among them the omnibus Committee on Public Information headed by the progressive journalist George Creel and charged with mobilizing public opinion behind the war. Perfecting the progressive technique of moral publicity, Creel encouraged a voluntary censorship program and turned to the new public relations industry for a national cadre of opinion shapers who launched a propaganda campaign of frightening proportions. Creel's committee also coordinated the work of local patriots, advising them and publicizing their activities as contributions to the war effort.

The second weapon in the government's domestic arsenal was an administrative technique inherited from prewar progressivism, deportation of undesirable

aliens and radicals. The efficiency of the deportation device lay in an administrative process not subject to judicial oversight, a form of executive justice that
provided maximum freedom for administrators and minimum safeguards
for the rights of the accused. The original mechanisms for the swift removal
of undesirables had been created by the Immigration Act of 1903, and the war
simply gave widened scope to these summary actions.

The main contributions of the federal government to the national hysteria
were the Espionage Act of 1917 and the Sedition Act of 1918, twin declarations
of bankruptcy, like the Federalist Alien and Sedition acts, by a society that
had reached its conceptual limits. The Espionage Act provided fines up to
$10,000 and twenty years in prison for anyone convicted of causing insubor-
dination, mutiny, or disloyalty in the armed forces by "false reports or false
statements." The law also empowered the postmaster general to withhold mailing
privileges to newspapers and periodicals deemed subversive, a power that
Wilson's appointee, Albert S. Burleson, turned into a formidable weapon against
dissent. With Wilson's knowledge if not always with his approval, Burleson
wielded discretionary power with a vengeance in banning Socialist periodicals
like *The Masses* and Victor Berger's *Milwaukee Leader* and even a Single-Tax
journal for suggesting that more revenue be raised through taxation. If Eugene
Debs was convicted and sentenced to ten years in prison under the Sedition
Act for telling a Socialist audience that the master class causes wars while the
subject class fights them, most of the victims of such heresy hunting were faceless
people guilty of nothing more scurrilous than the opinion that John D. Rockefeller was a son of a bitch who helped start a capitalist war.

The Sedition Act of the following year was designed to close the few loopholes
in the Espionage Act through which thousands of "spies" and "traitors" were
presumed to have escaped. The new law provided punishment for anyone
who should "utter, print, write or publish any disloyal, profane, scurrilous,
or abusive language about the form of government in the United States, or the
uniform of the Army or Navy" or any sentiments intended to bring the government or the military "into contempt, scorn, contumely, or disrepute." More
than 1500 Americans were tried and more than 1000 convicted under these
laws. As Senator Hiram Johnson pointed out, this meant simply, "You shall not
criticize anything or anybody in the Government any longer or you shall go
to jail."

In some measure the war hysteria constituted an aberration, a sudden departure from good sense and a betrayal of progressive ideals. But at a deeper
level most of the excesses were traceable to original progressive sins, either of
omission or commission. Discretionary power vested in administrative agencies,
which was a progressive innovation, supplied the flexibility and promptness
considered essential, but only at the expense of regular processes amenable to
judicial oversight. Used to facilitate policymaking and to free administrators
from constant interference by the legislature, the progressive device had its

merits. But applied indiscriminately to the ideas and opinions of citizens, the new administrative process forcibly illustrated all the dangers inherent in a policy cut adrift from accountability and control.

The war crisis lowered the principle of administrative autonomy to the level of license. In the case of Postmaster General Burleson, for example, even the President was unable to check misguided enthusiasm and the personal conviction that no American should be allowed to "say that this Government got into the war wrong." "It is a false statement," Burleson insisted, "a lie, and it will not be permitted." Such arbitrary power lodged either in the federal bureaucracy or in the lower echelons of state and local administrations inevitably fostered an alarming national irresponsibility by subjecting opinion and expression to the whims and caprices of petty officials freed, as one of them boasted, from "exaggerated sentimentalism [or] a misapplied reverence for legal axioms."

It would have been difficult in any case for Wilson's administration to have curbed the patriotic passions of a generation preoccupied with rescuing a sense of national unity from the repeated onslaughts of a vigorous cultural pluralism. But the wartime policy of the federal government was tantamount to issuing wholesale hunting licenses to superpatriots in tracking down and destroying dissent—in Christian pacifists, liberal reformers, socialists, anarchists, but also in a host of cultural as well as political radicals opposed to the war. The origins of this cultural rebellion against genteel restraints and nineteenth-century pieties lay deep in the prewar experience. The war simply brought to the surface cultural conflicts that since the turn of the century had pitted a moralistic progressive elite against a vanguard of intellectual and artistic radicals. By 1917 a major shift in the intellectual life of the country had already been documented in a series of confrontations, some symbolic and others real, between an inherited system of unified truth and the powerful forces of cultural revolt.

The Little Rebellion: Progressivism and the Challenge of Culture

On February 17, 1913, the International Exhibition of Modern Painting opened in the cavernous Sixty-ninth Regimental Armory on Twenty-sixth street in New York City. To the music of a military band, beneath rafters festooned with huge banners and pine boughs visitors strolled through a maze of sixteen hundred paintings, drawings, prints, and pieces of sculpture. The Armory Show, two years in the planning, took for its motto "The New Spirit," which was emblazoned on a mammoth replica of the Massachusetts Pine Tree Flag, a message that many American viewers translated as "the harbinger of universal anarchy." A non–juried show organized by practicing artists to display works "usually neglected," the exhibition had been originally conceived of as a strictly American affair, and it was actually dominated numerically by American work, which made up three-quarters of the show. The initial plans had been scrapped, however, for the more ambitious idea of a vast international retrospective tracing the rise of modernism from its nineteenth-century sources in Goya, Ingres, and Delacroix through the French realist Courbet to impressionism and the bewildering canvases of post-impressionists, expressionists, and cubists. It was not the dark looming shapes of Albert Pinkham Ryder that outraged progressive patrons, or the realistic cityscapes of the "New York Eight" with their conventional images and brushwork, but what one critic called "the imported ideology" of the new European artists—Picasso, Matisse, Brancusi, Picabia, Leger, Rouault, Kandinsky, Duchamp, and Lehmbruk. Their collective impact on the progressive eye carried the force of revolution. The staid art critic Kenyon Cox, a reliable guide for many a confused progressive, admitted to spending "an appalling morning"

at the show, where he had witnessed the "total destruction of the art of painting." "To have looked at it is to have passed through a pathological museum where the layman has no right to go. One feels that one has seen not an exhibition, but an exposure."

The Armory Show collected into a single public symbol the disparate meaning of European modernism. In the bold, thin colors of Matisse's *The Red Studio* or the splashes of one of Kandinsky's *Improvisations* or the frozen motion of Duchamp's *Nude Descending a Staircase,* Americans registered the results of a perceptual revolution that had transformed the European intellectual and artistic world and now threatened to overrun the United States. Here made visible were the effects of the revolt against nineteenth-century positivism and formalism—in Nietzsche, Bergson, Sorel, Freud, Ibsen, Strindberg—the all too apparent fruits of recent explorations into the unseen and unknown, the irrational and the relative, yielding new definitions of time, energy, force, and will. For those progressives who chose to examine the work of the modernists, the Armory Show took on the dimensions of a crisis.

The progressive crisis rose directly out of the challenge to a comfortable realism and moralism in the outlook of the average American, who firmly be-

THE ARMORY SHOW MAKES NEWS

Autographed menu for the dinner given by Armory artists for members of the press; below left, *Chicago Record-Herald* news story; below right, "Seeing New York with a Cubist: The Rude Descending a Staircase—Rush Hour on the Subway." (*Menu from Walt Kuhn Papers, Archives of American Art, Smithsonian Institution.*)

MAY BAR YOUNGSTERS FROM CUBISTS' SHOW

"Crazy-Quilt" Art Is Not for School Children's Eyes, Says Teacher.

USES MANY HARSH WORDS

Chicago Record-Herald

Instructor Declares Exhibit Is Nasty, Lewd, Immoral and Indecent.

3/27/13

Public school children of Chicago, always urged by their teachers to view the beauties of the Art Institute, may be asked by the same teachers to stay away from the building—and all because of cubist art.

Nasty, obscene, indecent, immoral, lewd and demoralising were a few of the adjectives used yesterday by W. C. Strauss, art instructor of Waller High School, Orchard and Center streets, after a careful inspection of the international exhibition of modern art.

SEEING NEW YORK WITH A CUBIST

The Rude Descending a Staircase
(Rush Hour at the Subway)

lieved in the solid reality of the objective social world and in the power of "good art" to represent it. Socially useful art, most progressives believed, was the art of representation, if not always laden with a moral at least carrying an educative function. There was a lingering idealism in the progressive world view that rested uneasily with the new pragmatic techniques of social analysis. These two halves of the progressive outlook were held together by the firm conviction that science and the scientific method, complicated and baffling as they might seem to the layman, would ultimately prove the unity of truth and reinforce an inherited doctrine of progress. The Armory Show upset this unexamined progressive assumption.

Progressivism had reluctantly come to terms with the "Ashcan School," the group of New York realists whose paintings of street scenes and city types drew from the same sources as those of the urban progressive reformers. Like Whitman with his cosmic self, the New York Eight sought to encompass the whole urban scene with their illustrator's techniques and documentary style. The social realism of the Eight most progressives had learned to understand and accept—a direct involvement with the pictorial aspects of twentieth century urban life; the casting out of the twin devils of Puritanism and Philistinism; and the celebration of the role of the artist as the protean Whitmanesque figure spending "delightful days drifting among people" and recording his "independent personal evidence" of the wonders of democracy. "The tramp sits on the edge of the curb," the Eight's spokesman, Robert Henri, explained. "He is huddled up. His body is thick. His underlip hangs. His eyes look fierce. . . . He is not beautiful, but he could well be the motive for a great and beautiful work of art." Progressives engaged in similar explorations of city life agreed, for they shared Henri's insistence on "fundamental law" and those universal axioms "controlling all existence." By 1910 realism had broken the Genteel Tradition's grip on the American imagination without, however, dissolving its view of objective reality.

It was just this sense of the manageability of their world that gave progressives the confidence to reform and improve it. Experimenting with the new tools of social and psychological analysis and new definitions of change helped sharpen the progressive method, but they also strengthened the belief that the world was plastic after all and could be molded into a controlled environment. The recent knowledge explosion in American universities had shaken but not destroyed the progressive faith in what Theodore Roosevelt called "realizable ideals" and the belief that "the great facts of life are simple." The conviction that at bottom art and politics amounted to the same thing made the Armory Show a troubling spectacle for most American viewers because it threatened not simply aesthetic preference but belief in the possibilities of planning and social control. The "detestable things" wrought by Picasso, Matisse and Duchamp—"degraded, indecent, and insane"—seemingly disclosed the lurking presence of the unpredictable and the unmanageable, of flux and formlessness. A Matisse painting reminded Gelett Burgess of the havoc a "sanguinary" girl of eight, "half-crazed with gin," might wreak on a blank wall with a box of crayons. In choosing a revolutionary theme for their exhibition the organizers of the Armory Show were only following the path their European counterparts had taken for over a century, but American viewers took their political challenge literally and responded in kind. As one hostile critic announced: "The exploitation of a theory of discords, puzzles, ugliness and clinical details is to art what anarchy is to society, and the practitioners need not so much a critic as an alienist." Artistic madness would surely lead to barbarism.

There was a natural flow of antimodernism from aesthetic into political channels. "The United States is invaded by aliens," warned the archconservative Royal Cortissoz, "thousands of whom constitute so many acute perils to the health of the body politic. Modernism is of precisely the same heterogeneous alien origin and is imperiling the republic of art in the same way." Like the millions of new immigrants, modernism had swept away "normal conventions" and eternal verities with anarchistic doctrines "prompted by types not yet fitted for their first papers in aesthetic naturalization—the makers of true Ellis Island art." The Armory Show showed clearly the dangers of leaving the aesthetic gates ajar.

Modernism in the Armory Show presented progressive viewers with a symbolic dilemma: how to ensure the improvement of American society without underwriting revolution. Once again as in all other matters American, it was Theodore Roosevelt who had the last word on the Armory Show. "It is vitally necessary," the retired President reminded his followers, "to move forward to shake off the dead hand of the reactionaries; and yet we have to face the fact that there is apt to be a lunatic fringe among votaries of any forward movement." Still, the problem remained—how to give support to the sane and deny it to the dangerous.

On a June evening less than four months after the Armory Show this problem acquired renewed urgency. At the Battery in New York City one thousand silk workers from Paterson, New Jersey, stepped off the ferry and marched in a solid phalanx up Broadway and into Madison Square Garden. There, before a crowd of 15,000, they proceeded to reenact the events of their prolonged strike against the mill owners. Spectators watched a new form of proletarian art, social drama as participatory ritual. The Paterson Pageant was the brainchild of the young radical journalist John Reed and a handful of socialist intellectuals and artists, who dreamed of fashioning a new mass art out of working class grievances and the formal protest of the intellectuals.

The Paterson strike had been triggered by the decision of the mill owners to increase the work load for unskilled silk weavers and dyers already living on the edge of destitution. Most of the workers in the Paterson dye houses and mills, some 25,000 in all, were new immigrants from Italy, Russia, and eastern Europe, a large number of them young girls earning an average wage of $6 or $7 a week. The IWW entered the town in the winter of 1913 to help organize this unpromising material around the immediate issues of shorter hours and higher wages. "Big Bill" Haywood, fresh from his triumph in the Lawrence textile workers' strike, joined the young Wobbly agitator Elizabeth Gurley Flynn and the romantic syndicalist Carlo Tresca in teaching the Paterson workers that it was "far better to starve fighting than to starve working." By February they had succeeded in uniting the unskilled workers and shutting down the town.

The AFL, in trying to break the strike with their skilled workers, fed the progressive tendency to identify the immigrant with radicalism. Yet throughout the spring the ranks of the strikers held firm. Forming committees, appointing pickets, and arranging rallies, the Wobblies held their forces together against mounting retaliation. The mill owners fought back, stirring up hatred of "outside agitators," enlisting the services of the clergy and the merchants of the town, and dispatching police to break up picket lines and disperse meetings. "The IWW preaches sabotage; the AFL practices it," one observer noted acidly. By spring the police had arrested nearly 2000 strikers, put an end to the Sunday marches, and were indulging themselves liberally in clubbings and beatings. "There's a war in Paterson," John Reed reported to his fellow intellectuals. "But it's a curious kind of war. All the violence is the work of one side—the Mill Owners."

Reed had reason to know. Like many of the Greenwich Village socialists and radicals, he had made the Sunday excursion to Paterson to see for himself the clash between the workers and the bosses. Reed, whom Walter Lippmann once accused of the inordinate desire to get himself arrested, did just that and spent a few days in the Paterson lockup before returning to New York to write his indictment of the owners for Max Eastman's *The Masses*. A volatile cultural radical without any clear sense of ideological direction as yet, Reed dreamed of rallying the artists and intellectuals to the side of the strikers as the beginning of a permanent alliance of forces for the radical reconstruction of American life. This was the idea he brought back to the socialite Mabel Dodge's salon, the gathering place of New York's radical literati: An "oppressed" minority of cultural radicals must unite with other outsiders in progressive America under the banner of cultural revolution and proceed to make the world over.

Out of the plannning sessions at Mabel Dodge's evenings and out of recesses of her pocketbook came the plans for a gigantic pageant to raise money for the strike fund and educate liberal fellow travelers in the lessons of solidarity. Reed threw himself headlong into the project, spending eighteen hours a day on the script, drilling a thousand performers into a theatrical company, designing the massive sets with John Sloan and Robert Edmond Jones. By June he was ready, Sloan's huge factory scenes and red curtains in place, and his cast primed for performance.

The pageant caught the spirit of solidarity that Reed had sensed on his visit to Paterson. As it opened, throngs of workers moved down the center aisle to linger in front of the huge gray mills before entering to the sound of whirring machines. Suddenly the chant began— "Strike! Strike!"—growing louder and more insistent until the workers came pouring out of the factory doors and life moved outside the empty, dark mills. In front of the dead industrial husks the workers reenacted the scenes of the strike—mass picketings, police harassment, the clash between strikers and scabs where a worker was killed, the climactic funeral procession.

The audience, many of them workers admitted at 25¢ a seat, joined in booing the police, chanting strike slogans and lustily singing the *Internationale.* "This kind of thing," exclaimed the liberal journalist Hutchins Hapgood, "makes us hope for a real democracy, where self-expression in industry and art among the masses may become a rich reality, spreading a human glow over the whole of humanity." For a brief moment it seemed to Reed and his radical cultural critics that they had succeeded where progressives had signally failed in forging new weapons for social justice out of the materials of mass art.

But life did not imitate art, and the pageant brought a cresting of radical hopes for cultural reconstruction that quickly receded. The spectacle, originally intended to replenish the strike fund, actually yielded a check for $150. The 24,000 strikers who had not participated began to question the dubious benefits bestowed on them by the intellectuals. "Bread was the need of the hour," Elizabeth Gurley Flynn complained, "and bread was not forthcoming." The gulf between art and politics could not be bridged by ceremonial: in the summer the skilled workers broke ranks and returned to the mills. Then the mill owners in a series of shop-by-shop settlements that conceded nothing to the unskilled workers shattered their morale and routed the IWW leadership. By summer's end the Paterson workers were back at work on their employers' terms. Reed's script for the oppressed workers of America acting out "the wretchedness of their lives and the glory of their revolt" had failed to close the distance between the intellectual vanguard and the working class.

Artists and Scientists: Critics of Progressivism

Other critics of progressivism before the First World War perceived different divisions in American society and suggested other ways of closing them. In 1914 Walter Lippmann published his *Drift and Mastery*, and a year later Van Wyck Brooks his caustic essay *America's Coming-of Age*, two demands for an immediate reassessment of progressive aims and aspirations. Lippmann and Brooks, with their manifestos of modernism, represented a new intellectual type, the publicist directing his criticism towards a diversified group of fellow intellectuals, political leaders, and opinion shapers who composed the progressive elite. Neither journalists in a traditional sense nor philosophers, they saw themselves as cultural commentators whose task it was to direct the flow of American life through channels of publicity and informed criticism towards new national goals. They represented a new fraternity of cultural critics who sought to elevate their roles to the realms of public power through their analysis of American society.

Van Wyck Brooks, who had recently graduated from Harvard, where he studied under William James and George Santayana, was first and foremost a spokesman for the "Little Renaissance" in American art and culture that swept across the country after 1912. By the time Brooks issued his challenge to progressivism the signs of cultural rebellion against the Genteel Tradition were everywhere. Harriet Monroe had begun publishing her *Poetry: A Magazine of Verse* and introducing the work of new poets like Hart Crane, T. S. Eliot, Ezra Pound, Robert Frost, Carl Sandburg, and Amy Lowell. In Margaret Anderson's *Little Review* readers could sample themes ranging from anarchism to sexual freedom. In the same year that Brooks issued his summons to progressivism, the Provincetown Players were experimenting with the one-act plays of Eugene O'Neill. Theodore Dreiser had already completed his naturalistic explorations of American business in *The Financier* (1912) and *The Titan* (1914). Edgar Lee Masters's *Spoon River Anthology* appeared in 1915; Edwin Arlington Robinson's *Man Against the Sky* and Sherwood Anderson's first novel, a year later. Brooks joined the growing circle of artists and intellectuals in Greenwich Village following a brief teaching career at Stanford and at the Worker's Educational Association in Cambridge, England. In the Village he met Lippmann, who urged him to add his share to the literary renaissance by scrutinizing the "noble dream" of an American democratic culture in the light of the "actual limitations of experience" in the early twentieth century. Brooks promptly obliged with what he called an address to his own "homeless generation" of artists and intellectuals.

Brooks defined the basic American duality as the cultural split between "Highbrow" and "Lowbrow" a fatal division that had paralyzed the creative will of the nation. The American dilemma, he was convinced, stemmed from the conflict between a "quite unclouded, quite unhypocritical assumption of transcendent theory" and the "catchpenny realities" of a business civilization. Between these poles lay a cultural wasteland in which no true community could thrive. Brooks traced the roots of this American schizophrenia to the original sin of Puritanism, "the all-influential fact in the history of the American mind." To Puritanism in its many forms could be attributed both the "fastidious refinement" of current tastes and the predatory "opportunism" of American moneymakers.

Like the progressive historian Vernon L. Parrington, who was compiling the materials for the first volume of *Main Currents of American Thought,* at the same time, Brooks presented sets of paired opposites to prove his case: Jonathan Edwards and Benjamin Franklin, Henry Wadsworth Longfellow and Mark Twain, James Russell Lowell and Walt Whitman. These were the products of a binary culture, figures standing on opposite sides of an "unbridgeable chasm between literate and illiterate America." Throughout the nineteenth century the

WORLD WAR I POSTER

(*The New-York Historical Society.*)

divorce of the real and the ideal had resulted in an "orgy of lofty examples, moralized poems, national anthems and baccalaureate sermons" until the average progressive citizen was now "charged with all manner of ideal purities, ideal honorabilities, ideal femininities, flag-wavings and skyscrapings of every sort." In the meantime the American progressive landscape had become "a stamping ground" for every greedy commercial impulse of every individual businessman who held that "society is fair prey for what he can get out of it."

Brooks peered below the political surface of American society and pointed to the shortcomings of the progressive approach to reform. Progressivism with its moral certainties and good-government shibboleths had failed to solve the fundamental problem of modern industrial society, the "invisible government" of business. So far, the efforts of well-meaning reformers to alter American priorities had amounted to "the attainment of zero." Progressivism had simply consolidated the rule of "commercialized men." Of what use was it to tinker with political mechanisms, indulge a social conscience, or "do any of the other easy popular contemporary things" unless the quality of American life could also be improved? "To cleanse politics is of the least importance if the real forces of the people cannot be engaged in politics; and they cannot be so engaged while the issues behind politics remain inarticulate."

Here Brooks reached the core of the cultural radical critique of progressivism: Meaningful improvement of American society would require more than rationalizing a business system, more than the cheerful cooperation of business and government whether in the name of the New Nationalism or the New Freedom. "Business," Brooks declared, "has traditionally absorbed the best elements of the American character, it has been cowed by no sense of subjection, it has thriven in a free air, it has received all the leaven, it has occupied the centre of the field." Nothing would answer now but the massive shift of American energies "from the plane of politics to the plane of psychology and morals"; otherwise progressivism would have failed in its regenerative mission. When the First World War broke out, Brooks still had hopes for the cultural rebellion of which he was a spokesman. Three years later, America's entrance into the war broke these hopes on the rocks of the war state.

Walter Lippmann also discerned a split in twentieth-century American life that progressivism had failed to repair, but his definition concerned the conflict between the "sterile tyranny of taboo" bequeathed by the nineteenth century and his own generation's desire "to be awake during their own lifetime." For Lippmann the problem reduced itself to acquiring an education in the "discipline of democracy." "Drift" resulted from the capricious rule of old "bogeys"; "mastery meant applying the scientific method to politics. Like Brooks, though for different reasons, Lippmann faulted progressive reformers for their lack of rigorous thought. The New Nationalism, although it had examined some of the worst abuses of industrialism, still spoke the language of an outmoded moralism, and the New Freedom continued to make false promises of a return to an era of competition. "You would think that competitive commercialism was really a generous, chivalrous, high-minded stage of human culture," Lippmann scoffed, instead of "an antiquated, feeble, mean, and unimaginative way of dealing with the possibilities of modern industry." Unlike Brooks and the cultural radicals, Lippmann championed the cause of business consolidation and the rule of industrial statesmen who in their own way sought to transcend politics by lifting decision making out of the marketplace to the level of scientific management. "They represent the revolution in business incentives at its very heart. For they conduct gigantic enterprises and they stand outside the higgling of the market, outside the shrewdness and strategy of competition. The motive of profit is not their personal motive. That is an astounding change."

Lippmann agreed with Brooks on the need for relocating American energies outside politics, but he differed dramatically on the means. Whereas the cultural radicals sought to challenge and hopefully destroy the rule of big business, Lippmann hoped to rationalize and reform it. First, "You have to go about deliberately to create a large class of professional businessmen." Next, "You have to encourage the long process of self-education in democracy through which unions can develop representative government and adequate leadership." And finally, "You have to devise a great many consumers' controls." Equipped with these three devices for depoliticizing industrial society, Americans could proceed to reconstruct the entire social and cultural order. Out of this recasting of priorities, he predicted, would come a true cooperative society, neither strictly capitalistic nor wholly collectivist, but a new commonwealth made up of managers, workers and consumers, each applying the instruments of measurement and control provided by science.

If American entrance into the First World War threatened the foundations of Van Wyck Brooks's radical reconstruction of American culture, it brought a welcome test for Lippmann's pragmatic liberalism and his plans for a businessmen's government. Brooks deplored the war as a betrayal of his dreams; Lippmann embraced it as an instrumentalist challenge. By 1917 these two critical views of progressivism had been institutionalized in two very different magazines—*The Seven Arts*, which Brooks and his cultural radical friends Randolph Bourne and James Oppenheim founded in 1916 and nursed through a year of precarious existence; and *The New Republic*, which Lippmann together with the liberal nationalists Herbert Croly and Walter Weyl had launched in 1914. The war records of these two periodicals testified to the divergent fortunes of cultural radicalism and liberal nationalism under the conditions of war. *The Seven Arts* announced its intention of speaking to "that *latent* America, that *potential* America" lying beneath the "commercial-industrial national organization," and it lasted just a year before succumbing to the fervor of the patriots.

Brooks's mantle fell on the diminutive figure of Randolph Bourne, who more clearly than any of the other opponents of the war saw the coming defeat of "that America of youth and aspiration" standing below the battle. In "War and the Intellectuals," the most scathing of his attacks on Lippmann and the prowar liberals, Bourne ridiculed the "war technique" of liberal reform that had led the intellectuals to the illusion that they had willed the war "through sheer force of ideas." In accepting the war, Bourne charged, *The New Republic* editors had necessarily aligned themselves with the least democratic forces in American society, those neanderthal interests still clinging to mystical notions of the national state and economic privilege. The war, Bourne concluded, provided an escape hatch for progressives, who had become prisoners of their own conceptions of the good society. The collapse of *The Seven Arts* after a year of minority opposition and Bourne's untimely death marked the end of the cultural radical attempt to reconstruct progressivism by supplying it with higher priorities.

Lippmann and the other editors of *The New Republic* continued to cling to the belief that they could direct a democratic war and help write a liberal peace. The American entrance, Lippmann explained soon after Wilson's declaration of war, would prove "decisive in the history of the world," since the United States could now proceed to "crystallize and make real the whole league of peace propaganda." Nor did he fear the effects of war psychology on the prospects of liberalism: in October 1917 he offered his services to the administration and was appointed secretary of the Inquiry, Wilson's hand-picked body of experts charged with preparing the American position at the peace table. Croly, who remained in his editorial post at *The New Republic,* quickly became disillusioned as he realized the nature of the liberal impasse both at home and abroad. From inside the administration, Lippmann's hopes for the prospects for a liberal peace remained high. Congratulating Colonel House on the administration's "victory" in securing Allied support for Wilson's Fourteen Points, Lippmann hailed the achievement as "brilliant" and "prophetic." "The President and you have more then justified the faith of those who insisted that your leadership was a turning point in modern history." Eighteen months later, discouraged by the President's failure at Versailles, Lippmann joined the ranks of the "tired radicals" seeking to defeat the treaty.

The Ordeal of Woodrow Wilson

In his address to Congress on January 8, 1918—the low point in the American war effort—Woodrow Wilson outlined the steps the United States and its allies would have to take in order to ensure a postwar world "made fit to live in." Wilson's Fourteen Points presented a blueprint for peacemaking drawn to his progressive specifications. Central to his plan was the principle of "open covenants openly arrived at," the extension to the international scene of the New Freedom ideal of moral publicity. Balancing this first point in a moral equation was the fourteenth, calling for "a general association of nations . . . formed under specific covenants for the purpose of affording mutual guarantees of political

PRESIDENT WILSON EMBARKS FOR PARIS, DECEMBER
1918

(*Brown Brothers.*)

independence and territorial integrity to great and small states alike." The
main substantive points in Wilson's utopian calendar included a general disarmament, complete freedom of the seas, an equitable adjustment of colonial
claims in the interests of the populations involved, and a series of specific provisions based on the principle of linguistic nationalism for territorial settlements
throughout Europe. These were the lofty terms that Wilson, in the face of the
mounting opposition of his war partners, attempted to impose at the peace table.

   In trying to achieve his aims, Wilson was driven by his own intensely moral
nature as well as by circumstance to make several costly miscalculations. Part
of his predicament inhered in the Fourteen Points themselves. What, for example, did his principle of national self-determination mean and by what general
formula could it be applied? What adjustments might be required when linguistic nationalism failed to coincide with economic viability or strategic aims?
Then, how could a new Soviet regime with an exportable totalitarian ideology
be accorded "an unhampered and unembarrassed opportunity" for political
development? How, in short, could he as the self-declared representative of the
only disinterested power at the peace table establish in each and every instance
his claim on the enlightened conscience of mankind?

A related set of problems and misconceptions stemming from the same fervor concerned his political position at home. Who but Wilson himself could convert the Allies to his program and ensure the triumph of his cherished principle of collective security? Determined to play the dominant role at the Paris conference, he insisted on making his peace program a partisan issue in the fall elections of 1918 by warning that a Republican victory would constitute a repudiation of his leadership and his vision. Republicans, who already had grown restive under an unofficially nonpartisan war policy, now retaliated by accusing the President himself of partisan dealings. In 1918 they regained control of both houses of Congress. If the Republican victory did not quite constitute a vote of no confidence, it did serve notice on Wilson that the spirit of party politics had been revived and would be decisive in settling the fate of his program.

Even more serious was Wilson's refusal to include Republican leaders among his advisers. Former President Taft, Charles Evans Hughes, and a number of other party notables had expressed cautious interest in the idea of a league of nations, and their calculated exclusion isolated the President from the moderate internationalism he would so desperately need. On the eve of his departure for Europe in December 1918, there were already ominous signs of a growing presidential detachment from the realities of domestic politics, as Wilson began the retreat into the recesses of his moralistic nature. "Tell me what is right," he urged his advisers as he prepared for the conference, "and I'll fight for it."

THE COUNCIL OF FOUR

From left to right: Vittorio Orlando of Italy, David Lloyd George of England, Georges Clemenceau of France, Woodrow Wilson. (*National Archives.*)

Wilson fought tenaciously, even heroically, for his Fourteen Points against overwhelming odds. But in forgetting the first rules of politics and ignoring the domestic disarray he had left behind, he fatally compromised his position.

In Lloyd George of Great Britain, Clemenceau of France, and Orlando of Italy, the President confronted national leaders, who as he came to understand, spoke for their countrymen as he could not. The Allies had suffered grievously during the war, and their spokesmen could count on popular support at home for a punitive peace, one that would assign war guilt to Germany, strip it of all possessions, exact enormous reparations, and provide all the necessary safeguards against future aggression. To counter these narrow nationalistic aims, Wilson brought with him to Paris only the Fourteen Points and his vision of a new concert of power. Despite his initial popularity with the peoples of Europe his lone voice became increasingly lost in the clamor of competing chauvinisms. The American story of the peace deliberations was one of a moralist's mounting frustration and forced retreat from idealism.

The first of the Fourteen Points to be jettisoned was the utopian concept of "open covenants." Soon after the opening of the conference the plenary sessions gave way first to a Council of Ten dominated by the heads of state and their foreign ministers, and then to a Council of Four composed of Wilson, Lloyd George, Clemenceau, and Orlando, meeting behind closed doors. The press, barred from working sessions, became almost wholly dependent on news releases handed out after each plenary session. Wilson compounded his communications problems by withdrawing coldly from his colleagues on the council and ignoring most of his advisers, who also complained of his aloofness. Cut adrift from presidential oversight, the American staff floundered in confusion and frustration. Wilson, announcing that he had no desire "to have lawyers drafting the treaty of peace," played a lone hand at Paris and quickly spent all his reserves of moral capital.

On some of the specific issues of the peace settlement the President was partially successful in moderating the original demands of his partners. After an epochal battle of wills with the cynical Clemenceau, who likened his adversary to Jesus Christ bearing the Ten Commandments, Wilson forced France to agree to a multinational defense pact but at the cost of the immediate return to France of Alsace-Lorraine, the French occupation of the Rhineland, and huge reparations to be paid by Germany. On the question of the former German colonies he abandoned the principle of "impartial adjustment" but salvaged his plan for a mandate system under League auspices. For Poland he secured a corridor to the sea at the expense of linguistic nationalism, and in the Austrian Tyrol and Trentino he presided over the transfer of some 200,000 Germans to Italy. When he refused to agree to a similar transfer of a strip of the Dalmatian coast, he precipitated a crisis by appealing to the Italian people for national self-restraint over the heads of their representatives, a tactic that only hardened

nationalist resolves and further discredited him with his colleagues. Self-determination of peoples, a legacy of nineteenth-century romantic nationalism, was
honored in the breach at Paris as often as it was successfully applied.

But it was on reparations that Wilson suffered his most telling defeat. France
originally proposed the preposterous figure of $200 billion, and England seemed
unwilling to settle for much less. Clemenceau and Lloyd George, under heavy
pressure from their respective publics, overrode Wilson's objections to such
crippling demands and forced him to accept the inclusion of civilian damages
and military pensions in the final assessment of Germany. The President, pushed
beyond the limits of endurance, ill and confused, agreed to the principle of
massive repayments and allowed the fixing of the specific amount to be postponed.
A Reparations Commission in 1921 set the indemnity at $56 billion without
regard to Germany's ability to pay or to the political consequences to a struggling
Weimar Republic.

Throughout the agony of daily defeat Wilson was sustained by his hopes
for the League of Nations and the work of drafting the covenant. The League,
he told himself, would correct the mistakes and make good the deficiencies of
the peace settlement to which it must be firmly tied. "Settlements may be temporary, but the action of nations in the interest of peace and justice must be
permanent," he explained in presenting his handiwork to the plenary session
in February 1919:

> This document . . . is not a straitjacket, but a vehicle of life. A living thing is born . . . it
> is at one and the same time a practical document and a humane document. . . .

Wilson considered the League the vital center of the treaty: whatever the
failings of the peacemakers—and Wilson now realized they were legion—the
League would correct them. Moreover, by tying the League so closely to the
treaty, the President hoped to forestall his congressional opponents by presenting them with a complete legal package that they would have to accept or reject
as a whole. That they might succeed in rejecting his great work he never seriously
considered.

It was Article X, the "heart of the covenant" in Wilson's view, that became the
great symbolic issue that eventually destroyed his dream. Article X provided that

> the members of the League undertake to respect and preserve as against external aggres-
> sion the territorial integrity and existing political independence of all the Members of the
> League. In case of any such aggression or in case of any threat or danger of such aggres-
> sion the Council shall advise upon the means by which this obligation shall be fulfilled.

For Wilson, Article X represented the triumph of moral force. The details of
applying sanctions against future offenders concerned him less than the simple
recognition by the nations of the world of his principle of collective security.
This principle, at least, he had managed to rescue from the ruins of the treaty,
and he meant to defend it at all costs.

In part the League, on which Wilson pinned all his hopes, represented the application of the progressive idea of commission government to the field of international affairs. Like a federal commission designed to free policymaking from the whims of politicians, the League with its various branches and agencies would provide the means for defusing international crises and resolving conflicts through arbitration. But in another and more profound sense Wilson's League of Nations was simply the culmination of inherited nineteenth-century liberal principles and a doctrine of progress. In the President's mind the League symbolized the old American truths and moral assumptions that neither the sophisticated instrumentalism of a Walter Lippmann nor the scoffings of cultural radicals like Van Wyck Brooks had been able to unsettle. As American institutions and legal instruments reformed the rest of the world, so the myth declared, and as the beneficent workings of trade and commerce gathered peoples together in harmony and abundance, the old selfish national interests would gradually die out until some day a worldwide legal community would rise in place of the old system of balance of power. Wilson, having witnessed four years of international slaughter and stood by while the nationalists at the peace conference imposed a punitive peace on Germany, was convinced that the time had come for building such an international moral order. While he was willing to concede much—and in fact had conspicuously failed to control the peace conference—he was not prepared to compromise on the League of Nations nor on the question of the role his country would have to play in its creation.

Wilson's utopian commitment led him to overlook two fundamental problems. The first resulted from attaching the League to the treaty: in joining an international agency to a Carthaginian peace, the Allies had merely fashioned an instrument of enforcement and put it in the hands of the victors. Connected to this contradiction of means was a second question of intent. Was the League intended to facilitate change or to prevent it? Was it designed simply to enforce a victor's peace, or would it adjust shifting balances of national power, incorporate new members, and provide for ordered change? No amount of Wilsonian rhetoric about "the general moral judgment of mankind" could obscure the basic confusion of purpose in his attempt to replace international power relations with a utopian community of moral force.

Wilson returned in the summer of 1919 to a nation already in the throes of reaction. The shadow of the Russian Revolution, which had fallen over the peace table, now lengthened across the Atlantic. The threat of revolution strengthened the forces of the right everywhere in Europe as conservatives rushed to defend their states from the Bolshevik menace. To Americans the Soviet challenge appeared particularly ominous because it threatened to destroy their own revolutionary tradition. Here was no mere political rearrangement sensibly completed and solicitous of property rights and personal liberties, but a vast social upheaval with a collectivist ideology that was the antithesis of Western capitalist democracy. The immediate American response to the new Soviet regime was twofold: an abortive attempt to strengthen the counterrevolutionary forces in Russia by landing troops (soon withdrawn) at Murmansk and Vladivostok, and the tendency at home to see Reds everywhere. By the summer of 1919 the "Red Scare" had taken full possession of the public imagination as a wartime fear of subversion was suddenly transformed into dread of imminent revolution.

Wilson also felt the full force of a congressional reaction that had been building since the Armistice. War mobilization had concentrated unprecedented power in the executive branch of the government, thus completing the political cycle that had begun with Theodore Roosevelt's presidency. But now, with reconversion and demobilization, the pendulum began to swing the other way, as Congress moved firmly to reassert its control over foreign affairs as well as domestic policy.

The legislative resurgence had already acquired a highly partisan cast with the revival of the Republican party, which with forty-nine seats in the Senate now enjoyed a two-vote margin over its rivals. Presented with the opportunity to check Wilson's power by modifying the terms of American participation in the new League of Nations, they scarcely could be expected to resist. Republicans also were preparing themselves for rolling back wartime controls and curbing the regulatory power of federal agencies, whose activities they now tended to equate with socialism. They reasoned that if the wartime prosperity could be maintained and the gains to business ensured at the same time the supervisory powers of the federal government were curtailed, then an incoming Republican administration, on which they counted, might well build a new dynasty based on voluntary cooperation. The League was only the most obvious issue with which Republicans aimed to reestablish themselves in contention once again.

Yet on the question of acceptance of Wilson's treaty and American participation in the League of Nations, the Republican members of the Senate remained divided. On the right of the party stood some dozen or fifteen "Irreconcilable" stalwarts, isolationists opposed to nearly any continued international involvement. At the other end of the spectrum were the "Mild Reservationists," supporters of the League in principle but concerned with the extent of Wilson's commitment to collective security and anxious to reduce it. Ranged between these two ideological poles were the "Strong Reservationists," making up the majority faction and taking their orders from Henry Cabot Lodge. Lodge combined a cordial hatred of the President with a narrow nationalism that had not changed since the Spanish-American War. The "Strong Reservationists," willing to consider United States participation only on their own terms, were fully prepared to force on the President significant reservations limiting the extent of American commitments and making the Congress rather than the chief executive the final judge of their applicability. Within his own party, Wilson could count on solid internationalist support, but it was clear at the outset of the struggle that he would have to detach a sizable number of Republican moderates from Lodge's control if he were going to win acceptance for his project. By July 1919, Wilson faced a formidable but not an impossible task, one that would require great patience and even greater flexibility.

For his part, Lodge followed a clever strategy contrived to exploit every advantage over his adversary. He packed the Senate Foreign Relations Committee with his followers; conducted interminable hearings that gave a voice to every conceivable opponent of the League; courted right-wing businessmen like Henry Clay Frick and Andrew Mellon, who had swung over to his side; and loaded the Treaty down with amendments. By fall his original forty-five amendments had been reduced to fourteen reservations, one for each of Wilson's initial Fourteen Points. The first reserved to the United States the sole right to decide whether it had fulfilled its obligations under the covenant and gave the power of withdrawal from the League to Congress. The second, directed at the controversial Article X, was also aimed unerringly at Wilson's greatest weakness. It provided the primary check to the President's hopes for full American participation by stipulating that the United States would accept no obligation to enforce the collective security provisions of the covenant without the consent of Congress in each and every case. Other reservations rejected any mandates assignable to the United States; reserved the right to determine which questions involving American interests might be submitted to the League; and withdrew the Monroe Doctrine from the international arena altogether. Taken together, Lodge's reservations were significant though hardly crippling modifications, as the subsequent history of the League would show.

Yet, as Lodge hoped, Wilson believed otherwise; he consistently refused to make a realistic assessment of the damage done to his vehicle. He was unwilling to consider the specific circumstances under which the United States might be called on to apply sanctions, either economic or military, because basically he was convinced that full discussion and debate in the forum of the League would make any such drastic appeal unnecessary. For him the real question was simple: Was the United States prepared to make the significant moral gesture towards peace and international security? Would the American people see to it that the Senate carried out its obligation? Although the actual struggle with the Senate grew complicated with proposals and counterproposals, amendments, reservations, and interpretations, Wilson's position remained essentially the one he had taken in presenting the treaty to the Senate: "The stage is set, the destiny disclosed. . . . We cannot turn back. We can only go forward, with lifted eyes and freshened spirit, to follow the vision."

His own vision led him away from Washington on an 8000-mile tour of the nation, during which he gave forty speeches explaining to the American people the importance of the League to their future security and welfare. In taking his case to the country Wilson was violating one of his own precepts. "The Senate," he once wrote, "is not . . . immediately sensitive to [public] opinion and is apt to grow, if anything, more stiff if pressure of that kind is brought to bear upon it." Now President Wilson ignored Professor Wilson's stricture. His tour carried him further and further away from political reality and the central problem of securing the consent of the Senate. Although he referred frequently to specific issues and explained the limited nature of the American commitment, it was to the theme of principle that he returned obsessively as he reduced the question to one of conscience:

You have no choice, my fellow citizens. . . . You cannot give a false gift. . . . Men are not going to stand it. . . . There is nothing for any nation to lose whose purposes are right and whose cause is just. . . . The whole freedom of the world not only, but the whole peace of mind of the world, depends upon the choice of America. . . . I can testify to that. . . . The world will be absolutely in despair if America deserts it. . . .

Worn out and distraught, collapsing under the weight of his moral mission, Wilson suffered a stroke in Pueblo, Colorado, on September 25 and was rushed back to Washington where a week later a second stroke left him paralyzed. Isolated by his illness from his followers and advisers, locked in a private moral world, Wilson in effect had spoken his last word on the treaty. Loyal Democrats received their presidential orders: vote to reject the treaty with the Lodge reservations. On November 19, 1919, the treaty with the reservations failed of adoption by a vote of 39 for and 55 against, with loyal Democrats joining the Irreconcilables to defeat it. Wilson still hoped to make the presidential election of 1920 the occasion of a giant referendum on the League, but his advisers along with more objective observers knew the fight was over. The President's dream had died.

Domestic discord in 1919 mirrored the collapse of Wilson's moral world. A calendar of violence marked the decline of original progressive hopes.

In January shipyard workers in Seattle struck for higher wages, organized a general strike, and paralyzed the city. At the request of the mayor the federal government dispatched the Marines.

In May four hundred soldiers and sailors sacked the offices of the Socialist New York *Call* and beat up the staff.

In the summer of 1919, race riots erupted in 25 cities across the country, the most serious outbreak in Chicago where 38 were killed and over 500 injured.

In September the Boston police force struck for the right to unionize, and the city experienced a wave of looting and theft until leading businessmen and Harvard students restored order.

In September 350,000 steelworkers struck for the right to unionize and an eight-hour day.

In November a mob in Centralia, Washington dragged the IWW agitator Wesley Everest from jail and castrated him before hanging him.

In December agents of the Labor Department rounded up 249 Russian Communists and deported them to Finland.

THE WALL STREET BOMBING, 1920

(*Brown Brothers.*)

There were Americans in 1919 who recalled Wilson's definition of the progressive task six years earlier as "the high enterprise of the new day." "Our duty is to cleanse, to reconsider, to correct the evil without impairing the good, to purify and humanize every process of our common life without weakening or sentimentalizing it." For those who remembered there could be little doubt that the new day had ended.

Suggested Readings

Three good surveys of the military conduct of the war are Edward M. Coffman, *The War to End Wars: The American Military Experience in World War I* (1968); Hanson W. Baldwin, *World War I* (1962); and Russell F. Weigley, *The American Way of War* (1973). Fredric L. Paxon, *American Democracy and the World War* (3 vols., 1936–48) provides massive treatment of the war years at home and in the field. John G. Clifford, *The Citizen Soldiers: The Plattsburg Training Camp Movement, 1913–1920* (1972), describes the preparedness movement.

Immediately following the war the participants on the home front took the measure of their difficulties and accomplishments in numerous monographs useful for their impressions: Benjamin Hibbard, *Effects of the Great War Upon Agriculture in the United*

States and Great Britain (1919); Grosvenor Clarkson, *Industrial America in the World War* (1923); Gordon Watkins, *Labor Problems and Labor Administration in the United States during the World War* (1920); George Creel, *How We Advertised America* (1920). More recent studies are at once more accurate, better balanced, and generally critical. Robert Cuff, *The War Industries Board* (1973), discusses in detail the overwhelming problems confronting the board, and Charles Gilbert, *American Financing of World War I* (1970), carefully analyzes a difficult subject. Frank L. Grubbs Jr., *The Struggle for Labor Loyalty: Gompers, the A. F. of L., and the Pacifists, 1917–1920* (1968), describes the war efforts of labor leaders. Theodore Saloutos and John D. Hicks, *Agricultural Discontent in the Middle West, 1900–1939* (1951), contains an account of the growing plight of the farmers, as the opening section of George Soule, *Prosperity Decade* (1947), does for the American economy as a whole. Daniel R. Beaver, *Newton D. Baker and the American War Effort, 1917–1919* (1966), surveys the contributions of a great organizer. George T. Blakely, *Historians on the Homefront: American Propagandists for the Great War* (1970), is an unsettling account of misplaced patriotism. Seward W. Livermore, *Politics Is Adjourned: Woodrow Wilson and the War Congress, 1916–1919* (1966), recounts the fate of wartime bipartisanship.

The years since World War II have seen a growing number of incisive studies of American civil liberties during and after the First World War. Beginning with Zechariah Chafee, *Free Speech in the United States* (1941), the list includes Harry N. Scheiber, *The Wilson Administration and Civil Liberties, 1917–1921* (1960); Donald M. Johnson, *The Challenge to American Freedoms* (1963); H. C. Peterson and Gilbert Fite, *Opponents of the War, 1917–1918* (1957); William Preston, Jr., *Aliens and Dissenters: Federal Suppression of Radicals, 1903–1933* (1963); Robert K. Murray, *Red Scare: A Study of National Hysteria, 1919–1920* (1955); and Paul L. Murphy, *The Meaning of Freedom of Speech . . . Wilson to FDR* (1972). Stanley Cohen, *A. Mitchell Palmer* (1963), paints a portrait of a national villain.

For the effects on the social and cultural life of Americans during the war, see the selections in David F. Trask, ed., *World War I at Home: Readings on American Life, 1914–1920* (1969), and Arthur S. Link, ed., *The Impact of World War* (1969). Paul A. Carter, *The Decline and Revival of the Social Gospel* (1954), traces the history of a key religious concept through the war, and Ray Abrams, *Preachers Present Arms* (1933), describes the recruitment of segments of the ministry to the war state. A. Hunter Dupree, *Science and the Federal Government* (1957), considers how war cements ties between government and the scientific community, Arthur Waskow, *From Race Riot to Sit-In, 1919 and the 1960's* (1966), and William Tuttle, Jr., *Race Riot: Chicago and the Red Summer of 1919* (1970), analyze the most serious of the racial disturbances during and after the war. Robert L. Friedheim, *The Seattle General Strike* (1964) dissects an important event. Wesley M. Bagby, *The Road to Normalcy: The Presidential Campaign and Election of 1920* (1962) opens the political door on the Twenties.

The immediate shock of war as experienced by artists and intellectuals is described in Stanley Cooperman, *World War I and the American Novel* (1967), and its lingering effects in Malcolm Cowley, *Exiles Return: A Literary Odyssesy of the 1920's* (1951), and Frederick J. Hoffman, *The 20's* (1955). There are two good discussions of American art in the early twentieth century: Sam Hunter, *American Painting and Sculpture* (1959), and Barbara Rose, *American Art Since 1900: A Critical History* (1967), which should be read together with her *Readings in American Art Since 1900: A Documentary Survey* (1968). John I. H. Bauer, *Revolution and Tradition in Modern American Art* (1967) provides useful commentary on the Ashcan School. For the Armory Show, see Milton Brown, *The Story of the Armory Show* (1963), and also the best brief discussion of its revolutionary meaning for American art, Meyer Schapiro,"Rebellion in Art," in Daniel Aaron, ed., *America in Crisis* (1952). The confused response of one practitioner of the strenuous life can be found in Theodore Roosevelt, "A Layman's Views of an Art Exposition," *Outlook 29*, March 9, 1913.

The best approach to the intellectual history of the Progressive years is through the writers themselves. Significant works of social and political analysis, now considered classics, include Jane Addams, *Twenty Years at Hull House* (1910); Randolph Bourne, *Youth and Life* (1913) and a collection of Bourne's war pieces, *War and the Intellectuals* (1964), edited by Carl Resek; Louis Brandeis, *Other People's Money* (1914); Van Wyck Brooks, *America's Coming of Age* (1915); Charles H. Cooley, *Human Nature and the Social Order* (1922); Herbert Croly, *The Promise of American Life* (1909); John Dewey, *School and Society* (1899); W. E. B. DuBois, *Souls of the Black Folk* (1903); Charlotte Perkins Gilman, *Women and Economics* (1898); Walter Lippmann, *Drift and Mastery* (1914); John Reed, *Insurgent Mexico* (1914) and *Ten Days That Shook the World* (1919); Walter Weyl, *The New Democracy* (1912).

On the diplomacy of war and peacemaking, Arno J. Mayer, *Political Origins of the New Diplomacy, 1917–1918* (1959) and *Politics and Diplomacy of Peacemaking: Containment and Counterrevolution at Versailles, 1918–1919* (1967), are both ponderous and provocative. N. Gordon Levin, *Woodrow Wilson and World Politics: America's Response to War and Revolution* (1968), focuses on the presidential strategies as does Warren Kuehl, *Seeking World Order: The United States and World Organization to 1920* (1969). Two works by Thomas A. Bailey, *Woodrow Wilson and the Lost Peace* (1944) and *Woodrow Wilson and the Great Betrayal* (1945), detail Wilson's tragic postwar course. On the opposition to the League, Ralph A. Stone, *The Irreconcilables: The Fight Against the League of Nations* (1970), is admirable, and John Garraty, *Henry Cabot Lodge* (1953), offers a sympathetic but not uncritical appraisal of Wilson's archenemy. On Soviet-American relations, see George F. Kennan, *Russia Leaves the War* (1956), and *The Decision to Intervene: Prelude to Allied Intervention in the Bolshevik Revolution* (1958). Peter G. Filene, *Americans and the Soviet Experiment* (1967), and Christopher Lasch, *The American Liberals and the Russian Revolution* (1962), consider the varied American reactions to the Revolution. Betty M. Unterberger, *America's Siberian Expedition* (1956), explains the failure of that misguided action. Lawrence E. Gelfand, *The Inquiry: American Preparations for Peace, 1917–1919* (1963), is an account of the role of President's advisers at Versailles. Paul Birdsall, *Versailles: Twenty Years After* (1973), assesses the peacemaking from the perspective of a later crisis.

Chronology, 1890–1920

1890
In *Louisville, New Orleans, and Texas Railroad v. Mississippi*, Supreme Court upholds segregation in railroad cars.
Sherman Anti-Trust Act passed in attempt to regulate monopolies in restraint of trade.
Sherman Silver Purchase Act passed, resulting in depleted gold reserves.
Yosemite National Park created.
General Federation of Women's Clubs formed.
William James's *Principles of Psychology*; William Dean Howells's *A Hazard of New Fortunes.*
Force Bill.
McKinley Tariff raises duties to average 49.5 percent.

1892
Populists organize in Saint Louis and nominate General James B. Weaver for President.
Grover Cleveland elected President.
John Muir forms Sierra Club.
Homestead strike in Carnegie steel mills.

1893
Financial panic sends United States economy into four years of depression.
Repeal of Sherman Silver Purchase Act.
Conference for Good City Government inaugurates urban progressive reform movement.
Pullman strike; Eugene V. Debs jailed.
Attempt to annex Hawaii following American-engineered coup thwarted by Cleveland.
Chicago World's Fair opens.
Frederick Jackson Turner, in "The Significance of the Frontier in American History," announces closing of the frontier.

1894
"Coxey's Army" of unemployed marches on Washington, where it is quickly dispersed.
Pullman strike, one of 1894 strikes in this year, broken by General Managers Association and federal troops; Debs jailed.
Henry Demarest Lloyd, *Wealth against Commonwealth*, exposé of Standard Oil Company.
Wilson-Gorman Tariff lowers some tariffs, makes average rate 39.9 percent.

1895
In *U.S. v. E. C. Knight Co.*, government defeated in antitrust suit against sugar monopoly.

1902
Roosevelt launches antitrust action against Northern Securities Company.
Newlands Act establishes Bureau of Reclamation for financing irrigation projects.
Roosevelt settles anthracite coal strike through arbitration.
Oliver Wendell Holmes appointed to Supreme Court.
United States returns civil government to Republic of Cuba.

1903
Bureau of Corporations established within new Department of Commerce and Labor.
W. E. B. DuBois's *The Souls of the Black Folk.*
Hay-Herran Treaty with Republic of Colombia giving United States 99-year lease on Canal Zone is rejected by Colombia.
Roosevelt aids revolt in Panama.
Hay-Bunau-Varilla Treaty gives United States full sovereignty in Canal Zone.
United States-Cuba reciprocity treaty forms close economic ties between both countries.
Citizens Industrial Association formed to secure open shop in American industry.
Wright brothers make their first flight.

1904
Roosevelt corollary to Monroe Doctrine.
Lincoln Steffens's *The Shame of the Cities.*
Roosevelt reelected, defeating Democrat Alton B. Parker and Socialist Eugene V. Debs.
Anna Howard Shaw becomes head of National American Woman Suffrage Association.
Northern Securities case.

1905
Lochner v. New York; Supreme Court declares unconstitutional New York law regulating hours for bakers.
Niagara Movement formed to agitate for integration and civil rights for blacks.
Industrial Workers of the World formed.
Roosevelt mediates in Russo-Japanese War.

1906
Hepburn Act passed, strengthening powers of Interstate Commerce Commission.
Pure Food and Drug Act.
Meat Inspection Act.
Upton Sinclair's *The Jungle.*
John Spargo's, *The Bitter Cry of Children*, exposé of child labor.

1912
Woodrow Wilson elected President, defeating Republican regular William Howard Taft, Progressive "Bull Moose" Theodore Roosevelt, and Socialist Eugene Debs.
Lawrence (Massachusetts) Strike against American Woolen Company, led by IWW.

1913
Sixteenth and Seventeenth Amendments ratified, authorizing federal income tax and providing for direct election of senators.
Underwood Tariff lowering rates.
Federal Reserve System created.
Armory Show in New York City.
Dayton, Ohio, adopts first major city manager plan.
Patterson Strike.

1914
First World War begins; Wilson declares American neutrality.
Wilson orders occupation of Vera Cruz.
Clayton Anti-Trust Act.
Panama Canal opened.
Smith-Lever Act.
Federal Trade Commission created to regulate business practices.
"Ludlow Massacre"; National Guard attacks tent colony of strikers in Ludlow, Colorado, killing 11 women and 2 children.

1915
United States troops occupy Haiti.
United States recognizes Carranza government in Mexico.
Germans declare unrestricted submarine warfare and sink *Lusitania* with loss of American lives.
Preparedness movement.
D. W. Griffith's movie *The Birth of a Nation.*

1916
Wilson reelected, narrowly defeating Charles Evans Hughes.
House-Grey Memorandum on United States efforts for negotiated peace.
American troops occupy Dominican Republic.
Louis Brandeis appointed to Supreme Court.
Tariff Commission created.
Adamson Act establishing eight-hour day on interstate railroads.
Keating-Owen Act regulating child labor (later declared unconstitutional).
General John J. Pershing's expedition into Mexico.

invalidates federal income tax.
Booker T. Washington's Atlanta Exposition address.
United States intervenes in boundary dispute between Britain and Venezuela as Secretary of State Richard Olney declares nation "practically sovereign on this continent."
Spain sends troops to quell Cuban revolution.
Stephen Crane's *The Red Badge of Courage*.

1896
Cuban rebel leader Maceo murdered, resulting in American popular support for Cuba.
Plessy v. Ferguson establishes "separate but equal" doctrine.
McKinley elected President, defeating Bryan and "Free Silver."

1897
Delôme Letter calling McKinley "weak" and "a would-be politician" intercepted, worsening American and Spanish relations.
Dingley Tariff raises duties to new high of 57 percent.

1898
Spanish-American War: United States acquires Philippines, Puerto Rico, and Guam, and annexes Hawaii.

1899
Hay's "Open Door" notes to world powers calling for "equal and impartial trade" in China and preservation of "Chinese territorial and administrative" integrity.
Senate ratifies peace treaty with Spain.
John Dewey's *School and Society*, pioneer progressive education tract.
United States, Germany and Great Britain partition Samoa.

1900
Foraker Act establishes civil government in Puerto Rico.
McKinley reelected President, defeating Bryan once again.
Robert La Follette elected to his first term as progressive governor of Wisconsin.
Theodore Dreiser's *Sister Carrie*, naturalistic novel causes literary stir.
National Civic Federation founded by labor leaders and important industrialists.

1901
Hay-Pauncefote Treaty.
Theodore Roosevelt becomes President after McKinley assassinated.
Platt Amendment.
Formation of United States Steel Corporation.
Insular cases.

order.
Algeciras Conference with Roosevelt's help settles French-German conflict in Morocco.
Black troops accused of involvement in Brownsville, Texas, riot.

1907
Financial panic; Roosevelt turns to J. P. Morgan and the bankers for help.
William James's *Pragmatism*.
Roosevelt appoints Dillingham Commission to investigate immigration problem.

1908
William Howard Taft elected President, defeating Bryan and Debs.
Louis Brandeis argues sociological brief in *Muller v. Oregon* as Court upholds state law regulating hours for women.
Root-Takahira Agreement; United States recognizes Japan's interests in Manchuria.

1909
Payne-Aldrich Tariff raising rates to protect Eastern manufacturers provoke opposition of South and Midwest.
Taft inaugurates Dollar Diplomacy in China and Latin America.
United States intervenes in Haitian and Nicaraguan finances.
National Association for the Advancement of Colored People founded.
Herbert Croly's *The Promise of American Life.*

1910
Taft fires Gifford Pinchot, chief forester.
Woodrow Wilson elected New Jersey governor.
Roosevelt's "New Nationalism" speech at Osawatomie, Kansas.
Women enfranchised in state of Washington.
Mann-Elkins Act.

1911
Triangle Shirtwaist Factory fire in New York City's East Side kills 146 women, leading to investigation and revision of state factory code.
Frederick Winslow Taylor's *Principles of Scientific Management,* pioneer work on industrial efficiency.
Marines sent to Nicaragua.
"Dissolution" of Standard Oil and American Tobacco trusts.

Germans resume unrestricted submarine warfare and United States enters war.
Russian Revolution; "February Revolution" establishing provisional government; "October Revolution" engineered by Bolsheviks.
Draft Act.
Espionage Act.
Purchase of Danish Virgin Islands.
Creation of War Industries Board.
Lansing-Ishii Agreement.
First Pulitzer prizes awarded.

1918
Wilson's Fourteen Points outlining administration's peace aims.
United States troops at Belleau Wood.
Saint Mihiel salient, first United States offensive.
Meuse-Argonne offensive.
Sedition Act providing severe penalties for expressing "disloyal" opinions.
Armistice; Germany defeated.

1919
Schenck v. U.S., upholding Espionage Act and government curtailment of free speech during wartime.
Abrams v. U.S., upholding Sedition Act.
Eighteenth Amendment prohibits sale or manufacture of alcoholic beverages.
Steel strike.
Race riots in Chicago, East Saint Louis, and Washington.

1920
Great Red Scare.
Defeat of Versailles Treaty by Senate.
Nineteenth Amendment gives vote to women.
Warren G. Harding elected President, defeating James M. Cox and Eugene Debs.

"THREE FLAGS," BY JASPER JOHNS (1958)

During the late 1950s and the 1960s, Pop
artists such as Johns adopted images from
advertising, comic strips, and all forms of
popular culture as subjects for their work.
During the sixties the symbol of the
American flag was used in many guises to
rally both opponents and supporters of
government policy. (*Collection of Mr. and
Mrs. Burton Tremaine, Meridan, Connecticut.*)

PART SIX

Modernizing the Republic

1920 to the Present

ROBERT H. WIEBE

T he First World War shattered some hopes beyond repair. Never again would a cultural vanguard expect a sweeping, almost spontaneous revolution in values with such happy zest as the Greenwich Village radicals did on the eve of the war. Never again would Americans bring such a shining optimism to international affairs as they did when Woodrow Wilson called them to battle for universal democracy and justice. A certain faith in the world's moral wholeness and its natural improvement had been irreparably lost. Yet these casualties of the war were themselves an important preparation for the nation's future. As the high ideals of the progressive years deflated, Americans entered the 1920s with a sharper focus on material goals. The greater willingness of Americans to find salvation through the economy set them on the path into the modern era.

The core of modern American society was a national economy that acquired its basic form in the 1920s. Beginning with the industrial consolidations of the late nineteenth century, the main subdivisions of the economy—the business of production and distribution, the centers of finance, skilled labor, and commercial agriculture—had become increasingly organized, increasingly committed to nationwide cooperation, and increasingly alert to the usefulness of the government in Washington. The First World War accelerated these trends. By the middle of the 1920s, the components of America's modern economy had co-alesced into a national system, and during the next half-century the system's essential character did not fundamentally alter.

Along with this national economic system came four primary problems that shaped modern American history. The dramatic occurrences of the modern era—the Great Depression, the Second World War, the onset of the Cold War, and the upheaval of the 1960s—certainly influenced the ways in which Americans tried to solve these problems. So in a much smaller way did the changes of. Presidents and political parties in Washington. But as the nation swung from prosperity to depression, from peace to war, and from confidence to doubt, it was always this set of four problems that gave continuity to America's develop-ment.

First, how should Americans maintain a strong economy? In the 1920s, the new economic system seemed quite capable of running itself. Without direction, however, it ended in the ditch of depression, and a majority of Americans turned for help to the national government. Yet for a quarter of a century after the Great Crash of 1929, the nation's leaders failed to settle on a generally acceptable means of using the government's powers. Not until the early 1950s did Republicans and Democrats alike come to rely on Washington's fiscal authority, particularly the huge national budget, to guarantee a steady, healthy economy.

A fiscal solution gained bipartisan approval partly because it promised maxi-mum government support for the whole economy with minimum interference in private economic affairs. A similar combination of support and restraint answered a second primary problem in modern America. How should authority be divided between national and local politics? What made this problem so sensitive was a growing separation between the two levels. National politics concentrated more and more exclusively on national economic issues. Local politics, on the other hand, continued to be steeped in a variety of traditional ethnic and cul-tural concerns. Different leaders, different standards, and different needs at the two levels of politics threatened to disrupt government. During the 1930s, the Democratic party under Franklin Roosevelt struck a tacit bargain that gave national leaders a free hand in devising general economic policy and local leaders a wide discretion in setting cultural and ethnic rules for their domains. In 1953, as the Republican Dwight Eisenhower entered the White House, this compromise seemed even sturdier than it had been under the Democrats.

A third primary problem involved personal rather than political guidance. What values should govern the individual in modern society? Some Americans adapted their values to fit the specialized occupations in a modern economy. Others, finding little prestige in their routine jobs, looked elsewhere for meaning in their lives. Though almost all Americans participated in the expanding consumer economy, some did so wholeheartedly and some warily. A great many wondered if they could even survive as individuals in an impersonally organized society. Such a wide range of responses demanded an equally varied array of alternative answers, and by midcentury American society seemed to offer the individual an appropriate mixture of personal values.

America's economy made it the world's most powerful nation, yet America's tradition held it aloof from international commitments. What role should the United States play in world affairs? In resolving this fourth primary problem, Americans tried to find a middle ground between immersion and withdrawal. Even the Second World War did not destroy America's urge to balance the need for involvement with the tradition of detachment. After the war, however, America's leaders interpreted the challenge of Soviet communism as too critical to allow a peacetime detachment, and through the global policy of containment, they cast the nation's future with a worldwide involvement in international affairs.

By the early 1950s, an initial round of asking and answering was completed. In the process, Americans had greatly increased the burdens on their national government. What happened in Washington intimately affected this web of solutions, and any number of actions there might unravel the entire pattern, forcing a new search for answers. During the late 1950s and 1960s, the policies of the national government did precisely that. A drive for uniform racial and cultural standards, highlighted by the movement for black rights, disrupted the balance between national and local power. An attempt to determine the destiny of Indochina, producing the Viet Nam War, eroded popular support for containment. These conflicts, in combination with deepening doubts about the future of the individual, triggered an open revolt against modern American values, first among well-to-do youths and then among millions of wage earners and townspeople throughout the nation.

In the 1970s, just as the national government was experimenting with a new compromise between national and local power in domestic affairs and a new balance between detachment and involvement in world affairs, the economy lost its equilibrium. International forces caused the greatest disturbance, and no purely American policy could tame them. In approximately a ten-year span from the middle of the 1960s to the middle of the 1970s, therefore, all four primary problems in modern American history had reemerged to demand a fresh set of answers. These problems, so thoroughly embedded in American society, defied any final, absolute solution. Their history was the history of modern America, and as each generation provided new answers, it wrote another chapter in the continuing American story.

30

The Emergence of Modern Politics

As their first order of business in the 1920s, Americans wanted to settle the issues that had carried over from the war years. But while they were placing those issues to rest, they also began the long process of developing a new system of politics. The most striking quality of the new politics was its division of interests between national and local affairs. In national affairs, modern politics concentrated on economic matters, seeking a nationwide policy that would best serve the economy as a whole. In local affairs, on the other hand, politics continued to mix people's economic ambitions with their ethnic, cultural and moral concerns. These differences were masked for a time, first by a general enthusiasm for America's prosperity and then by a common preoccupation with America's depression. Yet throughout the late twenties and early thirties, the gap between national and local politics was widening. During Franklin Roosevelt's first term as President, the emerging system of modern politics faced its initial crisis. After years of depression, were America's leaders capable of finding a national policy that actually benefited the whole economy? And how could such a policy bridge the gap between national economic needs and the cultural sensitivities of local politics? By the midthirties, a crucial set of answers to these questions was beginning to materialize.

The Reactionary Impulse, 1920–1924

Rarely had the voters faced such a lackluster pair of presidential candidates as they did in 1920. Each of the two major parties, turning away from the late examples of a strong chief executive, nominated a political mediocrity from Ohio. For the Democrats, Governor James M. Cox offered the best alternative to the stricken but still ambitious President Wilson. The Republicans selected the weak, affable Senator Warren G. Harding in order to break a convention deadlock. During the campaign, Cox talked as if he had lost his way in national affairs, and Harding relied almost exclusively on empty platitudes. But the handsome senator at least showed Americans a warm smile and a friendly manner. In November 1920, that genial personality, along with a nationwide accumulation of grievances against the Democrats, gave Harding an overwhelming 61 percent of the popular vote. Cox carried no states outside the South.

An era, it seemed, had ended. America now had a passive, conservative President with no taste for reform and no ambition for either national or international ventures. Promising the nation a return to "normalcy," Harding entered the White House with no apparent goals of any sort. Some observers concluded that he was trying to recapture the spirit of the McKinley years, when the chief executive had watched benignly while other people ran the country. They might better have cited the spirit of the Grant administration, for Harding allowed a swarm of greedy men to infest the government, corrupt many of its offices, and ruin his own reputation.

PRESIDENT HARDING AND FRIEND

President Warren G. Harding said "yes" to his friends too often, and his administration ended in scandal. (*Brown Brothers.*)

In an inconspicuous house on K Street, members of an "Ohio gang" with connections in the justice department sold immunity from federal prosecution. Charles Forbes, a chance acquaintance whom Harding appointed director of the Veterans' Bureau, fled the country in 1923 to avoid punishment for misusing millions of public funds. Most sensational of all, a long congressional inquiry in 1923 and 1924 exposed the bribes and backroom deals behind the private leasing of government oil lands on Teapot Dome in Wyoming and Elk Hill in California. For his part in the "Teapot Dome Scandal," Secretary of the Interior Albert Fall, whose lean frame, broad-brimmed hat, and drooping handlebar moustache made him look for all the world like a Hollywood sheriff, became the first cabinet officer in history to serve a jail sentence. Harding's close associate Attorney General Harry Daugherty barely escaped being the second. By a measure of morality or energy or ideology, the contrast between Harding's crowd and the administrations of Theodore Roosevelt and Woodrow Wilson could not have been more striking.

Harding's promise of normalcy echoed the desire of millions to purge their country of troubles and reclaim a mythical, harmonious past. Adapting the nation's oppressive wartime tactics to peacetime needs, a host of private citizens and public officials set out to eliminate organized radicalism in the name of 100 percent Americanism. They completed the destruction of the Industrial Workers of the World (IWW). Legally elected members from the Socialist Party were not even allowed their seats in the House of Representatives and the New York Assembly. During the Great Red Scare of 1919–20, Attorney General A. Mitchell Palmer twice ordered extensive raids on America's fledgling Communist party and came very close to annihilating it. "America," the evangelist Billy Sunday proudly declared, "is not a country for a dissenter to live in."

Although some prominent citizens sharply condemned the excesses of the Red Scare, antiradicalism remained a powerful force early in the 1920s. One of its victims was the Non-Partisan League, an alliance of respectable farmers, lawyers, and merchants that was active in an arc of states around North Dakota. Seeking freedom from distant businessmen and bankers, the Non-Partisan League wanted to use the credit of the state government so that local farmers could store their crops and market them at the best prices. Yet after winning control of the North Dakota government, the Non-Partisan League discovered that private bankers would not buy and sell North Dakota's state bonds. During the recession of 1921–22, the bankers' boycott succeeded in undermining the League's "socialist" program.

Antiradicalism also contributed to the drives against organized labor. Immediately after the war, businessmen and their allies created "open shop" committees throughout the nation to smash the unions in the American Federation of Labor. The leaders of the AFL were themselves vigorous antiradicals, but they still could not protect their own unions from sweeping charges that all labor organizations were somehow socialist and un-American. The steel companies crushed an ambitious organizing drive in their industry in 1919, and two years later the biggest meat packers cleared the unions from their plants. Under heavy attack, union membership fell from a peak of over 5 million in 1920 to about 3.6 million in 1923. Union morale suffered even more than statistics could reveal.

Because radicalism was invariably called an alien influence, immigrants generally suffered in the climate of the early twenties. Sometimes radicals and aliens were merged in a single stereotype of the bewhiskered, bomb-throwing foreigner. But the rising hostility to immigration came mostly from another kind of concern about a lost racial and cultural purity. Before the First World War, many "native Americans"—white, Anglo-Saxon, and Protestant—became convinced that they needed special protection against the deluge of Catholics and Jews from southern and eastern Europe. Some accused the immigrants of flooding the labor market and lowering the American standard of living. Others, citing the newcomers' support of corrupt political bosses, declared them unfit to vote. Advocates of prohibition condemned their saloons, and urban reformers condemned their living habits By 1920, innumerable Americans were justifying these prejudices with racial theories that categorized the "dirty little dark people" of southern and eastern Europe as a genetically inferior breed who were mongrelizing the American population.

Despite a minority who defended both the immigrants and the American tradition of open gates, public debate in the early twenties largely focused on the best techniques for restriction. The government's first attempt, the Literacy Test of 1917, had failed because, contrary to common belief, most immigrants could read and write. The opponents of immigration soon adopted a much more effective device, annual immigration quotas by nationality. Between 1921 and 1924, Congress considered various formulas for these quotas. In 1921, it used 3 percent of the number of foreign-born in the 1910 census as the basis for each European country's quota. In the comprehensive National Origins Act of 1924, Congress substituted 2 percent of the foreign-born in the 1890 census as an interim measure until experts could prepare the long-range solution, an annual limit of 150,000 immigrants divided according to the percentage of each European nation's historical contribution to the white population in the United States.*

The justification for these laws was explicitly defensive and nostalgic. Restrictionists idealized the racial qualities of an earlier America. At each stage in the legislative sequence, Congress discriminated more harshly against southern and eastern Europe, where by far the largest number of potential immigrants lived. Not only did the act of 1924 place a ceiling on immigration that was less than

---

*The complicated calculations on national origins were not completed until 1929. Some version of this quota system remained in effect until 1965, when Congress in a new law used the nation's need for skills as the basis for deciding who should be admitted.

one-fifth of the normal prewar flow; it assigned the English, Germans, and Scandinavians higher quotas than they were able to fill and closed the door on the Italians, Polish, and Russians. In a direct slap at the Japanese, the law totally excluded Asiatics. Seldom had Congress managed to embitter so many people here and abroad with a single law.

Of all the reactionary movements in the early 1920s, none equaled the Ku Klux Klan. In 1920 two talented promoters, Edward Clarke and Elizabeth Tyler, took charge of a small Southern organization with a name famous from the days of Reconstruction. By capitalizing on the attractions of its fraternal secrecy, white-hooded rituals, and elaborate titles, they built the Ku Klux Klan into a nationwide organization of about 4 million members by 1924. Its primary enemies were alienism and immorality, and in fighting them, the Klan often resorted to intimidation and violence. The fiery cross and the midnight whipping became its symbols of justice.

Basically the Klan was a collection of local organizations that adapted their purposes to fight the particular enemies of each community. In the Oklahoma oil fields, a local Klavern boasted of transforming "'no counts' of men and females . . . almost [into] a 'Sunday-School class.'" Its counterpart in Calypso, North Carolina, announced, "All the Catholic gold in the universe can't buy our manhood and our liberty." In Denver, the Klan opposed labor unions and welfare programs. But the Klan also stretched its influence into state and national politics.

A KU KLUX KLAN INITIATION NEAR
BRUNSWICK, MARYLAND, JUNE 28, 1922

Ghostly rituals gave the fraternity of the fiery cross an aura of special power, but the KKK was rarely a well-mobilized force. (*Brown Brothers.*)

Early in the 1920s, its leaders claimed political control of states as varied as Oklahoma, Oregon, and Indiana. The Klan's national spokesmen supported every campaign against radicals and immigrants, and Klansmen regularly flooded their congressmen with letters. The most important issue at the Democratic National Convention of 1924 was the place of the Klan in that party's affairs.

Though the Klan quickly aroused a vigorous national opposition, it remained a formidable presence in American politics because it represented only an exaggerated, somewhat disreputable version of a common impulse. Its themes were a lost unity and a lost virtue. It pined openly for a mythical America of hard-working, churchgoing, small-town citizens, all of whom were white, Anglo-Saxon, and Protestant. Like other Americans in all walks of life, Klansmen expected public policy to reflect their cultural, moral dreams. And in a variety of areas, including such economically significant ones as immigration and labor organization, just this kind of concern was still shaping public policy in the early twenties.

The Modern Economy, 1920–1929

Running parallel to these reactionary trends were fundamental changes that prepared the way for America's future. Though no single change made dramatic headlines, they combined to complete an economic revolution that had been under way for more than a quarter of a century. An important cluster of these changes involved the organization of the economy. Since the turn of the century, a varied array of groups in business, labor, agriculture, finance, and the professions had been forming throughout the nation. Each group was organized according to the special economic function it performed—lumber companies, retail druggists, railroad workers, investment bankers, civil engineers, and the like. Each of them wanted to stabilize its own economic sphere with its own rules. Each expected long-range planning to increase its efficiency and its income. Each recognized the importance of linking its activities with the activities of other economic groups around it. Taken together, they created a nationwide system of interest groups that were integrated by a common national outlook, a common concern for the health of the whole economy, and a common belief in the value of cooperation and coordination.

The most successful means of business stabilization was oligopoly, the domination of an industry by a few large firms. By 1920, oligopolies controlled almost every basic industry needing a heavy investment of capital. In railroading, for example, a handful of corporations, approximately equal in strength, divided the nation's territory among themselves. In the automobile industry, Ford and General Motors set the standard for a much more competitive but highly profitable market. In steel, one huge firm, United States Steel, rose above the other corporations—which were called Little Steel—to become the industry's informal leader. No matter what the variations, however, oligopoly always simplified the problems of industrial coordination by limiting the number of companies that had to agree on a common business policy. To facilitate long-range planning, these large corporations were themselves organized into several specialized departments, such as purchasing, finance, and production. The giants of industry had come a long way since the railroad pioneer James J. Hill had declared, "No one man can run more than ten thousand miles of railroad." In the 1920s no one thought to try. Management teams, working through elaborate corporate structures, coordinated the nation's big business.

In industries such as clothing manufacture, building construction, and most branches of retailing, where many small firms competed, trade associations were an alternative way of minimizing competition. About two thousand trade associations already existed in 1920, and they continued to multiply. Ranging from secret price-fixing pacts to occasional lunch meetings, the trade associations shared a commitment to pooling information so that common knowledge might stabilize their industries and increase their profits. Although they seldom coordinated business affairs as effectively as the oligopolies did, the trade associations still represented a significant step in the same general direction of cooperation and planning.

Most businessmen expected their wage earners to participate in these movements toward coordination and cooperation. Unlike the captains of industry of the late nineteenth century, who had usually treated wage earners much as they did hunks of ore or gears in the machinery, the modern business managers considered laborers as human beings whose efficiency would increase as their morale and incentive improved. Specialists in personnel policy organized company recreational programs for the employees, prepared chatty company bulletins, and invited workers to suggest improvements in the firm's procedures. To encourage a cooperative group spirit, some corporations sponsored their own company unions and shop committees. More and more of the unions in the AFL and the Railroad Brotherhoods accepted such company policies in an effort to salvage a place for themselves in the economy of the twenties. Under an accommodating new president, William Green, the AFL in 1925 listed the improvement of industrial productivity as one of its primary objectives. "[The] new, suave, discreet unionism," as one commentator noted late in the 1920s, "talks the language of the efficiency engineer and busies itself about ways and means of increasing output."

For good reason, successful commercial farmers regarded themselves as businessmen. As chemical fertilizers and the gasoline engine were revolutionizing agriculture, only the wealthy investor, applying these resources on a large scale and purchasing the latest improvements, could expect substantial profit from modern farming. These "agribusinessmen," like their industrial counterparts, sought to coordinate their affairs, and they too organized. Local farm bureaus distributed information about scientific farming techniques and through the

In the 1920s, America's "agribusiness" became integrated
into a national economic system. *(Library of Congress.)*

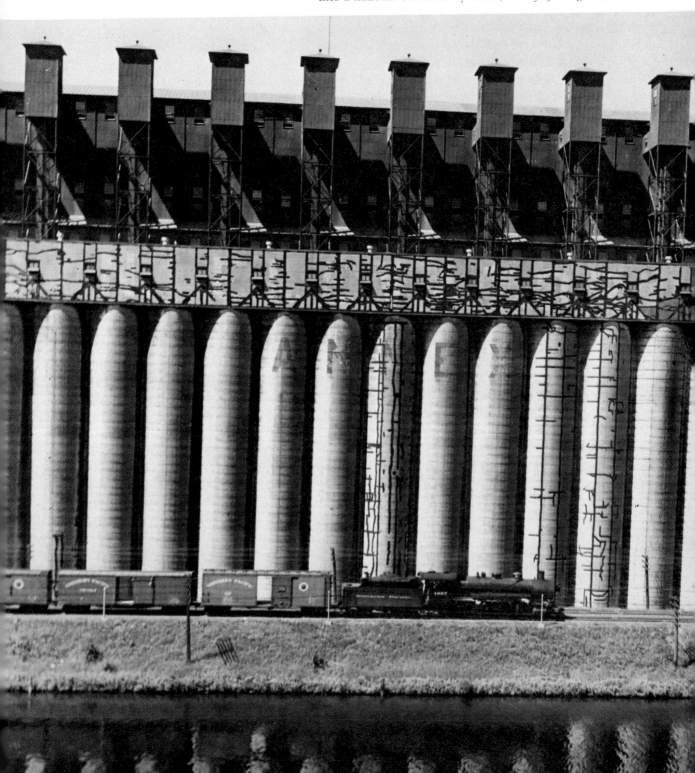

national organization, the American Farm Bureau Federation, lobbied for favorable government policies. In addition, cooperative marketing associations in such agricultural specialties as wheat and dairying tried to maintain a steady level of profits throughout the year for their members. The cooperatives acted so much like any other business organization that the same men who had staffed Bernard Baruch's War Industries Board in 1918 could become the most prominent advisers of the farm cooperatives during the 1920s.

Bankers acted as auxiliaries to these various business groups. The wizards of Wall Street no longer dominated American business as they had twenty years earlier. The regional structure of the new Federal Reserve System encouraged the development of other financial centers in such cities as Chicago, Minneapolis, and San Francisco. Bursts of prosperity after 1915, and again after 1923, not only hastened this financial decentralization but also increased the number of important corporations that could be their own bankers. During the 1920s, companies as diverse as Eastman Kodak, Aluminum Corporation of America, Ford, and Sears, Roebuck were routinely financing business expansion from their own vast profits. As a service agency, banking organized itself into specialized subdivisions that matched the needs of its business clients.

The professions formed a second band of auxiliaries to business. Lawyers had been specializing in contracts, taxation, and labor policy right along with the growth of modern business, and this close interaction between business needs and legal services continued during the 1920s. Engineering organizations, which had shown some interest in broad social reforms before the war, now concentrated their attention on business efficiency. A variety of economists, statisticians, psychologists, sociologists, and educators also adopted the stance of a willing helper to the nation's business. And where an important profession, such as chemistry, was not adequately developed, powerful industries encouraged its growth.

Changes in government came in tandem with the organization of these economic interests. Because the new network of groups was national in both scope and outlook, only the national government could meet its needs. But the government was expected to be a helper, not a director of the economy. Its tasks were to encourage the development of economic groups and smooth the cooperation among them.

The heaviest burdens of economic service fell on the executive branch. Even the election of an incompetent President did not seriously weaken the national executive. To the most critical executive posts, Harding appointed able men who were enthusiastic about the latest economic trends. Under Herbert Hoover, the Department of Commerce convinced manufacturers that they should standardize the production of items ranging from wood screws to fan belts, distributed business statistics to help the trade associations, enabled the major broadcasting companies to stabilize the new radio industry, and at every opportunity publicized the virtues of business cooperation. Secretary of Agriculture Henry C. Wallace was equally dedicated to the modern economy. He expanded his department's scientific research, its collection of agricultural data, and its promotion of orderly national and international marketing. The new Federal Power Commission, originally a collection of cabinet officials, did whatever it could to further the private development of America's hydroelectric resources, and such established departments as the Forestry and Fisheries Services and the Bureau of Mines also placed their skills at the disposal of their business constituents.

The independent commissions, which had expanded so impressively during the Progressive era, also adapted to assist business cooperation. Through the Transportation Act of 1920, the Interstate Commerce Commission received extensive authority over almost all areas of the railroad industry. But instead of using these broad powers to issue commands, the ICC certified the agreements that the major railroads and their organized business customers negotiated in the commission's offices. The Federal Trade Commission, which had exposed the monopolistic practices of large corporations during the war years, was transformed into a service agency for the trade associations, where businessmen met in private, agreed on a suitable method of cooperation, and departed with the government's blessing. Only the Federal Reserve Board, which Harding filled with cronies and deserving Republicans, failed to meet the new standards of government service. However, the New York Regional Board, under a reputable banker Benjamin Strong, substituted as headquarters for national banking policy.

The Supreme Court gave the modern economy the protection of the law. In *U. S. v. United States Steel* (1920), the Court allowed the nation's largest corporation to dominate its industry just as long as some competitors survived; and throughout the decade, the justices looked favorably on the oligopolies. Because the trade associations were a relatively new form of business cooperation, they posed a more complex problem for the Court. In 1921 and 1923, it condemned the associations' information pools as restraints of trade. Then in the *Maple Flooring Manufacturers' Association* case of 1925, the Court changed its mind: trade associations, like oligopolies, were legal if they did not eliminate all signs of competition in their areas of business. Meanwhile, the Court was placing narrow limits around the labor unions. Led by its new chief justice, William Howard Taft, whom Harding appointed in 1921, the Court sharply restricted organized labor's right to picket and boycott, and it watched approvingly as the lower courts expanded the use of injunctions against striking workers. In addition, the Supreme Court overturned a national child labor law in *Bailey* v. *Drexel Furniture Co.* (1922) and a state minimum wage law in *Adkins* v. *Children's Hospital* (1923).

Perhaps the government would have been a less willing helper if the modern economy had not performed miracles during the 1920s. As the interest groups and government services were forming a national network, the economy recovered from the sharp recession of 1921–22 and flourished grandly until late 1929. Manufacturing output as a whole rose 64 percent during the twenties, and after the postwar recession, the Gross National Product (GNP), one measure of the economy's overall strength, climbed a substantial 5 percent a year. The leaders of the boom were the automobile and construction industries. Both the number of automobile sales and the value of construction more than tripled between 1915 and 1925, then continued to rise. Moreover, these two leaders spread their benefits widely to such related industries as steel, petroleum, rubber, and cement.

How the economy worked impressed people even more than how much it produced. A broad range of manufacturing plants, following the lead of Henry Ford, introduced the moving assembly line, a revolution in factory procedure. Time and motion studies further refined the efficient use of labor. Through electricity in industry and the gasoline engine in agriculture, the amount of horsepower per worker rose well over 50 percent during the twenties. As a consequence of these changes, output per working hour increased an astonishing 35 percent, almost double the gains of the previous decade. America, it seemed, had answered all the riddles of economic growth. Throughout the decade, a stream of delegations came from abroad in hopes of discovering the secret of American productivity.

Contemporaries declared the arrival of a "New Era." Praise for the nationwide spirit of cooperation filled the air. As the number of strikes declined dramatically, spokesmen for the new industrial harmony boasted that America had resolved forever the conflict between labor and capital. Former critics of American society now became its ardent champions. Socialism was "reactionary," said John Spargo, once a leader of the Socialist party, and American capitalism offered "the greatest hope for mankind." "I can find no historic parallel, outside of the great religious revivals, with which [the New Era] has much in common," marveled a veteran of the social gospel. "Standards of ethics have probably changed more extensively than in any corresponding period in history." From the vantage point of the Great Depression, it would be easy to ridicule the most grandiose claims of the decade: poverty on the verge of abolition, a chicken in every pot and two cars in every garage, anyone with self-discipline and common sense a millionaire. But during the late 1920s, almost no one rose to challenge these visions.

The Politics of the New Era, 1924–1929

The first political test of confidence in the New Era began in August 1923 when President Harding, while touring the western states, died of a heart attack. Harding's Vice-President, Calvin Coolidge, an obscure Massachusetts politician of no apparent talents, suddenly inherited the White House. During his early months in office, the corruption that had spread through Harding's administration oozed to the surface and soon became public knowledge. Compounding the Republican party's troubles, a collection of dissident farm spokesmen, union officials, Socialists, and reformers nominated their own presidential candidate for 1924, the tough old progressive, Robert LaFollette, whose strongest appeal would be to normally Republican voters.

But as the journalist Bruce Blivin noted, most Americans reacted to the corruption among Harding's associates as nothing more than "a scandal of personality."

"Silent Cal" Coolidge, the model of small-town New England values, was able to overcome the crisis simply by demonstrating the old-fashioned Yankee virtues of tight-lipped integrity and tight-fisted frugality. At the Republican Convention of 1924, on a rising curve of prosperity and optimism, Coolidge's party nominated him for a full term. With scarcely any effort, Coolidge swamped his ineffectual Democratic opponent, the Wall Street lawyer John W. Davis, by 382 electoral votes to 136. Although LaFollette received an impressive personal tribute of almost 5 million popular votes, he carried only Wisconsin.

Coolidge's triumph coincided with a new calm in national affairs. The angry, volatile issues of the early twenties were rapidly subsiding. When Coolidge appointed the moderate Harlan Stone attorney general in 1924, the national government abandoned the cause of antiradicalism. The Communist party, practically outlawed early in the decade, appeared on the ballots of thirty-four states in 1928. As steady a voice of 100 percent Americanism as the *Saturday Evening Post* recalled the Red Scare almost apologetically as "nothing but the last symptom of war fever." At the annual meeting of the American Legion in 1925, one committee complained: "Americans have become apathetic to the monotonous appeal of the patriotic exhorter. The utmost ingenuity is frequently necessary to obtain publicity in the campaigns which the national convention has directed us to undertake." Vigilante activities also declined dramatically. Between 1922 and 1926, the American Civil Liberties Union reported, the number of disrupted public meetings dropped from 225 to 21.

The last public furor over the events of the Red Scare illustrated how much had changed since the early twenties. In 1921, two immigrant anarchists, Nicola

CALVIN COOLIDGE AND HERBERT HOOVER

No love was lost between Coolidge (left) and Hoover (right). Together, however, they symbolized solid values and sound leadership during the prosperous New Era. *(Culver Pictures, Inc.)*

Sacco and Bartolomeo Vanzetti, were tried for the murder of a paymaster in South Braintree, Massachusetts. In a courtroom echoing with antiradical rhetoric, the two anarchists were convicted and sentenced to death. For years, legal appeals delayed their execution. The bias of the trial, and the dignity and eloquence of the prisoners during their long ordeal, attracted a wide range of liberal and radical sympathizers, who fought fervently for their pardon. But the cause failed. As large crowds here and abroad mourned in public, Sacco and Vanzetti died in the electric chair in August 1927. Even more striking than the campaign of protest was the opposition to it. Now the conservatives were on the defensive. Prominent citizens who once would have screamed "Bolshevik!" remained remarkably quiet while an embarrassing legacy from the past ran its course. They considered the issues of immigrants and radicals already settled. It was time to enjoy the prosperous New Era.

Few Presidents have encountered as meek a Congress as Coolidge faced after 1924. Almost no one in Washington wanted to rock the cart. Although the costs of government in the New Era were about two and a half times higher than they had been in 1915, the President seldom had to justify his expenditures. The President's Bureau of the Budget, relying heavily on the advice of the United States Chamber of Commerce, decided on the level of government spending. After 1924, congressional appropriations were an almost perfect carbon for the bureau's recommendations. In 1926, even the controversial tax program of Secretary of the Treasury Andrew Mellon was enacted. To release more money for private investment, Congress lowered the rate of income tax for the very wealthy from 46 percent to 26 percent and cut inheritance taxes in half.

The only significant signs of a congressional rebellion came over farm policy. Commodity prices, which fell precipitously in 1921, revived sluggishly during the 1920s. In 1929, net farm income was still $3 billion lower than it had been in 1919. The farm lobby, demanding immediate assistance, proposed that the government sell part of the farmers' output in a protected, high-priced domestic market and dispose of whatever Americans did not buy in the lower-priced world market. In 1927 and again in 1928, Congress passed a McNary-Haugen bill to implement this program. Twice Coolidge vetoed it. Yet the actual difference between the farm lobby and the Coolidge administration was not very great. The administration's solution also sought to regulate the marketing of agricultural products. When prices fell, the commodity cooperatives would receive temporary government payments while they stored their products. As prices improved, the cooperatives would gradually sell their surplus and repay the government. The farm lobby, in fact, included this scheme in its second McNary-Haugen bill. Therefore, everyone appeared optimistic in 1929 when Congress created the Federal Farm Board, with an unprecedented $500 million in government credit to help the cooperatives market their products at the best prices.

But beneath the smooth surface of national economic politics, a very different spirit was bubbling away in local affairs. In the best years of the New Era, about two-thirds of the nation's families fell below an annual income of $2,500, which experts considered adequate in the twenties. These families had only an indirect stake in the economic system that was forming on the national level. Most wage earners were not union members, and most farmers never joined the agricultural organizations. Very small businesses everywhere—the neighborhood grocer, the secondhand shop, the little variety store—belonged to no economic league or trade association. Even a number of those Americans who were somewhat better off remained outside the New Era's organizational structure. The United States Chamber of Commerce discouraged membership in towns under 5000, and businessmen there kept largely to themselves. The Chicago Bar Association, the strongest of its kind in the nation, enrolled only half of the city's licensed lawyers in the late 1920s.

For most of these Americans, a neighborhood or a community bounded their lives. They cared very much about jobs and income, but they tried to manage such problems locally. Their networks were personal ones, woven through families, friendships, and contacts. They reinforced these strands with a high degree of cultural consciousness. Outside the cities, that usually meant pride in being white, Anglo-Saxon, and Protestant. These same qualities were also important in the cities, but there a great variety of groups were trying to preserve their

MAIN STREET, BINGHAM, UTAH, 1927

(Courtesy Utah State Historical Society.)

ethnic differences. Black, brown, yellow, or white skin, Italian, Polish, German, or Irish ancestors, Catholic, Protestant, or Jewish religion, all drew critical social lines.

Such tight local attachments made any kind of broad organization extremely difficult. The Ku Klux Klan had been an exception early in the twenties. Then in 1924 and 1925, widely publicized exposés of corruption in the Klan and the conviction of Indiana's leading Klansman, David Stephenson, for the sex murder of his secretary, demoralized that organization. By 1928 its membership fell to about 200,000. The Anti-Saloon League, once a formidable power in national politics, also collapsed in the late twenties. Equally important, few people in national affairs seemed to care any more about the cultural and moral standards that still mattered a great deal to millions of Americans. Although former members of the Klan did not discard their old beliefs about foreigners, Catholics, and radicals, no strong voice spoke for them in Coolidge's Washington. They became what the Klan had always claimed to be, an "Invisible Empire."

Local politics remained the one natural center for this mixture of economic, cultural, and moral concerns. In the towns and the countryside, they dominated innumerable county organizations in which friendship and family ties, not efficiency and expertise, determined who would receive most of the jobs and favors of local politics. In the wards of the large cities, similar private bargains tied individuals, families, and cultural groups into little political alliances. Another set of private bargains entwined government officials with a web of criminal activities in prostitution, gambling, and bootlegging. The boxer, Billy Conn, growing up on the streets of Pittsburgh, was twenty years old before he realized that the police were also paid by the city government. On a large scale, these many personal arrangements became political machines, which thrived during the 1920s. Though they were known by the names of the bosses—Tom Pendergast in Kansas City, Big Bill Thompson in Chicago, Ed Crump in Memphis, Frank Hague in Jersey City, and James Michael Curley in Boston—their roots were decentralized and popular.

During the New Era, it required an exceptionally powerful force to draw these insular, local alliances into national affairs. The strongest magnet was the Eighteenth, or "Prohibition," Amendment, which banned the production and sale of liquor. Put into effect in January 1920 and enforced by the strict Volstead Act, the Eighteenth Amendment began its career in an atmosphere of high optimism. Drinking, declared William Jennings Bryan, was as dead an issue as slavery. But countless Americans decided otherwise. An insatiable demand for liquor in the big cities and a considerable market elsewhere in the nation created a massive business out of illicit production and distribution. As one investigating commission ruefully noted, "Few things are more easily made than alcohol." A little machinery and a bathtub transformed any thirsty citizen into a distiller. Moreover, the long boundary of the United States was a sieve for illegal imports. To police these many violations, the Treasury Department employed about 2000 officials. Herbert Hoover later estimated that effective enforcement would have required at least 250,000.

Millions of locally oriented Americans considered Prohibition an insufferable violation of their rights. Not only did the "wets" make a travesty of the law in their neighborhoods and communities; they increasingly demanded action from state and national governments. In 1923, New York repealed its state law to enforce Prohibition. By 1930, six other states had followed New York's lead. With equal fervor, millions of locally oriented "drys" regarded Prohibition as the keystone of American morality. Not only did they give teeth to Prohibition in their localities; they sponsored stern state laws to uphold the "noble experiment." In Michigan, a fourth offense under the Prohibition law meant life imprisonment. Basically, the story of Prohibition was this stream of local passions pouring through the nation and battling in the name of irreconcilable truths.

From these same wells came the emotions that made Alfred E. Smith the most controversial politician of the 1920s. A capable governor of New York, who very much wanted to be President, Al Smith touched the nerve centers of local politics. He was a Catholic, a wet, and a self-taught immigrant's son who wore Tammany Hall's traditional brown derby askew and spoke in the accents of Manhattan's lesser known avenues. The thought of Al Smith in the White House roused feelings of wonder and horror across the nation. Self-conscious ethnic groups in the Northern cities gave him their fanatic devotion. White Protestant Democrats in the rural South looked on Smith as the Antichrist. At the Democratic National Convention of 1924, Smith's friends and enemies fought over his nomination for an incredible ninety-five ballots before turning in exhaustion on the one hundred and third to John W. Davis. Despite the absence of a serious competitor in 1928, Southern delegates allowed Smith's nomination for President with the most profound misgivings.

The election of 1928 provided a unique meeting ground for the conflicting spirits of national and local politics. To oppose Smith, the Republicans chose Herbert Hoover, by all odds the most important political spokesman for the New Era. After an impressive early success in business, Hoover won renown during the First

AL SMITH ON THE COVER OF "LIFE" MAGAZINE, 1928

Loyal to Tammany and hostile to Prohibition, Al Smith could never escape the image of the New York ward boss who had made good. *(Culver Pictures, Inc.)*

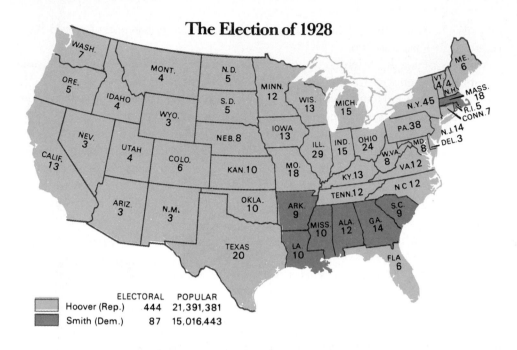

The Election of 1928

	ELECTORAL	POPULAR
Hoover (Rep.)	444	21,391,381
Smith (Dem.)	87	15,016,443

World War as an administrator, first of international relief, then of agriculture. There was already talk of Hoover as President in 1920. Instead, he served in the cabinets of Harding and Coolidge, and made himself the unofficial center of the executive branch: "Secretary of Commerce and assistant secretary of everything else." He was serious and shy, extremely proud and highly ambitious. Too formidable for Coolidge, who heartily disliked him, and too independent for many professional politicians, who preferred a weaker man, Hoover still went after the nomination with absolute confidence in his ability to be President. Successful Americans overwhelmingly supported him. Of those listed in *Who's Who,* for example, 87 percent endorsed his candidacy.

Al Smith wanted to pitch his campaign at the level of national policy. An essentially conservative man who later opposed the New Deal, the Democratic candidate thought of himself as an eminently qualified leader for the existing economic system, not as a product of New York City's Lower East Side. To oversee his campaign, Smith selected a prominent executive in General Motors, John J. Raskob, rather than a professional politician. The partisans of local politics, however, would not let Smith transcend his origins. In November 1928, Smith's name on the ballot drew large, jubilant majorities in the industrial cities, but it also sent millions of Protestant townspeople to the polls with literally a religious commitment to Hoover and put seven formerly Democratic Southern states in the Republican column. Hoover, the shining symbol of the New Era prosperity, swept to victory with 444 electoral votes against Smith's 87.

The Crisis of Depression, 1929–1935

Hoover had served at the creation of the New Era. Now, as President, he would preside at its triumph. At the inauguration of the "Great Engineer" in March 1929, who could have predicted that disaster was just six months ahead? By 1929, countless Americans were convinced that the nation was riding an escalator of unlimited progress, and increasing numbers of them were expressing this happy faith with investments in the stock market. If tomorrow would inevitably be more prosperous than today, why not buy some of tomorrow at today's prices? This reasoning had already pushed up prices on the New York Stock Exchange by 40 percent in 1927, then another 35 percent in 1928, to heights that bore no relation to the actual growth of the nation's corporations. Yet the Great Bull Market charged heedlessly onward. With scarcely a pause, stock prices continued to climb week after week until by September 1929 they stood a dizzying 400 percent above their level of only five years earlier.

Spasms of doubt shook the stock market in September and early October. Then on October 23, 1929, confidence died. For almost a week the stock exchange was a mad scene of frantic sellers, elusive buyers, and exhausted clerks struggling to record the wreckage. By October 29, all the paper profits of 1929 had been lost. Early in November the gains of 1928 disappeared, and during the summer of 1930 the hopes of 1927 also dissolved. Finally, on June 8, 1932, the stock market hit bottom, 50 percent below its modest level at the time of Coolidge's inauguration.

The collapse of the Great Bull Market had severe effects throughout the economy. Because the frantic speculation attracted a large portion of the nation's short-term credit, the heavy losses of late 1929 dried up the normal flow of loans to both individuals and companies. Banks, some of them deeply implicated in the speculation, sharply retrenched their activities and deepened the crisis. Retrenchment accentuated every weakness in the New Era economy. Because of a markedly unequal distribution of income, most Americans could buy only the bare necessities without credit. As purchases de-

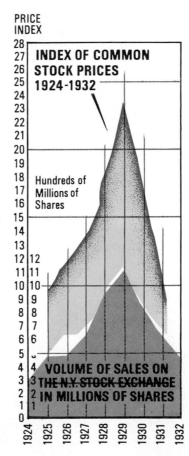

PRICE INDEX

INDEX OF COMMON STOCK PRICES 1924-1932

Hundreds of Millions of Shares

VOLUME OF SALES ON THE N.Y. STOCK EXCHANGE IN MILLIONS OF SHARES

1924 1925 1926 1927 1928 1929 1930 1931 1932

clined, thousands of small businesses, just making it in good times, now folded. Many farmers, also just making it before the crash, could no longer meet their mortgage payments. Business failures and farm foreclosures further sapped the resources of the banks that had been financing them. Soon the downward spiral was pulling the strong as well as the weak into a national depression.

During the next three years the economy, like a tin can in a vise, was relentlessly squeezed to half its size. Some indicators, such as labor income, salaries, and national income, fell somewhat less than 50 percent; others, such as industrial production, manufacturing wages, dividends, and farm income, somewhat more. The human costs were incalculably higher. Millions already living on the edge of poverty could afford no decline in farm income, no shorter hours of work. And the unemployed, about 30 percent of the labor force by early 1933, soon had nothing. The chicken once promised for every pot had gone into charity's soup kettle, and each year longer and longer lines of hungry, bewildered people formed in front of it with their empty bowls.

Hoover's response to depression was clear and firm. If the principles behind the New Era were correct, as everyone seemed to believe, Americans should follow them strictly and prosperity would surely be just around the corner. "Progress is born of Cooperation . . . ," the President reminded the nation. "The Government should assist and encourage these movements of collective self help by itself cooperating with them. . . ." For the large corporations, Hoover sponsored meetings at the White House to establish common industrial policies.

Depression struck Americans with a numbing force. Their savings irretrievably lost, customers mulled helplessly around the closed, empty banks. Where there were no jobs month after month, there was eventually no hope. Impoverished families took what shelter they could find, forming dismal shanty slums called "Hoovervilles." (*Brown Brothers, Library of Congress, Chicago Historical Society, Library of Congress.*)

For the trade associations, the Federal Trade Commission held a Trade Practices Conference to strengthen their stabilizing agreements. For labor, Hoover won a promise from business leaders to spread the work in their firms rather than simply fire some percentage of their employees. For agriculture, the new Federal Farm Board issued large amounts of credit so that the commodity cooperatives could keep their products off the market and halt the decline in farm prices. And for suffering Americans everywhere, Hoover used the President's office as clearinghouse and coordinator for private relief. Between 1929 and 1932, donations for relief increased about eightfold, a remarkable accomplishment by any previous standard.

Of all the President's problems, finance was the most difficult. Financiers had been expected to act as facilitators of business enterprise. Instead, they had fed the Great Bull Market. Hoover, who never trusted Wall Street bankers, took a certain grim satisfaction in the stock market crash, as his first terse announcement in October 1929 implied: "The fundamental business of the country—that is, the production and distribution of goods and services—is on a sound and prosperous basis." As the depression deepened, he insisted that the nation's big bankers fulfill their obligations to the economy by collecting a huge reservoir of credit for America's flagging industry. Financial leaders stalled, then refused. In 1932, the President reluctantly accepted the necessity of a new government credit agency, the Reconstruction Finance Corporation. That year, the RFC invested an astonishing $1.5 billion in private enterprise, mostly in a few large corporations that were considered the key to economic recovery. Hoover, who also watched Europe's banking disasters in 1931 intensify America's depression, left office with his original convictions unshaken. "We have been fighting for four years to preserve the system of production and distribution from . . . [the] failure of the financial and credit system."

From 1929 to 1932 the President acted positively, often vigorously, according to the principles of the New Era. If recovery had followed, he would have been a hero, tough enough in crisis to protect the American way. But in 1932 the national economy teetered on the edge of total collapse. Employers discarded their programs for spreading the work, and during the winter of 1932–33, another 3 million joined the over 12 million already without jobs. Relief inundated state and local governments without the funds to meet them. As commodity prices continued to fall, the Federal Farm Board simply ran out of credit and ceased to function. Farmers burned their corn and left their cotton unpicked because it no longer paid them to market the crop. In some Midwestern county seats, silent men with hunting rifles closed the courts so that their mortgages could not be foreclosed. More than five thousand banks had failed since 1930, and early in 1933 the entire financial structure of the nation began to crumble.

These signs of calamity brought out Hoover's poorest qualities. When thousands of war veterans marched to Washington in an appeal for bonuses, the President thought he heard revolution in their cries for a little cash, and in July

1932 he allowed the army to drive them away. Hoover's deep, personal antagonism to socialism kept him from supporting federal appropriations for state and local relief. Such narrow principles gave no comfort in a hungry land. "I have a remarkable job for you," the wry humorist Will Rogers had Hoover saying to his administrator of relief; "you are to feed the several million unemployed." "With what?" asked the official. "That's what makes the job remarkable." Even before the 1932 election, a majority of Americans had turned away from their President. The old prosperity slogans came back to haunt him. Now it was "a chicken in every garage." Clusters of makeshift hovels for the unemployed became "Hoovervilles."

Hoover's failure expressed the new, demanding standard by which Americans judged their President. During the New Era, when the economy appeared to operate by itself, relatively little was expected of the President as an individual. But the economy was now thoroughly national, and when it broke down, only the national government had the scope and authority capable of repairing it. Because the executive branch dominated the national government, people naturally looked there for help. Atop the executive branch stood the President, and the longer the depression lasted, the more he alone seemed the one person who could lead them out of the wilderness. By 1932 millions who had no other place to turn were blaming Hoover in a harsh, personal way for the nation's troubles.

Hoover, renominated at the gloomy Republican Convention of 1932, still refused to believe that the nation would reject him. But almost everyone else recognized 1932 as a Democratic year. The leading Democratic contender bore a magic name in American politics. Franklin D. Roosevelt, a distant cousin of

The Election of 1932

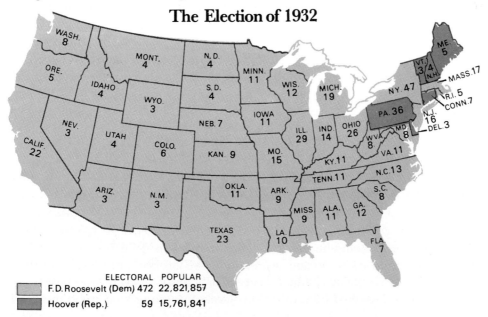

	ELECTORAL	POPULAR
F. D. Roosevelt (Dem)	472	22,821,857
Hoover (Rep.)	59	15,761,841

Theodore, had been assistant secretary of the navy in the Wilson administration and had then run as the vice-presidential candidate in the futile Cox campaign of 1920. Despite an attack of poliomyelitis in 1921 that paralyzed him from the waist down, Roosevelt had returned to public office in 1929 as governor of New York. Slow, careful preparation gave him a large bloc of delegates before the 1932 convention. A bargain with John Nance Garner of Texas, which made "Cactus Jack" the vice-presidential candidate, sealed his nomination. That November, riding to victory on the waves of popular sentiment that repudiated Hoover, Roosevelt received 472 electoral votes to the hapless Hoover's 59.

Once in office, Roosevelt revealed a unique capacity for leadership. Beneath an easy public style and a gracious private manner lay a keen, calculating mind that always sought to control people and events. Unlike Hoover, Roosevelt welcomed the challenge of selling his programs to a demoralized nation. A master of popular phrasing and simple analogies, he sent his strong, warm voice into millions of homes through radio "fireside chats" that were bits of genius in the use of a mass medium. Roosevelt made a great variety of people feel that he intuitively understood and sympathized with them. Always he radiated confidence. The tilt of Roosevelt's chin and the cocky angle of his cigarette holder invariably gave the sense of a man looking upward. The din of demands around his powerful office never ruffled him. To preserve his personal control, he waited just as long as possible before committing himself to a policy, serene in the faith that he could charm the impatient, make the decision, and soothe the disappointed.

Some critics later claimed that Roosevelt was a politician without any clear purpose in domestic affairs. They were wrong. Roosevelt entered the White House with as firm an attachment as Hoover's to the New Era, and until 1935 he remained extremely loyal to its principles. He wanted business to organize, industry by industry, and agriculture, commodity by commodity. With help from an efficient labor force and a supporting network of finance, he believed, these private groups could generate prosperity through their own natural patterns of cooperation. The government had only to assist them in regaining their strength and finding their proper places in the system.

What set Roosevelt so sharply apart from his predecessor was his willingness to experiment with a great variety of schemes to achieve this goal. Such openness in the nation's President attracted a wide range of newcomers to Washington and surrounded him with a curious but strikingly effective group of advisers. As secretary of the treasury, Roosevelt brought in his close friend and neighbor from Hyde Park, Henry Morgenthau, whose predictable loyalty and conscientiousness made him indispensable to the President. In agriculture Roosevelt appointed the son of Harding's secretary of agriculture, Henry A. Wallace, whose broad liberal vision compensated for his inattention to details. Another liberal Republican, Harold Ickes, became secretary of the interior and watched over his domain with a fierce jealousy and a scrupulous honesty. Along with Harry Hopkins, the tough, dedicated administrator of relief, these proved to be the President's most valuable assistants. But the new regime also drew kinds of people who had never before influenced government policy: an obscure Montana professor named M. L. Wilson with a proposal for limiting agricultural production; Raymond Moley, Rexford Tugwell, and Adolph Berle of Columbia University, the "Brains Trust" of Roosevelt's 1932 campaign, with ambitions to improve the economy's organization; and social workers with plans to aid the unemployed, the disabled, and the aged. These and many more recruits joined the veterans from the business and agricultural associations to help Roosevelt provide a "New Deal" for America's ailing economy.

An experimental President, an eager pack of advisers, and a receptive Congress combined to produce an explosion of government actions in 1933. (See chart page 1082.) They ranged from manipulations in the gold value of the dollar to emergency credit for farm mortgages, to a Civilian Conservation Corps (CCC), which gave jobs in rural conservation to unemployed urban youths. Two measures from this array formed the heart of the early New Deal. One was the National Industrial Recovery Act of June 1933. The less significant half of the law created the Public Works Administration (PWA), with a $3.3 billion appropriation that was supposed to generate jobs and invigorate the economy. But Secretary Ickes, its director, moved with such extreme caution that PWA had no appreciable effect on the depression. The far more important half of the National

PRESIDENT FRANKLIN ROOSEVELT VISITS A CIVILIAN CONSERVATION CORPS (CCC) CAMP

Hope at last! FDR's grand smile, infecting everyone around him, seemed to promise America a brighter future just ahead. Seated third from the left is Secretary Harold Ickes. On Roosevelt's left are Secretary of Agriculture Henry A. Wallace and Roosevelt's adviser, Rexford Tugwell. (*Associated Press.*)

Industrial Recovery Act authorized each specialized segment of business to prepare a code of self-governance and established the National Recovery Administration (NRA) to supervise the process.

As chief of NRA, the President chose General Hugh S. Johnson, a brash, noisy veteran in government affairs, who immediately launched a circus of a campaign to rally all Americans behind his program. Through parades, speeches, and assorted hoopla, Johnson made the Blue Eagle, NRA's emblem of cooperation, almost synonymous with the New Deal itself, and he counted on public opinion to make it almost synonymous with Americanism. "When every American Housewife understands that the Blue Eagle on everything that she permits to come into her home is a symbol of its restoration to security," the general roared in characteristic bombast, "may God have mercy on the man or group of men who attempt to trifle with this bird."

In NRA's first four months, business groups wrote over seven hundred constitutions to govern their affairs. Where one or more large firms dominated an industry, NRA relied on them to prepare the codes; where no firm dominated, NRA turned to a trade association. Although the codes varied from industry to industry, they usually included some agreement on prices, wages, and the acceptable limits of competition. The only integration among them was a common commitment to stabilization, a common freedom from antitrust prosecution, and a common dependence on the industrial groups themselves to regulate their own members. Johnson exalted the spirit of cooperation and swore at the "slackers," but never coerced the businessmen.

Section 7a of the National Industrial Recovery Act authorized workers to organize and bargain in their own behalf, and some labor leaders, notably John L. Lewis of the United Mine Workers, acted as though the government was now their sponsor:"THE PRESIDENT WANTS YOU TO JOIN THE UNION!"

THE NRA

The dream behind the National Recovery Administration (NRA) was progress through unity. In this cartoon, worker and manager look like loving brothers, and both like dutiful nephews of their Uncle Sam. *(Library of Congress.)*

Neither "union" nor "bargaining," however, had yet acquired a clear legal meaning. Company unions, many little organizations representing fractions of an industry's employees, and countless techniques for consultation between managers and workers fitted these elastic terms. The Roosevelt administration did not encourage an independent labor movement. When Ickes established the Labor Policy Board in the oil industry, for instance, he selected a company unionist, an independent unionist, and an economist. In fact, labor representatives rarely served on the governing boards that policed the industrial codes. Under NRA, labor remained dependent on management.

The second basic law of the early New Deal was the Agricultural Adjustment Act, which arrived in May 1933. By including almost every kind of farm program that had been proposed during the twenties and early thirties, the law constituted a grab bag of alternatives. There were provisions for marketing agreements, commodity loans, export subsidies, government purchases, and the latest favorite, a restricted allotment of acreage among farmers who raised a given crop. During its first months, the Agricultural Adjustment Administration (AAA) gave highest priority to cash relief and paid farmers to plow under their crops and slaughter their livestock in midseason, a bitter expedient with so much hunger in the nation. The long-term goal of the law, however, was to increase farm income to a level of "parity" with its income just before the First World War.

To achieve parity, AAA relied on the organized farmers in each subdivision of agriculture to select the program appropriate to their product. George Peek and Chester Davis, who headed AAA, were old friends of the farm associations and worked easily with them, especially the American Farm Bureau Federation. What looked like a concentration of power in Washington, therefore, was actually a scattering of powers among commercial farmers. Aside from temporary government coercion to limit the production of cotton and tobacco, the New Deal's farm policy preserved the essentials of the New Era. The national government delegated most of its authority to farm groups so that they could make their own decisions and largely administer them.

Elsewhere in the New Deal the same bustle, the same openness, and the same principles prevailed. Like Hoover, Roosevelt and many of his advisers considered finance particularly guilty of causing the depression. "The money changers have fled from their high seats in the temple of our civilization," the President bitingly said of the bankers in his inaugural address. While congressional investigations were revealing how bankers had speculated with their own institution's deposits, new laws sought to hold finance within proper bounds. Through the Glass-Steagall Act of 1933, Congress required banks to separate their investment in securities from normal commercial banking. The next year it placed the stock exchange under the regulation of the Securities and Exchange Commission (SEC). In 1935, Congress outlawed holding companies that had been formed in the 1920s for no other purpose than the sale of stock, and it gave the SEC authority to dissolve other questionable holding companies.

Aside from these punishments for past sins, however, finance received an impressive array of government assistance. Roosevelt, immediately after his inauguration in March 1933, declared a brief "Bank Holiday" in order to check a nationwide financial panic. The Reconstruction Finance Corporation then pumped loans into the banks that were still solvent. In addition, Congress created the Federal Deposit Insurance Corporation in 1933 so that ordinary citizens would no longer lose their savings when a bank failed. New executive agencies, especially the Home Owners Loan Corporation, underwrote farm and housing mortgages. In 1935, when Congress consolidated the regulatory powers of the Federal Reserve System in a centralized board of governors, the government had completed a national framework of supports around American finance. The effect of these laws was to place both the prestige and the credit of the government behind the everyday decisions of private bankers. Within a short time, even the SEC was depending on the more enlightened brokers and financiers themselves to stabilize the stock exchanges. As Chairman William O. Douglas stated in 1938, "Government regulation at its best should be residual."

The New Deal responded to the pressing problem of public relief with an equally restrained use of government power. Though Roosevelt did not hesitate about requesting funds in 1933, he shared a common belief that only desperate circumstances could justify national money for relief. The New Deal's first relief agency was appropriately named the Federal Emergency Relief Administration (FERA). During 1933 and 1934, Congress voted relief funds as if each new contribution would surely be the last. When an initial appropriation of $500 million for FERA proved inadequate, Roosevelt drew an additional $400 million from Ickes's PWA for a hastily devised program of work relief. In February 1934, Congress finally authorized more funds for FERA. Harry Hopkins, Roosevelt's administrator of relief, employing a small staff, relied on private groups and local governments to distribute most of the money. "Nothing in the new Federal Act was meant to change that local responsibility, nor did the Federal Administration have any intention of doing so," an expert on public relief con-

Trying to Revive the System
Principal New Deal Measures, 1933–1935

"Bank Holiday"	March 1933
Federal Emergency Relief Act, creating	
Federal Emergency Relief Administration (FERA)	May 1933
Agricultural Adjustment Act, creating	
Agricultural Adjustment Administration (AAA)	May 1933
Tennessee Valley Authority (TVA)	May 1933
Home Owners' Loan Corporation	June 1933
National Industrial Relations Act, creating	
National Recovery Administration (NRA)	June 1933
Federal Deposit Insurance Corporation	June 1933
Civil Works Administration (CWA)	November 1933
Securities and Exchange Commission (SEC)	June 1934
Public Utility Holding Company Act	August 1935

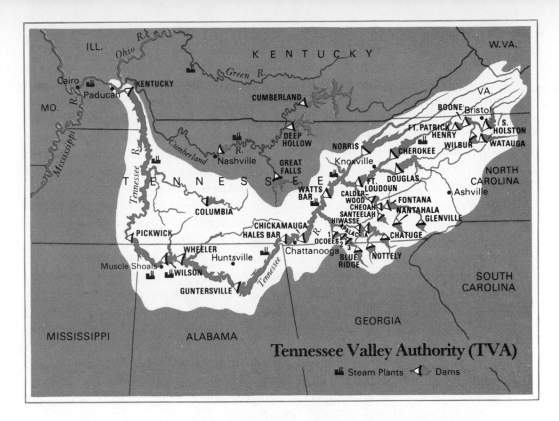

Tennessee Valley Authority (TVA)

Steam Plants ◄► Dams

cluded. To the starving, all that mattered was a little help had finally come.

The most daring government venture of the early New Deal was the Tennessee Valley Authority (TVA). Its origins lay in a long, inconclusive debate during the 1920s over the disposition of a dam at Muscle Shoals, Alabama, that the government had started to build in wartime but never completed. When Henry Ford, widely regarded in the 1920s as a great public benefactor, offered to lease and develop it, Senator George Norris of Nebraska, a tenacious old progressive, skillfully blocked the proposal and in time convinced a majority of his colleagues that the government itself should develop the dam. During the 1920s, however, no one anticipated the vast undertaking ahead. Beginning in 1933, Muscle Shoals became merely the point of departure for a new concept in regional rehabilitation, which soon gained international fame. The Tennessee Valley Authority, with sweeping administrative powers over a domain that wound through seven southern states, embarked on two decades of activity that created a network of dams and canals, rejuvenated the soil and protected it against floods, and harnessed electric resources to service millions of homes and thousands of new businesses.

From the outset, TVA challenged the customary rights of private enterprise by selling the electric power it generated. Because of this, conservatives probably hated it the most of all the New Deal programs. Nevertheless, TVA's directors had not completely abandoned the principles of the New Era. At every step, they worked through the existing, organized groups in their region. Chambers of commerce, leagues of bankers, commercial farming associations, and their local associates from the Department of Agriculture and the state agricultural colleges channeled the TVA's information, chose its demonstration farms, and distributed many of its political benefits. The same local groups were TVA's primary allies in the long legal battle with the private utility companies over the issue of public electricity, a battle that TVA did not fully win until 1939. Even such a striking departure as TVA, in other words, cooperated as closely as it could with the established private interests in the area.

In 1934, shortly before Raymond Moley left the New Deal to become its conservative critic, he commented, "This administration is as far from socialism or communism as any group ever assembled in a national government." The sheer quantity of government activities during 1933 and 1934 misled a good many people into believing that profound changes were under way. Despite the broadened range of government services, however, the fundamentals of the New Era remained intact. Subsequent speculation about a critical moment in March 1933 when American society might have taken a radical turn made little sense because the nation's leaders in March 1933 had no radical intentions. With fresh faces and tactics, through experiments and expedients, the New Deal fought to preserve a particular economic system that had formed during the 1920s and that continued to shape national policy after five grinding years of depression.

The New Deal at the Crossroads, 1935–1936

But the New Deal was not working. By late 1934, NRA was a shambles, the victim of the businessmen's self-serving codes, widespread violations of these same rules, and bitter criticism from almost every section of American society. The depression refused to lift. Though unemployment had declined since the darkest months of early 1933, it was about as bad as it had been the day Roosevelt was elected. Net farm income was a dismal 50 percent of its level in 1929, and the food shortages caused by a cruel drought on the Great Plains accounted for most of the price increases since 1933. Only corporate profits were making strong gains in 1934.

As confidence in the New Deal dwindled, millions of angry, suffering people appeared to be finding new leaders and new causes. From Louisiana came the shrewd, flamboyant Huey Long, who promised to make "every man a king." By appealing to the poor forgotten whites of his state, Long had become not only governor in 1929 but actually the ruler of Louisiana through an extensive, ruthless political machine. Elected to the Senate in 1930, the Louisiana Kingfish was soon using it as a forum to spread the gospel of Share Our Wealth, a simple, sweeping program that would expropriate the wealth of the very rich in order to provide all families with a $5,000 homestead and an annual income of about $2,500. From a suburb of Detroit came the rich radio voice of a Catholic priest, Charles Coughlin, who castigated Wall Street, called for the nationalization of the banks, and demanded an immediate, massive monetary inflation. From Long Beach, California, came Dr. Francis E. Townsend, who envisaged prosperity spreading to everybody through monthly government payments of $200 for each unemployed person over 60. All three campaigns were rapidly accelerating in late 1934 and early 1935.

Long, Coughlin, and Townsend spoke in the language of local politics, where the appeal of a popular, common sense economics had always remained strong. As years of depression eroded the hopes and evaporated the resources in countless neighborhoods and communities, the people whose lives were rooted there desperately sought ways of bringing opportunity back to their localities. To many of them, the neat, mechanical answers of Share Our Wealth, inflation, and old age pensions sounded just right. In the tradition of free silver in the 1890s and radical antimonopoly in the progessive years, these proposals promised at a stroke to give ordinary Americans a decent life without elaborate laws or government regimentation.

No one ever knew how many Americans accepted these formulas for prosperity. Though Long, Coughlin, and Townsend each claimed millions of adherents, none formed an effective organization. The imposing façades of Long's Share Our Wealth clubs, Coughlin's National Union for Social Justice, and Townsend's Old Age Revolving Pensions clubs covered a thoroughly scattered, locally oriented following that defied a head count. Partly because no one could estimate their strength, these movements caused considerable anxiety in Washington. The New Dealers in Congress and the White House had such nebulous, rumbling threats very much in mind as they considered their next moves against an obstinate depression.

In January 1935, Roosevelt set the New Deal into fresh winds by calling for a huge work relief program and a comprehensive social security measure. Three months later, Congress laid the foundation for the Works Progress Administration (WPA). The very size of the appropriation indicated how central the New Deal suddenly considered relief. With almost $5 billion, or ten times the amount originally given to FERA, the WPA absorbed about half the government's total expenditures. Like its predecessors, the act contained in its title the word *emergency*. By 1935, however, very few people thought that local or private contributions could ever again carry the burdens of relief in a depression. Hopkins, who administered the WPA, now emerged as Roosevelt's most powerful lieutenant. Through his large staff, the WPA supervised an extraordinary variety of projects, ranging from theatrical productions to road maintenance, that on the average employed over 2 million of American's jobless. Although WPA wages could not match Huey Long's $2,500, they were a blessed step above nothing.

The Social Security Act of August 1935 was more cautious in approach but more lasting in influence. It established a national system of old-age insurance that was funded by a tax on workers' wages and an equivalent tax on their

employers. The act also taxed employers to finance a varied set of state programs for unemployment compensation, and it offered the states matching
grants to aid dependent mothers and children and the disabled. In all, the
Social Security Act was a conservative version of schemes for social insurance
that had been discussed since the early 1900s. The poorest Americans, who had
no wages to tax or whose jobs fell outside the scope of the law, received no
protection at all. Payments did not even start until 1942. Nevertheless, if the
act did not equal the generosity of the Townsend Plan, it coped with the same
ills. Moreover, social security was an expandable formula, and later Congresses
gradually extended its range, until by the mid-1970s it covered almost all employees and many more of life's hazards.

Liberal congressmen produced a third basic law, which the President after
months of hesitation finally endorsed. The National Labor Relations Act, or
the Wagner Act, of July 1935 marked a startling shift in New Deal policy. Before
1935, the government had considered labor primarily as a dependent part of
industry. With the Wagner Act, however, the New Deal committed itself un-
equivocally to supporting unions that were independent of management. Not

SENATOR HUEY LONG OF LOUISIANA

Long, Roosevelt's most powerful
critic, expressed the anger and
frustration of poor people who
had not benefited from the early
New Deal. (*Culver Pictures, Inc.*)

only did the law bar company unions, but it also outlawed any form of company discrimination against members of an independent union. The National Labor Relations Board (NLRB), which was created to supervise the act, could conduct an election among a company's employees to ensure their free choice of a bargaining agent, and it could compel employers to comply with the new rules.

The first important consequence of these three ground-breaking acts was a powerful release of emotions. During 1935 and 1936, the New Deal, and above all Roosevelt himself, generated nationwide passions of hope and hate that would run like a high-voltage charge through the next two decades of American politics. If the New Deal neither cured the depression nor saved the nation from suffering, it communicated a humane concern when no one else seemed to care. The legislation of 1935, offering millions of hard-pressed Americans a bit of help, simultaneously held out the promise of much more to come. The Works Progress Administration kept innumerable families from a bottomless pit of despair. Social Security raised miraculous visions of a decent life in old age. The Wagner Act told countless wage earners that the government now stood with them instead of with their bosses.

What gave hope at the bottom of society spread horror at the top. Among many people with a strong stake in the existing system—bankers, lawyers, corporation executives, and doctors—these same laws created images of a chaotic society where demagogues were inciting the masses against everyone else's privileges. Year after year, an inability to explain what had gone wrong with the economy or predict what the government would do next had been deepening their frustration. Conservative doubts about the New Deal in 1933 turned into charges of incompetence in 1934, then outright hatred in 1935. No more irrational but much more powerful than the millions who loved Roosevelt, the wealthy foes of the New Deal had the means of making their feelings heard. They spoke from chambers of commerce and bar and medical and banking associations. They formed new organizations such as the American Liberty League, which spent millions to discredit the New Deal. Through newspapers, radio, and venomous little rumors ("Polio? Syphilis!"), they mounted a furious assault on the man even more than his administration.

Such an intense involvement with Roosevelt tended to obscure a second basic issue that accompanied the New Deal's economic policy. In destitute localities everywhere, the prospect of any assistance, of course, was a godsend. But how would it be distributed? By the efficiency standards of a distant bureaucracy or the personal judgments of local politicians? As the battles over Al Smith demonstrated, the Democratic party had been collecting a particularly combustible mixture of ethnic groups during the twenties. The elections of 1932 and 1934 added even more urban cultural blocs to the party's new majority. If the government's programs interfered with the sensitive, local standards of these groups, the New Deal coalition might disintegrate.

The Long and Coughlin movements, in the tradition of local politics, appealed directly to the Democratic majority's racial and religious feelings.* But the Roosevelt administration, national and economic in orientation, hoped to avoid all issues that might disturb these local cultures. After 1929, when hard times gave impetus to the drive against Prohibition, the national Democratic party had led the campaign for the Twenty-first Amendment, which in December 1933 repealed the Eighteenth and left the rules governing alcohol to local choice. Overjoyed to have Prohibition behind them, the New Dealers expected to concentrate exclusively on the problems of depression. It never dawned on them, for example, to revive the old Progressive wars against immigrant radicals or prostitution. Though Roosevelt selected the first woman to hold a cabinet post, Secretary of Labor Frances Perkins, neither Perkins nor Roosevelt's active wife, Eleanor, nor anyone else in the New Deal wanted to revive the movement for women's rights. By 1935, the old crusades were over, and no one in the Roosevelt administration was recommending a new one.

In many ways, the New Dealers were impressively liberal on matters of race and religion. Secretary of Interior Harold Ickes was a veteran member of the National Association for the Advancement of Colored People. Eleanor Roosevelt spoke eloquently for racial and religious equality. In the 1940s, Henry Wallace became one of the most prominent white champions of black rights. The President himself appointed a Jew as secretary of the treasury, an ironic reply to the anti-Semitic hallucination about a Jewish plot to control world finance. By inclination, however, all the New Dealers, including Ickes and Wallace, ignored ethnic problems as much as they could. They wanted to frame public policy in economic, not ethnic, terms and that predisposition prepared them to compromise with the values of their local constituents.

The pattern of decentralized administration that already characterized NRA and AAA supplied the broad formula for satisfying these local values. In return for the right to formulate general economic policy, national Democratic leaders would allow local politicians to distribute public funds in their own areas by their own standards. New Deal money in the South underwrote white Protestant cultures. In the large cities, its funds passed through urban political machines to the families and cultural groups who voted for them. Congress, by rejecting an amendment to the Wagner Act that would have required racial equality on the job, left the issue of bias in the unions to the labor leaders themselves. The immediate responses to these policies were politically heartening. Enthusiasm for the New Deal ran high in the South. In such cities as Pittsburgh and Kansas City, the New Deal's relief laws shored up the existing political machines, and in Chicago, WPA funds actually saved the budding Democratic

---

*Long himself was assassinated at the Louisiana State House in September 1935. Others, notably the Reverend Gerald L. K. Smith, tried to reach his national audience through religious and racial prejudice.

organization of Mayor Edward Kelley. These beneficiaries ranked among the Roosevelt administration's most dedicated supporters. Meanwhile organized labor declared Roosevelt its champion.

The primary political test of the New Deal's latest departures came in the elections of 1936. Roosevelt's Republican opponent was the honest, uninspired governor of Kansas, Alfred Landon. Coughlin, Townsend, and the remnants of Long's legions gathered to form the Union party and nominate Representative William Lemke of North Dakota for President. Although Coughlin personally promised 9 million votes for Lemke and the *Literary Digest* predicted Landon's election from a poll of those still able to afford telephones, most people expected Roosevelt to win. The margin of victory, however, would serve as the critical index to the New Deal's success. Experts laughed at the estimate of James Farley, Roosevelt's political aide and postmaster general, that the President would carry every state except Maine and Vermont. Yet in November exactly

ROOSEVELT SUPPORTER

By 1936, Roosevelt's devoted partisans saw him as
their personal, towering champion in the White
House. (*Library of Congress.*)

that happened. Along with huge Democratic majorities in Congress, the election gave Roosevelt a breathtaking 523 electoral votes to a mere 8 for Landon. The woebegone Union party did not even collect a million popular votes, and Coughlin announced his retirement from politics.

The Democratic triumph of 1936 ratified the New Deal's policies in the two most crucial areas of modern politics. First, it placed responsibility for the national economy squarely in the lap of the government. After 1936, most Americans looked to the leaders in Washington to guarantee their economic welfare, and the popular economics of people like Long, Coughlin, and Townsend never again won a mass following. The wealthy haters of Roosevelt had to bide their time and fight another day. Second, the landslide of 1936 justified the New Deal's balance between national and local power. Broad economic policy from Washington and local control over cultural matters proved a brilliantly successful formula. How federal funds were spent ranked on a par with how much was spent. Nevertheless, these two answers only set a general direction for political policy. No one had yet resolved precisely how the national government should exercise its authority over the economy. Nor could anyone foresee how future pressures might affect the New Deal's ad hoc, unwritten agreement on local autonomy in cultural and ethnic affairs. The election of 1936 was a point of departure to a destination still unknown.

Suggested Readings

The best general guide to national politics during the 1920s and 1930s is a combination of John D. Hicks, *Republican Ascendency, 1921–1933* (1960), and William E. Leuchtenburg, *Franklin D. Roosevelt and the New Deal, 1932–1940* (1963), an outstanding survey. Though less authoritative, George H. Soule, *Prosperity Decade* (1947), and Broadus Mitchell, *Depression Decade* (1947), provide an abundance of information on the national economy for these same years. Thomas C. Cochran, *American Business in the Twentieth Century* (1972), gives a clear overview of its subject, and Paul L. Murphy, *The Constitution in Crisis Times, 1918–1969* (1972), presents a full account of the Supreme Court's decisions. George B. Tindall, *The Emergence of the New South, 1913–1945* (1967), sets that region in a national context. A provocative interpretation of "The Age of Corporate Capitalism" appears in William Appleman Williams, *The Contours of American History* (1961).

Numerous books examine portions of the emerging modern economy. *Strategy and Structure: Chapters in the History of Industrial Enterprise* (1962), a pathbreaking volume by Alfred D. Chandler, Jr., analyzes the organization inside giant corporations, while Louis Galambos, *Competition and Cooperation: The Emergence of a National Trade Association* (1966), traces the pattern of organization among the scattered firms in cotton textiles. Allan Nevins and Frank Ernest Hill, *Ford: Expansion and Challenge, 1915–1933* (1957), covers the peak years of the flivver king's career. On labor the best study is Irving L. Bernstein's well-written *A History of the American Worker, 1920–1933: The Lean Years* (1960). Grant McConnell's *The Decline of Agrarian Democracy* (1953) centers on the American Farm Bureau Federation.

Robert K. Murray, *The Harding Era* (1969), and Donald R. McCoy, *Calvin Coolidge*

(1967), generously assess these Presidents and their policies. The major political scandal of the 1920s is explained in Burt L. Noggle, *Teapot Dome* (1962). David Burner's perceptive study, *The Politics of Provincialism* (1967), recounts the pulling and hauling in the Democratic party during the New Era, and William H. Harbaugh, *Lawyer's Lawyer: The Life of John W. Davis* (1973), evaluates the party's losing candidate in 1924. An interesting picture of the politics of natural resources emerges from Donald C. Swain, *Federal Conservation Policy, 1921–1933* (1963), and Norris Hundley, Jr., *Water and the West* (1975). The politics of commercial agriculture is the subject of Gilbert C. Fite's *George W. Peek and the Fight for Farm Parity* (1954). Theodore Saloutos and John D. Hicks, *Agricultural Discontent in the Middle West, 1900–1939* (1951), provides greater detail on farm groups and their programs. For the limitations of liberal reform, see LeRoy Ashby, *The Spearless Leader: Senator Borah and the Progressive Movement in the 1920's* (1972), Richard Lowitt, *George W. Norris: The Persistence of a Progressive, 1913–1933* (1971), and Arthur Mann, *LaGuardia: A Fighter against His Times, 1882–1933* (1959). In *Seedtime of Reform: American Social Service and Social Action, 1918–1933* (1963), on the other hand, Clarke A. Chambers discovers a maturing process during the twenties.

The best introduction to the ethnic and cultural issues of the twenties is John Higham's excellent *Strangers in the Land* (1955), which analyzes American nativism to 1925. David M. Chalmers, *Hooded Americanism* (1965), is a lively history of the Ku Klux Klan, and Kenneth T. Jackson, *The Ku Klux Klan in the City, 1915–1930* (1967), is an important supplement to the story. G. Louis Joughin and Edmund M. Morgan, *The Legacy of Sacco and Vanzetti* (1948), remains the richest account of events surrounding the trial of these men. The rise and fall of the "noble experiment" is traced in Andrew Sinclair, *Prohibition: The Era of Excess* (1962). Joseph R. Gusfield, *Symbolic Crusade* (1963), explores the emotional force behind Prohibition, and Norman F. Furniss, *The Fundamentalist Controversy, 1918–1931* (1954), reviews the antimodernist legislative campaigns. How cultural issues have been translated into politics is described generally in Oscar Handlin, *Al Smith and His America* (1958), and more specifically in J. Joseph Huthmacher, *Massachusetts People and Politics, 1919–1933* (1959).

John Kenneth Galbraith's clear essay, *The Great Crash, 1929* (3rd ed., 1972), marks the end of the New Era. Arthur M. Schlesinger, Jr., *The Crisis of the Old Order* (1957), the first volume of his *The Age of Roosevelt*, evokes the desperate confusion of economic depression, and so does the early portion of William Manchester's *The Glory and the Dream* (1974). In *The Lords of Creation* (1935), Frederick Lewis Allen captures the drama of the Wall Street debacle. More on the human meaning of the Great Depression can be found in Federal Writers' Project, *These Are Our Lives* (1939), and Studs Terkel, *Hard Times: An Oral History of the Great Depression* (1970). Joan Hoff Wilson's *Herbert Hoover: Forgotten Progressive* (1975) is the best general evaluation of that controversial President. Fuller accounts of government policy during Hoover's administration appear in Albert U. Romasco, *The Poverty of Abundance* (1965), Jordan A. Schwarz, *The Interregnum of Despair* (1970), and Harris G. Warren, *Herbert Hoover and the Great Depression* (1959).

Volumes 2 and 3 of Arthur Schlesinger's *The Age of Roosevelt—The Coming of the New Deal* (1958) and *The Politics of Upheaval* (1960)—provide a thorough and readable account of Franklin Roosevelt's first administration. The essays in John Braeman et al., eds., *The New Deal, I: The National Level* (1975), expand portions of the story; essays in the second volume, *The State and Local Levels* (1975), survey the experiences of government outside Washington. James T. Patterson, *The New Deal and the States* (1969), analyzes the tensions between national and state power. The most valuable work on the National Recovery Administration and other policies pertaining to business is Ellis W. Hawley, *The New Deal and the Problem of Monopoly* (1966). Organized labor's course is followed in

Irving Bernstein's *A History of the American Worker, 1933–1941: Turbulent Years* (1970). Val N. Perkins, *Crisis in Agriculture* (1969), details the beginning of the Agricultural Adjustment Administration. On the most innovative New Deal policy, C. Herman Pritchett, *The Tennessee Valley Authority* (1943), supplies basic information; Philip Selznick, *TVA and the Grass Roots* (1949), analyzes the Authority's social orientation; and Thomas K. McCraw, *TVA and the Power Fight, 1933–1939* (1971), traces the principal challenge to the Authority's program. Grace Abbott, *From Relief to Social Security* (1966), covers the record of public assistance, and Roy Lubove, *The Struggle for Social Security, 1900–1935* (1968), explains the origins of the Social Security Act. Michael E. Parrish, *Securities Regulation and the New Deal* (1970), is an illuminating monograph on that area of public policy. Two interesting studies — Paul K. Conkin, *Tomorrow a New World: The New Deal Community Program* (1959), and Jane DeHart Mathews, *The Federal Theater, 1935–1939* (1967) — suggest the breadth of interests affected by the New Deal. A sample of the sharp historical debates over the New Deal is collected in Alonzo L. Hamby, ed., *The New Deal* (1969).

On Roosevelt himself, the best study for the New Deal years is James MacGregor Burns, *Roosevelt: The Lion and the Fox* (1956). Frank Freidel's massive biography, *Franklin D. Roosevelt* (4 vols. to date, 1952–73), has carried FDR through his first critical months in the White House. Additional insights into the Roosevelt household appear in Alfred B. Rollins, Jr., *Roosevelt and Howe* (1962), and Joseph P. Lash, *Eleanor and Franklin* (1971). Among the many published journals and memoirs by participants in the New Deal, Raymond Moley's critical *After Seven Years* (1939) and Rexford G. Tugwell's appreciative *The Democratic Roosevelt* (1957) are especially useful. J. Joseph Huthmacher, *Senator Robert F. Wagner and the Rise of Urban Liberalism* (1968), and Paul A. Kurzman, *Harry Hopkins and the New Deal* (1974), are complimentary accounts of these important men. Otis L. Graham, Jr., *An Encore for Reform* (1967), explores the generally unfavorable responses of the old progressives to the New Deal, and George Wolfskill, *The Revolt of the Conservatives* (1962), describes the outrage of the American Liberty League.

The world of local politics appears largely in glimpses. In combination, John M. Allswang's *A House for All People: Ethnic Politics in Chicago, 1890–1936* (1971), Edward R. Kantowitz's *Polish-American Politics in Chicago, 1888–1940* (1975), and Humbert Nelli's *Italians in Chicago, 1880–1930* (1970) sketch an interesting picture for one big city. Arthur Mann, *LaGuardia Comes to Power: 1933* (1965), uses an important election in New York City to analyze its political roots. The relation between the New Deal and the local bosses is considered in Bruce M. Stave, *The New Deal and the Last Hurrah: Pittsburgh Machine Politics* (1970), and Lyle W. Dorsett, *The Pendergast Machine* (1968). Charles J. Tull, *Father Coughlin and the New Deal* (1965), and T. Harry Williams, *Huey Long* (1969), examine the New Deal's leading competitors in local politics, and David H. Bennett, *Demagogues in the Depression* (1969), chronicles their decline. The cultural values of the New Dealers themselves are summarized in E. Digby Baltzell, *The Protestant Establishment* (1964).

31

The Development of
Modern Politics

When the New Deal changed course in 1935, it abandoned the vision of
the economy that had dominated public policy since the First World War. During
the 1920s and early 1930s, policymakers sought harmony among the nation's
big economic units: business, labor, agriculture, and finance. With encouragement from Washington, it was assumed, business would lead the other units in
a coordinated march to prosperity. After 1935, these big economic blocs broke
into smaller and smaller subdivisions, each demanding its own policy to serve
its own interests. As the economy fragmented, government officials groped for
a new understanding of how the economy worked and how prosperity could
be achieved. The Second World War gave them a crucial clue. With a vast
increase in government spending during the war, the economy revived dramatically. Nevertheless, it took many more years of angry debate to settle on a
fiscal policy that would sustain an economy of countless special interests. Meanwhile, a growing number of Americans were insisting that the government
also tackle the nation's racial and cultural problems. As a new economic policy
developed in the 1950s, attention was already shifting to racial and cultural
issues that would mark the next phase of modern politics.

The New Deal Loses Its Way, 1936–1941

At the peak of his popularity in 1936, a confident Franklin Roosevelt prepared for a triumphant second term. His political base was secure. Federal assistance to wage earners, farmers, and the unemployed, in combination with a restrained use of national power in local affairs, had created a massive Democratic majority in Congress and attracted a passionate loyalty to the President himself. Now the challenge was to devise a policy expressing the government's broad responsibility for the American economy. Could the New Deal expand on the impressive but still tentative departures of 1935?

Roosevelt's first objective had already been dictated by the Supreme Court. In the tense climate of 1935 and 1936, as the New Deal was expanding its scope, the Court grew increasingly rigid. Drawing on precedents that in some instances had been conservative in the 1890s, a bare majority of five justices attacked the national government's primary source of power over the economy, regulation of interstate commerce. Mining and farming, in the Court's view, were local, not interstate, activities. By implication, these interpretations jeopardized a full range of the New Deal's policies in industry and agriculture. Moreover, a narrow construction of interstate commerce automatically cast doubts on the government's authority to regulate labor-management relations through the Wagner Act, and to tax employers and employees through the Social Security Act.

The most publicized of the Court's many decisions during 1935 and 1936 were the *Schechter* case (1935), striking down the National Recovery Administration (NRA), and *U. S.* v. *Butler* (1936), invalidating the tax on food processing in the Agricultural Adjustment Act. Neither decision crippled the New Deal. The NRA, a loosely worded delegation of powers to the executive that all nine justices condemned, was already dead by 1935. The Court's judgment merely gave it a decent burial. Following the *Butler* decision Congress continued the New Deal's basic farm program under the guise of soil conservation. But the Court's willingness to assault two such important laws, along with so many other threatening precedents in 1935 and 1936, forced a confrontation between the Roosevelt administration and the Supreme Court. As the President stated, the New Deal could not function with a "horse and buggy" conception of interstate commerce.

Reading his victory in 1936 as a mandate to storm this conservative outpost, Roosevelt submitted a judiciary reorganization bill to Congress in February 1937. The President requested the right to enlarge the Court from nine to a maximum of fifteen members if those justices over seventy years old did not voluntarily resign. Although Roosevelt's purpose was to create his own Court majority, he pretended that the issue was judicial efficiency. The existing Court, the President claimed, could not manage its heavy load of work, a charge that the magisterial Chief Justice Charles Evans Hughes easily refuted. To this deviousness, Roosevelt added an unusual ineptness. When Congress resisted his plan, Roosevelt refused either to negotiate or to compromise, and his heavy-handed pressure on the legislators strengthened the opposition. Instead of pitting the New Deal against the Court, Roosevelt's course set Congress against the President. By the summer of 1937, Roosevelt's bill was lost.

In the end, the conservatives did lose their judicial stronghold. During the congressional fight, the Court in *NLRB* v. *Jones and Laughlin Steel* (1937) upheld the Wagner Act by a margin of one vote. "A switch in time saved nine," the wags declared. A rapid sequence of retirements from the Court soon enabled the President to appoint a majority who were thoroughly committed to the New Deal. Beginning in 1937, the Court executed a dramatic reversal. By the time of *U. S.* v. *Darby* (1941), it had authorized a sweeping regulatory power over interstate commerce and validated all the principal legislation of the New Deal. But the price of victory was high. Roosevelt's clumsy attack on the Court severely tarnished his reputation as a leader. In the future, even Democratic congressmen would feel much freer to vote against the President.

The labor movement also strained the New Deal coalition. As the Wagner Act passed, the labor movement split into warring camps. John L. Lewis, president of the powerful United Mine Workers, led a group of dissident unions out of the craft-oriented AFL in order to organize the semiskilled and unskilled workers in the major mass production industries. The rebels eventually formed the Congress of Industrial Organizations (CIO), while the skilled trades remained in the AFL. Looking at the leaders of the two organizations, there seemed to

NINE OLD MEN, FROM "NEW MASSES," MARCH, 1937

The "Nine Old Men" of the Supreme Court as partisans of the New Deal saw them in 1937. Yet Roosevelt's attack on the court alienated many more Americans than it rallied to his cause. *(Brown Brothers.)*

be no contest. Lewis's dramatic flair and imaginative leadership made him a national attraction in the mid-1930s second only to Roosevelt, and the shaggy giant of the CIO appeared capable of demolishing the AFL's mild little William Green with words alone. "Explore the mind of Bill Green," the advocates of labor compromise had suggested to Lewis. "I have done a lot of exploring in Bill's mind," Lewis declared, "and I give you my word there is nothing there." But the AFL proved to be a resourceful enemy that mobilized local opposition to the CIO, collaborated with employers who were fighting the new unions, and helped antiunion congressmen brand the CIO a communist organization.

In addition, the CIO faced a formidable challenge from the unorganized industries themselves. Employers from the docks of San Francisco to the textile mills in North Carolina used murder, gas, beatings, and intimidation to demoralize their workers and block the CIO's unionizing efforts. The first crisis in this rough, uncertain struggle began in December 1936, when workers at a number of General Motors affiliates sat inside the company plants to gain recognition for their new organization, the United Auto Workers (UAW). Ignoring court orders to evacuate the buildings, receiving supplies from their friends outside, and turning back the police in "The Battle of the Running Bulls," the auto workers, with the help of cooperative state and national politicians, achieved the CIO's first great victory. In February 1937, General Motors and the UAW signed a peace pact. Illegal sit-down strikes quickly spread nationwide.

STEEL STRIKE RIOT, CHICAGO

Passions and dangers surrounded the organizing drives of the CIO. A movie camera captured this moment of terror when Chicago policemen assaulted steel strikers and their families in May 1937. *(Associated Press.)*

Meanwhile, a CIO drive in the steel industry won a second stunning success. In March 1937, U. S. Steel, the very symbol of the open shop in America's mass production industries, ended a bitter strike by recognizing the steelworkers' union. Almost all the corporations in "Little Steel," however, adamantly refused to follow suit, and bloody reprisals stalled the organizing campaign there. In the "Memorial Day Massacre" outside Republic Steel's plant in Chicago, for example, police shot into a fleeing crowd, killing or wounding dozens of strike sympathizers. In fact, there was an epidemic of industrial violence in 1937.

The turmoil of sit-down strikes and local warfare broke an uneasy truce over labor policy within the Democratic party. While an exasperated Roosevelt condemned management and labor alike by declaring "a plague on both your houses," Democratic factions in Congress angrily debated the sins of employers and unions. Fortunately for the CIO, a partisan National Labor Relations Board (NLRB) continued to fight vigorously in behalf of the new unions. By 1941, with almost 10 million members divided between the AFL and the CIO, the union movement had safely passed the first round of crisis. In the process, however, it had made a host of enemies, Democrats as well as Republicans.

A growing hostility to the labor movement decreased the likelihood that the government would assist other Americans to organize in their own behalf. Tenant farmers, for example, were particularly in need of the government's help. Always the poor relations in an era of commercial agriculture, they had suffered cruelly from depression and drought in the 1930s. The AAA, which distributed benefits only to landowners, offered the destitute tenants almost no relief. In 1935, when some of them formed the Southern Tenant Farmers' Union, landlords and sheriffs crushed their organization. When reformers in the Department of Agriculture argued the tenants' cause, they were fired.

Trying New Departures
Principal New Deal Measures, 1935–1938

Works Progress Administration (WPA)	May 1935
Wagner Act, creating National Labor Relations Board (NLRB)	July 1935
Social Security Act	August 1935
Bankhead-Jones Farm Tenancy Act, creating	
Farm Security Administration (FSA)	July 1937
Fair Labor Standards Act	June 1938

The first serious attempt to reverse this tide was the Bankhead-Jones Farm Tenancy Act of 1937. Through a new agency, the Farm Security Administration (FSA), the law provided credit with which tenants could purchase the farms they were working. In addition, the FSA explored ways to develop a diversified, cooperative community life for small farmers and to protect the interests of the forgotten farm laborers. The FSA was one logical extension of the New Deal's innovations in 1935, a rural counterpart of the program for organized labor. But in 1937, the opposition of the established agricultural organizations and the flagging reform spirit in Congress kept its budget small and its future precarious.

The only solid expansion of the New Deal came in the Fair Labor Standards Act of 1938. After much wrangling, Congress established a minimum wage level and an official rate of time and a half for overtime work, and it abolished child labor. With wholesale exemptions in agriculture, special dispensations for Southern employers, and minimum wage scales that were meager even by a depression standard, this law, like the Social Security Act, was neither general in its coverage nor generous in its provisions. Yet in combination with Social

Security and the Works Progress Administration (WPA), the Fair Labor Standards Act reinforced a fundamental new assumption. The national government should protect the economic welfare of its poorer citizens.

By 1938, the New Deal was obviously drifting. Its thin list of accomplishments in two years reflected above all the absence of a clear purpose. Once Roosevelt and his advisers had lost faith in the ability of organized business to bring back prosperity, they simply could not decide where to lay the foundations for a sound economy. None of the available alternatives seemed very promising. Roosevelt did sign two laws strengthening the rights of small businessmen. The Robinson-Patman Act of 1936 sought to protect independent retailers against such huge chains as A & P and Woolworth, and the Miller-Tydings Act of 1937 legalized "fair trade" agreements, or fixed retail pricing, in behalf of similar small firms. The President also authorized the justice department to bring more antitrust suits against big business. Yet Roosevelt never longed for the old days of small-unit competition, and the administration's new antitrust policy did not try to destroy giant corporations. Some advisers suggested a closer alliance between the New Deal and the unions, but Roosevelt neither understood organized labor's raw battles nor trusted John L. Lewis, its outstanding leader. The President also refused to believe that government spending could cure the depression. He even helped to cause a new economic crisis in 1937 by sharply reducing the government budget. Although Roosevelt

The burdens of the thirties crushed America's tenant farmers. In the dust bowl of the Great Plains, drought was as devastating as depression. *(Library of Congress, United States Department of Agriculture, Library of Congress.)*

was profoundly disturbed by the vision of "one-third of a Nation ill-nourished, ill-clad, ill-housed," he did not know how, in the long run, to solve the problem.

On Capitol Hill, an informal coalition of Republicans and conservative, largely Southern Democrats moved into the vacuum of leadership. With no clearer purpose than the liberals, they concentrated primarily on opposing "socialist" measures that would enlarge the national government's responsibilities, or "giveaway" programs that would expand its services. In the spirit of the 1920s, many of them still equated prosperity with a self-regulating economy. All of the conservatives used "New Dealer" as a dirty word. Roosevelt returned their feelings, but he could not check their rising power in Congress. When he tried to "purge" a few prominent opponents in his own party during the offyear elections of 1938, he not only failed but actually publicized his declining authority over the legislature.

In this confusion of uncertain purposes, vague rhetoric, and mutual suspicions, the one sharp focus fell on Roosevelt himself. Reformers, as their fortunes waned, considered him more important than ever. To conservatives, "that man in the White House" embodied the evils of their time. Roosevelt accentuated this tendency to personalize national politics. By 1939, the nation's parlor game was guessing whom the President might designate his successor. Characteristically, Roosevelt kept a serene silence, held the spotlight on himself, and at the last minute allowed the Democratic convention of 1940 to nominate him for an unprecedented third term. The prospect of a third term stirred all the latent emotions about Roosevelt, the aspiring dictator, and Roosevelt, the indispensable man. As the President knew very well, FDR would be the issue of the 1940 campaign.

This time, the Republicans selected a candidate able to challenge Roosevelt. Wendell Willkie, a former utilities executive who had once led the fight against TVA, was an inspired amateur in national politics. Liberal enough to attract independent voters yet conservative enough to satisfy most opponents of the New Deal, Willkie eagerly took on "the Champ" in a vigorous presidential campaign. With arms akimbo and eyes sparkling, he became the first Republican candidate in twenty years to

"Come along. We're going to the Trans-Lux to hiss Roosevelt." *(Library of Congress.)*

elicit a warm popular response as he toured the nation. "Well, muss my hair and call me Willkie!" a common saying in 1940, expressed an easy affection that almost no American had bestowed on solemn Herbert Hoover or bland Alfred Landon. But charm was also Roosevelt's special strength. Moreover, the New Deal's combination of national aid and local autonomy continued to be an extremely successful political formula. Though a few former allies, such as John L. Lewis and Vice-President Garner, deserted the President, most of the voters did not. In November 1940, Roosevelt and his new running-mate, Henry Wallace, won by a substantial margin, 449 electoral votes to 82 for Willkie.

Even before 1940, Roosevelt's attention had increasingly turned outward to the world, where wars in Asia and then in Europe were threatening to engulf the United States. Both Roosevelt and Willkie devoted as much time in their campaigns to foreign affairs as to domestic issues. Following the election, the President immersed himself in the problems that on December 7, 1941, would culminate in war. As Roosevelt later phrased it, he was already discarding the mantle of "Dr. New Deal" and preparing to don a new one, "Dr. Win-the-War." The passing of the New Deal left the government's economic role in limbo. Through humanitarian statements and innovative programs, the Roosevelt administration aroused nationwide expectations that the government would help the needy and support the economy. Yet the sum of the New Deal's efforts neither cured the depression nor established an economic policy. Other leaders would have to bridge the gap between popular hopes and government actions.

Wartime Prosperity and Postwar Confusion, 1941–1947

The Second World War solved the depression. Before the war was over, net farm income almost doubled and corporate profits after taxes climbed 70 percent. From a total of over 8 million unemployed in 1940, the curve dropped below a million by 1944. Moreover, an abundance of jobs and an industrial wage scale that rose 24 percent drew into the labor market an additional 7 million workers, half of whom were women. There had been no economic boom like it in American history.

Economic organization for a worldwide conflict required an extraordinary expansion of government power. The War Production Board, the Office of Price Administration, the War Manpower Commission, the Office of Defense Transportation, and the War Food Administration each had broad authority to manage its subdivision of the economy. Beginning in October 1942, the skillful South Carolina politician James F. Byrnes ruled above these agencies through the Office of Economic Stabilization, and subsequently the Office of War Mobilization.

The problems most bedeviling to the wartime agencies were allocating scarce resources and controlling inflation. Because the United States was blessed

BOEING AIRPLANE FACTORY

The Second World War sent America back to work.
(Library of Congress.)

with an abundance of natural resources, its own raw materials were sufficient for most wartime programs. When a shortage of rubber created a crisis, the rapid development of synthetic rubber soon resolved it. The shortage of skilled labor, however, defied solution. Not only did the armed services absorb over 15 million men and women, but civilians could not resist hopping from job to job in search of better wages. "Stabilization," or job-freeze, orders from Washington had little effect on labor turnover, and Roosevelt's proposal in 1944 to draft workers into an industrial army collapsed in the face of united opposition from employers and unions alike.

Prices soared during the early months of the war. The Office of Price Administration (OPA), under the able but politically obtuse economist Leon Henderson, lacked the power to control inflation because Congress refused to check the rise of agricultural prices. Only late in 1942, when James Byrnes took charge of the entire mobilization program, did a semblance of order begin to emerge. By mid-1943, a broad ceiling over prices, wages, and rents finally stopped the upward spiral. Although the cost of living increased about 33 percent during the war, relatively little of that occurred after the summer of 1943.

Finance posed a third basic wartime problem. Though more than half the costs of war accumulated as a national debt, massive new funds still had to be raised. The answer came in the revolutionary Revenue Act of 1942, which established America's modern structure of taxation. The heart of the measure was a steeply graduated income tax that for the first time covered most middle-income and lower-income groups. As a result, the number of families paying income tax quadrupled, and by 1945, revenues from the tax stood twenty times above their level in 1940. To ease the pain yet increase the flow, the government took most of these taxes directly from the paychecks rather than demand them in a lump once a year.

Inside the intricate framework of wartime rules, however, extreme decentralization prevailed. The tax laws contained numerous loopholes for the wealthy. Thousands of local draft boards decided who should fill the quotas for military service. To get the planes and tanks and beef and wheat it needed, the government simply offered to pay a lot of money. With industries, it signed lucrative contracts guaranteeing costs, profits, and large tax writeoffs. Companies negotiated these contracts through the various bureaus of the wartime government, then fought with one another for the labor and raw materials all of them needed. After the government allowed farm prices to skyrocket for a year, it continued to subsidize many farmers at a level above the market price for their products. Even the unpopular OPA, which rationed such scarce commodities as gasoline, meat, shoes, and sugar among a nation of grumbling consumers, exercised little control over the widespread violation of its rules. The government's chief administrators intervened only when the many small decisions below them had created a hopeless mess.

In the wartime scramble for advantage, reforms were pushed aside. The conservative coalition in Congress, growing a bit with each election, proceeded to trim the New Deal. As the unemployed came back to work, Congress in 1942 terminated the WPA. Calling the Farm Security Administration a "communist" center, its opponents abolished the FSA's social programs for the rural poor. The one child of the

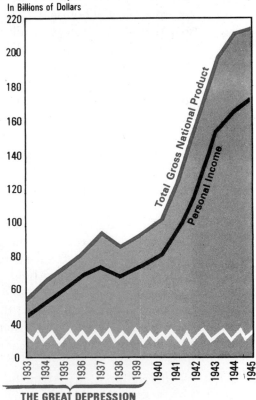

Recovery of the National Economy

In Billions of Dollars

thirties to thrive during the war was the revitalized union movement. In 1941, two more citadels of the open shop—Ford and the corporations in Little Steel— surrendered. During the war itself union membership rose 40 percent. Even more important, many employers, in an effort to hold their workers and maintain production, actually bargained with the unions for the first time. Yet here also the conservatives had their say. Although the number of strikes remained quite low between 1941 and 1945, important ones in the coal and railroad industries during 1943 triggered an angry public reaction, and Congress responded with the Smith-Connally Act, which authorized the President to postpone a strike for thirty days and seize a plant that had been struck. Strikers could be fined and imprisoned.

Above all, the conservatives fought every executive agency that tried to make economic plans for the postwar years. Not one of them survived the congressional budget cuts. As the war drew to a close, the only significant preparation for peace was the Servicemen's Readjustment Act of 1944, popularly known as the GI Bill, which provided unemployment compensation, medical care, mortgage funds, and educational subsidies for the returning veterans. Roosevelt, growing old and ill, did nothing to arrest the confusion. Investing all his energies in world problems, the President left the home front to his subordinates. When the Democrats nominated him for a fourth term in 1944, he campaigned listlessly against Thomas E. Dewey, the smooth, capable Republican governor of New York. Roosevelt still won handily, 439 to 99 electoral votes. Perhaps the nasty Democratic comment that no one wanted "little Tom Dewey sitting on two Washington telephone books" at a peace conference captured the essence of Roosevelt's strength. At a momentous juncture in world affairs, the President had an appropriately grand international prestige. But domestically, America had no leader at all entering 1945.

The man who actually presided over the nation's transition to peace was Harry S Truman. An able Missouri judge during the late 1920s and early 1930s, Truman came to the Senate in 1935 and built a reputation for hard work, party loyalty, and stubborn determination. At the 1944 convention, Democratic leaders selected the reliable, unobtrusive Truman to replace Vice-President Wallace, whose desire to expand the New Deal and usher in the "century of the common man" had alienated the conservatives in his party. Yet no one seemed to have considered Truman seriously as a possible President. Roosevelt, it appeared, would live forever. Then on April 12, 1945, only a few weeks after his fourth inauguration, the President died and an era ended. Millions mourned in public; thousands celebrated in their clubs; and Truman, no more prepared than the nation, suddenly found himself the chief executive.

The most experienced leader would have had difficulty guiding America's economy out of the war. Truman simply floundered. Even before Japan surrendered in August 1945, he could not withstand the popular pressures for a rapid demobilization of the armed forces and a rapid dismantling of most wartime regulations. Industries now made their own decisions in their own behalf, and during the first postwar year corporate profits shot up 20 percent. Strikes spread across the nation. By January 1946, 3 percent of the labor force, including auto, steel, electrical, and packinghouse workers, were simultaneously on strike. When a new round of strikes occurred that spring, a furious President went before Congress to threaten the railroad workers with an army draft even though the Railroad Brotherhoods had already cancelled the strike. The only broad national controls governed prices, and a feud between the President and Congress needlessly allowed these to end all at once in June 1946, producing the highest rate of inflation in the nation's history. Farm prices rose almost 14 percent in a month and nearly 30 percent before the end of the year. As the saying went, "To err is Truman." "Had Enough?" asked the Republicans.

Apparently many Americans had, for the offyear elections of 1946 cost the Democrats 11 seats in the Senate and 54 in the House. When the Eightieth Congress convened in 1947, the Republicans were the majority party for the first time since Hoover's administration. With the cooperation of conservative Democrats, they could even override the President's veto. Yet the Eightieth Congress had little to offer as an alternative to Truman's erratic policies. Its primary contribution was the Taft-Hartley Act of 1947, a culmination of the congressional antagonism toward unions that had been growing for a decade. A complicated law, Taft-Hartley required financial reports from the unions, restricted their political activities, and prohibited a list of "unfair" labor practices. It also empowered the President to postpone a major strike for an eighty-day "cooling off" period and allowed state governments to pass antiunion "right to work" laws. But despite these new rules and the howls they brought from the unions, labor-management relations proceeded much the same after Taft-Hartley as before.

The paralysis in public policy that was afflicting the government had far deeper causes than political quarrels in Washington. Fundamental changes were occurring in the economy, and no one yet knew how to deal with them. By 1936, it was no longer practical to picture the economy in terms of big inter-dependent units: business, labor, agriculture, and finance. Government officials, instead of trying to design one policy for each of these large blocs, increasingly responded to the special claims of much smaller economic units. After 1936, there were no more NRAs for all of American business, just a "little NRA" for coal, another program for oil, particular legislation for retailers, a special anti-trust policy for oligopolies, and on and on. Civil war in the labor movement publicized the very different grievances separating carpenters from steelworkers, from longshoremen from hatmakers—a decentralization of interests far greater than just a division between the AFL and the CIO. By the late 1930s, wheat growers and dairy farmers and cotton producers and cattle grazers were all demanding programs specifically designed for their commodities. It became more and more difficult to pretend that there was any unified, national agricultural interest.

The Second World War hastened this fragmentation. Beneath a shell of administrative centralization, innumerable special interests fought for the government's favors. The stakes were high, the rules loose, and the results chaotic. Each economic interest grew accustomed to caring for itself in the Washington jungle. By the end of the war, the big economic blocs of an earlier era were in thorough disarray. Such broad organizations as the U. S. Chamber of Commerce, the National Association of Manufacturers, and the American Bankers Association, once the voices of basic economic groups, now spoke for no one in particular. The American Farm Bureau Federation was rapidly losing strength, and the Department of Agriculture came to rely less and less on it to administer the government's farm programs. As the AFL and the CIO began making peace and preparing for their merger in 1955, both organizations were experiencing a similar decentralization. Strong industrial unions in the CIO exercised the same kind of independence that the affiliates of the AFL had long enjoyed, and neither central headquarters had much success trying to discipline such stubborn organizations of the Longshoremen and the Teamsters. Even the oligopolies were less integrated than they had once been. The latest wave of corporate consolidations, which eventually produced such conglomerates as Litton Industries, Textron, and Kaiser Industries, favored purely financial combinations of distinct and often very different kinds of business firms.

Paralleling this fragmentation of interests, a permanent, professional bureaucracy formed in Washington to deal with each specialized subdivision of the

The Growth of Union Membership

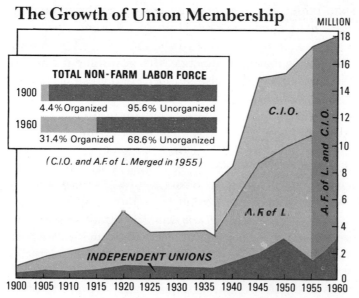

economy. Before 1935, when the national government acted largely as a service center, administrators tended to behave as if they were temporary and would soon leave the government to follow private careers. By 1936, however, the government had become the economy's vital center, and its new responsibilities appeared likely to remain for a long time. Officials in the Works Progress Administration (WPA), the enlarged bureaus of agriculture, the growing Tennessee Valley Authority (TVA), and many other agencies settled in for the duration. Then during the war, the government bureaucracy swelled to four times its size in 1939. In a hubbub of crash programs and quick decisions, no one closely supervised its myriad economic activities. Even after demobilization, the number of civilian employees more than doubled the government's prewar level. Administrators had grown accustomed to running their own little domains and protecting them from higher authorities. Almost every office along the miles of Washington corridors was linked to some private group and a few friendly congressmen. In sum, these many alliances between public officials and private interests made a broad public policy extremely difficult to create.

As this pattern of decentralization developed, the economic importance of the national government loomed larger than ever. No one could miss the intimate connection between government policy and the nation's phenomenal economic growth during the war. America's Gross National Product (GNP) rose a breathtaking 67 percent. Government expenditures accounted for an equally astonishing 40 percent of the total GNP. *Government*—singular and capitalized—arrived as an everyday term to designate this huge center of money and power. With the shadow of the Great Depression still across people's thoughts, the national government's vast authority became inseparably connected with long-term, peacetime prosperity. In the Full Employment Act of 1946, Congress accepted the government's responsibility for maintaining a healthy economy. But Congress carefully avoided specifying how. This sprawling, government-oriented economy had been changing too rapidly, and neither the Democrats nor the Republicans had found a satisfactory technique for managing it.

Local Politics Comes to Washington, 1936–1947

While leaders in Washington were grappling with the problems of the economy, the racial and cultural concerns of local politics gradually rose again to influence national affairs. For a time, it appeared that the informal bargain between the New Deal and local Democrats might keep the two levels separate. By granting local politicians wide authority over the distribution of federal funds, the Roosevelt administration did insulate itself from most local pressures during its second term. James Farley, Roosevelt's master of patronage, managed government appointments with a keen eye to the needs of both the administration and local politics, and the Democratic city bosses continued to give Roosevelt their loyal support. A diffuse anti-Semitism spread through the Great Plains and the northern industrial cities, but it never surfaced in national politics. Although some Southern whites considered the Farm Security Administration and the new industrial unions a threat to local rights, the FSA's programs for black tenant farmers never really materialized, and the CIO received little help trying to organize workers in the towns and small cities of the South. Nor did the New Deal's principal reforms in Indian affairs disturb local politics. After decades of government neglect and hostility to Indian culture, the Roosevelt administration sponsored the Indian Reorganization Act of 1934, an attempt to allow Indians tribal self-government and at least some economic autonomy. Nevertheless, the law required no change in local white policies toward Indians.

The Second World War broke this deceptive calm in national affairs. As the power of the national government rapidly expanded, it inevitably became entangled with local politics. The most shocking example occurred on the West Coast immediately after the Japanese attack at Pearl Harbor. A large majority of whites along the West Coast continued to nurse a traditional hostility toward Asiatics. Following a surprise attack on American territory, they readily believed rumors of a Japanese "fifth column" in the United States that was planning extensive sabotage and communicating with enemy submarines off America's shore. The government, they cried, must destroy the danger from within. These popular, bipartisan emotions found a willing servant in Lieutenant General John DeWitt, who headed the Army's Western Defense Command. Responding to DeWitt's request, Washington gave the general broad powers in February 1942 to solve the Japanese problem as he chose.

At the outset, DeWitt planned to use stronger measures against the 40,000 alien Japanese (immigrants who by law were denied the right to become American citizens) than against the 70,000 who were American citizens by birth. But that distinction quickly disappeared. Early in 1942, DeWitt ordered all Japanese Americans along the coast of Washington, Oregon, and California and from southern Arizona to abandon their homes. From temporary stockades, they were transported to ten island centers where the Army Relocation Authority guarded them for the duration. In *Korematsu* v. *U. S.* (1944), the Supreme Court upheld these policies on grounds of national security. Along with their liberty, Japanese Americans lost about $350 million in property and income.

Concentration camps for 110,000 Japanese Americans were an embarrassment to the Roosevelt administration, which was simultaneously fighting to empty the Nazi concentration camps in Europe. Officially, the Japanese Americans were in "relocation centers." After the initial wave of panic passed, government officials discussed ways of reversing their policy and releasing the prisoners. Once again, local hostilities prevailed. The Roosevelt administration was told that no communities would accept the Japanese Americans. As the common argument went, Japanese Americans would be mobbed if the government did not protect them inside the camps. Instead, the Army compromised during 1943 and 1944 by issuing extended leaves to 35,000 Japanese Americans. Finally, in January 1945, the gates were opened to everyone.

A second challenge came from black Americans who were losers in local politics. Between the two world wars, racial problems that had once been considered peculiarly Southern became clearly national. Close to a million blacks left the South during the 1920s, almost double the number who had emigrated in the previous decade. Even in depression, when the unemployed crowded the large cities, 400,000 more came North. Then during the early 1940s alone, another million responded to the wartime jobs that beckoned from Los Angeles to Boston. By 1950, approximately one-third of America's black population lived outside the South.

In two important respects, the Northern urban experience altered black attitudes. First, it encouraged their assertiveness. During the same years that whites argued over the racial merits of immigration, urban blacks were also manifesting a stronger racial consciousness. Claude McKay, Langston Hughes,

"RELOCATION"

A relatively prosperous Japanese-American family awaits its fate early in 1942. Imprisonment during the war cost them everything. (*Library of Congress.*)

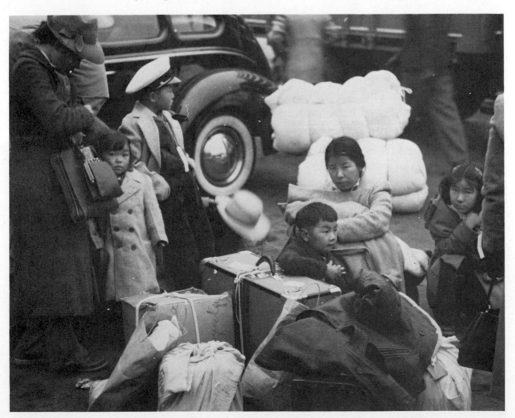

Black Population, 1920-1930

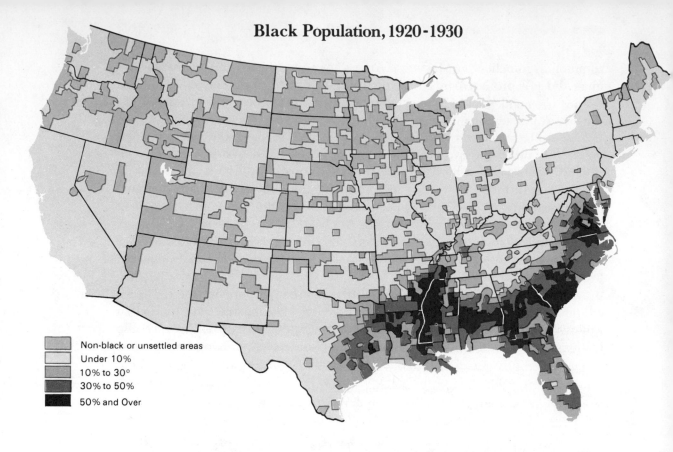

Legend:
- Non-black or unsettled areas
- Under 10%
- 10% to 30°
- 30% to 50%
- 50% and Over

Countee Cullen, and other contributors to the "Harlem Renaissance" of the 1920s wrote eloquently about the black spirit. Early in the twenties, millions of blacks found inspiration in the African nationalism of Marcus Garvey, an immigrant from Jamaica whose Universal Negro Improvement Association promised racial glory in the Empire of Africa.* Moreover, in some cities, blacks secured a place for themselves in the urban political machines. Under Tom Pendergast in Kansas City and Big Bill Thompson in Chicago, for example, black bosses represented their wards and negotiated with organized crime much as the white bosses were doing.

Second, the Northern urban experience stimulated a national movement for black rights. Each large city contained a core of black leaders who were aware of the modern nationalizing trends around them and eager to use them in behalf of their own people. Their primary organization was the National Association for the Advancement of Colored People (NAACP), and their primary spokesman was Walter White, the talented writer and persistent lobbyist who in 1931 began his long tenure as national secretary for the NAACP. When the Great Depression made it clear that only the national government could signifi-

---

*Garvey's conviction in 1923 for mail fraud disorganized his movement, and nothing comparable arose to take its place.

cantly improve the position of blacks in America, the NAACP pressed two kinds of arguments on the government's leaders. One, appealing to their conscience, demanded racial equality. The other, appealing to their political interests, offered to trade black votes for black rights. Unlike the Southern cotton fields, the Northern cities lay in competitive, two-party states with large electoral votes, and the NAACP tried to convince the Democratic party in particular that urban blacks could tip the balance in these states.

The New Deal's response was extremely disappointing. In matters of personal discrimination, Roosevelt's circle responded with sensitivity and imagination. In 1939, when the world-famous contralto Marian Anderson was denied the use of Constitution Hall in Washington because she was black, Harold Ickes arranged for a dramatic concert at the steps of the Lincoln Memorial. Eleanor Roosevelt's warmth and kindness to people of all races made her a national institution. But in basic matters of civil and economic rights, the Roosevelt administration changed very little. It refused to take a strong stand against lynching. Without special protection for black wage earners, the New Deal's labor policies sometimes resulted in even fewer jobs for blacks. Its agricultural programs in the South were administered through white channels and did nothing to loosen the bonds of black peonage. In the Department of Agriculture, black county agents who complained about white favoritism were fired. Although blacks did benefit from national relief, they often stood last in line. The New Deal left blacks to fight for their share through local politics, where their rewards were meager.

With these frustrations in the background, A. Philip Randolph, the shrewd president of the Brotherhood of Sleeping Car Porters, introduced a new tactic in the fight for blacks rights. Early in 1941, as the economy was mobilizing in anticipation of war, Randolph rallied blacks throughout the nation for a mass march on Washington that would publicize America's racial discrimination around the world and possibly disrupt the early stages of war production. Randolph's price for canceling the march was President Roosevelt's intervention in behalf of black workers. Despite his irritation at Randolph's threat, Roosevelt on June 25, 1941, issued a precedent-setting executive order that banned discriminatory hiring "because of race, creed, color, or national origin," both within the national government and throughout its expanding scheme of war-related contracts. The executive order also established the Fair Employment Practices Committee (FEPC) to oversee these rules.

But it was the need for labor, not the weak FEPC, that expanded economic opportunities for blacks during the war. Both in the war industries and in the armed services, Jim Crow rules gradually weakened under the pressure of an increasingly severe manpower shortage. Meanwhile, racial tensions were mounting, especially over access to housing and public facilities in the swollen industrial areas of the large cities. During the summer of 1943, these emotions exploded from coast to coast in a series of violent racial encounters. The worst of the riots occurred in Detroit, a primary center of war production, where 500,000 newcomers, including 60,000 blacks, had been squeezed in since 1940. On a hot Sunday in June 1943, a fight between teenage whites and blacks ignited two days of guerrilla warfare and widespread looting. Twenty-five blacks and nine whites were killed, hundreds wounded, and millions of dollars in property lost. By then, some Democrats were openly worrying about "the Negro vote." Yet every national election between 1936 and 1944 seemed to verify the political wisdom of Democratic policies. If blacks were really discontented, why did they vote as heavily Democratic.as any other urban group? Wait until after the depression, the Roosevelt administration had told its black critics. Wait until after the war, it told them in the early 1940s.

After the war, impatient black leaders insisted that the time had finally come. They had two reasons to feel some optimism. First, they were joined by a growing number of Northern whites who had committed themselves to a movement for equal black rights. This alliance had produced a string of FEPC laws in such states as New York, New Jersey, Massachusetts, and Connecticut, and now it

The migration of the blacks started from the fields and towns of the South and took them to the slums of the northern cities. Although still on the bottom rung, they at least found opportunities in the North to protest, as this call for a demonstration in the mid-forties illustrates. A civil rights movement was forming. *(Library of Congress, Chicago Historical Society.)*

was mobilizing for a national campaign against racial discrimination. Second, the elections of 1946, returning Republican majorities in several Northern states that had previously been Democratic, gave new force to the old argument of the NAACP. Black votes might indeed make the critical difference in a closely balanced national election. The shifting tides of party politics had invested a racial group with the same kind of importance that the economic groups in labor, agriculture, and business traditionally held. In the future, national campaigns would have to adapt to this distinctive political bloc.

Solving the Riddle of Economic Policy, 1948–1954

Although most Democratic leaders prayed that Truman would not run for President in 1948, he did. With little choice, less enthusiasm, and no hope, the national convention dutifully nominated him. The odds against Truman's success were prohibitive. Liberal Democrats judged him too conservative, and conservative Democrats judged him too liberal. Both considered him weak. Immediately after Truman was nominated, two additional parties appeared to attract the votes of dissident Democrats. The Progressive party, in the tradition of American parties with that name, depended on the reputation of one man, Henry Wallace. As former secretary of agriculture, Vice-President, and secretary of commerce under Roosevelt, he brought to the Progressives the prestige of the New Deal. And because Wallace's liberalism had flowered during the 1940s, he contributed his own fervent calls for world peace and domestic reform. In Birmingham, a new States' Rights Democratic party formed out of a general dislike for the New Deal legacy and a specific hostility to the regular party's appeal to the blacks. The "Dixiecrats" nominated Governor J. Strom Thurmond of South Carolina and dreamed of carrying the entire South. Above all, Truman faced a formidable Republican opponent in Governor Dewey of New York, who had done better against the indomitable Roosevelt in 1944 than any of the three Republican candidates preceding him. The only argument among the experts was the margin of Dewey's victory.

Truman made fools of the experts in 1948 because he responded so shrewdly

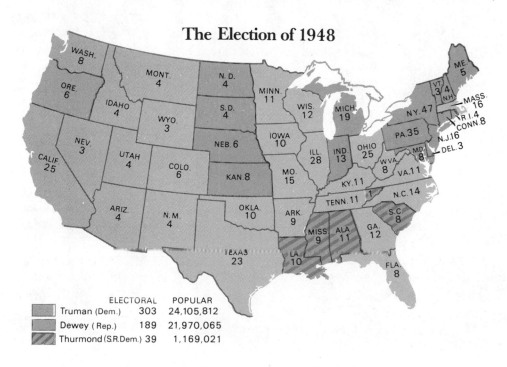

The Election of 1948

	ELECTORAL	POPULAR
Truman (Dem.)	303	24,105,812
Dewey (Rep.)	189	21,970,065
Thurmond (S.R.Dem.)	39	1,169,021

to the prevailing disorganization in political and economic affairs. In a nation of innumerable, scattered interest groups, no one knew how to provide effective leadership. Using a carefully devised strategy, the President shifted the blame for weak leadership to the Republican majority in the Eightieth Congress, which he scorned as the "Do-Nothing Congress." After the nominating conventions, he called Congress into special session and challenged the Republicans to enact their program. Of course little happened. The general paralysis in public policy appeared to be specifically a Republican malady.

Without a systematic program of his own, Truman compiled a long list of favors and promises. He reminded the unions that he had vetoed the Taft-Hartley Act of 1947 and that Republican votes had overridden him. He reminded business groups of tax benefits and government contracts. He promised parity to everything a farmer could produce. He recommended enlarging the TVA, increasing public housing, and broadening Social Security. He favored government aid to education. At the national convention in 1948, Mayor Hubert Humphrey of Minneapolis had led the successful drive for a firm platform on black rights, including a permanent FEPC and federal laws against lynching and poll taxes. Truman not only endorsed this platform; he took the cause to Harlem, where no presidential candidate had ever campaigned. Even more striking, the President embarked in 1948 on the long, difficult course of desegregating the armed forces.

Dewey took the high road, blandly promising a sound, sane administration. But the bantam rooster from Missouri, fighting his way through an arduous cross-country campaign, ran for President like a county politician. His remark to one audience told the meaning of the entire campaign: "Vote your own interests." In 1948, Truman's provincialism was sophisticated national politics. By November, Wallace, who increasingly seemed the candidate of the Communist party, had lost almost all support. Thurmond kept only the four Southern states which he had controlled in July. And Truman, with 303 electoral votes to Dewey's 189, scored the most stunning upset in modern politics.

Truman's victory demonstrated how many groups now looked to the national government for assistance. His second term revealed the constraints on the government in responding to them. Truman gave his many promises a name, the "Fair Deal," but few of them survived the next four years. Congress rejected federal aid to education, national health insurance, and a permanent FEPC. Although the President held to his purpose of desegregating the armed forces, he did not lead a general campaign for blacks' rights. In 1950, when the Supreme Court ruled against segregation in interstate commerce, neither Truman nor the Interstate Commerce Commission seriously tried to implement it. Most of Thurmond's Dixiecrats returned to the regular Democratic party without severe strain.

The laws that did pass minimized the national government's influence in guiding social change. The Housing Act of 1949, which renewed a program that had started during the New Deal, made Washington a financier, but not a planner, of public housing. Local governments and private groups decided who would get the benefits from public housing in their areas. Legislation subsidizing hospitals and medical research followed this same pattern. Appropriately, these bills carried the names of such conservative or moderate senators as Robert Taft of Ohio and Lister Hill of Alabama, for each law followed the safe tradition of a detached and indirect government support.

By the end of the 1940s, therefore, two basic conditions for a successful economic policy had been clarified. Such a policy had to meet the needs of innumerable small interest groups, and it had to remove the national government as far as possible from the affairs of these groups. The ideal means did lie immediately at hand. The government's fiscal powers expanded remarkably during the 1940s. Although national expenditures dropped with the end of the war, they still remained six or seven times greater than in the 1930s, and double the New Deal's percentage of the GNP. The wartime tax laws and their successors bound almost all Americans into the government's financial network. By 1946, the national debt had also risen sevenfold above the level of 1939, and funding this giant debt automatically made the government a dominant force in the nation's credit system. Moreover, the Federal Reserve's Board of Governors in Washington exercised an important general control over the nation's monetary affairs.

Adjusting the national budget, funding the national debt, regulating national monetary policy—here were precisely the mechanisms that the postwar economy could tolerate. The fiscal machinery operated just as effectively with any number of small interests. It did not require direct government interference with private groups or individuals. At the same time, it formed a broad national authority over the whole economy. If the economy faltered, the government could ease credit, lower taxes, and increase its deficit. If an economic boom threatened inflation, the government could tighten credit, raise taxes, and shrink the deficit.

Truman, however, was not the person to shape the government's fiscal powers into an acceptable public policy. First, neither the President nor his closest advisers felt free to manipulate government finance. Truman, much like Roosevelt before him, disliked budget deficits on principle and periodically led stern attacks on government spending. His narrow secretary of the Treasury, John Snyder, refused to consider the national debt as anything besides an unfortunate government expense. Second, Truman's prestige as a leader collapsed. The Korean War, beginning in June 1950, brought a sharp inflation and growing frustration over international affairs. In 1951 and 1952, evidence of corruption among Truman's associates and in the Justice Department sullied the administration's reputation. The President's own combative, unpredictable behavior added to the discontent. According to opinion polls in 1952, less than one in four Americans approved of his presidency.

Broad bipartisan approval for a policy of fiscal controls required a new President with a fresh start. The Republicans, looking toward the 1952 elections, vowed that this time they would be the ones to name the new President. The two important candidates for the Republican nomination were the brusque, efficient Robert Taft, son of a President and leader of his party in the Senate, and Dwight D. Eisenhower, hero of the Second World War and favorite of the party's moderates. Taft had established a long record of opposition to Washington bureaucracies and government interference with business. At the same time, as a practicing politician, he accepted the primary results of the New Deal and acknowledged a government responsibility to protect the economy. Eisenhower, on the other hand, had established his record in the army, where the general demonstrated an impressive talent for diplomacy as well as command.

DWIGHT D. EISENHOWER

In Ike, the Republicans finally found a winner. A war hero with such a smile was unbeatable in the fifties. *(Magnum.)*

Though Eisenhower said he favored a "balanced budget," the code words of conservative Republicanism, his attitude on domestic affairs was largely a mystery.

In a bitter contest, Eisenhower defeated Taft for the Republican nomination in 1952. Despite Taft's impressive strength among party regulars, the Republicans could not resist an immensely popular war hero. The Democrats had even more difficulty finding a candidate. A folksy campaign by the liberal Tennessee senator, Estes Kefauver, replete with handshakes, barbecues, and coonskin caps, gave him an early lead in a crowded field, but Truman refused his blessing. Instead, the Democrats finally drafted the circumspect governor of Illinois, Adlai E. Stevenson. That fall, against an eloquent but outclassed Stevenson, the general transformed his radiant smile, unaffected manner, and shining reputation into an overwhelming 442 electoral votes to Stevenson's 89.

By November, it was becoming clear that Eisenhower, even more than the conservative Taft, retained a nostalgic attachment to an earlier age. An army career had spared Eisenhower the kinds of policy adjustments that Taft had been making in the 1930s and 1940s, and the general had never abandoned the principles of the New Era. He prized individualism and visualized its operation through private groups—"political, industrial, church, school, labor," as he put it. "It has been a group effort, freely undertaken, that has produced the things of which we are so proud," Eisenhower announced, and he expected his administration to serve this "American way of life." "Free enterprise," "private initiative," and the dangers of "regimentation" peppered his conversations. He regarded TVA as "creeping Socialism." On election night, 1952, when Eisenhower finally broke loose from the happy mob, he placed his first telephone call to Herbert Hoover.

Eisenhower gathered so many wealthy opponents of the New Deal into his cabinet that it was popularly described as "nine millionaires and a plumber"— and the "plumber," Secretary of Labor Martin Durkin, soon resigned. The President and most of his cabinet shared a common purpose. They agreed that rich deposits of oil just off America's shore should be relinquished to the states, and in 1953, Congress passed such a law. They also proposed distributing federal revenues to the states. In cooperation with Secretary of the Treasury George Humphrey, the President set out to slash the national budget and minimize the government's influence in the economy. Eisenhower had no disagreement with the statement of Secretary of Defense Charles E. Wilson, former president of General Motors, that "what was good for our country was good for General Motors, and vice versa." Nor did he object when Secretary of Commerce Sinclair Weeks tried to fire the chief of the Bureau of Standards for reporting that a useless commercial battery additive, AD-2X, was useless. Secretary Weeks thought it should be allowed a "test of the marketplace."

Nevertheless, Eisenhower's attempt to revive the past quickly failed. Private groups welcomed favors, but almost none of them wanted responsibilities.

Bipartisan leagues of businessmen, union leaders, and professionals demanded more money and more assistance, not less, from Washington. The farm associations were horrified when Eisenhower recommended phasing out their subsidies. State and local governments recoiled at the thought of managing their own little economies.

Public confidence broke during a recession in 1953 and 1954. When Eisenhower responded with a firm assurance of no more New Deals and a willingness to wait for prosperity's return, he met a nationwide hue and cry. Reluctantly but realistically, the President reconsidered. By March 1954, the Eisenhower administration had committed itself to protecting the economy with fiscal countermeasures, and when the recession had passed, the President gave due credit to "the automatic workings of the fiscal system."

A stamp of approval from these impeccably conservative Republicans largely ended debate over the government's new approach to economic maintenance. By 1954, substantial majorities in Congress stood ready to support the economy by adjusting taxes and federal spending. The Federal Reserve Board and the Treasury Department both agreed that they should fund the national debt and regulate interest rates so that credit would expand in a weak economy and contract during inflation. In fact, the secretary of the Treasury now ranked with the secretaries of state and defense as government leaders. So many people accepted these fiscal techniques so fast because they seemed so neutral. They did not inhibit the stream of favor-seeking and favor-dispensing that flowed through Washington's busy offices. Liberals could still plan to expand government services and conservatives could still hope to preserve the government's detachment. For the Invisible Hand that had guided Hoover's cooperative commonwealth in the 1920s, the national government of the 1950s substituted the Barely Visible Hand of fiscal manipulation, and in the process it temporarily solved one of the knottiest problems in modern politics.

Local and National Politics Collide
1948–1954

As the government was unraveling the economic puzzle, the second fundamental problem in modern politics, national-local relations, grew more and more tangled. The prominence of black rights in the campaign of 1948 made race relations the most likely source of tension between national and local politics. But during his second term, Truman defused the issue by proceeding very cautiously on civil rights. Adlai Stevenson, the Democratic candidate in 1952, was more moderate on the subject than Truman. In addition, the NAACP was concentrating its primary energies on the Supreme Court, which attracted far less attention than the President or Congress. In *Smith* v. *Allwright* (1944), the Court had outlawed all-white primary elections in the South. Then in *Sweatt*

v. *Painter* (1950), it broadened an earlier ruling against segregated professional schools. The NAACP, behind its chief counsel, Thurgood Marshall, quietly prepared a legal assault on all segregated facilities.

Instead of black rights, it was anticommunism that disrupted the balance between national and local politics. A new wave of antiradicalism began to build after 1935, when enemies of the New Deal accused it of adopting communist ideas, and patriotic groups attacked the public schools for teaching radical doctrines. The House Committee on Un-American Activities, established in 1938, gave lurid publicity to the charge that communists dominated the new industrial unions. Congress captured the spirit of this vague antiradicalism in the Smith Act of 1940, which set criminal penalties for teaching or advocating violent revolution, or for belonging to an organization that did either. Despite the wartime alliance with the Soviet Union, anticommunist rhetoric remained fairly common during the early 1940s, and immediately after the war, both the House Un-American Activities Committee and numerous state antisubversive committees moved into action against an ever widening range of ideological dangers.

In 1947, the Truman administration declared international communism the enemy of the United States. Prominent Americans of both parties echoed the alarm. Between 1947 and 1949, communist governments spread across Eastern Europe and China, and in 1949 the Soviet Union exploded its first atomic bomb. Throughout the nation—in government, in the labor unions, in the communications industries, in public and private education—a variety of oaths and reviews screened those who were suspected of communist sympathies. The Justice Department, using both the Smith Act and the new Internal Security Act of 1950, prosecuted some members of the Communist party and forced the rest to disband. After a dramatic series of public hearings, Alger Hiss, once a respected official in the State Department, was convicted of perjury in January 1950 for denying that he had passed government information to a Soviet agent. In June came the shock of the Korean War, followed by arrests that eventually led to the execution of Julius and Ethel Rosenberg as Soviet spies. America seemed to be a monolith of anticommunism.

But inside this apparent consensus lay two profoundly different anticommunisms. One expressed the natural preoccupations of national politics. Appearing in strength around 1947, this anticommunism sought to defend the United States against an international challenge: the Soviet Union, the league of communist countries it headed, and the espionage system it directed. Abroad, this anticommunism tried to contain the power of the Soviet Union. At home, it concentrated above all on communists in government, because the enemy's agent at a crucial spot in the government could seriously damage the nation's defense. Hence, the revelations about Alger Hiss greatly aggravated these worries.

The other anticommunism expressed the fears and frustrations of locally oriented Americans. Their communism was a pervasive web of dangers that might appear in the guise of atheism, sexual freedoms, strange accents, civil rights, or whatever most threatened a particular group's sense of security. Although this anticommunism also spoke of national defense and international conflict, it equated these issues with threats to a locality's cultural and moral standards. The actual sources of danger might well be some of the leaders in national politics. Splintered, diffuse, and eruptive, this was the truly popular anticommunism.

These two anticommunisms, the one emphasizing power and the other emphasizing sin, were irreconcilable. From a national vantage point, the many state and local committees that in the name of anticommunism attacked textbooks and library catalogues and civil libertarians were part of an aimless witch-hunt. What possible relevance could these matters have to an international contest with Soviet Communism? As one lawyer summarized the work of the Broyles Commission in Illinois, it "almost completely skirted . . . the operations of the Communist party in Illinois," and it failed totally "to uncover evidence of actual subversion within the state." But such committees in Illinois, California, New York, Maryland, and elsewhere were not looking for that kind of communism. As the Broyles Commission stated, "Liberalism" was its enemy, and the educational system, the commission's primary target, was an excellent place to begin the battle. Sophisticated "Eastern internationalists" in the State Department were an equally logical target. The State Department's opposition to the Soviet Union did not affect such judgments, for they relied on a local definition of communism.

In February 1950, a month after the conviction of Alger Hiss, an undistinguished first-term Republican senator from Wisconsin, Joseph McCarthy, elbowed forward to make anticommunism his personal crusade. For more than four years, this canny politician frightened government officials with charges of communist infiltration in their departments, staged melodramatic investigations of suspected enemy agents, exercised a powerful influence over government appointments, and won a large following. According to a national poll early in 1954, three out of five Americans with an opinion about McCarthy favored his activities.

McCarthy opened his campaign by claiming he had a list of authentic communists who were still employed by the State Department. Some thought he said 205. The senator later settled on 57. During Truman's administration, he continued a scattergun attack on the State Department and helped to make "communism" a noisy issue in the elections of 1952. After Eisenhower's inauguration, McCarthy broadened his anticommunist fire until he hit the army itself early in 1954. Few politicans cared to risk an encounter with the Wisconsin slugger, because McCarthy quickly acquired a reputation for defeating his political enemies at the polls. Eisenhower also refused to engage him, saying privately, "I will not get into the gutter with that guy."

SENATOR JOSEPH MCCARTHY UNDER A HALO OF
LIGHTS AND HIS AIDE ROY COHN AT THE ARMY-
MCCARTHY HEARINGS IN 1954

To millions of Americans in the early fifties, these
were fearless patriots who defended the nation
against an insidious network of communists. (*Wide
World.*)

The key to McCarthy's success was his ability to use the national issue of communists in government as a source of strength in the Senate, and the local issue of domestic subversion as a source of strength among millions of citizens. McCarthy repeatedly claimed that the sole purpose of his investigations was the exposure of communists in government, and after the Hiss conviction, no one in Washington could lightly dismiss that possibility. As cool a head as Senator Taft endorsed McCarthy's freewheeling search for spies. When McCarthy failed to find any Soviet agents, however, he shifted his attack to the books that his suspects had written, the reforms that they had supported, and the people who had associated with them. McCarthy invariably identified communism as "Godless" and usually discovered its American disciples among the wellborn, well educated, and well placed.

Despite the special attention that McCarthy attracted, others used even more extreme language. In 1952, Senator William Jenner of Indiana declared, "I charge that this country today is in the hands of a secret inner coterie which is directed by agents of the Soviet Union." Democrats, including Truman, made important contributions to the harsh anticommunist climate. What set "McCarthyism" apart was its capacity to bring a rough-hewn version of local politics inside the national government. Violating the customary procedures of the Senate, McCarthy impugned the personal integrity of his critics and called them "gutless." The State Department, instead of selecting officials for their knowledge and skills, had to listen when it was told to "get rid of the alien-minded radicals and moral perverts."

Years of such confusion in the standards of government eventually became intolerable. When McCarthy attacked the upper echelons of the army in 1954, his growing opposition in Washington began to organize. The senator and his aides did not fare well in a televised series of "Army-McCarthy" hearings. In August 1954, the Senate created a select committee to review charges of senatorial misconduct against McCarthy, and that December, by a vote of 67 to 22, his colleagues condemned him. Without authority in the Senate, McCarthy faded into obscurity.

McCarthyism was simultaneously unique and representative. The special style of the Wisconsin senator and the special circumstances encouraging its success were passing matters. But the collision that McCarthyism caused between national and local politics would occur again and again in later years. By 1954, the centrality of the national government in American life was an indisputable fact. The scope and significance of its powers made it a magnet for almost every ambitious group in American society. Washington irresistibly attracted those issues that had once been hidden in the nation's neighborhoods and communities. If the national government could solve America's economic problems, why could it not also solve America's racial and cultural problems? As the national government fulfilled the New Deal's promise in economic management, therefore, it critically altered the New Deal's balance between national and local authority, and ushered in a new phase of modern politics.

Suggested Readings

William E. Leuchtenburg's *Franklin D. Roosevelt and the New Deal, 1932–1940* (1963) stands alone as a guide to the late years of the New Deal. However, Paul K. Conkin's essay, *The New Deal* (rev. ed., 1975), offers a shrewd assessment of its limitations. Joseph Alsop and Turner Catledge, *The 168 Days* (1938), reports the battle over the Supreme Court, and Paul L. Murphy, *The Constitution in Crisis Times, 1918–1969* (1972), reviews the relevant Court decisions. On the struggles of organized labor, the best survey is Irving L. Bernstein, *Turbulent Years* (1970). More information on the institutional warfare among the unions appears in Walter Galenson's detailed *The CIO Challenge to the AFL* (1960) and Philip Taft's sympathetic *The A. F. of L. from the Death of Gompers to the Merger* (1959). Sidney Fine, *Sit-Down* (1969), captures the drama of a crucial strike in the automobile industry, and Jerold S. Auerbach, *Labor and Liberty: The LaFollette Committee and the New Deal* (1966), examines one form of government assistance to the new unions. The bottom of the rural economy is explored in David E. Conrad, *The Forgotten Farmers: The Story of Sharecroppers in the New Deal* (1965), in Pete Daniel, *The Shadow of Slavery: Peonage in the South, 1901–1969* (1972), and most feelingly in James Agee and Walker Evans, *Let Us Now Praise Famous Men* (1941). Sidney Baldwin's *FSA* (1968) is an appealing history of the New Deal's major effort to help the rural poor. Barry Dean Karl, *Executive Reorganization and Reform in the New Deal* (1963), and Richard Polenberg, *Reorganizing Roosevelt's Government: The Controversy over Executive Reorganization, 1936–1939* (1966), discuss an important political struggle in the late thirties. These studies along with two other fine books— Richard S. Kirkendall's *Social Scientists and Farm Politics in the Age of Roosevelt* (1966) and James T. Patterson's *Congressional Conservatism and the New Deal* (1967)—help to explain the decline of reform.

The domestic side of the Second World War has received little attention from historians. Richard Polenberg, *War and Society: The United States, 1941–1945* (1972), provides a useful overview. Something of the relations between government and business is revealed in Bruce Catton, *The War Lords of Washington* (1948), and Donald M. Nelson, *Arsenal of Democracy: The Story of American War Production* (1946). Joel Seidman, *American Labor from Defense to Reconversion* (1953), deals primarily with government policy. On the other hand, William Henry Chafe, *The American Woman: Her Changing Social, Economic, and Political Roles, 1920–1970* (1972), includes a valuable discussion of women in the wartime economy. Roland A. Young, *Congressional Politics in the Second World War* (1956), reviews the legislative record. On specific laws, Davis R. B. Ross, *Preparing for Ulysses* (1969), explains the GI Bill, and Stephen K. Bailey, *Congress Makes a Law* (1957), analyzes the Full Employment Act.

A growing literature examines the place of racial minorities in modern America. Two surveys—John Hope Franklin, *From Slavery to Freedom* (3rd ed., 1969), and August Meier and Elliott M. Rudwick, *From Plantation to Ghetto* (rev. ed., 1970)—ably cover the years after 1920. Nathan Irvin Huggins, *Harlem Renaissance* (1971), minimizes the cultural significance of its subject. On the very different aspirations of Marcus Garvey and his followers, the best assessments are E. David Cronon, *Black Moses* (1955), and Thomas G. Vincent, *Black Power and the Garvey Movement* (1971). St. Clair Drake and Horace R. Cayton, *Black Metropolis* (2 vols., rev. ed., 1962), remains a valuable study of the Chicago ghetto. Raymond Wolters, *Negroes and the Great Depression* (1970), tells a grim story of the thirties, and Dan T. Carter's smoothly written *Scottsboro* (1969) recounts the most notorious abuse of justice in the South during that decade. The most important organizations serving blacks are discussed in Langston Hughes, *Fight for Freedom: The Story of the NAACP* (1962), and Nancy J. Weiss, *The National Urban League, 1910–1940* (1974). Also see Walter White's autobiography, *A Man Called White* (1948). Richard M. Dalfiume's *Desegregation of the United States Armed Forces* (1969), traces the most striking public gain for blacks during the Truman years. In *Black Bourgeoisie* (1957), E. Franklin Frazier offers a sharp analysis of relatively well-to-do blacks. Roger Daniels, *Concentration Camps, USA* (1971), is a brief study of the persecution of Japanese Americans during the Second World War; Jacobus ten Broek et al., *Prejudice, War and the Constitution* (1954), provides many of the details. Wilcomb E. Washburn, *The Indian in America* (1975), is a solid survey with an extensive bibliography.

Although there is no authoritative account of Harry Truman's administration, Cabell Phillips, *The Truman Presidency* (1966), is a reasonable introduction. Merle Miller, *Plain Speaking: An Oral Biography of Harry S. Truman* (1974), helps in understanding the President's quality of mind. A considerably more sophisticated study, Alonzo L. Hamby's *Beyond the New Deal: Harry S. Truman and American Liberalism* (1973), analyzes the place of the Truman administration in a modern democratic tradition. A good place to begin exploring the election of 1948 is Samuel Lubell, *The Future of American Politics* (1952). Susan M. Hartmann, *Truman and the 80th Congress* (1971), covers important background in Washington. The meaning of Henry A. Wallace's third-party candidacy is evaluated in Norman D. Markowitz, *The Rise and Fall of the People's Century* (1973), and detailed in Allen Yarnell, *Democrats and Progressives* (1974). V. O. Key, Jr., *Southern Politics in State and Nation* (1949), is a mine of information on its subject. On particular areas of public policy, William C. Berman, *The Politics of Civil Rights in the Truman Administration* (1970), and Richard O. Davies, *Housing Reform during the Truman Administration* (1966), are both careful studies. Allen J. Matusow's *Farm Policies and Politics in the Truman Years* (1967) makes a thorough assessment in its field. More critical appraisals of the President appear in Barton J. Bernstein, ed., *Politics and Policies of the Truman Administration* (1970), especially the essays by Bernstein himself. J. Joseph Huthmacher, ed., *The Truman Years* (1972), contains an excellent bibliography.

The best source on the growing Republican challenge to the Democrats is James T. Patterson's appreciative biography of Robert A. Taft, *Mr. Republican* (1972). Herbert S. Parmet, *Eisenhower and the American Crusades* (1972), is a good general account of the Eisenhower presidency, and Gary W. Reichard, *The Reaffirmation of Republicanism* (1975), contains a fuller examination of Eisenhower's early years in office. *The Ordeal of Power* (1963), a thoughtful appraisal of Eisenhower's presidency by Emmet John Hughes, is also most valuable on the early years. Additional material appears in Robert J. Donovan's chatty *Eisenhower: The Inside Story* (1956) and Sherman Adams's *Firsthand Report* (1961), the memoir of Eisenhower's chief domestic aide. The momentous changes in the government's fiscal powers and policies are discussed in Herbert Stein, *The Fiscal Revolution in America* (1969). For a dissent from the new fiscal orthodoxy, see Milton Friedman and Anna J. Schwartz, *A Monetary History of the United States, 1867–1960* (1963).

No domestic subject since the New Deal has attracted such scholarly attention as the anticommunist issue after the Second World War. Robert Griffith and Athan Theoharis, eds., *The Specter: Original Essays on the Cold War and the Origins of McCarthyism* (1974), Earl Latham, *The Communist Controversy in Washington* (1966), and Walter Gellhorn, ed., *The States and Subversion* (1952), suggest the wide range of topics and interests that were involved. Athan Theoharis, *Seeds of Repression* (1971), and Richard M. Freeland, *The Truman Doctrine and the Origins of McCarthyism* (1972), place a heavy responsibility for the rise of popular anticommunism on the Truman administration, and Alan D. Harper, *The Politics of Loyalty: The White House and the Communist Issue, 1946–1952* (1969), significantly tempers that judgment. Robert Griffith, *The Politics of Fear* (1970), analyzes McCarthy's sources of power in the Senate. In *The Intellectuals and McCarthy* (1967), Michael Paul Rogin blames conservative academicians for inflating the record of McCarthy's popular appeal. On the most sensational espionage cases, see Walter and Miriam Schneir, *Invitation to an Inquest* (1965), which explores the Rosenberg case, and Allen Weinstein, *Perjury! The Hiss-Chambers Conflict* (1977).

32

Modern Culture

As the economy was modernizing, so were the everyday lives and hopes and worries of countless Americans. A national consumer market, a revolution in transportation, and new means of mass communication guaranteed that almost everyone would feel the effects of this modernizing process. But the response to it varied widely. From the most positive of these responses came a set of values that gave Americans a new understanding of their lives and a new morality for guiding behavior. The old-fashioned ways, however, refused to capitulate. Adjusting to survive in the twentieth century, America's traditional values continued to fight for a place in the modern era. The most consistent common denominator between these competing sets of values was concern for the individual. Where in an organized, mechanized modern society did the individual fit? This disturbing question proved so difficult to manage that a series of clear answers did not develop until midcentury.

The Consumer Paradise

During the 1920s, a cornucopia of consumer delights spread before the nation. Abandoning the time-honored rules to buy cautiously, fear debt, and save each small surplus, Americans made consumer credit a national necessity, and it soon became available through a great variety of convenient, local outlets.

To one visitor from abroad, the entire nation was a "rapturous whirl of making and spending."

The most prized of the consumer treasures was the automobile. By 1920, new techniques of automobile production and heavy investments in plant equipment had prepared the way for mass marketing, and by the end of the decade, the number of registered cars almost equaled the number of families. For innumerable Americans, it was a case of love at first sight. Talk about the car, care of the car, accessories for the car occupied them as much as using the car. It emancipated people from a set of channels fixed by their homes, neighborhood shops, and jobs. Once the front porch had been the family gathering place on a pleasant evening. Now families piled into the car, and the new houses no longer had front porches. When a country housewife was asked why her family had a car but not a bathtub, she replied, "Bathtub? You can't go to town in a bathtub!" Indeed, a whole range of new freedoms came with the car. One horrified old-timer called it a "House of Prostitution on wheels."

A second group of consumer goods relied on the spread of electricity into family dwellings. The Midwestern utilities magnate Samuel Insull pioneered the revolutionary process of selling a metered electrical service to households, and other companies soon recognized the genius of his scheme. Though Insull's unwieldy empire of utility companies collapsed after the Crash of 1929, his influence lived on in millions of American homes. By the end of the twenties, two out of three households had electricity, in contrast to one out of five before the war. By 1940, with help from the New Deal's Rural Electrification Administration (REA), the proportion had risen to four out of five households.

Into the new electrical outlets, Americans plugged lamps, refrigerators, washing machines, and toasters, each a special object of joy and discussion during the twenties. Above all, electricity brought the radio. In November 1920, the crackling sounds of America's first radio station, KDKA at East Pittsburgh, opened a modern era of personal mass communication. By 1923, over 500 stations with much improved equipment were broadcasting to the nation. Most homes with electricity had radio sets. Other Americans gathered to listen at their local bars or clubhouses. While the car was dispersing Americans in search of their individual pleasures, the radio was bringing them back home on schedule to catch their favorite shows.

Consumer services as well as consumer goods poured from the cornucopia of the 1920s. Personal expenditures for recreation more than doubled between 1919 and 1929. Across an entire range of public entertainment—theatres, sports, amusement houses—the twenties were bonanza years, in part because the family car rapidly broadened the scope of potential customers. The lord of the entertainment world was a relative newcomer, motion pictures, which during the twenties grew from a scattering of nickelodeon shows and occasional full-length features to a systematized $2 billion industry with a steady flow of films and a dazzling array of stars. Not only did "movie houses" appear in

ROADSIDE BILLBOARDS, 1929

Sexual and racial stereotypes
abounded in standardized ads for
the national consumer market.
(*State Historical Society of
Wisconsin*)

almost every town and neighborhood in the nation; their ornate grandeur
marked them as centers of community life. By 1929, the average weekly attendance at these palaces of culture exceeded 80 million.

The pattern of modern consumerism, once set, did not appreciably change
during the next twenty years. A shortage of money in the thirties, and a shortage of material in the early forties, slowed the consumers' purchases without
significantly altering their preferences. Attendance at the movies and other
kinds of public entertainment dropped slightly in the 1930s but quickly returned to its earlier level in the following decade. At the beginning of the depression, most Americans clung tenaciously to their old cars. Only in the late
thirties did they again begin to purchase new ones in quantity. Then after the
war temporarily halted automobile production, Americans rushed to buy an
unprecedented number of new cars during the late forties. The sale of most
household appliances followed a similar curve. The number of radio sets, however, multiplied throughout the depression, and during the thirties and early
forties, the stars of radio enjoyed their golden age of popularity.

In its broad effects, modern consumerism nationalized America's sounds
and sights and experiences. Millions heard the same broadcasts, watched the
same movies, and bought the same kinds of cars. Moreover, the few corporations that dominated the major consumer industries increasingly homogenized
the output. In radio, the formation of the National Broadcasting Company in
1926 and the Columbia Broadcasting System in 1927 superimposed network
programming over a previously decentralized industry. The number of local

radio stations actually declined after 1927. From a handful of gigantic studios such as Warner Brothers and Metro-Goldwyn-Mayer came the standardized films that were characteristically "Hollywood" productions. Ford, General Motors, and Chrysler, which made 83 percent of America's automobiles by 1930, were soon synchronizing industrywide shifts in car styling. Along with a rapid expansion of chain stores and a continuing consolidation of newspaper ownership, these strong oligopolistic trends were systematizing everything in the consumer market from nuts to news. A flourishing industry of advertising made its friendly radio voices a part of American family life, and they transformed such nationally distributed products as Campbell soups and Pepsodent toothpaste into household words.

Modern Values

Among the images coming out of these national centers of communication was a new model for the good life. As the modern economy developed, it relied more and more heavily on the efficient fulfillment of specialized tasks. Some specialties, including those in such business-related occupations as management, banking, merchandising, and advertising and such professions as law, medicine, engineering, and economics, became so important to the economy that success in any of these careers was itself the source of a person's prestige in modern America. In the 1920s, perhaps 3 million Americans had the skills, or the success, to claim membership in these exalted ranks. In addition, as the nation's population grew from 106,466,000 to 123,077,000, or about 15 percent, during the twenties, the number of white collar workers rose 40 percent to over 14 million. Many of these white collar workers also thought of themselves as part of a specialized economic system.

The greater the emphasis on occupational success, the less people felt bound by traditional rules of behavior. What happened away from work increasingly belonged to a separate realm of individual discretion. From this crucial division of occupational life from private life came a new, often exhilarating freedom to enter the consumer market and simply enjoy oneself. During leisure hours, clothes became a matter of personal taste rather than an expression of solid character. The styles of the 1920s, appropriate to their modern meaning, emphasized freedom: the arrival of new colors and patterns for men, the departure of corsets and hobbling long skirts for women. Both men and women now smoked casually in public, and cigarette sales climbed 250 percent during the decade. The symbol of the exciting new freedom was the "Flapper." With hair bobbed, face painted, and cigarette in hand, she airily waved goodbye to yesterday's rules. Her flattened breasts, loose-fitting clothes, and short skirt gave her the appearance of a modern Peter Pan, seizing the pleasure of the moment in the spirit of eternal youth.

Nothing more clearly announced a new attitude toward private freedom than the changing responses of successful Americans to Prohibition. In 1920, most national spokesmen dutifully endorsed the Eighteenth Amendment. By 1924, however, such prominent citizens as the industrialist Pierre du Pont, the dean of the settlement workers Graham Taylor, and the philanthropist John D. Rockefeller, Jr., were leading a widespread defection from the cause. In 1926, an insignificant group, the Association against the Prohibition Amendment, was reorganized with a board of directors that read like a roster of the national elite. Soon a great many city and state organizations were arguing the case for repeal before chambers of commerce, bar associations, and other professional groups. By 1932, about three-fourths of the readers of *Literary Digest,* a rough index to the opinion of successful Americans, favored repeal of Prohibition.

The reasoning of these prominent citizens was simple. By making illegal an act that millions refused to consider wrong, Prohibition artificially created a new class of criminals, spread disrespect for the law, and then increased taxes to pay for the enforcement. Repeal of the Eighteenth Amendment would return the authority over liquor to state and local governments, where it be-

A FLAPPER AND A SPORT, SOME BOOZE, A FLIVVER, AND A SMOKE

For successfu' Americans, the sins of the nineteenth century became the pleasures of the twentieth. *(Culver Pictures, Inc)*

NEW YEAR'S NUMBER!

JANUARY 3, 1925

PRICE 15 CENTS

JUDGE

1925

"THEY'RE OFF!"

longed. On the surface, it was a weak argument. Many other unpopular laws increased the crime rate and were far more expensive to police. Because the enforcement of Prohibition was always haphazard, its costs had little effect on taxes. In other areas, the opponents of Prohibition welcomed the expansion of national authority over state and local powers. Actually, their entire case depended on a single assumption. It simply did not matter very much if people drank. Prohibition, in Pierre du Pont's phrase, was "a nuisance and menace"— or, more accurately, a menace *because* it was merely a nuisance. In a proper state of affairs, using alcohol would be an individual choice.

As the areas of private discretion expanded, leisure in general came to have a new meaning. Free time acquired a therapeutic purpose. Leisure activities no longer had to be justified as morally beneficial but simply as a salutary way for individuals to release their tensions and return refreshed to their jobs. The best expression of the new meaning for leisure was the annual vacation, a segregated bloc of time specifically for recuperation. Once the prerogative of a very small, prosperous minority, the annual vacation became widely accepted during the twenties. Early in the 1920s, according to a study by the sociologists Robert and Helen Lynd, most white-collar employees in Muncie, Indiana, assumed for the first time in their lives that they had a right to an annual vacation, and many received one with pay. As a rule, the movement to conserve natural resources fared poorly during the 1920s, but the notable exception was an enlargement in the National Park Service. Parks were now a valuable public facility, where the nation's city dwellers could turn once a year for revitalization.

A higher premium on personal freedom meant a lower premium on sin. Although church membership increased a striking 31 percent between 1916 and 1926, so did the emphasis in white-collar congregations on a soothing, largely undemanding religion that stressed good human relations rather than sin and salvation. Not every liberal Protestant welcomed Bruce Barton's best-selling *The Man Nobody Knows* (1925), which transformed Jesus into a vigorous executive who had taken "twelve men from the bottom ranks of business and forged them into an organization that conquered the world." Nevertheless, few liberal Protestants during the twenties expressed much concern of any kind for theological details or even denominational distinctions. To many of them, Catholicism now seemed less an evil religion than an odd but purely private choice. The anti-Catholic furor surrounding Al Smith's presidential campaign in 1928 simply makes no sense from a modern Protestant perspective.

Nor did the long-standing association between sex and sin. During the twenties, a variety of psychologists, including the American disciples of Sigmund Freud, told Americans to consider sex a human need to fulfill: the more complete the satisfaction, the healthier the individual. Repression and guilt only warped the personality. Public displays of affection no longer implied loose morals. Even premarital sex was a legitimate subject for discussion. Margaret

Sanger, America's pioneer advocate of birth control who had once been a pariah in respectable circles, now won the approval and even the financial support of many well-to-do Americans. Though too much "petting" remained a parental worry and any hint of "free love" was sharply condemned, sex emerged in the twenties as a subject for rational examination instead of moral taboo.

The new values covering recreation, religion, and sex found their strongest support in metropolitan areas. During the 1920s, cities of 100,000 or over grew more than twice as fast as the population as a whole. White-collar workers, who were increasing in numbers at about the same rate, congregated in and around these cities and reinforced one another's values. An urban way of life became their standard of America's progress, and they used it to judge the rest of the nation. Instead of praising the little red schoolhouses in the countryside, urban educators recommended their consolidation to lower costs and modernize instruction. Efficiency experts wrote despairingly about the incompetence of county governments. The farther that life was removed from the styles of the big city, the less attractive it appeared. The descriptions of the small town as a prison in Sherwood Anderson's *Winesburg, Ohio* (1919) and Sinclair Lewis's *Main Street* (1920) met a warm reception from urban readers.

The new urban standard was particularly hard in its judgment of the South. In 1925, Henry L. Mencken, the critic, essayist, and high priest of the new urban culture, visited Dayton, Tennessee to report on the trial of a high school biology instructor, John Scopes, who had broken a state law by teaching Darwin's theory of evolution. Because the trial pitted the famous criminal lawyer Clarence Darrow against William Jennings Bryan, the aging champion of evangelical Protestanism, it became a national spectacle. An urban audience, unable to comprehend why anyone would legislate against science, treated the Scopes trial like a carnival of freaks. As Mencken described the "anthropoid rabble" of Tennessee protecting themselves "from whatever knowledge violated their superstitions" and climaxing an outdoor religious revival with a sex orgy, the modern caricature of the South was taking shape. Sharecropping, soil leaching, and unmechanized farming retarded Southern agriculture. A crude racism appeared to dominate its society, and a narrow Protestant theology seemed to tyrannize its spirit. Both support for Prohibition and opposition to Al Smith thrived there. When Erskine Caldwell's *Tobacco Road* appeared in 1932, many successful Americans were already prepared to accept this picture of a stunted life on Georgia's barren soil as the true South.

Modern Families and Careers

Modern values also reshaped the role of the family in American life. In the white-collar world around the cities, men no longer relied heavily on the family to maintain their reputations. Occupations were their primary sources of prestige, and they brought their reputations home from their offices. Extramarital sex, especially in the large cities, became increasingly acceptable. Even in Sinclair Lewis's small city of "Zenith," the hero of *Babbitt* (1922) could have a brief affair without damaging his career. Wives, on their part, were expected to counter their husbands' drift away from the family. Advertisements promised miraculous results from a better dinner, a cleaner house, or any number of enticing domestic surprise. Advice columns revealed how to soothe a tense, weary man at the end of the workday. Accompanying the new explicitness about sex, a thriving cosmetics industry encouraged wives to enhance their charms as a means of holding husbands within the home.

Unlike the nineteenth-century wife, who had been solemnly charged with preserving society's morals, her modern counterpart had no such high responsibilities. And in a system of values that honored expertise, her talents as a homemaker could never compete with the claims of business and the professions. As women's traditional sphere shrank, however, other opportunities beckoned. The residential areas that men from their downtown offices called "bedroom towns" became uniquely female domains, where women moved and talked and acted much as they chose during the daytime hours. With radically less

The life of the modern woman mixed tradition with change. She remained chief cook and bottle washer, but new appliances dramatically altered her kitchen. She was still responsible for rearing the children, but she had greater control over the number of children. Mass media fed her with fantasies about love and beauty, but mass transportation expanded her freedom of movement and activities. *(State Historical Society of Wisconsin, Culver Pictures, Inc.)*

Margaret Sanger dares to tell the truth about Birth Control

For centuries the world has played a game of "hush" about the one most important fact of marriage. Even to-day tens of thousands of women are doomed to a life of hopeless, helpless drudgery—and their children are doomed to privation and neglect because the mother simply cannot give so many of them the proper care or support.

Words alone cannot tell the terrible sacrifice in wasted bodies and blasted lives that has been exacted from women every year. Words alone cannot express the untold suffering tens of thousands

"Why is it," Mrs. Sanger asks, "that the women of Australia, New Zealand, Holland, France, and many other nations are permitted to know the truths that can save them from this terrible suffering while the women of America must still endure the agonies to which they are

...argaret Sanger ...he intelligence ... to deny to ...h has brought ..., and life it- ...other nations. ... the storms of

this daring and heroic author points out that women who cannot afford to have more than one or two children, should not do so. It is a crime to herself, a crime to her children, a crime to society.

A Priceless Possession

Now Margaret Sanger's message to all women, contained in "Woman and the New Race," is made available to the public. A special edition of this vital book has been published in response to the overwhelming demand. Order your copy of this wonderful book at once, at the special edition price of only $2. Then if after reading it you do not treasure it as a priceless possession return it to us and your money will be refunded.

It is not even necessary to send a penny now. Just the coupon will bring your copy of "Woman and the New Race." It is bound in handsome, durable gray cloth, printed in clear readable type on good quality book paper and contains 286 pages, sent to you in a plain wrapper.

When the book is delivered at your home, pay the postman the special low price of $2 plus the few cents postage But mail the coupon at once. Tear it off before you turn this page.

Partial List of Contents

*Woman's Error and Her Debt
Cries of Despair
*When Should a Woman Avoid Having Children
Two Classes of Women
Birth Control—a Parent's Problem or Woman's
*Continence — Is it Practical or Desirable
Women and the New Morality
*Are Preventive Means Certain
Legislating Women's Morals
*Contraceptives or Abortion
Progress We Have Made

*Any one of these chapters is alone worth many times the

Truth Publishing Company
Dept. TA-144, 1658 Broadway
New York City

die. "Ignorance on this all-important subject has put me where I am."

Is the Husband or Wife to Blame?

birth control. It is a startling revelation of a new truth that will open the eyes of

surveillance than their grandmothers had experienced, they purchased the bulk of the family's consumer goods, and consequently their preferences had a powerful influence on the local consumer market.

Modern mothers and fathers reared their children to enter the same kind of occupationally oriented world in which they lived. The home, it was assumed, could provide very little of the knowledge that children would later need to make their way in twentieth-century society. Modern Americans looked outside the home for expert advice on almost every subject, from maintaining the family car to balancing the family budget. With the founding of *Reader's Digest* in 1922 and *Time* in 1923, they even had convenient, expert summaries of the latest news and views about their contemporary world. Hence, as parents, they were expected to be intermediaries between their children and an array of specialists who did know about their children's psyches, health and education.

Because parents had a relatively small part in equipping their children for successful adult careers, they had to prepare their sons and daughters to accept directions from outside the home. The preparations began early. Parents in the twenties and thirties were warned against the dangers of an excessive emotional attachment to their children or a domineering authority over them. Mothers heard about the perils of the Oedipus complex. Manuals on child care gave specific instructions on cuddling and comforting. Playwrights such as Sidney Howard and Tennessee Williams made the clutching, overbearing mother a central character in the American theater. In the movies of the 1930s and 1940s, such actors as Lewis Stone and Spencer Tracy modeled the modern role of the father: a superficially gruff, basically agreeable man who footed the bills, fussed with his pride, and eventually allowed the children to have their way.

The critical phase in the children's preparation for adulthood occurred during adolescence. Beginning in the 1920s, a well-developed and widely publicized youth culture provided adolescents with an acceptable means of rebelling against their parents and declaring themselves ready for the occupational world. Although the details varied decade by decade, the essentials remained the same. Along some sensitive frontier of values—sex during the 1920s, for example, or social reform during the 1930s—adolescents stepped just across the adult boundary and derided their lagging parents. When parents objected, their children accused them of hypocrisy or irrelevance. To divide the ages further, adolescents adopted their own special jargon, and they made very effective uses of dance and dress. Unlike the square dances and waltzes of the nineteenth century that had combined the generations, the Charleston in the 1920s and jitterbugging in the 1930s and 1940s required such limber joints that older people risked catastrophe if they tried it. Young men chose sufficiently outlandish clothes to make father look foolish in them. Young women chose sufficiently revealing ones to contrast their firm flesh with mother's signs of age. Modern parents not only subsidized the youth culture; they were told to worry if their children did not fully participate.

At each stage in child rearing, schools exercised a greater and greater influence. During the twenties and thirties, the public school system underwent a considerable expansion and adaptation. The elementary grades, which changed the least, increasingly served as feeders into the high schools, now important institutions in their own right. Enrollment in secondary schools doubled during the 1920s, and then rose another 50 percent during the 1930s. In 1920, one-sixth of America's adult population had high school diplomas; in 1940, one-half held them. Indeed, secondary education became so significant to white-collar families that some of them chose a place to live on the basis of the local high school's reputation. The Winnetka System under Carleton Washburne, for example, made that Illinois community nationally famous.

What modern families sought in a school system was a combination of instruction in the basic skills and socialization for modern America. The current trends in "progressive" education favored precisely this combination. The modern high school tried to prepare young minds that, as one committee of educational experts stated in 1929, "will be suited to the changing situations" of modern society. Even ethics "differed in different occupations," the journalist Lincoln Steffens noted in 1931. "And an ethical practitioner formed and fitted into one occupation . . . is apt to be disqualified thereby for another occupation, morally as well as technically." Therefore, the more progressive high schools taught

THE JUKEBOX CULTURE AROUND 1940

Modern adolescents used music and dance to create their own world apart from prying adults. (*Library of Congress.*)

general methods of thinking and a general open-mindedness rather than a specific body of truths and moral absolutes.

If young people could make a successful adjustment in high school, it was assumed, they would be prepared for a happy, rewarding life in modern America. Aptitude tests and counseling centers, both suddenly prominent in the high schools of the 1920s, guided them into the proper occupational areas, or for an increasing number, to college for further specialization. Those who then entered the best white-collar occupations had the satisfaction of discovering that they had acquired a superior mental power. According to a variety of publicists during the twenties, individuals who mastered a specialty in business or the professions developed a general capacity for rational thought that placed them in a select minority. By implication, the majority of Americans, in Mencken's blunt but revealing term, were "boobs," a highly suggestive public that could be manipulated by a foresighted few.

Along with this belief came a popular psychology called behaviorism, which contained a simple, persuasive formula for mass manipulation. As the psychologist John B. Watson explained the human personality, a clear stimulus produced in the individual a predictable response, and the regular repetition of such stimuli established a habit that with occasional reinforcement made the response self-generating. With the right message and the right means of communication, therefore, a rational minority who understood this process could influence an almost limitless number of people.

During the 1920s, behaviorism became an article of faith among successful Americans and gave many of them extraordinary confidence in their powers of social control. A number of otherwise routine white-collar jobs, particularly selling, now seemed fraught with significance. The insights into mass manipulation even offered a fresh view of history. "Galileo failed because he was an investigator and not a salesman," one psychologist revealed in 1925. "Consequently, he could not get his goods marketed . . . . His competitors, Aristotle, Moses, and the church fathers, had monopolized the market, and their stockholders would not let him do business." Advertising developed into an especially honored field. A new group of experts in personnel management also used the same basic formula of mass manipulation to guarantee employers a loyal and productive work force.

Successful Americans of many different persuasions accepted this assumption of a two-tiered society: a minority of manipulators and a mass to be manipulated. Neither liberal nor conservative, it simply came with America's modern values. What Republican businessmen in the 1920s applied to the sale of their goods, New Dealers in the 1930s applied to the sale of their reforms. In return for a sincere interest in the public welfare, the Roosevelt administration expected popular support, not popular demands. By the Second World War, these habits of modern leadership were so ingrained that businessmen and reformers alike automatically went about the tasks of "selling" the war, "conditioning" the public for bad news from the battlefront, and experimenting with better ways to improve American "morale."

Response of the Traditionalists

From the lower of these two tiers, modern America looked quite different. Most people's jobs did not belong in the specialized upper ranks of the economy and therefore brought very little national prestige. Moreover, mass communication made it impossible to ignore the disparity between their own lives and the lives of successful Americans. Millions of Americans with unskilled or routine jobs did hope that they, or their children, would eventually rise on the occupational ladder. Yet almost all of them found the modern values unacceptable to some degree. They chose instead to follow a long American tradition and live by local values. In a rural community or a city neighborhood, they judged one another by family reputations, church preferences, work habits, and a variety of other personal characteristics that established a standard of prestige and a scale of morality specifically designed for their own locality.

The pattern of resistance to the modern ways varied a great deal from place to place and even from individual to individual. During the twenties and thirties, some local pockets of opposition, particularly in the countryside, confronted the new values directly and repudiated them wholesale. Condemning the new liberalism in dressing, drinking, dancing, smoking, and sex, they refused to consider such behavior a matter of private choice and set firm rules against the modern hedonism. The most common agency of moral discipline was the church. As membership in the Protestant churches expanded, a large majority continued to belong to the evangelical denominations. Many Baptist and Methodist congregations, with a history of serious concern about their members' public behavior, banned the new ways as sins. Smaller bodies of Lutherans and Seventh-Day Adventists were even stricter about such practices as dancing and smoking. From evangelical Protestantism came the political pressure behind Tennessee's antievolutionary law of 1925, which precipitated the famous Scopes trial. In other Southern states as well, including Texas and Mississippi, state officials cooperated in keeping Darwin's theories out of the classroom. In the northern cities, the Catholic church often set its considerable weight against modern values, especially those on sex. Like the public schools in areas where evangelical Protestantism predominated, the Catholic parochial system carefully instructed its pupils in religious morality. According to nationwide studies in the late 1920s and 1930s, a majority of American schoolchildren were still receiving this kind of traditional, moral education.

"CHURCH SUPPER," *painting by James B. Turnball*

In reaction to modern values, millions of Americans
idealized an older, simpler society that was rooted in the
family, the church, and the community. *(Courtesy of
Mr. & Mrs. Carroll Martin.)*

Nevertheless, only a minority of Americans in a few localities totally rejected the new ways. A compromise between modern and traditional values was much more common. Almost all Americans wanted some share in the new culture, but a great many of them hoped to participate without feeling that it would corrupt them. At the beginning of the twenties, for example, motion pictures were exploiting sex so avidly that a majority of state legislatures threatened to censor them. In 1922, the movie industry responded with the Hays Office, Hollywood's center for self-censorship, which designated what parts of the female anatomy had to be covered, what language was taboo, and how justice must triumph in the end. These moral formulas created just the right aura of respectability. Without basically altering the movies, they appeased the critics and assured a mass audience.

Other mass media also enhanced their popularity by catering to traditional values. Magazines and newspapers told countless stories of how the time-honored virtues of honesty, thrift, and perseverance had enabled ordinary people to weather their troubles and win in the end. To vast daytime audiences, such radio soap operas as *Ma Perkins' Family* and *Just Plain Bill* recounted the trials and tribulations of familiar, local individuals who preserved their simple goodness under the most extraordinary hardships. Norman Rockwell's famous covers for the *Saturday Evening Post,* depicting the comforts of life in the family and the small town, ennobled many of the same traditional values.

In a traditional local setting, trusting other people required a feeling of intimacy with them. Sunday supplements responded to this need with articles on the private lives and endearing habits of prominent Americans, and radio stations featured informal, personal interviews with a variety of otherwise anonymous leaders. The popularity of both Franklin and Eleanor Roosevelt benefited immeasurably from the warm, friendly personalities they communicated to a traditionalist public. The President's battle with polio, his hobbies, and his anecdotes, all gave indispensably human qualities to the nation's leader. Far more than any other President's wife, Eleanor Roosevelt traveled throughout America to express her own personal concern for the needs of its citizens. Her syndicated newspaper column, *My Day,* an unpretentious account of her thoughts and affairs, significantly lessened the distance between the nation's First Lady and a large, attentive body of readers.

Perhaps the most important need of those Americans whose jobs neither carried much prestige nor paid very well was some evidence that they could still succeed without abandoning their values. During the 1920s, an abundance of publicity assured them that the avenue upward was not only broad but especially well-traveled by individuals of solid character and good habits. Salesmanship offered a particularly enticing route because it held out the prospect of success without a highly specialized training. Throughout the twenties, a popular passion for the salesman's skills was fed by numerous manuals, lectures, and correspondence courses that promised to reveal the secrets of the art to any ambitious American. The example of certain businessmen encouraged hopes of an even more dramatic rise to riches. If immigrants such as the utilities magnate Samuel Insull, the banking king A. P. Giannini, and the movie mogul Samuel Goldwyn could make it to the top, American society must still be rewarding the traditional virtues of hard work and high ambition.

No one's reputation benefited more grandly from such reasoning than Henry Ford's. Here was a country boy who had turned a mechanical genius and dogged persistence into a fabulous fortune and international fame. He had mastered the modern economy so thoroughly that everyone came to him to learn the best techniques of mass production and distribution. Yet he had never capitulated to the slick ways around him. He attacked the evils of Wall Street, belittled the significance of higher education, and demanded strict moral standards from his workers. He could even give new values the sound of old truths: "One day some one brought to us a slogan which read: 'Buy a Ford and Save the Difference.' I crossed out the 'save' and inserted 'spend'—'Buy a Ford and Spend the Difference.' It is the wiser thing to do. Society lives by circulation, and not by congestion."

The depression seriously damaged this American dream. After 1929, Ford's popularity declined drastically, and no businessman ever replaced him. Not even the prosperous 1940s revived the vision of a simple rise from humble origins to the pinnacle of the corporate system. A great many Americans still retained their commitment to the old-fashioned virtues. During the 1930s, for example, the child actress Shirley Temple became the movie industry's most valuable property for projecting an image of triumphant innocence amidst widespread corruption—both the imaginary corruption of the screen play and the publicized corruption of life in Hollywood. But the avenues to fame and fortune were increasingly obscure. Dale Carnegie's phenomenally popular *How to Win Friends and Influence People* (1936), the counterpart for the 1930s of the salesmen's manuals of the 1920s, promised wonders for its readers if they would only master an elementary set of rules. Yet unlike the literature of salesmanship, Carnegie's book was quite vague about where the ambitious but poor individual should look for his success. A critical element of hope was dwindling in the lives of millions of Americans.

Dangers to the Individual

The dimming prospects for individual success were only one part of a large, complicated problem that disturbed the followers of modern and traditional ways alike. How could individuals in any walk of life preserve their integrity in a nationalized, systematized society? Here, in a general sense, was a problem for all modern America. Signs of a new concern for the individual were already appearing before 1920. The American Civil Liberties Union, which had originated as an emergency committee to defend dissenters during the First World

War, remained after the war as a permanent center to protect the individual's freedom of speech, religion, assembly, and press under the First Amendment. Even before the war, America's most creative poets, Ezra Pound and T. S. Eliot, had started a trek to Europe of young writers and artists who felt stifled by American culture. A Lost Generation, the writer Gertrude Stein called these intellectual exiles. In 1920, America's greatest playwright, Eugene O'Neill, won the first of four Pulitzer Prizes for *Beyond the Horizon*, launching his long, agonizing exploration into the power of irrational forces over the individual's fate. From such scattered beginnings developed a broader and broader survey of the dangers for the individual in modern society.

The first danger to receive serious attention was the dehumanizing quality of modern society's organization. During the 1920s, the best of the so-called antiwar novels—John Dos Passos's *The Three Soldiers* (1921), e. e. cummings's *The Enormous Room* (1922), and Ernest Hemingway's *A Farewell to Arms* (1929)—said relatively little about war itself. Instead, they used the war as a means of portraying the individual's jeopardy inside an impersonally mobilized society. In 1923, critics gave a warm reception to the American version of Karel Capek's play *R. U. R.*, introducing the robot as modern society's citizen, and to *The Adding Machine*, Elmer Rice's biting comedy on the effects of dull, routine work.

Of all the routine tasks in modern America, intellectuals considered work on the assembly line the most threatening to the individual. In fact, it was less wearing than a fruit harvest, less demanding than a sweatshop, and less dangerous than a coal mine. But factory labor combined monotony and mechanization in a way that communicated a special danger to people who were already worried about modern society's depersonalization. After Sherwood Anderson had exposed the evils of the small town in *Winesburg, Ohio,* he turned to the assembly line, where he found the conveyer belt a relentless master over its wage slaves. Henry Ford's plant produced cars at the price of humanity, the young pastor Reinhold Niebuhr noted in his journal. One of the most acclaimed scenes in an American movie was Charlie Chaplin's rebellion in *Modern Times* against the intolerable discipline of the assembly line and his glorious escape through a maze of giant gears and monstrous machinery. America's great challenge, the cultural critic Lewis Mumford wrote in 1934, was to make "the machine . . . our servant, not our tyrant." By the 1930s, it became commonplace for intellectuals to condemn everything about the factory as ugly and alien.

Critics were also disturbed about an all-consuming passion for goods and money. The New Era, Suzanne La Follette acidly concluded, was testing the proposition "that human beings can live a generally satisfactory life . . . so long as they are kept powerfully under the spell of a great number of mechanical devices. . . ." During the 1920s, old progressives as dissimilar as the moralistic Westerner George Norris and the patrician Easterner Gifford Pinchot warned of the corrosive influence that the pursuit of money was having on American values. John Dos Passos made this corrupting passion a central theme in his

CHARLIE CHAPLIN IN "MODERN TIMES"

Charlie Chaplin, a Pied Piper for the working stiffs, romps
through the dehumanizing machinery of a modern factory.
(Culver Pictures, Inc.)

powerful, rambling trilogy *USA* (1930–36). In the 1930s, the nineteenth-century
pioneers of corporate enterprise received the indelible label "robber barons."
No part of the nation's heritage suffered more severely at the hands of American
writers than the success ethic, which such important novels as F. Scott Fitzgerald's
The Great Gatsby (1925) and Theodore Dreiser's *An American Tragedy* (1925)
attacked for its destructive effects on the individual. In *I'll Take My Stand* (1930),
twelve Southern intellectuals combined the worship of money with "the tempo
of industrial life" and the cult of machinery to prove that their region's agrarian
tradition offered the sole "defense of the individual" in modern America. To
the surprise of both authors and publisher, the book won an enthusiastic national
following.

  As urgent as many of these critics sounded, they were rarely either desperate or radical. They located danger spots in America's industrial order. Rather

Varieties of Reality

The meaning of art in modern America expanded and blurred. A profusion of photographs, illustrations, movies, buildings, landscapes, fashions, and handicrafts hopelessly muddied the traditional questions about the appropriate subjects of art, the necessary training for artists, and the proper cultivation of the viewers. Could advertising qualify as art? Were the creators of comic strips artists? Did mass production destroy artistic taste or generate new forms of democratic art? Yet the endless quarreling over these unanswerable questions could not hide the timeless qualities of the debate. Now as before, each aspiring artist tried to determine *what* people saw and *how* they saw it. Each of these many images promised its viewers a special insight into what was real, rather than merely superficial or transient. And these competing visions of reality, in turn, reflected the main lines of tension in modern American culture.

Images, like other modern goods, were mass distributed, and however unwittingly, Americans consumed them along with the myriad products of their society. As Americans took sides in a cultural conflict, therefore, they received images that helped them to understand their choices. During the 1920s and 1930s, for example, an aversion to city life was visualized in small groups of country people: a warm family gathering, an easy intimacy among friends, a mutual support between generations. The images of urban-industrial progress, on the other hand, were oriented toward things rather than people. Long, dramatic views of a factory, skyscraper, or center city communicated the expansive grandeur of American technology. Americans came to know these images so well that in the 1960s environmentalists needed only a slight shift in focus to make ironic statements about modern progress. A tip of the camera accentuated the smoke belching from the factory. A longer view of the city juxtaposed its skyline with urban blight. By the sixties, the country town was slipping from memory, and the visual alternative to the city leaped past civilization to the wilderness. The image of pure nature, however, was a study in contemporary American frustration, for it also offered no human comfort. As soon as people entered the virgin wilderness, they defiled it.

Erich Hartmann/Magnum.

For Americans without personal knowledge of small-town life, Norman Rockwell's famous drawings defined it as simple, friendly; and unaffected. In this fashion, Rockwell's imaginary town became part of modern America's reality. In contrast to Rockwell's cozy, vibrant town, the untouched wilderness had no place for people. Beneath this beautiful vision ran an undercurrent of hopelessness about modern American society.

Another group of artists sought reality in a complex relation between the emotions of the viewers and the essential components of what they saw. They probed the same subjects of nature and urban-industrial society, but they rephrased these issues in abstract images. The flowering of American abstraction came in the years after the Second World War when Willem de Kooning was expressing the dynamism of modern life in rugged blocks and explosive colors, and the controversial Jackson Pollack was extending visual horizons with his flowing lines and subtle uses of depth. Then in the 1960s, as many Americans rebelled against the clutter and complexity around them, painters of the "minimalist" and "op art" schools responded to these new yearnings with simple geometric abstractions.

Abstract artists, like other modern experts, developed techniques of expression that required special training simply to understand, let alone to use. Significantly, their strongest defenders were professional and business people whose own success depended on expertise. Every subdivision of knowledge, they assumed, had special rules for understanding. But modern abstractionists, unlike the pioneers of the Armory Show in 1913, reached a nationwide audience. For millions of skeptical Americans abstract art was an incomprehensible jumble of shapes and colors. In art as in other areas of knowledge, they demanded a common sense reality that anyone could grasp.

"Ashville," Willem de Kooning, *The Phillips Collection, Washington.*

"*Cathedral*," Jackson Pollock,
Dallas Museum of Fine Arts.

Willem de Kooning, a major contributer to America's renaissance in painting after the Second World War, gave new vitality to the European cubist tradition. More innovative than de Kooning, Jackson Pollock was particularly ingenious in adapting modern technology to his art, as the aluminum paint on this canvas demonstrates. In the 1960s the trends moved away from Pollock's complexity toward a simple, almost photographic reality. The reputation of Edward Hopper, whose best paintings had been completed three decades earlier, rose impressively. Almost no signs of life intruded on Hopper's brilliant, haunting scenes, and the loneliness of his stark art touched widespread anxieties about the individual's survival during the sixties.

"*House by the Railroad*," Edward Hopper,
The Museum of Modern Art.

The popular arts satisfied these demands. Through constant repetition the popular arts drilled a few simple images of truth and beauty into the American consciousness. The most familiar of all was the smooth, sexy, welcoming woman. From the Hollywood vamp of the twenties to the Petty girl of the forties to the *Playboy* centerfold of the sixties, a composite model of female beauty shaped men's assumptions about women and women's assumptions about themselves. The popular arts also celebrated the virtues of certain occupations. Under the auspices of the New Deal, for example, public murals and bas-relief sculptures glorified manual labor with scenes of proud, muscular men and women in the fields and factories.

Photo by Milton H. Greene.

Sex and violence—sometimes singly, sometimes in combination—dominated the popular arts after the Second World War. Mass-marketed stereotypes of sex and beauty reached their peak with the era of Marilyn Monroe, who exercised an extraordinary influence over American dreams and behavior. The vision of history's most horrible weapon as an awesome fantasy of color and clouds greatly strengthened the modern connection between violence and beauty.

During the Second World War these handsome titans became soldiers and sailors. In fact, the Second World War introduced an elaborate esthetic of violence that made instruments of destruction into objects of beauty: the gleaming fleets of battleships and bombers, then the eerie majesty of the atomic bomb's mushroom cloud. The beauty of violence remained after the war as an important theme of the popular arts. A particularly striking example appeared in the climactic scene of the movie *Bonnie and Clyde,* which transformed the mutilation of the heroine's body into an arresting, slow-motion dance of death.

U.S. Energy Research and Development Administration.

In reaction against these mass-produced images, some Americans swung to the other extreme and praised the beauty of almost anything unique. The market for handicrafts and homemade art objects thrived during the 1960s and 1970s. What popular primitivism lacked in refinement it contributed in personal expression, and its proponents contrasted the reality of a rough-hewn people's art with the artificiality of a slick commercial art. The urge for self-expression also spread into "street art," a new public outlet for the emotions of assertive, often angry city dwellers. None of the older art forms had to give way for the newcomers. A contemporary people's art simply added to the artistic variety of modern America.

Subway Graffitti. Was it art or vandalism? The answer lay in the cultural standards of the beholder.

Naar/Alskog/Photo Researchers, Inc.

than demand an end to modern society, they usually cautioned the individual to keep a safe distance from its most threatening centers. The individual's protection, in other words, was an intelligent detachment. The clearest summary of this view appeared in Hemingway's *A Farewell to Arms,* where Lieutenant Frederic Henry, an American who had volunteered for the Italian ambulance corps early in the First World War, watched the impersonal forces of the war devour more and more people around him until they verged on swallowing him, too. He deserted—a sane and courageous act as Hemingway described it. Escaping to Switzerland, he found fulfillment briefly in a love affair with Catherine Barkley. Yet even when her death left Frederic Henry absolutely alone, his core of inner strength enabled him to survive in an insensitive universe.

The individual's lonely detachment failed to satisfy a growing number of Americans who in some fashion felt overwhelmed by the forces surrounding them. The response to these feelings of powerlessness was an elaborate set of images and myths, a special culture of compensations that spun a dreamlike web of strength around the individual. Some of them envisaged a perfect defense for the otherwise vulnerable individual. During the depression, for example, a flood of advertisements promised males a physical strength so great that no one would dare to challenge it. The most famous of these appeals, a mail-order course in "Dynamic Tension," guaranteed that any man could relive the fairy tale of its sponsor's life. Charles Atlas, a huge man whose mound of muscles rippled from every ad, had himself been "a 97-pound weakling" before he discovered the secret he would now divulge.

The new mass media created a striking array of fantasies about the perfect defense. Some were comic: Charlie Chaplin's carefree little tramp weaving his way among bullies and cops and puffing, pompous officials; a dutiful, intent Buster Keaton wheeling and spinning past impossible dangers to complete the appointed task; the infinitely resilient pseudoblacks in *Amos 'n Andy,* the most popular radio program of the 1930s, who were always scheming, always losing, but always ready to try again. Or the fantasies might be brutal. The cult of the movie antihero surrounding James Cagney in *Public Enemy* and Edward G. Robinson in *Little Caesar* idolized a swaggering ruthlessness that cleared every obstacle with a Tommy gun. The most popular fantasy of toughness continued to be the classic Western hero, brave and handsome, who killed faceless bad men in the good man's cause and faceless Indians in the white man's cause. During the Second World War, in the midst of bombs, tanks, and machine gun blasts, Hollywood's Westerner-as-GI even overcame the awesome threats of modern warfare.

No clear line divided Charles Atlas from the Western hero, or the Western hero from Superman, yet somewhere along the way the meaning of the fantasy shifted from the perfect defense of the individual to the individual's vaulting leap into a wonder world of success. America's new culture of compensation was also filled with images of an all-conquering power. As public restraints on the subject of sex relaxed, both the movies and the popular magazines spread a modern version of the traditional rags-to-riches tale. In its nineteenth-century form, the hero had won the rich man's daughter through his sterling character and her father's approval. In the modern variation, however, physical charm alone catapulted the hero to the top. The rich man's daughter, finding the poor but virile man irrisistible, convinced an angry father that she could not live without him. The mirror image of this tale, a sexually charged Cinderella story, sent the poor but beautiful woman into the arms of a rich, adoring husband.

The "star" system that came to dominate the entertainment industry during the 1920s reflected this popular involvement with an all-conquering power. The stars themselves seemed to have such powers; the irresistible lover Rudolph Valentino thrilling millions of moviegoers; the "Galloping Ghost" Red Grange scoring five touchdowns in one game; the courageous young Gertrude Ederle swimming the English Channel; even the publicized flagpole sitters staying awake and alive days on end. Accentuating the personal qualities of success, American audiences showed a strong preference for the idiosyncratic star who ignored many of the usual rules of the game. Fans loved the erratic slugger Jack Dempsey more than the boxing machine Gene Tunney, and the high-living, casual "Sultan of Swat," Babe Ruth, more than the intense, consistent batting champion, Ty Cobb.

Against this background Charles Lindbergh, the star of stars, rose to fame. In May 1927, while liberally financed and elaborately organized competitors were stalled on the ground, this unknown pilot became the first person to complete a solo airplane flight from New York to Paris. Americans instantly made the quiet, handsome Midwesterner a national idol. Lindbergh's triumph, as millions interpreted it, was the accomplishment of an indomitable individual. Both literally and figuratively, the "Lone Eagle" had soared beyond the ordinary individual's constraints to his purely personal success. Moreover, Lindbergh's sudden fame did not appear to affect his traditional virtues of modesty, simplicity, and self-reliance. Of all the decade's stars, Lindbergh had the greatest and most lasting popularity.*

The star system also encouraged Americans to picture themselves, or their children, leaping to fame and fortune. The entertainment world not only made its stars fabulously rich; it also seemed to reward them instantaneously. Stars, according to popular mythology, were "discovered." As the prospects of an immediate success in business or the professions dimmed, the vision of boys as athletes and girls as actresses shaped more and more American dreams. The fewer the alternatives, the more passionate the involvements. In the late 1930s, the heavyweight champion Joe Louis was almost worshipped in the black

---

*The tragic kidnaping and death of Lindbergh's son produced a new surge of public interest in 1932. Then in 1941, Lindbergh's advocacy of a negotiated settlement with Hitler's Germany sharply diminished his popularity.

CHARLES LINDBERGH AND THE "SPIRIT OF ST. LOUIS"

An adoring public believed that Lindbergh, through strength of character, had achieved a personal triumph over his society's impersonal forces. *(Culver Pictures, Inc.)*

ghettos. In some urban neighborhoods, the kings of organized crime, who emerged in the 1920s with Prohibition, were equally compelling models of power and success.

One threat to the individual, the emptiness of old age, required a separate cluster of compensations. For two reasons, the problems of the aged were growing more severe in modern times. First, as the average life expectancy for an American rose from 47 years in 1900 to 68 years in 1950, the proportion of old people increased dramatically. Second, as the numbers expanded, the sources of self-respect for the aged were shrinking. Wherever America's modern values prevailed, old people could scarcely avoid feeling useless. Knowledge in a specialized society was supposed to be advancing too rapidly for an older generation to master. Only the young could keep pace with America's highly technical and increasingly complex progress. As children reached adulthood, therefore, parents had good reason to feel that their best years were gone and that the future, which belonged to the young, opened a huge void before them.

Beginning in the 1920s, many older Americans earnestly set about the task of tricking the fates and staying young. The market for bright clothes and beauty aids, cosmetic surgery and dentistry, wigs and elixirs, all thrived. After 1922, F. Scott Fitzgerald recalled, the revelry of the Jazz Age "was a children's party taken over by elders." At the same time, a veil fell over the process of dying. Pictures of old people invariably showed them smiling, alert, and vigorous. A special literature, including Walter Pitkin's very popular *Life Begins at Forty* (1932), told Americans to think positively about their later years, and a multiplying number of settlements for old people, particularly in Florida and California, promised a happy, relaxed retirement for those who could afford to buy it. Despite these compensations, however, Americans occasionally heard a cry of resentment from their abandoned elders. During the 1930s, the Townsend movement for old-age pensions, which drew its greatest strength from the retirement communities of California, was both an expression of economic need and a demand for attention. Although Social Security responded to the economic problem, nothing was done about the human importance of these forgotten Americans.

Answers for the Individual

During the twenties and thirties, the individual received a good deal of general advice and a variety of palliatives. But what failed to appear was a clear statement of the individual's situation and future prospects in modern society. A new round in search of an answer to this problem began rather vaguely in the depression, when a number of public leaders and intellectuals tried to conceive of the individual as part of a broad social enterprise. New Deal enthusiasts attacked the evils of "rugged individualism" and foresaw a new age of social responsibility. The reputation of the philosopher John Dewey, America's leading advocate of a social ethic, rose impressively during the 1930s. Moreover, as depression crippled America, one group of intellectuals looked abroad to the Soviet Union as a model of the healthy society. A few of them also took the next logical step and applied Karl Marx's theories of class conflict to American society. Only through class consciousness, they argued, could the individual find security. But in most cases, the affair between American intellectuals and the Soviet Union was a brief infatuation. Never willing to relinquish the individual in favor of the class, they were revolted by the bloody Soviet "purge" of the late thirties, and increasingly they became convinced that Americans would have to develop their own kind of social consciousness.

At best, the search of the thirties offered a hope for tomorrow, but not a solution for today. John Steinbeck, who had once been attracted by Marxism and who continued to have a strong social conscience, captured this tentative quality at the end of his finest novel, *The Grapes of Wrath* (1939). Steinbeck told the grim story of an impoverished Oklahoma farm family, the Joads, tracing them from their uprooting early in the depression through their futile quest for a fresh start in California. Then on the last page of his poignant novel, Steinbeck sketched in a few sentences a vision of a new fellow feeling just beginning to surface in America.

For a great many Americans, that spirit of a collective endeavor finally arrived with the Second World War. In 1940, Hemingway's hero from the 1920s reappeared in *For Whom the Bell Tolls* as Robert Jordan, who was no longer alone because he had found a social commitment. This time Hemingway's hero was fighting in the Spanish Civil War. Instead of deserting, as Frederic Henry had done in *A Farewell to Arms*, Robert Jordan chose to die for human values in the battle against fascism. A year later, the former pacifist Robert E. Sherwood, winner of four Pulitzer Prizes, announced his conversion to the same crusade in his play *There Shall Be No Night*.

After the attack on Pearl Harbor in December 1941, the sense of a shared enterprise spread throughout America. In ways that no government propaganda could have achieved, all kinds of people linked all kinds of activities to a common cause: welding for the war effort, waking an hour early for the car pool, keeping tin cans for the scrap metal drive, saving war

"Just gimme a coupla aspirin. I already got a Purple Heart."

(*Drawings copyrighted 1944, renewed 1972, Bill Mauldin; reproduced by courtesy of Bill Mauldin.*)

stamps for a war bond. Nothing eliminated the conflicts in a complex society, yet to a remarkable degree, whatever an American did had a larger social meaning attached to it. For a brief period, the individual seemed to require no special reinforcements. Even in the midst of military combat, Bill Mauldin's extremely popular cartoons of the grunts Willie and Joe pictured them slogging through the muck of war with their sense of reality and their instinct for survival firmly intact.

Then as soon as the war ended, the spirit of a common cause dissolved. The news told only of selfish strikers, business profiteers, and greedy farmers. The government seemed no more than an arena for squabbling interests. Where were the truly national goals? According to *The Best Years of Our Lives*, Hollywood's outstanding movie of the 1940s, the soldiers, who had sacrificed the most, had to fight still another battle at home to preserve their dignity in an ungrateful society. In fact, what had the war meant? In its aftermath, total war raised questions about the threat of a technological barbarism that could no longer be confined simply to the evils of fascism.

In these sobering postwar years, four answers emerged to define the place of the individual in modern American society. Though each of the four communicated a very different message, all of them dealt in some way with the clash between modern and traditional values, and all of them responded in some fashion to the issues and images of the vulnerable individual. Taken together, these four answers were a creative summary of the central problems in modern American culture.

One answer told the individual to learn the rules of the modern occupational system, abide by them, and succeed. The wartime economy intensified the demand for greater numbers of specialists with higher levels of skill, and immediately after the war, Americans turned to the schools to fill this demand. Bands of citizens campaigned to improve instruction in the basic skills. Funds flowed freely into the entire educational system. Between 1945 and 1950, expenditures in the public schools more than doubled; even more impressive, enrollment in higher education doubled. Just as the importance of the high school had dominated the 1920s and 1930s, so the importance of higher education dominated the years after the Second World War. Now only colleges and graduate schools could satisfy a complex economy's need for specialized training. The greatest single impetus to college enrollment came from the GI Bill of 1944, which eventually subsidized the education of about 8 million former servicepeople. Along with the sheer numbers it funded, the GI Bill helped to democratize opportunities in higher education and hence in the upper ranks of business and the professions as well.

In *Death of a Salesman* (1949), the young playwright Arthur Miller created a brilliant morality tale of why and how to use these broadening opportunities. Miller's drama was immediately acclaimed one of America's greatest plays. Through the story of Willy Loman, it provided an excruciating lesson on how to fail in modern America. Willy lived by a weakened, vulgarized version of the traditional American dream of success. In the 1920s, when salesmanship had seemed the right avenue for a self-made man, Willy chose that career with visions of a swift rise to wealth and importance. Instead, he became trapped in the endless, weary rounds of meager sales, humiliating failures, and interminable debts. Willy desperately hoped that his sons, who idolized him, could still realize his dream of quick riches, and he taught them the only values he knew: a personal style, a winning appearance, and an eye for the main chance would achieve the miracle of success. Under their father's guidance, Biff and Hap approached manhood athletic, shallow, and morally stunted. Biff, discovering the fraud of Willy's life, turned in impotent rage on his father. Hap became a petty cheat. Willy, broken and psychotic, completed his dream by committing suicide, under the pathetic delusion that his life insurance payment would somehow catapult Biff to greatness.

During the hopeful years, while Willy and the boys were polishing the car and talking of Biff's future as an athlete, Bernard, the scrawny kid next door, mooned after the popular Loman boys. But Bernard was also winning the highest grades in his high school class. As the Loman nightmare unfolded, Bernard left to learn a specialty and returned a self-possessed, well-balanced adult, who was sufficiently eminent as a young lawyer to argue a case before the Supreme Court. His father Charley, cool and clear-eyed, had simply relinquished his son to

America's system of specialized occupations. "And you never told him what to do, did you?" a bewildered Willy asked his neighbor. "You never took any interest in him." Instead of an embittered Biff to plague him, Charley enjoyed an easy, warm relation with the adult Bernard, who dropped by whenever his busy schedule allowed. Bernard's success explained Willy's failure. Modern America's avenue upward had been there all the while, but Willy's dream had hidden the only legitimate path to success.

The second of the postwar answers began by acknowledging that the individual did indeed face serious problems in the modern world. Like the earlier critics of America's machine culture, a variety of intellectuals, educators, and publicists now warned that science and technology by themselves were amoral. Like the defenders of America's traditional values, they declared that the individual would have to find an anchor of values outside of science. Such a task, they said, required finding the fundamental principles in civilized life, and only the humanists — the philosophers and poets and theologians — could lead that search.

The quest for basic values was a nationwide preoccupation in the late forties. Some scholars explored the American past to discover its essentially American qualities, giving special attention to such brooding spirits as Thoreau, Melville, and the Puritans. Others examined the far richer resources of the Western tradition. Adults were guided along the peaks of that tradition in well-received classes on the "Great Books" of Western civilization. In colleges throughout the country, new and often required courses tried to distill wisdom not only from a long span of time but also from a breadth of subjects, such as an interdisciplinary examination of American culture or a humanistic understanding of science. The most intriguing innovation in college education was Chancellor Robert Hutchins's program at the University of Chicago that integrated the entire subject matter of the undergraduate curriculum in a unified course of study.

The fascination with fundamentals produced a strong reaction against the pragmatist's faith in an experimental, evolving truth. John Dewey, who more than any other intellectual leader was identified with a scientific method in ethics, became a particular target of attack in the late 1940s. Dewey's old friends, such as the philosopher Sidney Hook, joined his old enemies, such as the journalist Walter Lippmann, in condemning the effects of scientific relativism. Others blamed Dewey for the intellectual deficiencies they found in American public education. Dewey's critics wanted certainties in place of his open-ended pursuit of truth. In foreign policy, for example, they sought to define a single, unwavering "national interest" to guide America's international affairs. In civil liberties, they assigned to the freedoms of the First Amendment an absolute, timeless meaning that no judiciary, they asserted, should ever alter.

The critics of scientific relativism accused it of arrogance as well as fuzziness. The human mind, they claimed, was incapable of solving all of the world's problems through a scientific method. This line of opposition, which acquired the name realism, found its most effective spokesman in Reinhold Niebuhr, a theologian who in his own career had moved from an optimistic Christian socialism to the humbling doctrines of Martin Luther. Niebuhr began by placing ultimate truth beyond the human reach in God's inscrutable wisdom. Therefore, all actions reflected an inevitable human fallibility, and all choices involved moral risks. Nevertheless, people could not throw up their hands and quit. Individuals had a moral responsibility to choose among alternatives and to act on their choices. The necessity of choosing from an inherently imperfect knowledge defined the human predicament. Americans, Niebuhr declared, must learn to accept these human limits and abandon their simple faith in a man-made progress. Instead, they should meet each situation as it arose, and without arrogance, commit themselves to a course that held the best promise of fulfilling their moral obligations. Niebuhr's complex commandments were praised more than they were studied. But in the simplified image of the sober individual strengthened through self-knowledge and humility, his message had a remarkably wide appeal during these anxious years.

The third of the postwar answers was a defiant statement in behalf of the sovereign individual. Setting the individual at odds with modern society, it told him to overcome the dangers around him through his own powers. In a few instances, this answer was addressed to the specialist. Ayn Rand's best-selling novel *The Fountainhead* (1943), for example, glorified the right of the creative professional to discard society's ordinary rules in order to realize his genius, and in the postwar years, Rand cults mushroomed on college campuses. Usually, however, the hero had no special training and no resources except his core of inner strength. During the forties, a mass audience learned about this hero through the movies, particularly those starring Humphrey Bogart, and through a flood of inexpensive paperbacks that suddenly covered the drug stores and newsstands.

Soon after the publication of his first book in 1947, Mickey Spillane became the undisputed king of this new paperback market. In less than a decade, 30 million copies of his novels had been sold, a record far surpassing any competitor's. His initial title revealed his central theme: *I, the Jury*—and judge and executioner. Spillane's hero was a tough, resourceful private detective named Mike Hammer, who radiated an irresistible power. Good people willingly helped him; weak ones crumbled before him. Beautiful, sensuous women, looking past his lumpy face to the inner man, desired him. Though often battered, he always survived through a "gimmick" or a bit of Hammer luck. Enemies understood that nothing would deter him. When Hammer set upon organized crime, for example, the entire Mafia quaked, for they knew that he would bring them a personal, bloody justice.

Although Spillane drew on a full tradition of fantasies about the all-conquering individual, he more than any of his predecessors gave them a contemporary urban setting. The metropolis, Mike Hammer declared, was a formless "monster," teeming with ominous forces. City culture was dehumanized and city government corrupt. In the urban jungle, Spillane's hero had no alternative but to devise his own code of values. It required an exceptional courage, an extraordinary effort of will, to break free from this threatening human mass. Those who succeeded, however, became true individuals and survived. Obviously, Spillane's message had touched a popular nerve. Not only the sale of his books but also the number of his imitators indicated that his, of all the postwar answers, found the widest audience.

The fourth of the postwar answers was the most pessimistic. It expressed such despair that it seemed to forecast the individual's destruction. In the late forties, Americans were listening for the first time to those Europeans who had already peered inside a soulless society and found no individuals there. Franz Kafka's nightmares of man as vermin, of a nameless subject wandering through a fathomless system to a death he came to welcome, were suddenly relevant. A much larger public responded so attentively to the accounts of a devouring social organization in Aldous Huxley's *Brave New World* (1932), Arthur Koestler's *Darkness At Noon* (1941), and George Orwell's *1984* (1949) that their contents became clichés. Because Orwell and Koestler were describing a communist system, Americans had a choice of reading their books as justifications for a free Western society. Instead, many Americans used them as a frame of reference for discussing the dangers in their own lives.

The Second World War, as it was viewed in retrospect, contributed significantly to this new spirit of despair. The best of the American war novels—Norman Mailer's *The Naked and the Dead* (1948), Irwin Shaw's *The Young Lions* (1948), and James Jones's *From Here to Eternity* (1951)—did not simply surround their characters with danger, as the war novels of the 1920s had done. Now individuals were sucked into the very center of destruction, and all characters were equally exposed to the stray bullet. No personal choice or inner strength affected these human specks that were being tossed by the fates.

Above all, "The Holocaust" and "The Bomb" posed the most profoundly disturbing problems of the postwar years. After Germany's surrender in 1945, the numbing facts about the Nazi's Jewish policy began to filter back to the United States. Rationally and efficiently, the German government had applied the best techniques of modern organization to systematically destroy 5 million human beings. Had the Germans, in the process, revealed an essential truth about the impersonal mobilization of power in modern society? Again in 1945, American atomic bombs demolished the Japanese cities Hiroshima and Nagasaki. The bomb juxtaposed scientific genius and human annihilation so sharply, challenged the concept of civilization so directly, and symbolized the terrors of death so vividly that it left even the most resolute Americans unable to express its import.

The uniquely American way of expressing despair about the individual's lot appeared in a new image, "the Southern." In 1949, the Southerner William

HIROSHIMA, 1945

Was modern society on the brink of suicide?
The awful power of the atomic bomb raised
fundamental questions about the meaning of
science, progress, and civilization. *(U.S. Air Force.)*

Faulkner, with his finest writing already behind him, received the Nobel Prize
for literature. He had recently risen to public prominence, and a favorite intellectual game of the late forties was unraveling the family histories in Faulkner's
Yoknapatawpha County, the fictional Mississippi setting for his greatest works.
A year earlier, the young Tennessee Williams had been awarded a Pulitzer Prize
for *A Streetcar Named Desire*, the second of two stunning dramatic successes in the
1940s that established him as a leading playwright. These two, along with other
gifted Southern writers such as Carson McCullers and Flannery O'Connor,
created a composite image unlike anything Americans had ever encountered.

Understanding the Southern depended on an appreciation of the Western,
for intentionally or not the Southern was a systematic attack on America's oldest

myth of individual strength. In the Western, one man entered an open plain that was as stripped of constraining institutions as he himself was of a constraining past. There he confronted a direct challenge, and by a clear moral choice he overcame it. He was the pure individual: a man alone, a man of simple, sovereign convictions, a man of action whose problem, once met, dissolved in a cleansing rite of violence. Not only had the movies, the radio, comics, and pulp fiction expanded the audience for this myth since the 1920s; such thoughtful writers as Hemingway had borrowed from it. The Western hero continued to stand tall in postwar America.

Like the Western, the Southern also used a regional stereotype to communicate a national message. Just as countless Americans associated the West with a new, formless land, many regarded the South as a decaying, backward region. This popular caricature helped Southern writers reach a national audience. In contrast to the Western's openness, the world of the Southern was a suffocating prison —a town or household or room in which the inmates were held by invisible shackles they could never break. Dreams and memories bound them to the dead as well as the living. Unlike the direct challenge in the Western, the hovering, atmospheric problems in the Southern were impalpable. The Southern world was filled with human vulnerability. Children were caught in a whirl of adult terror and adults locked in a desperate battle for sanity; amorality was in power and sadism at large; bodies were deformed and brains addled. In these struggles, contrary to the gun fights of the Western, women managed more effectively than men. Maleness and impotence were common companions in the Southern.

Where the Western hero acted, the characters in the Southern talked. They stabbed one another with words, searched in vain for the meaning of their lives with words, and covered their own anguish with words. Occasionally someone's hopelessness or passion would explode in violence, but violence only complicated the problems that no one would ever resolve. In *A Streetcar Named Desire*, Tennessee Williams let loose a caricature of the Western hero, the physical-sexual-nonverbal Stanley Kowalski, and he wrecked the fragile human defenses around him. Perhaps no more than a small minority listened carefully to the agonizing message of the Southern. Nevertheless, an exceptionally talented cluster of modern writers had finally questioned whether or not the individual could survive.

At midcentury, Americans reached a pause in the process of creating a modern culture. Their commitment to mass consumerism was firmly established. So was a widespread concern for the fate of the individual. Beyond these general areas of agreement, however, American culture remained a loose cover over a great variety of attitudes and aspirations. Both modern and traditional values still had their adherents. Some Americans were trying to combine elements of the two, as the postwar search for fundamental values illustrated. But a new clarity in the debate over the individual's place in modern America actually sharpened the differences among competing camps. It was questionable if Arthur Miller's

Bernard, Reinhold Niebuhr's Moral Man, Mickey Spillane's Mike Hammer, and Tennessee Williams's Stanley Kowalski all belonged to the same human race. To coexist, these conflicting beliefs required a good deal of mutual tolerance—or mutual indifference. Whether or not an increasingly nationalized American society would contain such leeway became one of the crucial problems for the next quarter-century to resolve.

Suggested Readings

America's modern culture is explored in detail in Daniel J. Boorstin, *The Americans: The Democratic Experience* (1973). Another broad study, Rowland Berthoff's *An Unsettled People* (1971), emphasizes the deficiencies in American individualism. William E. Leuchtenburg, *The Perils of Prosperity, 1914–32* (1958), has particularly revealing chapters on the consumer culture of the twenties and the changes in values accompanying it, subjects that are also covered in Frederick Lewis Allen's *Only Yesterday* (1931). There is a perceptive analysis of the new sexual morality in Christopher Lasch's *The New Radicalism in America [1889–1963]* (1965). Isabel Leighton, ed., *The Aspirin Age* (1949), contains a lively set of essays on the culture of the twenties, and Freda Kirchway, ed., *Our Changing Morality* (1924), offers a sample of present-day ponderings on the new values. A broad picture of the city's dominance in twentieth-century society appears in Zane L. Miller, *The Urbanization of Modern America* (1973); some of the effects of urbanization on suburban values are discussed in Peter J. Schmitt, *Back to Nature* (1969). Carl Bode, *Mencken* (1969), assesses the leading spokesman for the new urban culture. An intriguing section in Gilman M. Ostrander, *American Civilization in the First Machine Age: 1890–1940* (1970), defines the place of youth in modern society, and John R. Seeley et al., *Crestwood Heights* (1956), examines the importance of the schools in modern suburban life. Three books evaluate women's part in the new culture. William L. O'Neill, *Everyone Was Brave: The Rise and Fall of Feminism in America* (1969), and William Henry Chafe, *The American Woman* (1972), trace the decline of earlier trends toward emancipation, while J. Stanley Lemons, *The Woman Citizen: Social Feminism in the 1920s* (1973), concentrates on women's continuing action after the First World War. In *Birth Control in America* (1970), David M. Kennedy adds a critical analysis of Margaret Sanger's career.

Several books illuminate the values of important institutions and occupations. James W. Prothro, *Dollar Decade* (1954), summarizes the attitudes of businessmen during the twenties; Morrell Heald, *The Social Responsibilities of Business, Company, and Community, 1900–1960* (1970), views them from a longer perspective. Otis Pease, *The Responsibilities of American Advertising* (1958), covers developments in a thriving business. The engineer's dedication to business values is the subject of Edwin T. Layton, Jr., *The Revolt of the Engineers* (1971), and the social scientists' dedication to the same values is the subject of Loren Baritz, *The Servants of Power* (1960). Roy Lubove, *Professional Altruists* (1965), describes the businesslike efficiency of social workers. The section on the United States in Reinhard Bendix's *Work and Authority in Industry* (1956) investigates the strategy of the new specialists in personnel management. Also see Milton Derber, *The American Idea of Industrial Democracy, 1865–1965* (1970). The effects of the new culture on education are analyzed in Patricia Albjerg Graham, *Progressive Education from Arcady to Academe: A History of the Progressive Education Association, 1919–1955* (1967), August Hollingshead, *Elmtown's Youth* (1949), and Solon Kimball and James E. McClellan, Jr., *Education and the New America* (1962). Edward A. Krug, *The Shaping of the American High School, 1920–1941* (1972), provides basic information on the modern high school, and Christopher Jencks and David Riesman, *The Academic Revolution* (1968), explores the modern university.

Traditional values in modern America have attracted much less scholarly attention. Two interesting books analyze these values under challenge: Ray Ginger's *Six Days or Forever? Tennessee v. John Thomas Scopes* (1958), and Don S. Kirschner's *City and Country: Rural Responses to Urbanization in the 1920s* (1970). *Middletown* (1929) and *Middletown in Transition* (1937), classic studies of Muncie, Indiana, by Robert S. Lynd and Helen Merrell Lynd, reveal a mixture of traditional and modern values. Lawrence Chenoweth, *The American Dream of Success* (1974), describes the modern version of a traditional quest, and Donald B. Meyer, *The Positive Thinkers* (1965), examines modern variations of the equally traditional doctrine of self-help. Other books cast light on traditional values through the study of popular heroes. In *The Hero* (1959), Kenneth S. Davis discusses the fame of Charles Lindbergh. Reynold M. Wik, *Henry Ford and Grass-Roots America* (1972), explains the automobile magnate's powerful appeal, and Keith T. Sward, *The Legend of Henry Ford* (1948), contrasts the public image with the actual record.

The best account of modern relativism is Morton G. White, *Social Thought in America: The Revolt against Formalism* (rev. ed., 1957). Three excellent books discuss early discontents with relativism and various quests for certainty: Donald B. Meyer, *The Protestant Search for Political Realism, 1919–1941* (1960), Edward A. Purcell, Jr., *The Crisis of Democratic Theory: Scientific Naturalism & the Problem of Values* (1973), and David A. Hollinger, *Morris R. Cohen and the Scientific Ideal* (1975). The appeal of another kind of authority is examined in John P. Diggins, *Mussolini and Fascism: The View from America* (1972). Several fine books explore the intellectual consequences of the Depression: Charles C. Alexander, *Nationalism in American Thought, 1930–1945* (1969), Arthur A. Ekirch, *Ideologies and Utopias: The Impact of the New Deal on American Thought* (1969), R. Alan Lawson, *The Failure of Independent Liberalism, 1930–1941* (1971), Richard H. Pells, *Radical Visions and American Dreams: Culture and Social Thought in the Depression Years* (1973), and William Stott, *Documentary Expression and Thirties America* (1973). Other studies trace ideas in creative writing. Alfred Kazin, *On Native Grounds: An Interpretation of Modern American Prose Literature* (1942), is a stimulating essay. Frederick J. Hoffman, *The Twenties* (rev. ed., 1966), discusses American fiction in an artistically critical decade. The strains of both modern society and depression are revealed in Maxwell Geismar's *Writers in Crisis: The American Novel, 1925–1940* (1942), and Daniel Aaron's *Writers on the Left* (1961). Thomas R. West, *Flesh of Steel* (1967), deals with the effects of the machine on the literary imagination. Of course, the creative writers themselves remain our indispensable sources. The best survey of the fine arts is Oliver W. Larkin, *Art and Life in America* (rev. ed., 1960). On architecture, see John Burchard and Albert Bush-Brown, *The Architecture of America* (1961).

The ferment in values after the Second World War has yet to find a historian. Something of the concern for the individual is communicated in two important sociological studies, David Riesman et al., *The Lonely Crowd: A Study of the Changing American Character* (1950), and C. Wright Mills, *White Collar: The American Middle Class* (1951). Alexander Meiklejohn, *Free Speech and Its Relation to Self-Government* (1948), and Hans J. Morgenthau, *In Defense of the National Interest* (1951), illustrate the demand for fixed values. Also see Carl L. Becker, *Freedom and Responsibility in the American Way of Life* (1945). Robert M. Hutchins, *The Conflict in Education in a Democratic Society* (1953), and Arthur E. Bestor, Jr., *Educational Wastelands: The Retreat from Learning in Our Public Schools* (1953), discuss the place of fundamentals in education. The new tough-minded approach to social values is revealed in Arthur M. Schlesinger, Jr., *The Vital Center* (1949), Max Ascoli, *The Power of Freedom* (1949), and Reinhold Niebuhr, *The Irony of American History* (1952).

33

International

Power

The last, great thrust of modernization occurred in America's international relations. It came last because nothing between 1920 and 1940 forced the United States to make a fundamental change in its approach to world affairs. Without doubt, the United States was already the world's greatest power in 1920. In agriculture, industry, and finance, it towered above its competitors. Invulnerable itself to serious attack, the United States had the military potential to punish almost any nation it selected. The officials who conducted America's foreign relations during the twenties and thirties recognized, moreover, an inevitable connection between the security and prosperity of their own nation and the actions of other nations throughout the world. Yet an overwhelming majority of Americans, including the nation's leaders, had not abandoned the traditional belief that the United States should stand apart in the family of nations, carefully preserving the right to make its own decisions and to cooperate with other nations only as it chose.

The challenge that the nation's leaders faced, therefore, was to find a policy compatible with both their awareness of an interconnected world and their urge to retain America's freedom of action. Although opponents within the government accused one another of being "internationalists" or "isolationists," almost all shared a common desire to strike some reasonable balance between America's involvement and its detachment. It was the Second World War that disrupted this consensus. During the war and its troubling aftermath, the United States became far more enmeshed than it had ever been in world affairs, and Americans groped for a way to reconcile their vast international authority with their tradition of detachment. But the old balance was lost. By the early 1950s, the United States had committed itself to a systematic, worldwide containment of communism. With that commitment, America turned away from the tradition of detachment and entered a new era in foreign affairs.

A New International Order, 1920–1929

Immediately after the First World War, the strongest influences on America's foreign policy were pulling it out of international affairs. The war itself, disillusioned Americans were saying, had exposed the extensive moral rot in European civilization. This same sickness was now destroying the chances for a just peace. Some Americans feared that bolshevism would spread from Russia throughout the continent because European society was too weak to resist it. The widespread desire to insulate America from these European diseases drastically diminished support for President Wilson's League of Nations. After March 1920, when the Senate finally rejected the League, few Americans seemed to mourn its passing. As the perceptive Protestant minister John Haynes Holmes noted in 1920, "We still regard international affairs as existing in a realm altogether removed from our ordinary . . . standards."

Once the issue of the League had been settled, however, the American government demonstrated that it certainly was not withdrawing altogether from international affairs. As the Harding administration took office in 1921, the most threatening area of the world was the Far East, where friction between the United States and Japan had been mounting for several years. Not only were American leaders worried about Japan's imperial ambitions on the mainland of Asia, and possibly in the Philippine Islands, but they also fretted over Japan's longstanding defensive alliance with Great Britain, which linked a European friend to their Asian rival. With the Far East in mind, Charles Evans Hughes, Harding's austere and able secretary of state, used the growing concern over a worldwide naval armament race as justification for calling an international conference.

During the winter of 1921–22, representatives from industrial nations with interests in East Asia, except for the Soviet Union, met in Washington. To everyone's surprise, Hughes insisted that the delegates act as well as talk. Consequently, the Washington Conference produced three important agreements. All of them sought in some way to freeze the existing balance of power and privileges in East Asia. One, the critical Four-Power Treaty of nonaggression among the United States, Japan, Great Britain, and France, superseded the troublesome Anglo-Japanese Alliance. A second agreement, the Five-Power

Even in a group Harding's Secretary of State Charles Evans Hughes seemed to stand alone. But at the Washington Conference of 1921–1922, that tough independence got results. *(Wide World.)*

Treaty, added Italy to the big four and established tonnage limitations on major warships according to a ratio approximating the current strength of these nations. Finally, the Nine-Power Treaty committed all imperial nations to the principle of equal opportunity inside an independent China—the American doctrine of the "Open Door."

Through this new framework, the United States hoped to stabilize relations in the Far East in such a way that America could act as a world power without elaborate diplomatic involvements or military investments. By signing these treaties, the United States acknowledged a crucial interconnection among the policies of the world's industrial nations. But these agreements also minimized the need for close international cooperation. Although the treaties included provisions for mutual consultation, they were basically a structure of rules rather than a system for collective action. Americans assumed that once these rules were established, they would allow the United States to pursue its own objectives in its own way.

To a very different set of problems in Europe, the United States applied a similar formula of stabilization and limited participation. The Harding administration signed treaties with each of the defeated Central Powers that copied the settlements of the Paris Peace Conference—with one primary exception. These treaties excluded any commitment to international enforcement. At the same time, the United States was demanding that its former European allies repay the large loans it had granted them during the war. European nations deeply resented this interpretation of the war debts as a business transaction. They tried to convince the United States that at the very least, they should repay American loans only to the extent that Germany was paying them the war reparations promised in the Versailles Treaty. Officially, the United States refused to acknowledge any connection between the debts and reparations. Unofficially, however, the American government did take the lead in organizing financial assistance for Germany's weakened economy through the Dawes Plan (1924) and the Young Plan (1929). As Germany recovered sufficiently to pay reparations, the former Allied Powers then made some payments on their war debts, and the United States did not press them very hard for more. In other words, the United States was willing to help manage a complex problem in international finance just so long as it did not involve a formal government commitment.*

That same aversion to new commitments surfaced repeatedly during the twenties. America's relations with the League of Nations remained very cautious and strictly unofficial. After a prolonged debate over whether or not the United States should enter the World Court, the League's unintimidating judicial arm, the Senate finally voted to join in 1926. But the Senate attached so many special conditions to America's participation that the other members of the World Court refused the terms. A year later, the French government publicly invited the United States to negotiate a bilateral renunciation of war. The Coolidge administration, however, considered the prospect of such a treaty too close to an alliance with France. Coolidge's secretary of state, Frank B. Kellogg, instead insisted on an extremely broad statement outlawing war and an invitation for all nations to sign it. More than sixty governments eventually ratified the Paris Peace Pact of 1928.** "An international kiss," snorted Missouri's sour Senator James Reed. Nevertheless, the Paris Peace Pact, with no mention of enforcement, was extremely popular in the United States.

A similar mixture of involvement and detachment characterized Washington's role in America's economic expansion. During the 1920s, assistance in developing foreign markets ranked high among the new areas of government service. As the budget for the Department of Commerce grew sixfold between 1921 and 1932, the department invested heavily in surveys of foreign markets, advisory personnel for business groups abroad, and publicity on the opportunities

---

*The depression of the 1930s, by stopping this flow of investments, reparations, and debt payments, once again made the war debts a bitter issue.

**The Paris Peace Pact of 1928 was sometimes called the Kellogg-Briand Peace Pact.

for economic expansion. It even competed with the Department of Agriculture in trying to enlarge the international market for farm products. Beginning in 1922, the State Department also introduced a new service for international investors. Bankers could submit their proposed loans to foreign governments for the State Department's review. The department would then evaluate them and issue judgments of "objection" or "no objection." The State Department rarely opposed these loans, and its statements of "no objection" appeared to be a government stamp of approval in marketing the foreign bonds.

At the same time, government officials almost always acted as though America's private business activities, once under way, would take care of themselves. In Latin America, the economic interests of the United States spread extensively during the 1920s, and the government, like the internationally minded businessmen, hoped that the United States would have a near monopoly on foreign investments there. But the government's leaders grew increasingly unwilling to support these interests with force. Washington was gradually repudiating the "Roosevelt Corollary" to the Monroe Doctrine, which had made the United States a policeman over Latin America's unstable, defaulting governments. American policymakers much preferred using persuasion to using the marines. Some government officials, particularly Herbert Hoover, even tried to discourage the most risky private loans to Latin America for fear that United States military forces might later be asked to collect such loans.

The desire to stabilize world affairs took precedence over America's private economic expansion. Where Washington committed itself to a policy, businessmen had to fit their interests within that policy. For example, the United States operated from a somewhat misty conviction that the future of China would determine the future of East Asia. Though American trade and investment overwhelmingly favored Japan, not China, the government continued to view Japan as the greatest threat to its Asian policy. After all, foreign trade remained about 5 percent of the national income during the 1920s, and foreign investments never reached 3 percent of the nation's total assets. It was difficult to argue that the health of the American economy required drastic diplomatic measures abroad. Only where the United States had no other clear goals did business interests predominate. In the Middle East, for instance, the government allowed American oil companies to conduct their own diplomacy during the twenties. When they negotiated a place for themselves in the world petroleum cartel, Washington ratified the results.

Overall, the United States used its great power quite cautiously during the twenties. The tentative quality of its international involvement was best revealed in the attitudes of the most influential official in Washington, Herbert Hoover. Despite his impressive efforts as secretary of commerce to assist business abroad, Hoover firmly believed that America had to rely on the strength of its domestic economy. Against the advice of many economists and big businessmen, he favored the high Fordney-McCumber Tariff of 1922 and the higher

Hawley-Smoot Tariff of 1930, both formidable barriers to international commerce. The solution to America's farm problems lay at home, he said, for the United States would soon be consuming its entire agricultural output. An admirer of Woodrow Wilson, Hoover blamed Europe for the failure to make a constructive peace in 1919, and he never altered his poor opinion of America's wartime allies. Hoover doubted that the United States and Japan could reach a lasting accommodation in the Far East. Yet he abhorred war and would have sacrificed almost anything to avoid it. It required no leap of the imagination for Hoover, at the outbreak of the Second World War, to advocate a detached and defensive "Fortress America."

International Disintegration, 1930–1941

The Great Depression of the thirties was worldwide. By 1931, the German economy was virtually bankrupt, the British credit system was tottering, and the foundation beneath every other industrial nation was badly shaken. By 1933, whatever faint chances had once existed for a cooperative international response to the depression disappeared, and each major power looked to its own resources for a solution. Economic nationalism thrived, as government after government moved first to protect its weakened domestic interests from outside competition. Simultaneously, some powers also tried to renew their strength through military imperialism.

The first of the military imperialists to strike was Japan. When depression pinched its lifelines of commerce, Japan looked more avidly than ever to its most natural area for economic expansion, the Asian mainland. But Japan could expect little profit in China as long as it was plagued by civil wars and carved into many spheres of foreign influence. Beginning in September 1931, Japan's Kwantung Army, which was stationed in Manchuria, took the initiative by seizing all of this rich northern province. Twelve months later, Manchuria became the Japanese puppet state of Manchukuo. Tokyo then sought to extend its sway southward by making a vassal of China's most successful warlord, Chiang Kai-shek. Chiang, whose first priority was defeating the Chinese Communists under Mao Tse-tung, eluded the Japanese until the summer of 1937, when the Japanese government released its impatient army to conquer all of China. By October 1938, Japan had occupied China's most important cities. Both Chiang's Nationalists and Mao's Communists, however, kept resistance alive in the countryside.

An even more formidable imperialism emerged in Germany. Against a background of economic chaos, the National Socialist party worked its way into the German government early in 1933, established its leader Adolf Hitler as dictator, and proceeded to eliminate its opponents. For a time, outsiders refused to take the militaristic pomp, the crude racism, and the ranting leaders of the Nazis seriously. But the new government proved ingenious in attracting German

ADOLF HITLER REVIEWING TROOPS

Goose-stepping soldiers and Nazi salutes symbolized a
new German power that shook the foundations of
Europe in the late 1930s. *(Brown Brothers.)*

loyalties and mobilizing its economic resources. As the Nazis consolidated their
power at home, they also asserted it abroad. Hitler, repudiating the Versailles
Treaty as a "stab in the back," pulled Germany out of the League of Nations
in 1933 and two years later announced that Germany would rearm. In 1936,
German troops occupied the Rhineland provinces, which the Versailles Treaty
had demilitarized. In March 1938, demanding the political unification of all
German people, Hitler sent his soldiers into Austria, and Germany annexed it.
That September, the Sudeten territory of Czechoslovakia fell to Germany. In
March 1939, Hitler seized the rest of Czechoslovakia and took aim at the former
German lands along the Baltic Sea. By early summer of 1939, the German
military was poised at the border of Poland.

As a minor accompaniment, Italy also joined the new imperialists. The Fascist Benito Mussolini, who had arisen as Italy's dictator in 1922, longed to make his nation the great power of the Mediterranean. But the opportunistic Duce had to settle for lesser glory. In October 1935, hoping to distract Italians from their economic woes at home, Mussolini ordered his army into Ethiopia, and the following May, Italy annexed it as a colony. Two months later, civil war in Spain offered Mussolini another chance to extend Italy's influence in the Mediterranean. Between 1936 and 1938, Italian military intervention in behalf of General Francisco Franco's army, more than matching the assistance that France and the Soviet Union gave to the Spanish Republicans, made a critical difference in this war. By 1939, Franco's reactionary Falange ruled Spain. The canny Franco, however, remained independent of both Mussolini and Hitler, who had also aided his cause. The alliance that did emerge during the Spanish Civil War was the Rome-Berlin Axis, which firmly bound those two dictatorships by 1939.

None of the mechanisms for international stabilization so optimistically developed during the 1920s could halt these waves of violence. The Washington Conference's limitations on naval armament, which had been restated at the London Naval Conference of 1930, were now discarded in the rush for more power. Japan's expansion into China erased the Open Door doctrine of the Nine-Power Treaty. In 1933, Japan and then Germany simply walked out of the League of Nations. The League's attempt to impose economic sanctions against Italy for its invasion of Ethiopia failed abysmally, and in 1937, Italy also withdrew from the League. Even the normal channels of diplomacy were clogged with accusations, suspicions, and deceptions.

Consequently, each nation that felt threatened by the new imperialism adopted its own course. No European power had the energy to confront Japan. Britain and France, though fretful about their own imperial interests in Asia, neither condoned nor seriously challenged Japan's conquests. The Soviet Union and France were particularly vehement in condemning Hitler's advances. Yet neither trusted the other sufficiently to take an effective joint stand. Moreover, both Hitler and Mussolini, by keeping the hopes for compromise alive with hints of moderation, discouraged a collective retaliation. It was British Prime Minister Neville Chamberlain who most earnestly explored these prospects of a peaceful settlement. Unlike France and the Soviet Union, England reacted very mildly to Italy's intervention in Spain. When Hitler's demand for the Sudetenland precipitated a European crisis, Chamberlain carried the primary burdens of diplomacy that culminated in the Munich Conference of September 1938. At Munich, England and France agreed that Germany and other Central European states could divide about one-third of Czechoslovakia among themselves. In the wake of the Munich Conference, Chamberlain returned to London with promises of "peace in our time."

When Hitler devoured the rest of Czechoslovakia in March 1939, Chamberlain's illusion of peace dissolved. Britain and France committed themselves to a defense of Poland and frantically prepared for war. Then in August 1939, Germany and the Soviet Union, Europe's most implacable foes, shocked the world by signing a nonaggression pact. With the Nazi Wehrmacht prepared to strike at Poland, all eyes fixed on Berlin.

America's mixture of involvement and detachment had no way of reckoning with military imperialism. Either the United States would have to expand its commitments and cooperate with other nations, or it would have to separate itself even farther from the new centers of danger. Hoover's secretary of state, Henry L. Stimson, tried the first alternative and failed. When Japan occupied Manchuria in 1931 and 1932, an outraged Stimson explored ways by which the United States could join in a collective international response. As an outsider, however, the United States could not collaborate effectively with the League of Nations. And the Nine-Power Treaty on the Open Door in China, a vague document at best, contained no sanctions against a violator. Hoping at least to keep the path open for a stronger American policy in the future, Stimson this time was blocked by the President. Hoover publicly declared that the United States would participate in neither military nor economic sanctions against Japan. What emerged was a purely American and purely moral condemnation of Japan. The "Hoover-Stimson Doctrine" of 1932, relying on the Paris Peace Pact's repudiation of war, stated that the United States would refuse diplomatic recognition to a military aggressor's territorial gains.

A second way to expand international cooperation was to bypass the imperialists themselves and concentrate instead on lifting the depression. President Hoover tried to follow this route. By declaring a moratorium on war debts in 1931, he eased the impact of an international crisis in finance. Then as Hoover was leaving the White House in 1933, he contended that the United States must take the lead at a forthcoming London Economic Conference in order to stabilize the world's chaotic finances. Hoover's successor disagreed. Roosevelt, by refusing America's cooperation in the middle of the negotiations, destroyed the London Conference and aligned himself with the popular sentiment at home that the United States could solve its depression alone. Democrats preferred a far less demanding form of international cooperation, lower tariffs. They argued that by increasing the flow of trade, international tensions would ease and the prospects of world peace improve. With Secretary of State Cordell Hull in command, Congress passed the Reciprocal Trade Agreement Act of 1934, so that the State Department could negotiate these lower tariffs with other nations. Although the United States signed many such agreements, they had no effect on either the worldwide depression or the rise of militarism.

In the mid-thirties American sentiment appeared overwhelmingly to favor a greater detachment from a troubled world. Congress expressed this opinion on several occasions. The Tydings-McDuffie Act of 1934, which set a schedule of independence for America's Philippine colony, promised to remove a particularly dangerous outpost of American responsibility. The Johnson Debt-Default Act of 1934, establishing the narrowest possible definition of America's friends and enemies abroad, denied American credit to any foreign government that had not honored its war debt. Then between 1935 and 1937, Congress enacted a series of neutrality laws to close off the routes that had led into the previous war. It embargoed arms and munitions to belligerents, banned using American vessels to ship them, prohibited arming American merchant ships, and proscribed extending credit to belligerents. Later, the neutrality laws would be ridiculed as a scheme to "Keep America Out of the First World War." Americans, not yet knowing any other war, praised these laws as their protection against the madness of a world in arms.

As the pace of the new imperialism accelerated between 1937 and 1939, American attitudes began to change in two important respects. First, a growing majority of Americans concentrated their feelings of horror and hatred on Japan and Germany. The full-scale invasion of China in 1937 gave Americans their first appalling revelations of what a modern air force could do to an urban population. On the eve of the Second World War, the bombing of China's cities produced the same kind of humanitarian outcry in America that bayoneted babies had roused during the First World War. Although most Americans would not realize until the mid-1940s how literally the Nazis sought to exterminate the Jews, news about mass arrests and concentration camps increasingly identified Hitler's anti-Semitism as a threat to all civilized values. Japan and Germany, a majority of Americans concluded, were the centers of an insane barbarism.

A second change in attitudes involved the potential danger from Germany and Japan. Americans who understood their own society as a system of interest groups thought of the world also in terms of interrelated national interests and international spheres of influence. Many of them believed that the United States and Latin America formed a sphere of reciprocal interests, with the United States investing in the Latin American economies, processing their raw materials, and selling finished products in their markets. Early in the thirties, some Americans were willing to accept Japan and Manchuria as a comparable sphere. The more vigorously the new imperial systems grew, however, the more they seemed bent on absorbing the whole world. If Japan controlled all China, would its sphere not expand throughout the western Pacific and Southeast Asia? If Germany dominated Europe, how could it possibly be excluded from the Western Hemisphere? By lumping all of the expansive powers together as "fascist," Americans increasingly found themselves pondering the ultimate danger. Could America itself survive in a world of fascist spheres?

One natural reaction to these worries was to consolidate America's power in the Western Hemisphere. Under Roosevelt's "Good Neighbor Policy," the United States formally abandoned any claim to intervene in a Latin American state. The State Department actively pursued reciprocal trade in Latin America,

THE NAZI THREAT

(Library of Congress.)

and this region was exempted from the new prohibitions governing American neutrality. As Germany and Japan became ever more menacing, the United States sponsored agreements in 1936 and 1938 that made an external threat to one nation in the hemisphere the common concern of them all. At least the United States would protect the "American sphere."

In September 1939, Germany invaded Poland. As Hitler prepared to divide that unhappy land with the Soviet Union, Britain and France declared war on Germany. That winter the world waited. Then in April 1940, Germany began a lightning sweep through Western Europe, taking Norway, Denmark, the Netherlands, and Belgium. By June, France itself had fallen. Only Britain remained. Though German bombers devastated its cities and German submarines squeezed its lifeline of supplies, an invasion of England never came. Instead, the Nazis turned eastward late in 1940 and, with feeble assistance from their Italian ally, conquered the Balkans. In June 1941, Hitler launched the fateful thrust of the war, an attack into Russia. The Nazi-Soviet pact of 1939 had been a calculated expedient between enemies, enabling Hitler to conquer the heart of Europe and the Russians to seize a portion of Poland, the Baltic states of Latvia, Lithuania, and Estonia, and a slice of Finland. Now the Nazis were ready to smash their last great opponent on the continent, and the German war machine roared across a broad eastern front against Russia's primary cities.

While Germany was swallowing Europe, Japan extended its authority southward into French Indochina—ostensibly to tighten the blockade of China but actually to control a new area rich in natural resources. Just ahead lay the precious oil and rubber of Southeast Asia. In September 1940, Japan joined the Axis powers in a defensive Tripartite Pact. It was a tentative connection. Many Japanese leaders never trusted Hitler or wanted their nation's destiny tied to a European power. Yet from the outside, Tokyo's link with Berlin and Rome gave the impression of a unified fascist force rolling toward global domination.

Before September 1939, President Roosevelt seemed to be a firm believer in America's detachment from the world's turmoil. In 1932, to increase his chances for the presidential nomination, he abandoned the cause of America's entry into the League of Nations. Soon after taking office, he undermined the London Economic Conference. In fact, Roosevelt showed little interest in any foreign affairs outside the Western Hemisphere. The President did not seriously contest the neutrality laws of the mid-thirties, and he seldom hazarded an opinion of any kind about the state of the world. Although his private concerns obviously rose toward the end of the decade, his public statements remained very broad. In October 1937, Roosevelt did use the suggestive word *quarantine* in a speech on the evils of war and aggression. But when commentators took it to imply coercion or collective action against the fascist powers, the President angrily denied any such thought. After the Munich Conference in 1938, Roosevelt congratulated the leaders in England and France for their efforts to keep the peace.

Because the President's influence over foreign policy was always very strong in a time of crisis, even the subtle shades in Roosevelt's thinking became critically important after September 1939. Early in his career, Roosevelt came to believe that a great power such as the United States should play an important role in world affairs. His background and training equated Anglo-American culture with civilization, and his instincts told him that Germany was the nation's enemy. Unlike many of his contemporaries, Roosevelt never questioned either the wisdom or the justice of America's entry into the First World War. As foreign affairs occupied more and more of the President's attention, these attitudes increasingly shaped American policy. Characteristically, Roosevelt avoided hard commitments as long as he could, and in the process kept personal control over the government's decisions. The selfless Harry Hopkins, moving into the White House as Roosevelt's intimate adviser and mirroring his ideas on world affairs, was FDR's favorite envoy.

Between the outbreak of war in 1939 and Germany's "Blitzkrieg" in 1940, America hugged its shore. In 1939, the United States induced the nations of Latin America to join it in declaring a huge neutrality zone between Europe and the Western Hemisphere. Although England and France purchased war materials in the United States, the terms were "cash and carry." By law, Americans could provide neither credit nor shipping for a belligerent. Almost everyone hoped a major war would never develop. When Germany's conquest of Western Europe destroyed that hope, a new pattern of American opinion began to form. During 1940 and 1941, a rising majority of Americans wanted the United States to stand behind Britain's resistance to Hitler. At the same time, a declining but substantial majority wanted the United States to remain at peace. The rough guideline became "all aid short of war."

For a time, Roosevelt followed these potentially conflicting sentiments. During the presidential campaign of 1940, the "Battle of Britain" raged furiously as German bombers and submarines swarmed around the isolated isles. Roosevelt, despite a hard contest with the Republican Wendell Willkie, risked a dramatic violation of traditional neutrality in an effort to relieve the British. In September 1940, the President announced an exchange of fifty old American destroyers for the lease of British bases in the Western Hemisphere. The Destroyer Deal formally declared America's commitment to the British cause. Nevertheless, the Roosevelt administration resisted close diplomatic or military cooperation with Britain and generally refused to prepare for a wartime alliance.

But the pressure of events was forcing a hard choice between involvement and detachment. By the winter of 1940–41, Britain's situation appeared desperate and a German invasion imminent. Britain's dwindling assets in the United States could not begin to pay for the war materials it needed. Roosevelt, with growing popular support behind him, chose involvement. Describing the United States as the "arsenal of democracy," Roosevelt proposed an almost unlimited British access to American production and credit. An "America First" movement, which attracted such prominent men as Robert E. Wood of Sears, Roebuck, the labor leader John L. Lewis, and the hero of the twenties Charles Lindbergh, fought frantically against the legislation. Nevertheless, in March 1941, Congress passed the open-ended Lend-Lease Act, wiping out the last traces of American neutrality. Lend-lease, its opponents cried, was a Grim Reaper's AAA that would "plow under every fourth American boy." Publicly, Roosevelt tried to calm these fears of war. In private, however, he knew that the United States and Britain were now partners, pooling resources and coordinating plans against a common foe.

To ensure the delivery of these essential supplies, American convoys carried them closer and closer to the British Isles. In April 1941, the United States extended its patrols to the mid-Atlantic. Then in July, following Germany's invasion of Russia, American convoys moved a big step closer to the English ports by escorting the supplies as far as Iceland. A month later, the American navy expanded its protection to cover British merchant ships as well as American. Meanwhile, along the Atlantic sealanes, the Americans and British collaborated in locating and attacking German submarines. In September, one German submarine, as it fled from the U.S.S. *Greer*, fired at the American destroyer. Roosevelt, pretending that the submarine had been the aggressor and likening German power to a "rattlesnake" that was coiled to strike at the Western Hemisphere, ordered American ships to "shoot on sight." By October, Congress authorized convoys to land in Britain. "All aid" to Britain could not stop "short of war." Though most Americans did not yet know it, their second world war had already begun.

During these crucial months of 1940 and 1941, Asian affairs appeared to be less volatile and less important. Most Americans agreed that Japanese imperialism posed some kind of threat, but few could define it. Roosevelt himself did not have precise objectives in Asia, and he left the negotiations with Japan largely to his crusty secretary of state, Cordell Hull. Hull insisted that Japan honor the Nine-Power Treaty of 1922 on the Open Door. In effect, that meant a Japanese withdrawal from the mainland of Asia. As leverage, the United States imposed an increasingly tight embargo on trade with Japan, a policy that did indeed have a sharp effect on the Japanese economy. During most of 1941, conciliatory forces in the Japanese government under Prince Fuminaro Konoye, the prime minister, sought some way of mollifying the United States short of a complete Japanese capitulation. Although Konoye would not reopen the question of Manchuria, he proposed a Japanese military withdrawal elsewhere on the Asian mainland in exchange for a friendly Chinese government and American economic cooperation. But Hull was unrelenting. Before serious negotiations could begin, he insisted, Japan must first declare its acceptance of the Open Door throughout the area of Japanese expansion.

By the summer of 1941, the two nations were drifting towards war. In July, Japan completed its occupation of Indochina, and Roosevelt retaliated by freezing Japanese assets in the United States. Appraising their limited resources, Japan's leaders realized that if they had to fight the United States for their empire, the time had come. Though Prince Konoye continued to explore various formulas of compromise, his power at home was waning. Washington remained unresponsive. In October 1941, the more militant Hideki Tojo replaced Konoye as prime minister, and Japan prepared for war. As Japan mobilized, one last effort at negotiations failed. Meanwhile, because American intelligence had broken Japan's secret code, Washington knew that a Japanese attack of some kind was pending. Roosevelt's inner circle guessed that it would strike in Southeast Asia. But no one anticipated what was to come, and no one was ready. At dawn on December 7, Japanese planes roared across the naval base at Pearl Harbor, Hawaii and crippled America's Pacific force. By waiting instead of negotiating, Roosevelt had been given an event that dissolved the nation's doubts and propelled it into total war.*

---

*Within a few days after the attack on Pearl Harbor, an exchange of war declarations— Britain with Japan, Germany and Italy with the United States—completed the alignment of powers until August 1945, when the Soviet Union entered the war against Japan.

PEARL HARBOR, DECEMBER 7, 1941

Out of the wreckage of Pearl Harbor came a powerful
American commitment to win the war. *(Official Navy
Photograph.)*

World War, 1941–1945

Between December 1941 and May 1945, the United States, unlike its allies,
was continuously engaged in two very different wars. In the Pacific theater,
where victory hinged on control of the seas, the United States fought almost
alone. In the European theater, where victory could be won only on the continent, the United States contributed to a complex, collective effort.

During the early months of the war, both theaters offered a dismal picture
of retreat and jeopardy. Japanese units swept away the remnants of resistance
in Southeast Asia, occupying the Netherland East Indies (Indonesia), capturing
the British base at Singapore, and penetrating to the frontier of India. Japan's
naval victory in the Java Sea assured its control of the western Pacific. In May
1942, the last of America's small, isolated force in the Philippines surrendered
to the Japanese. Germany's successes were even more ominous. Its fleet of
submarines, which had been held in check before December 1941, unleashed
a devastating attack on the Atlantic supply lines. The Nazi's mechanized divisions under General Erwin Rommel drove across North Africa into Egypt,
threatening the Suez Canal. Above all, a renewed offensive in Russia spread

German troops from the outskirts of Leningrad in the north to the gates of Stalingrad in the south. Into the late fall of 1942, the greatest disaster, a Soviet collapse, loomed as a strong possibility.

How could the United States best use its massive resources to alter the balance of the war? In broad strategic matters, the answers came quickly and clearly. The European theater had priority over the Pacific. Food and war materials, which under lend-lease had been moving to Russia before Pearl Harbor, were the immediate contributions that the United States could make to Soviet survival. Despite the menace of the German submarines, the quantity of these supplies swelled each month. Finally, to relieve the pressure on the Soviet army, American and British forces had to launch a "second front" as soon as possible somewhere in the west.

The men who ultimately made these decisions were President Roosevelt and Prime Minister Winston Churchill, Britain's brilliant, calculating war leader. Their personal collaboration had begun at the Atlantic Conference of August 1941, which declared to the world that the United States and Great Britain stood together against the Axis. From December 1941 to January 1943, through a series of private meetings, the two men grew closer. Although Russia's fate also hung on the decisions that Roosevelt and Churchill made, the Soviet Union remained a distant ally, declaring its needs and awaiting a response from the Western powers.

The initial American impulse was to open at least a token second front in Western Europe during 1942. Sobered by the logistical difficulties of a quick attack on France, however, Roosevelt and his advisers reluctantly accepted Churchill's alternative of a North African campaign. In November 1942, an

SIEGE OF LENINGRAD

Their city surrounded by German troops, citizens of Leningrad dip water from a broken main. More than 600,000 died of starvation during the two-year seige. (*Associated Press.*)

Anglo-American force under General Dwight D. Eisenhower invaded French Morocco and Algiers and by the following May eliminated Axis power throughout North Africa. Meanwhile the Soviet Union had won the pivotal engagement of the European war. In an effort to crack Russia's resistance before another winter froze his army in place, Hitler gambled recklessly on an assault against Stalingrad. During the winter's war of 1942–43, a relentless Soviet counterattack not only saved Stalingrad but actually cost Germany half a million troops. The following summer, the Soviet army took the initiative and began its drive westward toward Berlin.

In 1943, Churchill again convinced Roosevelt to postpone an attack on France. That July, in the most dubious strategic decision of the war, an allied force landed in Sicily, then in September crossed into Italy. Although Italy immediately surrendered, German troops filled the vacuum from the north and stalled the allied army. It was not the second front that the Soviet Premier, Josef Stalin, thought he had been promised. Russian soldiers continued to bear the primary burden of the ground war against Germany, and Stalin was furious.

Not until June 6, 1944, did the United States and Britain finally establish a successful second front in France. Under General Eisenhower, the allies executed a brilliant landing at Normandy. Then in August, another force invaded southern France, and that same month Paris fell. In September, British and

FRANCE, 1944

The photographer Robert Capa captures the horrors of war and joys of peace: the Normandy invasion, a wounded soldier, liberated Paris. *(All from Robert Capa*, Images of War, *Copyright © 1964.)*

American troops entered Germany itself. Even before the Normandy landing, the Russian army was pressing toward Poland, East Prussia, and the Balkans. Except for a desperate Nazi counterattack at the German-Belgian border—the "Battle of the Bulge" in December 1944—Germany's army collapsed inside the allied vise. By the end of April, Russian troops were fighting in the streets of Berlin. Following Hitler's suicide, German officers capitulated on May 7, 1945.

The critical contributions to victory in Europe had been Russian lives and American productivity. About 16 million citizens of the Soviet Union died in the conflict with Germany. By contrast, British losses were about half a million, and American losses in both theaters of war about 250,000. The United States had indeed served as the arsenal of democracy. By 1942, America's war production equaled the combined output of the Axis powers; by 1944, it doubled the enemy's total. In 1943 and 1944, when Germany could no longer slow the delivery of American goods, the Nazis fell beneath a crushing wave of war materials. America's schedule of production became Germany's timetable of defeat.

In Asia, the United States confronted a weaker but more remote foe. Because Congress had authorized a program of naval construction well before Pearl Harbor, the American fleet was able to return in strength to the Pacific less than a year after Japan's devastating surprise attack. In May 1942, even as Japan was absorbing the Philippines, a successful American attack on Japanese shipping in the Coral Sea secured Australia. A month later, a Japanese naval force was repulsed near Midway Island, west of Hawaii. Then in November 1942, the American navy won a three-day battle off the Solomon Islands near Australia, and the balance of sea power shifted back to the United States.

Still, the pace of the Pacific war remained slow during 1943. The European theater continued to have priority, and the logistics of the Pacific campaign denied any chances for a sudden, grand success. On the assumption that only an occupation of Tokyo itself could end the war, naval forces under Admiral Chester Nimitz and a combination of American, Australian, and New Zealand ground forces under General Douglas MacArthur began a grim, two-pronged assault toward the Japanese mainland. Nimitz's command had to sweep the myriad islands in the central Pacific. From the south, MacArthur's command had to struggle through the jungles of New Guinea, then converge with Nimitz's on the Philippines.

Early in 1944, as America's productive capacities expanded to serve both the European and the Pacific wars, the drive to Japan gained momentum. By summer, the United States controlled the central Pacific. Then in October, with General MacArthur dramatically leading his troops to the site of a humiliating defeat early in the war, American forces invaded the Philippines. That same month, in the Battle of Leyte Gulf, Japanese naval power was destroyed. Ferocious Japanese resistance continued to keep casualties high. As late as March 1945, a month's fight for the tiny island of Iwo Jima left 20,000 Americans dead and wounded. But Japan itself now lay open to systematic bombing.

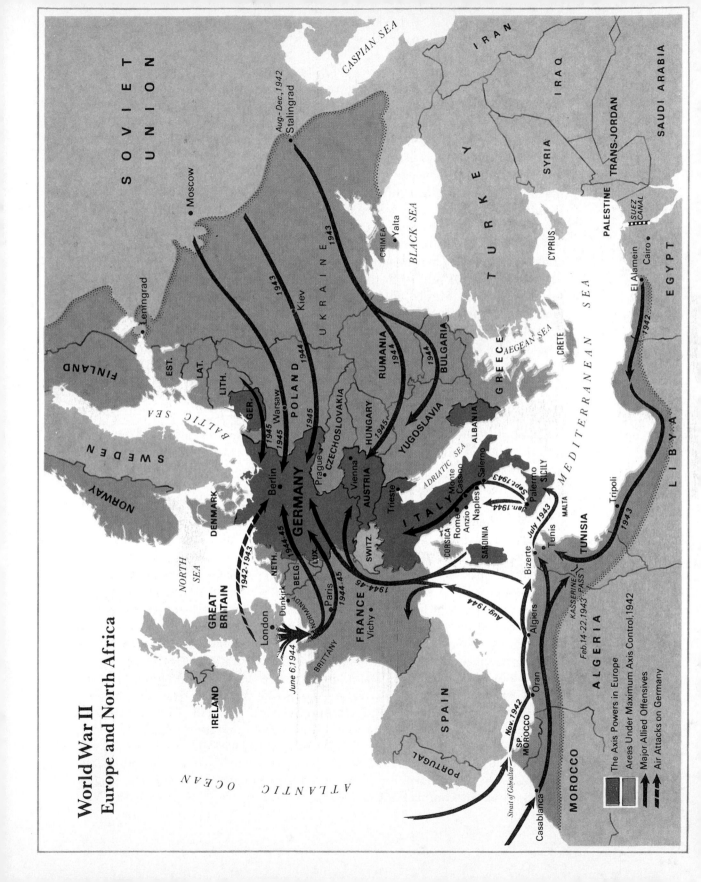

World War II
Europe and North Africa

S O V I E T   U N I O N

Moscow

Leningrad

CASPIAN SEA

Stalingrad
Aug.–Dec., 1942

BLACK SEA

Yalta
CRIMEA

UKRAINE

1943

Kiev

1943

I R A N

I R A Q

SAUDI ARABIA

SYRIA

TRANS-JORDAN

PALESTINE

SUEZ CANAL

Cairo

E G Y P T

El Alamein

1942

T U R K E Y

CYPRUS

AEGEAN SEA

GREECE

CRETE

BULGARIA
1944

RUMANIA
1944

1944

YUGOSLAVIA
1945

ALBANIA

MEDITERRANEAN SEA

L I B Y A

Tripoli

1943

FINLAND

EST.

LAT.

LITH.

GER.

BALTIC SEA

SWEDEN

NORWAY

Warsaw
1945

P O L A N D
1944

1945

1945

Berlin
1945

1945

Prague

CZECHOSLOVAKIA

G E R M A N Y

Vienna

HUNGARY
1945

AUSTRIA

SWITZ.

Trieste

ADRIATIC SEA

Monte Cassino

Salerno
Sept. 1943

Rome

Anzio
Jan. 1944

Naples

Palermo
July 1943

SICILY

MALTA

Tunis

Bizerte

TUNISIA

1943

NORTH SEA

DENMARK

NETH.

BELG.
1944-45

LUX.

Dunkirk

London

GREAT BRITAIN

1942-1943

Paris

F R A N C E
Vichy

1944-45

1944-45

BRITTANY

June 6, 1944

Aug. 1944

CORSICA

SARDINIA

KASSERINE PASS
Feb. 14-22, 1943

Algiers

Oran

Nov. 1942

A L G E R I A

IRELAND

ATLANTIC OCEAN

SPAIN

PORTUGAL

SP. MOROCCO

Casablanca

Strait of Gibraltar

MOROCCO

Legend

- The Axis Powers in Europe
- Areas Under Maximum Axis Control, 1942
- Major Allied Offensives
- Air Attacks on Germany

Napalm raids burned its compact cities, one by one. In March 1945, a single attack on Tokyo killed more than 80,000. When Germany surrendered in May 1945, an utterly exposed Japan was already tottering.

Strangely enough, the climactic blow of the Asian war had been in preparation even before Pearl Harbor and had been originally aimed at Germany, not Japan. In 1939, refugee physicists from Europe, fearing the potential of Germany's military technology, began urging the American government to explore the possibility of an awesome new atomic bomb before the Nazis could develop it. Within a year the project was under way. In utmost secrecy, groups of scientists at separate laboratories struggled against time to master the secrets of the atom. They learned to control a chain reaction of atomic fission so that it would generate enormous power. Then they translated this discovery into a technically practical military device. In July 1945, the task was finally completed at a lonely center in Los Alamos, New Mexico, under the direction of the physicist J. Robert Oppenheimer. By then, however, Germany had fallen. A new, inexperienced President, Harry Truman, sat in the White House. An array of military and civilian advisers counseled the President to use the new weapon against Japan, and Truman agreed. On August 6, a single bomb demolished the city of Hiroshima, immediately killing about 80,000 and maiming and poisoning thousands more. Three days later, just as the Soviet Union declared war on Japan, a second bomb razed Nagasaki. On August 14, Japan agreed to surrender.

Although Roosevelt did not live to celebrate the final victory, his leadership set the nation's course to the eve of surrender. At two levels, that leadership was notably effective. Roosevelt was an inspired spokesman of hope, not only for Americans but also for yearning people throughout the world. Even before Pearl Harbor, Roosevelt and Churchill had sketched ideals for the postwar world in the Atlantic Charter, which drew heavily on the Wilsonian principles of political self-determination, free economic exchange, and international cooperation. Roosevelt's broad goal of the "Four Freedoms"—freedom from want and fear, freedom of speech and religion—met an enthusiastic international response.

On a very practical level, Roosevelt was also a skilled mediator among quarreling, competing wartime interests. He maneuvered among the many military demands of Americans and allies alike, giving a little, taking a little, but never losing command. Of all the challenges to these negotiating talents, the greatest was the Soviet premier, Josef Stalin. Between the Bolshevik Revolution of 1917 and the German invasion of Russia in 1941, Soviet-American relations had been an almost unrelieved story of mutual hostility. Until 1933, the United States did not even recognize the Soviet Union. Americans responded in disgust to the Nazi-Soviet pact of 1939 and the Russian war against Finland that winter. Even after the United States and the Soviet Union became wartime allies, their exchanges were often sharp, especially over the delays in a second front. Stalin's suspicious nature complicated each problem.

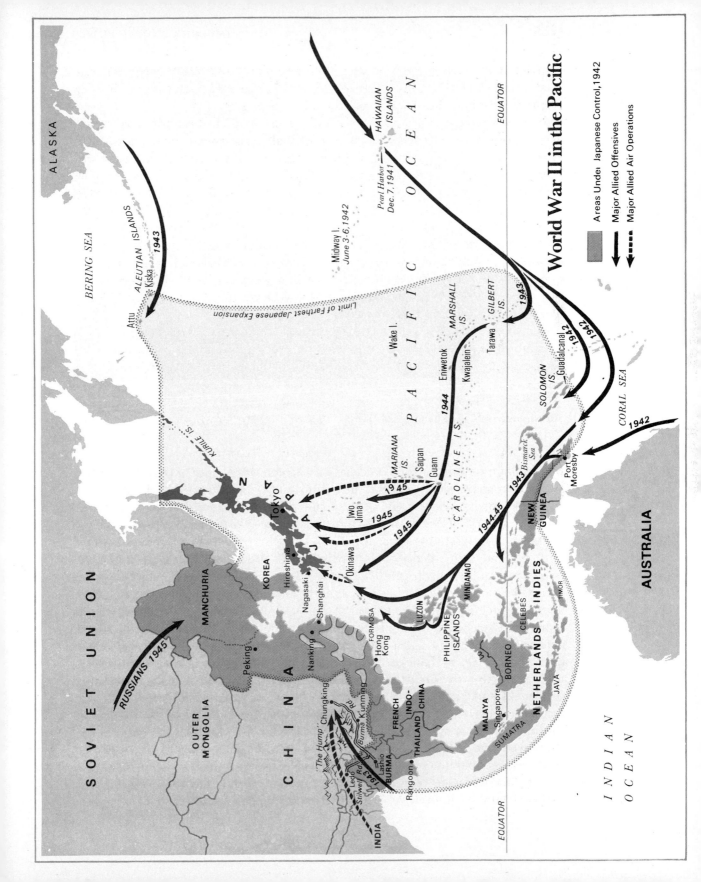

World War II in the Pacific

Areas Under Japanese Control, 1942

Major Allied Offensives

Major Allied Air Operations

ALASKA

BERING SEA

ALEUTIAN ISLANDS

Kiska **1943**

Attu

Limit of Farthest Japanese Expansion

HAWAIIAN ISLANDS

Pearl Harbor Dec. 7, 1941

EQUATOR

P A C I F I C   O C E A N

Midway I. June 3-6, 1942

Wake I.

MARSHALL IS.

Eniwetok

Kwajalein

GILBERT IS.

Tarawa **1943**

Guadalcanal **1942**

SOLOMON IS.

CORAL SEA **1942**

Port Moresby

1944 CAROLINE IS.

1945

MARIANA IS.

Saipan

Guam

Iwo Jima **1945**

1945

Okinawa

1945

J A P A N

TOKYO

Hiroshima

Nagasaki

Shanghai

KOREA

KURILE IS.

SOVIET UNION

MANCHURIA

RUSSIANS 1945

OUTER MONGOLIA

C H I N A

Peking

Nanking

Hong Kong

FORMOSA

LUZON

PHILIPPINE ISLANDS

MINDANAO

1944-45

NEW GUINEA

1943 Bismarck Sea

CELEBES

BORNEO

NETHERLANDS INDIES

JAVA

TIMOR

AUSTRALIA

"The Hump" Chungking

Kunming

Burma Rd.

Lashio

Ledo

Stilwell Rd. **1943**

BURMA

Rangoon

THAILAND

FRENCH INDO-CHINA

MALAYA

Singapore

SUMATRA

INDIA

I N D I A N   O C E A N

EQUATOR

THE SURRENDER OF JAPAN

At the microphone a magisterial Douglas
MacArthur presides as Japan surrenders. *(U.S. Army
Photograph.)*

Although no one person could have overcome this history of obstacles, Roosevelt did manage to open a dialogue with the Soviet dictator. At the depths of
Russia's wartime doubts in 1943, Stalin, Churchill, and Roosevelt arranged
their first joint meeting, which took place that November and December in
Tehran. During the conference, Roosevelt distanced himself from Churchill
and responded in a conciliatory way to Stalin's proposals. When the Big Three
met again at the much more important Yalta Conference of February 1945,
the American President adopted a similar stance toward his colleagues.

As an architect of national policy, however, Roosevelt was extremely vague.
The President was thoroughly committed to the allied policy of "unconditional
surrender," and he tried as best he could to bury the long-range problems of
the postwar world beneath the short-term needs of a military victory. But
fighting a war to win it did not establish an international program. Unlike
Churchill and Stalin, Roosevelt had almost no traditional goals that he could
actually transfer to a map of the postwar world. Moreover, the President had no
inclinations to draw one. In his wartime exchanges with Churchill and Stalin,
Roosevelt chided the British on the sins of their empire, talked of future Soviet-
American cooperation, but whenever possible, avoided specific commitments.

Only on the issue of international organization did the Roosevelt administration show itself decisive. At the Bretton Woods Conference of 1944, the

United States took the lead in developing a program for international monetary stabilization. The American dollar became the basis for most monetary transactions. To facilitate international finance, the conference planned two new agencies, the World Bank and the International Monetary Fund. The International Monetary Fund, in turn, belonged to a far more elaborate organization that was also developing during the war, a new league of nations. Once again, it was the Roosevelt administration that led the movement for another attempt at worldwide collective security.

Cordell Hull, tenaciously devoted to the concept of world organization, deserved the primary credit for negotiating a postwar United Nations (UN). Recalling Woodrow Wilson's disaster, the secretary of state wooed the Senate and included prominent Republicans in the planning of a new league. At every opportunity, Hull pressed America's wartime allies for firm commitments to an international organization. When the secretary retired in 1944, the hardest work had been done. Despite British fears for its empire and Soviet fears for its security, their representatives joined delegates from forty-six other nations in San Francisco to found a world organization. Overcoming a final Soviet resistance, the delegates signed the Charter for the United Nations in June 1945. The heart of the UN lay in the small Security Council, where the important decisions were made and each great power had a veto. The General Assembly, representing all members, served as an arena for discussion and broad pronouncements. Surrounding this legislative core, a host of agencies fulfilled specialized international functions; and presiding over the entire structure, the Secretary-General's office administered the UN's programs. In July 1945, the United States Senate overwhelmingly approved America's participation.

International organizations were only mechanisms, not policies, and the war did not create a new American foreign policy. What it did change was America's orientation toward international affairs. The primary lesson of the war, as almost every American leader interpreted it, was the importance of power. In the past, they argued, American diplomacy had relied far too exclusively on moral principles and good intentions. The ultimate guarantee of a just cause was an adequate military force and the will to use it. Blaming the Second World War on the failure of democratic nations before 1939 to confront the fascist aggressors, Americans made *Munich* and *appeasement* synonymous with diplomatic suicide.

By itself, this reasoning encouraged neither a greater international involvement nor a detachment from world affairs. It could justify both Wendell Willkie's expansive plea for "One World" and Congresswoman Clare Booth Luce's inturning rebuttal—"Globaloney!" Many Americans continued to hope that without sacrificing America's military strength, the nation could regain its traditional balance between involvement and detachment. Air power became the most popular means of achieving that goal. Even during the war, the presence of American troops abroad seemed fundamentally unnatural. Almost everyone expected the soldiers to come home and stay home after the war. For emotional as well as logistical reasons, therefore, Americans increasingly favored a powerful air force to provide a maximum of protection with a minimum of involvement. As the fighting came to an end, the Chief of Staff, General George C. Marshall, was planning the nation's postwar defense in these terms.

Roosevelt's thoughts about a new league of nations also reflected the recent emphasis on power. As a young man, Roosevelt had accepted the Wilsonian vision of an evolving general plan for world organization that would express an international consensus about peace and justice. By the Second World War, however, the President shifted his focus to some form of regional policing. He even settled on the international policemen: the United States, the Soviet Union, Great Britain, and China. In other words, the heart of Roosevelt's conception was no longer a "solemn covenant," just four strong, alert nations enforcing the peace in their natural regions of influence. Later, when the great powers could not cooperate inside the UN and the United States bypassed it in favor of military alliances, America altered Roosevelt's tactics without violating his assumptions about the connection between power and collective security.

Cold War, 1945–1950

On April 12, 1945, a change in Presidents made a critical difference in the nation's foreign affairs. Roosevelt had paid no attention to Harry Truman, the Vice-President who was pushed on him at the 1944 convention. Senator Robert Taft once said, in rejecting the office, that the Vice-President had nothing to do except "inquire about the President's health." Truman had not even done that. Stunned by Roosevelt's death, he suddenly found himself chief executive without adequate knowledge about America's international involvements or a clear postwar policy to guide him.

Within two years after Truman took office, the United States and the Soviet Union were engaged in a "Cold War" along a line approximating the location of their victorious armies in the summer of 1945. Though no experienced observer expected a placid transition from war to peace, relatively few people seemed to have anticipated or welcomed such bitter animosity. Despite an apparent desire in the United States and the Soviet Union for some accommodation, a core of problems between the two nations proved so intractable that they destroyed the capacity to compromise on any other issue. The underlying causes of this rift were extremely complex, and for decades reasonable people would differ sharply over their meaning. The immediate source of conflict, however, was obvious to everyone. What should be the postwar disposition of Germany and Eastern Europe?

At the Yalta Conference Roosevelt, Churchill, and Stalin took an initial step toward resolving this complicated package of problems. Stalin stated the Soviet position in detail. For Germany, which had invaded Russia twice in thirty years, he demanded a harsh settlement that would strip it of the potential to make war and send massive reparations in machinery and labor to the Soviet Union. In Eastern Europe, which had been Germany's avenue for invasion, Stalin wanted friendly governments from Poland in the north to the edge of Greece in the south. Where Stalin was rigid and determined, Roosevelt was vague and agreeable. The gravely ill President seemed to accept Stalin's argument that these measures were essential to Russian security. It was Churchill, not Roosevelt, who futilely resisted $20 billion as an estimate for German reparations. Again it was Churchill, more than Roosevelt, who forced the insertion of "free and unfettered elections" into the Yalta agreement on the postwar Polish government. Neither Churchill nor Roosevelt challenged a general Soviet sphere of influence covering Hungary, Rumania, Bulgaria, and Yugoslavia.

All parties regarded the agreements at Yalta as no more than the outline for a later settlement. But instead of proceeding toward a full-scale peace treaty, the Soviet Union and the United States each began reshaping the Yalta decisions to suit its own ends. Stalin made it clear that the elections in Poland would have to choose his candidates. Truman not only attacked Russia's coercion of Poland; he now challenged the entire concept of a Soviet sphere in Eastern Europe. Meanwhile, the United States abandoned plans for a harsh peace in Germany and tried to preserve its remaining economic strength. As a temporary measure, Germany had been divided into American, British, French, and Russian zones of military

ROOSEVELT AND CHURCHILL AT YALTA

Between 1941 and 1943, Roosevelt and Prime Minister Winston Churchill developed an exceptionally close wartime partnership. (Library of Congress.)

occupation. By treating these zones as self-contained administrative units, the United States was able to shield the western industrial portions of Germany from most Soviet demands for reparations.

By summer, Soviet-American tensions were so high that any meeting between Stalin and Truman was in doubt. In July 1945, however, the two did confer at Potsdam. Although the allied leaders issued bland statements of unity and Stalin renewed a promise to declare war on Japan, it was an unhappy conference. The crucial exchanges concerned Germany. Unable to find a common ground, the great powers accepted the separate ground that each one already held. The Soviet Union could set its own policy in the eastern zone of Germany; the United States, Great Britain, and France would determine policy in their western zones. The divisive issue of German reparations was cast vaguely into the future. After Potsdam, neither Truman nor Stalin sought another summit meeting.

There were many other sources of Soviet-American friction in 1945 and 1946. At the San Francisco conference to found the United Nations, the Russian delegates came close to disrupting the proceedings. The Soviet Union continued to view the UN as a league of potential enemies and often obstructed its work. Moreover, to contest American and British influence in the Middle East, Russia kept its troops in Iran and withdrew them early in 1946 only after strong protests. On its part, the United States abruptly ended economic aid to the Soviet Union after Germany's defeat, despite Russia's desperate need for assistance. Bluntly, Truman made any future aid dependent on a Soviet acceptance of American policies. In addition, the United States excluded Russia from the occupation government of Japan, as it already had from the occupation government of Italy.

Yet each of these problems by itself was either negotiable or tolerable. Only the issues of Germany and Eastern Europe defied any accommodation. In what Soviet officials construed as an assault on their vital interests, the Truman administration pursued a policy of reconciliation with Germany and demanded independent governments throughout Eastern Europe. The German zones rapidly became permanent eastern and western spheres; the Soviet Union tightened its authority over Poland and the Balkans. "From Stettin in the Baltic to Trieste in the Adriatic," Churchill declared in a speech at Fulton, Missouri, "an iron curtain has descended across the Continent." More and more stories of mass killings, deportations, and labor camps filtered through that curtain. Although there were moments of hope for a year after the Potsdam conference, the main trend in Soviet-American relations ran strongly toward suspicion and anger. By late 1946, even the occasional hopes disappeared.

What led the United States to confront the Soviet Union in Europe? The answer had four parts. The most elusive but perhaps the most important element was a powerful tradition of mutual distrust. There was a natural inclination in both the United States and the Soviet Union to regard the other nation as the "communist" or "capitalist" enemy. Because leaders in each nation viewed their Soviet or American counterparts as inherently expansionist, feelings of distrust easily turned into fears of aggression. Moreover, the wartime habit of dividing the world into diametrically opposing camps encouraged people to understand their postwar problems through similar concepts. By substituting *communism* for *fascism,* many Americans found a convenient answer to a perplexing, worldwide array of problems. In the process, this way of thinking made each little conflict still another sign of fundamental differences. After a clash with Russia's delegates over the charter for the UN, the influential Republican senator, Arthur Vandenberg, noted in his diary: "The basic trouble is that we are trying to unite two incompatible ideologies."

The second part of the answer concerned American expectations following a victorious war. It seemed that the United States, never before so paramount above all other nations, should be able to control the terms of a postwar settlement. Indeed, some saw no limit to America's influence. An "American Century" is commencing, declared the prominent publisher Henry Luce. It was difficult to accept the conflicts and confusions of the postwar world as normal. It was doubly irritating to meet the rigid opposition of a former ally, the Soviet Union. Because most Americans assumed that an able President could manage those international problems, a very heavy burden fell on the inexperienced Truman. Such a high level of popular expectations and low level of popular patience made a hard line in foreign affairs increasingly probable in 1945 and 1946.

The third element in America's postwar policy was Truman's personal inclination toward a hard line. By temperament, he was a fighter. Reporting his first sharp exchange with Soviet Foreign Minister Molotov, Truman wrote with obvious relish, "I gave it to him straight 'one-two to the jaw.' " The same man who thoroughly enjoyed his "Give 'em Hell, Harry" campaign for the presidency in 1948 also found it natural to "get tough" with the Russians in 1945 and 1946. In a characteristically Truman manner, the President wrote his secretary of state in January 1946, "I'm tired of babying the Soviets." Moreover, Truman took pride in his ability to reach a decision promptly, then hold to it firmly. After a meeting with J. Robert Oppenheimer over the moral implications of the atomic bomb, the President snapped: "Don't ever bring the damn fool in here again. He didn't set that bomb off. I did. This kind of snivelling makes me sick." With the unyielding Russians on one side and the pugnacious Truman on the other, the possibilities of a compromise were always slender.

Truman's advisers made the fourth contribution to America's postwar foreign policy. In his bewildering first months as President, Truman had three groups of counselors in foreign affairs. He inherited one group from the Roosevelt administration. Secretary of War Henry Stimson, Secretary of Commerce Henry Wallace, and Roosevelt's personal aide Harry Hopkins all considered themselves experts in world affairs. Whenever they looked at Truman, they saw the giant shadow of FDR behind him. Understandably, the new President found it hard to fit these advisers into a distinctively Truman administration, and one by one they dropped away. Hopkins and Wallace, who shared Roosevelt's optimism about postwar cooperation between the United States and the Soviet Union, were particularly unhappy about Truman's hard line with Stalin. By the fall of 1945, Hopkins was lamenting, "we are doing almost everything we can to break with Russia, which seems so unnecessary to me." After a long period of strain, Wallace finally cut his ties with the Truman administration in September 1946, when he declared in an important speech: " 'Getting tough' never brought anything real and lasting—whether for school yard bullies or businessmen or world powers. The tougher we get, the tougher the Russians will get."

By choice, Truman turned for advice to a group of political associates from his days in Congress. One of these, James Byrnes, became secretary of state in July 1945. Following an impressive career in Congress, on the Supreme Court, and as "Assistant President" in charge of America's wartime mobilization, Byrnes took his new office on the assumption that he would guide both the President and the nation into the postwar world. Though Byrnes was a firm anticommunist, he was also a bargainer. As a professional politician, he had emphasized mediation and adjustment, not flat commands. As secretary of state, he preferred a similar approach. In his scheme of things, Stalin was the international counterpart to a stubborn city boss. As long as Byrnes prevailed, an element of flexibility remained in America's relations with the Soviet Union.

Discreetly at hand stood a third group of advisers, whose base of operations was the State Department. As America's world affairs increasingly demanded a wider range of diplomatic services, the State Department emerged as a significant center of government power, with extensive connections in those business, military, and publishing circles that affected its work. The expanding department attracted an able and strong-minded set of leaders, including W. Averell Harriman, the son of a railroad magnate and ambassador to Great Britain and the Soviet Union, George Kennan, a career diplomat with special talents as a writer and planner, and Dean Acheson, a wellborn lawyer who had found his true calling in the State Department. Through such men as Harriman, Kennan, and Acheson, the department offered Truman something that his other advisers failed to provide, the outlines for a systematic world policy.

As the leaders in the State Department interpreted Soviet behavior, the Russians were following a long-term plan to destroy all capitalist societies. Communist ideology made them fanatics. Despite the needs of their war-ravaged nation, Soviet officials kept a large army mobilized after Germany's surrender. State Department leaders thought that if weakness in a neighboring country gave the Russians the opportunity, they would brutally use this military might. The Soviet army had already attempted such a probe in Iran. From its base in Central Europe, it could strike at any time into the devastated, chaotic nations of Western Europe. To counter this broad threat, the United States, too, needed a long-term plan. American power had to meet Soviet power on a global scale. Otherwise, as Harriman warned, the Russians would pursue their goal of world domination by continuing to build "tiers [of satellites], layer on layer," until they crushed the forces of freedom. Only a firm stand could stop them. As the history of fascism proved, appeasement merely whetted a dictator's appetite.

By the end of 1946 as the United States hovered at a momentous turn in its foreign policy, Truman was ready to follow the State Department's guidance. Unlike Secretary Byrnes, who never completely downed a feeling that Byrnes, rather than Truman, really should have been Roosevelt's successor, the leaders in the State Department invariably acted as obedient servants. Truman, who came to take great pleasure in his office, resented his secretary's independent ways and welcomed this respectful advice from the State Department. With the patrician Dean Acheson, the earthy President developed a beautifully synchronized relationship. Above all, Truman and the department's spokesmen agreed that it was high time to get even tougher with Russia.

In January 1947, Byrnes was replaced as secretary of state by General George Marshall, a man of flawless integrity but limited imagination who funneled ideas from the State Department. In February, one of Roosevelt's four policemen, Great Britain, informed Washington that it was retiring from the force. American, not British, aid would have to save the conservative government in Greece, which was racked with civil war. President Truman, addressing Congress in March on aid to both Greece and Turkey, dramatically announced the new "Truman Doctrine." "At the present moment in world history nearly every nation must choose between alternative ways of life," Truman declared. One alternative was freedom and democracy.

The second way of life is based upon the will of a minority forcibly imposed upon the majority. It relies upon terror and oppression, a controlled press and radio, fixed elections, and the suppression of personal freedoms. I believe that it must be the policy of the United States to support free peoples who are resisting attempted subjugation by armed minorities or by outside pressures.

Simultaneously, the State Department was preparing strategy for a general European defense "against totalitarian pressures." The Marshall Plan, which took shape in the summer of 1947, eventually sent more than $12 billion in American aid to its European allies, including West Germany, and enabled their shattered economies to achieve a minor miracle in recovery. Though the communist nations of Europe were officially invited to participate, the price was a breach in Russia's security system for Eastern Europe. American leaders expected the Russians to refuse. Bitterly denouncing its Western enemies, the Soviet Union obliged, and it demanded the same of its own European allies. Hungary in May, then Rumania in December, fell absolutely under Russian control.

In February 1948, turmoil inside Czechoslovakia, the very symbol of a liberated Europe, allowed the Communist party there to take power. Communications across the Iron Curtain virtually ceased. That spring, rumors raced through

THE BERLIN AIRLIFT

In 1948 the Berlin airlift expressed America's resolve to
keep any further European territory from communist
control. *(Black Star.)*

Washington that a real war was imminent. Instead, between April and June 1948,
the Soviet Union cut the transportation lines to Berlin. Buried deep in the Russian section of Germany, the former capital, like the country as a whole, was
administered through zones. Now the American, British, and French zones of
Berlin were under seige. The United States responded with an impressively
organized air lift that brought essential supplies to the citizens in these isolated
zones. In May 1949, the Russians finally abandoned the blockade. More than any
other event, the Berlin Blockade seemed to verify the Truman administration's
warnings about Soviet aggression. Domestic opposition to the Cold War collapsed
beneath the weight of the blockade, and anti-Soviet sentiments spread in Western
Europe

Riding the momentum of these changes at home and abroad, the Truman
administration completed negotiations for the North Atlantic Treaty, a pact of
mutual assistance among twelve nations that was signed in April 1949.* Although

*The eleven other nations were Belgium, Canada, Denmark, England, France, Holland,
Iceland, Italy, Luxembourg, Norway, and Portugal. Greece, Turkey, and West Germany
soon joined.

the wording of the treaty was general, almost everyone interpreted it as the guarantee of American military support in case of a Soviet attack in Europe. In January 1949, Dean Acheson, the primary architect of Truman's European program, became secretary of state and received proper credit for this sweeping commitment of American power. Meanwhile, the Federal Republic of Germany emerged out of the western zones of occupation and was set on its way to independence. To each of these steps, the Soviet Union responded with a countermeasure: the German Democratic Republic in the east, then the Warsaw Pact with its European satellites.

With breathtaking speed, the United States had fundamentally changed its role as a peacetime world power. Between March 1947 and April 1949, an entire structure of precedents collapsed. During the rise of fascism in the 1930s, the United States had withdrawn more and more tightly into the Western Hemisphere. Now through the Truman Doctrine, the United States made an open-ended offer of assistance to nations everywhere in the world. Instead of demanding payment of its war debts, as the United States had done after the First World War, the government devised the Marshall Plan to underwrite the economies of Western Europe. In 1940, even the fall of continental Europe had not brought the United States into the Second World War. In 1948, danger to the single city of Berlin threatened to trigger a third world war. In 1927, Americans had shied away from a simple bilateral renunciation of war with France. In 1949, the North Atlantic Treaty placed eleven other nations under the shelter of American power.

In spite of these profound changes, however, the United States still did not have a clear foreign policy. What areas of the world did the Truman Doctrine cover? Under Acheson's guidance, the Truman administration concentrated on Europe and left the rest of the world in limbo. How did the United States plan to defend the nations that fell under its protection? No one expected American troops to spread throughout the world. Some people, including the influential columnist Walter Lippmann, hoped that American economic aid would enable groups of nations to organize their own regional leagues of defense. In his inaugural address of 1949, the President encouraged this kind of vision. "Point Four" of that address raised the possibility of exporting more technological skills and fewer weapons to the world's needy nations.

Two critical events of 1949 underlined the importance of these unresolved problems. One occurred in Asia, where Mao Tse-tung's Communists poured out of Manchuria, drew popular support as they moved, and swept through China, driving Chiang Kai-shek's tattered remnants to the island of Formosa (Taiwan). Even before the end of the Second World War, American officials began their futile attempts to mediate between Chiang's Nationalists and Mao's Communists. Special American missions, including a highly publicized one in 1945 and 1946 under General Marshall, warned Chiang about the corruption in his government, dangled the prospect of economic assistance before the two camps, and struggled to arrange a truce between their armies. Unwilling to force a compromise on

Chiang yet unable to intervene effectively in his behalf, the United States invested some military aid and much larger amounts of hope in his cause. By 1949, the Truman administration could only say that its tactics had not worked.

The old American assumption that China held the key to all Asia exposed the Truman administration to charges of criminal neglect. Because America was the world's preeminent power, many argued, it could have saved China. By a reasonable construction of the Truman Doctrine, the United States should have. Instead, a vast territory and huge population had fallen to the enemy. Adding China to the Soviet sphere in Eastern Europe produced an appalling total effect. Simple maps blacked out the recent losses, and simple arithmetic summarized the human costs. When Congressman Richard Nixon of California totaled the people inside and outside the communist domain, he concluded that "in 1944 . . . the odds were 9 to 1 in our favor. Today . . . the odds are 5 to 3 against us."

Before the communist victory in China, Americans had been comforted by the belief that people elsewhere, once free to choose, would select something like the American way. The struggle against evil persisted, but as that sturdy liberal senator, Robert Wagner of New York, said, "History is on our side." In the administration's most cogent justification for the Truman Doctrine, George Kennan of the State Department relied on these premises to outline what would happen if the United States applied a steady, patient pressure along the perimeter of the com-

PRESIDENT TRUMAN WITH DEAN ACHESON ON HIS RIGHT AND
GEORGE MARSHALL ON HIS LEFT

The creators of America's containment policy remained in office to grapple with the Korean War. *(Wide World.)*

munist sphere. In time, the communist domain would erode from its own weaknesses, and gradually more and more people would select freedom. The Chinese Revolution struck at the heart of this faith. For another quarter-century, the United States not only refused to recognize the communist government of China; many Americans also clung to the belief that the Chinese, given a choice, would still follow the tough old warlord Chiang.

The second critical event of 1949 was the detonation of an atomic bomb by the Soviet Union. In 1945 and 1946, mutual distrust between the United States and the Soviet Union destroyed the chances for an international control over atomic weapons. The bomb remained exclusively American, and its monopoly enabled the United States to expand its international commitments without spreading its military forces abroad. The Truman Doctrine seemed to say that American aid alone could protect its allies. The bomb would deter a large-scale Soviet intervention. A few months before the Soviet's atomic test, Secretary Acheson told the Senate Foreign Relations Committee that the North Atlantic Treaty Organization (NATO) would require no more than token American soldiers in Europe. Truman gave this claim the ring of truth in 1949 by insisting on a reduced military budget. No American leader seriously contemplated using the bomb. Nor did any of them want the monopoly broken. Just having the bomb was enough.

How thoroughly the United States had relied on its monopoly in atomic weapons became clear after that monopoly was broken. The United States itself was suddenly, terribly vulnerable. America's new security program for Europe no longer had teeth. In the scramble for alternatives, some government officials actually did suggest a preemptive atomic strike at the Soviet Union. Moreover, if Soviet society was inherently inferior, as Americans had been repeatedly told, how had it manufactured its own bomb so soon? Spies must have stolen American secrets. The Federal Bureau of Investigation proceeded to uncover Julius and Ethel Rosenberg, who were charged with passing information about the bomb to the Soviet Union, found guilty, and executed. Judge Irving Kaufman who sentenced the Rosenbergs to death in 1951, expressed the anger of a nation that had been stripped of its primary protection:

. . . your conduct in putting into the hands of the Russians the A-bomb . . . has already caused, in my opinion, the Communist aggression in Korea, with the resultant [American] casualties exceeding fifty thousand and who knows but that millions more of innocent people may pay the price of your treason. Indeed, by your betrayal you undoubtedly have altered the course of history. . . .

Containment, 1950–1953

The Korean War, beginning in June 1950, completed America's global policy of "containment." As the problems of 1949 demonstrated, neither the geographical extent of America's anticommunism nor the methods enforcing it had been carefully examined. Without firm solutions on both of these issues, the

United States would continue to stumble from incident to incident. Appropriately, the place of decision was East Asia, where the Chinese Revolution had just forced Americans to rethink both the scope and the tactics of their foreign policy.

In 1945, during the Soviet Union's brief war against Japan, Russian troops moved across Manchuria into the Korean peninsula before American troops could land from the sea. The two armies hastily agreed to occupy northern and southern halves of the peninsula, divided at the 38th parallel, until their governments could settle the fate of this Japanese territory. As so often happened after the war, delays, Soviet-American tensions, and then the Cold War transformed a momentary convenience into a permanent solution. Under the auspices of the UN, which assumed responsibility for a Korean settlement, the United States backed one government in South Korea. The Soviet Union sponsored a rival government in North Korea. Each Korean government claimed the whole of the peninsula, and each was itching to fight for it. Because Korea had little significance in the complex contest between the Soviet Union and the United States, neither power closely supervised its dependent government before 1950.

As if in spite, the Korean pawns moved themselves in June 1950. Under circumstances that remain obscure, the two Korean armies clashed, and the superior northern force began rolling southward. Although the Truman administration had not prepared for a crisis in Korea, it was ready to act. After sending the South Koreans light reinforcements from Japan, the United States took advantage of Russia's absence from the Security Council of the United Nations to place America's cause under the authority of the UN. On June 27, the Security Council endorsed intervention. Officially, therefore, the United States did not fight a war in Korea; it cooperated in a UN police action.

The Shifting Front in Korea

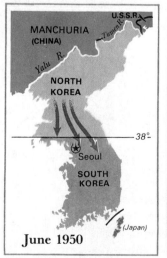 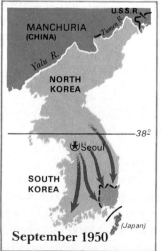 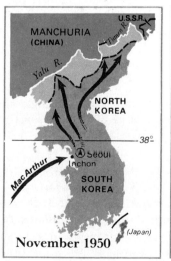 

Within a few days American troops were struggling to stem the South Korean retreat. During the summer, America's military power under General Douglas MacArthur did reverse the battle and drove the North Korean army past the 38th parallel back through its own territory to the Chinese border. The original purpose of the war had been protection of South Korea's territory. Now the goal seemed to be unification of the entire Korean peninsula. In November, large Chinese reinforcements surprised the American forces and pushed them once again below the 38th parallel. By early 1951, the war settled into a grudging, bloody struggle along the original boundary. Shortly after Eisenhower's inauguration in 1953, an armistice between the opposing armies more or less reestablished the division at the 38th parallel. A formal peace never came.

Though this stalemate war aroused widespread resentment in the United States, the range of opposition was quite narrow. Critics filled the air with might-have-beens and should-have-beens that censured Truman and Acheson as shortsighted, fumbling leaders, but they almost never questioned the appropriateness of American military intervention. Nor did the administration's critics rally much support for a big war against either China or Russia. The center of such ambitions was the imperious General MacArthur, whose belligerent and insubordinate behavior after China's entry into the war forced Truman to recall him from Korea in April 1951. As the hero of two wars and the successful director of America's occupation government in postwar Japan, MacArthur received an adoring welcome home after his recall. As the advocate of Asian conquest, however, MacArthur won no important endorsements. Even the free-swinging Joe McCarthy knew enough to avoid that crusade. In response to a thoroughly unpopular war, the large majority of Americans repudiated their President but ratified his policy.

The elections of 1952 solidified this point. Foreign policy loomed larger than in any presidential campaign since 1916, and discontent with the Korean War dominated these concerns. According to the opinion polls, only one in four Americans thought that the United States was winning the Cold War; only one in four approved of Truman's presidency. Yet neither the Republicans nor the Democrats broke from the administration's Korean policy. Both Eisenhower and Governor Adlai Stevenson supported the concept of a limited war. Both promised to settle it as promptly as possible. After declaring that he would "go to Korea" himself in an effort to end the fighting, Eisenhower took office in a climate of expectations that he, far better than Truman, could make Truman's policy work.

With the Korean War came answers to the two most perplexing questions in America's international affairs. After several years of hesitation, the government interpreted the words in the Truman Doctrine literally. Any nation willing to cooperate with America's worldwide anticommunist policy became a member of the Free World. Some of these members, such as England and Canada, were old and trusted democratic friends. Others were recent enemies. West Germany was now preparing to enter NATO. In 1951, over the vehement protests of the Soviet

Union, the United States signed a formal peace with Japan and incorporated it, along with Australia, New Zealand, and the Philippines, in America's expanding scheme of defensive alliances. Still other members of the Free World, such as Spain and South Korea, were authoritarian states. Nevertheless, as John Foster Dulles, the Republican party's leading expert on foreign affairs, said to the government of South Korea, its nation formed one "part in the great design of human freedom." Even a desire to remain neutral in the Cold War indicated an indifference to "human freedom."

Officially, every member of the Free World had equal importance in America's global policy. Before June 1950, both General MacArthur in Japan and Secretary Acheson in Washington had suggested that South Korea fell outside America's primary line of defense. War followed, and the government vowed never to repeat that mistake. Viewing the communist camp as one interrelated whole and the Free World as another, American policymakers interpreted a weakness in either bloc as the sign of greater changes to come. Yugoslavia's refusal to accept Soviet dictation after 1948, for example, kindled hopes for the

THE PENTAGON

The Pentagon in Washington was the imposing symbol of America's new military establishment, a crucial link in the containment policy. *(Library of Congress.)*

liberation of all Eastern Europe. Korea, as the expression went, pointed like a dagger at Japan. Clusters of free nations were likened to rows of dominoes, where the tipping of one toppled the rest. From these concerns came the cardinal rule that would dominate the next two decades of American foreign policy. The Free World must not relinquish a single additional piece of territory. No more Munichs; no more Chinas.

Just as firmly, the United States resolved the problem of tactics. Containment depended primarily on military power. Years of debate about the best way of assisting friendly nations ended in a resounding victory for military aid, which Congress not only increased but also distributed throughout the Free World. In Western Europe, the United States pressed its allies, including West Germany, to rearm and integrate their military strength. At home, the United States embarked on a long-range program of military preparedness that included the development of tactical units against local aggression, elaborate surveillance systems to gather military intelligence, and the construction of a far more lethal nuclear weapon, the hydrogen bomb. In addition, it explored better means for delivering a nuclear attack by air, from the sea, and through a network of foreign bases. Lacking a monopoly of nuclear weapons, Americans sought a clear military advantage over the Soviet Union, because ultimately, the proponents of containment argued, communist totalitarianism would respond only to power. The Department of Defense, which the National Security Act of 1947 had created to coordinate the army, navy, and air force, participated closely in decisions on foreign affairs. And the Central Intelligence Agency (CIA), which had also been established by the National Security Act, came of age as an important center of secret international relations.

Containment was a popular policy. An almost continuous string of international crises since the Second World War argued the necessity of a broad, consistent approach to world affairs. Moreover, Americans had several years to grow accustomed to the idea of a new policy. Beginning with the Truman Doctrine in 1947 and culminating in the Korean War, the nation's leaders prepared the way through stages of greater and greater international responsibility. Each additional step received widespread publicity and extensive explanation. By the early 1950s, a global program of military preparedness seemed the most sensible means of protecting the Free World and actually lessening the risks of nuclear holocaust.

Various groups of Americans found other reasons for endorsing containment. Intellectuals who were horrified by the communist controls over free expression welcomed the new policy. National leaders who thought naturally in terms of long-range planning and stability admired containment as an example of sound international management. Under the containment policy, corporations with foreign interests received a more consistent government support than ever before. Almost by definition, the links between American business and a foreign nation strengthened the cohesion of the Free World. Cultural and religious groups whose compatriots abroad were persecuted under communism gave containment a particularly zealous support.

Finally, containment appealed to the powerful American tradition of personal courage. The widely acclaimed movie *High Noon,* a parable on the Cold War, illustrated this connection. The hero (sober, freedom-loving America) discovered that the citizens of a western town who had once fought for their freedom (allies from the Second World War) lacked the stamina for another confrontation with a band of terrorists (fascism once, communism now). Although the hero was opposed by his pacifist bride (America's well-meaning but misguided critics of force), he knew his duty and went to meet the gunmen. At a critical moment, his bride saw the light and shot the last of the villains. The two of them (America united) then drove away, leaving the shamed townspeople with a security they had done nothing to preserve. As statesmen of the Cold War from Arthur Vandenberg to Richard Nixon said, it took "guts" to hold the line.

Government officials, citing the alternative of total war, called containment a moderate policy. Yet no one could deny that it was an astonishing departure from the past. Instead of a cautious balance between involvement and detachment, the United States had chosen wholesale, worldwide involvement. Containment required the government to concern itself not only with the foreign policy but also with the domestic affairs of a great variety of nations. In response to almost every international issue, the United States applied the same general test. What would help the communists and what would strengthen anticommunism? Critics abroad considered that test too narrow to deal with the world's diversity. America, they complained, was the first nation in history to move directly from childhood to senility in its foreign policy. But Americans replied that the solution to all other problems hinged on the outcome of this global contest between communism and freedom. There would be ample time to test these conflicting viewpoints, for the United States had set its course in world affairs for the next twenty years.

Suggested Readings

L. Ethan Ellis, *Republican Foreign Policy, 1921–1933* (1968), is a sound introduction to the postwar years. However, the most influential work on America's international affairs is William Appleman Williams, *The Tragedy of American Diplomacy* (rev. ed., 1962), an essay on the dominance of economic expansion in the nation's foreign policy. Joan Hoff Wilson's excellent book, *American Business and Foreign Policy, 1920–1933* (1971), analyzes this process of economic expansion, and Herbert Feis, *The Diplomacy of the Dollar: First Era, 1919–1932* (1950), provides insight into the State Department. Harold G. Moulton and Leo Pasvolsky, *War Debts and World Prosperity* (1932), follows a difficult subject in considerable detail. The best discussion of the London Economic Conference appears in Frank Freidel's *Franklin D. Roosevelt: Launching the New Deal* (1973). Lloyd C. Gardner's *Economic Aspects of New Deal Diplomacy* (1964) emphasizes an insatiable urge for profits.

A clear, reliable survey of United States policy in East Asia is presented in Warren I.

Cohen, *America's Response to China* (1971). Akira Iriye's *After Imperialism: The Search for a New Order in the Far East, 1921–1933* (1965) places American policy in an international setting. The crucial postwar treaties on Asia are covered in Thomas H. Buckley, *The United States and the Washington Conference, 1921–1922* (1970). In *Herbert Hoover's Latin American Policy* (1951), Alexander DeConde finds a liberalizing trend. Peter G. Filene, *Americans and the Soviet Experience, 1917–1933* (1967), traces responses from the Bolshevik Revolution to America's recognition of the Soviet Union, and Robert Paul Browder, *The Origins of Soviet-American Diplomacy* (1953), describes the frustrated hopes for economic gain accompanying recognition.

America's reaction to the early imperialist crisis in Asia is explored in Sara R. Smith, *The Manchurian Crisis, 1931–1932* (1948), Richard N. Current, *Secretary Stimson* (1954), and Robert H. Ferrell, *American Diplomacy in the Great Depression: Hoover-Stimson Foreign Policy, 1929–1933* (1957). Dorothy Borg's *The United States and the Far Eastern Crisis of 1933–1938* (1964) continues the story into the full-scale Sino-Japanese War. The title of Arnold A. Offner's *American Appeasement: United States Foreign Policy and Germany, 1933–1938* (1969), indicates the author's approach to the years when Hitler was consolidating power. Alton Frye, *Nazi Germany and the American Hemisphere, 1933–1941* (1967), minimizes Hitler's transatlantic ambitions.

The most thorough account of diplomatic events leading to the Second World War is the two-volume study by William L. Langer and S. Everett Gleason, *The Challenge to Isolation, 1937–1940* (1952), and *The Undeclared War, 1940–1941* (1953), a detailed justification of American policy. Herbert Feis, *The Road to Pearl Harbor* (1950), is a much more limited version from the same point of view, and Robert A. Divine's two volumes, *The Illusion of Neutrality* (1962) and *The Reluctant Belligerent* (1965), are only slightly more critical. In the last hurrah of a great historian, Charles A. Beard, *President Roosevelt and the Coming of the War, 1941* (1948), indicts FDR for maneuvering the nation into war. Manfred Jonas, *Isolation in America, 1935–1941* (1966), and Wayne S. Cole, *America First: The Battle against Intervention, 1941–1941* (1953), present the basic facts about the domestic opposition to the government's policies, and Warren F. Kimball, *The Most Unsordid Act: Lend-Lease, 1939–1941* (1969), discusses the issue that aroused the fiercest resistance. Complexities that the Roosevelt administration ignored are examined in Paul W. Schroeder's *The Axis Alliance and Japanese-American Relations, 1941* (1958), and the official in Tokyo who reported these complexities is the subject of Waldo H. Heinrichs, Jr., *American Ambassador: Joseph C. Grew and the Development of the United States Diplomatic Tradition* (1966). Roberta Wohlstetter, *Pearl Harbor: Warning and Decision* (1962), analyzes the controversy surrounding the Japanese strike at Hawaii.

Gordon Wright, *The Ordeal of Total War, 1939–1945* (1968), gives an overview of the European theater during the Second World War; A. Russell Buchanan, *The United States in World War II* (2 vols., 1964), covers America's military activities in both the European and the Pacific theaters. A famous naval historian, Samuel Eliot Morison, tells of the conflict at sea in *The Two-Ocean War* (1963). Morison's *Strategy and Compromise* (1958) and Kent Roberts Greenfield's *American Strategy in World War II: A Reconsideration* (1963), evaluate broad questions of military policy. Forrest C. Pogue, *George C. Marshall* (3 vols. to date, 1963–73), has followed the career of Roosevelt's chief of staff to 1945. The best introduction to America's foreign relations during these years is Gaddis Smith, *Diplomacy during the Second World War, 1941–1945* (1965). Herbert Feis, *Churchill, Roosevelt, and Stalin* (1957), examines the critical issues besetting the grand alliance. Two useful books—Robert A. Divine, *Second Chance: The Triumph of Internationalism in America during World War II* (1967), and Diane Shaver Clemens, *Yalta* (1970)—chart paths into the postwar years. Specifically on the President's leadership, the concluding volume of James MacGregor

Burns's biography, *Roosevelt: The Soldier of Freedom* (1970), finds a good deal of drift in the White House. Robert A. Divine, *Roosevelt and World War II* (1969), is a keen and generally favorable appraisal. Valuable material on two of Roosevelt's advisers appears in Robert E. Sherwood, *Roosevelt and Hopkins* (rev. ed., 1950), and John Morton Blum, ed., *From the Morgenthau Diaries: Years of War, 1941–1945* (1967). H. Bradford Westerfield, *Foreign Policy and Party Politics: Pearl Harbor to Korea* (1958), deals with the contribution of Congress. On the development of the atomic bomb, see Walter S. Schoenberger, *Decision of Destiny* (1969). Martin J. Sherwin, *A World Destroyed: The Atomic Bomb and the Grand Alliance* (1975), and Barton J. Bernstein, *The Atom Bomb: The Critical Issues* (1976), explore its international implications.

The history of the Cold War is a caldron of controversy. Two judicious guides are John Lewis Gaddis, *The United States and the Origins of the Cold War, 1941–1947* (1972), which tends to justify American policies, and Walter LaFeber, *America, Russia, and the Cold War, 1945–1966* (1967), which tends to criticize them. For a pungent taste of the battle, however, read on the one hand Herbert Feis, *From Trust to Terror: The Onset of the Cold War, 1945–1950* (1970), the last in his series of volumes explaining modern American diplomacy; and on the other hand Gabriel Kolko, *The Politics of War: The World and United States Foreign Policy, 1943–1945* (1968), and Joyce and Gabriel Kolko, *The Limits of Power: The World and United States Foreign Policy, 1945–1954* (1972), a thorough condemnation of Washington's policy. A number of careful, recent studies have added substantially to our knowledge of the critical problems dividing the United States and the Soviet Union immediately after the war: Thomas M. Campbell, *Masquerade Peace: America's UN Policy, 1944–1945* (1973), Lynn Etheridge Davis, *The Cold War Begins: Soviet-American Conflict over Eastern Europe* (1974), George C. Herring, Jr., *Aid to Russia, 1941–1946* (1973), Bruce Kuklick, *American Policy and the Division of Germany: The Clash with Russia over Reparations* (1972), and Thomas G. Paterson, *Soviet-American Confrontation: Postwar Reconstruction and the Origins of the Cold War* (1973). On issues that hardened the pattern of the Cold War, see Joseph I. Lieberman, *The Scorpion and the Tarantula: The Struggle to Control Atomic Weapons, 1945–1949* (1970), W. Phillips Davison, *The Berlin Blockade* (1958), and Robert E. Osgood, *NATO* (1962). The origins and the course of America's postwar policy in East Asia are discussed in Kenneth E. Shewmaker, *Americans and Chinese Communists, 1927–1945* (1971), Herbert Feis, *The China Tangle* (1953), Tang Tsou, *America's Failure in China, 1941–1950* (1963), and Akira Iriye, *The Cold War in Asia* (1974).

Lloyd C. Gardner, *Architects of Illusion: Men and Ideas in American Foreign Policy, 1941–1949* (1970), is a perceptive essay on the men who won control of America's postwar foreign policy, and Thomas G. Paterson, ed., *Cold War Critics: Alternatives to American Foreign Policy in the Truman Years* (1971), is a collection of essays on the men who lost. Additional information on the shapers of American policy appears in George Curry, "James F. Byrnes," in Vol. 14 of *American Secretaries of State and Their Diplomacy* (1965), Robert H. Ferrell, *George C. Marshall* (1966), which is Vol. 15 of the same series, Gaddis Smith, *Dean Acheson* (1972), which is Vol. 16, and Arnold A. Rogow, *James Forrestal* (1964), a study of the first secretary of defense. The writings of the participants themselves include these particularly useful books: Dean Acheson, *Present at the Creation* (1969), Lucius Clay, *Decision in Germany* (1950), George F. Kennan, *Memoirs, 1925–1950* (1967), and Arthur H. Vandenberg, Jr., ed., *The Private Papers of Senator Vandenberg* (1952).

For the background to the Korean War, see Leland M. Goodrich, *Korea: A Study of U. S. Policy in the United Nations* (1956). The policy struggles accompanying the war are discussed in John W. Spanier, *The Truman-MacArthur Controversy and the Korean War* (1959), and Trumbull Higgins, *Korea and the Fall of MacArthur* (1960). The indefatigable journalist I. F. Stone raises some intriguing questions in *Hidden History of the Korean War* (1952).

34

The Consequences of Modernization

The process of modernization that dominated American history during the second quarter of the twentieth century was also a process of nationalization. Modern politics drew more and more problems, and hence more and more public attention, into the orbit of *national* affairs. America's modern culture established *national* values in such areas as the meaning of success, the right to a private freedom, and the way to rear children, and it gave *national* voice to the plight of the individual in modern society. As international turmoil was producing America's worldwide policy of containment in the late forties and early fifties, foreign affairs became a matter of general *national* importance.

By the early 1950s, these modernizing, nationalizing forces integrated American society far more tightly than ever before. But the hope that integration meant unity, and that a united American society guaranteed a smooth, stable progress, proved to be illusory. Instead, nationalization created a critical imbalance in the lives of a growing number of Americans. New national rules in racial and cultural affairs threatened the traditional local autonomy of millions of white citizens. Other Americans rebelled against the nation's extensive international involvements, particularly its war in Viet Nam. Still others believed that nationalization was crushing them as individuals.

"National" usually meant "the national government." Just as Washington had become the center for more and more of the ambitions in modern America, so it now became the focus for more and more of the discontents with modern society. Nationalization, in other words, politicized America's hopes and hates. Even those who feared for their survival as individuals increasingly blamed their problems on the policies of the national government. During the late 1960s, a powerful surge of these many emotions poured into national politics and precipitated a crisis. The nation's political leaders had their hands full just trying to identify what had gone wrong, and at the end of the sixties, it was still not clear that they would be able to surmount this crisis.

Unity and Progress

In retrospect, Americans tended to scorn the 1950s as a time of mass conformity and bad taste. Where was the urge to reform, they asked? Did people want nothing more than a house in the suburbs and a job with a pension? What kind of standards glorified plastic, chrome, and neon? Questions like these missed too much of the decade. The 1950s, like the 1920s, were years of fulfillment. The large problems of the past seemed to be solved. As the bitter strikes and angry rhetoric of the postwar years subsided, so did most worries about a selfish, fragmented society. Despite two recessions during the decade, the

SUBURBAN DEVELOPMENT

Sometimes the sewers went in and sometimes they did not, but in the 1950s nothing could halt the stampede to the suburbs. (*State Historical Society of Wisconsin.*)

GNP rose by 50 percent. Never before had America offered its citizens such a grand array of services for their health, welfare, and pleasure. Echoing the claims of the 1920s, the publicist Peter Drucker told Americans that their society had passed *"beyond Capitalism and Socialism."* Millions believed that in solving the problems of the past, they had also learned how to solve the problems of the future. Not only had they constructed the good society; they knew how to maintain it as well.

This sense of control over America's destiny drew on three primary sources of strength. One was the resurgence of mass consumerism. After the economic frustrations of the Great Depression and the material shortages of the Second World War, the consumer extravaganza of the 1950s gave Americans their most persuasive evidence of a healthy, progressive society. In a variety of ways, its effects seemed increasingly democratic and unifying. The sheer quantity of services and goods suggested a more democratic consumer market. By the 1950s, leisure activities were absorbing 15 percent of the GNP. Between 1945 and 1957, the amount of consumer credit rose a breathtaking 800 percent, and as it swelled, it brought a full complement of revolving charge accounts, easy payment plans, and credit cards. The widespread use of such light, relatively inexpensive materials as plastics, aluminum, and transistors reinforced the belief in consumerism's democratic qualities. Not only did these new materials expand the range of inexpensive goods; they created a mass market for the duplicates of goods that

had once been luxury items, like silk stockings and fine-grained furniture. Because cheaper materials led to a much more rapid turnover of approximately the same products, critics complained of a shabby industrial policy of "planned obsolescence." All Americans felt the consequences in such mundane ways as the accumulation of consumer trash and the decline in repair services. But these were side effects that the consumer society of the 1950s appeared quite willing to tolerate.

Another sign of democratization was the nationwide rush to the suburbs. An extensive development of urban highways and a record level of automobile sales enabled many different kinds of Americans to pursue their dreams outside the city limits. The construction industry faced an almost insatiable demand for housing. During the depression and war years, the number of new dwellings had averaged about 300,000 a year. During the fifties, the average ran almost four times higher. Instead of the "bedroom towns" of the 1920s that had relied on the services of the inner city, the suburbs of the 1950s provided their residents with an increasingly self-contained life. Business firms, following the rush to the suburbs, displayed their wares along miles of commercial avenues and inside countless shopping plazas. By the late 1960s, there were even more jobs in the suburbs than in the cities. To encompass this sprawling, cloverleaf culture, Americans used a new word, *suburbia*.

In its broad effects, the consumerism of the fifties appeared to be drawing Americans closer together. A network of highways was quickly spreading across the nation. Between 1946 and 1956, state governments tripled their investment in road construction, and the Federal Highway Act of 1956 committed the national government to subsidizing over 40,000 miles of superhighways that would connect America's major cities. In the high-powered, postwar cars, Americans found their range of travel greatly expanded. The airplane shrank distances even more dramatically. Between 1947 and 1957, as passenger service grew fourfold, the airlines became a normal, accepted means of travel. Most impressive of all, television was transformed from a curious new toy into a staple of the American home. Fourteen thousand families had TV sets in 1947; ten years later 35 million families owned them. By driving, flying, or simply watching at home, Americans were discovering one another, it was assumed. Nobody, no place, needed to be strange or distant in a land of rapid transportation and instant communication.

Moreover, Americans appeared to unite just by acting as consumers. Common cars and clothes, common houses and vacations, common foods and recreations, gave the impression of a single national commitment to the same good life. In 1933, the Roosevelt administration had issued a three-cent postage stamp to symbolize unity in a society of large, economic blocs: a farmer, a businessman, a laborer, and a housewife, each in distinctive dress, marched shoulder to shoulder "in common determination." In the consumer society of the 1950s, a comparable image of unity would have shown an assortment of shoppers in the same style of clothes filling their carts with the same standardized products.

By the 1950s, consumerism had become a way of thinking. At a Moscow trade exhibit in 1959, Vice-President Richard Nixon engaged Soviet Premier Nikita Khrushchev in a famous "kitchen debate" inside a model American home. To each of Khrushchev's arguments about the superiority of communism to capitalism, the Vice-President pointed to the consumer goods immediately at hand, and back in the United States, a large majority of Americans applauded Nixon's logic. Consumerism also enabled Americans to evaluate the state of their society. An old device, "standard of living," won a wide new popularity in the 1950s because it could survey the entire population by measuring consumption. How much could a family purchase? What way of life did these purchases represent? How did one family's purchases compare with the purchases of other families? Standard of living and its cousin, "cost of living," became the most common American techniques for identifying public problems and formulating their solutions.

A second broad source of public confidence was faith in the experts. Following the awesome discoveries in atomic physics, the mass distribution of "wonder drug" antibiotics, and the conquest of poliomyelitis, scientists reached a new peak of prestige. More eagerly than ever, Americans looked to the nation's experts for personal guidance. Psychoanalysis achieved its pinnacle of popularity. Counseling specialists and home beautification advisers, tourist handbooks and sports manuals, all flourished. "Culture vultures" joined record and book clubs, studied brochures on the mysteries of painting, and subscribed to theater series so that they could experience the best of the arts. After a partial eclipse during the depression, advertising and public relations returned to full public favor. Scarcely a government program appeared without an attractive acronym like HUSKY, SHAPE, or VISTA. Farm subsidies became thrifty investments in a "soil bank," and the recession in 1953 a "rolling readjustment."

Like mass consumerism, faith in the experts had long been a standard part of modern society, and it continued to express itself in standard ways. The campaign to improve the educational system, for example, gained even greater momentum during the 1950s. Attacking the vagueness of the schools' "life adjustment" programs, reformers demanded rigorous instruction in the basic skills of the experts. Curricular "tracks" in the best suburban and private schools were linked so well with higher education that the brightest high school students, especially in science and mathematics, were able to prepare themselves for advanced college work. Between 1940 and 1960, costs per student more than quadrupled in the public schools, and expenditures in higher education rose more than sixfold. With the National Defense Education Act of 1958, the national government also invested in the education of scientists and engineers who seemed in dangerously short supply. In all, it was another impressive vote of confidence in the social value of expertise.

The distinctive new element in the 1950s was a faith in the unique powers of massed expertise. Reflecting the modern sense of an integrated society, an increasing number of Americans looked on the experts as a vast, national pool of

MAN AND MACHINE

Although very few understood the mysteries of modern technology, Americans banked their future on the computerized knowledge of the expert. *(Henri Cartier-Bresson/Magnum.)*

skills that could be used in various combinations to suit particular problems. Scientifically coordinated teams, rather than just scientifically trained individuals, held the key to the future. It required precisely such a cluster of specialists to harness the atom, to operate on the human heart, to measure public opinion, or to run a giant corporation. Moreover, these teams now had a marvelous new technological aid, the computer, which promised impartial answers to the world's most complicated questions. No lone genius could match the scientific range of computerized team research.

A gamut of images about science, management, and success was altered along with this new faith. The clearest expression of these changes came in response to America's space program. In 1957, the Soviet Union shocked Americans with the successful launching of a "Sputnik" spacecraft. After considerable public discussion about the weaknesses in American policy and technology, President John Kennedy countered the Soviet challenge in 1961 by promising to place a man on the moon before 1970. Amply financed and widely publicized, the Mercury program to orbit the earth, the Gemini program to maneuver in space, then the Apollo program to reach the moon filled the decade with televised countdowns, blastoffs, reentries, and splashdowns. Americans of all ages watched with fascination as scurrying teams of specialists readied the crafts and clicking computers monitored their flights. The climax of the Apollo flights occurred on July 20, 1969, as Neil Armstrong descended to the surface of the moon before a billion television witnesses, declaring it "one small step for man, one giant leap for mankind."

In the midst of these extremely intricate operations sat the crews of astronauts—trained, disciplined, yet relaxed. They were the group heroes of the 1960s. Even their personalities seemed to merge into a composite of the healthy, balanced American male. Various Americans saw what they wanted in the flight of the astronauts: the interplanetary Western, the verification of a science-fiction future, the triumph of ordinary American virtues, or the waste of national resources. For a good many Americans, however, the astronauts exemplified the values of massed expertise. In the 1920s, the nation had idolized Charles Lindbergh as the "Lone Eagle" who transcended his impersonally organized society. Inside the fantastic gear of the space explorer, his counterparts in the 1960s were cheered for achieving glory through an incredibly complicated team effort.

A third source of confidence during the fifties was government management. Once again, the popular faith in government management derived from a modern sense of the nation's wholeness, and this vision of wholeness made Washington the natural overseer of America's welfare. Clearly, the government's most important obligation was to maintain a healthy economy. By 1954, it stood ready to fulfill this task by adjusting the national budget, funding the national debt, and controlling national monetary policies. Beyond a general obligation to the economy, however, effective government management did not require systematic plans for the entire nation. On the contrary, the government usually responded to the demands of private groups, trying to give something to all of them without capitulating fully to any one of them.

Under President Dwight Eisenhower's light rein, the government followed these guidelines at a cautious pace. Indeed, the unspectacular qualities of government during the Eisenhower years contributed to a feeling of security among the nation's major interest groups. Many businessmen who had once been mortal enemies of a big bureaucracy enjoyed easy and profitable relations with the government during the fifties. Farm groups, after being frightened in 1953 by talk of a free market for agricultural products, soon learned that their subsidies would not disappear. During the early 1950s, as during the 1940s, the debates over farm policy mostly revolved around the exact level of government price supports for specific agricultural products. Farm groups continued to seek a guarantee of "parity," which was their estimate of a just price for their output. Then in 1956, the emphasis in farm policy shifted with the introduction of the soil bank, a government program that paid farmers to remove land from cultivation. For those scientifically advanced farmers who could grow more and more on less and less acreage, the soil bank proved a bonanza. The merger of the AFL and the CIO in 1955 under a tough, conservative president, George Meany, strengthened the political position of a third set of interests, organized labor. Although most unions were unenthusiastic about the Eisenhower administration itself, the AFL-CIO continued to have many allies in Congress. Minor restrictions on their financial affairs in the Landrum-Griffin Act of 1959, like the earlier restrictions in the Taft-Hartley Act, scarcely affected the unions' policies.

Changes in government management reflected the changes in American society. As the importance of the experts and mass consumerism rose, for example, government officials grew more sensitive to their needs. By the early 1950s, physicists, chemists, biologists, engineers, hospital administrators, and a variety of other scientific groups had become part of the Washington establishment. During the fifties, professionals ranging from pediatricians and vocational rehabilitaters to experts in race relations and urban planning found secure places for themselves in the government bureaucracy. The clearest new response to consumers came from the federal judiciary. In the *Schwegmann* decision of 1951, the Supreme Court struck down a basic part of the "fair trade" law of 1937, which had enabled merchants to maintain fixed retail prices regardless of the competition. When Congress enacted the new Federal Fair Trade Act in 1952, the courts made it so difficult to enforce that it steadily lost authority. By the 1960s, price-cutting retail chains and discount houses spread nationwide. Moreover, the Supreme Court also broadened the consumer's right to claim damages from the manufacturers of defective consumer products. A long tradition of legal issues between big business and small business was being overshadowed by a modern set of legal issues between business and the consumer.

No one coordinated Washington's vast apparatus of government. On paper, it looked as though the executive branch was the center of control. In 1950, Congress added to its extensive powers by giving the President the right to appoint his own chairmen to the independent regulatory commissions. Now each new administration could have an immediate influence on the policies of the "Big Six": the Civil Aeronautics Board, the Federal Communications Commission, the Federal Power Commission, the Federal Trade Commission, the Interstate Commerce Commission, and the Securities and Exchange Commission. Then in 1953, the new Department of Health, Education and Welfare (HEW) combined a great variety of services and programs under one executive chief. Nevertheless, the larger the executive branch grew, the more its authority was scattered among innumerable offices and subdivisions. As powerful a politician as President Eisenhower's principal domestic aide, Sherman Adams, could do no more than respond to the issues of government one at a time as they came to him. Fortunately for the President, the tests of good management required only a strong economy and a satisfied constituency of private interest groups. By these standards, the government functioned very well during the 1950s. Although Americans often grumbled about incompetent bureaucrats, they generally approved the results of bureaucratic government.

World Order

In foreign policy, as in domestic affairs, the United States presented a new face of national unity and common purpose during the fifties. After the Korean War, no significant group of Americans challenged the basic outlines of the nation's containment policy. Both Republicans and Democrats defined international communism as a worldwide conspiracy that was directed from its headquarters in

Moscow. The United States, they told the nation, must gird for a long, taxing struggle against the enemy.

The consensus on foreign policy covered strategy as well. Containment envisaged a worldwide league of so-called free nations encircling communist territory and sealing off its avenues of expansion. To complete this circle, the United States negotiated a variety of agreements with nations outside Europe. The most ambitious of these was the Southeast Asia Treaty Organization (SEATO) of 1955, which allied France, Great Britain, and the United States with Australia, New Zealand, Pakistan, the Philippines, and Thailand. In addition, the United States encouraged its allies in the Middle East to form the Central Treaty Organization (CENTO) of 1959.* As some critics promptly noted, neither organization was strong or comprehensive. Of the countries on the mainland of Southeast Asia, only Thailand entered SEATO. No Arab nation belonged to CENTO. Nevertheless, in combination with the North Atlantic Treaty Organization (NATO), these treaties formed a symbolic global ring around the communist domain. Formidable or not, they were a logical expression of containment's purposes.

America's reliance on military power to contain communism went almost unchallenged. Although Democrats and Republicans hotly debated the adequacy of each other's defense proposals, they were trying to prove themselves even more committed than their opponents to military preparedness. The Eisenhower administration, borrowing a term from women's fashions, proposed a "New Look" in America's military program. Politically, it appealed to the economy-minded, who were promised, in Secretary of Defense Charles Wilson's blunt phrase, "more bang for the buck." But militarily, the New Look represented only a slight shift away from ground and naval forces in favor of air and missile power. Some critics of the New Look, such as Professor Henry Kissinger of Harvard University, charged that the Eisenhower administration's heavy reliance on nuclear weapons removed too much flexibility from the nation's military policy and left it unable to meet a variety of small, local communist thrusts. Other critics, including Senator John Kennedy of Massachusetts, warned of a general decline in the nation's military power. Not many Americans paid attention to these complaints, and not much changed after Kennedy became President in 1961.

The popular confidence in containment relied on a broad faith in government management and massed expertise. The wonders of science figured just as prominently in international as in national affairs. The latest developments in ballistic missiles, supersonic jets, and nuclear-powered submarines became standard parts of the American vocabulary and standard images of American defense. Under President Eisenhower, the United States established a worldwide, electronic Distant Early Warning System (DEW Line) that would alert the nation's

---

*The members of CENTO were Great Britain, Iran, Pakistan, and Turkey.

military power in case of an enemy attack. Under President Kennedy, a "Hot Line" was installed in 1963 to provide instant communication between the White House and the Kremlin in case of the ultimate emergency. Abroad as at home, skillful managers plus modern technology equaled national security.

But foreign and domestic affairs were linked by much more than this abiding faith in managers and experts. Unlike any other peacetime era, military expenditures now dominated the national budget. Their size alone, fluctuating around 60 percent of the government's total costs, made military expenditures crucial to maintaining a healthy economy. In addition, the government's military contracts were concentrated in the scientifically sophisticated areas of industry. Directly or indirectly, the military program financed the research behind America's most important technological innovations. Moreover, such giant corporations as General Electric, General Motors, and Douglas Aircraft subcontracted portions of their military work, creating a much wider web of economic dependence around the government's initial investment. If the government terminated a big defense contract, therefore, it might send shock waves through a large section of the economy and undo the government's efforts to sustain prosperity.

A former general first popularized the phrase that most Americans used to describe these arrangements. President Eisenhower, always unhappy over the accumulation of power in Washington and always skeptical of budget demands from the military, devoted part of his final State of the Union address to warn the nation about this "military-industrial complex." During the sixties, more and more Americans came to picture the military-industrial complex as a diabolical force directing the nation's foreign policy. Actually, the government awarded military contracts in the same piecemeal fashion as it did the rest of its benefits, and the military-industrial complex remained much too decentralized to act in concert. But the sum of its influences was profound. In the past, mobilizing the nation for war had disrupted the economy. Now disarming the nation for peace threatened to disrupt the economy even more.

"Multinational" corporations formed a second new strand connecting the domestic economy with world affairs. Before the Second World War, almost all the subdivisions that American corporations established abroad had remained small dependent outposts of the parent companies. After the Second World War, however, corporate expansion entered a new phase. From soft drinks to automobiles to electronics, American industries gravitated to the capital-poor nations of the postwar world, where production costs were low, governments encouraging, and ready markets inviting. Even more important than the quantity of foreign subsidiaries were their special qualities. An increasing proportion of them duplicated the parent company's full corporate structure and dropped roots in the societies where they were planted. By the 1950s, these corporate offshoots were thriving on every continent, with a particularly large number in Canada and the economically advanced countries of Western Europe. Still tied to their parent companies in the United States yet assimilated into the lives of foreign nations, they gave a new transnational cast to the American economy.

Multinational corporations were only the most striking part of a massive business expansion after the Second World War. In 1946, America's private investments abroad approximated their level in 1929. During the next decade, foreign investments tripled. By the end of the 1960s, they stood almost ten times higher than in 1946. Much of this money went in search of minerals that the United States either lacked or used at a faster rate than it produced. Oil alone accounted for more than a third of these investments. The spread of American capital abroad, taken as a whole, expressed the economy's increasing dependence on resources and markets and government policies around the world.

A clear purpose in international affairs, a managerial approach to international problems, and a growing economic stake in international stability all contributed to the continuity in American foreign policy during the Eisenhower and Kennedy administrations. John Foster Dulles, who as secretary of state between 1953 and 1959 was largely responsible for the conduct of American policy, moved naturally with these currents. His experience in diplomacy began in 1907. As Eisenhower commented, only half in jest, "Foster has been studying to be secretary of state since he was five years old." During his legal career Dulles had worked sympathetically with some of America's most internationally oriented businessmen. Moreover, he was religiously anticommunist.

Foreign affairs continued to follow the primary lesson of the Truman years: lose no more people or territory to communism. Secretary Dulles subscribed so deeply to this lesson that he was willing to risk thermonuclear war in its behalf. To resolve any doubts on the subject, Dulles reminded the world in January 1954 that behind America's policy lay a "great capacity to retaliate, instantly, by means and at places of our own choosing." The first test of the secretary's "brinkmanship" began only a few months later in 1954. China opened a bombardment of several islands less than ten miles from its coast that Chiang Kai-shek, over a hundred miles away on Formosa (Taiwan), had fortified as his outposts. In the Formosa Resolution of January 1955, Congress authorized the President to protect both Formosa and these offshore islands. For brief periods in 1955 and again in 1958, there was at least a possibility of thermonuclear war over two rocky dots in the Formosa Strait named Quemoy and Matsu. But China did not press the attack, and the principle of containment was preserved.

Far closer to home, another crisis arose as Eisenhower was completing his second term. In 1959, an intensely nationalistic and charismatic Cuban, Fidel Castro, toppled the dictator Fulgencio Batista and set about breaking Cuba's economic dependence on the United States. Castro's assertiveness and Washington's hostility to his revolution produced a quick rupture. The Eisenhower administration established the main lines of a policy that its successor then continued: an economic boycott of Cuba, an attempt to isolate it politically in the Western Hemisphere, and an encouragement for Cuban counter-revolutionaries. There were also secret American plans to assassinate Castro. Castro came to rely

FIDEL CASTRO AND
NIKITA KHRUSHCHEV.

It was a happy moment for Castro
and Khrushchev but an ominous
one in Washington, where their
embrace was interpreted as a
grave threat to containment.
(Wide World.)

much more on Soviet assistance than he had anticipated, and soon the Cuban government formally committed itself to communism. Not only had the cardinal rule of containment been violated; the breach had occurred just off the Florida coast.

Castro became an American obsession. President Kennedy, who controlled his administration's foreign policy and shared Dulles's commitment to containment, entered office in 1961 with a powerful urge to eliminate Castro. When the CIA promised a successful counterrevolution in Cuba if it could only land a cadre of Castro's opponents on the island, Kennedy allowed the CIA to continue training a small army of Cuban émigrés in preparation for such an attack. On April 17, 1961, an ill-equipped émigré force of 1400 made a disastrous thrust at Cuba through the Bay of Pigs, where the invaders and America's reputation promptly sank together. As sponsor of the invasion, the United States was guilty of violating another nation's basic rights. As manager of America's foreign policy, the President was vulnerable to charges that he had done either too much or too little in assisting the émigré army.

The Bay of Pigs was background to a much graver crisis a year later. After the émigré attack, both Castro and Soviet Premier Khrushchev, a tough but erratic gambler, calculated that missile bases in Cuba would improve their bargaining positions with the United States. Secretly, a flow of Soviet materials and technicians began moving by supply ships to Cuba. American intelligence learned about the missile sites in 1962 as they were being constructed. The existing arsenals of intercontinental missiles defined the balance of military power between the Soviet Union and the United States, and Soviet missiles in Cuba did not alter that balance. As one American official phrased it, the Cuban missile sites had a "psychological and political rather than military" meaning. Kennedy, rejecting advice to bomb the sites at once, announced on October 22, 1962, that the United States would set a naval blockade around Cuba and demanded an immediate halt to the missile traffic. The world held its breath. Then a day after the blockade went into effect a dozen Soviet supply ships turned from their course and went home. Russia dismantled the bases, America promised to honor Cuba's sovereignty, and in the United States, Kennedy emerged from the ordeal a hero.

Khrushchev also designated another point of crisis. The rough-hewn Soviet premier came to full power in 1958 determined to break the stalemate of the Cold War. He especially bridled at the impasse over Berlin, the sole Western outpost in the Soviet sphere. In an effort to force a new settlement for Berlin, he not only threatened to restrict Western access to the city, he declared that the Soviet Union and East Germany might have to decide Berlin's future by themselves. Off and on between 1958 and 1962, that isolated city once again became a potential center of war. The peak of danger occurred in the summer and fall of 1961, when the communists erected a wall across Berlin to seal their section of the city. Kennedy responded with the preliminary moves toward a war mobilization. The President called for military reserves, increased civil defense, and reinforced the American garrison in Berlin. Although the Berlin Wall remained, the crisis passed. By 1962, neither side wanted to press the other on the issue of Berlin.

In each area of crisis—the offshore islands, Cuba, and Berlin—the United States basically sought to preserve the status quo. Indeed, American policy expressed a general opposition to major changes and upheavals. In 1958, that urge led Eisenhower to land fourteen thousand American troops in Lebanon, in an attempt to keep the bitter, tangled rivalries of the Middle East from toppling governments that were friendly to the United States. Between 1960 and 1964, a similar impulse lay behind the financial and diplomatic assistance that the United States gave to a United Nations police force in the Congo (Zaire), where a chaotic civil war was racking this former Belgian colony. American policy outside of Europe was accurately described as antirevolutionary. In even broader terms, it was antidisruptive. In July 1956, for example, President Gamal Nasser of Egypt vented his anger at the Western powers by seizing the Suez Canal. From a mixture of motives and a mistaken impression that the United States would support them, England, France, and Israel coordinated military forces in October to humble Nasser and retake the canal. The United States, however, broke from its

BUILDING THE BERLIN WALL

With the wall came the threat of war.
(Magnum.)

allies. Coldly cooperating with the Soviet Union, the Eisenhower administration worked through the United Nations to halt the war and return the canal to Egypt.

This strong desire to stabilize international affairs tempered America's foreign policy throughout the Eisenhower and Kennedy years. Despite loose Republican promises during the 1952 campaign to "roll back the iron curtain" in Europe and "unleash" Chiang Kai-shek's army on China, the Eisenhower administration carefully avoided either course. When East Germans rioted in 1953 and Hungarians revolted against their government in 1956, the United States did nothing to provoke a wider conflict. In East Asia, the United States made an explicitly defensive treaty with Formosa in 1955, and on several other occasions Secretary Dulles assured Americans that the leash on Chiang Kai-shek was very tight indeed. Eastern Europe and China, already lost to the enemy, would have to await the long-range successes of containment.

The longer America's containment policy lasted, the more it acquired the characteristics of a ceaseless international game that should be played according to a careful set of rules. The first, tentative moves to regularize the competition of the Cold War occurred soon after President Eisenhower took office. Stalin's death in 1953, coinciding with a new administration in Washington, reopened the possibility for some exchange between the Soviet and American governments, which since 1947 had been yelling at one another half way around the world. Very gingerly, diplomats from the two superpowers began to explore a number of delicate problems, including a settlement for Germany and a limitation on armaments. In 1955, they actually signed a peace treaty for Austria.

The symbol of hope for a new era of "peaceful coexistence" was the summit conference between Soviet and American heads of state, comparable to the ones Roosevelt, Churchill, and Stalin had held during the Second World War. World-wide pressures for such a conference grew too strong for either great power to resist. In July 1955, for the first time in ten years, the President of the United States and the Premier of the Soviet Union, along with their counterparts from Britain and France, sat down together at a meeting in Geneva. Less formally, Eisenhower and Khrushchev met again at Camp David, Maryland, in September 1959. Although Americans spoke optimistically about a new "spirit of Geneva" in 1955 and then a new "spirit of Camp David" in 1959, the next two summit conferences were disasters. Just before an eagerly anticipated meeting at Paris in 1960, an American U-2 spy plane had been downed far inside Russia and its pilot, Francis Gary Powers, displayed to the world as proof of America's hostile intentions. Khrushchev's angry attacks at Eisenhower wrecked the Paris meeting. Then at Vienna in 1961, the distrust between Khrushchev and Kennedy ruined the chances for an effective conference. For a time, the vogue of the summit ended.

Nevertheless, the underlying forces for stabilization continued to operate. Both the United States and the Soviet Union found the management of their inter-national spheres a complicated, frustrating, and expensive task. Both had poor success appealing to the so-called neutral countries outside the two spheres. Both were deeply committed to consumer satisfactions at home. Moreover, as the weapons of nuclear annihilation piled higher and higher in the arsenals of both nations, their leaders were to some degree sobered by the incredible power they could unleash. "We have arrived at that point," Eisenhower acknowledged in 1954, "where war does not present the possibility of victory or defeat." His counterpart in the Soviet Union, Georgi Malenkov, had already admitted as much a year earlier. Each of these parallel developments applied a slight brake of caution to the diplomacy of the Cold War. Gradually, the trends seemed to be moving from a volatile Cold War to a predictable Cold Peace.

Presidential Leadership

Each additional step in the process of modernization placed a heavier burden of management on the President. The responsibilities for maintaining a sound economy that had arrived with the Great Depression never left the White House. During the 1940s, world war and cold war also made the President the focus of America's international security. Although foreign affairs had traditionally been his special duty, never before had they carried such profound consequences. In

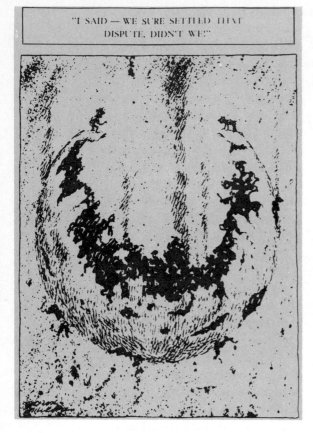

"I SAID — WE SURE SETTLED THAT DISPUTE, DIDN'T WE!"

(Frank Miller cartoon in the Des Moines Register
May 6, 1963. Wide World.)

the thermonuclear age, international relations became literally a matter of life and death. By the 1950s, the President alone seemed capable of ensuring the nation's unity, stability, and progress.

Under this massive weight of responsibilities, the meaning of the presidency changed in two important respects. First, the office was separated from the normal patterns of electoral politics. Beginning with Eisenhower's triumph in 1952, the vote for President no longer followed the same curve as the nationwide vote for other Democratic and Republican candidates. Franklin Roosevelt's rising and falling majorities had roughly paralleled the majorities of the Democratic party. Even Harry Truman's surprising victory in 1948 had coincided with a similar Democratic revival. After 1952, however, the presidential vote set a course of its own. In 1954, the Democrats recaptured both houses of Congress and continued to hold them, usually by substantial majorities. By contrast to this steady, partisan line, the presidential returns swung in big loops that expressed specific, quadrennial choices between individuals.

As Americans detached their President from party politics, they were developing a new relation with him that had relatively little to do with the electoral process. Its crucial components were television and national opinion polls. The President spoke personally to all the people through television; they responded directly to him through opinion polls. The entire nation and America's indispensable leader, it seemed, were engaged in a unique, continuous dialogue. A presidential election was merely the most formal and dramatic moment in the dialogue. Between elections, a string of opinion polls charted results that were widely interpreted as substitute elections, continually measuring the success of the nation's leader. Any overwhelming endorsement of the President, such as Eisenhower's runaway victories in the 1952 and 1956 elections or Kennedy's impressive ratings in the opinion polls of 1961 and 1962, became a sign of national strength. By the same token, a sharp drop in Truman's ratings during 1951 and 1952 signaled a severe national problem. Americans, in other words, made their month-by-month judgments of the President into a bedside graph of America's health.

The second significant change in the presidency involved the requirements for effective national leadership. The complex nature of the President's tasks forced him to act simultaneously as a mobilizing leader for the whole nation and as a cautious manager of America's intricate foreign and domestic affairs. As early as the 1930s, Roosevelt had understood this need for an inspiring moderation. FDR, however, served during a bitterly partisan period when no one could hope to transcend parties and represent all the people. Moreover, his leadership was identified not with steady management but with great emergencies: depression, then war. Truman was the last of the openly partisan Presidents. The Missouri scrapper seldom allowed anyone to forget that he was a Democrat, and his quick temper, sharp tongue, and unpredictable ways clashed with the image of a smooth manager.

Eisenhower was the first to meet the modern demands on the President. The general's background allowed him to appear a man above the clamor of special interests. Each landmark in his military career—wartime commander of the Allied armies of Europe, Chief of Staff, and commander of NATO's forces— suggested the highest level of nonpartisanship. Even as President, Eisenhower liked to think of himself as a nonpartisan leader. He projected an instinctive fairness that promised to reunite the nation after the harsh years of Truman and McCarthy. Although his temper and tongue could match Truman's, Eisenhower held them in public. Eisenhower never mastered the art of a formal television speech, but he was irresistibly attractive in casual shots. His incomparable smile, strong stride, and easy yet authoritative manner made him everybody's Ike. In a special sense, Eisenhower seemed able to speak to all Americans at home and speak for them abroad.

Eisenhower strengthened his position as national leader by delegating much of the controversial work of his administration. While his secretary of state used the militant language of the Cold War, the President spoke in a moderate, conciliatory tone. The world identified Dulles with "brinkmanship." It identified Eisenhower with "Atoms for Peace," a program to share America's scientific knowledge that the President first proposed in 1953 and then elaborated in 1955. In election years, Eisenhower almost always took the high ground of broad, bland pronouncements. Vice-President Nixon was the administration's partisan voice, and every two years he flayed the Democrats with a rawhide campaign rhetoric.

The Eisenhower formula was unbeatable. In the campaign of 1956, the Democrats again set the cultivated phrasemaker Adlai Stevenson of Illinois against the President, and again Eisenhower easily defeated him, 457 electoral votes to 73. As long as Eisenhower remained in the White House, no one else seemed very important as a national leader. At the nominating conventions of 1960, the men who filled this vacuum were Richard Nixon and John Kennedy. The choice of Nixon established a logical corollary to the modern presidency. The Vice-President, borrowing a reflected glory from the nation's one, indispensable leader, became the President's natural successor. Muting his earlier partisanship, Nixon conducted his campaign like the heir apparent who would continue the

The Election of 1960

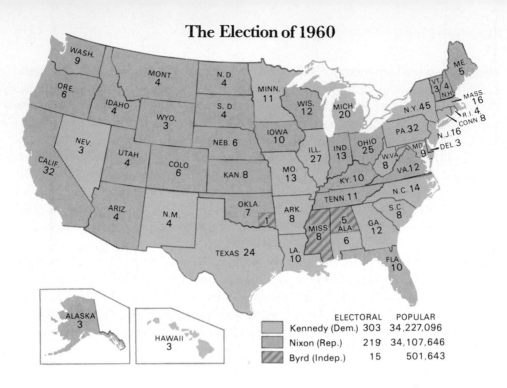

	ELECTORAL	POPULAR
Kennedy (Dem.)	303	34,227,096
Nixon (Rep.)	219	34,107,646
Byrd (Indep.)	15	501,643

policies of Eisenhower's popular rule. The Democrats, sensing the need for a new name to replace Stevenson, chose the youthful senator from Massachusetts, whose well-organized and liberally financed primary campaign gave him a considerable edge over his competitors. In the closest presidential race since the late nineteenth century, the inexperienced Kennedy received a scant 100,000 votes more than the uninspired Nixon.

When Kennedy entered the White House in 1961, the modern role of the President was already well defined. In place of his predecessor's nonpartisan background, Kennedy's large family fortune conveyed a similar detachment from the scramble of economic interests. In place of Eisenhower's reputation for fairness, Kennedy's record of personal courage in the Second World War suggested that he, too, would make a strong, even-handed leader. Like the combination of Dulles and Eisenhower, Kennedy also tried to balance militancy and moderation in his foreign policy. After the Cuban missile crisis of 1962, for example, came the Test Ban Treaty of 1963, in which the Soviet Union and the United States agreed to stop contaminating the atmosphere with their nuclear tests. Kennedy was particularly imaginative in associating the President's office with broad national goals. Under Kennedy's sponsorship, a wide assortment of studies and reports attempted to define America's primary objectives. It was Kennedy who recognized the special attraction of a journey to the moon as a truly national enterprise that would stand apart from domestic jealousies and make sense to Americans of all types and ages. Beginning in 1961, the President's Peace Corps, through which American volunteers took their skills to the world's poor nations, had a somewhat comparable appeal.

INAUGURATION OF JOHN F. KENNEDY

Presidents past and future gathered in 1961 as Chief
Justice Earl Warren administered the oath of office to John
Kennedy. Adlai Stevenson on the far left and Associate
Justice William O. Douglas on the far right, both of whom
had wanted the office, watched solemnly from the fringes.
Dwight Eisenhower, Lyndon Johnson, and Richard Nixon
stood in the front row. *(Wide World.)*

Kennedy's most impressive contributions to the new leadership involved the
intangibles of style and charm. He made a striking appearance on television, as
he had already demonstrated in his televised debates with Nixon during the 1960
campaign. As President, Kennedy continued to make excellent use of the
medium, both formally and informally. The youngest elected President in history
at forty-three, he radiated health and vigor. Appropriate to his administration's
image of youthful adventure, Kennedy's program acquired the name of the New
Frontier. At times, the handsome President's private affairs seemed to loom
larger across the nation than his public actions. Through the eager cooperation
of the news industry, the President and his stunningly attractive, photogenic
family entered everybody's lives as their familiars: Jack and his wife Jackie, their
children Caroline and John, Jr., the President's brother Bobby, and the rest of
the vibrant Kennedy clan.

Nothing better illustrated this intimate bond between Kennedy and the public
than America's response to the President's assassination in Dallas on November
22, 1963. For a long, mournful weekend, the nation immersed itself in every

detail of the tragedy and its aftermath. Through television, Americans traced the President's motorcade, saw Kennedy jarred by an explosion of shots, shared the vigil outside the hospital, witnessed the incredible murder of the prime suspect Lee Harvey Oswald, and then followed the doleful state funeral through the gray streets of Washington. No event had ever been so thoroughly national and yet so intensely personal. More than a decade later, with important questions about the assassination still unanswered, millions could re-create those "six seconds in Dallas" as if their lives, too, had hung in the balance.

After Kennedy's successor, Lyndon B. Johnson, had been in office only a few months, the Democratic party nominated him for a presidential term in his own right. Although Johnson had neither the towering prestige of Eisenhower nor the brilliant charm of Kennedy, he did have a long record of moderate congressional management and a brief but striking record of presidential leadership. To challenge Johnson in 1964, the Republicans selected the deeply conservative senator from Arizona, Barry Goldwater, along with an equally conservative candidate for Vice-President. Goldwater represented a wing of the Republican party that opposed city bosses and government bureaucrats, labor unions and farm subsidies, welfare payments and poverty programs. That fall, the Arizona senator, an honest, articulate man, spoke his mind freely. He promised thorough, drastic changes in government policy, including a considerably more aggressive foreign policy. Johnson skillfully kept his campaign within the standard presidential mold of dynamic temperateness. If anyone had doubted the popular appeal of the modern presidential model, this election must have settled the issue. In a remarkably clear contest between the images of unifying moderation and factional extremism, Johnson overwhelmed Goldwater, 43 million votes to 27 million.

The Crisis in National–Local Relations

The confidence of the fifties had created such optimism about the powers of national management that some Americans came to believe that every problem had a national, managerial solution. Most followers of this faith were successful Americans, whose careers flowed with the currents of modernization. National in orientation and outlook, they turned naturally to the government in Washington for the skills and authority necessary to solve America's problems. But a fine line separated their optimism from arrogance. As the national government enlarged the scope of its responsibilities, it generated new problems faster than it solved old ones. The first sign of these unexpected consequences appeared in an increasingly angry clash between an expansive national government and a threatened world of local white power.

One of President Eisenhower's earliest appointments was a new chief justice of the Supreme Court. He chose the affable California Republican, Earl Warren, who had been an extremely popular governor and the party's vice-presidential candidate in 1948. Although Warren was classified a "liberal Republican," he was also a skilled mediator who had no record of interest in social experimentation. He had even participated in the drive to intern Japanese Americans during the Second World War. His appointment seemed to augur a safe, middle-of-the-road Court.

As Earl Warren became chief justice in 1953, the most significant issue pending before the Supreme Court was racial segregation in the public schools. Precedents that challenged the doctrine of "separate but equal" educational facilities for blacks had been accumulating for more than a decade, but the Supreme Court had phrased them in cautious, narrow terms. Many observers expected a similar wording from the moderate new chief justice. Instead, in the unanimous decision of *Brown* v. *Board of Education* (1954), Warren boldly declared separate educational facilities inherently unequal and inhumane. The long legal march of the National Association for the Advancement of Colored People had reached its objective. At a stroke, the Court undercut the entire structure of Jim Crow laws.

SEGREGATED CAFÉ AND CIVIL RIGHTS DEMONSTRATOR

The discipline, drama, and fellowship of the civil rights movement won it nationwide support in the late fifties and early sixties. *(Left, Denny Lyman/ Magnum; right, Bruce Davidson/Magnum.)*

Few successful white Americans could debate Warren's conclusions. No ethnic standard had a logical place in their occupational world, and a rigid pattern of Jim Crow drinking fountains and bus seats seemed particularly irrational. In the postwar years, segregation had become an obvious affront to America's modern values. At home, it clashed with the ideal of an open society, in which citizens were free to acquire all the skills they could learn and buy all the goods they could earn. Abroad, it jeopardized America's chances of bringing people with brown or black or yellow skin into a worldwide anticommunist league. Prominent Southern liberals increasingly joined the critics of segregation. By the 1950s, nationally minded Americans regarded Jim Crow as an anachronism that a modern society could no longer tolerate.

They considered education an excellent place to begin racial desegregation. Because successful Americans were sensitive to the relation between skills and success, they immediately recognized the serious consequences of an inferior education. Moreover, they believed that completely dismantling the caste system would require slow, careful adjustments over many years. If children in integrated schools grew up free of prejudice, these new generations, coming one after another, would eventually eliminate the last traces of racial hate. Time and the power of education lay on the side of progress. In this spirit of optimistic caution the Supreme Court declared in 1955 that school desegregation should proceed "with all deliberate speed."

During the next decade, the conflicts over racial segregation reinforced these initial desires to abolish it. It was the opponents of segregation who could almost always claim to be law-abiding, orderly, and moderate. Southern whites, on the other hand, threw all manner of legal obstacles in the path of integration, ranging from the novel constitutional doctrine of "state interposition" between the national government and its citizens to the substitution of private segregated schools for the public system. With increasing firmness, the federal courts removed each one. In 1957, when Governor Orval Faubus of Arkansas defied a court order to desegregate the schools of Little Rock, it required a wall of soldiers to protect the thin line of black children from a taunting crowd of adult whites. Individual blacks faced a roughly comparable experience as they tried to enter the state universities in Alabama and Mississippi. In 1957 and 1960, Congress passed two mild civil rights laws that allowed the federal courts to intervene in behalf of disfranchised blacks. A number of Southern politicians reacted as if the right to vote were a subversive doctrine.

During the same years, blacks and whites also confronted each other directly over segregation. Blacks took the initiative, and their movement quickly became identified with the particular style of an intense, eloquent young minister from Montgomery, Alabama, Martin Luther King, Jr. Not yet twenty-seven years old, he emerged in 1955 as the nationally publicized leader of a local boycott against Montgomery's segregated buses. Through words and example, King provided blacks with a creative combination of the Christian love that their churches taught, the strategy of peaceful mass resistance that the Hindu, Mahatma Gandhi, had formulated, and the self-discipline that relatively well-to-do blacks had long used to defend their rights in America's caste system. While King was inspiring his fellow blacks, he was also attracting wide support among successful whites. Non-violent protest suited their standards of orderly behavior and peaceful change so well that many of them heralded King as one of America's statesmen.

In 1960, black students throughout the cities of the South applied King's tactics in a dramatic wave of "sit ins" that desegregated numerous restaurants, then a variety of other public accommodations. The following year the Congress on Racial Equality (CORE), an even older center of peaceful resistance, sponsored black and white "Freedom Riders" on a harrowing bus trip into the South that publicized the illegal segregation in interstate travel. This pillar of Jim Crow also toppled. As in the case of Little Rock, the violent responses to these protests strengthened the bond between successful whites and black moderates. In 1963, when King led a movement against segregation in Birmingham, Alabama, na-tional television vividly recorded the cattle prods, fire hoses, and snarling dogs that local police used to intimidate the blacks. Murders relating to the civil rights movement that year in Birmingham and the next summer in Mississippi could not be prosecuted in the Southern courts. King's Southern Christian Leadership Conference (SCLC) and its offspring, the Student Non-Violent Coordinating Committee (SNCC), seemed the embodiment of rationality by contrast to the revived Ku Klux Klan, the raucous rhetoric of local Southern politics, and the partiality of Southern white justice.

The accelerating pace of events gave the movement for black rights a new tempo and a new urgency. White sympathy for King's inspired moderation con-tinued to rise in the summer of 1963 when a quarter million Americans drama-tized the plight of the blacks by marching peacefully through Washington and gathering at the Lincoln Memorial. There they heard King's moving message of hope: "I have a dream that one day [in the Deep South] . . . little black boys and black girls will be able to join hands with little white boys and white girls and walk together as sisters and brothers."

What was missing was strong political leadership. The White House had largely held aloof from the civil rights movement. President Eisenhower, who later cursed his choice of Earl Warren as chief justice, stated privately "that the Supreme Court decision [on school desegregation] *set back* progress in the South at least fifteen years. . . . We can't demand *perfection* in these moral questions." No one was less happy than Eisenhower when the posturing Governor Faubus forced the President to intervene in Little Rock. Kennedy, though much less attached to local customs than his predecessor, was equally cautious as he began his term. Despite campaign promises to end racial discrimination in public hous-ing with "a stroke of the presidential pen," he delayed almost two years before signing the appropriate executive order. In 1963, Kennedy delivered an im-portant address in support of black rights and called for new legislation in their

behalf. However, Kennedy's pressure on Congress still lagged behind his words.

Lyndon Johnson filled the void in leadership. Always a restless soul, he had pushed his way out of the Texas hills as a youth, entered Congress in the 1930s, then moved up to the Senate in 1949. During Eisenhower's two terms, Johnson was generally regarded as the most powerful Democrat in Washington. An exceptionally skillful legislative director, he combined a relentless energy, a keen understanding of politics, and a driving ambition for greatness. A good many people were surprised in 1960 when Johnson accepted the nomination for Vice-President. But the shrewd Texan, who had watched Nixon step from that office to the Republican presidential nomination, knew just what he was doing.

By temperament, Johnson was always prepared to lead. With Kennedy's grave scarcely sealed in November 1963, the new President was already mobilizing for action, and during his first two years in office he compiled an astonishing record. Some of the measures he sponsored had originated with the Kennedy administration. Others were Johnson's own. Declaring a "War on Poverty," the President convinced Congress to invest billions of dollars in training the unemployed, supporting community development, reviving impoverished regional economies, and expanding educational services in the slums. As headquarters for the war, Congress in 1964 created the Office of Economic Opportunity (OEO). In addition, the Education Act of 1965 marked the beginning of massive federal aid to the public and parochial schools. Finally, after decades of discussion, medical insurance (Medicare) was included under Social Security.

In each of these two extraordinary years, President Johnson guided an important civil rights law through Congress. The Civil Rights Act of 1964, emphasizing coverage more than enforcement, deepened the national executive's involvement in almost every area of the expanding movement for equality: voting, public accommodations, schools, employment. The Civil Rights Act of 1965, concentrating on the franchise, made it possible for the national government to act as official registrar for black voters in the South. Under the provisions of the new law, the lists of eligible black voters rapidly expanded. Johnson, who cherished the tradition of the New Deal, assumed that his administration could facilitate the rise of black Americans much as the Roosevelt administration had assisted the poor thirty years earlier. In effect, the War on Poverty was a selective anti-depression program, and a high proportion of these impoverished Americans were blacks. The Civil Rights Acts of 1964 and 1965 completed a framework for racial reform that in many ways resembled the New Deal's labor policies of the late 1930s. They established a uniform structure of rules, centralized the admin-

BLACK AND WHITE TOGETHER

Massive yet orderly, the March on Washington in 1963 gave a powerful impetus to the biracial civil rights movement. (*Bob Adelman/Magnum.*)

"You Mean These Apply To The Riff-Raff Too?"

(From the Herblock Gallery, *Simon and Schuster, 1968.)*

istration of these rules, and relied on a sympathetic federal judiciary to enforce them.

Johnson's legislative success ended one phase of the movement for black rights. Its rationale had actually been stated in 1944 by Gunnar Myrdal's *An American Dilemma*, which dominated the understanding of race relations for the next twenty years. In this massive study that Myrdal prepared for the Carnegie Foundation, the Swedish scholar defined antiblack prejudice as the one great contradiction to the "American Creed," a nationally accepted set of beliefs in equality, opportunity, and justice for everybody. Behind the civil rights movement lay a faith that this American Creed would inevitably triumph over its antiblack contradictions. The Warren Court depended on the creed to give social authority to its legal rulings against segregation. Martin Luther King depended on the creed as a national white conscience that his strategy of civil disobedience could stir. The Johnson administration depended on the creed to rally the last holdouts behind a national program to eliminate racial inequalities from American life. Because of their common faith in the creed, a disciplined black minority and a well-to-do white minority had been able to work together in the cause of black rights. As a climax to the biracial civil rights movement, successful whites enthusiastically applauded in 1964 when King rose in Oslo to receive the Nobel Prize for Peace.

Contrary to the hopes of the civil rights movement, millions of whites understood the American Creed not as a common system of national values but as a justification for their particular set of local values. Turning inward, they continued to build their lives around family networks, cultural identities, and special local ways. In the 1960s, about half of America's white wage earners still lived in "ethnic, religious, and social enclaves relatively untouched by [the postwar years] and emphatically personal in character." Even those who had moved tried to stay within traveling distance of "home" and often retained very close ties with their families and old friends. Christianity in local America ranged from a ritualistically rich Catholicism, to the kind of evangelical Protestantism that made the revivalist Billy Graham a national hero, to such fundamentalist denominations as Jehovah's Witnesses. Beneath the glare of national TV, the gossipy, personal AM radio stations reflected these local values. Sports provided another outlet for a fierce local attachment. When the Chicago Black Hawks played in Detroit, or the New York Knicks in Boston, they were openly, honestly hated. In Brooklyn, nothing could ease the deep sense of cheat when the Dodgers—"dem Bums!"—departed in 1958 for Los Angeles.

Attempts to draw local Americans into a uniform system of national rules arrived like an enemy invasion. In most cases, local Americans could not grasp the legal and bureaucratic procedures behind such rules. As a study in 1970 revealed, a majority of Americans were "functionally illiterate" in the face of tax forms, insurance claims, credit contracts, and similar fine print. In the 1950s and 1960s, plans for urban improvement seldom took into account the local ways of life they were disrupting. The acronym for one local organization spoke the feelings of innumerable Americans from the inner city: SOUR—Stamp Out Urban Renewal. In the countryside as well as the city, it was becoming harder each year for Americans to protect their local networks.

In many localities skin color was a primary means of separating insiders from outsiders. White wage earners increasingly worked with people of other colors but still refused to accept such people in their neighborhoods, schools, parks, and taverns. During the fifties, these insular feelings exploded in anger throughout the South, where the civil rights movement first concentrated. But temperatures were also rising in the North. During the 1950s, every Northern city suffered from a housing shortage that dated from the slowing of home construction late in the 1920s. Indeed, there was a growing pressure on all kinds of city resources, partly as a result of new migrations. Rural blacks and whites who had been replaced by mechanical cotton pickers, consolidated farms, and mechanized coal mining poured into the city slums. So did Mexican Americans and Puerto Ricans, who were trying to escape their own grinding poverty. In a crowded arena of competitors, racial antagonisms turned into hate. When King took his civil rights campaign north in 1964, the ferocity of the white reaction matched anything he had encountered in the South.

By itself, the civil rights movement would have tipped modern America's delicate balance between national and local authority. Establishing national rules in such an extremely sensitive area of local white privilege guaranteed a local revolt. But civil rights did not come alone. A broader movement for national uniformity accompanied the movement for black rights and threatened an array of traditionally local powers. Because the Supreme Court figured so prominently in this nationalizing process, the Warren Court came to symbolize a wholesale assault on local America, and "Impeach Earl Warren" was its popular slogan of resistance. Between 1956 and 1965, the Court significantly narrowed the local power to censor obscenity. Beginning with the *Mallory* decision of 1957 and culminating in the *Escobedo* and *Miranda* decisions of 1964 and 1965, it set standards of police procedure to protect the rights of suspected criminals. In 1962 and 1964, the

ONE ANSWER TO NATIONAL AUTHORITY

(Danny Lyon/Magnum.)

Court outlawed prayers and Bible readings in the public schools. During these same years, notably in *Baker* v. *Carr* (1962), the Court also required the creation of state election districts that would approximate the rule of "one person, one vote."

Each of these changes challenged a basic local right. Censorship of movies, pornography, and schoolbooks was a widely used means of preserving local values. As the fear of street crime spread in the cities, many people thought they could no longer walk in their neighborhoods if the police were hobbled in pursuit of suspected criminals. The local truths of religion, a majority of Americans continued to believe, belonged in the schools just as they did in the home. Gerrymandering the cities was the customary way for small towns to ensure that the state legislature would protect their rights against outside intrusions.* In some instances, city dwellers wanted to gerrymander the suburbs for similar reasons.

The period of acute crisis in local power commenced in 1957. That year, Congress passed the first civil rights law since Reconstruction, federal troops entered Little Rock to enforce school desegregation, and the Warren Court embarked on its most active period. By 1965, the local barriers against national

---

*Gerrymandering is the drawing of grossly unequal election districts.

power appeared to be smashed. Washington officials were registering black voters in the rural South. The Warren Court had defined its broad national domain. As local governments complained of a budget squeeze, fresh funds for the war on poverty were bypassing almost all of the white neighborhoods in favor of the people economically below them. Not only did the public welfare rolls swell enormously in the mid-1960s, but some agents of OEO were even organizing welfare recipients to demand more. Until 1964, the President and Congress indicated from time to time that they had not completely forsaken the old balance. But when President Johnson called for a Great Society in January 1965, he officially committed his administration to a vigorous national management over matters that once were privileges of the locality. That year, Congress responded with large majorities for the President's program.

Nationally oriented Americans had convinced themselves that their understanding of equality, opportunity, and justice was everybody's American Creed. As they used this creed to make national policy, they assumed that no one would seriously question the new policy's impartiality. Everyone, they believed, would soon accept it as a nonpartisan, nonpolitical fact of life. But this nationalizing process had just the opposite effect. Instead of creating a nonpolitical consensus, it ignited a fresh political conflict. Actually by 1965 not a great deal had changed in the local white world. Only a small percentage of black children attended integrated classes. Many communities still found ways of keeping Christianity in and alien books out of their schools. Police procedures altered very little. Nevertheless, when locally oriented whites saw a solid phalanx in the national government arrayed against them, they prepared to fight for their traditional rights.

The Decline of Containment

A second crisis in Washington's management occurred in international affairs. Here also the nation's leaders tried to impose their understanding of events on people who lived by very different values. In this case, it was the doctrine of containment that clashed with other people's aspirations, and it was a variety of nations throughout the world that challenged America's right to thwart their own, distinctive ambitions.

From the beginning, containment was a specifically American policy. Relatively few other nations gave anticommunism the same overriding importance that the United States assigned to it. The more the Cold War stabilized and the more economically independent America's allies became, the more these allies resisted America's particular interpretation of world affairs. In Europe, France led the resistance. By refusing to join an integrated continental military force in 1954, France destroyed America's plans for a European Defense Community (EDC). Then after 1958, the Paris government under its imperial President, Charles de Gaulle, furnished a continuing center for European criticism of American policy. More subtly, Japan also maneuvered for greater independence from the United

States. No sooner had the American occupation ended in 1951 than Japan sought full control over its territory and policies. Here, as in Western Europe, the desire to trade with communist nations contributed to the tension, for the United States opposed almost all economic relations between the two international spheres.

Although the world's agrarian nations had a meager share in the prosperity of the 1950s, many of them, too, were marking their own separate paths. The electric names in Africa and Asia were fervent nationalists such as Gamal Nasser of Egypt, Kwame Nkrumah of Ghana, Jawaharlal Nehru of India, and Sukarno of Indonesia. In a variety of ways, these leaders struggled to develop their nations without sacrificing independence to either side in the Cold War. Extremely sensitive to pressures from the great powers, they retaliated in anger when the United States or the Soviet Union appeared to dangle economic aid as an incentive to enter its camp. Because the United States was allied to their former imperial masters in Europe, the recently emancipated colonies especially set themselves against a future that would be known as the "American Century."

In the face of these nationalist assertions, Secretary Dulles held tenaciously to the principles of containment. He threatened France with an "agonizing reappraisal" of America's support, and he condemned the trend toward neutralism among the agrarian nations. As best he could, he minimized the importance that such countries as India and Pakistan, or Greece and Turkey, assigned to their own feuds. After Dulles's retirement in 1959, however, the world's variety started to break through the monolithic conceptions of the Cold War. With Kennedy's inauguration, officials in Washington began exploring ways of responding to these diverse international ambitions. The new President, who expected to build his reputation in foreign affairs, encouraged fresh ideas about America's policies. He promised to accept the new nations of Africa and Asia on their own terms and to negotiate with the established nations as equals. In 1961, Kennedy announced the "Alliance for Progress" with Latin America that would use economic aid from the United States to improve the quality of life in this hemisphere. The Peace Corps also placed local human needs above international military policy.

Nevertheless, in the day-to-day conduct of foreign affairs, Kennedy, his primary adviser on foreign policy, McGeorge Bundy, and his secretary of state, Dean Rusk, gave priority to the containment of international communism. During the 1960 campaign, Kennedy had claimed that Soviet military advances left the United States at the wrong end of a "missile gap." Though no one ever found the gap, the new President still worked hard to expand America's military capabilities. Twice he demanded and received substantial increases in the military budget. Moreover, military assistance continued to dominate the budget for foreign aid. In Latin America, the guide to American policy was not the Alliance for Progress but isolating Castro's Cuba and insulating other countries against a similar revolution.

Under Kennedy's successor, even the exploration of alternatives dwindled. Johnson came to office in 1963 with a longstanding, firm commitment to containment, and he showed little patience with new ideas on world policy. Unlike Kennedy, he relied heavily on his advisers in foreign affairs. By backing the requests from the Pentagon and the State Department, Johnson hoped they would manage international problems while he concentrated on domestic affairs.

With this cast of mind, Johnson met the primary international challenge of his administration, a civil war in Viet Nam. America's involvement in Viet Nam dated from 1950, when the United States first supplied aid to the French in their attempt to recapture their Indochinese colony. France still lost the battle of the jungles to Ho Chi Minh's communist army, and in 1954 an international conference at Geneva created three independent states from the former French territory: Laos, Cambodia, and Viet Nam. Viet Nam was temporarily divided between a communist north and a noncommunist south pending national elections and unification.

After the French defeat, the United States assumed responsibility for containing communism throughout Indochina. As Dulles explained, one primary reason for sponsoring the Southeast Asia Treaty Organization in 1955 was to provide a "cover" over Indochina. With American support, the leaders in the southern portion of Viet Nam repudiated the Geneva plan for national elections and established a permanent state, South Viet Nam. As Kennedy took office, the anticommunist governments in both South Viet Nam and neighboring Laos were in jeopardy. South Vietnamese guerrillas who had been fighting the corrupt government in Saigon consolidated their forces as the National Liberation Front (NLF). Kennedy responded by expanding America's covert military assistance, including the organization of raids inside North Viet Nam, where some of the rebels were trained and supplied. The conflict in Laos stabilized, but not the one in South Viet Nam. The more American the war in Viet Nam became, the broader the guerrilla resistance to Saigon grew.

Johnson rode the momentum of America's involvement into a major war. In 1964, he inflated a small naval encounter off the Vietnamese coast as a calculated attack by North Viet Nam on an American ship, and in the "Gulf of Tonkin" Resolution the Senate granted the President wide discretion in defending America's forces in Viet Nam. Starting seriously in 1965, Johnson enlarged the American contingent in Viet Nam until by 1968 it exceeded half a million men. Under the code name Operation Rolling Thunder, massive bombing raids struck North Viet Nam, which now sent its own troops into the south. Squads of American planes followed the winding jungle trails of Indochina in an attempt to block the flow of troops and supplies from the north. Johnson abruptly dismissed each overture to compromise.

Johnson's plan in Viet Nam grew out of a central assumption in America's containment policy. As Kennedy's military adviser General Maxwell Taylor stated it, the communists had to be taught that a war for national liberation was "costly," not "cheap." Or in Dulles's words of 1954, communist guerrillas had to "suffer damage outweighing any possible gains from aggression." Johnson's strategy was to increase the level of punishment until the price of continuing the war became too high and the enemy would quit. Because the guerrilla foe was so difficult to locate, the military relied more on broad coverage than precise assaults. America's tactics included chemical defoliants, carpet bombing, and napalm. Inevitably they took a terrible civilian toll in search of the hidden enemy. Meanwhile, the Johnson administration issued optimistic statements about the progress of the war.

The Vietnamese did not respond according to plan. Under increasing attack, neither North Viet Nam nor the NLF weakened. During January and February of 1968, in a dramatic demonstration of their continuing strength, the communists launched the "Tet Offensive" into the primary cities of South Viet Nam, which had been considered well beyond the reach of the guerrilla armies. Even before the Tet Offensive, American opposition to the war had already been rising. Like Hoover's prosperity, Johnson's victory in Viet Nam stayed just around the corner too long. In the jargon of the sixties, the "credibility gap" had spread too wide. Saigon eventually reported a count of communist casualties that exceeded the total Vietnamese population. As the military draft quotas mounted each year, so did the number of evaders. In 1968, draft resistance erupted nation-

WAR IN VIETNAM

Who was the enemy in Viet Nam? Perhaps this Vietnamese woman knew, but increasing numbers of Americans could not say. (Magnum.)

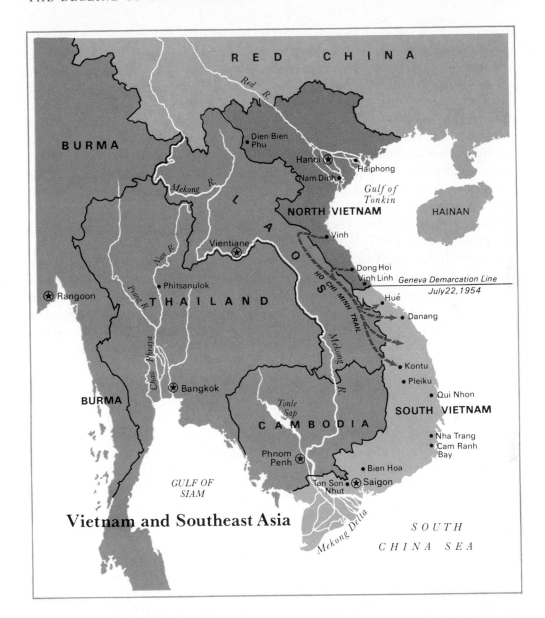

Vietnam and Southeast Asia

wide. J. William Fulbright, the chairman of the Senate Foreign Relations Committee, who had once trusted Johnson to conduct the war in his own way, became
one of its sharpest critics, and a growing body of disillusioned Democrats sided
with Fulbright against the President. With the Tet Offensive, television coverage
and news dispatches increasingly emphasized the futility and brutality of the
war. "Bombing, bombing! Why do you always write bombing?" an angry officer
demanded at a military briefing for reporters in Saigon. "It's air support, not
bombing!" On March 31, 1968, a frustrated Johnson turned the corner. Before
a nationwide television audience, he announced an end to the escalation of the

war and a new willingness to negotiate. Then in a stunning postscript, the subdued President said that he would not seek reelection.

Once a popular faith in containment would have strengthened American
support for the war. By the late 1960s, however, the Viet Nam crisis just accelerated the general decline of America's global policy. Communism, according
to the logic of containment, was a single international system directed from
Moscow. Yet throughout the 1960s, astonished Americans had been learning
more and more about a bitter hostility between China and the Soviet Union.
The Soviet-Chinese feud not only shattered a cardinal principle behind the
Cold War; it also contributed to the growing American awareness of a highly
diverse, subdivided world. The Viet Nam War, instead of being an integral
part of America's global policy, increasingly seemed a separate issue that could
be solved by itself.

In one more way Viet Nam hastened the decline of containment. Foreign
governments that had been harboring resentment against the world's greatest
power took the war as an occasion to express these feelings and declare their
independence of Washington. Even yesterday's imperialists in Western Europe
joined in the worldwide criticism of American policy in Viet Nam. No nation
altered its basic relations with the United States. But America's isolation over
Viet Nam did hurry the international decentralization that had been under
way for more than a decade.

By 1968, the American policy of containment was disintegrating. As the Viet
Nam War demonstrated, containment could not deal effectively with the rising
nationalist passions among the world's agrarian peoples. Nor could it respond
adequately to the growing independence among the world's industrial nations.
In the early fifties, containment had appeared to be a model of global management. Now this outworn policy, which the United States seemed unable to use
or to abandon, had become a manager's nightmare.

The Lament of the Individual

Meanwhile a third crisis was brewing among the very Americans who were
supposed to be the primary beneficiaries of modern society. In the 1950s,
a well-trained and well-paid minority, holding jobs with national prestige in
business and the professions, presumably sat atop American society and epitomized its confidence. Yet the same nationalizing forces that gave them power
and prestige also shrank their importance as individuals. The more systematized their society, the less significant, or even distinguishable, any one person
was in its operations. Perhaps, as the most critical voices of the late forties had
implied, there really were no individuals in a modern, bureaucratic society.

During the 1950s, successful Americans told one another to find their personal security in the impersonal forces governing their society. They praised
the unifying effects of mass consumerism. They expected the computer to make

sense out of the complex social problems around them. Sufficient megatons of "nuclear deterrent," they said, would preserve the Free World. The publicist Peter Drucker asked Americans to picture the "Industrial Enterprise" as their social model. According to the economist John Kenneth Galbraith, huge "countervailing powers," or nationwide interest groups, maintained the healthy balance inside American capitalism.

But where were the individuals in this scheme of abstractions? The countercurrents of doubt began to swell. One source was a set of images particularly associated with the thermonuclear age. Such popular novels and movies as *On the Beach* and *Fail-Safe* touched the deep fears of a world dying in its contaminated atmosphere and a flaw in the computerized balance of terror triggering the ultimate holocaust. The audience for a dehumanizing science fiction expanded. The most intriguing new American writer of the 1950s, J. D. Salinger, and the most talented new American dramatist of the 1960s, Edward Albee, both emphasized the individual's agonizing, inescapable vulnerability in modern society. Many young writers accentuated the individual's isolation by using ordinary conversation as a way of hiding rather than communicating their

RUSH HOUR, NEW YORK CITY

Routinized jobs in impersonal institutions made even successful Americans wonder about the meaning of their lives. A thousand clowns, one popular movie of the sixties called them. *(Abigail Hayman/Magnum.)*

characters' feelings. Only when the characters talked to themselves in lonely, interior monologues did they honestly express their emotions. Novelists such as Saul Bellow and Joseph Heller relieved their own grim assessments with a wild laughter at the individual's preposterous fate in modern society. The escape through humor found its most popular common denominator in the "sick joke" of the 1960s.

The malaise that these writers expressed was also affecting attitudes toward work. During the 1950s, employers noted that white-collar employees were inquiring more often about fringe benefits like vacations, company cars, and retirement plans than about the challenges of the job itself. By the 1960s, many corporations were discovering a new problem of morale among those executives who ran the company's daily affairs. Rising rates of absenteeism and declining rates of efficiency expressed the refusal of "middle managers" to devote themselves to jobs that no longer seemed to reward them. Indeed, white-collar efficiency had become a pervasive problem. Studies revealed that, on the average, an office of white-collar employees devoted about 50 percent of their potential labor to the job. In the fifties, large audiences followed the television series *Ben Casey*, whose utterly dedicated doctor-hero never shed his white coat or left his patients. By the 1960s, Ben Casey had become a grind. Somewhere outside of the job lay an elusive something called "fulfillment," and more and more successful Americans set out to find it.

It was a wide-ranging quest. Some cultivated their avocations instead of their vocations. It became increasingly common for well-to-do Americans to find their primary satisfactions from boating or bridge or travel or tennis. With the rise of avocationalism came a redefinition of leisure as something much more basic in life than simply a means to recuperate. A cult of the wilderness, condemning the artificiality of modern society and praising experiences with raw nature, enjoyed a new vogue. The glorification of nature was in part a reaction against the biological devastation that an indiscriminate use of insecticides was causing throughout America. In a chilling best-seller, *Silent Spring* (1962), Rachel Carson eloquently publicized this modern blight. Reaction against the taste and quality of mass-produced goods helped to generate an interest in personal craftsmanship. From a modest beginning in the "do-it-yourself" kits of the 1950s, this involvement with manual skills made workmanship an increasingly important part of white-collar America's full life.

The most general expression of the individual's modern quest was a nationwide fascination with personal power. Human manipulations that had once been considered ethically questionable became matters of public pride in the fifties and sixties. Experts explained how they had "sold" political candidates to the voters. Books coached Americans on games of "one upmanship" in their everyday relations with friends and acquaintances. Commentators and historians praised the "strong" Presidents. Because the preoccupation with power was a mass phenomenon, it found a variety of popular outlets. The crunching game of football arrived as America's leading sport. Its competitors adapted as best they could through shortened fences and livelier balls in baseball, the "big game" in tennis, the "dunk" in basketball, and the "power play" in hockey. High-speed auto racing attracted more and more fans. By the 1960s, everybody's car could be a personal vehicle of power: Cougar, Wildcat, Thunderbird, Stingray, Mustang. Promises of power suffused the advertising of everything from perfumes to breakfast foods. Its values saturated the movies and television, most drippingly in the James Bond shows and their many "superspy" imitators but just as thoroughly in the children's cartoons and the movies' technicolor shots of mutilation and bloodshed. According to some experts, the most common cause of alcoholism, the nation's greatest addiction, was a compensation for the feelings of powerlessness.

Against this background of doubting and searching, bands of well-to-do white youths came into the streets as the hippies and flower children and dropouts and rebels of the 1960s. Though a minority of their age group, they were so obvious and so audible that they always seemed far more numerous than they actually were. They clustered in the parks to smoke and sing. They crowded the sidewalks around college campuses. They became the most committed white partisans of black rights and the bulwark of a marching, chanting peace movement. Beginning with the Free Speech Movement at Berkeley in 1964 and culminating in the nationwide, decentralized Students for a Democratic Society (SDS), their protest groups rallied many more young people behind specific campaigns for student rights and social justice. Suburban high school students copied both their programs and their tactics. By 1967 and 1968, student strikes were commonplace. So were the pockets of young people who collected to experiment with communal life, drugs, and poverty. In the late 1960s, the largest of these colonies occupied much of the Haight-Ashbury district of San Francisco.

In many ways, these young dissenters were carrying out just one more variation of the modern adolescent rebellion. All the standard elements of the past forty years were there. Increasingly hard, acid rock set a musical barrier between the generations. Adults were accused of hypocrisy, and adult authority was condemned. Trust no one over thirty, the rebels declared. Even their primary areas of rebellion—dress, language, drugs, and sex—were the familiar ones from the 1920s. When young people in the 1960s wore workclothes or exotic clothes or no clothes, screamed four-letter words, substituted narcotics for alcohol, and claimed the right of sexual intercourse on demand, they were extending the very domains of personal freedom that well-to-do Americans of four decades earlier had explored.

At the same time, this noisy rebellion supplied a penetrating commentary on the contemporary life of successful Americans. It focused on the most sensitive problems of the individual in modern society. In response to a dehumanizing bureaucracy, the young dissenters assaulted the nation's important institutions: the government, the political party, the corporation, and the university.

Some of them ostentatiously rejected the products of these institutions—the government's laws, the party's candidates, the corporation's goods, the university's degrees—and many more young people cheered them on. In response to the individual's feelings of loneliness, they emphasized community and loyalty and love. Rejecting professionalism, they exalted individual fulfillment. Craftsmanship, nature, and a "whole earth" were almost holy causes. A few rebels tried to build an entire life around these new values in self-sufficient rural communes. The young dissenters even reflected their society's preoccupation with power. The abuse of power, they claimed, lay at the root of America's social evils. "Power to the people" would bring a new era of justice.

As they probed the primary doubts in their parents' lives, the young rebels split an older generation. A minority defended the right of their sons and daughters to a dissenting life style. Often these adults found courage to act out their own feelings. Some marched for civil rights and peace. Others, acknowledging the need for a new intimacy in human relations, experimented with "encounter" and "sensitivity" groups and greater sexual freedom. A few joined the dropouts. But a majority of successful adults opposed the new youth movement. By pushing their private anxieties into public, the young rebels threatened the balance that older people were maintaining between adult responsibility and its discontents. The more extreme the adolescent rebellion, the more widespread the opposition became. By 1970 the young radicals had lost almost all their sympathizers.

The most lasting outgrowth of the rebellious sixties was the movement for women's rights. No rational grounds existed for excluding women from a full range of white-collar occupations. Like race or culture, gender was irrelevant to a skills standard. Yet only in the private realm away from work did women enjoy anything approximating the freedom of successful men. As dressing styles, leisure activities, and public behavior increasingly became "unisex," men continued to keep the best jobs. By the 1960s, close to half of the women in America held paying jobs, partly because close to half the marriages in America ended in divorce. A significant proportion of women received lower salaries or wages than men did for the same work, and an even larger percentage of women were blocked somewhere along the ladder of promotion in their occupations. Meanwhile, women's responsibilities at home scarcely changed. The widespread concerns about individual fulfillment, the anxieties about powerlessness, and the increasing doubts about the quality of American consumerism, all had particularly sharp application in the lives of women. In the critical climate of the 1960s, some of them began to strike out against restraints and indignities.

In 1963, Betty Friedan's *The Feminine Mystique* broke the silence. By the end of the decade, a host of books and articles was analyzing the evils of the modern doll's house. The drive for black rights contributed a vocabulary to communicate women's feelings of oppression and, in 1966, the acronym for a

WOMEN DEMAND THEIR RIGHTS

Justice on the job represented the mild side of a broad and varied women's movement. *(Magnum.)*

new pressure group, the National Organization for Women (NOW). ("What do you want?" the civil rights marchers chanted. "FREEDOM!" "When do you want it?" "NOW!") The recent emphasis on personal power helped women to identify and expose a "machismo" cult of swaggering masculinity. Moreover, it justified their own demands for more power. Young women in particular were determined to start with a new set of rules, and some of them insisted on immediate, wholesale changes in the relations between men and women. A few even tried physical assaults on the "male chauvinist pigs." But this temporary phase was far less important to the success of the women's movement than America's modern occupational values. Where a standard of skills prevailed, women's rights to an equal opportunity was an unquestionable claim. Quite promptly, both the federal courts and the national executive committed themselves to enforcing equal access to jobs, and equal pay for equal work.

Early in 1968, the forces of protest and reform seemed on the verge of capturing the national government. The summer before, a quarter million Americans had marched quietly through Washington in behalf of peace in Viet Nam. Both their number and their discipline gave the movement a new respectability. The inheritor of this strength was a thoughtful, enigmatic Democratic senator from Minnesota, Eugene McCarthy, who in November 1967 opened his campaign for President on a peace platform. In January and February 1968, as the

Tet Offensive exposed the military failure of America's policy in Viet Nam, McCarthy was touring New Hampshire in preparation for the first presidential primary. That March, the quixotic candidate no one had taken seriously received almost as many votes as President Johnson himself.

Within a few weeks after the New Hampshire primary, Johnson quit the race. A second peace candidate, Robert Kennedy, entered the lists. The boyish Bobby Kennedy, who had been attorney general in John Kennedy's administration and then senator from New York, attracted an even more zealous following than his older brother had, and a majority of Americans assumed that in time he also would be President. The favorite of the youth movement, however, was still McCarthy. His willingness to fight a lonely battle and his cool, moral style converted tens of thousands of college students, "Clean for Gene" with shaves and neckties, into campaign workers. Meanwhile, through sit ins, rallies, and strikes, more radical students were applying heavy pressure on the major universities to support a great variety of causes for social justice.

Actually, the ground beneath the reform movement was already eroding. In April 1968, a sniper caught Martin Luther King on the balcony of a Memphis hotel. At the news of his assassination, black ghettos across the country erupted in violence. In death as in life, King could not channel the emotions of the Northern ghettos toward peaceful resistance. Although King gathered many loyal partisans in the Northern cities, he also encountered a very different, angry spirit, especially among younger blacks. This, in a broad sense, was the spirit of Black Power. At one level, Black Power was a reasoned explanation of American race relations. In *Black Power* (1967), for example, Stokely Carmichael and Charles Hamilton denied the existence of the American Creed, which had underpinned the civil rights movement. On the contrary, they argued, white values were best expressed in a self-serving institutional structure that made blacks a colonial people inside American society. Only a racially proud movement that was exclusively black could hope to break these institutional shackles. At another, more popular level, however, Black Power was a volatile expression of ghetto frustrations, a release of raw feelings that sometimes struck in fury at the most immediate sources of oppression in the ghettos themselves.

Less than a week after the adoption of the Civil Rights Act of 1965, the ghetto area of Watts in Los Angeles exploded in riot and flames. More black riots scorched almost every major city during the next three years, burned miles of the Detroit ghetto in 1967, and spread nationwide at the word of King's murder in 1968. Meanwhile, new black leaders were demanding exclusive control over the movement for black rights and draining support from King's biracial civil rights campaign. In place of King's cause, the spreading spirit of Black Power strengthened such groups as the ascetic, business-minded Black Muslims and the militant, socially minded Black Panthers. Successful whites were left in confusion. Some of them still read the autobiographies of Malcolm X and Claude Brown as moving accounts of how individual blacks had survived against extraordinary odds. These were also triumphs by white values. But the slashing ghetto despair that burned people's own homes belonged to another world, and fiery assaults from the unknown just frightened them.

The people who could best appreciate this rage were locally oriented whites, who were also rising in retaliation against outside domination. As the national threats to local power intensified, these whites struck back along two lines. One was an attempt to reassert control over what they regarded as their own local institutions. In the Northern cities, they fought against the racial integration of the schools, especially when integration meant busing black and white children. Numerous white Catholics in such cities as New Orleans, Philadelphia, and Boston actively resisted their church's policies of integration. Urban politicians attacked the local agencies of OEO and lobbied in Washington to disband it. In the towns as well as the cities, bumper stickers reading "Support Your Local Police" signaled a growing opposition to judicial restraints and supervisory review boards. The Crime Control Act of 1968, which generally endorsed strong police action, was considered a significant victory in this cause. In many white communities, Mayor Richard Daley of Chicago became a hero when it was reported that he had instructed the police to maim looters and kill arsonists during a ghetto riot.

The second line of counterattack was aimed at the youth rebellion. In the tradition of community control, locally oriented whites set out to suppress a wide range of unacceptable behavior. "Sideburns . . . shall not extend lower than the bottom of the ear opening and shall be uniform width," the regulations of the Louisville Fire Department stated. "Beards, goatees or any other extraneous facial hair will not be permitted." Opinion polls showed consistently large majorities favoring severe punishment for drug users, including marijuana smokers. By 1968, the Viet Nam War was unpopular throughout the United States. But in almost every locality, waving a Viet Cong flag or burning an American one, as television reported some radicals doing, ranked as a far greater evil than the war. By local values, affluent students had no right to insult their nation or squander its educational privileges. The New York police who cracked heads while breaking a campus strike at Columbia University in 1968, the townsmen who took a crowbar to the flower children, or the construction workers who roamed lower Manhattan beating up long-haired youths were expressing the feelings of innumerable fellow citizens. In May 1970, when four students at Kent State University were killed for no apparent reason by the National Guard, a nationwide poll tallied four out of five Americans on the side of the guardsmen.

Kent State typified the ending of the decade. University administrators relied more and more on the local police to control student unrest. Law enforcement agencies killed, jailed, or scattered the leadership of the Black Panthers. After 1967, the peace marches in Washington were battling, antagonistic affairs, and the peace organizations, always a quarreling lot, fragmented. Occasionally a happy episode broke the pattern. In the summer of 1969, "the nation of Woodstock," perhaps 400,000 young people, gathered at White Lake, New York, for a rock festival and a holiday frolic. But a few months later in Altamont, California, an attempt to repeat the joys of Woodstock dissolved in bloodshed.

These rising waves of anger swept over the presidential campaign of 1968. In June, while celebrating an important victory in the California primary, Robert Kennedy was assassinated by a moody young Jordanian, Sirhan Sirhan. Eugene McCarthy, now the sole leader of the peace movement, unaccountably allowed his own drive for the presidential nomination to lose momentum. That August in Chicago, while policemen were banging their way through a parkful of young demonstrators outside convention headquarters, the Democrats nominated a very different Minnesota politician, the talkative, middle-of-the-road Vice-President, Hubert Humphrey. The most vital force in the fall campaign was Governor George Wallace of Alabama, candidate of the American Independent party. As the advocate of "poor folks" against invading bureaucrats and decent citizens against subversive youths, Wallace gave local whites their first authentic spokesman in a presidential contest since Al Smith. Even more impressive than the 10 million votes Wallace eventually received, the nationwide enthusiasm for Wallace's cause revealed the depth of America's discontent.

In general, harsh and negative feelings dominated the campaign of 1968.

Richard Nixon, who had returned to win another Republican nomination, promised to impose law and order on a permissive society. The Democrat Humphrey likened the peace marchers to the appeasers of Hitler. In striking contrast to the fifties and early sixties, no one spoke any longer for a common American purpose. America's nationalizing trends had divided people into hostile camps, and for a time, no national manager could win the confidence of a broad majority. Except for the economy, which remained strong, the old problems of modernization had simply returned in new forms. As they converged in the politics of the late sixties, some Americans wondered if their society could survive the onslaught.

STUDENTS AND POLITICS, 1968

College students entered national politics with an unprecedented passion in 1968. Their fervor gave electric vitality to Eugene McCarthy s primary campaigns. Then at the Democratic convention in August, delegate votes and police clubs silenced McCarthy's youth brigade. In the gloomy aftermath, young radicals had the last word. *(Left, Robert Azzi/Nancy Palmer Photo Agency; middle, Mallock/Magnum; right, Costa Manos/Magnum.)*

Suggested Readings

William E. Leuchtenburg, *A Troubled Feast: American Society since 1945* (1973), is a lively introduction to the postwar years and contains a good bibliography. The confidence of the 1950s glows from *U. S. A., the Permanent Revolution* (1951) by the Editors of *Fortune* and from *The Big Change: America Transforms Itself, 1900–1950* (1952) by Frederick Lewis Allen. A similar confidence, with minor reservations, appears in the writings of various intellectuals: Peter F. Drucker, *The New Society* (1950), John Kenneth Galbraith, *American Capitalism* (1952), Daniel J. Boorstin, *The Genius of American Politics* (1952), and Daniel Bell, *The End of Ideology* (1960). From a more critical perspective, four books are particularly useful in assessing the contemporary political economy. C. Wright Mills, *The Power Elite* (1956), explores what later came to be called the military-industrial complex. Grant McConnell, *Private Power and American Democracy* (1966), and Theodore J. Lowi, *The End of Liberalism* (1969), analyze the dangers to the public interest from pressure-group politics. John Kenneth Galbraith, *The New Industrial State* (1967), examines the influence of corporate managers in national economic policy.

The history of politics during the confident years focuses largely on the presidency. Herbert S. Parmet, *Eisenhower and the American Crusades* (1972), and more briefly Charles C. Alexander, *Holding the Line: The Eisenhower Era, 1952–1961* (1975), cover the general's two terms. Marquis W. Childs, *Eisenhower: Captive Hero* (1958), gives valuable background. Both James MacGregor Burns, *John Kennedy* (1960), and Theodore C. Sorensen, *Kennedy* (1965), are useful political biographies. On Kennedy's administration, Arthur M. Schlesinger, Jr., *A Thousand Days* (1965), is appreciative and revealing. Jim F. Heath, *John F. Kennedy and the Business Community* (1969), emphasizes the President's conservative inclinations. In *The Promise and the Performance: The Leadership of John F. Kennedy* (1975), Lewis J. Paper tries to strike a balanced judgment. Rowland Evans and Robert Novak, *Lyndon B. Johnson* (1966), helps to explain the powerful chief executive. For legislation during the fifties and sixties, James L. Sundquist, *Politics and Policy: The Eisenhower, Kennedy and Johnson Years* (1968), is indispensable. John Barlow Martin's *Stevenson of Illinois* (1976), the first volume of a biography, examines the hero of the liberals who twice lost to Eisenhower. Theodore H. White's *The Making of the President, 1960* (1961) includes shrewd observations on Nixon's losing campaign. Barry Goldwater speaks for himself in *The Conscience of a Conservative* (1960). In a deceptively entitled study, *Revolt of the Moderates* (1956), Samuel Lubell explains moderate voting behavior that affected presidential politics. Richard E. Neustadt, *Presidential Power* (1960), is an analysis of leadership that reputedly influenced John Kennedy. Insights into the political turmoil of the late sixties appear in Eric F. Goldman, *The Tragedy of Lyndon Johnson* (1969), Tom Wicker, *JFK and LBJ* (1968), Penn Kimball, *Bobby Kennedy and the New Politics* (1968), and Lewis Chester et al., *An American Melodrama: The Presidential Campaign of 1968* (1969).

Donald R. Matthews, *U.S. Senators and Their World* (1960), and William S. White, *Citadel: The Story of the U.S. Senate* (1957), contain interesting material on another center of political power. John D. Weaver, *Warren* (1967), and Leo Katcher, *Earl Warren* (1967), praise the controversial chief justice, and Milton R. Konvitz, *Expanding Liberties* (1966), evaluates some of the Warren Court's important decisions. How the national government has affected modern urban affairs is analyzed in Mark I. Gelfand, *A Nation of Cities* (1975). A crucial new political bloc is examined in Robert Gilpin and Christopher Wright, eds., *Scientists and National Policy-Making* (1964), and Don K. Price, *The Scientific Estate* (1965).

John W. Spanier, *American Foreign Policy since World War II* (rev. ed., 1973), is a clear, largely favorable summary. On the internationalization of American business, see Raymond Vernon, *Sovereignty at Bay: The Multinational Spread of U. S. Enterprise* (1971), and

Mira Wilkins, *The Maturing of Multinational Enterprise: American Business Abroad from 1914 to 1970* (1974). In *The Politics of Oil*, Robert Engler examines some effects of internationalization. Paul Y. Hammond, *Organizing for Defense* (1961), discusses the place of the military in twentieth-century America; Warner R. Schilling et al., *Strategy, Politics, and Defense Budgets* (1962), analyzes specific decisions in military policy. Maxwell D. Taylor, *The Uncertain Trumpet* (1960), is a prominent general's appraisal of the Eisenhower years that influenced the Kennedy administration. The sources and consequences of America's military foreign policy are explored in Richard J. Barnet, *Roots of War* (1972), and Alexander L. George and Richard Smoke, *Deterrence in American Foreign Policy* (1974).

Michael A. Guhin, *John Foster Dulles* (1972), praises one architect of American foreign policy for his flexibility, and Herman Finer, *Dulles over Suez* (1964), gives a detailed account of the international furor that the secretary of state raised in 1956 and 1957. A dangerous issue that spanned the Eisenhower and Kennedy administrations is examined in Jack M. Schick, *The Berlin Crisis, 1958–1962* (1971). Richard J. Walton's *Cold War and Counterrevolution* (1972) takes a negative view of Kennedy's foreign policy. The decline of Kennedy's Alliance for Progress is traced in Jerome Levinson and Juan de Onís, *The Alliance That Lost Its Way* (1970). On the Cuban missile crisis, Henry M. Pachter, *Collision Course* (1963), provides a basic summary, and Graham T. Allison, *Essence of Decision* (1971), offers an intriguing set of alternative explanations.

Most writers on the war in Southeast Asia condemn the United States. *The Indochina Story* (1970) by the Committee of Concerned Asian Scholars is a particularly striking example, while Donald S. Zagoria, *Vietnam Triangle: Moscow, Peking, Hanoi* (1967), is one of the relatively few defenses of American policy. Henry Brandon, *Anatomy of Error: The Inside Story of the Asian War on the Potomac, 1954–1969* (1969), and Arthur M. Schlesinger, Jr., *The Bitter Heritage: Vietnam and American Democracy, 1941–1966* (1967), seek a middle ground. David Halberstam's fascinating *The Best and the Brightest* (1972) dissects the policy-making in Washington, and Frances Fitzgerald's excellent *Fire in the Lake* (1972) analyzes the consequences of this policy in Vietnam. J. William Fulbright, *The Arrogance of Power* (1967), expresses the opposition from Congress. A notorious massacre of civilians in Vietnam and the official attempts to hide it are exposed in Seymour M. Hersh, *My Lai 4* (1970).

The hopes and concerns of the civil rights movement are revealed in Martin Luther King, Jr., *Why We Can't Wait* (1964); Howard Zinn's account of young activists, *SNCC: The New Abolitionists* (1964); and Charles E. Silberman's *Crisis in Black and White* (1964), a liberal white's summary of the issues. The sources of black militancy emerge from *The Autobiography of Malcolm X* (1965), Charles V. Hamilton and Stokely Carmichael, *Black Power* (1967), Eldridge Cleaver, *Soul on Ice* (1968), and James Forman, *The Making of Black Revolutionaries* (1972). Claude Brown, *Manchild in the Promised Land* (1965), is an eloquent statement on life and survival in the ghetto. On the travail of civil rights leaders, see Chandler Davison, *Biracial Politics: Conflict and Coalition in the Metropolitan South* (1972), David L. Lewis, *King: A Critical Biography* (1970), and August Meier and Elliott Rudwick, *CORE* (1973), the account of an organization transformed by the sweep of events. *Report of the National Advisory Commission on Civil Disorders* (1968) and Robert M. Fogelson, *Violence as Protest* (1971), reflect the sense of complexity that came to surround the issue of black rights. Two important studies of poverty in America are Michael Harrington, *The Other America* (1962), and Harry M. Caudill, *Night Comes in the Cumberlands* (1963).

The literature of the youth rebellion begins with Jack Kerouac's *On the Road* (1957) and more or less ends with Charles A. Reich's *The Greening of America* (1971). The world against which these well-to-do youths rebelled is discussed in William H. Whyte, *The Organization Man* (1956), and Scott Donaldson, *The Suburban Myth* (1969). Theodore

Roszak, *The Making of a Counter-Culture* (1969), attempts to probe the rebellion's inner meaning, and Abbie Hoffman, *Steal This Book* (1971), expresses something of its style. Philip E. Slater's *The Pursuit of Loneliness* (1970) contrasts the rebel culture with establishment culture. In *Young Radicals* (1968), Kenneth Keniston analyzes leaders in the rebellion. Kirkpatrick Sale, *SDS* (1973), is a sympathetic study of its most prominent campus organization. Tom Wolfe comments on the culture of Haight-Ashbury in *The Electric Kool-Aid Acid Test* (1968). There are perceptive essays on radicalism in Joseph Boskin and Robert A. Rosenstone, eds., *Seasons of Rebellion* (1972). The most enduring portion of the rebellion, the movement for women's rights, is examined in William Henry Chafe's *The American Women* (1972). Three outstanding books — Betty Friedan, *The Feminine Mystique* (1963), Kate Millett, *Sexual Politics* (1970), and Robin Morgan (comp.), *Sisterhood is Powerful* (1970) — suggest the range and force of the movement.

Sources on the resistance to national liberalism and young radicalism are scattered. Arthur B. Shostak's *Blue-Collar Life* (1969) summarizes an array of studies on white urban wage earners and their families. Bennett M. Berger, *Working-Class Suburb* (1960), Herbert J. Gans, *The Levittowners* (1967), and William Kornblum, *Blue-Collar Community* (1974), add substantially to this analysis. Herbert J. Gans, *The Urban Villagers* (1962), and Sam Bass Warner, Jr., *The Urban Wilderness* (1972), include perceptive accounts of how government policies have damaged inner-city life. In *Small Town in Mass Society* (1958), Arthur J. Vidich and Joseph Bensman describe the defenses of townspeople against external authority. Peter Binzen, *Whitetown, U. S. A.* (1970), discusses urban dwellers in rebellion against such authority, and Numan V. Bartley, *The Rise of Massive Resistance* (1969), and Neil R. McMillen, *The Citizens' Council* (1971), trace an earlier rebellion in the South. The new explicitness about ethnic identities is explored in Michael Novak's *The Rise of the Unmeltable Ethnics* (1972).

35

Stabilization

By election time 1968, such broad, optimistic visions as John Kennedy's New Frontier and Lyndon Johnson's Great Society seemed part of a distant past. The news was a daily bombardment of conflicts: teachers versus students, hawks versus doves, professionals versus hard hats, men versus women, whites versus blacks. Countless Americans were preparing for even more trouble. Elementary schools taught children to be wary of strangers, particularly the friendly ones. Gun sales continued to climb. So did the hiring of private police.

In this climate of suspicion, political leaders changed both their style and their objectives. Rather than speak the confident language of unity and progress, they acknowledged America's divisions and tried to fit some of its pieces into a stable coalition. The most important of these new leaders was the victor in the presidential race of 1968, Richard Nixon. Entering the White House with scarcely more than 43 percent of the popular vote, Nixon began at once to broaden his political base. Four years later, he had satisfied the popular desires for "law and order" and "peace" so ably that he ranked among the most successful Presidents of the twentieth century. It was an astonishing political triumph. Although economic and personal disasters soon toppled Nixon, his new departures in both domestic and foreign affairs continued to dominate American policy in the mid-seventies.

National and Local Power

Richard Nixon first attracted national attention in the late 1940s when as a congressman from California, he helped to link the former State Department official Alger Hiss with communist espionage. That success, in addition to his reputation as a reliable Republican, made him a senator, then the Vice-President under Dwight Eisenhower. After his fractional loss to John Kennedy in 1960 and his failure to become governor of California in 1962, Nixon suffered a temporary eclipse. But he fought tenaciously to win a second presidential nomination in 1968. This time, in another extremely close contest, he defeated the Democrat Hubert Humphrey and George Wallace, the third-party candidate.

Nixon took office under a cloud. A minority President and a stiff, uninspiring speaker, he also attracted a particularly deep hostility from his opponents. Intellectuals nursed a hatred for "Tricky Dick" Nixon unlike anything a new President had faced in this century. In a short time, however, the shrewd chief executive was surprising enemies and friends alike with his political skills. The first item on the new President's agenda was to redress the balance between national and local power. Through policies that were sometimes called a "Southern strategy" and sometimes an appeal to the "Silent Majority," Nixon immediately set about allaying fears that the national government was antagonistic to local control. He started with the Supreme Court. Four vacancies offered Nixon the best opportunity since Franklin Roosevelt's second term to recast its philosophy. And because the Democratic Senate rejected two of his early

The Election of 1968

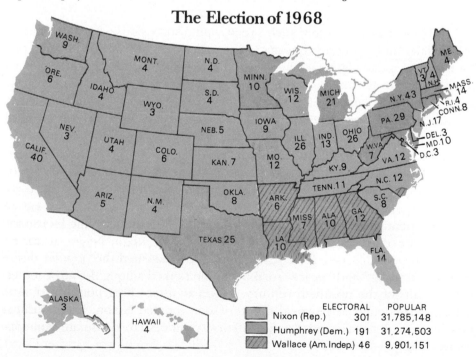

	ELECTORAL	POPULAR
Nixon (Rep.)	301	31,785,148
Humphrey (Dem.)	191	31,274,503
Wallace (Am. Indep.)	46	9,901,151

RICHARD NIXON

There was little warmth in his political style, but
Nixon proved to be an extraordinarily successful
President during his first term. *(Newsweek/Wally
McNamee.)*

nominees who had dubious, segregationist credentials, the President's intention of creating a conservative judiciary received nationwide attention.

Beginning with a new chief justice, the politically astute Minnesota Republican Warren Burger, Nixon's appointments did reorient the Supreme Court. Gradually it turned back toward the principles of local autonomy. The police received wider latitude in dealing with suspected criminals. After a period of doubt about the legality of the death penalty, the Burger Court in *Furman* v. *Georgia* (1972) decided that state legislatures only needed to be more specific about which crimes deserved the death sentence.

One of the most volatile issues of the seventies, busing schoolchildren to achieve racial integration, required more time to manage. The Supreme Court had established a long, consistent record of support for desegregation, including a crucial endorsement of busing in 1971. The first signs of an accommodation did not occur until 1974. That July, in *Milliken* v. *Bradley,* the Burger Court ruled against a busing plan for metropolitan Detroit that would have incorporated the suburban schools, 98 percent white, with the city schools, 65 percent black. "No single tradition in public education is more deeply rooted than local control over the operation of schools," the chief justice declared in the spirit of the old balance. The national government would "deprive the people of local control" if it imposed its authority across the jurisdictional boundaries of the metropolitan area. Nevertheless, even after this decision, the federal courts continued to enforce busing in Boston, where crowds of angry whites fought against the legal orders, and in Louisville, where the city and its suburbs were, in fact, part of a common plan.

Meanwhile members of the Nixon adminstration were echoing the values of local America. When a presidential commission recommended minimal supervision over pornography, Nixon dismissed its findings as "morally bankrupt." The President also condemned current trends in sexual freedom and demanded stern punishment for drug offenders. Through Attorney General John Mitchell, the administration publicized its cooperation with local police forces, and in May 1970, when tens of thousands of antiwar protesters came to Washington, the Justice Department responded with mass arrests and makeshift detention corrals. Nixon, who had once been the partisan voice of the Eisenhower administration, used Vice-President Spiro Agnew in a similar way. Through Agnew, the administration heaped scorn on "an effete corps of impudent . . . intellectuals," accused the television networks of news distortion, and locked horns with such nationally prominent newspapers as the New York *Times* and the Washington *Post*. In the previous twenty-five years, only Joseph McCarthy and George Wallace had expressed the popular hostility to modern values as effectively as Agnew did.

The administration's assault on modern values was part of a general effort to redress the balance between national and local authority. The new balance of the seventies tried to assure different groups in American society that they had domains of their own. The proud declaration of a Polish or Italian or Jewish identity became increasingly acceptable. From West Virginia to North Dakota, rural communities reasserted their right to control the local schools and censor the books they used. Through the programs of revenue sharing and block grants that the Nixon administration introduced, local governments received additional federal money to manage more or less as they chose. At the same time, nothing significantly abridged the privileges of successful Americans. The leading suburban and private schools operated as they always had. National economic policy remained the province of a national elite. In fact, the personal freedoms of well-to-do Americans continued to expand, most notably as a result of the Burger Court's decision in *Roe* v. *Wade* (1973), which legalized abortions.

The balance of the seventies did, however, halt new national programs in behalf of racial minorities. Early in the 1970s, for example, groups of Indians

CÉSAR CHAVEZ AND THE NATIONAL
FARM WORKERS

Despite the iron determination of
Chavez, the cause of the Chicano
farm workers declined in the
seventies. *(Michael Dobo/Stock
Boston.)*

drew attention to their history of oppression and ostracism by temporarily
occupying a number of public places that were linked with their past. Some
of these protests were peaceful, as at Fort Sheridan, Illinois, and some were
violent, as at Wounded Knee, South Dakota. Neither tactic won concessions
from the national government. During the sixties, Mexican Americans who
labored in California's "farm factories" had formed the National Farm Workers
Association under the patient and persistent César Chavez, and the new organization received considerable support from reformers and unionists. Robert
Kennedy had been its outstanding national partisan. But after Kennedy's
death, the Chicanos found no prominent champion in Washington. Beset by
the combined opposition of commercial farmers and a rival Teamsters union,
the fortunes of the National Farm Workers Association dwindled during the
seventies.

In addition, the Nixon administration dismantled the Office of Economic
Opportunity, which had been encouraging local black organizations, and announced a period of "benign neglect" in the government's policies for racial
equality. As the percentage of black pupils in all-black schools dropped below
20 percent, a rising percentage in Congress opposed busing as a way of achieving a closer racial balance in the schools. President Nixon, by expressing his

personal dislike for busing, strengthened this opposition. The only inviting avenues to a greater black power were now local, not national, and blacks did try to follow them. Early in the seventies, blacks became mayors of several important cities, including Cleveland, Atlanta, Los Angeles, and Detroit. Yet the big cities, in turn, were suffering from a severe budget squeeze. During the fall of 1975, for example, New York City almost went bankrupt. Hence, this kind of political power was diminishing just as blacks were acquiring it.

The new balance received a broad popular approval. Opinion polls in the mid-seventies registered two out of three Americans against busing, two out of three for the death penalty, three out of four against legalized marijuana, and almost everyone for greater protection against crime. These attitudes were crucial to Nixon's overwhelming reelection in 1972. That summer, a serious, liberal senator from South Dakota, George McGovern, won the Democratic nomination for President following his success in the primaries. Everything about McGovern's candidacy suggested danger to the new balance. He wanted to renew the war on poverty and use the government's authority in behalf of black rights. His support among well-to-do college students was as enthusiastic as Eugene McCarthy's had been four years earlier. McGovern refused to endorse harsh measures against street crimes and drug violations, and he appeared indifferent to such issues as Bibles in the schools and the suppression of obscenity. In November 1972, only Massachusetts and the District of Columbia gave majorities to McGovern. With 521 of 538 electoral votes, Nixon, a marginal leader less than four years before, scored one of the most impressive political victories of modern times.

A Flexible Diplomacy

Stability at home depended on stability abroad. The bitter controversy over Viet Nam continued as Nixon took office in 1969, and he knew that, one way or another, he had to end the war. Like his predecessors, Nixon was committed to containing communism in Southeast Asia. But to this task, the President brought his own assumptions about a sound policy. Remembering Eisenhower's settlement of the Korean conflict in 1953, Nixon concluded that in an unpopular war most Americans would choose the withdrawal of their own troops over a clear-cut military victory. Second, the President believed that the United States should be willing to increase the punishment of a stubborn enemy considerably above the levels the Johnson administration had inflicted.

Nixon's strategy in Southeast Asia, therefore, combined a wider, freer use of military power with a gradual removal of American troops. Initially, the President hoped that a more daring application of ground forces could still shift the military balance in Viet Nam. Through tactical invasions of Cambodia in 1970 and Laos in 1971, the American command tried to cut the supplies and disperse the armies that the enemy was concentrating in South Viet Nam.

When a coup established a friendly government in Cambodia, the United States equipped its army. Now it was openly an Indochinese war. But an Indochinese war merely created an Indochinese guerrilla opposition without affecting the balance of power in Viet Nam. The longer Nixon managed the war, the more he came to rely on bombing raids that exceeded even the massive ones under Johnson.

Meanwhile, the President was reducing the number of American troops in Viet Nam from over half a million in 1969 to under 100,000 in 1972. The South Vietnamese army, the President said, would soon be capable of fighting the ground war alone. Because these withdrawals significantly lessened American criticism of the war, they gave Nixon more time to reach some kind of settlement with the North Vietnamese. He needed the leeway, for the failure of his Indochinese strategy strongly argued for compromise. During the final months of Johnson's presidency, the United States and North Viet Nam had opened a forum for these negotiations in Paris, and after 1969, delegates from the two nations used it alternately to storm at one another and to explore the possibilities of peace.

The crisis in the negotiations occurred just after the election of 1972, when the scale of America's air attacks implied that it might indeed try to bomb North Viet Nam "back into the Stone Age." In January 1973, both sides modified their demands just enough to sign a peace agreement. In effect, the settlement allowed the war to continue without American troops. Through a tortured use of the language, Nixon was able to call the agreement "peace with honor" because technically it satisfied the standard rule of containment. No new territory had been relinquished to the communists. But the Indochinese paid an appallingly high cost in blood and misery for that honor. In two more years, even the illusion of containing communism dissolved. After appearing to hold their own against the communist armies, America's allies in South Viet Nam and Cambodia collapsed abruptly in the early months of 1975. Suddenly, communist governments ruled everywhere on the mainland of Southeast Asia except Thailand, and American power was eliminated. Once the shock of surprise had passed, few Americans tried to keep the issue of Indochina alive. Hawks and doves alike agreed that the war had been the most disastrous in American history.

During the final years of the Indochinese War, the Nixon administration was also responding to the worldwide problem of containment's crumbling structure. Here it showed exceptional imagination. In the most important series of events during Nixon's presidency, the United States dramatically improved its relations first with China, then with the Soviet Union. The deepening hostility between China and Russia, and the desire in each of these two nations to devote more energy to internal affairs, raised the possibility that one or both of them might welcome an accommodation with the United States. Early in 1971, Nixon seriously began investigating this opportunity. Feelers indicated that China was receptive to an American overture. While leaders in

SAIGON, MAY 1975

As the communist armies rolled toward Saigon, Americans
fought off their own allies in the panic to evacuate.
(Associated Press.)

Washington and Peking made small public gestures of moderation, Nixon's
adviser Henry Kissinger was meeting secretly in China with Premier Chou En-lai.
In the summer of 1971, the President broke the astonishing news that he personally would visit China.

After turning its back to the People's Republic of China for more than twenty
years, the United States acknowledged its existence with the chief executive's
presence. The entire affair was international theater at its best. In a rush of
discovery, millions of Americans learned something of the revolution that had
been transforming the world's largest nation. Then they watched on television
as their President crossed containment's invisible barrier in February 1972 to
shake hands with the leaders of "Red China." Though relations between the
two governments remained cautious, the United States finally abandoned the
cause of Chiang Kai-shek, accepted China in the United Nations, and prepared
the way for a broader interchange.

Also during 1971, the administration was moving silently toward détente with Russia. The Soviet Premier, Leonid Brezhnev, who was anxious to limit the range of Russia's international involvements, willingly grasped a chance to lessen the tensions with its chief rival. Once again, private diplomatic discussions on the possible areas of agreement came first. Once again, the President surprised the world by announcing a visit to the Soviet Union in May 1972. Nixon picked up a thread that had been lost at the futile summit conferences of 1960 and 1961. Soon after his trip to China, he traveled to Moscow, where he had an extremely cordial meeting with the very officials whom Americans had recently considered the masterminds of international conspiracy.

Like the new relations with China, the Soviet-American détente yielded few specific returns. The two nations reached some agreement on regulating their nuclear weapons, welcomed each other's citizens more liberally, and negotiated a sale of American wheat to Russia that unfortunately occurred just on the eve of a sharp rise in the American price for grain. And except for Brezhnev's reciprocal visit to the United States in 1973 and another wheat deal in 1975, nothing more concrete emerged from détente during the next few years. Many of the old antagonisms proved to be very much alive. Nevertheless, beginning in 1972, longstanding fears of thermonuclear war eased. The world's super powers were prepared to confer about any serious international problem.

The fresh departures with China and the Soviet Union, in turn, were part of an even broader reorientation of American diplomacy. The world's heterogeneity that the Kennedy administration recognized and the Johnson administration tried to ignore became the starting point in foreign relations during the Nixon administration. The new diplomacy relied on principles similar to those prevailing in America's domestic politics: bargain with a group at a time, work to minimize the friction among allies, keep promises as loose as possible, and assume the need for continuing renegotiations. Just as these techniques were used to manage varied interest groups at home, so they were expected to deal with an equally diverse set of international interests. In domestic affairs, Americans tested their effectiveness by such traditional guidelines as the victory of a political party or a rise in the standard of living. In world affairs, however, Americans had no comparable way of measuring the success or failure of these bargaining tactics. By the mid-1970s, America had moved full circle around the years of containment and operated once more without a systematic policy in its foreign relations.

Nixon's collaborator in this transformation was Henry Kissinger, a German-born professor from Harvard who first served as the President's adviser and then in 1973 became secretary of state. Kissinger personified the new diplomacy of evolving bargains and ad hoc arrangements. Under both Nixon and his successor Gerald Ford, Kissinger was the man in motion, negotiating the Paris accord with North Viet Nam, preparing the way for Nixon's visits to Peking and Moscow, shuttling between Israel and the Arab nations, touring the capitals of Europe, and searching for a settlement of the Cyprus War between Greece and Turkey. The substance of the nation's foreign policy seemed to be Kissinger grappling with one problem after another. As a result, many Americans held this one man responsible for the ups and downs of world affairs. In the summer of 1974, when international problems appeared to be abating, Kissinger was acclaimed the one indispensable man in Washington. Six months later, when détente with the Soviet Union was losing its freshness, hostilities were threatening in the Middle East, and Southeast Asia was falling to the communist armies, disillusioned critics called the secretary of state an utter incompetent. In another six months, Kissinger was presiding over a historic agreement between Egypt and Israel, and once again his reputation soared.

Kissinger's incessant travels gave the impression that the United States was immersed in every one of the world's problems. Actually, the trend ran in the opposite direction. During the era of containment, the slightest change anywhere on the globe had some meaning for America's anticommunist policy. By the 1970s, however, a great many international events no longer mattered very much. In 1974, Washington remained quite calm when new leaders and governments suddenly appeared in an array of countries throughout the world, including France, Germany, Israel, Greece, and Japan. In September 1975, when the Organization of American States (OAS) in the Western Hemisphere lifted its boycott of Cuba, few Americans even knew about this break in the chain of containment.

Each event, in effect, had to prove its own importance. Nothing better illustrated the new approach than the Nixon administration's response to the collapse of the Bretton Woods agreement, which since 1944 had regulated international monetary exchanges by the American dollar. Instead of scrambling to reassert its leadership of the Free World, the United States decided to let all national currencies fluctuate in price on an open world market. Beneath the hustle of the new diplomacy, the United States was reclaiming some of its old heritage, a detachment from international affairs. Above all, a large majority of Americans wanted to avoid "another Viet Nam." During the winter of 1975–76, for example, foreign intervention in the new African nation of Angola set the Soviet Union and Cuba against the United States and South Africa on opposite sides of a civil war. Congress, with a strong public sentiment behind it, moved promptly to place tight limits around America's involvement.

Despite these changes in orientation, many of the traditional assumptions behind containment continued to shape America's foreign affairs. National security was still equated with a full arsenal of nuclear weapons. Beginning in 1969, the United States and the Soviet Union engaged in lengthy Strategic Arms Limitation Talks (SALT), but the pattern of the arms race did not significantly change. In fact, the political opposition to disarmament was rising late in 1975. The United States still preferred firmly anticommunist governments as

its allies, and particularly in Latin America, it still considered aggressive reformers an international danger. Using the familiar language of the Cold War,
President Ford justified America's sponsorship of a military coup in Chile as
"in the best interest of the people in Chile and certainly in our best interest."
The critical difference was that these actions no longer belonged to a cohesive
global policy. They had become pieces of an old policy in search of a new framework.

An Erratic Economy

One of the few remaining areas of confidence during the late 1960s had
been the state of the economy. Yet no sooner did Nixon take office than this,
too, posed serious problems of stabilization. Because Congress had lowered
taxes just as the heaviest financing of the Viet Nam War was about to begin, the
government's policy generated a great surge of purchasing power that practically
guaranteed inflation. Prices were already rising sharply as Nixon became President. At the same time, the economy grew sluggish. From 1969 to early 1971,
as the percentage of unemployed increased to about 6 percent, the GNP scarcely
changed, its worst record in more than a decade. Late in 1971, the pinch eased.
For several months, the GNP rose impressively, unemployment eventually fell
below 5 percent, and the rate of inflation, while still disturbingly steep, showed
some signs of abating. Then in 1973 a crisis struck. Inflation took off at an
annual rate of about 10 percent, unemployment mounted until it also approached
10 percent, the GNP slumped almost 5 percent a year, and the stock market
dropped precipitously. Now the economy recalled memories of the thirties.

Almost every American blamed the President for these troubles. After all,
he was the manager of the national economy. By the 1970s, however, the scope
of the President's economic power had appreciably narrowed. The government
manipulated the national budget, the national debt, and national monetary
policy on the assumption that these domestic actions would produce a predictable
set of domestic reactions. To combat inflation, the government taxed surplus
income and tightened credit. To stimulate economic growth, it increased the
national deficit and lowered interest rates. But the wave of inflation that swept
over the United States in 1973 also flooded the world, overwhelming all national economies and bringing rates of increase elsewhere that were considerably
higher than America's. Basic resources ranging from grains and sugar to oil
and aluminum soared in price. The United States could not control any of them.
When world inflation was superimposed on an American recession, the standard
techniques of economic management no longer worked. Attacking the recession risked an even wilder inflation. Attacking inflation risked an even deeper
depression. In an earlier day, America's economy had dominated the rising
and falling curves of the international cycle. Now the United States was just

one of several great powers, and it tossed in the same winds that were shaking the rest of the world.

No President, therefore, could satisfy the popular demands that were placed on him. Both Nixon and Ford relied heavily on psychological tactics, both hoped that time would operate on their side, and both, when forced to choose, emphasized the problem of inflation over the problem of recession. In 1971, Nixon dramatically opened his battle against inflation with a temporary freeze on wages and prices, which publicized the administration's concern and prepared the way for a long-term program. In what was called Phase II, the freeze was lifted from most of the economy, and the executive applied intensive persuasion to hold wages and prices to modest rates of increase. By 1973, it was assumed, the executive could largely withdraw, set broad guidelines, and let the economy function normally in Phase III. Fortunately for the President, Phase II coincided with an economic revival and a steadying rate of inflation. Unfortunately for Nixon, Phase III began just as international inflation was ready to skyrocket, and a hastily devised Phase IV was lost in the updraft.

President Ford took office in midflight. After a futile try at positive thinking, which included the distribution of WIN (Whip Inflation Now) buttons, Ford reluctantly accepted the need for tax cuts and a sizable budget deficit early in 1975. The Democratic Congress enthusiastically endorsed these antidepression measures. In the long run, however, Ford insisted that Congress pair tax cuts with spending cuts, and he used his veto again and again to reduce appropriations. That combination no longer qualified as an antidepression policy. With prices still rising about 10 percent a year, Ford concentrated his attention on inflation. Opinion polls late in 1975 indicated that about three out of four Americans agreed with his priorities.

While the nation was wrestling with recession and inflation, two other trends emerged from these economic hardships. One involved the so-called ecology movement, which had spread during the 1960s in an effort to halt an urban-industrial society's damage to the physical environment. Images of an uncontaminated earth where man and nature were once again in harmony aroused a deeply embedded set of emotions. In a crescendo of cries, more and more successful Americans of all ages demanded relief from the dangers of chemical sprays, industrial wastes, and automobile exhaust. Veteran conservationists found an eager, new audience. "Organic" foods and "recyclable" products became increasingly popular in the consumer market. Beginning with the Clean Air Act of 1963, the national government responded by establishing a series of antipollution standards to protect both the atmosphere and the water ways.

In local America, however, the ecology crusade had a very mixed, sometimes hostile reception. Higher antipollution standards usually implied higher costs and perhaps fewer jobs. In America's vacation lands, environmental pres-

WIN (WHIP INFLATION NOW)

In his first months as President, Gerald Ford hoped that a
higher public morale would lower the rate of inflation.
(*UPI photo.*)

ervation often seemed the rich person's way of stopping latecomers from making
their fortunes. As the economy faltered, the ecology movement stumbled with
it. Neither Nixon nor Ford sympathized with the movement, and they willingly
gave precedence to profits and jobs over purification. Local governments, which
carried the primary burdens of enforcement, bent to the wishes of their local
industries, which usually led the opposition to the antipollution standards.
Although a widespread awareness and a continuing set of national guidelines
guaranteed that the ecology movement would not disappear, it became subordinated to the issues of inflation and recession.

The second of these trends was a movement toward national self-sufficiency,
which had been growing while America's commitment to the Cold War diminished. As the United States had to share more and more of its world power,
it could exercise less and less control over its international economic relations.
One of the primary threats that Cuba posed in the 1960s, for example, was its
encouragement for other agrarian countries to nationalize American-owned

assets. Beginning in the early 1960s, the United States suffered periodically from an adverse balance of payments, with too much capital leaving the country and not enough coming in. Though the United States had once helped European nations solve a comparable problem, no one offered to return the favor.

These vague, nagging irritations about an unreliable world came sharply into focus with the energy crisis of 1973–74. The immediate cause of the crisis was another round in the Middle Eastern conflict between Arabs and Israelis. After decades of clear military superiority over any combination of Arab opponents, Israel suddenly found the balance of forces much closer to even in a bloody, protracted war that began late in 1973. A primary reason for the new military balance was the financial support that the oil-producing Arab nations now gave to the war against Israel. To underline their commitment, these nations imposed a producers' boycott on petroleum in behalf of the Arab cause. That winter, every important industrial nation, except the Soviet Union, suffered an oil shortage. When a pause in the war occurred early in 1974 and the boycott ended, the Arab producers more than doubled the price of oil and in one

THE GAS CRISIS, 1973

(Allan Tannenbaum photo)

bold stroke altered the flow of international finance. Years before, the columnist Joseph Alsop had warned that hands from the Middle East pressed on Europe's jugular. Industrial nations everywhere felt the pressure in 1974, and in response to this awesome Arab power, they began withdrawing diplomatic support from Israel.

During the winter of 1973–74, millions of Americans feared that they might not have enough oil to heat their homes. Morning after morning, weary commuters scoured the city for an open service station, then waited in line for a few gallons of gasoline. Though the policy of American oil companies was more responsible for these domestic shortages than the boycott, the most publicized villains were the petroleum-rich Arab nations. The United States government seemed utterly helpless. Neither bluster nor persuasion affected the Arab producers. Because only the United States held reasonably fast in support of Israel, many Americans also worried about the possibility of being drawn into a Middle Eastern war just as they were escaping a Southeast Asian war. Such a striking lesson in America's vulnerability, coupled with the tendency in hard times to draw people's attention toward domestic problems, gave a strong impetus to the movement for American self-sufficiency. Total isolation was inconceivable, but a maximum degree of economic autonomy became one of the most popular national objectives.

A Cloudy Horizon

The early seventies, like the late forties, were years for sober reassessment. In ways reminiscent of the period just after the Second World War, Americans of many different kinds were demanding a return to the basics. Professions that had been subjected to radical pressures during the late sixties renewed their exclusive commitment to the values of expertise. "Permissive" child rearing fell into disrepute, and parents pledged their allegiance to clear authority and salutary discipline in the home. Yet unlike the postwar years, the 1970s revealed no new sources of strength. By now, the miracle cures of the 1950s had become thoroughly entangled in the very problems that people were struggling to resolve. The computer, rather than answering the big social questions, seemed only to verify the complexity and intractability of the nation's primary challenges: racial inequality, the culture of poverty, drugs, violence, crime. Neither desegregation nor the war on poverty had improved the relative economic standing of America's black population, which suffered severely in the recession of the 1970s. Even consumerism was suspect. To beat inflation and conserve energy, Americans were told, they should buy less, eat less, drive less, and heat less.

Early in the 1970s, prominent Americans also discovered a new, personal danger in the manipulative techniques that were originally meant to influence the masses. Through Daniel Ellsberg, a disillusioned expert from the Department of Defense, the nation's leading newspapers received classified documents exposing the government's secret maneuvers and systematic lies about the Indochinese War. Although the Nixon administration fought to suppress them, these documents were published serially during 1971, then compiled as *The Pentagon Papers.* Ellsberg himself became the target of a bizarre government plot of character defamation that included burglarizing his psychiatrist's office. Each year, more such stories appeared. President Johnson had approved the electronic surveillance of Martin Luther King, Robert Kennedy, and Spiro Agnew. Kissinger had requested wiretaps on his own aides and President Nixon had authorized one on his own brother. Military intelligence had spied on an array of liberal politicians and the FBI had compiled dossiers on an even longer list of them. The director of the FBI, J. Edgar Hoover, had waged a personal vendetta against King. The Internal Revenue Service had audited income tax returns on the basis of a citizen's political activities. The unfolding record revealed a technique gone berserk, or perhaps just democratic. People who had once thought they belonged to a minority of manipulators now saw themselves as part of the mass to be manipulated.

One widespread effort to protect the individual against manipulation was the consumer movement of the 1960s. In 1965, a zealous young lawyer named Ralph Nader emerged as the movement's chief spokesman with the publication of *Unsafe At Any Speed*, a detailed analysis of the automobile hazards being manufactured in Detroit. A shabby attempt by General Motors to discredit him only enlarged his fame. Through the efforts of young volunteers called "Nader's Raiders," a variety of additional exposés rapidly followed. By the end of the decade, innumerable journalists, scientists, and local committees were spreading the gospel of consumer standards, and polls indicated a large majority behind the cause. Millions of Americans even thought Nader should be President. Yet in spite of new legal guidelines in such areas as automobile safety, credit contracts, product labeling, and food adulteration, the consumer movement dwindled in the 1970s. There were many protests against inflation, but they had little cohesion or consistency. Consumers were everybody in general and nobody in particular—and exceedingly hard to organize. Nothing arose to replace the movement.

The soul searching of the late 1940s had inspired a new faith in "realism." Many Americans had concluded that if they accepted the world's complexity and the human mind's limitations, they could move step by step toward sounder,

CITY SMOG

The sickly haze of the cities was a subject of talk far more than action in the seventies. *(Elliott Erwitt/Magnum.)*

wiser policies. But the reassessments of the early 1970s seemed only to produce fatalism, a feeling that vast national and international problems defied solution. The novelist Kurt Vonnegut captured the mood in an exchange between two middle-aged men who were pondering a prospective world population of 7 billion:

> "I suppose they will all want dignity," I said.
> "I suppose," said O'Hare.

That same sense of the individual trapped in a web of forces characterized such important novels as Joyce Carol Oates' *Them* (1969) and Joseph Heller's *Something Happened* (1974), as well as a number of fine movies.

Americans at least discovered that the mightiest individuals were not necessarily more secure then they. One of the most publicized series of events during the Nixon years was the fall of the great men. Each new scandal in the sequence was more shocking than the last, and each punishment set a historic precedent. First came Abe Fortas, an associate justice of the Supreme Court whom President Johnson, in his final days, tried to make Earl Warren's replacement as chief justice. When a congressional inquiry in 1969 revealed that Fortas had profited unduly from his office, the pressure forced him to resign from the Court. Fortas was followed by Judge Otto Kerner, a liberal Democrat with an unusually high reputation for integrity, who had chaired the important Presidential Advisory Commission on Civil Disorders. Found guilty of accepting bribes while he had been governor of Illinois, Kerner went directly from his place on the circuit court to jail.

Next came Vice-President Agnew, national champion of law and order and current favorite to win the Republican nomination for President in 1976. Early in 1973, the Justice Department reconstructed a long history of secret payments that engineering firms, in return for government contracts, had been making to Agnew throughout his rise in Maryland politics. Couriers even sat in the Vice-President's anteroom waiting to deliver the cash. After a frantic attempt to save his career, the Vice-President suddenly resigned in October as part of a bargain with the Justice Department. Agnew received a light sentence for evading income tax but avoided the much more serious penalties for extortion and bribery.

The loss of the Vice-President was stunning enough. Yet Agnew was only the prologue. As he fell, the President himself was toppling. In June 1972, five men were arrested for burglarizing Democratic headquarters at the Watergate Apartments in Washington, D. C. After a flurry of attention, the story slipped from sight. Despite the connection between the burglars and the Republican Committee to Reelect the President, Nixon's Democratic opponent, Senator McGovern, could rouse little interest in the incident during the fall campaign. Then in the spring of 1973, one of the burglars decided to cooperate with the

THE FALL OF VICE-PRESIDENT SPIRO AGNEW

(Oliphant © 1973 Denver Post.)

government investigators. As he was talking, John Dean, a close presidential adviser, joined him. Behind these two, a longer line of penitents began to form.

The stories they told spread in two directions. One traced a variety of activities through the executive's most powerful offices: the use of campaign contributions to win government favors, the illegal handling of those funds, devious techniques for making the President a millionaire, and assorted tactics of political sabotage to ensure Nixon's reelection. Although it was a sordid view through the keyhole of national politics, it attracted far less attention than the second trail of evidence, which carried the planning and suppressing of the Watergate burglary to Nixon's inner staff—John Dean, Attorney General John Mitchell, and a pair of hard, ascetic organization men, H. R. Haldeman and John Ehrlichman, who were the President's principal domestic aides. Would the trail lead to the President's desk?

For more than a year, Nixon fought to block it. In public, the President repeatedly declared his innocence. In private, he plotted ways of obstructing a grand jury under the tenacious Judge John Sirica and a Senate investigating committee under the skeptical old-timer, Sam Ervin of North Carolina. Forced to accept a special Watergate prosecutor within the Justice Department, Nixon in October 1973 fired the first one, Archibald Cox of the Harvard Law School, because Cox was preparing to sue for the evidence that the President would not relinquish. Cox's replacement, the conservative Houston lawyer Leon Jaworski, proved just as dogged and carried his demand for the evidence to the Supreme Court.

JOHN DEAN TESTIFYING BEFORE THE SENATE SELECT
COMMITTEE

(Magnum.)

The evidence in question lay in a vault of tapes recording almost every conversation that had been held in President Nixon's private office. These tapes,
which Nixon strangely chose to clutch rather than destroy, eventually wrecked
his defenses. Someone tried erasing portions of the tapes. The White House
issued an edited transcript from them. Finally, the President decided to withhold them altogether. But in July 1974, the Supreme Court unanimously awarded
the tapes to Judge Sirica's grand jury and, through the grand jury, to all the
hounds at bay. As the House of Representatives was preparing to vote articles
of impeachment against the President, Nixon acknowledged much of what
the tapes would verify about his involvement in the Watergate affair almost
from the day of the burglary. Admitting the facts but denying any guilt, Nixon
resigned as President on August 9, 1974.

The last and mightiest fall set the most astonishing precedents. After receiving 97 percent of the electoral vote, the President—the indispensable leader—
had been driven from office in midterm. Moreover, his replacement had been

elected to no office higher than representative from the Fifth Congressional District of Michigan. Gerald Ford, whom Nixon selected in 1973 to replace the departed Agnew, had a mandate for national leadership only from the two houses of Congress. What might have caused an upheaval actually calmed the nation, for the prestige of the President now relied more on opinion polls than on election returns. Well before Nixon's capitulation, the most persuasive proof that he should resign lay in a steady stream of reports that only about one in four Americans was supporting his presidency.

Ford responded to the challenge of public confidence with just the right tactics. In his initial address as President, he promised to represent almost everyone except the atheists. His manner was unaffected, amiable, and open— a perfect contrast to Nixon's. Though temperamentally and ideologically conservative, he knew the ways of political compromise from his years as minority leader in the House of Representatives. Rather than adopt a bold executive brand of leadership, Ford retained his own cautious, congressional style. His programs, offering a little for this group, a little for that one, read like committee reports to the House. When opinion polls showed three out of four Americans behind the new President, Ford had weathered the crisis.

An equally important reason for the smooth transition between Presidents was a nationwide cynicism about all Washington politics. During the presidential crisis, no message appeared more clearly in the opinion polls. When a majority first expressed the belief that Nixon was lying about Watergate, four out of five also judged him no more corrupt than his predecessors. On the eve of his resignation, one out of two wanted the Senate to impeach Nixon but only one out of four thought it would. Much the same spirit prevailed during the election of 1974, when scarcely more than a third of the eligible voters cast their ballots.

As if to counteract this widespread cynicism, the news media presented Nixon's fall as a morality play. They focused on the individual, Richard Nixon, and interpreted his disgrace as a lesson to prove that even the most exalted would suffer for the sin of pride. Such an orientation also eased the transition between Presidents, because it made Nixon's resignation the solution to the nation's outstanding problem. Many people who subscribed to this interpretation sharply criticized President Ford late in 1974 for issuing a blanket pardon to Nixon and thus blocking legal action against the former chief executive. At the very least, the argument went, Nixon should confess his guilt before he earned a pardon. As one after another of Nixon's associates stood trial and received punishment, the curtain slowly fell on the morality play. Appropriately, the New York *Times* summarized the prison sentences for Mitchell, Haldeman, and Ehrlichman in February 1975 by calling them "The Price of Arrogance."

As Americans celebrated their bicentennial, they might have taken satisfaction from two centuries of constitutional government, a century of remarkable economic development, half a century of national security in a war-plagued world, and a quarter of a century of expanding minority rights. Instead, the

OPERATION SAIL, NEW YORK HARBOR, JULY 4, 1976

The most popular exhibit on the bicentennial Fourth of July
said nothing about America's revolutionary heritage, its
unique institutions, or its future promise. *(Associated Press.)*

prevailing tone was quiet. A bumper sticker neatly caught the tentative, drifting mood: "Yesterday sex was dirty and the air was clean." Economic troubles, which had dampened the centennial celebration in 1876, the Columbian Exposition in 1893, and the "Century of Progress" World's Fair in 1933, once again muted the cheers. The talk of an American Century in the forties, the voices of national confidence in the fifties, and the cries for social reform in the sixties had all subsided. Americans appeared to be waiting for someone, or something, to define a new set of objectives that would mark the path into a new era.

Suggested Readings

Accounts of Richard Nixon include a favorable one in Earl Mazo and Stephen Hess, *Nixon: A Political Portrait* (1968), and an unfavorable one in Garry Wills, *Nixon Agonistes* (1970). In *Kissinger* (1974), Marvin and Bernard Kalb raise Nixon's reputation in foreign affairs by deflating claims that Kissinger dominated the President. Harland B. Moulton, *From Superiority to Parity: The United States and the Strategic Arms Race, 1961–1971* (1973), discusses some preliminary moves toward détente. The presidential records of Lyndon Johnson and Nixon have stirred interest in the office of chief executive. Among recent books on the subject are George E. Reedy, *The Twilight of the Presidency* (1970), Arthur M. Schlesinger, Jr., *The Imperial Presidency* (1973), which is sharply critical of Nixon, and Otis L. Graham, Jr., *Toward a Planned Society: From Roosevelt to Nixon* (1976), which contrasts Nixon's approach to planning with the approach of Franklin Roosevelt. The Watergate affair has generated a special group of studies. Carl Bernstein and Bob Woodward, the reporters who helped to expose the affair, tell a fascinating tale of investigation and deception in *All the President's Men* (1974). Their sequel, *The Final Days* (1976), deals with Nixon during the year before his resignation. Jonathan Schell, *The Time of Illusion* (1976), is also illuminating on the Watergate period.

A number of fine books argue the need for reconsideration after the sixties. Christopher Lasch, *The Agony of the American Left* (1969), analyzes the limitations of contemporary radicalism, Alexander M. Bickel, *The Supreme Court and the Idea of Progress* (1970), the limitations of the judiciary, Robert L. Heilbroner, *An Inquiry into the Human Prospect* (1974), the limitations of the world economy, and Andrew Hacker, *The End of the American Era* (1970), the limitations of Washington's managerial leadership. On the other hand, Daniel Bell is reasonably confident about America's future in *The Coming of Post-Industrial Society* (1973). On two controversial issues, Martin Hoffman's *The Gay World: Male Homosexuality and the Social Creation of Evil* (1968) presents the case for homosexuals, and David F. Musto's *The American Disease* (1973) traces the history of federal policy on narcotics. A general account of a minority that has failed to find support in Washington is Matt S. Meier and Feliciano Rivera, *The Chicanos: A History of Mexican Americans* (1972).

Chronology, 1920 to the present

1920
Suspected radicals arrested in Palmer raids, height of Red Scare.
Senate rejects Versailles Treaty and U.S. entry in League of Nations.
Nineteenth Amendment guarantees women's suffrage.
First commercial radio station begins operation.
Sinclair Lewis's *Main Street* published.
Warren G. Harding elected President defeating James M. Cox.

1921
First bill restricting immigration passed.
Washington Conference limits naval tonnage among major powers.
Collapse of farm prices precipitates serious recession.

1922
Nationwide coal strike accompanied by violence.
Fordney-McCumber Tariff raises protective rates.
Recovery from 1921 recession begins.
Supreme Court strikes down child labor laws.

1923
U.S. Steel agrees to abandon twelve-hour day.
Teapot Dome, other Harding administration scandals exposed.
Harding dies in San Francisco; Calvin Coolidge becomes President.
Supreme Court strikes down minimum wage for women.

1924
Founding of *Reader's Digest* and *Time Magazine*.
Bonus Bill enacted, providing benefits to First World War veterans.
National Origins Act sets restrictive immigration quotas.
Snyder Act guarantees U.S. citizenship to American Indians.
Calvin Coolidge elected President defeating John W. Davis.

1925
John T. Scopes convicted of violating Tennessee law against teaching evolution.
F. Scott Fitzgerald's *The Great Gatsby* published.

1926
U.S. "joins," then quits World Court in treaty dispute.
Revenue Act lowers taxes on corporations, wealthy individuals.
First scheduled commercial airplane flights begin.
National Broadcasting Company, first radio network, formed.
Ernest Hemingway's *The Sun Also Rises* published.

1934
Frazier-Lemke Bankruptcy Act helps farmers regain lost property.
Federal Housing Administration founded to insure home mortgages.
Father Charles Coughlin, Detroit "radio priest," starts National Union for Social Justice.
Dr. Francis Townsend wins wide support for old age pension plan.
Works Progress Administration funds public works.
Public Utilities Holding Company Act attacks utilities trusts.
Supreme Court, in Schechter decision, strikes down NRA.
Wagner Act affirms collective bargaining rights, sets up NLRB.

1935
First Social Security Act adopted.
Revenue Act of 1935 increases taxes on wealthy.
Senator Huey P. Long of Louisiana leads national "Share Our Wealth" movement until assassinated in Baton Rouge.
Congress of Industrial Organizations begins rift of industrial unions from American Federation of Labor.
Senate rejects U.S. membership on World Court again.
Italy invades Ethiopia.

1936
Supreme Court strikes down AAA and New York minimum wage law.
CIO. sit down strikes paralyze rubber, auto industries.
Playwright Eugene O'Neil receives Nobel Prize for Literature.
Spanish Civil War erupts.
Roosevelt elected President defeating Alfred Landon in landslide.

1937
Roosevelt proposes courtpacking scheme; Congress buries it.
Supreme Court, reversing earlier positions, upholds Wagner Act.
CIO. officially expelled from AF of L.
Ten killed in "Memorial Day Massacre" during Chicago steel strike.
Bankhead-Jones Farm Tenancy Act helps tenants and small farmers.
Japan invades China.

1945
First electronic digital computer completed.
Roosevelt defeats Thomas E. Dewey to win fourth term as President.
FDR, Churchill, Stalin meet at Yalta, agree to divided occupation of Germany; further agreements reached at Potsdam.
Americans recapture Philippines.
Roosevelt dies; Harry S Truman becomes President.
U.S. drops atomic bombs on Hiroshima and Nagasaki in Japan.
Germany and Japan surrender.
Fifty nations meet in San Francisco to sign United Nations charter.

1946
Military demobilization brings major reductions in army, navy.
Wage and price controls end.
Evangelist Billy Graham holds first mass revival meeting.

1947
Taft-Hartley Act restricts power of unions.
National Security Act consolidates military under Defense Department.
Truman Doctrine promises U.S. support to "free peoples," establishing "containment" policy and marking start of Cold War.
U.S. launches Marshall Plan to help rebuild Western Europe.
Jackie Robinson becomes first black to play major league baseball.

1948
Truman integrates armed forces by executive order.
U.S. airlifts supplies to West Berlin during communist blockade.
Organization of American States established.
U.S. first nation to recognize new state of Israel.
Truman elected President defeating Dewey in surprising upset.

1949
Housing Act authorizes government slum clearance, urban renewal.
William Faulkner receives Nobel Prize for Literature.
Chinese Communists defeat Nationalists, win control of nation.
Soviet Union detonates its first atomic bomb.
U.S., Western Europe form North Atlantic Treaty Organization.

1950
Senator Joseph McCarthy launches crusade against communists in government.

1927
Nicola Sacco and Bartolomeo Vanzetti executed amid wide protests.
Charles Lindbergh makes first solo trans-Atlantic airplane flight.
The Jazz Singer, first feature sound film, released.

1928
Kellogg-Briand Pact outlaws war "as instrument of national policy."
Stock market boom begins.
Herbert Hoover elected President defeating Al Smith.

1929
William Faulkner's *The Sound and the Fury* and Thomas Wolfe's *Look Homeward Angel* published.
Stock market crashes.
Agricultural Marketing Act starts federal farm price stabilization.

1930
Smoot-Hawley Tariff raises protective barriers.
Sinclair Lewis becomes first American writer to receive Nobel Prize for Literature.
Stimson Doctrine establishes U.S. opposition to Japanese expansion.

1931
European financial collapse worsens Depression in U.S.
Japan invades Manchuria.

1932
Bonus Army of unemployed veterans dispersed by federal troops during march on Washington.
Riots among unemployed break out in Dearborn, Michigan.
Reconstruction Finance Corporation founded to help troubled businesses.
Franklin D. Roosevelt elected President defeating Hoover.

1933
Emergency Banking Act halts major national banking crisis.
Glass-Steagall Act establishes Federal Deposit Insurance Corporation.
National Industrial Recovery Act authorizes wage-price codes for industries and funds public works.
Agricultural Adjustment Act begins modern policy of farm supports.
Civilian Conservation Corps provides public employment for youths.
Tennessee Valley Authority, government power project, established.
Prohibition repealed by Twenty-first Amendment.

1938
Administration launches major anti-trust campaign.
Hitler seizes Austria; England concedes Czechoslovakia to Germany at Munich.
Vinson Naval Expansion Act authorizes U.S. naval growth.

1939
Germany invades Poland, starting Second World War.
Roosevelt declares American neutrality.
Russia, Germany sign pact, demoralizing U.S. Communist Party.
Neutrality Act authorizes "cash and carry" sale of munitions.
John Steinbeck's *The Grapes of Wrath* published.
First commercial trans-Atlantic air service begins. NBC begins first commercial television broadcasts.

1940
Germany captures Belgium, Holland, France.
German invasion of England thwarted in Battle of Britain; Winston Churchill becomes prime minister.
Congress approves new funds for American preparedness.
Roosevelt defeats Wendell Wilkie, wins third term.

1941
Congress approves Lend-Lease, American supplies to Allies.
American rearmament accelerates.
Roosevelt bans racial discrimination in government and defense industry hiring.
Germany invades Soviet Union.
FDR, Churchill meet in Atlantic Conference to prepare Anglo-American alliance.
Japan attacks Pearl Harbor; U.S. enters war.
Penicillin used effectively in treating humans.

1942
U.S. forms alliance with Britain, USSR, 23 other nations.
Government wage and price controls established.
Federal government evacuates 110,000 Japanese-Americans from California.
American troops driven from Philippines.
U.S. inflicts first major defeat on Japan at Battle of Midway.

1943
Race riot in Detroit leaves 34 dead.
FDR, Churchill plan Allied campaigns at Casablanca.
FDR, Churchill, Stalin meet for first time at Teheran.
Soviets defeat Germans at Stalingrad.
Allies invade Italy.
Americans drive Japanese from Guadalcanal.

1944
U.S. Navy defeats Japan in Battle of Leyte Gulf.
Allies invade France; recapture France, Belgium, Luxembourg.
"G.I. Bill of Rights" guarantees education and other benefits to veterans.

1951
Alger Hiss convicted of perjury in relation to espionage charges.
Communist troops invade South Korea; United States leads UN military force in opposing them. UN troops in Korea push communists back above original border.
Chinese enter war in Korea, push UN forces South.
Twenty-second Amendment limits Presidents to two terms.
War in Korea bogs down; peace talks begin at Panmunjom.
Truman removes Douglas MacArthur from command in Korea.

1952
Supreme Court invalidates government seizure of steel mills after strike.
U.S. completes development of hydrogen bomb.
Peace talks in Korea break down.
General Dwight D. Eisenhower elected President defeating Adlai Stevenson.

1953
Armistice signed, ending Korean War.
Earl Warren named Chief Justice of Supreme Court.
Julius and Ethel Rosenberg executed as spies, sparking wide protests.

1954
Supreme Court, in *Brown v. Board of Education of Topeka*, orders integration of all public schools.
First White Citizens Councils formed in South to resist integration.
Senate censures McCarthy after Army-McCarthy hearings.
Massive retaliation doctrine increases U.S. reliance on nuclear weapons.
U.S. joins Asian nations in anti-communist Southeast Asia Treaty Organization.

1955
Martin Luther King, Jr., leads bus boycott in Montgomery, Alabama.
AF of L, CIO merge, electing George Meany president.
Eisenhower and Soviet Premier Bulganin meet in Geneva.
Salk polio vaccine introduced.

1956
Highway Act begins construction of interstate highway system.
Soviet troops crush Hungarian Revolution.
Israelis and Arabs open hostilities; Britain, France occupy Suez.
Eugene O'Neill's play *Long Day's Journey Into Night* produced.
Eisenhower again defeats Stevenson for President.

1957
Federal troops enforce school desegregation in Little Rock, Arkansas.
Civil Rights Commission created to investigate racial discrimination.
Eisenhower Doctrine promises U.S. aid to Middle East against communists.
Soviet Union launches Sputnik, first man-made satellite.

1958
Agricultural Act lowers price supports for farmers.
First commercial jet airplanes begin operation.
Economic recession begins, helping Democrats to election victories.

1959
Alaska, Hawaii admitted to Union.
Fidel Castro overthrows Fulgencio Batista, controls Cuban government.

1960
Civil Rights Act expands court power over state voting laws.
Blacks stage first sit-in, at Greensboro, North Carolina lunch counter.
American U-2 spy plane shot down over USSR, destroying scheduled Eisenhower-Khrushchev summit meeting in Paris.
Cuban-American relations deteriorate; Castro develops ties to USSR.
First birth control pills marketed.
John F. Kennedy defeats Richard M. Nixon for President.

1961
U.S. breaks diplomatic relations with Cuba.
Peace Corps established.
American-backed invasion of Cuba at Bay of Pigs fails.
Freedom rides begin in South, challenging segregation.
Communists erect wall between East and West Berlin.
U.S. increases military aid to South Viet Nam.
Joseph Heller's Catch-22 published.

1962
Supreme Court, in Baker v. Carr, subjects legislative apportionment to federal scrutiny.
Federal marshals help James Meredith enroll at University of Mississippi.
Rachel Carson's Silent Spring warns of environmental dangers of pesticides.
John Glenn becomes first American to orbit earth.
Kennedy orders naval blockade of Cuba, forcing Soviets to remove offensive missiles from island.

1963
Nuclear Test Ban Treaty ratified.
Supreme Court in Gideon v. Wainwright guarantees right to defense counsel.
Betty Friedan's The Feminine Mystique launches new women's rights movement.
Kennedy assassinated; Lyndon B. Johnson becomes President.

1964
King receives Nobel Prize for Peace.
Civil Rights Act bans discrimination in public accommodations.
Gulf of Tonkin Resolution authorizes President to retaliate against aggression in South Viet Nam.
Johnson announces national War on Poverty.
Twenty-fourth Amendment bans poll tax.
Johnson elected President defeating Barry Goldwater in landslide.

1965
Congress approves flurry of Great Society legislation, including Medicare, federal aid to education, urban renewal funds.
Civil rights demonstrators clash with police in Selma, Alabama.
Race riot in Watts section of Los Angeles leaves 28 dead.
Ralph Nader's Unsafe at Any Speed launches consumer advocacy movement.
Johnson sends American combat troops to Viet Nam; bombing of North begins.

1966
Supreme Court, in Miranda v. Arizona, requires police to inform suspects of rights upon arrest.
Black Panther Party formed.

1967
Thurgood Marshall becomes first black appointed to Supreme Court.
Twenty-fifth Amendment provides for appointment of new Vice-President in case of vacancy.
Race riots in Newark, Detroit leave 66 dead.

1968
National Advisory Commission on Civil Disorders warns of "two societies, one black, one white—separate and unequal."
Columbia University paralyzed by student disorders.
Johnson withdraws from presidential race.
Martin Luther King, Jr. assassinated.
Senator Robert F. Kennedy assassinated.
Poor Peoples Campaign sets up tent city in Washington.
Civil Rights Act forbids housing discrimination.
Police and demonstrators clash during Democratic Convention in Chicago.
Richard Nixon defeats Hubert Humphrey in close presidential election.

1969
Nuclear Non-proliferation Treaty, banning spread of atomic weapons, ratified.
Supreme Court orders immediate school integration.
Two Americans first to land on moon.

1970
Environmental Protection Agency established.
American Indian Movement founded.
American forces invade Cambodia; four students killed in Ohio during nationwide campus protests.

1971
Supreme Court paves way for forced busing to achieve integration in Swann v. Charlotte-Mecklenburg Board of Education.
New York Times, Washington Post print previously secret Pentagon Papers, study of U.S. involvement in Viet Nam.
Twenty-sixth Amendment lowers voting age to 18.
Amtrak establishes government corporation to run passenger trains.
U.S. stops convertibility of dollar into gold, ending run on dollar.
Wage-price freeze and controls imposed.

1972
Nixon visits China, Soviet Union in effort to better relations.
Congress approves Equal Rights Amendment, guaranteeing women's rights; sends it to states for ratification.
Supreme Court, in Furman v. Georgia, bans death penalty as presently administered.
Five men arrested burglarizing Democratic headquarters in the Watergate; Washington Post ties them to high White House aides.
Nixon reelected in landslide over George McGovern in presidential election.

1973
Treaty of Paris halts fighting in Viet Nam; U.S. troops and prisoners of war return to U.S.
Senate Watergate Committee begins hearings on Nixon scandals; existence of tapes of presidential conversations disclosed.
Vice-President Agnew resigns after charges of bribe-taking; Gerald Ford appointed to succeed him.
Supreme Court, in Roe v. Wade, strikes down anti-abortion laws.
Arab oil boycott of U.S. creates energy shortage.
Nixon fires Watergate Special Prosecutor Archibald Cox.
Members of American Indian Movement occupy Wounded Knee, South Dakota.

1974
Worst economic recession since 1930s.
Supreme Court orders Nixon to release subpoenaed tapes.
House Judiciary Committee recommends impeachment on three counts.
Nixon resigns the presidency; Ford becomes President.
Ford pardons Nixon.

1975
South Viet Nam and Cambodia fall to communist governments.

1976
United States celebrates 200th anniversary of independence.
Supreme Court, in Gregg v. Georgia, upholds death penalty under certain conditions.
Carter defeats Ford in presidential election.

Declaration of Independence

IN CONGRESS, JULY 4, 1776

THE UNANIMOUS DECLARATION OF THE THIRTEEN UNITED STATES OF AMERICA

When, in the course of human events, it becomes necessary for one people to dissolve the political bands which have connected them with another, and to assume, among the powers of the earth, the separate and equal station to which the laws of nature and of nature's God entitle them, a decent respect to the opinions of mankind requires that they should declare the causes which impel them to the separation.

We hold these truths to be self-evident: That all men are created equal; that they are endowed by their Creator with certain unalienable rights; that among these are life, liberty, and the pursuit of happiness; that, to secure these rights, governments are instituted among men, deriving their just powers from the consent of the governed; that whenever any form of government becomes destructive of these ends, it is the right of the people to alter or to abolish it, and to institute new government, laying its foundation on such principles, and organizing its powers in such form, as to them shall seem most likely to effect their safety and happiness. Prudence, indeed, will dictate that governments long established should not be changed for light and transient causes; and accordingly all experience hath shown that mankind are more disposed to suffer, while evils are sufferable, than to right themselves by abolishing the forms to which they are accustomed. But when a long train of abuses and usurpations, pursuing invariably the same object, evinces a design to reduce them under absolute despotism, it is their right, it is their duty, to throw off such government, and to provide new guards for their future security. Such has been the patient sufferance of these colonies; and such is now the necessity which constrains them to alter their former systems of government. The history of the present King of Great Britain is a history of repeated injuries and usurpations, all having in direct object the establishment of an absolute tyranny over these states. To prove this, let facts be submitted to a candid world.

He has refused his assent to laws, the most wholesome and necessary for the public good.

He has forbidden his governors to pass laws of immediate and pressing importance, unless suspended in their operation till his assent should be obtained; and, when so suspended, he has utterly neglected to attend to them.

He has refused to pass other laws for the accommodation of large districts of people, unless those people would relinquish the right of representation in the legislature, a right inestimable to them, and formidable to tyrants only.

He has called together legislative bodies at places unusual, uncomfortable, and distant from the depository of their public records, for the sole purpose of fatiguing them into compliance with his measures.

He has dissolved representative houses repeatedly, for opposing, with manly firmness, his invasions on the rights of the people.

He has refused for a long time, after such dissolutions, to cause others to be elected; whereby the legislative powers, incapable of annihilation, have returned to the people at large for their exercise; the state remaining, in the mean time, exposed to all the dangers of invasions from without and convulsions within.

He has endeavored to prevent the population of these states; for that purpose obstructing the laws for naturalization of foreigners; refusing to pass others to encourage their migration hither, and raising the conditions of new appropriations of lands.

He has obstructed the administration of justice, by refusing his assent to laws for establishing judiciary powers.

He has made judges dependent on his will alone, for the tenure of their offices, and the amount and payment of their salaries.

He has erected a multitude of new offices, and sent hither swarms of officers to harass our people and eat out their substance.

He has kept among us, in times of peace, standing armies, without the consent of our legislatures.

He has affected to render the military independent of, and superior to, the civil power.

He has combined with others to subject us to a jurisdiction foreign to our constitution, and unacknowledged by our laws, giving his assent to their acts of pretended legislation:

For quartering large bodies of armed troops among us;

For protecting them, by a mock trial, from punishment for any murders which they should commit on the inhabitants of these states;

For cutting off our trade with all parts of the world;

For imposing taxes on us without our consent;

For depriving us, in many cases, of the benefits of trial by jury;

For transporting us beyond seas, to be tried for pretended offenses;

For abolishing the free system of English laws in a neighboring province, establishing therein an arbitrary government, and enlarging its boundaries, so as to render it at once an example and fit instrument for introducing the same absolute rule into these colonies;

For taking away our charters, abolishing our most valuable laws, and altering fundamentally the forms of our governments;

For suspending our own legislatures, and declaring themselves invested with power to legislate for us in all cases whatsoever.

He has abdicated government here, by declaring us out of his protection and waging war against us.

He has plundered our seas, ravaged our coasts, burned our towns, and destroyed the lives of our people.

He is at this time transporting large armies of foreign mercenaries to complete the works of death, desolation, and tyranny already begun with circumstances of cruelty and perfidy scarcely paralleled in the most barbarous ages, and totally unworthy the head of a civilized nation.

He has constrained our fellow-citizens, taken captive on the high seas, to bear arms against their country, to become the executioners of their friends and brethren, or to fall themselves by their hands.

He has excited domestic insurrection among us, and has endeavored to bring on the inhabitants of our frontiers the merciless Indian savages, whose known rule of warfare is an undistinguished destruction of all ages, sexes, and conditions.

In every stage of these oppressions we have petitioned for redress in the most humble terms; our repeated petitions have been answered only by repeated injury. A prince, whose character is thus marked by every act which may define a tyrant, is unfit to be the ruler of a free people.

Nor have we been wanting in our attentions to our British brethren. We have warned them, from time to time, of attempts by their legislature to extend an unwarrantable jurisdiction over us. We have reminded them of the circumstances of our emigration and settlement here. We have appealed to their native justice and magnanimity; and we have conjured them, by the ties of our common kindred, to disavow these usurpations, which would inevitably interrupt our connections and correspondence. They, too, have been deaf to the voice of justice and of consanguinity. We must, therefore, acquiesce in the necessity which denounces our separation, and hold them, as we hold the rest of mankind, enemies in war, in peace friends.

We, therefore, the representatives of the United States of America, in General Congress assembled, appealing to the Supreme Judge of the world for the rectitude of our intentions, do, in the name and by the authority of the good people of these colonies, solemnly publish and declare, that these United Colonies are, and of right ought to be, FREE AND INDEPENDENT STATES; that they are absolved from all allegiance to the British crown, and that all political connection between them and the state of Great Britain is, and ought to be, totally dissolved; and that, as free and independent states, they have full power to levy war, conclude peace, contract alliances, establish commerce, and do all other acts and things which independent states may of right do. And for the support of this declaration, with a firm reliance on the protection of Divine Providence, we mutually pledge to each other our lives, our fortunes, and our sacred honor.

JOHN HANCOCK [President]
[and fifty-five others]

Constitution of the United States of America

PREAMBLE

We the people of the United States, in order to form a more perfect union, establish justice, insure domestic tranquillity, provide for the common defense, promote the general welfare, and secure the blessings of liberty to ourselves and our posterity, do ordain and establish this CONSTITUTION for the United States of America.

ARTICLE I

Section I

All legislative powers herein granted shall be vested in a Congress of the United States, which shall consist of a Senate and a House of Representatives.

Section II

The House of Representatives shall be composed of members chosen every second year by the people of the several States, and the electors in each State shall have the qualifications requisite for electors of the most numerous branch of the State Legislature.

No person shall be a Representative who shall not have attained to the age of twenty-five years, and been seven years a citizen of the United States, and who shall not, when elected, be an inhabitant of that State in which he shall be chosen.

Representatives and direct taxes shall be apportioned among the several States which may be included within this Union, according to their respective numbers, *which shall be determined by adding to the whole number of free persons, including those bound to service for a term of years and excluding Indians not taxed, three-fifths of all other persons.* The actual enumeration

---

NOTE: Passages that are no longer in effect are printed in italic type.

shall be made within three years after the first meeting of the Congress of the United States, and within every subsequent term of ten years, in such manner as they shall by law direct. The number of Representatives shall not exceed one for every thirty thousand, but each State shall have at least one Representative; *and until such enumeration shall be made, the State of New Hampshire shall be entitled to choose three, Massachusetts eight, Rhode Island and Providence Plantations one, Connecticut five, New York six, New Jersey four, Pennsylvania eight, Delaware one, Maryland six, Virginia ten, North Carolina five, South Carolina five, and Georgia three.*

When vacancies happen in the representation from any State, the Executive authority thereof shall issue writs of election to fill such vacancies.

The house of Representatives shall choose their Speaker and other officers; and shall have the sole power of impeachment.

Section III

The Senate of the United States shall be composed of two Senators from each State, *chosen by the legislature thereof,* for six years; and each Senator shall have one vote.

Immediately after they shall be assembled in consequence of the first election, they shall be divided as equally as may be into three classes. The seats of the Senators of the first class shall be vacated at the expiration of the second year, of the second class at the expiration of the fourth year, and of the third class at the expiration of the sixth year, so that one-third may be chosen every second year; *and if vacancies happen by resignation or otherwise, during the recess of the legislature of any State, the Executive thereof may make temporary appointments until the next meeting of the legislature, which shall then fill such vacancies.*

No person shall be a Senator who shall not have attained to the age of thirty years, and been nine years a citizen of the United States, and who shall not, when elected, be an inhabitant of that State for which he shall be chosen.

The Vice-President of the United States shall be President of the Senate, but shall have no vote, unless they be equally divided.

The Senate shall choose their other officers, and also a President *pro tempore*, in the absence of the Vice-President, or when he shall exercise the office of President of the United States.

The Senate shall have the sole power to try all impeachments. When sitting for that purpose, they shall be on oath or affirmation. When the President of the United States is tried, the Chief Justice shall preside: and no person shall be convicted without the concurrence of two-thirds of the members present.

Judgment in cases of impeachment shall not extend further than to removal from office, and disqualification to hold and enjoy any office of honor, trust or profit under the United States: but the party convicted shall nevertheless be liable and subject to indictment, trial, judgment and punishment, according to law.

Section IV

The times, places and manner of holding elections for Senators and Representatives shall be prescribed in each State by the legislature thereof; but the Congress may at any time by law make or alter such regulations, except as to the places of choosing Senators.

The Congress shall assemble at least once in every year, and such meeting *shall be on the first Monday in December, unless they shall by law appoint a different day.*

Section V

Each house shall be the judge of the elections, returns and qualifications of its own members, and a majority of each shall constitute a quorum to do business; but a smaller number may adjourn from day to day, and may be authorized to compel the attendance of absent members, in such manner, and under such penalties, as each house may provide.

Each house may determine the rules of its proceedings, punish its members for disorderly behavior, and with the concurrence of two-thirds, expel a member.

Each house shall keep a journal of its proceedings, and from time to time publish the same, excepting such parts as may in their judgment require secrecy; and the yeas and nays of the members of either house on any question shall, at the desire of one-fifth of those present, be entered on the journal.

Neither house, during the session of Congress, shall, without the consent of the other, adjourn for more than three days, nor to any other place than that in which the two houses shall be sitting.

Section VI

The Senators and Representatives shall receive a compensation for their services, to be ascertained by law and paid out of the treasury of the United States. They shall in all cases except treason, felony and breach of the peace, be privileged from arrest during their attendance at the session of their respective houses, and in going to and returning from the same; and for any speech or debate in either house, they shall not be questioned in any other place.

No Senator or Representative shall, during the time for which he was elected, be appointed to any civil office under the authority of the United States, which shall have been created, or the emoluments whereof shall have been increased, during such time; and no person holding any office under the United States shall be a member of either house during his continuance in office.

Section VII

All bills for raising revenue shall originate in the House of Representatives; but the Senate may propose or concur with amendments as on other bills.

Every bill which shall have passed the House of Representatives and the Senate, shall, before it become a law, be presented to the President of the United States; if he approve he shall sign it, but if not he shall return it with objections to that house in which it originated, who shall enter the objections at large on their journal, and proceed to reconsider it. If after such reconsideration two-thirds of that house shall agree to pass the bill, it shall be sent, together with the objections, to the other house, by which it shall likewise be reconsidered, and, if approved by two-thirds of that house, it shall become a law. But in all such cases the votes of both houses shall be determined by yeas and nays, and the names of the persons voting for and against the bill shall be entered on the journal of each house respectively. If any bill shall not be returned by the President within ten days (Sundays excepted) after it shall have been presented to him, the same shall be a law, in like manner as if he had signed it, unless the Congress by their adjournment prevent its return, in which case it shall not be a law.

Every order, resolution, or vote to which the concurrence of the Senate and House of Representatives may be necessary (except on a question of adjournment) shall be presented to the President of the United States; and before the same shall take effect, shall be approved by him, or being disapproved by him, shall be repassed by two-thirds of the Senate and House of Representatives, according to the rules and limitations prescribed in the case of a bill.

Section VIII
The Congress shall have power

To lay and collect taxes, duties, imposts, and excises, to pay the debts and provide for the common defense and general welfare of the United States; but all duties, imposts and excises shall be uniform throughout the United States;

To borrow money on the credit of the United States;

To regulate commerce with foreign nations, and among the several States, and with the Indian tribes;

To establish an uniform rule of naturalization, and uniform laws on the subject of bankruptcies throughout the United States;

To coin money, regulate the value thereof, and of foreign coin, and fix the standard of weights and measures;

To provide for the punishment of counterfeiting the securities and current coin of the United States;

To establish post offices and post roads;

To promote the progress of science and useful arts by securing for limited times to authors and inventors the exclusive right to their respective writings and discoveries;

To constitute tribunals inferior to the Supreme Court;

To define and punish piracies and felonies committed on the high seas and offenses against the law of nations;

To declare war, grant letters of marque and reprisal, and make rules concerning captures on land and water;

To raise and support armies, but no appropriation of money to that use shall be for a longer term than two years;

To provide and maintain a navy;

To make rules for the government and regulation of the land and naval forces;

To provide for calling forth the militia to execute the laws of the Union, suppress insurrections, and repel invasions;

To provide for organizing, arming, and disciplining the militia, and for governing such part of them as may be employed in the service of the United States, reserving to the States respectively the appointment of the officers, and the authority of training the militia according to the discipline prescribed by Congress;

To exercise exclusive legislation in all cases whatsoever, over such district (not exceeding ten miles square) as may, by cession of particular States, and the acceptance of Congress, become the seat of government of the United States, and to exercise like authority over all places purchased by the consent of the legislature of the State, in which the same shall be, for the erection of forts, magazines, arsenals, dock-yards, and other needful buildings; — and

To make all laws which shall be necessary and proper for carrying into execution the foregoing powers, and all other powers vested by this Constitution in the government of the United States, or in any department or officer thereof.

Section IX

The migration or importation of such persons as any of the States now existing shall think proper to admit shall not be prohibited by the Congress prior to the year 1808; but a tax or duty may be imposed on such importation, not exceeding $10 for each person.

The privilege of the writ of habeas corpus shall not be suspended, unless when in cases of rebellion or invasion the public safety may require it.

No bill of attainder or ex post facto law shall be passed.

No capitation, or other direct, tax shall be laid, unless in proportion to the census or enumeration herein before directed to be taken.

No tax or duty shall be laid on articles exported from any State.

No preference shall be given by any regulation of commerce or revenue to the ports of one State over those of another; nor shall vessels bound to, or from, one State, be obliged to enter, clear, or pay duties in another.

No money shall be drawn from the treasury, but in consequence of appropriations made by law; and a regular statement and account of the receipts and expenditures of all public money shall be published from time to time.

No title of nobility shall be granted by the United States: and no person holding any office of profit or trust under them, shall, without the consent of the Congress, accept of any present, emolument, office, or title, of any kind whatever, from any king, prince, or foreign state.

Section X

No State shall enter into any treaty, alliance, or confederation; grant letters of marque and reprisal; coin money; emit bills of credit; make anything but gold and silver coin a tender in payment of debts; pass any bill of attainder, ex post facto law, or law impairing the obligation of contracts, or grant any title of nobility.

No State shall, without the consent of Congress, lay any imposts or duties on imports or exports, except what may be absolutely necessary for executing its inspection laws: and the net produce of all duties and imposts, laid by any State on imports or exports, shall be for the use of the treasury of the United States; and all such laws shall be subject to the revision and control of the Congress.

No State shall, without the consent of Congress, lay any duty of tonnage, keep troops or ships of war in time of peace, enter into any agreement or compact with another State, or with a foreign power, or engage in war, unless actually invaded, or in such imminent danger as will not admit of delay.

ARTICLE II

Section I

The executive power shall be vested in a President of the United States of America. He shall hold his office during the term of four years, and, together with the Vice-President, chosen for the same term, be elected as follows:

Each State shall appoint, in such manner as the legislature thereof may direct, a number of electors, equal to the whole number of Senators and Representatives to which the State may be entitled in the Congress; but no Senator or Representative, or person holding an office of trust or profit under the United States, shall be appointed an elector.

The electors shall meet in their respective States, and vote by ballot for two persons, of whom one at least shall not be an inhabitant of the same State with themselves. And they shall make a list of all the persons voted for, and of the number of votes for each; which list they shall sign and certify, and transmit sealed to the seat of government of the United States, directed to the President of the Senate. The President of the Senate shall, in the presence of the Senate and House of Representatives, open all the certificates, and the votes shall then be counted. The person having the greatest number of votes shall be the President, if such number be a majority of the whole number of electors appointed; and if there be more than one who have such majority, and have an equal number of votes, then the House of Representatives shall immediately choose by ballot one of them for President; and if no person have a majority, then from the five highest on the list said house shall in like manner choose the President. But in choosing the President the votes shall be taken by States, the representation from each State having one vote; a quorum for this purpose shall consist of a member or members from two-thirds of the States, and a majority of all the States shall be necessary to a choice. In every case, after the choice of the President, the person having the greatest number of votes of the electors shall be the Vice-President. But if there should remain two or more who have equal votes, the Senate shall choose from them by ballot the Vice-President.

The Congress may determine the time of choosing the electors and the day on which they shall give their votes; which day shall be the same throughout the United States.

No person except a natural-born citizen, *or a citizen of the United States at the time of the adoption of this Constitution,* shall be eligible to the office of President; neither shall any person be eligible to that office who shall not have attained to the age of thirty-five years, and been fourteen years a resident within the United States.

In case of the removal of the President from office or of his death, resignation, or inability to discharge the powers and duties of the said office, the same shall devolve on the Vice-President, and the Congress may by law provide for the case of removal, death, resignation, or inability, both of the President and Vice-President, declaring what officer shall then act as President, and such officer shall act accordingly, until the disability be removed, or a President shall be elected.

The President shall, at stated times, receive for his services a compensation, which shall neither be increased nor diminished during the period for which he shall have been elected, and he shall not receive within that period any other emolument from the United States, or any of them.

Before he enter on the execution of his office, he shall take the following oath or affirmation:—"I do solemnly swear (or affirm) that I will faithfully execute the office of the President of the United States, and will to the best of my ability preserve, protect and defend the Constitution of the United States."

Section II

The President shall be commander in chief of the army and navy of the United States, and of the militia of the several States, when called into the actual service of the United States; he may require the opinion, in writing, of the principal officer in each of the executive departments, upon any subject relating to the duties of their respective offices, and he shall have power to grant reprieves and pardons for offenses against the United States, except in cases of impeachment.

He shall have power, by and with the advice and consent of the Senate, to make treaties, provided two-thirds of the Senators present concur; and he shall nominate, and by and with the advice and consent of the Senate, shall appoint ambassadors, other public ministers and consuls, judges of the Supreme Court, and all other officers of the United States, whose appointments are not herein otherwise provided for, and which shall be established by law: but Congress may by law vest the appointment of such inferior officers, as they think proper, in the President alone, in the courts of law, or in the heads of departments.

The President shall have power to fill up all vacancies that may happen during the recess of the Senate, by granting commissions which shall expire at the end of their next session.

Section III

He shall from time to time give to the Congress information of the state of the Union, and recommend to their consideration such measures as he shall judge necessary and expedient; he may, on extraordinary occasions, convene both houses, or either of them, and in case of disagreement between them, with respect to the time of adjournment, he may adjourn them to such time as he shall think proper; he shall receive ambassadors and other public ministers; he shall take care that the laws be faithfully executed, and shall commission all the officers of the United States.

Section IV

The President, Vice-President and all civil officers of the United States shall be removed from office on impeachment for, and on conviction of, treason, bribery, or other high crimes and misdemeanors.

ARTICLE III

Section I

The judicial power of the United States shall be vested in one Supreme Court, and in such inferior courts as the Congress may from time to time ordain and establish. The judges, both of the Supreme and inferior courts, shall hold their offices during good behavior, and shall, at stated times, receive for their services a compensation which shall not be diminished during their continuance in office.

Section II

The judicial power shall extend to all cases, in law and equity, arising under this Constitution, the laws of the United States, and treaties made, or which shall be made, under their authority; — to all cases affecting ambassadors, other public ministers and consuls; — to all cases of admiralty and maritime jurisdiction; — to controversies to which the United States shall be a party; — to controversies between two or more States; — *between a State and citizens of another State;* — between citizens of different States; — between citizens of the same State claiming lands under grants of different States, and between a State, or the citizens thereof, and foreign states, citizens or subjects.

In all cases affecting ambassadors, other public ministers and consuls, and those in which a State shall be party, the Supreme Court shall have original jurisdiction. In all the other cases before mentioned, the Supreme Court shall have appellate jurisdiction, both as to law and fact, with such exceptions, and under such regulations, as the Congress shall make.

The trial of all crimes, except in cases of impeachment, shall be by jury; and such trial shall be held in the State where the said crimes shall have been committed; but when not committed within any State, the trial shall be at such place or places as the Congress may by law have directed.

Section III

Treason against the United States shall consist only in levying war against them, or in adhering to their enemies, giving them aid and comfort. No person shall be convicted of treason unless on the testimony of two witnesses to the same overt act, or on confession in open court.

The Congress shall have power to declare the punishment of treason, but no attainder of treason shall work corruption of blood, or forfeiture except during the life of the person attainted.

ARTICLE IV

Section I

Full faith and credit shall be given in each State to the public acts, records, and judicial proceedings of every other State. And the Congress may by general laws prescribe the manner in which such acts, records, and proceedings shall be proved, and the effect thereof.

Section II

The citizens of each State shall be entitled to all privileges and immunities of citizens in the several States.

A person charged in any State with treason, felony, or other crime, who shall flee from justice, and be found in another State, shall on demand of the executive authority of the State from which he fled, be delivered up, to be removed to the State having jurisdiction of the crime.

No person held to service or labor in one State, under the laws thereof, escaping into another, shall, in consequence of any law or regulation therein, be discharged from such service or labor, but shall be delivered up on claim of the party to whom such service or labor may be due.

Section III

New States may be admitted by the Congress into this Union; but no new State shall be formed or erected within the jurisdiction of any other State; nor any State be formed by the junction of two or more States, or parts of States, without the consent of the legislatures of the States concerned as well as of the Congress.

The Congress shall have power to dispose of and make all needful rules and regulations respecting the territory or other property belonging to the United States; and nothing in this Constitution shall be so construed as to prejudice any claims of the United States, or of any particular State.

Section IV

The United States shall guarantee to every State in this Union a republican form of government, and shall protect each of them against invasion; and on application of the legislature, or of the executive (when the legislature cannot be convened), against domestic violence.

ARTICLE V

The Congress, whenever two-thirds of both houses shall deem it necessary, shall propose amendments to this Constitution, or, on the application of the legislatures of two-thirds of the several States, shall call a convention for proposing amendments, which, in either case, shall be valid to all intents and purposes, as part of this Constitution, when ratified by the legislatures of three-fourths of the several States, or by conventions in three-fourths thereof, as the one or the other mode of ratification may be proposed by the Congress; provided *that no amendments which may be made prior to the year one thousand eight hundred and eight shall in any manner affect the first and fourth clauses in the ninth section of the first article;* and that no State, without its consent, shall be deprived of its equal suffrage in the Senate.

ARTICLE VI

All debts contracted and engagements entered into, before the adoption of this Constitution, shall be as valid against the United States under this Constitution, as under the Confederation.

This Constitution, and the laws of the United States which shall be made in pursuance thereof; and all treaties made, or which shall be made, under the authority of the United States, shall be the supreme law of the land; and the judges in every State shall be bound thereby, anything in the Constitution or laws of any State to the contrary notwithstanding.

The Senators and Representatives before mentioned, and the members of the several State legislatures, and all executive and judicial officers, both of the United States and of the several States, shall be bound by oath or affirmation to support this Constitution; but no religious test shall ever be required as a qualification to any office or public trust under the United States.

ARTICLE VII

The ratification of the conventions of nine States shall be sufficient for the establishment of this Constitution between the States so ratifying the same.

Done in Convention by the unanimous consent of the States present, the seventeenth day of September in the year of our Lord one thousand seven hundred and eighty-seven and of the Independence of the United States of America the twelfth. In witness whereof we have hereunto subscribed our names.

[Signed by]
Gᵒ WASHINGTON
Presidt and Deputy from Virginia
[and thirty-eight others]

AMENDMENTS TO THE CONSTITUTION

ARTICLE I*

Congress shall make no law respecting an establishment of religion, or prohibiting the free exercise thereof; or abridging the freedom of speech, or of the press; or the right of the people peaceably to assemble, and to petition the government for a redress of grievances.

ARTICLE II

A well-regulated militia being necessary to the security of a free State, the right of the people to keep and bear arms shall not be infringed.

ARTICLE III

No soldier shall, in time of peace, be quartered in any house without the consent of the owner, nor in time of war, but in a manner to be prescribed by law.

ARTICLE IV

The right of the people to be secure in their persons, houses, papers, and effects, against unreasonable searches and seizures, shall not be violated, and no warrants shall issue but upon probable cause, supported by oath or affirmation, and particularly describing the place to be searched, and the persons or things to be seized.

ARTICLE V

No person shall be held to answer for a capital, or otherwise infamous crime, unless on a presentment or indictment of a grand jury, except in cases arising in the land or naval forces, or in the militia, when in actual service in time of war or public danger; nor shall any person be subject for the same offense to be twice put in jeopardy of life or limb; nor shall be compelled in any criminal case to be a witness against himself, nor be deprived of life, liberty, or property, without due process of law; nor shall private property be taken for public use without just compensation.

ARTICLE VI

In all criminal prosecutions, the accused shall enjoy the right to a speedy and public trial, by an impartial jury of the State and district wherein the crime shall have been committed, which district shall have been previously ascertained by law, and to be informed of the nature and cause of the accusation; to be confronted with the witnesses against him; to have compulsory process for obtaining witnesses in his favor, and to have the assistance of counsel for his defense.

ARTICLE VII

In suits at common law, where the value in controversy shall exceed twenty dollars, the right of trial by jury shall be preserved, and no fact tried by a jury shall be otherwise re-examined in any court of the United States, than according to the rules of the common law.

---

*The first ten Amendments (Bill of Rights) were adopted in 1791.

ARTICLE VIII

Excessive bail shall not be required, nor excessive fines imposed, nor cruel and unusual punishments inflicted.

ARTICLE IX

The enumeration in the Constitution, of certain rights, shall not be construed to deny or disparage others retained by the people.

ARTICLE X

The powers not delegated to the United States by the Constitution, nor prohibited by it to the States, are reserved to the States respectively, or to the people.

ARTICLE XI [Adopted 1798]

The judicial power of the United States shall not be construed to extend to any suit in law or equity, commenced or prosecuted against one of the United States by citizens of another State, or by citizens or subjects of any foreign state.

ARTICLE XII [Adopted 1804]

The electors shall meet in their respective States, and vote by ballot for President and Vice-President, one of whom, at least, shall not be an inhabitant of the same State with themselves; they shall name in their ballots the person voted for as President, and in distinct ballots the person voted for as Vice-President, and they shall make distinct lists of all persons voted for as President, and of all persons voted for as Vice-President, and of the number of votes for each, which lists they shall sign and certify, and transmit sealed to the seat of government of the United States, directed to the President of the Senate;—the President of the Senate shall, in the presence of the Senate and House of Representatives, open all the certificates and the votes shall then be counted;—the person having the greatest number of votes for President shall be the President, if such number be a majority of the whole number of electors appointed; and if no person have such majority, then from the persons having the highest numbers not exceeding three on the list of those voted for as President, the House of Representatives shall choose immediately, by ballot, the President. But in choosing the President, the votes shall be taken by States, the representation from each State having one vote; a quorum for this purpose shall consist of a member or member from two-thirds of the States, and a majority of all the States shall be necessary to a choice. And if the House of Representatives shall not choose a President whenever the right of choice shall devolve upon them, before *the fourth day of March* next following, then the Vice-President shall act as President, as in the case of the death or other constitutional disability of the President.

The person having the greatest number of votes as Vice-President shall be the Vice-President, if such number be a majority of the whole number of electors appointed; and if no person have a majority, then from the two highest numbers on the list the Senate shall choose the Vice-President; a quorum for the purpose shall consist of two-thirds of the whole number of Senators, and a majority of the whole number shall be necessary to a choice. But no person constitutionally ineligible to the office of President shall be eligible to that of Vice-President of the United States.

ARTICLE XIII [Adopted 1865]

1. Neither slavery nor involuntary servitude, except as a punishment for crime whereof the party shall have been duly convicted, shall exist within the United States, or any place subject to their jurisdiction.

2. Congress shall have power to enforce this article by appropriate legislation.

ARTICLE XIV [Adopted 1868]

1. All persons born or naturalized in the United States, and subject to the jurisdiction thereof, are citizens of the United States and of the State wherein they reside. No State shall make or enforce any law which shall abridge the privileges or immunities of citizens of the United States; nor shall any State deprive any person of life, liberty, or property, without due process of law; nor deny to any person within its jurisdiction the equal protection of the laws.

2. Representatives shall be apportioned among the several States according to their respective numbers, counting the whole number of persons in each State, excluding Indians not taxed. But when the right to vote at any election for the choice of Electors for President and Vice-President of the United States, Representatives in Congress, the executive and judicial officers of a State, or the members of the legislature thereof, is denied to any of the male inhabitants of such State, being twenty-one years of age and citizens of the United States, or in any way abridged, except for participation in rebellion, or other crime, the basis of representation therein shall be reduced in the proportion which the number of such male citizens shall bear to the whole number of male citizens twenty-one years of age in such State.

3. No person shall be a Senator or Representative in Congress, or Elector of President and Vice-President, or hold any office, civil or military, under the United States, or under any State, who, having previously taken an oath, as a member of Congress, or as an officer of the United States, or as a member of any State legislature, or as an executive or judicial officer of any State, to support the Constitution of the United States, shall have engaged in insurrection or rebellion against the same, or given aid or comfort to the enemies thereof. But Congress may, by a vote of two-thirds of each house, remove such disability.

4. The validity of the public debt of the United States, authorized by law, including debts incurred for payment of pensions and bounties for services in suppressing insurrection or rebellion, shall not be questioned. But neither the United States nor any State shall assume or pay any debt or obligation incurred in aid of insurrection or rebellion against the United States, or any claim for the loss or emancipation of any slave; but all such debts, obligations, and claims shall be held illegal and void.

5. The Congress shall have power to enforce, by appropriate legislation, the provisions of this article.

ARTICLE XV [Adopted 1870]

1. The right of citizens of the United States to vote shall not be denied or abridged by the United States or by any State on account of race, color, or previous condition of servitude.

2. The Congress shall have power to enforce this article by appropriate legislation.

ARTICLE XVI [Adopted 1913]

The Congress shall have power to lay and collect taxes on incomes, from whatever source derived, without apportionment among the several States, and without regard to any census or enumeration.

ARTICLE XVII [Adopted 1913]

1. The Senate of the United States shall be composed of two Senators from each State, elected by the people thereof, for six years; and each Senator shall have one vote. The electors in each State shall have the qualifications requisite for electors of [voters for] the most numerous branch of the State legislatures.

2. When vacancies happen in the representation of any State in the Senate, the executive authority of such State shall issue writs of election to fill such vacancies: Provided, that the Legislature of any State may empower the executive thereof to make temporary appointments until the people fill the vacancies by election as the Legislature may direct.

3. This amendment shall not be so construed as to affect the election or term of any Senator chosen before it becomes valid as part of the Constitution.

ARTICLE XVIII [Adopted 1919; Repealed 1933]

1. *After one year from the ratification of this article the manufacture, sale, or transportation of intoxicating liquors within, the importation thereof into, or the exportation thereof from the United States and all territory subject to the jurisdiction thereof, for beverage purposes, is hereby prohibited.*

2. *The Congress and the several States shall have concurrent power to enforce this article by appropriate legislation.*

3. *This article shall be inoperative unless it shall have been ratified as an amendment to the Constitution by the legislatures of the several States, as provided by the Constitution, within seven years from the date of the submission thereof to the States by the Congress.*

ARTICLE XIX [Adopted 1920]

1. The right of citizens of the United States to vote shall not be denied or abridged by the United States or by any State on account of sex.

2. The Congress shall have power to enforce this article by appropriate legislation.

ARTICLE XX [Adopted 1933]

1. The terms of the President and Vice-President shall end at noon on the 20th day of January, and the terms of Senators and Representatives at noon on the 3d day of January, of the years in which such terms would have ended if this article had not been ratified; and the terms of their successors shall then begin.

2. The Congress shall assemble at least once in every year, and such meeting shall begin at noon on the 3d day of January, unless they shall by law appoint a different day.

3. If, at the time fixed for the beginning of the term of the President, the President-elect

shall have died, the Vice-President-elect shall become President. If a President shall not have been chosen before the time fixed for the beginning of his term, or if the President-elect shall have failed to qualify, then the Vice-President-elect shall act as President until a President shall have qualified; and the Congress may by law provide for the case wherein neither a President-elect nor a Vice-President-elect shall have qualified, declaring who shall then act as President, or the manner in which one who is to act shall be selected, and such persons shall act accordingly until a President or Vice-President shall have qualified.

4. The Congress may by law provide for the case of the death of any of the persons from whom the House of Representatives may choose a President whenever the right of choice shall have devolved upon them, and for the case of the death of any of the persons from whom the Senate may choose a Vice-President whenever the right of choice shall have devolved upon them.

5. Sections 1 and 2 shall take effect on the 15th day of October following the ratification of this article.

6. This article shall be inoperative unless it shall have been ratified as an amendment to the Constitution by the Legislatures of three-fourths of the several States within seven years from the date of its submission.

ARTICLE XXI [Adopted 1933]

1. The eighteenth article of amendment to the Constitution of the United States is hereby repealed.

2. The transportation or importation into any State, Territory, or Possession of the United States for delivery or use therein of intoxicating liquors, in violation of the laws thereof, is hereby prohibited.

3. This article shall be inoperative unless it shall have been ratified as an amendment to the Constitution by conventions in the several States, as provided in the Constitution, within seven years from the date of submission thereof to the States by the Congress.

ARTICLE XXII [Adopted 1951]

1. No person shall be elected to the office of President more than twice, and no person who has held the office of President, or acted as President, for more than two years of a term to which some other person was elected President shall be elected to the office of President more than once. But this article shall not apply to any person holding the office of President when this article was proposed by the Congress, and shall not prevent any person who may be holding the office of President, or acting as President, during the term within which this article becomes operative from holding the office of President or acting as President during the remainder of such term.

2. This article shall be inoperative unless it shall have been ratified as an amendment to the Constitution by the legislatures of three-fourths of the several States within seven years from the date of its submission to the States by the Congress.

ARTICLE XXIII [Adopted 1961]

1. The District constituting the seat of Government of the United States shall appoint in such manner as the Congress may direct:
   A number of electors of President and Vice-President equal to the whole number of

Senators and Representatives in Congress to which the District would be entitled if it were a State, but in no event more than the least populous State; they shall be in addition to those appointed by the States, but they shall be considered for the purposes of the election of President and Vice-President, to be electors appointed by a State; and they shall meet in the District and perform such duties as provided by the twelfth article of amendment.

2. The Congress shall have the power to enforce this article by appropriate legislation.

ARTICLE XXIV [Adopted 1964]

1. The right of citizens of the United States to vote in any primary or other election for President or Vice-President, for electors for President or Vice-President, or for Senator or Representative in Congress, shall not be denied or abridged by the United States or any State by reason of failure to pay any poll tax or other tax.

2. The Congress shall have the power to enforce this article by appropriate legislation.

ARTICLE XXV [Adopted 1967]

1. In case of the removal of the President from office or of his death or resignation, the Vice President shall become President.

2. Whenever there is a vacancy in the office of the Vice President, the President shall nominate a Vice President who shall take office upon confirmation by a majority vote of both Houses of Congress.

3. Whenever the President transmits to the President pro tempore of the Senate and the Speaker of the House of Representatives his written declaration that he is unable to discharge the powers and duties of his office, and until he transmits to them a written declaration to the contrary, such powers and duties shall be discharged by the Vice President as Acting President.

4. Whenever the Vice President and a majority of either the principal officers of the executive departments or of such other body as Congress may by law provide, transmit to the President pro tempore of the Senate and the Speaker of the House of Representatives their written declaration that the President is unable to discharge the powers and duties of his office, the Vice President shall immediately assume the powers and duties of the office as Acting President.

Thereafter, when the President transmits to the President pro tempore of the Senate and the Speaker of the House of Representatives his written declaration that no inability exists, he shall resume the powers and duties of his office unless the Vice President and a majority of either the principal officers of the executive department[s] or of such other body as Congress may by law provide, transmit within four days to the President pro tempore of the Senate and the Speaker of the House of Representatives their written declaration that the President is unable to discharge the powers and duties of his office. Thereupon Congress shall decide the issue, assembling within forty-eight hours for that purpose if not in session. If the Congress, within twenty-one days after receipt of the latter written declaration, or, if Congress is not in session, within twenty-one days after Congress is required to assemble, determines by two-thirds vote of both Houses that the President is unable to discharge the powers and duties of his office, the Vice President shall continue to discharge the same as Acting President; otherwise, the President shall resume the powers and duties of his office.

ARTICLE XXVI [Adopted 1971]

1. The right of citizens of the United States, who are eighteen years of age or older, to vote shall not be denied or abridged by the United States or by any State on account of age.

2. The Congress shall have power to enforce this article by appropriate legislation.

ARTICLE XXVII [Sent to States, 1972]

1. Equality of rights under the law shall not be denied or abridged by the United States or by any State on account of sex.

2. The Congress shall have the power to enforce, by appropriate legislation, the provisions of this article.

3. This amendment shall take effect two years after the date of ratification.

Growth of U. S. Population and Area

CENSUS	POPULATION OF CONTIGUOUS U. S.	PERCENT OF INCREASE OVER PRECEDING CENSUS	LAND AREA, SQUARE MILES	POPULATION PER SQUARE MILE
1790	3,929,214		867,980	4.5
1800	5,308,483	35.1	867,980	6.1
1810	7,239,881	36.4	1,685,865	4.3
1820	9,638,453	33.1	1,753,588	5.5
1830	12,866,020	33.5	1,753,588	7.3
1840	17,069,453	32.7	1,753,588	9.7
1850	23,191,876	35.9	2,944,337	7.9
1860	31,443,321	35.6	2,973,965	10.6
1870	39,818,449	26.6	2,973,965	13.4
1880	50,155,783	26.0	2,973,965	16.9
1890	62,947,714	25.5	2,973,965	21.2
1900	75,994,575	20.7	2,974,159	25.6
1910	91,972,266	21.0	2,973,890	30.9
1920	105,710,620	14.9	2,973,776	35.5
1930	122,775,046	16.1	2,977,128	41.2
1940	131,669,275	7.2	2,977,128	44.2
1950	150,697,361	14.5	2,974,726*	50.7
†1960	178,464,236	18.4	2,974,726	59.9
1970	204,765,770 (including Alaska and Hawaii)			

*As remeasured in 1940.

†Not including Alaska (pop. 226,167) and Hawaii (632,772).

Presidential Elections*

ELECTION	CANDIDATES	PARTIES	POPULAR VOTE	ELECTORAL VOTE
1789	GEORGE WASHINGTON	No party designations		69
	John Adams			34
	Minor Candidates			35
1792	GEORGE WASHINGTON	No party designations		132
	John Adams			77
	George Clinton			50
	Minor Candidates			5
1796	JOHN ADAMS	Federalist		71
	Thomas Jefferson	Democratic-Republican		68
	Thomas Pinckney	Federalist		59
	Aaron Burr	Democratic-Republican		30
	Minor Candidates			48
1800	THOMAS JEFFERSON	Democratic-Republican		73
	Aaron Burr	Democratic-Republican		73
	John Adams	Federalist		65
	Charles C. Pinckney	Federalist		64
	John Jay	Federalist		1
1804	THOMAS JEFFERSON	Democratic-Republican		162
	Charles C. Pinckney	Federalist		14
1808	JAMES MADISON	Democratic-Republican		122
	Charles C. Pinckney	Federalist		47
	George Clinton	Democratic-Republican		6
1812	JAMES MADISON	Democratic-Republican		128
	DeWitt Clinton	Federalist		89
1816	JAMES MONROE	Democratic-Republican		183
	Rufus King	Federalist		34
1820	JAMES MONROE	Democratic-Republican		231
	John Q. Adams	Independent Republican		1
1824	JOHN Q. ADAMS (Min.)†	Democratic-Republican	108,740	84
	Andrew Jackson	Democratic-Republican	153,544	99
	William H. Crawford	Democratic-Republican	46,618	41
	Henry Clay	Democratic-Republican	47,136	37
1828	ANDREW JACKSON	Democratic	647,286	178
	John Q Adams	National Republican	508,064	83
1832	ANDREW JACKSON	Democratic	687,502	219
	Henry Clay	National Republican	530,189	49
	William Wirt	Anti-Masonic	33,108	7
	John Floyd	National Republican		11
1836	MARTIN VAN BUREN	Democratic	762,678	170
	William H. Harrison	Whig		73
	Hugh L. White	Whig	736,656	26
	Daniel Webster	Whig		14
	W. P. Mangum	Whig		11

*Candidates receiving less than 1% of the popular vote are omitted. Before the 12th Amendment (1804) the Electoral College voted for two presidential candidates, and the runner-up became Vice-President. Basic figures are taken primarily from *Historical Statistics of the United States, 1789–1945* (1949), pp. 288–290; *Historical Statistics of the United States, Colonial Times to 1957* (1960), pp. 682–683; and *Statistical Abstract of the United States, 1969* (1969), pp. 355–357.

†"Min." indicates minority President—one receiving less than 50% of all popular votes.

Presidential Elections (Contd.)

ELECTION	CANDIDATES	PARTIES	POPULAR VOTE	ELECTORAL VOTE
1840	WILLIAM H. HARRISON	Whig	1,275,016	234
	Martin Van Buren	Democratic	1,129,102	60
1844	JAMES K. POLK (Min.)*	Democratic	1,337,243	170
	Henry Clay	Whig	1,299,062	105
	James G. Birney	Liberty	62,300	
1848	ZACHARY TAYLOR (Min.)*	Whig	1,360,099	163
	Lewis Cass	Democratic	1,220,544	127
	Martin Van Buren	Free Soil	291,263	
1852	FRANKLIN PIERCE	Democratic	1,601,274	254
	Winfield Scott	Whig	1,386,580	42
	John P. Hale	Free Soil	155,825	
1856	JAMES BUCHANAN (Min.)*	Democratic	1,838,169	174
	John C. Frémont	Republican	1,341,264	114
	Millard Fillmore	American	874,534	8
1860	ABRAHAM LINCOLN (Min.)*	Republican	1,866,452	180
	Stephen A Douglas	Democratic	1,375,157	12
	John C. Breckinridge	Democratic	847,953	72
	John Bell	Constitutional Union	590,631	39
1864	ABRAHAM LINCOLN	Union	2,213,665	212
	George B. McClellan	Democratic	1,802,237	21
1868	ULYSSES S. GRANT	Republican	3,012,833	214
	Horatio Seymour	Democratic	2,703,249	80
1872	ULYSSES S. GRANT	Republican	3,597,132	286
	Horace Greeley	Democratic and Liberal Republican	2,834,125	66
1876	RUTHERFORD B. HAYES (Min.)*	Republican	4,036,298	185
	Samuel J. Tilden	Democratic	4,300,590	184
1880	JAMES A. GARFIELD (Min.)*	Republican	4,454,416	214
	Winfield S. Hancock	Democratic	4,444,952	155
	James B. Weaver	Greenback-Labor	308,578	
1884	GROVER CLEVELAND (Min.)*	Democratic	4,874,986	219
	James G. Blaine	Republican	4,851,981	182
	Benjamin F. Butler	Greenback-Labor	175,370	
	John P. St. John	Prohibition	150,369	
1888	BENJAMIN HARRISON (Min.)*	Republican	5,439,853	233
	Grover Cleveland	Democratic	5,540,309	168
	Clinton B. Fisk	Prohibition	249,506	
	Anson J. Streeter	Union Labor	146,935	
1892	GROVER CLEVELAND (Min.)*	Democratic	5,556,918	277
	Benjamin Harrison	Republican	5,176,108	145
	James B. Weaver	People's	1,041,028	22
	John Bidwell	Prohibition	264,133	
1896	WILLIAM McKINLEY	Republican	7,104,770	271
	William J. Bryan	Democratic	6,502,925	176
1900	WILLIAM McKINLEY	Republican	7,207,923	292
	William J. Bryan	Democratic; Populist	6,358,133	155
	John C. Woolley	Prohibition	208,914	

*"Min." indicates minority President—one receiving less than 50% of all popular votes.

Presidential Elections (Contd.)

ELECTION	CANDIDATES	PARTIES	POPULAR VOTE	ELECTORAL VOTE
1904	THEODORE ROOSEVELT	Republican	7,623,486	336
	Alton B. Parker	Democratic	5,077,911	140
	Eugene V. Debs	Socialist	402,283	
	Silas C. Swallow	Prohibition	258,536	
1908	WILLIAM H. TAFT	Republican	7,678,908	321
	William J. Bryan	Democratic	6,409,104	162
	Eugene V. Debs	Socialist	420,793	
	Eugene W. Chafin	Prohibition	253,840	
1912	WOODROW WILSON (Min.)*	Democratic	6,293,454	435
	Theodore Roosevelt	Progressive	4,119,538	88
	William H. Taft	Republican	3,484,980	8
	Eugene V. Debs	Socialist	900,672	
	Eugene W. Chafin	Prohibition	206,275	
1916	WOODROW WILSON (Min.)*	Democratic	9,129,606	277
	Charles E. Hughes	Republican	8,538,221	254
	A. L. Benson	Socialist	585,113	
	J. F. Hanly	Prohibition	220,506	
1920	WARREN G. HARDING	Republican	16,152,200	404
	James M. Cox	Democratic	9,147,353	127
	Eugene V. Debs	Socialist	919,799	
	P. P. Christensen	Farmer-Labor	265,411	
1924	CALVIN COOLIDGE	Republican	15,725,016	382
	John W. Davis	Democratic	8,386,503	136
	Robert M. La Follette	Progressive	4,822,856	13
1928	HERBERT C. HOOVER	Republican	21,391,381	444
	Alfred E. Smith	Democratic	15,016,443	87
1932	FRANKLIN D. ROOSEVELT	Democratic	22,821,857	472
	Herbert C. Hoover	Republican	15,761,841	59
	Norman Thomas	Socialist	881,951	
1936	FRANKLIN D. ROOSEVELT	Democratic	27,751,597	523
	Alfred M. Landon	Republican	16,679,583	8
	William Lemke	Union, etc.	882,479	
1940	FRANKLIN D. ROOSEVELT	Democratic	27,244,160	449
	Wendell L. Wilkie	Republican	22,305,198	82
1944	FRANKLIN D. ROOSEVELT	Democratic	25,602,504	432
	Thomas E. Dewey	Republican	22,006,285	99
1948	HARRY S TRUMAN (Min.)*	Democratic	24,105,812	303
	Thomas E. Dewey	Republican	21,970,065	189
	J. Strom Thurmond	States' Rights Democratic	1,169,063	39
	Henry A. Wallace	Progressive	1,157,172	
1952	DWIGHT D. EISENHOWER	Republican	33,936,234	442
	Adlai E. Stevenson	Democratic	27,314,992	89
1956	DWIGHT D. EISENHOWER	Republican	35,590,472	457
	Adlai E. Stevenson	Democratic	26,022,752	73
1960	JOHN F. KENNEDY (Min.)*	Democratic	34,226,731	303
	Richard M. Nixon	Republican	34,108,157	219

*"Min." indicates minority President—one receiving less than 50% of all popular votes.

Presidential Elections (Contd.)

ELECTION	CANDIDATES	PARTIES	POPULAR VOTE	ELECTORAL VOTE
1964	**LYNDON B. JOHNSON**	Democratic	43,129,484	486
	Barry M. Goldwater	Republican	27,178,188	52
1968	**RICHARD M. NIXON** (Min.)*	Republican	31,785,480	301
	Hubert H. Humphrey, Jr.	Democratic	31,275,166	191
	George C. Wallace	American Independent	9,906,473	46
1972	**RICHARD M. NIXON**	Republican	45,767,218	520
	George S. McGovern	Democratic	28,357,668	17
1976**	**JIMMY CARTER**	Democratic	40,276,040	297
	Gerald Ford	Republican	38,532,630	241

*"Min." indicates minority President—one receiving less than 50% of all popular votes.

**Unofficial count from *The New York Times*, November 5, 1976.

Presidents and Vice-Presidents

TERM	PRESIDENT	VICE-PRESIDENT
1789–1793	George Washington	John Adams
1793–1797	George Washington	John Adams
1797–1801	John Adams	Thomas Jefferson
1801–1805	Thomas Jefferson	Aaron Burr
1805–1809	Thomas Jefferson	George Clinton
1809–1813	James Madison	George Clinton (d. 1812)
1813–1817	James Madison	Elbridge Gerry (d. 1814)
1817–1821	James Monroe	Daniel D. Tompkins
1821–1825	James Monroe	Daniel D. Tompkins
1825–1829	John Quincy Adams	John C. Calhoun
1829–1833	Andrew Jackson	John C. Calhoun (resigned 1832)
1833–1837	Andrew Jackson	Martin Van Buren
1837–1841	Martin Van Buren	Richard M. Johnson
1841–1845	William H. Harrison (d. 1841) John Tyler	John Tyler
1845–1849	James K. Polk	George M. Dallas
1849–1853	Zachary Taylor (d. 1850) Millard Fillmore	Millard Fillmore
1853–1857	Franklin Pierce	William R. D. King (d. 1853)
1857–1861	James Buchanan	John C. Breckinridge
1861–1865	Abraham Lincoln	Hannibal Hamlin
1865–1869	Abraham Lincoln (d. 1865) Andrew Johnson	Andrew Johnson
1869–1873	Ulysses S. Grant	Schuyler Colfax
1873–1877	Ulysses S. Grant	Henry Wilson (d. 1875)
1877–1881	Rutherford B. Hayes	William A. Wheeler

Presidents and Vice-Presidents (Contd.)

TERM	PRESIDENT	VICE-PRESIDENT
1881–1885	James A. Garfield (d. 1881)	Chester A. Arthur
	Chester A. Arthur	
1885–1889	Grover Cleveland	Thomas A. Hendricks (d. 1885)
1889–1893	Benjamin Harrison	Levi P. Morton
1893–1897	Grover Cleveland	Adlai E. Stevenson
1897–1901	William McKinley	Garret A. Hobart (d. 1899)
1901–1905	William McKinley (d. 1901)	Theodore Roosevelt
	Theodore Roosevelt	
1905–1909	Theodore Roosevelt	Charles W. Fairbanks
1909–1913	William H. Taft	James S. Sherman (d. 1912)
1913–1917	Woodrow Wilson	Thomas R. Marshall
1917–1921	Woodrow Wilson	Thomas R. Marshall
1921–1925	Warren G. Harding (d. 1923)	Calvin Coolidge
	Calvin Coolidge	
1925–1929	Calvin Coolidge	Charles G. Dawes
1929–1933	Herbert C. Hoover	Charles Curtis
1933–1937	Franklin D. Roosevelt	John N. Garner
1937–1941	Franklin D. Roosevelt	John N. Garner
1941–1945	Franklin D. Roosevelt	Henry A. Wallace
1945–1949	Franklin D. Roosevelt (d. 1945)	Harry S Truman
	Harry S Truman	
1949–1953	Harry S Truman	Alben W. Barkley
1953–1957	Dwight D. Eisenhower	Richard M. Nixon
1957–1961	Dwight D. Eisenhower	Richard M. Nixon
1961–1965	John F. Kennedy (d. 1963)	Lyndon B. Johnson
	Lyndon B. Johnson	
1965–1969	Lyndon B Johnson	Hubert H. Humphrey, Jr.
1969–1974	Richard M. Nixon	Spiro T. Agnew (resigned 1973);
	(resigned 1974)	Gerald R. Ford
1974–1976	Gerald R. Ford	Nelson Rockefeller
1976–	Jimmy Carter	Walter Mondale

Index

ABC Powers, 1006
Aberdeen, Lord, 600
Abilene (Kan.), 785
Abolitionists, 529, 530–32, 548–58, 578, 580, 597, 599, 876; post–1850, 558–63, 620, 636, 672
Abortions, 1248
Absenteeism, 1234
Acheson, Dean, 1186, 1187, 1189, 1191, 1194
Act Concerning Religion, 113–14
Act of Settlement, 153
Adams, Brooks, 985
Adams, Charles Francis, 672, 713
Adams, Henry, 713, 806, 925, 985
Adams, Herbert Baxter, 946
Adams, John, 2, 230, 234, 259, 263, 266, 267, 271, 276, 289, 292, 297, 308, 324, 327, 330, 347, 366; vice pres., 344; Pres., 356, 360, 372, 466; later, 366, 386
Adams, John Quincy, 366, 367, 379, 381, 471, 594, 595–97; Pres., 467, 473, 475, 487, 494; later, 599
Adams, Samuel, 259, 295, 297, 307, 315, 325, 330
Adams, Samuel Hopkins, 907
Adams, Sherman, 1206
Addams, Jane, 890, 894, 910, 959, 963–65
Adelantados, 14
Adkins v. Children's Hospital, 1065
Admiralty courts, 131, 250, 254, 267
Adults, post–1960, 1236
Advertising, 1138
AFL-CIO (merged), 1205. See also American Federation of Labor; Congress of Industrial Organizations
Africa, 76, 164, 205, 207, 1228. See also Barbary pirates; Blacks
Afro-American culture, 572–73, 575
Agassiz, Louis, 759
Age, average, in 1850, 435
Age of Reason (Paine), 405
Aged, 1147–48
Agnew, Spiro, 1248, 1260, 1262
Agricultural Adjustment Act, 1081, 1094, 1097

Agricultural Adjustment Administration, 1081
Agricultural Adjustment Association, 1088
Agricultural Wheel, 851
Agriculture, early, 178, 309, 394, 398, 443–44, 446–50, 452–55; post–1860, 695, 745–47, 786, 792–94, 797, 828, 846, 849–56; post–1890, 829–30, 862, 875, 877, 976; post–1920, 1062–64, 1068, 1076; post–1930, 1094, 1097–98, 1106; post–1940, 1101, 1103, 1115; post–1950, 1205
Aguinaldo, Emilio, 994–95
Airlift, Berlin, 1188
Air power, 1167, 1181–82
Air travel, 1202
Alabama, 371, 399, 438, 446, 567, 762
Alabama, 694, 712, 733, 775
Alamance (N. C.), 237
Alaska, 775–76
Albany (N. Y.), 204, 206
Albany Evening Journal, 488
Albee, Edward, 1233
Albemarle, Duke of, 72
Alcoholism, 1235
Aldrich, Sen. Nelson, 873, 926, 930, 933, 942
Alexander, Gen. E. P., 734
Alexander II, 776
Algeciras Conference, 997
Algiers, 1175
Alien and sedition acts, 359, 363
Aliens, 1108
Allen, Ethan, 405
Allen, James Lane, 819
Alliance for Progress, 1228
Allied war debts, 1161, 1166, 1167. See also Reparations
Allies (World War I), 1008, 1010, 1014, 1040, 1041, 1043, 1161
Alsace-Lorraine, 1041
Alsop, Joseph, 1259
Altamont (Calif.), 1240
Altgeld, Gov. John P., 882
Alton (Ill.), 555
Aluminum Corporation of America, 1064

Amalgamated Iron and Steel Workers Union, 881–82
American Anti-Anarchy Association, 1024
American Bankers Association, 1106
American Century, 1228, 1266
American Civil Liberties Union, 1067, 1142–43
American Colonization Society, 549
American Compromise, the, 768–98, 800
American Creed, 1224
American Defense Society, 1024
American Dilemma, An, 1224
American Farm Bureau Federation, 855, 1064, 1081, 1106
American Federation of Labor (AFL), 785, 858–59, 1032, 1058, 1062, 1095–96, 1106
American First movement, 1170
American Freedmen's Inquiry Commission, 737
American Independent Party, 1240
American Legion, 1067
American Liberty League, 1087
American Missionary Association, 738
American Museum, 307
American Party, 465, 490, 491–94
American Philosophical Society, 411, 412, 414
American Phrenological Journal, 519
American Plan, 859
American Railway Union, 848, 882
American Renaissance, 523–25
American Revolution, 229–30, 244–51, 263–89
American Steel and Wire Company, 840
American Sugar Refining Company, 840, 848
American Tobacco Company, 830, 840, 927
American Tract Society, 548
Amherst, Lord Jeffrey, 206–7, 208, 247
Amnesty, 730
Amos 'n Andy, 1145
Anabaptists, 114
Ancient Order of Hibernians, 796–97

Anderson, Joseph, 696
Anderson, Major Robert, 655
Anderson, Margaret, 1034
Anderson, Marian, 1111
Anderson, Sherwood, 1034, 1133, 1143
Andersonville prison, 731, 732
Andover Theological Seminary, 544
Andrew, John A., 720
Andros, Sir Edmund, 129–30, 148, 150
Anglo-American culture, 153–55, 216–22
Anglo-American relations, 208, 388
Anglo-American society, 4
Anglo-Japanese Alliance, 1159
Angola, 1254
Annapolis Royal (Nova Scotia), 142
Anthracite Coal Strike Commission, 928
Anticommunism. See Containment
Antietam, Battle of, 682
Anti-expansionists, 982, 986
Anti-Federalists, 335, 340
Anti-imperialists, 990, 992, 993
Anti-Masonic crusade, 545, 876
Anti-Masonic Party, 465, 487–90, 494
Antimonopolists, 843–48
Antipollution standards, 1256–57
Antiradicalism, 1058–59, 1120–23
Anti-Saloon League, 1070
Anti-Semitism, 1108, 1167
Antislavery movement, 554–55, 618–19, 624–26. See also Abolitionists; Blacks; Free Soil Party; Slavery
Antitrust suits, 1099
Antiwar protesters, 1248
Anthony, Susan B., 557
Apache Indians, 441, 442, 779
Apollo flights, 1204
Appleton, Nathan, 491
Apprenticeship, 399–400, 499
Arabs, 1253, 1258–59
Arapaho Indians, 779
Arbitration, 775
Argentina, 7, 1006
Argonne Forest, 1015
Argyll, Duke of, 674
Aristocracy, Anglo-American, 134–47, 232–33; mercantile, 137–38, 177–79
Arkansas, 391, 448, 567, 577, 585, 654–55, 657, 660, 762
Armament, 1159, 1165
Armories, 667
Armory Show, 1027–31
Arms embargo (1935), 1167
Armstrong, Neil, 1204
Army, U.S., 349, 359, 653, 678, 709

Army-McCarthy hearings, 1121, 1123
Army Relocation Authority, 1108
Arnold, Benedict, 278
Art, 415–18, 523, 1027–31. See also Painting; Theater
Arthur, Pres. Chester A., 801, 806
Articles of Confederation, 301–5, 325–29, 330
Ashley, James M., 756
Asia, 1001, 1165, 1176, 1178, 1179, 1189, 1228, 1254. See also countries by individual names
Asiatics, 1108
Assassination of Presidents, 801, 807, 921, 1217–18
Assembly line, 1066, 1143
Associations, voluntary, 401–2
Astor, John Jacob, 391, 459
Astronauts, 1204–5
Atchison, Sen. David R., 628
Atkinson, Edward, 992
Atlanta (Ga.), 723
Atlantic Charter, 1178
Atlantic Conference (1941), 1173
Atlantic Monthly, The, 818
Atlas, Charles, 1145
Atomic bomb, 1120, 1153, 1178, 1191
Atoms for Peace, 1215
Audiencias, 11
Austin, David, 404
Australia, 1176, 1194, 1207, 1213
Australian ballot, 811
Austria, 202, 206, 1008, 1164
Austria-Hungary, 1014, 1015
Automobile, 1061, 1066, 1096, 1127, 1128, 1135
Avocationalism, 1234
Axis powers, 1169, 1173. See also Hitler, Adolf; Mussolini, Benito
Aztec empire, 5, 16

Babcock, Orville F., 805
Babson, Roger, 839
Backus, Isaac, 405
Bacon, Nathaniel, 148–50
Bacon's Rebellion, 148–50
Baer, George, 928
Bailey v. Drexel Furniture Co., 1065
Baker, Ray Stannard, 905, 906–7, 950
Baker v. Carr, 1226
Balance of payments, 209–13; post-1960, 1258. See also Gold
Balance of power, 1211
Balboa, Vasco, 5
Baldwin, Roger, 971
Baldwin, Theron, 507–8

Balkans, 1168, 1176, 1184
Ballinger, Richard, 942
Baltimore, Lords, 60–64, 81
Baltimore (Md.), 178–79, 400, 452, 657–58
Baltimore and Ohio Railroad, 783, 797
Bank Holiday, 1082
Bank of North America, 311, 325
Bank of the United States (BUS), First, 346, 348, 353, 384, 477–81, 484, 487, 494; Second, 426, 696
Bank War, 479
Bankhead-Jones Farm Tenancy Act (1937), 1097
Banking, 215, 698, 780–81, 794, 839, 882; post-1910, 841, 943, 974, 1008; post-1920, 1058, 1064, 1076, 1081–82, 1162. See also Bank of the U.S.; Currency; Federal Reserve System
Bankruptcy, 145, 795
Banks, Gen. N. P., 691, 738
Baptist church, 506, 1139
Baptists, 181, 241, 404–5, 407, 512, 546–47
Barbary pirates, 364
Barbary states, 328
Barlow, Joel, 342, 395, 413
Barrington, Lord, 255
Barton, Bruce, 1132
Bartram, William, 413
Baruch, Bernard, 1020–21, 1023, 1064
Bascom, John, 915
Bates, Edward, 717
Batista, Fulgencio, 1209
Battle of Britain, 1170
Battle of the Bulge, 1176
Battle of the Running Bulls, 1096
Bay of Pigs, 1210
Bayard, James A., 366
Beard, Charles A., 895
Beauregard, Gen. P. G. T., 656, 677–78, 763
Beaver, 444
Beecher, Lyman, 409, 497, 510, 530, 540, 545–46, 549, 553–54
Beef, 453
Beef Trust, 927
Beekman, Henry, 209
Behaviorism, 1130, 1138–39
Belcher, Andrew, 142, 147
Belgium, 202, 434, 1168
Belknap, William W., 805
Bell, Alexander Graham, 781, 842
Bell, John, 640, 652
Bellamy, Edward, 842

Bellow, Saul, 1234
Belmont, August, 884
Benevolent Empire, 541, 544–48
Benjamin, Judah P., 665, 672, 713, 715
Bennington (Vt.), 285
Bentley, Arthur F., 895
Benton, Thomas Hart, 602, 921
Benton, Sen. Thomas Hart, 478
Berger, Victor, 969
Berkeley, Lord John, 72, 77
Berkeley, Sir William, 43, 139–40, 148–49, 158–59
Berkman, Alexander, 882
Berle, Adolph, 1079
Berlin, 1176
Berlin Blockade, 1188
Berlin Wall, 1211
Bermuda, 29
Bermuda Company, 31
Bernard, Gov., 255
Berrien, John M., 485
Best Years of Our Lives, The, 1149
Beveridge, Sen. Albert J., 981, 993
Bibb, Henry, 559
Bible Commonwealth. *See* Massachusetts Bay Colony
Bicameralism, 324
Bicentennial, 1265–66
Biddle, Nicholas, 479, 480–81
Big Four, 1160
Big Three, 1180
Bigelow, Jacob, 415, 516
Bill of Rights, 342
Bill of Rights (English), 153
Bills of credit, 213
Birmingham (Ala.), 1221
Birney, James G., 490, 553, 558, 603
Birth control, 1133, 1135
Birth rate, 431–32
Black Codes, 749–50
Black family, 745
Black Hills, 779
Black mobility, 744
Black Muslims, 1238
Black Panthers, 1238, 1239
Black Power, 1238, 1250
Black Reconstruction. *See* Reconstruction
Black Republicans, 626, 637
Black rights. *See* Civil rights movement
Blacks, abolitionists, 599–61; in Civil War, 705–6, 709–11, 716, 731; disfranchisement, 913, 953; education, 503, 739, 765, 795, 1219, 1239; family, 745; free, 458, 486, 506, 544,

549, 578, 580, 586–87, 618, 629; introduced into colonies, 17; migration, 950, 956, 1109; mobility, 744; population, 136, 164, 168; post–1715, 136; post–1865, 811–13; post–1875, 808, 811–13; post–1900, 950, 953–58; post–1920, 1109; post–1941, 1111–13; in Southern writing, 819–20, 1109–10; suffrage, 730, 752, 754, 760, 762; Reconstruction, 713, 734–47, 749–55, 759–66, 811–13; vote, 1112–13. *See also* Black Power; Civil rights movement; Slavery; South
Blaine, Rep. James G., 698
Bland, Giles, 149
Blitzkreig, 1169
Blivin, Bruce, 1066
Block grants, 1248
Blockade, China, 1169; Cuba, 1211; paper, 1009; Union, 669, 670, 672, 674, 675, 692, 694, 700; War of 1812, 384–85; World War I, 1009
Blodget, Samuel, 415
Blount, William, 342–43
Blue Eagle, 1080
Board of Customs, American, 254
Board of Trade and Plantations, 124–25
Boggs, L. W., 533
Bolivia, 7
Bombing raids, 1230, 1251
Bonds, 669, 698–99
Book of Mormon, The, 532
Booth, John Wilkes, 720, 731
Bootlegging, 1070. *See also* Prohibition
Border states, Civil War, 654–61
Boston, 29, 36, 54, 129–30, 138, 147, 164, 204, 254, 258, 280, 460, 1046, 1248
Boston Massacre, 256
Boston Tea Party, 258
Bounty-jumping, 704
Bourne, Randolph, 952, 1037–38
Bowderly, Terence V., 857
Bowdoin, Gov. James, 307–8
Bowdoin College, 503
Boxer Rebellion, 996
Boy Spies of America, 1024
Boycott, 255, 1209–10, 1254
Braddock, Major Gen. Edward, 205
Bradford, William, 46, 48–49, 50–51
Bragg, Gen. Braxton, 682, 691
Brain Trust, 1079
Bray, Rev. Thomas, 183

Brazil, 7, 570, 572, 1006
Breastworks and entrenchments, 686
Breckinridge, John C., 638, 639–40
Bretton Woods Conference, 1180–81
Brewster, William, 46
Brezhnev, Leonid, 1253
Bridge of ships, 1016
Bridges, 450
Brief Account, A, 217
Bright, John, 712
Brinksmanship, 1209, 1215
Britain's Remembrancer, 222
British West Indies, 211, 285, 547, 549, 587–88
Broadcasting industry, 1064
Brooks, Preston, 628
Brooks, Van Wyck, 1034–36, 1037–38, 1043
Brotherhood of Sleeping Car Porters, 1111
Brown, Claude, 1238
Brown, John, 628, 636–37
Brown, Dr. John, 222
Brown, Gov. Joseph E., 702, 715
Brown, Moses, 241–42
Brown, William Wells, 559
Brown University, 186
Brown v. *Board of Education,* 1219
Brownson, Orestes, 770, 771
Broyles Commission, 1121
Bruce, Blanche K., 763
Bryan, William Jennings, 851, 869, 881, 885–86, 889, 983–84; post–1912, 983–84, 1003, 1070, 1133
Bryce, Lord, 981
Bubble Act, 215
Buchanan, James, 609, 624; Pres., 493, 536, 627, 629, 631, 632, 640
Budenz, Louis, 971
Budget, U.S., 1099, 1116, 1118, 1208, 1228, 1255. *See also* National debt
Buell, Gen. Don Carlos, 678, 682, 688
Buffalo, 444
Buffon, Georges de, 219, 410, 411–12
Bulgaria, 1183
Bull Moose Party, 966
Bull Run, Battles of, 677, 678, 682, 687
Bundy, McGeorge, 1228
Bunker Hill, Battle of, 280
Bureau of the Budget, 1068
Bureau of Corporations, 927
Bureau of Mines, 1065
Bureaucracy, 364, 1023–24, 1101, 1106–7, 1206
Burger, Warren, 1247

Burgess, Gelett, 1031
Burgess, John W., 895
Burgh, James, 222
Burgoyne, Gen. John, 280, 283–85
Burke, Edmund, 173, 248, 267, 269
Burleson, Albert S., 1026, 1027
Burlington Railroad, 833, 846
Burnside, Ambrose E., 687
Burr, Aaron, 360, 370–71, 400
Bushnell, Horace, 759
Business, 395–96, 783–84, 828, 836–42, 1061–62, 1099, 1115, 1205. *See also* Business, regulation of; Foreign trade
Business, regulation of, 913, 927–31, 939, 943, 975–76; post-1917, 1020–23, 1069; post-1932, 1080, 1094, 1099, 1103. *See also* Trade
Busing, 1239, 1247–48, 1250
Bute, Lord, 245, 247–48
Butler, Andrew, 628
Butler, Gen. Benjamin F., 686, 722
Byrd, William, II, 134
Byrnes, James, 1186, 1187

Cabeza de Vaca, Alvar, 75
Cabilda, 12
Cabinet, 1118. *See also individually listed departments*
Cable, George Washington, 819
Cabot, Sen. George, 356
Cabot, John, 18
Cabot, Sebastian, 18
Cagney, James, 1145
Caldwell, Erskine, 1133
Calhoun, John C., 367, 471, 473, 477, 482, 484–85, 583, 588, 601, 619–20
California, 5, 598–99; post-1840, 608–9, 611, 617–18, 619, 621, 623, 758–59
Calvert, Cecilius, 60, 115–16
Calvert, Leonard, 60–64, 115–16
Calvinism, 406–407, 520
Cambodia, 1250, 1251
Camden (S. C.), 286
Cameron, Simon, 663–64, 706
Camp meetings, 508
Canada, 18, 22–29, 29, 141–42, 207, 246, 278, 280, 611, 1193
Canal, construction, 426, 450–52, 476. *See also* Erie Canal; Panama Canal
Candidates, The, 244
Canning, George, 596
Capek, Karel, 1143
Careers, 1138, 1141–42

Caribbean, 205, 997, 1005
Carlisle Commission, 285
Carmichael, Stokely, 1238
Carnegie, Andrew, 696, 783, 836, 992, 1004
Carnegie, Dale, 1142
Carolinas, 70–77, 124, 129, 130, 150, 170, 171, 182. *See also* North Carolina; South Carolina
Carpetbaggers, 763
Carranza Venustiano, 1006, 1008
Carranza Venustiano, 1006, 1008
Carroll, Charles, 234, 297
Carson, Rachel, 1234
Cartels, 837–38, 848
Carter, Landon, 173
Carter, Jimmy, 1269
Carter, Robert, 136–37
Carteret, Sir George, 77
Cartwright, Peter, 508
Casa de Contratacion, 9–10
Cass, Lewis, 614, 615, 624
Castro, Fidel, 1209–11, 1288
Catholic immigrants, 492–94, 497, 500–501
Catholics. *See* Roman Catholics
Castile, monarch of, 8
Catt, Carrie Chapman, 965, 966
Cattle industry, 76, 785
Censorship, 1025, 1226, 1248
Census, 412, 745; (1840), 601–2; (1848), 536; (1890), 777–78
Central America, 5–7, 18, 611, 708. *See also* Caribbean; Latin America
Central Intelligence Agency (CIA), 1195, 1210
Central Pacific Railroad, 778, 782
Central Powers, 1161
Central Treaty Organization (CENTO), 1207
Chamberlain, Neville, 1165
Chancellorsville, Battle of, 687
Channing, William Ellery, 518
Chaplin, Charlie, 1143, 1145
Charge accounts, 1201
Charities, private, 795, 909
Charles I, 29, 71
Charles II, 71, 80–81, 124, 171
Charles River Bridge Company, 395–96
Charleston (S. C.), 36, 75, 138, 164, 286, 454, 655–56, 693
Charlestown (Mass.), 54
Charlotte Temple, 417
Charter of Freedoms and Exemptions, 67

Chase, Salmon P., 654, 667–71, 699, 718, 720, 755
Chase, Samuel, 373
Chattanooga (Tenn.), 688–90
Chavez, César, 1249
Chemical defoliants, 1230
Cherokee Indians, 236, 437–41, 657
Chesapeake region, agriculture, 178; population, 87; Scottish merchants, 174; tobacco economy, 95–98
Chevalier, Michel, 466
Cheyenne Indians, 779
Chiang Kai-shek, 1163, 1189–90, 1212, 1252
Chicago, 831
Chicago Bar Association, 1069
Chicago Commons, 962, 964–65
Chicago *Tribune*, 750
Chicanos. *See* Mexican Americans
Chickamauga, Battle of, 688
Chickasaw Indians, 437, 657
Chicopee (Mass.), 455
Child, Dr. Robert, 58–59
Child labor, 455, 499, 833, 907, 916–19, 962, 976, 1065
Children, role of, 88, 104, 105, 107, 1136–37, 1147
Chile, 7, 986, 1006, 1255
China, 310, 453; post-1890, 994, 1005; post-1900, 995, 999, 1002; post-1920, 1160, 1162, 1163, 1165; post-1936, 1167; post-1941, 1182; post-1945, 1189–91; post-1950, 1209; post-1970, 1251–52
Chinese Exclusion Act, 759
Chinese immigrants, 758–59
Chinese Revolution, 1191, 1192
Choate, Joseph, 985
Choctaw Indians, 437, 657
Chou En-lai, 1252
Church. *See* Religion; *and individually listed names of denominations*
Church of England, 45, 52, 115–16, 130, 189–90, 242–43, 245, 404, 405; Society for the Propagation of the Gospel in Foreign Parts, 111, 183; in Virginia, 109–12, 181, 240–41, 403, 405
Church of Jesus Christ of Latter Day Saints. *See* Mormons
Churchill, Winston, 1173, 1175, 1178, 1180, 1182–83, 1184
Cider tax, 247
Cincinnati, 390
Circular Letter, 255
Cities, blacks in, 956, 958; immigrants

in, 434, 949–51; post–1865, 830–32; post–1893, 882–84, 889, 892–901; post–1900, 861; post–1920, 1109–10; post–1924, 1069–70; post–1941, 1111; post–1950, 1225; post–1960, 1239; post–1970, 1250

Citizens Industrial Association, 859

Civil Aeronautics Board, 1206

Civil liberties, 755, 1024–26

Civil Liberty and Self-Government, On, 772

Civil Rights Act (1866), 752–53; (1957), 1226; (1964), 1223; (1965), 1223, 1238

Civil rights movement, 561, 1055, 1110, 1111–13, 1115, 1119, 1219–27, 1238. *See also* Blacks; Civil Rights Act; Desegregation; Housing; Schools

Civil Service Reform Commission, 806

Civil War, 649–83, 685–95, 720–27, 779

Civilian Corps (CCC), 1079

Claiborne, 113

Claredon, Earl of, 72

Clark, "Champ," 944

Clark, George Rogers, 342–43

Clark, William, 369–70

Clarke, Edward, 1060

Class consciousness, 460–61

Clay, Henry, 471, 473, 476, 584, 586, 591; post–1832, 479, 483, 484, 489; post–1850, 459, 619; post–1860, 650

Clayton Antitrust Act, 848, 975

Clean Air Act (1963), 1256

Cleburne, Gen. Patrick R., 709

Clemenceau, Georges, 1041, 1042

Clemens, Samuel L., 787, 817, 1035

Cleveland, Grover, 789, 802; Pres., 847, 882–85, 980, 986

Cleveland (O.), 783

Clinton, De Witt, 366, 468–70, 494

Clinton, George, 355

Clinton, Sir Henry, 285

Clipper ship, 453–54

Clocks, 415

Clothes, 92, 457, 1062, 1130

Coal production, 780, 927–28

Cobb, Frank, 1011

Cobb, Ty, 1146

Coercive Acts, 258–59

Cohens v. *Virginia,* 374

Coinage Act of 1873, 791

Cold Harbor, Battle of, 721

Cold War, 1182–91, 1192, 1193, 1212–13, 1227

Cole, Thomas, 523

Colfax, Schuyler, 805

College of William and Mary, 113, 159–160

Colleges, 406, 697, 1150, 1151. *See also individual colleges and universities*

Colleton, Sir John, 71–72

Colonization, British, 19–24, 27–31, 36–64, 70–83; Dutch, 64–70; financing, 29–31; Spanish, 5–18

Collinson, Peter, 219

Colombia, 201, 999–1000

Colonial officers, 133–36, 211

Colonization Society, 559

Columbia (S. C.), 723

Columbia Broadcasting, 1128

Columbia University, 895, 1239

Columbiad, 395

Columbus, Christopher, 5

Columbus (N. M.), 1006

Comanche Indians, 779

Commander, Lydia, 960

Commerce, post–1770, 238, 310; post–1800, 382, 454–55. *See also* Business; Foreign trade; Industry; Trade

Commission government, 1043

Committee on Public Information, 1025

Committees of correspondence, 258

Commodity cooperatives, 1068, 1076

Commodity prices, 1068

Common Sense, 275, 278

Commonwealth v. *Hunt,* 461

Communal life, 1235, 1236

Communication, 400–1, 781–82, 1120. *See also* Mass communication; Radio industry; Telegraph; Telephone; Television; Transportation

Communism, 1055, 1120, 1121, 1163, 1185, 1210. *See also* Communist Party; Containment; Russia; Viet Nam War

Communist Party, 1058, 1067

Compromise of 1850, 616–24, 631

Computer, 1232, 1259

Concentration camps, 1108

Concepción, 7

Concord (Mass.), 54, 277, 280

Confederacy, 647–48, 652, 656–63, 666–83, 685–706, 709–12, 714–15, 720–27. *See also* Civil War; South

Conglomerates, 1106

Congo (Zaire), 1211

Congregationalism, 114, 117, 180–82, 242, 406–407

Congress, Confederate, 652, 656, 657, 666, 692, 700, 702–704, 711, 717

Congress, U.S., First Continental, 259–60, 271–72, 313; Second Continental, 276–77, 297, 301, 325; post–1791, 302, 344, 354; post–1800, 367, 546, 617, 623; post–1860, 628–29, 697, 704, 748–58, 802–803; post–1909, 942; post–1924, 1068; post–1935, 1090, 1094, 1100, 1166–67; post–1941, 1103; Eightieth, 1105, 1115; post–1953, 1214; post–1974, 1254; post–1975, 1256

Congress of Industrial Organizations (CIO), 1095–97, 1106, 1108

Congress on Racial Equality (CORE), 1221

Conkling, Sen. Roscoe, 806–7

Connecticut, 54, 59, 117, 129, 135, 170, 197

Connecticut Compromise, 335

Connecticut Yankees, 237–38

Conquistadores, 5–7

Conscription, 666, 702–705, 706–12, 714

Conservation, 444–45, 931–32, 1132. *See also* Natural resources; Soil conservation

Conservative Republicans, 718. *See also* Republican Party

Considerations on the Propriety of Imposing Taxes, 269

Constitution, English, 298

Constitution, Federal, 328, 330–41, 353, 373, 621, 629, 637

Constitution, state, 317

Constitutional amendments, 641; First, 405, 1143; first ten, 342; 12th, 360; 13th, 729, 730, 731, 749; 14th, 730, 731, 750–53, 754, 761; 15th, 731; 18th, 1070, 1130; 19th, 967; 21st, 1088

Constitutional conventions, 318

Constitutional theory, 828

Constitutional Union Party, 640

Constitutionalism, 735–41

Construction industry, 1062, 1066, 1202

Consumer, 838

Consumer credit, 1201

Consumer education, 1021

Consumer movement, 929, 969

Consumer services, 1127

Consumerism, 1126–29, 1143, 1201–2, 1206, 1232, 1259, 1260

Containment, 1055, 1120–23, 1191–96, 1207, 1209–11, 1227–32, 1250–55

Continental Army, 281, 325

Continental Congress. *See* Congress, U.S.

Contrabands, 706, 708

Contrabands, 686–87

Convention, nominating, (1924), 1061; (1940), 1100; (1960), 1215

Convoy system, 1016, 1170–71

Cooden, Richard, 712

Cooke, Jay, 699, 790

Cooley, Charles Horton, 828

Coolidge, Pres. Calvin, 1066–67

Coolidge, Pres. Calvin, 1066–67, 1068, 1072, 1161

Cooper, Anthony Ashley, 72–73

Cooper, James Fenimore, 444, 523

Cooper, Peter, 415, 795

Cooperatives, producers, 853–55, 858

Copper industry, 127, 788

Coral Sea, Battle of, 1176

Corinth, Battle of, 680

Corn, 446, 452, 780

Cornbury, Lord, 131, 140

Cornwallis, Lord, 287, 288

Coronado, Francisco, 5

Corporate capitalism, 840–41

Corporations, 830, 840, 910, 1023; post–1920, 1061–62, 1064; post–1933, 1074, 1084; post–1940, 1101, 1105; post–1950, 1195, 1208, 1234. *See also* Business; Business, regulation of

Corrupt practices act, 943

Corruption, post–1865, 764–65, 803–7, 885, 915; post–1920, 1057–58, 1066; post–1950, 1116, 1262–64

Corsi, Edward, 950

Cortés, Hernándo, 5

Cortissoz, Royal, 1031

Cosmetics industry, 1134

Cosmopolitan, 907

Cost of living, 1103

Cost-plus contract, 1023

Cotton, 76, 127, 392, 398, 446–47, 457, 478, 568; post–1861, 672, 695, 747, 849; post–1932, 1081

Cotton, John, 101–2

Cotton gin, 446

Cotton Whigs, 616

Coughlin, Charles, 1084–85, 1088, 1089, 1090

Council of Fifty, 534, 535

Council of Four, 1041

Council of the Indies, 10–12

Council of National Defense, 1020, 1025

Council for New England, 49–50

Council of Ten, 1041

Country Life Commission, 856

County fair, 394

Courtiers, 295

Courts, 333–34, 1094–95, 1206. *See also* Admiralty courts; Supreme Court

Cox, Archibald, 1263

Cox, George, 892

Cox, James, 1057

Cox, Kenyon, 1028–29

Coxey, Jacob, 883–84

Coxey's Army, 883–84

Craft, Ellen, 559

Craftsmanship, 1234, 1235

Crane, Hart, 1034

Crawford, William H., 367, 471

Crazy Horse, 779

Credibility gap, 1230

Credit, 238, 454, 1119, 1126–27, 1167, 1169, 1170, 1255. *See also* Currency

Credit cards, 1201

Credit Mobilier, 804–5

Creditor-merchants, 239

Creek Indians, 436, 437, 657

Creel, George, 1025

Creoles, 17, 216

Crime, 1132, 1226, 1247, 1250. *See also* Criminals

Crime Control Act (1968), 1239

Crime of '73, 791

Criminals, 1225, 1247. *See also* Crime

Crittenden, John J., 485, 641, 652

Croly, Herbert, 938, 1037

Cromwell, Oliver, 71

Crop failures, 878

Crosby, Ernest, 907

Crown Point, 207

Crump, Ed, 1070

Crystal Palace exhibition, 456

Cuba, 208, 593, 600, 611, 615–16, 773–74; post–1895, 985, 986, 993, 994, 998; post–1917, 1005; post–1958, 1209–11, 1228, 1254, 1257. *See also* Cuban missile crisis

Cuban missile crisis, 1216

Cullen, Countee, 1110

Culpeper, John, 150

Culpeper's Rebellion, 148, 150

Cultural radicalism, 1036–37, 1043

Culture, Afro-American, 572–73, 575; post–1800, 410–19, 522–25; post–1912, 1027–34

Cumings, Henry, 405

cummings, e. e., 1143

Curley, James Michael, 1070

Currency, 213–15; post–1775, 277–78,

310–11, 325, 333, 347; post–1856, 478, 670–71, 699, 780–81, 790–92; post–1913, 974. *See also* Banking; Gold; Greenbacks; Inflation; Silver

Currency Act, 215, 240

Curtis, Benjamin, 632

Curtis, George William, 806

Custer, George A., 779

Customs collectors, 131, 209, 211, 250, 255, 257

Customs duties, 129, 250–51, 254, 257, 346. *See also* Tariffs

Cyprus War, 1254

Czechoslovakia, 1164, 1165–66, 1187

Dairying, 849, 1064

Daley, Richard, 1239

Dana, Richard Henry, Jr., 750

Danish West Indies, 773, 776

Darrow, Clarence, 1133

Dartmouth College, 186, 396, 503

Darwin, Charles, 759, 1133

Daugherty, Harry, 1058

Davenport, James, 185

Davies, Samuel, 185

Davis, Chester, 1081

Davis, Henry Winter, 720

Davis, Jeff, 913

Davis, Jefferson, 614, 637; pres. of Confederacy, 649–53, 655–56, 661, 664–66, 671–72, 674, 675, 681, 685, 691–92, 697–98, 706, 710, 713, 720, 723, 725–26, 731–33

Davis, John W., 1067, 1071

Dawes Act (1887), 779

Dawes Plan (1924), 1161

Dean, John, 1263

Death penalty, 1247

Death rate, 88

Death of a Salesman, 1150

Debs, Eugene V., 848, 882, 928, 968, 970–71, 1026

Debtor relief legislation, 329. *See also* Bankruptcy

Declaration of Independence, 278–79, 301, 629

Declaratory Act (1766), 271

Defense of the Realm Act, 1017

DeForest, John W., 813–15

DeForest, Robert W., 894

de Gaulle, Pres. Charles, 1227

Deism, 405

DeLancey, Stephanus, 143

Delaney, Martin, 561

Delaware, 324, 577, 655, 657, 660

De la Warr, Lord, 40

Demobilization, 736, 1044, 1104–1105

Democratic Party, 465–66, 468, 470, 476–77, 482, 486–87, 612, 614; post–1850, 483, 491–92, 626, 630, 637–40; post–1860, 637, 717, 748–49, 866–74; post-1896, 881–90; post–1900, 913, 939, 944–46; post–1920, 1087–88, 1171–72; post–1930, 1054, 1111, 1214; post–1950, 1115, 1118; post–1960, 1215–16, 1240. *See also* Elections, congressional; Elections, presidential; Jackson, Andrew; Jeffersonian Republicans; New Deal

Dempsey, Jack, 1146

Denmark, 1168

Department of Agriculture, 1097, 1106, 1111, 1162

Department of Commerce, 1161

Department of Defense, 1195

Department of Forestry and Fisheries Services, 1065

Department of Health, Education and Welfare (HEW), 1206

Deportation, 1025, 1046

Depressions, (1780s), 322; (1790s), 359; (1819), 471; (1837), 547; (1857), 512; (1873), 758, 785, 791, 795, 835; (1893), 835, 881; (1894), 882–84. *See also* Great Depression; Unemployment

Derby, E. H., 319

Desegregation, 1115, 1219–20, 1226, 1247–48, 1259. *See also* Blacks; Civil rights movement; Housing; Schools; Segregation

Desertion, 716

de Soto, Hernando, 5

Destroyer Deal, 1170

Detroit, 831, 1112, 1238

Dew, Thomas R., 580

Dewey, Com. George, 989, 990

Dewey, John, 895, 952, 963, 972, 1148, 1151

Dewey, Thomas E., 1104, 1114–15

DeWitt, Benjamin Parke, 903

DeWitt, Lt. Gen. John, 1108

Diaz, Porfirio, 1006

Dickinson, Emily, 815

Dickinson, John, 221, 254–55, 277, 340

Diderot, Denis, 219

Digger Indians, 442

Diggs, Annie L., 878

Dillingham Commission, 953

Diplomatic corps, 380. *See also* Foreign policy

Discourse of Western Planting, 23

Discovery, 37

Disfranchisement, 953. *See also* Blacks; Civil rights movement

Disorder, popular, 315

Dissenters, 1236. *See also* Youth

Distant Early Warning System (DEW Line), 1207–8

District of Columbia, 490, 559, 591, 619, 621, 708, 760. *See also* Washington, D. C.

Divorce, 1236

Dixiecrats, 1114, 1115

Dodd, Samuel C. T., 838, 839

Dodge, Mabel, 1032

Dollar diplomacy, 1002–3, 1005. *See also* Foreign policy

Dominican Republic, 774, 776, 999, 1005

Dominion of New England, 129, 148, 150–52

Donnelly, Ignatius, 878, 879, 881

Do-Nothing Congress. *See* Congress, U.S., Eightieth

Doolittle, Sen. James R., 718

Dorr, Rheta Childe, 962

Dorr Rebellion (1843), 467

Dos Passos, John, 1143–44

Douglas, Frederick, 559, 561, 705, 741

Douglas, Stephen, 614, 621, 622, 624, 626, 628; post-1858, 630–36, 637–38, 726, 753

Douglas, William O., 1082

Douglas Aircraft, 1208

Douglass, Dr. William, 190–91

Doves, 1251

Dow, Neal, 558

Downing, George, 153

Draft resistance, 1230–31

Drake, Francis, 21, 23

Drayton, William, 297

Dred Scott case, 750

Dreiser, Theodore, 1034, 1144

Dropouts, 1235

Drucker, Peter, 1201, 1233

Drugs, 1235, 1248

DuBois, William E. B., 958

Duchamp, Marcel, 1029

Dueling, 400

Duke's Law (1665), 114

Dulany, Daniel, 269, 274, 276

Dulles, Sec'y John Foster, 1194, 1210, 1215, 1228, 1229

Dunmore, Lord, 236

Dunning, William A., 895

DuPont, Pierre, 1130, 1132

DuPont, Samuel F., 692

Durand, Asher B., 523

Durkin, Martin, 1118

Dutch, 64–70. *See also* Netherlands; New Netherland

Dutch Reformed Church, 114

Dutch West India Company, 65–70, 114

Dwight, Louis, 544

Dwight, Timothy, 342, 413

Dyes, 127

Early, Gen. Jubal A., 722, 734

East, 453. *See also* New England; Sectionalism

East Asia, 1159, 1192, 1212. *See also* Asia; *and countries by individual names*

East Germany, 1212. *See also* Germany; West Germany

East India Company, 21, 258

East Prussia, 1176

Eastland Company, 21

Eastman, Max, 971, 1032

Eastman Kodak, 1064

Eaton, John, 738

Ecology movement, 1256–57

Economic laissez-faire, 741–47

Economy, post–1600, 90–98; post–1700, 172–81, 238–39, 309; post–1793, 391; post–1820, 429–31, 457–60, 462; post–1860, 695–98, 777–86, 829, 835; post–1919, 1061–66, 1129, 1161; post–1935, 1093–1101; post–1940, 1101–7, 1116, 1150; post–1950, 1118, 1205; post–1960, 1255; post–1970, 1053–54, 1055

Ecuador, 7

Ederle, Gertrude, 1146

Edgeworth, Maria, 418

Edison, Thomas, 842

Education, 154–61, 238; post-1776, 304; post–1790, 415, 427, 497–504, 508; post-1827, 497–504; post-1865, 739, 795; post–1920, 1137–38, 1139; post-1940, 1115, 1120, 1150, 1151, 1203; post-1953, 1219, 1223; post–1960, 1223, 1239. *See also* Colleges; Schools

Education Act (1965), 1223

Edwards, Jonathan, 183–84, 544–45, 1035

Edwards, Justin, 544

Eggleston, Edward, 817

Egypt, 1172, 1228, 1254

Ehrlichman, John, 1263, 1265

Eight box law, 811

Eight-hour day, 784, 928, 1022
Eisenhower, Gen. Dwight D., 1175;
    Pres., 1054, 1117–18, 1121, 1193,
    1205, 1206, 1207–8, 1209, 1211–
    12, 1213, 1215, 1218, 1221
Elections, congressional, 468; (1862),
    717; (1863), 715; (1874), 802; (1934),
    1087; (1938), 1100; (1946), 1105,
    1113; (1974), 1265
Elections, local, 333
Elections, presidential, (1796), 356;
    (1800), 360–62; (1824), 471–73;
    (1828), 467–68, 473–75; (1832), 468,
    479; (1836), 489; (1840), 558–59, 561;
    (1844), 559, 602–604; (1848), 490–91,
    615; (1856), 626–27; (1860), 637–40,
    653; (1864), 718–19, 726; (1868), 791,
    801; (1872), 801; (1876), 801, 808–9,
    871; (1880), 801, 811–12, 870–71;
    (1884), 871; (1888), 871; (1892), 852–
    53, 870, 881; (1896), 869, 881–90,
    988; (1900), 968; (1904), 971; (1908),
    971; (1912), 939, 944–46, 966, 971;
    (1918), 1040; (1920), 1057; (1924),
    1067; (1928), 1067, 1071; (1932),
    1077–78, 1187; (1936), 1089–90;
    (1940), 1100–1; (1944), 1104; (1952),
    1117–18, 1193, 1214; (1956), 1214;
    (1960), 1216, 1246; (1964), 1218;
    (1968), 1237–38, 1240–41, 1245, 1246;
    (1972), 1250; (1976), 1269
Electoral college, 473, 475, 809
Electoral process, 910
Electric industry, 834, 1083–84
Electricity, 1066, 1127
Electronic surveillance, 1260
Eliot, T. S., 1034, 1143
Elizabeth I, of England, 20, 26
Ellsberg, Daniel, 1260
Emancipation, 705–6, 712
Emancipation Proclamation, 709, 716–
    17
Embargoes, 381–82, 392, 1167, 1171
Emergency Fleet Corporation, 1022
Emergency Relief Administration
    (FERA), 1082
Emerson, Joseph, 404
Emerson, Ralph Waldo, 516, 519–22,
    561, 616, 647, 815, 828
Emery, Sarah, 878
Emigrant Aid Society, 628
Emigrants, 17, 25–26
Encomienda, 18
Encyclopaedia Americana, 772
Endowment for International Peace,
    1004

Energy crisis, 1258–59
Enforcement Acts, 803
England. See Great Britain
English literature, 264–68
Enlightenment, the, 219–21
Entertainment industry, 1146. See also
    Movie industry; Radio industry;
    Television
Episcopalians, 512. See also Church of
    England
Era of Good Feelings, 387, 466
Ericsson, John, 693
Erie Canal, 435, 450–52
Erie Railroad, 783
Ervin, Sam, 1263
Escobedo decision, 1225
Esopus (N. Y.), 65
Espionage, 1120
Espionage Act (1917), 1026
Essex County (Mass.), 295
Estimate of the Manners and Prin-
    ciples of the Times, An, 222
Estonia, 1168
Ethiopia, 1165
Ethnic problems, 1088
Europe, post-1760, 240; post-1778,
    295; post-1820, 431–36, 459, 522–23,
    611–12, 613; post-1860, 671–74, 712–
    13; post-1870, 850, 980–81; post-
    1914, 1008; post-1919, 1043, 1160–
    61; post-1932, 1076; post-1940, 1101;
    post-1945, 1182–84; post-1947, 1120,
    1195
European Defense Community (EDC),
    1227
European theater, 1172–75, 1176, 1177.
    See also World War II
Evangelism, 407–8, 542, 547
Evans, George Henry, 461
Evans, Oliver, 415
Evarts, Jeremiah, 544
Everest, Wesley, 1046
Evolution, theory of, 1133, 1139
Ex parte Milligan, 755
Excess profits tax, 698, 1023
Exchange rates, 240
Excise tax, 346, 698
Exclusion Crisis, 79
Executive branch of government,
    1044, 1064–65, 1077, 1206
Executive office, 333, 335, 344, 353,
    385, 730, 929–30, 933–34, 1213–18
Expansionism, 235–36, 426, 593–604,
    775–77, 981–86
Expansionists, 611, 614, 615
Experimental communities, 531–32

Experiments and Observations on
    Electricity, 219
Experts, and public confidence, 1203–
    4
Exposition, 588
Extralegalism, 1024–26

Factories, 660, 666, 667, 696
Fagan, Mark, 893
Fair Deal, 1115
Fair Employment Practices Commit-
    tee (FEPC), 1111, 1112
Fair Oaks, Battle of, 681
Fair Labor Standards Act (1938),
    1098–99
Fair trade agreements, 1099. See also
    Commerce; Trade
Fair trade law (1937), 1206
Fairfax, Lord, 171
Fall, Albert, 1058
Fallen Timbers, Battle of, 349
Family, role of, post-1600, 104–5,
    107; post-1805, 399; post-1920, 1069,
    1133–38
Far East, 995, 997, 1002, 1159–60,
    1163. See also China; Japan; Open
    Door; Philippines
Farewell to Arms, A, 1145
Farley, James, 1089, 1107
Farm lobby, 1068. See also Agriculture
Farm Security Administration (FSA),
    1097, 1103–4, 1108
Farmers. See Agriculture
Farmers' Mutual Benefit Association,
    855
Farragut, David Glasgow, 680, 692–93,
    723
Faubus, Gov. Orval, 1220, 1221
Faulkner, William, 747, 1153–54
Federal Bureau of Investigation (FBI),
    1260
Federal Communications Commission,
    1206
Federal Deposit Insurance Corpora-
    tion, 1082
Federal Fair Trade Act (1952), 1206
Federal Farm Board, 1068, 1076
Federal Highway Act (1956), 1202
Federal Power Commission, 1065,
    1206
Federal Republic of Germany, 1189.
    See also Germany
Federal Reserve Act, 974–75
Federal Reserve Board, 1023, 1065,
    1116, 1119

Federal Reserve System, 974–75, 1064, 1082

Federal Steel Company, 840

Federal Trade Commission, 848, 975, 976, 1023, 1065, 1076, 1206

Federalist, The, 337–38, 348, 353, 363, 375

Federalists, 330–50, 352–60; post–1800, 360–77; post–1812, 377–87, 417, 594

Feminist movement, 557–58, 874–75, 878, 959–67. *See also* Women's rights movement

Fessenden, William Pitt, 699, 750

Fillmore, Pres. Millard, 483, 621

Filmer, Robert, 105

Findley, William, 316

Finland, 1168, 1178

Finley, Rev. Robert, 545

Finney, Charles Grandison, 509–10, 511, 545

Fireside chats, 1078

First National Bank of New York, 841–42

Fish, Hamilton, 773–74, 775, 776

Fisher, Samuel, 512

Fishing, 19, 49, 93

Fiske, John, 925, 985

Fitch, John, 415

Fitzgerald, F. Scott, 1015, 1144, 1148

Fitzhugh, George, 581

Fitzhugh, William, 136

Five-Power Treaty, 1159–60

Flagler, Harry, 783

Fletcher, Benjamin, 140–41

Fletcher v. *Peck*, 374

Florida, 5, 201, 208, 235, 246, 349, 438, 567, 594, 762

Florida, C. S. S., 712

Flour, 457

Flower children, 1235

Flynn, Elizabeth Gurley, 1032, 1033

Food, 453, 695, 849, 1021, 1094

Food Administration, 1021

Food shortages, 1084

For Whom the Bell Tolls, 1149

Foraker Act, 993

Forbes, Charles, 1058

Force Bill, 812

Ford, Henry, 1066, 1142, 1143

Ford, Pres. Gerald, 1253, 1255, 1256, 1257, 1265, 1269

Ford Motor Company, 1061, 1064, 1104

Fordney-McCumber Tariff, 1163

Foreign Bible Society, 542

Foreign affairs. *See* Foreign policy

Foreign policy, 377–87, 426; post–1844, 592–604; post–1860, 671–75; post–1865, 773–77; post–1890, 979–1111; post–1919, 1159–63; post–1933, 1166–67, 1169–82; post–1945, 1182–91; post–1950, 1191–96, 1206–7, 1209–13, 1227–28; post-1960, 1216, 1228–32; post–1969, 1250–55

Foreign trade, 478, 981, 995, 1161–62. *See also* Commerce; Tariffs

Formosa (Taiwan), 1189, 1209, 1212

Formosa Resolution (1955), 1209

Forrest, Gen. Nathan Bedford, 731

Fort Donelson, 678

Fort Duquesne, 204, 205, 207

Fort Fisher, 693

Fort Frontenac, 206

Fort Henry, 678

Fort Herkimer, 206

Fort Laramie, 442

Fort Monroe, 680

Fort Niagara, 206

Fort Orange, 65

Fort Oswego, 206

Fort Pickens, 655

Fort San Carlos, 999

Fort Sheridan (Ill), 1249

Fort Sumter, 655–56

Fort Ticonderoga, 206–7, 278, 283, 285

Fort William Henry, 206

Fortas, Abe, 1262

Fortress America, 1163

Fortress Monroe, 720

Foster, John, 146–47

Four-Power Treaty, 1159

Fourteen Points, 1016–17, 1038–39, 1041

Fowler, Lorenzo, 518

Fowler, Orson, 518

Fox Indians, 439

Frame of Government, 80

France, 202; post–1776, 280, 285; post–1861, 672, 674, 712; post–1905, 1002; post–1914, 1010, 1014, 1017; post–1918, 1014, 1159, 1161; post–1930, 1165; post–1939, 1168, 1169; post–1943, 1175; post–1950, 1207, 1211; post–1954, 1227, 1228; post–1974, 1254

Franco, Gen. Francisco, 1165

Frankfurter, Felix, 1022

Franklin, Benjamin, 82, 205, 218–21, 237, 285, 289, 1035

Franklin (Mass.), 392–93

Franklin (Tenn.), Battle of, 723

Fredericksburg, Battle of, 687

Free silver, 869, 881, 884, 988. *See also* Silver

Free Soil Party, 490, 559, 561, 618, 626, 876. *See also* Abolitionists

Free Speech Movement, 1235

Free World, 1193–95, 1233

Freedmen, 737–41, 742–45, 749, 751, 753, 762

Freedmen's Bureau, 738–41, 743, 752

Freedom fighter, 993

Freedom Riders, 1221

Freehold tenure, 170–71

Freeport Doctrine, 636

Frelinghuysen, Theodore, 545

Fremont, Capt. John C., 609, 613, 626–27, 659, 664, 705, 720

French and Indian War, 204–9, 245, 247

French Indochina, 1169

French Morocco, 1175

French Revolution, 355

French West Indies, 380. *See also* West Indies

Freud, Sigmund, 1132

Frick, Henry Clay, 881–82, 1045

Friedan, Betty, 1236

Fries, John, 259

Frontier towns, 785

Frost, Robert, 427, 1034

Fuel Administration, 1022

Fugitive slave laws, 561, 620, 621–22, 624, 635. *See also* Slavery

Full Employment Act (1946), 1107

Fullbright, J. William, 1231

Fulton, Robert, 416

Fur trade, 49, 66, 67, 76, 92–93, 127, 140, 246, 443. *See also* West

Furley, Benjamin, 217

Furman v. *Georgia*, 1247

Gag rule, 590–91

Gage, Thomas, 259, 280

Gale, Zona, 971

Gall, Franz Joseph, 518

Gallatin, Albert, 364, 393

Galloway, Joseph, 259–60

Gambling, 1070

G.A.R. (Grand Army of the Republic), 871

Gardoqui, Diego de, 327

Garfield, Harry A., 1022

Garfield, James A., 805, 810; Pres., 801, 806–807

Garland, Hamlin, 855–56, 879

Garner, John Nance, 1078, 1101

Garnet, Henry Highland, 559–60

Garrison, William Lloyd, 541, 550, 551–53, 555, 559, 560–61, 737, 875
Garvey, Marcus, 1110
Gary, Judge Elbert, 840
Gasoline engine, 1066
Gaspee, 258
Gates, Gen. Horatio, 285, 286–87
Gates, John W., 840
Gemini program, 1204
General Electric, 830, 1208
General Federation of Women's Clubs, 961
General Motors, 848, 1061, 1096, 1208
General Order No. 100, 772
Genet, Citizen, 355
George, Henry, 795, 842, 852, 877, 921
George, Lloyd, 1041, 1042
George III, 200, 208, 216, 245, 278, 279
Georgia, 182, 202, 323, 438–39, 492, 575, 762, 763
Gerard, Stephen, 391
Germain, Lord George, 283
German Democratic Republic, 1189. *See also* Germany
German immigrants, 491
Germans, 1060
Germantown (Pa.), 81
Germany, 165, 167–68, 434; post–1890, 986, 997, 999; post–1914, 1008, 1014–16, 1041–42, 1043, 1161, 1163–65, 1167–70; post–1941, 1172–73, 1178; post–1945, 1153, 1182, 1188–89; post–1974, 1254. *See also* Berlin; East Germany; Hitler; West Germany
Geronimo, 779
Gerrymandering, 1226
Gettysburg, Battle of, 687, 692
Ghana, 1228
Ghettos, 861, 956, 1238
Giannini, A. P., 1142
GI Bill. *See* Servicemen's Readjustment Act
Gibraltar, 288
Giddings, Franklin, 952–53
Gilbert, Sir Humphrey, 21–23, 27
Gilbert, W. S., 801
Gilded Age, 787, 789, 791–92, 801–7, 836, 867–69, 871–73, 934
Giles, William Brand, 372
Gilman, Charlotte Perkins, 959, 960
Ginger, 76, 127
Gladstone, William, 973
Glass, Carter, 812
Glass-Steagall Act, 1081

Glorious Revolution (1688), 148, 189
Godkin, E. L., 806
Gold, 444, 454, 617–18, 790, 791; post–1893, 850, 884, 887
Goldmark, Josephine, 962
Goldmark, Pauline, 962
Goldwater, Barry, 1218
Goldwyn, Samuel, 1142
Gompers, Samuel, 858–60, 928
Gooch, William, 132
Good Neighbor Policy, 1167
Goodnow, Frank, 895
Goodspeed, 37
Gordon, Sen. John B., 810
Gordon, Thomas, 264, 293
Gorgas, Gen. Josiah, 665–66
Gorman, Arthur P., 873
Gould, Jay, 858
Government, colonial, 26, 41–42, 43; post–1920, 1064–65, 1068; post–1950, 1205. *See also* Articles of Confederation
Governors, 193–96, 254, 258–59, 273–74; post–1776, 299, 322–23; post–1900, 913–16
Graham, Billy, 1224
Grain, 174, 178, 452, 695, 794
Grand Ohio Company, 247
Grange, Red, 1146
Granger laws, 846
Granger movement, 792–94, 842, 851, 853
Grant, Gen. Ulysses S., 678, 680, 689–91, 721–25, 736, 738–39, 756; Pres., 773, 776, 777, 789, 791, 801–3, 805–6, 808
Granville, Earl, 130, 171
Granville District, 130
Grapes of Wrath, The, 1148
Grasse, Admiral de, 288
Great Awakening, 179–87, 406-10
Great Britain, 12–13, 19–31, 89, 105–7, 124–34, 138, 141–42; post–1720, 170, 178, 188–91, 193, 201–9, 211–12, 214, 221–22; post–1760, 244–58, 263–90; post–1780, 310, 327, 349, 355; post–1812, 342, 434, 542–43, 608–9, 615; post–1860, 672–74, 712–13, 773, 775, 981; post–1900, 995–97, 1002; post–1914, 1008, 1014, 1017; post–1919, 1159, 1163; post–1930, 1165, 1168–70; post–1941, 1173, 1175–76, 1182, 1187; post–1950, 1193, 1207, 1211
Great Bull Market, 1073, 1076
Great Depression, 1054, 1073–84, 1085, 1097, 1099, 1101, 1110–11, 1142,

1145, 1161, 1163, 1166. *See also* Depressions
Great Northern Railroad, 833
Great powers, 1182, 1184, 1228
Great Revival, 505
Great Society, 1227
Greece, 1183, 1187, 1228, 1254
Greeks, 862
Greeley, Horace, 461, 489, 801
Green, Duff, 600
Green, William, 1062, 1096
Green Mountain Boys, 237
Greenback Party, 795–96, 842, 877
Greenbacks, 670–71, 699, 702, 792. *See also* Currency
Greene, Nathanael, 287–88
Greenough, Horatio, 523
Greenspring Faction, 140
Grenville, George, 248, 251
Grimke, Angelina, 555–56
Grimke, Sarah, 555–56
Griswold, Roger, 356, 366
Gross National Product (GNP), post–1920, 1065; post–1930, 1107, 1116; post–1950, 1201; post–1969, 1255
Grosvenor, W. M., 799
Guadeloupe, 210
Guam, 993
Guatemala, 6, 1003
Guerrilla warfare, 993, 1229, 1251
Guinea Company, 20
Guiteau, Charles, 807
Gulf of Tonkin Resolution, 1229

Hague, Frank, 1070
Hague Court, 1004
Haines, Charles G., 415
Haiti, 570, 593, 708, 774, 1003, 1005
Hakluyis, Richard, 23
Haldeman, H. R., 1263, 1265
Halfway house, 963
Halleck, Gen. Henry W., 680, 686, 687
Hamilton, Alexander, 325, 338, 340, 342, 363, 375, 378; Treasury Sec'y, 344–50, 353–54, 356; later, 371, 400
Hamilton, Charles, 1238
Hammond, James, 591
Hampton, Gen. Wade, 734, 811
Hancock, John, 255–56
Hancock, Thomas, 233
Hanna, Mark, 886, 893, 921, 999
Harding, Pres. Warren G., 1057–58, 1064–65, 1066, 1159–60
Harlem Renaissance, 1109–10
Harper, Robert Goodloe, 366
Harper, William Rainey, 895

Harpers Ferry, 636, 683
Harper's Monthly Magazine, 818
Harper's Weekly Magazine, 731, 804
Harriman, W. Averell, 1186–87
Harrington, James, 292
Harris, Gov. Isham, 657
Harris, Joel Chandler, 819, 820
Harrison, Jesse Burton, 580
Harrison, Pres. Benjamin, 922
Harrison, William Henry, 390, 436, 483, 489
Hat Act, 212
Hat industry, 392–93
Harte, Bret, 816–17
Hartford, 54
Harvard College, 59–60, 503
Haverhill, 54
Hawaii, 774, 986, 988, 990, 993
Hawkins, John, 21
Hawks, 1251
Hawley-Smoot Tariff, 1163
Hawthorne, Nathaniel, 525, 650–51
Hay, John, 817, 985, 989, 996–97, 1001, 1002
Hay-Herran Treaty of 1903, 999
Hayes, John L., 788, 789
Hayes, Pres. Rutherford B., 758–59, 782, 792, 797, 801, 806, 809, 810, 813
Hayne, Paul Hamilton, 817
Hayne, Robert Y., 589, 591
Haywood, "Big Bill," 969, 970, 1032
Headright system, 41, 62–63, 73, 140, 170
Hearst, William Randolph, 944, 987
Heathcote, Sir Gilbert, 96
Helper, Hinton Rowan, 580–81
Hemans, Felicia, 418
Hemp, 448
Henderson, Leon, 1102
Heller, Joseph, 1234, 1262
Hemingway, Ernest, 1143, 1145, 1149
Hendricks, Sen. Thomas A., 719
Henri, Robert, 1030
Henry VIII, of England, 18, 19, 27
Henry, Patrick, 241, 252, 259, 273, 275–76, 330–31, 333
Henry Street Settlement, 962
Hepburn, Rep. William P., 930
Hepburn Act, 930
Herndon, William H., 718
Hewitt, Abram S., 836, 921
High Noon, 1196
Highways, 1202. *See also* Transportation; Turnpikes
Higginson, Thomas Wentworth, 820
Hill, Benjamin H., 650

Hill, David, 873
Hill, James J., 1062
Hill, Lester, 1116
Hillquit, Morris, 858, 969
Hillsborough, Lord, 257
Hippies, 1235
Hiroshima, 1153, 1154, 1178
Hiss, Alger, 1120, 1246
Hitler, Adolph, post–1930, 1163–64, 1165–66, 1168; post–1941, 1175, 1176
Ho Chi Minh, 1229
Hoar, George F., 992
Hogs, 849
Holding companies, 838, 1081
Holmes, John Haynes, 1159
Holmes, Oliver Wendell, 418
Holmes, Oliver Wendell, Jr., 940–42
Home Owners Loan Corporation, 1082
Home Rule, 808–12
Homestead (Pa.), 881–82
Homestead Act, 639, 697, 778
Honduras, 8, 1003
Hood, John B., 723
Hook, Sidney, 1151
Hooker, "Fighting Joe," 687
Hoover, Herbert, 1021, 1071–72; Commerce Sec'y, 1064, 1162–63; Pres., 1073, 1075–78, 1166
Hoover-Stimson Doctrine, 1166
Hoovervilles, 1077
Hopkins, Harry, 1078, 1082, 1085, 1169, 1185–86
Hopkins, Samuel, 404
Housatonic, 693
House, Colonel, 1038
House of Burgesses, 241, 243–44, 252, 273
House of Commons, 268–69
House of Morgan, 841
House of Representatives, 334, 473, 617, 871, 1120. *See also* Elections, congressional
Housing, 462; post–1900, 861, 1115–16; post–1950, 1202, 1221, 1223
Housing Act (1949), 1115–16
Houston, Gen. Sam, 598, 614
Howard, Oliver O., 738–41
Howard, Sidney, 1136
Howe, Admiral Richard, 282
Howe, Frederick, 892, 900
Howe, Gen. William, 280, 282–84
Howe, Julia Ward, 769
Howe, Samuel Gridley, 531, 737
Howe, Sen. Timothy O., 760
Howells, William Dean, 815–16

Hudson Bay Company, 603
Hudson River Railroad, 783
Huerta, Victoriano, 1006
Hughan, Jessie Wallace, 971
Hughes, Bishop John, 500
Hughes, Charles Evans, 869, 913, 1040, 1095, 1159
Hughes, Langston, 1109
Huguenots, 164
Hukuang Railway, 1002
Hull, Cordell, 1166, 1171, 1181
Hull House, 890, 894, 895, 962
Hull House Maps and Papers, 894
Hume, David, 337
Humphrey, George, 1118
Humphrey, Hubert, 1115, 1240, 1246
Hungary, 1183, 1187, 1212
Hunley, H. L., 693
Hunter, Gen. David, 706
Hunter, Robert M. T., 134, 672
Hurd, J. C., 771
Hutchins, Robert, 1151
Hutchinson, Anne, 56–57, 119
Hutchinson, Gov. Thomas, 195, 252, 258
Huxley, Aldous, 1153
Hydrogen bomb, 1195

Ickes, Harold, 942, 1078, 1079, 1082, 1088, 1111
I'll Take My Stand, 1144
Illinois, 371, 397, 439
Illinois Central Railroad, 445
Illiteracy, 1225
Immigration, 86–89, 164–67, 235, 359, 390; post–1840, 431–36, 455, 490, 533; post–1865, 725, 777–78, 780, 830, 832, 833, 862, 871; post–1890, 912, 948–51, 953, 963; post–1900, 1020, 1031, 1059–60, 1108, 1109. *See also various nationalities by individual listings*
Immigration Act of 1903, 1026
Impeachment, 373, 756–58
Impending Crisis of the South, 580–81
Imperialism, 1163–71
Imports, 138, 238, 429
Impressment, 378–80, 381, 706
Impressment Act (1863), 698
Incan Empire, 6, 16
Income, 448–49, 458, 850, 856–57, 863, 1068, 1069, 1101
Income tax, 698, 940, 943, 974, 1068
Indentured servants, 44, 136, 567–68
Independent Treasury, 481, 483

India, 29, 205, 1172, 1228
Indian Appropriations Act, 442
Indian Reorganization Act (1934), 1108
Indiana, 371, 397
Indians, 16, 34–36, 42, 69, 216–17; post–1680, 76, 148–49; post–1775, 206, 236, 246; post–1780, 307, 348–49, 368, 390, 411; post–1812, 436–42, 458, 477, 532, 621, 624, 627, 629; post–1861, 657, 779, 820; post–1934, 1108; post–1970, 1248–49
Indigo, 76, 127, 136
Indochina, 1055, 1171
Indochinese War, 1251. See also Viet Nam War
Indonesia, 1172, 1228, 1229
Industrial accident compensation, 795
Industrial codes, 1081
Industrial Commission, 860, 861
Industrial Revolution, 830–36. See also Manufacturing; Textiles
Industrial Workers of the World (IWW), 858, 969–70, 1025, 1032, 1033, 1058
Industrialization, 347, 430, 443
Industry, 392–93, 457, 695–96, 830, 1128. See also Agriculture; Depressions; Industrial Revolution; Manufacturing
Inflation, 311, 325; post–1860, 695, 696, 698–702; post–1913, 1023, 1085; post–1940, 1101–3, 1105, 1116; post–1960, 1255; post–1970, 1255, 1256, 1259
Ingersoll, Charles Jared, 496
Inland Waterways Commission, 933
Institutional liberty, 722–73, 777, 799
Insull, Samuel, 1127, 1142
Insurance programs, industrial, 920
Intercollegiate Socialist Society (ISS), 971
Interest groups, 1253
Internal Revenue Service, 1260
Internal Security Act (1950), 1120
International Exhibition of Modern Painting. See Armory Show
International monetary exchange, 1254
International Monetary Fund, 1181
International Silver Company, 842
Interest rates, 1255
Interstate commerce, regulation of, 846, 930–31, 1065, 1094, 1115, 1206
Interstate Commerce Act (1887), 846

Interstate Commerce Commission, 930–31, 1065, 1115, 1206
Investment capital, 833–34
Investment houses, 835
Investment, foreign, 1209
Involuntary servitude, 729
Iowa, 441
Iran, 1184, 1186, 1207
Ireland, 27–29, 266
Irish immigration, 434, 462, 491, 594, 715
Iron, 42, 91–92, 448, 660, 675, 696, 706. See also Steel industry
Iron Act, 212
Iron Curtain, 1184, 1187. See also Russia
Ironclads, 693–95
Iroquois Confederacy, 36, 203
Israel, 1211, 1253, 1254, 1258
Italian immigration, 862
Italy, post–1918, 1041–42, 1160, 1165; post–1940, 1168, 1175, 1184
Iwo Jima, 1176

Jackson, Andrew, 383, 385; Pres., 368, 439, 441, 471–84, 550, 590, 591, 598. See also Democratic Party
Jackson, Gen. T. J. ("Stonewall"), 681, 687
Jackson (Miss.), 689
Jacobi, Mary Putnam, 965
Jacobites, 164
Jamaica, 588
James I, 29
James II, 124, 128–30, 148
James, Henry, 815
James, William, 972, 992–93, 1034
Jamestown (Va.), 7, 29, 37–38, 39–40, 149
Japan, 994, 995, 997; post–1919, 1159, 1162, 1163, 1165; post–1929, 1163, 1166, 1167, 1169, 1171; post–1941, 1172, 1176, 1178, 1184; post–1950, 1194, 1227–28; post–1974, 1254
Japanese Americans, 1108–1109
Japanese fifth column, 1108
Japanese immigrants, 1060
Jarratt, Rev. Devereux, 185, 232
Java Sea, 1172
Jaworski, Leon, 1263
Jay, John, 289, 327, 332, 338, 349, 355, 366
Jay Cooke and Company, 795, 835
Jefferson, Thomas, 266, 267, 271, 273, 277, 278, 288, 295, 298–99, 317–18; post–1780, 323, 326, 329, 330, 345,

354, 356, 359–60, 411; Pres., 230, 360–68, 370, 375, 382, 593–94; post–1819, 393, 396, 437, 471, 583, 596. See also Jeffersonian Republicans
Jeffersonian Republicans, 357, 360–68, 465. See also Democratic Republican Party; Jefferson, Thomas; Republican Party
Jehovah's Witnesses, 1224
Jenkins, Capt. Robert, 201
Jenner, Sen. William, 1122
Jerseys (East and West), 70, 77–79, 130
Jews, 114, 434, 462, 862, 949, 1059, 1153, 1167
Jim Crow, 1219–20, 1221
Jingo, 985, 988–89, 993
Johnson, Albert Sidney, 536
Johnson, Andrew, 505, 720; Pres., 730, 736, 741, 748, 752–54, 756–58, 760, 761, 773–74, 777, 806
Johnson, Gen. Hugh S., 1080
Johnson, Pres. Lyndon B., 1218, 1223–24, 1227, 1228–31, 1238, 1251, 1260
Johnson, Patience, 744
Johnson, Reverdy, 775
Johnson, Sen. Hiram, 869, 1026
Johnson, Tom, 893
Johnson Debt Default Act (1934), 1167
Johnston, Gen. Albert Sidney, 678
Johnston, Gen. Joseph E., 677–78, 680, 689, 691, 709, 715, 723
Joint-stock companies, 30–31, 38–39
Jomini, Baron Henry, 676–77, 678, 686, 687, 721
Jones, "Golden Rule," 893
Jones, J. B., 701
Jones, James, 1153
Jones, Robert Edmond, 1032
Joseph, Chief, 779
Juarez, Benito, 775
Judiciary Act (1801), 373
Judicial review, 371–77
Judson, Adoniram, 544
Jungle, The, 929
Julian, Rep. George W., 760
Justice Department, 1120, 1262

Kafka, Franz, 1153
Kaiser Industries, 1106
Kaiser Wilhelm II. See Wilhelm II
Kandinsky, Vasili, 1029
Kansas, 462, 626–31, 636, 878
Kansas-Nebraska Act, 491, 625–26, 627, 631, 633, 634

Kansas Pacific Railroad, 785
Kant, Immanuel, 519–20
Kaufman, Irving, 1191
Kean, Robert, 714
Kearney, Dennis, 758
Kearny, Stephen W., 613
Keaton, Buster, 1145
Kefauver, Estes, 1118
Kelley, Edward, 1089
Kelley, Florence, 962
Kelley, Oliver Hudson, 792
Kellogg, Frank B., 1161
Kellogg, William, 641
Kellogg-Briand Peace Pact. *See* Paris Peace Pact (1928)
Kendall, Amos, 478, 555
Kennan, George, 1186, 1190
Kennedy, John F., 1207; Pres., 1204, 1208–12, 1214–18, 1221, 1223, 1228
Kennedy, Robert, 1238, 1240, 1249, 1260
Kennedy family, 1217
Kenner, Duncan F., 713
Kent, James, 408, 514
Kent, William, 920
Kent State University, 1239
Kentucky, 236, 307, 359, 390, 577, 655, 659, 660–61
Kerner, Otto, 1262
Key, David M., 811
Khrushchev, Nikita, 1203, 1210–11, 1213
Kiefft, Willem, 68–70
King, Martin Luther, Jr., 1220–21, 1224, 1225, 1238, 1260
King, Rufus, 366, 587
King George's War, 204–206
King Philip's War, 142
King William's War, 142
Kingsley House, 962
King's Mountain (S. C.), 287
Kirby-Smith, Edmund, 691, 723
Kissinger, Henry, 1207, 1252, 1253
Kitchen Cabinet, 477, 478
Kitchen debate, 1203
Knight, E. C., case, 847, 927
Knights of the Golden Circle, 715
Knights of Labor, 785, 853, 857–58
Knowles, Commodore, 203–4
Know-Nothing Party, 465, 483, 491–94. *See also* American Party
Knox, Henry, 346, 348
Knox, Philander, 1002
Knox, William, 271
Koestler, Arthur, 1153
Konoye, Fuminaro, 1171

Korea, 997. *See also* Korean War
Korean War, 1116, 1120, 1191–93, 1195
Korematsu v. *U.S.*, 1108
Ku Klux Klan, 765–66, 803, 1060–61, 1070, 1221
Kwantung Army, 1163

Labor, 44, 107, 136, 177, 212; post–1819, 393, 433, 455, 462, 499, 700–701, 706; post–1865, 784–85, 795–98, 833, 862, 916–19; post–1900, 862, 907, 959–60, 962, 965, 976, 1022; post–1920, 1058, 1062, 1076, 1139, 1143; post–1935, 1089, 1095–97, 1099, 1105; post–1950, 1205. *See also* Unions, labor
Labor-management relations, 1094
Labor Policy Board, 1081
Labor unions. *See* Unions, labor
Labrador, 18
Local politics, post–1920, 1054, 1068–70, 1109; post–1934, 1085, 1088; post–1936, 1107–13
Lafayette, Marquis de, 288
LaFollette, Robert, 848, 869, 913, 915–16, 931, 933, 944, 1066–67
LaFollette, Suzanne, 1143
Lake Champlain, 203, 385
Lake Erie, 384
Lake Ontario, 384
Lamar, L. Q. C., 810
Land banks, 213–15
Land grants, 135, 140–41, 247, 741
Land ownership, 134, 170–71
Land policy, 304, 368, 426, 437, 441
Land, public, 429, 443, 445–46, 481
Land speculation, 175, 238, 246, 346, 445–46
Land warrants, 170
Land, western, 303–5, 432, 444, 777–79
Landlordism, 171–72
Landon, Alfred, 1089
Landrum-Griffin Act (1959), 1205
Lane, Ralph, 27
Lane Theological Seminary, 553
Lanier, Sidney, 817
Laos, 1250
Larkin, Thomas, 609, 613
Latin America, 5, 7, 18, 310; post–1890, 994, 1002; post–1902, 998–1001, 1002, 1005; post–1919, 1162; post–1936, 1167–68, 1169; post–1960, 1228; post–1974, 1255. *See also* Central America; *and names of individually listed countries*
Latvia, 1168

Laurens, Henry, 257
Law, 211, 513–18, 828
Lawes Divine, Morall and Martiall, 40
Lawes and Libertyes, The, 56
Lawrence, Abbott, 491, 518
Lawrence (Kan.), 628
Lawyers, 1064
League of Armed Neutrality, 285
League of Nations, 1040–43, 1044–45, 1159, 1161, 1164–66, 1169
Learned and scientific societies, 411, 412, 414
Lease, Mary E., 878
Lebanon, 1211
Lecompton constitution, 630–31, 634
Lecky, W. E. H., 165
Lectures on the Millennium, 404
Lee, Arthur, 325
Lee, Gen. Robert E., 681–83, 686, 687, 691, 692, 711, 721, 725, 734, 736
Lee, Richard Henry, 259, 273, 297, 300, 325, 330, 335
Legislative reference bureau, 916
Legislatures, state, 299–300, 315, 322
Leisler, Jacob, 150–52
Leisler's Rebellion, 148, 150–52
Lemke, William, 1089
Lend-lease, 1173
Lend-Lease Act (1941), 1170
Leningrad, 1173
Letcher, Gov. John, 657
Letters from a Farmer in Pennsylvania, 254–55, 270
Levant Company, 21
Lever Act, 1021
Lewelling, Gov. Lorenzo D., 879
Lewis, George C., 674
Lewis, John L., 1080, 1095, 1099, 1101, 1170
Lewis, Meriwether, 369–70
Lewis, Sinclair, 1133, 1134
Lexington, Battle of, 277
Leyte Gulf, Battle of, 1176
Liberal Republican Party, 777
Liberator, The, 551, 737
Liberia, 544, 549
Liberty, civil. *See* Civil liberties; Civil Rights Act; Civil rights movement
Liberty Party, 490, 558–59, 561, 626
Lieber, Francis, 771–73, 777, 799
Lillie, Samuel, 145, 147
Lincoln, Abraham, 632–36, 639; Pres., 537, 611, 619, 652, 653–58, 661, 664, 666, 671–72, 680, 685, 687–91, 698, 705–706, 708, 712–13, 715–21, 723, 725, 729, 731, 738, 755, 758, 770, 783

Lincoln, Gen. Benjamin, 286
Lincoln-Douglas debates, 635
Lima, 6
Lindbergh, Charles, 1146, 1170, 1205
Lippincott's Magazine, 817–18
Lippmann, Walter, 971, 1032, 1034, 1036–38, 1043, 1151, 1189
Literacy Bill (1913), 953
Literacy tests, 812, 953, 1057
Literary Digest, 1089
Literary and Philosophical Society, 414
Literature, post–1791, 417–18; post–1819, 523–25; post–1850, 519–22; post–1865, 813–20; post–1920, 1133, 1136, 1143–45, 1148–49; post–1945, 1150–56; post–1950, 1233–34; post–1963, 1236, 1238; post–1969, 1262
Lithuania, 1168
Little, Frank, 1025
Little Big Horn, Battle of, 779
Little Rock, 1220, 1221, 1226
Little Steel, 1097, 1104
Litton Industries, 1106
Livestock, 174
Livingston, Robert, 140–41, 370
Livingston, William, 322
Livingston Manor, 140
Lloyd, Henry Demarest, 846
Lochner case, 941–42
Locke, John, 73, 219
Lodge, Sen. Henry Cabot, 812, 985, 988, 993, 1044–45
Log Cabin, The, 489
London Economic Conference (1933), 1166, 1169
London Naval Conference (1930), 1165
Long, Huey, 1084–85, 1086, 1088, 1089, 1090
Longfellow, Henry Wadsworth, 418, 523, 1035
Longshoremen, 1106. *See also* Labor; Unions
Longstreet, Gen. James A., 692, 763
Lopez, Narciso, 615
Lords of Trade, 124
Los Alamos (N. M.), 1178
Lost Generation, 1143
Loudon, Lord, 206
Louis XVI, of France, 285
Louis, Joe, 1146–47
Louisbourg, 204–5, 206
Louisiana, 371, 447, 448, 458, 567, 569–70, 575, 746, 762, 764–65
Louisiana Territory, 369–70
Louisville, 1248

L'Ouverture, Toussaint, 570
Lovejoy, Elijah P., 555
Lowell, Amy, 1034
Lowell, James Russell, 418, 523, 613, 815, 1035
Lowell, Josephine Shaw, 962
Lowell (Mass.), 455
Loyal Publication Society, 772
Loyalists, 308–9, 314
Luce, Cong. Clare Booth, 1181
Luce, Henry, 1185
Lumbering, 443, 448, 457, 932, 933. *See also* Timber products
Lundy, Benjamin, 598
Lusitania, 1009
Lutherans, 114, 1139
Lyceums, 516–17, 519–20
Lynch, Col. Charles, 314
Lynd, Helen, 1132
Lynd, Robert, 1132
Lyon, Matthew, 356–57, 359
Lyon, Nathaniel, 658

MacArthur, Gen. Douglas, 1176, 1180, 1193, 1194
Macdonough, Capt. Thomas, 385
Mackintosh, Sir James, 543
Maclay, Sen. William, 348
Macon, Nathaniel, 384
Macon's Bill No. 2, 382
Madero, Francisco, 1006
Madison, James, 273; post–1780, 316–17, 323–24, 325, 329, 331, 334–35, 337–38; post–1788, 342, 353, 359–60, 375; Pres., 382; post–1827, 596
Magazines, 905–907
Magruder, Gen. John B., 680
Mahan, Capt. Alfred Thayer, 983–85
Mahan, Dennis Hart, 676
Mail delivery, 364, 545, 555
Mailer, Norman, 1153
Maine, 54, 170, 235, 585–86
Maine, 988, 991
Malcolm X, 1238
Male, sex role, 524–25
Malenkov, Georgi, 1213
Mallory, Stephen R., 692, 693
Mallory decision, 1225
Man Nobody Knows, The, 1132
Manchu dynasty, 995
Manchukuo, 1163
Manchuria, 997, 1002, 1163, 1166, 1167, 1189, 1192
Manhattan Island, 65
Manifest Destiny, 611, 613, 774, 979, 985

Manila, Battle of, 989
Mann, Horace, 392, 501–502, 518
Manufacturing, 213–14; post–1808, 392–93; post–1820, 430, 455–57; post–1920, 1064, 1065, 1066. *See also* Industrial Revolution
Mao Tse-tung, 1189
Maple Flooring Manufacturers' Association case, 1065
Marbury v. *Madison*, 373–74, 375
Marcy, William L., 470
Marine insurance, 178
Marion, Francis, 287
Markham, Edwin, 907
Marshall, Gen. George C., 1182, 1187, 1189
Marshall, John, 372–75, 396, 439
Marshall, Thomas, 579–80
Marshall, Thurgood, 1120
Marshall Plan, 1187, 1189
Martial law, 803
Martin, Thomas, 873
Martinique, 210
Marx, Karl, 461, 1148
Maryland, 60–64, 129, 130, 140; post–1700, 152, 170–71, 182–83, 274; post–1800, 446, 577, 655, 657–58, 660
Mason, George, 331
Mason, James M., 674, 713
Mass communication, 554, 1127, 1128, 1139, 1155. *See also* Communication; Newspapers
Mass media, 1145–46
Massachusetts, 129, 213, 255–57, 309, 322–23, 329, 487, 491
Massachusetts Bay Colony, 50, 53–56, 90, 101–4
Massachusetts Bay Company, 52–53
Massachusetts General Court, 54–56, 156–158, 202, 271
Masters, Edgar Lee, 1034
Mather, Cotton, 157
Matisse, Henri, 1029
Matsu, 1209
Mauldin, Bill, 1149
Maurer, James Hudson, 969
Maximilian, Archduke, 775
Mayflower, 47
Mayflower Compact, 50
Mayhew, Jonathan, 200, 242–43
Mayors, reform, 892–93
Maysville Road Bill, 476
McCarthy, Eugene, 1237, 1240, 1250
McCarthy, Joseph, 1121–23, 1193, 1215, 1248
McCarthyism, 1121–23

McClellan, Gen. George B., 678, 680–83, 686, 687, 718, 726
McClernand, John A., 689
McClure, S. S., 905
McClure's, 906
McCormick, Cyrus Hall, 452, 695, 786, 797
McCullers, Carson, 1154
McCulloch, Hugh, 790, 791
McCulloch v. *Maryland,* 374, 479
McDowell, Gen. Irwin, 677
McGovern, George, 1250, 1262
McGuffey's readers, 502
McKay, Claude, 1109
McKay, Donald, 454
McKay, Gordon, 696
McKinley, Pres. William, 829, 847, 869, 887, 921, 987, 993
McLean, John, 631, 632
McManes, Maines, 874
McMillan, James, 873
McNary-Haugen Bill, 1068
Meade, George Gordon, 687, 721
Meat Packing Act, 929
Meat packing industry, 834, 838, 929–30
Mechanicsville, Battle of, 681
Medicare, 1223
Meiklejohn, Alexander, 971
Mellon, Andrew, 1045, 1068
Melting Pot, The, 952
Melville, Herman, 477, 525, 641–42, 813, 815
Memorial Day Massacre, 1097
Memminger, Christopher G., 668, 670, 700
Memphis, 753
Mencken, Henry L., 1133, 1138
Mercantilism, 126–28
Mercenaries, German, 281
Merchants, 177–79, 309, 430
Mercury program, 1204
Merger movement, 830, 834–35, 837–39, 848, 927
Merriam, Charles, 895
Merriam, Robert, 900
Merrimac. See Virginia
Mesmerists, 518
Mestizos, 18
Methodists, 180, 185, 241, 407, 506, 508, 512, 1139
Metro-Goldwyn-Mayer, 1129
Mexican Americans, 1225, 1249
Mexican War, 558, 608–16, 980
Mexico, 5, 597–99, 609–11, 613–14, 773–75, 1005–8

Mexico City, 613
Michigan, 439
Middle Atlantic states, 477–78
Middle-class home, 427
Midway Islands, 775, 1176
Midwest, 817, 913. *See also* West
Middle East, 1162, 1184, 1207, 1211, 1254. *See also* Israel
Migration, 235–38, 307, 390–91, 426, 462
Milbourne, Jacob, 150–51
Military-industrial complex, 1208
Military law, 772
Military preparedness, 1195, 1207–8
Military Reconstruction Act, 754, 756, 761–62, 765
Military service, universal, 1020
Militia, 349, 384, 797
Mill, John Stuart, 712, 947
Mill Springs, Battle of, 678
Millennialism, 404, 419
Miller, Arthur, 1150–51, 1155–56
Miller, Joaquim, 817
Miller-Tydings Act of 1937, 1099
Millerites, 538
Milligan, Lambdin P., 755
Milliken v. *Bradley,* 1247–48
Mills, Samuel, 544, 545
Milton, John, 292
Minerals, 444
Mining, 443, 448, 1094
Minorities, 648, 1248. *See also* Asiatics; Blacks; Indians; Jews; Mexican Americans
Minuit, Peter, 65
Miranda decision, 1225
Miss Ravenel's Conversion from Secession to Loyalty, 813–15
Missile gap, 1228
Missionaries, 528, 529, 530, 533, 980
Missionary diplomacy, 1003–5
Mississippi, 5, 235, 390, 399, 437–38, 446, 458, 567, 575, 763
Mississippi River, 342, 349, 370, 446, 810–11
Missouri, 391, 441, 470, 577, 586, 654–55, 658, 660
Missouri Compromise, 582–87, 619, 623, 624, 625, 626, 629
Mitchell, Atty. Gen. John, 928, 1248, 1263, 1265
Mitchell, Wesley C., 1020
Mobile (Ala.), 693
Mobilization program, 1017, 1020–23, 1101–2
Moby Dick, 641–42

Moderate Republicans, 748–58
Molasses, 127, 210, 254
Molasses Act, 211, 251
Moley, Raymond, 1079, 1084
Molly Maguires, 796–97
Molotov, Vyacheslav, 1185
Money. *See* Currency
Mongolia, 997
Monitor, 693
Monroe, Harriet, 1034
Monroe, James, 356, 367, 381, 385, 437; Pres., 466, 470, 471, 596. *See also* Monroe Doctrine
Monroe Doctrine, 596–97, 604, 608, 774–75, 999
Montcalm, Marquis de, 208
Monterrey, 612
Montesquieu, Baron, 218
Montezuma, 5
Montgomery, Richard, 278
Montgomery (Ala.), 1220
Montgomery convention, 650
Moore, Thomas, 363
Morality, 416. *See also* Sex
Morgan, J. P., 841–42, 848, 859, 884, 927
Morganthau, Henry, 1078
Mormon War, 536–37
Mormons, 529–30, 532–41, 556
Morrill, Justin, 873
Morrill Act (1862), 697
Morrill Tariff, 669
Morris, Gouverneur, 331, 921, 925
Morris, Robert, 311, 323, 325, 346
Morse, Jedediah, 413
Morse, Samuel F. B., 416
Morton, Gov. O. P., 748
Moscow trade exhibit, 1203
Motley, John Lothrop, 654
Mothers, role of, 427. *See also* Women
Mott, Lucretia, 557
Movie industry, 1025, 1127–28, 1129, 1136, 1143, 1145–46, 1152, 1233
Muckrakers, 892, 905–8, 929, 956
Mugwumps, 871
Muir, John, 931, 932
Mulford, Rev. Elisha, 770
Muller v. *Oregon,* 917
Multinational corporations, 1208–9. *See also* Corporations
Mumford, Lewis, 1143
Munford, Robert, 244
Munich Conference (1938), 1165, 1167
Munitions embargo (1935), 1167
Munn v. *Illinois,* 794
Munsey, Frank, 905, 944

Murfree, Mary Noaihes, 819
Murfreesboro, Battle of, 688
Murphy, Edgar Gardner, 953
Muscle Shoals, 1083. *See also* Tennessee Valley Authority
Muscovy Company, 21
Mussolini, Benito, 1165
Muste, A. J., 971
My Day, 1141
Myrdal, Gunnar, 1224

Nader, Ralph, 1260
Nader's Raiders, 1260
Nagasaki, 1153, 1178
Napalm, 1178, 1230
Napoleon Bonaparte, 360, 370, 380, 712
Napoleon III, of France, 774–75
Nashville, Battle of, 723
Nasser, Pres. Gamal, 1211, 1228
Nasson, Samuel, 338
Nast, Thomas, 804
Nathan, Maude, 965
Nation, The, 742, 770, 805
National American Woman Suffrage Association, 965, 966
National Association for the Advancement of Colored People (NAACP), 958, 1088, 1110, 1113, 1119–20, 1219
National Association of Manufacturers (NAM), 859, 1106
National Banking Act of 1864, 780
National Broadcasting Company, 1128
National Child Labor Act, 976
National Child Labor Committee, 962
National Civic Federation, 860, 911
National Conservation Congress, 931
National Consumer's League (NCL), 962
National Country Life Commission, 932–33
National debt, post-1780, 325, 327, 345–46, 353, 355; post-1810, 364–65, 699; post-1868, 791; post-1941, 1103; post-1946, 1116; post-1952, 1119; post-1970, 1255. *See also* Budget
National Defense Education Act (1958), 1203
National Farm Workers Association, 1249
National Farmers Alliance, 851
National Guard, 1239
National Independent Party, 795–96
National Industrial Recovery Act, 1079–81

National Labor Relations Act, 1086–87
National Labor Relations Board (NLRB), 1087, 1097
National Labor Union, 784–85, 857
National Liberation Front (NLF), 1229
National Municipal League, 898, 911
National Organization for Women (NOW), 1237
National Origins Act, 1059–60
National Park Service, 1132
National Recovery Administration (NRA), 1080–81, 1084, 1088, 1094
National Reform Association, 461
National Republican Party, 468, 474, 475, 487. *See also* Whig Party
National security, 1024–25, 1195, 1254–55
National Security Act (1947), 1195
National Security League, 1024–25
National Socialist Party, 1163
National Union Convention, 753
National War Labor Board (WLB), 1022
National Women's Party, 965, 966
National Women's Trade Union League, 965
Nationalism, 769–73, 877, 1163, 1199–1200
Nativism, 492–93, 532, 639
Natural History of Man, 410
Natural resources, 235, 444, 446, 776, 931–32, 1102, 1132. *See also* Conservation
Naturalization laws, 167, 363
Nauvoo (Ill.), 533–34
Navajo Indians, 442
Navigation acts, 127–28, 327
Navigation system, 250
Navy, U. S., 127, 364, 384–85, 675, 1170
Nazi-Soviet pact (1939), 1168, 1178
Nazis, 1163–64, 1166, 1168, 1176. *See also* Germany; Hitler, Adolph
Nebraska, 624, 626, 878
Negroes. *See* Blacks
Nehru, Jawaharlal, 1228
Nelson, Admiral Horatio, 360
Neofederalism, 933–35
Netherland East Indies. *See* Indonesia
Netherlands, the, 1168
Neutrality, 355, 378, 674, 1008, 1009
Neutrality laws, 713, 1167, 1168, 1169
New Amsterdam, 65–66
New Bern (N. C.), 692
New Deal, 1079–90, 1093–1101, 1108,

1111, 1127, 1148. *See also* Roosevelt, Franklin D.
New England, 29, 88–89, 90–95, 100–4, 115–16, 117–120, 134–35, 154–61; post-1700, 170, 180–85, 214, 215, 235, 238, 242, 382; post-1812, 385, 452, 456–57, 491
New England Freedmen's Aid Society, 738
New England Non-Resistance Society, 555
New England Tract Society, 544
New Era, 1066, 1068–70, 1083, 1143
New France, 142, 207. *See also* Canada
New Freedom, 939, 972–76, 1036–37
New Frontier, 1217
New Guinea, 1176
New Hampshire, 54, 129, 164, 170, 235, 273, 315, 322, 324; presidential primary (1968), 1238
New Jersey, 129, 131, 171–72, 183, 283, 567, 846
New London, 54, 138
New Mexico, 442, 609, 613, 617, 623, 625
New Nationalism, 938, 943, 946, 1017, 1020, 1036
New Netherlands, 64–70, 114. *See also* New York; New York City
New Orleans, 208, 370, 385, 447, 448, 680, 753
New Panama Canal Company, 999
New Republic, The, 1037, 1038
New York, 64–70, 124, 129, 132, 140, 150–52, 171–72, 183; post-1732, 183, 300, 322; post-1800, 439, 452, 460, 487, 1071
New York Central Railroad, 783, 833
New York City, 36, 138, 164, 280, 447; post-1860, 435, 704–5, 803–4, 874, 950–51; post-1900, 831, 956; post-1970, 1250
New York Eight, 1028, 1030
New York *Herald*, 637
New York Public School Society, 499
New York Regional Board, 1065
New York Stock Exchange, 839, 882, 1073
New York *Sun*, 804
New York *Times*, 743, 803–4
New York *Tribune*, 461, 632
New Zealand, 1176, 1194, 1207
Newburyport (Mass.), 462, 499
Newcastle, Duke of, 245
Newfoundland, 18, 29, 288
Newport, 36, 138, 158

Newspapers, 358–59, 401, 803–4, 1141, 1248

Nez Percé Indians, 779

Nicaragua, 1003

Nicholson, Francis, 150

Niebuhr, Reinhold, 1143, 1151–52, 1156

Nimitz, Adm. Chester, 1176

Nine-Power Treaty, 1160, 1165, 1166, 1171

Nixon, Richard M., 1190, 1196, 1246; vice-pres., 1203, 1215; Pres., 1241, 1245, 1246–53, 1255, 1256, 1262–65

Nkrumah, Kwame, 1228

NLRB v. *Jones and Laughlin Steel*, 1095

Nobel Prize, 1154, 1224

Nonimportation Act (1806), 381

Nonintercourse Act, 382

Nonintervention, 997

Non-Partisan League, 1058

Normandy, 1175

Norris, Sen. George, 1083, 1143

North, 309, 313, 354, 393–95, 450, 470; post–1834, 486, 490, 528–30, 559–61; post–1850, 616–24, 626, 637–38; post–1860, 695, 701, 704–5, 715–16, 724–25, 760, 813–16; post–1900, 956, 958, 1109–10, 1225, 1239

North, Lord, 249, 258, 276

North Africa, 997, 1172–73, 1175

North American Review, 411, 417–18

North Atlantic Treaty, 1188–89

North Atlantic Treaty Organization (NATO), 1191, 1193, 1207

North Carolina, 73–76, 171, 233–35, 403, 438, 654, 657, 660, 762–63. *See also* Carolinas

North Korea, 1192. *See also* Korea; Korean War

North Viet Nam, 1229–30. *See also* Viet Nam War

Northeast, 434, 448, 453, 492, 499–501, 619. *See also* East

Northern Pacific Railroad, 833, 848

Northern Securities case, 848

Northern Securities Company, 927

Northrup, Solomon, 559

Northwest, 314, 327. *See also* West

Northwest Ordinance, 304–5

Norton, Andrews, 418

Norton, Charles Eliot, 992

Norway, 1168

Notes on Virginia, 295, 413

Nott, Eliphalet, 404

Nova Scotia, 18, 22–23, 29, 141, 206

Noyes, John Humphrey, 532

Nuclear weapons, 1195, 1207, 1253, 1254

Nullification, 588–92

Oates, Joyce Carol, 1262

Oberlin College, 503, 554

Obscenity, 1225

Obsolescence, planned, 1202

O'Connor, Flannery, 1154

O'Connor, John, 704

Office of Defense Transportation, 1101

Office of Economic Opportunity (OEO), 1223, 1239, 1249

Office of Economic Stabilization, 1101

Office of Price Administration (OPA), 1101, 1102, 1103

Office of War Mobilization, 1101

Ohio, 371, 390, 397

Ohio gang, 1058

Ohio Idea, 791

Ohio River, 204, 452

Oil industry, 829, 834, 1081, 1118, 1209, 1259. *See also* Petroleum industry

Oklahoma, 439, 585

Old age pensions. *See* Social Security acts

Old Northwest, 390, 393–95, 397. *See also* Northwest

Oligopolies, 1061, 1065, 1106

Olive Branch Petition, 277–78

Oliver, Andrew, 252

Olney, Richard, 847–48, 985, 986

Oneida community, 532

O'Neill, Eugene, 1034, 1143

Onis, Luis de, 595–96

Open door policy, 996–97, 999, 1002–3, 1160, 1165, 1166, 1171

Open shop, 882, 1104

Operation Rolling Thunder, 1229

Opinion polls, 1214, 1250, 1265

Oppenheim, James, 1037

Oppenheimer, J. Robert, 1178, 1185

Order of American Knights, 715

Order of the Cincinnati, 307

Order of the Heroes, 714

Order of the Star-Spangled Banner, 491

Oregon, 442, 601–3, 608, 612, 618

Oregon Trail, 603

Organic Act (1900), 993

Organization of American States (OAS), 1254

Origin of Species, 759

Orkney, Lord, 131–32

Orlando, Vittorio Emanuel, 1041

Orleans Territory, 391

Orwell, George, 1153

Osborn, Sir Danvers, 132

Ostrogorski, Moisei, 873

Oswald, Lee Harvey, 1218

Otis, James, 270

Ottawa Indians, 236

Ovington, Mary, 958

Pacific theater, 1172, 1176, 1178–79. *See also* World War II

Pacific Ocean, 5

Pacific Railroad Act, 698

Pacifism, 556

Page, Thomas Nelson, 819

Paine, Thomas, 275, 278, 405

Painting, 417. *See also* Art

Pakistan, 1207, 1228

Palerston, Lord, 673–74

Palmer, A. Mitchell, 1058

Palmer, Elihu, 405

Panic, (1819), 471; (1837), 481, 533; (1857), 458; (1873), 795, 835; (1893), 881. *See also* Depressions

Pankhurst, Emmeline, 966

Panama, 5, 994, 999–1001. *See also* Panama Canal

Panama Canal, 773, 1005

Paoli, Pascal, 266

Papacy, the, 15

Paris, 1175

Paris Peace Conference, 1040–43

Paris Peace Pact (1928), 1161

Parity, 1115, 1205

Parker, Theodore, 559

Parliament (British), 127, 252, 258, 266, 270, 298. *See also* Great Britain

Parsons, Theophilus, 514, 515

Parrington, Vernon L., 1035

Paterson, William, 333

Paterson, Pageant, 1031–33

Patronage, political, 139, 152, 193; post–1810, 364–65, 470, 475, 490; post–1862, 718, 720, 810; post–1880, 873, 874, 914; post–1912, 974; post–1936, 1107–8

Patronage system, British, 132, 133, 295

Patrons of Husbandry, 792–93, 846

Patroonship, 67–68

Patterson, John H., 912

Paul, Alice, 965, 966

Pauw, Corneille de, 410

Paxton Boys, 237

Payne-Aldrich Act, 942

Pea Ridge, Battle of, 680
Peace Corps, 1216, 1228
Peace with honor, 1251
Peace movement, 1004–5
Peace of Paris (1763), 249
Peal, Charles Willson, 412, 414
Pearl Harbor, 1108, 1171, 1176
Peek, George, 1081
Peffer, Sen. William A., 879
Peking, 996
Pemberton, John Clifford, 689, 691
Pendergast, Tom, 1070, 1110
Pendleton Act, 807
Peninsula campaign, 680–81, 686
Penn, William, 77, 79–83, 165, 191, 217–18
Pennsylvania, post–1679, 79–83; post–1700, 130, 171, 183, 191, 217–18, 220; post–1750, 213, 229, 235, 237, 241–42, 323; post–1800, 452, 487, 567
Pennsylvania Dutch, 444
Pennsylvania Prison Discipline Society, 549
Pennsylvania Railroad, 783, 833
Pentagon Papers, The, 1260
People of New York v. Ruggles, The, 408
Pepperrell, Col. William, 202–3
Perkins, Frances, 962, 1088
Perkins, George E., 859
Perkins, George W., 944
Perry, Com. Matthew C., 453
Perry Lane & Company, 97
Perryville (Tenn.), Battle of, 682
Pershing, Gen. John J., 1006–7, 1015
Personnel management, 1062, 1138
Peru, 7
Petroleum cartel, 1162
Petroleum industry, 696, 700, 783
Phelan, Sen. James, 703
Philadelphia, 36, 81, 138; post–1700, 164, 176, 178; post–1750, 254, 283–84, 285; post–1800, 459, 509–10
Philadelphia Convention, 330–35
Philadelphia Society of Friends, 738
Philippine Organic Act (1902), 995
Philippines, 205, 990, 993, 994–95; post–1919, 1159, 1167; post–1940, 1172, 1176, 1194, 1207
Phillips, David Graham, 905, 907
Phillips, Wendell, 563
Philosophical Letters, 218
Phrenology, 518–19
Physicians, 781–82
Pickens, Gov. Francis, 656
Pickering, John, 373

Pickering, Timothy, 366
Pierce, Pres. Franklin, 493, 616, 624, 625–26, 630
Pietism, 180, 867, 876–78, 885
Pike, Albert, 657
Pike, Lt. Zebulan, 369
Pilgrims, 45–51, 116
Pinchot, Gifford, 931, 942, 1143
Pinckney, Charles, 583–84
Pinckney, Charles Cotesworth, 366
Pinckney, Thomas, 349
Pinckney, William, 381
Pine tree shilling, 213
Pingree, Hazen, 892–93
Pioneer Stage Line, 546
Pioneers, The, 444
Pitkins, Walter, 1148
Pitt, William, 206–9, 245, 249
Pittsburgh, 393
Pittsburgh Survey, 894
Pizarro, Francisco, 6
Plains of Abraham, 208
Plains Indians, 657
Plantation, 28–29, 36, 172–74, 430, 743–47
Planter, 706, 708
Planter oligarchy, 577–78
Platt, Tom, 873
Platt Amendment, 994
Plumer, William, 366
Plunkitt, George Washington, 872, 874
Pluralism, 939, 952, 971, 976
Plymouth, 29, 48, 49, 89
Poe, Edgar Allan, 525
Poland, 1041, 1164, 1166, 1168, 1176, 1183, 1184
Police, 1225, 1247
Polish immigrants, 862, 1060
Political parties. See names of individually listed parties
Political reformers, 868–69
Political writings, 264–68
Politics, post–1700, 188–198; post–1775, 243–44, 268–76, 315; post–1784, 366, 397–99, 465–66; post–1860, 713–20, 801–7, 828, 869–76; post–1920, 1054, 1068–70, 1109; post–1934, 1085, 1088; post–1936, 1107–13
Politics, machine, 866, 872–74, 891, 900, 1070, 1088–89
Polk, Pres. James K., 477, 483, 490, 493, 603–4, 608–16
Poll tax, 811, 812, 953, 1115
Polygamy, 534, 536, 539, 541
Ponce de León, Juan, 5
Pontiac Indians, 249

Poole, Ernest, 971
Pope, Alexander, 264
Pope, Gen. John, 682, 687
Popish Plot, 79
Popular sovereignty, 622, 624–26, 630, 631–32, 634–38
Population, 17–18; post–1600, 34, 36, 86–89, 91; post–1720, 164–68, 235–38, 306–7, 390–91, 393; post–1820, 431–36, 675, 725, 780; post–1920, 1129. See also Birth control; Birth rate
Populism, 812, 842, 851–53, 869, 875–81, 884–90
Pornography, 1248
Port Royal, 72–73, 692
Portsmouth Treaty, 997
Portugal, 7
Post offices, 401. See also Mail delivery
Potsdam, 1184
Pottawatomie Creek massacre, 628
Pound, Ezra, 1034, 1143
Poverty, 147, 176; post–1850, 459–60, 492–93; post–1900, 861; post–1929, 1075; post–1960, 1235
Powder factories, 667
Powderly, Terence V., 785
Power, personal, 1234–35
Powers, Francis Gary, 1213
Powers, Johnny, 964
Pratt, Orson, 538
Presbyterians, 77, 116–17, 184, 241, 404–5, 406–7, 512, 547
Presidencias, 11
Press, freedom of, 716
Price controls, 1102. See also Parity; Price supports
Price fixing, 838, 842, 846, 848, 1021
Price supports, 1022, 1205. See also Price controls
Primogeniture, 107–8
Princeton University, 186, 946
Prison reform, 530–31, 544–45
Private property, right of, 295, 742
Privateers, 384
Privy Council, 124
Process of Government, 895
Proclamation of 1763, 249
Professional organizations, 895, 908–9
Progress and Poverty, 795
Progressive movement, 903–35. See also Progressivism
Progressive Movement, The, 903
Progressive Party, 944, 946, 1114
Progressive Republican League, 942–43

Progressivism, 855, 869, 889–901, 910–21, 939, 942, 959, 972–76, 1014–47. *See also* Progressive movement

Prohibition, 877, 1020, 1070–71, 1088, 1130–32. *See also* Temperance movement

Promise of American Life, The, 938

Promontory Point (Utah), 782

Propaganda, 217

Prophet, the, 390

Proprietary manors, 61–62

Prosperity, wartime, 700

Prostitution, 1070

Protectionism, 477–78, 789–90

Protestant Association, 148, 152

Protestantism, 20, 52, 397, 402–4, 500, 504–12, 1132, 1139, 1224. *See also* Religion

Providence Island Company, 31

Provincetown Players, 1034

Prussia, 206

Public debt. *See* National debt

Public Works Administration (WPA), 1079–81, 1082

Publishing, 815–16, 818–19

Puerto Ricans, 1225

Puerto Rico, 990, 993

Pulitzer, Joseph, 987

Pulitzer Prize, 1143, 1154

Pullman, George, 882

Pullman strike, 882

Pure Food and Drug Law, 929

Puritans, 25, 45, 51–59, 100–2, 114–16, 155–61, 297

Quakers, 77, 79–83, 114, 116, 179, 181, 183, 217–18, 220, 241–42, 313, 542

Quantrill, William C., 659

Quarantine, 1169

Quartering Act (1765), 254

Quebec, 203, 207–8, 250, 279

Quebec Act (1774), 250

Queen Anne's War, 142

Quemoy, 1209

Quincy, Josiah, 298

Quorum of the Twelve Apostles, 535

Quota system, 953

Race riots, 753, 956, 1046, 1112, 1238. *See also* Blacks

Racism, 549, 561, 578, 618, 708–9, 758–66, 992, 1088

Radical Reconstruction. *See* Reconstruction

Radical Republicans, 718, 720, 741, 748–58. *See also* Republican Party

Radicalism, 1026, 1027, 1032, 1058, 1235–36, 1239

Radio industry, 1064, 1127, 1145

Railroad Brotherhoods, 1064

Railroads, post-1820, 426, 448, 451–53, 458, 512; post-1860, 667, 697–98, 724–25, 741, 780, 797, 832–33, 844, 846, 848; post-1900, 914, 927, 930, 1002; post-1917, 1021, 1061. *See also* Transcontinental railroads

Railroads War Board, 1021

Raleigh, Sir Walter, 23, 27

Ramsay, David, 296, 413

Rand, Ayn, 1152

Randolph, A. Philip, 1111

Randolph, Edmund, 275–76, 331, 356

Randolph, George Wythe, 665

Randolph, John, 373, 586

Raskob, John J., 1072

Raymond, Daniel, 584

Raynal, Abbe, 410

Reactionary movements, 1058–61

Reader's Digest, 1136

Reaper, 452, 695, 786. *See also* McCormick, Cyrus Hall

Reason the Only Oracle of Man, 405

Rebellion, 147–53, 359

Recall, 910

Recession (1884), 835; (1921–22), 1058, 1065; (1953–54), 1119, 1200, 1202; post-1970, 1255, 1256

Reciprocal Trade Agreement Act (1934), 1166

Reconcentration program, 988

Reconciliation, 800–20

Reconstruction, 648, 719, 729–66, 770, 774

Reconstruction Finance Corporation (RFC), 1076, 1082

Reconversion, 1044

Recreation, 1132, 1133

Red China, 1252. *See also* China

Red Cloud, Chief, 779

Red River, 369

Red Scare, 1044, 1058, 1067–68

Redeemers, 808, 812

Reed, John, 1031–33

Reed, Sen. James, 1161

Re-export trade, 380. *See also* Commerce; Foreign trade; Trade

Reform movements, 528–63, 866–69. *See also* Abolitionists; Progressive movement; Prohibition; Temperance movement; Women's suffrage

Regional rehabilitation, 1083

Regulators, 237

Reid, Whitelaw, 747

Relief, private, 1076; public, 1080–83, 1085, 1088. *See also* Welfare

Religion, 15, 108–21, 179–87, 501; post-1916, 1132, 1133, 1139–40; post-1960, 1224, 1226. *See also* Religion, freedom of; *and individually listed denominations*

Religion, freedom of, 45–59, 62, 68, 75, 79, 112, 403–4; post-1820, 408, 1088. *See also* Religion

Religious revivalism, 490, 491, 504–12

Remond, Charles Lenox, 560

Rensselaerswyck (N. Y.), 67–68, 140

Rent controls, 1102

Reparations, 1042, 1183, 1184. *See also* Allied war debts

Reparations Commission, 1042

Republic Steel, 1097

Republican Committee to Reelect the President, 1262

Republican Party, 354–87, 405–6, 471, 492; post-1850, 533, 626, 632, 637–40, 641; post-1862, 718–20, 725–26; post-1865, 730, 748–58, 763, 770, 866–74, 876; post-1875, 808–13; post-1890, 885–89, 913; post-1910, 938–39, 942–44; post-1918, 1040, 1044; post-1924, 1066, 1071; post-1946, 1105, 1113; post-1952, 1117; post-1964, 1218. *See also* Liberal Republican Party; Progressive Republican League; Radical Republicans

Republicanism, 291–319, 322

Reservationists, Strong, 1044–45

Resumption Act, 792

Retailing, 1062, 1099. *See also* Business

Revels, Hiram R., 763

Revenue Act (1764). *See* Sugar Act

Revenue Act (1942), 1103

Revenue sharing, 1118, 1248

Revolution of 1800 (Jeffersonian), 352–87

Rhett, Edmund, 744

Rhineland, 1041, 1164

Rhode Island, 54, 58–59, 129, 183, 214, 337, 467

Rhodes, James Ford, 925

Rice, 127, 136, 447

Rice, Elmer, 1143

Richmond (Va.), 660, 680–81, 687, 721, 722

Riis, Jacob, 922

Riley, James Whitcomb, 817

Riots, 315, 400, 704–5. *See also* Race riots
Ritchie, Thomas, 471
River gods, 232
Roads, 426, 450, 476. *See also* Highways; Transportation
Roanoke Island, 23, 27, 692
Robber barons, 783, 1144
Robertson, William, 410
Robins, Margaret Dreier, 965
Robinson, Edward G., 1145
Robinson, Edwin Arlington, 1034
Robinson, James Harvey, 895
Robinson-Patman Act (1936), 1099
Rochambeau, Comte de, 288
Rochester (N. Y.), 509, 545
Rockefeller, John D., 696, 783, 829, 834
Rockefeller, John D., Jr., 1130
Rockefeller, William, 783
Rockhill, William, 985
Rockwell, Norman, 1141
Roe v. *Wade*, 1248
Roebling, John, 832
Roebling, Washington, 832
Rogers, Will, 1077
Rollin, Charles, 293
Roman Catholics, 15, 17, 60–64, 182–83; post–1822, 531, 532; post–1926, 1132, 1139, 1239. *See also* Catholic immigrants; Religion
Rome-Berlin Axis, 1165
Rommel, Gen. Erwin, 1172
Roosevelt, Eleanor, 1088, 1141
Roosevelt, Pres. Franklin D., 1054, 1077–83, 1094–95, 1097, 1099–1101, 1132, 1166; post–1936, 1107, 1111, 1138, 1167, 1169–71, 1173, 1178, 1180, 1182–83. *See also* Fireside chats; New Deal
Roosevelt, Pres. Theodore, 848, 869, 985, 988, 990, 991; post–1910, 938–39, 942, 946, 952, 966, 1030, 1031; post–1914, 1004
Root, Elihu, 997, 1001
Root, Jesse, 376
Root-Takahira Agreement, 997
Rosecrans, W. S., 688
Rosenberg, Ethel, 1120, 1191
Rosenberg, Julius, 1120, 1191
Ross, Chief John, 657
Rough Riders, 922–23, 990, 991
Rousseau, Jean Jacques, 219
Rowley (Mass.), 92
Rowson, Susannah, 417
Rubber shortage, 1102

Ruffin, Edmund, 656
Ruins of Empire, 405
Rum, 210
Rumania, 1183, 1187
Rural Electrification Administration (REA), 1127
Rush, Dr. Benjamin, 295, 411, 414
Rusk, Dean, 1228
Russell, Charles Edward, 907
Russell, Lord John, 649, 674, 712
Russia, 285; post–1900, 997, 1008, 1014; post–1918, 1039, 1043–44; post–1930, 1148, 1165–66; post–1939, 1168, 1170; post–1941, 1172–73, 1175–76, 1178, 1182; post–1945, 1120–21, 1182–94; post–1950, 1228, 1232; post–1960, 1210–13, 1216; post–1970, 1251, 1253. *See also* Communism; Stalin, Joseph
Russian Revolution, 1043–44
Rutgers University, 186
Ruth, Babe, 1146
Ryder, Albert Pinkham, 1028

Sabbatatian movement, 545–46
Sac Indians, 439
Sacco, Nicola, 1067–68
Saigon, 1230
Saint Domingue, 570
Salem (Mass.), 54
Salesmen, 1141, 1150
Salinger, J. D., 1233
Salt, 42
Salt Lake City, 536
Samoa, 986
San Francisco, 1181, 1235
San Francisco conference, 1184
San Juan, 990
Sandburg, Carl, 1034
Sandys, George, 153
Sandys, Sir Edwin, 40–41, 47
Sanger, Margaret, 1132–33, 1135
Santa Anna, Antonio Lopez de, 598, 610, 613
Santa Fe, 680, 777
Santa Fe Trail, 598
Santa Ysabel, 1006
Santayana, George, 1034
Santiago, 7, 990
Santo Domingo, 210, 314, 773, 803
Sarah Constant, 37
Saratoga, 285
Savannah, 164, 286, 723
Say and Sele, Lord, 101
Saybrook Platform (1708), 181

Scalawags, 763
Scandinavian immigrants, 1060
Schechter case, 1094
Schiff, Jacob, 841–42
Schools, 503, 765, 1203, 1219, 1223, 1225, 1226, 1239, 1248. *See also* Colleges; Desegregation; Education
Schurz, Carl, 672, 802, 986, 992
Schuyler, Philip John, 143
Schwegmann decision, 1206
Scientific reformers, 898–901
Scientific relativism, 1151–52
Scientists, 414–15
Scopes, John, 1133
Scotch-Irish immigrants, 165, 166–67, 237
Scott, Dred, 629–30, 631, 634, 637
Scott, Thomas A., 783
Scott, Winfield, 489, 612, 613
Scottish factors, 240–41
Scottish merchants, 174
Screw press, 446
Scribner's, 817–18
Sea Islands, 739–41
Sears, Roebuck, 1064
Secession, 640, 654, 657–60. *See also* Nullification
Second Bank of the United States, 426, 471
Second front, 1173. *See also* World War II
Sectionalism, 612, 616–25, 626, 647–48
Securities and Exchange Commission (SEC), 1081, 1206
Security Council (UN), 1192. *See also* United Nations
Sedalia (Mo.), 785
Seddon, James A., 665, 715
Sedgwick, Catherine, 397
Sedition Act (1918), 1026
Segregation, 709, 950, 976, 1120, 1219–20. *See also* Desegregation; Housing
Seligman, Edwin, 895
Seminole Indians, 437, 439, 595, 657
Semmes, Raphael, 694
Senate, U. S., 334, 335, 619, 1123. *See also* Congress; *and names of specific treaties individually listed*
Senates, state, 300
Separatists, 47, 116, 299, 324
Servitude, 105–7
Servicemen's Readjustment Act (GI Bill), 1104, 1150
Settlement house, 961, 962–65
Seven Arts, The, 1037, 1038
Seven Days campaign, 681

Seven Years War. *See* French and Indian War

Seventh-Day Adventist Church, 1139

Seville, Archdeacon of, 9

Seward, Sen. William H., 487, 489, 621, 625, 637, 639, 654; post–1860, 671, 712, 718, 748, 773, 774–76

Sex, 524–25, 1132–33, 1134, 1136, 1146, 1235, 1236, 1248

Seymour, Gov. Horatio, 704, 791

Shafter, Gen. William R., 990

Shakers, 538

Share Our Wealth, 1084

Sharecropping, 745–47

Sharpe, Gov. Horatio, 253

Shaw, George Bernard, 972

Shaw, Irwin, 1153

Shawnee Indians, 436

Shays, Daniel, 329

Shenandoah Valley campaign, 681

Shepherd, Alexander, 874

Sheridan, Philip H., 722

Sherman, Gen. William T., 686, 689, 693, 722–23, 740, 741

Sherman, Sen. John, 732, 791–92, 810, 880

Sherman Antitrust Act, 846–47, 848, 927, 975

Sherman Silver Purchase Act, 884

Sherwood, Robert E., 1149

Shiloh Meeting House, Battle of, 678–80, 686

Shipbuilding, 212

Shipping, 391, 773, 1022, 1169

Shirley, Gov. William, 202, 206, 234

Shoe industry, 457, 696

Shopping plazas, 1202

Shute, Col. Samuel, 132

Sibley, Gen. Henry Hopkins, 680

Sidell, John C., 609, 610, 614, 672, 674

Sidney, Algernon, 80, 292

Silk, 42, 76

Silent Majority, 1246

Silent Spring, 1234

Sillman, Benjamin, 518

Silver, 215, 444, 791, 884. *See also* Currency; Free silver

Simms, William Gilmore, 523

Simons, Algie, 969

Sims, Capt. F. W., 724

Sinclair, Upton, 907, 929, 971

Singapore, 1172

Sioux Indians, 442, 779

Sirhan, Sirhan, 1240

Sirica, John, 1263

Sit-ins, 1221

Sitting Bull, 779

Slave codes, 44–45, 637. *See also* Slavery

Slave Power, 494, 608, 612, 617, 626, 634. *See also* Slavery

Slave revolts, 570, 588, 593. *See also* Slavery

Slave trade, 142, 313, 543, 547, 593. *See also* Slavery

Slavery, 17, 36, 44–45, 76, 136, 168–69, 309, 312–14; post–1820, 427–28, 443, 446, 448, 458, 490–93, 506–7, 566–604, 613; post–1851, 616–42, 648, 672, 686–87, 692, 705–12, 725; post–1865, 731, 743. *See also* Abolitionists; Blacks; Slave codes; Slave Power; Slave revolts; Slave trade; South

Sloan, John, 1032

Sloughter, Henry, 150

Slums, 459, 460, 861, 1225

Small, Albion, 895

Smalls, Robert, 706

Smith, Alfred E., 1071–72, 1132

Smith, Capt. John, 39

Smith, Gen. Edmund Kirby, 682

Smith, Gerald L. K., 1088

Smith, Hoke, 913

Smith, J. Allan, 895, 898

Smith, Joseph, Jr., 532–35

Smith, Melancton, 338

Smith, Sir Thomas, 37

Smith, William, 194

Smith Act (1940), 1120

Smith-Connally Act, 1104

Smuggling, 201, 209, 211

Social Democratic Party, 968

Social Gospelists, 877

Social Security acts, 1085–86, 1087, 1094, 1098, 1115, 1148, 1223

Socialism, 795, 968–72, 1026. *See also* Socialist Labor Party

Socialist Labor Party, 968–69, 1058. *See also* Socialism

Society, post–1600, 85–121; post–1720, 163–198; post–1750, 231–44; post–1775, 295–96, 306–14; 343–44, 393–96; post–1820, 426–27; post–1865, 735–66; post–1920, 1054, 1142–48; post–1939, 1148–56; post–1948, 1115–16; post–1950, 1205–6; post–1960, 1232–37

Society of the Cincinnati, 348

Society of Friends. *See* Quakers

Society of Jesus, 113

Society for the Propagation of the Gospel in Foreign Parts, 183

Soil, 235, 446

Soil banks, 1205

Soil conservation, 445–46, 1094. *See also* Conservation; Natural resources

Solomon Islands, 1176

Some Account of the Province of Pennsylvania, 217

Sons of Liberty, 252

Souls of the Black Folk, 958

South, post–1684, 136–37, 139, 168–69, 172–74, 185, 214, 272, 285–88, 314; post–1780, 309, 354, 398–99, 437–41; post–1820, 443, 446–50, 458, 474, 493, 506–507, 567–82, 618, 626, 695, 701; post–1861, 702–4, 736–66, 777, 808–13, 817–20; post–1880, 873, 878, 913, 953–58; post–1920, 1109, 1133, 1139; post–1935, 1088; post–1950, 1220, 1225. *See also* Confederacy; Democratic Party

South Africa, 1254

South America. *See* Latin America

South Carolina, 76–77, 164, 183, 202, 236, 237, 323; post–1820, 477, 575, 587–92, 640; post–1820, 587–92, 640, 763

South Dakota, 878

South Korea. *See* Korea; Korean War

South End House, 962

South Viet Nam. *See* Viet Nam War

Southeast Asia, 1251. *See also* individually listed countries

Southeast Asia Treaty Organization (SEATO), 1207, 1229

Southern Christian Leadership Conference (SCLC), 1221

Southern Democrats, 748–49, 764. *See also* Democratic Party

Southern Tenant Farmers' Union, 1097

Southwest, 327, 390–91, 398–99, 443, 446, 749. *See also* West

Sovereignty, doctrine of, 271–72

Soviet-American detente, 1253–54

Soviet-Chinese feud, 1232

Soviet Union. *See* Russia

Snyder, John, 1116

Space program, 1204–5

Spain, 4, 5–18, 19–20, 201, 208; post–1779, 285, 288, 327, 349, 593–96, 610, 615; post–1895, 986, 1165, 1194

Spanish-American War, 983, 989–92, 993

Spanish Civil War, 1165

Spanish Republicans, 1165

Spanish West Indies, 201
Spargo, John, 971, 1066
Special interest groups, 1205
Specie, 325, 478, 669–70, 790, 791, 803
Specie Circular, 481
Speech, freedom of, 556. *See also* Bill of Rights
Speedwell, 47
Spillane, Mickey, 1152–53, 1156
Spirit of American Government, The, 895
Spooner, Senator, 993
Sports, 1235
Spotswood, Alexander, 132
Spotsylvania, Battle of, 721
Spurzheim, Johann Gasper, 518
Sputnik, 1204
Square Deal, 926–33, 943
Squatters, 445–46
St. Augustine, 142
St. Clair, Gen. Arthur, 348
St. Joseph (Mo.), 452
St. Lawrence River, 206
St. Leger, Lt. Col. Barry, 283–84
St. Louis (Mo.), 658
St. Mary's (Md.), 62
Stalin, Joseph, 1175, 1178, 1180, 1182. *See also* Communism; Russia
Stalingrad, 1173, 1175
Stamp Act, 248, 251–54, 268
Stamp Act Congress, 251, 268
Standard of living, 458, 1203
Standard Oil Company of Ohio, 783–84, 829, 838, 840
Standardization of production, 1064
Stanton, Edwin M., 664, 757–58
Stanton, Elizabeth Cady, 557
Stanton, Henry B., 514, 687
Staple Act (1663), 127–28
Stark, John, 285
Starr, Ellen Gates, 894
State capitals, 315–16
State constitutions, 317, 322–24
State Department, 1121, 1162, 1186–87
State governments, 296–300, 314, 315, 324, 332, 913
States' rights, 770, 771. *See also* Nullification; Secession
States' Rights Democratic Party, 536, 1114. *See also* Democratic Party
Steamboats, 415, 446, 454, 512
Steel industry, 780, 783, 830, 834, 838, 840, 1023, 1061
Steele, Gen. Frederick, 691
Steffens, Lincoln, 892, 905, 906, 907, 1137

Stein, Gertrude, 1143
Steinbeck, John, 1148
Stephens, Alexander H., 485, 670, 705, 714–15, 731, 749, 750, 761
Stephenson, David, 1070
Stevens, Thaddeus, 718, 741, 742, 749, 750, 751, 753, 757
Stevens, Uriah, 785
Stevenson, Adlai E., 1118, 1119, 1193, 1215
Steward, Ira, 784
Stiles, Ezra, 316, 411
Stimson, Henry L., 1166, 1185
Stock exchanges, 1082
Stock market, 837, 1073
Stone, Harlan, 1067
Stone, Lewis, 1136
Stone, Lucy, 557
Story, Joseph, 514, 518
Stowe, Harriet Beecher, 622
Strasser, Adolph, 858
Strategic Arms Limitation Talks (SALT), 1254–55
Streetcar Named Desire, A, 1155
Strikes, labor, 176–77, 400, 797, 858, 881–83; post–1900, 927–28, 969, 1022, 1046, 1066, 1096, 1104, 1105
Strikes, student, 1235, 1239
Strong, George Templeton, 673, 704
Strong, Josiah, 985
Stuart, Charles, 549–50
Student Non-Violent Coordinating Committee (SNCC), 1221
Students for a Democratic Society (SDS), 1235
Stuyvesant, Peter, 68–70, 114
Submarine warfare, 693, 1009–10, 1016, 1022, 1168, 1170, 1172, 1173
Subsidies, 1205
Suburbs, 832, 912, 1201, 1202. *See also* Housing; Urbanization
Sudbury (Mass.), 54
Sudetenland, 1164, 1165
Suez Canal, 1172, 1211–12
Suffrage, 195, 196, 274, 397, 467. *See also* Blacks; Women's suffrage
Sugar, 127, 210, 211, 447, 593
Sugar Act, 250–51
Sukarno, 1228
Sullivan, Louis, 832
Sullivan, Roger, 945
Sumner, Sen. Charles, 628–29, 705, 717–18, 741, 750; post–1870, 751, 753–54, 757, 759, 770, 775–76, 802–3
Sumner, William Graham, 742
Sunday school movement, 497, 547

Supreme Court, 344, 395–96, 629–30, 631, 755–56, 846, 847–48, 927; post–1800, 372–75, 939–42; post–1920, 1065, 1094–95, 1108, 1115, 1119–20, 1206; post–1953, 1218–20, 1221, 1225–26, 1246–48, 1264
Susquehanna Company, 235
Sussex, 1009
Sweatt v. *Painter*, 1119–20
Swift, Ezpheniah, 376
Swift, Gustavus, 838
Swift, Jonathan, 264
Switzerland, 434
Sylvis, William H., 784
Symmes, John Cleves, 397

Taft, Sen. Robert, 1116, 1117–18, 1122, 1182
Taft, Pres. William Howard, 848, 938, 942, 944, 945, 993, 997, 1002–3; post–1914, 1022, 1040, 1065
Taft-Hartley Act (1947), 1105, 1115
Taiwan. *See* Formosa
Tallmadge, James, Jr., 583
Tammany Hall, 872
Taney, Roger B., 395–96, 480, 629, 632, 716, 755
Tappan, Lewis, 552–54
Tarbell, Ida, 905, 906–7
Tariff of Abominations, 474. *See also* Tariffs
Tariff Commission, 976. *See also* Tariffs
Tariffs, 211, 347, 429; post–1825, 474; post–1832, 477–78, 588–59, 639, 741; post–1865, 787–89, 988; post–1908, 942, 974, 976; post–1920, 1162–63, 1166
Tarleton, Col. Banastre, 287
Taxation, 110, 114, 156, 208, 247, 251–56, 258; post–1780, 334, 428–29, 669; post–1913, 1023; post–1935, 1094, 1103; post–1948, 1116; post–1960, 1255; post–1947, 1256. *See also* Excise tax; Tariffs
Taylor, Gen. Maxwell, 1229
Taylor, Graham, 962, 1130
Taylor, John, 363, 377
Taylor, John W., 585
Taylor, Nathaniel William, 408
Taylor, Zachary, 483, 489, 610, 612–13; Pres., 615, 621
Tea Act, 258
Teamsters, 1106. *See also* Unions, labor
Teapot Dome Scandal, 1058

Technology, 415

Tecumseh, 390

Tehran conference, 1180

Telegraph, 512, 781, 833. *See also* Communication

Telephone, 781–82. *See also* Bell, Alexander Graham; Communication

Television, 1202, 1214, 1217–18, 1231, 1234, 1248

Teller Amendment, 990

Temperance movement, 409, 510, 531, 532, 544, 546, 548, 557–58. *See also* Prohibition

Temperance Society, 548

Temple, Shirley, 1142

Ten-Hour Law, 962

Tenant farmers, 1097, 1108. *See also* Agriculture

Tender Is the Night, 1015

Tenement-House Problem, 894

Tennant, Gilbert, 184–85

Tennessee, 438, 577, 654, 657, 660

Tennessee Valley Authority (TVA), 1083–84, 1107, 1115

Tenure of Office Act, 756–58

Test Ban Treaty, 1216

Tet Offensive, 1230, 1238

Texan Revolution, 598–99

Texas, 441, 568, 597–602, 610; post–1845, 448, 490, 604, 617, 619, 763, 878

Texas Pacific Railroad, 858

Textiles, 212, 448, 455, 457, 478, 666, 1031–33. *See also* Industrial Revolution; Manufacturing

Textron, 1106

Thailand, 1207, 1251

Theater, 1136

Theory of Our National Existence, The, 771

Third parties, 876–77. *See also party names by individual listings*

Thomas, Gen. George H., 678, 688, 690, 723

Thomas, William I., 895

Thompson, Big Bill, 1070, 1110

Thompson, George, 553

Thoreau, Henry David, 525

Thurmond, Gov. J. Strom, 1114, 1115

Tilden, Gov. Samuel J., 795, 808

Tillman, Ben, 884, 913, 953, 956

Timber products, 42, 76, 93, 127, 444. *See also* Lumbering

Timrod, Henry, 817

Tippecanoe, 390

Tobacco, 62, 76, 95–98, 110, 127, 136–37, 139, 174, 240–41, 309, 446, 447, 695; post–1865, 747, 830, 1081

Tocqueville, Alexis de, 401, 425–26, 435–36, 444, 459, 505

Todd, Rev. John, 518

Tojo, Hideki, 1171

Tokyo, 1178

Toombs, Robert, 485, 652, 655, 671

Tories. *See* Loyalists

Tories in England, 264, 265

Torpedoes, 693

Town meeting, 135

Towns, 102–4, 393, 1070. *See also* Town meeting

Townsend, Dr. Francis E., 1085, 1088, 1089, 1090

Townsend movement, 1148

Townshend, Charles, 249, 254

Townshend duties, 254–58

Tracy, Spencer, 1136

Trade, 213, 238–39, 245, 250–51, 310, 327, 330, 453–54, 461, 1167–68. *See also* Commerce; Foreign trade; Trade associations

Trade associations, 837–38, 1062, 1065, 1076, 1080

Trade Practices Conference, 1076

Trading licenses, 140

Trans-National America, 952

Transactions, 411

Transcendentalism, 519

Transcontinental railroads, 624, 639, 698, 782, 811, 832–33. *See also* Railroads

Transcontinental Treaty, 596

Transportation, 178–79, 212, 446, 450, 453; post–1860, 675, 697, 724, 782–83, 832–83, 832–33, 892. *See also* Air travel; Automobile; Canal, construction; Railroads; Turnpikes

Transportation Act (1920), 1065

Travels, 413

Treasury Department, 668, 1070–71

Treaty of Ghent, 484

Treaty of Greenville, 349

Treaty of Guadalupe Hidalgo, 614

Treaty of Hartford, 68

Treaty of Tordesillas, 20

Treaty of Utrecht, 142

Treaty of Washington, 775

Trenchard, John, 264

Trenholm, George, 700

Trent affair, 674

Tripartite Pact, 1169

Trist, Nicholas, 614

Truman, Pres. Harry S, 1104, 1114–16, 1118–22, 1178, 1182, 1184, 1185–90, 1192–93, 1214, 1215

Truman Doctrine, 1187, 1189, 1190, 1191, 1193, 1195

Trusts, 838–39, 843, 859, 910, 926–28; post–1912, 945, 973–74, 975. *See also* Business; Business, regulation of

Tudor, William, 417–18

Tugwell, Rexford, 1079

Tunney, Gene, 1146

Turkey, 1207, 1228, 1254

Turner, Frederick Jackson, 461, 983

Turner, George Kibbe, 907

Turner, Nat, 549, 570

Turnpikes, 450. *See also* Highways; Transportation

Twain, Mark. *See* Clemens, Samuel

Tweed, William Marcy, 803–4, 874

Twenty Years at Hull House, 959

Two Penny Acts, 241

Tyler, Elizabeth, 1060

Tyler, John, 483, 489; Pres., 599–604

Tydings–McDuffie Act (1934), 1166–67

U-boat. *See* Submarine warfare

U-2 spy plane, 1213

Ulster plantation, 29

UN. *See* United Nations

Uncle Tom's Cabin, 622

Unemployment, 512, 795, 882; post–1929, 1075, 1076, 1084; post–1934, 1084, 1101; post–1969, 1255. *See also* Depressions

Unemployment compensation, 1086

Underground Railroad, 560

Underhill, Capt. John, 69

Underwood, Sen. Oscar, 945

Underwood Tariff, 974

Union and Civil War, 647–48, 650, 654, 657–63, 666–83, 685–707, 723, 726, 796. *See also* North

Union League, 735, 762

Union Pacific Railroad, 725, 778, 782–83

Union Party, 1089

Union of Soviet Socialist Republics (U.S.S.R.). *See* Russia

Unions, labor, 795, 848, 1022, 1058, 1062, 1065; post–1935, 1086–87, 1095–97, 1099, 1120; post–1941, 1104, 1105, 1106; post–1970, 1249. *See also* AFL-CIO; American Federation of Labor; Congress of Industrial Organizations; Labor; Lewis, John L.

Unitarians, 512

United Auto Workers (UAW), 1096.
    See also Labor
United Mine Workers Union, 927,
    1095. *See also* Labor; Lewis, John L.
United Nations (UN), 1181, 1184,
    1192, 1211, 1252
Union Pacific Railroad, 804–5, 833,
    848
United States Chamber of Commerce,
    1069, 1106
United States Railroad Administra-
    tion, 1021–22
United States Steel, 830, 840, 927,
    1061, 1097
United States Review, 457
Universal Negro Improvement Asso-
    ciation, 1110
Universities, 895, 1030. *See also* Col-
    leges; *and universities listed in-
    dividually*
University of Chicago, 895, 1151
University Settlement, 895, 962
University of Washington, 895
Unsafe At Any Speed, 1260
Upshur, Abel P., 599, 601
Urbanization, 177, 443, 455, 459, 830–
    32, 861. *See also* Housing; Suburbs
U.S. v. Butler, 1094
U.S. v. Darby, 1095
U.S. v. United States Steel, 1065
Utah, 536, 623, 625, 777
Ute Indians, 779
Utilitarianism, 415

Valdivia, Pedro de, 7
Valentino, Rudolph, 1146
Values, individual, 1129, 1139–42,
    1151–56
Van Buren, Martin, 468–71, 475, 477,
    478, 489, 490–91; Pres., 489, 591, 599
Van Rennselaer, Kiliaen, 69
Van Twiller, Wouter, 68
Van Wyck, Charles H., 879
Vancouver Island, 612
Vandenberg, Sen. Arthur, 1185, 1196
Vanderbilt, Cornelius, 783
Vanzetti, Bartolomeo, 1068
Veblen, Thorstein, 963, 972
Veiller, Lawrence, 894
Venezuela, 986
Vera Cruz, 1003, 1006
Vermont, 172, 235, 324, 343
Versailles Treaty, 1161, 1164
Vesey, Denmark, 570
Veterans, 1076–77. *See also* Grand
    Army of the Republic

Veto, presidential, 477
Viceroyalty, 11, 17
Vicksburg, Battle of, 688–89, 691, 692
Victoria, Queen, 674, 773
Viet Nam War, 1055, 1229–32, 1238–
    39, 1250–51
Vigilantes, 237, 314, 377, 765–66,
    1024–26, 1067
Villa Pancho, 1006
Villard, Oswald Garrison, 958
Vincent, Rev. Marvin R., 769
Violence, 400
Virginia, 693–94
Virginia, 37–45, 109–12, 131–32, 139–
    41, 148–50; post–1700, 164, 170, 171,
    182, 197, 235, 236, 239, 240–41; post–
    1750, 243–44, 273, 295, 359, 398, 403;
    post–1820, 405, 446, 492, 577, 580,
    654, 655–57, 659–60, 763, 803
Virginia Company, 31, 37–45, 47, 217
Virginia Dynasty, 367, 385
Virginia plan, 331–33, 335
Volny, Compto de, 405
Vonnegut, Kurt, 1262
Volstead Act, 1070
Voltaire, 217–18, 219
Voluntary associations, 401–2
Volunteers, Civil War, 661–66
Voting, 731, 811–13, 869–71, 934, 1226.
    See also Suffrage; Women's suffrage

Wade, Sen. Benjamin F., 720, 760
Wade-Davis bill, 720
Wadsworth, Jeremiah, 311
Wage controls, 1102, 1256
Wages, 455, 459–60, 462, 950; post–
    1912, 1022, 1031, 1065. *See also*
    Wage controls
Wagner, Robert, 1190
Wagner Act, 1086–87, 1088, 1094, 1095
Walden, 525
Walker, David, 549
Walker, Leroy P., 663
Walker Tariff, 478
Wall Street, 839
Wallace, Gov. George, 1240, 1246, 1248
Wallace, Henry A., 1078, 1088, 1101,
    1104, 1114, 1115, 1185–86
Wallace, Henry C., 1064–65
Wallas, Graham, 972
Walling, William English, 969
Walpole, Robert, 178, 201, 265
Walpose, Horace, 267
Walsh, Frank P., 1022
Waltham (Mass.), 455
War of Austrian Succession, 202

War debts. *See* Allied war debts
War of 1812, 230, 377–85, 392, 484, 592
War Food Administration, 1101
War Industries Board, 1020, 1064
War of Jenkins' Ear, 201–2
War Labor Policies Board, 1022
War of the League of Augsbury, 141–
    42
War Manpower Commission, 1101
War materials, 1169–70, 1173
War on Poverty, 1223, 1259
War production, 1176
War Production Board, 1101
War Raw Materials Department, 1017
War of the Spanish Succession, 143–44
Warner, Charles Dudley, 787
Warner Brothers, 1128
Warren, Chief Justice Earl, 1218–20,
    1221, 1225–26
Warren, Com. Peter, 202–3
Warsaw Pact, 1189
Warships, 712–13
Washburne, Carleton, 1137
Washington, Booker T., 956
Washington, George, 204–6, 233, 249,
    266; post–1775, 280–83, 296, 326;
    Pres., 341–42, 348, 349, 353, 355, 357,
    409; post–1790, 359
Washington (D. C.), 353, 363, 385, 386,
    416, 586–87, 874; post–1932, 1076–77,
    1221; post–1963, 1221, 1222, 1237,
    1239, 1248. *See also* District of Co-
    lumbia
Washington   Conference,   1159–60,
    1165
Water power, 457
Watergate, 1262–64
Watie, Gen. Stand, 657
Watson, Elkanah, 394–95
Watson, John B., 1138
Watson, Thomas, 812, 878
Wayne, Gen. Anthony, 307, 349
Wealth, 397, 829, 863
Weather charts, 411
Webster, Daniel, 478, 484, 487; post–
    1830, 489, 589, 599, 620–22
Webster, Noah, 352
Webster Ashburton Treaty, 599
Weed, Thurlow, 487–89, 490, 494, 626
Weeks, Sinclair, 1118
Weems, Parson, 409–10
Weld, Theodore Dwight, 549–50, 553
Welfare, 1138; post–1960, 1227. *See
    also* Relief; Social Security
Welles, Gideon, 667, 695, 748
Wells, David A., 787

Wells, H. G., 972
Wentworth, Gov. Benning, 273
West, 368, 426, 433, 436, 442–44, 452–53, 457, 476, 492–93, 507–508, 617; post–1860, 777–79, 816–17. *See also* Land, western
West Africa, 544
West Coast, 1108. *See also* West
West Germany, 1193. *See also* Germany
West Indies, 21, 76, 93, 210–11, 310, 378, 575. *See also* British West Indies; French West Indies
West Point (Military Academy), 676
West Virginia, 660
Western Front, 1014–15. *See also* World War II
Western Hemisphere, 1167–68
Western Union Telegraph Company, 781
Westinghouse, George, 842
Weston, Thomas, 47
Wethersfield (Conn.), 54
Weyl, Walter, 953, 1037
Wheat, 446, 452, 849, 1064
Wheat deal (1975), 1253
Whig Party (U.S.), 266, 300; post–1820, 465–66, 468, 470, 483–94, 599; post–1850, 616, 624, 625, 626
Whigs (British), 264, 265
Whiskey distillers, 837–38
Whiskey Ring, 805
White, Gov. John, 23–24
White, Hugh, 489
White, Walter, 1110
White, William Allen, 910
White-collar workers, 1129–30, 1132, 1133, 1234
Whitefield, George, 184–85
Whitlock, Brand, 893, 900
Whitman, Walt, 525, 813, 815–16, 1035
Whittier, John Greenleaf, 523, 534, 621
Wholesale price index, 836
Wilberforce, William, 544
Wilderness, Battle of the, 721
Wiley, Calvin H., 733
Wiley, Henry, 929

Wilhelm II, 1016
Wilkes, Capt. Charles, 674
Wilkinson, Gen. James, 342–43, 370
William III, 133, 152
Williams, Israel, 260
Williams, Roger, 56, 58, 116, 119, 153
Williams, Tennessee, 1136, 1154, 1156
Willkie, Wendell, 1100–1, 1170, 1181
Wilmington (N. C.), 693
Wilmot, David, 617
Wilmot Proviso, 617, 618–19
Wilson, Alexander, 416
Wilson, Charles E., 1118, 1207
Wilson, Jabes, 264
Wilson, James, 266, 271, 323, 331, 334–35, 339
Wilson, M. L., 1079
Wilson, Woodrow, 935, 939, 944; Pres., 848, 945–48, 966–67, 972–76, 1003–11, 1015–17, 1020–23, 1038–47, 1053
Wilson's Creek, Battle of, 659
WIN (Whip Inflation Now) buttons, 1256
Windsor (Conn.), 54
Wine production, 42, 76
Winnetka System, 1137
Winning of the West, 925
Winthrop, John, 53, 99, 119, 231
Winthrop, John, Jr., 91, 154
Wire Nail Association, 837
Wirt, William, 479
Wirtz, Major Henry, 732
Wisconsin, 439, 915–16
Wise, Rev. John, 130
Wobblies. *See* Industrial Workers of the World (IWW)
Wolfe, James, 206–8
Women, 89, 109, 399; post–1830, 501, 503, 548, 555; post–1867, 792–94, 874–75, 890, 894, 961; post–1920, 1134, 1136. *See also* Feminist movement; Women in labor force; Women's rights movement; Women's suffrage
Women in labor force, 455, 462, 700–1, 833, 917, 959–60, 965, 1101
Women's rights movement, 1088, 1236–37. *See also* Feminist movement

Women's suffrage, 795, 961, 965–67, 1020
Wood, Robert, 1170
Woodstock, 1240
Wool industry, 19, 452, 478, 788
Woolen Act, 211–12
Woolman, John, 571
Woolsey, Theodore Dwight, 773
Woolson, Constance Fenimore, 817
Working Men's Party, 499
Worcester v. *Georgia*, 438–39
Workman's compensation act, 976
Works Progress Administration (WPA), 1085, 1087–89, 1098, 1103, 1107
Workweek, 856
World Anti-Slavery Convention, 599
World Bank, 1181
World Court, 1161
World War I, 1008–10, 1014–17, 1019–20, 1041
World War II, 1055, 1101, 1153, 1172–82
Wormley, James, 810
Wormley agreement, 810–11
Wounded Knee (S. D.), 1249
Wright, Frances, 393
Wythe, George, 318

XYZ affair, 356

Yale College, 160
Yalta Conference, 1180, 1182–83
Yancey, William L., 663, 672
Yates, Abraham, 316
Yazoo Company, 371
Yellow fever, 410–11
Yorktown, Battle of, 288
Young, Brigham, 535–36, 538
Young Plan, 1161
Youth, revolt of, 1136, 1235–36, 1239–40
Yucatán Peninsula, 614
Yugoslavia, 1183, 1194

Zaire. *See* Congo
Zangwill, Israel, 952